ENCYCLOPEDIA OF
AMERICAN HISTORY

Revised Edition

Comprehensive Index

VOLUME XI

ENCYCLOPEDIA OF
AMERICAN HISTORY
Revised Edition

Volume I
THREE WORLDS MEET
Beginnings to 1607

Volume II
COLONIZATION AND SETTLEMENT
1608 to 1760

Volume III
REVOLUTION AND NEW NATION
1761 to 1812

Volume IV
EXPANSION AND REFORM
1813 to 1855

Volume V
CIVIL WAR AND RECONSTRUCTION
1856 to 1869

Volume VI
THE DEVELOPMENT OF THE INDUSTRIAL UNITED STATES
1870 to 1899

Volume VII
THE EMERGENCE OF MODERN AMERICA
1900 to 1928

Volume VIII
THE GREAT DEPRESSION AND WORLD WAR II
1929 to 1945

Volume IX
POSTWAR UNITED STATES
1946 to 1968

Volume X
CONTEMPORARY UNITED STATES
1969 to the Present

Volume XI
COMPREHENSIVE INDEX

ENCYCLOPEDIA OF AMERICAN HISTORY

Revised Edition

Comprehensive Index

VOLUME XI

Facts On File
An imprint of Infobase Publishing

Encyclopedia of American History, Revised Edition
Comprehensive Index

Editorial Director: Laurie E. Likoff
Editor in Chief: Owen Lancer
Chief Copy Editor: Michael G. Laraque
Associate Editor: Dorothy Cummings
Maps and Illustrations: Dale E. Williams

Facts On File, Inc.
An imprint of Infobase Publishing
132 West 31st Street
New York NY 10001

Library of Congress Cataloging-in-Publication Data
Encyclopedia of American history / Gary B. Nash, general editor. — Rev. ed.
p. cm.
Includes bibliographical references and index.
Contents: v. 1. Three worlds meet, beginnings to 1607 — v. 2. Colonization and settlement, 1608 to 1760 — v. 3. Revolution and new nation, 1761 to 1812 — v. 4. Expansion and reform, 1813 to 1855 — v. 5. Civil War and Reconstruction, 1856 to 1869 — v. 6. The development of the industrial United States, 1870 to 1899 — v. 7. The emergence of modern America, 1900 to 1928 — v. 8. The Great Depression and World War II, 1929 to 1945 — v. 9. Postwar United States, 1946 to 1968 — v. 10. Contemporary United States, 1969 to the present — v. 11. Comprehensive index. ISBN 978-0-8160-7136-4 (set : hc : alk. paper) — ISBN 978-0-8160-7137-1 (v. 1 : hc : alk. paper) — ISBN 978-0-8160-7138-8 (v. 2 : hc : alk. paper) — ISBN 978-0-8160-7139-5 (v. 3 : hc : alk. paper) — ISBN 978-0-8160-7140-1 (v. 4 : hc : alk. paper) — ISBN 978-0-8160-7141-8 (v. 5 : hc : alk. paper) — ISBN 978-0-8160-7142-5 (v. 6 : hc : alk. paper) — ISBN 978-0-8160-7143-2 (v. 7 : hc : alk. paper) — ISBN 978-0-8160-7144-9 (v. 8 : hc : alk. paper) — ISBN 978-0-8160-7145-6 (v. 9 : hc : alk. paper) — ISBN 978-0-8160-7146-3 (v. 10 : hc : alk. paper) — ISBN 978-0-8160-7147-0 (v. 11 : hc : alk. paper) 1. United States—History—Encyclopedias. I. Nash, Gary B.
E174.E53 2009
973.03—dc22   2008035422

About the Editors

General Editor: Gary B. Nash received a Ph.D. from Princeton University. He is director of the National Center for History in the Schools at the University of California, Los Angeles, where he teaches American history of the colonial and Revolutionary era. He is a published author of college and precollegiate history texts. Among his best-selling works are the coauthored *American People: Creating a Nation and Society* (Longman, 1998), now in its seventh edition; *American Odyssey: The U.S. in the Twentieth Century* (McGraw-Hill/Glencoe, 1999), now in its fourth edition; and *The Atlas of American History,* coauthored with Carter Smith (Facts On File, 2006).

Nash is an elected member of the Society of American Historians, the American Academy of Arts and Sciences, the American Antiquarian Society, and the American Philosophical Society. He has served as past president of the Organization of American Historians in 1994–95 and was a founding member of the National Council for History Education. His latest books include *First City: Philadelphia and the Forging of Historical Memory* (University of Pennsylvania Press, 2002), *The Unknown American Revolution: The Unruly Birth of Democracy and the Struggle to Create America* (Viking, 2005), and *The Forgotten Fifth: African Americans in the Era of Revolution* (Harvard University Press, 2006).

Volume I Editor: Peter C. Mancall is professor of history and anthropology at the University of Southern California (USC) and director of the USC–Huntington Early Modern Studies Institute. He received a Ph.D. from Harvard University and is an elected member of the American Antiquarian Society. He is the author of several books, including *Deadly Medicine: Indians and Alcohol in Early America* (Cornell University Press, 1995), *Hakluyt's Promise: An Elizabethan's Obsession for an English America* (Yale University Press, 2007), and *Fatal Journey: The Final Expedition of Henry Hudson* (Basic Books, 2009), and the editor of eight books, including *Travel Narratives from the Age of Discovery* (Oxford University Press, 2006) and *The Atlantic World and Virginia, 1550–1624* (University of North Carolina Press, 2007).

Volume II Editor: Billy G. Smith, Montana State University, received a Ph.D. from the University of California, Los Angeles. He has published numerous books, including *The "Lower Sort": Philadelphia's Laboring People, 1750–1800* (Cornell University Press, 1990), *Down and Out in Early America* (Pennsylvania State Press, 2004), and *Class Matters: Early North America and the Atlantic World* (University of Pennsylvania Press).

Volume III Editor: Paul A. Gilje, is professor of history, Samuel Roberts Noble Foundation Presidential Professor, and a George Lynn Cross Research Professor at the University of Oklahoma. After graduating with a B.A. in history from Brooklyn College, CUNY, he earned an M.A. and Ph.D. from Brown University. He is the author of several books, including *The Making of the American Republic, 1763–1815* (Upper Saddle River, N.J.: Prentice Hall, 2006); *Liberty on the Waterfront: American Maritime Society and Culture in the Age of Revolution,* 1750–1850 (Philadelphia: University of Pennsylvania Press, 2004); *Rioting in America* (Bloomington: Indiana University Press, 1996); *The Road to Mobocracy: Popular Disorder in New York City, 1763 to 1834* (Chapel Hill: University of North Carolina Press for the Institute of Early American History and Culture, Williamsburg, 1987). In 2004 *Liberty on the Waterfront* won both the Society for Historians of the Early American Republic Best Book Award and the North American Society for Oceanic History John Lyman Book Award for best book on U.S. maritime history. Gilje served as president of the Society for Historians of the Early Republic in 2008–2009.

Volume IV Editor: Malcolm J. Rohrbough, University of Iowa, holds a Ph.D. from the University of Wisconsin. He is the author of several books, including *Days of Gold: The California Gold Rush and the American Nation* (University of California Press, 1996), and is coeditor of a 10-volume history of the trans-Appalachian frontier published by Indiana University Press.

Volume V Editor: Joan Waugh is a professor of history at the University of California, Los Angeles, where she specializes in the Civil War and Reconstruction periods. She is the author of *Unsentimental Reformer: The Life of Josephine Shaw Lowell* (Harvard University Press, 1998) and the forthcoming *Ulysses S. Grant, American Hero, American Myth* (University of North Carolina Press, 2009). Recently published books include (with Alice Fahs) *The Memory of the Civil War in American Culture* (University of North Carolina Press, 2004) and (with Gary W. Gallagher) *Wars within a War: Controversy and Conflict over the American Civil War* (University of North Carolina Press, 2009).

Volume VI Editor: Ari Hoogenboom, professor emeritus, Brooklyn College, City University of New York, received a Ph.D. from Columbia University. He is the coeditor of *The Gilded Age* (Prentice Hall, 1967) and the author of *Rutherford B. Hayes: Warrior and President* (University Press of Kansas, 1995), among other books and articles. His latest book is *Gustavus Vasa Fox of the Union Navy: A Biography* (Johns Hopkins University Press, 2008).

Volume VII Editor: Elizabeth Faue, Wayne State University, received a Ph.D. from the University of Minnesota. She is the author of *Community of Suffering and Struggle: Women, Men, and the Labor Movement in Minneapolis, 1915–1945* (University of North Carolina Press, 1991) and *Writing the Wrongs: Eva Valesh and the Rise of Labor Journalism* (Cornell University Press, 2002).

Volume VIII Editor: John W. Jeffries, dean of arts, humanities, and social sciences at the University of Maryland, Baltimore County, received a Ph.D. from Yale University. He is the author of several books, including *Wartime America: The World War II Home Front* (Ivan Dee, 1996).

Volume IX Editors: Allan M. Winkler, Miami University of Ohio, received a Ph.D. from Yale University. He is the author of several books, including *Life under a Cloud: American Anxiety about the Atom* (Oxford University Press, 1993) and a best-selling textbook, *The American People: Creating a Nation and Society* (with Gary B. Nash), now in its seventh edition.

Charlene Mires, Villanova University, edited revisions and additions to the current edition. She received a Ph.D. from Temple University and is the author of *Independence Hall in American Memory* (University of Pennsylvania Press, 2002).

Volume X Editor: Donald T. Critchlow, St. Louis University, received a Ph.D. from the University of California, Berkeley. He is the author of several books, including *Intended Consequences: Birth Control, Abortion, and the Federal Government in Modern America* (Oxford University Press, 1999), *Phyllis Schlafly and Grassroots Conservatism: A Woman's Crusade* (Princeton University Press, 2005), and *The Conservative Ascendancy: How the GOP Right Made Political History* (Harvard University Press, 2007).

Foreword

The Encyclopedia of American History series is designed as a handy reference to the most important individuals, events, and topics in U.S. history. In 10 volumes, the encyclopedia covers the period from the 15th century, when European explorers first made their way across the Atlantic Ocean to the Americas, to the present day. The encyclopedia is written for precollegiate as well as college students, for parents of young learners in the schools, and for the general public. The volume editors are distinguished historians of American history. In writing individual entries, each editor has drawn upon the expertise of scores of specialists. This ensures the scholarly quality of the entire series. Articles contributed by the various volume editors are uncredited.

This 11-volume encyclopedia of "American history" is broadly conceived to include the historical experience of the various peoples of North America. Thus, in the first volume, many essays treat the history of a great range of indigenous people before contact with Europeans. In the same vein, readers will find essays in the first several volumes that sketch Spanish, Dutch, and French explorers and colonizers who opened up territories for European settlement that later would become part of the United States. The venues and cast of characters in the American historical drama are thus widened beyond traditional encyclopedias.

In creating the eras of American history that define the chronological limits of each volume, and in addressing major topics in each era, the encyclopedia follows the architecture of *The National Standards for United States History, Revised Edition* (Los Angeles: National Center for History in the Schools, 1996). Mandated by the U.S. Congress, the national standards for U.S. history have been widely used by states and school districts in organizing curricular frameworks and have been followed by many other curriculum-building efforts.

Entries are cross-referenced, when appropriate, with *See also* citations at the end of articles. At the end of most entries, a listing of articles and books allows readers to turn to specialized sources and historical accounts. In each volume, an array of maps provide geographical context, while numerous illustrations help vivify the material covered in the text. A time line is included to provide students with a chronological reference to major events occurring in the given era. The selection of historical documents in the back of each volume gives students experience with the raw documents that historians use when researching history. A comprehensive index to each volume also facilitates the reader's access to particular information.

In each volume, long entries are provided for major categories of American historical experience. These categories may include: African Americans, agriculture, art and architecture, business, economy, education, family life, foreign policy, immigration, labor, Native Americans, politics, population, religion, urbanization, and women. By following these essays from volume to volume, the reader can access what might be called a mini-history of each broad topic, for example, family life, immigration, or religion.

—Gary B. Nash
University of California, Los Angeles

Foreword to the Revised Edition

"History has to be rewritten in every generation because, although the past does not change, the present does," writes Lord Christopher Hill, one of Great Britain's most eminent historians. "Each generation asks new questions of the past, and finds new areas of sympathy as it re-lives different aspects of the experiences of its predecessors." It is this understanding, that the pursuit of historical knowledge requires new research and new reflections on the past, that undergirds a revised and extended edition of the Encyclopedia of American History.

The individual volume editors of this revised edition have made important additions and revisions to the original edition published in 2003. Most important, they have added many new entries—several hundred for the entire 11-volume set. This puts more meat on the bone of what was already a comprehensive encyclopedia that presented four centuries of American history in all its diversity and complexity. For the 10th volume, covering the period from 1969 to the present, new entries cover momentous events and important figures of the last six years. For the other volumes, new entries increase the diversity of Americans covered by biographical accounts as well as events that new scholarship shows have had greater importance than recognized heretofore.

In addition, careful attention has been given to correcting occasional errors in the massive number of entries in the first edition. Also, many entries have been revised to add further details while making adjustments, based on new scholarship, to the interpretation of key events and movements. Consonant with that effort to make the encyclopedia as fresh and usable as possible, the volume editors have added many new recently published books to the "Further Reading" notes at the ends of the entries, and new full-color historical maps help put history in its geographical context.

—Gary B. Nash

Index

Boldface roman numerals denote volume number. **Boldface** page numbers denote extensive treatment of a topic. *Italic* page numbers refer to illustrations; *c* refers to the chronology; and *m* indicates a map.

A

AA (American Association) **VI**:26
AAA. *See* Agricultural Adjustment Act; Agricultural Adjustment Administration
AAAS. *See* American Association for the Advancement of Science
AABA. *See* American Anti-Boycott Association
AALL. *See* American Association for Labor Legislation
AAPA (Association against the Prohibition Amendment) **VII**:274
Aaron, Henry L. "Hank" **IX**:5; **X**:1, 330, 377*c*
AARP (American Association of Retired Persons) **X**:222
AASS. *See* American Anti-Slavery Society
Aataentsic **I**:1, 171–172
ABA (American Bar Association) **VI**:294; **X**:364
ABA (American Basketball Association) **X**:331
Abakua **I**:51
Abbas, Mahmoud **X**:56
Abbe, Cleveland **VI**:387
Abbey, Edwin Austin **VI**:183
Abbott, Grace **VII**:1, 2
    Addams, Jane **VII**:3
    Hamilton, Alice **VII**:133
    peace movements **VII**:256
    women's network **VIII**:421
Abbott and Costello **VIII**:245
ABC. *See* American Broadcasting Company
'Abd-al-'Azîz (ruler of Fez) **I**:176
Abdul Enterprises, Ltd. **X**:5
Abell, John **III**:118
Abenaki **I**:1–2
    Acadia **I**:2
    Duston, Hannah Emerson **II**:105

    Maliseet **I**:227
    New Hampshire **II**:259, 260
    Passamaquoddy **I**:287
    Vermont **II**:398
Abercromby, James **II**:167; **III**:171
Aberdeen, Lord (George Hamilton-Gordon) **IV**:287–288
Abernathy, Ralph
    Birmingham confrontation **IX**:39
    King, Martin Luther, Jr. **IX**:174
    SCLC **IX**:292
"Abide with Me" **V**:273
Abilene, Kansas **VI**:64
Abington School District v. Schempp **IX**:273, 355*c*
AbioCor artificial heart **X**:320
Ableman v. Booth **V**:443*c*
ABMs. *See* anti-ballistic missile systems
ABM Treaty. *See* Anti-Ballistic Missile Treaty
abolition/abolitionism **II**:*1*, 1–2; **III**:1–3, *25*, 25–27, 460*c*; **IV**:1–5, *2*, 412*c*–415*c*; **V**:1–4, *2*
    ACS **IV**:17
    Act Abolishing the Slave Trade in the District of Columbia **IV**:449
    African Americans **III**:8; **IV**:9–10
    American Anti-Slavery Society **IV**:15–16
    American Missionary Association **V**:8
    antislavery **III**:25, 26
    "Appeal to the Christian Women of the South" (Grimke) **IV**:430–434
    Atkinson, Edward **VI**:21
    Beecher, Henry Ward **VI**:30
    Benezet, Anthony **II**:35–36
    Brown, John **V**:43–45
    Cary, Mary Ann Shadd **V**:58

    Chase, Salmon P. **V**:62
    Civil War **V**:73, 74
    Compromise of 1850 **IV**:103, 104
    Confiscation Acts **V**:87
    Coxe, Tench **III**:125
    Crittenden Compromise **V**:98
    Dana, Charles A. **V**:102
    Democratic Party **IV**:118
    Dickinson, Anna E. **V**:111
    Douglass, Frederick **V**:115–116
    Easton, Hosea **IV**:129
    Emancipation Proclamation **V**:130–132
    Emerson, Ralph Waldo **IV**:140
    entertainment, popular **VI**:116
    Equiano, Olaudah **III**:156
    female antislavery societies **IV**:147–148
    Fifteenth Amendment **V**:141, 142
    Finney, Charles Grandison **IV**:151
    Forbes, John Murray **VI**:132
    Forten, James **III**:170
    Foster, Abigail Kelley **IV**:161–162
    Fourteenth Amendment **V**:157
    Franklin, Benjamin **III**:174
    fugitive slave laws **IV**:168
    Fuller, Margaret **IV**:169
    Garnet, Henry Highland **IV**:174
    Garrison, William Lloyd **V**:164–165
    Genius of Universal Emancipation **IV**:175
    Greeley, Horace **V**:177
    Grimké, Angelina and Sarah **IV**:180

    Hall, Prince **III**:205
    Harper, Frances Ellen Watkins **V**:184; **VI**:159–160
    Harpers Ferry, West Virginia **V**:185–186
    Harvard Regiment **V**:186
    Hicks, Elias **IV**:189
    Hicks, Thomas H. **V**:188
    Higginson, Thomas Wentworth **V**:189; **VI**:171, 172
    Howe, Julia Ward **V**:198
    Jay, John **III**:230
    Johnson, Andrew **V**:212
    Joint Committee on the Conduct of the War **V**:215
    Jones, Absalom **III**:237–238
    journalism **IV**:209
    Julian, George Washington **V**:219
    Juneteenth **V**:219
    Kelley, William D. **V**:222
    King, Rufus **III**:246
    Kościuszko, Tadeusz **III**:249
    Lay, Benjamin **II**:203
    Liberia **IV**:225
    Liberty Party **IV**:226
    literature **IV**:228
    Lovejoy, Elijah **IV**:229–230
    lyceum movement **IV**:231
    Madison, James **III**:284
    Massachusetts Emigrant Aid Society **IV**:241–243
    Methodism **III**:296–297
    Mott, Lucretia **IV**:265
    Negro Convention movement **IV**:279
    NWSA **V**:277
    Paine, Thomas **III**:329
    Paul, Nathaniel **IV**:295
    Peale, Charles Willson **III**:333

abolition/abolitionism *(continued)*
  Pennington, James William
    Charles **V:**300–301
  personal liberty laws **IV:**298
  Phillips, Wendell **IV:**299
  Pickering, Timothy **III:**335
  Port Royal Experiment
    V:311–312
  Quakers **III:**351, 352
  Quok Walker Case **III:**354–
    355
  race and race relations
    IV:311
  religion **IV:**317; **V:**331;
    VI:306
  Republican Party **IV:**322
  Seneca Falls convention
    IV:341
  slavery **III:**390, 391; **V:**362,
    363
  slave trade **III:**393
  Society of Friends **V:**364
  Stanton, Edwin M. **V:**368
  Stanton, Elizabeth Cady
    V:369
  Stevens, Thaddeus **V:**372
  Stowe, Harriet Beecher
    V:374
  Sumner, Charles **V:**376, 377
  Tappan, Arthur and Lewis
    IV:366
  temperance movement
    IV:369
  Thirteenth Amendment
    V:388
  Thoreau, Henry David
    IV:376
  Truth, Sojourner **V:**392–394
  Underground Railroad
    V:397
  Vallandigham, Clement L.
    V:413
  Van Lew, Elizabeth **V:**414
  Wade, Benjamin Franklin
    V:421
  Wade-Davis Bill **V:**421
  Weld, Theodore Dwight
    IV:395–396
  Wheatley, Phillis **III:**439
  Williams, Peter, Jr. **IV:**402
  Wilson, Henry **V:**433
  Women's National Loyal
    League **V:**434
  women's status and rights
    IV:404; **V:**436
  Wright, Fanny **IV:**405
abortion **II:**126; **X:1–5,** 2, 3*t,*
  376*c,* 379*c,* 382*c*
  *Akron v. Akron Center for
    Reproductive Health*
    X:20–21
  birth control **X:**43, 44
  birthrates **X:**44
  Brennan, William J., Jr.
    X:48
  Burger, Warren E. **X:**51
  capital punishment **X:**67

Christian Coalition **X:**73
Clinton, William J. **X:**80
conservative movement
  X:93
feminism **X:**132–134
Ford, Gerald R. **X:**139
Ginsburg, Ruth Bader
  X:152–153
Gore, Albert, Jr. **X:**157
Helms, Jesse A., Jr. **X:**165
House of Representatives
  X:171
Kennedy, Edward M. **X:**197
Libertarian Party **X:**209
marriage and family
  VIII:231
McGovern, George S. **X:**217
Moral Majority **X:**234
NOW **X:**247, 248
O'Connor, Sandra Day
  X:265
political parties **X:**276
Powell, Lewis **X:**288
pro-life/pro-choice
  movements **X:**288–289
Reagan, Ronald W. **X:**299,
  300
Rehnquist, William H.
  X:305
Roberts, John G. **X:**311
Roe v. Wade **X:**311–312,
  385–386
Scalia, Antonin **X:**316
Schlafly, Phyllis **X:**317
sexual revolution **X:**322
socialism **VI:**336
Souter, David **X:**324
Supreme Court **X:**338, 339
UN **X:**355
WEAL **IX:**345, 346
*Webster v. Reproductive
  Health Services* **X:**368–
  369
White, Byron R. **X:**369
women's status and rights
  IX:348; **X:**371
"Abortion and the Conscience of
  the Nation" (Reagan) **X:**4
Abou-Ishaq Ibrahim Es Saheli
  I:359
Abraham **I:**238
Abraham Levitt and Sons
  VIII:379
Abraham Lincoln, USS **X:**185
Abraham Lincoln: A History
  (Nicolay and Hay) **VI:**147
Abraham Lincoln Brigade
  VIII:304, 369–370
Abrams, Jacob **VII:**58
Abrams v. United States
  censorship **VIII:**65
  civil liberties **VII:**58
  Holmes, Oliver Wendell
    VII:141
  Schenck v. U.S. **VII:**313
  Sedition Act **VII:**319
  Supreme Court **VII:**343

*Abridgment of the Debates of
  Congress from 1789 to 1856*
  (Benton) **IV:**54
ABS. *See* American Bible Society
Absalom! Absalom! (Faulkner)
  V:240; **VIII:**128, 220
Abscam **X:5–6**
abstract art **VII:**25
abstract expressionism **VIII:**31
Abu Bakr **I:**140
Abu Ghraib prison **X:**188
Abwehr **VIII:**187
Abyssinian Baptist Church **VI:**4;
  IX:261
Abzug, Bella
  feminism **X:**134
  Friedan, Betty **IX:**127
  NOW **X:**247
AC. *See* alternating current
academic tests **X:**114. *See also*
  standardized testing
Acadia **I:2–3**
Acadians **II:2–3,** 437*c*
  Canada **III:**77
  Creole **II:**82
  French colonies **II:**138
  Monckton, Robert **II:**241
  Paris, Treaty of (1763)
    III:331
  Queen Anne's War **II:**324
  Seven Years' War **II:**348
Acamapitchtli **I:**18
Acapulco **I:**269, 325
accessibility issues **X:**24–25
*Account of an Expedition from
  Pittsburgh to the Rocky
  Mountains* (Long) **IV:**145
Account of Denmark (Molesworth)
  III:103
Account of Slaves, Servants, and
  Witches (Moraley) **II:**443–444
Account of the Puritan-Pequot
  War (Mason) **II:**439–440
Acheson, Dean **IX:**1, 1–2, 352*c*
  Asia **IX:**21
  Hiss, Alger **IX:**147
  Korean War **IX:**177
  military-industrial complex
    IX:216
  NATO **IX:**247
  NSC-68 **IX:**247
  White Paper **IX:**343
Acheson-Lilienthal report
  VIII:217
Achille Lauro (ship)
  foreign policy **X:**142
  North, Oliver L. **X:**258
  terrorism **X:**345
acid rain **X:**232
ACLU. *See* American Civil
  Liberties Union
Ácoma pueblo
  art and architecture **I:**13
  New Mexico **I:**266; **II:**263
  Oñate, Juan de **I:**279
  Pueblo **I:**305; **II:**317
Acosta, Jorge **I:**364

Acosta, José de **I:3,** 215
acquired immune deficiency
  syndrome (AIDS) **X:6–7,** 378*c*
  Africa **X:**17
  African Americans **X:**13
  Bush, George W. **X:**56
  disease/epidemics **I:**108
  gay and lesbian rights
    movement **X:**149
  sexual revolution **X:**323
ACS. *See* American Colonization
  Society
Act Abolishing the Slave Trade
  in the District of Columbia
  IV:449
Act Against Papists (England)
  I:121
Act Concerning Religion
  (Maryland) **II:**151, 335
"Act for Establishing Religious
  Freedom" (Jefferson) **III:**282
Act for More Effectual Suppression
  of Piracy (England) **II:**296
Act in Restraint of Appeals
  (England) **I:**75
ACTION agency **IX:**333
Act of Interposition (Arkansas)
  IX:118
Act of Supremacy (1534) **II:**21
Act of Supremacy and Uniformity
  (1559)
  Church of England **I:**75
  Elizabeth I **I:**120
  Reformation **I:**317
Act of the Six Articles (England)
  I:75
Actor's Lab **IX:**222
Acts of Trade and Navigation
  II:3–4, 436*c*
  British Empire **II:**48
  mercantilism **II:**231
  monarchy, British **II:**240
  Randolph, Edward **II:**326
  rum trade **II:**338
  smuggling **II:**364
  Vice-Admiralty Courts
    III:424
Act to Combat International
  Terrorism (1984) **X:**345–346
ACTU (Association of Catholic
  Trade Unionists) **VIII:**22
Acuff, Roy, and His Smoky
  Mountain Boys **VIII:**250
ACW. *See* Amalgamated Clothing
  Workers of America
ADA. *See* Americans for
  Democratic Action; Americans
  with Disabilities Act
Adair, James **II:**4
Adal sultanate
  Dengel, Lebna **I:**105
  Djibouti **I:**109
  Ethiopia **I:**124–125
Adams, Abigail **II:**118; **III:3–4**
  Adams, John **III:**4
  Jefferson, Thomas **III:**233,
    234

Tyler, Royall **III**:417
Warren, Mercy Otis **III**:427
Washington, George
III:429
Adams, Ansel **VII**:258; **VIII**:30
Adams, Brock **X**:321
Adams, Charles Francis
Bulloch, James D. **V**:49
Liberal Republican Party
VI:222
Seward, William H. **V**:347
Adams, Hannah **III**:4
Adams, Henry **VI**:1–2
Brooks, Phillips **VI**:50
Exodusters **VI**:123
King, Clarence **VI**:208
La Farge, John Frederick
Lewis Joseph **VI**:217,
218
literature **VI**:225
Saint-Gaudens, Augustus
VI:321
Victorianism **VI**:374
Adams, Herbert **VI**:327
Adams, John **III**:4–7, 5, 460c–
464c
Adams, Abigail **III**:3
Adams, Samuel **III**:8
Alien and Sedition Acts
III:14
art **III**:33
Attucks, Crispus **III**:38
Bache, Benjamin Franklin
III:39
Barbary Wars **III**:45
Boston Massacre **III**:58
Callender, James T. **III**:74
Common Sense **III**:103
constitutions, state **III**:110
Continental Congress, First
III:113
Continental Congress,
Second **III**:115
Continental navy **III**:117
Conway Cabal, the **III**:118
Declaration of
Independence **III**:133
Democratic Party **IV**:116–
117
Duane, James **III**:140
education **III**:148
election of 1800 **III**:149,
150
Enlightenment, American
II:118
Federalist Party **III**:164
foreign affairs **III**:168
Franklin, Benjamin **III**:174
Fries's Rebellion **III**:180,
181
Gerry, Elbridge **III**:194
Haiti **III**:203
Hamilton, Alexander
III:207, 208
Harrison, William Henry
IV:184
Jay, John **III**:229

Jefferson, Thomas **III**:232–
235
Judiciary Act (1801) **III**:242
Loyal Nine **III**:276
Lyon, Matthew **III**:277
Marbury v. Madison
III:285
Marshall, John **III**:290
Paris, Treaty of (1783)
III:331, 332
Pickering, Timothy **III**:335
Quasi War **III**:353
Quincy, Josiah **III**:354
religion **III**:360
Rodney, Caesar **III**:373
suffrage **III**:401
Taylor, John, of Caroline
III:408
U.S. Military Academy at
West Point **V**:409
Virginia dynasty **III**:425
Warren, Joseph **III**:427
Warren, Mercy Otis **III**:427,
428
Washington, D.C. **III**:428
Washington, George **III**:431
wolves **II**:422
writs of assistance **III**:448,
449
XYZ affair **III**:451
Adams, John Quincy **IV**:5–6,
411c, 412c
abolitionism **IV**:4
Adams, Abigail **III**:4
Adams, John **III**:6
Adams-Onís Treaty **IV**:6
American Anti-Slavery
Society **IV**:15
American System **IV**:20
Amistad incident **IV**:22
Calhoun, John C. **IV**:69
Clay, Henry **IV**:96, 97
Cuba **IV**:111
Democratic Party **IV**:117,
118
election of 1828 **IV**:135
election of 1840 **IV**:139
elections, presidential **X**:117
Era of Good Feelings
IV:141
Florida **III**:167
foreign affairs **III**:169
foreign policy **IV**:154
Harrison, William Henry
IV:185
Jackson, Andrew **IV**:206, 207
King, Rufus **III**:246
Monroe Doctrine **IV**:259,
260
political parties **III**:339
Polk, James K. **IV**:301
Tappan, Arthur and Lewis
IV:367
Tyler, John **IV**:383
Van Buren, Martin **IV**:385
Whigs **IV**:396
Adams, New York **IV**:150

Adams, Samuel (1722–1803)
III:7–8, 460c
alcohol **III**:13
Ames, Fisher **III**:19
anti-Federalists **III**:24
Boston Massacre **III**:58
Boston Tea Party **III**:59
Cincinnati, Order of **III**:90
committees of
correspondence **III**:101
Constitution, ratification of
the **III**:105
Continental Congress, First
III:113
Continental Congress,
Second **III**:115
Conway Cabal, the **III**:118
Gerry, Elbridge **III**:194
Hancock, John **III**:208
King George's War **II**:192
Lee, Arthur **III**:258
Lexington and Concord,
Battles of **III**:264, 266
Loyal Nine **III**:276
Old South Church **III**:323,
324
Suffolk Resolves **III**:400
Warren, Joseph **III**:427
Adams, Samuel Hopkins (1871–
1958) **VII**:198
Adams Memorial (Saint-Gaudens)
VI:321
Adamson Act **VII**:1–2
AFL **VII**:12
Democratic Party **VII**:74
elections **VII**:91
lobbying **VII**:181
muckrakers **VII**:217
New Freedom **VII**:236
Railroad Administration
VII:291
Wilson, Thomas Woodrow
VII:383, 384
Adams-Onís Treaty **IV**:6, 411c,
422–423
Adams, John Quincy **IV**:5
Austin, Moses **IV**:39
Florida **III**:167; **IV**:152
foreign affairs **III**:169
foreign policy **IV**:154
Native Americans **IV**:274
Oregon Treaty of 1846
IV:286
Seminole **IV**:338
Seminole War, First/Second
IV:339
Texas **IV**:371
Adarand Constructors Inc. v. Pena
X:159, 305
Adawiyya, Rabi' a al- **I**:348
ADC. *See* Aid to Dependent
Children
ADD. *See* Attention Deficit
Disorder
Addams, Jane **VI**:410c; **VII**:2–3,
406c
Atkinson, Edward **VI**:22

criminal justice **VII**:66–67
Hamilton, Alice **VII**:133
immigration **VI**:186
Kelley, Florence **VII**:164
NAACP **VII**:224
New Woman **VII**:240
NWTUL **VII**:230
peace movements **VII**:256
progressivism **VI**:294
religion **VII**:297
settlement houses **VI**:327
social work **VII**:329
"Why Women Should Vote"
VII:420–424
WILPF **VII**:386
women's status and rights
VII:389
Addis Ababa, Ethiopia **VIII**:118
*Address to the People of Great
Britain* (Jay) **III**:229
"Address to the Slaves of the
United States of America"
(Garnet) **IV**:174
adelantado **I**:3–4
Columbus, Bartholomew
I:83
Ojeda, Alonso de **I**:277
Ponce de León, Juan **I**:296
Adelphia Communications **X**:59
Adena **I**:253
ADHD (Attention Deficit and
Hyperactivity Disorder) **X**:223
Adirondack Forest Preserve **VI**:81
Adirondack Mountains **IV**:28
Adja kingdom **I**:132
adjustable rate mortgages (ARMs)
X:60
Adkins v. Children's Hospital
VII:3–4, 100, 343, 408c
Adler, Dankmar **VI**:347
Adler, Felix **VI**:120, 205, 408c
Administration of Justice Act
III:100, 460c
Admission Act (1959) **IX**:143
admissions policies
affirmative action **X**:10
Bakke case **X**:40–41
*Gratz v. Bollinger/Grutter v.
Bollinger* **X**:158–159
adobe **I**:12, 327
Adobe Walls, Battle of **IV**:82
*Adolescence, Its Psychology and
Its Relation to Physiology,
Anthropology, Sociology, Sex,
Crime, Religion and Education*
(Hall) **VI**:158
Adolf of Nassau (archbishop of
Mainz) **I**:148
Adorno, Rolena **I**:40, 147
Adrian, Robert **III**:384
Adrian VI of Utrecht (pope) **I**:205
Adriatic Sea **I**:374
adultery **II**:425–426
adulthood **I**:20–21
Adult Literacy and Lifeskills
Survey (2003) **X**:210

Advanced Research Projects Agency (ARPA) **X:**181
Adventism **IV:**319–320; **VI:**69, 307
Adventures of Dolly, The (film) **VII:**131, 215
Adventures of Huckleberry Finn, The (Twain) **VI:**409c
  cotton culture **IV:**108
  literature **V:**240; **VI:**226
  Twain, Mark **VI:**367–368
Adventures of Tom Sawyer, The (Twain) **V:**240; **VI:**367
advertising **VI:**2, 2–3; **VII:**4, 4–5; **VIII:**1–2; **IX:**2, 2–3, 354c, 357c; **X:**7–9, 8, 376c
  art **VII:**24
  business **VII:**46; **VIII:**58; **IX:**47
  chain stores **VI:**65
  childhood **IX:**55
  children **VII:**400
  cosmetics and beauty industry **VII:**65
  credit cards **IX:**79
  economy **IX:**97
  elections **IX:**103
  FCC **VIII:**131
  Food, Drug, and Cosmetic Act **VIII:**140
  GM **IX:**133
  illustration, photography, and graphic arts **VI:**183
  journalism **VII:**158–159
  Life magazine **VIII:**217
  literature **IX:**194
  McDonald's **IX:**208
  McPherson, Aimee Semple **VII:**196–197
  media **X:**217, 219
  miracle drugs **IX:**218
  newspapers **VI:**265, 266
  Packard, Vance **IX:**253
  popular culture **VIII:**301
  postwar planning **VIII:**306
  POUR **VIII:**310
  public opinion polls **VIII:**312
  radio **VII:**289, 290
  service sector **IX:**289
  sexuality **VII:**322
  shopping centers **IX:**289
  sports and recreation **VII:**335; **X:**332
  suburbanization/suburbs **VIII:**379
  teenagers **IX:**314
  television **IX:**315
  tobacco suits **X:**351, 352
  trade, domestic and foreign **VII:**354
  U.S. Shipping Board **VII:**360
  Wanamaker, John **VI:**382
  war bonds **VIII:**412
  World War II home front **VIII:**434
  yellow journalism **VI:**405

Advertising Council
  advertising **VIII:**1–2
  commemoration **IX:**66
  Freedom Train **IX:**125
advice and consent **III:**107
"Advice to My Country" (Madison) **III:**284
Advisory Committee on Uranium **IX:**250
AEC. *See* Atomic Energy Commission
Aëdes aegypti **II:**431
AEF. *See* American Expeditionary Force
Aegyptopithecus **IX:**286
AEI (American Enterprise Institute) **X:**349
AERA. *See* American Equal Rights Association
Aeronautics, Bureau of **VIII:**201, 202
Aesthetic movement **VI:**3, 19, 313
AFDC (Aid to Families with Dependent Children) **X:**128
affirmative action **X:**9–10, 376c, 381c
  African Americans **X:**13
  Bakke case **X:**40–41
  Brennan, William J., Jr. **X:**48
  Byrd, Robert **X:**61
  Civil Rights Act (1991) **X:**77
  education, higher **X:**112
  feminism **X:**134
  Gore, Albert, Jr. **X:**157
  Gratz v. Bollinger/Grutter v. Bollinger **X:**158–159
  liberalism **X:**208
  militia movement **X:**231
  NAACP **X:**245
  Powell, Lewis **X:**288
  race and race relations **X:**297
  Rehnquist, William H. **X:**305
"affluent society" **IX:**98
Affluent Society, The (Galbraith) **IX:**129, 354c
Afghanistan, Soviet invasion of (1979) **X:**378c
  Carter, James Earl, Jr. **X:**69
  cold war, end of **X:**85, 86
  defense policy **X:**100
  détente **X:**104
  foreign policy **X:**141
  Middle East **X:**228–229
Afghanistan War (2001–) **X:**10–13, *11*
  Africa **X:**16
  Bush, George W. **X:**55–56
  defense policy **X:**103
  economy **X:**110
  elections, presidential **X:**118
  foreign policy **X:**143
  Powell, Colin L. **X:**287
  Reagan, Ronald W. **X:**301
  Rice, Condoleezza **X:**309

Rumsfeld, Donald **X:**313
  Senate, U.S. **X:**322
  terrorism **X:**346, 347
  UN **X:**356
AFL. *See* American Federation of Labor; American Football League
AFL-CIO. *See* American Federation of Labor-Congress of Industrial Organizations
Afognak Forest and Fish-Culture Reserve **VI:**82
Afonso V (king of Portugal) **I:**148
Africa **II:**4–5; **IX:**3–4, 354c; **X:**15–17. *See also* colonization; *specific countries, e.g.:* Liberia
  African Americans **II:**5
  Akan **I:**5
  Amistad incident **IV:**21, 22
  art and architecture **I:**12
  Asante **I:**13–14
  Azores **I:**17
  blues **VII:**39
  Bunche, Ralph **IX:**45
  Cadamosto, Alvise de **I:**49
  Canary Islands **I:**56–57
  casta paintings **I:**64
  castas **I:**65
  cold war **IX:**63
  cold war, end of **X:**85
  Columbian Exchange **I:**81
  Dias, Bartholomeu **I:**105–106
  Dutch West India Company **II:**107
  Fernando Póo **I:**129
  foreign policy **VI:**133, 134
  Fulani **I:**135
  Gao **I:**137–138
  Garvey, Marcus **VII:**121
  Gedi **I:**138
  Ghana **I:**139–140
  gold **I:**141
  Gold Coast **I:**143
  Gomes, Diogo **I:**143
  Gonja **I:**143
  Gorée Island **I:**144
  Guinea-Bissau **I:**148
  horses **I:**169
  Ibn Khaldûn, 'Abd-ar-Rahmân Abû Zayd ibn Muhammad ibn Muhammad **I:**176
  invention and technology **I:**184
  Islam **I:**189
  Kotoko **I:**200–201
  Leo Africanus **I:**210–211
  Luba **I:**217
  Luhya **I:**217
  Mali **I:**225–226
  mestizaje **I:**241
  Muslims **II:**247–248
  New Spain **I:**269
  Niger River **I:**271
  Peace Corps **IX:**255
  plague **I:**294

Point Four Program **IX:**257
  population trends **I:**298
  Príncipe **I:**302
  Ramusio, Giovanni Battista **I:**313
  religion, African-American **II:**328
  Sahara **I:**323–324
  salt trade **I:**324–325
  São Tomé **I:**328
  slavery **I:**336–338; **II:**355–356
  slave trade **I:**339–340; **II:**358–360
  smallpox **I:**340, 341
  Songhai **I:**341–342
  Soviet Union **IX:**295
  Téké **I:**353
  Timbuktu **I:**359–360
  Tuareg **I:**370
  UN **X:**355
  wars of national liberation **IX:**338, 339
  Williams, George Washington **VI:**396
  witches/witchcraft **I:**385
  yellow fever **II:**431
  Yoruba **I:**389
  zambo **I:**391–392
Africa, Horn of **I:**109, 124
African Affairs, Bureau of (U.S. State Department) **IX:**3, 354c
African-American churches, growth of **VI:**3–5, 7, 306
African-American Church of God **VII:**298
African-American musical theater **VI:**257
African-American regiments **V:**4–5
  Cary, Mary Ann Shadd **V:**58
  Corps d'Afrique **V:**96
  Douglass, Frederick **V:**116
  54th Massachusetts Regiment **V:**142–144
  Taylor, Susie King **V:**385
  Truth, Sojourner **V:**393
  volunteer army **V:**419
African Americans **I:**299; **II:**5–8, 6, 438c; **III:**8–10, 462c, 464c, 465c; **IV:**6–10, 7, 9m, 415c; **V:**445c, 446c; **VI:**5–8, 6, 407c, 409c, 412c; **VII:**403c, 404c, 406c, 408c, 409c; **VIII:**2, 2–5, 4, 443c–449c; **IX:**4–6, 6, 351c, 354c, 355c, 357c; **X:**13–15, 377c, 379c–381c, 383c, 384c
  Aaron, Henry L. "Hank" **X:**1
  abolitionism **II:**1, 2; **III:**1, 2; **IV:**1–4; **V:**1–4
  abortion **X:**3
  ACS **IV:**16–17
  AFL **VI:**13
  African-American churches, growth of **VI:**3–5
  African Methodist Episcopal Church **V:**5

agriculture **IV:**11; **VII:**7
AIDS **X:**7
aircraft industry **VIII:**15
alcohol **III:**13
Alice **II:**19
Allen, Richard **III:**15–16
American Anti-Slavery
  Society **IV:**15–16
American Missionary
  Association **V:**8
American Revolution **III:**19
Amistad incident **IV:**21–22
amnesty, acts of **V:**9
Angelou, Maya **X:**25–26
Anglican Church **II:**21
antilynching legislation
  VIII:22
antislavery **III:**25–27
Army, U.S. **VIII:**26
art and architecture **III:**27;
  IV:29; **VII:**24–25;
  VIII:30; **X:**31
assassination of Abraham
  Lincoln **V:**21
assassinations **IX:**22
"Atlanta Compromise"
  Speech (Washington)
  VI:432–433
Attucks, Crispus **III:**37–38
automobile industry
  VIII:37
Baker, Ella Josephine
  IX:32–33
Baldwin, James **IX:**34–35
banks **III:**42
Banneker, Benjamin
  III:43–44
Baptists **II:**33
baseball **VII:**33, 34
Bates, Edward **V:**31
Beckwourth, Jim **IV:**50
Benezet, Anthony **II:**35
Bethune, Mary McLeod
  VIII:43–44
bicycling **VI:**35–36
big bands **VIII:**44
birthrates **X:**44–45
Black Cabinet **VIII:**45–46
Black Codes **V:**34–35
Black Panthers **IX:**40–41
Black Power **IX:**41–42
Blair, Francis Preston, Jr.
  V:36
Boas, Franz Uri **VII:**40
Bridges, Harry **VIII:**53
Brotherhood of Sleeping Car
  Porters **VIII:**54
Brown, John **V:**44, 45
Brown, William Wells **V:**46
Brownsville Riot **VII:**42
*Brown v. Board of
  Education* **IX:**43–44
Bruce, Blanche Kelso
  V:46–47
Buffalo Soldiers **VI:**54
Burger, Warren E. **X:**51
Burns, Anthony **IV:**65–66

Butler, Benjamin Franklin
  V:53
Byrnes, James F. **VIII:**60
camp followers **III:**77
Canada **III:**77, 78
Carmichael, Stokely
  IX:49–50
Carney, William Harvey **V:**55
carpetbaggers **V:**56
Carver, George Washington
  VI:63
Cary, Mary Ann Shadd **V:**58
Catholics **VIII:**64
Catto, Octavius V. **V:**58–59
CCC **VIII:**71
Charleston **II:**64
childhood **II:**67
CIO **VIII:**82
cities and urban life **III:**91–
  92; **VII:**54, 55; **VIII:**70;
  IX:56
citizenship **III:**92, 95;
  VII:57
civil rights **VIII:**72–73
Civil Rights Act (1866) **V:**70
Civil Rights Act (1875) **V:**71
Civil Rights Act (1957)
  IX:59
Civil Rights Act (1960)
  IX:59, 60
Civil Rights Cases **VI:**72
Civil War **V:**75
Civil War centennial **IX:**62
Clark, William **III:**97
class consciousness **VI:**73
cold war, end of **X:**84
Colored National Labor
  Union **V:**77
Communist Party **VII:**61
Communists **VIII:**77–78
conservative coalition
  VIII:86
Constitution, United States
  III:106
consumerism **IX:**76
corruption, political **VI:**83
cosmetics and beauty
  industry **VII:**66
cotton **III:**122
Coxe, Tench **III:**125
crime and punishment **X:**97
Crummell, Alexander
  VI:86–87
Cuffe, Paul **III:**127–128
dance **II:**90
Dartmoor Prison **IV:**113
Davis Bend, Mississippi,
  freedmen's colony
  V:106–107
Delany, Martin Robinson
  V:107–108
Democratic Party **V:**109,
  110; **VIII:**92, 93
disease/epidemics **II:**97, 98,
  100; **III:**138
Douglass, Frederick
  V:115–116

Dred Scott decision **V:**116–
  118
DuBois, W.E.B. **VII:**80–81
due process clause **VI:**101
Dunbar, Paul Laurence
  VI:101–102
Dunmore, John Murray, earl
  of **III:**142
Eastman, George **VI:**105
economy **IV:**129
education **II:**112; **IV:**135;
  V:124–125; **VI:**108;
  VIII:106; **IX:**100
education, federal aid to
  VI:110
education, higher **VI:**111
Eisenhower, Dwight D.
  IX:101
election of 1932 **VIII:**109
election of 1936 **VIII:**110
elections **IX:**103
elections, conduct of **VI:**113
elections, presidential
  X:118
Ellington, Duke **VIII:**111–
  112
Elliot, Robert Brown **V:**127
emancipation **V:**127–130
Emerson, Ralph Waldo
  IV:139
employment **V:**133
enemy aliens **VIII:**114–115
Enlightenment, American
  II:118–119
entertainment, popular
  VI:116, 117; **VII:**96
Equiano, Olaudah **III:**156–
  157
ethnocentrism **II:**121–122
Executive Order 8802
  VIII:120, 465–466
Exodusters **VI:**122–123
exploration **IV:**145
Fair Deal **IX:**115
Fair Labor Standards Act
  VIII:124
family life **X:**127
Farmer, James L. **X:**128–
  129
Farrakhan, Louis A. **X:**129
female antislavery societies
  IV:147
FEPC **VIII:**123–124
fertility **II:**125–126
Field, Stephen Johnson
  VI:127
FMP **VIII:**134
Forbes, John Murray
  VI:132
Forrest, Nathan Bedford
  V:152
Forten, James **III:**169–170
Fort Mose **II:**132
Fort Pillow **V:**153, 154
Foster, Stephen C. **V:**156
Fourteenth Amendment
  V:156, 157

Freedmen's Bureau **V:**159–
  161
Freedmen's Savings Bank
  V:159
Freedom Train **IX:**125
Freeman, Elizabeth **III:**176
FSA **VIII:**127
fugitive slave laws **IV:**168
Gabriel's Rebellion **III:**185–
  186
Garnet, Henry Highland
  IV:174
Garvey, Marcus **VII:**121
gender **II:**145
Georgia Expedition **III:**193
Grant, Ulysses S. **V:**175, 176
Great Awakening **II:**156
Great Depression **VIII:**159
Great Migration **VII:**127–
  129
*Griggs v. Duke Power
  Company* **X:**160
Grimké, Charlotte Forten
  V:178–179
Gullah **II:**158–159
Haiti **III:**204
Hall, Prince **III:**205
Hamer, Fannie Lou **IX:**141–
  142
Hancock, Winfield Scott
  V:184
Harlem Renaissance
  VII:135–136
Harper, Frances Ellen
  Watkins **V:**184; **VI:**159–
  160
Harpers Ferry, West Virginia
  V:185, 186
Harrington, Michael **IX:**142
Hayes, Rutherford B.
  VI:167
*Heart of Atlanta Motel v.
  U.S.* **IX:**145–146
Helms, Jesse A., Jr. **X:**165
Hemings, Sally **III:**210–211
Hicks, Elias **IV:**189
Higginson, Thomas
  Wentworth **V:**189
Hill, Anita Faye **X:**165–166
Holiday, Billie **VIII:**169
homefront **V:**193
Horton, Willie **X:**168–169
Howard, Oliver Otis **V:**197
Hull, Agrippa **III:**216–217
Hurricane Katrina **X:**174
Hurston, Zora Neale
  VIII:180–181
indentured servitude **II:**175
invention and technology
  VII:149
Irish Americans **VIII:**188
Islam **X:**189
Jackson, Jesse, L. **X:**191–
  192
jazz **VII:**153; **VIII:**194
Jefferson, Thomas **III:**232
Jim Crow laws **VI:**203–204

African Americans (*continued*)
Johnson, Andrew **V:**212, 213
Johnson, Anthony **II:**186
Johnson, Jack **VII:**154–156
Jones, Absalom **III:**237–238
Joplin, Scott **VII:**158
journalism **IX:**166
Juneteenth **V:**219
Kennedy, John F. **IX:**170
KKK **IX:**179
Knights of Labor **VI:**209
Ku Klux Klan **V:**223;
    VII:165
Ku Klux Klan Act **V:**225
labor/labor movements
    III:252; **VI:**7; **VIII:**205,
    207; **IX:**182
labor trends **VI:**217
land **II:**202
Langston, John Mercer
    VI:218–219
lead mines **IV:**223
Levitt, William J. **IX:**189
Lewis, John **IX:**190–191
liberalism **VIII:**214, 216;
    IX:191
Liberia **IV:**225; **VI:**223–224
Libertarian Party **X:**209
Liberty Party **IV:**226
literature **II:**206; **IV:**227,
    228; **V:**239–240; **VI:**225;
    VII:180–181; **VIII:**218,
    219; **IX:**193, 194; **X:**210
lobbying **VII:**182
Locke, Alain LeRoy
    VII:183
lost cause, the **V:**245
Louis, Joe **VIII:**223–224
Louisiana **II:**210–211
Lovejoy, Elijah **IV:**230
LWV **IX:**187
lynching **VI:**229–231
malaria **II:**213–214
Mann Act **VII:**189–190
March on Washington
    Movement **VIII:**227–228
mariners **II:**215
Marines, U.S. **VIII:**230
marriage and family **II:**218–
    219; **III:**288–289; **IV:**239;
    VIII:230, 231; **IX:**202
Mason-Dixon Line **V:**250
Medal of Honor **V:**255
medicine **III:**296; **VII:**200;
    VIII:236
Memphis riot (1866)
    V:259–260
Methodism **III:**296, 297
Middletown **VII:**206
midwives **II:**234
migration **VII:**207;
    VIII:239, 240; **IX:**215
miscegenation **II:**237; **V:**261
modernism **VII:**212
Moravians **III:**302
Morrill Land-Grant Act
    V:269

mortality **II:**244
movie industry **VII:**215
movies **X:**236
Muhammad, Elijah **IX:**226–
    227
Murray, Pauli **IX:**227–228
music **III:**308, 309; **IV:**269;
    V:274; **VI:**255–258;
    VII:218, 219; **VIII:**249–
    252; **X:**238
Myrdal, Gunnar **VIII:**252–
    253
NAACP **VII:**224; **VIII:**255–
    256; **IX:**232; **X:**244–245
NACW **VI:**259–260;
    VII:225
National Origins Act
    VII:227
Nation of Islam **X:**249–250
Native Americans **IV:**274
nativism **VII:**234
Navy, U.S. **VIII:**265
Negro Convention
    movement **IV:**279
Negro Plot of 1741 **II:**255
New Deal **VIII:**270
New Netherland **II:**266
New Orleans riot **V:**282
Newport **II:**267
news media **VIII:**271
newspapers **VI:**266
New York City draft riots
    V:284
Niagara Movement **VII:**240
Niagara Movement
    Declaration of Principles
    VII:415–417
NYA **VIII:**263
Obama, Barack Hussein
    X:263–264
Operation Dixie **IX:**249
Osceola **IV:**289
Owens, Jesse **VIII:**288–289
OWI **VIII:**286
Parks, Rosa **IX:**254–255
Paul, Alice **VII:**254
Paul, Nathaniel **IV:**295
Payne, Francis **II:**282–283
PCSW **IX:**262
Pennington, James William
    Charles **X:**300–301
People's Party **VI:**282
Phillips, Wendell **IV:**299
photography **VIII:**296
Pinchback, P. B. S. **V:**307
Pinchot, Gifford **VII:**260
Plessy v. Ferguson **VI:**284–
    285, **433–438**
politics (Roosevelt era)
    VIII:298, 299
popular culture **VII:**265;
    IX:258; **X:**280
population trends **II:**303;
    III:342, 343; **VI:**286;
    VII:266; **VIII:**305; **X:**282
Port Huron Statement
    IX:260

poverty **X:**285, 286
Powell, Adam Clayton
    IX:261
Powell, Colin L. **X:**286–288
POWs **VIII:**311
Prince, Lucy Terry **II:**311
prisons **V:**314–315
race and race relations
    II:325–326; **III:**357–358;
    IV:310–312; **V:**319–320;
    VII:282, 283; **VIII:**317–
    319; **IX:**269–271;
    X:295–298
radicalism **VII:**286–287
Radical Republicans
    V:320–321
radio **VII:**289, 290
railroads **V:**322
Rainey, Joseph H. **V:**322–
    323
Randolph, A. Philip
    VIII:321
Rapier, James T. **V:**323
Ray, Charlotte **V:**323–324
Reconstruction **V:**326
Reconstruction Acts **V:**327,
    328
recreation **VIII:**328
redemption **V:**328, 329
Red Scare **VII:**296
refugees **V:**330
relief **VIII:**333
religion **II:**327–328;
    III:361; **IV:**317–318, 321;
    V:331–332; **VIII:**335;
    IX:272, 273
Revels, Hiram R. **V:**335
Rhinelander case **VII:**301
Rhode Island **II:**333
Rhodes, James Ford **VI:**312
Rice, Condoleezza **X:**309–
    310
Rickey, Branch **IX:**277
Robeson, Paul **VIII:**341–
    342
Robinson, Jackie **IX:**277–
    278
rock and roll **IX:**278
Roosevelt, Eleanor
    VIII:343
Roosevelt, Franklin D.
    VIII:345, 346
Rosie the Riveter **VIII:**347
rural areas **VIII:**348
rural life **III:**375
Savannah **II:**343
SCLC **IX:**292–294
Scottsboro Boys **VIII:**353–
    354
Second Great Awakening
    IV:337
segregation **VII:**319–321;
    IX:287–288
Selective Service **VIII:**358
Seminole **IV:**338
Seminole War, First/Second
    IV:339

sharecropping **V:**349
Sherman, William T. **V:**356
Sherman's March through
    Georgia **V:**357
shipbuilding **VIII:**359
Singleton, Benjamin
    V:361–362
slave codes **II:**352
slavery **III:**390–392; **IV:**345;
    V:362–364
slave trade **III:**393
Smith, Venture **II:**363–364
SNCC **IX:**302–303
Social Security Act
    VIII:364
South **VIII:**366, 367
South Carolina **II:**369–370
southern demagogues
    VII:332
Special Field Order No. 15
    V:365–366
SPG **II:**368
sports and recreation
    VII:333; **VIII:**371, 372;
    IX:298–299; **X:**331–332
States' Rights Party **IX:**299
STFU **VIII:**368
Stimson, Henry L. **VIII:**375
Stowe, Harriet Beecher
    V:373–374
suburbanization/suburbs
    VIII:380; **IX:**305–306
suffrage **II:**380; **III:**401
Supreme Court **IV:**362;
    VIII:381, 383
Sweet trial **VII:**344–345
Taney, Roger B. **IV:**366
Tanner, Benjamin Tucker
    VI:351–352
Tarbell, Ida Minerva
    VII:349
Taylor, Susie King **V:**384–
    385
teenagers **IX:**314, 315
Terrell, Mary Eliza Church
    VII:352
Thomas, Clarence **X:**350
Till, Emmett Louis **IX:**318
Tin Pan Alley **VII:**353
Trotter, William Monroe
    VII:357
Truth, Sojourner **V:**392–394
Tubman, Harriet **V:**394–395
Turner, Henry McNeal
    VI:366
Underground Railroad
    V:397–398
unemployment **VIII:**399
UNIA **VII:**361
Union League **V:**404
Union navy **V:**405
Urban League **IX:**325–326
U.S. Naval Academy at
    Annapolis **V:**410
U.S. v. Cruikshank **V:**411–
    412
veterans **IX:**329

Vietnam War **IX:**331
violence and lawlessness **VI:**375
Virginia **II:**402
Voting Rights Act of 1965 **IX:**333–334
WAC **VIII:**420
Wagner, Robert F. **VIII:**410
Walker, David **IV:**389
Wallace, George C. **X:**364
War on Poverty **IX:**335
Warren, Earl **IX:**337
Warren Court **IX:**338
Washington, Booker T. **VI:**383–384
WASP **VIII:**419
Watterson, Henry **VI:**386
Watts uprising **IX:**339–340
WAVES **VIII:**418
Welles, Orson **VIII:**414
Wells-Barnett, Ida Bell **VI:**387–388
Wheatley, Phillis **III:**438–439
White, Walter **VIII:**416
Wilkins, Roy **IX:**344–345
Williams, Fannie Barrier **VI:**394–395
Williams, George Washington **VI:**395–396
Williams, Peter, Jr. **IV:**402
woman suffrage **VII:**384
Women's National Loyal League **V:**434, 435
women's status and rights **II:**423, 426; **III:**446–448; **IV:**402; **V:**436, 437; **VII:**389; **VIII:**423, 424; **IX:**348; **X:**370
World's Columbian Exposition **VI:**403
World War II **VIII:**427–429
World War II home front **VIII:**432, 433
WPA **VIII:**425
Wright, Richard **VIII:**437
Young, Brigham **IV:**408
zoot-suiters **VIII:**441, 442
African-American soldiers, Union. *See also* African-American regiments
    Butler, Benjamin Franklin **V:**53
    emancipation **V:**129
    Milliken's Bend, Battle of **V:**260
    Petersburg campaign **V:**302
    Pinchback, P. B. S. **V:**307
    prisons **V:**314
    Union army **V:**403
African-American suffrage **V:**445c, 446c; **V:**407c, 411c
    African Americans **VI:**5
    African Methodist Episcopal Church **V:**5
    Bowles, Samuel **VI:**43
    Catto, Octavius V. **V:**59

Douglass, Frederick **V:**116
    elections **V:**125
    Enforcement Acts **V:**133
    Fifteenth Amendment **V:**141–142
    Fourteenth Amendment **V:**156, 157
    Freedmen's Bureau **V:**161
    grandfather clause **VI:**152
    Harper, Frances Ellen Watkins **VI:**160
    impeachment of Andrew Johnson **V:**202
    Johnson, Andrew **V:**212, 213
    Julian, George Washington **V:**219
    Kelley, William D. **V:**222
    NAACP **VII:**224
    race and race relations **VII:**282
    Reconstruction **V:**325, 326
    Reconstruction Acts **V:**328
    Schurz, Carl **VI:**324
    Stone, Lucy **VI:**346
    Tillman, Benjamin Ryan **VI:**358
    Tubman, Harriet **V:**394–395
    U.S. v. Cruikshank **V:**411–412
African Dorcas Association **IV:**402
African Free School **IV:**174; **VI:**86
African Intelligencer, The **IV:**225
African Lodge No. 459 **IV:**389
African Masonic Lodge **III:**205
African Meeting House **VI:**4
African Methodist Church **IV:**388
African Methodist Episcopal (AME) Church **II:**156; **V:**5
    ACS **IV:**17
    African-American churches, growth of **VI:**4–5
    African Americans **III:**9; **VI:**7; **X:**14
    Allen, Richard **III:**15
    Liberia **VI:**223
    Methodism **III:**297
    Negro Convention movement **IV:**279
    religion **IV:**318
    slavery **IV:**347
    Tanner, Benjamin Tucker **VI:**351, 352
    Tubman, Harriet **V:**395
    Turner, Henry McNeal **VI:**366, 367
    Walker, David **IV:**389
African Methodist Episcopal Zion (AMEZ) Church
    African-American churches, growth of **VI:**5
    African Americans **VI:**7
    religion **IV:**318
African National Congress (ANC) **X:**16, 325
African Repository, The **IV:**17

African Society for Mutual Relief **IV:**402
Afrika Korps **VIII:**278
Afro-American Steamship and Mercantile Company **VI:**223
Afrocentrism **X:**237
AFSCME. *See* American Federation of State, County, and Municipal Employees
"After Black Power, Women's Liberation" (Steinem) **X:**334
afterlife **I:**21
"After the Ball" (Harris) **VII:**353
Agadja. *See* Fon
"Against the Murderous and Plundering Hordes of the Peasants" (Luther) **I:**219
"Against the Papacy in Rome Founded by the Devil" (Luther) **I:**219
Agassiz, Alexander **VII:**210
Agassiz, Louis
    Fiske, John **VI:**129
    Mitchell, Maria **VI:**247
    race and race relations **IV:**310, 311
    Walcott, Charles Doolittle **V:**379
age discrimination **X:**17
Age Discrimination Act (1975) **X:17–18,** 131
Age Discrimination in Employment Act (1967) **X:**131
Agee, James **VIII:**296
Agee, Philip **VIII:**120
Agency for International Development **IX:**255, 257
Agent Orange **IX:**90
Age of Discovery **I:**106, 225
Age of Enlightenment. *See* Enlightenment, the
Age of Reason **III:**217; **IV:**248–249
Age of Reason (Paine)
    deism **III:**135
    Morse, Jedidiah **III:**307
    Paine, Thomas **III:**330
Age of the Common Man **IV:**130, 248
AGF. *See* Army Ground Forces
aging **X:**39, 40
Agnew, Spiro T. **X:18,** 138, 256, 257, **376c**
agnosticism **VI:**193
Agricultural Adjustment Act (AAA) **VIII:5–7, 444c, 445c**
    Agricultural Adjustment Administration **VIII:**7
    Agricultural Marketing Act **VIII:**8
    agriculture **VIII:**9–10; **IX:**7–8
    Communists **VIII:**77
    Congress **VIII:**79
    conservatism **VIII:**84
    FHA **VIII:**126
    First New Deal **VIII:**138

Hughes, Charles Evans **VII:**142
New Deal **VIII:**269
OPA **VIII:**282
socialists **VIII:**362
South **VIII:**366
Supreme Court **VIII:**382
taxation **VIII:**387–388
wage and price controls **VIII:**409
Wallace, Henry A. **VIII:**411
Agricultural Adjustment Administration (AAA) **VIII:7–8**
    African Americans **VIII:**3
    Agricultural Adjustment Act **VIII:**5, 6
    agriculture **VIII:**9–11
    America First Committee **VIII:**17
    Baruch, Bernard M. **VII:**32; **VIII:**42
    Brain Trust **VIII:**51
    Byrnes, James F. **VIII:**60
    economy **VIII:**104
    FHA **VIII:**126
    First New Deal **VIII:**138
    liberalism **VIII:**215
    New Deal **VIII:**269
    rural areas **VIII:**348
    South **VIII:**366
    Tugwell, Rexford G. **VIII:**397–398
    unemployment **VIII:**399
agricultural and mechanical (A&M) colleges **VI:**8
Agricultural and Mechanical Colleges Acts. *See* Morrill Land-Grant Act
agricultural colleges **VII:**89
agricultural cooperatives **VII:**49
agricultural depression (1920s) **VII:**48
Agricultural Economics, Bureau of **VIII:**210
Agricultural Marketing Act **VII:5–6; VIII:8, 443c**
    Agricultural Adjustment Act **VIII:**5
    agriculture **VII:**8; **VIII:**9
    Congress **VIII:**79
    FCA **VIII:**125–126
    Hoover presidency **VIII:**173, 174
Agricultural Society, U.S. **IV:**12
Agricultural Workers Organization **VII:**147
Agriculture, Bureau of **VIII:**210
Agriculture, U.S. Department of (USDA)
    agriculture **IV:**12; **V:**6; **VI:**8; **IX:**8
    Capper-Volstead Act **VII:**49
    CCC **VIII:**71
    Congress **V:**89
    conservation/environmentalism **VI:**81, 82

Agriculture, U.S. Department of
(*continued*)
environment **VIII:**115
FCA **VIII:**126
Forest Reserve Act **VI:**134
Meat Inspection Act
VII:198
medicine **VI:**244
Pure Food and Drug Act
VII:277
victory gardens **VIII:**405–
406
Wallace, Henry A. **VIII:**411
agriculture and horticulture
I:395*c;* **II:8–14,** *10;* **III:10–12,**
466*c;* **IV:10–13; V:5–7; VI:8–**
10, *9,* 411*c;* **VII:6–8,** *7,* 407*c;*
VIII:8–11, 443*c*–445*c,* 447*c;*
IX:6–8, 351*c,* 353*c;* **X:18–20,**
19
abolitionism **IV:**1
Acadians **II:**2
African Americans **IV:**7;
VI:6
Agricultural Adjustment Act
VIII:5
Agricultural Adjustment
Administration **VIII:**7–8
Agricultural Marketing Act
VII:5–6; **VIII:**8
agriculture **II:**14
Algonquin **II:**18
Amazon River **I:**9
animals **II:**23
Apalachee **I:**11
Arawak **I:**11
Asian Americans **VIII:**32
Azores **I:**17
Bankhead-Jones Farm
Tenant Act **VIII:**39
barbed wire **VI:**24
Bidwell, John **IV:**56
braceros **IX:**42–43
Brain Trust **VIII:**51
Brook Farm **IV:**65
business **VIII:**58; **IX:**46
business cycles **VI:**57, 58
cacao **I:**47–49
California **IV:**71
Capper-Volstead Act
VII:48–49
Carib **I:**60
Carver, George Washington
VI:63
Champlain, Samuel de
II:62
Chávez, César Estrada
IX:53–54
child labor **VII:**51–52
children **VIII:**67
chinampas **I:**73
class **II:**69–70
Colombian Exchange **I:**81
Communists **VIII:**78
Connecticut **II:**77
Coolidge, Calvin John **VII:**65
corn **II:**80–81

cotton **III:**122–123
Crime of '73 **VI:**86
Currency Act **VII:**68
Deere, John **IV:**115–116
Delaware **II:**96
Democratic Party **VIII:**92
"Discourse Concerning
Western Planting"
(Hakluyt) **I:423–425**
dust bowl **VIII:**97–99
Economic Opportunity Act
(1964) **IX:**95
economy **II:**109; **IV:**131;
V:121, 123; **VII:**83, 85;
VIII:102
education, federal aid to
VI:110–111
education, higher **VI:**111–
112
election of 1936 **VIII:**109
employment **V:**132
environment **II:**119;
III:153–155; **VII:**98;
VIII:116
Erie Canal **IV:**142
Fair Labor Standards Act
VIII:124
fairs, agricultural **III:**161
farmers' alliances **VI:**125–
126
Federal Farm Loan Act
VII:106
FHA **VIII:**126
First New Deal **VIII:**138
Florida **I:**131
food **II:**130
foreign policy **VI:**133;
VII:116
frontier, the **III:**181
George III **III:**192
GI Bill of Rights **VIII:**149
Great Depression **VIII:**157
Great Migration **VII:**127–
128
Great Plains **III:**197
hacienda **I:**149–150
Haiti **III:**203
Handsome Lake **III:**209
Harding, Warren Gamaliel
VII:135
Hawaii **IV:**188–189
Hawley-Smoot Tariff Act
VIII:163
Hispaniola **I:**162–163
Hohokam **I:**164
homefront **V:**193
Hoover presidency
VIII:173
Hopi **I:**167
Huron **I:**172
immigration **V:**199; **VI:**185;
VIII:184
indentured servitude **II:**174
Indian Affairs, Bureau of
IV:196
Indian Affairs, Office of
VI:190

Indian Removal Act **IV:**198
Indian Reorganization Act
VIII:186
indigo **II:**177
industrialization **IV:**201
investments, foreign, in the
United States **VI:**197
IRCA **X:**177
Iroquois **I:**185, 186
Italian Americans **VIII:**190
Japanese Americans,
relocation of **VIII:**194
Johnson, Hiram Warren
VII:154
Kalm, Peter **II:**191
labor/labor movements
II:197–199; **IX:**181
Latino movement **IX:**185
literature **VIII:**219
lobbying **VII:**181–182
Madeira **I:**222
Maine **II:**213
marriage and family
III:289; **VIII:**230
Maryland **II:**220
Maya **I:**234
McCormick, Cyrus Hall
IV:243–245
McGillivray, Alexander
III:294
McNary-Haugen Farm Bill
VII:195–196
Mexican Americans
VIII:237
Mexican immigration
VII:203
Mexican Invasion **VII:**203
Mexican Revolution
VII:204
migration **VII:**207;
VIII:239–240; **IX:**215
Mississippian **I:**244, 245
Morrill Land-Grant Act
V:269
Mossi **I:**253
National Reclamation Act
VII:228–229
Native Americans **II:**251;
III:311; **VII:**231
New Freedom **VII:**236
New Frontier **IX:**243
New Mexico **I:**263
New Spain **I:**269–270
North Carolina Regulation
III:320–321
Nullification Controversy
IV:282
Omaha platform **VI:**272
Owen, Robert **IV:**291
panic of 1837 **IV:**294
Pennsylvania **II:**287
Permanent Indian Frontier
IV:298
Pinckney, Elizabeth Lucas
III:336
Point Four Program
IX:258

politics (Roosevelt era)
VIII:298
population trends **VII:**267
potato **II:**304–305
presidency **VII:**269
primogeniture and entail
II:310
Puerto Ricans **IX:**267
race and race relations
III:357
radicalism **VII:**286–287
REA **VIII:**349–350
Resettlement Administration
VIII:338–339
Rhode Island **II:**333
rural areas **VIII:**348–349
rural life **III:**375; **VII:**306–
307
Sandys, George **II:**343
São Tomé **I:**328
science and technology
III:385
Secotan **I:**329
service sector **IX:**288, 289
slavery **II:**355; **III:**390;
IV:347
socialists **VIII:**362
society, British American
II:366
South **VIII:**366, 367
South Carolina Regulation
III:395
Spanish colonies **II:**371
STFU **VIII:**367–368
Sudan **I:**347
Sunbelt **VIII:**380
Taino **I:**352
tariffs **VII:**349, 350
Taylor, John, of Caroline
III:408
technology **VIII:**389
tenants **II:**386–387
Tennessee Valley Authority
VIII:393
Texas **IV:**371
Timucua **I:**360
Tláloc **I:**361
tobacco **I:**363–364
trade, domestic and foreign
III:415
Trail of Tears **IV:**377
Tugwell, Rexford G.
VIII:397
UFW **IX:**324–325
unemployment **VIII:**399
victory gardens **VIII:**405–
406
wage and price controls
VIII:409
Wallace, Henry A. **VIII:**411
Wilson, Thomas Woodrow
VII:383
women's status and rights
II:423
World War II **VIII:**428
World War II home front
VIII:434

Agriculture Labor Relations Act
(California, 1975) **X**:20
Aguado, Juan **I**:86
Aguilar, Francisco de **I**:4
Aguilar, Gerónimo de **I**:4–5,
94–95, 147
Aguilar, Martín de **IV**:103
Aguinaldo, Baldomero **IX**:256
Aguinaldo, Emilio **VII**:8–9, 403*c*
Army Act **VII**:22
Filipino insurrection **VI**:127,
128
foreign policy **VII**:113
Jones Act (1916) **VII**:156
Aguirre, Lope de **I**:119
Agustín I (emperor of Mexico)
IV:329
ahaws **I**:236, 237
AHF. *See* American Heritage
Foundation
Ahmad I al-Mansur (sultan of
Morocco) **I**:138, 342
Ahmeek Mining Company **VII**:210
Ahuitzotl **I**:19, 361
Aideed, Muhammad Farah **X**:81,
102, 380*c*
Aid for Dependent Children
IX:95
AIDS. *See* acquired immune
deficiency syndrome
Aid to Dependent Children
(ADC)
mothers' pensions **VII**:213,
214
Social Security Act
VIII:363–365, 454–455
women's network **VIII**:421
Aid to Families with Dependent
Children (AFDC) **X**:128
Aid to the Blind **VIII**:363–365
AIG (American International
Group) **X**:61
AIM. *See* American Indian
Movement
Ainsworth, Henry **II**:247
Ainsworth Psalter (Ainsworth)
II:247
"Ain't Nobody's Business If I Do"
(Waters) **VII**:220
AIP. *See* American Independent
Party
AIPO (American Institute for
Public Opinion) **VIII**:312
Air America **X**:220
airbags **X**:320
Aircall Corporation (New York)
IX:286
Air Commerce Act **VII**:29, 165
air conditioning
automobile industry **IX**:26
migration **IX**:215
technology **IX**:313
Aircraft Battle Force **VIII**:202
aircraft carriers **VIII**:11–13, *12*
convoys **VIII**:87
Coral Sea, Battle of the
VIII:87

Halsey, William F. **VIII**:161
Navy, U.S. **VIII**:265
Okinawa **VIII**:287
Pearl Harbor **VIII**:292, 293
Philippine Sea, Battle of the
VIII:295
aircraft industry **VIII**:13–15, *14,*
446*c*
automobile industry **VIII**:37
business **VIII**:58
CIO **VIII**:82
economy **VIII**:104
labor/labor movements
VIII:207
mobilization **VIII**:242
South **VIII**:367
Sunbelt **VIII**:381
technology **VIII**:389, 397
Air Force, Royal Canadian
VIII:128
Air Force, U.S. **IX**:351*c*
Meredith, James **IX**:213
Mitchell, William (Billy)
VII:211
science and technology
IX:285
Air Force, U.S. Department of the
IX:238
airline deregulation **X**:196
airliners. *See* jet airliners
airlines, commercial **VII**:28, 29
Air Mail Act **VII**:29
airplanes. *See* aircraft
air pollution **X**:379*c*
airport security **X**:55
air power **VIII**:15–16
Army Air Forces, U.S.
VIII:26
Arnold, Henry H. "Hap"
VIII:27–28
blitzkrieg **VIII**:47
bombing **VIII**:48
Britain, Battle of **VIII**:53–
54
convoys **VIII**:87
demobilization (WWII)
VIII:91
Forrestal, James V. **VIII**:143
Guadalcanal **VIII**:160
Navy, U.S. **VIII**:265
North African campaign
VIII:278
Pearl Harbor **VIII**:293
Solomon Islands **VIII**:365
World War II European
theater **VIII**:431
Air Quality Act (1967) **IX**:109,
357*c*
air quality standards **X**:375*c*
air raid alarms **VIII**:281
air-surveillance systems **X**:101
air traffic controllers strike (1981)
X:202, 378*c*
air travel. *See* aviation
Aja people **I**:125
Akan **I**:5–6, 13–14, 143
Akerman, Amos **V**:225

Akimel Au Authm **II**:176
Akron, Ohio **VIII**:399
*Akron v. Akron Center for
Reproductive Health* **X**:20–21,
265
Alabama **IX**:356*c. See also*
Birmingham, Alabama
African Americans **VIII**:3
agriculture **IV**:10; **V**:6
Alamo, The **IV**:14
Black, Hugo L. **VIII**:45
Creek **III**:125
Dow, Lorenzo **IV**:126
economy **IV**:130
Evans, Walker **VIII**:120
Florida **IV**:151
freedom rides **IX**:123
Hastings, Lansford W.
IV:187
Horseshoe Bend, Battle of
IV:190
Indian Removal Act **IV**:197
Jackson, Andrew **IV**:205
McIntosh, William **IV**:247
migration **IV**:254
Mobile campaign **V**:264
NAACP **IX**:232
Native Americans **IV**:274
panic of 1819 **IV**:293
popular sovereignty **IV**:305
race and race relations
VIII:317, 318
railroads **IV**:314, 316
Rapier, James T. **V**:323
Reynolds v. Sims **IX**:276
Scottsboro Boys **VIII**:353
Seminole **IV**:338
Sequoyah **IV**:342
slave trade, internal **IV**:348,
349
SNCC **IX**:303
southern demagogues
VII:332
States' Rights Party **IX**:299
Sunbelt **VIII**:381
Tennessee Valley Authority
VIII:392–393
Trail of Tears **IV**:378
Travis, William Barret
IV:379
Wallace, George C. **X**:363–
364
White Citizens' Councils
IX:342
Alabama, CSS **V**:7
Canada **VI**:61
Confederate navy **V**:84
foreign policy **V**:151
Semmes, Raphael **V**:346
Seward, William H. **V**:348
Sumner, Charles **V**:378
Union navy **V**:405
Washington, Treaty of
VI:385
Alabama, USS **VIII**:201
Alabama Midland case **VI**:57, 303
Alabama River **IV**:277

Aladdin oven **VI**:22
alafins **I**:281
Alamance, Battle of **III**:12, 321,
460*c*
Alamo, The **IV**:13–15, 413*c*
Austin, Stephen F. **IV**:40
Bowie, James **IV**:62, 63
Crockett, Davy **IV**:111
foreign policy **IV**:155
Gadsden Purchase **IV**:173
Houston, Sam **IV**:191
Mexican-American War
IV:251
San Jacinto, Battle of
IV:328
Santa Anna, Antonio López
de **IV**:330
Texas **IV**:372
Texas Revolution **IV**:375
Travis, William Barret
IV:380
Alamogordo, New Mexico
atomic bomb **VIII**:34–35
Hiroshima and Nagasaki
VIII:166
Manhattan Project **VIII**:227
Oppenheimer, J. Robert
IX:251
alarm systems **X**:318, 320
Alaska **I**:260; **II**:14–15, 17;
III:12–13; **V**:446*c*; **VII**:404*c*
abortion **X**:2
Bering, Vitus Jonassen **II**:36
California **III**:74
conservation/
environmentalism **VI**:82;
X:92
foreign policy **V**:151
Green Party **X**:159
Harding, Warren Gamaliel
VII:135
Klondike gold rush **VI**:208–
209
marriage and family **X**:215
Monroe Doctrine **IV**:260
Native Americans **X**:250–
251
Oregon Treaty of 1846
IV:286
Russia in **II**:14–15
Russian settlements **II**:338
Seward, William H. **V**:348
WAVES **VIII**:418
Alaska Commercial Company
VI:34
Alaska Native Claim Settlement
Act (ANSCA) **X**:21, *21*, 250
Alaska Natives **X**:21, 282
Alaska statehood **IX**:8–9
Albanian rebels **X**:199
Albany, Georgia **IX**:292–293, 302
Albany, New York **II**:264
anti-Masonry **IV**:25
Burgoyne, Sir John **III**:68
Conkling, Roscoe **VI**:80
economy **IV**:131
Erie Canal **IV**:141

Albany, New York *(continued)*
  Free-Soil Party **IV:**163
  Hudson Highlands
    campaign **III:**216
  industrialization **IV:**200
  Judaism **VI:**205
  Lafayette, Marie-Joseph-
    Paul-Yves-Roch-Gilbert
    de Motier, marquis de
    III:253
  Liberty Party **IV:**226
  Paul, Nathaniel **IV:**295, 296
  railroads **IV:**314, 316
  Shakers **III:**387
  Yates, Abraham **III:**453–454
  Young, Thomas **III:**457
Albany African Church
  Association **IV:**295
Albany Congress **II:**14–15, *15,*
  93; **III:**173, 218
Albee, Edward (playwright)
  IX:193
Albee, Edward F. (theater owner/
  booker) **VI:**117
Albert (cardinal elector of Mainz)
  I:218
Albert, Carl B. **X:**21–22, 138,
  169
Albright, Horace **VII:**228
Albright, Madeleine K. **X:**22,
  381*c*
  defense policy **X:**102
  feminism **X:**134
  Fourth World Conference
    on Women speech
    X:405–407
  UN **X:**357
  women's status and rights
    X:371
Albuquerque, Alfonso de **I:**6,
  299, 331
Albuquerque, New Mexico **IV:**26
alcaldes **I:**41
Alcatraz occupation and protest
  (1971) **IX:**13; **X:**250, 375*c*
Alcoa, Inc. **VIII:**57–58
alcohol **II:**15–16; **III:**13–14,
  464*c*; **VII:**406*c,* 407*c*
  animals **III:**22
  cities and urban life **V:**67
  debt, national **III:**132
  French colonies **II:**136
  fur trade **II:**141, 142
  Grant, Ulysses S. **V:**174
  Hamilton, Alexander
    III:207
  immigration **V:**200
  Jemison, Mary **II:**184
  marriage and family **II:**218
  Massachusetts **II:**225
  medicine **V:**257
  Native Americans **III:**314
  political parties, third
    VI:286
  popular culture **III:**340–341
  Powderly, Terence Vincent
    VI:287

Prohibition Party **VI:**295–
  296
Prophet, the Shawnee
  III:349
Sugar Act **III:**401
taverns and inns **II:**384;
  III:407
temperance movement
  III:410
Valley Forge **III:**422
Alcohol, Tobacco, and Firearms,
  Bureau of (ATF)
  Branch Davidians **X:**46
  militia movement **X:**231
  Reno, Janet **X:**309
alcoholism
  Dix, Dorothea **IV:**124
  Native Americans **VIII:**264
  Owen, Robert **IV:**291
  Permanent Indian Frontier
    IV:297–298
  temperance movement
    IV:369
Alcorn, James L. **V:**339
Alcorn County, Mississippi
  VIII:349–350
Alcorn University **V:**335
Alcott, Bronson
  Alcott, Louisa May **VI:**10
  Fuller, Margaret **IV:**169
  literature **IV:**228
  Peabody, Elizabeth Palmer
    VI:279
  transcendental movement
    IV:378, 379
Alcott, Louisa May **V:**446*c;*
  VI:10
Alcott, William **IV:**122
Alden, John **II:**16, 17, 376
Alden, Priscilla **II:**16–17, 376
Alder Creek **IV:**126
Alderson Prison, West Virginia
  VII:110
Aldie, Battle of **V:**99
Aldine Press **I:**376
Aldrich, Nelson W.
  Allison, William Boyd **VI:**11,
    12
  Congress **VI:**80
  corruption, political **VI:**83
  lobbying **VI:**228
  Payne-Aldrich Tariff Act
    VII:255
  Republican Party **VII:**299
  tariffs **VI:**352; **VII:**349
Aldrich, Thomas Bailey **VI:**225
Aldrin, Edwin "Buzz" **X:**326
Aleman, Arnoldo **X:**255
Aleut **II:**17; **X:**379*c*
  Alaska **II:**12
  ANSCA **X:**21
  Inuit **II:**177
  Russian settlements **II:**338–
    339
Aleutian Islands **VIII:**20
Alexander, Charles **IV:**210
Alexander, Cosmo **III:**399

Alexander, Edward P. **V:**7–8
  Balloon Corps **V:**26
  Confederate army **V:**81
  Gettysburg, Battle of **V:**168
Alexander, Harold R. L. G.
  VIII:278, 360
Alexander, James **II:**433
Alexander, John White **VII:**23
Alexander, Mary Spratt Provoost
  II:17–18
Alexander, William (Lord Stirling)
  (1726–1783) **IV:**258
Alexander, Sir William (1567–
  1640) **I:**3
Alexander, Will W. (FSA
  administrator) **VIII:**127
Alexander I (czar of Russia)
  IV:260
Alexander II (czar of Russia)
  VII:126
Alexander III the Great (king of
  Macedonia) **I:**348
Alexander VI (pope) **I:**6, 396*c*
  Grotius, Hugo **I:**146
  Leo X **I:**210
  Requerimiento **I:**318
  Tordesillas, Treaty of **I:**367
  Vitoria, Francisco de **I:**379
"Alexander's Ragtime Band"
  (Berlin) **VII:**219, 353
Alexandra (princess of England)
  IX:117
Alexandria, Egypt **VIII:**118
Alexandria, Virginia **IV:**349
Alexandria Confederate Memorial
  V:268
Alexie, Sherman **X:**211
Alfonso (king of Kongo) **I:**200
Alfred P. Murrah Federal
  Building, Oklahoma City
  X:266, 381*c*
  militia movement **X:**231
  Oklahoma City bombing
    X:267
  terrorism **X:**346
Alger, Horatio **VI:**10–11, 99
Algeria **III:**462*c*
  Barbary Wars **III:**45, 46
  Barlow, Joel **III:**46
  Chauncey, Isaac **III:**86
  foreign affairs **III:**169
  North African campaign
    VIII:277
  OPEC **X:**267
  POWs **III:**346
  World War II European
    theater **VIII:**431
Algiers **IV:**115
Algonquian Indians **I:**398*c*
  architecture **II:**24
  Chesapeake Bay **II:**65, 66
  Columbian Exchange **I:**82
  Connecticut **II:**75
  disease/epidemics **II:**98
  Dutch-Indian Wars **II:**105–
    106
  ethnocentrism **II:**121

Glaize, meeting at the
  III:195
Harriot, Thomas **I:**155
Kieft, Willem **II:**192
Logan, James **II:**209
Mantoac **I:**229
Maryland **II:**219
Massachusetts **II:**222
Native American religion
  I:261
Native Americans **II:**251
New Hampshire **II:**259
New York **II:**269, 270
North Carolina **II:**274
Pennsylvania **II:**284
population trends **I:**298
Powhatan **II:**305–306
Powhatan Confederacy
  II:307
religion **II:**330
Roanoke **I:**321
sachems **II:**341
Secotan **I:**329
Squanto **II:**376
wampum **II:**406
werowance **I:**383
White, John **I:**383
women's status and rights
  II:422, 426
Algonquian language **I:**6–7
  Algonquin Indians (Ottawa
    Valley) **II:**18
  architecture **II:**24
  Eliot, John **II:**115
  Harriot, Thomas **I:**154
  Massachusett **I:**233
  Montagnais-Naskapi **I:**250
  Passamaquoddy **I:**287
  Powhatan **I:**300, 301
  sachems **II:**341
Algonquin Indians (Ottawa Valley)
  II:18
  Brébeuf, Jean de **II:**46
  French colonies **II:**137
  religion **II:**331
Algonquin park wolf **II:**421
Ali (caliph) **I:**188
Ali (film) **IX:**10
Ali, Laila **IX:**10
Ali, Muhammad **IX:**5–6, 9, 9–10,
  298, 356*c,* 357*c*
Alianza Federal de Mercedes
  IX:186, 317, 318, 357*c*
Alice (slave and historian) **II:**19
Alien and Sedition Acts (1798)
  III:14, 464*c*
  Adams, John **III:**6
  Anarchist Immigration Act
    VII:14
  Bill of Rights **III:**51
  Catholics **III:**83
  Democratic Party **IV:**117
  Democratic-Republican
    Party **III:**136
  Duane, James **III:**140
  Federalist Party **III:**164
  Fries's Rebellion **III:**180

Gallatin, Albert **III**:188
journalism **III**:241
liberty tree **III**:268
Quasi War **III**:353
Sedition Act **VII**:318
states' rights **III**:397
Virginia and Kentucky
  Resolutions **III**:424
Alien Enemies Act **III**:14, 464*c*
Alien Exclusion Act. *See*
  Immigration Act (1917)
Alien Registration Act. *See* Smith
  Act
alimony **X**:123
Alito, Samuel
  Clinton, Hillary Rodham
    X:78
  gun control **X**:162
  O'Connor, Sandra Day
    X:265
All about Eve (film) **IX**:222
Allah **I**:188, 238
Allakoi (king of Mali) **I**:225
All-America Football Conference
  IX:298
All-American Baseball League
  IX:299
Allegheny City, Pennsylvania
  VI:62, 63
Allegheny College (Pennsylvania)
  VII:349
Allegheny County Buildings
  (Pittsburgh, Pennsylvania)
  VI:313
Allegheny Mountains
  art and architecture **IV**:29
  Baltimore & Ohio Railroad
    IV:43
  National Road **IV**:271
  railroads **IV**:313, 316
Allegheny River **VI**:119
Allen, Charles H. **VII**:110
Allen, Ethan **II**:398; **III**:14–15,
  460*c*, 461*c*
  Arnold, Benedict **III**:30
  deism **III**:135
  Fort Ticonderoga **III**:171
  Green Mountain Boys
    III:199
  Lyon, Matthew **III**:277
Allen, Florence **VIII**:422
Allen, James **V**:25
Allen, Leroy **IX**:39
Allen, Paul **X**:147
Allen, Richard **III**:15–16, 464*c*
  abolitionism **V**:1
  ACS **IV**:17
  African-American churches,
    growth of **VI**:4
  African Americans **III**:9
  African Methodist Episcopal
    Church **V**:5
  antislavery **III**:26–27
  Benezet, Anthony **II**:35
  Great Awakening **II**:156
  Haig, Alexander M., Jr.
    X:163

Jones, Absalom **III**:238
  Negro Convention
    movement **IV**:279
  religion **IV**:318
  Walker, David **IV**:389
Allen, Steve **IX**:283
Allen, Thad W. **X**:174
Allen, William "Foghorn Bill"
  IV:287
Allen, William Francis **VI**:255
Allende, Salvador **X**:205, 377*c*
Allgemeines Krankhaus (Vienna,
  Austria) **VII**:126
All God's Chillun Got Wings
  (O'Neill) **VIII**:341
Alliance
  Barry, John **III**:47
  Continental navy **III**:117
  Jones, John Paul **III**:239
Alliance for Progress **IX**:10–11,
  354*c*
  Kennedy, John F. **IX**:170
  Latin America **IX**:184; **X**:205
  Peace Corps **IX**:255
  wars of national liberation
    IX:339
Allied Combined Bomber
  Offensive **VIII**:16
Allied Control Council **VIII**:307;
  IX:38
Allied Forces Headquarters
  VIII:278, 360
Allied Powers/Allies. *See* Grand
  Alliance
All in the Family **X**:343
Allison, Emma **VI**:284
Allison, William Boyd **VI**:11–12,
  42
Allison Amendment **VI**:12
All My Pretty Ones (Sexton)
  IX:195
All My Sons (Miller) **IX**:193
Allouez Mining Company **VII**:210
All Quiet on the Western Front
  (film) **VIII**:301
All-Star Games **VIII**:370
Allston, Washington
  art and architecture
    IV:27–28
  Morse, Samuel F. B. **IV**:264
  West, Benjamin **III**:436
All the King's Men (Warren)
  IX:193–194
Almagro, Diego de **I**:285, 292,
  293
almanacs **III**:43
Almanac Singers **VIII**:160
Almoravids
  Ghana **I**:140
  Islam **I**:189
  Mali **I**:225
  marabout **I**:231
  Sahara **I**:324
almshouses **II**:19–20
  architecture **II**:25
  Philadelphia **II**:293
  poverty **III**:344

Almy, Brown & Slater **IV**:199
Almy, William **III**:146, 389
Alpert, Richard **IX**:187, 196
Alpha Suffrage Club **VI**:388
Alsace **VII**:370
Alsberg, Henry **VIII**:136–137
Alsop, Joseph **IX**:13, 14
Alsop, Stewart **IX**:13, 14
Alston, Melvin **IX**:291
Alta California **I**:51–52
Altair 8800 computer **X**:147, 318
Altamont Speedway Free Festival
  IX:259
alt-country music **X**:239
altepetl
  Aztecs **I**:19
  Nahua **I**:257
  Tlaxcala **I**:361–362
alternating current (AC) **VI**:353,
  354, 410*c*; **VII**:92
alternative education **X**:115
alternative rock **X**:238
Altgeld, John Peter **VI**:12–13
  Darrow, Clarence Seward
    VII:69–70
  Debs, Eugene Victor
    VII:73
  Haymarket riot **VI**:169
  Pullman Strike **VI**:297
Althing **I**:177
Altman, Robert **X**:279
Alton, Illinois **IV**:3, 230–231
Alton Observer **IV**:230
aluminum **VIII**:354
Alvarado, Hernando de **I**:93
Alvarado, Juan Bautista **IV**:222
Alvarado, Pedro de **I**:7–8, 8
  Aguilar, Francisco de **I**:4
  Aztecs **I**:22
  Cuitláhuac **I**:101
  Las Casas, Bartolomé de
    I:205, 206
  Maya **I**:235
  New Spain **I**:267
  Tezcatlipoca **I**:357
  Tlaxcala **I**:362
Álvares, Francisco **I**:125
Alvord, John W. **V**:159
Alzheimer's disease **X**:301
AMA. *See* American Medical
  Association; American
  Missionary Association
Amadas, Philip
  Barlowe, Arthur **I**:28
  Manteo **I**:229
  North Carolina **II**:274
  Roanoke **I**:320–321
  Wanchese **I**:382
  Wingina **II**:417
Amalgamated Association of
  Iron, Steel, and Tin Workers
  VI:411*c*
  Carnegie, Andrew **VI**:62
  Homestead Strike **VI**:175,
    176
  steel industry **VII**:337
  U.S. Steel **VII**:365, 366

Amalgamated Association of
  Miners **VI**:73
Amalgamated Clothing and Textile
  Worker's Union **VIII**:188
Amalgamated Clothing Workers of
  America (ACW) **VIII**:16
  AFL **VII**:11
  CIO **VIII**:81
  Dubinsky, David **VIII**:97
  Hillman, Sidney **VIII**:165,
    166
  Jews **VIII**:195
  labor/labor movements
    VII:170
  Lewis, John L. **VIII**:213
  NWTUL **VII**:231
Amalgamated Copper **VII**:242
Amalgamated Trades and Labor
  Assembly **VI**:213
amalgamation **I**:391; **V**:261
Amana Church Society **IV**:320
Amana Community **VI**:371
Amateur Athletic Union **VIII**:223
"Amazing Grace" (Newton)
  II:247
Amazing Stories (magazine)
  IX:287
Amazon River **I**:8–9
  Andes Mountains **I**:9
  Brazil **I**:33, 34
  Carib **I**:60
  Hastings, Lansford W.
    IV:187
  tobacco **II**:391
Amazons (female warriors) **I**:103,
  132
Ambassador Hotel (Los Angeles,
  California) **IX**:23
Ambassadors, The (James)
  VII:179
Amboise, Charles d' **I**:211
Ambrister, John **III**:167
ambulance corps **V**:257
AMCA (American Medical
  College Association) **VI**:244
Amda Siyon (ruler of Ethiopia)
  I:124
AME Church. *See* African
  Methodist Episcopal Church
AME Church Review, The **VI**:351
Amelia Court House **V**:14
Amelia Island **III**:167
Amendments to the U.S.
  Constitution **X**:22–24,
  123–124. *See also specific
  amendments, e.g.:* First
  Amendment
America (Ginsberg) **IX**:135
"America" (song) **V**:273
America 2000 **X**:115
America and the World War
  (Roosevelt) **VII**:267
America First Committee
  VIII:16–17, 447*c*
  conservatism **VIII**:85
  destroyers-for-bases deal
    VIII:95

America First Committee
(*continued*)
Hoover, Herbert C.
VIII:172–173
isolationists **VIII:**190
Johnson, Hugh S. **VIII:**197
Neutrality Acts **VIII:**268
Wheeler, Burton K.
VIII:416
American, The (James) **VI:**200,
226
American Aborigine **IX:**241
American Academy of Arts and
Sciences **III:**384, 462*c*; **IV:**335;
VI:247
American Academy of Fine Arts
IV:28
American Academy of Sciences
VI:82
American Airlines **VII:**165
American Almanac **IV:**134
American and Foreign Anti-
Slavery Society
abolitionism **IV:**3; **V:**3
American Anti-Slavery
Society **IV:**16
Tappan, Arthur and Lewis
IV:367
Weld, Theodore Dwight
IV:396
American and Foreign Bible
Society **IV:**320
American Anti-Boycott
Association (AABA)
Buck's Stove **VII:**42
Danbury Hatters **VII:**69
labor/labor movements
VII:169
National Civic Federation
VII:226
open shop movement
VII:247
American Anti-Imperialist League
Platform (1899) **VI:441–442**
American Antiquarian Society
VII:140
American Anti-Slavery Society
(AASS) **IV:15–16,** *16,* 413*c*
abolitionism **IV:**3; **V:**3
Anthony, Susan B. **VI:**16
female antislavery societies
IV:147, 148
Foster, Abigail Kelley
IV:161
Garrison, William Lloyd
V:164, 165
Liberty Party **IV:**226
Lovejoy, Elijah **IV:**230
Mott, Lucretia **IV:**265
Phillips, Wendell **IV:**299
religion **IV:**317
Seneca Falls convention
IV:341
Society of Friends **V:**364
Stone, Lucy **VI:**345
Tappan, Arthur and Lewis
IV:366

Weld, Theodore Dwight
IV:396
Williams, Peter, Jr. **IV:**402
*American Architect and Building
News* **VI:**166
American Art Union (New York
City) **IV:**28
American Association (AA) **VI:**26
American Association for Labor
Legislation (AALL) **VI:**115;
VII:392
American Association for the
Advancement of Science (AAAS)
Mitchell, Maria **VI:**247
professional organizations,
rise of **VI:**294
science and technology
IV:334
American Association of
Advertising Agencies **VII:**4, 5;
IX:3, 357*c*
American Association of Colored
Youth **VI:**160
American Association of
Education of Colored Youth
V:184
American Association of Medical
Colleges **VI:**244
American Association of
Petroleum Geologists **X:**155
American Association of Retired
Persons (AARP) **X:**222
American Association of Social
Workers **VII:**330
American Association of
University Women **VI:**313
American Atheists **IX:**273; **X:**307
American Bandstand **X:**239
American Baptist **VI:**388
American Baptist Anti-Slavery
Convention **V:**331
American Baptist Home Mission
Society **V:**331
American Bar Association (ABA)
VI:294; **X:**364
American Basketball Association
(ABA) **X:**331
American Bell **VI:**192
American Bible Society (ABS)
humanitarianism **III:**217
Morse, Jedidiah **III:**308
religion **IV:**317, 320
American Biograph Company
VII:131
American Board of
Commissioners for Foreign
Missions
Choctaw **IV:**87
Indian Removal Act **IV:**198
Morse, Jedidiah **III:**307
Whitman, Marcus **IV:**398
American Bridge **VII:**336
American Broadcasting Company
(ABC) **IX:**65; **X:**344
American Bund **VIII:**25
American Capitalism (Galbraith)
IX:129

American Catholic Church
VI:307, 308
"American Century, The" (Luce)
VIII:224
American Chemical Society
VI:294
American Citizens Equal Rights
Association **V:**307
"American Civilization" (Emerson)
IV:140
American Civil Liberties Union
(ACLU) **VII:9–10; VIII:17–
18,** 443*c*
Abscam **X:**6
Asian Americans **VIII:**32
Baldwin, Roger Nash
VII:31
Bork, Robert **X:**45–46
civil liberties **VII:**58;
VIII:72
Darrow, Clarence Seward
VII:70
Engel v. Vitale **IX:**107
Escobedo v. Illinois **IX:**111
flag burning **X:**136
Hamilton, Alice **VII:**133
Korematsu v. U.S. **VIII:**203
*McCreary County v. ACLU/
Van Orden v. Perry* **X:**216
pornography **X:**284
Rankin, Jeannette **VII:**292
Scopes Trial **VII:**316
Thomas, Norman **VIII:**394
USA PATRIOT Act **X:**359
American Club Woman **VII:**367
American Colonization Society
(ACS) **IV:16–17,** 411*c*
abolitionism **IV:**1–3; **V:**1
American Anti-Slavery
Society **IV:**16
Cuffe, Paul **III:**128
Forten, James **III:**170
*Genius of Universal
Emancipation* **IV:**175
Jones, Absalom **III:**238
Liberia **IV:**225; **VI:**223
Paul, Nathaniel **VI:**295
Pennington, James William
Charles **V:**300
race and race relations
IV:311
religion **IV:**317
slavery **V:**362
Turner, Henry McNeal
VI:366
American Commonwealth, The
(Bryce) **VI:**53, 410*c*
American Communist Party
VII:61
American Conflict (Greeley)
VI:242
American Convention of Abolition
Societies **IV:**17
American Council of Learned
Societies **IX:**235
American Council on Race
Relations **VIII:**319

American Defense Society
VII:267
American Democrat, The **IV:**210
American Dental Association
IX:265
*American Dictionary of the
English Language, An*
(Webster) **III:**434
American Dilemma, An (Myrdal)
VIII:448*c*
African Americans **VIII:**5
civil rights **VIII:**73
liberalism **VIII:**216
Myrdal, Gunnar **VIII:**252,
253
race and race relations
VIII:317, 319
American Diplomacy (Kennan)
IX:167
American dream **VIII:**62
American Duties Act **III:**401
American Economic Association
VI:115, 294
American embassies **X:**346
American Emigrant Company
VI:82
American Enterprise Institute
(AEI) **X:**349
American Equal Rights
Association (AERA)
Anthony, Susan B. **VI:**16
Brown, Olympia **VI:**51
Stone, Lucy **VI:**346
women's status and rights
V:436, 437
*American Exodus, An: A Record
of Human Erosion* (Lange)
VIII:98, 210
American Expeditionary Force
(AEF) **VII:**10, 10–11
American Legion **VII:**13
armed forces **VII:**20
conscription **VII:**62
Jones Act (1917) **VII:**157
Pershing, John Joseph
VII:257
Selective Service Act
VII:321
veterans **VII:**371
Wilson, Thomas Woodrow
VII:383
World War I **VII:**393, 394
American Express **IX:**79
American Farm Bureau **VII:**407*c*
Capper-Volstead Act **VII:**49
lobbying **VII:**181
McNary-Haugen Farm Bill
VII:195
politics (1900–1928)
VII:261
rural life **VII:**306, 307
American Farm Bureau
Federation **IX:**351*c*
Agricultural Adjustment
Administration **VIII:**7
agriculture **IX:**7
FSA **VIII:**127

American Federationist
  Buck's Stove **VII**:43
  radical and labor press
    VII:285
  Valesh, Eva McDonald
    VII:367
American Federation of Labor
  (AFL) **VI**:**13**, 409*c;* **VII**:**11–**
  12; VIII:**18–19,** 445*c,* 446*c;*
  IX:**11–12,** 353*c*
  ACW **VIII**:16
  anticommunism **VIII**:22
  Bridges, Harry **VIII**:53
  Brotherhood of Sleeping Car
    Porters **VIII**:54
  Buck's Stove **VII**:43
  CIO **VIII**:81; **IX**:71, 72
  Clayton Antitrust Act
    VII:59
  Coolidge, Calvin John
    VII:64
  Democratic Party **VII**:74
  Dubinsky, David **VIII**:97
  economy **IX**:97
  employment **V**:133
  Fair Labor Standards Act
    VIII:124
  Foster, William Zebulon
    VII:116, 117
  Gompers, Samuel **VI**:151
  Haywood, William Dudley
    VII:137
  Hillman, Sidney **VIII**:165–
    166
  Homestead Strike **VI**:175
  ILGWU **VIII**:187
  immigration restrictions
    VI:187
  Industrial Relations
    Commission **VII**:145
  Irish Americans **VIII**:189
  IWW **VII**:146, 147
  Knights of Labor **VI**:210
  labor, radical **VI**:213
  labor/labor movements
    VII:170–172; **VIII**:205–
    207; **IX**:182; **X**:201
  labor organizations
    VI:216
  Lawrence Strike **VII**:173
  Lewis, John L. **VIII**:213
  lobbying **VII**:181
  McNary-Haugen Farm Bill
    VII:196
  Mitchell, John **VII**:211
  Murray, Philip **VIII**:249
  NAM **VII**:225, 226
  National Civic Federation
    VII:226
  New Unionism **VII**:237
  NLRB **VIII**:259
  Norris–La Guardia Act
    VIII:277
  NWLB **VII**:229; **VIII**:261
  Passaic Strike **VII**:253
  Paterson Strike **VII**:253
  Perkins, Frances **VIII**:293

  professional organizations,
    rise of **VI**:293
  Pullman Strike **VI**:298
  radical and labor press
    VII:285
  radicalism **VII**:287
  Railroad Administration
    VII:291
  Reuther, Walter **VIII**:340;
    IX:275
  Seattle General Strike
    VII:317
  Shirtwaist Makers Strike
    VII:324
  Socialist Labor Party **VI**:336
  steel industry **VII**:337
  Steel Strike of 1919
    VII:338–339
  strikes **VIII**:377, 378
  Teamsters Union **IX**:310
  UMWA **VIII**:401–402
  union movement **IX**:323
  Valesh, Eva McDonald
    VII:367
  WFM **VII**:381, 382
  Workmen's Compensation
    Act **VII**:392
American Federation of Labor–
  Congress of Industrial
  Organizations (AFL-CIO)
  IX:354*c;* **X**:381*c*
  AFL **IX**:11
  CIO **IX**:72
  Economic Opportunity Act
    (1964) **IX**:95
  ERA **X**:124
  labor/labor movements
    X:201, 203, 204
  Randolph, A. Philip
    VIII:321
  Reuther, Walter **VIII**:340;
    IX:275
  Teamsters Union **IX**:310,
    311
  UFW **IX**:325
  union movement **IX**:323,
    324
American Federation of State,
  County, and Municipal
  Employees (AFSCME) **IX**:182,
  324; **X**:203
American Federation of Teachers
  X:114
American Folksongs (Guthrie)
  VIII:448*c*
American Football League (AFL)
  IX:298; **X**:330
American Football League Players
  Association **X**:196
American Freedmen's Inquiry
  Commission **V**:160
American Free Trade League
  VI:227
American Friends Service
  Committee **VII**:257
American Fund for Public Service
  VII:10

American Fur Company **III**:465*c;*
  IV:**18–19**
  Ashley, William Henry
    IV:32–33
  Astor, John Jacob **IV**:33,
    35
  Astoria **IV**:35
  Beckwourth, Jim **IV**:51
  Bent, Charles **IV**:51
  Bodmer, Karl **IV**:60
  Bridger, James **IV**:64
  Catlin, George **IV**:84
  Chouteau family **IV**:88
  Fort Laramie **IV**:156
  Fort Vancouver **IV**:158
  fur trade **III**:183; **IV**:171
  Missouri Fur Company
    IV:258
  mountain men **IV**:266, 267
  rendezvous **IV**:321
  Rocky Mountain Fur
    Company **IV**:324, 325
  St. Vrain, Céran **IV**:328
  Wyeth, Nathaniel J. **IV**:406
American Geography, The
  (Morse) **III**:307
American Gothic (Wood) **VIII**:31
American Guide (FWP series)
  VIII:137
American Hebrew **VI**:219
American Heritage Foundation
  (AHF) **IX**:66, 125
American Heritage Rivers
  Initiative **X**:290
American Historical Association
  history **VII**:140
  professional organizations,
    rise of **VI**:294
  White, Andrew Dickson
    VI:391
American Home Economics
  Association **VI**:313
American Hospital Association
  IX:115
American Hotel **IV**:242
American Idol **X**:239
American Independent Party
  (AIP) **X**:**24,** 364
American Indian Center (Chicago)
  IX:241
American Indian Defense
  Association **VII**:233, 351
American Indian Movement
  (AIM) **IX**:*12,* **12–13,** 241–242,
  319, 357*c;* **X**:250, 376*c*
American Indian Religious
  Freedom Act (1978) **X**:250
American Indians. *See* Native
  Americans
"American Individualism" (Hoover)
  VIII:171
American in Paris, An (film)
  IX:225
American in Paris, An (Gershwin)
  VII:125, 220
American Institute for Public
  Opinion (AIPO) **VIII**:312

American Institute for Social
  Service **VI**:335
American Institute of Architects
  VI:18
American Institute of Mining
  Engineers **VI**:247
American Institutionalist school
  IX:129
American International Group
  (AIG) **X**:61
American Iron and Steel
  Association **VI**:228
Americanism
  Espionage Act **VII**:101
  religion **VI**:308
  Roman Catholicism **VI**:316
Americanization **VII**:**12–13**
  citizenship **VII**:57
  globalization **X**:154
  Immigration Act (1917)
    VII:145
  Jones Act (1917) **VII**:157
  nativism **VII**:233–234
  Rhinelander case **VII**:301
  Trading with the Enemy Act
    VII:355
American Jewish Congress
  VIII:196
American Jockey Club **VI**:177, 178
American Journal of Education
  IV:134
American Journal of Science and
  Arts **IV**:334; **VI**:144, 145
American Labor Party **VIII**:97
American Law Review **VII**:140
American League
  baseball **VII**:32–33
  DiMaggio, Joe **VIII**:95, 96
  sports and recreation
    VII:334; **VIII**:370
American Legion **VII**:**13–14**
  anticommunism **VIII**:22
  citizenship **VII**:57
  commemoration **IX**:66
  GI Bill of Rights **VIII**:149
  lobbying **VII**:181
  Soldiers' Bonus **VII**:331
  veterans **VII**:371, 372
American Liberty League
  VIII:19
  conservatism **VIII**:84
  Democratic Party **VIII**:93
  Republican Party **VIII**:337
American Library Association
  IX:175
American Magazine **VII**:217, 349
American Medical Association
  (AMA) **VII**:403*c*
  Fair Deal **IX**:115
  FSA **VIII**:127
  lobbying **VII**:181
  Meat Inspection Act
    VII:198
  Medicare **IX**:209
  medicine **IV**:250; **VI**:244;
    VII:199, 200; **VIII**:235,
    236

American Medical Association
(*continued*)
    professional organizations,
        rise of **VI:**293
    public health **VII:**274;
        IX:265
    Pure Food and Drug Act
        VII:277
    science and technology
        IV:334
American Medical College
    Association (AMCA) **VI:**244
American Mercury **VII:**179, 180,
    201
American Missionary Associa-
    tion (AMA) **IV:**367; **V:**7–8;
    VI:112
American Missionary Society
    VI:111
American Motors **IX:**25
American Museum of Natural
    History (New York City)
    Boas, Franz Uri **VII:**39
    Catlin, George **IV:**85
    Mead, Margaret **VII:**197
    New York City **V:**282
American Mutoscope and
    Biograph Company **VII:**214
American National Baptist
    Convention **VI:**5
American National Exhibition
    (Moscow, 1959) **IX:**65, 121
"American Negro, The"
    (Moynihan) **X:**127
American Negro Academy **VI:**87,
    412*c*
American News Company **VI:**99
American Newspaper Guild
    VIII:271
American Newspaper Publishers
    Association **VI:**267
American Party (1840s–1850s).
    See Know-Nothing Party
American Party (1969) **X:**24
American Peace Society **V:**46,
    295; **VII:**255
American People's Money, The
    (Donnelly) **VI:**90
American Philosophical Society
    II:20; **III:**17–18, 460*c*
    Bartram, John **II:**34
    Bond, Thomas **II:**38
    Crèvecoeur, J. Hector St.
        John de **III:**127
    education **IV:**133
    Franklin, Benjamin
        III:173
    Philadelphia **II:**293
    Rittenhouse, David **III:**372
    science and technology
        III:384
American Plan **VII:**14, 247,
    407*c*
American Political Science
    Association **VI:**294
American Professional Football
    Association **VII:**333

American Protective Association
    (APA) **VI:**13–14, 410*c*
    immigration restrictions
        VI:186
    nativism **VI:**264
    religion **VI:**308
    Roman Catholicism **VI:**315
American Protective League
    VII:63
American Protestant Episcopal
    Church **III:**387
American Psychiatric Association
    (APA) **X:**376*c*
    gay and lesbian rights
        movement **X:**148
    science and technology
        IV:334
American Psychological
    Association **VI:**294
American Public Health
    Association **VI:**245, 407*c*
American Quarterly Review
    IV:210
American Radiator Building (New
    York City) **VIII:**28
American Railroad Journal **IV:**44
American Railway Union (ARU)
    Cleveland, Grover **VI:**75
    Debs, Eugene Victor
        VII:72, 73
    Lloyd, Henry Demarest
        VI:227
    Pullman Strike **VI:**297, 298
American Recovery and
    Reinvestment Act (2009) **X:**61,
    384*c*
American Red Cross **VI:**409*c*
    Barton, Clara **V:**29–30
    disease/epidemics **V:**112
    photography **VII:**259
    recreation **VIII:**329
American Red Cross Liberty
    Fund **X:**232
American Register, The **IV:**209
American Relief Administration
    VIII:171, 385
American Renaissance
    art and architecture **VI:**19
    literature **VI:**227
    Saint-Gaudens, Augustus
        VI:321
    sculpture **VI:**326
    White, Stanford **VI:**392
American Renaissance, An (Kemp)
    X:196
American Republican Party
    IV:196
American Revolution **III:**18–19.
    See also Revolutionary War
    abolitionism **II:**2
    African Americans **III:**8
    Algonquin **II:**18
    American Philosophical
        Society **III:**17
    Anglican Church **III:**21
    antislavery **III:**25
    Arnold, Benedict **III:**30–31

art **III:**32
Attakullakulla **II:**29
Billings, William **III:**50
Brackenridge, Hugh Henry
    III:60
Burgesses, House of **II:**51
Catholics **III:**83
Delaware **II:**96
Democratic-Republican
    societies **III:**137
Dunmore, John Murray, earl
    of **III:**142
education **III:**147, 148
Ely, Samuel Cullick **III:**151
environment **III:**154
French Revolution **III:**178
frontier, the **III:**181
Hancock, John **III:**208
iron manufacturing **II:**178
labor/labor movements
    IV:217
lawyers **III:**256
militia movement **X:**230
Olive Branch Petition
    III:324
Ostenaco **II:**280
Paine, Thomas **III:**329
popular culture **III:**341–342
race and race relations
    III:357
Randolph, Edmund **III:**358
religion **III:**360, 361
religious liberty **III:**362,
    363
riots **III:**371
Rittenhouse, David **III:**372
Rodney, Caesar **III:**373
Shippen, William, Jr. **II:**351
slave trade **III:**393
Warren, Mercy Otis **III:**427,
    428
Whigs **III:**439; **IV:**396
Wright, Fanny **IV:**405
American Rights Committee
    VII:267
American Right to Life Action
    X:289
American River **IV:**176
American Samoa **VII:**197
"American Scholar, The"
    (Emerson) **IV:**140, 228
American School of Ethnology
    IV:311
Americans for Democratic Action
    (ADA) **IX:**13–14
    Eagleton, Thomas F. **X:**107
    Henderson, Leon **VIII:**164
    Reuther, Walter **VIII:**339
    Roosevelt, Eleanor
        VIII:344
American Slavery As It Is (Weld)
    American Anti-Slavery
        Society **IV:**15–16
    Weld, Theodore Dwight
        IV:396
American Smelting and Refining
    VII:242

American Socialist **VII:**356
American Social Science
    Association (ASSA)
    Lieber, Francis **V:**234
    professional organizations,
        rise of **VI:**294
    Villard, Henry **VI:**375
American Society for the
    Promotion of Temperance
    IV:369
American Society of Composers,
    Authors, and Publishers
    (ASCAP) **VI:**171
American Sociological Association
    VI:294, 382
American Spelling Book (Webster)
    III:434, 462*c*; **IV:**134
American Sugar Refining
    Company
    business and government
        VI:57
    Congress **VI:**80
    corruption, political **VI:**83
    Northern Securities Case
        VII:242
American Sunday School Union
    (ASSU) **IV:**317, 321
Americans with Disabilities Act
    (ADA) **X:**24–25, 25, 53, 379*c*,
    403–405
American System **IV:**19–21
    Clay, Henry **IV:**96
    internal improvements
        IV:203
    Lincoln, Abraham **V:**235
    National Road **IV:**271
    Polk, James K. **IV:**302
    tariffs **V:**383
    Whigs **IV:**396–397
American System of Manufactures
    VII:150
American Telegraph Company
    V:385
American Telephone and
    Telegraph (AT&T) **VII:**406*c*
    business **VIII:**57
    FCC **VIII:**131
    Industrial Revolution,
        Second **VI:**192
    invention and technology
        VII:151
    Morgan, John Pierpont
        VI:251
    popular culture **VII:**265
    pornography **X:**283
    radio **VII:**288–290
American Temperance Society
    (ATS) **IV:**317, 369
American Temperance Union
    (ATU) **IV:**317, 370
American Tract Society **IV:**317
American Union against
    Militarism (AUAM) **VII:**31,
    256, 257
American Unitarian Association
    III:419; **IV:**318
American West Indian News **IX:**32

American Woman Suffrage
Association (AWSA) **VI:**410c
Anthony, Susan B. **VI:**16
Bradwell, Myra Colby **VI:**47
Brown, Olympia **VI:**51
Harper, Frances Ellen
Watkins **VI:**160
NWSA **V:**277
Stanton, Elizabeth Cady
V:370
Stone, Lucy **VI:**346
women's status and rights
V:436, 437; **VI:**399
American Women (PCSW report)
IX:262
American Woolen Company
VII:147, 174
American Youth Congress
VIII:130
American Zionist Emergency
Council **VIII:**441
America's Cup **V:**367
America's Funniest Home Videos
X:343
America's Most Wanted **X:**343
"America Speaks" (film series)
VIII:56
"America's Place in World History"
(Fiske) **VI:**129
America Tertia Pars (de Léry)
I:59
Ames, Adelbert **V:**55
Ames, Fisher **III:**19, 269
Ames, Iowa **VI:**63
Ames, Mary Clemmer **VI:**266
Ames, Oakes **V:**97
AMEZ Church. *See* African
Methodist Episcopal Zion
Church
Amherst, Sir Jeffrey **II:**348, 349
Fort Ticonderoga **III:**171
Gage, Thomas **III:**186
Native Americans **III:**312
Pontiac's War **III:**339, 340
Amherst College/University
Coolidge, Calvin John
VII:63
Trotter, William Monroe
VII:357
Webster, Noah **III:**434
Amiens, Peace of **III:**415
amillennialism **X:**125
Amistad Committee **IV:**21
Amistad incident **IV:21–22,** 22,
413c
Adams, John Quincy **IV:**6
American Missionary
Association **V:**8
Story, Joseph **III:**399
Tappan, Arthur and Lewis
IV:366–367
*U.S. v. Libellants and
Claimants of the Schooner
Amistad* **IV:434–438**
Amity and Commerce, Treaty of
(1778) **III:**413
Ammons, Elias **VII:**187

Ammonscossittee **II:**280
amnesty **X:**175, 368
amnesty, acts of (Reconstruction)
V:8–9, 446c
Congress **V:**89, 90
desertion **V:**111
loyalty oaths **V:**246
Proclamation of Amnesty
and Reconstruction
V:461–462
Amnesty Act (1872) **VI:**407c
Amnesty Proclamation (1865). *See*
Proclamation of Amnesty
Amoco **VII:**245, 336
Amos 'n' Andy Show **VII:**265, 288,
290, 409c; **VIII:**301, 302, 320
amphibious warfare **VIII:19–20,**
20
Higgins, Andrew J.
VIII:165
Italian campaign **VIII:**191
King, Ernest J. **VIII:**202
Marines, U.S. **VIII:**229
Navy, U.S. **VIII:**265
Nimitz, Chester W.
VIII:274
Normandy, invasion of
VIII:275–276
Philippine Sea, Battle of the
VIII:295
shipbuilding **VIII:**359
Sicily **VIII:**360
Tarawa **VIII:**386
World War II Pacific theater
VIII:436
amusement parks **VII:**293–294
Anaconda Mining Company
VII:85, 210
Anaconda Plan
Civil War **V:**73
Lincoln, Abraham **V:**237
Scott, Winfield **IV:**336
tactics and strategy **V:**381
Union army **V:**403
Anacostia Flats, Washington, D.C.
VIII:48
Anacostia River **V:**426
Anaheim, California **VII:**166
Anahuac, Mexico **IV:**374, 379,
380
Analco pueblo **I:**327
Anarchist Immigration Act
VII:14–15, 56, 144
anarchists/anarchism
Ely, Richard Theodore
VI:115
Goldman, Emma **VII:**125
Haymarket riot **VI:**168, 169
Homestead Strike **VI:**176
Howells, William Dean
VI:180
labor, radical **VI:**213
Pan-American Exposition
VII:252
radicalism **VII:**287
Warren, Josiah **IV:**392–393
anarchosyndicalists **VI:**213

Anasazi **I:**264, 395c; **II:**330
ANC. *See* African National
Congress
Anchisaurus **IV:**335
Ancient Order of Hibernians
(AOH) **V:**201; **VI:**248, 249
Ancon, Treaty of (1883) **VI:**67
Andalusia **I:**332–333; **II:**375
Anderson, James **VI:**62
Anderson, John B. **X:25,** 378c
Carter, James Earl, Jr. **X:**69
political parties **X:**277, 278
Reagan, Ronald W. **X:**300
Anderson, Joseph Reid **V:**392
Anderson, Kenneth A. N.
VIII:278
Anderson, Laurie **X:**31
Anderson, Margaret
Greenwich Village **VII:**131
literature **VII:**179
modernism **VII:**212
radical and labor press
VII:285
Anderson, Marian **VIII:**3, 255,
446c
Anderson, Mary **VIII:**421
Anderson, Richard H.
Antietam, Battle of **V:**13
Spotsylvania, Battles of
V:367–368
Wilderness, Battle of the
V:432
Anderson, Robert **V:9–10,** 154,
155, 354, 444c
Anderson, Terry **X:**345
Anderson, Thomas **X:**24
Anderson, William "Bloody Bill"
V:52, 317
Andersonville Prison, Georgia
V:10–11
Barton, Clara **V:**29
monuments **V:**268
prisons **V:**314, 315
Wallace, Lew **VI:**381
Andes Copper Mining Company
VII:210
Andes Mountains **I:9**
Amazon River **I:**8
khipu **I:**199
Machu Picchu **I:**221
Peru **I:**289
Potosí **I:**300
silver **I:**336
Andover Theological Seminary
III:307
André, John **III:19–20**
Arnold, Benedict **III:**31
theater **III:**411
Trumbull, John **III:**416
West Point **III:**437
Andreessen, Marc **X:**182, 319
Andrew, John A.
Carney, William Harvey
V:55
54th Massachusetts
Regiment **V:**142
Harvard Regiment **V:**186

Andrews, Eliza **V:**129
Andrews, George **IX:**108
Andrews, James J. **V:**11
Andrews, Samuel **VII:**335
Andrews, Stephen Pearl **VI:**400,
401
Andrews, T. Coleman **IX:**300
Andrews Sisters **VIII:403**
Freedom Train **IX:**125
music **VIII:**252
USO **VIII:**403
Andrews's Raid **V:**11, 255
Andros, Sir Edmund **II:20–21,**
436c
Dominion of New England
II:102
government, British
American **II:**152
Massachusetts **II:**223
Mather, Cotton **II:**227
Andrus, Leonard **IV:**115
anesthesia **IV:**333; **V:**257–258,
343; **VI:**244; **VIII:**351
Angel Island (San Francisco,
California) **V:**200; **VI:**184;
VIII:32
Angell, James Burrill **VI:14–15,** 27
Angelou, Maya **X:25–26**
Angelus Temple (Los Angeles,
California) **VII:**196
Anglican Church (Church of
England) **I:74–76; II:21–22;
III:20–22**
antislavery **III:**26
Baptists **III:**44
Bland, Richard **III:**53
Boucher, Jonathan **III:**59
Catholics **III:**83
Connecticut **II:**78
Dutch Reformed Church
II:107
Elizabeth I **I:**120
Enlightenment, American
II:118
Great Awakening **II:**154–
155
Henry VIII **I:**159
James I **I:**192
Johnson, Samuel **II:**187
King's College **II:**194, 195
Pilgrims **II:**293
Pinckney, Charles
Cotesworth **III:**336
Protestantism **II:**315
Puritans **I:**307
Randolph, Edward **II:**326
Reformation **I:**316–317
religion **III:**360, 361
religion, Euro-American
II:329, 330
religious liberty **III:**362,
363
Roman Catholicism **II:**335–
336
Virginia **II:**401
Weems, "Parson" Mason
Locke **III:**435

Anglican Church (*continued*)
Whitefield, George **II:**413
women's status and rights
II:425
Anglo-American Food Committee
VIII:11
Anglo-American relations
VIII:20–21
Arnold, Henry H. "Hap"
VIII:28
foreign policy **VIII:**142
Grand Alliance **VIII:**155
Italian campaign **VIII:**191
Anglo-Cherokee War **II:28–29,**
378
Anglo-Dutch wars **II:**270, 271
Anglo-French Wars **III:**79
Anglo-Iranian Oil Company
IX:214
Anglo-Normans **I:9–11,** 12, 120,
395*c*
Anglo-Powhatan War
Opechancanough **II:**278,
279
Powhatan **II:**306
Powhatan Confederacy
II:308
Angola
Africa **X:**15–16
cold war, end of **X:**84–85
Nzinga **I:**274–275
slave trade **I:**340
animal husbandry **I:**150, 270
animal rights **X:**20
animals **II:22–23; III:22–23**
agriculture **II:**11–14; **III:**11;
V:6
Colombian Exchange **I:**81
Colombian Exchange **I:**81
environment **II:**119; **III:**153
food **II:**130
science and technology
III:384
wolves **II:**421
"Annabelle Lee" (Poe) **IV:**229
Annan, Kofi **X:***356*
Annapolis Convention **III:23,**
462*c*
Constitutional Convention
III:108
Dickinson, John **III:**137
Hamilton, Alexander
III:206
Madison, James **III:**282
Annapolis Naval Academy. *See*
United States Naval Academy
at Annapolis
Anne (queen of Great Britain and
Ireland) **II:**240
annexation **IV:**414*c;* **VI:**163, 323
"Annexation" (O'Sullivan) **IV:**234
annexation of Texas **IV:438–439**
Anniston, Alabama **IX:**123
Another Country (Baldwin)
IX:34–35
Another Side of Bob Dylan
IX:92

ANSCA. *See* Alaska Native Claim
Settlement Act
Anshutz, Thomas **VII:**23
Anson, Cap **VI:**26
Antarctica **IV:**411*c*
exploration **IV:**146
global warming **X:**155
Wilkes expedition **IV:**400
Antelope Station, Nebraska
VI:240
Anthony, Daniel **V:**211
Anthony, Henry B. **VI:**14
Anthony, Susan B. **V:**446*c;* **VI:***15,*
15–16, 408*c;* **VII:**403*c*
abolitionism **V:**3
Blackwell, Antoinette Brown
VI:39
Bloomer, Amelia **IV:**59–60
Brown, Olympia **VI:**51
economy **IV:**131
Fourteenth Amendment
V:157
Gage, Matilda Joslyn **VI:**137
Hooker, Isabella Beecher
VI:176
NAWSA **VII:**223
NWSA **V:**277
Philadelphia Centennial
Exposition **VI:**284
prostitution **V:**316
Shaw, Anna Howard
VI:328–329
Speech on Woman Suffrage
VI:413
Stanton, Elizabeth Cady
V:369, 370
Stone, Lucy **VI:**346
temperance movement
IV:370
Williams, Fannie Barrier
VI:395
woman suffrage **VII:**384,
385
Women's National Loyal
League **V:**434
women's status and rights
V:436–438; **VI:**399
Woodhull, Victoria **VI:**401
World's Columbian
Exposition **VI:**402
Anthracite Coal Strike **VII:15–16,**
403*c*
Darrow, Clarence Seward
VII:70
labor: strikes and violence
VI:213
Mann-Elkins Act **VII:**190
mining **VII:**208–209
Mitchell, John **VII:**211
muckrakers **VII:**217
National Civic Federation
VII:226
New Unionism **VII:**238
presidency **VII:**268
Roosevelt, Theodore
VII:304
UMWA **VII:**360

Anthracite Coal Strike
Commission **VII:**209, 211
anthrax **X:**383*c*
anthropology **VIII:**353
"A'n't I a Woman?" speech
(Sojourner Truth) **IV:**415*c*
anti-ballistic missile systems
(ABMs) **X:**29, 99
Anti-Ballistic Missile (ABM)
Treaty **X:26–28,** *27,* 383*c*
arms race **X:**29–30
Bush, George W. **X:**55
détente **X:**103–104
SALT I/SALT II **X:**336
SDI **X:**337
antibiotic(s)
medicine **V:**256; **VIII:**234;
IX:211; **X:**222
miracle drugs **IX:**217–218
population trends **IX:**260
science and technology
VIII:351
technology **IX:**313
antibiotic resistance **X:**222
anti-Catholicism
American Protective
Association **VI:**13–14
Catholics **III:**82, 83
nativism **V:**280
anti-Catholic riots **IV:22–24,** *23*
immigration **IV:**195–196
Know-Nothing Party
IV:214
religion **IV:**320
Seton, Elizabeth Ann
IV:344
anti-Chinese agitation, rise of
IV:24
gold **IV:**178
immigration **IV:**196
race and race relations
IV:312
Anti-Comintern Pact **VIII:**225
anticommunism **VIII:22; IX:14–**
15, 352*c*
Americans for Democratic
Action **IX:**13, 14
antiwar movement, Vietnam
X:29
Army-McCarthy hearings
IX:18
Bridges, Harry **VIII:**53
Bunche, Ralph **IX:**45
cold war **IX:**63
communism **IX:**67–68
conservatism **VIII:**85;
IX:74, 75
Dulles, John Foster **IX:**91
elections **IX:**103
Federal Employee Loyalty
Program **IX:**119
folk music revival **IX:**121
Gallup Poll **IX:**131
Hollywood Ten **IX:**149
Hoover, J. Edgar **IX:**149,
150
HUAC **IX:**150–151

Internal Security Act (1950)
IX:157–158
Latin America **IX:**184
McCarthy, Joseph R.
IX:206–207
movies **IX:**223
Nixon, Richard M. **X:**256
Polish Americans **VIII:**297
religion **VIII:**335
Reuther, Walter **VIII:**339–
340
SEATO **IX:**292
Truman Doctrine **IX:**322,
359–361
union movement **IX:**323
Wallace, Henry A. **VIII:**411,
412
Anti-Defamation League **VIII:**25
antidepressants **X:**223
Anti-Drug Abuse Act (1986) **X:**97,
243
Antietam National Battlefield
V:276, 304
Antietam/Sharpsburg, Battle of
V:*12,* **12–14,** 444*c*
Armistead, Lewis A. **V:**17
Burnside, Ambrose E. **V:**52
Civil War **V:**74
desertion **V:**110
Early, Jubal A. **V:**119
Emancipation Proclamation
V:131
Garnett, Richard B. **V:**164
Gordon, John B. **V:**170
Harpers Ferry, West Virginia
V:186
Harvard Regiment **V:**186
Hill, Ambrose P. **V:**190
Hollywood Cemetery **V:**192
Holmes, Oliver Wendell
VII:140
Hood, John Bell **V:**196
Hooker, Joseph **V:**196
Howard, Oliver Otis **V:**197
Irish-American regiments
V:205
Jackson, Thomas J.
"Stonewall" **V:**210
Lee, Robert E. **V:**231
Longstreet, James **V:**242
McClellan, George Brinton
V:252
McKinley, William **VI:**240
McLaws, Lafayette **V:**253
Meade, George Gordon
V:253
medicine **V:**257
science and technology
V:340–341
Stuart, J. E. B. **V:**376
Toombs, Robert A. **V:**389
women soldiers **V:**435
Zouaves **V:**441
anti-Federalists **III:23–25**
Adams, Samuel **III:**8
Bank of the United States,
First **III:**41

Bill of Rights **III:**50
Clinton, George **III:**98–99
Constitution, ratification of the **III:**105, 106
Constitutional Convention **III:**109
Henry, Patrick **III:**211, 212
Lee, Richard Henry **III:**260
Madison, James **III:**283
Mason, George **III:**292
political parties **III:**338
states' rights **III:**397
Taylor, John, of Caroline **III:**408
Yates, Abraham **III:**453–454
Anti-Imperialist League **VI:16–17**
Atkinson, Edward **VI:**22
Higginson, Thomas Wentworth **VI:**172
Platform (1899) **VI:**441–442
southern demagogues **VII:**332
Antilles **I:**81
antilynching legislation **VIII:22–23**
African Americans **VIII:**2
Bethune, Mary McLeod **VIII:**44
Byrnes, James F. **VIII:**60
civil rights **VIII:**72
Democratic Party **VIII:**93
NAACP **VIII:**255
race and race relations **VIII:**317
Robeson, Paul **VIII:**342
Roosevelt, Eleanor **VIII:**343
South **VIII:**367
STFU **VIII:**368
Thomas, Norman **VIII:**394
Wagner, Robert F. **VIII:**410
White, Walter **VIII:**416
anti-Masonry **IV:25,** 149, 397
antimiscegenation laws **X:**213
antimissile defense system **X:**157
antimonopoly *VIII:23,* **23–24**
Frankfurter, Felix **VIII:**144
Henderson, Leon **VIII:**163
liberalism **VIII:**215
National Recovery Administration **VIII:**259
New Deal **VIII:**270
PUHCA **VIII:**313
recession of 1937–1938 **VIII:**324
Second New Deal **VIII:**356
TNEC **VIII:**391
Antinomianism
Cotton, John **II:**82
Hooker, Thomas **II:**165
Hutchinson, Anne Marbury **II:**170
Rhode Island **II:**333
anti-nuke movement **X:**377c
Antioch College **IV:**237

Antipodes **I:**84
antipoverty programs
Economic Opportunity Act (1964) **IX:**95
Harrington, Michael **IX:**142
VISTA **IX:**333
antiques **VI:**3
Antiquities Act **VII:16,** 404c
National Park Service **VII:**228
property rights **X:**290
Roosevelt, Theodore **VII:**304
Anti-Saloon League (ASL)
lobbying **VII:**181
Prohibition **VII:**272
Prohibition Party **VI:**295, 296
Volstead Act **VII:**374
anti-satellite systems (ASAT) **X:**101
anti-Semitism **VII:16–18,** *17;* **VIII:24–25**
America First Committee **VIII:**17
conservatism **VIII:**84
Coughlin, Father Charles E. **VIII:**88
Donnelly, Ignatius Loyola **VI:**100
Ford, Henry **VII:**112
Goldman, Emma **VII:**126
Hearst, William Randolph **VII:**138
Hillman, Sidney **VIII:**166
Holocaust **VIII:**170
immigration **VIII:**184
Jackson, Jesse, L. **X:**192
Jews **VIII:**195, 196
Judaism **VI:**205
Leo Frank case **VII:**176
Mencken, Henry Louis **VII:**202
postwar planning **VIII:**307
race and race relations **VIII:**318
refugees **VIII:**329
Union Party **VIII:**401
World War II **VIII:**427
World War II home front **VIII:**433
Zionism **VIII:**441
antiseptic surgery **V:**256, 258; **VI:**244
antislavery. *See* abolition/abolitionism
Anti-Slavery Convention of American Women **IV:**180, 265
Anti-Slavery Record **IV:**16
anti-suffragists **VII:18,** 384
Anti-Terrorism Act (1987) **X:**346
Anti-Terrorism Act (1990) **X:**346
Anti-Terrorism and Effective Death Penalty Act (1996) **X:**346

antitrust law **VII:**408c; **X:**381c–383c. *See also* Clayton Antitrust Act; Sherman Antitrust Act
business **X:**59
Capper-Volstead Act **VII:**49
computers **X:**87
Gates, William Henry, III **X:**147–148
Antitrust Paradox, The (Bork) **X:**45
antiunion movement **X:**203
antiwar movement (Vietnam era) **X:28–29**
Asian-American movement **IX:**21–22
civil disobedience **IX:**58
Dylan, Bob **IX:**92
folk music revival **IX:**121
Hayden, Tom **IX:**144
McCarthy, Eugene **IX:**205–206
New Left **IX:**244
popular culture **IX:**259
SDS **IX:**304
sexual revolution **X:**322
Vietnam War **IX:**331
Weathermen/Weather Underground **IX:**341
Antony and Cleopatra (Barber) **IX:**228
Antwerp, Belgium **VIII:**54
Anuszkiewicz, Richard **X:**30
"anxious bench" **IV:**151
Anzio, Italy
amphibious warfare **VIII:**20
Italian campaign **VIII:**191
World War II European theater **VIII:**431
AOH. *See* Ancient Order of Hibernians
APA. *See* American Protective Association; American Psychiatric Association
Apache Indians **VI:**407c, 409c
Armijo, Manuel **IV:**26
Carson, Kit **IV:**82
Colt revolver **IV:**102
Geronimo **VI:**142–143
Great Plains **III:**197
Howard, Oliver Otis **V:**197–198
Indians of the desert Southwest **II:**176
Lone Wolf v. Hitchcock **VII:**185
Native American religion **I:**261
Native Americans **IV:**276
Navajo **II:**254
New Mexico **I:**264
New Spain, northern frontier of **III:**318
Pershing, John Joseph **VII:**258
St. Vrain, Céran **IV:**328
Santa Fe **I:**327
Texas **IV:**371

Apache War **VI:17–18,** 409c, 410c
Geronimo **VI:**143
Indian Rights Association **VI:**190
Native Americans **VI:**261–262
Apalachee Indians **I:11,** 342; **II:**323
Apalachicola River, Battle of **IV:**338
apartheid **X:**16, 324–325, 379c
Apes, William **IV:**227
A. Philip Randolph Institute **VIII:**321
Apollo 8 (spacecraft) **IX:**297
Apollo 11 (spacecraft) **IX:**285, 297; **X:**375c
Apollo 13 (spacecraft) **IX:**231
Apollo space program **IX:**357c
NASA **IX:**231
science and technology **IX:**285
space exploration **IX:**297
space policy **X:**326
technology **IX:**312, 313
Apologetica Historia (Las Casas) **I:**207
Appalachia **IX:15–16,** *16,* 142
Appalachian Mountains
agriculture **IV:**10
Batts, Thomas **II:**34
Bonus Bill **IV:**62
canal era **IV:**79
Cherokee **IV:**85
gold **IV:**176
internal improvements **IV:**202
migration **IV:**253, 254
mining **VII:**207
National Road **IV:**271
Native Americans in the War of 1812 **IV:**276
Virginia **II:**401
Appalachian Regional Development Act (1965) **IX:**15, 142, 357c
Appalachian Spring (Copland) **VIII:**251
Appalachian Trail **IX:**239
Appeal in Favor of that Class of Americans Called Africans, An (Child) **V:**2
Appeal to Reason (journal)
radical and labor press **VII:**284, 285
Sinclair, Upton **VII:**325
socialism **VII:**327
Trading with the Enemy Act **VII:**356
"Appeal to the Christian Women of the South" (Grímke) **IV:430–434**
female antislavery societies **IV:**148
Grímké, Angelina and Sarah **IV:**180
women's status and rights **IV:**404

Appeal to the Colored Citizens of the World (Walker) **IV:**412c
  abolitionism **V:**2
  ACS **IV:**17
  Walker, David **IV:**389
Apple Computers **X:**87
Applegate, Jesse **IV:26**
Apple II computer **X:**318
Appleton, Daniel **VI:**242
appliances **VII:**93–94
Appomattox campaign **V:14**
  Appomattox Court House, Virginia **V:**15
  Ewell, Richard Stoddert **V:**136
  Five Forks, Battle of **V:**147
Appomattox Court House, Virginia **V:14–16,** *15,* 445c
  Appomattox campaign **V:**14
  Chamberlain, Joshua L. **V:**60
  Civil War **V:**74
  Confederate States of America **V:**87
  fire-eaters **V:**146
  Gordon, John B. **V:**170
  Grant, Ulysses S. **V:**174
  Harvard Regiment **V:**187
  Lee, Robert E. **V:**232
  Longstreet, James **V:**242
  marine corps **V:**248
  Parker, Ely Samuel **V:**295
  Sheridan, Philip H. **V:**353
apportionment **IX:**355c, 357c
  Baker v. Carr **IX:**33–34
  LWV **IX:**187
  Reynolds v. Sims **IX:**276
  Voting Rights Act of 1965 **IX:**334
  Warren, Earl **IX:**337
  Warren Court **IX:**338
apprentices **II:23–24**
  artisans **II:**27; **III:**35
  childhood **II:**67
  education **II:**112; **III:**147
  Garrison, William Lloyd **V:**164
  journeymen **II:**190
  labor/labor movements **II:**197, 200; **III:**252
  lawyers **III:**256
  marriage and family **III:**288
  medicine **V:**256
  NYA **VIII:**262–263
  poverty **III:**344
"Apres-Midi d'un Faune, L'" (Faulkner) **VIII:**128
Aquidneck Island **III:**369, 370
Aquinas. *See* Thomas Aquinas
Aquit family **I:**25
Arab-Israeli conflict **IX:**214; **X:**227. *See also* Israel; Palestine
Arab-Israeli War (1967) (Six-Day War)
  Camp David accords **X:**65
  Israel **IX:**160
  Jews and Judaism **X:**193

Middle East **X:**227
  Soviet Union **IX:**295
Arab-Israeli War (1973) (October War; Yom Kippur War) **X:**376c
  Camp David accords **X:**65
  cold war, end of **X:**84
  economy **X:**109
  energy **X:**120
  Jews and Judaism **X:**193
  Middle East **X:**227
  OPEC **X:**268
Arab-Israeli War (1948) **IX:**352c
Arab nationalism **IX:**214
Arafat, Yasir **X:**229, 230
Aragón
  Castile **I:**66
  Charles V **I:**70
  Ferdinand and Isabella **I:**127
  Reconquista **I:**314
Arapaho Indians **V:**443c, 445c
  Bent's Fort **IV:**55
  Chouteau family **IV:**88
  Native Americans **IV:**276
Arator (Taylor) **III:**408
Araucania **I:**373
Arawak **I:**11, 85; **II:**58
Arawakan speakers **I:**352
Arbeiter Zeitung **VII:**285
Arbenz Guzmán, Jacobo **IX:**91, 184, 353c
arbitration **VI:**209, 276
Arbuckle, Fatty **VII:**160
Arbuthnot, Alexander **III:**167
archaeological classicism **X:**31
archaeology **IV:**335
Archangel, Russia **VII:**324
Architectural Barriers Act (1968) **X:**24–25
architecture **II:**24, **24–26,** *25;* **III:27–30,** *28;* **VII:18–20.** *See also* art and architecture
  art **VII:**23, 25
  Aztecs **I:**22
  Bulfinch, Charles **III:**65
  Copán **I:**90
  Enlightenment, American **II:**118
  Harrison, Peter **II:**163
  Hearst, William Randolph **VII:**138
  housing **II:**166–167
  invention and technology **I:**184; **VII:**150
  Jefferson, Thomas **III:**233
  L'Enfant, Pierre-Charles **III:**260–261
  Machu Picchu **I:**221
  Olmecs **I:**278
  Palenque **I:**283
  Pan-American Exposition **VII:**251
  Shakers **III:**387
  Smith, Robert **II:**363
  society, British American **II:**367
  Wright, Frank Lloyd **VII:**395

Architecture for Country Houses (Downing) **IV:**31
arc lamps **VI:**353
Arctic Ocean **I:**272, 273
Arctic region **II:**177
Ardennes Forest, Belgium
  blitzkrieg **VIII:**47
  Bradley, Omar N. **VIII:**51
  Bulge, Battle of the **VIII:**54–55
Arecibo Observatory (Puerto Rico) **IX:**296
Are Men Gay Deceivers? (Leslie) **VI:**222
"Are You Politically Correct" (*New York* magazine) **X:**276
Argall, Samuel **II:**285
Argentina **I:**168
  Good Neighbor policy **VIII:**152
  Latin America **X:**206
  Monroe Doctrine **IV:**259, 261
Argonne Forest, France **VII:**11, 258, 407c
Arguim **I:**49
Argus (newspaper) **VII:**134
Arikara Indians **IV:**413c
  Ashley, William Henry **IV:**31
  disease/epidemics **IV:**123
  Native Americans **IV:**276
  Smith, Jedediah Strong **IV:**350
Aristide, Jean-Bertrand
  Clinton, William J. **X:**81
  defense policy **X:**102
  Haiti **X:**164
Aristotle
  Las Casas, Bartolomé de **I:**206
  lyceum movement **IV:**231
  medicine **V:**256
  science and technology **II:**345
  Sepúlveda, Juan Ginés de **I:**330
  slavery **II:**354
Arizona **II:**437c; **IV:**414c
  agriculture **II:**8–9
  Alvarado, Pedro de **I:**7
  Apache War **VI:**17
  Bilingual Education Act **X:**42
  Deseret, State of **IV:**120
  Goldwater, Barry **IX:**135, 136
  Hastings, Lansford W. **IV:**187
  Hohokam **I:**164
  Hopi **I:**167
  immigration **IV:**193
  Indians of the desert Southwest **II:**176
  Japanese Americans, relocation of **VIII:**193, 194
  Johnson, Hugh S. **VIII:**196

Lamy, Jean Baptiste **IV:**222
  Mexican immigration **VII:**203
  mining **VII:**209
  Native Americans **IV:**276; **X:**250
  overland mail **IV:**290
  Sunbelt **X:**338
  Texas **X:**372
  WFM **VII:**381
Arizona, USS **VIII:**292
Arizona City (Yuma), Arizona **IV:**187
Arkansas
  Austin, Stephen F. **IV:**39
  Clinton, Hillary Rodham **X:**77
  Clinton, William J. **X:**79–80
  Cody, William Frederick **VI:**76
  Faubus, Orval **IX:**117–118
  governors **V:**172
  Japanese Americans, relocation of **VIII:**194
  Jim Crow laws **VI:**204
  Ku Klux Klan **V:**223
  Liberia **VI:**223
  migration **IV:**254
  Mississippi River **V:**262
  Missouri Compromise **IV:**257
  Osceola **IV:**289
  overland mail **IV:**290
  race and race relations **VIII:**318
  slave trade, internal **IV:**348
  southern demagogues **VII:**332
  Taylor, Zachary **IV:**367
  Texas **IV:**370
  workers' compensation **VII:**392
Arkansas, CSS **V:**264
Arkansas National Guard **IX:**118
Arkansas River
  Pike, Zebulon Montgomery **IV:**300
  St. Vrain, Céran **IV:**328
  Santa Fe Trail **IV:**331, 332
  Sequoyah **IV:**343
Arkansas Volunteers **IV:**179
Arlington National Cemetery **V:16–17;** **VII:**258; **IX:**23
Armada Portrait **I:**122
Armageddon
  evangelical Christians **X:**125
  religion **VI:**307
  Tanner, Benjamin Tucker **VI:**351
Armco **IX:**300
armed forces **VII:20–21.** *See also specific branches, e.g.:* Army, U.S.
Armey, Dick **X:**170
Armies of the Night, The (Mailer) **IX:**194

Armijo, Manuel **IV:26–27**
  Bent, Charles **IV:**52
  Magoffin, James W. **IV:**233
  St. Vrain, Céran **IV:**328
  Santa Fe Trail **IV:**332
Arminianism **III:**20
Arminius, Jacob **II:**315
Armistead, Lewis A. **V:17–18,** 183, 184
Armistice Day **VII:**11
Armored Forces **VIII:**385
Armory Show **VII:21,** 405c
  art **VII:**23
  Ashcan School **VII:**26
  Greenwich Village **VII:**130
  modernism **VII:**212
Armour, Philip D. **VI:**243
Armour and Company **VII:**198
ARMs (adjustable rate mortgages) **X:**60
arms control **X:**376c–379c
  ABM Treaty **X:**27
  Bush, George H. W. **X:**53
  defense policy **X:**100
  foreign policy **X:**142
  Gore, Albert, Jr. **X:**157
  INF Treaty **X:**179–181
  Kemp, Jack F. **X:**196
  Kissinger, Henry A. **X:**198
  Reagan, Ronald W. **X:**301
Arms Control and Disarmament Agency **X:**336
arms embargo
  Neutrality Acts **VIII:**267, 268
  South Africa **X:**325
  Spanish civil war **VIII:**370
arms parity **VIII:**225
arms race **IX:**17, 17, **17–18;** **X:29–30.** See also arms control
  Catholic Bishops' Letter **X:**70
  cold war **IX:**64
  hydrogen bomb **IX:**152
  Korean War **IX:**177
  Limited Test Ban Treaty of 1963 **IX:**192
  Mills, C. Wright **IX:**217
  Republican Party **IX:**274
  SALT I/SALT II **X:**336
  SANE **IX:**283
Armstrong, Edwin **VII:**151
Armstrong, Lance **X:**384c
Armstrong, Louis **VII:**409c; **VIII:**251
  big bands **VIII:**44
  Holiday, Billie **VIII:**169
  jazz **VII:**153
  music **VII:**219, 220; **VIII:**250, 251
Armstrong, Neil **IX:**231; **X:**326, 375c
Armstrong, Samuel C. **VI:**111, 383
Armstrong, Scott **X:**51
Army, Confederate. See Confederate army

Army, Union. See Union army
Army, U.S. **VII:**409c; **VIII:25–26; IX:**351c
  AEF **VII:**10–11
  African Americans **VIII:**3
  amphibious warfare **VIII:**20
  armed forces **VII:**20, 21
  Army Act **VII:**22
  Army-McCarthy hearings **IX:**18
  Asian Americans **VIII:**32
  Atkinson, Henry **IV:**36
  Axis **VIII:**38
  Bourke-White, Margaret **VIII:**50
  Bradley, Omar N. **VIII:**50
  Capra, Frank **VIII:**62
  censorship **VIII:**65
  Cherokee **III:**87
  Cody, William Frederick **VI:**76
  Confederate army **V:**79
  conscription **VII:**63
  demobilization (WWII) **VIII:**91; **IX:**84
  DiMaggio, Joe **VIII:**96
  Drayton, William H. **IV:**127
  foreign policy **VI:**133
  Frémont, John C. **IV:**166
  gays and lesbians **VIII:**148
  Guadalcanal **VIII:**159
  Hamilton, Alexander **III:**208
  Harrison, William Henry **IV:**184
  Hershey, Lewis B. **VIII:**164
  Hood, John Bell **V:**196
  intelligence tests **VII:**148
  Japanese Americans, relocation of **VIII:**194
  King, Ernest J. **VIII:**202
  Landon, Alfred M. **VIII:**209
  Leyte Gulf, Battle for **VIII:**214
  MacArthur, Douglas **IX:**197, 198
  March on Washington Movement **VIII:**227
  Marshall, George C. **VIII:**232–233
  Mason, Richard B. **IV:**241
  Mauldin, Bill **VIII:**233
  Mitchell, William (Billy) **VII:**211
  mobilization **VIII:**241
  Mormon War **IV:**262
  National Park Service **VII:**228
  Nimitz, Chester W. **VIII:**274
  Normandy, invasion of **VIII:**275
  North African campaign **VIII:**277
  Okinawa **VIII:**287
  OSS **VIII:**284
  Pearl Harbor **VIII:**292

Pershing, John Joseph **VII:**257–258
  Philippines **VIII:**294
  Pike, Zebulon Montgomery **IV:**299–300
  Presley, Elvis **IX:**263
  Santa Fe Trail **IV:**332
  Scott, Winfield **IV:**335–336
  second front **VIII:**355
  Selective Service **VIII:**358
  Solomon Islands **VIII:**365–366
  steel industry **VIII:**374
  strikes **V:**375
  tanks **VIII:**385
  Tarawa **VIII:**386
  Union army **V:**400
  WAC **VIII:**419–421
  War Production Board **VIII:**414
Army, U.S. Department of the **IX:**238
Army Act **VII:**20, **22,** 22
Army Air Corps **VII:**21
Army Air Forces, U.S. (USAAF) **VIII:26–27,** 27
  aircraft industry **VIII:**14
  air power **VIII:**15
  Army, U.S. **VIII:**25–26
  Arnold, Henry H. "Hap" **VIII:**27–28
  Atlantic, Battle of the **VIII:**33–34
  bombing **VIII:**47
  Bourke-White, Margaret **VIII:**50
  demobilization (WWII) **VIII:**91
  Hiroshima and Nagasaki **VIII:**167
  Marshall, George C. **VIII:**233
  Okinawa **VIII:**287
  OSS **VIII:**285
  WAC **VIII:**420
  WASP **VIII:**418
Army Air Service **VII:**211–212
Army Appropriation Act (1901) **VI:**88
army chief of staff **VIII:**233
Army Corps of Engineers. See United States Army Corps of Engineers
Army Ground Forces (AGF) **VIII:**25, 420
Army Life in a Black Regiment (Higginson) **V:**189; **VI:**171
Army-McCarthy hearings **IX:18–19,** 353c
  Eisenhower, Dwight D. **IX:**101
  McCarthy, Joseph R. **IX:**207
  television **IX:**316
Army Medical Bureau (Union) **V:**256, 257
Army of New Mexico **V:**82

Army of Northern Virginia
  Antietam, Battle of **V:**12
  Appomattox campaign **V:**14
  Appomattox Court House, Virginia **V:**15
  Chancellorsville, Battle of **V:**60–62
  Cold Harbor, Battle of **V:**76–77
  Confederate army **V:**82
  Confederate States of America **V:**87
  Davis, Jefferson **V:**105
  Gettysburg, Battle of **V:**166–168
  Gordon, John B. **V:**170
  Halleck, Henry Wager **V:**182
  Hancock, Winfield Scott **V:**183
  Hill, Ambrose P. **V:**190
  Jackson, Thomas J. "Stonewall" **V:**210
  Lee, Robert E. **V:**230–231
  Longstreet, James **V:**241
  Louisiana Tigers **V:**245
  McClellan, George Brinton **V:**251, 252
  Meade, George Gordon **V:**254
  Oates, William C. **V:**287
  Overland campaign **V:**290
  Stuart, J. E. B. **V:**376
  tactics and strategy **V:**381, 382
  Zouaves **V:**441
Army of Tennessee (Confederate)
  Appomattox campaign **V:**14
  Atlanta campaign **V:**21, 22
  Bragg, Braxton **V:**42
  Chattanooga, Battle of **V:**64
  Chickamauga, Battle of **V:**64
  Confederate army **V:**82
  Cumming, Kate **V:**98
  Hood, John Bell **V:**195, 196
  Johnston, Joseph E. **V:**215
  Longstreet, James **V:**242
  Murfreesboro/Stones River, Battle of **V:**271, 272
  Orphan Brigade **V:**288
  Wheeler, Joseph **V:**428
Army of Texas **V:**48
Army of the Cumberland
  Atlanta campaign **V:**21
  Chattanooga, Battle of **V:**63
  Chickamauga, Battle of **V:**64
  Hooker, Joseph **V:**197
  Rosecrans, William S. **V:**337
  Sheridan, Philip H. **V:**353
  Thomas, George H. **V:**389
  Union army **V:**403
Army of the James
  Appomattox campaign **V:**14
  Butler, Benjamin Franklin **V:**53
  Union army **V:**403

Army of the Mississippi **V:**337
Army of the Ohio
    Atlanta campaign **V:**22
    Shiloh, Battle of **V:**358, 359
    Thomas, George H. **V:**388,
      389
    Union army **V:**403
Army of the Potomac **V:**444*c*,
    445*c*
    Antietam, Battle of **V:**12
    Appomattox campaign **V:**14
    Buell, Don C. **V:**48
    Burnside, Ambrose E. **V:**51,
      52
    Chancellorsville, Battle of
      V:60–62
    Cold Harbor, Battle of
      V:76–77
    Fredericksburg, Battle of
      V:157
    Gettysburg, Battle of
      V:166–168
    Hancock, Winfield Scott
      V:183
    Harvard Regiment **V:**186
    homefront **V:**193
    Hooker, Joseph **V:**196, 197
    Howard, Oliver Otis **V:**197
    Jackson, Thomas J.
      "Stonewall" **V:**210
    Lookout Mountain, Battle
      of **V:**243
    McClellan, George Brinton
      V:250, 251
    McDowell, Irvin **V:**252
    Meade, George Gordon
      V:253–254
    Overland campaign **V:**290,
      291
    Peninsular campaign **V:**298,
      299
    Petersburg campaign **V:**301
    Shenandoah Valley:
      Jackson's campaign
      V:349
    Sheridan, Philip H. **V:**353
    Stuart, J. E. B. **V:**375
    tactics and strategy **V:**381,
      382
    Union army **V:**403, 404
    Wilderness, Battle of the
      V:432
Army of the Shenandoah
    Appomattox campaign **V:**14
    Custer, George A. **V:**99
    Shenandoah Valley:
      Sheridan's campaign
      V:351
    Sheridan, Philip H. **V:**353
Army of the Tennessee (Union)
    Howard, Oliver Otis **V:**197
    Lookout Mountain, Battle
      of **V:**243
    Sherman, William T. **V:**355
    Union army **V:**403
    Vicksburg campaign **V:**417,
      418

Army of the Trans-Mississippi
    V:82
Army of the West **V:**32, 82
Army of Vicksburg **V:**82
Army of Virginia **V:**252
Army Relief Society **VIII:**223
Army Service Forces (ASF)
    VIII:420
Army Signal Corps, U.S. **V:**385;
    IX:280
Army Signal Intelligence Service,
    U.S. **VIII:**76, 284
Army Signal Service **VI:**387
Army War College
    armed forces **VII:**20
    Hershey, Lewis B. **VIII:**164
    National Defense Act
      VII:227
    Preparedness **VII:**267
Arnarson, Ingólfur **I:**177, 272
Arnold, Benedict **III:**30, **30–31**,
    461*c*, 462*c*
    Allen, Ethan **III:**15
    André, John **III:**19, 20
    Burr, Aaron **III:**69
    Canada **III:**78
    Carleton, Guy **III:**81
    Conway Cabal, the **III:**118
    Fort Ticonderoga **III:**171
    Jefferson, Thomas **III:**232
    Loyalists **III:**275
    Montgomery, Richard
      III:301
    Morgan, Daniel **III:**303
    Quebec, Battle of **III:**353
    Saratoga, surrender at
      III:380, 382
    U.S. Military Academy at
      West Point **V:**408
    Valcour Island, Battle of
      III:421
    West Point **III:**437
    Yorktown, surrender at
      III:454
Arnold, Henry H. "Hap" **VIII:27–**
    28
    Army, U.S. **VIII:**25–26
    Army Air Forces, U.S.
      VIII:26
    Marshall, George C.
      VIII:233
    photography **VIII:**296
Arnold, Matthew **VI:**19, 203
Arnold, Samuel **V:**19
Arnold, Thurman **VIII:**24; **X:**145
Aroostook War **IV:27**
    Caroline affair **IV:**81
    foreign policy **IV:**154
    Webster-Ashburton Treaty
      IV:394
ARPA (Advanced Research
    Projects Agency) **X:**181
ARPANET **X:**181, 182
Arrangement in Gray and Black:
    Portrait of the Artist's Mother
    (Whistler) **VI:***389*, 390
Arrowsmith (Lewis) **VII:**180

arsenals
    Confederate army **V:**81
    governors **V:**172
    Jackson, Claiborne F. **V:**209
art and architecture **I:***12*, **12–13;**
    II:*26*, **26–27;** **III:31–33,** *32;*
    IV:27–31, *28*, 414*c;* **V:***18*,
    18–19; **VI:18–20,** *19*, 409*c;*
    VII:23–25, *25*, 404*c*, 405*c;*
    VIII:28–31, *29*, *30;* **IX:19–20,**
    20; **X:30–32,** *32. See also*
    architecture
    Africa **II:**5
    Armory Show **VII:**21
    Ashcan School **VII:**25–26
    Audubon, John James
      IV:37–38
    Bierstadt, Albert **VI:**36–38
    Bodmer, Karl **IV:**60–61
    Bourke-White, Margaret
      VIII:50
    Brook Farm **IV:**65
    Burnham, Daniel Hudson
      VI:54–56
    Cassatt, Mary **VI:**63–64
    Chase, William Merritt
      VI:65–66
    Copley, John Singleton
      III:118
    Dürer, Albrecht **I:**114
    Eakins, Thomas **VI:**103–105
    Earle, Ralph **III:**145
    environment **VI:**120
    Evans, Walker **VIII:**119–
      120
    exploration **IV:**145
    FAP **VIII:**128–129
    Great Depression **VIII:**159
    Great Migration **VII:**129
    Greenwich Village **VII:**130
    Harlem Renaissance
      VII:135–136
    Hayden, Sophia Gregoria
      VI:165–166
    Hearst, William Randolph
      VII:138
    Homer, Winslow **VI:**173–
      175
    illustration, photography,
      and graphic arts **VI:**183–
      184
    La Farge, John Frederick
      Lewis Joseph **VI:**217–
      218
    literature **VII:**179
    Massachusetts **II:**225
    McCrea, Jane **III:**293
    modernism **VII:**212
    Morse, Samuel F. B. **IV:**264
    movie industry **VII:**215
    NEA **IX:**234
    Olmecs **I:**278–279
    Oyo **I:**282
    painting. *See* painting
    Palenque **I:**283
    Peale, Charles Willson
      III:332–333

    photography **VII:**258–259;
      VIII:296
    popular culture **VII:**263;
      VIII:301
    recreation **VIII:**327
    Remington, Frederic
      VI:310
    Richardson, Henry Hobson
      VI:313
    Ryder, Albert Pinkham
      VI:319–320
    Saint-Gaudens, Augustus
      VI:321
    Sargent, John Singer
      VI:323–324
    sculpture **VI:**326–327
    Stuart, Gilbert **III:**399–400
    Sullivan, Louis H. **VI:**347–
      348
    Theus, Jeremiah **II:**389–390
    Tiffany, Louis Comfort
      VI:356
    Toltecs **I:**366–367
    Trumbull, John **III:**416–417
    Venice **I:**375
    Victorianism **VI:**374
    West, Benjamin **III:**435–
      436
    Whistler, James Abbott
      McNeill **VI:**388–390
    White, Stanford **VI:**392
Art Deco **VII:**24
Arte de Navigae **I:**118
Arthur, Chester Alan **VI:***20*,
    20–21, 409*c*
    Barton, Clara **V:**29
    civil service reform **VI:**73
    Congress **VI:**80
    Conkling, Roscoe **VI:**81
    Hayes, Rutherford B.
      VI:167
    immigration **VI:**68
    presidency **VI:**290
    Reid, Whitelaw **VI:**305
    tariffs **VI:**352
    Williams, George
      Washington **VI:**396
Arthur Anderson LLP **X:**59, 315
Arthur Merwyn (Brown) **III:**64
Articles of Confederation **III:33–**
    35, *34*, 461*c*–463*c*, **469–473**
    American Revolution **III:**18
    Annapolis Convention
      III:23
    anti-Federalists **III:**24
    citizenship **III:**93
    Constitution, ratification of
      the **III:**104
    Constitution, United States
      III:107
    Constitutional Convention
      III:108, 109
    Continental Congress,
      Second **III:**115
    debt, national **III:**130
    Federalist Papers **III:**163
    Federalists **III:**165

Fiske, John **VI:**129
King, Rufus **III:**245
Lee, Richard Henry **III:**260
Madison, James **III:**282
Monroe, James **IV:**258–
Morris, Gouverneur **III:**303
Northwest Ordinances
    III:321–322
Randolph, Edmund **III:**358
Sherman, Roger **III:**389
states' rights **III:**397
Articles of Impeachment for
    President William Jefferson
    Clinton **X:409–411**
Articles of Religion (England)
    I:75
"Articles on the Organization of
    Church and Worship" **I:**53
artificial organs **X:**224, 320
artillery
    battle flags **V:**31
    Confederate army **V:**80–81
    Garnett, Richard B. **V:**163
    Lincoln, Abraham **V:**237
    science and technology
        V:342
    tactics and strategy **V:**379
    Union army **V:**401
    Washington, D.C. **V:**426
Art Institute of Chicago **VI:**218
artisans **II:27–28; III:35–36,**
    462*c*
    Aesthetic movement **VI:**3
    African Americans **VI:**7
    American Philosophical
        Society **II:**20
    apprentices **II:**23–24
    architecture **III:**29
    art **II:**26–27
    banks **III:**42
    Burgis, William **II:**51
    cities and urban life
        III:90–92
    class **II:**70
    Copley, John Singleton
        III:118
    cotton **III:**123
    crafts **II:**82
    deism **III:**135
    Dummer, Jeremiah **II:**104
    economy **II:**110
    education **III:**147
    Feke, Robert **II:**125
    freemasonry **III:**176
    Hesselius, John **II:**164–165
    indentured servitude **II:**175
    Industrial Revolution
        III:225
    Jews **III:**236
    Johnston, Henrietta Deering
        II:188
    Keith, William **II:**191
    Kuhn, Justus Engelhardt
        II:196
    labor/labor movements
        II:200; **III:**252
    limners **II:**205

MacIntosh, Ebenezer
    III:279
Massachusetts **II:**225
Mauldin, Bill **VIII:**233–234
Pelham, Peter **II:**283
Pennsylvania **II:**288
pewter **II:**291
Philadelphia **II:**292
Phyfe, Duncan **III:**334
religion, Euro-American
    II:330
Rittenhouse, David **III:**372
Smibert, John **II:**361
Spanish colonies **II:**374
Tammany Society **III:**405
Theus, Jeremiah **II:**390
Tiffany, Louis Comfort
    VI:356–357
trade, domestic and foreign
    III:415
Trumbull, John **III:**416–417
Virginia **II:**401
West, Benjamin **III:**435–
    436
women's status and rights
    II:423
Artist Fund Society (Philadelphia)
    IV:28
Artist's Letters from Japan, An (La
    Farge) **VI:**218
*Artist's Wife and His Setter Dog,
    The* (Eakins) **VI:**105
art music **VI:**254–255
Art Nouveau **VI:**19–20
Arts and Crafts movement **VII:**19
Art Students League of New York
    VI:66
Art Students' League of
    Philadelphia **VI:**104
ARU. *See* American Railway
    Union
Aryan Nations **X:**297
Asante **I:13–14,** 143
ASAT (anti-satellite systems)
    X:101
Asbury, Francis **III:36,** 36
    camp meetings **III:**77
    Methodism **III:**297
    religion **IV:**317
ASCAP (American Society of
    Composers, Authors, and
    Publishers) **VI:**171
Asche Building (New York City)
    VII:356
ASF (Army Service Forces)
    VIII:420
ASGP (Association of Green
    Parties) **X:**159
Ashbrook, John **X:**93
Ashburton, Lord. *See* Baring,
    Alexander
Ashby, Turner **V:**350
Ashcan School **VII:**23, **25–26,**
    130, 405*c*
Ashcroft, John
    independent counsel **X:**179
    tobacco suits **X:**353

USA PATRIOT Act **X:**358
*Webster v. Reproductive
    Health Services* **X:**368
Ashe, John **III:**63, 64
Ash Hollow (Blue Water Creek)
    IV:276
Ashkenazim **I:**196; **VI:**308
Ashley, John **III:**176
Ashley, William Henry **IV:31–33,**
    32*m*
    American Fur Company
        IV:18
    Astor, John Jacob **IV:**35
    Atkinson, Henry **IV:**36
    Beckwourth, Jim **IV:**50
    Bridger, James **IV:**64
    exploration **IV:**144
    fur trade **IV:**171
    McLoughlin, John **IV:**248
    Missouri Fur Company
        IV:258
    mountain men **IV:**266
    rendezvous **IV:**321
    Rocky Mountain Fur
        Company **IV:**324
    Smith, Jedediah Strong
        IV:350
Ashley fur trading expedition
    IV:411*c*
Ashley River **III:**84
Ashmun, Jehudi **IV:**225
*Ashwander v. Tennessee Valley
    Authority* **VIII:**392–393
Asia **IX:20–21**
    cold war **IX:**63
    Columbus, Christopher
        I:84, 85
    dollar diplomacy **VII:**79
    domino theory **IX:**89
    foreign policy **VI:**133, 134
    globalization **X:**155
    immigration **IX:**155
    Immigration Act (1965)
        IX:156
    Kennan, George F. **IX:**167
    Manchuria **VIII:**225–226
    Peace Corps **IX:**255, 256
    Point Four Program **IX:**257
    SEATO **IX:**291–292
    Silk Road **I:**335
    wars of national liberation
        IX:338
"Asia after Vietnam" (Nixon)
    X:256
Asian-American movement
    IX:21–22
Asian Americans/Asian
    immigration **VIII:31–33,** 32;
    X:32–34
    cities and urban life **IX:**56
    civil rights **VIII:**72
    elections, presidential **X:**118
    immigration **VIII:**184
    literature **X:**210, 211
    McCarran-Walter Act
        IX:204, 205
    multiculturalism **X:**236

National Origins Act
    VII:228
nativism **VII:**233, 234
population trends **IX:**260;
    X:282
Quota Act **VII:**279
race and race relations
    VII:281, 282; **X:**295
suburbanization/suburbs
    VIII:380
Asian Exclusion League **VIII:**32
Asiatic Barred Zone
    immigration **VII:**144
    Immigration Act (1917)
        VII:145
    nativism **VII:**234
Asiatic cholera **IV:**121–122
Asiatic Fleet **VIII:**265
asiento **I:**269
Asimov, Isaac **IX:**287
Askia Dawud (Songhai emperor)
    I:253
Askia dynasty **I:**138
Askia Ishak (Songhai emperor)
    I:342
Askia Muhammad I (Songhai
    emperor) **I:**14
    Gao **I:**138
    Mossi **I:**253
    Songhai **I:**342
    Timbuktu **I:**359–360
ASL. *See* Anti-Saloon League
Asphalt Jungle, The (film) **IX:**222
Aspin, Les **X:**81, 101, 102
Aspirations of Nature (Hecker)
    VI:316
ASSA. *See* American Social
    Science Association
assassination of Abraham Lincoln
    V:19–21, *20,* 446*c*
    amnesty, acts of **V:**9
    Johnson, Andrew **V:**211
    photography **V:**304
    Seward, William H. **V:**348
    theater **V:**386
assassinations **X:34,** **34–35,** 378*c*
    1960s **IX:22–24,** *23,*
        355*c*–357*c*
    African Americans **IX:**6
    Democratic Party **IX:**85
    gun control **X:**161
    journalism **IX:**165
    Kennedy, Jacqueline **IX:**169
    Kennedy, John F. **IX:**169,
        171
    Kennedy, Robert F. **IX:**171,
        172
    King, Martin Luther, Jr.
        IX:175
    Oswald, Lee Harvey **IX:**252
    race and race relations
        X:295
    Reagan, Ronald W. **X:**300
    television **IX:**315
assault weapons **X:**97, 161
Assemblies of God **VII:**298;
    VIII:335

assembly lines. *See* mass
production
Assertive Multilateralism policy
X:80
assimilation
immigration **V**:200
Native Americans **VIII**:263,
264
Polish Americans **VIII**:297
World War II home front
VIII:433
Assiniboine Indians
Bodmer, Karl **IV**:60
Lewis and Clark Expedition
III:263
Native Americans **IV**:276
Assistant Secretary of the Treasury
VIII:422
Associated Artists **VI**:356
Associated Catholic Charities
VII:102
Associated Jewish Charities
VII:102
Associated Press
Iwo Jima **VIII**:192
journalism **IV**:209; **V**:217;
VII:160
McCarthy, Joseph R. **IX**:206
Association, the **III**:36–37, 460*c*
Continental Congress, First
III:114
Declaration of
Independence **III**:132
Industrial Revolution
III:224
Sherman, Roger **III**:389
Association against the Prohibition
Amendment (AAPA) **VII**:274
Association for the Advancement
of Women **VI**:39, 248
Association of Advertising Clubs
of America **VII**:4
Association of American Medical
Colleges **VI**:410*c*
Association of American Painters
and Sculptors **VII**:23
Association of Catholic Trade
Unionists (ACTU) **VIII**:22
Association of Green Parties
(ASGP) **X**:159
Association of the Army of
Northern Virginia **V**:244, 415
Association of the Army of
Tennessee **V**:415
ASSU. *See* American Sunday
School Union
Astaire, Fred **VII**:124; **VIII**:246
Astor, John Jacob **II**:142;
III:465*c*; **IV**:33–35, *34*
American Fur Company
IV:18–19
Ashley, William Henry
IV:32–33
Astoria **IV**:35
Chauncey, Isaac **III**:86
Chouteau family **IV**:88
Columbia River **IV**:103

economy **IV**:131
Fort Vancouver **IV**:158
fur trade **III**:183; **IV**:171
Girard, Stephen **III**:195
Missouri Fur Company
IV:258
mountain men **IV**:266
Oregon Trail **IV**:285
Oregon Treaty of 1846
IV:287
Rocky Mountain Fur
Company **IV**:325
Astoria (Fort George) **IV**:35–36
American Fur Company
IV:18
Astor, John Jacob **IV**:34
Columbia River **IV**:103
Fort Vancouver **IV**:158
Oregon Trail **IV**:285
Penobscot campaign
III:333, 334
Scott, Winfield **IV**:336
Smith, Jedediah Strong
IV:350
War of 1812 **IV**:391
Astor Research Library **VI**:224
Astounding Stories (magazine)
IX:287
astrolabe **I**:15, 99, 334
astrology **II**:230, 345
astronauts **IX**:231, 355*c*, 357*c*;
X:326–329, 378*c*, 384*c*
astronomy **II**:345; **III**:463*c*
Mitchell, Maria **VI**:247–248
Rittenhouse, David **III**:372
science and technology
III:384; **VI**:325–326;
VII:314; **VIII**:352
Aswan High Dam (Egypt) **IX**:295,
306, 307
Atahualpa (Inca emperor) **I**:*15*,
15–16, 397*c*
gold **I**:142
Inca **I**:180
Pizarro, Francisco **I**:293
Soto, Hernando de **I**:342
Atchison, David Rice **V**:37, 221
ATF. *See* Alcohol, Tobacco, and
Firearms, Bureau of (ATF)
Athabascan **II**:176
Athens, Greece **IV**:231
Athens, Ohio **IV**:246
Atkinson, Edward **VI**:21–22
Atkinson, Henry **IV**:36, 57, 327
Atkinson, Samuel C. **IV**:210
Atkinson, Ti-Grace **X**:247
Atkins v. Virginia **X**:67
Atlanta, CSS **V**:151
Atlanta, Georgia
blues **VII**:39
Joplin, Scott **VII**:158
King, Martin Luther, Jr.
IX:173, 174
Ku Klux Klan **VII**:165
race and race relations
VII:283
Sunbelt **VIII**:381

Atlanta campaign **V**:**21–23**, *22*,
445*c*
Blair, Francis Preston, Jr.
V:36
Cleburne, Patrick R. **V**:75
Copperheads **V**:95
Davis, Jefferson **V**:105
elections **V**:126
emancipation **V**:129
Gone With the Wind **V**:170
homefront **V**:193, 194
Hood, John Bell **V**:196
Hooker, Joseph **V**:197
Johnston, Joseph E. **V**:215
Petersburg campaign **V**:302
Sherman, William T. **V**:355
Sherman's March through
Georgia **V**:356
Thomas, George H. **V**:389
Union army **V**:403
Atlanta Compromise **VI**:7, 384,
411*c*, **432–433**
Atlanta Cotton Exposition **VI**:384
Atlanta University **VI**:112
Atlantic, Battle of the **VIII**:*33*,
33–34
Casablanca Conference
VIII:62
cash-and-carry **VIII**:63
convoys **VIII**:87
destroyers-for-bases deal
VIII:94
Navy, U.S. **VIII**:265
shipbuilding **VIII**:359
submarines **VIII**:378
Atlantic and Pacific Railroad
VI:100
Atlantic and Pacific Tea Company
(A&P) **VII**:85
Atlantic Charter **VIII**:34, 447*c*,
461
Africa **IX**:3
Anglo-American relations
VIII:21
Arnold, Henry H. "Hap"
VIII:28
foreign policy **VIII**:142
Grand Alliance **VIII**:155
OWI **VIII**:286
propaganda **VIII**:311
Soviet-American relations
VIII:368, 369
UN **VIII**:402
Welles, Sumner **VIII**:415
Atlantic Coast. *See also* east coast/
eastern United States
ACS **IV**:17
agriculture **IV**:12
foreign policy **IV**:153
Forty-niners **IV**:160
Atlantic Fleet **VIII**:265
Atlantic Monthly
Eliot, Charles William **VI**:113
Harte, Bret **VI**:162
Hersey, John R. **VIII**:164
Higginson, Thomas
Wentworth **VI**:171

Howells, William Dean
VI:179
James, Henry **VI**:200
Jewett, Sarah Orne **VI**:202,
203
literature **VI**:225
Lloyd, Henry Demarest
VI:227
Norton, Charles Eliot
VI:269
Atlantic Monthly Press **VIII**:283
Atlantic Ocean
Azores **I**:17–18
dust bowl **VIII**:98
foreign policy **IV**:154
icebergs **I**:176–177
invention and technology
VII:150
Panama Canal **VII**:250
Atlantic Richfield **VII**:245, 336
Atlantic Squadron **VIII**:265
Atlantis (space shuttle) **X**:327
Atlantis: The Antediluvian World
(Donnelly) **VI**:100
atlas **I**:32, 241
Atlas Shrugged (Rand) **X**:93
atomic bomb **VIII**:**34–35**, 447*c*,
449*c*; **IX**:352*c*. *See also* nuclear
weapons
AEC **IX**:24
air power **VIII**:16
Anglo-American relations
VIII:21
arms race **IX**:17
Axis **VIII**:38
Bush, Vannevar **VIII**:57
business **VIII**:59
civil defense **IX**:56
cold war **IX**:64
Communists **VIII**:78
demobilization (WWII)
VIII:91; **IX**:84
Dennis v. U.S. **IX**:86
Einstein's Letter OF 1939
to President Franklin D.
Roosevelt **VIII**:**460–461**
ENIAC **IX**:105
espionage **VIII**:118
foreign policy **VIII**:142
Forrestal, James V. **VIII**:143
Grand Alliance **VIII**:155,
156
Hersey, John R. **VIII**:164
Hiroshima and Nagasaki
VIII:166, 469–471
hydrogen bomb **IX**:152
intelligence **VIII**:187
Iwo Jima **VIII**:192
Jews **VIII**:196
Korean War **IX**:177
Lilienthal, David E.
VIII:217
MacArthur, Douglas **IX**:198
Manhattan Project
VIII:226–227
Mariana Islands **VIII**:229
marriage and family **IX**:202

military-industrial complex **IX:**216
mobilization **VIII:**242
NSC-68 **IX:**247
Oppenheimer, J. Robert **IX:**250, 251
OSRD **VIII:**283, 284
Potsdam Conference **VIII:**308
Roosevelt, Franklin D. **VIII:**346
SANE **IX:**283
science and technology **VIII:**352; **IX:**285
Soviet-American relations **VIII:**368
Stimson, Henry L. **VIII:**375
technology **VIII:**389; **IX:**311–312
Tennessee Valley Authority **VIII:**393
Truman, Harry S. **IX:**320
Truman Doctrine **IX:**322
Truman's Announcement of the Atomic Bombing of Hiroshima **VIII:**469–471
V-J Day **VIII:**406
Wallace, Henry A. **VIII:**411
World War II **VIII:**427, 428
World War II Pacific theater **VIII:**437
atomic energy. *See* nuclear power
Atomic Energy Act (1946) **IX:**24, 351*c*
Atomic Energy Act (1954) **IX:**25, 353*c*
Atomic Energy Commission (AEC) **IX:**24, **24–25**
hydrogen bomb **IX:**152
Lilienthal, David E. **VIII:**217
medicine **IX:**210
Oppenheimer, J. Robert **IX:**251
technology **IX:**311
atomic power **VIII:**352
Atoms for Peace initiative **X:**261
"Atoms for Peace" speech (Eisenhower) **IX:**25, 353*c*
"atom smasher" **VIII:**352
ATS. *See* American Temperance Society
AT&T. *See* American Telephone and Telegraph
Attakullakulla **II:28–29,** 378
Attention Deficit and Hyperactivity Disorder (ADHD) **X:**223
Attention Deficit Disorder (ADD) **X:**218, 223
Attlee, Clement *VIII:*307, 448*c*
atomic bomb **VIII:**34–35
Grand Alliance **VIII:**156
Potsdam Conference **VIII:**307, 308
A. T. Stewart department store **VI:**382

Attucks, Crispus **III:**9, **37–38,** 56
ATU. *See* American Temperance Union
Atwater, Lee **X:**168
Atwood, Charles **VI:**55
Atzerodt, George **V:**19–21
AUAM. *See* American Union against Militarism
Auburn Penitentiary **III:**347
audiencia **I:16–17; II:**371
Council of the Indies **I:**97
Ferdinand and Isabella **I:**128
New Spain **I:**268
Philip II **I:**291
Zumárraga, Juan de **I:**392
Audubon, John James **IV:**37, **37–38,** 335, 412*c*; **VII:**98
Audubon Ballroom (New York City) **IX:**23, 199
Audubon Society **VI:**82
Augsburg, Peace of **I:**219, 315
Augusta **III:**135
Aum Shinrikyo **X:**346
Aurora
Duane, James **III:**140
Duane, William **III:**140
journalism **III:**241
Auschwitz-Birkenau camp **VIII:**170
Austin, Hudson **X:**160
Austin, Moses **IV:38–39**
Austin, Stephen F. **IV:**39
lead mines **IV:**223
Texas Revolution **IV:**373
Austin, Stephen F. **IV:39–41**
Alamo, The **IV:**14
Austin, Moses **IV:**38
Houston, Sam **IV:**191
lead mines **IV:**223
Santa Anna, Antonio López de **IV:**329
Santa Fe Trail **IV:**330
Texas **IV:**371–372
Texas Revolution **IV:**373–374
Austin, Texas **IV:**222, 370–371
Austinville mine (Virginia) **IV:**223
Australia **IX:**353*c*
Bridges, Harry **VIII:**52
Coral Sea, Battle of the **VIII:**87
evolution **VI:**122
Flynn, Edward J. **VIII:**139
Guadalcanal **VIII:**159
investments, foreign **VII:**152
Jefferson, Joseph, III **VI:**202
Johnson, Jack **VII:**154
MacArthur, Douglas **IX:**197
Midway, Battle of **VIII:**238
SEATO **IX:**291, 292
sports and recreation **VII:**333

UN **X:**356
Wilkes expedition **IV:**400
World War II Pacific theater **VIII:**435
Australian ballot. *See* secret ballot
Austria
Baldwin, Roger Nash **VII:**32
Harding, Warren Gamaliel **VII:**135
Holocaust **VIII:**169
investments, American, abroad **VI:**197
isolationists **VIII:**189
League of Armed Neutrality **III:**257
Monroe Doctrine **IV:**260
peace movements **VII:**256
population trends **VII:**266
Siberian Expedition **VII:**324
World War I **VII:**393
World War II European theater **VIII:**432
Austria-Hungary
foreign policy **VII:**114–115
Lilienthal, David E. **VIII:**217
peace movements **VII:**256
population trends **VII:**266
Trading with the Enemy Act **VII:**355
Versailles, Treaty of **VII:**369, 370
Autobiography (Franklin) **III:**175, 268
Autobiography (Jefferson) **VI:**202
Autobiography of an Idea (Sullivan) **VI:**347
Autobiography of Malcolm X, The (Malcolm X with Alex Haley) **IX:**6, 199, 356*c*
auto-da-fé **I:**17, 182
Auto-Lite Plant **VIII:**377
Automat (New York City) **IX:**121
automobile(s) **VI:**411*c*
cities and urban life **VII:**54–55
food **IX:**121–122
Ford, Henry **VII:**112
Fuel Administration **VII:**119
GM **IX:**132–133
Interstate Highway Act of 1956 **IX:**158–159
Middletown **VII:**206
National Park Service **VII:**228
recreation **VII:**295; **VIII:**328; **IX:**271
science, invention, and technology **VII:**150; **X:**320
sexuality **VII:**322
shopping centers **IX:**290
suburbanization/suburbs **VII:**340–341
teenagers **IX:**314

automobile industry **VII:26–28,** 27, 405*c*; **VIII:35–37,** 36, 445*c*; **IX:25–27,** 26, 27, 354*c*; **X:35–37,** 36
African Americans **VIII:**3
business **VIII:**57, 58
CIO **VIII:**82
Communists **VIII:**78
consumerism **IX:**76
economy **VII:**84; **VIII:**102; **IX:**97; **X:**111
Ford, Henry **VII:**111–112
Ford Motor Corporation **IX:**122–123
GM **IX:**132–133
Great Depression **VIII:**157
Interstate Highway Act of 1956 **IX:**159
invention and technology **VII:**150
labor/labor movements **VIII:**205–207; **X:**202
Lewis, John L. **VIII:**213
literature **IX:**194
mass production **VII:**195
mining **VII:**210
mobilization **VIII:**241
Murray, Philip **VIII:**249
Nader, Ralph **X:**241
National Traffic and Motor Vehicle Safety Act of 1966 **IX:**238
New Unionism **VII:**237
occupational health and safety **VII:**243
oil industry **VII:**245
Pure Food and Drug Act **VII:**276
rationing **VIII:**322, 323
Reuther, Walter **IX:**275
steel industry **VII:**337–338; **VIII:**373, 374
suburbanization/suburbs **VII:**340–341; **IX:**306
technology **VIII:**389; **IX:**313
tourism **IX:**318
transportation **VIII:**396
urban transportation **VII:**364
War Production Board **VIII:**414
automobile racing **VIII:**328
Autry, Gene **VIII:**246, 250
Avery, Henry **II:**296
Avery, Oswald **X:**224
Avery, Sewell L. **VIII:**19
Avery, Waightstill **II:**383
aviation **VII:28–29,** 404*c*, 409*c*; **VIII:**443*c*; **IX:27–29,** 28
Kelly Air Mail Act **VII:**165
Lindbergh, Charles Augustus **VII:**177–179
Marines, U.S. **VIII:**230
Navy, U.S. **VIII:**265
Preparedness **VII:**267

aviation (*continued*)
 science, invention, and
  technology **VI:**196–197;
  VII:150; **IX:**285; **X:**319–
  320
 scrap drives **VIII:**354
 technology **IX:**313
 WAC **VIII:**420
 WASP **VIII:**419
 WAVES **VIII:**418
 Wright Brothers **VII:**395–
  396
aviation industry. *See* aircraft
 industry
Ávila, Pedro Arias de **I:**342
Avilés, Pedro Menéndez de
 Calusa **I:**52
 Caroline, Fort **I:**61
 Florida **I:**131; **II:**128
 St. Augustine **II:**341
Avis Rent-A-Car **IX:**3
Awatixa **I:**162
Awatovi **I:**168
Awaxawi **I:**162
AWSA. *See* American Woman
 Suffrage Association
Axis **VIII:37–38,** 38, 447*c*, 448*c*
 African Americans **VIII:**4
 America First Committee
  VIII:17
 Army, U.S. **VIII:**25
 atomic bomb **VIII:**34
 Britain, Battle of **VIII:**53
 Casablanca Conference
  VIII:62–63
 code breaking **VIII:**76
 conservatism **VIII:**85
 enemy aliens **VIII:**114
 espionage **VIII:**117–118
 Ethiopia **VIII:**118
 FBI **VIII:**130
 FCC **VIII:**131
 foreign policy **VIII:**141,
  142
 Four Freedoms **VIII:**143
 German Americans
  VIII:149
 Good Neighbor policy
  VIII:152
 Hiroshima and Nagasaki
  VIII:167
 Hopkins, Harry L. **VIII:**177
 Hull, Cordell **VIII:**180
 isolationists **VIII:**189–190
 Italian campaign **VIII:**191
 Knox, Frank **VIII:**202
 Lend-Lease **VIII:**211
 Luce, Henry R. **VIII:**224
 North African campaign
  VIII:278
 OSS **VIII:**284, 285
 POWs **VIII:**310, 311
 Teheran Conference
  VIII:390
 UN **VIII:**402
 World War II **VIII:**427,
  428

World War II European
 theater **VIII:**429–432
World War II Pacific theater
 VIII:435
Yalta Conference **VIII:**439
"axis of evil" **X:**56
Axtell, James **I:**225
Ayde (ship) **I:**134–135
Ayer, F. Wayland **VI:**2; **VII:**4
Ayers, Bill **X:**367, 368
ayllu **I:**289
Aytch (Watkins) **V:**239
azayr **I:**324, 325
Azcapotzalco
 Aztecs **I:**18
 Tacuba **I:**352
 Tlacacla **I:**361
Azores **I:**17–18, 145, 396*c*
Aztecs **I:18–23,** *19,* 397*c*; **II:**330
 Aguilar, Francisco de **I:**4
 Aguilar, Gerónimo de **I:**5
 Alvarado, Pedro de **I:**7
 art and architecture **I:**13
 Aztlán **I:**23
 black legend **I:**31
 Cacamatzin **I:**47
 cacao **I:**47, 48
 chinampas **I:**73
 Cholula **I:**74
 Codex Mendoza **I:**77–78
 Columbian Exchange **I:**82
 conquistadores **I:**88
 Cortés, Hernán **I:**96
 Cuauhtémoc **I:**99–100
 Cuitláhuac **I:**101
 Díaz del Castillo, Bernal
  I:106
 Durán, Diego **I:**114
 Escalante, Juan de **I:**123
 Florentine Codex **I:**130
 flowery wars **I:**131
 gold **I:**142
 Grijalva, Juan de **I:**145
 Huitzilopochtli **I:**171
 invention and technology
  I:184
 Itzcóatl **I:**189–190
 khipu **I:**199
 Malinche **I:**227
 Maya **I:**235
 Mexico **I:**242
 Moctezuma II Xocoyotzin
  I:245–246
 Nahua **I:**257
 Nahuatl **I:**258
 Native American religion
  I:260
 Quetzalcoatl **I:**309
 Sahagún, Bernardino de
  I:323
 Sandoval, Gonzalo de **I:**325
 smallpox **I:**341
 Tabasco **I:**351
 Tacuba **I:**352
 Tarascan **I:**353
 Tenochtitlán **I:**354–356
 Teotihuacán **I:**356

Tezcatlipoca **I:**357
Tláloc **I:**361
Tláloc **I:**361
Tlaxcala **I:**361, 362
Toltecs **I:**365, 367
Velázquez, Diego de **I:**374
Veracruz **I:**376
Aztlán **I:18, 23,** 354
Azusa Street Revival **VII:**298

B

B-1 bomber **X:**101
B-17 Flying Fortress
 air power **VIII:**15—16
 bombing **VIII:**47
 WAC **VIII:**420
 WASP **VIII:**419
B-24 Liberator **VIII:**15, 33–34
B-25 Mitchell **VIII:**419
B-26 Marauder **VIII:**419
B-29 Superfortress
 aircraft industry **VIII:**14
 air power **VIII:**16
 Army Air Forces, U.S.
  VIII:27
 atomic bomb **VIII:**35
 bombing **VIII:**48
 Hiroshima and Nagasaki
  VIII:166
 Iwo Jima **VIII:**192
 World War II Pacific theater
  VIII:437
B-52 (aircraft) **IX:**285
Baath Party (Iraq) **X:**187
Baba, Ahmad **I:**25
Babbitt (Lewis) **VII:**180;
 VIII:218
Babbitt, Irving **VIII:**84
Babcock, Orville E.
 foreign policy **V:**151
 Grant, Ulysses S. **V:**175
 Santo Domingo, proposed
  annexation of **VI:**323
 Whiskey Ring **V:**429
Babes in Toyland (Herbert)
 VII:95, 219
Babur, Zahiruddin Muhammad
 I:181
Baburnama (Babur) **I:**181
baby boom **IX:31–32,** *32,* 351*c*
 business **IX:**47
 childhood **IX:**54, 55
 commemoration **IX:**66
 economy **IX:**97
 marriage and family **IX:**201
 NEH **IX:**234–235
 New York World's Fair
  (1964) **IX:**246
 population trends **VIII:**305;
  IX:259
 shopping centers **IX:**290
 Spock, Benjamin **IX:**297
 suburbanization/suburbs
  IX:305
 teenagers **IX:**314

women's status and rights
 VIII:423
World War II **VIII:**428
World War II home front
 VIII:433
baby boomers **X:39–40**
 Amendments to the U.S.
  Constitution **X:**23
 birthrates **X:**44
 sexual revolution **X:**322
Bacall, Lauren **IX:**224
Bacchante and Infant Faun
 (MacMonnies) **VI:**327
Bach, J. S. **II:**247
Bache, Benjamin Franklin **III:**39
 Alien and Sedition Acts
  III:14
 Duane, William **III:**140
 journalism **III:**241
Bachelet, Verónica Michelle
 X:206
Bacher, Robert F. **IX:**24
Backenridge, William **IV:**400
backlash **X:**93, 134
Backus, Isaac **II:**33; **III:39–40,**
 44
Bacon, Francis **VI:**100
Bacon, Henry **VI:**327
Bacon, Nathaniel
 Bacon's Rebellion **II:**31–
  32
 Berkeley, Lady Frances
  II:36
 Berkeley, Sir William **II:**37
 Charges against the Virginia
  Governor **II:441–442**
 crowd actions **II:**86
 "Declaration in the Name of
  the People of Virginia"
  II:441–442
 Jamestown **II:**183
 Virginia **II:**400
Bacon's Rebellion **II:31–32,** *32,*
 436*c*
 Berkeley, Lady Frances
  II:36
 Berkeley, Sir William **II:**37
 Burgesses, House of **II:**51
 class **II:**70
 crowd actions **II:**86
 Jamestown **II:**183
 Powhatan Confederacy
  II:308
 Susquehannock War
  II:380
 Virginia **II:**400
bacteria **X:**222
Bad Axe River, Battle of
 Atkinson, Henry **IV:**36
 Black Hawk War **IV:**58
 Native Americans **IV:**274
 Sac and Fox **IV:**327
 Taylor, Zachary **IV:**367
Badlay, Ahmad **I:**124
Badnarik, Michael **X:**118
Badoglio, Pietro **VIII:**118
Badr, battle of **I:**238

Baehr v. Miike **X**:215
Baer, George **VII**:208–209
Baez, Buenaventura **VI**:323
Baez, Joan
    Dylan, Bob **IX**:92
    folk music revival **IX**:121
    March on Washington
      (1963) **IX**:201
    music **IX**:229
    popular culture **IX**:259
    Savio, Mario **IX**:284
Baghdad, Iraq **X**:187, 188
Bahamas **II**:384; **VIII**:181
Bahía **I**:25–26, 35
Baikal, Lake (Russia) **VII**:325
Bailey, James A. **VI**:25, 117–118
Bailey, Joseph **V**:311
*Bailey v. Drexel Furniture
    Company* **VII**:408*c*
bailouts
    automobile industry **X**:37
    business **X**:61
    Chrysler Corporation Loan
      Guarantee Act **X**:74–75
    New York City (1974)
      X:253–254
Bainbridge, William **III**:46
Baja California **I**:51–52
Baker, Charles **IX**:33
Baker, Ella Josephine **IX**:32–33
    King, Martin Luther, Jr.
      IX:174
    NAACP **VIII**:256
    SNCC **IX**:302
Baker, Howard **X**:320, 321
Baker, James **X**:163
Baker, Ray Stannard
    journalism **VII**:159
    muckrakers **VII**:217
    Steffens, Lincoln **VII**:339
    Tarbell, Ida Minerva
      VII:349
Baker, Theodore **VI**:255
Baker v. Carr **IX**:33–34, 338,
    355*c*; **X**:48
Baker v. Vermont **X**:215–216
Bakeshop Act **VII**:182, 183
Baki **I**:349–350
Bakke, Allan **X**:40, 158
Bakke case (*Regents of the
    University of California v.
    Allan Bakke*) **X**:40–41, 377*c*
    affirmative action **X**:9
    Brennan, William J., Jr.
      X:48
    Gramm-Rudman-Hollings
      Act **X**:159
    *Gratz v. Bollinger/Grutter v.
      Bollinger* **X**:158
    NAACP **X**:245
    Powell, Lewis **X**:288
Bakker, Jim **X**:234, 342
Bakri, al- **I**:139–140
Balaguer, Joaquin **IX**:184
Balanced Budget and Emergency
    Deficit Control Act. *See*
    Gramm-Rudman-Hollings Act

Balboa, Vasco Núñez de **I**:26, 397*c*
    adelantado **I**:4
    conquistadores **I**:88
    Panama **I**:284
    Soto, Hernando de **I**:342
Baldanzi, George **IX**:249
Baldwin, Chuck **X**:118
Baldwin, James **IX**:34, 34–35,
    353*c*
    African Americans **IX**:5
    literature **IX**:194
    March on Washington
      (1963) **IX**:201
Baldwin, Matthias **IV**:333
Baldwin, Roger Nash **VII**:9,
    31–32, 58
Baldwin, Roger Sherman **IV**:21,
    367
Baldwin Locomotive Works
    IV:333
Bali **VII**:197
Balinese Character (Fortune and
    Mead) **VII**:197
Balkans **VIII**:431, 432
Ball, George W. **X**:357
Ballinger, Richard Achilles
    Pinchot, Gifford **VII**:260
    Progressive Party **VII**:270
    Taft, William Howard
      VII:348
ballistic missiles
    ABM Treaty **X**:27
    arms race **IX**:17
    aviation **IX**:29
    Bush, George H. W. **X**:53
    computers **IX**:71
    Cuban missile crisis **IX**:81
    defense policy **X**:99–101
    ICBMs **IX**:17
    INF Treaty **X**:180
Balloon Corps **V**:25–26
balloons **V**:341, 380
ballot stuffing **VI**:83
Ball's Bluff, Battle of
    Harvard Regiment **V**:186
    Holmes, Oliver Wendell
      VII:140
    Joint Committee on the
      Conduct of the War
      V:215, 216
Balmaceda, José Manuel **VI**:67
Baltic States **VIII**:266
Baltimore, Archdiocese of **IV**:344
Baltimore, Battle of **IV**:43
    Key, Francis Scott **IV**:213
    Madison, James **III**:284
    War of 1812 **IV**:392
Baltimore, Maryland
    ACS **IV**:17
    anti-Catholic riots **IV**:24
    anti-Masonry **IV**:25
    baseball **VII**:33
    Butler, Benjamin Franklin
      V:53
    Catholics **III**:83
    Continental Congress,
      Second **III**:116

Democratic Party **IV**:119
disease/epidemics **IV**:122
education, philanthropy and
    VI:112
Free-Soil Party **IV**:163
*Genius of Universal
    Emancipation* **IV**:175
immigration **IV**:194; **VI**:184
industrialization **IV**:200
Judaism **VI**:205
Marshall, Thurgood **IX**:202
McCulloch v. Maryland
    IV:245
Morse, Samuel F. B. **IV**:264
Polk, James K. **IV**:302
population trends **III**:343
railroads **IV**:314
religion **IV**:318
riots (1861) **V**:26, 53, 426
Seton, Elizabeth Ann
    IV:344
slave trade, internal **IV**:349
trade, domestic and foreign
    III:414–415
Washington, D.C. **V**:426
Baltimore, USS **VI**:67
Baltimore Daily Advertiser
    IV:208
Baltimore Morning Herald
    VII:201
Baltimore & Ohio Railroad (B&O)
    IV:43–44, 412*c*
    economy **IV**:131
    Great Strike of 1877 **VI**:154
    industrialization **IV**:200
    internal improvements
      IV:202–203
    Mosby, John Singleton
      V:271
    National Road **IV**:273
    railroads **IV**:314, 316
    science and technology
      IV:333
    transportation **V**:391;
      VIII:396
Baltimore Sun
    cities and urban life **IV**:92
    journalism **IV**:208, 210
    Mencken, Henry Louis
      VII:201
Balzac v. Puerto Rico **VII**:408*c*
Banai, Eddie Benton **IX**:12, 357*c*
Bancroft, Anne **IX**:226
Bancroft, George
    McMaster, John Bach
      VI:242
    Peabody, Elizabeth Palmer
      VI:279
    Social Darwinism **VI**:334
bandeirantes **I**:35
Banister, Marion Glass **VIII**:422
banjos **II**:247
BankAmericard **IX**:79
Bankhead, John H. **VIII**:11, 39
Bankhead Bill (1935) **VIII**:39
Bankhead-Jones Farm Tenant Act
    (1937) **VIII**:39, 107, 127, 445*c*

banking, investment **VI**:23–24,
    375
Banking Act of 1933 (Glass-
    Steagall Act) **VIII**:40–41,
    444*c*
    banking **VIII**:40
    Banking Act (1935) **VIII**:41
    FDIC **VIII**:132
    Hoover presidency
      VIII:174
    monetary policy **VIII**:243
    New Deal **VIII**:269
Banking Act of 1935 **VIII**:41
    banking **VIII**:40
    Banking Act (1933) **VIII**:41
    Eccles, Marriner S.
      VIII:101
    FDIC **VIII**:132
    monetary policy **VIII**:243
    New Deal **VIII**:269
banking and currency **II**:32–33;
    III:42–43; **IV**:44–48, 45; **V**:26–
    28, 27; **VII**:406*c*; **VIII**:39–40,
    443*c*, 444*c*. *See also* national
    banking system
    agriculture **III**:11
    American System **IV**:19–20
    Austin, Moses **IV**:38–39
    Banking Act (1933) **VIII**:40–
      41
    Banking Act (1935) **VIII**:41
    Bank of the United States,
      Second **IV**:48
    Benton, Thomas Hart
      IV:53–54
    Berle, Adolf A., Jr. **VIII**:43
    Bonus Bill **IV**:62
    business **VIII**:57; **X**:57
    business cycles **VI**:59
    Chase, Salmon P. **V**:63
    Coughlin, Father Charles E.
      VIII:88
    Democratic Party **IV**:118;
      V:108; **VII**:74
    economy **III**:146; **IV**:129,
      131–132; **V**:121–123;
      VII:84–85; **VIII**:103
    elderly **VIII**:107
    election of 1840 **IV**:138
    Emergency Banking Act of
      1933 **VIII**:112–113
    Era of Good Feelings
      IV:141
    farmers' alliances **VI**:125
    FCA **VIII**:125
    FDIC **VIII**:132
    FHA **VIII**:126
    Freedmen's Savings Bank
      V:159
    Gallatin, Albert **III**:188
    Girard, Stephen **III**:195
    Gould, Jay **VI**:151
    government **VIII**:152
    Great Depression **VIII**:157
    HOLC **VIII**:170–171
    Hoover presidency
      VIII:174

banking and currency *(continued)*
 housing **VI:**179
 Jones, Jesse H. **VIII:**197
 Kennedy, Joseph P.
  VIII:199
 Morgan, John Pierpont
  VI:250–251
 Morris, Robert **III:**305
 national banking system
  VI:260–261
 panic of 1837 **IV:**295
 panic of 1857 **V:**294
 RFC **VIII:**325
 stock market crash
  VIII:376
 trade, domestic and foreign
  III:414
 USA PATRIOT Act **X:**359
 USHA **VIII:**404
 Wilson, Thomas Woodrow
  VII:383
Banking and Currency Committee
 VIII:356
Bank of America **IX:**208
Bank of England
 Bank of the United States,
  First **III:**40
 commonwealthmen **III:**103
 debt, national **III:**130
 panic of 1837 **IV:**294
Bank of New York
 banks **III:**42
 Hamilton, Alexander
  III:206
 McDougall, Alexander
  III:294
 panic of 1792 **III:**330
 trade, domestic and foreign
  III:414
Bank of North America **III:40,**
 462*c*
 banks **III:**42
 Bingham, William **III:**51
 Morris, Gouverneur **III:**304
 Morris, Robert **III:**305
 trade, domestic and foreign
  III:414
Bank of Pennsylvania **III:**462*c*
 banks **III:**42
 Carey, Mathew **III:**80
 Gallatin, Albert **III:**188
Bank of the United States, First
 III:40–41, *41,* 463*c,* 466*c*
 banking **IV:**45
 banks **III:**42
 Carey, Mathew **III:**80
 Duer, William **III:**141
 economy **III:**146; **IV:**132
 Federalist Party **III:**164
 Gallatin, Albert **III:**188
 Girard, Stephen **III:**195
 Hamilton, Alexander
  III:207
 King, Rufus **III:**245
 McCulloch v. Maryland
  IV:245
 panic of 1792 **III:**330

states' rights **III:**397
trade, domestic and foreign
 III:414
War of 1812 **IV:**390–391
Bank of the United States, Second
 IV:48–49, 411*c,* 413*c*
 American System **IV:**19–21
 art and architecture
  IV:29–30
 banking **IV:**46
 Benton, Thomas Hart **IV:**54
 Bonus Bill **IV:**62
 Calhoun, John C. **IV:**68
 Clay, Henry **IV:**97
 Democratic Party **IV:**118
 economy **IV:**132
 election of 1828 **IV:**137
 election of 1840 **IV:**138
 Era of Good Feelings
  IV:141
 Girard, Stephen **III:**195
 Jackson, Andrew **IV:**207
 Madison, James **III:**284
 Marshall, John **III:**290
 Martin, Luther **III:**291
 McCulloch v. Maryland
  IV:245–246
 Monroe, James **IV:**259
 national banking system
  VI:260
 panic of 1819 **IV:**293
 panic of 1837 **IV:**294
 Polk, James K. **IV:**301
 Taney, Roger B. **IV:**366
 Van Buren, Martin **IV:**385
 Webster, Daniel **IV:**393
 Whigs **III:**397
bankruptcy **X:**384*c*
 agriculture **X:**20
 automobile industry **X:**37
 business **X:**59, 60
 business cycles **VI:**58
 railroads **VI:**302
 Sarbanes-Oxley Act **X:**315
bankruptcy (New York City)
 X:377*c*
bankruptcy law **III:**291
Banks, Dennis **IX:**12, 357*c*
Banks, Nathaniel P. **V:28–29**
 Cedar Mountain, Battle
  of **V:**59
 Jackson, Thomas J.
  "Stonewall" **V:**210
 Mississippi River war **V:**264
 Peninsular campaign **V:**298
 Red River campaign **V:**329
 Shenandoah Valley:
  Jackson's campaign **V:**349,
  350
 Union army **V:**401
 Vicksburg campaign **V:**418
 Zouaves **V:**442
Bank War
 Democratic Party **IV:**118
 economy **IV:**132
 panic of 1837 **IV:**294
Bannan, Benjamin **VI:**248, 249

Banneker, Benjamin **III:***43,*
 43–44, 463*c*
Banthine **IX:**211
Bantu **I:**26–27, 56, 217
Bao Dai (emperor, ruler of South
 Vietnam) **IX:**330
Baptismal Scene (Rothko)
 VIII:31
Baptism in Kansas (Curry)
 VIII:31
Baptists **II:33–34; III:44–45**
 African-American churches,
  growth of **VI:**4
 African Americans **VI:**7;
  X:14
 antislavery **III:**26
 Backus, Isaac **III:**40
 evangelical Christians **X:**125
 female antislavery societies
  IV:147
 Great Awakening **II:**156
 migration **VII:**207
 Rauschenbusch, Walter
  VII:292–293
 religion **III:**360–362;
  IV:317–320; **V:**331;
  VII:298; **VIII:**335
 religion, African-American
  II:328
 religion, Euro-American
  II:329
 religious liberty **III:**363,
  364
 Second Great Awakening
  IV:337
 Virginia **II:**402
 Willard, Samuel **II:**415
 Williams, Roger **II:**416
baraka **I:**348
Baraka, Amiri **IX:**6, 356*c*
Baramendana (king of Mali)
 I:225, 226
Baranov, Alexander **II:**338
Baratarian Coast **IV:**220
Barbadoes, James G. **IV:**15
Barbados **I:**27, 349; **II:**369;
 III:436
Barbary Wars **III:45–46**
 Chauncey, Isaac **III:**86
 Decatur, Stephen **IV:**115
 foreign affairs **III:**168, 169
 Rowson, Susanna Haswell
  III:374
barbed wire **VI:**24, 65, 376, 408*c*
Barbee, George **VI:**177
Barber, Samuel **IX:**228
Barber of Seville, The
 (Beaumarchais) **III:**48
Barbie doll **IX:**55
Barbizon school **VI:**217
"Barcelona Letter" of 1493
 (Columbus) **I:**303, 368,
 402–404
Barclay, Robert **IV:**220–221
Bard, John **III:**295
Bardeen, John **X:**86
Barents, Willem **I:**115, 273

Baring, Alexander (1st baron
 Ashburton) **IV:**394, 414*c*
Baring Brothers **VI:**59
Barkley, Alben **VIII:**80
Barletta, Nicolas Ardito **X:**269
Barlow, Francis Channing **V:**419
Barlow, Joel **III:46–47**
 Barbary Wars **III:**45
 Connecticut Wits **III:**104
 environment **III:**154
Barlowe, Arthur **I:28**
 Manteo **I:**229
 North Carolina **II:**274
 Roanoke **I:**320–321
 Wanchese **I:**382
 Wingina **II:**417
Barnard, George Gray **VI:**327
Barnard, George N. **V:**304–305
Barnard, Henry **IV:**133; **V:**120
Barnard College
 Goldmark, Josephine Clara
  VII:127
 Hurston, Zora Neale
  VIII:181
 Mead, Margaret **VII:**197
Barnburners **IV:**163; **VI:**357
Barnes, Clifford **X:**168
Barnett, Ferdinand **VI:**388
Barnett, Ross **IX:**213
Barnett, Samuel **VI:**327
Barnum, Phineas T. **VI:24–25,**
 25, 407*c*
 cities and urban life **IV:**92
 entertainment, popular
  VI:117–118
 music **IV:**269
Barnwell, John **II:**395
Baronov, Aleksandr Andreyevich
 III:12
Baroody, William, Jr. **X:**349
Baroody, William, Sr. **X:**349
Barr, Bob **X:**118
Barré, Isaac **III:**443
Barrett, James **III:**266
Barrington, Lord Thomas **III:**49
barrios **VIII:**237
Barron, Frank **IX:**187
Barron, James
 Chesapeake-Leopard affair
  III:88
 Decatur, Stephen **IV:**115
 Jefferson, Thomas **III:**235
Barron v. Baltimore **IV:**413*c*
Barry, John **III:47,** 461*c*
Barry, Leonora Marie **VI:**215
bars **VIII:**328
"Bars Fight" (Terry) **II:**206
barter **I:**362
Barth, Karl **VIII:**335
Barthelme, Frederick **X:**211
Bartholdi, Auguste **VI:**344
Bartholdi Pedestal Fund **VI:**219
"Bartleby the Scrivener" (Melville)
 IV:229
Bartlett, Charlie **IX:**168
Bartók, Béla **VIII:**252
Barton, Benjamin Smith **III:**385

Barton, Bruce **VII:**5
Barton, Clara **V:29–30,** *30;*
    VI:409*c*
    Andersonville Prison,
        Georgia **V:**11
    disease/epidemics **V:**112
    Johnstown flood **VI:**204
    nurses **V:**285
    women soldiers **V:**435
Barton, W. P. C. **III:**385
Bartram, John **II:34**
    American Philosophical
        Society **II:**20; **III:**17
    animals **II:**23
    Kalm, Peter **II:**191
    Pennsylvania **II:**287
    science and technology
        II:345; **III:**385
Bartram, William **III:47–48,** *48,*
    385, 463*c*
Baruch, Bernard Mannes **VII:32;**
    VIII:41–42
    Byrnes, James F. **VIII:**60
    cold war **IX:**62
    dollar-a-year men **VIII:**96
    Johnson, Hugh S. **VIII:**196
    Preparedness **VII:**267
    reconversion **VIII:**326
    religion **VIII:**335
    War Industries Board
        VII:378
Baruch-Hancock Report
    VIII:326
bascule bridge **VI:**48
baseball **VI:25–27,** *26;* **VII:32–**
    34, *33;* **VIII:**445*c–447c;*
    IX:351*c,* 354*c;* **X:**380*c,* 384*c*
    Aaron, Henry L. "Hank"
        X:1
    African Americans **IX:**5
    DiMaggio, Joe **VIII:**95–96
    Gay Nineties **VI:**140
    Japanese Americans,
        relocation of **VIII:**194
    movies **X:**236
    popular culture **VII:**263–
        264
    recreation **VII:**293, 295;
        VIII:328; **X:**302
    Rickey, Branch **IX:**276–277
    Robinson, Jackie **IX:**277–
        278
    sports and recreation
        V:366–367; **VII:**332–334;
        VIII:370–371; **IX:**298,
        299; **X:**329–330
    Sunday, William Ashley, Jr.
        VII:341–342
    urban transportation
        VII:364
Baseball Hall of Fame and
    Museum (Cooperstown, New
    York) **VIII:**370; **IX:**277
BASIC programming language
    IX:285; **X:**147
Basie, William "Count"
    African Americans **VIII:**3

big bands **VIII:**44
    Holiday, Billie **VIII:**169
    music **VIII:**250
basketball **VI:**343; **VII:**334;
    VIII:371; **X:**331–332
Basques **I:**77, 250
bas relief **VI:**321
Bastogne, Belgium **VIII:**54–55
Bataan Death March *VIII:42,*
    42–43, 447*c*
    Hiroshima and Nagasaki
        VIII:167
    Philippines **VIII:**295
    POWs **VIII:**311
Bataan Peninsula, Philippines
    VIII:294
Batavia, New York **IV:**25
Bates, Edward **V:30–31,** 333
Batista, Fulgencio **IX:**35, 64
Batman **VIII:**303
Baton Rouge, Louisiana **IV:**6;
    VIII:223
Battel, Andrew **I:28,** 307
Battle above the Clouds. *See*
    Lookout Mountain, Battle of
"Battle Cry of Freedom" **V:**273
battle flags **V:***31,* **31–32,** *32*
"Battle Hymn of the Republic"
    (Howe)
    Howe, Julia Ward **V:**198
    music **V:**273
Battle of Bunker Hill (Trumbull)
    III:416
"battle of the riders" **VI:**168
*Battles and Leaders of the Civil
    War* (Gilder) **V:**239; **VI:**147
battleships
    Navy, U.S. **VIII:**265
    Pearl Harbor **VIII:**292, 293
    Philippine Sea, Battle of the
        VIII:295
Batts, Thomas **II:34–35,** 124
Bauer, Gary **X:**94
Baugh, Sammy **VIII:**371
Baum, L. Frank **VI:**90
Bavarian Illuminati **III:**307
Baxter, Irving **VI:**359
Bayard, James A. **III:**151, 373
Bayard, Thomas Francis **VI:**15,
    27–28, 34
Bayard-Chamberlain Treaty
    VI:34
Bayh, Birch **X:**123
Bayley, Richard **IV:**343
Bay of Pigs **IX:35–36,** 355*c*
    CIA **IX:**52
    cold war **IX:**64
    Cuban missile crisis **IX:**80
    journalism **IX:**166
    Kennedy, John F. **IX:**170
    Limited Test Ban Treaty of
        1963 **IX:**192
    military-industrial complex
        IX:216
    New Frontier **IX:**243
    Operation Mongoose
        IX:250

Bay Psalm Book
    Day, Stephen **II:**92
    Eliot, John **II:**115
    Massachusetts **II:**223
    music **II:**247
    printing and publishing
        II:311
Baze v. Rees **X:**67
BBC (British Broadcasting
    Corporation) **VIII:**312
BBN (Bolt Beranek and Newman,
    Inc.) **X:**181
BE (Bureau of Ethnology) **VI:**141
Beach, Alfred **VI:**361
Beach, Amy Marcy Cheney
    VI:28–29, 254–255
Beacon Hill (Boston) **III:**118
Beadle, Erastus **V:**239; **VI:**98
Beadle, Irwin **V:**239
Beagle, HMS **VI:**122
Beale, Fred **VII:**122
Beall, Lloyd J. **V:**248
Beal v. Doe **X:**3
Beame, Abraham **X:**253, 254
Bean, James Baxter **V:**258
Beanes, William **IV:**213
Beard, Charles
    debt, national **III:**131
    history **VII:**139–140
    industrial development
        V:204
    Lend-Lease **VIII:**211
    literature **VII:**180
    modernism **VII:**212
Beard, Mary
    history **VII:**140
    industrial development
        V:204
    literature **VII:**180
    modernism **VII:**212
Bear Flag Revolt **IV:**49*m,* **49–50**
    Bidwell, John **IV:**56
    California **IV:**71
    Carson, Kit **IV:**82
    exploration **IV:**145
    Frémont, John C. **IV:**167
    Larkin, Thomas Oliver
        IV:223
Bear Lake **IV:**325
Bear Stearns **X:**61
Beat Generation **IX:36–37,** 353*c*
    counterculture **IX:**78
    gays and lesbians **IX:**132
    Ginsberg, Allen **IX:**134–135
    Kerouac, Jack **IX:**173
    Leary, Timothy **IX:**187
    literature **IX:**194
    marriage and family **IX:**202
    music **IX:**229
    religion **IX:**272
    teenagers **IX:**314
Beatles, The **IX:37–38,** *38,* 356*c*
    counterculture **IX:**79
    Ginsberg, Allen **IX:**135
    LSD **IX:**196
    movies **IX:**225
    music **IX:**229–230; **X:**238

popular culture **IX:**259
    rock and roll **IX:**279
    teenagers **IX:**314
    television **IX:**315
beatniks
    Beat Generation **IX:**37
    counterculture **IX:**78
    Kerouac, Jack **IX:**173
Beattie, Ann **X:**211
Beatty, Warren **IX:**226
Beaufort, Battle of **III:**236
Beaulieu, Priscilla **IX:**263
Beaumarchais, Pierre-Auguste
    Caron de **III:48–49**
Beaumont, Texas **VII:**245
Beaumont, William **IV:**249
Beauregard, Pierre Gustave
    Toutant **V:32,** 444*c*
    Alexander, Edward P. **V:**7–8
    Anderson, Robert **V:**10
    Appomattox Court House,
        Virginia **V:**16
    Boyd, Belle **V:**40
    Buell, Don C. **V:**48
    Bull Run/Manassas, First
        and Second Battles of
        V:50
    Confederate army **V:**82
    Davis, Jefferson **V:**105
    Fort Sumter **V:**154, 155
    Greenhow, Rose O'Neal
        V:178
    H.L. Hunley, CSS **V:**191
    Johnston, Albert Sidney
        V:214
    Johnston, Joseph E. **V:**214
    literature **V:**239
    Shiloh, Battle of **V:**359, 360
    Wigfall, Louis T. **V:**431
"Beautiful River" (Lowry) **VI:**257
*Beautiful Women of Twelve
    Epochs* (Leslie) **VI:**222
beauty industry **VII:65–66**
Beaux, Cecilia **VII:**23
Beaux Arts style **VI:**326, 392,
    409*c*
Beaver Island **IV:**358
Beaver Wars **II:35,** 169, 179
bebop **VIII:**195, 251
Beccaria, Cesare **III:**346; **IV:**296
Bechet, Sidney **VII:**153
Beck (Hansen) **X:**239
Beck, Dave **IX:**310, 311, 323
Beck, Martin **VI:**117
Becker, Carl **VII:**139–140, 212
Becknell, William **IV:50,** 145,
    330, 331
Beckwourth, Jim **IV:50–51,** 411*c*
    exploration **IV:**144, 145
    mountain men **IV:**266
    Rocky Mountain Fur
        Company **IV:**324
Beckwourth Pass **IV:**145
Bedini, Gaetano **IV:**24
Beecher, Catharine
    cities and urban life **IV:**93
    education **IV:**134, 135

Beecher, Catharine *(continued)*
  female antislavery societies
    IV:148
  Stowe, Harriet Beecher
    V:373
  women's status and rights
    IV:403
Beecher, Henry Ward **IV:**414*c;*
  VI:29, **29–30**
  Beecher-Tilton scandal
    VI:30
  Dana, Charles A. **VI:**92
  Darwinism and religion
    VI:93
  Hooker, Isabella Beecher
    VI:176
  Ingersoll, Robert Green
    VI:193
  music **VI:**255
  religion **VI:**306, 307
  Social Darwinism **VI:**334
  Winnemucca, Sarah **VI:**397
Beecher, Lyman
  anti-Catholic riots **IV:**23
  nativism **V:**280
  religion **IV:**317
  temperance movement
    III:410
Beecher-Tilton scandal **VI:30**
  Beecher, Henry Ward **VI:**30
  Dana, Charles A. **VI:**92
  Woodhull, Victoria **VI:**401
"Beef Trust" **VI:**243
beer **I:**60; **III:**13
Beethoven, Ludwig van **III:**309
Begin, Menachem
  Camp David accords **X:**64,
    66
  Carter, James Earl, Jr. **X:**69
  Middle East **X:**228
Behaim, Martin **I:28–29**
Behe, Michael **X:**306–307
Beiderbecke, Bix **VII:**153
Beijing, China **VI:**273; **VII:**40
Beirut Marine barracks bombing
  (1983) **X:**378*c*
  foreign policy **X:**142
  Middle East **X:**229
  terrorism **X:**345
Belafonte, Harry **IX:**201, 283
Belarus **X:**142
Belasco, David **VI:**355
"Bel-Gem Waffle" **IX:**246
Belgian Congo **IX:**339
Belgium **VII:**408*c;* **VIII:**448*c*
  Africa **IX:**4
  blitzkrieg **VIII:**47
  Bulge, Battle of the **VIII:**54
  Hoover, Herbert C.
    VIII:171
  peace movements **VII:**256
  Preparedness **VII:**267
  Versailles, Treaty of **VII:**370
  Washington Conference
    on Naval Disarmament
    VII:379
  World War I **VII:**393

Belknap, Jeremy **III:**155
Belknap, William Worth **V:**175
Bell, Alexander Graham **VI:31,**
  31, 408*c*
  communications **VI:**78
  eugenics **VII:**102
  Franklin Institute **IV:**163
  Philadelphia Centennial
    Exposition **VI:**284
  science, invention, and
    technology **VI:**194, 196;
    VII:315
  telegraph **V:**386
Bell, Derrick **X:**15
Bell, James Thomas "Cool Papa"
  VII:335
Bell, John **V:32–33,** 443*c*
  Harlan, John Marshall
    VI:159
  Republican Party **IV:**323
  Vance, Zebulon B. **V:**414
Bellamy, Black Sam **II:**296
Bellamy, Edward **VI:32**
  business cycles **VI:**58
  Higginson, Thomas
    Wentworth **VI:**172
  literature **VI:**226
  politics (1900–1928) **VII:**261
  socialism **VI:**336
  Socialist Party **VI:**337
  utopianism **VI:**371
  Willard, Frances **VI:**394
Bellamy, Joseph **III:**316, 317
Belle Boyd in Camp and Prison
  (Boyd) **V:**239
Bellecourt, Clyde **IX:**12, 357*c*
Belle Isle Prison **V:**314
Bell for Adano, A (Hersey)
  VIII:164
Bell Laboratories **IX:**70, 311
Bellotti v. Baird **X:**20
Bellow, Saul **VIII:**221
Bellows, George **VII:**25
Bellows, Henry **V:**227, 228, 411
Bell Telephone Company **X:**377*c*
  Bell, Alexander Graham
    VI:31
  computers **X:**86
  science, invention, and
    technology **VI:**196;
    X:319
Bell Telephone Laboratories **X:**86
Bell XP-59 (jet fighter) **VIII:**14
Belmont, August **VI:**177; **VII:**226
Belmont Stakes **VI:**177
Belmont v. Belmont **X:**247
Beloved (Morrison) **X:**210
Belzec death camp, Poland
  VIII:169–170
Bemis Heights, Battle of **III:**31,
  380, 381*m,* 382
Benadryl **IX:**211
Benchley, Robert **VII:**180
Benedict, Ruth
  Boas, Franz Uri **VII:**39
  literature **VII:**181
  Mead, Margaret **VII:**197

Benezet, Anthony **II:35–36**
  abolitionism **II:**2
  African Americans **II:**7
  education **II:**112
  Quakers **II:**323
  Woolman, John **II:**426
Ben Gurion, David **IX:**160
Ben-Hur (Wallace) **VI:**381
benign neglect **II:**48, 154
Benin **I:29–30; II:**359
  Dahomey **I:**103–104
  Fon **I:**132
  Gold Coast **I:**143
  slavery **I:**337
  slave trade **I:**340
"Benito Cereno" (Melville) **IV:**229
Benjamin, Judah P. **V:33,** 85, 203
Bennett, James Gordon, Jr.
  VI:32–34, 266, 359
Bennett, James Gordon, Sr.
  IV:208; **V:**217
Bennett, Ned **IV:**388
Bennett, Rolla **IV:**388
Bennett, S. Fillmore **VI:**257
Bennett, William J. **X:41**
  conservative movement **X:**94
  crime and punishment **X:**97
  Kemp, Jack F. **X:**196
  NEA/NEH **X:**245, 246
  neoconservatism **X:**252
Bennington, Battle of
  Burgoyne, Sir John **III:**68
  Fort Ticonderoga **III:**172
  Saratoga, surrender at
    III:380
Benny, Jack **VII:**95; **VIII:**301,
  302, 443*c*
Bent, Charles **IV:51–52**
  Bent, William **IV:**52
  Bent's Fort **IV:**54
  Kearny, Stephen Watts
    IV:212
  St. Vrain, Céran **IV:**328
  Smith, Jedediah Strong
    IV:351
Bent, St. Vrain, and Company
  IV:51, 54
Bent, William **IV:52–53**
  Bent, Charles **IV:**51
  Bent's Fort **IV:**54
  Bridger, James **IV:**64
  Smith, Jedediah Strong
    IV:351
Benteen, Frederick **V:**241
Benting v. Oregon **VII:**343
Benton, Jesse Hart **V:**209
Benton, Thomas Hart **IV:**53,
  53–54
  American Fur Company
    IV:18
  art and architecture **VIII:**31
  Astor, John Jacob **IV:**34–35
  exploration **IV:**145
  Frémont, Jesse Benton
    IV:165
  Frémont, John C. **IV:**166
  Manifest Destiny **IV:**234

panic of 1837 **IV:**294
public land policy **IV:**306
Santa Fe Trail **IV:**330
Truman, Harry S. **IX:**321
Bentonville, Battle of **V:**34, 190
Bentsen, Lloyd **X:**52, 105
Bent's Fort **IV:54–55**
  Beckwourth, Jim **IV:**51
  Bent, Charles **IV:**51
  Fort Laramie **IV:**156
  St. Vrain, Céran **IV:**328
  Santa Fe Trail **IV:**332
Benzoni, Girolamo **I:**32
Berbers **I:**189
Berg, Paul **X:**224
Berger, Samuel R. "Sandy" **X:**102
Berger, Victor
  socialism **VII:**327
  Socialist Party **VI:**337
Bergman, Ingrid **VIII:**447*c;*
  IX:224
Bergmann, Carl **IV:**195
Beriah Green Oneida Institute
  IV:174
Bering, Vitus Jonassen **II:36**
  Alaska **III:**12
  Alaska, Russia in **II:**14
  exploration **II:**124
  Inuit **II:**177
  literature **II:**206
Bering Sea dispute **VI:34**
  Bayard, Thomas Francis
    VI:27–28
  Canada **VI:**61
  Harlan, John Marshall
    VI:159
  Harrison, Benjamin **VI:**161
Bering Strait **I:**81, 297, 395*c;*
  II:177
Berkeley, California **VII:**66, 154.
  See also University of California
  at Berkeley
Berkeley, Lady Frances **II:**36
Berkeley, George **II:**429
Berkeley, John (first Barton
  Stratton) **II:**152, 261
Berkeley, Sir William **II:36–37**
  Bacon's Rebellion **II:**31–32
  Berkeley, Lady Frances
    II:36
  Burgesses, House of **II:**51
  printing and publishing
    II:311
  Virginia **II:**400
Berkman, Alexander
  Frick, Henry Clay **VI:**136
  Goldman, Emma **VII:**126
  Homestead Strike **VI:**176
  labor, radical **VI:**213
  radical and labor press
    VII:285
Berkshire Agricultural Society
  III:161
Berle, Adolf A., Jr. **VIII:43,** 51
Berlin, Germany **VIII:**445*c,* 448*c*
  bombing **VIII:**47–48
  Britain, Battle of **VIII:**53–54

cold war, end of **X**:84
détente **X**:103
education, philanthropy and
  VI:112
Ely, Richard Theodore
  VI:115
espionage **VIII**:118
Ethical Culture movement
  VI:120, 121
Open Door Notes **VI**:272–
  273
Soviet Union **IX**:295
sports and recreation
  VIII:372
World War II European
  theater **VIII**:432
Yalta Conference **VIII**:439
Zimmermann telegram
  VII:401
Berlin, Ira **II**:7, 325
Berlin, Irving
  Freedom Train **IX**:125
  Gershwin, George **VII**:124
  music **VII**:218, 219;
    VIII:252
  Tin Pan Alley **VII**:353
Berlin Academy (Berlin,
  Connecticut) **IV**:400
Berlin airlift **IX**:39, 352c
Berlin blockade **IX**:38–39, 352c
  cold war **IX**:63
  NATO **IX**:247
  Truman, Harry S. **IX**:320
Berlin Decree **III**:49
  Bonaparte, Napoleon **III**:55
  Cadore Letter **III**:73
  embargo of 1807 **III**:152
  foreign affairs **III**:169
  Milan Decree **III**:297
  Orders in Council **III**:325
Berlin Wall **IX**:355c; **X**:379c
  Bush, George H. W. **X**:52
  cold war, end of **X**:84, 86
  Iron Curtain, collapse of
    X:189
  Soviet Union **IX**:295
Berman v. Parker **X**:195
Bermuda **I**:30
  destroyers-for-bases deal
    VIII:95
  Gates, Sir Thomas **II**:143
  tobacco **II**:391
Bermuda Company **I**:30–31, 326
Bermuda Conference **VIII**:170
Bermúdez, Juan **I**:30
Bernadotte, Folke **IX**:45
Bernanke, Ben **X**:60, 111
Bernard, Sir Francis **III**:49–50,
  56, 58
Berners-Lee, Tim **X**:182, 319
Bernstein, Carl **X**:219, 233
Bernstein, Leonard **VII**:220;
  VIII:448c; **IX**:228, 228
Berrio, Antonio de **I**:119
Berry, Carrie **V**:192
Berry, Chuck **IX**:37
Berwanger, Jay **VIII**:371

Berwick Academy (Maine)
  VI:202
Besant, Annie Wood **VI**:309
Bessemer, Henry **VI**:34
Bessemer process **VI**:34–35
  bridges **VI**:47
  Carnegie, Andrew **VI**:62
  Industrial Revolution,
    Second **VI**:191
  steel **VI**:345
Bessie, Alvah **IX**:147, *148*
Best, Pete **IX**:37
Bethany Sunday School **VI**:381
Bethlehem Crossroads, Virginia
  IV:380
Bethlehem Steel
  Murray, Philip **VIII**:249
  steel industry **VII**:337;
    VIII:373; **IX**:300
  Taylor, Frederick Winslow
    VII:350–351
Bethune, Mary McLeod **VIII**:43–
  44
  African Americans **VIII**:3
  Black Cabinet **VIII**:45, 46
  Democratic Party **VIII**:93
  NYA **VIII**:263
  Roosevelt, Eleanor
    VIII:343
  Terrell, Mary Eliza Church
    VII:352
  WPA **VIII**:425
Bethune-Cookman College
  VIII:44
Beveridge, Albert J. **IV**:236
Beverley, Robert **II**:37, 182
Bewick, Moreing and Company
  VIII:171
Bhagavad Gita **VIII**:166
BIA. *See* Indian Affairs, Bureau of
Biafra, Bight of **I**:340
Biberman, Herbert **IX**:147, *148*
Bible, the **I**:396c
  book, the **I**:33
  Common Sense **III**:101, 102
  Darwinism and religion
    VI:93
  deism **III**:135
  education **III**:147
  Eliot, John **II**:115
  Finney, Charles Grandison
    IV:150
  Gutenberg, Johannes
    Gensfleisch zum **I**:148
  literature **III**:268
  marriage and family **II**:218–
    219
  Mercator, Gerhardus **I**:240
  race and race relations
    IV:310–311
  Reformation **I**:315, 317
  religion **VI**:306, 307;
    VII:297; **IX**:272
  The Tempest **I**:353–354
  Unitarianism **III**:419
Bible colleges **VIII**:335
Bible societies **III**:217

Bibliotheca universalis (Gesner)
  I:139
Bickerdyke, Mary Ann **V**:34
bicycling **V**:367; **VI**:35–36, *36*,
  140
Biddle, Francis **VIII**:193
Biddle, Nicholas
  banking **IV**:46
  Bank of the United States,
    Second **IV**:48
  election of 1840 **IV**:138
Biden, Joseph **X**:41–42
Bidlack Treaty **IV**:98, 414c
Bidwell, John **IV**:55–56, 77;
  VI:296
Bienville, Jean-Baptiste Le Moyne,
  sieur de **II**:37–38, 210; **IV**:223
Bierce, Ambrose **VI**:226
Bierstadt, Albert **V**:18, 443c;
  VI:36–38, 275
big bands **VIII**:44–45, 446c
  Ellington, Duke **VIII**:112
  Goodman, Benny **VIII**:150–
    151
  jazz **VIII**:195
  music **VIII**:250–252
  popular culture **VIII**:301
  recreation **VIII**:328
Big Bethel, Virginia **V**:190
Big Black River, Battle of **V**:298,
  418
Big Bopper, the **IX**:279
Bigelow, Jacob **III**:385
Bigelow v. Virginia **X**:3
Big Foot **VI**:331
Big Four (railroad magnates)
  VI:180–181
Big Horn Basin **VI**:76–77
Bighorn Mountains **VI**:85
Bighorn River **IV**:257
Big Money, The (Dos Passos)
  VIII:218, 219
"big science" **VII**:151
Big Shanty, Georgia **V**:11
Big Six (meatpacking companies)
  VI:243
Big Sleep, The (Chandler)
  VIII:220
Big Sleep, The (film) **IX**:224
"Big Steel" **IX**:300. *See also* U.S.
  Steel
Big Stick diplomacy **VII**:34–36,
  35, 305
"Big Three" (United States, Soviet
  Union, Great Britain)
  Cairo Conference **VIII**:61
  Potsdam Conference
    VIII:307
  Soviet-American relations
    VIII:368
  World War II European
    theater **VIII**:430
"Big Three" automakers
  automobile industry **VII**:27;
    IX:26
  economy **VII**:84
  technology **IX**:313

Big Three Conference (Potsdam).
  See Potsdam Conference
Big Tree, Treaty of **II**:184
Bikini Atoll **IX**:24
Biko, Stephen **X**:325
Bilbo, Theodore **VII**:332
bilingual education **X**:166, 210
Bilingual Education Act (1968)
  X:42
Bill and Melinda Gates
  Foundation **X**:148
Billboard magazine **IX**:37
Billing, George **II**:261
Billings, John **V**:239
Billings, Warren **VII**:213
Billings, William **III**:50, 308, 309;
  VI:254
*Billings and Holden Collection of
  Ancient Psalmody* **IV**:268
Billingsport, Delaware **III**:135
"Billion Dollar Congress" **VI**:161,
  162
Bill of Rights **III**:50–51, 461c,
  463c; **IV**:413c. *See also specific
  amendments, e.g.:* First
  Amendment
    Amendments to the U.S.
      Constitution **X**:23
    anti-Federalists **III**:23, 24
    Brennan, William J., Jr.
      X:47, 48
    Catholics **III**:83
    civil liberties **VIII**:71
    civil liberties, Union **V**:69
    civil rights **VIII**:72
    commemoration **IX**:66
    Constitution, ratification of
      the **III**:105
    Constitution, United States
      III:107
    constitutions, state **III**:110
    Federalists **III**:166
    Four Freedoms **VIII**:144
    Freedom Train **IX**:125
    Gideon v. Wainwright
      IX:133
    Henry, Patrick **III**:212
    Jews **III**:236
    Lee, Richard Henry **III**:260
    Mason, George **III**:292
    states' rights **III**:397
Bill of Rights (England) **II**:149
Billy Budd (Melville) **IV**:229;
  VI:226
Billy the Kid **VI**:376
Billy the Kid (Copland) **VIII**:251
Biloxi, Mississippi **II**:253, 254
Biloxi Indians **II**:253
Bimbia people **I**:56
bimetallism **VI**:38
  Bland-Allison Act **VI**:41
  Crime of '73 **VI**:86
  currency issue **VI**:88
  McKinley, William **VI**:241
binders **VI**:8
Binet, Alfred **VII**:148
Bingham, Arthur **III**:269–270

Bingham, Eula **X**:264
Bingham, George Caleb **IV**:414*c*
　art **IV**:29; **V**:18
　Boone, Daniel **III**:56
　painting **VI**:275
Bingham, William **III:51–52**
bingo **VIII**:328
bin Laden, Osama **X**:383*c*
　Afghanistan War **X**:10–12
　Clinton, William J. **X**:83
　defense policy **X**:102, 103
　foreign policy **X**:143
　Hamdan v. Rumsfeld **X**:164
　Middle East **X**:229
　Powell, Colin L. **X**:287
　terrorism **X**:347
biological hazards **X**:264
Biological Survey, Bureau of
　VI:82
Biological Weapons Anti-
　Terrorism Act (1989) **X**:346
Biologics Control Act (1902)
　IX:235
biology **VIII**:352, 353; **X**:171–172
Bipartisan Campaign Finance
　Reform Act (1997) **X**:63–64
Bipartisan Campaign Finance
　Reform Act (2002) **X**:64, 275
"Bird in a Gilded Cage, A"
　VII:218
Birdsall, Mary **IV**:60
Birds of America (Audubon)
　IV:38, 335, 412*c*
Birmingham, Alabama
　　Black, Hugo L. **VIII**:45
　　freedom rides **IX**:123
　　Sunbelt **VIII**:381
Birmingham, Alabama, church
　bombing (1963) **IX**:6, 355*c*
Birmingham, Alabama,
　confrontation (1963) **IX**:39–
　40
　　civil disobedience **IX**:58
　　Civil Rights Act (1964)
　　　IX:60
　　journalism **IX**:166
　　King, Martin Luther, Jr.
　　　IX:174
　　"Letter from Birmingham Jail"
　　　(King) **IX:366–373**
　　March on Washington
　　　(1963) **IX**:200–201
　　race and race relations
　　　IX:269
　　SCLC **IX**:293
Birmingham, USS **VIII**:11
Birmingham Meeting House
　III:62
Birney, James **IV**:226, 302
birth control **VII:36–37**, 406*c*,
　407*c*; **X:42–44**. *See also* "The
　Pill"
　　abortion **X**:3
　　birthrates **X**:44
　　Brennan, William J., Jr.
　　　X:48
　　Catholics **VIII**:64

Ellis, Henry Havelock
　VII:95
eugenics **VII**:103
family life **X**:127
feminism **X**:132, 134
fertility **II**:126
Flynn, Elizabeth Gurley
　VII:110
Goldman, Emma **VII**:126
Greenwich Village **VII**:131
marriage and family **V**:249;
　VII:191
NOW **X**:247
population trends **VII**:266
pro-life/pro-choice
　movements **X**:289
prostitution **V**:316
public health **VII**:275, 276
Roe v. Wade **X**:311, 312
Sanger, Margaret **VII**:312–
　313
science and technology
　VII:314
sexuality **VII**:322
sexual revolution **X**:322
socialism **VII**:327
White, Byron R. **X**:369
women's status and rights
　VII:387, 388
Birth Control Review **VII**:36, 103
Birth of a Nation, The (film)
　VII:37–38, 406*c*
　　entertainment, popular
　　　VII:96
　　Griffith, David Wark
　　　VII:131
　　Herbert, Victor August
　　　VI:170
　　Ku Klux Klan **VII**:165
　　movie industry **VII**:215
　　NAACP **VII**:224
　　popular culture **VII**:265
　　race and race relations
　　　VII:283
　　Rhinelander case **VII**:301
　　Trotter, William Monroe
　　　VII:357
birthrates **X:44–45**
　　family life **X**:127
　　marriage and family **VIII**:231
　　population trends **VIII**:304–
　　　306
　　women's status and rights
　　　VIII:423
　　World War II home front
　　　VIII:433
Bishop, Maurice **X**:159, 160
bishops **III**:20, 21
bison. *See* buffalo
Bitterroot Mountains **III**:263
Bittner, Van **IX**:249
Black, Brown and Beige
　(Ellington) **VIII**:112, 251
Black, Hugo L. **VIII**:45, 445*c*;
　IX:336
　　Baker v. Carr **IX**:33
　　Dennis v. U.S. **IX**:86

Engel v. Vitale **IX**:107
Fair Labor Standards Act
　VIII:124
Gideon v. Wainwright
　IX:134
*Heart of Atlanta Motel v.
　U.S.* **IX**:146
Korematsu v. U.S. **VIII**:203
Supreme Court **VIII**:383
Black, Jeremiah Sullivan **V**:147
Black Abolitionist Papers, The
　IV:402
Black Arts Movement **IX**:6
Black Arts Repertory Theatre
　IX:6, 356*c*
Blackbeard. *See* Teach, Edward
Blackberry **X**:319
Blackberry Winter (Mead)
　VII:197
Black Boy (Wright) **VIII**:219, 437
Blackburn, Robin **II**:359
Blackburn's Ford **V**:241
Black Cabinet **VIII:45–46**
　　African Americans **VIII**:3
　　Bethune, Mary McLeod
　　　VIII:44
　　civil rights **VIII**:72
　　Democratic Party **VIII**:93
　　NYA **VIII**:263
Black Codes **V:34–35**, 446*c*
　　Civil Rights Act (1866) **V**:70
　　Democratic Party **V**:109
　　Fifteenth Amendment
　　　V:141
　　Fourteenth Amendment
　　　V:157
　　Freedmen's Bureau **V**:161
　　Johnson, Andrew **V**:212, 213
　　Reconstruction Acts **V**:327
　　Thirteenth Amendment
　　　V:388
Black Crook, The **VI**:257, 354
Black Death. *See* plague
Blackfeet Indians
　　American Fur Company
　　　IV:18
　　Astor, John Jacob **IV**:35
　　Bent, Charles **IV**:51
　　Bodmer, Karl **IV**:60
　　Catlin, George **IV**:84
　　Missouri Fur Company
　　　IV:258
Blackfriars Theatre **I**:334
"Black Friday" (September 24,
　1869) **VI**:151, 315
Black Hawk **III**:466*c*; **IV**:57, 411*c*,
　413*c*
　　Black Hawk War **IV**:56–58
　　Keokuk **IV**:213
　　Native Americans **IV**:274
　　Sac and Fox **IV**:327
Black Hawk War **IV:56–58**, 57,
　413*c*
　　Anderson, Robert **V**:9
　　Atkinson, Henry **IV**:36
　　Davis, Jefferson **V**:103
　　disease/epidemics **IV**:122

Johnston, Albert Sidney
　V:213
Johnston, Joseph E. **V**:214
Keokuk **IV**:213
lead mines **IV**:223
Lincoln, Abraham **V**:235
Mason, Richard B. **IV**:241
Native Americans **IV**:274
Taylor, Zachary **IV**:367
Black Hills
　　exploration **IV**:145
　　Little Bighorn, Battle of
　　　V:240–241
　　Smith, Jedediah Strong
　　　IV:350
　　treaty rights **IX**:319
Black Hills, War for the
　　Crazy Horse **VI**:85–86
　　Native Americans **VI**:261,
　　　263
　　Red Cloud **VI**:303
Black Hills gold rush **VI**:38–39,
　408*c*
　　Crazy Horse **VI**:85
　　Sioux wars **VI**:331
　　Sitting Bull **VI**:332
"Black International" **VI**:213
"Black Justice" (ACLU pamphlet)
　VIII:17, 443*c*
black legend **I:31–32**
　　Las Casas, Bartolomé de
　　　I:204
　　printing press **I**:303
　　Sepúlveda, Juan Ginés de
　　　I:331
blacklisting
　　folk music revival **IX**:121
　　Hollywood Ten **IX**:148, 149
　　HUAC **IX**:150
　　movies **IX**:223
　　NLRA **VIII**:257
　　Robeson, Paul **VIII**:342
black lung **VII**:392
black market **VIII:46–47**
　　OPA **VIII**:282
　　rationing **VIII**:322
　　wage and price controls
　　　VIII:410
　　World War II **VIII**:427
　　World War II home front
　　　VIII:432
"Black Monday" (May 27, 1935)
　VIII:351, 382
"Black Monday" (May 17, 1954)
　IX:294
Black Monday (Brady) **IX**:342
Blackmun, Harry **X**:232, 311–312,
　387–390
Black National Convention **IV**:15
Black Nationalism
　　Carmichael, Stokely **IX**:49
　　CORE **IX**:74
　　Garvey, Marcus **VII**:121
Black Panthers **IX**:40, 40–41, 357*c*
　　African Americans **IX**:6
　　Baldwin, James **IX**:35
　　birth control **X**:43

Black Power **IX:**41
Carmichael, Stokely **IX:**49,
50
Meese, Edwin C., III **X:**225
race and race relations
IX:271
SNCC **IX:**303
Weathermen/Weather
Underground **IX:**341
Black Power **IX:41–42,** *42,* 357*c*
African Americans **IX:**6
Carmichael, Stokely **IX:**49
conservative movement
X:93
CORE **IX:**74
Great Society **IX:**139
Lewis, John **IX:**190
Meredith, James **IX:**213
race and race relations
IX:271
SNCC **IX:**303
Black Republicanism
Grant, Ulysses S. **V:**175
Reconstruction **V:**326
redemption **V:**328
Black Riders, The (Crane) **VI:**85,
227
Black Sea **VI:**204
black separatism
African Americans **IX:**6;
X:15
Farrakhan, Louis A. **X:**129
Muhammad, Elijah **IX:**226
Nation of Islam **X:**249–250
race and race relations
IX:271
Wilkins, Roy **IX:**345
Black Sox scandal **VII:**33, 334,
407*c*
Black Star Line **VII:**121, 122, 361
Blackstone, Sir William **III:52,**
459*c;* **IV:**239, 303
Black Swan Records **VII:**220
"Black Thursday" (October 24,
1929) **VIII:**376
"Black Tuesday" (October 29,
1929) **VIII:**376, 443*c*
Black Warrior (steamer) **IV:**112
Blackwater **X:**188
Blackwell, Alice Stone **VII:**385
Blackwell, Antoinette Brown
VI:39–40
Brown, Olympia **VI:**50, 51
Women's National Loyal
League **V:**434
women's status and rights
VI:399, 400
Blackwell, Elizabeth **IV:**415*c;*
VI:40
disease/epidemics **V:**112
ladies aid societies **V:**227,
228
medicine **IV:**250
nurses **V:**285
prostitution **V:**316
women's status and rights
VI:400

Blackwell, Henry
Higginson, Thomas
Wentworth **VI:**171
NAWSA **VII:**223
Stone, Lucy **VI:**346
Bladensburg, Battle of **IV:**392
Blaeu, Willem **I:32–33**
Blaine, James Gillespie **VI:40–41,**
409*c*
Chilean-American relations
VI:67
Civil Rights Act (1875)
V:71
Cleveland, Grover **VI:**74
Congress **VI:**79–80
Conkling, Roscoe **VI:**81
corruption, political **VI:**83
Crédit Mobilier **V:**97
environment **VI:**119
Garfield, James Abram
VI:139
Harrison, Benjamin **VI:**161
Ingersoll, Robert Green
VI:193
Mafia incident **VI:**234–235
mugwumps **VI:**252
newspapers **VI:**266
Pan-American Union
VI:276
presidential campaigns
(1870–1899) **VI:**293
Radical Republicans **V:**320
Reid, Whitelaw **VI:**305
Republican Party **V:**334;
VI:311
Blair, Francis Preston, Jr. **V:35–
36**
governors **V:**172
peace movements **V:**296
Blair, Henry (1807–1860) **IV:**333,
413*c*
Blair, Henry W. (1834–1920)
VI:110
Blair, James
Andros, Sir Edmund **II:**20
Anglican Church **II:**21
College of William and Mary
II:74
Blair, John **III:**403
Blair, Montgomery **V:**36; **VI:**78
Blair, Tony **X:**10
Blake, Arthur "Blind" **VII:**220
Blake, Eubie **VII:**96, 219
Blake, John Lauris **IV:**183
Blakely, Georgia **V:**267
Blake's Lands, South Carolina
IV:388
Blakey, G. Robert **X:**298
Blalock, Alfred **VIII:**234
Blanchard, Joshua P. **V:**295
Blanck, Max **VII:**356
Blanco, Kathleen **X:**173
Bland, Edward **II:**124
Bland, Richard (1710–1776)
III:52–53
Bland, Richard P. (1835–1899)
VI:41

Bland-Allison Act **VI:41–42,**
408*c*
Allison, William Boyd
VI:11–12
bimetallism **VI:**38
Congress **VI:**80
Crime of '73 **VI:**86
currency issue **VI:**89
Free-Silver movement
VI:135
Hayes, Rutherford B.
VI:168
Blashfield, Edwin Howland
VI:276
Blast, The (journal) **VII:**285
Blatch, Harriot Eaton Stanton
VII:38, 385
Blavatsky, Helena Petrovna
VI:309, *309*
Blease, Cole **VII:**332
Bleeding Kansas **V:36–38,** *37,*
443*c*
abolitionism **V:**4
Douglas, Stephen A. **V:**114
Higginson, Thomas
Wentworth **V:**189; **VI:**171
Kansas-Nebraska Act **V:**222
Republican Party **V:**333
slavery **V:**363
Blennerhassett, Harman **III:**70
Blind Fiddler, The (Krimmel)
IV:29
Bliss, Philemon **VI:**218
Bliss, Philip P. **VI:**257
Blithedale Romance, The
(Hawthorne) **IV:**229, 379
blitzkrieg **VIII:47,** 446*c*
aircraft industry **VIII:**13
air power **VIII:**15
Anglo-American relations
VIII:21
Britain, Battle of **VIII:**53
CDAAA **VIII:**77
election of 1940 **VIII:**110
mobilization **VIII:**241
refugees **VIII:**330
Selective Service **VIII:**357
tanks **VIII:**385
World War II European
theater **VIII:**429, 431
Blitzstein, Marc **VII:**220
Bliven, Bruce **VII:**430–432
Blix, Hans **X:**187
Block, Adriaen **II:**75
blockade
Civil War **V:**74
Confederate navy **V:**84
Congress, Confederate **V:**88
Dahlgren, John A. B. **V:**101
food riots **V:**148
foreign policy **V:**150
Lincoln, Abraham **V:**236,
237
Mallory, Stephen R. **V:**247
medicine **V:**258
Mobile campaign **V:**265
Monitor-Merrimack **V:**265

Porter, David Dixon **V:**311
Semmes, Raphael **V:**346
Seward, William H. **V:**348
Union navy **V:**405
War of 1812 **IV:**390
Welles, Gideon **V:**428
blockade runners **V:**83–84, 163
"blockbuster" movies **X:**278–279
"blockbuster" novels **X:**212
block grants **X:**97
blockhouses **V:**141
blogs **X:**182–183
blood banks **VIII:**234
blood transfusions **X:**6
"Bloody Angle" **V:**291, 368
Bloody Marsh, Battle of **II:**278
"Bloody Massacre perpetrated in
King Street, The" **III:**366
Bloody Run, Battle of **III:**340
Bloody Sunday **IX:**293
Bloom, Allan **X:**94
Bloom, Harold **X:**26
Bloomer, Amelia **IV:**59, **59–60,**
414*c*
Seneca Falls convention
IV:341
temperance movement
IV:370
women's status and rights
IV:404
*Bloudy Tenent of Persecution,
for Cause of Conscience, The*
(Williams) **II:**416
Blount, James H. **VI:**163
Blount, William **III:53,** 222
Blow, Kurtis **X:**238
Blow, Peter **V:**116
"Blowin' in the Wind" (Dylan)
IX:121, 229
Blow Up (film) **X:**278
BLS. *See* Labor Statistics, Bureau
of
bluebacks **V:**122
Blue Cross **VIII:**236
bluegrass music **VIII:**250
Blue Jacket (Shawnee chief)
III:54
Fallen Timbers, Battle of
III:161
Greenville, Treaty of
III:200
Harrison, William Henry
IV:184
Blue Licks, Battle of **III:54,** 56,
314
Bluemner, Oscar **VII:**25
Blue Mountains **IV:**285, 286
Blue Ridge Mountains **II:**124
Blue Shield **VIII:**236
blues music **VII:39**
entertainment, popular
VII:97
Gershwin, George **VII:**124,
125
Great Migration **VII:**129
Harlem Renaissance
VII:136

blues music (*continued*)
jazz **VII:**153
migration **VII:**207
music **VI:**256; **VII:**218–220; **VIII:**250, 252
popular culture **VII:**265
Bluest Eye, The (Morrison) **X:**210
"Blue Suede Shoes" **IX:**263
Blum, Leon **VIII:**303
Blunt, John **II:**370
Blunt, Roy **X:**171
Bly, Nellie **VI:**266
Blyden, Edward **VI:**223
B-movies **IX:**224, 226
B'nai B'rith **VIII:**195
Board of Admiralty **III:**116
Board of Associated Loyalists **III:**176
Board of Control and Labor Standards for Army Clothing **VIII:**165
Board of Economic Warfare **VIII:**411
Board of Education of Westside Community Schools v. Mergens **X:**122
Board of Health (Washington, D.C.) **VI:**219
Board of Mediation, U.S. **VII:**409c
Board of Trade **II:**437c
Board of Treasury **III:**116
Board of War
Continental Congress, Second **III:**116
Gates, Horatio **III:**190
Pickering, Timothy **III:**334
Board of War and Ordnance **III:**4
Boas, Franz Uri **VII:39–40,** 405c
Hurston, Zora Neale **VIII:**181
literature **VII:**181
Locke, Alain LeRoy **VII:**183
Mead, Margaret **VII:**197
race and race relations **VII:**282, 283
Boating Party, The (Cassatt) **VI:**64
Bobadilla, Francisco de
Columbus, Bartholomew **I:**83
Columbus, Christopher **I:**86
bobbysoxers **VIII:**361
Bockscar (B-29 bomber) **VIII:**166
Bodmer, Karl **IV:60–61,** 413c
Boehm, John Philip **II:**149
Boehner, John **X:**171
Boeing 247 **VIII:**13
Boeing 707 **IX:**28, 29, 313
Boeing 747 **VII:**179; **X:**319
Boeing B-17 Flying Fortress. See B-17 Flying Fortress
Boeing B-24 bombers. See B-24 Liberator

Boeing B-29 Superfortress. See B-29 Superfortress
Boeing B-47 (aircraft) **IX:**285
Boeing B-52 (aircraft) **IX:**285
Boeing Company **VIII:**14, *14;* **IX:**313
Boesky, Ivan **X:**58, 59
Bogardus, James **IV:**333–334
Bogart, Humphrey **VIII:**246, 447c; **IX:**147, 224
Boggs, Hale **IX:**159; **X:**267
Boggs, Lillburn W. **IV:**89
Boggs company **IV:**125
Bohemian Charitable Association **VII:**102
bohemianism
Greenwich Village **VII:**130–131
The Masses **VII:**193
Tin Pan Alley **VII:**353
Bohlen, Charles **IX:**167
Bohr, Niels **IV:**163
Boies, David **X:**147
Boise City, Oklahoma **VIII:**98
Bok, Edward W. **VI:**235
Boker, George **VI:**225
Boland, Edward **X:**45, 183
Boland Amendment **X:45,** 378c
cold war, end of **X:**85
contras **X:**95
Iran-contra affair **X:**183
North, Oliver L. **X:**258
War Powers Act **X:**365
Boldt, George **IX:**319
Boleyn, Anne
Church of England **I:**74
Elizabeth I **I:**120
Henry VIII **I:**160
Mary I **I:**232
Bolingbroke, Lord **III:**338
Bolívar, Simón **IV:**186
Bolivarian Alternative for the Americas **X:**207
Bolivia **I:**300
Bush, George H. W. **X:**52
Chilean-American relations **VI:**67
Latin America **X:**206
Bolling, Richard **X:**89
"Boll Weevils" **X:**169
bolometer **VI:**326
Bolotowsky, Ilya **VIII:**31
Bolsec, Jérome **I:**54
Bolshevik Revolution. See Russian Revolution
Bolsheviks **VII:**407c
communism **IX:**67
Red Scare **VII:**296
Reed, Jack **VII:**296, 297
Russian Revolution **VII:**308
Bolt Beranek and Newman, Inc. (BBN) **X:**181
bolting cloth **II:**235
Bolton, Herbert Eugene **II:**39
Bolton, John R. **X:**357
Bombay, India **VIII:**52
Bomber, Daniel **I:**195

bombing (WWII) **VIII:47–48**
air power **VIII:**15–16
Army Air Forces, U.S. **VIII:**26
Arnold, Henry H. "Hap" **VIII:**28
atomic bomb **VIII:**35
Britain, Battle of **VIII:**53–54
foreign policy **VIII:**141
Hiroshima and Nagasaki **VIII:**166–168
Iwo Jima **VIII:**192
Japanese Americans, relocation of **VIII:**193
Kennedy, Joseph P. **VIII:**200
movies **VIII:**246
news media **VIII:**272
Normandy, invasion of **VIII:**275
Pearl Harbor **VIII:**292
World War II **VIII:**428
World War II Pacific theater **VIII:**437
bomb shelters. See fallout shelters
Bonafacio, Andres **IX:**256
Bonaparte, Napoleon **III:54–55,** 464c
Barlow, Joel **III:**46–47
Berlin Decree **III:**49
Cadore Letter **III:**73
embargo of 1807 **III:**152
foreign affairs **III:**168, 169
French Revolution **III:**179
Fulton, Robert **III:**183
Haiti **III:**203
Jomini, Antoine-Henri, baron de **V:**217
Kościuszko, Tadeusz **III:**249
Louisiana Purchase **III:**273
Milan Decree **III:**297
Orders in Council **III:**325
Quasi War **III:**353
tactics and strategy **V:**379
Talleyrand-Périgord, Charles-Maurice de **III:**405
Bond, Julian **IX:**191; **X:**245
Bond, Thomas **II:38**
Bond, W. C. **III:**384
bonds (financial instrument)
banking **V:**28
banking, investment **VI:**23, 24
Chase, Salmon P. **V:**63
Confederate States of America **V:**86
Congress, Confederate **V:**88
economy **V:**121–123
investments, foreign, in the United States **VI:**197
national banking system **VI:**260
panic of 1857 **V:**294
Bonds, Barry **X:**330

Bonfire of the Vanities (Wolfe) **X:**370
Bonhomme Richard **III:**117, 239
Bon Marché, Paris **VI:**96
Bonner, Robert **VI:**98
Bonner, Thomas D. **IV:**51
Bonnet, Stede **II:38–39,** 296, 385
Bonneville Dam **VIII:**199
Bonney, Anne **II:**296
Bonnie and Clyde **VIII:**130
Bonnie and Clyde (film) **IX:**226
"Bonny Blue Flag, The" **V:**273
Bonus Army **VIII:48–49,** 49, 444c
election of 1932 **VIII:**108
Hoover presidency **VIII:**175
Patton, George S., Jr. **VIII:**291
relief **VIII:**332
Soldiers' Bonus **VII:**331
veterans **VII:**373
Bonus Bill **III:**284; **IV:62,** 271
Bonus March (1932). See Bonus Army
boogie-woogie **VIII:**250
"Boogie-Woogie Bugle Boy of Company B, The" **VIII:**252
book, the **I:33,** 113, 303
bookmaking (horse racing) **VI:**178
Book of Common Prayer
Anglican Church **II:**21
Church of England **I:**75
Protestantism **II:**315
Puritans **I:**307
"Book of General Laws and Libertyes, The" **II:**151
Book of Kells **I:**33, 328
Book of Martyrs (Foxe) **I:**132
Book of Mormon
Deseret, State of **IV:**119
Mormon Church **VI:**251
religion **IV:**319; **VI:**308
Smith, Joseph, Jr. **IV:**352
Young, Brigham **IV:**407
Book-of-the-Month Club **VIII:**328–329
books **X:**218–219. See also literature
bookstores **X:**212
boondoggles **VIII:**74, 426
Boone, Daniel **II:**124; **III:55, 55–56,** 459c, 461c
Blue Licks, Battle of **III:**54
Dragging Canoe **III:**139
frontier, the **III:**181
Wilderness Road **III:**442
Boone, Pat **IX:**278
Boonesborough **III:**56, 442, 461c
Booth, Edwin
Booth, John Wilkes **V:**38
theater **V:**387
Winnemucca, Sarah **VI:**397
Booth, John Wilkes **V:38–39,** 39, 446c
assassination of Abraham Lincoln **V:**19–21
espionage **V:**135

Seward, William H. **V**:348
theater **V**:386, 387
Booth, Junius Brutus **V**:38, 387
Booth, Lionel F. **V**:153
Borah, William E. **VII**:*114;*
VIII:49–50
antimonopoly **VIII**:23–24
Darrow, Clarence Seward
VII:70
isolationists **VIII**:189
Republican Party **VIII**:336,
337
Borden, Gail **IV**:334
Borden, Lizzie **VI**:375
border control **X**:359
borderlands **II:39–40**
Byrd family **II**:53
ethnocentrism **II**:122
Oglethorpe, James Edward
II:277
Border Patrol **VII**:144, 203, 408*c*
border ruffians **V**:37, 38
border states
Civil War **V**:73
Confiscation Acts **V**:87
emancipation **V**:129
Emancipation Proclamation
V:131
governors **V**:172
Union League **V**:404
Borgia family **I**:6
Bork, Robert **X:45–46,** 379*c*
abortion **X**:4
conservative movement **X**:94
Cox, Archibald, Jr. **X**:95
Nixon, Richard M. **X**:257
Reagan, Ronald W. **X**:300
Ruckelshaus, William D.
X:312
Senate, U.S. **X**:321
Supreme Court **X**:339
Watergate scandal **X**:366
"born again" **X**:124–125
Borneo **VIII**:437
Borresen, Kari **IX**:273
Bosch, Juan **IX**:184, 339
Bosnia-Herzegovina **X**:381*c*
Clinton, William J. **X**:81
Dayton accords **X**:99
defense policy **X**:102
Fellowship of Reconciliation
VII:109
Bosnian Serbs **X**:99, 102
Bosomworth, Mary Musgrove
II:40–41, 392
Boss, Charlotte **IX**:264
Bosserman, Alden **V**:68
Boston (Sinclair) **VII**:326
Boston, Massachusetts **II:41–43,**
42*m*
abolitionism **IV**:3
ACS **IV**:17
Adams, John **III**:4
Adams, John Quincy **IV**:5
Adams, Samuel **III**:7
African Americans **III**:9;
IV:9

agriculture **IV**:12
American Anti-Slavery
Society **IV**:15
Andros, Sir Edmund **II**:20
anti-Catholic riots **IV**:23, 24
art and architecture **IV**:30
Attucks, Crispus **III**:37–38
Boylston, Zabdiel **II**:43
Brandeis, Louis Dembitz
VII:41
Burgoyne, Sir John **III**:67
Catholics **III**:83
cities and urban life **III**:90;
VI:71; **IX**:56
committees of
correspondence **III**:101
Constitution, USS **III**:108
Coolidge, Calvin John
VII:64
crowd actions **II**:86
disease/epidemics **II**:99,
100; **IV**:122
Dix, Dorothea **IV**:124
Dorchester Heights
III:138–139
dust bowl **VIII**:98
Edison, Thomas Alva
VI:107
education **IV**:135
entertainment, popular
VI:117
female antislavery societies
IV:147
Finney, Charles Grandison
IV:151
food riots **III**:167
French Alliance **III**:178
fugitive slave laws **IV**:168
Fuller, Margaret **IV**:169
Hamilton, Alice **VII**:133
Hancock, John **III**:208–209
Harris, Benjamin **II**:162–
163
Howe, Sir William **III**:215
Howells, William Dean
VI:179
immigration **IV**:194, 196;
VI:184, 186
industrialization **IV**:199–201
invention and technology
VI:194, 196
Irish Americans **VIII**:188
Jackson, Helen Hunt
VI:199
Jewett, Sarah Orne **VI**:202
Knox, Henry **III**:247–248
labor, radical **VI**:213
La Farge, John Frederick
Lewis Joseph **VI**:217
Larkin, Thomas Oliver
IV:222
lotteries **II**:210
MacIntosh, Ebenezer
III:279
Malcolm X **IX**:198
Mann, Horace **IV**:237
Massachusetts **II**:224

music **VII**:219
NWTUL **VII**:230
Old South Church **III**:323–
324
Parkman, Francis **IV**:113
Phillips, Wendell **IV**:299
printing and publishing
II:311
railroads **IV**:313, 314
religion **IV**:317
Revere, Paul **III**:366, 367
Revolutionary War **III**:367
riots **III**:371
Sewall, Samuel **II**:350
smallpox **II**:361
sports and recreation
VII:334–335
Stewart, Maria **IV**:356–357
Sullivan, John **III**:402
taverns and inns **II**:384
temperance movement
IV:369
transportation, urban
VI:360, 361
Trotter, William Monroe
VII:357
Unitarianism **III**:419
urban transportation
VII:363
Walker, David **IV**:389
Washington, George
III:430
Webster, Daniel **IV**:393
Wheelwright, John **II**:412
Winthrop, John **II**:418
witches/witchcraft **II**:419
wolves **II**:421
yellow fever **II**:431
Young, Thomas **III**:457
Boston, USS **IV**:189; **VI**:163
Boston American **VII**:138
Boston Anarchist **VI**:213
Boston Associated Charities
VII:330
Boston Associates **III**:226
Boston Bicycling Club **VI**:35
Boston Caucus **II**:80
"Boston classicists" **VI**:254
Boston Common **II**:41; **V**:268
Boston Court House **V**:189
Boston Daily Advertiser **IV**:208
Boston Daily Record **IX**:253
Boston Daily Times **IV**:208
Boston Female Anti-Slavery
Society
African Americans **IV**:9
American Anti-Slavery
Society **IV**:15
Phillips, Wendell **IV**:299
Boston Gazette **III**:4
Boston Guardian **VII**:357
*Boston Handel and Haydn Society
Collection of Church Music*
(Mason) **IV**:268
Boston Harbor **III**:65
"Boston Hymn" (Emerson)
IV:140

Bostonians, The (James) **VI**:200,
280
Boston Journeymen Bootmakers'
Society **IV**:218–219
Boston Latin School **IV**:140, 299
Boston Manufacturers' Mutual
Fire Insurance Company
VI:22
Boston Manufacturing Company
IV:199
Boston Massacre **III:56–58,** 57,
460*c*
Adams, John **III**:5, 6
African Americans **III**:9
Attucks, Crispus **III**:37–38
Hancock, John **III**:209
Hutchinson, Thomas
III:219
popular culture **III**:341
Quincy, Josiah **III**:354
Townshend Duties **III**:413
Warren, Joseph **III**:427
Young, Thomas **III**:457
Boston News-Letter **II**:268, 437*c*
Boston Philosophical Society
II:43
Boston Port Bill **III**:460*c*
Coercive Acts **III**:100
Continental Congress, First
III:113
Dunmore, John Murray, earl
of **III**:142
Mason, George **III**:292
Boston Public Library **VI**:224,
392
Boston Red Sox **VII**:334
Boston School of Oratory **VI**:139–
140
Boston School of Social Work
VII:330
Boston Social Club **VII**:64
Boston Spectator **IV**:183
Boston Symphony Orchestra
VI:28, 29, 233
Boston Tea Party **III:58–59,**
460*c*
artisans **III**:35
committees of
correspondence **III**:101
Dickinson, John **III**:137
Hancock, John **III**:209
Hutchinson, Thomas
III:219
North, Frederick, Lord
III:320
Old South Church **III**:323–
324
Quincy, Josiah **III**:354
Revere, Paul **III**:366
riots **III**:371
Tea Act **III**:409
Warren, Joseph **III**:427
Young, Thomas **III**:457
Boston University **IX**:173
Boston Vigilance Committee
VI:171
Bosworth Field, Battle of **I**:159

botany
  Bartram, John **II:**34
  Colden, Jane **II:**73
  Kalm, Peter **II:**191
  Pennsylvania **II:**287
  science and technology
    II:345; **III:**384–385
Botany Woolen Mill **VII:**253
Botts, John M. **V:**68
Boucher, Jonathan **III:59–60**
Boucicault, Dion **V:**387; **VI:**202, 355
Boudin, Kathy **IX:**341; **X:**368
Boudinot, Elias **IV:61–62**
  Cherokee **IV:**86
  religion **IV:**320
  Ridge, John **IV:**323, 324
Bougainville Island **VIII:**366
Boughton, George **VI:**275
Boulder Dam **VIII:**115
Boundary 2 (journal) **X:**211
boundary disputes **VI:**407*c;*
    VII:404*c*
  Bayard, Thomas Francis
    VI:28
  Canada **III:**79
  Jay's Treaty **III:**231
  Mason-Dixon Line **V:**250
  Rittenhouse, David **III:**372
  Washington, Treaty of
    VI:385
bounty system **V:39–40,** 400
Bouquet, Henry **II:**58, 349
Bourbon dynasty **II:**372
Bourbons (Democratic party
    faction) **VI:**95, 96
"Bourbon Triumvirate" **V:**45
Boure gold fields **I:**226
Bourgeois, Louise **IX:**19
Bourgeois, Marie Thérèse **IV:**87
Bourke-White, Margaret **VIII:50**
  Life magazine **VIII:**217
  news media **VIII:**272
  photography **VIII:**296
  popular culture **VIII:**303
Bourne, Randolph **VII:**193
Boutwell, George S. **VI:**17
bovine tuberculosis **VIII:**10
Bow, Clara **VII:***96,* 97
Bowdoin, James **III:**377, 417
Bowdoin College **IV:**412*c;* **V:**60
Bowen, Harold **VIII:**283
Bower Hill **III:**440
Bowers, Henry F. **VI:**13, 410*c*
Bowers v. Hardwick **X:**48, 369,
    379*c*
Bowie, Duncan **VI:**359
Bowie, James **IV:62–63**
  Alamo, The **IV:**14
  Texas Revolution **IV:**375
  Travis, William Barret
    IV:380
Bowlegs, Billy **IV:**338, 339
Bowles, Charles S. **VII:**344
Bowles, Chester **VIII:**283
Bowles, Samuel **VI:42–43,** 97
bowling **VIII:**328

Boxer, C. R. **I:**335
Boxer Rebellion **VII:40–41,** 403*c*
  foreign policy **VI:**133;
    VII:113
  Leahy, William D. **VIII:**210
  McKinley, William **VI:**241
  Open Door Notes **VI:**273
  Open Door Policy **VII:**246
boxing **VI:43–45,** *44;* **VII:**405*c,*
    407*c;* **VIII:**446*c*
  African Americans **IX:**5
  Ali, Muhammad **IX:9–10**
  Dempsey, William Harrison
    "Jack" **VII:75–76**
  Johnson, Jack **VII:154–156**
  Louis, Joe **VIII:**223–224
  recreation **VII:**295;
    VIII:328
  sports and recreation **V:**367;
    VII:332, 333; **VIII:**371;
    IX:298
boy bands **X:**238
Boyce, Neith **VII:**131, 375
boycotts **VII:**405*c;* **VIII:**444*c. See
    also* Montgomery bus boycott
  AFL **VI:**13
  agriculture **X:**20
  Chávez, César Estrada
    IX:54
  civil disobedience **IX:**58
  Continental Congress, First
    III:113, 114
  Danbury Hatters **VII:**69
  King, Martin Luther, Jr.
    IX:174
  labor/labor movements
    VII:170
  Norris–La Guardia Act
    VIII:277
  Pullman Strike **VI:**297
  Taft-Hartley Act **IX:**309
  UFW **IX:**324
  White Citizens' Councils
    IX:342
Boyd, Belle **V:**40, 135, 239
Boyd, John P. **III:**411, 412
Boyer, Elizabeth **IX:**345
Boyer, Herbert **X:**224
Boyers, Peggy **X:**211
Boyers, Robert **X:**211
Boyle, Robert **II:**74
Boylston, Thomas **III:**414
Boylston, Zabdiel **II:43,** 99, 361
Boy Scouts
  children **VIII:**67
  Japanese Americans,
    relocation of **VIII:**194
  recreation **VIII:**329
Boy Scouts of America v. Dale
    X:382*c*
Boyz in the Hood **X:**236
Bozell, Brent **X:**49, 50
Bozeman Trail, War for the
  Crazy Horse **VI:**85
  Native Americans **VI:**263
  Red Cloud **VI:**303
Bozo people **I:**109

BP (Brotherhood of Professional
  Base Ball Players) **VI:**26
Brace, Charles Loring **VI:45–46**
braceros/bracero program
  VIII:447*c;* **IX:42–43,** 352*c*
  immigration **VIII:**184
  Latino movement **IX:**185
  Mexican Repatriation
    Program **VIII:**238
Brackenridge, Hugh Henry
  III:60–61, 179, 269
Bracton, Henry **III:**256
Bradbury, John **IV:**379
Bradbury, Ray **IX:**195
Braddock, Edward **II:43–44,**
    437*c*
  Boone, Daniel **III:**55
  Cornplanter **III:**119
  Franklin, Benjamin **III:**173
  Pennsylvania **II:**287
  Seven Years' War **II:**348
  Washington, George
    III:429
Braddock, James **VIII:**223
Bradford, Andrew **II:**268
Bradford, Cornelia Smith **II:**44
Bradford, David **III:**440
Bradford, Sarah **V:**395
Bradford, William (governor)
  II:44
  alcohol **II:**15–16
  Mayflower Compact **II:**228
  Morton, Thomas **II:**244
  Pilgrims **II:**293
  Plymouth **II:**298
  Zenger, John Peter **II:**433
Bradford, William (printer) **II:45;**
  III:17
Bradford, William E. (Union
  officer) **V:**153
Bradford Patent **II:**298
Bradley, Bill **X:**157
Bradley, Joseph **VI:**72, 400
Bradley, Omar N. **V:**17; **VIII:50–**
  51, 448*c;* **IX:**216
Bradley, Will **VI:**184
Bradstreet, Anne Dudley **II:**45
Bradwell, Myra Colby **VI:46–47,**
  400
Bradwell v. Illinois **VI:**47, 400,
  408*c*
Brady, James S. **X:**35, 161
Brady, Mathew B. **V:40–42,** *41,*
  304, 305; **VI:**147
Brady, Thomas J. **VI:**343, 344
Brady, Thomas P. **IX:**342
Brady, William **VI:**376
Brady Handgun Violence
  Prevention Act **X:**380*c,* 381*c*
  crime and punishment
    X:97
  federalism **X:**131
  gun control **X:**161
Bragg, Braxton **V:**42
  Atlanta campaign **V:**22
  Beauregard, Pierre Gustave
    Toutant **V:**32

Buell, Don C. **V:**48
Chattanooga, Battle of
  V:63
Chickamauga, Battle of
  V:64, 65
Confederate army **V:**82
Corinth, Battle of **V:**95
Davis, Jefferson **V:**105
Forrest, Nathan Bedford
  V:152
Hill, Daniel H. **V:**190
Lookout Mountain, Battle
  of **V:**243
Murfreesboro/Stones River,
  Battle of **V:**271, 272
Rosecrans, William S. **V:**337
Shiloh, Battle of **V:**358
Braham, Dave **VI:**257
Brainerd, David **II:45–46**
Braintree, Massachusetts **III:**3, 4
Braintree Instructions **III:**4
Brain Trust **VIII:51**
  Baruch, Bernard M. **VII:**32;
    VIII:42
  Berle, Adolf A., Jr. **VIII:**43
  Emergency Banking Act of
    1933 **VIII:**113
  First New Deal **VIII:**138
  Johnson, Hugh S. **VIII:**196
  London Economic
    Conference **VIII:**221
  Moley, Raymond C.
    VIII:243
  National Recovery
    Administration **VIII:**259
Branch Davidians **X:46–47,** 380*c*
  independent counsel **X:**179
  militia movement **X:**231
  Oklahoma City bombing
    X:267
  Reno, Janet **X:**309
  terrorism **X:**346
Brandeis, Louis Dembitz **VII:***41,*
  41–42, 406*c*
  antimonopoly **VIII:**23
  civil liberties **VII:**58
  court-packing plan **VIII:**89
  Douglas, William O.
    VIII:97
  Frankfurter, Felix **VIII:**144
  Goldmark, Josephine Clara
    VII:127
  Holmes, Oliver Wendell
    VII:140
  Muller v. Oregon **VII:**218
  New Nationalism **VII:**237
  religion **VIII:**335
  Supreme Court **VII:**343–
    344; **VIII:**382
Brandeis Brief **VII:**218
Brandeis University **IX:**228
Brandenburg Gate, Remarks at
  (Reagan) **X:396–399**
Brandenburg v. Ohio **X:**71
Brando, Marlon **IX:**224
Brandt, Willy **X:**84
Brandy Station, Battle of **V:**166

Brandywine, Battle of **III:**61*m*, **61–62,** 461*c*
 Cornwallis, Charles, Lord **III:**120
 Greene, Nathanael **III:**198
 Howe, Sir William **III:**215
 Knox, Henry **III:**248
 Knyphausen, Wilhelm, Baron von **III:**248
 Monroe, James **IV:**258
 Pinckney, Charles Cotesworth **III:**336
 Pulaski, Casimir **III:**350
 Revolutionary War **III:**368
Brannan, Samuel **IV:63–64**
Brant, John **IV:**277
Brant, Joseph **II:**412; **III:62–63,** *63,* 195, 228, 461*c*
Brant, Molly **II:**187; **III:**62
Brant, Sebastian **I:**249
Brantley, Etheldred T. **IV:**380
Branzburg v. Hayes **X:**376*c*
brass bands **V:**273
Brattain, Walter H. **X:**86
Brattle, Thomas **II:46,** 204
Brattle, William **II:**204
Brattle Street Church (Cambridge, Massachusetts) **II:**46, 204
Brave Men (Pyle) **VIII:**315
Brave One, The (film) **IX:**223
Bray, Thomas **II:**21, 112
Brazil **I:33–35,** *34,* 396*c*
 Amazon River **I:**9
 Bahía **I:**25–26
 Battel, Andrew **I:**28
 Berle, Adolf A., Jr. **VIII:**43
 Cabral, Pedro Álvares **I:**46
 cannibalism **I:**58
 castas **I:**65
 Clinton, William J. **X:**83
 Coelho, Jorge d'Albuquerque **I:**78
 Dutch West India Company **II:**107
 emancipation **V:**130
 French explorations of the Atlantic **I:**133, 134
 Hastings, Lansford W. **IV:**187
 Histoire d'un voyage faict en la terre du Bresil autrement dite Amerique (Léry) **I:418–423**
 John III **I:**197
 Latin America **IX:**184; **X:**206
 Léry, Jean de **I:**212, 213
 Magellan, Ferdinand **I:**223
 Portuguese seaborne empire **I:**300
 slavery **II:**354
 slave trade **II:**358
 smallpox **I:**341
 Stade, Hans **I:**346
 sugar **I:**348, 349
 Thevet, André **I:**357
 tobacco **I:**363

Tordesillas, Treaty of **I:**368
Tupinambá **I:**371
Vespucci, Amerigo **I:**378
Wise, Henry A. **V:**434
brazilwood **I:**25, 26, 35
Brazos River **IV:**371, 373
Brazos River Valley **IV:**39
breach of contract **X:**298
Bread-winners, The (Hay) **VI:**164
Breakfast at Tiffany's (Capote) **IX:**194
Brébeuf, Jean de **II:46–47**
Breckenridge, Henry **VII:**227, 267
Breckinridge, John C. **V:42–43,** 443*c*
 Chattanooga, Battle of **V:**63
 Democratic Party **IV:**119; **V:**109
 Murfreesboro/Stones River, Battle of **V:**271
 Orphan Brigade **V:**288
 Republican Party **IV:**323
Breed's Hill **III:**65, 67, 427
Breezing Up (Homer) **VI:**174–175
Breiner, Leo **VII:**345
Breintnall, Joseph **II:**34, 287
Bremer, Arthur H. **IX:**24
Bremer, L. Paul, III **X:**187
Brendan the Navigator, Saint **I:35–36**
Brennan, William J., Jr. **X:**47, **47–48**
 Baker v. Carr **IX:**33
 Burger, Warren E. **X:**51
 flag burning **X:**136
 Meese, Edwin C., III **X:**225
 Souter, David **X:**324
 Warren Court **IX:**337
Brennan, William J., Sr. **X:**47
Brent, Charles **VII:**222
Brent, Margaret Reed **II:47**
Breslaw, Elaine G. **II:**390
Brest, Battle of **I:**135
Brest-Litovsk, Treaty of **VII:**308
Brethren, The (Woodward and Armstrong) **X:**51
Bretton Woods Conference **VIII:52,** 448*c*
 Congress **VIII:**81
 Eccles, Marriner S. **VIII:**101
 economy **VIII:**105
 foreign policy **VIII:**142
 Morgenthau, Henry T., Jr. **VIII:**244
 postwar planning **VIII:**307
 Roosevelt, Franklin D. **VIII:**346
Brewer, David **VII:**218, 417–420
Brewster, Mary **VI:**328
Brewster, William **II:**75, 293
Breyer, Stephen **X:48–49**
 Gore, Albert, Jr. **X:**157
 gun control **X:**162
 Hamdan v. Rumsfeld **X:**164

McCreary County v. ACLU/ Van Orden v. Perry **X:**216
 Supreme Court **X:**339
Brezhnev, Leonid **X:**376*c,* 377*c*
 ABM Treaty **X:**26
 cold war, end of **X:**84, 85
 defense policy **X:**100
 détente **X:**103
 Europe **IX:**113
 Ford, Gerald R. **X:**139
 foreign policy **X:**141
 Lend-Lease **VIII:**212
 Nixon, Richard M. **X:**257
Briand, Aristide **VII:**49, 50, 164
Briar's Creek, Battle of **III:63–64**
bribery **X:**377*c*
 Agnew, Spiro T. **X:**18
 direct election of senators **VII:**78
 Foreign Corrupt Practices Act **X:**139
 Senate, U.S. **X:**321
Brice, Fanny **VII:**96
Brice's Crossroads, Battle of **V:**152
Bricker, John **VIII:**111
bridge (card game) **VIII:**328
Bridge and Structural Ironworkers **VII:**11
Bridger, James **IV:64–65**
 Astor, John Jacob **IV:**35
 Bent, William **IV:**53
 exploration **IV:**144, 145
 mountain men **IV:**266
 Rocky Mountain Fur Company **IV:**324
Bridger's Pass **IV:**145
bridges **VI:47–48,** *48*
 Bell, Alexander Graham **VI:**31
 Carnegie, Andrew **VI:**62
 Eads, James Buchanan **VI:**103
 transportation, urban **VI:**360
Bridges, Harry **VIII:52–53**
Bridges, Robert **III:**169
Bridgestone/Firestone **X:**203
Bridgman, Frederick **VI:**275
Brief Account of the Destruction of the Indies (Las Casas) **I:**31
Briefe and True Reporte of the New Found Land of Virginia (Harriot) **I:**398*c;* **II:**206
 Bry, Theodor de **I:**37
 Camden, William **I:**55–56
 Hakluyt, Richard, the Younger **I:**152
 Harriot, Thomas **I:**154–156
 Monardes, Nicholas **I:**247
 Native American religion **I:**261
 Picts **I:**292
 Roanoke **I:**321
 White, John **I:**383

Brierfield Iron Works **V:**171
brigade system **IV:**31–33
brigantine **I:36,** 184
Briggs, Charles A. **VI:**307
Briggs, Emily **VI:**266
Briggs, James S. **V:**93
Bright Eyes (Indian reform activist) **VI:48–49,** 199
Brimm, Benjamin **V:**412
Brims **II:**47
Bringing It All Back Home (Dylan) **IX:**92
Brinkley, David **IX:**315
Bristol **I:36–37,** 77
Bristow, Benjamin H. **V:**429; **VI:**159
Britain. *See* Great Britain
Britain, Battle of **VIII:53–54**
 air power **VIII:**15
 Anglo-American relations **VIII:**21
 destroyers-for-bases deal **VIII:**94
 Kennedy, Joseph P. **VIII:**200
 news media **VIII:**272
 radio **VIII:**320
 refugees **VIII:**330
Britannia (Camden) **I:**55, 56
British Aggressions in Venezuela or the Monroe Doctrine on Trial (Scruggs) **VI:**373
British army **III:**459*c,* 461*c*
 André, John **III:**19–20
 Arnold, Benedict **III:**31
 Boston Massacre **III:**56–58
 Bunker Hill, Battle of **III:**65–67
 Burgoyne, Sir John **III:**67–68
 Carleton, Guy **III:**81
 Charleston, siege of **III:**84–85
 cities and urban life **III:**90
 Clark, George Rogers **III:**95–96
 Clinton, George **III:**98
 Clinton, Sir Henry **III:**99
 Cornwallis, Charles, Lord **III:**119–121
 Cowpens, Battle of **III:**124
 Dorchester Heights **III:**138–139
 Gage, Thomas **III:**186–187
 Georgia Expedition **III:**192
 Golden Hill, Battle of **III:**196
 Guilford Courthouse, Battle of **III:**202
 Harlem Heights, Battle of **III:**210
 Howe, Sir William **III:**215–216
 Lexington and Concord, Battles of **III:**264–266
 Monmouth, Battle of **III:**299

British army (*continued*)
New York City, fire of
III:318
Penobscot campaign
III:333–334
Pontiac's War **III:**339
POWs **III:**346
Quartering Act **III:**352
Revolutionary War **III:**367–368
Saratoga, surrender at
III:380–382
Savannah, Battle of **III:**382–383
Savannah, siege of **III:**383
Tarleton, Banastre **III:**406–407
Yorktown, surrender at
III:454–457
British Broadcasting Corporation
(BBC) **VIII:**312
British colonies. *See* English
colonies
British Columbia **I:**150; **IV:**123;
VII:404*c*
British East India Company
I:117; **III:**460*c*
Boston Tea Party **III:**58,
59
China trade **III:**88–89
Coercive Acts **III:**100
Grotius, Hugo **I:**146
Hakluyt, Richard, the
Younger **I:**153
Hudson, Henry **II:**168
Linschoten, Jan Huygen van
I:215
North, Frederick, Lord
III:320
Sandys, Sir Edwin **I:**326
Spanish Armada **I:**345
Spice Islands **I:**345
Tea Act **III:**408–409
British Empire **II:**47–49
Fort Mose **II:**132
Johnson, Sir William
II:187–188
Massachusetts **II:**224
New York City **II:**272
Paxton Boys **II:**282
technology **II:**385
British Guiana **VI:**75, 373
"British Invasion" (pop music)
X:238
British Malaya **VII:**152
British Methodist Episcopal
Church **VI:**4–5
British navy
Chesapeake-Leopard affair
III:88
Delaware River forts
III:135
Howe, Richard, Lord
III:214
impressment **III:**222–223
Jersey, HMS **III:**235
POWs **III:**346

Rhode Island, Battle of
III:369, 370
Saintes, Battle of the
III:378–379
British North American Act
(1867) **VI:**61
British Petroleum **VII:**245, 336
"British Prison Ship, The"
(Freneau) **III:**180
British Royal Marines **VII:**325
Broaddrick, Juanita **X:**194
Broadway theater **VII:**408*c*
entertainment, popular
VII:95–96
Gershwin, George **VII:**124
music **VII:**218–220
popular culture **X:**280–281
sexual revolution **X:**322
Tin Pan Alley **VII:**353
Brock, Sir Isaac **IV:**192
Brody, Fawn **III:**210
brogans **V:**399
Broken Blossoms (film) **VII:**132
Brom and Bett vs. Ashley **III:**176
Bronzeville neighborhood
(Chicago) **IX:**4
Brooke, John Mercer **V:**83, 265
Brooker, William **II:**268
Brook Farm **IV:**65
Dana, Charles A. **VI:**91
Emerson, Ralph Waldo
IV:140
Fourier, Charles **IV:**162
Fuller, Margaret **IV:**169
literature **IV:**228
Peabody, Elizabeth Palmer
VI:279
religion **IV:**320
transcendental movement
IV:379
Brookings Institution **VIII:**263;
X:349
Brookline, Massachusetts **IX:**169,
171
Brooklyn, New York
birth control **VII:**36
environment **VI:**120
housing **VI:**179
Sanger, Margaret **VII:**312
sports and recreation
VIII:370
urban transportation
VII:364
White, Alfred Tredway
VI:390
Brooklyn Botanic Garden **VI:**391
Brooklyn Bridge **VI:**18, *48*, 409*c*
Brooklyn Bureau of Charities
VI:391
Brooklyn Children's Aid Society
VI:390
Brooklyn Dodgers **IX:**351*c*, 354*c*
African Americans **IX:**5
Rickey, Branch **IX:**276, 277
Robinson, Jackie **IX:**277, 278
sports and recreation
VIII:370; **IX:**298

Brooklyn Society for the
Prevention of Cruelty to
Children **VI:**390–391
Brooks, Garth **X:**238, 240, 280
Brooks, James **V:**97
Brooks, John W. **VI:**132
Brooks, Ned **IX:***316*
Brooks, Phillips **VI:50**, 306, 313
Brooks, Preston
abolitionism **V:**4
Bleeding Kansas **V:**37
slavery **V:**363
Sumner, Charles **V:**377
Brooks Brothers **VI:**96
Brookwood Labor College
VII:109
Brophy, Thomas D'Arcy **IX:**125
brothels **V:**316
Brotherhood of Locomotive
Firemen **VII:**72
Brotherhood of Professional Base
Ball Players (BP) **VI:**26
Brotherhood of Railway and
Airline Clerks **VIII:**54
Brotherhood of Railway Carmen
VII:117
Brotherhood of Railway
Engineers and Firemen
VII:291
Brotherhood of Sleeping Car
Porters **VIII:54**
African Americans **VIII:**4
Harlem Renaissance
VII:136
March on Washington
Movement **VIII:**227
Randolph, A. Philip
VIII:321
"Brotherhood of Thieves, or, A
True Picture Of The American
Clergy and Church" (Foster)
IV:161
brothers' war **V:**43, 71, 186
Broughton, William **IV:**103
Brouthers, Dan **VI:**26
Browder, Earl
Communists **VIII:**78
FBI **VIII:**130
Foster, William Zebulon
VII:117
Popular Front **VIII:**304
Thomas, Norman **VIII:**394
Brown, Charles Brockden **III:64,**
269; **IV:**209
Brown, Dan **X:**212
Brown, Dee **X:**375*c*
Brown, Earle **IX:**228
Brown, Edmund G. **VII:**213
Brown, Floyd **X:**168
Brown, Henry B. **VI:**284,
433–434
Brown, H. Rap **IX:**303
Brown, Jacob **IV:**336
Brown, James
music **X:**238
rock and roll **IX:**279, 280
Brown, Jerry **X:**20

Brown, John **V:43–45,** *44,* 443*c*
abolitionism **V:**4
Atkinson, Edward **VI:**21
Baltimore & Ohio Railroad
IV:44
Bleeding Kansas **V:**37
Booth, John Wilkes **V:**38
Bowles, Samuel **VI:**42
Civil War **V:**73
Cooper Union speech **V:**94
Douglass, Frederick **V:**116
Exodusters **VI:**122
Forbes, John Murray **VI:**132
Gaspée affair **III:**189
Harper, Frances Ellen
Watkins **VI:**160
Harpers Ferry, West Virginia
V:185–186
Higginson, Thomas
Wentworth **V:**189; **VI:**171
Langston, John Mercer
VI:218
Lee, Robert E. **V:**230
music **V:**273
Republican Party **IV:**323
slavery **V:**363
Stuart, J. E. B. **V:**375
Thoreau, Henry David
IV:376–377
Watterson, Henry **VI:**385
Wise, Henry A. **V:**434
Brown, John, Jr. **V:**211
Brown, Joseph Emerson **V:45**
Cobb, Howell **V:**76
Confederate States of
America **V:**86
conscription **V:**91
elections **V:**127
governors **V:**172
homespun **V:**194
peace movements **V:**296
states' rights **V:**370
Toombs, Robert A. **V:**389
Brown, Lewis **X:**349
Brown, Linda **IX:**338
Brown, Michael
Bush, George W. **X:**56
Hurricane Katrina **X:**174
New York World's Fair
(1964) **IX:**246
Brown, Moses **III:**463*c*
economy **III:**146
industrialization **IV:**199
Slater, Samuel **III:**389
Brown, Oliver **IX:**43–44, 227
Brown, Olympia **VI:50–51,** 176,
399, 400
Brown, Prentiss **VIII:**283
Brown, Ron **X:**194
Brown, Walter **VII:**29
Brown, William Wells **IV:**415*c;*
V:46
American Anti-Slavery
Society **IV:**16
54th Massachusetts
Regiment **V:**142
slavery **V:**362

Brown Berets **IX:**350
Browne, Edmund **II:**421
Browne, Richard **I:**181, 182
Browne, Robert **II:**75
Brownell, Herbert **X:**50
Brownhelm, Ohio **VI:**218
Brownie cameras **VI:**105; **VII:**258
Browning, Elizabeth **VI:**269
Browning, Robert **VI:**219, 269
Brownlow, William G. **V:**68, 223
Brownson, Orestes A.
    literature **IV:**228
    religion **VI:**308
    Roman Catholicism **VI:**316
Brownsville, Pennsylvania **IV:**271
Brownsville Raid, The (Weaver)
    VII:42
Brownsville Riot **VII:42**
Brown University
    Angell, James Burrill **VI:**14
    Baptists **III:**44
    Ward, Lester Frank **VI:**382
Brown v. Board of Education of
    Topeka **IX:43–44,** 353*c*
    African Americans **VIII:**5;
      IX:4–5
    civil rights **VIII:**72
    Eisenhower, Dwight D.
      IX:101
    Faubus, Orval **IX:**118
    freedom rides **IX:**123
    Latino movement **IX:**185
    Marshall, Thurgood **IX:**203
    Murray, Pauli **IX:**227
    Myrdal, Gunnar **VIII:**253
    NAACP **VIII:**256; **IX:**232
    race and race relations
      IX:269; **X:**297
    segregation **IX:**288
    sit-ins **IX:**290
    South Africa **X:**324
    Southern Manifesto **IX:**294
    Supreme Court **VIII:**383
    Till, Emmett Louis **IX:**318
    Tourgée, Albion W. **V:**390
    Warren, Earl **IX:**337
    Warren Court **IX:**338
    White Citizens' Councils
      IX:341–342
    Wilkins, Roy **IX:**344
Bruce, Blanche Kelso **V:46–47;**
    VI:5
Brulé, Étienne **II:49–50,** 123
Brulé Lakota Indians **IV:**276;
    VI:85
Brunner, Emil **VIII:**335
Brunswick, Georgia **VI:**223
Brush, Charles F. **VI:**194
Bry, Theodor de **I:37–38,** 38
    black legend **I:**32
    Camden, William **I:**55–56
    cannibalism **I:**58–59
    Harriot, Thomas **I:**155–156
    Native American religion
      I:261
    Picts **I:**292
    Secotan **I:**329

Stade, Hans **I:**346
White, John **I:**383
Bryan, William Jennings **VI:51–**
    53, *52,* 411*c;* **VII:***316,* 403*c,*
    405*c,* 409*c*
    Anti-Imperialist League
      VI:17
    bimetallism **VI:**38
    class consciousness **VI:**74
    Cleveland, Grover **VI:**75
    Congress **VI:**80
    "Cross of Gold" speech
      VI:438–441
    Currency Act **VII:**68
    currency issue **VI:**90
    Darrow, Clarence Seward
      VII:70
    Democratic Party **VI:**95–96;
      VII:74
    Donnelly, Ignatius Loyola
      VI:100
    elections **VII:**90, 91
    Free-Silver movement
      VI:135
    Hanna, Marcus Alonzo
      VI:158
    Lease, Mary Elizabeth
      Clyens **VI:**220
    McKinley, William **VI:**240,
      241
    Mencken, Henry Louis
      VII:202
    Narcotics Act **VII:**222
    New Nationalism **VII:**237
    People's Party **VI:**282
    presidential campaigns
      (1870–1899) **VI:**293
    Republican Party **VII:**299
    Scopes Trial **VII:**316, 317
    Simpson, Jerry **VI:**330
    Sunday, William Ashley, Jr.
      VII:342
    Taft, William Howard
      VII:347
    Watson, Thomas Edward
      VII:380
    Watterson, Henry **VI:**386
Bryan's Station **III:**54
Bryant, Carolyn **IX:**269, 318
Bryant, Louise **VII:**131, 296
Bryant, Roy **IX:**318
Bryant, William Cullen
    art and architecture **IV:**28
    Cooper Union speech **V:**93
    literature **IV:**228
    Massachusetts Emigrant Aid
      Society **IV:**242
Bryce, James (first viscount Bryce)
    VI:53, 410*c*
Bryne, Ethel **VII:**36
Bryn Mawr College
    education **VI:**109
    Goldmark, Josephine Clara
      VII:127
    social work **VII:**330
    Thomas, M. Carey **VI:**356
    women's colleges **VI:**398

Brzezinski, Zbigniew **X:**22
Bubble Act (England) **II:**370
Buber, Martin **VIII:**334
bubonic plague. *See* plague
buccaneers **II:**296
Buchanan, Franklin
    brothers' war **V:**43
    Confederate navy **V:**83
    H.L. Hunley, CSS **V:**191
    Monitor-Merrimack **V:**265,
      266
    U.S. Naval Academy at
      Annapolis **V:**409, 410
Buchanan, George **I:**191
Buchanan, James **V:***47,* **47–48,**
    443*c*
    Benton, Thomas Hart **IV:**54
    Bleeding Kansas **V:**38
    Breckinridge, John C. **V:**42
    Cass, Lewis **IV:**83
    Cobb, Howell **V:**76
    Democratic Party **IV:**118,
      119; **V:**109
    Deseret, State of **IV:**121
    Douglas, Stephen A. **V:**114
    education, federal aid to
      VI:110
    filibustering **V:**145
    foreign policy **V:**149, 150
    Fort Sumter **V:**154
    Frémont, John C. **IV:**167
    Homestead Act **V:**194
    Larkin, Thomas Oliver
      IV:223
    Manifest Destiny **IV:**235
    Mormon Church **IV:**90;
      VI:252
    Mormon War **IV:**263
    Morrill Land-Grant Act
      V:269
    nativism **V:**280
    Oregon Treaty of 1846
      IV:287
    Ostend Manifesto **V:**290
    popular sovereignty **IV:**304
    public land policy **IV:**307
    Republican Party **IV:**322–
      323; **V:**333
    Stanton, Edwin M. **V:**368
    Young, Brigham **IV:**408
Buchanan, McKean **V:**43
Buchanan, Patrick J. **X:**49
    conservative movement **X:**94
    Nader, Ralph **X:**242
    Reform Party **X:**304
    WTO **X:**372
Buchenwald concentration camp,
    Germany **VIII:**50
Buck, Carrie **VII:**43
Buck, Dudley **VI:**255
Buck, Pearl S. **VIII:**446*c*
Buck, Robert M. **VII:**286
Buckley, James
    Helms, Jesse A., Jr. **X:**165
    neoconservatism **X:**252
    New York City bailout
      X:254

Buckley, William F., Jr. **X:49–50**
    conservatism **IX:**74
    conservative movement
      X:93
    terrorism **X:**345
    YAF **IX:**349
Buckley v. Valeo **X:**63, 275
Buck's Stove and Range **VII:**43
Buck's Stove case **VII:**12, **42–43,**
    226
Buck v. Bell **VII:43–44,** 103, 141,
    409*c*
Budapest, Hungary **VII:**116;
    VIII:432
Buddhism
    Beat Generation **IX:**37
    religion **IV:**319; **IX:**272;
      X:306
    Vietnam War **IX:**330
Budge, Don **VIII:**372
Budget, Bureau of the
    Budget and Accounting Act
      VII:44
    Executive Reorganization
      Act **VIII:**121
    government **VIII:**153
    Harding, Warren Gamaliel
      VII:134
budget, federal **X:**377*c,* 382*c. See*
    also deficit, federal
    Clinton, William J. **X:**82
    Congressional Budget and
      Impoundment Control
      Act **X:**88–89
    economy **X:**109, 110
    Gingrich, Newton L. **X:**151
Budget, U.S. Office of the **VII:**71
Budget and Accounting Act
    VII:44, 134–135, 351, 408*c*
budget reform **VII:**71
budget surpluses **X:**382*c*
Buell, Don C. **V:48–49,** 358–360,
    389
Buena Vista, Battle of **IV:**252
    Bragg, Braxton **V:**42
    Davis, Jefferson **V:**103
    Gregg, Josiah **IV:**179
    McDowell, Irvin **V:**252
    Mexican-American War
      IV:252
    Santa Anna, Antonio López
      de **IV:**330
    Taylor, Zachary **IV:**368
buffalo **II:**127; **III:64–65**
    animals **III:**22–23
    extermination of **VI:53–54,**
      411*c*
    Great Plains **III:**197
    Native Americans **III:**315;
      VI:261, 263
Buffalo, New York
    cities and urban life **V:**67
    Cleveland, Grover **VI:**74
    disease/epidemics **IV:**122
    economy **IV:**131
    Erie Canal **IV:**141
    Free-Soil Party **IV:**163

Buffalo, New York (continued)
  Garnet, Henry Highland
    IV:174
  industrialization IV:200
  Liberty Party IV:227
  Massachusetts Emigrant Aid
    Society IV:242
  migration IV:254
  Pan-American Exposition
    VII:251
  railroads IV:316
  Scott, Winfield IV:336
Buffalo Bayou IV:328
Buffalo Bill. See Cody, William
  Frederick "Buffalo Bill"
Buffalo Bill: King of the Border
  Men (Buntline) VI:76
Buffalo Bill's Wild West Show
  VI:77, 409c
Buffalo Creek III:359
Buffalo Soldiers VI:54, 395
Buffett, Warren X:148
Buford, John V:166
Buick Motor Car Company
  automobile industry VII:26
  economy VII:84
  GM IX:132
building codes VI:179
building construction VII:84
Bulfinch, Charles III:29, 65
Bulgaria X:384c
  Axis VIII:38
  cold war IX:63
  Europe IX:112
  World War I VII:393
Bulge, Battle of the VIII:54–55,
  55, 448c
  Bradley, Omar N. VIII:51
  Patton, George S., Jr.
    VIII:291
  World War II European
    theater VIII:431–432
Bull, Dixey II:296
bullets V:340
Bullivant, Benjamin II:383
Bulloch, James D. V:7, 49, 150
Bull Run/Manassas, First Battle of
  V:49–50, 50, 444c
  Barton, Clara V:29
  Beauregard, Pierre Gustave
    Toutant V:32
  Brady, Mathew B. V:41
  Bull Run/Manassas, First
    and Second Battles of
    V:49–50
  Burnside, Ambrose E. V:52
  Civil War centennial IX:62
  Early, Jubal A. V:119
  espionage V:135
  homefront V:194
  Hooker, Joseph V:196
  Howard, Oliver Otis V:197
  Irish-American regiments
    V:205
  Jackson, Thomas J.
    "Stonewall" V:210
  Johnston, Joseph E. V:214

  Joint Committee on the Con-
    duct of the War V:215, 216
  McClellan, George Brinton
    V:250
  McDowell, Irvin V:252
  medicine V:256
  Sherman, William T. V:354
  Stuart, J. E. B. V:375
  tactics and strategy V:380,
    381
  uniforms V:398
  Union army V:401
  Zouaves V:442
Bull Run/Manassas, Second Battle
  of V:50–51, 444c
  Antietam, Battle of V:12
  Bull Run/Manassas, First
    and Second Battles of
    V:50–51
  Cedar Mountain, Battle
    of V:59
  Early, Jubal A. V:119
  Ewell, Richard Stoddert
    V:135
  German-American
    regiments V:166
  Harvard Regiment V:186
  Hill, Ambrose P. V:190
  homefront V:194
  Hood, John Bell V:196
  Jackson, Thomas J.
    "Stonewall" V:210
  Lee, Robert E. V:230, 231
  Longstreet, James V:242
  Louisiana Tigers V:245
  McClellan, George Brinton
    V:251
  Meade, George Gordon
    V:253
  Stuart, J. E. B. V:376
Bulwer, Henry Lytton V:98
Bunau-Varilla, Philippe VII:251,
  404c
Bunche, Ralph VIII:318; IX:44–
  45, 45, 201, 352c
Bundists VIII:71
Bundy, McGeorge X:49
Bunel, Joseph III:203
Bunker Hill, Battle of III:65–67,
  66m, 461c
  Clinton, Sir Henry III:99
  Dorchester Heights III:138
  Gage, Thomas III:187
  Howe, Sir William III:215
  Putnam, Israel III:350
  Warren, Joseph III:427
Bunker Hill Monument IV:313
Buntline, Ned (E. C. Judson)
  Bridger, James IV:64–65
  Cody, William Frederick
    VI:76
  entertainment, popular
    VI:118
Bureau(s), government. See under
  type of bureau, e.g.: Alcohol,
  Tobacco, and Firearms, Bureau
  of

Bureau of Motion Pictures
  VIII:55–56
  censorship VIII:66
  movies VIII:246
  OWI VIII:286
Burford, Anne Gorsuch X:300
Burger, Warren E. X:50–51, 375c
  Ford, Gerald R. X:138
  Meese, Edwin C., III X:225
  Supreme Court X:338, 339
  U.S. v. Nixon X:358
  Watergate scandal X:367
Burger Court X:152
Burgesses, House of II:50, 50–
  51, 435c; III:459c
  Bland, Richard III:52
  Byrd, William, II II:52
  committees of
    correspondence III:101
  Dunmore, John Murray, earl
    of III:142
  Henry, Patrick III:211, 212
  Jefferson, Thomas III:232
  Lee, Richard Henry III:260
  Mason, George III:292
  Parsons' Cause II:281, 282
  Stamp Act III:395
  Virginia II:399, 400
  Virginia Resolves III:425
  Washington, George
    III:430
Burgis, William II:51, 205
Burgoyne, Sir John III:67, 67–68,
  461c
  Beaumarchais, Pierre-
    Auguste Caron de III:48
  Brant, Joseph III:63
  Clinton, George III:98
  Deane, Silas III:129
  Fort Ticonderoga III:172
  Gates, Horatio III:190
  Howe, Sir William III:215
  Hudson Highlands
    campaign III:216
  McCrea, Jane III:293
  POWs III:346
  Revolutionary War III:368
  Saratoga, surrender at
    III:380, 382
Burgundy I:70
burial complex I:253
burial customs II:328
burial practices
  Cahokia I:50
  Hopewell culture I:167
  mound builders I:254
Burke, Edmund III:68–69
  North, Frederick, Lord
    III:320
  Paine, Thomas III:329
  political parties III:338
Burke, Fielding VII:122
Burke, Tom V:359
Burke Act VI:93; VII:44–45, 232,
  404c
Burkina Faso I:252
Burleigh, A. Peter X:357

Burleson, Albert S. VII:285
burlesque VI:117
Burlingame Treaty V:201; VI:15,
  68
Burlington Railroad VIII:396
Burlington Railroad Strike VI:213
Burlington Zephyr (train)
  VIII:396
Burma
  Cairo Conference VIII:61
  OSS VIII:285
  World War II Pacific theater
    VIII:435, 437
"Burmuda Pamphlets" I:353
burned-over district
  Erie Canal IV:143
  Second Great Awakening
    IV:337
  Smith, Joseph, Jr. IV:352
Burnham, Daniel Hudson VI:54–
  56, 55
  art and architecture VI:19
  Hayden, Sophia Gregoria
    VI:166
  World's Columbian
    Exposition VI:402
Burns, Anthony IV:65–66, 66,
  415c
  Dana, Richard Henry
    IV:113
  fugitive slave laws IV:168
  Higginson, Thomas
    Wentworth V:189; VI:171
Burns, Arnold X:225
Burns, George VII:95
Burns, Tommy VII:154, 333,
  405c
Burnside, Ambrose E. V:51,
  51–52, 444c
  Antietam, Battle of V:13
  Chancellorsville, Battle of
    V:60
  civil liberties, Union V:70
  Fredericksburg, Battle of
    V:157–159
  Joint Committee on the
    Conduct of the War
    V:216
  Lee, Robert E. V:231
  Lincoln, Abraham V:237
  McClellan, George Brinton
    V:252
  Vallandigham, Clement L.
    V:413
Burnside carbines V:51
"Burnside's Mud March" V:52
Burnt Corn, Battle of IV:190
Burr, Aaron II:311; III:69,
  69–70, 465c
  Adams, John III:6
  Amendment, Twelfth III:16
  Cass, Lewis IV:83
  Claiborne, William C. C.
    IV:94, 95
  Democratic Party IV:116–
    117
  dueling III:141

election of 1800 **III:**150, 151
Hamilton, Alexander **III:**208
Jefferson, Thomas **III:**234
Louisiana Purchase **III:**275
Madison, Dolley Payne Todd **III:**280
Pickering, Timothy **III:**335
Randolph, Edmund **III:**358
Wilkinson, James **III:**444
Burr, Esther Edwards **II:52**
Burriel, Juan **VI:**87–88, 377
Burritt, Elihu **V:**295
Burroughs, John **V:**431
Burroughs, William S. (adding machine inventor) **VI:**196
Burroughs, William S., II (writer)
Beat Generation **IX:**36–37
counterculture **IX:**78
Ginsberg, Allen **IX:**134
Kerouac, Jack **IX:**173
Leary, Timothy **IX:**187
literature **IX:**194
Burrows, Daniel **IX:**180
Burr's Conspiracy **IV:**95
burr stones **II:**235
Burton, Mary **II:**255
Burton, Phillip **X:**169
Bury My Heart at Wounded Knee (Brown) **X:**375*c*
bus boycott (Montgomery, Alabama). *See* Montgomery bus boycott
Bush, George H. W. **X:53–53**, 52, 85, 274, 379*c*, 380*c*
ABM Treaty **X:**28
abortion **X:**4
Africa **X:**16
Americans with Disabilities Act **X:**25
arms race **IX:**17; **X:**30
Bennett, William J. **X:**41
Brown v. Board of Education **IX:**44
Buchanan, Patrick J. **X:**49
Bush, George W. **X:**54
Cheney, Richard B. **X:**71, 72
Civil Rights Act (1991) **X:**76
Clinton, William J. **X:**80, 81
conservative movement **X:**94
crime and punishment **X:**97
defense policy **X:**101
Dole, Robert **X:**105
Dukakis, Michael S. **X:**105
economy **X:**110
education, primary/ secondary **X:**115
elections, presidential **X:**116
foreign policy **X:**142
Gore, Albert, Jr. **X:**157
Haig, Alexander M., Jr. **X:**163
Helms, Jesse A., Jr. **X:**165
Horton, Willie **X:**168

INF Treaty **X:**181
Latin America **X:**206
Mexico **X:**226
Middle East **X:**229
Mitchell, George **X:**232
narcotics **X:**243
North Vietnam **X:**260
Panama invasion (1989–1990) **X:**269
Persian Gulf War **X:**273
Powell, Colin L. **X:**286
pro-life/pro-choice movements **X:**289
Quayle, J. Danforth **X:**293
Reagan, Ronald W. **X:**300
Rice, Condoleezza **X:**309
Roberts, John G. **X:**311
SDI **X:**337
Souter, David **X:**324
South Africa **X:**325
Supreme Court **X:**339
Thomas, Clarence **X:**350
"Thousand Points of Light" speech **X:399–403**
UN **X:**357
veto (presidential) **X:**361
Walsh, Lawrence E. **X:**365
Bush, George W. **X:53–57**, 54, 383*c*, 384*c*
ABM Treaty **X:**28
abortion **X:**5
Afghanistan War **X:**10, 11
Africa **X:**17
automobile industry **X:**37
Bilingual Education Act **X:**42
business **X:**59
campaign finance **X:**64
Cheney, Richard B. **X:**71, 72
Clinton, Hillary Rodham **X:**78
conservation/ environmentalism **X:**92
conservative movement **X:**94
defense policy **X:**102
DHS **X:**167
economy **X:**110, 111
education, primary/ secondary **X:**115
elections, presidential **X:**116–118
federalism **X:**131
foreign policy **X:**143–144
gay and lesbian rights movement **X:**150
global warming **X:**156
Gore, Albert, Jr. **X:**157
House of Representatives **X:**170
Hurricane Katrina **X:**174
immigration **X:**176
independent counsel **X:**179
Iraq War **X:**185, 187, 188
Kelo v. City of New London **X:**195

Kennedy, Edward M. **X:**197
medicine **X:**224
Mexico **X:**226–227
Middle East **X:**229, 230
Nader, Ralph **X:**242
NEPA **X:**246
O'Connor, Sandra Day **X:**265
Oklahoma City bombing **X:**267
political parties **X:**276
Powell, Colin L. **X:**287
Presidential Address to a Joint Session of Congress and the American People (9/20/2001) **X:411–414**
Rehnquist, William H. **X:**305
Rice, Condoleezza **X:**309
Roberts, John G. **X:**311
Rumsfeld, Donald **X:**313
Sarbanes-Oxley Act **X:**315
SDI **X:**337
stem cell research **X:**335, 336
Supreme Court **X:**339
terrorism **X:**347
UN **X:**356
USA PATRIOT Act **X:**358, 360
veto (presidential) **X:**361
Bush, Vannevar **VIII:56**, **56–57**
Internet **X:**182
Manhattan Project **VIII:**226, 227
OSRD **VIII:**283–284
Bush Doctrine **X:**56, 143
Bushnell, Horace **IV:**319
Bush v. Gore **X:**383*c*
Ginsburg, Ruth Bader **X:**153
Gore, Albert, Jr. **X:**157
O'Connor, Sandra Day **X:**265
Rehnquist, William H. **X:**305
Scalia, Antonin **X:**316
Souter, David **X:**324
Supreme Court **X:**339
Thomas, Clarence **X:**350
Bush v. Vera **X:**381*c*
bushwhackers **V:52–53**
Bleeding Kansas **V:**36–38
jayhawkers **V:**211
Quantrill, William Clarke **V:**317
slavery **V:**363
business **VIII:57–59; IX:45–47;** **X:57–61**, 58, 58*t*, 60*m*
advertising **VIII:**1
AFL **VIII:**18; **IX:**11
African Americans **X:**14
America First Committee **VIII:**17
anticommunism **VIII:**22
antimonopoly **VIII:**23–24
Baruch, Bernard M. **VIII:**42

Berle, Adolf A., Jr. **VIII:**43
Borah, William E. **VIII:**49
Brain Trust **VIII:**51
Bridges, Harry **VIII:**53
CIO **IX:**71
Congress **VIII:**81
conservatism **VIII:**83, 85
Coughlin, Father Charles E. **VIII:**88
dollar-a-year men **VIII:**96
Economic Opportunity Act (1964) **IX:**95
economy **VIII:**102; **IX:**97–98
elections **IX:**104
Fair Labor Standards Act **VIII:**124
First New Deal **VIII:**138
fiscal policy **VIII:**138–139
foreign policy **VIII:**140
Full Employment Bill **VIII:**145
GI Bill of Rights **VIII:**149
globalization **X:**153–154
Good Neighbor policy **VIII:**151
government **VIII:**152
Great Depression **VIII:**157, 158
Harriman, W. Averell **VIII:**161
Henderson, Leon **VIII:**163
Hoover presidency **VIII:**174
Hopkins, Harry L. **VIII:**176
ILGWU **VIII:**187
isolationists **VIII:**189
Job Corps **IX:**161
Johnson, Hugh S. **VIII:**196
Johnson, Lady Bird **IX:**162
Jones, Jesse H. **VIII:**197
Kaiser, Henry J. **VIII:**199
Kennedy, Joseph P. **VIII:**200
labor/labor movements **VIII:**205
Levitt, William J. **IX:**188–190
liberalism **VIII:**214, 215
literature **VIII:**218
Long, Huey P. **VIII:**222
Luce, Henry R. **VIII:**224
McDonald's **IX:**208
mobilization **VIII:**242
movies **VIII:**247
National Recovery Administration **VIII:**259–260
New Deal **VIII:**269, 270
news media **VIII:**272
NIRA **VIII:**256
NLRA **VIII:**257
NLRB **VIII:**258–259
NWLB **VIII:**261–262
Nye committee **VIII:**278, 279
OPM **VIII:**283

business *(continued)*
  OWMR **VIII:**287
  Packard, Vance **IX:**253
  Progressive Party **IX:**264
  public opinion polls **VIII:**312
  PUHCA **VIII:**313
  recession of 1937–1938
    VIII:324
  Reciprocal Trade
    Agreements Act **VIII:**325
  reconversion **VIII:**326, 327
  Republican Party **VIII:**337
  Revenue Act of 1935
    VIII:340
  RFC **VIII:**326
  science and technology
    IX:285
  Second New Deal **VIII:**356
  shopping centers **IX:**290
  South **VIII:**367
  Soviet Union **IX:**295
  steel industry **VIII:**373
  strikes **VIII:**378
  Sunbelt **X:**338
  taxation **VIII:**387
  technology **VIII:**389;
    IX:311
  Third New Deal **VIII:**393
  TNEC **VIII:**391
  USHA **VIII:**404
  wage and price controls
    VIII:409
  Wagner, Robert F. **VIII:**410
  War Production Board
    VIII:414
  Willkie, Wendell L.
    VIII:417
  World War II home front
    VIII:432
Business Advisory Council
  VIII:161
business and government **VI:**56–
  57, 315
Business: A Profession (Brandeis)
  VII:41
business codes **VIII:**260
business cycles **VI:57–59,** 188, 261
"business necessity" **X:**51, 77
business schools **VII:**87–88
busing. *See* school busing
Bus Stop (film) **IX:**223, 225
Bustamante, Anastasio **IV:**329
Bute, John Stuart, earl of
  III:70–71
  George III **III:**192
  liberty tree **III:**267
  Paris, Treaty of (1763)
    III:331
Butler, Andrew P.
  Bleeding Kansas **V:**37
  Kansas-Nebraska Act **V:**221
  Sumner, Charles **V:**377
Butler, Benjamin Franklin **V:53,**
  445c
  Baltimore, Maryland, riots
    V:26
  Confiscation Acts **V:**87

contrabands **V:**92
Dana, Charles A. **VI:**92
Dana, Richard Henry **IV:**113
emancipation **V:**128
Grant, Ulysses S. **V:**175
Greenback-Labor Party
  VI:155
Hicks, Thomas H. **V:**188
Hill, Daniel H. **V:**190
Joint Committee on the
  Conduct of the War **V:**216
loyalty oaths **V:**246
New Orleans, Battle of
  V:281
prisons **V:**314
Union army **V:**401
Butler, John **III:**449
Butler, Matthew **VI:**223
Butler, Nicholas Murray **VI:**131;
  VII:49
Butler, Norman 3X **IX:**23
Butler, Pierce
  Buck v. Bell **VII:**43
  court-packing plan **VIII:**89
  Irish Americans **VIII:**188
  Supreme Court **VIII:**382
Butler, W. O. **V:**213
Butler, Zebulon **III:**449
butter **VIII:**322
Butterfield, Daniel **V:**254
Butterfield, John **IV:**290–291
Butterworth, Mary Peck **II:52**
Butz, Earl **X:**138
Byrd, Richard **VII:**409c
Byrd, Robert **X:**196, 320
Byrd, William, I **II:**53
Byrd, William, II **II:52–53**
  agriculture **II:**12
  Batts, Thomas **II:**34
  Byrd family **II:**53
  environment **III:**153–154
  travel **II:**393, 394
Byrd family **II:**53
Byrne, William **X:**272
Byrnes, James F. **VIII:60**
  Democratic Party **VIII:**93
  Hillman, Sidney **VIII:**166
  mobilization **VIII:**241
  OPA **VIII:**282
  OWM **VIII:**286
  OWMR **VIII:**287
  reconversion **VIII:**326
  wage and price controls
    VIII:409
  War Manpower Commission
    VIII:413
  War Production Board
    VIII:414

C

CAA. *See* Civil Aeronautics
  Authority
CAAA. *See* Comprehensive Anti-
  Apartheid Act
Cabet, Étienne **IV:67–68**

Cabeza da Vaca, Álvar Núñez
  IV:371
Cabeza de Vaca, Álvar Núñez
  I:39–40
  Coronado, Francisco **I:**92
  Narváez, Pánfilo de **I:**259
  New Mexico **I:**265
  Zuni **I:**394
cabildos **I:40–42; II:**371
  cacique **I:**49
  New Spain **I:**268
  Veracruz **I:**376
cabinetmaking **III:**334
cabinet of curiosities **I:**42, **42–43,**
  358
Cable, George Washington
  VI:225, 226
Cable, John **VII:**47
Cable Act **VII:47–48,** 408c
  citizenship **VII:**57
  ERA **VII:**100
  Expatriation Act **VII:**104
  women's status and rights
    VII:388–389
cable cars **V:**392; **VI:**360
Cable Communications Policy Act
  (1984) **X:**342
Cable News Network. *See* CNN
cable television
  movies **X:**236
  music **X:**239
  television **X:**342–344
cable TV **X:**236
Cabot, George **IV:**186–187
Cabot, John **I:43–44,** 396c;
  II:240
  Acadia **I:**2
  Bristol **I:**37
  Patent Granted by King
    Henry VII to John Cabot
    and his Sons (March
    1496) **I:404–405**
Cabot, Sebastian **I:44–46,** 45,
  396c
  Bermuda **I:**30
  Bristol **I:**37
  Cabot, John **I:**44
  cod **I:**77
  Eden, Richard **I:**118
  Northeast Passage **I:**272
  Northwest Passage **I:**273
Cabral, Gonçalo **I:**396c
Cabral, Pedro Álvares **I:46–47,**
  396c
  Brazil **I:**34
  Dias, Bartholomeu **I:**106
  Portuguese seaborne empire
    I:300
  Tordesillas, Treaty of **I:**368
Cabrillo, Juan Rodríguez **I:**51;
  IV:75
Cacamatzin (king of Texcoco) **I:**47
cacao **I:47–49,** 362
cacique **I:**49
  Díaz del Castillo, Bernal
    I:106
  Grijalva, Juan de **I:**145

Guerrero, Gonzalo **I:**147
Las Casas, Bartolomé de
  I:206
limpieza de sangre **I:**214
Taino **I:**352
CAD (computer-aided design)
  X:87
Cadamosto, Alvise de **I:49–50,**
  143
Caddo Indians
  Bowie, James **IV:**63
  Native Americans **V:**278,
    279
  Texas **IV:**371
Cadillac, Antoine de la Mothe
  II:37, 132
Cadillac Motor Company
  automobile industry **VII:**26
  Ford, Henry **VII:**111
  GM **IX:**132
  science and technology
    X:320
Cadman, Charles **VII:**219
Cadore Letter **III:73,** 169
*Caesar's Column: A Story of the
  Twentieth Century* (Donnelly)
  Donnelly, Ignatius Loyola
    VI:100
  literature **VI:**226
  utopianism **VI:**371
CAFTA (Central American Free
  Trade Agreement) **X:**259
Cage, John **VIII:**252; **IX:**19, 228
Cagney, James **VIII:**246
Cahan, Abraham **VI:**225;
  VII:285
Cahill, Holger **VIII:**129
Cahokia **I:50–51**
CAI (computer-aided instruction)
  X:87
Caine Mutiny, The (Wouk)
  VIII:220
Cairo, Illinois **IV:**230
Cairo Conference (November
  1943) **VIII:61**
  Harriman, W. Averell
    VIII:162
  Hopkins, Harry L.
    VIII:177
  Manchuria **VIII:**226
Cairo Conference, Second
  (December 1943) **VIII:**61
Cairo Conference Statement
  VIII:448c
Cairo Declaration **VIII:**61
Caitlin, George **V:**18
Cajun music **VIII:**250
Cajuns **II:**82
Calabar **I:**51
Calder, Alexander Milne **VI:**327;
  VIII:29, 31
Calderon, Felipe **X:**226
Caldwell, Erskine **VIII:**50, 219
Caldwell, John **III:**355; **IV:**69
Caldwell, Seth **III:**355
Caldwell v. Jennison **III:**355
Caledonian Games **VI:**359

calendars **I:**21
Calhoun, John C. **IV:***68*, **68–70,**
   412*c*, 415*c*
   American System **IV:**20
   Atkinson, Henry **IV:**36
   Benton, Thomas Hart **IV:**54
   Bonus Bill **IV:**62
   Clay, Henry **IV:**96
   Compromise of 1850
      IV:104
   Davis, Jefferson **V:**104
   Democratic Party **V:**108–
      109
   Drayton, William H. **IV:**127
   election of 1840 **IV:**137,
      139
   Fillmore, Millard **IV:**149–
      150
   foreign policy **IV:**155
   Indian Affairs, Bureau of
      IV:196
   Indian Affairs, Office of
      VI:188
   internal improvements
      IV:203
   National Road **IV:**271
   Nullification Controversy
      IV:282, 283
   railroads **IV:**314
   secession **V:**344
   tariffs **V:**383
   Taylor, Zachary **IV:**368
   Tyler, John **IV:**383
   Van Buren, Martin **IV:**385
   Virginia and Kentucky
      Resolutions **III:**424
   War Hawks **IV:**389
   Webster, Daniel **IV:**393
   Whigs **IV:**397
   Yancey, William Lowndes
      V:439
Calhoun, Patrick **IV:**68
Calhoun, Thomas **V:**22
Calicut **I:**46
California **I:**51–52, 398*c*; **III:**73–
   74; **IV:**70–72, 414*c*; **VIII:**448*c*;
   X:381*c*
   affirmative action **X:**9–10
   Agricultural Adjustment Act
      VIII:6
   agriculture **V:**6; **X:**20
   Applegate, Jesse **IV:**26
   Ashley, William Henry **IV:**31
   Asian Americans **VIII:**32
   Bear Flag Revolt **IV:**49
   Beckwourth, Jim **IV:**51
   Bidwell, John **IV:**55–56
   Bilingual Education Act
      X:42
   Brannan, Samuel **IV:**63
   Calhoun, John C. **IV:**69
   California missions **IV:**75
   California Trail **IV:**77
   Carson, Kit **IV:**82
   Catholics **VIII:**64
   cattle kingdom **VI:**64
   cities and urban life **X:**75

Clay, Henry **IV:**97
Clayton-Bulwer Treaty
   IV:98
Colorado gold rush **IV:**99,
   100
Comstock Lode **IV:**105
corruption, political **VI:**83
criminal justice **VII:**66
currency issue **VI:**89
Dana, Richard Henry
   IV:113
Davis, Jefferson **V:**103
Deseret, State of **IV:**120
disease/epidemics **IV:**122,
   123
Donner party **IV:**125
dust bowl **VIII:**98
economy **IV:**130, 132
energy **X:**121
exploration **IV:**144, 146
Field, Stephen Johnson
   VI:126
Figueroa, José **IV:**148
Fillmore, Millard **IV:**150
fire-eaters **V:**145
foreign policy **IV:**155
Fort Laramie **IV:**157
Fort Leavenworth **IV:**158
Forty-niners **IV:**159–160
Frémont, John C. **IV:**166,
   167
Gadsden Purchase **IV:**173
gay and lesbian rights
   movement **X:**149, 150
Gentlemen's Agreement
   VII:123
gold **IV:**176–179
Goodman, Benny **VIII:**150
Great White Fleet **VII:**130
Gregg, Josiah **IV:**179
Guadalupe Hidalgo, Treaty
   of **IV:**180, 181
Guthrie, Woody **VIII:**160
Harding, Warren Gamaliel
   VII:135
Harte, Bret **VI:**162
Hastings, Lansford W.
   IV:187
Hayden, Tom **IX:**144
Hearst, William Randolph
   VII:137, 138
Hispanic Americans **X:**167
Huntington, Collis Potter
   VI:180
immigration **IV:**193; **V:**201;
   VI:68; **X:**176
IRCA **X:**177
Jackson, Helen Hunt
   VI:199
Japanese Americans,
   relocation of **VIII:**193,
   194
Jefferson, Joseph, III
   VI:202
Johnson, Hiram Warren
   VII:154
Johnson, Hugh S. **VIII:**196

Kearny, Stephen Watts
   IV:212
Kennedy, Robert F. **IX:**172
Know-Nothing Party **IV:**215
Ku Klux Klan **VII:**166
Lamy, Jean Baptiste **IV:**222
La Raza Unida **IX:**183
Larkin, Thomas Oliver
   IV:222
Latino movement **IX:**186
Manifest Destiny **IV:**234,
   235
marriage and family **X:**213,
   216
Mason, Richard B. **IV:**241
McDonald's **IX:**208
medicine **X:**224
Meese, Edwin C., III **X:**225
Mexican Americans
   VIII:237
Mexican-American War
   IV:251–253
Mexican immigration
   VII:203
Mexican Repatriation
   Program **VIII:**238
migration **IV:**254, 255;
   VIII:239, 240; **IX:**215
mining **VII:**210
Monroe Doctrine **IV:**260
Mooney-Billings case
   VII:213
movie industry **VII:**216
multiculturalism **X:**236, 237
Murray, Pauli **IX:**227
Murrieta, Joaquín **IV:**267
narcotics **X:**244
Native Americans **III:**315;
   IV:275
New Spain, northern
   frontier of **III:**317
oil **VI:**271
oil industry **VII:**245
Oregon Trail **IV:**285
Oregon Treaty of 1846
   IV:286, 287
overland mail **IV:**290
Permanent Indian Frontier
   IV:297
"Pike's Peak or Bust" **IV:**301
Polk, James K. **IV:**302
popular sovereignty **IV:**306
population trends **X:**283
pro-life/pro-choice
   movements **X:**289
race and race relations
   VII:282, 283; **VIII:**318,
   319; **X:**297
Reagan, Ronald W. **X:**299
religion **IV:**319
Rocky Mountain Fur
   Company **IV:**325
Seattle General Strike
   VII:105
segregation **VII:**320
Siberian Expedition
   VII:324

Sinclair, Upton **VII:**326
Smith, Jedediah Strong
   IV:350
sports and recreation
   VIII:373
stem cell research **X:**335
Stockton, Robert Field
   IV:357–358
strikes **VIII:**377
Submerged Lands Act
   (1953) **IX:**305
Sunbelt **VIII:**380, 381;
   X:338
Taylor, Zachary **IV:**368
technology **VIII:**397
Texas **IV:**372
theme parks **IX:**317
Townsend, Francis E.
   VIII:394
UFW **IX:**324–325
violence and lawlessness
   VI:375
Warren, Earl **IX:**336–337
Wilkes expedition **IV:**400
World War II **VIII:**428
Young, Brigham **IV:**408
Zimmermann telegram
   VII:401
California Battalion **IV:**187
California Constitutional
   Convention **IV:**223
California gold rush **IV:**72–75,
   73, *74m*, *159*, *177*, 414*c*
   anti-Chinese agitation, rise
      of **IV:**24
   Beckwourth, Jim **IV:**51
   Bidwell, John **IV:**56
   Brannan, Samuel **IV:**64
   California **IV:**71–72
   California Trail **IV:**77–78
   Clayton-Bulwer Treaty
      IV:98
   Colorado gold rush **IV:**99,
      100
   Colt revolver **IV:**102
   Comstock Lode **IV:**104–105
   Dana, Richard Henry
      IV:113
   Deseret, State of **IV:**120
   disease/epidemics **IV:**122
   exploration **IV:**145–146
   Fort Laramie **IV:**156, 157
   Forty-niners **IV:**159–160
   gold **IV:**176–179
   Hastings, Lansford W.
      IV:187
   Huntington, Collis Potter
      VI:180
   immigration **IV:**193
   lead mines **IV:**224
   Mason, Richard B. **IV:**241
   migration **IV:**255
   Murrieta, Joaquín **IV:**267
   music **IV:**268
   Native Americans **IV:**275
   Oregon Trail **IV:**285
   "Pike's Peak or Bust" **IV:**300

California gold rush (*continued*)
    race and race relations
      IV:312
    religion **IV:**319
    Santa Fe Trail **IV:**332
    Strauss, Levi **IV:**359
    Vanderbilt, Cornelius
      IV:387
California Indians **II:**55, **55–56,**
  347
California Institute of Technology
  VIII:352; **IX:**311
California missions **IV:75–77**
    Figueroa, José **IV:**148–149
    gold **IV:**178
    Larkin, Thomas Oliver
      IV:222
Californian, the **VI:**162
California Rangers **IV:**268
California Star **IV:**64
California Trail **IV:77–78**
    Bidwell, John **IV:**56
    California **IV:**71
    California gold rush **IV:**72
    Colorado gold rush **IV:**99
    Donner party **IV:**125
    Fort Laramie **IV:**157
    mountain men **IV:**267
    Oregon Trail **IV:**285
    Smith, Jedediah Strong
      IV:350
Callender, James T. **III:**74
    Hamilton, Alexander
      III:207
    Hemings, Sally **III:**210, 211
    Jefferson, Thomas **III:**234
Call Home the Heart (Burke)
  VII:122
Calliope, HMS **VI:**323
Call of the Wild, The (London)
  VII:404*c*
Calloway, Cab **VIII:**3, 44
calmecac **I:**20, 100
calpulli **I:**19, 257
calumet **II:**56
Calumet and Hecla Mining
  Company **VII:**210, 382
Calumet Conglomerate Lode
  VII:209
Calumet Mining Company
  VII:209
Calusa **I:52–53**
Calvert, Cecilius (second Baron
  Baltimore) **II:**313, 335
Calvert, George (first Baron
  Baltimore) **II:56,** 435*c*
    government, British
      American **II:**151
    Maryland **II:**219
    proprietary colonies **II:**313
Calvert, Leonard (third Baron
  Baltimore) **II:56–57**
    Brent, Margaret Reed **II:**47
    government, British
      American **II:**151
    Maryland **II:**219, 220
    St. Mary's City **II:**342

Calvert family **V:**250
Calverton, V. F. **VII:**286
Calvin, John **I:**53, **53–55**
    Finney, Charles Grandison
      IV:150
    German Reformed Church
      II:148
    Huguenots **I:**170
    humanitarianism **III:**217
    Léry, Jean de **I:**212
    Presbyterians **II:**309
    printing press **I:**303
    Protestantism **II:**314
    religion **IV:**318
Calvinism
    Anglican Church **III:**20
    Dow, Lorenzo **III:**139
    education **II:**111; **III:**147
    Edwards, Jonathan **II:**113,
      114
    Finney, Charles Grandison
      IV:151
    Huguenots **I:**170
    Ingersoll, Robert Green
      VI:192
    James I **I:**192
    McCormick, Cyrus Hall
      IV:245
    Morse, Samuel F. B. **IV:**264
    New Divinity **III:**316, 317
    Osborn, Sarah Haggar
      Wheaten **II:**279
    Protestantism **II:**314
    religion **III:**360, 362;
      IV:318, 319; **IX:**272
    religion, Euro-American
      II:329
    Second Great Awakening
      IV:337
    Tappan, Arthur and Lewis
      IV:366
    Tennent, William, Sr.
      II:389
    Unitarianism **III:**419
CAM (computer-aided
  manufacturing) **X:**87
Cambodia **X:**375*c*, 377*c*
    cold war, end of **X:**84
    foreign policy **X:**140, 141
    Kent State protests **X:**197
    North Vietnam **X:**260
    SEATO **IX:**291
    Vietnam War **IX:**332
    Vietnam War, end of U.S.
      involvement **X:**361
Cambodian Americans **X:**33
Cambridge, England **VII:**108
Cambridge, Massachusetts
  VI:171, 172
Cambridge Platform **II:**75
Cambridge University **VI:**87;
  VIII:164
Camden, Battle of **III:74–76,**
  75*m*
    Cornwallis, Charles, Lord
      III:120
    Gates, Horatio **III:**190

    Greene, Nathanael **III:**198–
      199
    Kalb, Johann, baron de
      III:245
    Tarleton, Banastre **III:**407
Camden, New Jersey **IV:**316
Camden, South Carolina **III:**213–
  214
Camden, William **I:55–56**
    Drake, Sir Francis **I:**112
    Elizabeth I **I:**121
    London **I:**216
Camden & Amboy (C&A)
  Railroad **IV:**316
Camel News Caravan **IX:**315
"Camelot" **IX:**168, 169
cameras **VI:**105, 410*c*; **VII:**151
Camera Work **VII:**259
Cameron, Don **VI:**299, 300
Cameron, James **X:**279
Cameron, Simon **V:**424; **VI:**299
Cameroon **I:**56
    Bantu **I:**26
    Calabar **I:**51
    Fang **I:**127
    Fulani **I:**135
Caminha, Álvaro da **I:**328
Camm, John **II:**282
Camp, Walter **VI:**130–131
campaign finance **X:63–64,** 376*c*
    Clinton, William J. **X:**82
    Gore, Albert, Jr. **X:**157
    House of Representatives
      X:169, 171
    Internet **X:**183
    Judicial Watch **X:**194
    Nader, Ralph **X:**242
    NRA **X:**249
    Obama, Barack Hussein
      X:264
    PACs **X:**274–275
Campaign for an Economic
  Democracy **IX:**144
Campanella, Roy **IX:**277
Campann, Klass **X:**278
Campbell, Albert H. **V:**57
Campbell, Archibald **III:**63, 382,
  383
Campbell, John (*Boston News-
  Letter* publisher) **II:**312
Campbell, John W. (*Astounding
  Stories* editor) **X:**287
Campbell, Robert **IV:**156
Campbell, Thomas **IV:**18, **78,**
  319
Campbell, W. Glenn **X:**349
Campbellites **IV:**319
Campbell's Soup **VI:**2, 3
Campbelltown Academy **IV:**258
Camp Chase **V:**314
Camp David accords **X:64–66,**
  228, 234, 377*c*
Camp Douglas **V:**314
Camp Fire Girls **VIII:**329
Camp Floyd **IV:**263
camp followers **III:76–77**
    Molly Pitcher **III:**298

Revolutionary War **III:**369
  women's status and rights
    III:446
Camp Hill, Alabama **VIII:**353
camping **VII:**295
camp meetings **III:**77
    African Americans **IV:**8
    Dow, Lorenzo **III:**139;
      IV:126
    Methodism **III:**297
    popular culture **III:**341
    recreation **VII:**295
    Second Great Awakening
      IV:337, 337
Camp Morton **V:**314
Camp O'Donnell, Philippines
  VIII:42
Camp Robinson, Nebraska **VI:**86
Camp Traverse de Sioux **IV:**415*c*
Campus Crusade for Christ
  IX:272
Canaan, New Hampshire **IV:**174
Canada **II:**438*c*; **III:77–79,** 459*c*,
  466*c*; **VI:61; VII:**404*c*; **X:**380*c*
    agriculture **III:**11
    Algonquin **II:**18
    American Fur Company
      IV:18
    Arnold, Benedict **III:**30
    Aroostook War **IV:**27
    Astor, John Jacob **IV:**33
    Astoria **IV:**35
    atomic bomb **VIII:**34
    Bayard, Thomas Francis
      VI:27–28
    Bering Sea dispute **VI:**34
    Boas, Franz Uri **VII:**39
    Burgoyne, Sir John **III:**67
    Carleton, Guy **III:**81
    Caroline affair **IV:**80–81
    Cartier, Jacques **I:**61–62
    Champlain, Samuel de
      II:62
    Coercive Acts **III:**100
    *Cosmographie Universelle,
      La* (Thevet) **I:413–418**
    economy **X:**110
    embargo of 1807 **III:**152
    Europe **IX:**113
    foreign affairs **III:**168
    foreign policy **IV:**154; **X:**142
    Fort Ticonderoga **III:**171,
      172
    French colonies **II:**136,
      138–139
    Frobisher, Martin **I:**134
    frontier, the **III:**181
    fur trade **IV:**170
    Gage, Thomas **III:**186
    Gates, Horatio **III:**190
    Ghent, Treaty of **IV:**176
    Gilbert, Sir Humphrey
      I:141
    habitants **I:**149
    Hull, William **IV:**192
    Iberville, Pierre Le Moyne,
      sieur d' **II:**173

immigration **VII**:144;
  VIII:184
investments, American,
  abroad **VI**:197
investments, foreign
  VII:151, 152
Iroquois **III**:227, 228
Jesuits **II**:185
Johnson, Jack **VII**:154
Johnson, Sir John **III**:237
Kalb, Johann, baron de
  III:245
King William's War **II**:195
Lafayette, Marie-Joseph-
  Paul-Yves-Roch-Gilbert
  de Motier, marquis de
  III:253
Lafayette, marquis de
  III:253
Loyalists **III**:275, 276
McLoughlin, John **IV**:247
McPherson, Aimee Semple
  VII:196
migration **VII**:207
Montagnais-Naskapi
  I:249–250
Montgomery, Richard
  III:301
NAFTA **X**:259
Native Americans in the War
  of 1812 **IV**:277
NATO **IX**:246
New Orleans, Battle of
  IV:280
Oregon Treaty of 1846
  IV:286–288
Paris, Treaty of (1763)
  III:331
Paul, Nathaniel **IV**:295
population trends **VII**:266
Prophet, the Shawnee
  III:349
Protestantism **II**:314–315
Quebec, Battle of **III**:353
Queen Anne's War **II**:323,
  324
Red Jacket **III**:359
Revolutionary War **III**:368
St. Clair, Arthur **III**:377
Saratoga, surrender at
  III:380
Schuyler, Philip John **III**:384
sports and recreation
  VII:333–335
Thames, Battle of the
  IV:375
Tippecanoe, Battle of
  III:411, 412
Valcour Island, Battle of
  III:421
War Hawks **IV**:390
War of 1812 **IV**:391
Washington, Treaty of
  VI:384–385
Webster-Ashburton Treaty
  IV:394–395
West Indies **III**:436

Canada West **V**:58
Canadian River **IV**:145, 331
canal(s) **II**:9
  American Philosophical
    Society **III**:17
  cities and urban life **V**:66
  Fulton, Robert **III**:182
  Hohokam **I**:164
  investments, foreign, in the
    United States **VI**:197
  transportation **V**:390
  Venice **I**:374–375
canal era **IV**:79–80, 80m
  Clayton-Bulwer Treaty
    IV:98–99
  economy **IV**:130–131
  Erie Canal **IV**:141–143
  industrialization **IV**:200
  internal improvements
    IV:202
  National Road **IV**:271
  panic of 1837 **IV**:294
  railroads **IV**:313
  science and technology
    IV:333
"canal ring" **VI**:357
Canal Zone, Panama. *See* Panama
  Canal Zone
Canary Islands **I**:56–57
  Columbus, Christopher **I**:84
  Magellan, Ferdinand **I**:223
  sugar **I**:349
Canby, Edward **V**:265
Canby, William **III**:374
cancer
  Hopkins, Harry L. **VIII**:177
  Jackson, Helen Hunt
    VI:199
  medicine **VIII**:234, 235
  tobacco suits **X**:351
Cane (Toomer) **VII**:136, 181
Cane Ridge, Kentucky **III**:362;
  IV:337
Canis lupus **II**:421
canned goods
  business **VIII**:58
  OPA **VIII**:282
  rationing **VIII**:322
Cannery Row (Steinbeck)
  VIII:374
cannibalism **I**:57–59
  Aztecs **I**:18–19
  Fang **I**:127
  Laudonnière, René de
    I:208
  Léry, Jean de **I**:212
  Stade, Hans **I**:346
  Tupinambá **I**:371
Cannibals All! (Fitzhugh)
  Fitzhugh, George **V**:146,
    147
  literature **V**:239
  slavery **V**:362
Canning, George **III**:301; **IV**:260
cannon
  Confederate army **V**:81
  Dahlgren, John A. B. **V**:101

science and technology
  V:342
  Washington, D.C. **V**:426
Cannon, James P. **VII**:61
Cannon, Joseph Gurney **VII**:48,
  48, 404c
  Congress **VII**:62
  Democratic Party **VII**:74
  elections **VII**:91
  Meat Inspection Act
    VII:198
  National Reclamation Act
    VII:229
  Progressive Party **VII**:270
  Republican Party **VII**:300
  Taft, William Howard
    VII:347
Canonchet **II**:57
Canonicus **II**:57, 417
Canoy Indians **II**:413
Canterbury, Robert **X**:197
Canton, China **III**:88
Canton, Ohio **VII**:328
Canton Bulldogs **VII**:333
Cantonment Division **VII**:10
Cantor, Eddie **VI**:116–117;
  VII:96
Cantril, Hadley **VIII**:313
Cantwell v. Connecticut **VIII**:446c
Cão, Diogo **I**:200
CAP. *See* Community Action
  Program
Cape Blanc **I**:49
Cape Breton Island **II**:192
Cape Cod **VII**:375
Cape Cod (Thoreau) **IV**:377
Cape Esperance, Battle of
  VIII:366
Cape Fear, North Carolina **III**:83,
  301
Cape Finisterre, Battle of **III**:197
Cape Henlopen **II**:95
Cape Horn
  Astoria **IV**:35
  Dana, Richard Henry
    IV:113
  Forty-niners **IV**:159
Cape Montserado, Liberia **IV**:225
Cape of Good Hope **I**:105–106
Capes, Battle of the **III**:79–80
  Cornwallis, Charles, Lord
    III:121
  Grasse, François-Joseph-
    Paul, comte de **III**:197
  Yorktown, surrender at
    III:455
Cape Verde Islands **I**:49, 50
Cap-Français, Santo Domingo
  IV:387
Capital Airlines **IX**:27
capitalism
  business **IX**:47
  conservatism **IX**:75
  foreign policy **X**:143
  marriage and family **V**:248
  Marx, Karl **V**:249
  New Deal **VIII**:270, 271

popular culture **VIII**:301
  shopping centers **IX**:289
capital markets **VI**:364–365
capital punishment **X**:66–67, 376c
  Brennan, William J., Jr.
    X:48
  Kennedy, Edward M. **X**:197
  Oklahoma City bombing
    X:267
  prisons **III**:347
  Rehnquist, William H.
    X:305
  Supreme Court **X**:338, 339
Capitol building (Washington,
  D.C.) **IV**:411c
  art and architecture **III**:29;
    IV:30
  Bulfinch, Charles **III**:65
  L'Enfant, Pierre-Charles
    III:261
capitulación **I**:88
Capone, Al **VII**:67, 273
Capote, Truman **IX**:194, 357c
Capper, Arthur **VII**:49
Capper-Volstead Act **VII**:48–49,
  408c
  Agricultural Marketing Act
    VII:6
  agriculture **VII**:8
  Harding, Warren Gamaliel
    VII:135
  lobbying **VII**:181–182
Capra, Frank **VIII**:61–62, 246
captaincies
  Bahía **I**:25–26
  Brazil **I**:35
  John III **I**:197
Captain Planet and the Planeteers
  X:91
captivity **II**:57–58
  Deerfield Massacre **II**:93
  Jemison, Mary **II**:183–184
  literature **II**:206
  Rowlandson, Mary White
    II:336
Caracol **I**:359
caravel **I**:59, 59–60
  Columbus, Bartholomew
    I:83
  Gomes, Diogo **I**:143
  invention and technology
    I:184
caravela latina **I**:59
Carawan, Guy **IX**:121, 229
carbines **V**:237, 341
carbon dioxide detectors **X**:318
Cárdenas, García López de **I**:92,
  168
Cárdenas, Juan de **I**:48
card games **VIII**:328
Cardinal Mindszenty Foundation
  X:93
Cardozo, Benjamin N.
  court-packing plan **VIII**:89
  Frankfurter, Felix **VIII**:144
  Supreme Court **VIII**:381,
    382

Carey, Hugh **X:**253, 254
Carey, Mathew **III:80–81,** 435
Carib **I:60–61**
Arawak **I:**11
Barbados **I:**27
cannibalism **I:**58
Martinique **I:**232
Montserrat **I:**251
Taino **I:**352
Caribbean **II:58–60**
Acadians **II:**2
agriculture **II:**12
Atlantic, Battle of the
VIII:33
Barbados **I:**27
Big Stick diplomacy **VII:**34
Bonnet, Stede **II:**38, 39
Clayton-Bulwer Treaty
IV:98
Constitution, USS **III:**107
Creole **II:**82
destroyers-for-bases deal
VIII:95
dollar diplomacy **VII:**79
filibustering **V:**145
Florida **IV:**152–153
foreign policy **IV:**156;
V:149, 151; **VII:**113–114,
116
Garvey, Marcus **VII:**121
Great White Fleet **VII:**129
Haiti **III:**203
Hispaniola **I:**162
imperialism **VI:**187
investments, American,
abroad **VI:**197
labor/labor movements
II:199
Lafitte, Jean **IV:**220
Manifest Destiny **IV:**235
McKinley, William **VI:**241
miscegenation **II:**237
Pan-American Exposition
VII:252
Peace Corps **IX:**255
piracy **II:**296
population trends **I:**298
presidency **VII:**268
Saintes, Battle of the
III:378
slavery **II:**356
slave trade **II:**358
Spanish colonies **II:**371,
374
sugar **I:**349
tobacco **II:**391
trade, domestic and foreign
VII:354
UNIA **VII:**361
Velázquez, Diego de
I:373–374
Venezuela boundary dispute
VI:373
wars of national liberation
IX:338, 339
West Indies **III:**436–437
yellow fever **II:**431

Carleill, Christopher **I:**111
Carleton, Sir Guy (first baron
Dorchester) **III:**81
Carleton, James **V:**444c
Carlisle, Pennsylvania **VI:**109,
189–190
Carlisle commission **III:81–82**
Carlos, John **IX:**42
Carlton, James H. **IV:**82
Carlyle, Thomas
Emerson, Ralph Waldo
IV:140
Norton, Charles Eliot
VI:269
transcendental movement
IV:379
Carmel, California **VII:**197
Cameron, Simon **V:**368
Carmichael, Hoagy **VIII:**153
Carmichael, Stokely **IX:49–50,**
50, 357c
African Americans **IX:**6
Black Power **IX:**41, 42
freedom rides **IX:**124
King, Martin Luther, Jr.
IX:174
Lewis, John **IX:**190
Meredith, James **IX:**213
SNCC **IX:**303
women's status and rights
IX:347
Carnation, Lily, Lily Rose
(Sargent) **VI:**324
Carnegie, Andrew **VI:61–63,** *62,*
410c; **VII:**403c
business **VII:**45
class consciousness **VI:**73,
74
Frick, Henry Clay **VI:**135–
136
Homestead Strike **VI:**175
Industrial Revolution,
Second **VI:**191
Johnstown flood **VI:**204
labor/labor movements
VII:169
Morgan, John Pierpont
VI:251
Pan-American Union
VI:276
peace movements **VII:**255
Robber Barons, The **VI:**315
science and technology
VIII:352
Scott, Thomas Alexander
VI:326
Social Darwinism **VI:**334
steel **VI:**345
steel industry **VII:**336
trusts **VI:**365
U.S. Steel **VII:**365
Washington, Booker T.
VI:384
"Wealth (Gospel of Wealth)"
VI:423–426
workers' compensation
VII:391

Carnegie Corporation of New
York **VI:**63
Carnegie Endowment for
International Peace **VII:49–50**
Carnegie, Andrew **VI:**62
foreign policy **VII:**115–116
Kellogg-Briand Treaty
VII:164
peace movements **VII:**255
Carnegie Foundation for the
Advancement of Teaching
VII:199; **X:**113
Carnegie Hall (New York City)
VIII:446c
Ellington, Duke **VIII:**112
Goodman, Benny **VIII:**151
music **VII:**219; **VIII:**250
Carnegie Institute of Technology
(Pittsburgh) **VI:**63; **VIII:**163
Carnegie Institution (Washington,
D.C.)
Buck v. Bell **VII:**43
Bush, Vannevar **VIII:**56
Gilman, Daniel Coit **VI:**148
science and technology
VII:313–314
Walcott, Charles Doolittle
VI:380
Carnegie Steel Company **VI:**411c
business **VII:**45
Carnegie, Andrew **VI:**62
Frick, Henry Clay **VI:**136
Homestead Strike **VI:**175,
176
Industrial Revolution,
Second **VI:**192
Robber Barons, The **VI:**315
steel **VI:**345
steel industry **VII:**337
U.S. Steel **VII:**365
Carney, William Harvey **V:55,**
143, 255
Carolinas **II:**436c. *See also* North
Carolina; South Carolina
abolitionism **V:**1
animals **III:**22
class **II:**70
economy **II:**109
Gates, Horatio **III:**190
government, British
American **II:**151–152
Graffenried, Christopher,
baron de **II:**154
Hobkirk's Hill, Battle of
III:213
proprietary colonies **II:**313,
314
riots **III:**371
tactics and strategy **V:**382
trade, domestic and foreign
II:392
travel **II:**393, 394
Westo **II:**410, 411
Caroline affair **IV:80–81,** 154
Caroline Islands **VII:**408c
Carolingian Empire **I:**166
Carondelet, USS **V:**263

Carpenters Union **VIII:**213
carpetbaggers **V:55–57,** *56*
Reconstruction **V:**324
redemption **V:**329
Warmoth, Henry Clay **V:**425
Carr, Lois Green **II:**424
Carr, Lucien **IX:**36
Carr, Robert **II:**95
Carranza, Venustiano **VII:**406c
Big Stick diplomacy **VII:**35
foreign policy **VII:**114
Mexican Invasion **VII:**203,
204
Mexican Revolution
VII:204
Zimmermann telegram
VII:401
Carreño, Teresa **VI:**233
carriera de India **I:**334
Carroll, John **III:**82, 83
Carroll of Carrollton, Charles
III:82, 83
Carson, Christopher "Kit" **V:**444c
Carson, John **VII:**97
Carson, Kit **IV:81–82,** *82,* 414c
exploration **IV:**145
Frémont, Jesse Benton
IV:165
Frémont, John C. **IV:**166,
167
Rocky Mountain Fur
Company **IV:**324
St. Vrain, Céran **IV:**328
Carson, Rachel **IX:50–51,** *51,*
355c
business **IX:**47
conservation/
environmentalism **X:**89,
90
consumerism **IX:**76
environment **IX:**108–109
literature **IX:**194
NEPA **X:**246
science and technology
IX:286
Carson Valley, Nevada **IV:**104–
106, 120
Cartagena, Juan de **I:**223, 224
cartels **VIII:**75
Carter, Billy **X:**69
Carter, James Earl "Jimmy," Jr.
X:65, 67–70, *68,* 377c, 378c,
380c
Africa **X:**16
Anderson, John B. **X:**25
antiwar movement, Vietnam
X:29
arms race **IX:**17
Camp David accords **X:**65,
66
Chrysler Corporation Loan
Guarantee Act **X:**74
Clinton, William J. **X:**79, 81
cold war, end of **X:**85
conservative movement
X:93
defense policy **X:**100

détente **X:**104
Dole, Robert **X:**105
economy **X:**109
education, primary/
    secondary **X:**114
energy **X:**120
Energy, U.S. Department
    of **X:**122
ERA **X:**124
evangelical Christians **X:**125
Ford, Gerald R. **X:**137
foreign policy **X:**141
Haiti **X:**164
Helms, Jesse A., Jr. **X:**165
Humphrey, Hubert H.
    IX:152
independent counsel **X:**179
Iranian hostage crisis **X:**184,
    185
Koreagate **X:**199
Latin America **X:**205
Lewis, John **IX:**190
"Malaise" Speech **X:393–
    396**
Medal of Honor **V:**255
Middle East **X:**228
Mitchell, George **X:**232
Mondale, Walter F. **X:**233,
    234
neoconservatism **X:**252
NEPA **X:**246
Nicaragua **X:**254, 255
OMB **X:**266
O'Neill, Thomas "Tip" P., Jr.
    X:267
Panama Canal turnover
    X:270, 271
Peace Corps **IX:**256
political parties **X:**277
Reagan, Ronald W. **X:**300
Richardson, Elliot L. **X:**311
SALT I/SALT II **X:**336, 337
South Africa **X:**325
Supreme Court **X:**338
terrorism **X:**345
veto (presidential) **X:**361
Carter, Landon **II:60**
Carter, Nick **VI:**225
Carter, Robert "King" **II:12,
    60–61; III:**308–309
Carter Center (Emory University)
    X:70
Carter Coal case **VIII:**382
Carteret, George
    government, British
        American **II:**152
    New Jersey **II:**261
Carteret, Philip **II:61**
Carter Family, the **VIII:**250
Carthage, Illinois **IV:**119, 263
Cartier, Jacques **I:61–63, 397c;
    II:**135
    Acadia **I:**2
    French explorations of the
        Atlantic **I:**133
    Hochelaga **I:**163–164
    Iroquois **I:**186

Maliseet **I:**227
Montagnais-Naskapi **I:**250
Northwest Passage **I:**273
Ramusio, Giovanni Battista
    I:313
Thevet, André **I:**357
cartography
    Behaim, Martin **I:**28–29
    Blaeu, Willem **I:**32
    Columbus, Bartholomew
        I:83
    Herrman, Augustine **II:**164
    mappae mundi **I:**229–230
    Mercator, Gerhardus
        I:240–241
    Norumbega **I:**274
    Pennsylvania **II:**288
    Powell, John Wesley **VI:**288
    T-O maps **I:**367
    Waldseemüller, Martin
        I:381–382
    Wilkes expedition **IV:**399–
        400
cartoons, political **V:**275
Caruso, Enrico **VII:**219, *219*
Carver, George Washington
    VI:63, 384, 411c
Carver, John **II:**226, 294
Carver, Jonathan **IV:**103
Carver, Raymond **X:**211
Cary, Mary Ann Shadd **V:58**
CAS (Children's Aid Society)
    VI:45–46
Casablanca (film) **VIII:**246, 447c
Casablanca, Morocco **VIII:**277,
    431
Casablanca Conference *VIII:62,
    62–63,* 447c
    Arnold, Henry H. "Hap"
        VIII:28
    Hopkins, Harry L. **VIII:**177
    Italian campaign **VIII:**191
    second front **VIII:**355
    Sicily **VIII:**360
    World War II European
        theater **VIII:**431
    Yalta Conference **VIII:**439
Casa de Contratación **I:**63–64
    Council of the Indies **I:**97
    gold **I:**142
    Seville **I:**332, 333
Casals, Pablo **IX:**169
Cascade Range **IV:**119
"Cascades, The" (Joplin) **VII:**158
Case, Clifford **X:**29
casemates **V:**207
Case Western Reserve **VII:**127
Casey v. Planned Parenthood
    X:21
cash-and-carry **VIII:63,** 446c
    Anglo-American relations
        VIII:21
    CDAAA **VIII:**77
    foreign policy **VIII:**141
    Lend-Lease **VIII:**211
    Neutrality Acts **VIII:**267,
        268

cash crops **III:**10–11; **VI:**8–9
casinos
    advertising **X:**7
    Native Americans **X:**251
    recreation **X:**304
Casket **IV:**210
Casola, Pietro **I:**375
Casor, John **II:**186
Cass, Lewis **IV:82–84,** *83,* 414c
    American Fur Company
        IV:18
    Benton, Thomas Hart **IV:**54
    Polk, James K. **IV:**302
    popular sovereignty **IV:**304
    Taylor, Zachary **IV:**368
Cassady, Neal
    Beat Generation **IX:**36, 37
    counterculture **IX:**78
    Kerouac, Jack **IX:**173
Cassatt, Alexander **VI:**64
Cassatt, Mary **V:**19; **VI:63–64,**
    184, 409c
Cassell, John **VI:**149
Cassini, Oleg **IX:**117
casta paintings **I:**64, 214
castas **I:**64–65, 269
Castelar, Emilio **VI:**377
Castellion, Sébastien **I:**54
Castile **I:65–67**
    Charles V **I:**70, 71
    conquistadores **I:**87
    corregidor **I:**93
    Ferdinand and Isabella
        I:127–128
    Ibn Khaldûn, 'Abd-ar-
        Rahmân Abû Zayd
        ibn Muhammad ibn
        Muhammad **I:**176
    Philip II **I:**291
    Reconquista **I:**314
    Tordesillas, Treaty of **I:**367
Castillo, Alonso del **I:**40
Castillo, Carlos **IX:**184
Castillo, Diego del **II:61**
castizos **I:**241
Castle Garden (New York City)
    IV:194; **V:**200; **VI:**184
Castle Island (Boston) **III:**367
castles **I:**10
"Castle Thunder" Prison **V:**181
Casto, Don M. **IX:**306
Castro, Fidel **IX:354c; X:**205,
    378c
    anticommunism **IX:**14
    assassinations **X:**34
    Bay of Pigs **IX:**35, 36
    CIA **IX:**52
    cold war **IX:**64
    Cuban missile crisis **IX:**80,
        81
    Dulles, John Foster **IX:**91
    Grenada, invasion of **X:**159,
        160
    Hispanic Americans **X:**166
    immigration **IX:**156
    Immigration Act (1965)
        IX:156

Kennedy, John F. **IX:**170
    Latin America **IX:**184;
        X:204, 207
    Mills, C. Wright **IX:**217
    Operation Mongoose
        IX:250
    population trends **IX:**260
    Soviet Union **IX:**295
Castro, José **IV:**49
C. A. Swanson and Sons **IX:**122
Caswell, Richard **III:**302
Catawba **II:61–62**
    Native Americans **II:**252–
        253
    North Carolina **II:**273
    society, British American
        II:367
    South Carolina **II:**368
    Yamasee War **II:**430
Catch-22 (Heller) **IX:**193
Catcher in the Rye, The (Salinger)
    literature **IX:**194
    popular culture **IX:**258
    teenagers **IX:**314
Catchings, Waddill **VIII:**101
Catesby, Mark **II:62,** 421
Catfish Row (Charleston, South
    Carolina) **VII:**125
Cathay. *See* China
Cathay Company. *See* Company
    of Cathay
Cathedral (Carver) **X:**211
Cather, Willa **VI:**203; **VII:**179
Catherine de' Medici **I:**170
Catherine of Aragón **I:**397c
    Church of England **I:**74
    Henry VII **I:**159
    Henry VIII **I:**159–160
    Mary I **I:**232
    Reformation **I:**316–317
Catherwood, Frederick **I:**90;
    IV:146
cathode-ray tube (CRT) screen
    VII:151; **X:**87
Catholic Bishops' letter (*The
    Challenge of Peace*) **X:70**
Catholic Conference of Bishops'
    Division on Family Life **X:**289
Catholic Hour (TV series) **IX:**273
Catholic Interracial Council
    VIII:64
Catholicism/Catholics. *See* Roman
    Catholic Church/Catholics
Catholic schools **X:**115
Catholic University of America
    VI:316
Catholic Worker (newspaper)
    VIII:444c
Catlin, George **IV:**60, **84–85,**
    289
"Catlin's Indian Gallery" **IV:**84
Cato Institute **X:**209–210
Cat on a Hot Tin Roof (Williams)
    IX:193, 258
Cato's Letters (Trenchard and
    Gordon) **III:**103
Catskill Mountains **IV:**28, 29

Catt, Carrie Lane Chapman
   VII:50, 403c
      Hamilton, Alice **VII:**133
      NAWSA **VII:**223, 224
      peace movements **VII:**256
      Shaw, Anna Howard **VI:**329
      woman suffrage **VII:**384–385
      women's status and rights
         VII:388
cattle **II:**11–12, 14, 22–23
cattle fever **VI:**244
cattle kingdom **VI:**64, **64–65**
Catto, Octavius V. **V:58–59**
cavalry **I:**281–282
      battle flags **V:**31
      Confederate army **V:**80, 81
      Gettysburg, Battle of **V:**168
      Stuart, J. E. B. **V:**375, 376
      tactics and strategy **V:**379–380
      Union army **V:**401
      Wheeler, Joseph **V:**428
      Wilderness, Battle of the
         V:432
Cavern Club (Liverpool, England)
   IX:37
Cayor **I:69**
Cayuga **I:69**, 185, 186, 398c;
   III:449
Cayuse Indians **IV:**398–399
CBI theater. *See* China-Burma-
   India theater
CBN (Christian Broadcasting
   Network) **X:**342
CB&Q. *See* Chicago, Burlington
   & Quincy Railway Company
CBS (Columbia Broadcasting
   System)
      cold war culture **IX:**65
      Coughlin, Father Charles E.
         VIII:87
      entertainment, popular
         VII:97
      journalism **VII:**161; **IX:**165
      music **VII:**220
      popular culture **VII:**265
      radio **VIII:**321
      television **IX:**315; **X:**344
CBS Evening News **X:**344
CC. *See* Christian Coalition
CCA. *See* Citizens Councils of
   America
CCC. *See* Civilian Conservation
   Corps
CCW. *See* Joint Committee on the
   Conduct of the War
CDA. *See* Communications
   Decency Act
CDA (Committee to Defend
   America) **VIII:**77
CDAAA (Committee to Defend
   America by Aiding the Allies)
   VIII:76–77
CDC. *See* Centers for Disease
   Control
CDs. *See* compact discs

CEA. *See* Council of Economic
   Advisors
cease-fire agreement **X:**362
Ceau[s&cedilla]escu, Nicolae
   X:189
Cedar Creek, Battle of
      De Forest, John William
         V:107
      Shenandoah Valley:
         Sheridan's campaign
         V:352
      Sheridan, Philip H. **V:**353
Cedar Mountain, Battle of
   V:59–60
      Banks, Nathaniel P. **V:**29
      Bull Run/Manassas, First
         and Second Battles of
         V:50
      Hill, Ambrose P. **V:**190
      Jackson, Thomas J.
         "Stonewall" **V:**210
Cédras, Raoul **X:**81, 380c
*Celebrated Jumping Frog of
   Calaveras County, The* (Twain)
   VI:367
Celera Genomics **X:**172
celibacy **III:**257
Celler, Emanuel **X:**123
cell phones **X:**319
cemeteries
      Arlington National Cemetery
         V:16–17
      Civil Rights Act (1875) **V:**71
      Gettysburg, Battle of **V:**168
      Gettysburg Address **V:**169
      Hollywood Cemetery
         V:191–192
Cemetery Hill
      Early, Jubal A. **V:**119
      Ewell, Richard Stoddert
         V:136
      Gettysburg, Battle of **V:**167,
         168
      Howard, Oliver Otis **V:**197
      Longstreet, James **V:**242
      Meade, George Gordon
         V:254
      Zouaves **V:**442
Cemetery Ridge
      Armistead, Lewis A. **V:**17
      Gettysburg, Battle of **V:**167,
         168
      Hancock, Winfield Scott
         V:183
      Howard, Oliver Otis **V:**197
      Longstreet, James **V:**242
      Meade, George Gordon
         V:254
Cempoala **I:**96
cenote **I:**71, 390
censorship **VIII:65–66; X:70–71**
      ACLU **VIII:**17
      Catholics **VIII:**64
      censorship **VIII:**65, 66
      civil liberties **VIII:**71
      civil liberties, Confederate
         V:68

Coughlin, Father Charles E.
   VIII:88
      liberalism **X:**207
      Libertarian Party **X:**209
      movies **VIII:**245; **X:**235
      news media **VIII:**272
      OWI **VIII:**286
      popular culture **VIII:**301
      pornography **X:**284
      radical and labor press
         VII:285
      telegraph **V:**386
      television **X:**344
      World War II **VIII:**427
      World War II home front
         VIII:432
census, U.S. (general) **III:**106
census, U.S. (1790) **III:**26, 342,
   343, 463c
census, U.S. (1820) **III:**342, 343
census, U.S. (1830) **III:**26, 391
census, U.S. (1850) **V:**309, 310
census, U.S. (1880) **V:**309, 310
census, U.S. (1930) **VIII:**66
Census, U.S. (1990) **X:**213–214
Census, U.S. (2000)
      Asian Americans **X:**33
      marriage and family **X:**213
      poverty **X:**285
Census, U.S. (2002) **X:**213
Centennial Copper Company
   VII:210
Centennial Exposition **IV:**94;
   V:438
Center for Study of Responsive
   Law **X:**241
Centers for Disease Control
   (CDC) **IX:**351c
      AIDS **X:**6, 7
      medicine **IX:**211, 212
      public health **IX:**265
Central America **IV:**415c. *See
   also specific countries, e.g.:*
   Nicaragua
      Clayton-Bulwer Treaty
         IV:98–99
      filibustering **V:**145
      foreign policy **IV:**155, 156;
         X:142
      Gore, Albert, Jr. **X:**157
      Iran-contra affair **X:**183
      IRCA **X:**177
      Manifest Destiny **IV:**235
      Monroe Doctrine **IV:**259–
         261
Central American Court of Justice
   (Costa Rica) **VI:**62–63
Central American Free Trade
   Agreement (CAFTA) **X:**259
Central Americans **X:**167
Central Competitive Field
   VII:359
central government **III:**163
Central High School (Little Rock,
   Arkansas). *See* Little Rock,
   Arkansas school desegregation
Centralia, Washington **VII:**147

Central Intelligence Agency (CIA)
   VIII:447c; **IX:51–52**, 351c,
   353c; **X:**384c
      Bay of Pigs **IX:**35, 36
      Boland Amendment **X:**45
      cold war **IX:**64
      cold war, end of **X:**85
      domino theory **IX:**89
      intelligence **VIII:**187
      Iran-contra affair **X:**183
      Latin America **IX:**184;
         X:205
      LSD **IX:**195
      military-industrial complex
         IX:216
      National Security Act of
         1947 **IX:**237
      Nicaragua **X:**254
      Operation Mongoose
         IX:250
      OSS **VIII:**284, 285
      Reagan, Ronald W. **X:**301
      terrorism **X:**345, 347
      Truman, Harry S. **IX:**320
      U.S. v. Nixon **X:**358
      wars of national liberation
         IX:339
Central Labor Union **VI:**213
Central Pacific Railroad (CP)
   V:446c
      business and government
         VI:56
      Comstock Lode **IV:**105
      Crédit Mobilier **V:**97
      Huntington, Collis Potter
         VI:180–181
      lobbying **VI:**228
      Mormon Church **IV:**90
      Pacific Railroad Act **V:**293,
         294
      railroads **V:**321–322;
         VI:301
      transportation **V:**391
Central Park (New York City)
      cities and urban life **IV:**93;
         V:67
      New York City **V:**283
      New York City draft riots
         V:284
      Olmsted, Frederick Law
         V:287–288
Central Plains **IV:**145
Central Powers **VII:**393
Central Strike Committee
   VII:318
Central Trust Company **VII:**71
Central University of Nashville
   IV:387
Century Club Groups **VIII:**77
Century Monthly Magazine
      Gilder, Richard Watson
         VI:147
      illustration, photography,
         and graphic arts **VI:**183
      literature **VI:**225
Century of Dishonor, A (Jackson)
   VI:199, 409c, **414–416**

"Century of the Common Man"
 VIII:411
CEQ. *See* Council on
 Environmental Quality
ceramics **VI:**3
Ceremony (Silko) **X:**210
CERN (European Laboratory for
 Particle Physics) **X:**319
Cerro Gordo, Battle of **IV:**330;
 V:209
Cerro Rico **I:**300
CERT (Computer Emergency
 Response Team) **X:**182
Cervantes, Miguel de **III:**60
CES. *See* Committee on
 Economic Security
Chaco Canyon **I:**264
Chad **X:**17
CHADD (Children and Adults
 with ADD) **X:**223
Chadd's Ford **III:**62
Chadwick, George W. **VI:**254,
 255
Chaffee, Roger **IX:**231, 297
Chaffee, Zachariah **VII:**57
"chain migration" **V:**200
chain stores **VI:65; VII:**85
Chak (rain god) **I:**236
Chak Toh Ich'ak (Maya king of
 Tikal) **I:**358
Chaleur Bay **I:**61
Challenge of Peace, The (Catholic
 Bishops' Letter) **X:**70
Challenger disaster **X:**327, 378*c*
Chalmette Plantation **IV:**281
Chamberlain, George Earle
 VII:291
Chamberlain, John **I:**216
Chamberlain, Joshua L. **V:60**
 Appomattox Court House,
  Virginia **V:**16
 Gettysburg, Battle of **V:**167
 Union army **V:**401
 volunteer army **V:**419
Chamberlain, Neville
 Anglo-American relations
  VIII:21
 Kennedy, Joseph P.
  VIII:200
 Munich Conference
  VIII:248
Chamberlin, Thomas C. **VI:**325
Chamber of Commerce, U.S.
 anticommunism **VIII:**22
 Economic Opportunity Act
  (1964) **IX:**95
 Employment Act of 1946
  IX:106
 housing **VIII:**178
Chambers, Whittaker **IX:52–53,**
 53
 Hiss, Alger **IX:**146
 HUAC **IX:**150
 Nixon, Richard M. **X:**256
Chambliss, J. **VII:**438–440
Chamorro, Violeta Barrios de
 X:255

Chamorro people **I:**224
Champagny, Jean-Baptiste
 Nompere de **III:**73
Champion's Hill, Battle of **V:**298
Champlain, Lake **IV:**411*c*
 Arnold, Benedict **III:**30, 31
 Carleton, Guy **III:**81
 Erie Canal **IV:**141
 Fort Ticonderoga **III:**171,
  172
 Lyon, Matthew **III:**277
 Montgomery, Richard
  III:301
 Revere, Paul **III:**366
 Saratoga, surrender at
  III:380
 Valcour Island, Battle of
  III:421
 War of 1812 **IV:**391, 392
Champlain, Lake, Battle of
 IV:392
Champlain, Samuel de **II:62–63,**
 63, 435*c*
 Brûlé, Étienne **II:**50
 exploration **II:**123
 French colonies **II:**136
 Hochelaga **I:**164
 Iroquois **I:**187
 literature **II:**206
 Maliseet **I:**227
 Native Americans **II:**251
 New Hampshire **II:**259
 Passamaquoddy **I:**287
 Vermont **II:**398
Champlain Canal **IV:**141
Champotón **I:**95
Chamuscado, Francisco **I:**265
Chanca, Diego Álvarez **I:**57–58
Chancellor, Richard **I:**272–273
Chancellorsville, Battle of **V:60–**
 62, *61,* 445*c*
 Alexander, Edward P. **V:**8
 German-American
  regiments **V:**166
 Gordon, John B. **V:**170
 Hill, Ambrose P. **V:**190
 Howard, Oliver Otis **V:**197
 Jackson, Thomas J.
  "Stonewall" **V:**210
 Lee, Robert E. **V:**231
 McLaws, Lafayette **V:**253
 Meade, George Gordon
  V:253
 Sickles, Daniel E. **V:**361
 Ward, Lester Frank
  VI:382
Chandeleur Islands, Louisiana
 X:173
Chandler, Elizabeth **IV:**147
Chandler, Zachariah **V:**202, 215,
 216
Chaney, James **IX:**356*c*
 CORE **IX:**73
 MFDP **IX:**219
 race and race relations
  IX:270
channeling **X:**253

Channing, William Ellery
 Brook Farm **IV:**65
 Fuller, Margaret **IV:**169
 literature **IV:**228
 Peabody, Elizabeth Palmer
  VI:279, 280
 religion **IV:**318
 Unitarianism **III:**419
Chapel Hill, North Carolina
 IV:301
Chaplin, Charlie **VII:**407*c*
 Committee for Public
  Information **VII:**60
 entertainment, popular
  VII:96, 97
 movie industry **VII:**214, 216
 movies **VIII:**245
Chapman, J. Wilburn **VII:**342
Chapman, Mark David **X:**35
Chappaquiddick Island,
 Massachusetts **X:**196
Chappell, Warren **I:**303
Chapultepec, Act of **VIII:**448*c*
Chapultepec, Battle of
 Hill, Daniel H. **V:**190
 Jackson, Thomas J.
  "Stonewall" **V:**209
 Longstreet, James **V:**241
Chapultepec, Mexico **I:**365
Charbonneau, Toussaint **III:**263,
 377
Charge, A (Hall) **III:**205
Charges against the Virginia
 Governor (Bacon) **II:441–442**
Charismatic movement **IX:**272–
 273
charity
 humanitarianism **III:**217
 Mason, George **III:**292
 poverty **III:**344
 Washington Benevolent
  Societies **III:**433
Charlemagne **I:**166, 314
Charles I (king of Great Britain
 and Ireland) **II:**435*c*
 Common Sense **III:**102
 English Civil War **II:**116
 monarchy, British **II:**240
 North Carolina **II:**274
 South Carolina **II:**369
Charles I (king of Spain). *See*
 Charles V (Holy Roman
 Emperor)
Charles II (king of Great Britain
 and Ireland) **II:**436*c*
 Glorious Revolution **II:**149
 monarchy, British **II:**240
 North Carolina **II:**274
 Royal African Company
  II:337
 South Carolina **II:**369
Charles III (king of Spain)
 III:258
Charles V (Holy Roman Emperor)
 I:69–71
 cabildo **I:**41
 Cabot, Sebastian **I:**45

Castile **I:**66
 Council of the Indies **I:**97
 Holy Roman Empire **I:**166
 Las Casas, Bartolomé de
  I:205, 207
 Luther, Martin **I:**218, 219
 Magellan, Ferdinand **I:**223
 Mendoza, Antonio de **I:**239
 Oviedo y Valdés, Gonzalo
  Fernández de **I:**281
 Reformation **I:**315
 Sepúlveda, Juan Ginés de
  I:330
 Spanish Armada **I:**344
 Trent, Council of **I:**369
 Zumárraga, Juan de **I:**392
Charles Martel (Frankish ruler)
 I:314
Charles River Bridge **IV:**362
*Charles River Bridge v. Warren
 Bridge* **IV:**114, 366
Charleston (dance) **VII:**265
Charleston, siege of **III:84–85,**
 85, 462*c*
 Clinton, Sir Henry **III:**99
 Cornwallis, Charles, Lord
  III:120
 Estaing, Charles-Henri
  Theodat, comte d'
  III:158
 Greene, Nathanael **III:**198
 Jews **III:**236
 Pinckney, Charles
  Cotesworth **III:**336
 POWs **III:**346
 Revolutionary War **III:**368
Charleston, South Carolina **II:63–**
 64, 436*c;* **IV:**412*c*
 Beauregard, Pierre Gustave
  Toutant **V:**32
 Catholics **III:**83
 cities and urban life **II:**68
 Confederate navy **V:**83
 Dahlgren, John A. B. **V:**101
 Democratic Party **IV:**119
 disease/epidemics **II:**99,
  100; **IV:**123
 Drayton, William H. **IV:**127
 Fort Sumter **V:**154
 Frémont, John C. **IV:**166
 Gershwin, George **VII:**125
 Grimké, Angelina and Sarah
  IV:180
 H.L. Hunley, CSS **V:**191
 Jackson, Andrew **IV:**205
 Jim Crow laws **VI:**203
 Johnston, Henrietta Deering
  II:188
 Laurens, Henry **III:**255
 Liberia **VI:**223
 marine corps **V:**248
 Middleton, Arthur **II:**233
 miscegenation **II:**238
 Nullification Controversy
  IV:283
 Queen Anne's War **II:**323
 railroads **IV:**314

Charleston, South Carolina
(*continued*)
religion **IV:**318
slavery **IV:**347–348
slave trade, internal **IV:**350
smallpox **II:**361
Sons of Liberty **III:**394
South Carolina **II:**369
Stono Rebellion **II:**377–378
Stuart, John **II:**378
Teach, Edward **II:**385
Union navy **V:**405
Vesey, Denmark **IV:**387–388
Walker, David **IV:**389
yellow fever **II:**431
Charleston Daily Courier **V:**117
Charleston Expedition of 1776
III:83–84
Cornwallis, Charles, Lord
III:120
Lee, Charles **III:**258–259
Tarleton, Banastre **III:**407
Charleston Harbor **IV:**283
Charleston History Museum
V:191
Charleston Work House **IV:**388
Charlestown, Massachusetts
IV:23
Charlestown Peninsula **III:**65
Charlotte Temple (*Charlotte,
a Tale of Truth*) (Rowson)
III:269, 374; **IV:**229
charnel house **I:**253, 254
Charter of Privileges
(Pennsylvania) **II:**286
Chartist movement **VI:**61–62
Chase, Salmon P. **V:62–63**
assassination of Abraham
Lincoln **V:**21
banking **V:**28
Cooper Union speech
V:93–94
economy **V:**121
Fillmore, Millard **IV:**149
greenbacks **V:**177
impeachment of Andrew
Johnson **V:**203
Kansas-Nebraska Act **V:**222
national banking system
VI:260
Port Royal Experiment
V:312
Republican Party **V:**333
Wade, Benjamin Franklin
V:421
Chase, Samuel **III:85–86,** *86,*
465c
Constitution, ratification of
the **III:**105
Fries's Rebellion **III:**181
impeachment **III:**222
Marbury v. Madison
III:285
Marshall, John **III:**291
Randolph, John **III:**359
Rodney, Caesar **III:**373

Rodney, Caesar Augustus
III:373
Supreme Court **III:**403
Chase, William Merritt **VI:65–66,**
184, 275
Chase-Riboud, Barbara **III:**210
Chattanooga, Battle of **V:63–64,**
445c
Blair, Francis Preston, Jr.
V:36
Bragg, Braxton **V:**42
Hooker, Joseph **V:**197
Howard, Oliver Otis **V:**197
Lookout Mountain, Battle
of **V:**243
Sherman, William T. **V:**355
Thomas, George H. **V:**389
women soldiers **V:**435
Chattanooga, Tennessee **IV:**325
Chauncey, Isaac **III:**86
Chauncy, Charles **II:64; III:**419
Chautauqua Institute **VI:66–67**
Chautauqua movement **VI:**110,
306
Chauvin, Pierre **II:**135
Chávez, César Estrada **IX:53–54,**
54, 357c
agriculture **X:**19–20
braceros **IX:**43
Hispanic Americans **X:**166
Latino movement **IX:**186
UFW **IX:**324
union movement **IX:**324
Chávez, Hugo **X:**205, *206,* 207
Chavez, Mariano **IV:**26
Chavis, Benjamin **X:**245
Cheap Cotton by Free Labor
(Atkinson) **VI:**21
Cheatham, Benjamin **V:**359
"Checkers" speech **IX:**316, *353c;*
X:256
Checkley, John **II:**406
checks and balances **I:**97, 126
Chelsea Keramic Art Works **VI:**3
chemical industry **VII:**408c
Chemical Warfare Service
VIII:420
chemistry
Gibbs, Wolcott **VI:**144–145
Richards, Ellen Henrietta
Swallow **VI:**312–313
Rush, Benjamin **III:**375–376
science and technology
III:384; **VIII:**352
women's status and rights
VI:400
chemotherapy **VIII:**234
Cheney, Lynne **X:**245, 246
Cheney, Richard B. **X:71–73**
Bush, George W. **X:**54
elections, presidential
X:118
independent counsel **X:**179
Senate, U.S. **X:**321
Cher **X:**240
Chernomyrdin, Viktor **X:**157

Cherokee Advocate **IV:**86
Cherokee Constitution **IV:**325,
412c
Cherokee Indians **I:**187; **II:64–
65,** *438c;* **III:86–87,** *460c;*
IV:85–86, *412c–414c. See also*
Five Civilized Tribes
Adair, James **II:**4
animals **II:**23
Attakullakulla **II:**28–29
Black Hawk War **IV:**56
Boudinot, Elias **IV:**61
cotton culture **IV:**107–108
Dragging Canoe **III:**139
Fort Stanwix, Treaty of
III:170
Franklin, state of **III:**175
Frémont, John C. **IV:**166
Horseshoe Bend, Battle of
IV:190
Houston, Sam **IV:**191
Indian Affairs, Bureau of
IV:197
Indian Removal Act **IV:**197,
198
Iroquois **II:**180
Lamar, Mirabeau B. **IV:**222
Native Americans **III:**311,
313–315; **IV:**275; **V:**278–
279; **VIII:**264; **X:**250
Native Americans in the War
of 1812 **IV:**277, 278
North Carolina **II:**273
Nullification Controversy
IV:282
Ostenaco **II:**280
Priber, Christian Gottlieb
II:309–310
Ridge, John **IV:**323–324
Ross, John **IV:**325
Scott, Winfield **IV:**336
Sequoyah **IV:**342
slavery **IV:**346–347
South Carolina **II:**369
South Carolina Regulation
III:394
Stuart, John **II:**378
Trail of Tears **IV:**377
Ward, Nancy **II:**408
Watie, Stand **V:**427
Wilderness Road **III:**442
women's status and rights
III:446
Cherokee language **IV:**342–343,
412c
Cherokee National Council **IV:**324
Cherokee Nation v. Georgia
IV:412c
Jackson, Andrew **IV:**207
Native Americans **IV:**275
Trail of Tears **IV:**378
Cherokee Phoenix
Boudinot, Elias **IV:**61
Cherokee **IV:**85
Indian Removal Act **IV:**198
*Cherokee Phoenix and Indian
Advocate* **IV:**343

Cherokee Removal Act **IV:**324
Cherokee War **III:**87, 312
Cherry, Francis **IX:**117, 118
Cherry Creek, Colorado **IV:**300
Chertoff, Michael **X:**168
Chesapeake, USS
Free Trade and Sailor's
Rights **IV:**165
Ghent, Treaty of **IV:**175
War of 1812 **IV:**391
Chesapeake and Ohio Canal
IV:79, 93
Chesapeake and Ohio Railroad
(C&O) **VI:**181
Chesapeake Bay **II:**65m, **65–66,**
436c
abolitionism **V:**1
African Americans **II:**7
Anglican Church **II:**21
Annapolis Convention **III:**23
architecture **II:**25
Astor, John Jacob **IV:**33
Chesapeake-Leopard affair
III:88
class **II:**70
convict labor **II:**80
disease/epidemics **II:**98
domesticity **II:**101
economy **II:**109
education **II:**112
English immigrants **II:**117
Ghent, Treaty of **IV:**176
Grasse, François-Joseph-
Paul, comte de **III:**197
housing **II:**166
Howe, Sir William **III:**215
indentured servitude **II:**174,
175
Jamestown **II:**181
labor/labor movements
II:197–199
Lane, Ralph **I:**203
mortality **II:**243, 244
Mount Vernon **II:**245
population trends **II:**302–
303
Powhatan **I:**300–301
primogeniture and entail
II:310
religion, Euro-American
II:329
slavery **II:**356; **III:**390, 392
slave trade, internal **IV:**348,
349
Smith, John **II:**362
society, British American
II:365
tobacco **II:**391–392
Virginia **II:**398
War of 1812 **IV:**392
Westo **II:**411
Yorktown, surrender at
III:454
Chesapeake-Leopard affair
III:88, *465c*
Decatur, Stephen **IV:**115
embargo of 1807 **III:**152

foreign affairs **III**:169
Jefferson, Thomas **III**:234–235
Chesnut, Mary B. **V:64,** 239
Chesnutt, Charles W. **VI**:7, 225
Chester, Thomas Morris **IV**:17
Chestnut Street Theater
(Philadelphia) **III**:411
Chest of Chatham **I**:112, 157
Cheves, Langdon **IV**:46
Chevreul, Eugene **VI**:174
Chevrolet BelAir **IX**:133
Chevrolet Corvair
automobile industry **X**:35
GM **IX**:133
literature **IX**:194
Nader, Ralph **X**:241
National Traffic and Motor
Vehicle Safety Act of 1966
IX:238
Chevrolet Motor Company
IX:133
Chevron **VII**:245, 336
Cheyenne Indians **II**:166; **V**:443c,
445c; **VI**:408c
Beckwourth, Jim **IV**:51
Bent, William **IV**:52–53
Bent's Fort **IV**:55
Century of Dishonor, A
(Jackson) **VI:414–416**
Cody, William Frederick
VI:76
Colorado gold rush **IV**:100
Crazy Horse **VI**:86
Native Americans **IV**:276
Cheyenne River **IV**:146
Cheyney University of
Pennsylvania **VI**:112
Chiang Kai-shek (Jiang Jieshi)
IX:352c
Acheson, Dean **IX**:1
Asia **IX**:20
Cairo Conference **VIII**:61
cold war **IX**:63
Luce, Henry R. **VIII**:224
SEATO **IX**:292
Soviet Union **IX**:295
White Paper **IX**:343
World War II Pacific theater
VIII:435
Yalta Conference **VIII**:440
Chicago, Burlington & Quincy
Railway Company (CB&Q)
banking, investment **VI**:23
Forbes, John Murray
VI:132
Hill, James J. **VI**:172, 173
internal improvements
IV:203
Morgan, John Pierpont
VI:251
Northern Securities Case
VII:241
Chicago, Illinois
agriculture **IV**:11
America First Committee
VIII:17

Bethune, Mary McLeod
VIII:44
blues **VII**:39
Brotherhood of Sleeping Car
Porters **VIII**:54
Cassatt, Mary **VI**:64
cities and urban life **IV**:91;
VI:70, 71
Cody, William Frederick
VI:76
communications **VI**:78
Communist Party **VII**:61
criminal justice **VII**:66–67
"Days of Rage" riots (1969)
X:367, 368, 375c
disease/epidemics **IV**:122
Du Sable, Jean Baptiste
Pointe **II**:104
economy **IV**:131
entertainment, popular
VI:117
FAP **VIII**:129
fire (1871). *See* Chicago Fire
Foster, William Zebulon
VII:117
FTP **VIII**:136
Goodman, Benny **VIII**:150
Great Migration **VII**:129
Greenwich Village **VII**:131
Hamilton, Alice **VII**:133
Haymarket riot **VI**:168–169
Haywood, William Dudley
VII:137
Hillman, Sidney **VIII**:165
Ickes, Harold L. **VIII**:183
immigration **VI**:184, 186;
VII:144
industrialization **IV**:201
internal improvements
IV:203
invention and technology
VI:196
Irish Americans **VIII**:188
Japanese Americans,
relocation of **VIII**:194
jazz **VII**:153
Joplin, Scott **VII**:158
Kelley, Florence **VII**:164
King, Martin Luther, Jr.
IX:175
Ku Klux Klan **VII**:166
labor, radical **VI**:213
Lilienthal, David E.
VIII:217
Lloyd, Henry Demarest
VI:227–228
lumbering **IV**:231
Mann Act **VII**:189–190
McCormick, Cyrus Hall
IV:243
McDonald's **IX**:208
Meat Inspection Act
VII:198
meatpacking **VI**:243
Mexican Americans
VIII:237
migration **IV**:254

mining **VII**:209
Muhammad, Elijah **IX**:226
music **VII**:218, 219;
VIII:252
National Civic Federation
VII:226
New Woman **VII**:240
NWTUL **VII**:230–231
population trends **VI**:286;
VII:267
Prohibition **VII**:273
public housing **IX**:266, 267
Pullman Strike **VI**:297
Pure Food and Drug Act
VII:276–277
race and race relations
VII:283; **VIII**:319; **X**:295
riots (1966) **X**:295
Selective Service **VIII**:358
settlement houses **VI**:327
Sinclair, Upton **VII**:325
skyscrapers **VI**:333
socialism **VII**:327
sports and recreation
VII:334–335
steel industry **VII**:337
Steffens, Lincoln **VII**:339
Sunday, William Ashley, Jr.
VII:341, 342
Sweet trial **VII**:344
technology **VIII**:389
temperance movement
IV:370
transportation, urban
VI:360–361
urban reform **VII**:363
U.S. Steel **VII**:365
Vanderbilt, Cornelius
IV:387
Villard, Henry **VI**:374
Vorse, Mary Heaton
VII:375
Weathermen/Weather
Underground **IX**:341;
X:367, 368
women's status and rights
IX:348
Chicago, Milwaukee, and St. Paul
Railroad **IV**:203
Chicago *Alarm* **VI**:213
Chicago *American* **VII**:138
Chicago and Northwestern
Railroad **IV**:203
Chicago and Rock Island Railroad
IV:203
Chicago *Arbeiter Zeitung* **VI**:213
Chicago Bears **VIII**:371
Chicago Board of Censors
VIII:65
Chicago Cardinals **VIII**:371
Chicago Civic Federation
VII:226
Chicago Commons Settlement
VII:330
Chicago Cubs **VII**:334
Chicago *Daily News* **VII**:160;
VIII:202

Chicago Defender **VII**:129;
VIII:271
"Chicago Eight" **X:73,** 375c
Chicago *Examiner* **VII**:138
Chicago Fire (1871) **VI**:407c
Burnham, Daniel Hudson
VI:54
economy **V**:124
invention and technology
VI:196
Chicago Golf Club **VI**:343
Chicago Library Board **VI**:395
Chicago Museum of Science and
Industry **VI**:402
Chicago Public Library **VI**:224
Chicago riots (1966) **X**:295
Chicago school (architecture)
VI:18
Chicago School of Civics and
Philanthropy **VII**:330
Chicago Seven **IX**:144
Chicago Stock Exchange **VI**:347
Chicago Tribune **VI**:409c
elections **IX**:102
Ickes, Harold L. **VIII**:183
Ingersoll, Robert Green
VI:193
Lloyd, Henry Demarest
VI:227
lynching **VI**:229, 230
Villard, Henry **VI**:374
Chicago Vice Commission **VI**:215
Chicago White Sox **VII**:33, 341
Chicago Women's Club **VI**:395
Chicago Women's Liberation
Union **X**:132
Chicago World's Fair. *See* World's
Columbian Exposition
Chicano movement **X**:166
Chicanos. *See* Mexican Americans
Chicano Youth Liberation
conferences **IX**:137
Chicaza **I**:343
Chichén Itzá **I:71–73,** 72
Native American religion
I:260
Toltecs **I**:364
Yucatán Peninsula **I**:390
Chichimeca **I**:365
Chickamauga, Battle of **V:64–65**
Cleburne, Patrick R. **V**:75
Hill, Daniel H. **V**:190
homefront **V**:194
Hood, John Bell **V**:196
Longstreet, James **V**:242
Lookout Mountain, Battle
of **V**:243
Sheridan, Philip H. **V**:353
tactics and strategy **V**:380
Thomas, George H. **V**:388,
389
Chickamauga and Chattanooga
National Military Park **V**:276
Chickamauga Indians
Cherokee **III**:87
Dragging Canoe **III**:139–140

Chickamauga Indians (*continued*)
    Franklin, state of **III**:175
    Wilderness Road **III**:442
Chickasaw Indians **II:66; IV:86**.
    See also Five Civilized Tribes
    Adair, James **II**:4
    Bienville, Jean-Baptiste Le
        Moyne, sieur de **II**:38
    Choctaw **II**:68; **IV**:86
    Clark, William **III**:96
    Indian Removal Act **IV**:197
    Native Americans **II**:254;
        V:278, 279
    Trail of Tears **IV**:378
chiefdoms
    cacique **I**:49
    Calusa **I**:52–53
    Cofitachequi **I**:80
    Coosa **I**:89
    Mississippian **I**:245
    Powhatan **I**:300–301
Chief Joseph. *See* Joseph (chief of
    the Nez Perce)
Chihuahua City, Mexico
    Armijo, Manuel **IV**:27
    Magoffin, James W. **IV**:233
    Pike, Zebulon Montgomery
        IV:300
Child, Julia **IX**:122
Child, Lydia Maria
    abolitionism **V**:2
    Hale, Sarah Josepha **IV**:183
    literature **IV**:229
child abuse **X**:46, 308
childbed fever **IV**:123
childbirth **I**:20
    alcohol **II**:16
    fertility **II**:125–126
    marriage and family **II**:218
    medicine **VI**:244
    midwives **II**:234
    mortality **II**:244
    women's status and rights
        II:425
child care **VIII**:231; **X**:134
child custody rights **X**:123
childhood **II:66–67; IX:54–55**
    commemoration **IX**:66
    education **II**:111–112;
        IX:99
    marriage and family **II**:218
    television **IX**:315
    yellow fever **II**:431
child labor **VI:**211**, 211–212;
    VII:50–53,** 51, 406c, 407c
    Abbott, Grace **VII**:1
    Adamson Act **VII**:2
    AFL **VII**:12
    children **VII**:399, 400;
        VIII:67
    Democratic Party **VII**:74
    elections **VII**:91
    Ethical Culture movement
        VI:121
    Hamilton, Alice **VII**:133
    Keating-Owen Act **VII**:163
    Kelley, Florence **VII**:164

marriage and family
    VII:192
mothers' pensions **VII**:214
muckrakers **VII**:217
Muller v. Oregon **VII**:217
New Freedom **VII**:236
news media **VII**:271
Perkins, Frances **VIII**:293
photography **VII**:259
Progressive Party **VII**:270
progressivism **VII**:270
Smith, Alfred E. **VII**:326
Supreme Court **VII**:343
Valesh, Eva McDonald
    VII:367
Vorse, Mary Heaton
    VII:375
Child Labor Act **VII**:407c, 408c
*Child Labor Legislation
    Handbook* (Goldmark) **VII**:127
Child Online Protection Act
    (1998) **X**:284
children **I**:20; **VII:398–400,
    406c; VIII:66–67**
    *Akron v. Akron Center for
        Reproductive Health*
        X:20–21
    baby boomers **X**:39, 40
    big bands **VIII**:44
    Birmingham confrontation
        IX:39–40
    birthrates **X**:44–45
    Brace, Charles Loring
        VI:45–46
    Bush, George W. **X**:56
    Children's Bureau **VII**:53
    "Children's Era" Speech
        (Sanger) **VII:432–434**
    cities and urban life
        VII:55–56
    Clinton, Hillary Rodham
        X:78
    cosmetics and beauty
        industry **VII**:66
    criminal justice **VII**:66–67
    education **III**:147–148;
        V:124; **VIII**:105–107
    education, homeschooling
        X:112–113
    education, primary/
        secondary **X**:113–116
    Fair Labor Standards Act
        VIII:124
    family life **X**:127, 128
    FERA **VIII**:133
    Head Start **IX**:144–145
    homefront **V**:192, 193
    Hoover, Herbert C.
        VIII:173
    immigration **X**:175
    kindergarten **VI**:207
    labor/labor movements
        III:252
    literature **VIII**:219
    marriage and family **III**:287,
        288; **V**:248–249; **VII**:192–
        193; **VIII**:230, 231

media **X**:218
medicine **X**:223–224
music **III**:308, 309
Native Americans **VII**:233
NRA **X**:249
NYA **VIII**:262–263
popular culture **X**:278
population trends **IX**:260
pornography **X**:283
poverty **III**:344; **X**:285
public health **IX**:265, 266
recreation **VIII**:327
sexuality **VII**:322
Slater, Samuel **III**:389
Social Security Act
    VIII:363, 365, 454–456
Spock, Benjamin **IX**:297
television **X**:344
tobacco suits **X**:352
Vicksburg campaign **V**:418
victory gardens **VIII**:406
Wald, Lillian **VII**:377
White, Alfred Tredway
    VI:390–391
women's status and rights
    VIII:422
work, household **VII**:390
YMCA/YWCA **VII**:397, 398
children, unborn **X**:289, 368
Children and Adults with ADD
    (CHADD) **X**:223
Children's Aid Society (CAS)
    VI:45–46
Children's Bureau **VII:53–54**
    Abbott, Grace **VII**:1
    children **VIII**:66, 67
    Kelley, Florence **VII**:164
    mothers' pensions **VII**:214
    public health **VII**:276
    Sheppard-Towner Act
        VII:323
    Social Security Act
        VIII:364
    Wald, Lillian **VII**:377
    women's network **VIII**:421
"Children's Era" Speech (Sanger)
    VII:432–434
Children's Gun Violence
    Prevention Act (1998) **X**:161
Children's Health Act (1997)
    X:197
Chile **X**:377c
    Andes Mountains **I**:9
    Chilean-American relations
        VI:67–68
    Essex, USS **IV**:144
    Latin America **X**:205, 206
    mining **VII**:210
    Monroe Doctrine **IV**:259
    Monte Verde **I**:251
    Valdivia, Pedro de **I**:373
Chilean-American relations
    VI:67–68
Chimalpahin, Domingo Francisco
    de San Antón Muñón **I:73**
Chimayo, New Mexico **III**:29
Chimborazo Hospital **V**:297

China **I:67–69; IV:**414c;
    VII:403c, 407c, 408c;
    VIII:446c, 448c
    Angell, James Burrill **VI**:15
    Army Air Forces, U.S.
        VIII:27
    Asian Americans **VIII**:32
    Astoria **IV**:35
    Axis **VIII**:37
    bombing **VIII**:48
    Boxer Rebellion **VII**:40–41
    Cabot, Sebastian **I**:45, 46
    Cairo Conference **VIII**:61
    chain stores **VI**:65
    Chinese Exclusion Act
        VI:68
    class consciousness **VI**:73
    Company of Cathay **I**:87
    disease/epidemics **IV**:121
    dollar diplomacy **VII**:79
    Forbes, John Murray
        VI:131
    foreign policy **IV**:156;
        VI:133; **VII**:113;
        VIII:141–142
    Gentlemen's Agreement
        VII:123
    Great White Fleet **VII**:130
    Hay, John Milton **VI**:164
    Hughes, Charles Evans
        VII:142
    Hull, Cordell **VIII**:180
    Ibn Battuta **I**:175
    immigration **VI**:187;
        VIII:184
    imperialism **VI**:188
    invention and technology
        I:185
    Jesuits **I**:193
    League of Nations **VII**:176
    Leahy, William D. **VIII**:210
    Lend-Lease **VIII**:211–212
    Luce, Henry R. **VIII**:224
    Mahan, Alfred Thayer
        VI:236
    Ma Huan **I**:225
    Manchuria **VIII**:225, 226
    Marshall, George C.
        VIII:233
    McPherson, Aimee Semple
        VII:196
    National Origins Act
        VII:228
    nativism **VII**:234
    Open Door Notes **VI**:272–
        273
    Open Door Policy **VII**:246
    OSS **VIII**:285
    Perry, Matthew Calbraith
        IV:298
    Polo, Marco **I**:294–296
    printing press **I**:302
    Ricci, Matteo **I**:319–320
    segregation **VII**:320
    Silk Road **I**:335
    silver **I**:336
    sugar **I**:348

Taft, Robert A. **VIII**:385
trade, domestic and foreign
    VII:354
Tyler, John **IV**:383
UN **VIII**:403
Washington Conference
    on Naval Disarmament
    VII:379
WILPF **VII**:386
World War I **VII**:393
World War II Pacific theater
    VIII:435
Yalta Conference **VIII**:440
China, People's Republic of
    X:376c, 382c, 383c
    Acheson, Dean **IX**:1
    Asia **IX**:20, 21
    Carter, James Earl, Jr. **X**:69
    Clinton, William J. **X**:82
    cold war **IX**:63
    cold war, end of **X**:84, 85
    Dennis v. U.S. **IX**:86
    détente **X**:104
    Eisenhower, Dwight D.
        IX:100
    Ford, Gerald R. **X**:139
    foreign policy **X**:140, 141
    Kissinger, Henry A. **X**:198
    Korean War **IX**:177, 178
    labor/labor movements
        X:203
    Limited Test Ban Treaty of
        1963 **IX**:192
    MacArthur, Douglas
        IX:198
    McCarthy, Joseph R.
        IX:207
    Nixon, Richard M. **X**:257
    NSC-68 **IX**:247
    Peace Corps **IX**:256
    SEATO **IX**:292
    Soviet Union **IX**:295
    technology **IX**:312
    Truman Doctrine **IX**:322
    UN **VIII**:403
    White Paper **IX**:342–343
    WTO **X**:372
China, Republic of (Nationalist
    China) **IX**:352c
    Asia **IX**:20, 21
    Bush, George W. **X**:55
    cold war **IX**:63
    Luce, Henry R. **VIII**:224
    SEATO **IX**:292
    Soviet Union **IX**:295
    White Paper **IX**:343
China-Burma-India (CBI) theater
    VIII:435–436
chinampas **I**:18, **73**, 354
China trade **III**:88–89, 183, 414
Chinese Americans **IX**:349; **X**:33
Chinese Exclusion Act *VI*:68,
    68–69, 409c, **416–417**;
    VII:403c
    Arthur, Chester Alan **VI**:21
    Asian-American movement
        IX:21

citizenship **VII**:56
Gentlemen's Agreement
    VII:123
immigration **VII**:144
immigration restrictions
    VI:187
nativism **VII**:234
race and race relations
    VII:281
Root-Takahira Agreement
    VII:305
Chinese immigrants
    anti-Chinese agitation, rise
        of **IV**:24
    Asian Americans **VIII**:32
    Chinese Exclusion Act
        VI:68, **416–417**
    cities and urban life **V**:66
    citizenship **VII**:56
    Fifteenth Amendment
        V:141
    gold **IV**:178
    immigration **IV**:196; **V**:201;
        VI:68; **VII**:144; **VIII**:184
    Immigration Act (1917)
        VII:145
    immigration restrictions
        VI:187
    National Origins Act
        VII:228
    nativism **VII**:234
    Pacific Railroad Act **V**:293
    Quota Act **VII**:279
    race and race relations
        IV:312
    railroads **V**:322
Chinese Nationalists **IX**:20, 21
Chinese Revolution **IX**:352c
Chinook Indians **II**:275; **IV**:224
Chippewa Creek, Battle of
    Red Jacket **III**:360
    Scott, Winfield **IV**:336
    War of 1812 **IV**:392
Chippewa Indians **IV**:83, 192;
    X:250
Chirac, Jacques **X**:143
Chiricahua Apache Indians
    V:444c; **VI**:17, 143
Chirikov, Aleksei **II**:14, 36
Chisholm, Alexander **III**:403
Chisholm, Shirley **X**:129
Chisholm Trail **VI**:64
Chisholm v. Georgia **III**:463c
    Amendment, Eleventh
        III:16
    Jay, John **III**:230
    political correctness **X**:275
    Supreme Court **III**:403
Chita (Hearn) **VI**:169
chitlin circuit **VI**:117
Chitomachon **II**:413
Chivington, John M. **IV**:52–53,
    100; **V**:443c, 445c
chlorpromazine **X**:223
Choate, Pat **X**:304
chocolate. *See* cacao
Choctaw, USS **V**:260

Choctaw Indians **I**:343; **II**:67–68;
    III:89; **IV**:86–87. *See also* Five
    Civilized Tribes
    Adair, James **II**:4
    animals **III**:22
    Bienville, Jean-Baptiste Le
        Moyne, sieur de **II**:38
    Chickasaw **II**:66
    cotton culture **IV**:107–108
    Indian Removal Act **IV**:197
    Natchez Revolt **II**:250
    Native Americans **IV**:274–
        275; **VIII**:264
    Native Americans in the War
        of 1812 **IV**:277
    New Orleans, Battle of
        IV:281
    Pushmataha **IV**:307
    Red Shoes **II**:327
    Trail of Tears **IV**:377
Chodorov, Frank **X**:93
Choice, Not an Echo, A (Schlafly)
    X:317
Choiseul Island **VIII**:366
cholera
    disease/epidemics **IV**:121–
        122, 124
    immigration **IV**:194
    Mason, Richard B. **IV**:241
    medicine **VII**:198
    Oregon Trail **IV**:286
    public health **VII**:274
    science and technology
        VII:314
    Trail of Tears **IV**:377
cholera morbus **IV**:368
Cholula **I**:74
    Aztecs **I**:19, 21
    Cortés, Hernán **I**:96
    Malinche **I**:227
    Quetzalcoatl **I**:309
    Tlaxcala **I**:362
    Toltecs **I**:365
Chopin, Kate **VI**:225
Chorlton Twist Company **IV**:291
Chouteau, Auguste Pierre **IV**:88
Chouteau, Jean Pierre **IV**:87
Chouteau, Pierre, Jr. **IV**:18, 88
Chouteau, René **IV**:87
Chouteau family **IV**:87–88, 171,
    266
Christadelphians **IV**:320
Christenings Make Not Christians
    (Williams) **II**:417
Christian, William **II**:29
Christiana, Pennsylvania, riot
    V:65
Christian American **X**:74
Christian Anticommunist Crusade
    X:93
Christian Association of
    Washington **IV**:78, 319
Christian Broadcasting Network
    (CBN) **X**:342
Christian Church (Disciples of
    Christ)
    Campbell, Thomas **IV**:78

religion **IV**:318, 319
Smith, Joseph, Jr. **IV**:352
Christian Coalition (CC) **X**:73–
    74
    conservative movement
        X:94
    evangelical Christians **X**:125
    Moral Majority **X**:234
Christian Commonwealth, The
    (Eliot) **II**:115
Christian Crusade **X**:93
Christian Front **VIII**:25
Christianity. *See also specific*
    Christian religions, e.g.: Roman
    Catholic Church
    Africa **II**:5
    African-American churches,
        growth of **VI**:4–5
    African Americans **III**:10
    Anglo-Normans **I**:10
    auto-da-fé **I**:17
    camp meetings **III**:77
    Castile **I**:66
    conservatism **VIII**:84
    Cozumel **I**:99
    Darfur **I**:104
    Darwinism and religion
        VI:92–93
    Dutch Reformed Church
        II:106–107
    Ethiopia **I**:124, 125
    evangelical Christians
        X:124–125
    Handsome Lake **III**:209
    Iceland **I**:177
    Jews **I**:194–196
    Las Casas, Bartolomé de
        I:205
    Lisbon **I**:215
    London **I**:216
    Moral Majority **X**:234
    Morse, Jedidiah **III**:307
    Native Americans **II**:253
    New World **I**:271
    Nzinga **I**:274–275
    Powhatan Confederacy
        II:308
    praying towns **II**:308–309
    Prester John **I**:301
    race and race relations
        III:357
    Reconquista **I**:314
    Reformation **I**:315
    religion **VI**:307; **IX**:272;
        X:306
    religion, African-American
        II:328
    religion, Euro-American
        II:328
    religion, Native American
        II:331
    revitalization movements
        II:332
    Serra, Junípero **II**:347
    slavery **II**:356; **III**:392
    Tanner, Benjamin Tucker
        VI:352

Christianity *(continued)*
 televangelism **X:**341–342
 Trent, Council of **I:**369–370
 Willard, Samuel **II:**415
 women's status and rights
  II:424
Christianity and the Social Crisis
 (Rauschenbusch)
 Rauschenbusch, Walter
  VII:293
 religion **VII:**297
 Social Gospel **VI:**335
*Christian Liberty (The Freedom of
 a Christian)* (Luther) **I:**218
Christian Nurture (Bushnell)
 IV:319
Christian Realism **VIII:**334,
 335–336
Christian Recorder, The **VI:**351
Christian Right **X:**94
Christian Science **VI:69,** 105–
 106, 408*c*
Christian Science Association
 VI:69, 106
Christian Science Monitor
 VI:106; **VII:**47
Christian Science Sentinel
 VI:106
Christian Socialism **VI:**115;
 VIII:394
Christmas **III:**341; **V:**274
Christy, Arthur **X:**179
Chrysler, Walter P. **VII:**84
Chrysler Building (New York City)
 VIII:28
Chrysler Corporation **X:**384*c*
 automobile industry **VII:**27;
  VIII:35; **IX:**25, 26; **X:**35,
  37
 economy **VII:**84
 strikes **VIII:**377
 technology **IX:**313
Chrysler Corporation Loan
 Guarantee Act (1979) **X:74–
 75,** 378*c*
Church, Benjamin **II:**323; **III:**89–
 90, 295
Church, Frank **X:**29, 34
Church, Frederic Edwin **V:**18;
 VI:37
Church, William C. **X:**248
church and state, separation of
 X:94, 378*c*
Church and the Age, The
 (Hecker) **VI:**316
Churchill, Winston **VIII:***141, 162,
 440, 447c; 448c;* **IX:***321*
 Anglo-American relations
  VIII:21
 Army, U.S. **VIII:**25
 Arnold, Henry H. "Hap"
  VIII:28
 Atlantic Charter **VIII:**34,
  461
 Bourke-White, Margaret
  VIII:50
 Britain, Battle of **VIII:**54

Bulge, Battle of the **VIII:**55
Cairo Conference **VIII:**61
Casablanca Conference
 VIII:62
destroyers-for-bases deal
 VIII:94
foreign policy **VIII:**142
Grand Alliance **VIII:**155–
 156
Harriman, W. Averell
 VIII:162, *162*
Hopkins, Harry L. **VIII:**177
Iron Curtain, collapse of
 X:188
Lend-Lease **VIII:**211
Munich Conference
 VIII:248
North African campaign
 VIII:277
Pearl Harbor **VIII:**292
Potsdam Conference
 VIII:307
Roosevelt, Franklin D.
 VIII:346
second front **VIII:**355
Soviet-American relations
 VIII:368
Teheran Conference
 VIII:390
UN **VIII:**402
V-E Day **VIII:**405
World War II European
 theater **VIII:**430
Yalta Agreement **VIII:**467–
 469
Yalta Conference **VIII:**439
Church of Christ **IV:**337
Church of Christ, Scientist. *See*
 Christian Science
Church of England. *See* Anglican
 Church
Church of God in Christ **X:**14
Church of Jesus Christ of Latter-
 day Saints (Mormon Church)
 IV:88–90, 412*c;* **VI:251–252**
 Bowles, Samuel **VI:**43
 Brannan, Samuel **IV:**63–64
 Bridger, James **IV:**64
 Christian Science **VI:**69
 conservative movement
  X:93
 Deseret, State of **IV:**119–
  121
 ERA **X:**124
 exploration **IV:**145
 marriage and family **IV:**240
 migration **IV:**253, 255
 Mormon Trail **IV:**261–262
 Mormon War **IV:**262–264
 Native Americans **IV:**275
 Nauvoo **IV:**278
 polygamy **IV:**303
 pornography **X:**283
 religion **IV:**319; **VI:**308–
  309; **X:**306
 Second Great Awakening
  IV:337

Smith, Joseph, Jr. **IV:**352
Strang, James Jesse **IV:**358
Young, Brigham **IV:**407
Church of the Ascension (New
 York City) **VI:**217
Church of the Brethren **V:**295
Churchwell, William M. **VI:**221
Churchyard, Thomas **I:**140
Churubusco, Battle of **V:**17, 190
CIA. *See* Central Intelligence
 Agency
Cíbola **I:**397*c*
 Hopi **I:**168
 New Mexico **I:**265
 Zuni **I:**394
Cicero **IX:**57
Ciconicin Indians **II:**96
cider **III:**13
Cieza de León, Pedro **I:76,**
 261–262, 284
cigarettes **VIII:**322
Cigarmakers International **VI:**13,
 150–151
cihuacoatl
 flowery wars **I:**131–132
 Moctezuma II Xocoyotzin
  I:245
 Tlacacla **I:**361
Cimarron Desert **IV:**330, 332
cimarrones **I:**285
Cimarron River **IV:**325, 351
Cincinnati, Ohio
 agriculture **IV:**11
 American Anti-Slavery
  Society **IV:**15
 anti-Catholic riots **IV:**24
 Audubon, John James **IV:**37
 currency issue **VI:**89
 immigration **VI:**184
 industrialization **IV:**201
 internal improvements
  IV:202
 Johnson, Tom Loftin
  VII:156
 Judaism **VI:**205
 labor, woman **VI:**215
 Lamy, Jean Baptiste **IV:**222
 Liberal Republican Party
  VI:222
 Liberia **VI:**223
 meatpacking **VI:**243
 medicine **IV:**249
 music **VII:**219
 NAM **VII:**225
 popular sovereignty **IV:**305
 population trends **III:**343
 Prohibition **VII:**273
 religion **IV:**319
 sports and recreation
  VIII:370
 Sunday, William Ashley, Jr.
  VII:342
 Taft, Robert A. **VIII:**385
 Taft, William Howard
  VII:347
 Weld, Theodore Dwight
  IV:396

Cincinnati, Order of **III:90**
Cincinnati, USS (ironclad) **V:**263
Cincinnati, USS (light cruiser)
 VIII:201
Cincinnati College **IV:**246
Cincinnati *Commercial* **VI:**169,
 374
Cincinnati *Enquirer* **VI:**169
Cincinnati Gazette **VI:**304
Cincinnati Law School **VII:**347
Cincinnati Post **VII:**159–160
Cincinnati Reds **VII:**33, 334
Cincinnatus
 Cincinnati, Order of **III:**90
 presidential campaigns
  (1870–1899) **VI:**290
 republicanism **III:**365
 Washington, George **III:**431
cinema. *See* movie industry;
 specific films
cinematography **VII:**151
Cinerama **IX:**223
Cinqué, Joseph **IV:**21, 22, *22,*
 413*c*
CIO. *See* Congress of Industrial
 Organizations
Cipollone, Rose **X:**351
circuit chip. *See* integrated circuits
circuit courts
 Judiciary Act (1789) **III:**242
 Judiciary Act (1801) **III:**242
 Supreme Court **III:**404
circumnavigation of the globe
 Drake, Sir Francis **I:**110,
  111
 Magellan, Ferdinand **I:**223,
  224
 Pigafetta, Antonio **I:**292
circuses **VI:**24, 25, 117–118, 407*c*
Cisneros, Sandra **X:**211
Citadel, The (Charleston, South
 Carolina) **IV:**348; **V:**81
cities and urban life **II:68–69;
 III:90–92,** *91;* **IV:90–94,** *92;*
 V:65–68, *66;* **VI:69–72,** *70,*
 410*c;* **VII:54–56,** *55;* **VIII:68–
 70,** *69;* **IX:55–56; X:75–76**
 African Americans **IV:**7
 agriculture **V:**7
 AIM **IX:**12
 Americanization **VII:**12–13
 art and architecture **VI:**18;
  VII:19; **VIII:**28
 automobile industry **VII:**28
 Catholics **VIII:**63, 64
 Charleston **II:**63–64
 child labor **VII:**52
 Democratic Party **VIII:**92
 Dillingham Commission
  VII:77
 disease/epidemics **II:**99;
  III:138; **IV:**121; **V:**113
 economy **IV:**132
 education **V:**124; **VI:**108,
  109
 election of 1936 **VIII:**109
 election of 1940 **VIII:**111

environment **VII**:98
eugenics **VII**:102
Federal Housing
 Administration (FHA)
 VIII:134
Federalists **III**:166
FMP **VIII**:134
gays and lesbians **VIII**:147–
 148
GI Bill of Rights **VIII**:150
Great Depression **VIII**:159
HOLC **VIII**:171
homefront **V**:193
housing **VI**:178–179;
 VIII:178
immigration **VII**:143;
 IX:156
industrialization **IV**:200
Industrial Revolution
 III:225
Irish Americans **VIII**:188
Latino movement **IX**:185
literature **IV**:227; **VIII**:218
machine politics **VI**:234
Mann Act **VII**:189
marriage and family **IV**:240;
 VII:191
Maya **I**:234
medicine **VI**:245
Mexican Americans
 VIII:237
migration **VIII**:239; **IX**:215
movies **VIII**:245
music **VI**:254
New York City **V**:282–283
panic of 1857 **V**:294
penitentiary movement
 IV:296
Philadelphia **V**:303–304
Polish Americans **VIII**:297
popular culture **VIII**:301
population trends **III**:343;
 V:309; **VI**:286; **VIII**:305;
 X:282
poverty **III**:344
prostitution **V**:315–316
public housing **IX**:266
*Recent Social Trends in the
 United States* **VIII**:323
recreation **VII**:295;
 VIII:329
religion **VI**:306; **VIII**:334
Resettlement Administration
 VIII:339
Richmond, Virginia **V**:335–
 337
Roosevelt, Franklin D.
 VIII:345
skyscrapers **VI**:333
slavery **IV**:347
Social Gospel **VI**:335
socialism **VII**:327
social work **VII**:328–329
South **VIII**:367
suburbanization/suburbs
 VII:341; **VIII**:379
Sunbelt **VIII**:381

technology **IX**:313
teenagers **IX**:315
Tesla, Nikola **VI**:353
transportation **V**:390, 392
transportation, urban
 VI:360–361
unemployment **VIII**:399
Urban League **IX**:325–326
urban redevelopment
 IX:326
urban reform **VII**:362–363
urban transportation
 VII:363–365
USHA **VIII**:404
Watts uprising **IX**:339–340
work, household **VII**:389
World War II home front
 VIII:432
zoot-suiters **VIII**:442
Citizen Genêt. *See* Genêt,
 Edmond Charles
Citizen Kane (film) **VIII**:447*c*
 recreation **VIII**:328
 Welles, Orson **VIII**:414,
  415
Citizens Councils of America
 (CCA) **IX**:342, 354*c*
Citizens for Victory **VIII**:77
citizenship **III**:92–95, 464*c*;
 V:446*c*; **VII**:56–57, 403*c*,
 405*c*–408*c*
 African Americans **VI**:5
 Alien and Sedition Acts
  III:14
 Americanization **VII**:13
 amnesty, acts of **V**:9
 Articles of Confederation
  III:34
 Cable Act **VII**:47
 Civil Rights Act (1866) **V**:70
 Civil War **V**:72
 Constitution, United States
  III:106
 Dawes Severalty Act
  VI:93–94
 Democratic Party **V**:109
 Douglass, Frederick **V**:116
 Dred Scott decision **V**:116–
  118
 Expatriation Act **VII**:103–
  104
 Foraker Act **VII**:110
 Fourteenth Amendment
  V:156, 157
 Haiti **III**:203
 immigration **III**:221
 Jews **III**:236
 Jones Act (1917) **VII**:157
 Louisiana Purchase **III**:273
 Mariana Islands **VIII**:229
 Native Americans **VII**:231;
  VIII:263
 nativism **VII**:234
 Paine, Thomas **III**:329
 Reconstruction **V**:325
 social work **VII**:329
 Soldiers' Bonus **VII**:331

Supreme Court **VIII**:384
 women's status and rights
  VI:399
citizen-soldier **V**:68
 common soldier **V**:77
 Confederate army **V**:80
 governors **V**:171
 Union army **V**:400, 404
City Beautiful movement
 art and architecture **VI**:18
 Burnham, Daniel Hudson
  VI:56
 Olmsted, Frederick Law
  V:288
 World's Columbian
  Exposition **VI**:402
City College of New York
 education, higher **VI**:111
 Frankfurter, Felix **VIII**:144
 Sinclair, Upton **VII**:325
City Lights (film) **VII**:216
City Lights Bookshop (San
 Francisco) **IX**:78
city planning **VII**:19
city-states **I**:389
City Tavern (Philadelphia) **II**:383;
 III:407
Ciudad Hidalgo **I**:357
Civil Aeronautics Act **VIII**:446*c*
Civil Aeronautics Authority (CAA)
 VII:165; **VIII**:13
Civil Air Patrol **VIII**:27, 281
Civil Crusade (Panama) **X**:269
civil defense **IX**:56–57, 64–65,
 153, 355*c*
civil disobedience **IX**:57–58
 African Americans **IX**:5
 Parks, Rosa **IX**:254–255
 Randolph, A. Philip
  VIII:321
 sit-ins **IX**:291
"Civil Disobedience" (Thoreau)
 IV:414*c*, 443–446
 civil disobedience **IX**:57
 literature **IV**:228
 Peabody, Elizabeth Palmer
  VI:280
 Thoreau, Henry David
  IV:376
 transcendental movement
  IV:379
Civiletti, Benjamin **X**:5
Civilian Conservation Corps
 (CCC) **VIII**:70–71
 African Americans **VIII**:3
 Black Cabinet **VIII**:46
 Byrnes, James F. **VIII**:60
 children **VIII**:66
 Congress **VIII**:81
 conscientious objectors
  VIII:83
 conservatism **VIII**:84, 85
 education **VIII**:106
 environment **VIII**:116
 ERAA **VIII**:114
 marriage and family
  VIII:231

Native Americans **VIII**:264
New Deal **VIII**:269
NYA **VIII**:262
race and race relations
 VIII:318
relief **VIII**:332
Social Security Act
 VIII:363
civilian defense **VIII**:281–282
Civilian Production
 Administration **VIII**:414
Civilian Public Service (CPS)
 VIII:83
Civility (Indian leader) **II**:75
civil law **III**:256
civil liberties **VII**:57–58;
 VIII:71–72
 abortion **X**:1–5
 ACLU **VII**:9; **VIII**:17
 Asian Americans **VIII**:32
 Baldwin, Roger Nash
  VII:31
 Black, Hugo L. **VIII**:45
 Brandeis, Louis Dembitz
  VII:41–42
 civil rights **VIII**:73
 Confederate **V**:68–69
 Douglas, William O.
  VIII:97
 Espionage Act **VII**:100–101
 Fellowship of Reconciliation
  VII:109
 Frankfurter, Felix **VIII**:144
 free speech fights **VII**:118
 Gallatin, Albert **III**:187
 Greenwich Village **VII**:130,
  131
 Harlem Renaissance
  VII:136
 Holmes, Oliver Wendell
  VII:140, 141
 Korematsu v. U.S. **VIII**:203
 liberalism **VIII**:216
 Native Americans **X**:250
 Rankin, Jeannette **VII**:292
 Roosevelt, Eleanor **VIII**:343
 Roosevelt, Franklin D.
  VIII:346
 Schenck v. U.S. **VII**:313
 Scopes Trial **VII**:316
 Supreme Court **VII**:343–
  344; **VIII**:383–384
 Sweet trial **VII**:345
 Thomas, Norman **VIII**:394
 Union **V**:69–70
 USA PATRIOT Act **X**:358,
  359
 World War II **VIII**:427
 World War II home front
  VIII:432
Civil Liberties Act (1988) **X**:76,
 379*c*
civil rights **VII**:404*c*, 409*c*;
 VIII:72–74, 73, 447*c*, 449*c*;
 IX:354*c*; **X**:382*c*
 abolitionism **IV**:4
 abortion **X**:1–5

civil rights (continued)
    African Americans **IV**:8–10;
      VIII:5; **X**:14
    AIM **IX**:12–13
    AIP **X**:24
    Americans with Disabilities
      Act **X**:24–25, **403–405**
    Amistad incident **IV**:21
    antilynching legislation
      VIII:22
    Baker, Ella Josephine **IX**:32
    Bethune, Mary McLeod
      VIII:44
    Bill of Rights **III**:51
    Bright Eyes **VI**:49
    Bruce, Blanche Kelso **V**:47
    Byrnes, James F. **VIII**:60
    carpetbaggers **V**:56
    Catholics **VIII**:64
    Civil Rights Act (1991)
      X:76–77
    Civil Rights Cases **VI**:72
    Communists **VIII**:78
    conservatism **IX**:75
    consumerism **IX**:76
    CORE **IX**:72
    Cuffe, Paul **III**:127
    Democratic Party **VIII**:94
    Dickinson, Anna E. **V**:111
    Douglas, William O.
      VIII:97
    DuBois, W.E.B. **VII**:80, 81
    education **IX**:100
    election of 1944 **VIII**:111
    elections **IX**:103, 104
    elections, conduct of **VI**:113
    Elliot, Robert Brown **V**:127
    Enforcement Acts **V**:133
    Executive Order 8802
      VIII:120, 465–466
    Executive Order 9066
      VIII:121, 466–467
    Exodusters **VI**:122
    Fair Deal **IX**:115
    FEPC **VIII**:123–124
    Field, Stephen Johnson
      VI:127
    Fourteenth Amendment
      V:157
    Free Speech Movement
      IX:125–126
    fugitive slave laws **IV**:168
    Gallup Poll **IX**:130
    Garnet, Henry Highland
      IV:174
    Garrison, William Lloyd
      V:165
    gay and lesbian rights
      movement **X**:148–149
    Gonzáles, Rodolfo "Corky"
      IX:136
    Harlan, John Marshall
      VI:159
    Harper, Frances Ellen
      Watkins **V**:184
    Hayes, Rutherford B.
      VI:167, 168

    Hispanic Americans **X**:166
    Hoar, George F. **VI**:173
    Humphrey, Hubert H.
      IX:151
    impeachment of Andrew
      Johnson **V**:202
    Indian Rights Association
      VI:190
    Jim Crow laws **VI**:203–204
    Johnson, Andrew **V**:213
    Kamehameha I **IV**:211
    Kennedy, Robert F. **IX**:171
    labor/labor movements
      IV:217–218
    Latino movement **IX**:185
    Lewis, John **IX**:190–191
    liberalism **VIII**:216; **IX**:191;
      X:208
    Liberia **IV**:225; **VI**:223
    LWV **IX**:187
    marriage and family **IV**:240–
      241; **X**:213
    Marshall, Thurgood **IX**:202
    Myrdal, Gunnar **VIII**:253
    NAACP **VII**:224; **VIII**:255;
      IX:232; **X**:244–245
    Native Americans **VIII**:263
    New Deal **VIII**:270
    New Frontier **IX**:243
    New Left **IX**:243
    Niagara Movement **VII**:240
    Niagara Movement
      Declaration of Principles
      VII:415–417**
    Nixon, Richard M. **X**:256
    Phillips, Wendell **IV**:299
    Plessy v. Ferguson **VI**:284–
      285, **433–438**
    political parties **X**:276
    Powell, Adam Clayton
      IX:261
    race and race relations
      VIII:319
    Randolph, A. Philip
      VIII:321
    Roosevelt, Eleanor
      VIII:343
    Roosevelt, Franklin D.
      VIII:346
    Scottsboro Boys **VIII**:353–
      354
    Second Great Awakening
      IV:337–338
    Selective Service **VIII**:358
    Seneca Falls convention
      IV:340–342
    sexual revolution **X**:322
    South **IX**:367
    States' Rights Party **IX**:299,
      300
    Still, William **IV**:357
    Supreme Court **VIII**:383,
      384
    Third New Deal **VIII**:393
    Thomas, Norman **VIII**:394
    Tourgée, Albion W. **V**:390
    Truman, Harry S. **IX**:320

    Urban League **IX**:325–326
    Wagner, Robert F. **VIII**:410
    Wallace, Henry A. **VIII**:411
    War on Poverty **IX**:335
    Warren Court **IX**:338
    White, Byron R. **X**:369
    White, Walter **VIII**:416
    Wilkins, Roy **IX**:344
    Willkie, Wendell L.
      VIII:417
    women's status and rights
      III:447–448
    Wright, Richard **VIII**:437
Civil Rights Act (1866) **V**:70–71,
  446*c*
    carpetbaggers **V**:56
    impeachment of Andrew
      Johnson **V**:202
    Johnson, Andrew **V**:213
    Radical Republicans **V**:321
    Reconstruction **V**:325
    Reconstruction Acts **V**:327
    Thirteenth Amendment
      V:388
Civil Rights Act (1875) **V**:71;
  VI:408*c*, 409*c*
    African Americans **VI**:5, 7
    Butler, Benjamin Franklin
      V:53
    Civil Rights Cases **VI**:72
    Field, Stephen Johnson
      VI:127
    Grant, Ulysses S. **V**:176
    Jim Crow laws **VI**:203
    Langston, John Mercer
      VI:219
    Sumner, Charles **V**:378
    Thirteenth Amendment
      V:388
Civil Rights Act (1957) **IX**:58–59,
  354*c*
Civil Rights Act (1960) **IX**:59–60,
  354*c*
Civil Rights Act (1964) **IX**:60–61,
  61, 355*c*, 356*c*
    affirmative action **X**:9
    African Americans **IX**:5;
      X:13
    assassination of Abraham
      Lincoln **V**:21
    Bakke case **X**:40
    Black Power **IX**:41
    Civil Rights Act (1991) **X**:77
    Democratic Party **IX**:85
    EEOC **IX**:110
    ESEA **IX**:106
    feminism **X**:132
    FEPC **VIII**:124
    Goldwater, Barry **IX**:136
    Graham, Billy **IX**:138
    *Gratz v. Bollinger/Grutter v.
      Bollinger* **X**:158
    Great Society **IX**:139
    *Griggs v. Duke Power
      Company* **X**:160
    *Heart of Atlanta Motel v.
      U.S.* **IX**:145, 146

    Humphrey, Hubert H.
      IX:151
    Jim Crow laws **VI**:203–204
    Johnson, Lady Bird **IX**:162
    Johnson, Lyndon B. **IX**:163
    Kennedy, Robert F. **IX**:171
    King, Martin Luther, Jr.
      IX:174
    labor/labor movements
      IX:182
    liberalism **X**:208
    March on Washington
      (1963) **IX**:201
    NOW **IX**:236; **X**:247
    Powell, Adam Clayton
      IX:261
    race and race relations
      IX:270; **X**:295
    segregation **IX**:288
    SNCC **IX**:303
    Southern Manifesto **IX**:294
    WEAL **IX**:345
    White Citizens' Councils
      IX:342
    women's status and rights
      IX:346, 347; **X**:371
Civil Rights Act (1991) **X**:76–77,
  380*c*
    affirmative action **X**:9
    Bush, George H. W. **X**:53
    race and race relations
      X:297
Civil Rights Cases (1883) **VI**:72
    due process clause **VI**:101
    Field, Stephen Johnson
      VI:127
    Harlan, John Marshall
      VI:159
    Jim Crow laws **VI**:203
    Supreme Court **VI**:348
Civil Rights movement
    African Americans **IX**:4–6
    Asian-American movement
      IX:21–22
    Baker v. Carr **IX**:33
    Baldwin, James **IX**:35
    Black Power **IX**:41–42
    Carmichael, Stokely **IX**:49
    civil disobedience **IX**:58
    Civil Rights Act (1957)
      IX:58–59
    Civil Rights Cases **VI**:72
    Civil War centennial **IX**:62
    Faubus, Orval **IX**:117–118
    folk music revival **IX**:121
    freedom rides **IX**:123–124
    gay and lesbian rights
      movement **X**:148
    Graham, Billy **IX**:138
    Hamer, Fannie Lou **IX**:141–
      142
    Hayden, Tom **IX**:143
    Hoover, J. Edgar **IX**:149–
      150
    "I Have a Dream" Speech
      (King) **IX**:373–375**
    Jackson, Jesse, L. **X**:191

journalism **IX:**166
Kennedy, John F. **IX:**170
Kennedy, Robert F. **IX:**171
King, Martin Luther, Jr. **IX:**173–175
KKK **IX:**179
"Letter from Birmingham Jail" (King) **IX:366–373**
Lewis, John **IX:**190
literature **IX:**194
Malcolm X **IX:**198–199
March on Washington (1963) **IX:**199–201
Marshall, Thurgood **IX:**202–203
Meredith, James **IX:**213
MFDP **IX:**219–220
modern Republicanism **IX:**221
Muhammad, Elijah **IX:**227
multiculturalism **X:**236
Murray, Pauli **IX:**227
music **IX:**229
NAACP **IX:**232; **X:**244
NASA **IX:**231
Parks, Rosa **IX:**254–255
Puerto Ricans **IX:**267
race and race relations **IX:**269
religion **IX:**272
Robinson, Jackie **IX:**277, 278
Savio, Mario **IX:**284
SCLC **IX:**292–294
segregation **IX:**288
sit-ins **IX:**290–291
SNCC **IX:**302
sports and recreation **IX:**298–299
teenagers **IX:**315
Till, Emmett Louis **IX:**318
UFW **IX:**324
Wallace, George C. **X:**364
Watts uprising **IX:**340
World War II **VIII:**428
Civil Service Commission
civil liberties **VIII:**71
PCSW **IX:**262
Roosevelt, Theodore **VII:**303–304
Civil Service Department **X:**132
civil service reform **VI:72–73,** 409c
Adams, Henry **VI:**1
Arthur, Chester Alan **VI:**20
Atkinson, Edward **VI:**22
Bayard, Thomas Francis **VI:**27
Beecher, Henry Ward **VI:**30
Cleveland, Grover **VI:**74
Congress **VI:**79, 80
Conkling, Roscoe **VI:**81
corruption, political **VI:**84
elections, conduct of **VI:**113
Forbes, John Murray **VI:**132
foreign policy **VI:**133, 134

Garfield, James Abram **VI:**138
Godkin, Edwin Lawrence **VI:**149
Hanna, Marcus Alonzo **VI:**158
Harrison, Benjamin **VI:**161
Hayes, Rutherford B. **VI:**167
Liberal Republican Party **VI:**222
Lockwood, Belva Ann Bennett McNall **VI:**229
mugwumps **VI:**252
presidency **VI:**290
presidential campaigns (1870–1899) **VI:**293
Schurz, Carl **VI:**324
Villard, Henry **VI:**375
White, Andrew Dickson **VI:**391
civil unions **X:**149–150, 383c. *See also* same-sex marriage
Civil War **V:71–75,** 72m, 444c
abolitionism **V:**4
ACS **IV:**17
African Americans **IV:**7
agriculture **IV:**12; **V:**6
Alabama, CSS **V:**7
American Fur Company **IV:**19
amnesty, acts of **V:**8
Andersonville Prison, Georgia **V:**10–11
Anthony, Susan B. **VI:**16
Appalachia **IX:**15
Arlington National Cemetery **V:**16
art **V:**18, 19
Atkinson, Edward **VI:**21
Balloon Corps **V:**25–26
Baltimore & Ohio Railroad **IV:**44
banking **IV:**47; **V:**26–28
Barton, Clara **V:**29
battle flags **V:**31
Bennett, James Gordon, Jr. **VI:**32
Bickerdyke, Mary Ann **V:**34
Bidwell, John **IV:**56
Bierstadt, Albert **VI:**37
Birth of a Nation, The **VII:**37
Bloomer, Amelia **IV:**60
blues **VII:**39
Bowles, Samuel **VI:**42–43
Brady, Mathew B. **V:**41
bridges **VI:**47
brothers' war **V:**43
Brown, William Wells **V:**46
Burnside, Ambrose E. **V:**51–52
Canada **VI:**61
Carson, Kit **IV:**82
cartography **V:**57
Cassatt, Mary **VI:**63
cattle kingdom **VI:**64

Catto, Octavius V. **V:**59
Cherokee **IV:**86
cities and urban life **IV:**91, 93
citizenship **VII:**57
civil service reform **VI:**72
code breaking **VIII:**76
Cody, William Frederick **VI:**75
common soldier **V:**77–79
Compromise of 1850 **IV:**104
Congress **VI:**79; **VII:**61
conscription **V:**90–92; **VII:**62
conservation/environmentalism **VI:**81
contract labor **VI:**82
Corps d'Afrique **V:**96
cotton culture **IV:**107, 109
Creek **IV:**110
currency issue **VI:**88, 89
Dana, Charles A. **VI:**91
Davis Bend, Mississippi, freedmen's colony **V:**106
Deere, John **IV:**116
Delany, Martin Robinson **V:**108
Democratic Party **IV:**119; **V:**109; **VII:**74
desertion **V:**110–111
disease/epidemics **V:**112
Dix, Dorothea **IV:**125
Dred Scott decision **V:**116–118
Eads, James Buchanan **VI:**103
economy **V:**121–123
education **IV:**134, 135; **V:**124; **VI:**109
education, philanthropy and **VI:**112
elections **V:**125–126
Emerson, Ralph Waldo **IV:**139, 140
employment **V:**132–133
entertainment, popular **VI:**116, 117
Exodusters **VI:**122
exploration **IV:**146
federal income tax **VII:**106
Federal Reserve Act **VII:**107
field fortifications **V:**139–141
fire-eaters **V:**146
Forbes, John Murray **VI:**132
foreign policy **IV:**153, 156; **V:**149–151
Fort Laramie **IV:**158
Fort Leavenworth **IV:**158
Forty-niners **IV:**160
Foster, Abigail Kelley **IV:**162
Frémont, Jesse Benton **IV:**166

Frémont, John C. **IV:**167
fugitive slave laws **IV:**168, 169
fur trade **IV:**171
Garfield, James Abram **VI:**138
Garnet, Henry Highland **IV:**174
Garrison, William Lloyd **V:**165
German-American regiments **V:**165–166
Gettysburg Address **V:169, 461**
Godkin, Edwin Lawrence **VI:**149
Goldmark, Josephine Clara **VII:**127
governors **V:**171
Greeley, Horace **V:**177
Griffith, David Wark **VII:**131
Halleck, Henry Wager **V:**182
Harlan, John Marshall **VI:**159
Harper, Frances Ellen Watkins **V:**184; **VI:**160
Harrison, Benjamin **VI:**160
Hastings, Lansford W. **IV:**187
Hayden, Ferdinand Vandeveer **VI:**165
Hayes, Rutherford B. **VI:**166, 167
Higginson, Thomas Wentworth **VI:**171
Hollywood Cemetery **V:**192
Holmes, Oliver Wendell **VII:**140
homefront **V:**192–194
Homer, Winslow **VI:**174
Hood, John Bell **V:**195, 196
Houston, Sam **IV:**192
Huntington, Collis Potter **VI:**180
immigration **IV:**196; **V:**199–201
immigration restrictions **VI:**187
impressment **V:**203
Indian Affairs, Office of **VI:**189
industrial development **IV:**199; **V:**204–205
Ingersoll, Robert Green **VI:**193
Internal Revenue taxes **VI:**194
investments, American, abroad **VI:**197
investments, foreign, in the United States **VI:**197
Irish-American regiments **V:**205
ironclad oath **V:**206
ironclads **V:**207

Civil War (*continued*)
Jackson, Claiborne F. **V:**209
Jim Crow laws **VI:**203
Johnson, Andrew **V:**212
Joint Committee on the
Conduct of the War
V:215–216
Jomini, Antoine-Henri,
baron de **V:**216–217
journalism **IV:**210; **V:**217–
219
Ku Klux Klan **VII:**165
labor/labor movements
IV:219
ladies aid societies **V:**227
Langston, John Mercer
VI:218
Leslie, Frank and Miriam
Florence Follin **VI:**221
Letcher, John **V:**232
letters **V:**232–233
Liberal Republican Party
VI:222
Liberia **VI:**223
Lincoln, Abraham **V:**236
literature **V:**239; **VI:**224,
225
lobbying **VI:**228
lyceum movement **IV:**232
lynching **VI:**229
Magoffin, James W. **IV:**233
Manifest Destiny **IV:**236
marine corps **V:**248
The Masses **VII:**193
McClellan, George Brinton
V:250
McCormick, Cyrus Hall
IV:243–245
McDowell, Irvin **V:**252–253
McKinley, William **VI:**240
McLaws, Lafayette **V:**253
Medal of Honor **V:**255
medicine **V:**256–259
merchant marine **VI:**245
Mexican-American War
IV:253
mining **VII:**207
Mississippi River war **V:**263
Missouri Compromise
IV:257
Mobile campaign **V:**264–
265
Molly Maguires **VI:**248
monuments **V:**267–268
Moody, Dwight Lyman
VI:249
Morgan, John Pierpont
VI:250
Mormon Church **IV:**90
Mormon War **IV:**263
Morse, Samuel F. B. **IV:**265
Morton, Oliver P. **V:**270
Mott, Lucretia **IV:**266
music **V:**272–274
Nast, Thomas **V:**275
national banking system
VI:260

national military parks
V:276
Native Americans **V:**277–
279
NRA **X:**248
nurses **V:**285–286
occupational health and
safety **VII:**243
overland mail **IV:**291
Pacific Railroad Act **V:**293
panic of 1837 **IV:**295
Parkman, Francis **VI:**277
Phillips, Wendell **IV:**299
Pingree, Hazen S. **VII:**260
popular culture **VII:**263
Powell, John Wesley **VI:**287
presidency **VII:**268
Quantrill, William Clarke
V:317–318
Quay, Matthew Stanley
VI:299
race and race relations
IV:309, 311, 312
railroads **IV:**316
Reid, Whitelaw **VI:**304
religion **IV:**321; **VI:**306
Republican Party **IV:**322
Rhodes, James Ford **VI:**312
Ross, John **V:**325
rules of war **V:**338
St. Vrain, Céran **IV:**328
Santa Fe Trail **IV:**332
Schurz, Carl **VI:**324
science and technology
V:340–343
Scott, Thomas Alexander
VI:326
Scott, Winfield **IV:**336
segregation **VII:**319
Selective Service Act
VII:321
Seminole **IV:**338
Seminole War, First/Second
IV:339, 340
Seton, Elizabeth Ann
IV:344
slavery **III:**391; **IV:**344, 346;
V:363–364
Society of Friends **V:**364–
365
sports and recreation **V:**366–
367; **VII:**333, 334
strikes **V:**374–375
Supreme Court **IV:**362
Taney, Roger B. **IV:**367
Tappan, Arthur and Lewis
IV:367
taxation **V:**384
temperance movement
IV:370
Thirteenth Amendment
V:387–388
Tilden, Samuel Jones
VI:357
trade, domestic and foreign
VII:354
Truth, Sojourner **V:**393

Tubman, Harriet **V:**394
UMWA **VII:**359
U.S. Army Corps of
Engineers **V:**407
U.S. Military Academy at
West Point **V:**409
U.S. Naval Academy at
Annapolis **V:**410
Vallandigham, Clement L.
V:413
Vance, Zebulon B. **V:**414
Van Lew, Elizabeth **V:**414–
415
Vesey, Denmark **IV:**388
veterans **VII:**371
Villard, Henry **VI:**374
violence and lawlessness
VI:375–376
volunteer army **V:**418–420
Wakeman, Sarah Rosetta
V:422
Walker, Mary Edwards
V:422, 423
Wallace, Lew **VI:**381
Ward, Lester Frank **VI:**382
Washington, D.C. **V:**425–
427
Watterson, Henry **VI:**386
Weather Bureau, U.S.
VI:387
White, Andrew Dickson
VI:391
Williams, George
Washington **VI:**395
women soldiers **V:**435–436
women's status and rights
V:437
Young, Brigham **IV:**408
Zouaves **V:**441
Civil War Bench **V:**267
Civil War centennial **IX:**61–62
Civil War Soldier's Orphans Home
(Glenwood, Iowa) **VII:**341
Civil Works Administration
(CWA) **VIII:74, 444***c***
cities and urban life **VIII:**69
FERA **VIII:**133
Hopkins, Harry L. **VIII:**176
marriage and family
VIII:231
New Deal **VIII:**269
PWA **VIII:**314
relief **VIII:**332
Social Security Act
VIII:363
WPA **VIII:**425
Claflin, Tennessee **VI:**336
Claiborne, William C. C. **II:**219,
220; **IV:94–95**
claim clubs **IV:95–96**, 305–306
claim jumpers **IV:**56, 95
Clancy, Deirdre **IX:**117
Clan na Gael **V:**201
clans
Crow **II:**85
Huron **I:**172; **II:**169
Iroquois **I:**186

Mali **I:**226
Mpongwe **I:**255
sachems **II:**341
Clansman, The (Dixon)
Birth of a Nation, The
VII:37
Ku Klux Klan **VII:**165
Trotter, William Monroe
VII:357
Clarel (Melville) **VI:**227
Clarenbach, Kathryn **X:**247
Clarenbach, Kay **IX:**236
Clark, Dick **X:**239
Clark, Ellery **VI:**359
Clark, George Rogers **III:95,
95–96**, 461***c***
Clark, William **III:**96
Genêt, Edmond Charles
III:191
Native Americans **III:**314
Clark, Jonas Gilman **VI:**157
Clark, J. Reuben **VII:**58
Clark, Kenneth **IX:**44
Clark, Mamie **IX:**44
Clark, Mark (Black Panther party
member) **IX:**41
Clark, Mark W. (U.S. general)
VIII:191
Clark, Maurice **VII:**335
Clark, Thomas **IX:**86, 146
Clark, Tom C. **IX:**33
Clark, William **III:96–97**, 465***c***
American Philosophical
Society **III:**18
Astor, John Jacob **IV:**33
Astoria **IV:**35
Catlin, George **IV:**84
Clark, George Rogers **III:**95
Columbia River **IV:**103
exploration **IV:**144
Kearny, Stephen Watts
IV:212
Lewis, Meriwether **III:**261,
262
Lewis and Clark Expedition
III:262–264
Native Americans **IV:**273
Oregon Trail **IV:**285
race and race relations
IV:311
Reagan, Ronald W. **X:**301
Sacagawea **III:**377
temperance movement
III:410
Clarke, Arthur C. **IX:**287
Clarke, Herbert L. **VI:**339
Clarke, John
Baptists **II:**33
Rhode Island **II:**333
Williams, Roger **II:**416
Clark Institute for Deaf Children
VII:63
Clark Memorandum **VII:58–59**,
409***c***
Clarkson, Thomas **III:**127
Clark University **VI:**157–158;
VII:118

class **II:69–71**
  Aleut **II:**17
  Bacon's Rebellion **II:**31
  cities and urban life **II:**69
  clothing **II:**71
  consumption **II:**79
  Dale, Sir Thomas **II:**89
  dance **II:**90
  economy **II:**110
  education **II:**112
  English Civil War **II:**116
  ethnocentrism **II:**121, 122
  Georgia **II:**145
  Great Awakening **II:**156
  housing **II:**167
  labor/labor movements
    II:200
  marriage and family **II:**217
  Massachusetts **II:**224
  miscegenation **II:**237, 238
  slave resistance **II:**353
class-action lawsuits **X:**353
class consciousness **VI:73–74,**
  225, 374
classical architecture **VII:**18–20
classical art **X:**31
classical liberalism **X:**207–208
classical music **VII:**219–220;
  VIII:252; **X:**238
classicism **VI:**18, 19; **X:**31
Classic period (Mesoamerica)
  I:234–235
Claverack College **VII:**312
Clay, Cassius. *See* Ali, Muhammad
Clay, Henry **IV:96–98,** 97,
  412c–414c
  abolitionism **V:**1
  ACS **IV:**17
  Adams, John Quincy **IV:**5–6
  American System **IV:**19–21
  anti-Masonry **IV:**25
  banking **IV:**46
  Benton, Thomas Hart
    IV:53
  Bonus Bill **IV:**62
  Compromise of 1850
    IV:103, **446–449**
  Democratic Party **IV:**118
  election of 1828 **IV:**135
  election of 1840 **IV:**137,
    139
  Fillmore, Millard **IV:**149,
    150
  Free Trade and Sailor's
    Rights **IV:**165
  Harrison, William Henry
    IV:185
  internal improvements
    IV:203
  Jackson, Andrew **IV:**206
  Liberia **IV:**225
  Liberty Party **IV:**226
  Lincoln, Abraham **V:**235
  Mexican-American War
    IV:251
  Missouri Compromise
    IV:257

  music **IV:**269
  National Road **IV:**271
  Nullification Controversy
    IV:283
  Oregon Treaty of 1846
    IV:287
  Polk, James K. **IV:**302
  public land policy **IV:**306
  Tallmadge Amendment
    IV:365
  tariffs **V:**383
  Taylor, Zachary **IV:**368
  Tyler, John **IV:**382, 383
  War Hawks **IV:**389
  Webster, Daniel **IV:**393
  Whigs **IV:**396, 397
Clay, Lucius **IX:**159
Clay, Margaret Meuse **II:**33
Clayton, John **IV:**98
Clayton, Powell **V:**223
Clayton Antitrust Act **VII:59,**
  406c
  Adamson Act **VII:**2
  AFL **VII:**12
  business **VII:**46
  Capper-Volstead Act **VII:**49
  Democratic Party **VII:**74
  Federal Trade Commission
    Act **VII:**108
  labor/labor movements
    VII:170, 172
  lobbying **VII:**181
  muckrakers **VII:**217
  New Unionism **VII:**238
  progressivism **VII:**271
  Wilson, Thomas Woodrow
    VII:384
Clayton-Bulwer Treaty **IV:98–99,**
  415c
  foreign policy **IV:**154;
    V:149–150
  McKinley, William **VI:**241
  Panama Canal **VII:**250
Clean Air Act (1963) **IX:**47
Clean Air Act amendments (1990)
  X:53, 91, 379c
Clean Air Act Extension (1970)
  X:375c, **386**
  automobile industry **X:**35
  environment **IX:**109
  property rights **X:**290
Clean Water Act (1972) **X:**290,
  376c
"clear and present danger"
  VII:313, 407c; **IX:**86
Clear Skies Initiative **X:**56, 92
Cleaver, Eldridge **IX:**35, 41
Cleburne, Patrick R. **V:**63, 64,
  75, 419
Clem, Johnny **V:**273
Clemenceau, Georges **VII:**175,
  369
Clemens, Samuel Langhorne. *See*
  Twain, Mark
Clement VIII (pope) **I:**80
Clemson College **VI:**358
Clendinnen, Inga **I:**323

clerical occupations
  business **IX:**46, 47
  economy **IX:**97
  labor/labor movements
    IX:181
Clermont (steamboat) **III:**465c
  economy **IV:**130
  Fulton, Robert **III:**183
  science and technology
    III:385; **IV:**333
Cleveland, Grover **VI:74–75,** 75,
  95, 292, 409c–411c
  Alexander, Edward P. **V:**8
  Angell, James Burrill **VI:**15
  Atkinson, Edward **VI:**22
  Bayard, Thomas Francis
    VI:27, 28
  Blaine, James Gillespie
    VI:41
  Congress **VI:**80
  Cuba **VI:**88
  currency issue **VI:**89–90
  Dana, Charles A. **VI:**92
  Dawes Severalty Act **VI:**93
  Debs, Eugene Victor **VII:**73
  Democratic Party **V:**110;
    VI:95
  Forest Reserve Act **VI:**134
  Free-Silver movement
    VI:135
  Geological Survey, U.S.
    VI:141
  Grand Army of the Republic
    VI:152
  Harrison, Benjamin **VI:**161,
    162
  Hawaii **VI:**163
  Higginson, Thomas
    Wentworth **VI:**172
  immigration restrictions
    VI:187
  Morgan, John Pierpont
    VI:251
  mugwumps **VI:**252
  political parties, third
    VI:286
  presidency **VI:**290
  presidential campaigns
    (1870–1899) **VI:**293
  Pullman Strike **VI:**297
  Reid, Whitelaw **VI:**305
  Republican Party **VI:**311
  Samoa **VI:**323
  Schurz, Carl **VI:**325
  Statue of Liberty **VI:**344
  tariffs **VI:**352
  Tillman, Benjamin Ryan
    VI:358
  Van Lew, Elizabeth **V:**415
  Venezuela boundary dispute
    VI:373
  veterans **V:**415
  volunteer army **V:**420
  Watterson, Henry **VI:**386
Cleveland, Ohio
  Bourke-White, Margaret
    VIII:50

  currency issue **VI:**89
  Free-Soil Party **IV:**164
  Hanna, Marcus Alonzo
    VI:158
  internal improvements
    IV:202
  Johnson, Tom Loftin
    VII:156
  libraries, public **VI:**224
  music **VII:**219
  oil **VI:**271
  oil industry **VII:**244
  rust belt **X:**314
  Standard Oil **VII:**335
  urban reform **VII:**362
Cleveland Emigration Convention
  VI:218
Cleveland Foundation **VIII:**243
Cleveland Orchestra **VIII:**134
Cleveland Press **VII:**159–160
Clift, Montgomery **IX:**223
Clifton, New Jersey **VII:**253
climate
  Andes Mountains **I:**9
  Brazil **I:**33
  Peru **I:**289
Clinton, DeWitt **III:97–98;**
  IV:411c
  Catlin, George **IV:**84
  Erie Canal **IV:**141
  transportation **V:**390
  Willard, Emma **IV:**401
Clinton, George **III:**98, **98–99**
  Bank of the United States,
    First **III:**41
  Clinton, DeWitt **III:**97
  Constitution, ratification of
    the **III:**105–106
  Shays's Rebellion **III:**388
  Yates, Abraham **III:**453
Clinton, Sir Henry **III:99–100,**
  461c, 462c
  André, John **III:**20
  Burgoyne, Sir John **III:**67, 68
  Charleston, siege of **III:**84,
    85
  Charleston Expedition of
    1776 **III:**83–84
  Cornwallis, Charles, Lord
    III:120, 121
  Estaing, Charles-Henri
    Theodat, comte d'
    III:158
  Hudson Highlands
    campaign **III:**216
  Knyphausen, Wilhelm,
    Baron von **III:**248
  Monmouth, Battle of
    III:299–300
  Moore's Creek Bridge,
    Battle of **III:**301
  Revolutionary War **III:**368
  Saratoga, surrender at
    III:382
  Savannah, Battle of **III:**382
  Yorktown, surrender at
    III:454, 455

Clinton, Hillary Rodham **X:77–79**, *78*, 383*c*
  Clinton, William J. **X:**79, 82
  elections, presidential **X:**118
  Mitchell, George **X:**232
  Rumsfeld, Donald **X:**313
  Starr, Kenneth **X:**332
  women's status and rights **X:**371
Clinton, Joseph J. **VI:**5
Clinton, William (New York colonial governor) **II:**93
Clinton, William J., and administration **X:79–84**, *80*, 380*c*–382*c*
  ABM Treaty **X:**28
  abortion **X:**4–5
  Africa **X:**16
  Albright, Madeleine K. **X:**22
  Amendments to the U.S. Constitution **X:**23
  Angelou, Maya **X:**26
  Articles of Impeachment **X:409–411**
  baby boomers **X:**39
  Breyer, Stephen **X:**48
  Bush, George H. W. **X:**53
  campaign finance **X:**63
  capital punishment **X:**66
  Clinton, Hillary Rodham **X:77–79**
  conservative movement **X:**94
  crime and punishment **X:**97
  Dayton accords **X:**99
  defense policy **X:**101
  Dole, Robert **X:**105
  Dukakis, Michael S. **X:**106
  economy **X:**110
  education, primary/secondary **X:**115
  elections, presidential **X:**116
  federalism **X:**131
  feminism **X:**134
  foreign policy **X:**142, 143
  Galbraith, John Kenneth **IX:**130
  gay and lesbian rights movement **X:**149
  Ginsburg, Ruth Bader **X:**152
  Gore, Albert, Jr. **X:**156, 157
  gun control **X:**161
  Haiti **X:**164
  Helms, Jesse A., Jr. **X:**165
  House of Representatives **X:**170
  immigration **X:**177
  impeachment **X:**178
  Inaugural Address, Second **X:407–409**
  independent counsel **X:**179
  Iraq War **X:**186
  Judicial Watch **X:**194
  Korematsu v. U.S. **VIII:**203
  Kosovo **X:**199
  Latin America **X:**206

  Mexico **X:**226
  Middle East **X:**229
  Mitchell, George **X:**232
  Mondale, Walter F. **X:**234
  Nader, Ralph **X:**242
  neoconservatism **X:**252
  NEPA **X:**246
  North Vietnam **X:**260
  OMB **X:**266
  Parks, Rosa **IX:**255
  Perot, H. Ross **X:**273
  Persian Gulf War **X:**274
  political parties **X:**276
  pornography **X:**284
  Powell, Colin L. **X:**286–287
  pro-life/pro-choice movements **X:**289
  property rights **X:**290
  Reno, Janet **X:**308–309
  RFRA **X:**307
  SDI **X:**337
  Senate, U.S. **X:**321
  South Africa **X:**325
  Starr, Kenneth **X:**332, 333
  Supreme Court **X:**339
  tobacco suits **X:**353
  USA PATRIOT Act **X:**359
  veto (presidential) **X:**361
clipper ships **VI:**245
Cloak Makers' Strike (1910) **VII:**149
cloning, human **X:**172, 381*c*
Close, Chuck **X:**31
Closing Circle, The (Commoner) **X:**90
Closing of the American Mind, The (Bloom) **X:**94
Clotel, or the President's Daughter (Brown) **IV:**415*c*
cloth **I:**143
clothing **II:71–73**, *72*
  childhood **II:**67
  Confederate army **V:**81
  consumption **II:**79
  fashion **V:**138–139
  Flathead Indians **II:**127
  fur trade **II:**142
  homespun **V:**194
  industrial development **V:**204, 205
  Lewis, John L. **VIII:**213
  Muslims **II:**248
  rationing **VIII:**322
  society, British American **II:**367
Clovis Man **I:**263
Clovis people **I:**251
Club of Rome **X:**90
Clyburn, James **X:**171
Clyman, James **IV:**125
CNLU (Colored National Labor Union) **V:77**
CNN (Cable News Network) **X:**218, 280, 344
Coahuila-Texas, Mexico
  Austin, Stephen F. **IV:**40
  Houston, Sam **IV:**191

  Texas **IV:**372
  Texas Revolution **IV:**373, 374.
coal
  Hopi **I:**167–168
  industrialization **IV:**199
  mining **VI:**246, 247
Coal Arbitration Board **VIII:**75
coal industry **VIII:74–76**, 75
  Anthracite Coal Strike **VII:**15
  Frick, Henry Clay **VI:**135
  industrial development **V:**204
  Lewis, John L. **VIII:**213
  South **VIII:**366
Coalition for the Free Exercise of Religion **X:**307
coal miners **V:**374
Coast Guard, U.S.
  Hurricane Katrina **X:**173, 174
  Navy, U.S. **VIII:**265
  women's status and rights **VIII:**424
Cobain, Kurt **X:**238, 280
Cobb, David **X:**118
Cobb, Howell **V:75–76**
Cobb, Ty **VIII:**445*c*
Cobbett, William **III:**80
Cobden, Richard **V:**46
Coca-Cola Company **IX:**46
Coca-Cola Export Corporation **VIII:**125
cocaine **X:**243–244
cochineal **I:**269
Cochise **V:**444*c*
Cochran, Jacqueline **VIII:**419
Cochrane, Alexander **IV:**43
Cocke, Abraham **I:**28
Cocoanuts, The (film) **VIII:**443*c*
cod **I:76–77**, 272
Coddington, William **II:**73, 267, 333
Code and Cipher School (Bletchley Park) (MI-6) **VIII:**76, 187
code breaking **VIII:76**
  Atlantic, Battle of the **VIII:**33
  espionage **VIII:**117
  intelligence **VIII:**186
  Stimson, Henry L. **VIII:**375
  technology **VIII:**389
  WAVES **VIII:**418
Code for the Government of Armies, A (Lieber) **V:**234
code talkers **VIII:**264, *264*
Codex Aubin **I:**410
Codex Matritense. *See* Florentine Codex
Codex Mendoza **I:**77, **77–78**
  Mendoza, Antonio de **I:**239
  Nahuatl **I:**258
  Thevet, André **I:**358

Cody, William Frederick "Buffalo Bill" **VI:75–77**, *76*, *118*, 409*c*
  entertainment, popular **VI:**118
  literature **VI:**225
  Native Americans **VI:**263
  Sitting Bull **VI:**332
  Wild West shows **VI:**225
Coe, Conway **VIII:**283
Coelho, Anthony **X:**24–25, 373
Coelho, Jorge d'Albuquerque **I:78–79**, 334
Coercive Acts **III:100**, 460*c*
  Association, the **III:**37
  Boston Tea Party **III:**59
  Burke, Edmund **III:**69
  committees of correspondence **III:**101
  Continental Congress, First **III:**113
  Dickinson, John **III:**137
  Franklin, Benjamin **III:**173
  Gage, Thomas **III:**187
  Hutchinson, Thomas **III:**219
  Lexington and Concord, Battles of **III:**264
  North, Frederick, Lord **III:**320
  resistance movement **III:**366
  Revere, Paul **III:**367
  Suffolk Resolves **III:**400
  Wayne, Anthony **III:**433
Coeur d'Alene miners' strike **VI:77**, 213
coffee **I:79–80**
  alcohol **III:**13
  black market **VIII:**46
  OPA **VIII:**282
  rationing **VIII:**322
Cofitachequi **I:80–81**
cofradias **II:**373, 374
Cogswell, William **V:**34
cohabitation **X:**213–214
Cohan, George M.
  Committee for Public Information **VII:**60
  entertainment, popular **VII:**96
  music **VII:**219
  Tin Pan Alley **VII:**353
Cohen, Stanley **X:**224
Cohen, William **X:**102, 232
Cohen v. California **X:**369
Cohn, Roy **IX:**18
Co-Hong import-export monopoly **III:**88
COI (Coordinator of Information) **VIII:**284
coinage **IV:**413*c*; **V:**27
Coinage Act (1792) **IV:**47
Coinage Act (1834) **IV:**47
Coinage Act (1837) **IV:**47
Coinage Act (1873) **VI:**408*c*
  bimetallism **VI:**38
  Bland-Allison Act **VI:**41
  Crime of '73 **VI:**86
  currency issue **VI:**89

Coin's Financial School (Harvey)
 VI:90
Coit, Stanton **VI:**121, 327
coke (coal) **VI:**135, 136
Coke, Sir Edward **III:**256
Coke, Thomas **III:**36
Coker v. Georgia **X:**66
COLA. *See* cost-of-living
 adjustment
Colambu (king of Limasawa
 Island) **I:**224
Colbert, Claudette **VIII:**246
Colbert, Jean-Baptiste **II:**137
Colby, William **VIII:**285
Colden, Cadwallader **II:73,** 209,
 345
Colden, Jane **II:73–74**
Cold Harbor, Battle of **V:76–77**
 field fortifications **V:**141
 Grant, Ulysses S. **V:**174
 Hancock, Winfield Scott
  V:184
 Hill, Ambrose P. **V:**190
 homefront **V:**193
 Lee, Robert E. **V:**231
 Meade, George Gordon
  V:254
 Overland campaign **V:**291
Cold Mountain (Frazier) **V:**240
Cold Springs, New York **V:**374
cold war **IX:62–64,** 352c
 Acheson, Dean **IX:**2
 AEC **IX:**24
 Americans for Democratic
  Action **IX:**13
 anticommunism **IX:**14
 arms race **IX:**17
 Asia **IX:**20
 aviation **IX:**28
 Berlin blockade **IX:**38–39
 Catholic Bishops' Letter
  X:70
 Chambers, Whittaker **IX:**53
 CIA **IX:**52
 Civil War centennial **IX:**62
 communism **IX:**67
 conscription, end of **X:**89
 conservatism **VIII:**85; **IX:**75
 conservative movement
  X:93
 consumerism **IX:**75
 Dennis v. U.S. **IX:**86
 domino theory **IX:**89
 Dulles, John Foster **IX:**91
 DuPont Corporation **IX:**91
 elections **IX:**104
 Europe **IX:**112
 Fair Deal **IX:**115
 Federal Employee Loyalty
  Program **IX:**119
 Ford Motor Corporation
  IX:123
 foreign policy **X:**142
 Freedom Train **IX:**125
 Graham, Billy **IX:**138
 HUAC **IX:**150
 hydrogen bomb **IX:**152

immigration **IX:**155
Internal Security Act (1950)
 IX:157
Internet **X:**181
Interstate Highway Act of
 1956 **IX:**158
Johnson, Lyndon B. **IX:**164
journalism **IX:**166
Kennan, George F. **IX:**167–
 168
Kennedy, John F. **IX:**170–
 171
Korean War **IX:**177–179
Latin America **IX:**183
marriage and family **IX:**202
Marshall Plan **IX:**203–204,
 359–361
medicine **IX:**212
Middle East **IX:**214; **X:**227
military-industrial complex
 IX:216
movies **IX:**224
NASA **IX:**231
National Security Act of
 1947 **IX:**237
Native Americans **IX:**241
NATO **IX:**246; **X:**259
NEA **IX:**234
NEH **IX:**235
neoconservatism **X:**251
New Frontier **IX:**243
NSC-68 **IX:**247
OSRD **VIII:**284
OSS **VIII:**285
Peace Corps **IX:**255
Port Huron Statement
 IX:260
Potsdam Conference
 VIII:307
religion **VIII:**335, 336;
 IX:272
science fiction **IX:**287
SDS **IX:**303
shopping centers **IX:**289,
 290
Smith Act **VIII:**361
"Sources of Soviet Conduct"
 (Kennan) **IX:363–366**
Soviet Union **IX:**295
Suez crisis **IX:**307
technology **IX:**311
teenagers **IX:**314
treaty rights **IX:**319
Truman, Harry S. **IX:**320
Truman Doctrine **IX:**321–
 322, 351c, 359–361
UN **X:**355
Vietnam War **IX:**330
wars of national liberation
 IX:338
cold war, end of **X:84–86.** *See
 also* Soviet Union, breakup of
 ABM Treaty **X:**26
 Africa **X:**15
 arms race **X:**30
 Bush, George H. W.
  X:51–53

defense policy **X:**101
INF Treaty **X:**181
Iron Curtain, collapse of
 X:188–189
Latin America **X:**204
NATO **X:**260
space policy **X:**326
Vietnam War, end of U.S.
 involvement **X:**361
cold war culture **IX:64–65**
 Civil War centennial **IX:**62
 commemoration **IX:**65–66
 Native Americans **IX:**241
Cole, Lester **IX:**147, *148*
Cole, Thomas **IV:**28, 29; **V:**18
Cole, Timothy **VI:**147
Cole, USS **X:**10, 346, 383c
Colegrove v. Green **IX:**33
Coleman, Glenn **VII:**26
Coleridge, Samuel Taylor **IV:**379
Colfax Courthouse **V:**412
Colgate, William
 economy **IV:**131
 industrialization **IV:**199
 religion **IV:**320
Colgate Company **VII:**290
Colgate-Palmolive Company
 X:303
Colhuacan **I:**18
Coligny, Gaspard de **I:**208
collective bargaining **VIII:**445c
 AFL **VI:**13
 agriculture **IX:**7; **X:**20
 automobile industry
  VIII:36
 Fair Labor Standards Act
  VIII:124
 Higgins, Andrew J.
  VIII:165
 ILGWU **VIII:**187
 labor/labor movements
  VIII:206, 208; **X:**203
 Lewis, John L. **VIII:**213
 mining **VII:**209
 New Deal **VIII:**269
 NLRA **VIII:**257–258
 NLRB **VIII:**258–259
 Progressive Party **VII:**270
 progressivism **VII:**271
 Taft-Hartley Act **IX:**309
 UFW **IX:**325
 UMWA **VIII:**401
 Wagner, Robert F.
  VIII:410
college(s). *See also specific
 colleges and universities*
 African-American churches,
  growth of **VI:**4
 African Americans **VI:**7
 agriculture **VI:**8
 baby boomers **X:**40
 education **III:**148–149;
  VII:88–89
 education, higher **VI:**111;
  X:111, 112
 feminism **X:**133
 football **VI:**130–131

*Gratz v. Bollinger/Grutter v.
 Bollinger* **X:**158–159
 marriage and family
  VIII:231
 multiculturalism **X:**236, 237
 NYA **VIII:**263
 women's status and rights
  VIII:422
college admissions policies
 affirmative action **X:**10
 Bakke case **X:**40–41
 *Gratz v. Bollinger/Grutter v.
  Bollinger* **X:**158–159
College Entrance Examining
 Board **VI:**114
college football **VIII:**371
College of Charleston **IV:**166
College of New Jersey **III:**445.
 See also Princeton College/
 University
College of Philadelphia **II:74,**
 113
 Anglican Church **III:**20
 medicine **III:**295, 296
 Rush, Benjamin **III:**375
College of Physicians and
 Surgeons **IV:**184
College of William and Mary
 II:74
 Anglican Church **II:**22;
  III:20
 lawyers **III:**256
 Marshall, John **III:**289
 Monroe, James **IV:**258
 Randolph, Edmund
  III:358
 Virginia **II:**401
College Settlement Association
 VI:327
Collier, John
 Indian Reorganization Act
  VIII:185–186
 Native Americans **VII:**233;
  VIII:264
 race and race relations
  VIII:318–319
Collier's
 journalism **VII:**159
 literature **VII:**179
 The Masses **VII:**193
Colloquy of Regensburg **I:**98
Colman, Samuel **IV:**356
Colmer, William **VIII:**326
Colombia **IV:**414c; **VII:**404c,
 406c
 Big Stick diplomacy **VII:**34
 Bush, George H. W. **X:**52
 Bush, George W. **X:**56
 foreign policy **V:**149, 151;
  VII:114; **X:**144
 Harrison, William Henry
  IV:185–186
 Monroe Doctrine **IV:**259
 Panama Canal **VII:**251
Colón, Panama **VII:**251
Colonel Dismounted, The (Bland)
 III:53

Colonial Air Transport **VII:**28, 165
colonial period
    alcohol **III:**13
    citizenship **III:**92
    corporations **III:**121
    dueling **III:**140
    education **III:**147
    environment **III:**153–154
    Florida **III:**166–167
    foreign affairs **III:**168
    impeachment **III:**222
    impressment **III:**222–223
    Industrial Revolution **III:**224
    insurance **III:**227
    political parties **III:**338
    popular culture **III:**341
    prisons **III:**346
    privateering **III:**347
    race and race relations **III:**357
    religion **III:**360
    religious liberty **III:**362
    republicanism **III:**365
    resistance movement **III:**365–366
    science and technology **III:**384–385
    West Indies **III:**436
    Wilkes, John **III:**443
    women's status and rights **III:**446
Colonial Williamsburg, Virginia **IX:**66
colonization (African) **IV:**411*c*
    abolitionism **IV:**1–3; **V:**1
    ACS **IV:**16–17
    American Anti-Slavery Society **IV:**16
    Crummell, Alexander **VI:**87
    Delany, Martin Robinson **V:**107
    foreign policy **VI:**134
    Forten, James **III:**170
    Garnet, Henry Highland **IV:**175
    Garrison, William Lloyd **V:**164
    King, Rufus **III:**246
    Liberia **IV:**225
    Negro Convention movement **IV:**279, 280
    slavery **V:**362
    Socialist Party **VI:**337
    Williams, George Washington **VI:**396
colonization/colonists (European).
    See specific countries, e.g.:
    English colonization
Colony for Epileptics and Feebleminded **VII:**43
Colorado **IV:**414*c*
    Carson, Kit **IV:**82
    Cody, William Frederick **VI:**75
    Deseret, State of **IV:**120

dust bowl **VIII:**97
elections, conduct of **VI:**113
exploration **IV:**144
gay and lesbian rights movement **X:**149
gold **IV:**179
Haywood, William Dudley **VII:**137
immigration **IV:**193
Indian Rights Association **VI:**190
Japanese Americans, relocation of **VIII:**194
La Raza Unida **IX:**183
medicine **X:**223
mining **VII:**209
National Reclamation Act **VII:**229
Native Americans **IV:**275
Non-Partisan League **VII:**241
Pike, Zebulon Montgomery **IV:**300
population trends **X:**282
pro-life/pro-choice movements **X:**289
Santa Fe Trail **IV:**330
Texas **IV:**372
tourism **IX:**319
UMWA **VII:**360
Villard, Henry **VI:**374
woman suffrage **VII:**384
women's status and rights **VI:**399
Colorado Fuel and Iron Company **VII:**186
Colorado gold rush **IV:99–100**
    Beckwourth, Jim **IV:**51
    Bent, William **IV:**52
    Fort Laramie **IV:**158
    gold **IV:**179
    "Pike's Peak or Bust" **IV:**300
Colorado Plateau **IV:**144
Colorado Republican Federal Campaign Committee v. Federal Election Committee **X:**63
Colorado River
    Johnson, Hiram Warren **VII:**154
    Kaiser, Henry J. **VIII:**199
    Powell, John Wesley **VI:**288
    Smith, Jedediah Strong **IV:**350
    Texas **IV:**371
    Texas Revolution **IV:**373
Colorado River Valley **IV:**39
Colorado Springs, Colorado **VI:**199
Colored Farmers' National Alliance and Cooperative Union **VI:**125
Colored Methodist Episcopal Church **VI:**7
Colored National Labor Union (CNLU) **V:77**

Colored Woman's Progressive Franchise Association **V:**58
Colquitt, Alfred **V:**45
Colson, Charles **X:**357, 367
Colt, Samuel **IV:100–101**, *101*
    Colt revolver **IV:**102
    economy **III:**131
    industrialization **IV:**199
    science and technology **IV:**333; **V:**340
Colter, John **IV:**144
Colt Firearms Company **V:**340
Colt revolver **IV:**100, **102**, 199
Columbia (space shuttle) **X:**329, 378*c*, 384*c*
Columbia Broadcasting System (CBS). *See* CBS
Columbiad, The **III:**46
Columbia District **IV:**248
Columbia Fur Company **IV:**18
Columbia House **VI:**327, 390
Columbia Law School
    Berle, Adolf A., Jr. **VIII:**43
    Douglas, William O. **VIII:**96
    Lloyd, Henry Demarest **VI:**227
Columbian Exchange **I:81–83**
    cacao **I:**48
    conquistadores **I:**88
    Coosa **I:**89
    disease/epidemics **I:**107, 108
    Las Casas, Bartolomé de **I:**205
    Madeira **I:**222
    New Spain **I:**269
    population trends **I:**297
    potato **II:**304
    rice cultivation **II:**334
    smallpox **I:**340
    Soto, Hernando de **I:**343
    sugar **I:**349
Columbia Pictures **X:**235
Columbia Records **VII:**220
Columbia River **IV:102–103**
    American Fur Company **IV:**18
    Applegate, Jesse **IV:**26
    Astor, John Jacob **IV:**33, 34
    Astoria **IV:**35
    exploration **IV:**146
    Fort Vancouver **IV:**158
    fur trade **III:**183
    Lee, Jason **IV:**224
    Lewis and Clark Expedition **III:**263
    McLoughlin, John **IV:**247, 248
    migration **IV:**255
    National Reclamation Act **VII:**229
    Oregon Trail **IV:**285
    Oregon Treaty of 1846 **IV:**286–288
    Rocky Mountain Fur Company **IV:**325

Wilkes expedition **IV:**400
Wyeth, Nathaniel J. **IV:**406
Columbia River Fishing and Trading Company **IV:**406
Columbia University. *See also* King's College
    Anglican Church **III:**20
    Baruch, Bernard M. **VII:**32
    Boas, Franz Uri **VII:**39
    Brain Trust **VIII:**51
    counterculture **IX:**78
    Dewey, John **VII:**77
    Ellington, Duke **VIII:**112
    Ely, Richard Theodore **VI:**114
    Ethical Culture movement **VI:**120, 121
    football **VI:**130, 131
    foreign policy **VII:**116
    history **VII:**139
    Hurston, Zora Neale **VIII:**181
    Kearny, Stephen Watts **IV:**212
    Kellogg-Briand Treaty **VII:**164
    Kerouac, Jack **IX:**173
    La Farge, John Frederick Lewis Joseph **V:**217
    Lieber, Francis **V:**234
    Livingston, William **III:**271
    Lloyd, Henry Demarest **VI:**227
    MacDowell, Edward Alexander **VI:**233
    Mead, Margaret **VII:**197
    Meredith, James **IX:**213
    Mills, C. Wright **IX:**217
    mining **VI:**247
    Tugwell, Rexford G. **VIII:**397
    Weathermen/Weather Underground **IX:**341
Columbia University Law School **VII:**142
Columbine High School **X:**161–162, 382*c*
Columbus, Bartholomew **I:**4, **83**, 84, 86
Columbus, Christopher **I:83–87**, 85, 396*c*
    adelantado **I:**4
    animals **II:**23
    art and architecture **I:**13
    Azores **I:**18
    "Barcelona Letter" (1493) **I:402–404**
    Behaim, Martin **I:**29
    cabildo **I:**41
    cacao **I:**48
    Canary Islands **I:**57
    cannibalism **I:**57
    caravel **I:**59
    Cathay **I:**68
    Columbian Exchange **I:**81
    Columbus, Bartholomew **I:**83

conquistadores **I**:88
corn **I**:91, 92
cross staff **I**:99
Cuba **I**:100
Ferdinand and Isabella
 I:127, 128
Gama, Vasco da **I**:137
gold **I**:141–142
Hispaniola **I**:162
horses **I**:168; **II**:165
Jamaica **I**:191
Jews **I**:195; **II**:185
limpieza de sangre **I**:214
Ma Huan **I**:225
Mandeville, Sir John **I**:227,
 228
mappae mundi **I**:230
Montserrat **I**:251
navigation technology
 I:262
New World **I**:270, 271
Ojeda, Alonso de **I**:277
Oviedo y Valdés, Gonzalo
 Fernández de **I**:281
Papal Bull Inter Caetera of
 1493 **I**:**400–402**
Peter Martyr **I**:290
Ponce de León, Juan **I**:296
*Privileges and Prerogatives
 Granted by Their
 Catholic Majesties to
 Christopher Columbus—
 1492* **I**:**399–400**
Silk Road **I**:335
sugar **I**:349
Taino **I**:352
Tordesillas, Treaty of **I**:367
travel narratives **I**:368
Velázquez, Diego de **I**:374
Columbus, Diego **I**:85, 86, 100
Columbus, Hernando **I**:84
Columbus, New Mexico
 VII:406*c*
 Big Stick diplomacy **VII**:35
 foreign policy **VII**:114
 Mexican Invasion **VII**:203
Columbus, Ohio **IV**:202
Columbus Enquirer **IV**:221
Colwell, James **V**:233
Comanche Indians **II**:157;
 IV:413*c*
 Bent, Charles **IV**:51
 Bent's Fort **IV**:55
 Catlin, George **IV**:84
 Chouteau family **IV**:88
 Cody, William Frederick
 VI:75–76
 Colt revolver **IV**:102
 exploration **IV**:145
 Great Plains **III**:197
 Lamar, Mirabeau B. **IV**:222
 Lone Wolf v. Hitchcock
 VII:185
 New Spain, northern
 frontier of **III**:318
 Rocky Mountain Fur
 Company **IV**:325

 Santa Fe Trail **IV**:330
 Smith, Jedediah Strong
 IV:351
 Texas **IV**:371
Combating Terrorism Act (2001)
 X:347
combat propaganda **VIII**:311,
 312
Combined Bomber Offensive
 VIII:62, 191
Combined Chiefs of Staff
 Army, U.S. **VIII**:26
 Arnold, Henry H. "Hap"
 VIII:28
 Italian campaign **VIII**:191
Combined Food Board **VIII**:11
Combined Joint Task Forces
 X:260
comedy **VIII**:245, 246; **X**:343
Comenius, John Amos **VI**:207
Comet (British airliner) **IX**:28
Comey, James, Jr. **X**:179
Coming of Age in Samoa (Mead)
 VII:181, 197, 409*c*
Comintern. *See* Communist
 International
Command and General Staff
 College **VIII**:164
Command and Staff School
 (Fort Leavenworth, Kansas)
 IV:158
commemoration **IX**:65–67
Commencement of *the Liberator*
 (Garrison) **IV**:**428–429**
*Commentaries on the Laws of
 England* (Blackstone) **III**:52,
 459*c*
Commerce, Illinois **IV**:353
Commerce, U.S. Department of
 Children's Bureau **VII**:53
 FCC **VIII**:130
 Harding, Warren Gamaliel
 VII:134–135
 NAM **VII**:225
 Wallace, Henry A. **VIII**:411
commerce clause **IX**:145, 146,
 288
Commerce Court **VII**:190
Commerce of the Prairies (Gregg)
 IV:179
Commercial Convention of 1815
 IV:154
commissary system **II**:21
Commission on Civil Rights
 Civil Rights Act (1957)
 IX:58, 59
 Civil Rights Act (1960)
 IX:59
 Civil Rights Act (1964)
 IX:61
 Democratic Party **IX**:85
Commission on Economy and
 Efficiency **VII**:44
Commission on Immigration
 Reform, U.S. **X**:175
Commission on Industrial
 Relations **VII**:145

Commission on Interracial
 Cooperation
 antilynching legislation
 VIII:23
 postwar planning **VIII**:306
 race and race relations
 VIII:317, 319
Commission on Party Structure
 and Delegate Selection **X**:232
Commission on the Status of
 Women **X**:132
Committee for a Sane Nuclear
 Policy (SANE) **VIII**:394
Committee for Industrial
 Organization **VIII**:82, 249,
 445*c*, 446*c*
Committee for Public Information
 (CPI) **VII**:**59–60**, *60*, 407*c*
 advertising **VII**:5
 conscription **VII**:62
 Espionage Act **VII**:101
 Fuel Administration
 VII:119
 Palmer, Alexander Mitchell
 VII:249
 presidency **VII**:269
 Selective Service Act
 VII:321
 World War I **VII**:394
Committee for the First
 Amendment **IX**:147, 148
Committee for the Prevention of
 Tuberculosis **VII**:275
Committee for the Study of
 Nursing Education, Rockefeller
 Foundation **VII**:127
Committee for the Suppression of
 Legalized Vice **V**:316
Committee of Fifteen (New York
 City) **VI**:121
Committee of Fifty-one (New
 York State) **III**:294
Committee of Five (Virginia)
 III:292
Committee of Foreign Affairs
 III:116
Committee of Mechanics **III**:35
Committee of One Hundred
 (Gastonia, North Carolina)
 VII:122
Committee of One Hundred
 (New York State) **III**:294, 461*c*
Committee of Safety
 (Philadelphia) **III**:372
Committee of Safety (Virginia)
 III:52
Committee of Secret
 Correspondence **III**:116
Committee of Thirteen
 (Crittenden Compromise)
 V:97–98
Committee on Civil Rights
 IX:299
Committee on Economic Security
 (CES) **VIII**:293, 363, 364
Committee on Foreign Relations
 V:377

Committee on Human Rights
 VIII:449*c*
Committee on Maternal Health
 VII:37
Committee on Military Affairs
 V:433
Committee on the Present
 Danger **X**:100
committees of correspondence
 III:**101**, 460*c*
 Adams, Samuel **III**:7
 Association, the **III**:37
 Boston Tea Party **III**:59
 Church, Benjamin **III**:89
 citizenship **III**:93
 Clinton, George **III**:98
 Coercive Acts **III**:100
 Continental Congress, First
 III:114
 Continental Congress,
 Second **III**:116
 Henry, Patrick **III**:211
 Quincy, Josiah **III**:354
 Revere, Paul **III**:366–367
 Yates, Abraham **III**:453
 Young, Thomas **III**:457
Committee to Defend America
 (CDA) **VIII**:77
Committee to Defend America
 by Aiding the Allies (CDAAA)
 VIII:**76–77**
Committee to Re-Elect the
 President (CREEP)
 Mitchell, John N. **X**:233
 Nixon, Richard M. **X**:257
 Watergate scandal **X**:365
commodification **X**:237
Commodity Committees
 VII:378
Commodity Credit Corporation
 Agricultural Adjustment
 Administration **VIII**:7
 agriculture **VIII**:10
 RFC **VIII**:325
commodity prices **VII**:48–49
Common Council (Albany, New
 York) **III**:453
Commoner, Barry **X**:90
"common knowledge" **X**:351
common law **III**:142, 256–257
Commons, John R. **VI**:115;
 IX:129
Common School Journal (Mann)
 IV:133, 237
common schools **III**:147–148;
 IV:133
Common Sense (Paine) **II**:241;
 III:**101–103**, *102*, 461*c*
 corporatism **III**:122
 Declaration of
 Independence **III**:133
 Franklin, Benjamin **III**:174
 literature **III**:268
 Paine, Thomas **III**:329
 republicanism **III**:365
 resistance movement
 III:366

Common Sense Book of Baby and Child Care (Spock) **IX:**351*c*
baby boomers **X:**39
childhood **IX:**55
Spock, Benjamin **IX:**297
common soldier **V:77–79**
letters **V:**233
literature **V:**239
lost cause, the **V:**244
photography **V:**304
uniforms **V:**399
veterans **V:**416
Commonwealth and Southern (holding company) **VIII:**392, 417
commonwealthmen **III:103–104**
anti-Federalists **III:**24
Declaration of Independence **III:**133
Whigs **III:**439
Commonwealth of Independent States **X:**326
Commonwealth v. Hunt **IV:**218–219
communal farms **VIII:**339
communes **VI:**371
Communicable Disease Center **IX:**211
communications **VI:77–78**
business cycles **VI:**58
illustration, photography, and graphic arts **VI:**183
immigration **VI:**185–186
Industrial Revolution, Second **VI:**191
labor, woman **VI:**214
magazines **VI:**235
Pan-American Union **VI:**276
communications, command, and control systems (C3) **X:**100
Communications Act (1934) **VIII:**130, 131, 321, 444*c*
Communications Decency Act (CDA) **X:**381*c*
censorship **X:**71
Internet **X:**182
pornography **X:**284
Communications Security Unit (U.S. Navy) **VIII:**187
Communication Workers of America v. Beck **X:**63
communism **VII:**407*c*, 409*c*; **IX:67–68,** 352*c*–354*c*. *See also* Communists
Africa **IX:**3
Americans for Democratic Action **IX:**14
anticommunism **IX:**14–15
Asia **IX:**20
Asian-American movement **IX:**22
Bay of Pigs **IX:**36
CDAAA **VIII:**77
Chambers, Whittaker **IX:**52
CIO **IX:**72
cold war **IX:**62–64

cold war, end of **X:**84
cold war culture **IX:**64
commemoration **IX:**65, 66
conservatism **IX:**74, 75
conservative movement **X:**93
consumerism **IX:**75
contras **X:**95
Dennis v. U.S. **IX:**86
Disney, Walt **IX:**88
domino theory **IX:**89
Europe **IX:**113
foreign policy **X:**142
Gallup Poll **IX:**130–131
gays and lesbians **IX:**131
Graham, Billy **IX:**138
Hearst, William Randolph **VII:**138
Hiss, Alger **IX:**146–147
Hollywood Ten **IX:**147
HUAC **IX:**150, 151
Internal Security Act (1950) **IX:**157–158
Korean War **IX:**177, 178
labor, radical **VI:**212
Latin America **IX:**183; **X:**205
liberalism **X:**207
marriage and family **IX:**202
McCarran-Walter Act **IX:**205
McCarthy, Joseph R. **IX:**206
Middle East **IX:**214
military-industrial complex **IX:**216
movies **IX:**223, 224
NATO **IX:**246–247
Nixon, Richard M. **X:**257
NSC-68 **IX:**247–248
Operation Mongoose **IX:**250
Oppenheimer, J. Robert **IX:**251
Peace Corps **IX:**255
Point Four Program **IX:**258
Popular Front **VIII:**304
Progressive Party **IX:**264
propaganda **VIII:**311
radicalism **VII:**287
Reagan, Ronald W. **X:**299
religion **IX:**272
Rosenberg, Julius and Ethel **IX:**280
Russian Revolution **VII:**308
SANE **IX:**283
SDS **IX:**304
SEATO **IX:**292
shopping centers **IX:**289
Smith Act **VIII:**361–362
socialism **VII:**328
Soviet Union **IX:**295
television **IX:**316
Truman, Harry S. **IX:**320–321
Truman Doctrine **IX:**321, 322
veterans **IX:**329

Vietnam War **IX:**330
Vietnam War, end of U.S. involvement **X:**362
wars of national liberation **IX:**338, 339
White Paper **IX:**343
Communist International (Comintern) **VII:**407*c*, 409*c*
Communist Party **VII:**61
Communists **VIII:**77
Popular Front **VIII:**303, 304
Communist Labor Party
Communist Party **VII:**61
radicalism **VII:**287
Reed, Jack **VII:**297
Russian Revolution **VII:**308
Communist Manifesto (Marx) **V:**249; **VI:**401
Communist Party **VII:61,** 409*c*
anticommunism **IX:**15
Army-McCarthy hearings **IX:**18
Baldwin, Roger Nash **VII:**31
Bay of Pigs **IX:**35
Chambers, Whittaker **IX:**52
communism **IX:**67
Flynn, Elizabeth Gurley **VII:**110
Foster, William Zebulon **VII:**116, 117
Gallup Poll **IX:**131
Gastonia Strike **VII:**122
gays and lesbians **IX:**131
Hiss, Alger **IX:**146
Internal Security Act (1950) **IX:**157, 158
Iron Curtain, collapse of **X:**189
labor/labor movements **VII:**172
movies **IX:**223
Oppenheimer, J. Robert **IX:**251
Passaic Strike **VII:**253
Progressive Party **IX:**264
radical and labor press **VII:**286
radicalism **VII:**287, 288
Reagan, Ronald W. **X:**299
Red Scare **VII:**296
Reed, Jack **VII:**297
Rosenberg, Julius and Ethel **IX:**280
Russian Revolution **VII:**308
Sacco and Vanzetti **VII:**311
socialism **VII:**328
Soviet Union, breakup of **X:**326
Supreme Court **VII:**343
Warren, Earl **IX:**337
Communist Party of the United States of America (CPUSA)
Bridges, Harry **VIII:**53
Communist Party **VII:**61

Communists **VIII:**77–78
FBI **VIII:**130
Popular Front **VIII:**303, 304
race and race relations **VIII:**317
radicalism **VII:**287
Scottsboro Boys **VIII:**353
Wright, Richard **VIII:**437
Communists **VIII:77–78**
America First Committee **VIII:**17
anticommunism **VIII:**22
Bonus Army **VIII:**49
censorship **VIII:**65
CIO **VIII:**82
civil liberties **VIII:**71
election of 1932 **VIII:**109
election of 1944 **VIII:**111
FBI **VIII:**130
FTP **VIII:**136
FWP **VIII:**137
Harriman, W. Averell **VIII:**162
Hillman, Sidney **VIII:**166
ILGWU **VIII:**187
labor/labor movements **VIII:**207
Lewis, John L. **VIII:**213
liberalism **VIII:**215
literature **VIII:**218
Murray, Philip **VIII:**249
Nazi-Soviet Pact **VIII:**266
NLRB **VIII:**258, 259
politics (Roosevelt era) **VIII:**298
Popular Front **VIII:**303
race and race relations **VIII:**317–318
Scottsboro Boys **VIII:**353
socialists **VIII:**362
Spanish civil war **VIII:**369
Supreme Court **VIII:**384
Community Action Program (CAP) **IX:68–69,** 356*c*
cities and urban life **IX:**56
Great Society **IX:**139
Model Cities program **IX:**220
War on Poverty **IX:**335
Community Chest drives **VIII:**310
community colleges **X:**111
community schools **VI:**108–109
Community Services Organization (CSO) **IX:**53, 186
commutation **V:**81
compact discs (CDs)
music **X:**239
popular culture **X:**278, 279
science and technology **X:**318–320
Compagnie des Pasteurs **I:**54
Company of Cathay **I:87,** 134, 135
Company of Merchants Trading to Africa **II:**337

Company of One Hundred Associates **II:**136
Company of the Indies **II:**38
Company of the West **II:**266
Compendious Dictionary of the English Language, A (Webster) **III:**434
Compendium Physicae (Morton) **II:**345
competition, global **X:**35, 36
Compleat Book of Divinity, A (Willard) **II:**415
Comprehensive Anti-Apartheid Act (CAAA) **X:**16, 325, 379*c*
Comprehensive Crime Control Act (1984) **X:**97, 243, 378*c*
Comprehensive Drug Abuse Prevention and Control Act (1970) **X:**242–243
Compromise of 1850 **IV:103–104,** 415*c,* **446–449; V:**444*c*
   Bell, John **V:**32
   Benton, Thomas Hart **IV:**54
   Calhoun, John C. **IV:**70
   California **IV:**71
   Cass, Lewis **IV:**84
   Civil War **V:**73
   Clay, Henry **IV:**97–98
   Clayton-Bulwer Treaty **IV:**98
   Democratic Party **IV:**118; **V:**109
   Douglas, Stephen A. **V:**114
   Fillmore, Millard **IV:**150
   fire-eaters **V:**146
   Free-Soil Party **IV:**164
   Fugitive Slave Act **IV:447–449**
   fugitive slave laws **IV:**168
   Guadalupe Hidalgo, Treaty of **IV:**181–182
   Julian, George Washington **V:**219
   Know-Nothing Party **IV:**214
   Missouri Compromise **IV:**257
   Mormon War **IV:**263
   personal liberty laws **IV:**299
   Pierce, Franklin **V:**307
   popular sovereignty **IV:**304
   Rhodes, James Ford **VI:**312
   Seward, William H. **V:**347
   Stephens, Alexander Hamilton **V:**371
   Texas **IV:**372
   Texas and New Mexico Act **IV:446–447**
   Underground Railroad **V:**398
   Utah Act **IV:447**
   Vallandigham, Clement L. **V:**413
   Webster, Daniel **IV:**394
   Welles, Gideon **V:**428
   Whigs **IV:**398
Compromise of 1876 **V:**329
Compton, Arthur H. **IX:**250

Compton, Henry **II:**21
Compton, Karl **VIII:**283
compulsory education **VII:**85, 409*c;* **VIII:**66
computed tomography (CT) scan **X:**224
computer(s) **IX:69–71,** *70,* 351*c;* **X:***86,* **86–88,** *87*
   agriculture **X:**18, 19
   business **X:**57
   economy **X:**109
   ENIAC **IX:**104–105
   globalization **X:**153
   Internet. *See* Internet
   literature **X:**212
   media **X:**217, 219, 220
   medicine **X:**224
   movies **X:**235
   science and technology **IX:**285; **X:**317–319
   technology **IX:**311, 313
computer-aided design (CAD) **X:**87
computer-aided instruction (CAI) **X:**87
computer-aided manufacturing (CAM) **X:**87
computer chips. *See* integrated circuits
Computer Emergency Response Team (CERT) **X:**182
computer industry **X:**109
Computer Matching and Privacy Protection Act (1988) **X:**130
computer viruses **X:**182
Comstock, Anthony **VI:78–79,** 251
Comstock, William A. **VIII:**40
Comstock Laws **VI:**407*c*
   birth control **VII:**36
   Greenwich Village **VII:**131
   radical and labor press **VII:**285
   Sanger, Margaret **VII:**312
Comstock Lode **IV:**99, **104–106,** 179
Comte, Auguste **VI:**128
Conant, James **VIII:**283
Conant, Roger **II:**222
concentration camps **VIII:**169–170, 310
Concepción (ship) **I:**223, 224
Concerned Women for America **X:**125
Concerning Children (Gilman) **VII:**125
Concerning Women (La Follette) **VII:**388
concert bands **VI:**258
Concerto in F (Gershwin) **VII:**125
Concord, Battle of. *See* Lexington and Concord, Battles of
Concord, Massachusetts
   Emerson, Ralph Waldo **IV:**140
   literature **IV:**228

   religion **IV:**320
   Thoreau, Henry David **IV:**376
   transcendental movement **IV:**378
Concord Academy **IV:**376
Concorde (jet airliner) **IX:**27
Concord Sonata (Ives) **VII:**220
concrete **VI:**196; **VII:**19
concubinage **I:**64–65, 241; **II:**59
Condition, Elevation, Emigration, and Destiny of the Colored People of the United States, The (Delany) **V:**108
condoms **X:**42
Conecuh County, Alabama **IV:**379
Conestoga Indians **II:74–75,** 282
Conestoga wagon **II:**287; **IV:**273, 286
Coney Island, New York **VII:**293
Confederate army **V:79–83,** *80*
   Balloon Corps **V:**25–26
   Bentonville, Battle of **V:**34
   bounty system **V:**39
   Bragg, Braxton **V:**42
   brothers' war **V:**43
   Bull Run/Manassas, First and Second Battles of **V:**50–51
   Chattanooga, Battle of **V:**63
   conscription **V:**90
   Cumming, Kate **V:**98
   desertion **V:**110, 111
   disease/epidemics **V:**112
   Early, Jubal A. **V:**119
   field fortifications **V:**141
   foraging **V:**148–149
   Harpers Ferry, West Virginia **V:**186
   homefront **V:**193
   immigration **V:**200, 201
   ironclad oath **V:**206
   letters **V:**233
   McLaws, Lafayette **V:**253
   Medal of Honor **V:**255
   medicine **V:**256–258
   Milliken's Bend, Battle of **V:**260
   music **V:**274
   Native Americans **V:**278
   Pemberton, John C. **V:**298
   Price, Sterling **V:**313
   prisons **V:**314
   science and technology **V:**342, 343
   Shiloh, Battle of **V:**358–360
   uniforms **V:**398–400
   veterans **V:**415–416
   Vicksburg campaign **V:**417, 418
   volunteer army **V:**419
   war contracting **V:**423, 424
   Watterson, Henry **VI:**386
   Wilderness, Battle of the **V:**432
   Zouaves **V:**441

Confederate cavalry **V:**268
Confederate Cherokee Regiment of Mounted Rifles **V:**427
Confederate Constitutional Convention **V:**371
Confederated Southern Memorial Association **V:**229
Confederate Flag Pole **V:**267
Confederate Justice Department **V:**33
Confederate Medical Department **V:**256
Confederate navy **V:83–84**
   Alabama, CSS **V:**7
   ironclads **V:**207
   Mallory, Stephen R. **V:**247
   Mississippi River war **V:**263
   Monitor-Merrimack **V:**265
   New Orleans, Battle of **V:**280
   science and technology **V:**342
   Semmes, Raphael **V:**346
   Union navy **V:**405, 406
   war contracting **V:**424
Confederate Ordnance Department **V:**424
Confederate River Defense Fleet **V:**263
Confederate States of America **V:84–87,** *85,* 444*c*
   banking **V:**26–28
   cartography **V:**57
   Confederate army **V:**79
   Congress, Confederate **V:**88
   Constitution. *See* Constitution of the Confederate States of America
   Constitution of the Confederate States of America **V:456–457**
   Davis, Jefferson **V:**104
   Democratic Party **V:**109
   economy **V:**122–123
   elections **V:**126–127
   espionage **V:**134–135
   food riots **V:**147–148
   foreign policy **V:**150, 151
   habeas corpus, writ of **V:**181, 182
   homefront **V:**193
   Houston, Sam **IV:**192
   impressment **V:**203–204
   ladies aid societies **V:**227
   letters **V:**233
   Lincoln, Abraham **V:**236
   Mallory, Stephen R. **V:**247
   Memminger, Christopher G. **V:**259
   Native Americans **V:**278
   Nullification Controversy **IV:**283
   Republican Party **V:**333
   Richmond, Virginia **V:**335
   secession **V:**343

Confederate States of America
(continued)
    slavery **V:**363
    states' rights **V:**370
    Tredegar Iron Works **V:**392
Confederation Congress **IV:**258–
259
Confederation of Mexican Farm
Workers' and Laborers' Union
VIII:237
Conference for Progressive
Political Action (CPPA)
VII:105
Conference on the Negro in
National Defense **VIII:**227
Confession of Augsburg **I:**219
Confidence-Man, The (Melville)
IV:229
Confiscation Acts **V:**87–88, 444*c*
    contrabands **V:**92
    emancipation **V:**129
    Emancipation Proclamation
        V:130
    race and race relations
        V:319
    slavery **V:**364
Confucianism **IV:**319
Congo, Democratic Republic of
I:217
Congo Free State **VI:**396
Congolese civil war (1960–1964)
IX:4, 339
Congolese National Liberation
Council **IX:**4
Congo River **I:**200
congregaciones **II:**373
Congregationalists/
Congregationalism **I:**307;
    II:75
    Anglican Church **III:**21
    Backus, Isaac **III:**40
    Civil Rights Cases **VI:**72
    Connecticut **II:**78
    Cotton, John **II:**81–82
    Dwight, Timothy **III:**143
    female antislavery societies
        IV:147
    Great Awakening **II:**156
    imperialism **VI:**188
    Massachusetts **II:**223
    Morse, Jedidiah **III:**307,
        308
    New England Primer **II:**258
    Old South Church **III:**323
    Osborn, Sarah Haggar
        Wheaten **II:**279
    Pilgrims **II:**293
    Protestantism **II:**315
    religion **III:**360–362;
        IV:317, 318; **VI:**307
    religion, Euro-American
        II:329
    religious liberty **III:**363
    temperance movement
        III:410
    Unitarianism **III:**419
    Williams, Roger **II:**415–416

Congress, Confederate **V:**88–89
    Cobb, Howell **V:**76
    Confederate States of
        America **V:**85
    conscription **V:**90
    economy **V:**122
    habeas corpus, writ of **V:**181
    Letcher, John **V:**232
    Mallory, Stephen R. **V:**247
    Memminger, Christopher
        G. **V:**259
    taxation **V:**384
    Toombs, Robert A. **V:**389
    Wigfall, Louis T. **V:**431
    Yancey, William Lowndes
        V:439
Congress, United States **IV:**415*c*;
    V:89–90; **VI:**79–80, 407*c*;
    VII:61–62, 403*c*, 405*c*–407*c*;
    VIII:78–81, 80, 444*c*–448*c*;
    IX:351*c*, 354*c*, 356*c*, 357*c*;
    X:375*c*, 376*c*, 378*c*, 384*c*. *See
also* House of Representatives,
U.S.; Senate, U.S.
    abolitionism **V:**1
    abortion **X:**3
    Abscam **X:**5–6
    African Americans **VIII:**2
    Agricultural Adjustment Act
        VIII:6
    Agricultural Adjustment
        Administration **VIII:**7
    Agricultural Marketing Act
        VIII:8
    agriculture **VIII:**9
    Allison, William Boyd
        VI:11–12
    Amendment, Twelfth **III:**16
    Amendments to the U.S.
        Constitution **X:**22–23
    Ames, Fisher **III:**19
    antilynching legislation
        VIII:23
    antimonopoly **VIII:**23–24
    anti-Semitism **VIII:**25
    antiwar movement, Vietnam
        X:29
    Arnold, Henry H. "Hap"
        VIII:28
    Articles of Confederation
        III:33, 34
    Bankhead-Jones Farm
        Tenant Act **VIII:**39
    Banking Act (1933) **VIII:**40,
        41
    Banking Act (1935) **VIII:**41
    Baruch, Bernard M.
        VIII:42
    Bates, Edward **V:**30
    Blaine, James Gillespie
        VI:40–41
    Bonus Army **VIII:**48
    Budget and Accounting Act
        VII:44
    Bureau of Motion Pictures
        VIII:56
    Bush, George W. **X:**55

Byrnes, James F. **VIII:**60
Calhoun, John C. **IV:**68–69
Canada **VI:**61
Capper-Volstead Act
    VII:48–49
Carter, James Earl, Jr. **X:**69
cash-and-carry **VIII:**63
Cheney, Richard B. **X:**71,
    72
child labor **VII:**52
Children's Bureau **VII:**53
Chilean-American relations
    VI:67–68
citizenship **VII:**57
civil liberties **VII:**57–58
civil service reform **VI:**73
Cody, William Frederick
    VI:76
Comstock, Anthony **VI:**79
Congressional Budget and
    Impoundment Control
    Act **X:**89
Conkling, Roscoe **VI:**80
conservation/
    environmentalism **VI:**81
conservatism **VIII:**85; **IX:**74
conservative coalition
    VIII:85–86
conservative movement
    X:94
Constitution, United States
    III:106, 107
Constitutional Convention
    III:109
court-packing plan **VIII:**89
Coxey's Army **VI:**84
Crittenden Compromise
    V:98
Cuba **VI:**88
Declaration of
    Independence **III:**133
defense policy **X:**100
demobilization (WWII)
    VIII:91
Democratic Party **VIII:**92
Dix, Dorothea **IV:**125
Donnelly, Ignatius Loyola
    VI:99
Economic Bill of Rights
    VIII:102
education, federal aid to
    VI:110
election of 1932 **VIII:**108
election of 1936 **VIII:**109
election of 1940 **VIII:**110
election of 1944 **VIII:**111
elections **IX:**103, 104
elections, presidential
    X:118
Emergency Banking Act of
    1933 **VIII:**113
enemy aliens **VIII:**114
ERA **X:**123, 124
espionage **VIII:**117
Ethiopia **VIII:**118
Executive Order 9066
    VIII:121

Executive Reorganization
    Act **VIII:**121
Expatriation Act **VII:**103
Fair Deal **IX:**115
Fair Labor Standards Act
    VIII:124
FAP **VIII:**129
FCA **VIII:**126
FCC **VIII:**131
FDIC **VIII:**132
Federal Reserve Act
    VII:107–108
FEPC **VIII:**124
FERA **VIII:**132
Ferraro, Geraldine A. **X:**135
FMP **VIII:**134
Foraker Act **VII:**110
Ford, Gerald R. **X:**137
foreign policy **VIII:**142
Forest Reserve Act **VI:**134
Four Freedoms **VIII:**143
FSA **VIII:**127
Full Employment Bill
    VIII:145
FWP **VIII:**137
Garfield, James Abram
    VI:138
Garner, John Nance
    VIII:147
GI Bill of Rights **VIII:**149
gold standard **VIII:**150
Gore, Albert, Jr. **X:**157
government **VIII:**152
habeas corpus, writ of **V:**182
Hamilton, Alexander
    III:206
Hawaii **VI:**163
Hawley-Smoot Tariff Act
    VIII:163
Hayes, Rutherford B.
    VI:166
*Heart of Atlanta Motel v.
    U.S.* **IX:**145, 146
Henderson, Leon **VIII:**163
HOLC **VIII:**170
Holocaust **VIII:**170
Hoover presidency
    VIII:173
Hull, Cordell **VIII:**180
immigration **VI:**68, 184;
    VII:144; **VIII:**184
Immigration Act (1917)
    VII:145
immigration restrictions
    VI:187
imperialism **VI:**188
Indian Affairs, Office of
    VI:188, 189
Indian Reorganization Act
    VIII:186
Industrial Relations
    Commission **VII:**145–
146
internal improvements
    IV:202
Internal Revenue taxes
    VI:194

Internal Security Act (1950) **IX:**157

Interstate Highway Act of 1956 **IX:**159

invention and technology **VII:**150

Irish Americans **VIII:**188

isolationists **VIII:**189

Jackson, Helen Hunt **VI:**199

Japanese Americans, relocation of **VIII:**194

Jefferson, Thomas **III:**233

Jews **VIII:**196

Johnson, Tom Loftin **VII:**156

Jones, Jesse H. **VIII:**197

Jones Act (1916) **VII:**157

Kansas-Nebraska Act **V:**221–222

Keating-Owen Act **VII:**163

Kellogg-Briand Treaty **VII:**164

King, Rufus **III:**245

labor/labor movements **VIII:**205

La Guardia, Fiorello **VIII:**208, 209

Langston, John Mercer **VI:**219

lead mines **IV:**224

Leahy, William D. **VIII:**211

Letcher, John **V:**232

Lewis, John **IX:**191

Liberal Republican Party **VI:**222

Liberia **VI:**223

Lloyd, Henry Demarest **VI:**227–228

lobbying **VI:**228

Lockwood, Belva Ann Bennett McNall **VI:**229

London Economic Conference **VIII:**221

Luce, Henry R. **VIII:**224

Madison, James **III:**282

marriage and family **X:**215

McCarran-Walter Act **IX:**205

McCulloch v. Maryland **IV:**245–246

McNary-Haugen Farm Bill **VII:**195

Medicare **IX:**209, 210

medicine **IX:**210; **X:**224

Middle East **X:**229

military-industrial complex **IX:**216

Model Cities program **IX:**221

modern Republicanism **IX:**221

muckrakers **VII:**217

Native Americans **IX:**241

NEA **IX:**235

NEH **IX:**234

Neutrality Acts **VIII:**267–268

New Madrid earthquake **IV:**280

NLRA **VIII:**257–258

Norris, George W. **VIII:**276

NWP **VII:**230

NWTUL **VII:**231

occupational health and safety **VII:**243

overland mail **IV:**290

panic of 1819 **IV:**294

panic of 1837 **IV:**295

politics (1900–1928) **VII:**261

Polk, James K. **IV:**301

postwar planning **VIII:**306

Powell, Adam Clayton **IX:**261

Preparedness **VII:**267–268

presidency **VI:**289–290; **VII:**268, 269

presidential campaigns (1870–1899) **VI:**291–292

Progressive Party **VII:**269–270

public health **VII:**276

public housing **IX:**267

Quota Act **VII:**279

Randolph, Edmund **III:**358

Reciprocal Trade Agreements Act **VIII:**325

Reconstruction **V:**326

refugees **VIII:**329

relief **VIII:**331–333

religion **III:**361

Republican Party **IX:**274

Revenue Act of 1935 **VIII:**340

RFC **VIII:**325–326

Roosevelt, Franklin D. **VIII:**345

Sedition Act **VII:**318

Selective Service **VIII:**357

Smith Act **VIII:**361–362

Social Security Act **VIII:**363

Soldiers' Bonus **VII:**331

South **VIII:**366

Southern Manifesto **IX:**294

Supreme Court **VII:**343

Tallmadge Amendment **IV:**365

taxation **V:**384; **VIII:**387

Tennessee Valley Authority **VIII:**392

Third New Deal **VIII:**393

TNEC **VIII:**391

tobacco suits **X:**352–353

Townsend, Francis E. **VIII:**395

transportation **VIII:**395

treaty rights **IX:**319

Tyler, John **IV:**382–383

UN **X:**357

USHA **VIII:**404

Van Buren, Martin **IV:**385

Venezuela boundary dispute **VI:**373

Versailles, Treaty of **VII:**370–371

War Hawks **IV:**389–390

Whitman, Marcus **IV:**399

women's status and rights **VIII:**422; **X:**371

World War II home front **VIII:**434

Yazoo claims **III:**454

Congress, USS

brothers' war **V:**43

Essex, USS **IV:**144

Monitor-Merrimack **V:**266

Congressional Black Caucus **X:**296

Congressional Budget and Impoundment Control Act (1974) **X:88–89,** 158, 377*c*

Congressional Committee of NAWSA **VII:**385

Congressional Gold Medal

Kennedy, Robert F. **IX:**172

Parks, Rosa **IX:**255

Reagan, Ronald W. **X:**302

Congressional Medal of Honor. *See* Medal of Honor

congressional pages **X:**171

congressional pay raises **X:**23

congressional power **X:**357–358

Congressional Quarterly **IX:**107

Congressional Reconstruction **V:**325–327

Congressional Scorecard **X:**74

Congressional Union for Woman Suffrage **VII:**230, 385

Congress of Industrial Organizations (CIO) **VIII:81–82,** *82,* 446*c*; **IX:71–72,** 351*c,* 353*c. See also* American Federation of Labor-Congress of Industrial Organizations

AFL **VIII:**18–19; **IX:**11, 12

African Americans **VIII:**3

Amalgamated Clothing Workers of America (ACW) **VIII:**16

anticommunism **VIII:**22

automobile industry **VIII:**36, 37

Bridges, Harry **VIII:**53

Byrnes, James F. **VIII:**60

Communists **VIII:**78

conservative coalition **VIII:**86

Democratic Party **VIII:**94

Dubinsky, David **VIII:**97

economy **IX:**97

Hillman, Sidney **VIII:**166

ILGWU **VIII:**187

Irish Americans **VIII:**189

Jews **VIII:**195

labor/labor movements **VIII:**205–207; **IX:**182; **X:**201

Lewis, John L. **VIII:**213

Murray, Philip **VIII:**248

NLRB **VIII:**259

NWLB **VIII:**261

Operation Dixie **IX:**249–250

Polish Americans **VIII:**297

Popular Front **VIII:**304

Reuther, Walter **VIII:**339; **IX:**275

South **VIII:**366

strikes **VIII:**377

UMWA **VIII:**401

union movement **IX:**323

Congress of Industrial Organizations (CIO) Political Action Committee **VIII:**166, 207

Congress of Racial Equality (CORE) **VIII:**447*c;* **IX:72–74,** *73,* 355*c,* 356*c*

African Americans **IX:**5

Carmichael, Stokely **IX:**49

Farmer, James L. **X:**129

Fellowship of Reconciliation **VII:**109

freedom rides **IX:**123, 124

MFDP **IX:**219

NAACP **IX:**232

race and race relations **IX:**270

sit-ins **IX:**291

Voting Rights Act of 1965 **IX:**333

Congress of Vienna **III:**405

Congress's Own **III:**204

Conkling, Roscoe **VI:80–81**

Arthur, Chester Alan **VI:**20–21

civil service reform **VI:**73

Congress **VI:**80

Garfield, James Abram **VI:**139

Grant, Ulysses S. **V:**175

Hayes, Rutherford B. **VI:**167

Liberal Republican Party **VI:**222

newspapers **VI:**266

presidential campaigns (1870–1899) **VI:**293

Republican Party **VI:**311

Connally, John B. **IX:**22, 252

Connecticut **II:75–78,** *76,* 435*c*

abolitionism **III:**2

African Americans **III:**9

agriculture **II:**13; **VI:**8

Amistad incident **IV:**21

Anglican Church **II:**21

Baptists **III:**44

Canonchet **II:**57

Catlin, George **IV:**84

Colt, Samuel **IV:**100, 101

Comstock, Anthony **VI:**78

Constitution, ratification of the **III:**104–105

Continental army, mutinies of **III:**113

Connecticut *(continued)*
 Davenport, James **II**:91–92
 disease/epidemics **II**:100
 Dominion of New England
  II:102
 Dow, Lorenzo **III**:139
 Dummer, Jeremiah **II**:104
 Easton, Hosea **IV**:129
 economy **IV**:131
 Endecott, John **II**:116
 Foster, Abigail Kelley
  IV:161
 fugitive slave laws **IV**:168
 gay and lesbian rights
  movement **X**:149
 Ghent, Treaty of **IV**:176
 Hammon, Jupiter **II**:162
 Hartford Convention
  IV:186
 Hooker, Isabella Beecher
  VI:176
 Hooker, Thomas **II**:165
 indentured servitude **II**:175
 industrialization **IV**:199
 Kelo v. City of New London
  X:195
 Know-Nothing Party **IV**:214
 land **II**:201
 lead mines **IV**:223
 Maine Law **IV**:234
 Mason, John **II**:222
 Massachusetts **II**:223
 medicine **X**:223
 New Netherland **II**:265
 Pequot **II**:289
 personal liberty laws **IV**:298
 population trends **III**:343;
  X:282
 postal service **II**:304
 railroads **IV**:314
 religion, Euro-American
  II:329
 religious liberty **III**:363–
  364
 Seabury, Samuel **III**:386,
  387
 shipbuilding **II**:351
 slavery **III**:390
 stem cell research **X**:335
 Welles, Gideon **V**:427
 Wheelock, Eleazar **II**:412
 Willard, Emma **IV**:400
 witches/witchcraft **II**:419
 Wyoming Valley Wars
  III:450
 Yale, Elihu **II**:429
 Yale College **II**:429
Connecticut Compromise **III**:283,
 389, 463*c*
Connecticut Farms, Battle of
 III:248
Connecticut General Assembly
 III:389
Connecticut Observer **IV**:161
Connecticut Rangers **III**:204, 210
Connecticut Society for the
 Reformation of Morals **III**:410

Connecticut State Board of
 Education **VI**:347–348
Connecticut State Capitol
 Building **III**:65
Connecticut Wits **III:104**
 Barlow, Joel **III**:46
 Dwight, Timothy **III**:143
 literature **III**:268, 269
*Connecticut Yankee in King
 Arthur's Court, A* (Twain)
 V:240
Connie's Inn (Harlem, New York)
 VII:220
Connolly, John **VI**:359
Connolly, Richard B. **VI:**368,
 369
Connor, Eugene "Bull"
 Birmingham confrontation
  IX:39–40
 freedom rides **IX**:123
 race and race relations
  IX:269
Conquering Bear **IV**:276
Conquest of Labor and Souls
 II:371
Conquest of Mexico (Prescott)
 VI:381
conquistador(es) **I:87–89,** 88
 adelantado **I**:3–4
 Aguilar, Francisco de **I**:4
 Aguilar, Gerónimo de **I**:4–5
 Alvarado, Pedro de **I**:7–8
 Atahualpa **I**:15, 16
 Aztecs **I**:19, 21–22
 Balboa, Vasco Núñez de
  I:26
 Barbados **I**:27
 black legend **I**:31–32
 Cabeza de Vaca, Álvar
  Núñez **I**:39–40
 castas **I**:64
 Cieza de León, Pedro **I**:76
 Córdoba, Francisco
  Hernández de **I**:90–91
 Coronado, Francisco
  I:92–93
 Cortés, Hernán **I**:94–97
 encomienda **I**:122
 gender **II**:144
 gold **I**:142
 Grijalva, Juan de **I**:145
 hacienda **I**:149
 Hopi **I**:168
 Inca **I**:180
 Las Casas, Bartolomé de
  I:204, 205, 207–208
 Mabila **I**:221
 Maya **I**:237
 Mendoza, Antonio de **I**:239
 Moctezuma II Xocoyotzin
  I:245–246
 Narváez, Pánfilo de **I**:258–
  259
 New Mexico **I**:265
 Ojeda, Alonso de **I**:277
 Panama **I**:285
 Peru **I**:289

 Pizarro, Francisco **I**:292–
  293
 Ponce de León, Juan **I**:296
 Sandoval, Gonzalo de **I**:325
 Santa Fe **I**:327
 Sepúlveda, Juan Ginés de
  I:330
 smallpox **I**:341
 Soto, Hernando de **I**:342–
  343
 Spanish colonies **II**:371
 Spanish immigration
  II:374–375
 Tenochtitlán **I**:354, 356
 Tlaxcala **I**:362
 travel narratives **I**:369
 Valdivia, Pedro de **I**:373
 Velázquez, Diego de **I**:374
 Yucatán Peninsula **I**:390
 Zumárraga, Juan de **I**:392
Conrad, Johannes **VI**:115
Conrad, Joseph **VI**:85, 200
Conrad I (king of Germany)
 I:166
Conscience of a Conservative, The
 (Goldwater) **IX**:354*c*
 conservatism **IX**:74
 elections **IX**:104
 Goldwater, Barry **IX**:135
Conscience Whigs **IV**:163; **V**:376
conscientious objectors (COs)
 VIII:83; X:375*c*
 ACLU **VIII**:18
 civil liberties **VIII**:72
 Fellowship of Reconciliation
  VII:109
 peace movements **V**:295
 Selective Service **VIII**:358
 Society of Friends **V**:365
 Supreme Court **VIII**:384
 Thomas, Norman **VIII**:394
consciousness raising **X**:132
conscription **V:90–92,** *91;*
 VII:62–63, *63. See also* draft
 evasion; Selective Service
 bounty system **V**:39
 citizenship **VII**:57
 civil liberties, Confederate
  V:68, 69
 civil liberties, Union **V**:70
 Civil War **V**:74
 common soldier **V**:78
 Confederate army **V**:80
 Confederate States of
  America **V**:86
 Congress **V**:90
 Congress, Confederate **V**:88
 Davis, Jefferson **V**:104
 Eagleton, Thomas F. **X**:107
 elections **V**:126
 ERA **X**:124
 governors **V**:172
 habeas corpus, writ of **V**:181
 homefront **V**:193
 Jones Act (1917) **VII**:157
 Kennedy, Edward M. **X**:196
 Letcher, John **V**:232

 peace movements **V**:296
 race and race relations **V**:320
 Schenck v. U.S. **VII**:313
 Selective Service Act
  VII:321
 socialism **VII**:328
 Soldiers' Bonus **VII**:331
 states' rights **V**:370
 Stephens, Alexander
  Hamilton **V**:371
 Trading with the Enemy Act
  VII:355
 Union army **V**:400–401
 Wigfall, Louis T. **V**:431
conscription, end of **X**:89, 376*c*
Conscription Act of 1862
 (Confederacy) **V**:86, 90
Conscription Act of 1863 (Union)
 V:39, 283, 284
Conscription Act of 1864
 (Confederacy) **V**:90
Conseil Européen pour la
 Recherche Nucléaire (CERN)
 X:319
conservation, environmentalism,
 and environmental policy
 VI:81–82; IX:356*c,* 357*c;*
 X:89–92, *91,* 375*c*
 Antiquities Act **VII**:16
 art and architecture **X**:32
 automobile industry **X**:36
 CCC **VIII**:70–71
 Clinton, William J. **X**:81
 conservative movement
  X:93
 energy **X**:120
 environment **VI**:119–120;
  VII:98; **IX**:108
 global warming **X**:155–156
 Hurricane Katrina **X**:173
 Ickes, Harold L. **VIII**:183
 Johnson, Lady Bird **IX**:162,
  163
 Marsh, George Perkins
  VI:239
 Mitchell, George **X**:232
 Muir, John **VI**:254
 NAFTA **X**:259
 National Wilderness
  Preservation Act of 1964
  IX:240
 NEPA **X**:246
 Pinchot, Gifford **VII**:259,
  260
 property rights **X**:290–291
 recreation **IX**:271
 Walcott, Charles Doolittle
  VI:380
 Watt, James G. **X**:367
 Wild and Scenic Rivers Act
  of 1968 **IX**:343–344
conservatism **VIII:83–85;**
 IX:74–75
 American Liberty League
  VIII:19
 Americans for Democratic
  Action **IX**:13

Chambers, Whittaker **IX:**53
Congress **VIII:**80
conservative coalition
   VIII:86
court-packing plan **VIII:**89
election of 1936 **VIII:**110
elections **IX:**104
Goldwater, Barry **IX:**135,
   136
Great Society **IX:**139
Hiss, Alger **IX:**147
housing **VIII:**178
liberalism **IX:**191
New Deal **VIII:**270
politics (Roosevelt era)
   VIII:300
relief **VIII:**333
Republican Party **VII:**300;
   IX:274
States' Rights Party **IX:**299
Supreme Court **VIII:**382
unemployment **VIII:**400
World War II **VIII:**428
YAF **IX:**349–350
conservative coalition (1930s)
   VIII:85–86, 446c
CCC **VIII:**71
Congress **VIII:**79–80
conservatism **VIII:**85
court-packing plan **VIII:**89
Democratic Party **VIII:**93–
   94
Executive Reorganization
   Act **VIII:**121
Fair Labor Standards Act
   VIII:124
Full Employment Bill
   VIII:145
Garner, John Nance **VIII:**147
government **VIII:**153
liberalism **VIII:**216
New Deal **VIII:**270, 271
NRPB **VIII:**261
politics (Roosevelt era)
   VIII:300
postwar planning **VIII:**306
presidency **VIII:**309
recession of 1937–1938
   VIII:324
Republican Party **VIII:**337
Roosevelt, Franklin D.
   VIII:346
South **VIII:**367
Supreme Court **VIII:**383
Taft, Robert A. **VIII:**385
taxation **VIII:**388
Third New Deal **VIII:**393
World War II home front
   VIII:434
WPA **VIII:**426
Conservative Judaism **VIII:**334;
   X:193, 307
"Conservative Manifesto" **VIII:**446c
Congress **VIII:**80
conservatism **VIII:**85
conservative coalition
   VIII:86

Conservative Mind, The (Kirk)
   X:93
conservative movement **X:92–94**
African Americans **X:**14
Bennett, William J. **X:**41
Buchanan, Patrick J. **X:**49
Buckley, William F., Jr. **X:**49,
   50
capital punishment **X:**66
elections, presidential **X:**118
ERA **X:**123, 124
Helms, Jesse A., Jr. **X:**165
House of Representatives
   X:169
immigration **X:**177
Laffer curve **X:**204
liberalism **X:**207, 208
Moral Majority **X:**234
neoconservatism **X:**251–252
political correctness **X:**276
political parties **X:**276
pornography **X:**284
property rights **X:**290
Quayle, J. Danforth **X:**293
Reagan, Ronald W. **X:**300
Reaganomics **X:**302
Schlafly, Phyllis **X:**316
Supreme Court **X:**338, 339
Thomas, Clarence **X:**350
Conservative Party (Mexico)
   IV:330
Considerations on Keeping
   Negroes: Part Second
   (Woolman) **II:**427
Considerations on Paintings (La
   Farge) **VI:**218
Considerations on the Nature
   and Extent of the Legislative
   Authority of the British
   Parliament (Wilson) **III:**444
Considerations on the Propriety
   of Imposing Taxes in the British
   Colonies (Dulany) **III:**142,
   459c
Considerations Respecting the
   Helots of the United States
   (Tench) **III:**125
consistory **I:**54
Constantinople **I:**196
Constellation (U.S. frigate)
Barbary Wars **III:**45
Barry, John **III:**47
Quasi War **III:**353
Constitution, ratification of the
   III:104–106
anti-Federalists **III:**24
Chase, Samuel **III:**85
debt, national **III:**129
Federalist Papers **III:**162–
   163
Federalist Party **III:**164
Federalists **III:**165, 166
foreign affairs **III:**168
Hamilton, Alexander
   III:206
journalism **III:**240
Macon, Nathaniel **III:**280

Madison, James **III:**283
Paine, Thomas **III:**330
Penobscot campaign
   III:334
Wilson, James **III:**444
Constitution, USS ("Old
   Ironsides") **III:107–108,** 465c;
   IV:*391*
Barbary Wars **III:**45
Essex, USS **IV:**144
Holmes, Oliver Wendell
   VII:140
Quasi War **III:**353
Revere, Paul **III:**367
War of 1812 **IV:**391
Constitution Act **III:**79
Constitutional Convention
   III:108–110
Annapolis Convention
   III:23
anti-Federalists **III:**24
antislavery **III:**26
Articles of Confederation
   III:34
Blount, William **III:**53
Brackenridge, Hugh Henry
   III:60
debt, national **III:**131
Dickinson, John **III:**137
Federalist Papers **III:**162,
   163
Federalists **III:**166
Franklin, Benjamin **III:**174
Gerry, Elbridge **III:**194
Hamilton, Alexander
   III:206
Henry, Patrick **III:**212
impeachment **III:**222
Independence Hall **III:**223
King, Rufus **III:**245
Livingston, William **III:**270–
   271
Madison, James **III:**282
Martin, Luther **III:**291
Mason, George **III:**292
Missouri Compromise
   IV:256
Monroe, James **IV:**259
Morris, Gouverneur **III:**304
Pinckney, Charles
   Cotesworth **III:**336
Randolph, Edmund **III:**358
Sherman, Roger **III:**389
states' rights **III:**397
Washington, George **III:**431
Wilson, James **III:**444
Constitutional League **VII:**224
Constitutional Post **II:**304
Constitutional Unionist Party
   V:443c
Bell, John **V:**32
Harlan, John Marshall
   VI:159
Vance, Zebulon B. **V:**414
Constitutional View of the Late
   War Between the States, A
   (Stephens) **V:**372

Constitution Hall (Washington,
   D.C.) **VIII:**3
Constitution of Missouri **IV:424–
   425**
Constitution of the Confederate
   States of America **V:456–457**
civil liberties, Confederate
   V:68
Confederate States of
   America **V:**84–85
fire-eaters **V:**146
habeas corpus, writ of **V:**181
race and race relations
   V:319
Constitution of the United States
   III:106–107, 461c, 463c, **474–
   480; VIII:**444c, 446c, 448c;
   IX:356c; **X:**376c, 382c
abolitionism **IV:**1, 3; **V:**2–3
abortion **X:**2
Adams, John **III:**5, 6
Adams, Samuel **III:**8
African Americans **III:**9
Agricultural Adjustment
   Administration **VIII:**7
Albany Congress **II:**15
Amendment, Eleventh
   III:16
Amendment, Twelfth
   III:16–17
Amendments to the U.S.
   Constitution **X:**22–24
American Anti-Slavery
   Society **IV:**15
American Revolution **III:**18
American System **IV:**20, 21
Ames, Fisher **III:**19
amnesty, acts of **V:**9
anti-Federalists **III:**23–25
Articles of Confederation
   III:34
Backus, Isaac **III:**40
banks **III:**42
Bill of Rights **III:**50
Black, Hugo L. **VIII:**45
Brackenridge, Hugh Henry
   III:60
Carroll of Carrollton,
   Charles **III:**82
citizenship **III:**93
citizen-soldier **V:**68
civil liberties **VII:**57, 58
civil liberties, Union **V:**69
civil rights **VIII:**72
Clinton, George **III:**98–99
commemoration **IX:**66
Confederate States of
   America **V:**85
Congressional Budget and
   Impoundment Control
   Act **X:**88, 89
Constitution, ratification of
   the **III:**104–106
Constitutional Convention
   III:108
Continental Congress,
   Second **III:**115

Constitution of the United States
(*continued*)
　　Dartmouth College case
　　　IV:114
　　Dekanawideh **II:**93
　　Democratic Party **IV:**118;
　　　V:108
　　Dickinson, John **III:**137
　　economy **III:**146
　　election of 1800 **III:**150
　　elections, presidential
　　　X:116, 118
　　Equal Access Act **X:**122
　　Exodusters **VI:**122
　　federal income tax **VII:**107
　　federalism **X:**130, 131
　　Federalist Papers **III:**162,
　　　163
　　Federalists **III:**166
　　Foraker Act **VII:**110
　　Four Freedoms **VIII:**144
　　fugitive slave laws **IV:**168
　　Garrison, William Lloyd
　　　V:164, 165
　　Great Awakening **II:**156
　　habeas corpus, writ of
　　　V:181, 182
　　Hancock, John **III:**209
　　Heart of Atlanta Motel v.
　　　U.S. **IX:**145, 146
　　history **VII:**140
　　impeachment **III:**222
　　Indian Affairs, Bureau of
　　　IV:196
　　Industrial Revolution
　　　III:225
　　internal improvements
　　　IV:203
　　Internal Revenue taxes
　　　VI:194
　　Iroquois **I:**187
　　Jews **III:**236, 237
　　journalism **III:**240
　　Judiciary Act (1789) **III:**242
　　Judiciary Act (1801) **III:**242
　　King, Rufus **III:**245
　　Liberia **VI:**223
　　Louisiana Purchase **III:**273
　　Madison, James **III:**281
　　Mann Act **VII:**189
　　McCulloch v. Maryland
　　　IV:245–246
　　Meat Inspection Act
　　　VII:198
　　Meese, Edwin C., III **X:**225
　　Morris, Gouverneur **III:**303,
　　　304
　　Nullification Controversy
　　　IV:282
　　Patrons of Husbandry
　　　VI:279
　　Pennsylvania **II:**288
　　Pentagon Papers **X:**272
　　personal liberty laws **IV:**298
　　Phillips, Wendell **IV:**299
　　political parties **III:**338
　　popular sovereignty **IV:**304

Port Huron Statement
　　IX:260
Prohibition **VII:**272
pro-life/pro-choice
　　movements **X:**289
race and race relations
　　IV:309, 310, 312
Randolph, Edmund **III:**358
Randolph, John **III:**359
Reconstruction **V:**324
religion **III:**361; **IV:**316
religion, Euro-American
　　II:330
religious liberty **III:**364
republicanism **III:**365
Republican Party **IV:**323
Reynolds v. Sims **IX:**276
secession **V:**344
segregation **III:**319; **IX:**288
Sherman, Roger **III:**389
slavery **IV:**345–346
states' rights **III:**397; **V:**370
States' Rights Party **IX:**299–
　　300
suffrage **IV:**360
Supreme Court **III:**402–
　　403
tariffs **III:**406
taxation **VIII:**387
Thomas, Clarence **X:**350
trade, domestic and foreign
　　III:414
Twenty-sixth Amendment
　　X:354
Tyler, John **IV:**383
Volstead Act **VII:**374
Washington, George
　　III:432
Washington Benevolent
　　Societies **III:**433
Whigs **IV:**398
constitutions, state **III:**110–111,
　　461*c*
　　abolitionism **III:**1
　　Adams, John **III:**5
　　Adams, Samuel **III:**7
　　American Revolution **III:**18
　　Carroll of Carrollton,
　　　Charles **III:**82
　　Catholics **III:**83
　　citizenship **III:**93, 95
　　Constitution, ratification of
　　　the **III:**105
　　Ely, Samuel Cullick **III:**151
　　Gallatin, Albert **III:**187
　　Hancock, John **III:**209
　　Henry, Patrick **III:**212
　　impeachment **III:**222
　　Jay, John **III:**229
　　Jews **III:**237
　　Lyon, Matthew **III:**277
　　Mason, George **III:**292
　　Morris, Gouverneur **III:**303
　　Peale, Charles Willson
　　　III:333
　　Randolph, Edmund **III:**358
　　Rittenhouse, David **III:**372

suffrage **III:**400
Yates, Abraham **III:**453
Young, Thomas **III:**457
Construction Construed and
　　Constitutions Vindicated
　　(Taylor) **III:**408
constructionism **X:**311
Consular Service, U.S. **VII:**152
Consumer Advisory Board
　　VIII:139
consumer goods **VIII:**282,
　　322–323
consumerism **IX:75–76**
　　advertising **VI:**3; **IX:**2; **X:**7
　　baby boomers **X:**40
　　childhood **IX:**54, 55
　　cold war culture **IX:**64, 65
　　credit cards **IX:**79
　　literature **IX:**194
　　shopping centers **IX:**290
　　trade, domestic and foreign
　　　VI:359
Consumer Price Index (CPI)
　　COLA **IX:**76
　　OPA **VIII:**282
　　wage and price controls
　　　VIII:409, 410
consumer protection
　　business **IX:**47
　　Carter, James Earl, Jr. **X:**69
　　consumerism **IX:**76
　　economy **IX:**97
Consumer Reports **IX:**202
consumer rights movement **X:**241
Consumers Research, Inc. **VIII:**1
Consumers Union **VIII:**1
consumption. *See* tuberculosis
containment
　　domino theory **IX:**89
　　Dulles, John Foster **IX:**91
　　Europe **IX:**113
　　Kennan, George F. **IX:**167
　　Korean War **IX:**177
　　military-industrial complex
　　　IX:216
　　modern Republicanism
　　　IX:221
contempt of Congress
　　Hollywood Ten **IX:**147
　　HUAC **IX:**150, 151
　　impeachment of Richard M.
　　　Nixon **X:**178
"Contents of Children's Minds,
　　The" (Hall) **VI:**157
Continental army **II:**351;
　　III:111–112, *112,* 461*c*
　　African Americans **III:**9
　　alcohol **III:**13
　　Arnold, Benedict **III:**30–31
　　banks **III:**42
　　Beaumarchais, Pierre-
　　　Auguste Caron de **III:**48
　　Bingham, William **III:**51
　　Brandywine, Battle of
　　　III:62
　　Brant, Joseph **III:**63
　　Burgoyne, Sir John **III:**68

Burr, Aaron **III:**69
Camden, Battle of **III:**74–
　　76
camp followers **III:**76–77
Charleston, siege of **III:**84,
　　85
Charleston Expedition of
　　1776 **III:**84
Cincinnati, Order of **III:**90
Clinton, George **III:**98
Continental army, mutinies
　　of **III:**112–113
Continental Congress,
　　Second **III:**115
Conway Cabal, the **III:**118
Cowpens, Battle of **III:**124
debt, national **III:**130
Dragging Canoe **III:**139
dueling **III:**140–141
Dwight, Timothy **III:**143
Estaing, Charles-Henri
　　Theodat, comte d'
　　III:158
Federalists **III:**166
Fort Washington, capture of
　　III:172
freemasonry **III:**176
French Alliance **III:**177,
　　178
Gates, Horatio **III:**189–190
Georgia Expedition **III:**192
Germantown, Battle of
　　III:193, 194
Greene, Nathanael **III:**198–
　　199
Green Mountain Boys
　　III:199
Guilford Courthouse, Battle
　　of **III:**202
Hale, Nathan **III:**204
Hamilton, Alexander
　　III:205–206
Harlem Heights, Battle of
　　III:210
Hobkirk's Hill, Battle of
　　III:213
Howe, Richard, Lord
　　III:214
Howe, Sir William **III:**215
Hull, Agrippa **III:**217
Hull, William **IV:**192
Independence Hall **III:**223
Jews **III:**236
Kalb, Johann, baron de
　　III:245
King's Mountain, Battle of
　　III:247
Knox, Henry **III:**247
Kościuszko, Tadeusz
　　III:248
Lafayette, marquis de
　　III:253
Lee, Charles **III:**258–259
Lee, Henry **III:**259
Lee, Robert E. **V:**230
L'Enfant, Pierre-Charles
　　III:260

Long Island, Battle of
III:271–272
Lyon, Matthew **III**:277
Marion, Francis **III**:286
Marshall, John **III**:289
McDougall, Alexander
III:294
medicine **III**:295
Molly Pitcher **III**:298
Monmouth, Battle of
III:299–300
Monroe, James **IV**:258
Montgomery, Richard
III:301
Moore's Creek Bridge,
Battle of **III**:301
Morgan, Daniel **III**:303
Morristown encampment
III:306–307
music **III**:309
Native Americans **III**:312
Newburgh conspiracy
III:316
Ohio Company of Associates
III:323
Pickering, Timothy **III**:334
Pulaski, Casimir **III**:350
Putnam, Israel **III**:350
Quakers **III**:351
Red Bank, Battle of
III:359
Red Jacket **III**:359
Revere, Paul **III**:367
Revolutionary War **III**:368
Rhode Island, Battle of
III:370
Rush, Benjamin **III**:376
St. Clair, Arthur **III**:377–
378
Sampson, Deborah **III**:379–
380
Saratoga, surrender at
III:380–382
Savannah, Battle of **III**:382–
383
Steuben, Frederick, baron
von **III**:398
Stoney Point, Battle of
III:399
Sullivan, John **III**:402
Taylor, John, of Caroline
III:408
Trenton and Princeton,
Battles of **III**:416
Trumbull, John **III**:416
Valley Forge **III**:421–423
Washington, George
III:430–431
Wayne, Anthony **III**:433
White Plains, Battle of
III:440–441
Wilkinson, James **III**:443
women's status and rights
III:446
"Yankee Doodle" **III**:453
Yorktown, surrender at
III:457

Continental army, mutinies of
III:112–113
Continental army **III**:111
Continental Congress,
Second **III**:116
Morristown encampment
III:307
"Continental Army" (1916
Preparedness plan) **VII**:227,
267
Continental Association. *See*
Association, the
Continental Certificates **III**:130,
131, 305
Continental Congress, First
III:113–115, *114,* 460*c*
Adams, Samuel **III**:7
Association, the **III**:37
Bland, Richard **III**:52
Burke, Edmund **III**:69
Continental Congress,
Second **III**:115
Deane, Silas **III**:129
Declaration of
Independence **III**:132
Dickinson, John **III**:137
Galloway, Joseph **III**:188–
189
Jay, John **III**:229
Lee, Arthur **III**:258
resistance movement
III:366
Revere, Paul **III**:367
Rodney, Caesar **III**:373
Washington, George
III:430
Wilson, James **III**:444
Continental Congress, Second
III:115–117, 461*c*, 463*c*
Adams, John **III**:5
African Americans **III**:9
Annapolis Convention
III:23
antislavery **III**:26
Articles of Confederation
III:33
Bank of North America
III:40
Bingham, William **III**:51
Bland, Richard **III**:52
Burgoyne, Sir John **III**:68
Canada **III**:78
Carlisle commission **III**:82
Carroll of Carrollton,
Charles **III**:82
citizenship **III**:93
Clinton, George **III**:98
constitutions, state **III**:110
Continental army **III**:111
Continental navy **III**:117
Deane, Silas **III**:129
debt, national **III**:130, 132
Declaration of
Independence **III**:132–
133
Dickinson, John **III**:137
Duer, William **III**:141

Federalists **III**:165
Franklin, Benjamin **III**:174
French Alliance **III**:177
Galloway, Joseph **III**:189
George III **III**:191
Gerry, Elbridge **III**:194
Hancock, John **III**:209
Henry, Patrick **III**:211–212
Independence Hall **III**:223
Jay, John **III**:229
Lafayette, marquis de
III:253, 254
Laurens, Henry **III**:255
Lee, Arthur **III**:258
Lee, Charles **III**:258
Livingston, Philip **II**:207
Livingston, Robert R.
III:270
Madison, James **III**:281,
282
Martin, Luther **III**:291
Morris, Robert **III**:305
Newburgh conspiracy
III:316
Olive Branch Petition
III:324
Pitt, William **III**:337
POWs **III**:345
privateering **III**:347
Randolph, Edmund
III:358
Rodney, Caesar **III**:373
Rush, Benjamin **III**:376
Schuyler, Philip John
III:384
trade, domestic and foreign
III:413
Washington, George
III:430
Wilson, James **III**:444
Witherspoon, John **III**:445
Yates, Abraham **III**:453
Continental Divide
fur trade **IV**:171
Oregon Trail **IV**:285
"Pike's Peak or Bust" **IV**:301
Continental navy **III:117,** 461*c*
African Americans **III**:9
Barry, John **III**:47
Chauncey, Isaac **III**:86
Constitution, USS **III**:107–
108
Jones, John Paul **III**:238–
239
POWs **III**:346
Continental System **III**:49
contrabands **V:92–93**
Butler, Benjamin Franklin
V:53
Cary, Mary Ann Shadd
V:58
Eaton, John, Jr. **V**:120
emancipation **V**:128–129
Freedmen's Bureau **V**:160
Mason-Dixon Line **V**:250
Memphis riot (1866) **V**:259
nurses **V**:285

Port Royal Experiment
V:312
slavery **V**:364
Thirteenth Amendment
V:387
contraception. *See* birth control;
"The Pill"
contract bridge **VIII**:328
contracted immigration
Alamo, The **IV**:14
Austin, Moses **IV**:39
Austin, Stephen F. **IV**:39–40
foreign policy **IV**:155
Houston, Sam **IV**:191
Texas **IV**:371
Texas Revolution **IV**:373
Contraction Act (1866) **VI**:88–89
contract labor **VI:82**
immigration **VI**:184
immigration restrictions
VI:187
Knights of Labor **VI**:209
Contract Labor Act (1864) **VI**:82
contract law **IV**:361–362
Contract with America **X**:380*c*
Gingrich, Newton L. **X**:151
House of Representatives
X:170
NEPA **X**:246
Senate, U.S. **X**:321
Contract with America (Gingrich)
X:152
contras **X:94–95**
Boland Amendment **X**:45
cold war, end of **X**:85
foreign policy **X**:142
Gore, Albert, Jr. **X**:157
Iran-contra affair **X**:183
Nicaragua **X**:254–255
North, Oliver L. **X**:258
Contrast, The (Tyler) **III**:411,
417, 462*c*
Contreras, Battle of **V**:190, 209
*Contributions to the Ethnography
and Philology of the Indian
Tribes of the Missouri Valley*
(Hayden) **VI**:164–165
Controlled Materials Plan
VIII:242
Controlled Substance Act (1971)
X:242, 243, 375*c*
Conventional Armed Forces in
Europe Treaty **X**:379*c*
Convention of 1800 **III**:353, 415
Convention of 1818 **IV**:154, 286
Convention of London **IV**:411*c*
Conventuals **I**:133
Conversations on Common Things
(Dix) **IV**:124
conversos
auto-da-fé **I**:17
Ferdinand and Isabella
I:128
inquisition **I**:182
Jews **I**:195
Las Casas, Bartolomé de
I:205

convict labor **II**:79–80
    contract labor **VI**:82
    English immigrants **II**:117
    Hollywood Cemetery **V**:192
    indentured servitude **II**:174
    labor/labor movements
        III:251–252
    Scots immigrants **II**:346
convivencia **I**:128
convoys **VIII**:86–87
    America First Committee
        VIII:17
    Atlantic, Battle of the
        VIII:33
    North African campaign
        VIII:278
Conway, Martin F. **IV**:242
Conway, Thomas **III**:118, 141
Conway Cabal, the **III**:**118**
    dueling **III**:141
    Gates, Horatio **III**:190
    Valley Forge **III**:421
Conyers, John, Jr. **IX**:255
Coode, John
    Glorious Revolution **II**:149
    Maryland **II**:220
    St. Mary's City **II**:343
Cook, Clarence **VI**:3
Cook, James **I**:274
    Bering, Vitus Jonassen **II**:36
    Hawaii **III**:210; **IV**:188;
        VI:163
    Kamehameha I **IV**:211
    Northwest Coast Indians
        II:275
Cook, Will Marion **VI**:257; **VII**:219
Cook and Brother Armory **V**:424
Cook County, Illinois **VII**:67
Cooke, Alistair **VII**:5
Cooke, Elisha, Jr. **II**:**80**
Cooke, Jay **V**:**93**. *See also* Jay
    Cooke & Company
    banking, investment **VI**:23
    business cycles **VI**:58
    Chase, Salmon P. **V**:62
    Donnelly, Ignatius Loyola
        VI:100
    economy **V**:121
    Philadelphia **V**:303
Cooke, W. F. **IV**:333
cooks **V**:286
Cook v. Gralike **X**:131
Coolidge, Calvin John **VII**:63–65,
    64, 71, 408*c*
    advertising **VII**:5
    AFL **VII**:12
    agriculture **VIII**:9
    aviation **VII**:28–29
    conservatism **VIII**:84
    elections **VII**:91, 92
    environment **VIII**:115
    Garvey, Marcus **VII**:122
    Harding, Warren Gamaliel
        VII:135
    Hoover, Herbert C. **VIII**:172
    Hughes, Charles Evans
        VII:142

Kelly Air Mail Act **VII**:165
    Lindbergh, Charles
        Augustus **VII**:177
    McNary-Haugen Farm Bill
        VII:195–196
    Naval Disarmament
        Conference **VII**:235
    presidency **VII**:268, 269
    progressivism **VII**:271
    radicalism **VII**:288
    Republican Party **VII**:301
    socialism **VII**:328
    Tennessee Valley Authority
        VIII:392
    UNIA **VII**:362
    veterans **VII**:372
    Veterans Bureau **VII**:373
    WILPF **VII**:386
Coolidge, William **VII**:123
Cooper, Anthony Ashley **II**:274
Cooper, Douglas **V**:278
Cooper, Gary **IX**:147
Cooper, George **V**:156
Cooper, James Fenimore **IV**:412*c*
    Cowboys and Skinners
        III:123
    dime novels **VI**:98
    journalism **IV**:210
    literature **III**:268; **IV**:227,
        228
Cooper, Peter
    Baltimore & Ohio Railroad
        IV:44
    currency issue **VI**:89
    economy **IV**:131
    Greenback-Labor Party
        VI:155
    industrialization **IV**:200
    railroads **IV**:314
Cooper, William **III**:146
Cooper River **III**:84
Cooper Shop Volunteer
    Refreshment Saloon **V**:228
Cooperstown, New York **IV**:228;
    VII:33
Cooper Union (New York City)
    IV:135; **VII**:324
Cooper Union speech (Lincoln)
    V:93–94, 236, 443*c*
Cooper v. Aaron **X**:48
Cooper v. Boren **X**:48
Coordinator of Information (COI)
    VIII:284
Coors, Joseph **X**:93
Coosa **I**:89
Copán **I**:89–90, 356, 359
Cope, Edward **VI**:240, 325
Copland, Aaron **VI**:254; **VII**:220;
    VIII:134, 251; **IX**:228; **X**:238
Copley, John Singleton **II**:225;
    III:118
    art **III**:32, 33
    Peale, Charles Willson
        III:332
    Trumbull, John **III**:416
    West, Benjamin **III**:436
Coppage v. Kansas **VII**:406*c*

copper
    industrial development
        V:204
    Revere, Paul **III**:367
    scrap drives **VIII**:354
Copperheads **V**:94–95
    civil liberties, Union **V**:70
    Congress **V**:89
    Democratic Party **V**:109
    Harvard Regiment **V**:186
    homefront **V**:193
    Lincoln, Abraham **V**:236
    Morton, Oliver P. **V**:270
    Murfreesboro/Stones River,
        Battle of **V**:272
    Nast, Thomas **V**:275
    peace movements **V**:295–
        296
    Seymour, Horatio **V**:348
    Vallandigham, Clement L.
        V:413
    Women's National Loyal
        League **V**:434
copper mines **VI**:17, 246
Copper Queen mine **VI**:246
Coppola, Francis Ford **X**:279
copyrights/copyright law **VI**:411*c*;
    X:378*c*, 382*c*
    computers **X**:88
    Herbert, Victor August
        VI:171
    science and technology
        X:317
Coquibacoa **I**:277
Coral Sea, Battle of the **VIII**:**87**
    aircraft carriers **VIII**:12
    air power **VIII**:15
    Guadalcanal **VIII**:159
    Midway, Battle of **VIII**:238
    Navy, U.S. **VIII**:265
    Nimitz, Chester W.
        VIII:274
    Solomon Islands **VIII**:365
    World War II Pacific theater
        VIII:436
Coral Sea, USS **VIII**:12
Coralville, Iowa **IV**:262
Corbett, Boston **V**:39
Corbett, James J. **VI**:44, 45
Corby, William **V**:205
Corcoran, Michael **V**:205
Córdoba, Francisco Hernández
    de **I**:90–91, 145, 147
cordon strategy **V**:380
CORE. *See* Congress of Racial
    Equality
Coretta Scott King Award **IX**:175
Corey, Giles **II**:420
Corinth, Battle of **V**:95–96, 313,
    337
Corliss engine **VI**:284
corn **I**:*91*, 91–92, 395*c*; **II**:80–81
    agriculture **II**:8–11, 13, 14
    Akan **I**:5
    alcohol **III**:13
    Cahokia **I**:50
    Columbian Exchange **I**:81

Connecticut **II**:77
Crow **II**:85
Florida **I**:131
food **II**:130
Huron **I**:172
Iroquois **I**:185; **II**:180
Massachusett **I**:233
Mississippian **I**:244, 245
Native American religion
    I:260
New Mexico **I**:263
New Spain **I**:269–270
Roanoke **I**:321
Secotan **I**:329
Zuni **I**:393
Cornbury, Lord (Edward Hyde)
    II:107, **171**
Cornelius, Don **X**:239
Cornell, Ezra **VI**:112, 391
Cornell University
    Bourke-White, Margaret
        VIII:50
    education, philanthropy and
        VI:112
    Ely, Richard Theodore
        VI:115
    Ethical Culture movement
        VI:121
    Hughes, Charles Evans
        VII:142
    Kelley, Florence **VII**:164
    White, Andrew Dickson
        VI:391
corn harvester **IV**:333, 413*c*
Cornish, Samuel E. **IV**:8, 209,
    412*c*
Corn Laws **IV**:287
Cornplanter **III**:118–119, *119*,
    359–360; **IV**:277
Cornstalk **II**:81
Cornu, Sebastian **IV**:60
Cornwall, Connecticut **IV**:61
Cornwallis, Charles, Lord
    III:**119–121**, *120*, 462*c*
    Brandywine, Battle of
        III:62
    Camden, Battle of **III**:75,
        76
    Capes, Battle of the **III**:79,
        80
    Charleston, siege of **III**:84
    Charleston Expedition of
        1776 **III**:83, 84
    Clinton, Sir Henry **III**:99
    Cowpens, Battle of **III**:124–
        125
    Delaware River forts
        III:135
    Eutaw Springs, Battle of
        III:159
    Fort Washington, capture of
        III:172
    French Alliance **III**:177
    Grasse, François-Joseph-
        Paul, comte de **III**:197
    Greene, Nathanael **III**:198,
        199

Guilford Courthouse, Battle of **III:**201, 202
Jefferson, Thomas **III:**232
King's Mountain, Battle of **III:**246
Knyphausen, Wilhelm, Baron von **III:**248
Lafayette, marquis de **III:**253
Laurens, Henry **III:**255
Monmouth, Battle of **III:**299, 300
Revolutionary War **III:**368
Rochambeau, Jean-Baptiste-Donatien de Vimeur, comte de **III:**372
Tarleton, Banastre **III:**407
Trenton and Princeton, Battles of **III:**416
Yorktown, surrender at **III:**454–455, 457
Cornwallis, Edward **II:**2
Corolla Line **IX:**116
Coronado, Francisco Vásquez de **I:**92–93, 397*c;* **II:**317
Franciscans **I:**133
gold **I:**142
Hopi **I:**168
Narrative Relating to Francisco Coronado's explorations of the Southwest, 1540–1542 **I:**410–412
New Mexico **I:**265
Pueblo **I:**305
Texas **IV:**371
Zuni **I:**394
corporal punishment **III:**347
corporate relocations **X:**202–203
Corporation for National Service **IX:**333
corporations **III:**121; **VI:**410*c;* **VII:**403*c. See also specific corporations*
Bank of the United States, First **III:**41
business **X:**58, 59
economy **III:**146; **VII:**84, 85; **IX:**98
Field, Stephen Johnson **VI:**127
Foreign Corrupt Practices Act **X:**139–140
Galbraith, John Kenneth **IX:**129, 130
GE **IX:**132
GM **IX:**132–133
Hamilton, Alexander **III:**207
House of Representatives **X:**170–171
Industrial Revolution, Second **VI:**192
insurance **III:**227
Morgan, John Pierpont **VI:**251
railroads **V:**322

Revenue Act of 1935 **VIII:**340
Revenue Act of 1942 **VIII:**341
Rockefeller, John Davison **VII:**302
trusts **VI:**364
corporatism **III:**122, 338, 371
Corps d'Afrique **V:**96
Corps of Discovery **III:**262
Corps of Ordnance **V:**171
Corps of Topographical Engineers **IV:**145, 166
Corpus Christi, Texas **IV:**368
corrective advertising **X:**7
corregidor **I:**93–94
audiencia **I:**16
cabildo **I:**41
Mendoza, Antonio de **I:**239
New Spain **I:**268
Tlaxcala **I:**362
Corregidor Island, Philippines **VIII:**42, 294, 295
corregimientos **I:**93
Correll, Charles **VII:**290
corrupt bargain
Adams, John Quincy **IV:**6
Clay, Henry **IV:**97
election of 1828 **IV:**135
Jackson, Andrew **IV:**206
corruption **IX:**354*c. See also* political corruption
Crédit Mobilier **V:**97
Grant, Ulysses S. **V:**175
journalism **V:**219
Reconstruction **V:**326
Sickles, Daniel E. **V:**360
Teamsters Union **IX:**310
union movement **IX:**323
Warmoth, Henry Clay **V:**425
Whiskey Ring **V:**429, 430
Corrupt Practices Act (1925) **X:**63
Corso, Gregory **IX:**36, 195
Cortés, Hernán **I:**94–97, 95, 396*c,* 397*c;* **II:**374
Aguilar, Francisco de **I:**4
Aguilar, Gerónimo de **I:**5
Alvarado, Pedro de **I:**7
Aztecs **I:**21–22
black legend **I:**31
cabildo **I:**41
Cacamatzin **I:**47
castas **I:**64–65
Charles V **I:**70, 71
Cholula **I:**74
Columbian Exchange **I:**82
conquistadores **I:**88
Cozumel **I:**99
Cuauhtémoc **I:**99, 100
Díaz del Castillo, Bernal **I:**106
Escalante, Juan de **I:**123, 124
Franciscans **I:**133
Grijalva, Juan de **I:**145
horses **I:**168

Las Casas, Bartolomé de **I:**205
limpieza de sangre **I:**214
Malinche **I:**226–227
Mendoza, Antonio de **I:**239
Mexico **I:**242
Moctezuma II Xocoyotzin **I:**245, 246
Narváez, Pánfilo de **I:**258–259
New Spain **I:**267
Quetzalcoatl **I:**309
Sahagún, Bernardino de **I:**323
Sandoval, Gonzalo de **I:**325
smallpox **I:**341
Tabasco **I:**351
Tacuba **I:**352
Tenochtitlán **I:**354, 356
Tezcatlipoca **I:**357
Tlaxcala **I:**362
Toltecs **I:**364
Velázquez, Diego de **I:**374
Veracruz **I:**376
Xicotencatl the Elder **I:**387
Xicotencatl the Younger **I:**387
Corvair (Chevrolet). *See* Chevrolet Corvair
Corvo (brig) **IV:**100
Corynebacterium diphtheria **II:**100
COs. *See* conscientious objectors
Cos, Perfecto de **IV:**328, 329
Cosby, William
De Lancey, James **II:**93
Morris, Lewis **II:**243
New York **II:**271
Zenger, John Peter **II:**433
Cosby Show **X:**343
cosmetics and beauty industry **VII:**65–66; **VIII:**446*c*
cosmographers **I:**368–369
Cosmographia Universalis (Münster) **I:**57
Cosmographie de Levant (Thevet) **I:**357
Cosmographie Universelle, La (Thevet) **I:**358, 413–418
Cosmopolitan
Hearst, William Randolph **VII:**138
journalism **VII:**159
muckrakers **VII:**217
cosmopolitanism **VI:**18
Costa Rica **V:**145
Costigan, Joseph **VIII:**23
Costigan-Wagner antilynching bill **VIII:**72
cost-of-living adjustment (COLA) **IX:**76–77, 352*c*
business **IX:**47
CIO **IX:**72
economy **IX:**97
labor/labor movements **IX:**182
Cost of Living Council **X:**108

Coswall, Robert **II:**370
Cotopaxi Iron Works **IV:**243
Cottage Residences (Downing) **IV:**31
Cottier, Daniel **VI:**3
cotton **III:**122–123, 463*c*
African Americans **VI:**6
agriculture **III:**11; **IV:**13; **V:**5–6; **VI:**9; **VII:**7
Carver, George Washington **VI:**63
Confederate States of America **V:**86
Coxe, Tench **III:**125
Davis Bend, Mississippi, freedmen's colony **V:**107
economy **V:**121
foreign policy **V:**150
industrial development **IV:**199; **V:**204, 205
Industrial Revolution **III:**224
Mississippi River **V:**262
New South **VI:**265
New York City **V:**283
Port Royal Experiment **V:**312
Red River campaign **V:**329
Slater, Samuel **III:**389
slavery **III:**390; **V:**363
South **VIII:**366
trade, domestic and foreign **VI:**360
Whitney, Eli **III:**441–442
Cotton, John **II:**81, 81–82, 165, 416
Cotton Belt
abolitionism **IV:**1
economy **IV:**133
slave trade, internal **IV:**348
Cotton Bowl **VIII:**371
Cotton Club (Harlem, New York City)
big bands **VIII:**44
Ellington, Duke **VIII:**112
music **VII:**220
cotton culture **IV:**106–109, 107*m*
agriculture **IV:**11
economy **IV:**130, 133
Indian Removal Act **IV:**198
industrialization **IV:**201
migration **IV:**254
panic of 1837 **IV:**294, 295
slavery **IV:**347
slave trade, internal **IV:**348
Texas **IV:**370, 372
cotton gin **III:**463*c*
abolitionism **IV:**1; **V:**1
agriculture **III:**11; **IV:**10–12
cotton **III:**123
economy **III:**146
plantations **V:**308
science and technology **III:**385
slavery **III:**390
Whitney, Eli **III:**441–442
Cotton Is King (King) **IV:**106

cotton mills **VI:**21, 22
Cotton Pickers (Homer) **VI:**174
Cottonseed Trust **VI:**364
cotton speculation **VI:**92
Coughlin, Father Charles E.
VIII:87–88, *88*
America First Committee
VIII:17
anti-Semitism **VIII:**25
Catholics **VIII:**64
censorship **VIII:**65
conservatism **VIII:**84
election of 1936 **VIII:**109
Irish Americans **VIII:**188
Long, Huey P. **VIII:**223
religion **VIII:**334
Townsend, Francis E.
VIII:395
Union Party **VIII:**401
Council Bluffs, Iowa **IV:**36, 285
Council for Democracy **VIII:**77
Council Grove **IV:**331
Council of Appointment (New
York State) **III:**97
Council of Bishops (Baltimore,
Maryland) **VI:**109, 409*c*
Council of Censors (Pennsylvania)
III:110
Council of Economic Advisors
(CEA) **IX:**77–78, 351*c*
economy **IX:**96
Employment Act of 1946
IX:107
Full Employment Bill
VIII:145
Council of Federated
Organizations **IX:**219
Council of Foreign Ministers
VIII:307
Council of National Defense
VII:32
Council of Prairie du Chien
IV:412*c*
Council of Revision (New York
State) **III:**110
Council of Safety (South Carolina)
III:255
Council of State (Virginia)
III:110
Council of the Indies **I:**16, 17,
97–98, 291; **II:**371
Council of Trent **I:**98, 193
Council on African Affairs
VIII:342
Council on Environmental Quality
(CEQ) **X:**90, 246
Council on Foreign Relations
VII:115
counsel, right to. *See* right to
counsel
counterculture **IX:**78, **78–79,** *79,*
355*c*
Beat Generation **IX:**36–37
Beatles **IX:**37–38
Dylan, Bob **IX:**92
elections **IX:**104
environment **IX:**110

folk music revival **IX:**121
literature **IX:**194
LSD **IX:**195
marriage and family **IX:**202
movies **IX:**224–226
music **IX:**229
narcotics **X:**242
New Age movement **X:**253
New Left **IX:**244
religion **IX:**272
rock and roll **IX:**279
teenagers **IX:**315
Weathermen/Weather
Underground **IX:**341
Woodstock festival **X:**371–
372
counterfeiting **II:**52
Counterreformation **I:**98, 315,
317; **II:**185
counterterrorism **X:**258
country music **VIII:**250, 252;
X:238, 240, 280
Country of the Pointed Firs, The
(Jewett) **VI:**203
coups **X:**164
coureurs de bois
ethnocentrism **II:**122
French colonies **II:**137
fur trade **II:**141
Jolliet, Louis **II:**188, 189
Courses of Popular Lectures
(Wright) **IV:**405
Court of Federal Claims
(Washington, D.C.) **VI:**229
Court of Oyer and Terminer
II:420
court-packing plan **VIII:88–89,**
445*c*
Black, Hugo L. **VIII:**45
Borah, William E. **VIII:**49
Byrnes, James F. **VIII:**60
Congress **VIII:**80
conservatism **VIII:**85
conservative coalition
VIII:86
Democratic Party **VIII:**94
Executive Reorganization
Act **VIII:**121
Garner, John Nance
VIII:147
government **VIII:**152
Hoover, Herbert C.
VIII:172
Ickes, Harold L. **VIII:**183
isolationists **VIII:**189
Johnson, Hugh S. **VIII:**196–
197
La Follette, Robert M., Jr.
VIII:208
New Deal **VIII:**270
Norris, George W. **VIII:**276
politics (Roosevelt era)
VIII:300
Republican Party **VIII:**337
Roosevelt, Franklin D.
VIII:346
Supreme Court **VIII:**383

Third New Deal **VIII:**393
Wheeler, Burton K.
VIII:416
Courtship of Miles Standish
(Longfellow)
Alden, John **II:**16
Alden, Priscilla **II:**17
Standish, Myles **II:**376
courts-martial
Custer, George A. **V:**99
Lee, Charles **III:**258, 259
Putnam, Israel **III:**350
Schuyler, Philip John
III:384
Cousins, Norman **IX:**283
Couto, Diogo de **I:**334
Couture, Thomas **VI:**217
Covenant Chain **II:**20, 193
Covenanters **II:**346
Covenant Keeping (Willard)
II:415
Covered Wagon, The (film)
VII:215
covered wagons **IV:**412*c*
covert operations
CIA **IX:**52
cold war **IX:**64
foreign policy **X:**142
Operation Mongoose
IX:250
coverture **III:**445, 448
Covode, John **V:**215
Cowboys and Skinners **III:123–
124**
Cowell, Henry **VII:**124
Cowley, Malcolm **IX:**173
Cowpens, Battle of **III:**124*m,*
124–125, 462*c*
Cornwallis, Charles, Lord
III:120
Greene, Nathanael **III:**199
Guilford Courthouse, Battle
of **III:**201
Morgan, Daniel **III:**303
Revolutionary War **III:**368
Tarleton, Banastre **III:**407
Cowskin Prairie Council **V:**278
Cox, Archibald, Jr. **X:**95, 376*c*
independent counsel **X:**179
Jaworski, Leon **X:**193
Nixon, Richard M. **X:**257
Richardson, Elliot L.
X:310–311
Ruckelshaus, William D.
X:312
U.S. v. Nixon **X:**357
Watergate scandal **X:**366
Cox, James M. **VII:**408*c*
Coolidge, Calvin John
VII:64
elections **VII:**91
Harding, Warren Gamaliel
VII:134
Republican Party **VII:**301
Cox, Kenyon **VI:**276; **VII:**23
Cox, Samuel **V:**39
Coxe, Daniel **II:**261

Coxe, Tench **III:125,** 225
Coxey, Jacob S. **VI:**84, 411*c*
Coxey's Army **VI:**84, 411*c*
Cozumel **I:**94, **98–99**
Cozzens, James Gould **VIII:**220
CP. *See* Central Pacific Railroad
CPI. *See* Committee for Public
Information; Consumer Price
Index
CPPA (Conference for Progressive
Political Action) **VII:**105
CPS (Civilian Public Service)
VIII:83
CPS (Current Population Survey)
X:33
CPUSA. *See* Communist Party of
the United States of America
crafts **II:**82
apprentices **II:**23–24
artisans **II:**28
journeymen **II:**190
women's status and rights
II:423
Craftus, Richard **IV:**113
Craig, Larry E. **X:**177
Crampton's Gap **V:**190
Crane, Stephen **VI:84–85**
Crazy Horse **VI:**85
dime novels **VI:**99
Gilder, Richard Watson
VI:147
Howells, William Dean
VI:180
literature **V:**240; **VI:**226, 227
Cranfield, Edward **II:**260
Crania Americana (Morton)
IV:311
Cranmer, Thomas **I:**74, 75; **II:**315
Cranston, Alan **X:**321
Cranston, Samuel **II:**333
Crass, Lewis **IV:**164
Crater, Battle of the
Burnside, Ambrose E. **V:**52
field fortifications **V:**141
Joint Committee on the
Conduct of the War
V:215
Petersburg campaign **V:**302
Crawford, William H. **IV:**412*c*
election of 1828 **IV:**135
Jackson, Andrew **IV:**206
public land policy **IV:**305
Van Buren, Martin **IV:**385
Cray supercomputers **X:**87
"Crazy Blues" **VII:**219
Crazy Horse **VI:85–86,** 408*c*
Black Hills gold rush **VI:**39
Native Americans **VI:**261
Red Cloud **VI:**303
Sioux wars **VI:**331
Sitting Bull **VI:**332
creation cycles **I:**236
creationism **X:**306, 307
creation myths **II:**330
Aataentsic **I:**1
Aztecs **I:**18
Aztlán **I:**23

Maya **I:**236
Palenque **I:**283
Quetzalcoatl **I:**309
credit. *See* banking and currency
credit cards **IX:79–80**, 97, 352*c*
Credit Island **IV:**367
Crédit Mobilier **V:96–97**
    corruption, political **VI:**83
    Hoar, George F. **VI:**173
    railroads **VI:**302
    Whiskey Ring **V:**429
Cree Indians **I:**260; **IV:**60, 84
Creek Indians **III:125–126;**
    IV:109–110, 411*c*. *See also*
    Five Civilized Tribes
    Adair, James **II:**4
    animals **III:**22
    Bosomworth, Mary
      Musgrove **II:40–41**
    Brims **II:**47
    Cherokee **IV:**85
    Choctaw **IV:**86
    cotton culture **IV:107–108**
    Crockett, Davy **IV:**110
    Dragging Canoe **III:**139
    Florida **III:**167
    frontier, the **III:**182
    Georgia Expedition **III:**192
    Harrison, William Henry
      IV:185
    Horseshoe Bend, Battle of
      IV:189–190
    Indian Removal Act **IV:**197,
      198
    McGillivray, Alexander
      III:294–295
    McIntosh, William **IV:**247
    migration **IV:**253
    Native Americans **III:**311,
      314; **IV:**274
    Native Americans in the War
      of 1812 **IV:276–278**
    New Orleans, Battle of
      IV:280, 281
    popular sovereignty **IV:**307
    race and race relations
      IV:312
    Seminole **IV:**338
    Seminole War, First/Second
      IV:339
    Tecumseh **III:**409
    Trail of Tears **IV:**378
    War of 1812 **IV:**391
    Yamasee **II:**430
Creek War
    Cherokee **III:**86, 87
    Choctaw **III:**89; **IV:**86
    Creek **III:**126; **IV:**109
    McIntosh, William **IV:**247
    Pushmataha **IV:**307
    Ross, John **IV:**325
    Seminole **IV:**338
    Sequoyah **IV:**342, 343
Creel, George
    advertising **VII:**5
    Committee for Public
      Information **VII:**59

free speech fights **VII:**118
Selective Service Act
    VII:321
CREEP. *See* Committee to Re-
    Elect the President
Creole(s) **II:82–83**
    African Americans **II:**6
    Du Sable, Jean Baptiste
      Pointe **II:**104–105
    fertility **II:**125
    Gullah **II:**159
    slavery **II:**356
Cresson Medal **IV:**163
Cresswell, John A. J. **VI:**78
Crèvecoeur, J. Hector St. John de
    III:126–127, 462*c*
    environment **III:**154, 155
    literature **III:**268
    society, British American
      II:364, 368
Crick, Francis H. C. **IX:**285, 314
Crimea **VIII:**439
Crime Act (1994) **X:**380*c*
crime and punishment **II:83–84,**
    84; **X:95–98**, *96,* 96*t,* 375*c.* *See*
    also criminal justice
    African Americans **II:**8
    Butterworth, Mary Peck
      II:52
    cities and urban life **III:**91;
      V:67; **VIII:**70; **IX:**56
    Escobedo v. Illinois **IX:**111
    Ginsburg, Ruth Bader
      X:153
    gun control **X:**161
    Hoover, J. Edgar **IX:**149–
      150
    Horton, Willie **X:**168
    humanitarianism **III:**217
    Hurricane Katrina **X:**173
    indentured servitude **II:**174
    Leary, Timothy **IX:**187–188
    Molly Maguires **VI:**248
    narcotics **X:**242
    Native Americans **VIII:**264
    prisons **III:**346–347
    Reno, Janet **X:**308–309
    Richmond, Virginia **V:**335–
      336
    RICO **X:**298–299
    Rosenberg, Julius and Ethel
      IX:280
    South Carolina Regulation
      III:394–395
    women's status and rights
      II:425
Crimean War
    Godkin, Edwin Lawrence
      VI:149
    ironclads **V:**207
    medicine **V:**257
    Monitor-Merrimack **V:**265
    panic of 1857 **V:**294
    Zouaves **V:**441
Crime of '73 **VI:**86, 408*c*
    bimetallism **VI:**38
    Bland-Allison Act **VI:**41

Free-Silver movement
    VI:135
    Sherman, John **VI:**329
criminal justice **VII:66–67**, 409*c.*
    See also crime and punishment
    children **VII:**399
    journalism **VII:**159
    Leo Frank case **VII:**176
    Leopold and Loeb **VII:**176–
      177
    Mann Act **VII:**189
    Narcotics Act **VII:**223
    Teapot Dome **VII:**351
criollos **I:**268; **II:**371, 372
Cripple Creek miners' strike
    Haywood, William Dudley
      VII:137
    IWW **VII:**146
    WFM **VII:**381
Crisis (Paine) **III:**268
Crisis, The (NAACP journal)
    VII:405*c*
    DuBois, W.E.B. **VII:**80, 81
    Harlem Renaissance
      VII:136
    NAACP **VII:**224; **IX:**232
    Wilkins, Roy **IX:**344
*Critical Period of American
    History, The* (Fiske) **VI:**129
Crittenden, George **V:**43
Crittenden, John J. **V:**43, 98
Crittenden, Thomas **V:**43
Crittenden Compromise **V:**89,
    97–98, 431, 444*c*
Croatia **X:**99, 102, 381*c*
Croatoan Indians **I:**229, 322
Crockett, Davy **IV:***110,* 110**–111,**
    411*c*
    Alamo, The **IV:**14
    Bowie, James **IV:**63
    Disney, Walt **IX:**88
    Texas Revolution **IV:**375
    Travis, William Barret
      IV:380
Crockett, George **IX:**86
Croghan, George **II:84–85**
Croix-de-Lorraine **I:**335
Croly, David **V:**261
Croly, Herbert **VII:**237
Cromwell, Oliver
    Anglican Church **II:**21
    English Civil War **II:**116
    Scots immigrants **II:**346
Cronkite, Walter **IX:**315, 316;
    X:344
Crook, George
    Apache War **VI:**17
    Bright Eyes **VI:**48
    Crazy Horse **VI:**86
    Red Cloud **VI:**303
    Shenandoah Valley:
      Sheridan's campaign
      V:351–352
    Sioux wars **VI:**331
    Sitting Bull **VI:**332
Crooks, Ramsey **IV:**18–19
crop diversification **VI:**63

Crop Loan Act **VIII:**126
crop rotation **IV:**12
Cropsey, Jasper **VI:**275
croquet **V:**367
Crosby, Alfred **I:**81, 107, 108
Crosby, Bing **VIII:***251*
    Freedom Train **IX:**125
    Irish Americans **VIII:**188
    jazz **VIII:**195
    movies **VIII:**245
    music **VIII:***251,* 252
Cross, Temple of the **I:**283
cross-Channel invasion **VIII:**62
Cross Keys, Battle of **V:**210, 350
Cross Keys, Virginia **IV:**380
Crossley, Archibald **VIII:**312
"Cross of Gold" Speech (Bryan)
    VI:411*c*, **438–441**
    Bryan, William Jennings
      VI:52
    Currency Act **VII:**68
    Democratic Party **VII:**74
cross staff **I:99,** 262, 334
crossword puzzles **VII:**295
Crouching Tiger, Hidden Dragon
    (film) **X:**279
crowd actions (1600s–1700s)
    II:86–87, 202
Crowder, Enoch **VII:**62, 321
Crowe, William J. **X:**72
Crow Indians **I:**162; **II:85–86**
    Beckwourth, Jim **IV:**51
    Catlin, George **IV:**84
    exploration **IV:**145
    Native Americans **IV:**276
Croyable (privateer) **III:**353
Crozer Theological Seminary
    IX:173
CRT screen. *See* cathode-ray tube
    screen
Crucible, The (Miller) **IX:**193,
    258
crude oil **VI:**271
cruel and unusual punishment
    X:376*c*
    Bill of Rights **III:**51
    Brennan, William J., Jr.
      X:48
    capital punishment **X:**66, 67
Cruikshank case. *See United
    States v. Cruikshank*
cruise missiles **X:**100, 101, 180
Crummell, Alexander **VI:86–87,**
    412*c*
Crusade for Citizenship **IX:**32
Crusade for Justice **IX:**136, 183
Cruz, Juana Inés de la **II:**373
Cruzan v. Missouri **X:**305
Crying of Lot 49, The (Pynchon)
    X:211
crystal meth **X:**244
CSO. *See* Community Services
    Organization
CT (computed tomography) scan
    X:224
cuauhpipiltin **I:**20
Cuauhtémoc **I:**97, **99–100**

Cuba **I:100–101; IV:111–112;
  VI:87–88**, 412*c;* **VII:**403*c,*
  404*c;* **IX:**354*c;* **X:**383*c*
    Amistad incident **IV:**21
    Anti-Imperialist League
      VI:16–17
    Army Act **VII:**22
    assassinations **X:**35
    Atkinson, Edward **VI:**22
    Barbados **I:**27
    Bay of Pigs **IX:**35–36
    Big Stick diplomacy **VII:**34
    CIA **IX:**52
    Cleveland, Grover **VI:**75
    cold war **IX:**64
    Columbus, Christopher **I:**86
    Córdoba, Francisco
      Hernández de **I:**90
    Cortés, Hernán **I:**94
    Crane, Stephen **VI:**85
    Cuban missile crisis
      IX:80–81
    de Lôme Letter **VI:**94
    Democratic Party **V:**109
    Dulles, John Foster **IX:**91
    emancipation **V:**130
    Essex decision **III:**157
    Fillmore, Millard **IV:**150
    foreign policy **IV:**155, 156;
      V:149, 151; **VI:**134;
      VII:113–114; **X:**144
    Good Neighbor policy
      VIII:151
    Grijalva, Juan de **I:**145
    Hearst, William Randolph
      VII:137
    Hoar, George F. **VI:**173
    immigration **IX:**156
    Immigration Act (1965)
      IX:156
    imperialism **VI:**188
    investments, American,
      abroad **VI:**197
    Johnson, Jack **VII:**155
    Kaiser, Henry J. **VIII:**199
    Kennedy, John F. **IX:**170
    Knox, Frank **VIII:**202
    Las Casas, Bartolomé de
      I:205
    Latin America **IX:**184;
      X:205–207
    Maine, Remember the
      VI:237
    Manifest Destiny **IV:**235
    McKinley, William **VI:**241
    Mills, C. Wright **IX:**217
    Mitchell, William (Billy)
      VII:211
    Monroe Doctrine **IV:**260
    Narváez, Pánfilo de **I:**258
    Nicaragua **X:**254
    Operation Mongoose
      IX:250
    Ostend Manifesto **V:**289–
      290
    Pershing, John Joseph
      VII:258
    population trends **IX:**260
    Reagan, Ronald W. **X:**301
    Republican Party **IV:**322
    Roosevelt, Theodore
      VII:304
    Roosevelt Corollary
      VII:305
    Rough Riders **VI:**317
    slavery **II:**354
    Soto, Hernando de **I:**342
    Spanish-American War
      VI:340, 341
    Spanish colonies **II:**371,
      374
    sports and recreation
      VII:333
    Stevenson, Adali E. **IX:**302
    Taino **I:**352
    Velázquez, Diego de
      I:373–374
    Virginius affair **VI:**377
Cuban Americans **X:**166, 167,
  382*c*
Cuban embargo **X:**382*c*
Cuban missile crisis **IX:80,
  80–81,** 355*c*
    Acheson, Dean **IX:**2
    arms race **IX:**17
    cold war **IX:**64
    journalism **IX:**166
    Kennedy, John F. **IX:**171
    Limited Test Ban Treaty of
      1963 **IX:**192
    New Frontier **IX:**243
    Soviet Union **IX:**295
Cuban Revolution **VI:**310, 407*c;*
  X:204
cubism **VIII:**30, 31
Cudahy Meatpacking **VI:**243
Cueva, Doña Beatriz de la **I:**8
Cuffe, Paul **III:127–128,** 462*c*
Cuguano, Ottobah **II:**359
Cuicuilco **I:**356
Cuitláhuac **I:101**
    Aztecs **I:**22
    Cortés, Hernán **I:**96
    Cuauhtémoc **I:**100
Culberson, Charles **VII:**101, 318
Cullen, Countee **VII:**136
Culp, Wesley **V:**43
Culpeper, Thomas, Lord **II:87**
Culpeper, Virginia **V:**59
Culp's Hill
    brothers' war **V:**43
    Gettysburg, Battle of **V:**167,
      168
    Hancock, Winfield Scott
      V:183
    Meade, George Gordon
      V:254
culture, popular. *See* popular
  culture
Culture and Commitment (Mead)
  VII:197
*Culture and Democracy in
  the United States* (Kallen)
  VII:181
Cumberland, Maryland
    internal improvements
      IV:202
    migration **IV:**254
    National Road **IV:**271
Cumberland, USS (sailing frigate)
  V:266
Cumberland Law School
  (Birmingham, Alabama)
  VIII:180
Cumberland Road. *See* National
  Road
Cumberland Valley **III:**140
Cumming, Alexander **II:**28
Cumming, Alfred **IV:**121
Cumming, Kate **V:**98
Cummings, E. E. **VII:**179, 186,
  212
Cummings, Homer **VIII:**130
Cunard Line **VI:**186; **VII:**187
Cunningham, Andrew B. **VIII:**360
curia regis **I:**304
Curie, Marie **IV:**163
Curie, Pierre **IV:**163
Curley, James Michael **VIII:**188
Curran, Thomas J. *IX:*87
currency **VIII:**444*c. See also*
  banking and currency; fiat
  currency; gold standard; silver
  coinage/silver standard
    banking **V:**26–27
    Bank of the United States,
      First **III:**41
    banks **III:**42
    cacao **I:**48
    Confederate States of
      America **V:**86
    Congress **V:**89
    Congress, Confederate **V:**88
    debt, national **III:**130
    economy **III:**146; **V:**121–
      123
    gold **I:**141
    greenbacks **V:**177–178
    Massachusetts **II:**223
    Morris, Gouverneur **III:**303,
      304
    Revolutionary War **III:**369
    Tenochtitlán **I:**354–355
    Tlaxcala **I:**362
    trade, domestic and foreign
      III:413, 414
    wampum **II:**406–407
    Wilson, Thomas Woodrow
      VII:383
Currency Act (1764) **III:128,** 459*c*
    banks **III:**42
    debt, national **III:**130
    economy **III:**145
    Grenville, George **III:**200
Currency Act (1834) **IV:**413*c*
Currency Act (1900) **VII:68,** 83,
  299, 403*c*
currency issue (late 19th century)
  VI:88–90, 89, 408*c,* 410*c*
    Atkinson, Edward **VI:**22
    Bland-Allison Act **VI:**41–42
    Congress **VI:**80
    Coxey's Army **VI:**84
    Crime of '73 **VI:**86
    Democratic Party **VI:**95
    Free-Silver movement
      VI:135
    Greenback-Labor Party
      VI:154–155
    Hayes, Rutherford B.
      VI:168
    McKinley, William **VI:**241
    national banking system
      VI:261
    Omaha platform **VI:**272
    political parties, third
      VI:286
currency stabilization **VIII:**243,
  426
Current Population Survey (CPS)
  X:33
Curry, H. M. **VII:**292
Curry, John Steuart **VIII:**31
Curtin, Andrew Gregg **VI:**299
Curtis, Benjamin R. **V:**117, 203
Curtis, Charles **VIII:**108; **X:**123
Curtis, Cyrus H. K.
    advertising **VI:**2
    illustration, photography,
      and graphic arts **VI:**184
    magazines **VI:**235
Curtis, George William
    civil service reform **VI:**73
    Conkling, Roscoe **VI:**81
    Nast, Thomas **V:**275
    Norton, Charles Eliot
      VI:269
Curtis, Samuel R. **V:**209, 296, 297
Curtis, Tom **VI:**359
Curtis, William **V:**130
Curtis Act **VII:**232
Cushing, William **III:**355, 403
Cushman, Pauline **V:**134
Cushman, Robert **II:**294
Custer, George Armstrong **V:98–
  99,** 99; **VI:**408*c*
    Appomattox campaign **V:**14
    Appomattox Court House,
      Virginia **V:**15
    Black Hills gold rush **VI:**38
    Cody, William Frederick
      VI:77
    Crazy Horse **VI:**85
    entertainment, popular
      VI:118
    Five Forks, Battle of **V:**147
    Gettysburg, Battle of **V:**168
    Little Bighorn, Battle of
      V:240, 241
    Native Americans **VI:**261
    Red Cloud **VI:**303
    Shenandoah Valley:
      Sheridan's campaign
      V:352
    Sheridan, Philip H. **V:**353
    Sioux wars **VI:**331
    Sitting Bull **VI:**332
Custer, Tom **V:**255

Custis, George Washington Parke **V:**229
Custis, John Parke **III:**59
Custis, Mary Anne **V:**16, 229
Customs, U.S. **X:**167
customs duties **II:**3
customs regulations **III:**424
Cutler, Timothy **II:**194
Cuzco **I:**101–102
   Atahualpa **I:**15–16
   Cieza de León, Pedro **I:**76
   Native American religion
    I:261
CWA. *See* Civil Works
  Administration
Cyane, HMS **III:**108
cyclopes **I:**248
Cyclops Iron Company **VI:**62
cyclosporine **X:**224
cyclotron **VIII:**352
cynocephali **I:**248
Czechoslovakia
   cold war **IX:**63
   Europe **IX:**112, 113
   foreign policy **VIII:**141
   Iron Curtain, collapse of
    X:189
   isolationists **VIII:**189–190
   Munich Conference
    VIII:248
   Neutrality Acts **VIII:**267
   Siberian Expedition
    VII:324–325
   Soviet Union **IX:**295
   Suez crisis **IX:**307
   Versailles, Treaty of **VII:**370
Czech Republic **X:**337
Czolgosz, Leon **VII:**15, 252

D

2,4-D (herbicide) **VIII:**10
Dabney, Charles **VI:**250
Dabney, Morgan & Company
  VI:250
DaCosta, Isaac **III:**236
Dacron **IX:**91
Dade, Francis L.
   Osceola **IV:**289
   Seminole **IV:**338
   Seminole War, First/Second
    IV:339
Dagomba **I:**103, 252
daguerreotypes **V:**41
Dahlgren, John A. B. **V:**101, 342,
  405
Dahlgren gun **V:**101
Dahomey **I:**103–104, 132
Dahomey Village (World's
  Columbian Exposition) **VI:**403
Daily News Building (New York
  City) **VIII:**28
Daily Southern Argus **IV:**123
Daily Worker **VII:**61, 286
Daimler Chrysler **X:**58
dairy industry **VI:**8; **X:**20

"Daisy Bell" **VI:**35
"Daisy" commercial (election of
  1964) **IX:**3
Daisy Miller (James) **VI:**200, 226
Dakota Territory **VI:**190
Daladier, Edouard **VIII:**248
Dale, David **IV:**291
Dale, Sir Thomas **II:**10, **89–90,**
  143
Daley, Richard **IX:**144; **X:**73
Dallas, Alexander J. **III:**43
Dallas, Battle of **V:**22
Dallas, George M. **IV:**302
Dallas, Texas **IX:**22
Dallas-Fort Worth, Texas **IV:**370–
  371; **VIII:**381
Dallin, Alexander **X:**309
Daly, Maria Lydig **V:**102
Daly, Mary **IX:**273
Daly, Patrick **V:**102
Damadian, Raymond **X:**224
Damrosch, Walter **VI:**29
dams **VII:**98–99
"Dan, Dan, Dan-Butterfield,
  Butterfield" **V:**273
Dana, Charles Anderson **V:**102;
  VI:91–92
   Brook Farm **IV:**65
   McMaster, John Bach
    VI:242
   newspapers **VI:**265, 266
Dana, Francis **III:**82
Dana, James Dwight **IV:**400;
  VI:240
Dana, Richard Henry **IV:**113
   Burns, Anthony **IV:**66
   California **IV:**71
   California Trail **IV:**77
   journalism **IV:**210
Danbury Hatters case (*Loewe v.*
  Lawlor) **VII:69,** 405*c*
   AFL **VII:**12
   Buck's Stove **VII:**42
   labor/labor movements
    VII:170
dance **II:26,** 90
   cosmetics and beauty
    industry **VII:**66
   music **III:**309; **VII:**219
   Native Americans **VII:**233
   popular culture **III:**341;
    VII:265
dance halls **VII:**294
Dancing Rabbit Creek, Treaty of
  IV:87, 377
Danforth, John C.
   Branch Davidians **X:**46
   independent counsel **X:**179
   UN **X:**357
Daniel, Clifton **IX:**321
Daniel Boone Escorting Settlers
  (Bingham) **III:**56
Daniels, Josephus **VIII:**211, 418
Danish West Indies **VI:**223
Danites **IV:**89, 353
Danks, Hart Pease **VI:**257
D. Appleton & Co. **VI:**242

DAR. *See* Daughters of the
  American Revolution
Darby Lumber Co. v. United
  States **VIII:**124
Dare, Virginia **I:**398*c;* **II:90–91**
Dar es Salaam, Tanzania, embassy
  bombing. *See* embassy
  bombings
Darfur **I:**104; **X:**17, 56
Darfur Peace Agreement **X:**17
Darién settlement **I:**284
Dark Victory (film) **VIII:**246
Darlan, Jean **VIII:**277–278
Darlington, Pennsylvania **IV:**246
DARPA. *See* Defense Advanced
  Research Projects Agency
Darrow, Clarence Seward
  VII:69–70, 316, 409*c*
   ACLU **VII:**10
   Haywood, William Dudley
    VII:137
   Leopold and Loeb **VII:**177
   Mencken, Henry Louis
    VII:202
   Scopes Trial **VII:**316, 317
   Scottsboro Boys **VIII:**353
   Sweet trial **VII:**344, 345
Dartmoor Massacre **IV:**113
Dartmoor Prison **IV:113–114,**
  165
Dartmouth, Lord William
  III:264
Dartmouth College **II:91,** *91,*
  411, 412; **VI:**114
Dartmouth College case
  (*Dartmouth College v.*
  Woodward) **IV:114,** 393, 411*c*
Darwin, Charles
   Darwinism and religion
    VI:92
   eugenics **VII:**102
   evolution **VI:**122
   Fiske, John **VI:**128, 129
   imperialism **VI:**188
   literature **VI:**226
   Marsh, Othniel Charles
    VI:240
   Norton, Charles Eliot
    VI:269
   race and race relations
    IV:311
   religion **VI:**306
   science and technology
    VI:325
   Scopes Trial **VII:**316
   Social Darwinism **VI:**334
Darwin, Erasmus **VI:**122
Darwinism and religion **VI:92–93**
   Chautauqua Institute **VI:**66
   evolution **VI:**122
   religion **VI:**307
Darwin on Trial (Johnson) **X:**306
Darwin's Black Box (Behe)
  X:306–307
Das Capital (Marx) **V:**249
Daschle, Tom **X:**321, 383*c*
Dasemunkepeuc **II:**417

Dash for the Timber, A
  (Remington) **VI:**310
Datsun (Nissan) **IX:**27
Daugherty, Harry M.
   Coolidge, Calvin John **VII:**64
   Harding, Warren Gamaliel
    VII:135
   Railroad Shopmen's Strike
    VII:291–292
   Teapot Dome **VII:**351, 352
Daughter of the Middle Border, A
  (Garland) **VI:**140
Daughters of Bilitis (DOB)
  IX:131; **X:**322
Daughters of Charity **IV:**344
Daughters of Edwin D. Boit, The
  (Sargent) **VI:**324
Daughters of Saint Crispin
  VI:215
Daughters of the American
  Revolution (DAR) **VIII:**446*c*
   African Americans **VIII:**3
   education **VIII:**106
   history **VII:**140
   Ladies Memorial
    Associations **V:**229
Daughters of the Confederacy
  VII:140
DAV (Disabled American
  Veterans) **VII:**373
Davenport, Charles Benedict
  VII:102, 314
Davenport, James **II:91–92**
David (Michelangelo) **I:**243
David, Jacques-Louis **IV:**37
Davies, Arthur B. **VII:**23, 25
Davies, Ronald **IX:**118
Davies, Samuel **II:**92
Dávila, Pedrarias
   Balboa, Vasco Núñez de
    I:26
   Grijalva, Juan de **I:**145
   Panama **I:**284
DaVinci Code, The (Brown) **X:**212
Davis, Alexander Jackson **IV:**31
Davis, Andrew Jackson **IV:**320
Davis, Arthur P. **IX:**5
Davis, Benjamin O. **VIII:**375, 446*c*
Davis, Bette **VIII:**246; **IX:**13
Davis, Charles H. **V:**263, 264
Davis, Chester **VIII:**6
Davis, David **VI:**292
Davis, Dwight F. **VI:**342; **VII:**212
Davis, Edmund J. **V:**223
Davis, Edwin H. **IV:**335
Davis, Elmer **VIII:**286
Davis, Harry **VII:**96, 216, 404*c*
Davis, Henry Winter **V:**421–422
Davis, Isaac **IV:**188, 211
Davis, Jeff C. (Union general)
  V:357
Davis, Jefferson (Confederate
  president) **V:102–105,** *103,*
  444*c*
   assassination of Abraham
    Lincoln **V:**21
   Atlanta campaign **V:**22

Davis, Jefferson (*continued*)
  Beauregard, Pierre Gustave Toutant **V:**32
  Benjamin, Judah P. **V:**33
  Black Hawk War **IV:**58
  Bragg, Braxton **V:**42
  Bull Run/Manassas, First and Second Battles of **V:**50
  Chattanooga, Battle of **V:**63, 64
  Chesnut, Mary B. **V:**64
  civil liberties, Confederate **V:**68, 69
  Civil War **V:**74
  Confederate army **V:**79
  Confederate States of America **V:**84–87
  Congress, Confederate **V:**88
  conscription **V:**91
  Davis, Varina Howell **V:**105–106
  Davis Bend, Mississippi, freedmen's colony **V:**106, 107
  Democratic Party **V:**109
  elections **V:**126, 127
  filibustering **V:**145
  Fillmore, Millard **IV:**149–150
  food riots **V:**148
  foreign policy **V:**150
  Fort Sumter **V:**154, 155
  Freedmen's Bureau **V:**161
  Gadsden Purchase **IV:**173
  Gettysburg, Battle of **V:**166
  governors **V:**172
  Greeley, Horace **V:**177
  Greenhow, Rose O'Neal **V:**178
  habeas corpus, writ of **V:**181
  Heroes of America **V:**188
  Hill, Daniel H. **V:**190
  Hollywood Cemetery **V:**192
  homefront **V:**193
  Hood, John Bell **V:**195, 196
  Inaugural Address **V:454–456**
  Jackson, Claiborne F. **V:**209
  Jackson, Thomas J. "Stonewall" **V:**210–211
  Johnston, Albert Sidney **V:**214
  Johnston, Joseph E. **V:**214, 215
  journalism **V:**218
  Lee, Robert E. **V:**230
  Letcher, John **V:**232
  literature **V:**239
  Mallory, Stephen R. **V:**247
  Memminger, Christopher G. **V:**259
  Mexican-American War **IV:**252
  Milliken's Bend, Battle of **V:**260
  monuments **V:**268

  Morrill Land-Grant Act **V:**269
  Murfreesboro/Stones River, Battle of **V:**271, 272
  Pacific Railroad Act **V:**293
  peace movements **V:**296
  Rhodes, James Ford **VI:**312
  secession **V:**345
  Shiloh, Battle of **V:**358
  states' rights **V:**370
  Stephens, Alexander Hamilton **V:**371
  tactics and strategy **V:**380, 381
  Toombs, Robert A. **V:**389
  Vance, Zebulon B. **V:**414
  Vicksburg campaign **V:**416
  Wigfall, Louis T. **V:**431
  Yancey, William Lowndes **V:**439
Davis, John (explorer) **I:**144, 273
Davis, John P. (lawyer and activist) **VIII:**255
Davis, John W. (lawyer and presidential candidate) **VII:**408c
  American Liberty League **VIII:**19
  Brown v. Board of Education **IX:**44
  conservatism **VIII:**84
  Coolidge, Calvin John **VII:**64
  elections **VII:**91
Davis, Joseph Emory **V:**103, 106
Davis, Paulina Wright **IV:**404
Davis, Rennie **X:**73
Davis, Sammy, Jr. **IX:**201
Davis, Stuart **IX:**24; **VIII:**31
Davis, Varina Howell **V:105–106**
  Chesnut, Mary B. **V:**64
  Davis, Jefferson **V:**103
  Hollywood Cemetery **V:**192
Davis, Wild Jeff **VII:**332
Davis Bend, Mississippi, freedmen's colony **V:106–107,** 129, 161
Davis Cup **VI:**342
Dawes, Charles Gates **VII:70–71,** 71
  Budget and Accounting Act **VII:**44
  Coolidge, Calvin John **VII:**64
  Dawes Plan **VII:**72
  foreign policy **VII:**116
  Harding, Warren Gamaliel **VII:**134
Dawes, Henry L. **VI:**93, 94, 397–398
Dawes, William **III:**367, 427, 461c
Dawes Bank **VII:**71
Dawes Plan **VII:72**
  Coolidge, Calvin John **VII:**65
  economy **VII:**85

  foreign policy **VII:**116
  presidency **VII:**269
Dawes Severalty Act **VI:93–94,** 410c, **418–420**
  Burke Act **VII:**44
  Indian Affairs, Office of **VI:**190
  Indian Reorganization Act **VIII:**185
  Indian Rights Association **VI:**190
  Lone Wolf v. Hitchcock **VII:**185
  marriage and family **IV:**238
  Native Americans **VI:**261–263; **VII:**231–232; **VIII:**263
  presidency **VI:**290
  race and race relations **VIII:**318
  Red Cloud **VI:**303
  Sooners **VI:**339
  Winnemucca, Sarah **VI:**398
Dawit I (emperor of Ethiopia) **I:**124
Dawit II (emperor of Ethiopia) **I:105,** 125
Dawley, T. R. **V:**239
Dawson City **VI:**208, 209
Day, Benjamin **IV:**208
Day, Doris **IX:**259
Day, Dorothy **VIII:**444c
  Catholics **VIII:**64
  NWP **VII:**230
  religion **VIII:**334
Day, Stephen **II:92**
day care
  children **VIII:**67
  Clinton, Hillary Rodham **X:**78
  family life **X:**128
"Day of Doom, The" (Wigglesworth) **II:**415
"Day of Infamy" speech (Roosevelt) **VIII:466**
"Days of Rage" riots (Chicago, 1969) **X:**367, 368, 375c
Dayton, Ohio **IV:**202; **VIII:**399
Dayton, Tennessee **VIII:**316–317
Dayton accords **X:99,** 102, 381c
Daytona Normal and Industrial School for Negro Girls (Daytona Beach, Florida) **VIII:**44
DC (direct current) **VI:**353
DC-4 (Douglas C-54 Skymaster) **VIII:**397
D-day **VIII:**275–276, 355, 448c
DDT
  agriculture **VIII:**10
  Carson, Rachel **IX:**50, 51
  environment **IX:**109
  science and technology **IX:**286
Dead Indian Land Act **VII:**232
Dean, Dizzy **VIII:**303

Dean, Howard **X:**183
Dean, James
  movies **IX:**224
  popular culture **IX:**259
  teenagers **IX:**314
Dean, John **X:**365
Deane, Francis B. **V:**392
Deane, Silas **III:129**
  Beaumarchais, Pierre-Auguste Caron de **III:**48
  Kalb, Johann, baron de **III:**245
  Lee, Arthur **III:**258
Dearborn, Henry **IV:**336
Dearborn Independent **VII:**17, 112
death **I:**21
Death Comes for the Archbishop (Cather) **VII:**179
Death of a Salesman (Miller) **IX:**193, 258, 352c
Death of General Montgomery in the Attack on Quebec (Trumbull) **III:**416
Death of General Wolfe (West) **III:**32
death penalty **X:**168. *See also* executions
death rate **X:**221. *See also* life expectancy; mortality
Deaver, Michael **X:**300
debates, presidential. *See* presidential debate
DeBow's Review **IV:**210
Debs, Eugene Victor **VII:72–73,** 73, 403c, 407c
  Cleveland, Grover **VI:**75
  Communist Party **VII:**61
  Darrow, Clarence Seward **VII:**70
  elections **VII:**90
  Espionage Act **VII:**101
  Federal Trade Commission Act **VII:**108
  IWW **VII:**147
  Lloyd, Henry Demarest **VI:**227
  National Civic Federation **VII:**226
  politics (1900–1928) **VII:**262
  Pullman Strike **VI:**297, 298
  radicalism **VII:**287, 288
  Red Scare **VII:**296
  socialism **VII:**327, 328
  Socialist Party **VI:**337
  socialists **VIII:**362
Debs, In re **VI:**298
debt, national **III:129–132; IV:**130t
  banking, investment **VI:**23
  Bank of the United States, First **III:**40, 41
  Carroll of Carrollton, Charles **III:**82
  Constitution, United States **III:**107

economy **III:**145, 146;
X:108
Federalist Party **III:**164
Gallatin, Albert **III:**188
Hamilton, Alexander
III:206, 207
Jay, John **III:**230
Jay's Treaty **III:**231
Morris, Gouverneur
III:304
War Revenue Act **VII:**379
debt, state
debt, national **III:**130–132
Hamilton, Alexander
III:206
Shays's Rebellion **III:**388
debtors **III:**347
debt relief **X:**206
DEC (Digital Equipment
Corporation) **IX:**71
Decades (Peter Martyr) **I:**118,
353
Decades of the New Worlde, The
(Eden) **I:**118
Decatur, Stephen **IV:114–115**
Barbary Wars **III:**46
foreign affairs **III:**169
Fulton, Robert **III:**183
Decima, Japan **IV:**298
Declaration and an Address, A
(Campbell) **IV:**78
Declaration by United Nations
(1942) **VIII:**402
Declaration of Independence
III:132–134, *133,* **134,** 461*c,*
467–469
abolitionism **IV:**1
Adams, John **III:**5
Adams, Samuel **III:**7
American Revolution **III:**18
art **III:**33
Carroll of Carrollton,
Charles **III:**82
Catholics **III:**83
Chase, Samuel **III:**85
commemoration **IX:**66
Continental Congress,
Second **III:**115
corporatism **III:**122
Dickinson, John **III:**137
Forten, James **III:**170
Franklin, Benjamin **III:**174
French Alliance **III:**177
George III **III:**191, 192
Gerry, Elbridge **III:**194
Great Awakening **II:**156
Hancock, John **III:**209
immigration **III:**221
Independence Hall **III:**223
Jefferson, Thomas **III:**232
Livingston, Philip **II:**207
Livingston, Robert R.
III:270
Mason, George **III:**292
Pennsylvania **II:**288
Port Huron Statement
IX:260

race and race relations
IV:309
resistance movement
III:366
Rush, Benjamin **III:**376
Seneca Falls convention
IV:341
Sherman, Roger **III:**389
slave trade **III:**393
Wilson, James **III:**444
Witherspoon, John **III:**445
Declaration of Independence, The
(Trumbull) **III:**416
Declaration of Independence
bicentennial **X:**377*c*
Declaration of Independence for
Women **VI:**284
Declaration of Indian Purpose
IX:241
Declaration of Lima **VIII:**151–
152, 446*c*
"Declaration of Nathaniel Bacon
in the Name of the People of
Virginia" **II:441–442**
Declaration of Negro Rights
VII:122, 361
Declaration of Panama **VIII:**446*c*
Declaration of Paris (1856)
Confederate navy **V:**84
foreign policy **V:**150
neutrality **VII:**235
Declaration of Rights
(Massachusetts)
citizenship **III:**95
Freeman, Elizabeth **III:**176
Quok Walker Case **III:**355
Declaration of Rights (Virginia)
III:292
Declaration of Rights and
Grievances (First Continental
Congress) **III:**132
Declaration of Sentiments
(American Anti-Slavery
Society) **V:**164
Declaration of Sentiments
(Seneca Falls convention)
IV:441–443
Gage, Matilda Joslyn **VI:**137
marriage and family **IV:**240
Seneca Falls convention
IV:341–342
women's status and rights
IV:404; **V:**436, 438
"Declaration of the Causes and
Necessity of Taking up Arms,
A" **III:**324
Declaration of the Rights of Man
III:178
Declaration of Women's Rights.
See Declaration of Sentiments
(Seneca Falls convention)
Declaration on Liberated Europe
VIII:439
Declaratory Act **III:**68, **134,** 396
*Decline and Fall of the Roman
Empire* (Gibbon) **III:**365
DeConcini, Dennis **X:**321

deconstructionism **X:**32
Decoration Day. *See* Memorial
Day
Decter, Midge **X:**252
Deephaven (Jewett) **VI:**202
Deep Space I (spacecraft) **X:**329
Deere, John **IV:**11, **115–116,** 200
Deerfield Massacre **II:92–93,**
323
deerskin trade
animals **III:**22
Catawba **II:**61
fur trade **II:**141
Deerslayer, The (Cooper) **IV:**228
Defense, U.S. Department of
(DOD) **IX:**352*c*
Brownsville Riot **VII:**42
Cheney, Richard B. **X:**72
computers **X:**87
economy **IX:**97–98
migration **IX:**215
National Security Act of
1947 **IX:**238
NSC-68 **IX:**247, 248
Rumsfeld, Donald **X:**312–
313
Truman, Harry S. **IX:**320
Defense Advanced Research
Projects Agency (DARPA)
X:181, 182
defense budget **IX:83–84**
business **IX:**46
cold war, end of **X:**85
defense policy **X:**100, 101,
103
demobilization (WWII)
IX:84
economy **IX:**98; **X:**109
Gore, Albert, Jr. **X:**157
Reagan, Ronald W. **X:**300–
301
Defense Department
Appropriations Act (2006)
X:322
defense industry **VIII:**227, 228,
433, 447*c*
Defense of Brig. Gen. Wm. Hull
(Hull) **IV:**192
Defense of Marriage Act (DOMA)
X:149, 215
*Defense of the Constitutions of
the Government of the United
States* (Adams) **III:**5–6
Defense Plant Corporation
VIII:326
defense policy **X:99–103**
ABM Treaty **X:**26
conservative movement
X:94
Federal Information Act
X:130
Gore, Albert, Jr. **X:**157
Defense Supply Corporation
VIII:326
defensive warfare
Confederate navy **V:**83
Overland campaign **V:**291

tactics and strategy **V:**380–
381
Washington, D.C. **V:**426
deference **III:**122
deferments **VIII:**357, 413
Defiance, Mount **III:**172
Defiance, Ohio **III:**195
deficit, federal **X:**378*c,* 379*c*
Bush, George H. W. **X:**53
Clinton, William J. **X:**82
Congressional Budget and
Impoundment Control
Act **X:**88–89
economy **X:**109, 110
Gramm-Rudman-Hollings
Act **X:**158
Laffer curve **X:**204
New York City bailout
X:253–254
Reagan, Ronald W. **X:**300
Senate, U.S. **X:**321
deficit, trade **X:**109
deficit reduction **X:**80, 110
deficit spending
Morgenthau, Henry T., Jr.
VIII:244
New Deal **VIII:**269
PWA **VIII:**314
recession of 1937–1938
VIII:324
World War II home front
VIII:434
De Forest, John William **V:107,**
240; **VI:**225
De Forest, Lee **VII:**151
de Forest, Lockwood **VI:**356
Deganawida **I:**397*c*
Hiawatha **I:**161–162
Iroquois **I:**186
Mohawk **I:**246
Degas, Edgar **VI:**64
de Gaulle, Charles **IX:**113, 247
DeGolyer McClelland Company
VI:139
Deidesheimer, Philip **IV:**105
deism **III:134–135**
Allen, Ethan **III:**15
Enlightenment, American
II:118
Great Awakening **II:**156
Jefferson, Thomas
III:232
Morse, Jedidiah **III:**307
Paine, Thomas **III:**330
religion **III:**361
religion, Euro-American
II:329–330
religious liberty **III:**363
deities. *See* gods/goddesses
De jure belli ac pacis (Concerning
the law of war and peace)
(Grotius) **I:**146
Dekanawideh **II:**93
de Klerk, F. W. **X:**16, 325
de Kooning, Willem **VIII:**30, 31,
129; **IX:**19
Delagrange, Leon **VII:**28

De Lancey, James **II:93–94**
Cowboys and Skinners **III:**123
De Lancey family **II:**94,
Zenger, John Peter **II:**433
De Lancey family **II:**93, **94;** **III:**271
De Lancey's Cowboys **III:**123
Delancy, Peter **III:**140
Delany, Martin Robinson **V:107–108,** *108*
ACS **IV:**17
Douglass, Frederick **V:**115
54th Massachusetts Regiment **V:**142
Liberia **VI:**223
Negro Convention movement **IV:**279
Delaware **I:**105; **II:94–96**
abolitionism **V:**1
Constitution, ratification of the **III:**104
constitutions, state **III:**110
Dickinson, John **III:**137
disease/epidemics **II:**100
English immigrants **II:**117
Federalists **III:**166
Finney, Charles Grandison **IV:**151
industrialization **IV:**199
Know-Nothing Party **IV:**214, 215
Maine Law **IV:**234
Penn, William **II:**284
Pennsylvania **II:**285
Protestantism **II:**316
Rodney, Caesar **III:**373
Rodney, Caesar Augustus **III:**373, 374
Swedish colonies **II:**381
Underground Railroad **V:**397
Delaware, USS **III:**353
Delaware Assembly **III:**373
Delaware Bay **VI:**61
Delaware & Hudson (D&H) Canal Company **IV:**313
Delaware Indians **II:96–97**
Brainerd, David **II:**45, 46
Delaware **II:**95
Fallen Timbers, Battle of **III:**161
fur trade **II:**142
Gnadenhutten Massacre **III:**196
Greenville, Treaty of **III:**200
land **II:**201
Native Americans **III:**314; **IV:**273; **V:**278
Neolin **II:**255–256
New Jersey **II:**261
New York **II:**269
Pennsylvania **II:**284
revitalization movements **II:**332
Teedyuscung **II:**386

Walking Purchase **II:**405–406
Weiser, Johann Conrad **II:**409
Zeisberger, David **II:**433
Delaware River **III:**461c
agriculture **IV:**12
environment **III:**155
Monroe, James **IV:**258
Trenton and Princeton, Battles of **III:**416
Washington, George **III:**431
Delaware River forts **III:135–136**
Cornwallis, Charles, Lord **III:**120
Greene, Nathanael **III:**198
Hessians **III:**213
Howe, Richard, Lord **III:**214
Red Bank, Battle of **III:**359
De La Warr, Lord **I:104–105;** **II:**143
DeLay, Tom **X:**170, 171
De Leon, Daniel
IWW **VII:**147
labor, radical **VI:**213
radicalism **VII:**287
socialism **VI:**336; **VII:**327
Socialist Labor Party **VI:**336, 337
Delhi **I:**336
DeLisi, Charles **X:**171, 225
Dell, Floyd **VII:**130, 286
Delle Navigationi (Ramusio) **I:**152
Dellett, James **IV:**379
Dellinger, Dave **X:**73
Delmarva Peninsula **II:**95
de Lôme, Enrique Dupuy **VI:**88, 94
de Lôme Letter **VI:94,** 412c
Cuba **VI:**88
Maine, Remember the **VI:**237
Spanish-American War **VI:**340
De Long, George Washington **VI:**33
Delta blues **VIII:**250, 252
del Valle, Eric Arturo **X:**269
demerits **V:**409–410
De Mille, Cecil B. **VII:**216
demobilization, after World War II **VIII:91–92; IX:84–85**
elderly **VIII:**108
labor/labor movements **IX:**181
mobilization **VIII:**242
OWMR **VIII:**287
postwar planning **VIII:**306
reconversion **VIII:**326
strikes **VIII:**378
V-J Day **VIII:**407
WAC **VIII:**421
World War II home front **VIII:**434

democracy **II:**208
Carter, James Earl, Jr. **X:**69
foreign policy **X:**142–143
Latin America **X:**205, 206
Democracy and Education (Dewey) **VII:**76, 77
Democracy in America (Tocqueville) **IV:**335, 413c
Democratic-Farmer-Labor (DFL) Party **IX:**205; **X:**233
Democratic Leadership Council **X:**80
Democratic National Committee (DNC)
feminism **X:**134
Mitchell, George **X:**232
Nixon, Richard M. **X:**257
Watergate scandal **X:**365–366
Democratic National Convention (1876) **VI:**386
Democratic National Convention (1948) **IX:**299, 352c
Democratic National Convention (1964) **IX:**219, 220, 356c; **X:**233
Democratic National Convention (1968) **IX:**357c; **X:**375c
antiwar movement, Vietnam **X:**28
"Chicago Eight" **X:**73
counterculture **IX:**79
Democratic Party **IX:**85
Hayden, Tom **IX:**144
McCarthy, Eugene **IX:**206
MFDP **IX:**220
Democratic National Convention (1972) **X:**217
Democratic National Convention (2004) **X:**263
Democratic Party **IV:116–119,** *117;* **V:108–110,** 443c; **VI:94–96,** *95;* **VII:73–75,** 405c; **VIII:92–94,** 448c; **IX:85–86;** **X:**380c
abolitionism **V:**3
abortion **X:**4
Acheson, Dean **IX:**1
AFL **VIII:**18
African Americans **VIII:**2
Altgeld, John Peter **VI:**12
America First Committee **VIII:**17
American Liberty League **VIII:**19
Americans for Democratic Action **IX:**13
anticommunism **VIII:**22
anti-Masonry **IV:**25
antiwar movement, Vietnam **X:**29
Baruch, Bernard M. **VII:**32; **VIII:**42
Benton, Thomas Hart **IV:**54
Biden, Joseph **X:**42
Black Cabinet **VIII:**46

Blaine, James Gillespie **VI:**41
Blair, Francis Preston, Jr. **V:**36
Brain Trust **VIII:**51
Breckinridge, John C. **V:**42
Brown, Joseph Emerson **V:**45
Bryan, William Jennings **VI:**51
Byrd, Robert **X:**61
Byrnes, James F. **VIII:**60
Carter, James Earl, Jr. **X:**67
Cass, Lewis **IV:**83
Catholics **VIII:**63
"Chicago Eight" **X:**73
CIO **VIII:**82
cities and urban life **VIII:**68, 69; **X:**76
Civil Rights Act (1866) **V:**70
Civil Rights Act (1957) **IX:**58, 59
Civil War **V:**73
Clayton Antitrust Act **VII:**59
Cleveland, Grover **VI:**74
Cobb, Howell **V:**76
common soldier **V:**79
Congress **V:**89; **VIII:**79–81
conservatism **VIII:**84, 85; **IX:**74
conservative coalition **VIII:**85–86
conservative movement **X:**94
Coolidge, Calvin John **VII:**64
Copperheads **V:**94, 95
corruption, political **VI:**83
Crockett, Davy **IV:**110
Currency Act **VII:**68
currency issue **VI:**90
Davis, Jefferson **V:**103
Debs, Eugene Victor **VII:**72
Dewson, Mary **VIII:**95
Douglas, Stephen A. **V:**113, 114
Drayton, William H. **IV:**127
Dred Scott decision **V:**117
Eagleton, Thomas F. **X:**107
economy **X:**110
education, federal aid to **VI:**110
election of 1828 **IV:**135
election of 1840 **IV:**137, 139
election of 1932 **VIII:**108–109
election of 1936 **VIII:**109
election of 1940 **VIII:**110
election of 1944 **VIII:**111
elections (general) **V:**125, 126; **VII:**89–92; **IX:**102–104
elections, presidential **X:**118
enemy aliens **VIII:**115
ERA **X:**123, 124

Executive Reorganization Act **VIII:**121

Fair Deal **IX:**115

Farley, James A. **VIII:**125

farmers' alliances **VI:**126

Faubus, Orval **IX:**118

federal income tax **VII:**106–107

Ferraro, Geraldine A. **X:**135

Fillmore, Millard **IV:**149

fire-eaters **V:**146

fireside chats **VIII:**137

Flynn, Edward J. **VIII:**139

foreign policy **IV:**155

Free-Silver movement **VI:**135

Free-Soil Party **IV:**163, 164

Frémont, John C. **IV:**167

fugitive slave laws **IV:**168

Garner, John Nance **VIII:**147

gender gap **X:**150

German Americans **VIII:**148–149

global warming **X:**156

Hamer, Fannie Lou **IX:**141

Harding, Warren Gamaliel **VII:**134

Harriman, W. Averell **VIII:**161

Harrison, William Henry **IV:**186

Hawaii statehood **IX:**143

Hayes, Rutherford B. **VI:**167, 168

Henderson, Leon **VIII:**163–164

Hicks, Thomas H. **V:**188

Hillman, Sidney **VIII:**166

homefront **V:**193, 194

Hoover presidency **VIII:**175–176

Hopkins, Harry L. **VIII:**176

Horton, Willie **X:**168

House of Representatives **X:**169–171

Howe, Louis M. **VIII:**179

HUAC **IX:**150

Hull, Cordell **VIII:**180

immigration **VI:**184, 186; **X:**176

independent counsel **X:**179

Ingersoll, Robert Green **VI:**193

Internal Revenue taxes **VI:**194

Internal Security Act (1950) **IX:**157

Irish Americans **VIII:**188

isolationists **VIII:**189

Italian Americans **VIII:**190

Jackson, Claiborne F. **V:**209

Jackson, Jesse, L. **X:**192

Jackson, Thomas J. "Stonewall" **V:**210

Jews **VIII:**195–196

Johnson, Hugh S. **VIII:**196

Johnson, Lady Bird **IX:**162

Jones, Jesse H. **VIII:**197

Kansas-Nebraska Act **V:**221

Know-Nothing Party **IV:**214, 215

Ku Klux Klan **V:**223

labor/labor movements **IV:**218; **VII:**170–171; **VIII:**205; **X:**201

Latino movement **IX:**186

Lease, Mary Elizabeth Clyens **VI:**220

liberalism **VIII:**215, 216; **IX:**191; **X:**208

Liberal Republican Party **VI:**222

Lloyd, Henry Demarest **VI:**228

machine politics **VI:**234

Mallory, Stephen R. **V:**247

Manifest Destiny **IV:**234

marriage and family **X:**215

Marshall, Thurgood **IX:**203

McCarthy, Joseph R. **IX:**206

McClellan, George Brinton **V:**251, 252

McCormick, Cyrus Hall **IV:**245

McGovern, George S. **X:**216–217

McKinley, William **VI:**240, 241

Mexican-American War **IV:**251, 252

MFDP **IX:**219

Mitchell, George **X:**231–232

modern Republicanism **IX:**221

Morgenthau, Henry T., Jr. **VIII:**244

Mormon Church **IV:**89

Mormon War **IV:**263

Murray, Philip **VIII:**249

Nauvoo **IV:**278

neoconservatism **X:**251, 252

New Deal **VIII:**268

New Freedom **VII:**236

Ostend Manifesto **V:**290

PACs **X:**275

Palmer, Alexander Mitchell **VII:**249

panic of 1837 **IV:**295

Paul, Alice **VII:**254

peace movements **V:**295–296

Pelosi, Nancy **X:**271

People's Party **VI:**281–283

Pierce, Franklin **V:**306–307

Polish Americans **VIII:**297

political parties **X:**276–278

political parties, third **VI:**286

politics (1900–1928) **VII:**261

politics (Roosevelt era) **VIII:**297–300

Polk, James K. **IV:**301

popular sovereignty **IV:**304

presidential campaigns (1870–1899) **VI:**290–293

Progressive Party **VII:**269; **IX:**263

progressivism **VII:**271

pro-life/pro-choice movements **X:**289

public opinion polls **VIII:**312

race and race relations **V:**320

Reagan, Ronald W. **X:**299

Reconstruction **V:**326

redemption **V:**328, 329

Republican Party **IV:**322; **V:**333, 334; **VI:**311; **VIII:**336–338

Roosevelt, Eleanor **VIII:**343–344

Roosevelt, Franklin D. **VIII:**345

secession **V:**344

Senate, U.S. **X:**320–322

Shriver, Robert Sargent, Jr. **X:**324

Smith, Alfred E. **VII:**326

socialists **VIII:**362

Solid South **VI:**338

South **VIII:**367

southern demagogues **VII:**332

Stanton, Elizabeth Cady **V:**369, 370

States' Rights Party **IX:**299, 300

Stephens, Alexander Hamilton **V:**371

Stevenson, Adali E. **IX:**302

Sunbelt **X:**338

Taft, William Howard **VII:**347

Taney, Roger B. **IV:**365

tariffs **VI:**352; **VII:**349

Taylor, Zachary **IV:**368

Thirteenth Amendment **V:**388

Thomas, Norman **VIII:**394

Tilden, Samuel Jones **VI:**357

Triangle Shirtwaist Fire **VII:**356

Truman, Harry S. **IX:**320

Underwood-Simmons Tariff **VIII:**359

Vallandigham, Clement L. **V:**413, 414

Van Buren, Martin **IV:**385, 386

Versailles, Treaty of **VII:**370

violence and lawlessness **VI:**376

volunteer army **V:**420

Watson, Thomas Edward **VII:**380

Weathermen/Weather Underground **IX:**341

Whigs **IV:**396–398

Wilson, Thomas Woodrow **VII:**383

Wise, Henry A. **V:**434

women's status and rights **VIII:**422

World War II home front **VIII:**434

Wright, Fanny **IV:**406

Wright, James C., Jr. **X:**372

Zionism **VIII:**441

Democratic-Republican Party III:136, 463c–465c; **IV:**412c

Adams, Abigail **III:**4

Alien and Sedition Acts **III:**14

Amendment, Twelfth **III:**16–17

Ames, Fisher **III:**19

anti-Federalists **III:**25

artisans **III:**35

Bache, Benjamin Franklin **III:**39

Bank of the United States, First **III:**41

Bank of the United States, Second **IV:**48

Baptists **III:**44

Bill of Rights **III:**51

Bonus Bill **IV:**62

Brackenridge, Hugh Henry **III:**60

Burr, Aaron **III:**70

Callender, James T. **III:**74

Carey, Mathew **III:**80

Chase, Samuel **III:**86

cities and urban life **III:**90

citizenship **III:**93, 94

Clinton, George **III:**99

debt, national **III:**132

Democratic Party **IV:**116

Duane, William **III:**140

election of 1800 **III:**149–151

election of 1828 **IV:**135

embargo of 1807 **III:**152

Federalist Party **III:**164

foreign affairs **III:**169

French Revolution **III:**179

Fries's Rebellion **III:**180–181

Gallatin, Albert **III:**188

Hamilton, Alexander **III:**207

Hartford Convention **IV:**186

Hull, William **IV:**192

immigration **III:**221

impeachment **III:**222

Industrial Revolution **III:**226

Jackson, Andrew **IV:**206

Jay's Treaty **III:**231

Jefferson, Thomas **III:**233, 234

Democratic-Republican Party
(continued)
    journalism **III**:240, 241
    liberty tree **III**:268
    literature **III**:269
    Livingston, Robert R.
        III:270
    Louisiana Purchase
        III:273
    Lyon, Matthew **III**:277
    Macon, Nathaniel **III**:280
    Madison, James **III**:281
    Marbury v. Madison
        III:285
    Marshall, John **III**:290
    music **III**:309
    Non-Importation Act
        III:319
    Pickering, Timothy **III**:334
    political parties **III**:339
    popular culture **III**:341,
        342
    Quasi War **III**:353
    Randolph, John **III**:358,
        359
    religious liberty **III**:363–
        364
    riots **III**:372
    Rodney, Caesar Augustus
        III:373
    states' rights **III**:397
    Tammany Society **III**:405
    Taney, Roger B. **IV**:365
    tariffs **III**:406
    Taylor, John, of Caroline
        III:408
    Van Buren, Martin **IV**:385
    Virginia dynasty **III**:425
    War Hawks **IV**:389–390
    War of 1812 **IV**:390
    Washington, D.C. **III**:429
    West Point **III**:437
    Whiskey Rebellion **III**:440
    XYZ affair **III**:451
Democratic-Republican societies
    III:136–137
    artisans **III**:35
    Democratic-Republican
        Party **III**:136
    Whiskey Rebellion **III**:440
Democratic Review **IV**:210
Democratic Senatorial Campaign
    Committee **X**:232
Democratic Vistas (Whitman)
    VI:227
*Democratic Washington Union,
    The* **IV**:164
Demoiselle, La (Miami leader)
    II:201
Dempsey, William Harrison "Jack"
    VII:75–76, 76, 295, 333, 407*c*;
    VIII:371
DeMun, Jule **IV**:88
Demuth, Charles **VII**:24
DeMuth, Christopher **X**:349
Dengel, Lebna (emperor of
    Ethiopia) **I:105**, 125

dengue fever **IV**:123
Denison, Nathan **III**:449
Denison House **VI**:327–328
Denmark **I**:177
    blitzkrieg **VIII**:47
    Britain, Battle of **VIII**:53
    League of Armed Neutrality
        III:257
    Pingree, Hazen S. **VII**:260
    Versailles, Treaty of
        VII:370
Dennett, Mary Ware **VII**:36, 388
Dennie, Joseph **IV**:209
Dennis, Eugene **IX**:86
Dennis Miller Live **X**:343
Dennison, William **V**:171, 419
Dennis v. United States **VIII**:362;
    IX:86, 337, 352*c*
denominationalism **II**:315;
    III:361, 362
Densmore, Frances **VI**:255
Densmore, George **VI**:146
déntente
    cold war, end of **X**:84, 85
    conservative movement
        X:93
    Ford, Gerald R. **X**:139
    foreign policy **X**:140–142
    Helms, Jesse A., Jr. **X**:165
    Reagan, Ronald W. **X**:300
dentistry **V**:258
Denton, Michael **X**:306
Denver, Colorado
    Colorado gold rush **IV**:100
    gold **IV**:179
    Japanese Americans,
        relocation of **VIII**:194
    overland mail **IV**:290
    "Pike's Peak or Bust" **IV**:300
Denyankan kingdom **I**:330
De omni rerum fossilium (Gesner)
    I:139
De Orbe Novo (Peter Martyr)
    I:397*c*
Department for Negroes
    (Women's Christian
    Temperance Union) **VI**:160
Department of California **V**:253
Department of Dakota **V**:184
Department of Northeastern
    Virginia **V**:252
Department of Southwestern
    Virginia **V**:42, 269
Department of the Cumberland
    V:10
Department of the East **V**:253
Department of the Missouri
    V:182, 353
Department of the Ohio
    Buell, Don C. **V**:48
    Burnside, Ambrose E. **V**:52
    McClellan, George Brinton
        V:250
Department of the Pacific **V**:253
Department of the South **V**:253
Department of West Virginia
    V:184

department stores **VI:96–97**, 410*c*
    advertising **VI**:2
    cities and urban life **V**:67
    economy **X**:109
    mail-order houses **VI**:237
    radio **VII**:290
    Wanamaker, John **VI**:382
DePauw University **VIII**:217
Dependent and Disability Act
    (1890) **VI**:161
Dependents Pension bill **VI**:152,
    410*c*
deportation **X**:378*c*
depression (1857–1858) **VI**:58
depression (1870) **IV**:243
depression (1873–1878) **VI**:89,
    411*c*
    business cycles **VI**:58
    Chinese Exclusion Act
        VI:68
    Crime of '73 **VI**:86
    Democratic Party **V**:110
    economy **V**:124
    Frick, Henry Clay **VI**:135
    labor organizations **VI**:215
    National Labor Union
        V:276
    Pullman Strike **VI**:297
    Republican Party **V**:334
    strikes **V**:374
depression (1883–1886) **VI**:375
depression (1893) **VII**:260
depression (1893–1897)
    business cycles **VI**:58–59
    Cleveland, Grover **VI**:75
    Coxey's Army **VI**:84
    investments, American,
        abroad **VI**:197
depression (1907) **VII**:204
depression (1930s). *See* Great
    Depression
depression, agricultural (1920s)
    VII:48
DePriest, Oscar **VIII**:2–3
DePugh, Robert **X**:230
*De Rebus Oceanicis et Nove Orbe
    decades tres* (Peter Martyr)
    I:290
deregulation **X**:383*c*
    business **X**:57
    energy **X**:121
    federalism **X**:131
    Kennedy, Edward M. **X**:196
    labor/labor movements
        X:203
Dermot MacMurrough (king of
    Ireland) **I**:10
Description of New England, A
    (Smith) **II**:363
desegregation/integration
    IX:353*c*, 355*c*; **X**:375*c*
    African Americans **X**:14, 15
    Baker, Ella Josephine **IX**:32
    Brennan, William J., Jr.
        X:48
    *Brown v. Board of
        Education* **IX**:43–44

    Civil Rights Act (1964)
        IX:61
    Democratic Party **IX**:85
    Faubus, Orval **IX**:117, 118
    Federal Housing
        Administration **IX**:120
    freedom rides **IX**:123–124
    Kennedy, Robert F. **IX**:171
    liberalism **X**:207
    Malcolm X **IX**:199
    Meredith, James **IX**:213
    NAACP **VIII**:256; **IX**:232
    NYA **VIII**:263
    Parks, Rosa **IX**:254
    race and race relations
        IX:269; **X**:297
    SCLC **IX**:292–294
    SNCC **IX**:302, 303
    Southern Manifesto
        IX:294
    States' Rights Party **IX**:299
    Supreme Court **VIII**:383;
        X:338
    Thurmond, James Strom
        X:351
    Wallace, George C. **X**:364
    White Citizens' Councils
        IX:342
Deseret, State of **IV:119–121**
    migration **IV**:255
    Mormon Church **IV**:90
    religion **IV**:319
    Young, Brigham **IV**:408
Deseret National Bank **VIII**:101
desertion **V:110–111**
    Confederate States of
        America **V**:87
    Heroes of America **V**:188
    homefront **V**:193
    Lee, Robert E. **V**:231
    Louisiana Tigers **V**:245
    Revolutionary War **III**:369
    Valley Forge **III**:422
Desert News **IV**:121
deserts **I**:323–324
"deserving poor" **IX**:144
designer drugs **X**:244
Deslondes Rebellion **III**:204
De Smet, Pierre Jean **IV**:146
Des Moines, Iowa **VII**:362;
    VIII:126
Des Moines River **IV**:145
Des monstres et prodiges (Paré)
    I:248
destroyers
    Navy, U.S. **VIII**:265
    Pearl Harbor **VIII**:292
    Philippine Sea, Battle of the
        VIII:295
destroyers-for-bases deal
    VIII:94–95, 446*c*
    America First Committee
        VIII:17
    Anglo-American relations
        VIII:21
    Britain, Battle of **VIII**:53
    CDAAA **VIII**:77

foreign policy **VIII:**141
Knox, Frank **VIII:**202
Willkie, Wendell L.
VIII:417
Destruction of the Indies (Las
Casas) **I:**207
"Desultory Thoughts" (Murray)
III:308
Desverney, Peter Prioleau **IV:**388
Detective Story **VII:**160
détente **X:103–104**
defense policy **X:**99, 101
INF Treaty **X:**180
Nixon, Richard M. **X:**257
Detention Review Board **IX:**158
determinism **VI:**200, 201
Detroit, Michigan **II:**142;
VIII:448c
African Americans **VIII:**5
aircraft industry **VIII:**14–15
American Fur Company
IV:19
anti-Catholic riots **IV:**23
anti-Semitism **VIII:**25
blues **VII:**39
cities and urban life **VI:**70;
VIII:68
Ford, Henry **VII:**111
Ford Motor Corporation
IX:122
fur trade **IV:**170
immigration **VII:**144
libraries, public **VI:**224
migration **IV:**254
Muhammad, Elijah **IX:**226
Native Americans in the War
of 1812 **IV:**277
Pingree, Hazen S. **VII:**260,
261
population trends **VII:**267
Prohibition **VII:**272
public housing **IX:**267
race and race relations
VIII:318
social work **VII:**329
sports and recreation
VII:334–335
steel industry **VII:**337–338
Sweet trial **VII:**344–345
Thames, Battle of the
IV:375
unemployment **VIII:**399
urban reform **VII:**362
Volstead Act **VII:**374
zoot-suiters **VIII:**442
Detroit Automobile Company
VII:111
Detroit City Railways **VII:**260
Detroit Edison Company **VII:**111
Detroit *Free Press* **VI:**85
Detroit Independent **VII:**344
Detroit News **VII:**159–160
Detroit Tigers **VII:**334
Detroit Urban League **VII:**344
Devil's Den **V:**196, 304
Devil's Tower, Wyoming **VII:**16
Devin, Thomas A. **V:**147

Devine, Annie **IX:**219, 220
Dewey, George **VI:97,** 412c
Aguinaldo, Emilio **VII:**9
Filipino insurrection **VI:**127
Hawaii **VI:**163
Spanish-American War
VI:341
Dewey, John **VII:76–77**
education **VII:**85; **VIII:**105
Hall, Granville Stanley
VI:157
James, William **VI:**201
marriage and family
VII:193
NAACP **VII:**224
politics (1900–1928)
VII:261
pragmatism **VI:**289
Dewey, Thomas E. **VIII:**448c;
IX:86–88, 87, 352c
Americans for Democratic
Action **IX:**14
conservatism **IX:**74
Democratic Party **IX:**85
election of 1940 **VIII:**110
election of 1944 **VIII:**111
elections **IX:**102
Fair Deal **IX:**115
Full Employment Bill
VIII:145
Gallup Poll **IX:**130
Ickes, Harold L. **VIII:**183
politics (Roosevelt era)
VIII:300
Republican Party **VIII:**338;
IX:274
Taft, Robert A. **VIII:**385
Walsh, Lawrence E. **X:**364
Warren, Earl **IX:**337
"Dewey Defeats Truman" headline
IX:102
Dewing, Thomas Wilmer **VI:**392
De Witt, John L. **VIII:**193
DeWitt's Corner, Treaty of **III:**87
Dewson, Mary W. "Molly"
VIII:95
Democratic Party **VIII:**93
Perkins, Frances **VIII:**293
women's network **VIII:**421
women's status and rights
VIII:423
DFL Party. *See* Democratic-
Farmer-Labor Party
Dharma Bums, The (Kerouac)
IX:37, 173
DHS. *See* Homeland Security,
U.S. Department of
Dial, The
Emerson, Ralph Waldo
IV:140
Fuller, Margaret **IV:**169
Peabody, Elizabeth Palmer
VI:279, 280
Thoreau, Henry David
IV:376
transcendental movement
IV:379

Diallo, Amadou **X:**382c
"Dialogue Between a European
and an American Englishman,
A" (Hutchinson) **III:**219
Diamond, Jared **I:**16
Diana (Saint-Gaudens) **VI:**321
Diary from Dixie, A (Chesnut)
V:64, 239
Dias, Bartholomeu **I:105–106**
Cabral, Pedro Álvares **I:**46
caravel **I:**59
Gama, Vasco da **I:**137
invention and technology
I:184
Diaspora **X:**193
Díaz, Porfirio **VII:**405c
Big Stick diplomacy **VII:**35
investments, American,
abroad **VI:**197
Mexican immigration
VII:202
Mexican Revolution
VII:204
Díaz del Castillo, Bernal **I:106**
Charles V **I:**70–71
Grijalva, Juan de **I:**145
Tenochtitlán **I:**354
Díaz-Ordáz Bolaños, Gustavo
X:226
Dickinson, Anna E. **V:111**
Dickinson, Charles **III:**141
Dickinson, Daniel S. **IV:**304
Dickinson, Emily **VI:97–98,** 409c
Bowles, Samuel **VI:**43
Crane, Stephen **VI:**85
Higginson, Thomas
Wentworth **V:**188;
VI:171, 172
Howells, William Dean
VI:180
Jackson, Helen Hunt
VI:199
literature **VI:**227
Dickinson, John **III:137,** 459c
Articles of Confederation
III:33
Continental Congress, First
III:113
Galloway, Joseph **III:**189
Olive Branch Petition
III:324
Townshend Duties **III:**412
Dickinson, Preston **VII:**24
Dickinson, Robert Litou **VII:**37
Dickinson-Ayon Treaty **V:**151
Dickinson College **III:**137, 376
Dickpert, Joest **I:**248
Dickson, W. K. Laurie **VII:**214
dictatorships **X:**16
Didrikson, Mildred "Babe"
VIII:303, 372
Die Freiheit **VII:**126
Diem, Ngo Dinh
Dulles, John Foster **IX:**91
Vietnam War **IX:**330
wars of national liberation
IX:339

Dien Bien Phu, Vietnam **IX:**330
Dieppe, Battle of **VIII:**20
Dies, Martin
FTP **VIII:**136
FWP **VIII:**137
HUAC **IX:**150
diet
animals **II:**23
cacao **I:**48
corn **II:**80–81
Delaware Indians **II:**96
disease/epidemics **I:**107–
108
food **II:**130–131
Huron **I:**172
Natchez **I:**259
society, British American
II:367
Diet of Augsburg **I:**219
Diet of Worms **I:**218, 315
Dietrich, Marlene **VIII:**245
DiGerlando, Benedict **IX:**111
Diggio, John **III:**269
Digital Equipment Corporation
(DEC) **IX:**71
digital thermostats **X:**318
digital video cameras **X:**318, 319
digital video disk (DVD)
literature **X:**212
media **X:**220
recreation **X:**303
science and technology
X:318–320
Diller, Burgoyne **VIII:**31
Dillinger, John **VIII:**130; **IX:**149
Dillingham, William P. **VII:**77,
78, 144
Dillingham Commission **VII:77–
78**
Cable Act **VII:**47
immigration **VII:**144
Immigration Act (1917)
VII:145
National Origins Act
VII:227
race and race relations
VII:282
science and technology
VII:315
Dillingham Report **VII:**144, 405c
DiMaggio, Joe **VIII:95–96,** 447c
Monroe, Marilyn **IX:**223
recreation **VIII:**328
sports and recreation
VIII:370
dime novels **VI:98–99,** 99
Cody, William Frederick
VI:76
entertainment, popular
VI:118
journalism **VII:**160
literature **V:**239; **VI:**225
popular culture **VII:**265
Dimmock, Charles **V:**192
Dimond, Anthony **IX:**8
Diners Club **IX:**79, 352c
Dingell, John **X:**72

Dingley Tariff **VI**:412*c;* **VII**:405*c*
  Allison, William Boyd **VI**:12
  business and government
    VI:56
  Congress **VI**:80
  McKinley, William **VI**:241
  presidency **VI**:290
Dinosaur National Park **VII**:229
Dinwiddie, Robert
  Ohio Company of Virginia
    II:278
  Ostenaco **II**:280
  Washington, George
    III:429
Dinwiddie Court House, Virginia
  V:14, 99
Diogo I (king of Kongo) **I**:200
Dior, Christian **IX**:116
diphtheria **II**:100
  medicine **VII**:198, 200;
    X:222
  population trends **VII**:266
  public health **VII**:274
  science and technology
    VII:314
diplomacy **I**:382; **V**:443*c;* **VI**:407*c;*
  X:376*c,* 381*c*
  Adams, John **III**:5
  Adams, John Quincy **IV**:5
  Africa **X**:16
  Albright, Madeleine K. **X**:22
  Angell, James Burrill **VI**:15
  Attakullakulla **II**:28
  Barlow, Joel **III**:46
  Bunche, Ralph **IX**:44–45
  Camp David accords **X**:65
  Cass, Lewis **IV**:83
  Choctaw **III**:89
  Continental Congress,
    Second **III**:116
  Creek **III**:125
  Crèvecoeur, J. Hector St.
    John de **III**:127
  Deane, Silas **III**:129
  Dulles, John Foster
    IX:90–91
  foreign affairs **III**:168
  foreign policy **V**:149–152;
    X:141
  Gallatin, Albert **III**:187, 188
  Genêt, Edmond Charles
    III:190–191
  Habib, Philip C. **X**:163
  Harriman, W. Averell
    VIII:162
  Harrison, William Henry
    IV:185–186
  Harte, Bret **VI**:162–163
  Hay, John Milton **VI**:164
  Hendrick **II**:164
  Howells, William Dean
    VI:179
  Jackson, Jesse, L. **X**:192
  Jay, John **III**:229, 230
  Jay's Treaty **III**:231
  Kennan, George F. **IX**:167–
    168

Kennedy, Joseph P.
  VIII:200
King, Rufus **III**:245
Lamar, Mirabeau B. **IV**:222
Larkin, Thomas Oliver
  IV:222–223
Lee, Arthur **III**:257–258
Livingston, Robert R. **III**:270
Marsh, George Perkins
  VI:239
Mellon, Andrew William
  VII:201
Mondale, Walter F. **X**:234
Montour, Andrew **II**:241
Montour, Madame **II**:242
Nixon, Richard M. **X**:257
North Vietnam **X**:260–261
peace movements **V**:296
Red Jacket **III**:359
Rice, Condoleezza **X**:310
Roosevelt, Franklin D.
  VIII:346
Seward, William H. **V**:348
Stevenson, Adali E. **IX**:302
Talleyrand-Périgord, Charles-
  Maurice de **III**:405
Teedyuscung **II**:386
Vergennes, Charles Gravier,
  comte de **III**:423
Weiser, Johann Conrad
  II:409
XYZ affair **III**:451
"Direct Cinema" movement
  IX:223
direct current (DC) **VI**:353
direct election of senators **VII**:**78,**
  405*c*
  Johnson, Hiram Warren
    VII:154
  journalism **VII**:159
  La Follette, Robert M.
    VII:173
  New Freedom **VII**:236
  Pingree, Hazen S. **VII**:260
  politics (1900–1928)
    VII:261
  Progressive Party **VII**:270
  Wilson, Thomas Woodrow
    VII:384
direct mail marketing **X**:7
Direct Tax Act **III**:164, 180
DirecTV **X**:283
Dirksen, Everett McKinley **IX**:60,
  139
disabilities **X**:115–116, 379*c*
disability insurance **VIII**:365
disability rights movement
  X:24–25
Disabled American Veterans
  (DAV) **VII**:373
disarmament
  Carnegie Endowment for
    International Peace
    VII:50
  Catholic Bishops' Letter
    X:70
  foreign policy **X**:144

WILPF **VII**:386
  World Disarmament
    Conference **VIII**:426–
    427
disaster relief **X**:174
Disciples of Christ. *See* Christian
  Church
disco music **X**:238, 279
*Discourse Concerning Unlimited
  Submission and Non-Resistance*
  (Mayhew) **III**:293
"Discourse Concerning Western
  Planting" (Hakluyt) **I**:152
"Discourse Concerning Western
  Planting, A" (Hakluyt) **I**:**423–
  425**
*Discourse of a Discoverie for
  a New Passage to Cataia, A*
  (Gilbert) **I**:140
"Discourse on the Constitution"
  IV:69
Discourses on Women (Mott)
  IV:266
Discovery (space shuttle) **X**:329,
  384*c*
Discovery, HMS **IV**:188
*Discovery, Settlement and Present
  State of Kentucke, The* (Filson)
  III:56
discrimination **VI**:408*c;*
  VIII:447*c*
  AFL **VI**:13
  African Methodist Episcopal
    Church **V**:5
  carpetbaggers **V**:56
  civil rights **VIII**:73
  Civil Rights Act (1875) **V**:71
  Field, Stephen Johnson
    VI:127
  Fifteenth Amendment **V**:141
  Fourteenth Amendment
    V:157
  March on Washington
    Movement **VIII**:227, 228
  NAACP **VIII**:256
  race and race relations
    VII:282, 283; **VIII**:319
  Randolph, A. Philip
    VIII:321
  redemption **V**:328
  relief **VIII**:332–333
  Selective Service **VIII**:358
  Supreme Court **VIII**:383
  WAC **VIII**:419
  WASP **VIII**:419
  World War II home front
    VIII:432
  WPA **VIII**:426
  Wright, Richard **VIII**:437
disease and epidemics **I**:**106–109,**
  107, *107,* 108; **II**:**97–100,** 99,
  435*c;* **III**:**138,** 463*c;* **IV**:**121–
  124,** *122;* **V**:**112–113;** **VI**:408*c.*
  See also specific diseases, e.g.:
  tuberculosis
  Aataentsic **I**:1
  Abenaki **I**:1

African Americans **IV**:7
Alaska **III**:12
Allen, Richard **III**:16
animals **II**:23
Apalachee **I**:11
Aztecs **I**:22
Black Hawk War **IV**:58
Bonaparte, Napoleon **III**:55
Brown, Charles Brockden
  III:64
California **I**:52
California missions **IV**:76
Carey, Mathew **III**:80
Cartier, Jacques **I**:61
Catawba **II**:61–62
cities and urban life **III**:91;
  IV:92–93
Cofitachequi **I**:80
Columbian Exchange
  I:81–82
Coosa **I**:89
Dix, Dorothea **IV**:124
Duane, James **III**:140
economy **IV**:132; **V**:123
fur trade **IV**:171
George III **III**:192
Girard, Stephen **III**:195
Great Plains **III**:197
Hawaii **III**:210; **IV**:188
Hispaniola **I**:163
horses **I**:169
Iceland **I**:177
immigration **IV**:194
Jones, Absalom **III**:238
Las Casas, Bartolomé de
  I:205, 207
Léry, Jean de **I**:213
Madison, Dolley Payne
  Todd **III**:280
malaria **II**:213–214
Martinique **I**:232
medicine **II**:229–230;
  III:295, 296; **IV**:248, 249;
  V:257; **VI**:244, 245
Mexican-American War
  IV:252
Mississippian **I**:244, 245
Mississippi River war **V**:264
Natchez **I**:259
Native Americans **II**:250,
  252–253; **III**:315; **IV**:275
New Spain **I**:269
Oregon Trail **IV**:286
Permanent Indian Frontier
  IV:297–298
plague **I**:293–294
Pontiac's War **III**:340
population trends **I**:297–
  298; **II**:302
prisons **V**:313, 314
prostitution **V**:316
Pueblo Revolt **II**:318
rural life **III**:375
Rush, Benjamin **III**:376
Shiloh, Battle of **V**:358–359
slavery **I**:338
slave trade, internal **IV**:349

smallpox **I:**340–341;
II:360–361
Soto, Hernando de **I:**342,
343
sugar **I:**349
Taino **I:**352
Timucua **I:**360
Trail of Tears **IV:**377, 378
Union army **V:**401
Valley Forge **III:**422–423
Virginia **II:**398, 399
Warren, Joseph **III:**427
Webster, Noah **III:**434
Whitman, Marcus **IV:**398
Whitman, Narcissa **IV:**399
Wilkinson, James **III:**444
yellow fever **II:**431
disestablishmentarianism
Madison, James **III:**281
religious liberty **III:**363–
364
Disney, Walt **VIII:**446*c;* **IX:***88,*
88–89
Hollywood Ten **IX:**147
movies **VIII:**246, 247
New York World's Fair
(1964) **IX:**246
theme parks **IX:**317
Disney Channel **X:**344
Disney Corporation **X:**279
Disneyland (California)
Disney, Walt **IX:**88, 89
New York World's Fair
(1964) **IX:**246
theme parks **IX:**317
dispensationalism **X:**125
disposable income **X:**302
"Disquisition on Government"
(Calhoun) **IV:**69
Disraeli, Benjamin **VI:**204
*Dissertation on Canon and Feudal
Law, A* (Adams) **III:**4
Disston Company **IV:**199
Distinguished Flying Cross
VII:178
*Distinguishing Marks of a Work
of the Spirit of God, The*
(Edwards) **II:**114
Distribution-Preemption Act
(1841) **IV:**203, 306
District of Columbia. *See*
Washington, D.C.
District of Columbia School
Board **VII:**352
Di Varthema, Ludovico **I:**238–
239
Divers Voyages (Hakluyt) **I:**152
"Divinity School Address"
(Emerson) **IV:**320
Division of Negro Affairs
VIII:263, 425
Division of the Atlantic **V:**184
Division of the Potomac **V:**186
divorce **X:**375*c*
Blackwell, Antoinette Brown
VI:39
family life **X:**127, 128

feminism **X:**134
Jackson, Andrew **IV:**205
Kelley, Florence **VII:**164
marriage and family **III:**287;
IV:239–240; **V:**248;
VII:190, 192; **VIII:**231,
232; **X:**213, 216
population trends **VII:**266;
VIII:305
sexuality **VII:**322
women's status and rights
III:446, 448; **IV:**403;
VI:399; **X:**370
World War II home front
VIII:433
Wright, Fanny **IV:**405
Dix, Dorothea **IV:***124,* **124–125,**
414*c*
Mann, Horace **IV:**237
nurses **V:**285
penitentiary movement
IV:296
Dix, John A. **V:**313
Dix-Hill cartel **V:**313–314
"Dixie" **V:**273, 274
Dixiecrats. *See* State's Rights
Party
Dixon, George E. **V:**191
Dixon, Jeremiah **V:**250
Dixon, Thomas
Birth of a Nation, The
VII:37–38
Griffith, David Wark
VII:131
Ku Klux Klan **VII:**165
Trotter, William Monroe
VII:357
Djenne-Djeno **I:**14, **109**
Djibouti **I:109–110**
Dmytryk, Edward **IX:**147–149,
148
DNA (deoxyribonucleic acid)
Human Genome Project
X:171–172
medicine **X:**222, 224
science and technology
IX:285–286
technology **IX:**314
DNC. *See* Democratic National
Committee
DOB. *See* Daughters of Bilitis
Dobbs, Arthur **I:**273
Dobrynin, Anatoly **X:**336
Doctor Huguet (Donnelly)
VI:100
Doctor's Riot **III:**371
Dr. Strangelove (film) **IX:**65
doctrinero **I:**205
documentaries **VIII:**302–303
DOD. *See* Defense, U.S.
Department of
Dodd, Samuel C. T. **VI:**192, 362
Dodd, Thomas **IX:**283
Dodge, Grenville M.
Allison, William Boyd
VI:11
Bridger, James **IV:**64

Pacific Railroad Act **V:**293
Dodge, Henry **IV:**158
Dodge, Josephine **VII:**18
Dodge, Mabel **VII:**193
Dodge Brothers **VII:**84
DOE. *See* Energy, U.S.
Department of
Doeg Indians **II:**31
Doenitz, Karl **VIII:**33
Doe v. Bolton **X:**2, 289
dog racing **VIII:**328
dogs **II:**23
Dog's Life, A (film) **VII:***215*
Doheny, Edward **VII:**135, 351
Dohrn, Bernadine **IX:**341; **X:**367,
368
DOJ. *See* Justice, U.S.
Department of
Dolby Surround Sound speaker
systems **X:**235, 318
Dole, Elizabeth **X:**105, 165
Dole, Robert **X:104–105,** 381*c*
Buchanan, Patrick J. **X:**49
Bush, George H. W. **X:**52
Ford, Gerald R. **X:**139
immigration **X:**176
Kemp, Jack F. **X:**196
Senate, U.S. **X:**321
Dole, Sanford B. **IV:**189; **VI:**163
dollar-a-year men **VIII:**96
mobilization **VIII:**242
Nelson, Donald M.
VIII:266
technology **VIII:**390
World War II home front
VIII:434
dollar diplomacy **VII:79,** 114
DOMA. *See* Defense of Marriage
Act
Domestic Council **X:**266
Domestic Counter-Terrorism
Center **X:**346
domesticity (colonial era) **II:100–**
101, 423
domestic partners **X:**149
domestic policy
Bush, George H. W. **X:**53
Bush, George W. **X:**56
Clinton, William J. **X:**80
energy **X:**121
House of Representatives
X:171
liberalism **X:**207
Nixon, Richard M. **X:**256–
257
Reagan, Ronald W. **X:**300
domestic service
children **VIII:**67
Mexican Americans
VIII:237
women's status and rights
VIII:424
domestic terrorism **X:**346–347
domestic trade. *See* trade
(domestic and foreign)
domestic violence intervention
X:308

Dominican Republic **I:**163;
VII:404*c,* 406*c;* **IX:**356*c*
Big Stick diplomacy **VII:**35
foreign policy **VII:**113, 114
Latin America **IX:**184
Roosevelt Corollary **VII:**305
Stevenson, Adali E. **IX:**302
Dominicans **I:110; II:101**
Aguilar, Francisco de **I:**4
California **I:**51
Durán, Diego **I:**114
Las Casas, Bartolomé de
I:206
Porres, St. Martín de **I:**299
Dominion of New England
II:101–103, 102*m,* 436*c*
Andros, Sir Edmund **II:**20
Connecticut **II:**77
Dudley, Joseph **II:**103
Glorious Revolution **II:**150
King Philip's War **II:**193
Massachusetts **II:**223
monarchy, British **II:**240
New Hampshire **II:**260
New York **II:**271
Randolph, Edward **II:**326
domino theory **IX:**21, 35, **89**
Donahue, Thomas J. **X:**177
Donaldson, Joseph **III:**45
Donatário system **I:**35
Dongan, Thomas **II:**336
Donnacona **I:**61
Donnelly, Ignatius Loyola
VI:99–100
bimetallism **VI:**38
currency issue **VI:**90
literature **VI:**226
Omaha platform **VI:**272
Patrons of Husbandry
VI:278
People's Party **VI:**282
utopianism **VI:**371
Valesh, Eva McDonald
VII:367
Donner, George **IV:**125, 126
Donner, Jacob **IV:**125, 126
Donner party **IV:**77, **125–126,**
187
Donovan, Mike **VI:**44
Donovan, William J. **VIII:**284–
285, *285,* 447*c*
Don Quixote (Cervantes) **III:**60
"don't ask, don't tell" **X:**101, 149
"Don't Be Cruel" (Presley) **IX:**229
Doolittle, Amos **III:**145
Doolittle, Hilda. *See* H. D.
Doors of Perception, The (Huxley)
IX:195
Dorantes, Andrés **I:**40
Dorchester Heights **III:138–139,**
461*c*
Fort Ticonderoga **III:**171–
172
Knox, Henry **III:**248
Trumbull, John **III:**416
Washington, George
III:430

Dorr, Thomas **IV:**383
Dorr Rebellion (Dorr War)
 IV:383, 414*c*
Dorsey, Jimmy **VIII:**44, 250
Dorsey, Stephen W. **VI:**344
Dorsey, Tommy
 big bands **VIII:**44
 music **VIII:**250
 Sinatra, Frank **VIII:**361
DOS operating system **X:**147
Dos Passos, John **VII:**179, 180,
 186, 212; **VIII:**218–219
dot-coms **X:**110
Doubleday, Abner
 baseball **VII:**33
 Gettysburg, Battle of **V:**166,
 167
 Meade, George Gordon
 V:254
double predestination **I:**192
"Double V" campaign **VIII:**319
Douglas, Aaron **VII:**136
Douglas, Ann **VII:**180
Douglas, Helen Gahagan **X:**123,
 256
Douglas, Stephen A. **IV:**415*c;*
 V:*113,* **113–115,** 443*c*
 Bidwell, John **IV:**56
 Bleeding Kansas **V:**37
 Buchanan, James **V:**48
 Compromise of 1850
 IV:104
 Cooper Union speech **V:**94
 Crittenden Compromise
 V:98
 Davis, Jefferson **V:**104
 Democratic Party **IV:**118–
 119; **V:**109
 Fillmore, Millard **IV:**150
 Kansas-Nebraska Act **V:**221
 Letcher, John **V:**232
 Lincoln, Abraham **V:**236
 Pacific Railroad Act **V:**293
 popular sovereignty **IV:**304
 Republican Party **IV:**322,
 323; **V:**332
 Sumner, Charles **V:**377
 Taylor, Zachary **IV:**368
 Watterson, Henry **VI:**385
Douglas, William O. **VIII:96–97;**
 IX:*336*
 Baker v. Carr **IX:**33
 Dennis v. U.S. **IX:**86
 SEC **VIII:**357
 White, Byron R. **X:**369
Douglas Aircraft Company
 aircraft industry **VIII:**13
 aviation **IX:**27, 28
 technology **IX:**313
Douglas C-54 Skymaster (DC-4)
 VIII:397
Douglas DC-3 **VIII:**13, 389, *396*
Douglass, Frederick **IV:**413*c;*
 V:*115,* **115–116**
 abolitionism **V:**3, 4
 African Americans **IV:**9;
 VI:7

American Anti-Slavery
 Society **IV:**16
 Brown, John **V:**43, 44
 Brown, William Wells **V:**46
 Catto, Octavius V. **V:**59
 Delany, Martin Robinson
 V:107
 Dickinson, Anna E. **V:**111
 emancipation **V:**130
 Emancipation Proclamation
 V:131
 entertainment, popular
 VI:116
 Exodusters **VI:**122–123
 female antislavery societies
 IV:147
 54th Massachusetts
 Regiment **V:**142, 143
 Forten, James **III:**170
 Free-Soil Party **IV:**163
 Garnet, Henry Highland
 IV:174
 Garrison, William Lloyd
 V:164
 Harpers Ferry, West Virginia
 V:186
 Langston, John Mercer
 VI:218
 literature **IV:**228; **V:**239
 lyceum movement **IV:**232
 Negro Convention
 movement **IV:**279
 newspapers **VI:**266
 Pennington, James William
 Charles **V:**300
 race and race relations
 IV:311
 Seneca Falls convention
 IV:341
 slavery **V:**362
 Thirteenth Amendment
 V:388
 Truth, Sojourner **V:**393
 Washington, Booker T.
 VI:384
 Wells-Barnett, Ida Bell
 VI:388
 World's Columbian
 Exposition **VI:**403
Douglass, Lewis **V:**143
Dove, Arthur **VII:**25
Dow, Herbert **IX:**89, 90
Dow, Lorenzo **III:139;** **IV:126–**
 127
Dow, Neal **IV:**233, 234
Dow Chemical Corporation
 VII:150; **IX:89–90**
Dowding, Nancy **IX:**345
dower right **III:**446
Dow Jones Industrial Average
 VIII:324; **X:**59, 379*c*
Dowmetal pistons **IX:**90
"Downhearted Blues" **VII:**97
Downing, Andrew Jackson **IV:**31
downsizing **X:**201
Doyle, Arthur Conan **VII:**142
Doz, André **II:**139

draft. *See* conscription
draft evasion **IX:**357*c;* **X:**377*c*
 Ali, Muhammad **IX:**10
 antiwar movement, Vietnam
 X:28
 Clinton, William J. **X:**79
Dragging Canoe **III:139–140,**
 460*c*
 Cherokee **III:**87
 Franklin, state of **III:**175
 Native Americans **III:**314
 Wilderness Road **III:**442
Dragon's Gate (Laurence) **IX:**349
Dragon's Teeth (Sinclair) **VII:**326
Dragonwings (Laurence) **IX:**349
Drake, Daniel **IV:**249
Drake, Edwin L. **VI:**191, 271
Drake, Sir Francis **I:110–113,**
 111, 398*c*
 Elizabeth I **I:**121
 Frobisher, Martin **I:**135
 Grenville, Sir Richard **I:**145
 Hawkins, Sir John **I:**157
 Ingram, David **I:**181
 Lane, Ralph **I:**203
 New Mexico **I:**265
 North Carolina **II:**274
 Panama **I:**285
 Roanoke **I:**321
 St. Augustine **II:**341
 Spanish Armada **I:**344
Drake Manuscript **I:113–114,**
 134, 288
drama. *See* theater
Dramamine **IX:**211
Draper, Henry **VI:**325
Drayandi, Joh. **I:**346
Drayton, William H. **IV:127**
Dreams from My Father (Obama)
 X:263
Dred (Stowe) **V:**374
*Dred: A Tale of the Great Dismal
 Swamp* (Stowe) **IV:**229
Dred Scott decision (*Dred Scott
 v. Sandford*) **V:116–118,** *117,*
 443*c*
 abortion **X:**4
 Amistad incident **IV:**22
 Buchanan, James **V:**48
 Civil War **V:**73
 Fourteenth Amendment
 V:157
 popular sovereignty **IV:**304
 race and race relations
 IV:310
 Republican Party **IV:**323
 slavery **IV:**346; **V:**363
 Taney, Roger B. **IV:**366
Dreiser, Theodore
 cities and urban life **VII:**55
 Howells, William Dean
 VI:180
 literature **VI:**226; **VII:**179
 radical and labor press
 VII:285
Dresden, Germany **VII:**41
Dresden codice **I:**47

dress **VII:79–80**
 sexuality **VII:**322
 southern demagogues
 VII:332
 work, household **VII:**389
Drew, Charles **VIII:**234
Drew, Daniel **VI:**151
Drewry's Bluff **V:**248
Drexel, Morgan & Company
 VI:250
Drinker, Philip **VIII:**234
dropout rates **X:**13
drought. *See also* dust bowl
 Great Plains Indians **II:**157
 Jamestown **II:**181
 Popé **II:**301
 Pueblo Revolt **II:**318
Drouillard, George **IV:**144
drug crimes **X:**378*c*
Drug Enforcement Agency **X:**243
drugs, illicit **IX:**355*c*
 Bennett, William J. **X:**41
 crime and punishment **X:**96,
 97
 Ginsberg, Allen **IX:**135
 Kerouac, Jack **IX:**173
 Leary, Timothy **IX:**187, 188
 LSD **IX:**195–196
 medicine **X:**224
 Mexico **X:**226
 music **IX:**229
 narcotics **X:**242–244
drugs, pharmaceutical **X:**222. *See
 also* miracle drugs
drug testing **X:**339
drug trafficking
 Afghanistan War **X:**12
 Bennett, William J. **X:**41
 Bush, George H. W. **X:**52
 Bush, George W. **X:**56
 crime and punishment **X:**96
 narcotics **X:**243
drug treatment programs **X:**308
drug users **X:**6, 323
"Drummer Boy of Shiloh, The"
 V:273
drums **II:**247
Drums Along the Mohawk
 (Edmonds) **VIII:**220
Drum Taps (Whitman) **V:**430, 431
Drunkard's Looking Glass, The
 (Weems) **III:**435
Drysdale, Hugh **II:**153
Duala people **I:**56
Duane, James **III:**74, 114
Duane, William **III:140,** 241;
 IV:46
Dub[c&hacek]ek, Alexander
 IX:113; **X:**189
Dubinsky, David **VIII:**97
 CIO **VIII:**82
 Hillman, Sidney **VIII:**165–
 166
 ILGWU **VIII:**187
 labor/labor movements
 VIII:206
 Lewis, John L. **VIII:**213

DuBois, William Edward
Burghardt **II:**358; **VII:80–81,**
81, 404*c,* 405*c;* **VIII:**449*c*
African Americans **VI:**7
Boas, Franz Uri **VII:**40
education, philanthropy and
VI:112
Garvey, Marcus **VII:**122
Harpers Ferry, West Virginia
V:186
history **VII:**140
NAACP **VII:**224; **VIII:**255–
256; **IX:**232
Niagara Movement **VII:**240
radicalism **VII:**288
Rhinelander case **VII:**301
Trotter, William Monroe
VII:357
Washington, Booker T.
VI:384
Wells-Barnett, Ida Bell
VI:388
Williams, Fannie Barrier
VI:395
Williams, George
Washington **VI:**396
Dubuque, Iowa **IV:**223, 224
Dubuque, Julien **IV:**223
Duchamp, Marcel **VII:**24
"duck and cover" **IX:**57, 65
Dudingston, William **III:**189
Dudley, Joseph **II:103**
Dominion of New England
II:102
Mather, Increase **II:**228
Queen Anne's War **II:**323
Dudley, Thomas (1576–1653)
II:103, 418
Dudley, Thomas Haines (1819–
1893) **V:**49
dueling **III:140–141,** 465*c*
Burr, Aaron **III:**69, 70
Hamilton, Alexander
III:208
Johnston, Albert Sidney
V:213
due process
Abscam **X:**5
marriage and family **X:**213
pornography **X:**283
Supreme Court **VIII:**382
*Webster v. Reproductive
Health Services* **X:**368
due process clause **VI:100–101**
Bill of Rights **III:**51
Conkling, Roscoe **VI:**81
Cooper Union speech **V:**94
Patrons of Husbandry
VI:279
Supreme Court **IV:**362
women's status and rights
VI:399
Duer, William **III:141,** 330–331
Duet on Ice (Anderson) **X:**31
Dukakis, Michael S. **X:105–106,**
379*c*
Albright, Madeleine K. **X:**22

Bush, George H. W. **X:**52
Horton, Willie **X:**168–169
Duke, David **IX:**213
Duke of Stockbridge, The
(Bellamy) **VI:**32
Duke Power Company **X:**160
Duke's Laws **II:**152, 270
Dulany, Daniel **III:**142, 395, 437,
459*c*
Dulles, Allen Welsh **IX:***90*
Bay of Pigs **IX:**35, 36
modern Republicanism
IX:221
OSS **VIII:**285
Dulles, John Foster **IX:***90,* **90–91,**
292
Dumbarton Oaks Conference
VIII:402; **IX:**90
Dummer, Jeremiah **II:103–104**
Dunaway, Faye **IX:**226
Dunbar, Paul Laurence **VI:**7, *101,*
101–102
Dunbar Hospital (Paradise Valley,
Detroit) **VII:**344
Dun & Bradstreet **IV:**366
Dundy, Elmer S. **VI:**49
Dunkard Church **V:**13
Dunkirk **VIII:**47
Dunlap, William **III:**142, 411
Dunmore, John Murray, earl of
III:142–143, 460*c,* 461*c*
African Americans **III:**8
Murray, Judith Sargent
Stevens **III:**308
Native Americans **III:**312
Randolph, Edmund **III:**358
slavery **III:**391
Dunmore's Proclamation **III:**142,
461*c*
Dunmore's War
Clark, George Rogers
III:95
Native Americans **III:**312
Tecumseh **III:**409
Dunn, Willie **VI:**343
Dunnet Landing, Maine **VI:**203
DuPont, Éleuthère Irénée
DuPont Corporation **IX:**91
economy **IV:**131
industrialization **IV:**199
DuPont, Samuel F. **V:**405
DuPont brothers **VIII:**278
DuPont Corporation **IX:91**
business **VIII:**57
invention and technology
VII:150
music **IX:**228
New York World's Fair
(1964) **IX:**246
Nye committee **VIII:**278
technology **IX:**311
Durán, Diego **I:**114
Aguilar, Francisco de **I:**4
Aztecs **I:**21
Aztlán **I:**23
Durand, Asher B. **IV:**28, 29; **VI:**275
Durand-Ruel, Paul **VI:**64

Durant, William C.
automobile industry **VII:**26
economy **VII:**84
GM **IX:**132–133
Durenburger, Dave **X:**321
Dürer, Albrecht **I:**114
Durstine, Roy **VII:**5
Du Sable, Jean Baptiste Pointe
II:104–105
dust bowl **VIII:97–99,** *98,* 443*c*
agriculture **VIII:**9
Bourke-White, Margaret
VIII:50
environment **VIII:**115
Guthrie, Woody **VIII:**160
Ickes, Harold L. **VIII:**183
Lange, Dorothea **VIII:**210
marriage and family
VIII:230
Mexican Americans
VIII:237
migration **VIII:**239
photography **VIII:**296
popular culture **VIII:**301
religion **VIII:**335
rural areas **VIII:**348
Steinbeck, John **VIII:**374
technology **VIII:**397
Duston, Hannah Emerson
II:105
Dutch East India Company
I:115–116; **II:**167
Blaeu, Willem **I:**32
Brazil **I:**35
Spanish Armada **I:**345
Spice Islands **I:**345
Dutchess County, New York
IV:223
Dutch-Indian Wars **II:105–106,**
270
Dutchman (Baraka) **IX:**6
Dutch Protestants **III:**362
Dutch Reformed Church **II:***106,*
106–107
Frelinghuysen, Theodorus
Jacobus **II:**135
religion **VIII:**334
Stuyvesant, Peter **II:**379
Dutch trade and colonization
II:435*c*
Algonquin **II:**18
architecture **II:**25
Connecticut **II:**75
debt, national **III:**130–131
Delaware **II:**95
fur trade **II:**141
Gorée Island **I:**144
Grotius, Hugo **I:**145–146
Holland Land Company
III:214
invention and technology
I:184
Iroquois **I:**187; **II:**179
Minuit, Peter **II:**235–236
New Amsterdam **II:**256–
258
New Jersey **II:**261

New Netherland **II:**264–
266
New York **II:**269–270
New York City **II:**272
Stuyvesant, Peter **II:**379
women's status and rights
II:424
Dutch West India Company
I:115; **II:107**
Delaware **II:**96
Dutch Reformed Church
II:107
Minuit, Peter **II:**236
New Netherland **II:**264,
265
New York **II:**269, 270
New York City **II:**272
Stuyvesant, Peter **II:**379
duties **II:**3
Duval, Gabrial **III:**291
DVD. *See* digital video disk
Dvořák, Antonín **VI:**170, 255
Dwight, Louis **IV:**296
Dwight, Theodore **IV:**187
Dwight, Timothy **III:**104, **143;**
IV:317
dye **I:**17–18
Dyer, Leonids C. **VII:**408*c;*
VIII:22
Dyer, Mary **II:**108, *108,* 116, 322
Dylan, Bob **IX:**92, **92–93,** 355*c*
Beat Generation **IX:**37
counterculture **IX:**79
folk music revival **IX:**121
Ginsberg, Allen **IX:**135
March on Washington
(1963) **IX:**201
music **IX:**229
popular culture **IX:**259
rock and roll **IX:**279
teenagers **IX:**314
Weathermen/Weather
Underground **IX:**341
dynamic conservatism (modern
Republicanism) **IX:221–222**
Dynamic Sociology (Ward)
VI:334, 382
dynamite **VI:**247
dynamos **VI:**194
dysentery **II:**399
Bataan Death March
VIII:42
disease/epidemics **V:**112
Keokuk **IV:**213
Mississippi River war **V:**264
Sequoyah **IV:**343
Dyula **I:**226

E

Eads, James Buchanan **VI:**47,
62, **103**
Eads Bridge (St. Louis, Missouri)
VI:47, 62, 408*c*
Eagan, Thomas **VII:**225
Eagle Forum **X:**94, 316, 317

Eagleton, Thomas F. **X:107,** 217
Eaglewood, New Jersey **IV:**396
Eakins, Thomas **V:**18; **VI:103–105,** *104;* **VII:**23
Earhart, Amelia **VIII:**443*c*
Earle, Ralph **III:**32, 33, **145,** 436
Earle, Thomas **IV:**226
Early, Jubal A. **V:***119,* **119–120,** 445*c*
   Cedar Mountain, Battle of **V:**59
   Chancellorsville, Battle of **V:**61, 62
   Gordon, John B. **V:**170
   literature **V:**239
   Longstreet, James **V:**242, 243
   lost cause, the **V:**244
   Petersburg campaign **V:**302
   Shenandoah Valley: Sheridan's campaign **V:**351–352
   Washington, D.C. **V:**426
Early Sunday Morning (Hopper) **VIII:**31
earth art **X:**30–31
Earth Day **X:**90, 91, 375*c*
earthquakes **I:**9; **X:**380*c,* 384*c*
Easley, Ralph **VII:**226
East, Department of the **VII:**267
East, John **X:**165
East Bay Street lottery **IV:**387
East Cambridge House of Correction (Massachusetts) **IV:**124
east coast/eastern United States
   art and architecture **IV:**27
   Catt, Carrie Lane Chapman **VII:**50
   cattle kingdom **VI:**64
   Forty-niners **IV:**159, 160
   Free-Soil Party **IV:**164
   Indian Rights Association **VI:**190
   Jackson, Helen Hunt **VI:**199
   lead mines **IV:**224
   Lee, Jason **IV:**224
   medicine **IV:**249
   Mexican-American War **IV:**252
   migration **IV:**253, 255
   Morse, Samuel F. B. **IV:**264
   movie industry **VII:**216
   National Road **IV:**271
   Oregon Trail **IV:**285
   popular sovereignty **IV:**306–307
   population trends **VII:**266
   railroads **IV:**314
   religion **IV:**317
   Rocky Mountain Fur Company **IV:**325
   sports and recreation **VII:**335
   Texas **IV:**370, 371
   UMWA **VII:**360

Easter **III:**341
Easter massacre **V:**411–412
Eastern Europe **IX:**353*c*
   Europe **IX:**112
   Iron Curtain, collapse of **X:**188–189
   Marshall Plan **IX:**204
   Peace Corps **IX:**256
   Soviet Union **IX:**295
eastern European immigrants
   ILGWU **VII:**149
   immigration **VII:**144
   Immigration Act (1917) **VII:**145
   IWW **VII:**146
Eastern Lunatic Hospital **III:**296
Eastern Parkway, Brooklyn, New York **IV:**120
Eastern State Penitentiary **III:**347; **IV:**296
Easter Rebellion **III:**186
East Germany. *See* German Democratic Republic
East India Company. *See* British East India Company; Dutch East India Company
East Indies
   Albuquerque, Alfonso de **I:**6
   Essex, USS **IV:**144
   Gama, Vasco da **I:**137
   trade, domestic and foreign **III:**414
Eastman, Crystal **VII:**9, 31
Eastman, George **VI:105,** 410*c*
   invention and technology **VI:**196; **VII:**151
   photography **VII:**258
   Washington, Booker T. **VI:**384
Eastman, Max
   Greenwich Village **VII:**130
   The Masses **VII:**193
   modernism **VII:**212
   radical and labor press **VII:**285, 286
   Vorse, Mary Heaton **VII:**375
Eastman Kodak. *See* Kodak
East of Eden (film) **IX:**224
East of Eden (Steinbeck) **VIII:**375
Easton, Hosea **IV:129**
Eastwood, Mary **IX:**236
Easy Street (film) **VII:**216
Eaton, Amos **III:**384
Eaton, Dorman B. **VI:**80
Eaton, John, Jr. **V:120–121**
Eaton, William **II:**46
Eatonville, Florida **VIII:**180
Ebbetts Pass **IV:**144
Ebenezer Baptist Church, Atlanta **IX:**173, 175
Ebenezer Society **IV:**320
E bonds **VIII:**412
Ebony Concerto (Stravinsky) **VIII:**252

Ebony magazine **X:**219
Eccles, Marriner S. **VIII:101**
   banking **VIII:**40
   Banking Act (1935) **VIII:**41
   Henderson, Leon **VIII:**163
   Keynesianism **VIII:**200
   recession of 1937–1938 **VIII:**324
   TNEC **VIII:**391
Echeverría, Álvarez **X:**226
EchoStar Communications Corporation **X:**283
Eckert, John P., Jr. **IX:**70, 105
E. C. Knight case **VI:**364
Eclectic Readers (McGuffey) **IV:**134, 246
Eclectic Spelling Book (McGuffey) **IV:**246
École des Beaux-Arts (Paris) **VI:**63, 275
ecology
   Columbian Exchange **I:**81–83
   conservation/environmentalism **X:**90
   horses **I:**170
   Madeira **I:**222
Economic and Social Council (United Nations) **VIII:**402
Economic Bill of Rights **VIII:102**
   election of 1944 **VIII:**111
   Employment Act of 1946 **IX:**106, 107
   Full Employment Bill **VIII:**145
   liberalism **VIII:**216
   medicine **VIII:**236
   NRPB **VIII:**246
   Roosevelt, Franklin D. **VIII:**347
   Third New Deal **VIII:**393
Economic Cooperation Act **IX:**204
Economic Cooperation Administration **IX:**204
economic development **X:**195
economic models **X:**204
Economic Opportunity Act of 1964 **IX:95–96,** 356*c*
   CAP **IX:**68–69
   Great Society **IX:**139
   Harrington, Michael **IX:**142
   Job Corps **IX:**161
   Johnson, Lyndon B. **IX:**163
   labor/labor movements **IX:**182
   VISTA **IX:**333
   War on Poverty **IX:**335
Economic Ornithology and Mammalogy, Division of **VI:**82
economic recovery **VIII:**268
Economic Recovery Tax Act (1981) **X:**300
economic reform **VII:**383
Economic Research and Action Project (ERAP) **IX:**144, 304

economics
   Kemp, Jack F. **X:**196
   Laffer curve **X:**204
   liberalism **X:**207
   Reaganomics **X:**302
economic sanctions. *See* sanctions
Economic Security Bill **VIII:**363
Economic Stabilization Act (1942) **VIII:**282, 409
Economic Stabilization Act (1970) **X:**363
economic stimulus **VIII:**269
economies of scale **X:**19
economy **II:109–110; III:145–147; IV:129–133,** 130*t;* **V:***121,* **121–124; VII:83–86; VIII:102–105,** *103,* 446*c;* **IX:96, 96–98; X:107–111,** *108,* 383*c*
   abolitionism **III:**1; **IV:**1; **V:**4
   Acadians **II:**2
   Acts of Trade and Navigation **II:**3
   advertising **VIII:**1
   Africa **II:**4
   Agricultural Adjustment Act **VIII:**5
   Agricultural Marketing Act **VII:**5–6
   agriculture **II:**8–10; **III:**10–11; **IV:**10–13; **V:**5; **VII:**6–8; **VIII:**9, 11; **X:**18
   almshouses **II:**19
   American Liberty League **VIII:**19
   American System **IV:**19–21
   animals **III:**22
   antimonopoly **VIII:**24
   artisans **II:**27–28; **III:**35
   atomic bomb **VIII:**35
   Austin, Moses **IV:**38–39
   automobile industry **VIII:**35; **X:**37
   Aztecs **I:**22
   baby boom **IX:**31
   baby boomers **X:**39
   banking **II:**32–33; **VIII:**39–40
   Bank of the United States, First **III:**40, 41
   banks **III:**42–43
   Berle, Adolf A., Jr. **VIII:**43
   Bonus Army **VIII:**48
   Bonus Bill **IV:**62
   Boxer Rebellion **VII:**40
   Brain Trust **VIII:**51
   Bretton Woods Conference **VIII:**52
   Brown, Joseph Emerson **V:**45
   Budget and Accounting Act **VII:**44
   Bush, George W. **X:**55
   business **VII:**45, 46; **VIII:**57–58; **IX:**45–47
   business cycles **VI:**57–59
   California Indians **II:**55
   Canada **III:**77; **VI:**61

Caribbean **II**:59
carpetbaggers **V**:56
cash-and-carry **VIII**:63
cattle kingdom **VI**:65
CEA **IX**:77
Charleston **II**:63–64
Chase, Salmon P. **V**:63
childhood **II**:66
child labor **VII**:51
children **VII**:399, 400
cities and urban life **III**:91;
    VI:70–71; **VII**:54;
    VIII:68
civil liberties **VII**:57
Civil War **V**:74
class **II**:70
Clayton Antitrust Act
    VII:59
Clinton, George **III**:98
Clinton, William J. **X**:79–80
cold war **IX**:62
cold war culture **IX**:65
communications **VI**:78
Confederate navy **V**:84
Confederate States of
    America **V**:86, 87
Congress **VI**:80; **VIII**:79
Connecticut **II**:77
conservatism **VIII**:84
conservative coalition
    VIII:85, 86
consumerism **IX**:75
Coolidge, Calvin John
    VII:65
corporations **III**:121
cosmetics and beauty
    industry **VII**:65
cotton **III**:122–123
cotton culture **IV**:106, 108
counterculture **IX**:78
Coxe, Tench **III**:125
Coxey's Army **VI**:84
credit cards **IX**:79
Currency Act **III**:128
CWA **VIII**:74
Dawes Plan **VII**:72
Delaware **II**:96
demobilization (WWII)
    VIII:91
Democratic Party **IV**:118;
    V:110; **VII**:75; **VIII**:92–
    94
dollar-a-year men **VIII**:96
Eccles, Marriner S.
    VIII:101
Economic Bill of Rights
    VIII:102
education **VI**:109; **VIII**:105
education, primary/
    secondary **X**:113, 114
Eisenhower, Dwight D.
    IX:101
elderly **VIII**:108
election of 1840 **IV**:138
elections **IX**:103
Ely, Richard Theodore
    VI:115

embargo of 1807 **III**:152
Emergency Banking Act of
    1933 **VIII**:112–113
energy **X**:120
environment **II**:119
Era of Good Feelings
    IV:141
Ethical Culture movement
    VI:120
ethnic organizations
    VII:101
Executive Order 9066
    VIII:121
Farmer-Labor Party
    VII:105
FCA **VIII**:126
FDIC **VIII**:132
Federal Farm Loan Act
    VII:106
Federal National Mortgage
    Association **VIII**:135
Federal Reserve Act
    VII:107–108
Federal Trade Commission
    Act **VII**:108
FEPC **VIII**:123
FERA **VIII**:133
First New Deal **VIII**:138
fiscal policy **VIII**:138–139
fishing **II**:126
Florida **III**:167
Ford, Gerald R. **X**:139
Fordney-McCumber Tariff
    VII:112
foreign affairs **III**:169
foreign policy **VI**:133;
    VII:113–116; **VIII**:140
Georgia **II**:147
globalization **X**:153–155
Golden Hill, Battle of
    III:196
gold standard **VIII**:150
Good Neighbor policy
    VIII:151
government **VIII**:154
Great Depression **VIII**:156–
    159
Great Migration **VII**:127–
    128
greenbacks **V**:177
Gregg, Josiah **IV**:179
Harpers Ferry, West Virginia
    V:185
Hartford Convention
    IV:186
Hawley-Smoot Tariff Act
    VIII:162–163
Hepburn Act **VII**:138, 139
Holland Land Company
    III:214
homefront **V**:192–193
Hoover, Herbert C.
    VIII:172
Hoover presidency
    VIII:173–174
Hopkins, Harry L. **VIII**:176
horses **II**:166

Hull, Cordell **VIII**:180
Ickes, Harold L. **VIII**:183
immigration **IV**:193; **V**:199;
    VIII:184; **X**:176
imperialism **VI**:188
Inca **I**:179
industrial development
    IV:199–200; **V**:204
Industrial Revolution
    III:224
Industrial Revolution,
    Second **VI**:192
insurance **III**:227
investments, American,
    abroad **VI**:197
investments, foreign
    VII:151–152
investments, foreign, in the
    United States **VI**:197
Irish Americans **VIII**:189
Iroquois **I**:186
Jefferson, Thomas **III**:235
Jews **VIII**:196
journalism **IV**:210; **VII**:160
Kaiser, Henry J. **VIII**:199
Keynesianism **VIII**:200–201
labor, child **VI**:212
labor, radical **VI**:212
labor, woman **VI**:214–215
labor/labor movements
    II:200; **III**:251; **IV**:217;
    IX:181
Ladies Memorial
    Associations **V**:229
Larkin, Thomas Oliver
    IV:222
liberalism **VIII**:214–216
literature **VIII**:218, 220
London Economic
    Conference **VIII**:221
lumbering **II**:211–212
LWV **IX**:186, 187
marriage and family **V**:249;
    VII:190
Marshall Plan **IX**:203–204,
    359–361
Maryland **II**:220–221
Massachusetts **II**:224
mass production **VII**:194–
    195
Mbundu **I**:237
McCulloch v. Maryland
    IV:245
McNary-Haugen Farm Bill
    VII:195
Mellon, Andrew William
    VII:201
mercantilism **II**:230–231
Mexican immigration
    VII:202–203
Mexican Invasion **VII**:203
Mexican Revolution
    VII:204
migration **IV**:254; **IX**:215
military-industrial complex
    IX:216
Mississippi River **V**:261

mobilization **VIII**:241–242
movies **VIII**:247
Murray, Philip **VIII**:249
NAFTA **X**:259
NAM **VII**:225
National Recovery
    Administration **VIII**:259–
    260
Native Americans **II**:251
nativism **VII**:233
Navajo **II**:254
Naval Disarmament
    Conference **VII**:235
New Deal **VIII**:268, 269
New Hampshire **II**:259
New Jersey **II**:262
New Netherland **II**:266
New Orleans **II**:267
New Spain **I**:269–270
New Woman **VII**:238
New York **II**:271
New York City **V**:283
Non-Intercourse Act
    III:319
Non-Partisan League
    VII:241
NRPB **VIII**:261
NWLB **VIII**:261–262
NYA **VIII**:262–263
Obama, Barack Hussein
    X:264
oil industry **VII**:244–245
OPEC **X**:268
Orders in Council **III**:325
OWM **VIII**:286
OWMR **VIII**:287
Pan-American Exposition
    VII:252
panic of 1792 **III**:330–331
panic of 1819 **IV**:293–294
panic of 1837 **IV**:294–295
panic of 1857 **V**:294
Payne-Aldrich Tariff Act
    VII:255
Pennsylvania **II**:287
Pequot **II**:289
Philadelphia **II**:292; **V**:303
Pinchot, Gifford **VII**:260
Pingree, Hazen S. **VI**:263
Point Four Program **IX**:257
politics (Roosevelt era)
    VIII:298
population trends **IX**:260
Port Huron Statement
    IX:260
poverty **III**:344; **X**:286
presidency **VII**:268, 269
Progressive Party **VII**:269;
    IX:264
progressivism **VII**:270
public land policy **IV**:305
Pueblo **I**:305
Puerto Ricans **IX**:267
PWA **VIII**:314
Quota Act **VII**:279
radicalism **VII**:287
railroads **VI**:301

economy (continued)
  Reagan, Ronald W. **X:**300
  Reaganomics **X:**302
  *Recent Social Trends in the
    United States* **VIII:**323
  recession of 1937–1938
    VIII:323–324
  Reconstruction **V:**326
  reconversion **VIII:**326–327
  relief **VIII:**330
  Republican Party **VII:**300
  RFC **VIII:**325–326
  Rhode Island **II:**333
  Roosevelt, Franklin D.
    VIII:344
  rum trade **II:**338
  rural areas **VIII:**348
  St. Mary's City **II:**342
  Santa Fe Trail **IV:**332
  science and technology
    VII:315
  Second New Deal **VIII:**356
  segregation **VII:**319
  service sector **IX:**288–289
  slavery **II:**356–357; **III:**390;
    IV:344–345; **V:**363, 364
  slave trade, internal **IV:**349–
    350
  Smith, Alfred E. **VII:**327
  socialism **VII:**327–328
  Social Security Act
    VIII:363
  society, British American
    II:365, 366
  Soldiers' Bonus **VII:**331
  South Carolina Regulation
    III:394
  southern demagogues
    VII:332
  Soviet Union, breakup of
    X:326
  Spanish colonies **II:**371,
    373
  states' rights **V:**370
  steel industry **VII:**336, 337
  stock market crash **VIII:**376
  strikes **V:**374
  suburbanization/suburbs
    VII:340
  Sugar Act **III:**401
  Sunbelt **X:**338
  Supreme Court **VII:**342–
    343
  tariffs **VII:**349, 350
  taxation **VIII:**387, 388
  temperance movement
    IV:369–370
  Texas **IV:**370
  Third New Deal **VIII:**393
  TNEC **VIII:**391
  tobacco **II:**390–392
  Townsend, Francis E.
    VIII:394
  trade, domestic and foreign
    II:392–393; **III:**413–414;
    VII:353–354
  transportation **VIII:**395

  trusts **VI:**361–362
  Tugwell, Rexford G.
    VIII:397
  Underwood-Simmons Tariff
    VII:359
  UNIA **VII:**361
  union movement **IX:**324
  U.S. Shipping Board
    VII:360–361
  vaudeville **VII:**368
  Versailles, Treaty of **VII:**370
  veterans **VII:**371
  wage and price controls
    II:405
  Walker, David **IV:**389
  wampum **II:**407
  War Industries Board
    VII:377–378
  West Indies **III:**436
  World War II **VIII:**428
  World War II home front
    VIII:432–434
  Young, Brigham **IV:**408
ECT (electroconvulsive therapy)
  X:223
Ecuador **VI:**122; **X:**267
Eddy, Mary Baker **VI:**69, **105–
  106**, *106*, 408c
Eden, Charles **II:**385
Eden, Richard **I:117–118**, *290*,
  353
Eden, William **III:**82
Edgar Huntly (Brown) **III:**64
Edgefield Plan **VI:**358
Edgefield Real Estate and
  Homestead Association **V:**361
Edge of the Sea, The (Carson)
  IX:51
Edgerton, John **VII:**247
Edict of Nantes. *See* Nantes,
  Edict of
Edison, Thomas Alva **VI:106–
  107**, *107*, 408c, 409c; **VII:***314*
  banking, investment **VI:**24
  Bell, Alexander Graham
    VI:31
  Eads, James Buchanan
    VI:103
  Franklin Institute **IV:**163
  GE **VII:**123; **IX:**132
  Industrial Revolution,
    Second **VI:**191, 192
  music **VI:**258
  science, invention, and
    technology **VI:**194–196;
    VII:315
  Tesla, Nikola **VI:**353, 354
Edison Electric Illuminating
  Company **VI:**195
Edison Electric Light Company
  IX:132
Edison General Electric Company
  VI:375; **VII:**123
Edison Laboratories **VII:**214
Edison Lamp Company **VI:**375
Edison Machine Works **VI:**375
Edmonds, S. Emma **V:**134, 239

Edmund Pettus Bridge (Alabama)
  IX:303
Edmunds Act (1882) **VI:**252
Edmunds-Tucker Act **IV:**121;
  VI:252
Edo language **I:**29
EDS (Electronic Data Systems
  Corporation) **X:**272
Ed Sullivan Show, The **IX:**356c
  Beatles **IX:**37
  popular culture **IX:**259
  teenagers **IX:**314
  television **IX:**315
Educate America Act (Goals
  2000) **X:**115
education **II:110–113**, *111*,
  113m; **III:147–149**, *148*;
  IV:133–135, *134*, 412c; **V:124–
  125**; **VI:107–110**, *108*; **VII:86–
  89**, *87*, 409c; **VIII:105–107**,
  106, 448c; **IX:99–100**, 354c,
  356c
  Adams, John Quincy **IV:**5
  affirmative action **X:**9–10
  African Americans **II:**7;
    III:9; **IV:**7, 8; **VI:**5, 7;
    IX:4–5; **X:**13
  American Missionary
    Association **V:**8
  Angell, James Burrill
    VI:14–15
  Anglican Church **III:**20
  Appalachia **IX:**16
  Asian Americans **X:**33
  Aztecs **I:**20
  Baldwin, Roger Nash
    VII:31
  Benezet, Anthony **II:**35
  Bent, Charles **IV:**51
  Bidwell, John **IV:**56
  Bilingual Education Act
    X:42
  Black Panthers **IX:**40
  Blackstone, Sir William
    III:52
  Brant, Joseph **III:**62
  *Brown v. Board of
    Education* **IX:**43–44
  Bruce, Blanche Kelso **V:**46
  Bush, George W. **X:**56
  carpetbaggers **V:**56
  Carver, George Washington
    VI:63
  Catholics **VIII:**64
  Chase, William Merritt
    VI:66
  Chautauqua Institute
    VI:66–67
  child labor **VII:**52
  children **VII:**399–400;
    VIII:66, 67
  Christian Coalition **X:**73
  cities and urban life **IV:**93
  civil rights **VIII:**72
  Civil Rights Act (1964)
    IX:61
  Clinton, William J. **X:**79–80

  College of Philadelphia
    II:74
  College of William and Mary
    II:74
  computers **X:**87
  Connecticut **II:**78
  conservation/
    environmentalism **X:**91
  consumerism **IX:**76
  Crummell, Alexander **VI:**87
  Dartmouth College **II:**91
  Dewey, John **VII:**76–77
  Donnelly, Ignatius Loyola
    VI:99
  Dwight, Timothy **III:**143
  Eaton, John, Jr. **V:**120
  economy **VIII:**104
  education, federal aid to
    VI:110–111
  ESEA **IX:**105–106
  Ethical Culture movement
    VI:121
  feminism **X:**134
  Forbes, John Murray
    VI:132
  Franklin, Benjamin **III:**174–
    175
  Franklin Institute **IV:**162–
    163
  Freedmen's Bureau **V:**161
  Frémont, Jesse Benton
    IV:165
  FSA **X:**128
  GI Bill of Rights **VIII:**149
  Gilman, Daniel Coit **VI:**148
  Gonzáles, Rodolfo "Corky"
    IX:136
  Great Awakening **II:**156
  Great Society **IX:**139
  Grimké, Angelina and Sarah
    IV:180
  Grimké, Charlotte Forten
    V:178
  Hale, Sarah Josepha **IV:**183
  Hall, Granville Stanley
    VI:157–158
  Harper, Frances Ellen
    Watkins **V:**184; **VI:**159–
    160
  Harvard College **II:**163
  Hayes, Rutherford B.
    VI:168
  Head Start **IX:**144–145
  Hispanic Americans
    X:166–167
  House of Representatives
    X:170
  ILGWU **VII:**149
  Indian Affairs, Bureau of
    IV:196
  Indian Affairs, Office of
    VI:189–190
  Indian Removal Act **IV:**198
  Indian Rights Association
    VI:190
  Ingersoll, Robert Green
    VI:192–193

intelligence tests **VII:**148
Irish Americans **VIII:**189
Italian Americans **VIII:**191
Jackson, Helen Hunt
VI:199
James, Henry **VI:**199–200
James, William **VI:**200, 201
Japanese Americans,
relocation of **VIII:**194
Jefferson, Thomas **III:**232,
235
Jesuits **I:**193; **II:**185
Jewett, Sarah Orne **VI:**202
Jews **VIII:**195
Job Corps **IX:**161
Johnson, Hiram Warren
VII:154
Kelley, Florence **VII:**164
kindergarten **VI:**207
King's College **II:**193–195
labor, child **VI:**212
labor/labor movements
IV:219
Lamar, Mirabeau B. **IV:**221,
222
Latino movement **IX:**185
lawyers **III:**256
Lazarus, Emma **VI:**219
literature **IV:**229
Locke, John **II:**208
Lockwood, Belva Ann
Bennett McNall **VI:**228–
229
Long, Huey P. **VIII:**222
LWV **IX:**187
lyceum movement **IV:**231–
232
Mann, Horace **IV:**237–238
marriage and family **II:**218–
219; **III:**287; **VII:**192
Massachusetts **II:**223, 225
Massachusetts School Act
II:223, 226
McGuffey, William Holmes
IV:246–247
medicine **III:**295; **VII:**199
Memminger, Christopher
G. **V:**259
migration **VIII:**239
Model Cities program
IX:221
Morrill Land-Grant Act
V:269–270
mothers' pensions **VII:**214
multiculturalism **X:**236–237
Murray, Pauli **IX:**227
music **IX:**228–229
NAACP **VIII:**256; **IX:**232
Native Americans **VII:**231,
233; **IX:**242; **X:**250
NEH **IX:**234–235
New England Primer **II:**258
New Frontier **IX:**243
New Woman **VII:**239
New York World's Fair
(1939–1940) **VIII:**273
Niagara Movement **VII:**240

Northwest Ordinances
III:322
NWTUL **VII:**231
NYA **VIII:**262–263
PCSW **IX:**262
Peabody, Elizabeth Palmer
VI:279, 280
Pike, Zebulon Montgomery
IV:300
Princeton College **II:**311
professional organizations,
rise of **VI:**294
Protestantism **II:**316
Puerto Ricans **IX:**268
race and race relations
VII:282; **X:**297
refugees **V:**330
religion **IX:**274
religious liberty **III:**364
Republican Party **V:**333
Revels, Hiram R. **V:**335
Rhode Island **II:**334
Rockefeller, John Davison
VII:303
Rowson, Susanna Haswell
III:374
Rush, Benjamin **III:**375–
376
science and technology
VII:315
Scopes Trial **VII:**316
segregation **IX:**288
Seneca Falls convention
IV:340
Sequoyah **IV:**342, 343
service sector **IX:**289
slavery **IV:**345, 347
Smith, Jedediah Strong
IV:350
social work **VII:**329, 330
Society of Friends **V:**365
South **VIII:**366
Southern Manifesto **IX:**294
SPG **II:**368
Starbuck, Mary Coffin
II:377
Stevens, Thaddeus **V:**372
Stevenson, Adali E. **IX:**302
Sumner, William Graham
VI:347–348
Supreme Court **VIII:**383
Taft, Robert A. **VIII:**385
Taft, William Howard
VII:347
Taylor, Susie King **V:**385
technology **IX:**311
temperance movement
IV:369
Terrell, Mary Eliza Church
VII:352
Thomas, M. Carey **VI:**356
Thoreau, Henry David
IV:376
Tillman, Benjamin Ryan
VI:358
Tubman, Harriet **V:**394–
395

urban reform **VII:**362
utopianism **VI:**371
Virginia **II:**401
Wallace, Henry A. **VIII:**411
Ward, Lester Frank **VI:**383
Washington, Booker T.
VI:383–384
WEAL **IX:**345
Wheelock, Eleazar **II:**412
White, Alfred Tredway
VI:391
White, Andrew Dickson
VI:391
Willard, Emma **IV:**400–401
Williams, Peter, Jr. **IV:**402
Witherspoon, John **III:**445
women's colleges **VI:**398
women's status and rights
III:447, 448; **IV:**402;
VI:400; **VIII:**422, 424
work, household **VII:**390
Wright, Fanny **IV:**405
YMCA/YWCA **VII:**397
Young, Brigham **IV:**407
education, federal aid to **VI:**109,
110, **110–111**
education, higher **VI:111–112;**
X:111–112. *See also specific*
colleges and universities
African Americans **X:**13
Asian Americans **X:**33
baby boomers **X:**40
Eliot, Charles William
VI:113–114
feminism **X:**133
Gratz v. Bollinger/Grutter v.
Bollinger **X:**158–159
political correctness **X:**276
Title IX **X:386–387**
women's status and rights
X:370, 371
education, homeschooling
X:112–113
education, philanthropy and
VI:112–113
education, primary and secondary
X:113–116, *114,* 122–123
Education, U.S. Department of
Bennett, William J. **X:**41
Carter, James Earl, Jr. **X:**69
education, higher **X:**111
education, primary/
secondary **X:**114
Educational Policies Commission
VIII:106
Educational Problems (Hall)
VI:158
Education Amendments (1972)
X:112. *See also* Title IX
Education Flexibility Partnership
Act (1999) **X:**131
Education for Economic Security
Act (Equal Access Act, 1984)
X:122–123
Education of Henry Adams, The
(Adams) **VI:**1
Edward, HMS **III:**47, 461*c*

Edward VI (king of England) **I:**75,
232, 304; **II:**315
Edwards, Douglas **IX:**315
Edwards, John **X:**118
Edwards, Jonathan **II:113–114,**
114
Dwight, Timothy **III:**143
Edwards, Sarah Pierpont
II:115
Enlightenment, American
II:118
Finney, Charles Grandison
IV:150
Frelinghuysen, Theodorus
Jacobus **II:**135
Great Awakening **II:**154,
155
literature **II:**206
New Divinity **III:**316–317
Protestantism **II:**315
Puritans **II:**320
"Sinners in the Hands of an
Angry God" **II:442–443**
Edwards, Melvin **X:**31
Edwards, Sarah Emma E. **V:**435
Edwards, Sarah Pierpont **II:114–**
115, 155–156
Edwards v. Aguillard **X:**306
EEOC. *See* Equal Employment
Opportunity Commission
Effingham **III:**47
Egypt **IX:**354*c;* **X:**377*c*
Camp David accords
X:64–66
Carter, James Earl, Jr. **X:**69
cold war, end of **X:**84
Ethiopia **VIII:**118
foreign policy **X:**141
Israel **IX:**160
Lange, Dorothea **VIII:**210
Middle East **X:**227, 228
Soviet Union **IX:**295
Suez crisis **IX:**306–307
Versailles, Treaty of
VII:370
Egyptian art **VII:**24
Ehrlich, Paul **VII:**275
Ehrlichman, John
Mitchell, John N. **X:**233
U.S. v. Nixon **X:**357
Watergate scandal **X:**366,
367
Eichelberger, Clark M. **VIII:**77
E. I. DuPont de Nemours
and Company. *See* DuPont
Corporation
Eiffel, Gustave **VI:**344
"Eight, The" **VII:**23, 26, 405*c*
Eight Cousins (Alcott) **VI:**10
1819 Factory Act **IV:**291
Eighteenth Amendment
VII:407*c;* **VIII:**444*c*
criminal justice **VII:**67
elections **VII:**90
Maine Law **IV:**234
Prohibition **VII:**274
Prohibition Party **VI:**296

Eighteenth Amendment
(*continued*)
temperance movement
III:410
Volstead Act **VII:**374
Eighth Air Force, U.S.
air power **VIII:**15
Army Air Forces, U.S.
VIII:27
bombing **VIII:**47
Eighth Amendment **X:**48, 66, 67,
376*c*
Eighth Army (Great Britain)
VIII:191
8th Division **VII:**324
eight-hour day **VII:**406*c*
AFL **VII:**12
Haymarket riot **VI:**168
Railroad Administration
VII:291
Eight Men Out (film) **X:**236
Einhorn, David **VI:**205, 308
Einstein, Albert **VIII:**446*c*
atomic bomb **VIII:**34
Franklin Institute **IV:**163
hydrogen bomb **IX:**152
Letter of 1939 to Roosevelt
VIII:460–461
Manhattan Project **VIII:**226
Oppenheimer, J. Robert
IX:250
science and technology
VII:314; **VIII:**352
Einzatsgruppen **VIII:**169
Eisenhower, Dwight D. *VIII:275,
447c;* **IX:100–102,** *101,* **336,**
353*c,* 354*c*
AEC **IX:**25
agriculture **IX:**8
Alaska statehood **IX:**9
Amendments to the U.S.
Constitution **X:**22
Americans for Democratic
Action **IX:**14
Arlington National Cemetery
V:17
arms race **IX:**17
automobile industry **IX:**26
Baker v. Carr **IX:**34
Bay of Pigs **IX:**35
Brennan, William J., Jr.
X:47
*Brown v. Board of
Education* **IX:**44
Bunche, Ralph **IX:**45
Burger, Warren E. **X:**50
Byrnes, James F. **VIII:**60
CIA **IX:**52
civil defense **IX:**57
Civil Rights Act (1957)
IX:58, 59
Civil Rights Act (1960)
IX:59
Civil War centennial **IX:**61
cold war **IX:**64
commemoration **IX:**66
computers **IX:**70

defense budget **IX:**83
demobilization (WWII)
VIII:91
Democratic Party **IX:**85
Dewey, Thomas E. **IX:**87
domino theory **IX:**89
Dulles, John Foster **IX:**90
economy **VIII:**104; **IX:**97,
98
education **IX:**99
elections **IX:**103
environment **IX:**108
Faubus, Orval **IX:**118
Federal Employee Loyalty
Program **IX:**119
Federal Housing
Administration **IX:**120
Goldwater, Barry **IX:**135
government **VIII:**154
government, state/local
IX:137
Graham, Billy **IX:**138
Hawaii statehood **IX:**143
Hershey, Lewis B. **VIII:**164
hydrogen bomb **IX:**152
Indian Claims Commission
IX:157
Interstate Highway Act of
1956 **IX:**158, 159
Israel **IX:**160
journalism **IX:**165
Korean War **IX:**177–178
Latin America **IX:**184
liberalism **IX:**191
Limited Test Ban Treaty of
1963 **IX:**192
Lindbergh, Charles
Augustus **VII:**179
Luce, Henry R. **VIII:**224
McCarthy, Joseph R. **IX:**207
medicine **IX:**210
military-industrial complex
IX:216
Mills, C. Wright **IX:**217
mobilization **VIII:**242
modern Republicanism
IX:221, 222
NASA **IX:**231
New Deal **IX:**242
Nixon, Richard M. **X:**256
Normandy, invasion of
VIII:275
North African campaign
VIII:278
nuclear proliferation **X:**261
Patton, George S., Jr.
VIII:291
Point Four Program **IX:**257,
258
Powell, Adam Clayton
IX:261
public health **IX:**266
religion **IX:**272
Republican Party **IX:**274
Rosenberg, Julius and Ethel
IX:280–281
SANE **IX:**283

science and technology
IX:285
SEATO **IX:**292
second front **VIII:**355
segregation **IX:**288
Sicily **VIII:**360
Southern Manifesto **IX:**294
Stevenson, Adali E. **IX:**302
Submerged Lands Act
(1953) **IX:**305
Suez crisis **IX:**307
Taft, Robert A. **VIII:**385
Warren, Earl **IX:**337
Warren Court **IX:**337
White Citizens' Councils
IX:342
Eisenhower, Milton **VIII:**194
Eisenhower Doctrine **IX:**160,
354*c*
Eisenstadt v. Baird **X:**48
Eisenstein, Sergei **VIII:**342
ElBaradei, Mohammed **X:**187
elderly **VIII:107–108; X:**379*c*
election of 1936 **VIII:**109
FERA **VIII:**133
Great Depression **VIII:**159
marriage and family
VIII:230, 231
New Deal **VIII:**270
poverty **X:**286
Social Security Act
VIII:363, 364
Townsend, Francis E.
VIII:394–395
unemployment **VIII:**399
Union Party **VIII:**401
victory gardens **VIII:**406
World War II home front
VIII:432
El Dorado **I:**9, **118–119,** 142
Eldridge, Roy **VIII:**44
Eleanor Darnall (Kuhn) **II:**196
election(s) **V:125–127; VII:89–
92,** *90;* **IX:102, 102–104**
citizenship **VII:**57
Copperheads **V:**95
Currency Act **VI:**68
Democratic Party **V:**108
Emancipation Proclamation
V:131
Enforcement Acts **V:**133
Fifteenth Amendment
V:142
Johnson, Andrew **V:**212
New Freedom **VII:**236
New Nationalism **VII:**237
Pingree, Hazen S. **VII:**261
Progressive Party **VII:**270
secession **V:**345
Smith, Alfred E. **VII:**326–
327
Versailles, Treaty of
VII:370
volunteer army **V:**419
Election Assistance Commission
X:171
election of 1796 **III:**6, 207

election of 1800 **III:149–151,**
464*c*
Adams, Abigail **III:**3–4
Adams, John **III:**6
Adams, Samuel **III:**8
Alien and Sedition Acts
III:14
Amendment, Twelfth **III:**16
American Revolution **III:**19
Ames, Fisher **III:**19
artisans **III:**35
cities and urban life **III:**90
Claiborne, William C. C.
IV:94
Coxe, Tench **III:**125
Democratic Party **IV:**116–
117
Democratic-Republican
Party **III:**136
Federalist Party **III:**164
Fries's Rebellion **III:**181
Hamilton, Alexander
III:208
Jay, John **III:**230
journalism **III:**241
Monroe, James **IV:**259
Pinckney, Charles
Cotesworth **III:**336
Tammany Society **III:**405
election of 1804 **III:**246
election of 1808 **III:**246, 284
election of 1816 **III:**246; **IV:**259,
411*c*
election of 1820 **IV:**117
election of 1824 **IV:**412*c*
Adams, John Quincy **IV:**5
banking **IV:**46
Calhoun, John C. **IV:**69
Clay, Henry **IV:**96–97
Democratic Party **IV:**117
Era of Good Feelings
IV:141
Jackson, Andrew **IV:**206
Van Buren, Martin **IV:**385
Whigs **IV:**396
election of 1828 **IV:135–137,**
136*m,* 412*c*
American Revolution **III:**19
American System **IV:**20
banking **IV:**46
Benton, Thomas Hart **IV:**53
Clay, Henry **IV:**96
Democratic Party **IV:**118;
V:108
Harrison, William Henry
IV:185
Jackson, Andrew **IV:**206
Van Buren, Martin **IV:**385
Whigs **IV:**396
election of 1832 **IV:**413*c*
American System **IV:**21
banking **IV:**46
Bank of the United States,
Second **IV:**48
Clay, Henry **IV:**96
Harrison, William Henry
IV:185

Jackson, Andrew **IV**:206
Van Buren, Martin **IV**:385
Whigs **IV**:397
election of 1836 **IV**:413*c*
  banking **IV**:47
  Free-Soil Party **IV**:163
  Harrison, William Henry
    IV:186
  Van Buren, Martin **IV**:386
  Webster, Daniel **IV**:393
  Whigs **IV**:397
election of 1840 **IV**:137–139,
  138*m*, 413*c*
  banking **IV**:47
  Democratic Party **IV**:118
  Harrison, William Henry
    IV:186
  Liberty Party **IV**:226
  Mexican-American War
    IV:251
  panic of 1837 **IV**:295
  Tyler, John **IV**:382
  Van Buren, Martin **IV**:386
  Whigs **IV**:397
election of 1844 **IV**:414*c*
  banking **IV**:47
  Democratic Party **IV**:118
  Houston, Sam **IV**:191
  Liberty Party **IV**:226–227
  Manifest Destiny **IV**:234
  Mexican-American War
    IV:251
  Oregon Treaty of 1846
    IV:287
  Polk, James K. **IV**:301–302
  Tyler, John **IV**:383
  Whigs **IV**:397
election of 1848 **IV**:414*c*
  Cass, Lewis **IV**:83
  Democratic Party **IV**:118
  Fillmore, Millard **IV**:149
  Free-Soil Party **IV**:164
  Scott, Winfield **IV**:336
  Taylor, Zachary **IV**:368
  Whigs **IV**:397
election of 1850 **IV**:54
election of 1852 **IV**:415*c*
  Fillmore, Millard **IV**:150
  Free-Soil Party **IV**:164–165
  Scott, Winfield **IV**:336
  Whigs **IV**:398
election of 1854 **IV**:322
election of 1856 **V**:443*c*
  Fillmore, Millard **IV**:150
  Frémont, John C. **IV**:167
  Know-Nothing Party
    IV:215
  nativism **V**:280
  Republican Party **IV**:322
election of 1860 **V**:443*c*
  Civil War **V**:73
  Confederate States of
    America **V**:84
  Cooper Union speech **V**:94
  Democratic Party **V**:109
  Douglas, Stephen A. **V**:114
  elections **V**:125

Harlan, John Marshall
  VI:159
Homestead Act **V**:194
immigration **IV**:195
public land policy **IV**:307
Republican Party **V**:333
Welles, Gideon **V**:428
election of 1863 **V**:126, 270
election of 1864
  Harlan, John Marshall
    VI:159
  homefront **V**:193, 194
  McClellan, George Brinton
    V:252
  miscegenation **V**:261
  Nast, Thomas **V**:275
election of 1866 **V**:202
election of 1868 **V**:446*c*
  Democratic Party **V**:110
  Fifteenth Amendment
    V:141
  Greeley, Horace **V**:177
  Ku Klux Klan **V**:223
  Liberal Republican Party
    VI:222
  Radical Republicans **V**:321
election of 1872 **VI**:291, 296,
  407*c*
election of 1874 **VI**:95
election of 1875 **VI**:122
election of 1876 **VI**:408*c*
  African Americans **VI**:6
  corruption, political **VI**:83
  Dana, Charles A. **VI**:92
  Democratic Party **V**:110;
    VI:95
  elections **V**:127
  Grant, Ulysses S. **V**:176
  Hayes, Rutherford B.
    VI:166–167
  Ingersoll, Robert Green
    VI:193
  presidential campaigns
    (1870–1899) **VI**:291
  Reconstruction **V**:326
  Reed, Thomas Brackett
    VI:304
  Reid, Whitelaw **VI**:305
  Republican Party **V**:334;
    VI:311
  Tilden, Samuel Jones
    VI:357
  Wallace, Lew **VI**:381
election of 1878 **VI**:95
election of 1880
  Arthur, Chester Alan
    VI:20–21
  Hayes, Rutherford B.
    VI:168
  presidential campaigns
    (1870–1899) **VI**:292–293
  Socialist Labor Party **VI**:336
election of 1884 **VI**:292, 409*c*
  Cleveland, Grover **VI**:74
  Democratic Party **VI**:95
  Higginson, Thomas
    Wentworth **VI**:172

mugwumps **VI**:252
presidential campaigns
  (1870–1899) **VI**:293
election of 1886 **VI**:336
election of 1888 **VI**:95, 293, 410*c*
  Allison, William Boyd **VI**:12
  Cleveland, Grover **VI**:75
  Grand Army of the Republic
    VI:152
  Harrison, Benjamin **VI**:161
  Quay, Matthew Stanley
    VI:299
  Socialist Labor Party **VI**:336
election of 1890 **VI**:162, 352
election of 1892 **VI**:293, 411*c*
  Cleveland, Grover **VI**:75
  Hanna, Marcus Alonzo
    VI:158
  Harrison, Benjamin **VI**:162
  Populist Party Platform
    VI:430–432
  Prohibition Party **VI**:296
  tariffs **VI**:352
election of 1896 **VI**:293, 411*c*
  Allison, William Boyd **VI**:12
  Bryan, William Jennings
    VI:52
  class consciousness **VI**:74
  "Cross of Gold" Speech
    (Bryan) **VI**:438–441
  Democratic Party **VII**:74
  Hanna, Marcus Alonzo
    VI:158
  People's Party **VI**:282
  Republican Party **VII**:299
  Watson, Thomas Edward
    VII:380
election of 1900 **VI**:291, 293;
  VII:403*c*
  elections **VII**:90
  Hanna, Marcus Alonzo
    VI:158
  Platform of the American
    Anti-Imperialist League
    VI:441–442
  Republican Party **VII**:299
election of 1904 **VII**:90–91, 94,
  404*c*
election of 1908 **VII**:91, 405*c*
election of 1912 **VII**:405*c*
  Cannon, Joseph Gurney
    VII:48
  Democratic Party **VII**:74
  elections **VII**:91
  Republican Party **VII**:300
  Roosevelt, Theodore **VII**:304
  Wilson, Thomas Woodrow
    VII:383
election of 1916 **VII**:406*c*
  Democratic Party **VII**:74
  Republican Party **VII**:300
  Wilson, Thomas Woodrow
    VII:383
election of 1918 **VII**:75
election of 1920 **VII**:408*c*
  Democratic Party **VII**:75
  elections **VII**:91

election of 1924 **VII**:75, 92, 408*c*
election of 1928 **VII**:409*c*
  Congress **VIII**:78
  Democratic Party **VII**:75
  elections **VII**:92
  politics (Roosevelt era)
    VIII:297–298
  Republican Party **VIII**:336
election of 1930 **VIII**:79
election of 1932 **VIII**:**108–109**,
  444*c*
  Agricultural Adjustment Act
    VIII:5
  Agricultural Marketing Act
    VIII:8
  Amalgamated Clothing
    Workers of America
    (ACW) **VIII**:16
  Baruch, Bernard M.
    VIII:42
  Berle, Adolf A., Jr. **VIII**:43
  Bonus Army **VIII**:48
  Communists **VIII**:77
  Congress **VIII**:79
  conservatism **VIII**:84
  Coughlin, Father Charles E.
    VIII:88
  Democratic Party **VIII**:92
  economy **VIII**:103–104
  election of 1932 **VIII**:108
  Farley, James A. **VIII**:125
  Garner, John Nance **VIII**:147
  German Americans
    VIII:148–149
  Harriman, W. Averell
    VIII:161
  Hoover presidency
    VIII:173
  Howe, Louis M. **VIII**:179
  Hull, Cordell **VIII**:180
  La Follette, Robert M., Jr.
    VIII:208
  La Guardia, Fiorello
    VIII:209
  Lewis, John L. **VIII**:213
  Moley, Raymond C.
    VIII:243
  NAACP **VIII**:255
  New Deal **VIII**:268
  politics (Roosevelt era)
    VIII:298
  relief **VIII**:331
  Republican Party **VIII**:336
  Reuther, Walter **VIII**:339
  Roosevelt, Eleanor
    VIII:343
  Roosevelt, Franklin D.
    VIII:345
  socialists **VIII**:362
  Tennessee Valley Authority
    VIII:392
  Thomas, Norman **VIII**:394
  Tugwell, Rexford G.
    VIII:397
  Wallace, Henry A. **VIII**:411
  Willkie, Wendell L.
    VIII:417

election of 1934
  Congress **VIII**:79
  conservative coalition
    VIII:86
  New Deal **VIII**:270
  politics (Roosevelt era)
    VIII:298
  Republican Party **VIII**:337
  Roosevelt, Franklin D.
    VIII:345
election of 1936 **VIII**:109–110,
  445c
  AFL **VIII**:18
  American Liberty League
    VIII:19
  Black Cabinet **VIII**:46
  Borah, William E. **VIII**:50
  CIO **VIII**:82
  Communists **VIII**:78
  Congress **VIII**:79
  conservatism **VIII**:85
  conservative coalition
    VIII:86
  Coughlin, Father Charles E.
    VIII:87
  Democratic Party **VIII**:93
  Dubinsky, David **VIII**:97
  election of 1932 **VIII**:108–
    109
  Farley, James A. **VIII**:125
  Gallup Poll **IX**:130
  German Americans
    VIII:148–149
  Ickes, Harold L. **VIII**:183
  Jews **VIII**:195–196
  Kennedy, Joseph P.
    VIII:200
  Knox, Frank **VIII**:202
  labor/labor movements
    VIII:207
  La Follette, Robert M., Jr.
    VIII:208
  Landon, Alfred M. **VIII**:209
  Lewis, John L. **VIII**:213
  Long, Huey P. **VIII**:223
  Luce, Henry R. **VIII**:224
  NAACP **VIII**:255
  New Deal **VIII**:270
  politics (Roosevelt era)
    VIII:298, 300
  Popular Front **VIII**:304
  public opinion polls
    VIII:312
  Republican Party **VIII**:337
  Roosevelt, Franklin D.
    VIII:345
  socialists **VIII**:362
  South **VIII**:366
  Supreme Court **VIII**:383
  Thomas, Norman **VIII**:394
  Townsend, Francis E.
    VIII:395
  Union Party **VIII**:401
  Willkie, Wendell L.
    VIII:417
election of 1938
  Congress **VIII**:80

conservative coalition
    VIII:86
  politics (Roosevelt era)
    VIII:300
  Republican Party **VIII**:337
election of 1940 **VIII**:110–111,
  447c
  Byrnes, James F. **VIII**:60
  Congress **VIII**:81
  Democratic Party **VIII**:94
  destroyers-for-bases deal
    VIII:95
  election of 1944 **VIII**:111
  enemy aliens **VIII**:115
  Farley, James A. **VIII**:125
  Flynn, Edward J. **VIII**:139
  German Americans
    VIII:149
  Hopkins, Harry L. **VIII**:177
  isolationists **VIII**:190
  Italian Americans **VIII**:190–
    191
  Jews **VIII**:196
  Johnson, Hugh S. **VIII**:197
  Kennedy, Joseph P.
    VIII:200
  La Guardia, Fiorello
    VIII:209
  Lewis, John L. **VIII**:213
  Luce, Henry R. **VIII**:224
  Murray, Philip **VIII**:249
  Polish Americans **VIII**:297
  politics (Roosevelt era)
    VIII:300
  public opinion polls
    VIII:312
  Republican Party **VIII**:337–
    338
  Roosevelt, Franklin D.
    VIII:346
  Selective Service **VIII**:357
  socialists **VIII**:362
  Wallace, Henry A. **VIII**:411
  Willkie, Wendell L.
    VIII:417
  World War II home front
    VIII:434
election of 1942
  politics (Roosevelt era)
    VIII:300
  Republican Party **VIII**:338
  World War II home front
    VIII:434
election of 1944 **VIII**:111
  Congress **VIII**:81
  Democratic Party **VIII**:94
  Economic Bill of Rights
    VIII:102
  Farley, James A. **VIII**:125
  Flynn, Edward J. **VIII**:139
  Full Employment Bill
    VIII:145
  Higgins, Andrew J.
    VIII:165
  Hillman, Sidney **VIII**:166
  labor/labor movements
    VIII:207

politics (Roosevelt era)
    VIII:300
  Republican Party **VIII**:338
  Roosevelt, Franklin D.
    VIII:347
  Wallace, Henry A. **VIII**:411
  Willkie, Wendell L.
    VIII:417
  World War II home front
    VIII:434
  Zionism **VIII**:441
election of 1946
  elections **IX**:102
  Kennedy, John F. **IX**:169
  McCarthy, Joseph R. **IX**:206
  Republican Party **IX**:274
election of 1948 **IX**:352c
  Democratic Party **IX**:85
  Dewey, Thomas E. **IX**:87
  elections **IX**:102
  Fair Deal **IX**:115
  Gallup Poll **IX**:130
  McCarthy, Eugene **IX**:205
  Mondale, Walter F. **X**:233
  Progressive Party **IX**:264
  Republican Party **IX**:274
  States' Rights Party **IX**:300
election of 1950 **IX**:103
election of 1952 **IX**:353c
  computers **IX**:70
  Democratic Party **IX**:85
  Eisenhower, Dwight D.
    IX:100
  elections **IX**:103
  Korean War **IX**:177–178
  MacArthur, Douglas **IX**:198
  McCarthy, Joseph R. **IX**:207
  modern Republicanism
    IX:221
  Nixon, Richard M. **X**:256
  Progressive Party **IX**:264
  Republican Party **IX**:274
  States' Rights Party **IX**:300
  Stevenson, Adali E. **IX**:302
election of 1954 **IX**:117–118, 207
election of 1956 **IX**:354c
  Democratic Party **IX**:85
  elections **IX**:103
  Faubus, Orval **IX**:118
  Free Speech Movement
    IX:125
  modern Republicanism
    IX:221
  Perot, H. Ross **X**:273
  Stevenson, Adali E. **IX**:302
election of 1958 **IX**:103, 221,
  354c
election of 1960 **IX**:354c
  Democratic Party **IX**:85
  elections **IX**:103
  Humphrey, Hubert H.
    IX:151
  Johnson, Lady Bird **IX**:162
  Johnson, Lyndon B. **IX**:163
  journalism **IX**:165
  Kennedy, Jacqueline **IX**:168
  Kennedy, John F. **IX**:169

Kennedy, Robert F. **IX**:171
  King, Martin Luther, Jr.
    IX:174
  Nixon, Richard M. **X**:256
  Powell, Adam Clayton
    IX:261
  Republican Party **IX**:274
  Roosevelt, Eleanor
    VIII:344
  Stevenson, Adali E. **IX**:302
election of 1962 **IX**:104
election of 1964 **IX**:356c
  advertising **IX**:3
  Bush, George H. W. **X**:51
  conservatism **IX**:75
  elections **IX**:104
  Goldwater, Barry **IX**:135–
    136
  liberalism **IX**:191
  MFDP **IX**:219–220
  modern Republicanism
    IX:222
  Mondale, Walter F. **X**:233
  Republican Party **IX**:274
election of 1966 **IX**:139
election of 1968 **IX**:357c
  Agnew, Spiro T. **X**:18
  AIP **X**:24
  antiwar movement, Vietnam
    X:29
  assassinations **IX**:23
  Buchanan, Patrick J. **X**:49
  campaign finance **X**:64
  censorship **X**:71
  Cheney, Richard B. **X**:72
  "Chicago Eight" **X**:73
  Clinton, William J. **X**:83
  conservative movement
    X:93
  counterculture **IX**:79
  Democratic Party **IX**:85
  elections **IX**:104
  House of Representatives
    X:170
  Humphrey, Hubert H.
    IX:151
  Kennedy, Robert F. **IX**:171–
    172
  Kissinger, Henry A. **X**:198
  labor/labor movements
    X:201
  liberalism **IX**:191
  McCarthy, Eugene **IX**:205–
    206
  Meredith, James **IX**:213
  Mitchell, George **X**:231
  Mitchell, John N. **X**:233
  Nader, Ralph **X**:242
  Nixon, Richard M. **X**:256
  NRA **X**:249
  political parties **X**:277
  Reform Party **X**:304
  Republican Party **IX**:274
  SANE **IX**:284
  Senate, U.S. **X**:321
  Sunbelt **X**:338
  Wallace, George C. **X**:364

election of 1972 **X:**376c
  assassinations **IX:**23–24
  Bush, George H. W. **X:**51
  Eagleton, Thomas F. **X:**107
  McCarthy, Eugene **IX:**206
  McGovern, George S.
    X:216–217
  Mitchell, George **X:**232
  Mitchell, John N. **X:**233
  Mondale, Walter F. **X:**233
  Nixon, Richard M. **X:**257
  Shriver, Robert Sargent, Jr.
    X:324
election of 1974 **X:**232
election of 1976
  Carter, James Earl, Jr. **X:**67,
    68
  Ford, Gerald R. **X:**139
  McCarthy, Eugene **IX:**206
  Mondale, Walter F. **X:**233
election of 1980 **X:**378c
  Anderson, John B. **X:**25
  Carter, James Earl, Jr. **X:**69
  censorship **X:**71
  economy **X:**109
  Iranian hostage crisis **X:**185
  Meese, Edwin C., III **X:**225
  Mondale, Walter F. **X:**234
  Moral Majority **X:**234
  political parties **X:**277
  Reagan, Ronald W. **X:**300
election of 1984 **X:**378c
  abortion **X:**4
  Albright, Madeleine K. **X:**22
  Bush, George H. W. **X:**52
  Ferraro, Geraldine A. **X:**135
  Jackson, Jesse, L. **X:**191–
    192
  McGovern, George S. **X:**217
  Mondale, Walter F. **X:**234
  Reagan, Ronald W. **X:**300
election of 1986 **X:**232
election of 1988 **X:**379c
  Albright, Madeleine K. **X:**22
  Bush, George W. **X:**54
  censorship **X:**71
  Christian Coalition **X:**74
  Dukakis, Michael S. **X:**105–
    106
  Horton, Willie **X:**168–169
  Quayle, J. Danforth **X:**293
  "Thousand Points of Light"
    Speech (Bush) **X:**399–
    403
election of 1992 **X:**380c
  Albright, Madeleine K. **X:**22
  Angelou, Maya **X:**26
  Bush, George H. W. **X:**53
  Carter, James Earl, Jr. **X:**67,
    68
  Clinton, William J. **X:**80
  conservative movement
    X:93
  Dole, Robert **X:**105
  Dukakis, Michael S. **X:**106
  economy **X:**110
  Gore, Albert, Jr. **X:**157

House of Representatives
    X:170
  Libertarian Party **X:**209
  Meredith, James **IX:**213
  political parties **X:**277
election of 1996
  censorship **X:**71
  Dole, Robert **X:**104, 105
  Gore, Albert, Jr. **X:**157
  Green Party **X:**159
  immigration **X:**176
  Kemp, Jack F. **X:**196
  Libertarian Party **X:**209
  Nader, Ralph **X:**242
  NRA **X:**249
  Reform Party **X:**304
  Senate, U.S. **X:**321
  Sunbelt **X:**338
election of 2000 **X:**383c
  Bush, George W. **X:**54–55
  Cheney, Richard B. **X:**72
  Gore, Albert, Jr. **X:**157
  Green Party **X:**159
  immigration **X:**176
  Mexico **X:**226
  Supreme Court **X:**339
election of 2004 **X:**384c
  Bush, George W. **X:**56
  PACs **X:**275
  Senate, U.S. **X:**321
  Sunbelt **X:**338
election of 2008 **X:**384c
  Biden, Joseph **X:**42
  Clinton, Hillary Rodham
    X:79
  Internet **X:**183
  Obama, Barack Hussein
    X:264
  Senate, U.S. **X:**322
  Sunbelt **X:**338
elections (presidential) **X:116–119,**
  117. *See also specific election*
  years, e.g.: election of 1980
  advertising **X:**8–9
  cities and urban life **X:**76
elections, conduct of **VI:113**
elections, Iraqi **X:**384c
elective system **VI:**111, 114
electoral college
  Amendment, Twelfth **III:**16
  anti-Federalists **III:**24
  Bush, George W. **X:**55
  Constitution, United States
    III:107
  election of 1800 **III:**149, 150
  elections, presidential
    X:116, 118
  Gore, Albert, Jr. **X:**157
  Hamilton, Alexander
    III:207
  Morris, Gouverneur **III:**304
Electoral Commission Act
  Grant, Ulysses S. **V:**176
  presidential campaigns
    (1870–1899) **VI:**292
  Tilden, Samuel Jones
    VI:357

Electoral Count Act **VI:**292, 410c
electoral districts **X:**339
electoral votes **X:**116–118
electricity **VI:**410c; **VII:92–94,** 93
  agriculture **VIII:**10
  cities and urban life
    VII:54–56
  Edison, Thomas Alva
    VI:107
  Franklin, Benjamin **III:**173
  GE **VII:**123
  Industrial Revolution,
    Second **VI:**191
  invention and technology
    VI:194–196; **VII:**149
  mining **VII:**209, 210
  oil industry **VII:**245
  Pan-American Exposition
    VII:251
  Philadelphia Centennial
    Exposition **VI:**284
  REA **VIII:**349–350
  rural areas **VIII:**349
  technology **VIII:**389
  Tennessee Valley Authority
    VIII:393
  Tesla, Nikola **VI:**353–354
  urban transportation
    VII:363
Electric Kool-Aid Acid Test, The
  (Wolfe) **IX:**194, 196
electric motors **VI:**353; **VII:**93
electric power deregulation **X:**121
electric power generation **X:**122
Electric Tower (Pan-American
  Exposition) **VII:**251
electroconvulsive therapy (ECT)
  X:223
Electronic Data Systems
  Corporation (EDS) **X:**272
Electronic Numerical Integrator
  and Calculator (ENIAC)
  IX:104–105, 351c
  computers **IX:**69, 70; **X:**86
  science and technology
    IX:285
  technology **IX:**313
Electronic Privacy Information
  Center **X:**284
electronics **IX:**352c
  economy **IX:**98
  mobilization **VIII:**242
  science and technology
    IX:286; **X:**317
electronic surveillance. *See*
  surveillance, electronic
Elementary and Secondary
  Education Act of 1965 (ESEA)
  IX:105–106, 356c
  education **IX:**99
  education, primary/
    secondary **X:**115
  Great Society **IX:**139
  House of Representatives
    X:170
  Powell, Adam Clayton
    IX:261

Elements of Military Art and
  Science (Halleck) **V:**182
elestrostatic generators **VIII:**352
elevated trains **VI:**191, 360–361,
  407c
elevators **IV:**333; **VI:**196, 410c
11th Illinois Cavalry **VI:**193
Eleventh Amendment **III:16,**
  230, **403,** 464c
Eli Lilly & Company **VIII:**57;
  X:224
Eliot, Charles William **VI:113–**
  114
  Brooks, Phillips **VI:**50
  education, higher **VI:**111
  Fiske, John **VI:**129
  Gibbs, Wolcott **VI:**145
  Hall, Granville Stanley
    VI:157
  Hayden, Ferdinand
    Vandeveer **VI:**165
  medicine **VII:**199
  Norton, Charles Eliot
    VI:269
  Peirce, Charles Sanders
    VI:280
Eliot, John **II:115,** 253, 308–309
Eliot, T. S. **VII:**179, 212, 408c;
  IX:195
"Elite Syncopations" (Joplin)
  VII:158
Elixir of Sulfanilamide **VIII:**140
Elizabeth, New Jersey **III:**413
Elizabeth I (queen of England
  and Ireland) **I:119–122,** 120,
  397c, 398c
  Anglo-Normans **I:**10
  black legend **I:**32
  Camden, William **I:**55
  Church of England **I:**75
  Company of Cathay **I:**87
  De La Warr, Lord **I:**104
  Drake, Sir Francis **I:**111,
    112
  East India Company **I:**117
  Frobisher, Martin **I:**134,
    135
  Gilbert, Sir Humphrey
    I:140, 141
  Hakluyt, Richard, the Elder
    I:150, 151
  Hakluyt, Richard, the
    Younger **I:**151, 152
  Hawkins, Sir John **I:**157
  Henry VIII **I:**160
  James I **I:**191
  Lane, Ralph **I:**203
  Levant Company **I:**213
  London **I:**216
  Mary I **I:**232–233
  monarchy, British **II:**240
  North Carolina **II:**274
  Privy Council **I:**304
  Protestantism **II:**315
  Puritans **I:**307
  Ralegh, Sir Walter **I:**311
  Reformation **I:**317

Elizabeth I (*continued*)
Roanoke **I**:320
Shakespeare, William **I**:333, 334
Spanish Armada **I**:344
Walsingham, Sir Francis **I**:382
Elizabeth Cady Stanton, as Revealed in Her Letters, Diary and Reminiscences (Stanton) **VII**:38
Elizabeth Settlement **I**:75
Elk Hills, California **VII**:351
Elkhorn Tavern. *See* Pea Ridge/Elkhorn Tavern, Battle of
Elkins Act **VII**:**94**, 190, 304, 404*c*
Ellenton riot **VI**:358
Ellicott, Joseph **III**:214
Ellington, Edward Kennedy "Duke" **VIII**:**111–112**, *112*
African Americans **VIII**:3
big bands **VIII**:44
Goodman, Benny **VIII**:151
jazz **VII**:153; **VIII**:195
music **VII**:220; **VIII**:250–251
Elliot, Missy **X**:240
Elliot, Robert Brown **V**:**127**
Ellis, Henry (royal governor) **II**:147
Ellis, Henry Havelock **VII**:**94–95**
birth control **VII**:36
Freud, Sigmund **VII**:118–119
sexuality **VII**:322
women's status and rights **VII**:389
Ellis, Thomas **I**:177
Ellis Island, New York **V**:200; **VI**:184, 186; **VIII**:208
Ellison, Keith **X**:189
Ellison, Ralph **IX**:353*c*
African Americans **IX**:5
Juneteenth **V**:219–220
literature **IX**:194
popular culture **IX**:258
Ellsberg, Daniel
impeachment of Richard M. Nixon **X**:178
Pentagon Papers **X**:271–272
Watergate scandal **X**:365
Ellsworth, Elmer Ephraim **V**:441
Ellsworth, Oliver
Judiciary Act (1789) **III**:242
Judiciary Act (1801) **III**:242
Supreme Court **III**:403
Ellsworth, Solomon, Jr. **IV**:335
El Mansur. *See* Ahmad I al-Mansur
Elmer Gantry (Lewis) **VII**:180
El Mirador **I**:234
El Movimiento **IX**:185
El Paso, Texas
Magoffin, James W. **IV**:233
race and race relations **VIII**:318
Texas **IV**:371

El Portete **I**:392
El Salvador
Latin America **X**:206
Mexico **X**:226
North, Oliver L. **X**:258
Reagan, Ronald W. **X**:301
El Teatro Campesino **IX**:186
Ely, Eugene B. **VIII**:11
Ely, Richard Theodore **VI**:**114–116**, 148, 335
Ely, Samuel Cullick **III**:**151**
e-mail **X**:181
emancipation **III**:462*c*; **V**:**127–130**, *128*, 444*c*
abolitionism **III**:1; **V**:1, 2
African Methodist Episcopal Church **V**:5
Benjamin, Judah P. **V**:33
Chase, Salmon P. **V**:63
Civil War **V**:74
Congress **V**:90
conscription **V**:91
contrabands **V**:92, 93
Copperheads **V**:95
Democratic Party **V**:109
Douglass, Frederick **V**:115, 116
Dunmore, John Murray, earl of **III**:142
elections **V**:126
Forbes, John Murray **VI**:132
Garrison, William Lloyd **V**:164
Greeley, Horace **V**:177
Harvard Regiment **V**:186
impeachment of Andrew Johnson **V**:202
Johnson, Andrew **V**:212, 213
Joint Committee on the Conduct of the War **V**:216
Kelley, William D. **V**:222
King, Rufus **III**:246
Kościuszko, Tadeusz **III**:249
Lincoln, Abraham **V**:236
McClellan, George Brinton **V**:251
race and race relations **V**:320
Radical Republicans **V**:320
Republican Party **V**:334
rural life **III**:375
Stanton, Edwin M. **V**:368
Stevens, Thaddeus **V**:372
Sumner, Charles **V**:377
tactics and strategy **V**:381
Thirteenth Amendment **V**:388
Washington, George **III**:432
Welles, Gideon **V**:428
Women's National Loyal League **V**:434, 435
women's status and rights **V**:438

emancipation laws
abolitionism **III**:1–3
African Americans **III**:9
antislavery **III**:25
Emancipation Order (1861) **V**:444*c*
Emancipation Proclamation **V**:**130–132**, 445*c*, 460
African-American regiments **V**:4
Antietam, Battle of **V**:12
Blair, Francis Preston, Jr. **V**:36
Civil War centennial **IX**:62
Confiscation Acts **V**:87–88
Copperheads **V**:95
emancipation **V**:128, 129
Emerson, Ralph Waldo **IV**:140
54th Massachusetts Regiment **V**:142
foreign policy **V**:151
Freedom Train **IX**:125
governors **V**:172
homefront **V**:193
Lincoln, Abraham **V**:236
March on Washington (1963) **IX**:201
McClellan, George Brinton **V**:252
New York City draft riots **V**:284
race and race relations **V**:320
Reconstruction **V**:324
Sherman, William T. **V**:356
slavery **V**:364
Thirteenth Amendment **V**:387
Union army **V**:403
"Emancipation Proclamation of Preborn Children" (Reagan) **X**:4
Emancipator, The
American Anti-Slavery Society **IV**:15, 16
Genius of Universal Emancipation **IV**:175
Liberty Party **IV**:226
Tappan, Arthur and Lewis **IV**:366
embargoes **X**:382*c*
cold war, end of **X**:85
Haiti **X**:164
Nicaragua **X**:254
Persian Gulf War **X**:273
embargo of 1807 **III**:**151–153**, *152*, 465*c*
Adams, John Quincy **IV**:5
agriculture **III**:11
alcohol **III**:13
architecture **III**:29
Berlin Decree **III**:49
Bonaparte, Napoleon **III**:55
Chesapeake-Leopard affair **III**:88
economy **III**:147

Federalist Party **III**:164
foreign affairs **III**:169
foreign policy **IV**:153–154
Gallatin, Albert **III**:188
Hartford Convention **IV**:186
Industrial Revolution **III**:226
Jefferson, Thomas **III**:235
Macon's Bill No. 2 **III**:280
National Road **IV**:271
panic of 1819 **IV**:293
states' rights **III**:397
tariffs **III**:406
trade, domestic and foreign **III**:415
Wilkinson, James **III**:444
embassy bombings (Dar es Salaam, Tanzania, and Nairobi, Kenya, 1998) **X**:382*c*
Afghanistan War **X**:10
Clinton, William J. **X**:83
terrorism **X**:346
embedded journalists **X**:187
Emergency Banking Act of 1933 **VIII**:**112–113**, *113*, 444*c*
banking **VIII**:40
Banking Act (1933) **VIII**:41
Eccles, Marriner S. **VIII**:101
FDIC **VIII**:132
RFC **VIII**:325
Emergency Detention Act (1950) **IX**:158
Emergency Economic Stabilization Act (2008) **X**:61, 384*c*
Emergency Fleet Corporation **VII**:317, 360
Emergency Highway Energy Conservation Act (1974) **X**:130
Emergency Maternity and Infant Care (EMIC) **VIII**:67
Emergency Price Control Act **VIII**:282, 409, 447*c*
Emergency Relief and Construction Act **VIII**:310
Emergency Relief Appropriation Act (ERAA) **VIII**:**113–114**, 445*c*
Congress **VIII**:79
FAP **VIII**:128
liberalism **VIII**:215
REA **VIII**:349–350
relief **VIII**:332
Resettlement Administration **VIII**:338
Second New Deal **VIII**:356
Social Security Act **VIII**:363, 364
WPA **VIII**:425
Emerson, Edward **V**:142
Emerson, Irene Sanford **V**:116
Emerson, John **V**:116
Emerson, Ralph Waldo **IV**:**139–141**, *140*, 413*c*
Alcott, Louisa May **VI**:10
art and architecture **IV**:28–29

Brook Farm **IV:**65
Brown, John **V:**45
  environment **VII:**98
  54th Massachusetts
    Regiment **V:**142
  Forbes, John Murray
    VI:132
  Fuller, Margaret **IV:**169
  Howells, William Dean
    VI:179
  James, Henry **VI:**199–200
  journalism **IV:**210
  Lazarus, Emma **VI:**219
  literature **IV:**228
  lyceum movement **IV:**232
  Peabody, Elizabeth Palmer
    VI:279
  religion **IV:**318, 320
  Thoreau, Henry David
    IV:376
  transcendental movement
    IV:378, 379
  Whitman, Walt **V:**430
EMIC (Emergency Maternity and
  Infant Care) **VIII:**67
*Emigrant's Guide to Oregon and
  California* (Hastings) **IV:**125,
  187
emigration **III:**127; **V:**108
Emile, Adélaide Marie **III:**304
Emilio, Luis F. **V:**142
Emily's List **X:**134
eminent domain
  Kelo v. City of New London
    X:195
  Panama Canal turnover
    X:270
  property rights **X:**290
emissions
  Bush, George W. **X:**55
  conservation/
    environmentalism **X:**92
  global warming **X:**156
Emmett, Daniel Decatur **V:**273
Emmitsburg, Maryland **IV:**344;
  VI:217
Emmitsburg Road **V:**167
Emory University **X:**70
Emperor Jones (O'Neill) **VII:**179,
  408c
emphysema **X:**351
Empire State Building (New
  York City) **VII:**259; **VIII:**28,
  443c
employment **V:132–133**. *See also*
  unemployment
  African Americans **VI:**6, 7
  Appalachia **IX:**15–16
  Asian Americans **X:**33
  Black Codes **V:**35
  CCC **VIII:**70–71
  CEA **IX:**77
  children **VIII:**66–67
  cities and urban life **V:**67
  Civil Rights Act (1964)
    IX:61
  Civil War **V:**74

Colored National Labor
  Union **V:**77
  EEOC **IX:**110
  family life **X:**128
  gays and lesbians **IX:**131
  Great Society **IX:**139
  immigration **V:**199, 201
  March on Washington
    Movement **VIII:**227,
    228
  Mexican Americans
    VIII:237
  music **VIII:**251
  Native Americans **V:**278
  Puerto Ricans **IX:**268
  relief **VIII:**332
  service sector **IX:**288–289
  steel industry **VIII:**374
  WEAL **IX:**345
  women's status and rights
    VIII:422–424; **IX:**346;
    X:370–371
Employment Act of 1946 **IX:106–
107**, 351c
  CEA **IX:**77
  Economic Bill of Rights
    VIII:102
  economy **IX:**96
  Full Employment Bill
    VIII:145
  Keynesianism **VIII:**201
  Wagner, Robert F.
    VIII:411
employment discrimination
  IX:356c; **X:**380c
  affirmative action **X:**9
  Americans with Disabilities
    Act **X:**24–25, **403–405**
  EEOC **IX:**110
  feminism **X:**132, 133
  *Griggs v. Duke Power
    Company* **X:**160
  Urban League **IX:**325
Employment Division v. Smith
  X:307
Empower America **X:**196
empresarios
  Alamo, The **IV:**14
  Austin, Stephen F. **IV:**39
  Texas Revolution **IV:**373
Empress of China (ship) **III:**88
encomenderos **I:**93, 267
encomienda **I:122–123; II:**101
  Aguilar, Francisco de **I:**4
  Aguilar, Gerónimo de **I:**5
  Charles V **I:**70
  Cortés, Hernán **I:**94, 97
  Cuba **I:**100
  Ferdinand and Isabella
    I:128
  hacienda **I:**150
  Las Casas, Bartolomé de
    I:204–207
  limpieza de sangre **I:**214
  Mendoza, Antonio de **I:**239
  New Spain **I:**267
  Sandoval, Gonzalo de **I:**325

Sepúlveda, Juan Ginés de
  I:330
  Tlaxcala **I:**362
  Zumárraga, Juan de **I:**392
Encyclopedia Americana **V:**234
Endangered Species Act (1973)
  X:90, 290, 376c
Endeavor (space shuttle) **X:**328
Endecott, John **II:115–116**, 222,
  225
Ending Poverty in California
  (EPIC) **VII:**326
Endo, ex parte **VIII:**448c
End of Days **VI:**307
endorsements **X:**332
enemy aliens **VIII:114–115**
  civil liberties **VIII:**72
  Executive Order 9066
    VIII:121
  Expatriation Act **VII:**104
  Italian Americans **VIII:**191
  Smith Act **VIII:**361
enemy combatants **X:**188
energy **X:**56, 72, **119–121**, *120,
  121*
Energy, U.S. Department of
  (DOE) **X:122**
  Carter, James Earl, Jr. **X:**69
  energy **X:**120
  Human Genome Project
    X:171, 172
  medicine **X:**225
energy crisis (1973)
  economy **X:**109
  Energy, U.S. Department
    of **X:**122
  Ford, Gerald R. **X:**139
  foreign policy **X:**140
energy crisis (1979) **X:**69, 109
Energy Policy Act (1992) **X:**122
Energy Policy Act (2005)
  Bush, George W. **X:**56
  conservation/
    environmentalism **X:**92
  Energy, U.S. Department
    of **X:**122
  Senate, U.S. **X:**322
Energy Policy Office **X:**122
Energy Reorganization Act (1974)
  IX:25
Energy Research and Development
  Administration **X:**122
Enforcement Acts **V:133–134**
  elections, conduct of **VI:**113
  Ku Klux Klan **V:**223–225
  Ku Klux Klan Act **V:**225
  Ku Klux Klan cases **VI:**210
  Rainey, Joseph H. **V:**323
  Reconstruction **V:**326
  redemption **V:**328
  U.S. v. Cruikshank **V:**411–
    412
enforcement clause **V:**388
Engel, George **VI:**169
Engels, Friedrich
  communism **IX:**67
  Kelley, Florence **VII:**164

Marx, Karl **V:**249
  politics (1900–1928)
    VII:261
Engel v. Vitale **IX:107–108**, 274,
  337, 338, **355c**
England **II:**435c, 436c. *See also*
  Great Britain
  Cherokee **II:**64–65
  Chickasaw **II:**66
  convict labor **II:**79–80
  Delaware **II:**95
  economy **II:**109
  exploration **II:**124
  foreign policy **VII:**113
  forts **II:**133
  fur trade **II:**141
  King George's War **II:**192
  land **II:**201
  movie industry **VII:**216
  New Netherland **II:**266
  Open Door Policy **VII:**246
  piracy **II:**296
  privateering **II:**312
  Queen Anne's War **II:**323–
    324
  race and race relations
    II:325
  Seven Years' War **II:**348–
    350
  slave trade **II:**358
  South Sea Company **II:**370
  spinsters **II:**375
  tobacco **II:**391
  trade, domestic and foreign
    II:393
  War of Jenkins' Ear **II:**408–
    409
  wolves **II:**421
English Channel **I:**344, 345
  blitzkrieg **VIII:**47
  Casablanca Conference
    VIII:62
  Normandy, invasion of
    VIII:275, 276
  World War II European
    theater **VIII:**431
English Civil War **II:116**, 436c
  English immigrants **II:**117
  Maryland **II:**220
  Pennsylvania **II:**285
English Cod, An (Chase) **VI:**66
English colonies
  African Americans **II:**6
  Albany Congress **II:**15
  architecture **II:**25
  art **II:**26, 27
  banking **II:**32–33
  borderlands **II:**39–40
  British Empire **II:**48–49
  Burgesses, House of **II:**51
  class **II:**69–71
  Connecticut **II:**75–76
  disease/epidemics **II:**98
  education **II:**111
  English Civil War **II:**116
  ethnocentrism **II:**122
  fertility **II:**125–126

English colonies *(continued)*
  fishing **II:**126, 127
  food **II:**130–131
  forests **II:**131
  French colonies **II:**137–138
  Georgia **II:**145–147
  German immigrants
    II:147–148
  German Reformed Church
    II:148
  Great Awakening **II:**156
  Jamestown **II:**181
  journeymen **II:**190
  King Philip's War **II:**193
  Lutherans **II:**212
  manufacturing and industry
    II:214
  marriage and family **II:**216–
    217
  medicine **II:**230–231
  mulattoes **II:**246
  music **II:**247
  Native Americans **II:**252–
    254
  New Jersey **II:**261–262
  New York **II:**271–272
  North Carolina **II:**273–275
  pewter **II:**291
  Pilgrims **II:**293
  population trends **II:**302–
    303
  printing and publishing
    II:311
  privateering **II:**312, 313
  race and race relations
    II:325–326
  rice cultivation **II:**334
  science and technology
    II:345
  slavery **II:**354–358
  smallpox **II:**360
  society, British American
    II:364–368
  Spanish colonies **II:**372
  Stuyvesant, Peter **II:**379
  suffrage **II:**380
  technology **II:**385
  tenants **II:**387
  theater **II:**389
  trade, domestic and foreign
    II:392
  Tuscarora War **II:**395
  Virginia **II:**398
  war and warfare **II:**407
  Westo **II:**410–411
  Wingina **II:**417
  women's status and rights
    II:422, 425, 426
  Yamasee War **II:**430
English colonization/exploration
    I:395c, 396c, 398c
  Acadia **I:**2–3
  Anglo-Normans **I:**10
  art and architecture **I:**12
  Bermuda Company **I:**30–31
  black legend **I:**32
  Bristol **I:**36–37

  Cabot, Sebastian **I:**45, 46
  Camden, William **I:**55–56
  Drake, Sir Francis **I:**111–
    112
  Elizabeth I **I:**119–122
  Gilbert, Sir Humphrey
    I:140
  Grotius, Hugo **I:**146
  Hakluyt, Richard, the Elder
    I:150–151
  Hakluyt, Richard, the
    Younger **I:**151–153
  James I **I:**191–192
  Levant Company **I:**213
  London **I:**215–216
  Montserrat **I:**251
  Nevis **I:**263
  Parliament **I:**286
  Peckham, Sir George **I:**288
  population trends **I:**298
  Privy Council **I:**304
  Roanoke **I:**320–322
  Sandys, Sir Edwin **I:**326
  Spanish Armada **I:**344–345
  Walsingham, Sir Francis
    I:382
  White, John **I:**383
  witches/witchcraft **I:**384
English common law **II:**422, 423
English immigrants **II:116–117**
  indentured servitude **II:**173,
    174
  mortality **II:**244
  Oglethorpe, James Edward
    II:277–278
  Opechancanough **II:**278–
    279
  Ostenaco **II:**280
  redemptioners **II:**326–327
English language **X:**210
English language instruction
    VII:13, 381
English-only education **X:**42
English Protestants **I:**132
English Statute of Artificers
    II:405
English Vagrancy Act **I:**336
engraving **I:**37–38
  art **II:**27
  Dummer, Jeremiah **II:**104
  Pelham, Peter **II:**283
ENIAC. *See* Electronic Numerical
    Integrator and Calculator
Enigma machine **VIII:**76
Enlightenment, American
    II:117–119
  Great Awakening **II:**156
  journalism **II:**189
  Pennsylvania **II:**287–288
  Philadelphia **II:**293
  science and technology
    II:345
Enlightenment, the
  Beaumarchais, Pierre-
    Auguste Caron de **III:**48
  Common Sense **III:**101,
    102

  Crèvecoeur, J. Hector St.
    John de **III:**127
  deism **III:**134
  education **IV:**134–135
  environment **III:**153, 154
  freemasonry **III:**176
  frontier, the **III:**181
  Judaism **VI:**205
  literature **III:**268, 269
  New Divinity **III:**316, 317
  Paine, Thomas **III:**329
  penitentiary movement
    IV:296
  race and race relations
    III:357
  religion **IV:**319
  Revere, Paul **III:**366
  Rush, Benjamin **III:**375
  Unitarianism **III:**419
  Yates, Abraham **III:**453
Enlightenment Gallery **I:**43
Enola Gay (B-29 bomber)
    VIII:35, 166
Enormous Room, The (cummings)
    VII:179
Enovid **IX:**257
*Enquiring into the Effects of
  Public Punishments upon
  Criminals and upon Society,
  An* (Rush) **IV:**296
Enrollment Act **V:**90–91, 400–401
Enron Corporation **X:**383c
  business **X:**59
  economy **X:**110
  Sarbanes-Oxley Act **X:**315
entail. *See* primogeniture and entail
Enterprise, USS **VIII:**238, 314
Enterprise for the Americas
    Initiative **X:**206
"Entertainer, The" (Joplin)
    VII:158, 219, 403c
entertainment, popular **VI:116–
    119,** *118;* **VII:95–98,** *96*
  baseball **VII:**33
  blues **VII:**39
  Chautauqua Institute
    VI:66–67
  Gershwin, George **VII:**124–
    125
  Houdini, Harry **VII:**141–
    142
  invention and technology
    VI:196
  marriage and family
    VII:192–193
  movie industry **VII:**214
  popular culture **VII:**263–
    265
  radio **VII:**289–290
  sports and recreation
    VII:334–335
  theater **VI:**354
  Tin Pan Alley **VII:**353
  urban transportation
    VII:363–364
  vaudeville **VII:**368–369
  Victorianism **VI:**374

  entitlement liberalism **X:**208
entrada **I:**397c; **II:**263
  Apalachee **I:**11
  Escalante, Juan de **I:**123
  Inca **I:**180
environmental impact statements
    X:375c
environmental issues **II:119–121,**
    120; **III:153–156; VI:119–120,**
    120; **VII:**96, **98–100,** *99;*
    VIII:115–116, *116;* **IX:**355c
  Agricultural Adjustment
    Administration **VIII:**7
  agriculture **VIII:**9
  animals **III:**22
  automobile industry **IX:**27
  business **IX:**47
  Carson, Rachel **IX:**50, 51
  Catesby, Mark **II:**62
  CCC **VIII:**71
  consumerism **IX:**76
  Ickes, Harold L. **VIII:**183
  Johnson, Lady Bird **IX:**162–
    163
  Kalm, Peter **II:**191
  Marsh, George Perkins
    VI:239
  National Outdoor
    Recreation Review
    Commission **IX:**237
  National Park Service
    VII:228
  National Reclamation Act
    VII:228–229
  National Trails Act of 1968
    IX:239
  recreation **IX:**271
  science and technology
    VII:315; **IX:**286
  Spanish colonies **II:**371
  technology **IX:**313
environmental movement
    IX:108–110, *109,* 163, 286
environmental policy. *See*
    conservation, environmentalism,
    and environmental policy
Environmental Protection Agency
    (EPA) **X:**375c
  Carson, Rachel **IX:**50, 51
  conservation/
    environmentalism **X:**90,
    92
  environment **IX:**109
  NEPA **X:**246
  Ruckelshaus, William D.
    X:312
EPA. *See* Environmental
    Protection Agency
EPIC (Ending Poverty in
    California) **VII:**326
Epidemic Intelligence Service
    IX:211
epidemics. *See* disease and
    epidemics
Epidemiologic Intelligence
    Service **IX:**265
episcopacy **II:**21, 22

Episcopal Church **III:**465c
   Anglican Church **III:**21
   Brooks, Phillips **VI:**50
   Chautauqua Institute **VI:**66
   Ely, Richard Theodore
      VI:115
   Indian Rights Association
      VI:190
   Jones, Absalom **III:**238
   Murray, Pauli **IX:**228
   religion **IV:**318; **VIII:**335
   Seabury, Samuel **III:**386
   Seton, Elizabeth Ann
      IV:343
   Williams, Peter, Jr. **IV:**402
*Epistle of Caution and Advice,
   An* **II:**2
*Epistle to the Clergy of the South-
   ern States, An* (Grimké) **IV:**180
"Epistle to the Hebrews, An"
   (Lazarus) **VI:**219
Epperson v. Arkansas **VII:**317;
   IX:274, 357c
Eppes, Mary Jefferson **III:**4
Equal Access Act (1984) **X:**122–
   123
Equal Credit Opportunity Act
   (1974) **X:**377c
Equal Employment Opportunity
   Act (1972) **X:**376c
   affirmative action **X:**9
   education, higher **X:**112
   race and race relations
      X:297
Equal Employment Opportunity
   Commission (EEOC) **IX:**110,
   356c
   affirmative action **X:**9
   Civil Rights Act (1964)
      IX:61
   feminism **X:**132
   Hill, Anita Faye **X:**166
   NOW **IX:**236; **X:**247
   Thomas, Clarence **X:**350
   women's status and rights
      IX:347
equality
   citizenship **III:**92
   Forten, James **III:**170
   popular culture **III:**342
   race and race relations
      III:357–358
   Randolph, A. Philip
      VIII:321
   riots **III:**371–372
   Washington, Booker T.
      VI:384
Equality (Bellamy) **VI:**32
Equality League of Self-
   Supporting Women **VII:**38
equal opportunity **VIII:**319;
   IX:243
Equal Pay Act (1963) **IX:**355c
   EEOC **IX:**110
   feminism **X:**132
   women's status and rights
      IX:346; **X:**371

equal protection
   Bakke case **X:**40
   Ginsburg, Ruth Bader
      X:152–153
   NAACP **X:**245
   Plessy v. Ferguson **VI:**284,
      285
   Rehnquist, William H. **X:**305
   Thomas, Clarence **X:**350
Equal Rights (journal) **VII:**286
Equal Rights Amendment (ERA)
   VII:100, 408c; **X:123–124,**
   376c, 378c
   abortion **X:**4
   Amendments to the U.S.
      Constitution **X:**23
   Brennan, William J., Jr.
      X:48
   conservative movement
      X:93
   feminism **X:**132–134
   Ferraro, Geraldine A. **X:**135
   Ford, Gerald R. **X:**139
   Friedan, Betty **IX:**127
   Moral Majority **X:**234
   NAWSA **VII:**223–224
   NOW **IX:**236; **X:**247, 248
   NWP **VII:**230
   Paul, Alice **VII:**254
   PCSW **IX:**262
   pro-life/pro-choice
      movements **X:**289
   Schlafly, Phyllis **X:**316, 317
   Steinem, Gloria **X:**334
   WEAL **IX:**345
   women's network **VIII:**422
   women's status and rights
      VII:388; **VIII:**424;
      IX:346; **X:**371
Equal Rights Amendment
   (Hawaii) **X:**215
Equal Rights League **VI:**218
Equal Rights Party **VI:**229, 401
Equiano, Olaudah **III:**156, **156–
   157,** 463c
   Account of His Capture and
      Enslavement **II:446–
      448**
   religion, African-American
      II:328
   slavery **II:**355–356
   slave trade **II:**359
Equitable Life Insurance Society
   VII:159
Equity Society **VII:**241
E.R. (TV program) **X:**343
ERA. *See* Equal Rights
   Amendment
ERAA. *See* Emergency Relief
   Appropriation Act
ERAmerica **X:**124
Era of Good Feelings **IV:141**
   Democratic Party **IV:**117
   Democratic-Republican
      Party **III:**136
   foreign policy **IV:**154
   Monroe, James **IV:**259

ERAP. *See* Economic Research
   and Action Project
Erasmus **I:**330
Eratosthenes of Alexandria **I:**84
Erdrich, Louise **X:**210–211
Ericsson, John
   Mitchell, William (Billy)
      VII:211
   Monitor-Merrimack **V:**265
   science and technology
      V:342
Erie, Lake **I:**185
   agriculture **IV:**12
   Canada **III:**77
   disease/epidemics **IV:**122
   Erie Canal **IV:**141
   Glaize, meeting at the **III:**195
   migration **IV:**254
   railroads **IV:**314
   Smith, Jedediah Strong
      IV:350
   War of 1812 **IV:**391
Erie, Lake, Battle of **IV:**185,
   220–221, 221m, 391
Erie, Pennsylvania **IV:**220
Erie Canal **IV:141–143,** 142,
   411c, 412c
   agriculture **IV:**12
   Baltimore & Ohio Railroad
      IV:43
   Bonus Bill **IV:**62
   canal era **IV:**79
   Clinton, DeWitt **III:**97
   economy **IV:**130–131
   Finney, Charles Grandison
      IV:151
   industrialization **IV:**200
   internal improvements
      IV:202
   lead mines **IV:**224
   migration **IV:**254
   Morris, Gouverneur **III:**304
   railroads **IV:**313
   science and technology
      IV:333
   transportation **V:**390
Erie County, New York **VI:**74
Erie Railroad **V:**446c
   Baltimore & Ohio Railroad
      IV:44
   corruption, political **VI:**83
   Gould, Jay **VI:**151
   oil **VI:**271
   railroads **VI:**302
   Robber Barons, The **VI:**315
Eriksson, Leif. *See* Leif Eriksson
Erik the Red **I:**144, 272, 395c
Erlanger, Abraham **VI:**355
erosion **III:**155
Errors in Navigation (Wright)
   I:262
Ervin, Sam, Jr. **X:**376c
   Congressional Budget and
      Impoundment Control
      Act **X:**89
   ERA **X:**123–124
   Watergate scandal **X:**366

ESA (European Space Agency)
   X:329
Escalante, Juan de **I:123–124**
escalators **VI:**196
Esch-Cummins Act **VII:**408c
Escobedo, Daniel **IX:**111
Escobedo v. Illinois **IX:**111, 338,
   356c
ESEA. *See* Elementary and
   Secondary Education Act of
   1965
Eskimos. *See* Inuit
Esopus Wars **II:**105, 106
Espejo, Antonio de **I:**168
espionage **V:**134, **134–135;**
   VIII:116–118, 117; **IX:**352c
   André, John **III:**19–20
   anticommunism **IX:**15
   atomic bomb **VIII:**35
   Beaumarchais, Pierre-
      Auguste Caron de **III:**48
   Boyd, Belle **V:**40
   censorship **VIII:**65
   Church, Benjamin **III:**89
   CIA **IX:**52
   communism **IX:**67
   Communists **VIII:**78
   enemy aliens **VIII:**114
   FBI **VIII:**130
   FCC **VIII:**131
   German Americans
      VIII:149
   Greenhow, Rose O'Neal
      V:178
   Hale, Nathan **III:**204–205
   Heroes of America **V:**187–
      188
   Hiss, Alger **IX:**146–147
   Hoover, J. Edgar **IX:**149
   intelligence **VIII:**187
   Internal Security Act (1950)
      IX:157, 158
   OSS **VIII:**284
   Rosenberg, Julius and Ethel
      IX:280–281
   Soviet-American relations
      VIII:368
   Van Lew, Elizabeth **V:**414–
      415
Espionage Act (1917) **VII:100–
   101,** 407c
   ACLU **VII:**9
   Anarchist Immigration Act
      VII:15
   censorship **VIII:**65
   civil liberties **VII:**57–58
   Committee for Public
      Information **VII:**60
   conscription **VII:**63
   espionage **VIII:**117
   Fellowship of Reconciliation
      VII:109
   Fuel Administration
      VII:119
   Greenwich Village **VII:**131

Espionage Act *(continued)*
  Haywood, William Dudley
    VII:137
  IWW **VII:**147
  labor/labor movements
    VII:171
  New Unionism **VII:**238
  Palmer, Alexander Mitchell
    VII:249
  Rosenberg, Julius and Ethel
    IX:280
  Schenck v. U.S. **VII:**313
  Sedition Act **VII:**318
  socialism **VII:**328
  Supreme Court **VII:**343
  Trading with the Enemy Act
    VII:355
  World War I **VII:**394
Espiritu **I:**325
Es Saheli, Abou-Ishaq Ibrahim
  I:228–229
Essay on Crimes and Punishments
  (Beccaria) **IV:**296
*Essay on the Education of Female
  Teachers* (Beecher) **IV:**134
Essex, John **II:**90
Essex, USS (aircraft carrier)
  VIII:*12*
Essex, USS (sailing frigate)
  III:157–158; **IV:**143–144, 165
Essex decision **III:157–158,**
  465*c;* **IV:**165
Esso **VII:**245, 336
establishment clause
  Equal Access Act **X:**122
  *McCreary County v. ACLU/
    Van Orden v. Perry* **X:**216
  religion **X:**307
Estaing, Charles-Henri Theodat,
  comte d' **III:158,** *158*
  French Alliance **III:**177–
    178
  Howe, Richard, Lord
    III:214
  Rhode Island, Battle of
    III:370
  Savannah, siege of **III:**383
  Sullivan, John **III:**402
Estevanico
  Cabeza de Vaca, Álvar
    Núñez **I:**40
  Coronado, Francisco **I:**92
  New Mexico **I:**265
  Pueblo **I:**305
Estonia **X:**384*c*
  cold war **IX:**63
  Europe **IX:**112
  Teheran Conference
    VIII:390
  Versailles, Treaty of **VII:**370
Esty, Mary **II:**276
Ethan Frome (Wharton) **VII:**179
Ethical Culture movement
  VI:120–121, 205, 408*c*
ethics
  conservative movement
    X:93, 94

Dewey, John **VII:**76, 77
  family life **X:**128
  Human Genome Project
    X:172
  stem cell research **X:**335
  television **X:**343
Ethics and Public Policy Center
  X:350
Ethics in Government Act (1978)
  X:179
Ethics in Government Act (1994)
  X:179
ethics violations **X:**170, 225
Ethiopia **I:**105, **124–125;**
  VIII:118–119
  Anglo-American relations
    VIII:21
  coffee **I:**79
  cold war, end of **X:**85
  Dengel, Lebna **I:**105
  foreign policy **VIII:**141
  Liberia **VI:**223
  Manchuria **VIII:**225
  Prester John **I:**301
ethnic cleansing **X:**382*c*
  Clinton, William J. **X:**81, 83
  Dayton accords **X:**99
  defense policy **X:**102
  foreign policy **X:**143
  Kosovo **X:**199
ethnic communities **VI:**186
ethnic groups
  cities and urban life **VIII:**70
  conservative coalition
    VIII:86
  news media **VIII:**271
  Polish Americans **VIII:**297
ethnic organizations **VII:101–
  102**
ethnocentrism **II:121–123**
Ethnology, Bureau of (BE)
  VI:141
Ethnology Building (Pan-
  American Exposition) **VII:**252
Ettor, Joseph **VII:**109, 173, 174
Eucharist **I:**75, 315
eugenics **VII:102–103**
  anti-Semitism **VII:**17
  birth control **VII:**36–37
  Buck v. Bell **VII:**43–44
  Holmes, Oliver Wendell
    VII:141
  race and race relations
    VII:281–282
  Racial Integrity Act **VII:**284
  Sanger, Margaret **VII:**312
  science and technology
    VII:314, 315
  women's status and rights
    VII:388
Eugenics Record Office
  Buck v. Bell **VII:**43
  eugenics **VII:**102
  science and technology
    VII:314
Euphemia (Lennox) **II:**204
Eureka barge **VIII:**165

Europe **IX:***112,* **112–113,** 351*c.*
  See also specific countries
  art and architecture **I:**12,
    13
  cacao **I:**48
  coffee **I:**79–80
  cold war, end of **X:**84
  crowd actions **II:**86
  Delaware **II:**95
  ethnocentrism **II:**121–123
  Farewell Address of George
    Washington **III:**162
  feudalism **I:**129–130
  foreign policy **VI:**133
  horses **I:**169
  immigration **VII:**144;
    IX:155
  invention and technology
    I:184–185
  Islam **I:**189
  Jews **I:**194; **III:**236–237
  Kennan, George F. **IX:**167
  Marshall Plan **IX:**203–204,
    359–361
  Middle East **X:**227
  NATO **IX:**247; **X:**259
  navigation technology
    I:262
  Peace Corps **IX:**256
  plague **I:**294
  population trends **I:**297,
    298
  primogeniture and entail
    II:310
  printing press **I:**303
  slavery **I:**336–338
  smallpox **I:**340
  Soviet Union **IX:**295
  trade, domestic and foreign
    VI:360
  Truman Doctrine **IX:**322,
    359–361
  witches/witchcraft **I:**384,
    385
European Americans
  cities and urban life **III:**92
  Native Americans **III:**311–
    313
  race and race relations
    III:357–358
  Tecumseh **III:**409
  women's status and rights
    III:445–448
European Children's Fund
  VIII:171
European immigration **IX:**204
European Laboratory for Particle
  Physics (CERN) **X:**182
European Recovery Program. *See*
  Marshall Plan
European Space Agency (ESA)
  X:257
Eutaw Springs, Battle of
  III:159*m,* **159–160,** 199, 286
euthanasia **X:**305, 381*c*
Evacuation Day **III:**341
Evangelical Alliance **VI:**335, 347

evangelical Christians **X:124–125**
  Christian Coalition **X:**73–74
  conservative movement
    X:93
  education, homeschooling
    X:112
  ERA **X:**124
  Moral Majority **X:**234
  televangelism **X:**341–342
evangelicalism
  African Americans **IV:**8
  anti-Catholic riots **IV:**22–24
  anti-Masonry **IV:**25
  Baptists **III:**44
  camp meetings **III:**77
  Dow, Lorenzo **IV:**126–127
  Finney, Charles Grandison
    IV:150–151
  Protestantism **II:**315
  religion **IV:**317; **VII:**298,
    299; **VIII:**335
  Whitefield, George **II:**413–
    414
Evangelical Lutheran Ministerium
  of Pennsylvania **II:**212, 246
Evangeline (Longfellow) **IV:**414*c*
evangelism
  Graham, Billy **IX:**138
  McPherson, Aimee Semple
    VII:196
  Moody, Dwight Lyman
    VI:249–250
  religion **VI:**306; **IX:**271, 272
  Sunday, William Ashley, Jr.
    VII:342
Evans, George Henry **IV:**306
Evans, John **V:**443*c*
Evans, Linda **X:**368
Evans, Oliver **IV:**199, 313
Evans, Walker **VIII:***119,* **119–
  120**
  art and architecture **VIII:**30
  photography **VII:**258;
    VIII:296
  popular culture **VIII:**303
Evanston Academy at
  Northwestern University
  VII:342
Evanston College for Ladies
  VI:393
Eveready Hour **VII:**5
Everest, Wesley **VII:**147
Everett, Edward
  ACS **IV:**17
  Harlan, John Marshall
    VI:159
  journalism **IV:**210
  Wilson, Henry **V:**433
Everglades, Florida **IV:**338;
  VIII:181
Evergood, Philip **VIII:**31
Evers, Medgar **IX:**355*c*
  African Americans **IX:**6
  assassinations **X:**34
  race and race relations
    IX:269
Everybody's Magazine **VII:**193

evolution **VI:121–122; VII:**403*c*, 409*c*
  Baldwin, Roger Nash **VII:**31
  Beecher, Henry Ward **VI:**30
  Bryan, William Jennings **VI:**52
  conservatism **VIII:**84
  Darrow, Clarence Seward **VII:**70
  Darwinism and religion **VI:**92, 93
  Democratic Party **VII:**75
  eugenics **VII:**102
  Fiske, John **VI:**128, 129
  Gilman, Daniel Coit **VI:**148
  Hall, Granville Stanley **VI:**158
  Hayden, Ferdinand Vandeveer **VI:**164
  pragmatism **VI:**289
  religion **VI:**306, 307; **VII:**297–299; **X:**306–307
  Royce, Josiah **VI:**318
  science and technology **VI:**325; **VII:**314; **VIII:**352
  Scopes Trial **VII:**316–317
  Social Darwinism **VI:**334
  Sumner, William Graham **VI:**347
Evolution: A Theory in Crisis (Denton) **X:**306
"Evolution of Language, The" (Fiske) **VI:**128
E. W. Clark & Company **V:**93
Ewe **I:125–126**
Ewell, Richard Stoddert **V:135–136**
  Antietam, Battle of **V:**13
  Appomattox campaign **V:**14
  Bull Run/Manassas, First and Second Battles of **V:**51
  Gettysburg, Battle of **V:**166–168
  Longstreet, James **V:**242
  Shenandoah Valley: Jackson's campaign **V:**350
  Wilderness, Battle of the **V:**432
Ewing, Elizabeth **IX:**117
Ewuare the Great (king of Benin) **I:**29
Examination of the Constitution of the United States, An (Coxe) **III:**125
Excelsior Brigade **V:**360
exchange agreements **III:**346
exchange rate **VIII:**325
exclusionary policy **VI:**13
excommunication **I:**218
executions **II:**436*c*
  auto-da-fé **I:**17
  crime and punishment **II:**83–84
  Gabriel's Rebellion **III:**185

prisons **III:**346
witches/witchcraft **I:**384, 385; **II:**419, 420
Executive Boards **III:**116
Executive Office of the President
  Executive Reorganization Act **VIII:**121
  FEPC **VIII:**123
  government **VIII:**153
Executive Order 8802 **VIII:120, 447*c*, 465–466**
  African Americans **VIII:**4
  Brotherhood of Sleeping Car Porters **VIII:**54
  civil rights **VIII:**73
  enemy aliens **VIII:**114–115
  FEPC **VIII:**123
  Freedom Train **IX:**125
  March on Washington Movement **VIII:**227, 228
  NAACP **VIII:**256
  race and race relations **VIII:**319
  Randolph, A. Philip **VIII:**321
  Roosevelt, Franklin D. **VIII:**346–347
Executive Order 8905 **VIII:**65
Executive Order 9066 **VIII:120–121, 447*c*, 466–467**
  ACLU **VIII:**18
  Asian Americans **VIII:**32
  enemy aliens **VIII:**115
  Japanese Americans, relocation of **VIII:**193
  Korematsu v. U.S. **VIII:**203
Executive Order 9808 **IX:**351*c*
Executive Order 9981 **VIII:**54
Executive Order 11246 **X:**208
Executive Order 12612 **X:**131
Executive Order 12630 **X:**290
Executive Order 13083 **X:**131
Executive Order 13112 **X:**290
executive power **III:**107
executive privilege
  Burger, Warren E. **X:**51
  Cox, Archibald, Jr. **X:**95
  U.S. v. Nixon **X:**357–358
  Watergate scandal **X:**367
Executive Reorganization Act **VIII:121–122**
  Congress **VIII:**80
  FCA **VIII:**126
  government **VIII:**153
  liberalism **VIII:**215
  New Deal **VIII:**269
  NRPB **VIII:**260
  presidency **VIII:**309
  Third New Deal **VIII:**393
exemption clauses (Civil War draft laws)
  conscription **V:**91
  governors **V:**172
  New York City draft riots **V:**284
  peace movements **V:**296

plantations **V:**309
Union army **V:**401
exemptions (Selective Training and Service Act of 1940) **VIII:**358
exit polls **X:**117
Exodusters **V:**361; **VI:7, 122–123**
exoticism **VI:**18, 19
expansionism
  Adams-Onís Treaty **IV:**6
  agriculture **IV:**12
  Alamo, The **IV:**14
  American System **IV:**21
  art and architecture **IV:**28
  Ashley, William Henry **IV:**31–33
  Benton, Thomas Hart **IV:**53
  Blaine, James Gillespie **VI:**41
  Canada **VI:**61
  Colt revolver **IV:**102
  conservation/ environmentalism **VI:**81
  Democratic Party **IV:**118
  economy **IV:**130
  education **VI:**107
  environment **VI:**119–120
  Era of Good Feelings **IV:**141
  foreign policy **IV:**153, 155–156; **V:**149; **VI:**134
  Gadsden Purchase **IV:**173
  Guadalupe Hidalgo, Treaty of **IV:**181
  Hawaii **IV:**187
  Houston, Sam **IV:**191
  imperialism **VI:**187
  Indian Removal Act **IV:**197–198
  internal improvements **IV:**202–203
  literature **IV:**229
  Manifest Destiny **IV:**234–236
  Mexican-American War **IV:**251
  migration **IV:**253
  Native Americans **IV:**273–275
  Native Americans in the War of 1812 **IV:**276
  Nullification Controversy **IV:**282
  Oregon Treaty of 1846 **IV:**287
  Ostend Manifesto **V:**289
  panic of 1819 **IV:**293
  Polk, James K. **IV:**302
  popular sovereignty **IV:**304–307
  race and race relations **IV:**309, 311–312
  Smith, Joseph, Jr. **IV:**353
  states' rights **V:**370
  temperance movement **IV:**369
  Texas **IV:**371

Travis, William Barret **IV:**379
Walker, William **V:**423
War of 1812 **IV:**390, 392
Webster-Ashburton Treaty **IV:**394–395
Expatriation Act **VII:103–104, 405*c***
  Cable Act **VII:**47
  immigration **VII:**144
  nativism **VII:**234
Experimental Theatre (Vassar College) **VIII:**135
Experiments and Observations on the Gastric Juice and Physiology of Digestion (Beaumont) **IV:**249
exploration **II:123–124; IV:144–146**
  Amazon River **I:**9
  Applegate, Jesse **IV:**26
  Astor, John Jacob **IV:**33
  Batts, Thomas **II:**34
  Bering, Vitus Jonassen **II:**36
  Bristol **I:**37
  Brulé, Étienne **II:**49
  Cabot, John **I:**43–44
  Cabot, Sebastian **I:**44–46
  Cadamosto, Alvise de **I:**49–50
  Cartier, Jacques **I:**61–63
  Castillo, Diego del **II:**61
  Champlain, Samuel de **II:**62–63
  Clark, William **III:**96–97
  Columbus, Christopher **I:**83–87
  Dias, Bartholomeu **I:**105–106
  Dominicans **II:**101
  Florida **II:**128
  Frémont, John C. **IV:**166–167
  French colonies **II:**135
  French explorations of the Atlantic **I:**133–134
  Frobisher, Martin **I:**134–135
  Fuca, Juan de **II:**139
  Henry the Navigator **I:**160–161
  Hudson, Henry **II:**167–168
  Indians of the desert Southwest **II:**176
  La Salle, René-Robert Cavelier, sieur de **II:**202–203
  Lewis, Meriwether **III:**261–262
  Lewis and Clark Expedition **III:**262–264
  literature **II:**206
  Louisiana **II:**210
  Magellan, Ferdinand **I:**223–224
  Ma Huan **I:**225
  mariners **II:**214

exploration *(continued)*
  Marquette, Jacques **II:**215
  monarchy, British **II:**240
  mountain men **IV:**266–267
  New Mexico **I:**265
  New York **II:**269
  Nicolet, Jean **II:**273
  Norse **I:**272
  Oregon Trail **IV:**285
  Parmenius, Stephen **I:**286–287
  Pennsylvania **II:**285
  Pike, Zebulon Montgomery **IV:**299–300
  Portuguese seaborne empire **I:**299–300
  Powell, John Wesley **VI:**288
  Protestantism **II:**314–315
  Ralegh, Sir Walter **I:**311–312
  Sequeira, Diogo Lopes de **I:**331
  Smith, Jedediah Strong **IV:**350–351
  Walsingham, Sir Francis **I:**382
Explorer 1 (spacecraft) **IX:**296
Explosion (Lichtenstein) **IX:**20
Export-Import Bank **VIII:**325
exports
  agriculture **III:**11; **X:**19
  Continental Congress, First **III:**114
  economy **III:**146; **VII:**83–84
  embargo of 1807 **III:**152
  industrialization **IV:**199–200
  merchant marine **VI:**245
  trade, domestic and foreign **III:**414; **VI:**359, 360
Exquemelin, Alexander Olivier **II:**296
Extracts from the Virginia Charters (Mason) **III:**292
extremist groups **X:**230, 267
Exxon Valdez oil spill **X:**379c
Eyes on Russia (Bourke-White) **VIII:**50
e-zines **X:**220
Ezra Church, Battle of **V:**22

F

FAA. *See* Federal Aviation Administration
Fabian Society **VI:**394
Fable, A (Faulkner) **VIII:**128
FACE. *See* Freedom of Access to Clinic Entrances Act
factionalism **VI:**95, 311
Factor, Max **VII:**65
factories. *See also* industrialization
  Atkinson, Edward **VI:**22
  cities and urban life **V:**65, 66
  Coxe, Tench **III:**125
  homefront **V:**192–193

industrial development **V:**205
Industrial Revolution **III:**225, 226
  population trends **III:**343
  science and technology **V:**343
Factory Act (1819) **IV:**291
factory system **IV:**201, 243
Fair, Laura **VI:**146
Fair American (vessel) **IV:**211
Fairbanks, Douglas **VII:**60, 97
Fairbanks, Richard **II:**304
Fairbanks, Thaddeus **IV:**333
Fairchild Semiconductor **IX:**71
Fair Deal **IX:115–116,** 352c
  Democratic Party **IX:**85
  government, state/local **IX:**137
  New Deal **IX:**242
  States' Rights Party **IX:**299
  Truman, Harry S. **IX:**320
Fair Employment Practices Committee (FEPC) **VIII:123–124**
  African Americans **VIII:**4
  Brotherhood of Sleeping Car Porters **VIII:**54
  civil rights **VIII:**72–73
  Executive Order 8802 **VIII:**120
  Fair Deal **IX:**115
  March on Washington Movement **VIII:**227
  NAACP **VIII:**256
  New Deal **IX:**242
  race and race relations **VIII:**319
  Randolph, A. Philip **VIII:**321
  Roosevelt, Franklin D. **VIII:**347
  Urban League **IX:**325
  White, Walter **VIII:**416
Fairfax, Sally **III:**432
Fairfax Resolves **III:**292
Fair God, The (Wallace) **VI:**381
Fair Housing Amendments Act (1988) **X:**379c
Fair Information practices **X:**88
Fair Labor Standards Act (FLSA) **VIII:124,** 446c
  Adkins v. Children's Hospital **VII:**3
  Black, Hugo L. **VIII:**45
  children **VIII:**67
  Congress **VIII:**80
  government **VIII:**152
  Hillman, Sidney **VIII:**166
  New Deal **VIII:**269
  Perkins, Frances **VIII:**293
  transportation **VIII:**395
fairness doctrine **X:**220, 342
Fair Oaks, Battle of. *See* Seven Pines, Battle of
Fair Play for Cuba Committee **IX:**252

fairs, agricultural **III:161**
Faithful Narrative of the Surprising Work of God (Edwards) **II:**114
Faleiro, Rui **I:**223
Falkland Islands **IV:**261
Falkland Islands war **X:**164
Fall, Albert **VII:**408c
  Harding, Warren Gamaliel **VII:**135
  Native Americans **VII:**233
  Teapot Dome **VII:**351
Fallam, Robert **II:**124
Fallen Timbers, Battle of **III:161–162,** 464c
  Blue Jacket **III:**54
  Cherokee **III:**87
  Glaize, meeting at the **III:**195
  Greenville, Treaty of **III:**200
  Harrison, William Henry **IV:**184
  Jay's Treaty **III:**231
  Knox, Henry **III:**248
  Lewis, Meriwether **III:**261
  Native Americans **III:**314; **IV:**273
  Prophet, the Shawnee **III:**349
  Red Jacket **III:**360
  Wayne, Anthony **III:**434
Fallingwater (Frank Lloyd Wright house) **VII:**395; **VIII:**28, 445c
Fall of Babylon, The (film) **VII:**132
Fallon, George **IX:**159
fallout shelters **IX:**355c
  civil defense **IX:**57
  cold war culture **IX:**65
  hydrogen bomb **IX:**153
  marriage and family **IX:**202
Fall River, Massachusetts **VI:**375; **VII:**231
Falwell, Jerry
  abortion **X:**4
  conservative movement **X:**94
  feminism **X:**134
  Moral Majority **X:**234
  televangelism **X:**342
Family and Medical Leave Act (1993) **X:**80, 128, 380c
Family Entertainment Protection Act **X:**78
Family Law **X:**343 ·
family life **X:127–128.** *See also* marriage and family life
  Asian Americans **X:**33
  baby boomers **X:**39
  feminism **X:**134
Family Limitation (Sanger)
  birth control **VII:**36
  Sanger, Margaret **VII:**312
  women's status and rights **VII:**388
family planning **X:**1, 43

Family Planning Service and Population Research Act (1970) **X:**43
Family Research Council **X:**94
family reunification **X:**32
Family Support Act (FSA) **X:128**
"family values" **X:**128, 214
Famine Emergency Commission **VIII:**173
famines **V:**199
Fandino, Juan de Leon **II:**408
Faneuil Hall **III:**427
Fang **I:**56, **127**
Fannie Mae. *See* Federal National Mortgage Association
Fannin, James **IV:**221, 375
Fanning, Edmund **III:**321
Fanon, Frantz **IX:**40
Fantus, Bernard **VIII:**234
FAP. *See* Federal Art Project
Faraday, Michael **IV:**332, 334
Farazi, Al- **I:**139
Fard, Wallace D.
  Muhammad, Elijah **IX:**226
  Nation of Islam **X:**249
  religion **IX:**273
Far East
  foreign policy **X:**144
  imperialism **VI:**188
  Rice, Condoleezza **X:**310
Farel, Guillaume **I:**53, 54
Farewell Address of George Washington **III:162,** 464c
  Hamilton, Alexander **III:**207
  political parties **III:**338–339
  Washington, George **III:**431
Farewell to Arms, A (Hemingway) **VII:**185–186
Farewell to His Troops (Robert E. Lee) **V:463**
Fargo (film) **X:**279
Farías, Valentín Gómez **IV:**329
Farley, James A. **VIII:124–125**
  Catholics **VIII:**63
  Democratic Party **VIII:**93
  election of 1936 **VIII:**109
  Flynn, Edward J. **VIII:**139
  Irish Americans **VIII:**188
  recession of 1937–1938 **VIII:**324
  religion **VIII:**334
  Roosevelt, Franklin D. **VIII:**345
Farm Aid concerts **X:**20
farm bankruptcy **X:**20
Farm Bloc
  Capper-Volstead Act **VII:**49
  lobbying **VII:**181, 182
  McNary-Haugen Farm Bill **VII:**195, 196
Farm Bureau **IX:**95, 106
farm cooperatives **VII:**6, 8
Farm Credit Administration (FCA) **VIII:125–126**
  Agricultural Adjustment Act **VIII:**6
  agriculture **VIII:**10

HOLC **VIII**:171
Morgenthau, Henry T., Jr.
VIII:244
New Deal **VIII**:269
RFC **VIII**:326
Farmer, James L. **IX**:72–74;
X:**128–129**
Farmer-Labor Party **VII**:**105**
Non-Partisan League
VII:241
politics (1900–1928)
VII:262
Popular Front **VIII**:303–
304
progressivism **VII**:271
radical and labor press
VII:286
rural life **VII**:307
farmers' alliances **VI**:**125–126**
Donnelly, Ignatius Loyola
VI:100
Lease, Mary Elizabeth
Clyens **VI**:220
national banking system
VI:261
Omaha platform **VI**:272
Patrons of Husbandry
VI:278–279
People's Party **VI**:281–283
Simpson, Jerry **VI**:330
Watson, Thomas Edward
VII:380
Farmers Association (South
Carolina) **VI**:358
Farmer's Holiday Association
(FHA) **VIII**:**126**
Farmers Home Administration
VIII:127
farming/farmers. *See* agriculture
and horticulture
farm loans **VII**:8, 407*c*
Farm Mortgage Refinancing Act
VIII:126
Farm Security Administration
(FSA) **VIII**:**127**, 445*c*
advertising **VIII**:1
agriculture **VIII**:10
art and architecture
VIII:30
Bankhead-Jones Farm
Tenant Act **VIII**:39
Evans, Walker **VIII**:119–
120
Lange, Dorothea **VIII**:210
medicine **VIII**:235
New Deal **VIII**:269
photography **VIII**:296
rural areas **VIII**:348
farm subsidies **IX**:8, 353*c*, 356*c*
"farm system" **VIII**:370
Farm Tenancy Committee
VIII:127
Farnsworth, Philo **VII**:151
Farragut, David Glasgow **V**:*137*,
137–138, 444*c*, 445*c*
elections **V**:126
ironclads **V**:207

Mississippi River war **V**:263,
264
Mobile campaign **V**:265
monuments **V**:267
New Orleans, Battle of
V:280, 281
Porter, David Dixon **V**:311
Union navy **V**:405
Vicksburg campaign **V**:417
Welles, Gideon **V**:428
Farragut Monument (Saint-
Gaudens) **VI**:321
Farragut Square (Washington,
D.C.) **V**:267
Farrakhan, Louis A. **X**:**129**, 381*c*
African Americans **X**:14, 15
Hurricane Katrina **X**:174
Muhammad, Elijah **IX**:226
NAACP **X**:245
Nation of Islam **X**:249
race and race relations
X:297
Farrell, James T. **VIII**:188, 189,
219
Farwell, Arthur **VI**:255
Far West
cities and urban life **VI**:69
Crime of '73 **VI**:86
currency issue **VI**:89
fascism
Nazi-Soviet Pact **VIII**:266
OWI **VIII**:286
Popular Front **VIII**:303,
304
propaganda **VIII**:311
Spanish civil war **VIII**:369,
370
Stimson, Henry L.
VIII:375
fashion **V**:**138–139**, *139*; **IX**:**116–
117**, *117*
childhood **IX**:55
homespun **V**:194
New York City **V**:282
teenagers **IX**:314
Zouaves **V**:441
Faster Pussycat! Kill! Kill! (film)
IX:226
fast-food industry **IX**:352*c*
food **IX**:122
GE **IX**:132
McDonald's **IX**:208
"Fast for Life" **IX**:54
Fastow, Andrew **X**:59
Fatah **X**:230
"Fate" (Emerson) **IV**:140
"Father Abraham's Speech"
(Franklin) **II**:301
Father Knows Best
marriage and family **IX**:202
suburbanization/suburbs
IX:306
television **IX**:315
*Fatigue and Efficiency: A Study in
Industry* (Goldmark) **VII**:127
"Fat Man" (atomic bomb)
VIII:166, 227

Faubus, Orval **IX**:**117–118**, 354*c*
*Brown v. Board of
Education* **IX**:44
modern Republicanism
IX:221
segregation **IX**:288
Southern Manifesto **IX**:294
Faulkner, William **V**:240; **VII**:180;
VIII:**127–128**, *128*, 219, 220,
443*c*; **IX**:193, 352*c*
Fauntroy, Walter **X**:23
Fauset, Jessie **VII**:136
Fava, Francesco Saverio, Baron
VI:234
Favrile Glass **VI**:356
Fayette, New York **IV**:119, 319
Fayette County, Pennsylvania
III:187–188
FBI. *See* Federal Bureau of
Investigation
FBI National Academy **VIII**:130
FCA. *See* Farm Credit
Administration
FCC. *See* Federal
Communications Commission
FCDA. *See* Federal Civil Defense
Administration
FDA. *See* Food and Drug
Administration
FDIC. *See* Federal Deposit
Insurance Corporation
*Fear God and Take Your Own
Part* (Roosevelt) **VII**:267
Feast of the Dead **I**:172
FEC. *See* Federal Election
Commission
FECA. *See* Federal Election
Campaign Act
Federal Aid Highway Act (1956).
See Interstate Highway Act
of 1956
Federal-Aid Highway
Amendments (1974) **X**:130
Federal Aid Road Act **VII**:28,
340
Federal Art Project (FAP)
VIII:29–30, **128–129**, *129*,
332
Federal Aviation Administration
(FAA) **IX**:28, 354*c*
federal budget. *See* budget,
federal
Federal Bureau of Investigation
(FBI) **VII**:409*c*; **VIII**:**129–
130**
Abscam **X**:5–6
America First Committee
VIII:17
anticommunism **VIII**:22
black market **VIII**:46
Black Panthers **IX**:41
Branch Davidians **X**:46
Carmichael, Stokely **IX**:50
CIA **IX**:51
espionage **VIII**:117
FCC **VIII**:131
gays and lesbians **IX**:131

Hoover, J. Edgar **IX**:149–
150
HUAC **IX**:150, 151
impeachment of Richard M.
Nixon **X**:178
intelligence **VIII**:186–187
Japanese Americans,
relocation of **VIII**:194
Mann Act **VII**:190
MFDP **IX**:220
narcotics **X**:243
OPA **VIII**:282
OSS **VIII**:284
presidency **VII**:269
Reno, Janet **X**:309
Robeson, Paul **VIII**:342
Ruckelshaus, William D.
X:312
Selective Service **VIII**:357
terrorism **X**:347
U.S. v. Nixon **X**:358
Federal Cigarette Labeling and
Advertising Act (1965) **X**:351
Federal Civil Defense
Administration (FCDA) **IX**:56,
57
Federal Communications
Commission (FCC) **VIII**:**130–
132**, *131*, 444*c*
censorship **VIII**:65
New Deal **VIII**:269
news media **VIII**:272
radio **VIII**:321
science, invention, and
technology **VII**:151;
X:319
television **X**:342
Welles, Orson **VIII**:415
Federal Council of Churches
VI:335; **VII**:297
Federal Council on Negro Affairs
VIII:45
federal debt **VII**:379
Federal Deposit Insurance
Corporation (FDIC) **VIII**:**132**,
444*c*
banking **VIII**:40
Banking Act (1933) **VIII**:40,
41
Banking Act (1935) **VIII**:41
marriage and family
VIII:231
monetary policy **VIII**:243
New Deal **VIII**:269
Federal Election Campaign Act
(FECA) **X**:376*c*, 377*c*
campaign finance **X**:63
PACs **X**:274–275
political parties **X**:277
Federal Election Commission
(FEC)
campaign finance **X**:63, 64
Christian Coalition **X**:74
PACs **X**:275
Federal Emergency Management
Agency (FEMA)
Bush, George W. **X**:56

Federal Emergency Management
Agency *(continued)*
DHS **X:**167, 168
Hurricane Katrina **X:**173–
174
Federal Emergency Relief Act
(FERA) **VIII:**235
Federal Emergency Relief
Administration (FERA)
VIII:132–133, 444*c*
Byrnes, James F. **VIII:**60
cities and urban life **VIII:**69
Congress **VIII:**79
conservatism **VIII:**84
CWA **VIII:**74
elderly **VIII:**108
First New Deal **VIII:**138
FSA **VIII:**127
Hopkins, Harry L. **VIII:**176
New Deal **VIII:**269
NYA **VIII:**262
relief **VIII:**332
Resettlement Administration
VIII:338
RFC **VIII:**325
Social Security Act **VIII:**363
WPA **VIII:**425
Federal Employee Loyalty
Program **IX:119,** 351*c*
anticommunism **IX:**14
Truman, Harry S. **IX:**320
Truman Doctrine **IX:**322
Federal Energy Administration
X:122
Federal Farm Board **VIII:**443*c*
Agricultural Marketing Act
VIII:8
FCA **VIII:**125–126
Hoover presidency
VIII:173, 174
McNary-Haugen Farm Bill
VII:195
Morgenthau, Henry T., Jr.
VIII:244
Federal Farm Credit Board
VIII:126
Federal Farm Loan Act **VII:106,**
407*c*
agriculture **VII:**8
New Freedom **VII:**236
rural life **VII:**306
Wilson, Thomas Woodrow
VII:383
Federal Farm Loan Board
VII:106; **VIII:**125–126
federal funding
abortion **X:**3, 4
birth control **X:**43, 44
NEA/NEH **X:**245–246
stem cell research **X:**335–
336
*Webster v. Reproductive
Health Services* **X:**368
federal government. *See*
government
Federal Highway Act (1921)
VII:28

Federal Home Loan Bank Act
VIII:170, 174
Federal Housing Administration
(FHA) **VIII:133–134,** 445*c;*
IX:119–120
business **X:**60
Democratic Party **IX:**85
Eccles, Marriner S.
VIII:101
Federal National Mortgage
Association **VIII:**135
housing **VIII:**177
Italian Americans **VIII:**191
New Deal **VIII:**269
RFC **VIII:**326
shopping centers **IX:**290
suburbanization/suburbs
VIII:379, 380; **IX:**305
USHA **VIII:**404
federal income tax. *See* income
tax, federal
Federal Information Act (1974)
X:129–130, 377*c*
Federal Intelligence Surveillance
Act (FISA) **X:**359
federalism **X:130–131,** 230, 290
Federalism Impact Assessments
X:130, 131
Federalist Papers **III:162–163,**
463*c*
Federalists **III:**166
Hamilton, Alexander
III:206
Jay, John **III:**229
journalism **III:**240
Madison, James **III:**283
political parties **III:**338
Supreme Court **III:**403
Federalist Party **III:164–165,**
464*c*
Adams, John **III:**6
Adams, John Quincy **IV:**5
Adams, Samuel **III:**8
Alien and Sedition Acts
III:14
Amendment, Twelfth **III:**16,
17
American Revolution
III:18
Ames, Fisher **III:**19
anti-Federalists **III:**23, 24
artisans **III:**35
Bache, Benjamin Franklin
III:39
Bank of the United States,
First **III:**41
Bill of Rights **III:**51
Callender, James T. **III:**74
Carroll of Carrollton,
Charles **III:**82
cities and urban life **III:**90
citizenship **III:**93–94
Clinton, DeWitt **III:**97
Connecticut Wits **III:**104
debt, national **III:**132
Democratic Party **IV:**116–
117

Democratic-Republican
Party **III:**136
Drayton, William H. **IV:**127
Dwight, Timothy **III:**143
election of 1800 **III:**149–
151
election of 1828 **IV:**135
embargo of 1807 **III:**152
French Revolution **III:**179
Fries's Rebellion **III:**180,
181
Hamilton, Alexander
III:207, 208
Hartford Convention
IV:186–187
immigration **III:**221
impeachment **III:**222
Industrial Revolution
III:226
Jackson, Andrew **IV:**206
journalism **III:**240, 241
King, Rufus **III:**245
Lee, Henry **III:**259
Louisiana Purchase **III:**273
Lyon, Matthew **III:**277
Madison, James **III:**283,
284
Marbury v. Madison
III:285
Marshall, John **III:**289, 290
Martin, Luther **III:**291
Morse, Jedidiah **III:**307
music **III:**309
Otis, Harrison Gray **III:**326
panic of 1819 **IV:**294
Phyfe, Duncan **III:**334
Pickering, Timothy **III:**335
Pinckney, Charles
Cotesworth **III:**336
political parties **III:**338, 339
popular culture **III:**341
Quasi War **III:**353
Randolph, John **III:**359
religious liberty **III:**363,
364
riots **III:**372
St. Clair, Arthur **III:**378
states' rights **III:**397
Taney, Roger B. **IV:**365
tariffs **III:**406
Virginia dynasty **III:**425
War of 1812 **IV:**390
Washington, D.C. **III:**428
Washington Benevolent
Societies **III:**433
Webster, Daniel **IV:**393
Webster, Noah **III:**434
West Point **III:**437
XYZ affair **III:**451
Federalists **III:165–166**
Bill of Rights **III:**50
citizenship **III:**93
Constitution, ratification of
the **III:**104–106
Constitutional Convention
III:109
Coxe, Tench **III:**125

Democratic Party **IV:**117
Federalist Party **III:**164
Madison, James **III:**283
political parties **III:**338
Shays's Rebellion **III:**388
Federal Land Banks
agriculture **VII:**8
Federal Farm Loan Act
VII:106
rural life **VII:**306
Federal Marriage Amendment
X:78
Federal Music Project (FMP)
VIII:134–135, 250, 251, 332
Federal National Mortgage
Association (Fannie Mae)
VIII:135, 171; **X:**60–61
Federal One
FAP **VIII:**129
FMP **VIII:**134
FTP **VIII:**135
FWP **VIII:**136
Federal Open Market Committee
VIII:41
Federal Power Commission **X:**122
Federal Radio Act **VIII:**321
Federal Radio Commission
VIII:130–131
Federal Reserve Act **VII:107–
108,** 406*c*
Banking Act (1935) **VIII:**41
Democratic Party **VII:**74
economy **VII:**83, 85
elections **VII:**91
New Freedom **VII:**236
Wilson, Thomas Woodrow
VII:383, 384
Federal Reserve Banks **VIII:**40
Federal Reserve Board
banking **VIII:**40
Banking Act (1933) **VIII:**40,
41
Banking Act (1935) **VIII:**41
Eccles, Marriner S.
VIII:101
economy **X:**109
Federal Reserve Act
VII:107
Great Depression **VIII:**157
monetary policy **VIII:**243
New Freedom **VII:**236
SEC **VIII:**357
stock market crash **VIII:**376
Wilson, Thomas Woodrow
VII:383
Federal Reserve System
business and government
VI:57
economy **X:**109, 111
FDIC **VIII:**132
national banking system
VI:261
Federal Steel Company
Industrial Revolution,
Second **VI:**192
steel industry **VII:**336
U.S. Steel **VII:**365

Federal style **III:**27
Federal Suffrage Association
VI:399
Federal Theatre Project (FTP)
VIII:*135*, **135–136**
popular culture **VIII:**303
relief **VIII:**332
Welles, Orson **VIII:**414
WPA **VIII:**425, 426
Federal Trade Commission (FTC)
VII:108
advertising **X:**7
business **IX:**46
Federal Trade Commission
Act **VII:**108
SEC **VIII:**356
Federal Trade Commission Act
VII:108, 406*c*
advertising **VII:**4
Democratic Party **VII:**74
New Freedom **VII:**236
progressivism **VII:**271
Wilson, Thomas Woodrow
VII:383
Federal Water Pollution Control
Act (1972) **X:**290
Federal Water Quality
Administration **IX:**139
Federal Writers' Project (FWP)
VIII:136–137
literature **VIII:**220–221
music **VIII:**250
relief **VIII:**332
Wright, Richard **VIII:**437
Federated Press **VII:**286, 375
Federated Trades of San Diego
VII:118
Federation of American Zionists
VI:205
Federation of Colored Catholics
VIII:64
Federation of Islamic Associations
X:189
Federation of Organized Trades
and Labor Unions of the
United States (FOOTALU)
VI:168, 215–216
feebleminded
eugenics **VII:**103
intelligence tests **VII:**148
Racial Integrity Act
VII:284
Feingold, Russell **X:**63
Feke, Robert **II:125**, 165
Fell, Margaret **II:**285, 321
Fellowship for Christian Social
Order **VII:**115, 116
Fellowship of Reconciliation
VII:108–109, 133, 257
felonies **X:**97
Fels-Naptha soap **VI:**2
FEMA. *See* Federal Emergency
Management Agency
Female Academy (Middlebury,
Vermont) **IV:**400
female antislavery societies **IV:**9,
147–148, 161

Female Anti-Slavery Society of
Philadelphia **IV:**265, 341
Female Medical College **VI:**400
Female Quixote, The (Lennox)
II:204
feme covert/feme sole **II:**422;
III:446
Feminine Mystique, The (Friedan)
IX:355*c*
counterculture **IX:**78
family life **X:**127
feminism **X:**132
Friedan, Betty **IX:**126, 127
literature **IX:**194
NOW **IX:**236; **X:**247
women's status and rights
IX:346; **X:**371
feminism **II:**47; **X:131–135**
abolitionism **V:**3
Brennan, William J., Jr.
X:48
conservative movement
X:93
counterculture **IX:**78
Dickinson, Anna E. **V:**111
family life **X:**127
fashion **V:**139
Fifteenth Amendment
V:141, 142
Fourteenth Amendment
V:157
Friedan, Betty **IX:**126–127
Gilman, Charlotte Perkins
VII:125
Ginsburg, Ruth Bader
X:152
Harper, Frances Ellen
Watkins **VI:**160
NOW **IX:**236; **X:**247, 248
NWP **VII:**230
Paul, Alice **VII:**254
political parties **X:**276
pornography **X:**284
pro-life/pro-choice
movements **X:**289
religion **IX:**273
Sanger, Margaret **VII:**312–
313
spiritualism **IV:**355
Spock, Benjamin **IX:**297
Steinem, Gloria **X:**334
Stewart, Maria **IV:**356–357
Thomas, M. Carey **VI:**356
women's status and rights
V:436–437; **IX:**346, 348;
X:371
Fenians **VI:**61
Fenno, John **III:**180, 240, 463*c*
Fenton, William **VII:**217
Fenwick, John **II:**261
FEPC. *See* Fair Employment
Practices Committee
FERA. *See* Federal Emergency
Relief Administration
FERA (Federal Emergency Relief
Act) **VIII:**235
Ferber, Edna **VII:**180

Ferdinand VII (king of Spain)
IV:329
Ferdinand and Isabella (king and
queen of Castile and Aragón)
I:127–128, *128*, 396*c*
Cabot, Sebastian **I:**45
Castile **I:**66
Cathay **I:**68
Columbus, Bartholomew
I:83
Columbus, Christopher
I:84–86
corregidor **I:**93
Franciscans **I:**133
Jews **I:**194–195
Peter Martyr **I:**290
Reconquista **I:**314
Tordesillas, Treaty of **I:**367
Ferguson, Patrick **III:**246–247
Ferlinghetti, Lawrence **IX:**78,
195
Fermi, Enrico
hydrogen bomb **IX:**152
Manhattan Project **VIII:**227
Oppenheimer, J. Robert
IX:251
Fernandez-Armesto, Felipe **I:**85
Fernando Póo **I:**129
Ferraro, Geraldine A. **X:**134, **135**,
234, 378*c*
ferries **II:**394
Ferris wheel **VI:**403
fertility **II:125–126**
fertilizers **X:**20
Fessenden, William Pitt **V:**327
festivals **I:**21
fetal tissue research **X:**4, 5
Fetherstone, Henry **I:**306
feudalism **I:129–130**
entail **I:**123
John III **I:**197
Parliament **I:**286
feudal privileges
North Carolina **II:**274
primogeniture and entail
II:310
proprietary colonies **II:**313
South Carolina **II:**369
Feulner, Edwin J. **X:**93, 349
Fever River **IV:**223
Fez **I:**176
FHA. *See* Federal Housing
Administration
FHA (Farmer's Holiday
Association) **VIII:**126
Fhimah, Al Amin Khalifa **X:**383*c*
fiat currency
banking **V:**27, 28
economy **V:**122
greenbacks **V:**177–178
Fibber McGee and Molly
VIII:301
fiber optics **X:**319, 377*c*
fiction **X:**211
fiefdoms **I:**129–130; **II:**310
Field **X:**211
Field, Cyrus West **V:**443*c*; **VI:**126

Field, David Dudley, Jr. **VI:**126
Field, James G. **VI:**282
Field, Marshall **VI:**96
Field, Stephen Johnson **VI:**101,
126–127, 348
Fielden, Samuel **VI:**169
field fortifications **V:139–141,**
140
Field Foundation **IX:**190
Fielding, Fred F. **X:**311
Fielding, Lewis **X:**365
field music **V:**272, 273
Field of Dreams (film) **X:**236
Fields, Annie Adams **VI:**203
Fields, James T. **VI:**202
Fields, W. C.
entertainment, popular
VII:95
movies **VIII:**245
vaudeville **VII:**368
Fieldston School **VI:**121
15th Air Force, U.S. **VIII:**27
Fifteenth Amendment **V:141–**
142, 446*c*, 464; **VI:**407*c*;
VIII:448*c*
African Americans **VI:**5
American Anti-Slavery
Society **IV:**16
Anthony, Susan B. **VI:**16
Civil Rights Act (1957)
IX:58–59
Douglass, Frederick **V:**116
elections **V:**125
elections, conduct of **VI:**113
grandfather clause **VI:**152
Harrison, Benjamin **VI:**161
Hayes, Rutherford B.
VI:166, 168
Hoar, George F. **VI:**173
NAACP **VII:**224
NWSA **V:**277
race and race relations
IV:309
Reconstruction **V:**326
Republican Party **V:**334
segregation **VII:**319
Thirteenth Amendment
V:388
Truth, Sojourner **V:**394
U.S. v. Cruikshank **V:**411,
412
women's status and rights
V:437; **VI:**399
Fifth Amendment
Army-McCarthy hearings
IX:18
Bill of Rights **III:**51
Cooper Union speech **V:**94
*Heart of Atlanta Motel v.
U.S.* **IX:**145, 146
Hollywood Ten **IX:**147
HUAC **IX:**150–151
Kelo v. City of New London
X:195
Marshall, Thurgood **IX:**203
Miranda v. Arizona **IX:**218–
219

Fifth Amendment (*continued*)
 Scalia, Antonin **X**:316
 Supreme Court **IV**:362;
  VII:343; **VIII**:382
 Warren Court **IX**:338
5th Amphibious Corps **VIII**:386
Fifth Army, U.S. **VIII**:191
Fifth Cavalry **VI**:76
"fifth column" **VIII**:330
Fifth Fleet (U.S. Navy) **VIII**:202
Fifth Military District **V**:184
Fifth War Loan Drive **VIII**:138
55th Massachusetts Colored
 Regiment **V**:143
"fifty-four forty or fight" **IV**:287
54th Massachusetts Regiment
 V:142–144, *143,* 445*c*
 African-American regiments
  V:4
 Brown, William Wells **V**:46
 Carney, William Harvey
  V:55
 Douglass, Frederick **V**:116
 ladies aid societies **V**:227
 Medal of Honor **V**:255
 monuments **V**:268
Fight for the Waterhole
 (Remington) **VI**:310
Fighting 99th Pursuit Squadron
 VIII:3–4
Figueroa, José **IV:148–149**
Fiji Islands **IV**:400
Filene, Edward **VI**:96
Filene's **VI**:96
file sharing **X**:239–240
filibuster (legislative obstruction)
 X:320
filibustering (military expeditions)
 V:144–145
 Cuba **IV**:111–112; **VI**:87
 Fillmore, Millard **IV**:150
 foreign policy **IV**:156
 Lamar, Mirabeau B. **IV**:222
 Manifest Destiny **IV**:235
 Ostend Manifesto **V**:290
 Walker, William **V**:423
Filipino Americans **X**:32, 33
Filipino insurrection **VI:127–128,**
 412*c*
 Aguinaldo, Emilio **VII**:8–9
 Anti-Imperialist League
  VI:17
 Army Act **VII**:22
 Atkinson, Edward **VI**:22
 Hay, John Milton **VI**:164
 McKinley, William **VI**:241
 Spanish-American War
  VI:341
Filipino Revolution **IX**:256
Fillmore, Millard **IV:**149, **149–**
 150, 415*c*
 Compromise of 1850
  IV:104
 Deseret, State of **IV**:120
 foreign policy **IV**:156
 Frémont, John C. **IV**:167
 immigration **IV**:196

Know-Nothing Party **IV**:214
 Mormon Church **VI**:252
 nativism **V**:280
 Perry, Matthew Calbraith
  IV:298
 Republican Party **IV**:322
 Taylor, Zachary **IV**:368
 Webster, Daniel **IV**:394
 Whigs **IV**:397–398
film. *See* movie industry; *specific*
 films
Filson, John **III**:56
Final Settlement with Respect to
 Germany, Treaty on **X**:379*c*
finance. *See* banking
financial bailouts. *See* bailouts
Finland
 Nazi-Soviet Pact **VIII**:266
 Soviet-American relations
  VIII:368
 Versailles, Treaty of **VII**:370
Finley, Clement A. **V**:256, 257
Finney, Charles Grandison
 IV:150–151
 Foster, Abigail Kelley
  IV:161
 religion **IV**:317
 Second Great Awakening
  IV:337
 Weld, Theodore Dwight
  IV:395
firearms **II**:436*c. See also* gun
 control; muskets; rifles
 AEF **VII**:10
 Dahlgren, John A. B. **V**:101
 forts **II**:133
 fur trade **II**:142
 Great Plains Indians **II**:157
 industrial development
  V:204
 Industrial Revolution
  III:225–226
 New Spain, northern
  frontier of **III**:318
 NRA **X**:248–249
 Supreme Court **X**:339
 Whitney, Eli **III**:442
fire departments **III**:91; **V**:67
fire-eaters **V:145–146**
 secession **V**:344, 345
 Wigfall, Louis T. **V**:431
 Yancey, William Lowndes
  V:439
fire inspection **VI**:22
fire insurance **III**:227
Fire Island, New York **IV**:169
Fire Next Time, The (Baldwin)
 IX:35, 194
fireships **I**:344
fireside chats **VIII:137–138,**
 447*c*
 banking **VIII**:40
 Emergency Banking Act of
  1933 **VIII**:113
 Lend-Lease **VIII**:211
 New Deal **VIII**:269
 news media **VIII**:272

popular culture **VIII**:301
 radio **VIII**:320
 Roosevelt, Franklin D.
  VIII:345
 scrap drives **VIII**:354
 technology **VIII**:389
Firestone Company **X**:37, 203
Firing Line **X**:50
1st South Carolina Volunteer
 Infantry **V**:189
1st U.S. Dragoons **IV**:241
First Amendment **VIII**:446*c*;
 X:376*c,* 378*c,* 379*c,* 382*c. See*
 also freedom of speech; freedom
 of the press; free speech fights
 abolitionism **V**:3
 advertising **X**:7
 Alien and Sedition Acts
  III:14
 Army-McCarthy hearings
  IX:18
 Bill of Rights **III**:51
 Brandeis, Louis Dembitz
  VII:42
 Brennan, William J., Jr. **X**:47
 campaign finance **X**:63, 64
 censorship **VIII**:65, 66;
  X:70, 71
 civil liberties **VII**:57, 58;
  VIII:71
 Engel v. Vitale **IX**:107
 flag burning **X**:135, 136
 Hollywood Ten **IX**:147, 148
 Holmes, Oliver Wendell
  VII:141
 HUAC **IX**:150
 Jews **III**:237
 Madison, James **III**:282
 McCreary County v. ACLU/
  Van Orden v. Perry
  X:216
 PACs **X**:275
 Pentagon Papers **X**:272
 pornography **X**:283, 284
 religion **III**:361; **X**:307
 religious liberty **III**:364
 Schenck v. U.S. **VII**:313
 Supreme Court **VII**:343–
  344; **VIII**:384; **X**:339
 Warren, Earl **IX**:338
First Army, U.S. **VIII**:50–51, 55
First Great Awakening
 Anglican Church **III**:21
 Baptists **III**:44
 religion **III**:360, 362
 religious liberty **III**:362–
  363
 Scots-Irish **III**:386
First Massachusetts Heavy
 Artillery Regiment **VII**:260
First Modern Suite (MacDowell)
 VI:409*c*
First National Conference of
 Chicanas **IX**:348
First New Deal **VIII:138**
 antimonopoly **VIII**:23
 Brain Trust **VIII**:51

Congress **VIII**:79
 conservatism **VIII**:84
 Coughlin, Father Charles E.
  VIII:88
 economy **VIII**:104
 Executive Reorganization
  Act **VIII**:121
 FERA **VIII**:132
 liberalism **VIII**:215
 Long, Huey P. **VIII**:222
 Moley, Raymond C.
  VIII:243
 National Recovery
  Administration **VIII**:259
 New Deal **VIII**:269, 270
 NIRA **VIII**:256
 PWA **VIII**:314
 relief **VIII**:332
 Roosevelt, Franklin D.
  VIII:345
 Schechter Poultry
  Corporation v. U.S.
  VIII:351
 Second New Deal **VIII**:356
 Social Security Act
  VIII:363
 Wallace, Henry A. **VIII**:411
First Security Corporation
 VIII:101
First Texas Heavy Artillery **V**:255
First Virginia Cavalry **V**:270, 271
FISA (Federal Intelligence
 Surveillance Act) **X**:359
fiscal conservatives **VII**:299, 301
fiscal policy **VIII:138–139**
 Eccles, Marriner S.
  VIII:101
 Economic Bill of Rights
  VIII:102
 economy **VIII**:104
 Full Employment Bill
  VIII:145
 government **VIII**:154
 Hopkins, Harry L. **VIII**:176
 Keynesianism **VIII**:200,
  201
 liberalism **VIII**:215–216
 mobilization **VIII**:242
 monetary policy **VIII**:244
 Morgenthau, Henry T., Jr.
  VIII:244
 New Deal **VIII**:269, 270
 NRPB **VIII**:261
 postwar planning **VIII**:306
 recession of 1937–1938
  VIII:324
 taxation **VIII**:386–388
 Third New Deal **VIII**:393
 TNEC **VIII**:391
 unemployment **VIII**:400
 World War II **VIII**:428
 World War II home front
  VIII:434
Fischl, Eric **X**:31
Fish, Hamilton
 Canada **VI**:61
 foreign policy **V**:151

Grant, Ulysses S. **V:**175
  Santo Domingo, proposed
    annexation of **VI:**323
  Virginius affair **VI:**377
  Washington, Treaty of
    VI:385
Fisher, Bernice **IX:**72
Fisher, Carrie **X:**279
Fisher, Fred **IX:**18
Fisher, Irving **VIII:**243
Fisheries, U.S. Bureau of
  IX:50–51
Fisher's Hill **V:**352
fishing **II:***126,* **126–127**
  Acadians **II:**2
  Aleut **II:**17
  Algonquin **II:**18
  animals **II:**22
  cod **I:**76–77
  Columbia River **IV:**102
  Delaware Indians **II:**96–97
  environment **II:**119
  food **II:**130
  French colonies **II:**135
  Iberville, Pierre Le Moyne,
    sieur d' **II:**173
  Iroquois **I:**185
  Maine **II:**213
  mariners **II:**214
  Mount Vernon **II:**245
  Newfoundland **II:**258
  Northwest Coast Indians
    II:275
  Passamaquoddy **I:**287
  recreation **VIII:**327
fishing rights **VI:**407*c*
  Bayard, Thomas Francis
    VI:27
  Native Americans **X:**250
  Washington, Treaty of
    VI:385
Fisk, Clinton Bowen **VI:**111, 296
Fisk, James **V:**446*c*
  Bowles, Samuel **VI:**43
  corruption, political **VI:**83
  Gould, Jay **VI:**151
  violence and lawlessness
    VI:375
Fiske, John **VI:128–129,** 408*c*
  Darwinism and religion
    VI:93
  Eliot, Charles William
    VI:114
  religion **VI:**306
  Social Darwinism **VI:**334
Fiske, Robert B., Jr. **X:**380*c*
  Clinton, Hillary Rodham
    X:77
  Clinton, William J. **X:**82
  independent counsel **X:**179
Fisk University **V:**446*c*
  education, higher **VI:**111
  education, philanthropy and
    VI:112
  music **VI:**255
  race and race relations
    VIII:318

Fisk University Jubilee Singers
  VI:7, 255
Fitch, Clyde **VI:**355
Fitchburg, Massachusetts **IV:**314
Fitchburg Railroad **IV:**316
Fithian, Philip **II:**112
Fitzgerald, Ella **VIII:**195
Fitzgerald, F. Scott **VII:**180, 186,
  186; **VIII:**189, 220; **IX:**192
Fitzgerald, John "Honey Fitz"
  IX:169
Fitzgerald, Patrick **X:**179
Fitzgerald, Zelda **VII:***186*
Fitzhugh, George **V:146–147,**
  239, 362
Fitzpatrick, John **VII:**337,
  338–339
Fitzpatrick, Thomas
  Astor, John Jacob **IV:**35
  Bidwell, John **IV:**56
  Bridger, James **IV:**64
  Fort Laramie **IV:**156
  mountain men **IV:**266
Fitzsimmons, Frank **IX:**311
Five Civilized Tribes **IV:**412*c*
  Cherokee **IV:**85
  Chickasaw **IV:**86
  Choctaw **IV:**86
  cotton culture **IV:**108
  Creek **IV:**109
  Dawes Severalty Act **VI:**93
  Indian Removal Act **IV:**197
  Jackson, Andrew **IV:**207
  Native Americans **IV:**275;
    V:278, 279
  religion **IV:**317
  slavery **IV:**346–347
  Trail of Tears **IV:**377
Five Dollar Day
  Americanization **VII:**13
  economy **VII:**84
  welfare capitalism **VII:**380
Five Forks, Battle of **V:147**
  Appomattox campaign **V:**14
  Appomattox Court House,
    Virginia **V:**15
  Chamberlain, Joshua L.
    V:60
  Custer, George A. **V:**99
  Lee, Robert E. **V:**232
  Sheridan, Philip H. **V:**353
Five Nations of the Iroquois
  Confederation. *See* Iroquois
  Indians
"Five of Hearts Club" **VI:**208
Five-Power Pact (1922) **VII:**379
527 groups **X:**64, 275
Flack, Audrey **X:**31
Flacks, Dick **IX:**260
flag, U.S. **III:**374
flag burning **X:135–136,** *136,*
  379*c*
  Brennan, William J., Jr.
    X:48
  Supreme Court **X:**339
  White, Byron R. **X:**369
Flagler, Henry M. **VII:**335

Flag Protection Act (1989) **X:**136
flags. *See* battle flags
Flanagan, Hallie **VIII:**135, 136
Flanagan, John **VI:**359
Flanders **I:**240
Flanders campaign **III:**215
"Flapper Jane" (Bliven) **VII:430–
  432**
Flash Gordon (TV series) **IX:**287
flatboats **V:**262
Flathead Indians **II:127–128**
  Bridger, James **IV:**64
  Lee, Jason **IV:**224
  Whitman, Marcus **IV:**398
Flathead Lake **IV:**350
Flatiron Building (New York City)
  VI:55
Flat Swamps, Virginia **IV:**380
Flaubert, Gustave **VI:**200, 225
fleas **I:**293–294
Fleet Marine Force **VIII:**229
Fleming, Alexander
  agriculture **VIII:**10
  medicine **VIII:**234
  miracle drugs **IX:**218
Fleming, J. L. **VI:**388
Fletcher, Alice **V:**255
Fletcher, William **V:**239
Fletcher v. Peck **III:**466*c*
  Marshall, John **III:**291
  Supreme Court **III:**403
  Yazoo claims **III:**454
Flexner, Abraham **VI:**244;
  VII:199–200, 329
Flexner, Bernard **VII:**31
Flexner, Eleanor **VII:**223
flex time **X:**128
Flint, Michigan **VIII:**206
flintlock muskets **V:**358
Florence, Italy
  Italian campaign **VIII:**191
  Laudonnière, René de
    I:208
  Leonardo da Vinci **I:**211
  Michelangelo **I:**243
  World War II European
    theater **VIII:**431
Florentine Codex **I:**130
  Aztecs **I:**20
  Nahuatl **I:**258
  Sahagún, Bernardino de
    I:323
Florida **I:130–131,** 396*c,* 397*c;*
  II:128–130, *129;* **III:166–167,**
  462*c,* 464*c;* **IV:151–153,** 152*m,*
  411*c,* 413*c*
  Adams-Onís Treaty **IV:**6
  Apalachee **I:**11
  architecture **II:**25
  Blount, William **III:**53
  Cabeza de Vaca, Álvar
    Núñez **I:**39
  Calusa **I:**52–53
  Caroline, Fort **I:**61
  cities and urban life **X:**75
  Creek **III:**126
  Cuba **IV:**111; **VI:**87

Drake, Sir Francis **I:**112
economy **IV:**130
election of 1840 **IV:**138
elections, presidential
  X:117–118
embargo of 1807 **III:**152
Era of Good Feelings **IV:**141
FBI **VIII:**130
foreign affairs **III:**168, 169
foreign policy **IV:**153, 154
Fort Mose **II:**132
French explorations of the
  Atlantic **I:**133, 134
Gore, Albert, Jr. **X:**157
Horseshoe Bend, Battle of
  IV:190
Hurston, Zora Neale
  VIII:181
Indian Removal Act **IV:**197
Jackson, Andrew **IV:**206
Jefferson, Joseph, III
  VI:202
Jim Crow laws **VI:**204
Le Moyne, Jacques **I:**209–
  210
Liberia **VI:**223
Louisiana Purchase **III:**273
Mallory, Stephen R. **V:**247
Massachusetts Emigrant Aid
  Society **IV:**243
migration **IV:**254; **VIII:**239
Monroe, James **IV:**259
Narváez, Pánfilo de **I:**259
Native Americans **II:**253;
  III:311; **IV:**274
Native Americans in the War
  of 1812 **IV:**277, 278
Oglethorpe, James Edward
  II:278
Osceola **IV:**289
Paris, Treaty of (1763)
  III:331
Paris, Treaty of (1783)
  III:332
Pinckney Treaty **III:**336,
  337
Ponce de León, Juan **I:**296
population trends **X:**283
Proclamation of 1763
  III:348
public land policy **IV:**305
race and race relations
  VIII:317
railroads **IV:**316
Randolph, John **III:**359
Reno, Janet **X:**308
St. Augustine **II:**341–342
science and technology
  III:385
segregation **VII:**320
Seminole **IV:**338
Seminole War, First/Second
  IV:339
Soto, Hernando de **I:**342
Stono Rebellion **II:**377
Submerged Lands Act
  (1953) **IX:**305

Florida *(continued)*
   Sunbelt **VIII:**380; **X:**338
   Taylor, Zachary **IV:**367, 368
   Texas **IV:**371
   Thevet, André **I:**358
   Timucua **I:**360
   tobacco suits **X:**352
   War of 1812 **IV:**390
   War of Jenkins' Ear **II:**408, 409
Florida, CSS **V:**151
flour milling **VI:129–130**
Flower, Enoch **II:**112
"flower children" **IX:**244
Flowers, Gennifer **X:**194
flowery wars **I:131–132**
   Aztecs **I:**18
   Cuauhtémoc **I:**100
   Huitzilopochtli **I:**171
   Tlacacla **I:**361
   Tlaxcala **I:**362
Floyd, Charles Arthur "Pretty Boy" **IX:**149
Floyd, John **IV:**277
FLSA. *See* Fair Labor Standards Act
Flushing Meadows Park (Queens, New York) **IX:**244, 246
flute ships **I:**184
Flyer I (airplane) **VII:***150*
Flying Dutchmen **V:**166
Flynn, Edward J. **VIII:139**
   Catholics **VIII:**63
   Democratic Party **VIII:**94
   Irish Americans **VIII:**188
Flynn, Elizabeth Gurley **VII:109–110,** *110,* 405*c*
   Baldwin, Roger Nash **VII:**31
   free speech fights **VII:**117–118
   Haywood, William Dudley **VII:**137
   IWW **VII:**147
   Lawrence Strike **VII:**174
   New Unionism **VII:**238
   Paterson Strike **VII:**253
   Sanger, Margaret **VII:**312
FMP. *See* Federal Music Project
FNLA (Frente Nacional de Libertação de Angola) **X:**85
FOIA. *See* Freedom of Information Act
Foley, Mark **X:**151, 171
Foley, Thomas S. **X:136–137,** 170, 380*c*
Foliated Cross, Temple of the **I:**283
folk music **VI:**255–256, *256;* **VIII:**250
folk music revival **IX:***120,* **120–121**
   Dylan, Bob **IX:**92
   music **IX:**229
   popular culture **IX:**259
Follett, Ken **X:**273
Follies, The **VII:**95, 405*c*

Folsom Man **I:**263
Fon **I:**103, 125, **132**
Fonda, Jane **IX:**144
Fonda, Peter **IX:**225
food **II:130–131; IX:121–122**
   agriculture **II:**8
   Andersonville Prison, Georgia **V:**11
   Chesapeake Bay **II:**65
   Confederate army **V:**81
   crowd actions **II:**86
   Delaware Indians **II:**96
   disease/epidemics **V:**112
   fishing **II:**126
   impressment **V:**204
   McDonald's **IX:**208
   Muslims **II:**248
   Northwest Coast Indians **II:**275
   potato **II:**304–305
   prisons **V:**314
   refugees **V:**330
   Smith, John **II:**362
   taverns and inns **II:**383
Food, Agriculture, Conservation, and Trade Act (1990) **X:**20
Food, Drug, and Cosmetic Act **VIII:1, 139–140,** 235, 446*c*
Food Administration, U.S.
   Blatch, Harriot Eaton Stanton **VII:**38
   Taft, Robert A. **VIII:**385
   World War I **VII:**393
Food and Agriculture Act (1965) **IX:**8, 356*c*
Food and Drug Administration, U.S. (FDA) **IX:**354*c*; **X:**382*c*
   advertising **VIII:**1
   FCC **VIII:**131
   Food, Drug, and Cosmetic Act **VIII:**139–140
   medicine **IX:**212; **X:**222–223
   "The Pill" **IX:**257
   Pure Food and Drug Act **VII:**277
Food for Peace **X:**217
Food Materials and Their Adulterations (Richards) **VI:**313
food riots **III:167–168; V:147–148**
   employment **V:**132
   homefront **V:**192
   women's status and rights **V:**437
Food Stamp Act (1964) **IX:**8
Food Stamp program **IX:**335
Fool's Errand, A (Tourgée) **V:**389
FOOTALU. *See* Federation of Organized Trades and Labor Unions of the United States
football **VI:***130,* **130–131,** 408*c*
   Gay Nineties **VI:**140
   Kemp, Jack F. **X:**196
   recreation **VII:**295; **VIII:**328; **X:**302

   sports and recreation **V:**367; **VII:**333; **VIII:**371; **X:**330–331
   television **X:**344
Foote, Andrew H. **V:**263
Foote, Arthur **VI:**255
Foote, Henry Stuart **V:**103
Foote, Shelby **V:**240
foraging **V:148–149,** 166, 356–357
Foraker, Joseph Benjamin **VII:**42, 110
Foraker Act **VII:110–111,** 157, 403*c*
Foran Act (1885) **VI:**82
Forbes, Charles
   Harding, Warren Gamaliel **VII:**135
   Teapot Dome **VII:**352
   Veterans Bureau **VII:**373
Forbes, George **VII:**357
Forbes, John (1710–1759) **II:**348; **III:**430
Forbes, John Murray (1813–1898) **VI:131—132,** 269
Force Bill **IV:**283; **VI:**161
forced labor **I:**26, 318
Ford, Gerald R. **X:137–139,** *138,* 376*c,* 377*c*
   Angelou, Maya **X:**26
   assassinations **X:**35
   Bush, George H. W. **X:**51
   Carter, James Earl, Jr. **X:**67, 68
   Cheney, Richard B. **X:**71, 72
   conservative movement **X:**93
   defense policy **X:**100
   détente **X:**104
   Dole, Robert **X:**104, 105
   economy **X:**109
   ERA **X:**124
   federalism **X:**130
   foreign policy **X:**141
   Haig, Alexander M., Jr. **X:**163
   Helms, Jesse A., Jr. **X:**165
   Kissinger, Henry A. **X:**198
   New York City bailout **X:**254
   Nixon, Richard M. **X:**257
   Owens, Jesse **VIII:**289
   Reagan, Ronald W. **X:**300
   Remarks on Taking the Oath of Office **X:392–393**
   Richardson, Elliot L. **X:**311
   Rumsfeld, Donald **X:**312
   SALT I/SALT II **X:**336
   Scalia, Antonin **X:**316
   Supreme Court **X:**338
   veto (presidential) **X:**361
Ford, Harrison **X:**279
Ford, Henry **VI:**411*c;* **VII:***111,* **111–112,** 405*c*
   aircraft industry **VIII:**14–15
   America First Committee **VIII:**17

   Americanization **VII:**13
   anti-Semitism **VII:**17
   architecture **VII:**19
   automobile industry **VII:**26
   business **VII:**45
   CIO **VIII:**82
   economy **VII:**84
   Ford Motor Corporation **IX:**122
   labor/labor movements **VIII:**205
   mass production **VII:**195
   rural life **VII:**306
   science, invention, and technology **VI:**196; **VII:**150; **VIII:**352
   technology **VIII:**389
   Tennessee Valley Authority **VIII:**392
   urban transportation **VII:**364
   welfare capitalism **VII:**381
Ford, Henry, II **IX:**122
Ford, James **VIII:**77
Ford, John **VIII:**301; **IX:**223, 224
Ford, Theodosia **III:**307
Ford, William Clay **X:**36
Ford Bill (New York) **VII:**304
Ford Edsel **IX:**123
Ford Foundation **VIII:**210
Fordham Law School **VIII:**139
Fordham University **VI:**217; **VII:**197
Ford Highland Park Plant. *See* Highland Park Ford Plant
Ford Motor Company of Canada **VII:**152
Ford Motor Corporation **IX:122–123.** *See also* Model T Ford
   automobile industry **VII:**26, 27; **VIII:**35; **IX:**25, 26; **X:**36–37
   aviation **VII:**29
   business **X:**58
   Chrysler Corporation Loan Guarantee Act **X:**74
   cities and urban life **VII:**54
   economy **VII:**85
   Ford, Henry **VII:**111
   GM **IX:**133
   Reuther, Walter **VIII:**339; **IX:**275
   strikes **VIII:**377
   technology **IX:**313
   welfare capitalism **VII:**380
Ford Mustang **IX:**123
Fordney-McCumber Tariff **VII:112–113,** 408*c*
   economy **VII:**85
   Hawley-Smoot Tariff Act **VIII:**163
   tariffs **VII:**350
Ford's Theatre (Washington, D.C.)
   assassination of Abraham Lincoln **V:**19–20
   Booth, John Wilkes **V:**38–39
   theater **V:**386

Ford Trimotor aircraft **VII:**29
foreclosures **VIII:**445*c;* **X:**60, 111
foreign affairs **III:168–169,** 463*c*–465*c*
  Articles of Confederation **III:**33
  Barbary Wars **III:**45–46
  Cadore Letter **III:**73
  Chesapeake-Leopard affair **III:**88
  citizenship **III:**94
  Continental Congress, Second **III:**116
  Democratic-Republican societies **III:**137
  economy **III:**146–147
  embargo of 1807 **III:**151–153
  Essex decision **III:**157–158
  Farewell Address of George Washington **III:**162
  Federalist Party **III:**164
  Florida **III:**166–167
  Franklin, Benjamin **III:**174
  French Revolution **III:**178–179
  Jay, John **III:**229–230
  Jay-Gardoqui Treaty **III:**230–231
  Jay's Treaty **III:**231
  Jefferson, Thomas **III:**233, 234
  King, Rufus **III:**245
  Lee, Arthur **III:**258
  Little Belt incident **III:**269–270
  Livingston, Robert R. **III:**270
  Macon's Bill No. 2 **III:**280
  Monroe-Pinkney Treaty **III:**300–301
  Neutrality Proclamation **III:**315–316
  Non-Importation Act **III:**319
  Non-Intercourse Act **III:**319–320
  Orders in Council **III:**325–326
  Paris, Treaty of (1783) **III:**331–332
  Pinckney Treaty **III:**336–337
  Quasi War **III:**352–353
  tariffs **III:**406
  trade, domestic and foreign **III:**413, 415
  Vergennes, Charles Gravier, comte de **III:**423
  West Indies **III:**436–437
  XYZ affair **III:**451
Foreign Affairs, Committee of **III:**116
foreign aid **IX:**354*c*
  abortion **X:**4
  Africa **X:**17

Alliance for Progress **IX:**10–11
  cold war **IX:**63
  contras **X:**95
  Europe **IX:**113
  Point Four Program **IX:**257–258
  South Africa **X:**325
  Suez crisis **IX:**307
  UN **X:**355
Foreign Anti-Slavery Society **V:**165
Foreign Conspiracy Against the Liberties of the United States (Morse) **IV:**195
Foreign Corrupt Practices Act (1977) **X:139–140,** 377*c*
Foreign Economic Administration **IX:**302
Foreign Miners Tax **IV:**268
foreign policy **IV:153–156; V:149–152; VI:133–134; VII:113–116,** *114;* **VIII:140–143,** *141,* 449*c;* **IX:**357*c;* **X:140–144,** *141*
  Africa **IX:**3–4; **X:**15–17
  Albright, Madeleine K. **X:**22
  America First Committee **VIII:**16–17
  Americans for Democratic Action **IX:**14
  Anglo-American relations **VIII:**21
  anticommunism **IX:**14
  Anti-Imperialist League **VI:**17
  antiwar movement, Vietnam **X:**28–29
  Atlantic Charter **VIII:34, 461**
  Axis **VIII:**38
  Biden, Joseph **X:**42
  Big Stick diplomacy **VII:**34–36
  Black Cabinet **VIII:**46
  Blaine, James Gillespie **VI:**41
  Borah, William E. **VIII:**49
  Boxer Rebellion **VII:**40–41
  Britain, Battle of **VIII:**53
  Buchanan, Patrick J. **X:**49
  Bush, George H. W. **X:**52
  Bush, George W. **X:**55, 56
  Canada **VI:**61
  Carnegie Endowment for International Peace **VII:**49, 50
  Carter, James Earl, Jr. **X:**69
  cash-and-carry **VIII:**63
  Cheney, Richard B. **X:**72
  Chilean-American relations **VI:**67–68
  Clinton, William J. **X:**80, 81, 83
  cold war **IX:**62
  cold war, end of **X:**84–86
  Congress **VIII:**80, 81

conservatism **VIII:**85; **IX:**74
  conservative movement **X:**93–94
  Coolidge, Calvin John **VII:**65
  Cuba **IV:**111
  defense policy **X:**99–103
  demobilization (WWII) **VIII:**91
  destroyers-for-bases deal **VIII:**94, 95
  détente **X:**103–104
  dollar diplomacy **VII:**79
  Eisenhower, Dwight D. **IX:**100–101
  election of 1940 **VIII:**110, 111
  election of 1944 **VIII:**111
  elections **VII:**91; **IX:**103, 104
  elections, presidential **X:**118
  FBI **VIII:**130
  Federal Information Act **X:**130
  Fillmore, Millard **IV:**150
  Foraker Act **VII:**110
  Ford, Gerald R. **X:**139
  Foreign Corrupt Practices Act **X:**139
  foreign policy **VIII:**141
  German Americans **VIII:**149
  glasnost **X:**153
  Good Neighbor policy **VIII:**151–152
  Gore, Albert, Jr. **X:**157
  government **VIII:**154
  Grant, Ulysses S. **V:**175
  Great White Fleet **VII:**129–130
  Grenada, invasion of **X:**159–160
  Haig, Alexander M., Jr. **X:**163, 164
  Harding, Warren Gamaliel **VII:**135
  Harriman, W. Averell **VIII:**161–162
  Harrison, Benjamin **VI:**161–162
  Hay, John Milton **VI:**164
  Hoover, Herbert C. **VIII:**172–173
  Hoover presidency **VIII:**174
  Hull, Cordell **VIII:**180
  imperialism **VI:**188
  Iran-contra affair **X:**183–184
  isolationists **VIII:**189–190
  Israel **IX:**160
  Italian Americans **VIII:**190–191
  Jews **VIII:**196
  jingoes **VI:**204
  Johnson, Hiram Warren **VII:**154

Johnson, Hugh S. **VIII:**196–197
  Johnson, Lyndon B. **IX:**163, 164
  Jones Act (1916) **VII:**156–157
  Jones Act (1917) **VII:**157
  Kennedy, Edward M. **X:**197
  Kennedy, John F. **IX:**170–171
  Kissinger, Henry A. **X:**198
  labor/labor movements **VIII:**207
  La Follette, Robert M., Jr. **VIII:**208
  Landon, Alfred M. **VIII:**209
  Latin America **X:**204–207
  League of Nations **VII:**175–176
  Lend-Lease **VIII:**211, 212
  Lewis, John L. **VIII:**213
  liberalism **VIII:**216
  Lodge, Henry Cabot **VII:**184
  London Economic Conference **VIII:**221
  London Naval Conference **VIII:**222
  Manchuria **VIII:**225–226
  modern Republicanism **IX:**221
  Monroe Doctrine **IV:**259–261, **425–427**
  Morgenthau, Henry T., Jr. **VIII:**244
  NATO **IX:**247
  neoconservatism **X:**252
  Neutrality Acts **VIII:**267–268, 457–460
  New Deal **VIII:**270
  New Frontier **IX:**243
  Nicaragua **X:**254–255
  Nixon, Richard M. **X:**256, 257
  Norris, George W. **VIII:**276–277
  NSC-68 **IX:**247–248
  Nye committee **VIII:**278–279
  Open Door Notes **VI:**272–273
  Open Door Policy **VII:**245–246
  Oregon Treaty of 1846 **IV:**286–288
  Panama Canal **VII:**251
  Peace Corps **IX:**255
  peace movements **VII:**256–257
  Point Four Program **IX:**257–258
  Polish Americans **VIII:**297
  Polk, James K. **IV:**302
  postwar planning **VIII:**306, 307
  Preparedness **VII:**267
  presidency **VII:**268, 269

foreign policy (*continued*)
  Progressive Party **IX**:264
  public opinion polls
    VIII:313
  Reagan, Ronald W. **X**:301
  Reciprocal Trade
    Agreements Act
    VIII:324–325
  Republican Party **VIII**:337
  Roosevelt, Franklin D.
    VIII:346
  Roosevelt, Theodore
    VII:304
  Roosevelt Corollary
    VII:304–305
  Root-Takahira Agreement
    VII:305–306
  Samoa **VI**:322–323
  Santo Domingo, proposed
    annexation of **VI**:323
  Senate, U.S. **X**:321
  Seward, William H. **V**:348
  Siberian Expedition
    VII:324–325
  South Africa **X**:324–325
  Soviet-American relations
    VIII:368–369
  Spanish-American War
    VI:340–341
  Spanish civil war **VIII**:369–
    370
  Stimson, Henry L. **VIII**:375
  Sumner, Charles **V**:376–378
  Taft, Robert A. **VIII**:385
  terrorism **X**:348
  TNEC **VIII**:391
  trade, domestic and foreign
    VII:353–355
  Truman, Harry S. **IX**:320
  Truman Doctrine **IX**:321,
    322, 359–361
  Tyler, John **IV**:383
  UN **VIII**:402–403
  Versailles, Treaty of
    VII:369–370
  veterans **VII**:371, 373
  Vietnam War **IX**:332
  Wallace, Henry A. **VIII**:411
  War of 1812 **IV**:390
  wars of national liberation
    IX:338–339
  Washington Conference
    on Naval Disarmament
    VII:379
  Welles, Sumner **VIII**:415
  Wheeler, Burton K.
    VIII:416
  Willkie, Wendell L.
    VIII:417
  Wilson, Thomas Woodrow
    VII:383, 384
  World War II **VIII**:427, 428
Foreign Policy Association (FPA)
  VII:49, 115
foreign students **X**:359
foreign trade. *See* trade (domestic
  and foreign)

Foreman, George **IX**:10
Forerunner, The (journal)
  VII:125
Forest Leaves (Harper) **V**:184
Forest Management Act (1897)
  VI:134, 411*c*
Forest Reserve Act **VI**:81–82,
  134–135, 411*c*
Forestry Commission **VI**:254
Forestry Division (U.S.
  Department of Agriculture)
  VI:81, 134
forests **II**:119, 120, **131**, 211–
  212; **III**:153–155
Forest Service, U.S.
  National Trails Act of 1968
    IX:239
  National Wilderness
    Preservation Act of 1964
    IX:240
  Pinchot, Gifford **VII**:259–
    260
  Progressive Party **VII**:270
  Taft, William Howard
    VII:348
  Walcott, Charles Doolittle
    VI:380
For God and the People
  (Rauschenbusch) **VII**:293
"Forgotten Man" **VIII**:301
Forlorn Hope Expedition **IV**:126
Formosa (Taiwan). *See* China,
  Republic of
Forrest, Edwin **V**:387
Forrest, Nathan Bedford **V:152–
  153**, *153*, 445*c*
  Confederate army **V**:81
  Fort Pillow **V**:153, 154
  Ku Klux Klan **V**:223;
    VII:165
  Ku Klux Klan cases **VI**:210
  prisons **V**:314
Forrestal, James V. **VIII**:143, 265
Forrester Research Group **X**:283
Forsberg, Randall **X**:261
fort(s) **II:133–134**
  Bacon's Rebellion **II**:31
  Florida **II**:129
  Native Americans **II**:254
  Oglethorpe, James Edward
    II:278
  Ohio Company of Virginia
    II:278
  Royal African Company
    II:337
Fortas, Abe **IX**:133, 338; **X:144–
  145**, 375*c*
Fort Atkinson **IV**:36
Fort Beauséjour **II**:2
Fort Benning, Georgia **VIII**:50,
  233
Fort Blakely **V**:265
Fort Bliss **IV**:233
Fort Bridger
  Bridger, James **IV**:64
  Deseret, State of **IV**:120
  Donner party **IV**:125

exploration **IV**:145
Mormon Trail **IV**:262
Mormon War **IV**:263
Oregon Trail **IV**:285
Fort Brown **VII**:42, 404*c*
Fort Caroline **I:61**, 397*c*; **II**:128
  Florida **I**:131
  French explorations of the
    Atlantic **I**:134
  Laudonnière, René de
    I:208
  Le Moyne, Jacques **I**:209
Fort Clark **IV**:60
Fort Clinton **III**:350
Fort Constitution **III**:216
Fort Cumberland **III**:440
Fort Dearborn **IV**:277, 391
Fort Detroit **II**:132; **III**:459*c*
  Harrison, William Henry
    IV:185
  Hull, William **IV**:192
  Lake Erie, Battle of **IV**:220
  Native Americans **IV**:274
  Pontiac's War **III**:340
  War of 1812 **IV**:391
  Wilkinson, James **III**:443
Fort Dix **X**:348
Fort Donelson **VI**:381
Fort Donelson, Battle of
  Forrest, Nathan Bedford
    V:152
  Grant, Ulysses S. **V**:174
  Halleck, Henry Wager
    V:182
  Union navy **V**:406
Fort Dunmore **III**:142
Fort Duquesne **II**:438*c*
  Braddock, Edward **II**:43–44
  forts **II**:133
  Franklin, Benjamin **III**:173
  French colonies **II**:138
  Gage, Thomas **III**:186
  Gates, Horatio **III**:189
  Ohio Company of Virginia
    II:278
  Seven Years' War **II**:348
  Washington, George
    III:430
Forten, James **II**:35; **III:169–
  170**, 464*c*
  abolitionism **IV**:3
  ACS **IV**:17
  African Americans **III**:10
  antislavery **III**:26
  Jones, Absalom **III**:238
Fort Erie **IV**:392
Fort Fisher, Battle of **V**:215, 216,
  311
Fort Frontenac **II**:438*c*; **III**:98
Fort Gaines **V**:248
Fort George. *See* Astoria
Fort Gibson **IV**:241; **V**:278, 279
Fort Gibson, Treaty of **IV**:289
Fort Griswold **III**:31
Fort Hall
  Applegate, Jesse **IV**:26
  California Trail **IV**:78

exploration **IV**:145
Oregon Trail **IV**:285
Wyeth, Nathaniel J. **IV**:406
Fort Harmar Council **III**:378
Fort Harrison **IV**:367
"For the Dear Old Flag I Die"
  V:273
Fort Henry
  Ashley, William Henry
    IV:31, 32
  Grant, Ulysses S. **V**:174
  Halleck, Henry Wager
    V:182
  rendezvous **IV**:321
  Rocky Mountain Fur
    Company **IV**:324
  Shiloh, Battle of **V**:358
For the Union Dead (Lowell)
  IX:195
Fort Jackson **V**:263
Fort Jackson, Treaty of
  cotton culture **IV**:108
  Creek **III**:126; **IV**:109
  McIntosh, William **IV**:247
Fort James **II**:271
Fort Jenkins **III**:449
Fort Kaskaskia **III**:95
Fort King **IV**:289
Fort Knox **IV**:300
Fort La Galette **III**:186
Fort Laramie **IV:156–158**, *157*
  California Trail **IV**:77
  Donner party **IV**:125
  foreign policy **IV**:156
  Mormon Trail **IV**:262
  Native Americans **IV**:275–
    276
  Oregon Trail **IV**:285
Fort Laramie, Treaty of **IV**:157–
  158; **V**:446*c*; **VI**:408*c*
  Black Hills gold rush **VI**:38
  Crazy Horse **VI**:85
  Little Bighorn, Battle of
    V:240, 241
  Native Americans **VI**:263
  Red Cloud **VI**:303
  Sioux wars **VI**:331
  Sitting Bull **VI**:332
  treaty rights **IX**:319
Fort Leavenworth **IV:158**
  Atkinson, Henry **IV**:36
  Cody, William Frederick
    VI:75
  Frémont, John C. **IV**:167
  Kearny, Stephen Watts
    IV:212
  Stuart, J. E. B. **V**:375
Fort Lee
  Fort Washington, capture of
    III:172
  Greene, Nathanael **III**:198
  Howe, Sir William **III**:215
Fort Loudoun **II**:280; **IV**:342
Fort Mackinac
  American Fur Company
    IV:18
  medicine **IV**:249

Native Americans in the War
of 1812 **IV:**277
War of 1812 **IV:**391, 392
Fort Macon **V:**52
Fort McHenry **IV:**213; **V:**189
Fort McKenzie **IV:**18, 60
Fort Meigs **IV:**185, 277
Fort Mercer **III:**135, 359
Fort Miami **III:**161–162
Fort Mifflin **III:**135, 359
Fort Mims
McIntosh, William **IV:**247
Native Americans **IV:**274
Native Americans in the War
of 1812 **IV:**277
Fort Monroe
contrabands **V:**92
Davis, Jefferson **V:**105
Peninsular campaign **V:**298
Fort Montgomery **III:**216, 350
Fort Mose **II:132, 408, 409**
Fort Moultrie
Anderson, Robert **V:**9–10
Charleston, siege of **III:**84
Fort Sumter **V:**154
Marshall, George C.
VIII:233
Osceola **IV:**289
Van Buren, Martin **IV:**386
Fort Necessity **II:132–133, 278;**
III:429
Fort Niagara
Gage, Thomas **III:**186
Native Americans **III:**314
Native Americans in the War
of 1812 **IV:**277
War of 1812 **IV:**391
Fort Nisqually **IV:**400
Fort Orange **II:**256
Fort Oswego **III:**68, 345
Fort Patrick Henry **III:**139
Fort Peck Dam, Montana
VIII:50
Fort Phil Kearny **VI:**85
Fort Pickering **IV:**367; **V:**259
Fort Pillow, Tennessee **V:153–**
154, 445c
Forrest, Nathan Bedford
V:152
Joint Committee on the
Conduct of the War
V:215, 216
Mississippi River war **V:**263
Fort Pitt **II:133; III:**340, 377
Fort Prince George **III:**323
Fort Pulaski **V:**342; **VII:**16
Fort Rosalie **II:**250
Fort Sackville **III:**95
Fort St. George **II:**278
Fort St. Philip **V:**263
Fort Sam Houston **VII:**212
Fort Sanders **V:**253
Fort San Mateo **I:**61
Fort Schlosser **IV:**79
Fort Scott **IV:**339
Fort Severn **V:**409
Fort Smith **IV:**290

Fort Snelling **V:**116
Fort Stanton **VI:**376
Fort Stanwix, Treaty of **II:**188;
III:170–171, 460c, 462c
Cornplanter **III:**119
Iroquois **III:**228
Native Americans **III:**312
Ohio Company of Virginia
III:323
Red Jacket **III:**359
Fort Stedman
Appomattox campaign **V:**14
Gordon, John B. **V:**170
Petersburg campaign **V:**303
Fort Stephenson **IV:**185
Fort Sumter, South Carolina
V:154–155, 155, 444c
Anderson, Robert **V:**10
Beauregard, Pierre Gustave
Toutant **V:**32
Bowles, Samuel **VI:**42
Cass, Lewis **IV:**84
Civil War **V:**73
Civil War centennial **IX:**62
Confederate States of
America **V:**84
Davis, Jefferson **V:**104
Douglas, Stephen A. **V:**114
54th Massachusetts
Regiment **V:**144
fire-eaters **V:**146
Forbes, John Murray
VI:132
foreign policy **IV:**156
Hicks, Thomas H. **V:**188
journalism **V:**217, 218
Leslie, Frank and Miriam
Florence Follin **VI:**221
Lincoln, Abraham **V:**236
Manifest Destiny **IV:**236
secession **V:**345
Wigfall, Louis T. **V:**431
Fort Supply **IV:**120
Fort Sutter
Bidwell, John **IV:**56
Brannan, Samuel **IV:**64
Donner party **IV:**125, 126
Wilkes expedition **IV:**400
Fort Ticonderoga **III:171, 171–**
172, 461c
Allen, Ethan **III:**15
Arnold, Benedict **III:**30
Gates, Horatio **III:**190
Green Mountain Boys
III:199
Knox, Henry **III:**248
Kościuszko, Tadeusz
III:248
Lyon, Matthew **III:**277
Montgomery, Richard
III:301
Quebec, Battle of **III:**353
St. Clair, Arthur **III:**378
Saratoga, surrender at
III:380
Schuyler, Philip John
III:384

Valcour Island, Battle of
III:421
Wayne, Anthony **III:**433
Fortune, Reo **VII:**197
Fortune, Timothy Thomas
African Americans **VI:**7
Civil Rights Cases **VI:**72
newspapers **VI:**266
Wells-Barnett, Ida Bell
VI:387, 388
Fortune magazine
Bourke-White, Margaret
VIII:50
Evans, Walker **VIII:**120
Luce, Henry R. **VIII:**224
public opinion polls
VIII:312
Fort Union **IV:**18
Fort Vancouver **IV:158–159**
Astoria **IV:**36
Columbia River **IV:**103
Lee, Jason **IV:**224
McLoughlin, John **IV:**248
Oregon Trail **IV:**285–286
Rocky Mountain Fur
Company **IV:**325
Smith, Jedediah Strong
IV:351
Wyeth, Nathaniel J. **IV:**406
Fort Wagner
African-American regiments
V:4
Carney, William Harvey
V:55
54th Massachusetts
Regiment **V:**142–144
marine corps **V:**248
Fort Washington **IV:**184, 300
Fort Washington, Battle of
III:248
Fort Washington, capture of
III:172, 441
Fort Wayne, Treaty of **IV:**184–
185
Fort William **IV:**247
Fort William Henry **III:**127, 171
Fort William Henry Massacre
II:134; III:312, 345
Fort Wilson riot **III:**444
Fort Wintermoot **III:**449
48ers **IV:**193; **V:**165
Forty Fort **III:**449
Forty-niners **IV:159, 159–161**
California Trail **IV:**77, 78
Fort Laramie **IV:**157
gold **IV:**177–178
lead mines **IV:**224
migration **IV:**255
Native Americans **IV:**275
Oregon Trail **IV:**285
42nd Parallel, The (Dos Passos)
VIII:219
42nd "Rainbow" Division **IX:**197
Forum magazine **VII:**24
For Whom the Bell Tolls
(Hemingway) **VIII:**220, 369
fossil fuels **X:**155

Foster, Abigail Kelley **IV:**16,
161–162
Foster, David **X:**303
Foster, Ezola **X:**304
Foster, Jodie **X:**35
Foster, Stephen C. (songwriter)
V:156; VI:257
Foster, Stephen Symonds **IV:**161
Foster, Vincent **X:**77, 82
Foster, William T. (economist)
VIII:101
Foster, William Zebulon (union
organizer) **VII:116–117**
Communist Party **VII:**61
Communists **VIII:**77
IWW **VII:**147
steel industry **VII:**337
Steel Strike of 1919
VII:338–339
Fothergill, John **III:**47
Foucault, Jean-Bernard-Léon
IV:332
Founding Fathers
alcohol **III:**13
Hamilton, Alexander
III:205–208
Madison, James **III:**281,
284
Fountainhead, The (Rand) **X:**93
Fountain of Age (Friedan) **IX:**127
4-H Clubs **VIII:**67; **IX:**8
Four Freedoms **VIII:143–144,**
*144, 286, 303, **461–465***
442nd Regimental Combat Team
(U.S. Army) **VIII:**32, 194
Fourier, Charles **IV:**65, 162
Four-Minute Men **VII:**60
Four Mothers Society **VII:**233
Four Power Pacific Treaty (Four-
Power Pact, 1921) **VII:**379,
408c
"Fourteen Points" speech (Wilson)
VII:407c, 427–430
Democratic Party **VII:**74
League of Nations **VII:**175
peace movements **VII:**256
progressivism **VII:**271
Trading with the Enemy Act
VII:355
Versailles, Treaty of **VII:**369,
370
Wilson, Thomas Woodrow
VII:383
Fourteenth Amendment **V:156–**
157, 446c, 463–464; VI:408c,
410c; VIII:446c; X:376c
amnesty, acts of **V:**9
Anthony, Susan B. **VI:**16
Bakke case **X:**40
banking **V:**28
Black, Hugo L. **VIII:**45
Brown, Joseph Emerson
V:45
*Brown v. Board of
Education* **IX:**43, 44
citizenship **III:**93
Civil Rights Cases **VI:**72

Fourteenth Amendment
(*continued*)
Constitution, United States
III:106
Douglass, Frederick **V:**116
due process clause **VI:**100–
101
Escobedo v. Illinois **IX:**111
Field, Stephen Johnson
VI:127
Fifteenth Amendment **V:**141
Gideon v. Wainwright
IX:133–134
Hayes, Rutherford B.
VI:168
impeachment of Andrew
Johnson **V:**202, 203
Johnson, Andrew **V:**213
Ku Klux Klan cases **VI:**210
Lochner v. New York
VII:182, 183
marriage and family **X:**213
Morton, Oliver P. **V:**270
NAACP **VII:**224
Patrons of Husbandry
VI:279
PCSW **IX:**262
Plessy v. Ferguson **VI:**284
pornography **X:**283
race and race relations
IV:309
Radical Republicans **V:**321
Reconstruction **V:**325
Reconstruction Acts **V:**327,
328
Rehnquist, William H.
X:305
Republican Party **V:**334
Reynolds v. Sims **IX:**276
Scalia, Antonin **X:**316
segregation **VII:**319
Stevens, Thaddeus **V:**372
Supreme Court **VI:**348;
VII:343; **VIII:**382, 383
Thirteenth Amendment
V:388
Thomas, Clarence **X:**350
U.S. v. Cruikshank **V:**412
veterans **V:**415
women's status and rights
V:437; **VI:**399
Fourth Amendment **III:**51;
IX:203
Fourth Ward Republican Club
V:307
*Four Weeks among Some of the
Sioux Tribes* (Welsh) **VI:**190
four-wheel drive (4WD) **X:**36
Fowler, Charles Henry **VI:**393
Fowlstown **IV:**339
Fox, Catherine **IV:**320; **VI:**309
Fox, Charles James **III:**320
Fox, George
abolitionism **II:**1
Pennsylvania **II:**285
Protestantism **II:**316
Quakers **II:**321, 322

Fox, Gustavus Vasa **V:**428
Fox, Kate **IV:**354, 355
Fox, Leah **IV:**320
Fox, Margaret **IV:**320, 354, 355;
VI:309
Fox, Richard Kyle **VI:**44
Fox, Vicente
Bush, George W. **X:**56
Latin America **X:**206
Mexico **X:**226
Foxe's Book of Martyrs **I:**132–
133
foxholes **V:**141
Fox Hunt, The (Homer) **VI:**174
Fox Indians. *See* Sac and Fox
Indians
Fox News
media **X:**217
popular culture **X:**280
television **X:**344
FPA. *See* Foreign Policy
Association
Frame of Government **II:**152
France **II:**436c; **III:**459c, 461c–
463c, 465c; **VII:**407c, 408c;
VIII:446c, 448c; **IX:**352c–354c;
X:384c. *See also* French *entries*;
Vichy France
Acadia **I:**2, 3
Adams, John **III:**6
Adams, John Quincy **IV:**5
AEF **VII:**11
aircraft industry **VIII:**13
art and architecture **VI:**18
Atlantic, Battle of the
VIII:33
Bache, Benjamin Franklin
III:39
Beaumarchais, Pierre-
Auguste Caron de
III:48–49
Berlin blockade **IX:**38
Berlin Decree **III:**49
blitzkrieg **VIII:**47
Bodmer, Karl **IV:**61
Bonaparte, Napoleon
III:54–55
Borah, William E. **VIII:**50
Boxer Rebellion **VII:**40
Bradley, Omar N. **VIII:**51
Brazil **I:**35
British Empire **II:**48
Bulge, Battle of the
VIII:54
Cabet, Étienne **IV:**67
Cadore Letter **III:**73
Canada **III:**78
Capes, Battle of the
III:79–80
Carlisle commission **III:**82
Casablanca Conference
VIII:62
cash-and-carry **VIII:**63
Cass, Lewis **IV:**83
Cassatt, Mary **VI:**63, 64
Cayor **I:**69
CDAAA **VIII:**77

Chesapeake-Leopard affair
III:88
Chickasaw **II:**66
Choctaw **II:**68
Clinton, Sir Henry **III:**99
cold war **IX:**63
Committee for Public
Information **VII:**59
Confederate States of
America **V:**86
Continental Congress,
Second **III:**116
Cuba **IV:**111, 112
Dawes Plan **VII:**72
debt, national **III:**129–131
disease/epidemics **IV:**121
domino theory **IX:**89
embargo of 1807 **III:**151–
152
Essex decision **III:**157
Estaing, Charles-Henri
Theodat, comte d'
III:158
Ethiopia **VIII:**118–119
Europe **IX:**113
exploration **II:**123–124
fashion **IX:**116
Florida **IV:**151, 152
foreign affairs **III:**168, 169
foreign policy **IV:**153, 154;
V:149–151; **VII:**113–116;
VIII:141
forts **II:**133
Foster, William Zebulon
VII:116
Fourier, Charles **IV:**162
Franklin, Benjamin **III:**174
Fulton, Robert **III:**182–
183
fur trade **IV:**171
Gage, Thomas **III:**186
Genêt, Edmond Charles
III:190–191
Ghent, Treaty of **IV:**175
Haiti **III:**203, 204
Hamilton, Alexander
III:207–208
Holocaust **VIII:**170
Holy Roman Empire **I:**166
Hoover, Herbert C.
VIII:171
immigration **III:**221;
VIII:184
investments, American,
abroad **VI:**197
ironclads **V:**207
isolationists **VIII:**189–190
Israel **IX:**160
Italian Americans **VIII:**190
Italian campaign **VIII:**191–
192
James, Henry **VI:**200
Jay, John **III:**229
Jay's Treaty **III:**231
Jefferson, Thomas **III:**233,
234
Johnson, Jack **VII:**155

Kalb, Johann, baron de
III:245
Kellogg-Briand Treaty
VII:164
King George's War **II:**192
Knox, Frank **VIII:**202
Kościuszko, Tadeusz
III:248, 249
Lafitte, Jean **IV:**220
Laudonnière, René de
I:208
League of Armed Neutrality
III:257
League of Nations **VII:**175
Lee, Arthur **III:**258
Lend-Lease **VIII:**212
Leonardo da Vinci **I:**211–
212
Léry, Jean de **I:**212–213
London Economic
Conference **VIII:**221
London Naval Conference
VIII:222
Louisiana Purchase **III:**273
Macon's Bill No. 2 **III:**280
Marshall Plan **IX:**204
medicine **IV:**249
Mexican-American War
IV:251
"Micmac Indian Responds to
the French" **II:440–441**
Middle East **IX:**214
Milan Decree **III:**297
Mitchell, William (Billy)
VII:211
Monroe Doctrine **IV:**260
Montserrat **I:**251
Munich Conference
VIII:248
Native Americans **III:**312
NATO **IX:**247
Naval Disarmament
Conference **VII:**235
Nazi-Soviet Pact **VIII:**266
neutrality **VII:**235
Normandy, invasion of
VIII:275–276
North African campaign
VIII:277, 278
Ohio Company of Virginia
III:323
Open Door Policy **VII:**246
Orders in Council **III:**325
Oregon Trail **IV:**285
Paine, Thomas **III:**329–330
Panama Canal **VII:**250
Paris, Treaty of (1763)
III:331
Paris, Treaty of (1783)
III:332
Patton, George S., Jr.
VIII:291
peace movements **VII:**256
Pershing, John Joseph
VII:258
Pinckney, Charles
Cotesworth **III:**335

Pontiac's War **III:**339
Popular Front **VIII:**303
privateering **II:**313;
  III:347–348
Quasi War **III:**352–353
SEATO **IX:**291, 292
second front **VIII:**355
Seven Years' War **II:**348–
  350
Seward, William H. **V:**347,
  348
Siberian Expedition
  VII:324
Spanish civil war **VIII:**369
Statue of Liberty **VI:**344
Suez crisis **IX:**307
Talleyrand-Périgord, Charles-
  Maurice de **III:**405
technology **IX:**312
Teheran Conference
  VIII:390
Thevet, André **I:**357–358
trade, domestic and foreign
  III:413, 415; **VII:**354
UN **VIII:**403; **X:**356
V-E Day **VIII:**405
Versailles, Treaty of **VII:**369,
  371
Vietnam War **IX:**330
War of 1812 **IV:**390, 391
wars of national liberation
  IX:338
Washington Conference
  on Naval Disarmament
  VII:379
West Indies **III:**436
Wilson, Thomas Woodrow
  VII:383, 384
World Disarmament
  Conference **VIII:**426
World War I **VII:**393
World War II European
  theater **VIII:**430, 431
World War II Pacific theater
  VIII:435
Wright, Fanny **IV:**406
XYZ affair **III:**451
Yalta Conference **VIII:**439
franchise operations
  economy **IX:**98
  food **IX:**122
  McDonald's **IX:**208
Francis (duke of Guise) **I:**170
Francis, Sam **IV:**381
Francis, Will **IV:**381
Francis I (king of France)
  Calvin, John **I:**53
  Leo X **I:**210
  Leonardo da Vinci **I:**212
  Verrazano, Giovanni da
    I:377
Franciscans **I:133**
  Apalachee **I:**11
  Azores **I:**18
  California **I:**51, 52; **III:**73,
    74
  Calusa **I:**52

Florentine Codex **I:**130
Florida **I:**131; **II:**129
  Hopi **I:**168
  missions **II:**239
  Native Americans **II:**253
  New Mexico **I:**265, 266;
    II:263
  New Spain, northern
    frontier of **III:**318
  Pueblo **II:**317
  reducción **I:**314
  Sahagún, Bernardino de
    I:323
  Santa Fe **I:**327
  Serra, Junípero **II:**347
  Timucua **I:**360
  Yucatán Peninsula **I:**390
  Zumárraga, Juan de **I:**392
Francis of Assisi, Saint **I:**133
Francke, August **II:**245
Franco, Francisco
  foreign policy **VIII:**141
  Popular Front **VIII:**303,
    304
  Spanish civil war **VIII:**369,
    370
Franco-American Convention
  (1800) **III:**464*c*
Franco-American Treaty of 1778
  III:451
Franco-Prussian War (1870–1871)
  V:29
Frank, Jerome **VIII:**6
Frank, Leo **VII:**176
Franken, Al **X:**220
Frankenstein (Shelley) **IX:**287
Frankenthaler, Helen **IX:**19
Frankfurt, Germany **VIII:**91
Frankfurter, Felix **VIII:144–145;**
  IX:*336
  Acheson, Dean **IX:**1
  antimonopoly **VIII:**23
  Baker v. Carr **IX:**33
  Brennan, William J., Jr. **X:**47
  Engel v. Vitale **IX:**107
  Holmes, Oliver Wendell
    VII:140
  Lilienthal, David E.
    VIII:217
  religion **VIII:**335
  Sacco and Vanzetti **VII:**311
  Zionism **VIII:**441
Frank Leslie's Chimney Corner
  VI:221
Frank Leslie's Gazette of Fashion
  V:138
*Frank Leslie's Illustrated
  Newspaper*
  journalism **IV:**210; **V:**218
  Leslie, Frank and Miriam
    Florence Follin **VI:**221
  magazines **VI:**235
  Nast, Thomas **V:**275
Frank Leslie's Illustrated Weekly
  VI:221
Frank Leslie's Ladies Gazette
  IV:210; **VI:**221

Frank Leslie's Lady's Journal
  VI:221
Frank Leslie's Lady's Magazine
  VI:221
Franklin, Ann Smith **II:**134
Franklin, Battle of **V:**389
Franklin, Benjamin **I:**187;
  II:437*c;* **III:172–175,** *173,*
  461*c–*463*c*
  abolitionism **V:**1
  Albany Congress **II:**15
  American Philosophical
    Society **II:**20; **III:**17
  Bache, Benjamin Franklin
    III:39
  Bond, Thomas **II:**38
  College of Philadelphia
    II:74
  Continental Congress,
    Second **III:**115
  Deane, Silas **III:**129
  Declaration of
    Independence **III:**133
  deism **III:**134
  disease/epidemics **II:**99
  education **II:**112–113
  Enlightenment, American
    II:118
  environment **III:**155
  Federalists **III:**166
  Franklin, Deborah Read
    II:134
  Franklin, William **III:**175,
    176
  Franklin Institute **IV:**162–
    163
  French Alliance **III:**177
  fugitive slaves **II:**140
  Galloway, Joseph **III:**188
  Godfrey, Thomas **II:**150
  Hutchinson, Thomas
    III:218
  insurance **III:**227
  Jay, John **III:**229
  journalism **II:**189
  Kalm, Peter **II:**191
  labor/labor movements
    III:252
  land **II:**202
  Lee, Arthur **III:**258
  literature **III:**268
  medicine **IV:**248
  New England Primer **II:**258
  newspapers **II:**268
  Oliver, Andrew **III:**325
  Paine, Thomas **III:**329
  Paris, Treaty of (1783)
    III:331, 332
  Paxton Boys **II:**282
  Pennsylvania **II:**288
  Philadelphia **II:**293
  Poor Richard's Almanack
    II:300–301
  postal service **II:**304
  Protestant work ethic
    II:317
  Quartering Act **III:**352

  religion, Euro-American
    II:330
  Rittenhouse, David **III:**372
  science and technology
    II:345; **III:**384
  smallpox **II:**361
  society, British American
    II:364, 368
  technology **II:**385
  travel **II:**394
  Webster, Noah **III:**434
  Weems, "Parson" Mason
    Locke **III:**435
  Whately, Thomas **III:**437
  Whitefield, George **II:**414
  witches/witchcraft **II:**420–
    421
Franklin, Deborah Read **II:134**
Franklin, James **II:**268, 312
Franklin, John Hope **VI:**396
Franklin, Massachusetts **III:**415
Franklin, Missouri **IV:**331
Franklin, Rosalind **IX:**285
Franklin, state of **III:175**
Franklin, Stella **VII:**231, 285
Franklin, Tennessee **V:**196
Franklin, William **III:**173,
  175–176
Franklin County, Massachusetts
  IV:227
Franklin Delano Roosevelt
  Library **IX:**66
Franklin D. Roosevelt, USS
  VIII:12
Franklin Institute **III:**175;
  IV:162–163
Franklin Medal **IV:**163
Franks, Bobby **VII:**70, 176–177
Franks, David **III:**236
Fraser, Simon **III:**382
Frauds Exposed (Comstock) **VI:**79
Frazier, Charles **V:**240
Frazier, Joe **IX:**10
Frazier-Lemke Farm Bankruptcy
  Act **VIII:**382, 445*c*
Freddie Mac **X:**60–61
Fredendall, Lloyd R. **VIII:**277
Frederick, Harold **VI:**225
Frederick, Maryland **V:**12
Frederick II (king of Prussia)
  V:216
Frederick III the Wise (elector of
  Saxony) **I:**218
Frederick Douglass Center
  VI:395
Fredericksburg, Battle of **V:157–**
  159, *158,* 444*c*
  Alexander, Edward P. **V:**8
  Burnside, Ambrose E. **V:**52
  Confederate army **V:**81
  Early, Jubal A. **V:**119
  Hancock, Winfield Scott
    V:183
  Harvard Regiment **V:**186
  Hill, Ambrose P. **V:**190
  Holmes, Oliver Wendell
    VII:140

Fredericksburg, Battle of
  (continued)
    Hooker, Joseph **V:**196
    Irish-American regiments
      V:205–206
    Jackson, Thomas J.
      "Stonewall" **V:**210
    Joint Committee on the
      Conduct of the War
      V:215
    Lee, Robert E. **V:**231
    Longstreet, James **V:**242
    McLaws, Lafayette **V:**253
    Meade, George Gordon
      V:253
    Pickett, George Edward
      V:306
    Quay, Matthew Stanley
      VI:299
    Sickles, Daniel E. **V:**361
Fredonia Academy (Fredonia,
  New York) **VI:**114
Free African Society **III:**9, 238,
  463*c*
Free Baptist Church **IV:**295
free blacks
    abolitionism **IV:**1–3
    ACS **IV:**16–17
    African Americans **III:**9;
      IV:8–9
    American Anti-Slavery
      Society **IV:**15, 16
    antislavery **III:**26
    exploration **IV:**145
    Liberia **IV:**225
    literature **IV:**228
    Missouri Compromise
      IV:257
    Paul, Nathaniel **IV:**295
    race and race relations
      IV:311
    slavery **IV:**346
    Taney, Roger B. **IV:**366
    Vesey, Denmark **IV:**387–
      388
    Walker, David **IV:**389
    Williams, Peter, Jr. **IV:**402
Free Church of Worcester **VI:**171
Freed, Alan
    music **IX:**229
    rock and roll **IX:**278–279
    teenagers **IX:**314
freedmen
    African Americans **III:**8, 9
    antislavery **III:**26
    Black Codes **V:**34–35
    citizenship **III:**95
    Civil Rights Act (1866) **V:**71
    Cuffe, Paul **III:**127–128
    Eaton, John, Jr. **V:**120
    emancipation **V:**129–130
    Freedmen's Bureau **V:**159–
      161
    Haiti **III:**203, 204
    Howard, Oliver Otis **V:**197
    Hull, Agrippa **III:**216–217
    Johnson, Anthony **II:**186

Jones, Absalom **III:**238
Payne, Francis **II:**283
population trends **V:**310
Reconstruction **V:**326
redemption **V:**328
sharecropping **V:**349
slavery **II:**357; **V:**364
Smith, Venture **II:**364
Special Field Order No. 15
  V:366
Stanton, Edwin M. **V:**369
Sumner, Charles **V:**378
Truth, Sojourner **V:**394
Freedmen's Bureau **V:159–162,**
  160*m,* 446*c*
    Black Codes **V:**35
    Congress **V:**90
    contrabands **V:**93
    Davis Bend, Mississippi,
      freedmen's colony **V:**106
    Delany, Martin Robinson
      V:108
    Eaton, John, Jr. **V:**120
    education **V:**124
    education, higher **VI:**111
    education, philanthropy and
      VI:112
    emancipation **V:**130
    Fifteenth Amendment
      V:141
    Howard, Oliver Otis **V:**197
    impeachment of Andrew
      Johnson **V:**202
    Johnson, Andrew **V:**212, 213
    Kelley, William D. **V:**222
    Langston, John Mercer
      VI:218
    Memphis riot (1866) **V:**259
    Radical Republicans **V:**321
    Reconstruction **V:**326
    Revels, Hiram R. **V:**335
    Society of Friends **V:**365
    Thirteenth Amendment
      V:388
Freedmen's Relief Association
  V:178
Freedmen's Savings Bank **V:47,**
  159, 323
Freedom 7 (spacecraft) **IX:**231,
  296
Freedom Ballot (Mississippi)
  IX:302
"freedom dues" **II:**27, 173
Freedom of Access to Clinic
  Entrances Act (FACE) **X:**4,
  289
freedom of assembly **VIII:**71
Freedom of Information Act
  (FOIA) **X:**129–130, 194
freedom of religion. *See* religious
  liberty
freedom of speech **X:**379*c,* 381*c*
    Baldwin, Roger Nash
      VII:31
    Bill of Rights **III:**51
    Brennan, William J., Jr. **X:**47
    campaign finance **X:**63

censorship **VIII:**65; **X:**70,
  71
civil liberties **VIII:**71
Equal Access Act **X:**122
Espionage Act **VII:**101
Flynn, Elizabeth Gurley
  VII:109
Foster, William Zebulon
  VII:116
Internet **X:**182
PACs **X:**275
pornography **X:**283, 284
freedom of the press
    Abscam **X:**5
    censorship **VIII:**65; **X:**70,
      71
    citizenship **III:**93
    civil liberties **VIII:**71
    Pentagon Papers **X:**272
    pornography **X:**283
Freedom of the Will (Edwards)
  II:114
freedom rides **IX:123–124,** *124,*
  355*c*
    African Americans **IX:**5
    Birmingham confrontation
      IX:39
    Carmichael, Stokely **IX:**49
    CORE **IX:**72, 73
    education **IX:**100
    Lewis, John **IX:**190
    NAACP **IX:**232
    race and race relations
      IX:269
    sit-ins **IX:**291
    SNCC **IX:**302
Freedom's Journal
    ACS **IV:**17
    African Americans **IV:**8
    Crummell, Alexander **VI:**86,
      87
    Forten, James **III:**170
    journalism **IV:**209
    Paul, Nathaniel **IV:**295
    Walker, David **IV:**389
    Williams, Peter, Jr. **IV:**402
Freedom Tower at Ground Zero
  X:384*c*
"Freedom Train" (Berlin) **IX:**125
Freedom Train exhibition (1947–
  1949) **IX:**66, **124–125**
freedwomen **V:**34–35, 369
Free Enquirer **IV:**405
free exercise clause **V:**412; **X:**122
free labor
    Atkinson, Edward **VI:**21
    employment **V:**132–133
    Port Royal Experiment
      V:312
    Republican Party **V:**333
free love **VI:**407*c*
    socialism **VI:**336
    spiritualism **IV:**355
    Woodhull, Victoria **VI:**400,
      401
Freeman, Elizabeth **III:**176
Freeman, Mary Wilkins **VI:**225

Freeman, Orville I. **X:**233
Freeman, the (journal) **VI:**387–
  388
Freeman's Farm, Battle of
  III:380, 381*m,* 382
Freeman's Journal **III:**180
free market economics **X:**93
freemasonry (Masons) **II:**283;
  III:176–177
    African Americans **III:**9
    anti-Masonry **IV:**25
    Hall, Prince **III:**205
    Revere, Paul **III:**366
    Walker, David **IV:**389
"Freeport Doctrine" **V:**114
Free Press, Detroit **VI:**85
Freer Gallery **VI:**380
Free-Silver movement **VI:135**
    Altgeld, John Peter **VI:**12
    Anti-Imperialist League
      VI:17
    Bryan, William Jennings
      VI:51–52
    Cleveland, Grover **VI:**75
    Congress **VI:**80
    Crime of '73 **VI:**86
    currency issue **VI:**90
    Democratic Party **VI:**95
    elections **VII:**90
    farmers' alliances **VI:**125
    Hanna, Marcus Alonzo
      VI:158
    Lease, Mary Elizabeth
      Clyens **VI:**220
    national banking system
      VI:261
    Omaha platform **VI:**272
    People's Party **VI:**282
    political parties, third
      VI:286
    presidential campaigns
      (1870–1899) **VI:**293
Free Society of Traders **II:**152
Free-Soil Party **IV:163–165,** *164,*
  415*c*
    abolitionism **IV:**4; **V:**3, 4
    Bleeding Kansas **V:**36
    Brown, John **V:**44
    Cass, Lewis **IV:**83
    Chase, Salmon P. **V:**62
    Civil War **V:**73
    Clay, Henry **IV:**97
    Dana, Richard Henry
      IV:113
    Democratic Party **IV:**118
    Higginson, Thomas
      Wentworth **VI:**171
    Hoar, George F. **VI:**173
    Julian, George Washington
      V:219
    Kansas-Nebraska Act **V:**222
    Liberty Party **IV:**226, 227
    Mann, Horace **IV:**237
    public land policy **IV:**306
    Republican Party **IV:**322;
      V:332, 333
    slavery **V:**362, 363

Sumner, Charles **V:**376
Taylor, Zachary **IV:**368
Welles, Gideon **V:**428
Whigs **IV:**398
Free Speech and Headlight
   VI:388, 411*c*
free speech clause **X:**122. *See also*
   freedom of speech
free speech fights **VII:117–118**
   Baldwin, Roger Nash
      VII:31
   Espionage Act **VII:**101
   Flynn, Elizabeth Gurley
      VII:109
   Foster, William Zebulon
      VII:116
Free Speech Movement **IX:125–
126**
   civil disobedience **IX:**58
   counterculture **IX:**78
   education **IX:**100
   Savio, Mario **IX:**284
   SDS **IX:**304
   sit-ins **IX:**291
Free-State Hotel (Lawrence,
   Kansas) **IV:**243
Free Synagogue, New York City
   VII:298
free trade
   Atkinson, Edward **VI:**22
   Bayard, Thomas Francis
      VI:28
   Lease, Mary Elizabeth
      Clyens **VI:**220
   Liberal Republican Party
      VI:222
   Villard, Henry **VI:**375
Free-Trade Agreement
   Implementation Act (1988)
      X:379*c*
free-trade agreements
   economy **X:**110
   Latin America **X:**206
   Mexico **X:**226
Free Trade and Sailor's Rights
   IV:165
free-trade zone **X:**206
Freewheelin' Bob Dylan, The
   IX:92
free will **III:**316, 317
freeze-dried food **X:**327
Freie Arbeiter Shtimme **VII:**285
Freiheit, New York **VI:**213
Frelinghuysen, Frederick **VI:**67,
   68
Frelinghuysen, Theodorus
   Jacobus **II:135,** 155, 315
Frelinghuysen, Thomas **IV:**149
Frémont, Jesse Benton **IV:165–
166**
   Benton, Thomas Hart **IV:**54
   Frémont, John C. **IV:**166
   Harte, Bret **VI:**162
Frémont, John Charles **IV:166–
168, 167,** 414*c;* **V:**443*c,* 444*c*
   Bates, Edward **V:**31
   Bear Flag Revolt **IV:**49

Benton, Thomas Hart **IV:**54
Bidwell, John **IV:**56
Buchanan, James **V:**48
California **IV:**71
California Trail **IV:**77
Carson, Kit **IV:**81–82
Confiscation Acts **V:**87
Donnelly, Ignatius Loyola
   VI:100
exploration **IV:**145
Frémont, Jesse Benton
   IV:165
Greeley, Horace **V:**177
Halleck, Henry Wager
   V:182
Hastings, Lansford W.
   IV:187
Jackson, Thomas J.
   "Stonewall" **V:**210
Kearny, Stephen Watts
   IV:212
Know-Nothing Party **IV:**215
Larkin, Thomas Oliver
   IV:223
Mason, Richard B. **IV:**241
nativism **V:**280
Oregon Trail **IV:**285
Peninsular campaign **V:**298
Republican Party **IV:**322;
   V:333
Shenandoah Valley:
   Jackson's campaign **V:**349,
   350
Union army **V:**401
Watterson, Henry **VI:**385–
   386
French, Daniel Chester **VI:**327
French, William **V:**13
French Academy of Sciences
   IV:245
French alliance **III:177–178,**
   461*c,* 464*c*
   Catholics **III:**83
   Deane, Silas **III:**129
   Federalist Party **III:**164
   Franklin, Benjamin **III:**174
   French Revolution **III:**178
   Lafayette, marquis de
      III:253–254
   Lee, Arthur **III:**258
   Neutrality Proclamation
      III:315
   Quasi War **III:**353
   Revolutionary War **III:**368–
      369
   Rhode Island, Battle of
      III:369–370
   Rochambeau, Jean-Baptiste-
      Donatien de Vimeur,
      comte de **III:**372–373
   Vergennes, Charles Gravier,
      comte de **III:**423
French and Indian War (Seven
   Years' War) **II:348–350,** *349,*
   437*c,* 438*c;* **III:**459*c*
   Adams-Onís Treaty **IV:**6
   Algonquin **II:**18

American Revolution **III:**18
Astor, John Jacob **IV:**33–35
Boston Massacre **III:**56
Braddock, Edward **II:**43–44
Bute, John Stuart, earl of
   III:71
Canada **III:**78
captivity **II:**58
Carleton, Guy **III:**81
Cherokee **II:**65; **III:**87
Choctaw **III:**89
Clinton, George **III:**98
Clinton, Sir Henry **III:**99
Cornwallis, Charles, Lord
   III:119, 120
Creek **III:**125
Crèvecoeur, J. Hector St.
   John de **III:**126–127
Croghan, George **II:**85
debt, national **III:**130
De Lancey, James **II:**93, 94
economy **III:**145
exploration **II:**124
Florida **III:**166; **IV:**151
foreign affairs **III:**168
Fort Ticonderoga **III:**171
Fort William Henry
   Massacre **II:**134
Franklin, Benjamin **III:**173
French colonies **II:**137–139
frontier, the **III:**181
fur trade **III:**183; **IV:**171
Gage, Thomas **III:**186
Gates, Horatio **III:**189
George III **III:**192
Howe, George Augustus
   II:167
Howe, Richard, Lord
   III:214
Howe, Sir William **III:**215
Johnson, Sir William **II:**188
Marion, Francis **III:**286
Massachusetts **II:**224
McDougall, Alexander
   III:294
Monckton, Robert **II:**241
Montgomery, Richard
   III:301
Moravians **III:**302
Morgan, Daniel **III:**303
National Road **IV:**271
Native Americans **III:**311,
   312
New Hampshire **II:**260
New Spain, northern
   frontier of **III:**317
Ohio Company of Virginia
   II:278; **III:**323
Ostenaco **II:**280
Paris, Treaty of (1763)
   III:331
Pennsylvania **II:**286–287
Pitt, William **III:**337
Pontiac's War **III:**339
POWs **III:**345
privateering **II:**313
Putnam, Israel **III:**350

Quakers **III:**351
Revere, Paul **III:**366
Roman Catholicism **II:**336
St. Clair, Arthur **III:**377
Schuyler, Philip John
   III:384
society, British American
   II:367
South Carolina **II:**369
Walking Purchase **II:**406
Washington, George
   III:429–430
West Indies **III:**436
Wolfe, James **II:**421
writs of assistance **III:**448
Yates, Abraham **III:**453
French army
   French Alliance **III:**178
   Haiti **III:**204
   Rhode Island, Battle of
      III:370
   Rochambeau, Jean-Baptiste-
      Donatien de Vimeur,
      comte de **III:**372–373
   Savannah, siege of **III:**383
   Yorktown, surrender at
      III:454, 455, 457
French Clinical School **IV:**249
French colonies **II:135–139,**
   138*m,* 436*c*
   art **II:**27
   Bienville, Jean-Baptiste Le
      Moyne, sieur de **II:**37–38
   Champlain, Samuel de
      II:62–63
   Cherokee **II:**65
   Creole **II:**82–83
   Fort Detroit **II:**132
   Louisiana **II:**210
   Massachusetts **II:**223
   mulattoes **II:**246
   Natchez Revolt **II:**249–250
   Native Americans **II:**254
   Newfoundland **II:**259
   New Orleans **II:**266
   Ohio Company of Virginia
      II:278
   Roman Catholicism **II:**336
   Spanish colonies **II:**372
   trade, domestic and foreign
      II:392
   war and warfare **II:**407
French explorations of the
   Atlantic **I:133–134**
   Acadia **I:**2–3
   Brazil **I:**35
   Canary Islands **I:**57
   Caroline, Fort **I:**61
   Cartier, Jacques **I:**62
   Iroquois **I:**186–187
   Laudonnière, René de
      I:208
   Le Moyne, Jacques **I:**209–
      210
   Natchez **I:**259
French Foreign Legion **V:**441;
   VII:325

French immigrants **II:139,** 173
French impressionism **VI:**275
French Indochina **VIII:**435
French National Convention **III:**203
French navy **III:**197, 378–379
French Protestants. *See* Huguenots
French Resistance **VIII:**285
French Revolution **III:178–179**
   Adams, Abigail **III:**3
   Adams, John Quincy **IV:**5
   agriculture **III:**11
   Ames, Fisher **III:**19
   artisans **III:**35
   Bache, Benjamin Franklin **III:**39
   Beaumarchais, Pierre-Auguste Caron de **III:**48–49
   Burke, Edmund **III:**69
   Canada **III:**79
   citizenship **III:**94
   Democratic-Republican Party **III:**136
   Democratic-Republican societies **III:**136–137
   Dwight, Timothy **III:**143
   Federalist Party **III:**164
   foreign affairs **III:**168
   Free Trade and Sailor's Rights **IV:**165
   French Alliance **III:**178
   Genêt, Edmond Charles **III:**190, 191
   George III **III:**192
   Haiti **III:**203
   immigration **III:**221
   King, Rufus **III:**245
   Lafayette, marquis de **III:**253, 254
   Morris, Gouverneur **III:**304
   Paine, Thomas **III:**329–330
   Pinckney Treaty **III:**337
   popular culture **III:**341
   Priestley, Joseph **III:**345
   Rochambeau, Jean-Baptiste-Donatien de Vimeur, comte de **III:**373
   Talleyrand-Périgord, Charles-Maurice de **III:**405
   trade, domestic and foreign **III:**414
   Washington, George **III:**431
   "Yankee Doodle" **III:**453
"French Revolution in small, an Age of Reason in a patty pan, a" (Emerson) **IV:**140
French Romanesque **VI:**313
Frenchtown, Michigan **IV:**185
French traders
   Algonquin **II:**18
   fur trade **II:**141
   Great Plains Indians **II:**157
   métis **II:**232–233
   Native Americans **II:**251

Freneau, Philip **III:179–180**
   Brackenridge, Hugh Henry **III:**60
   Duer, William **III:**141
   Hamilton, Alexander **III:**207
   journalism **III:**240
   literature **III:**268–269
Frente Nacional de Libertação de Angola (FNLA) **X:**85
frescoes **I:**244
Freud, Sigmund **VII:118–119**
   Ellis, Henry Havelock **VII:**94
   Gilman, Charlotte Perkins **VII:**125
   Hall, Granville Stanley **VI:**157
   modernism **VII:**212
   sexuality **VII:**322
   social work **VII:**330
   women's status and rights **VII:**389
Frick, Henry Clay **VI:135–136**
   Carnegie, Andrew **VI:**62
   Goldman, Emma **VII:**126
   Homestead Strike **VI:**175, 176
   Industrial Revolution, Second **VI:**192
   Johnstown flood **VI:**204
   labor, radical **VI:**213
   open shop movement **VII:**247
   Robber Barons, The **VI:**315
   U.S. Steel **VII:**365
Frickey, Edwin **VI:**191
Friedan, Betty **IX:126–127,** *127,* 355*c,* 357*c*
   counterculture **IX:**78
   family life **X:**127
   feminism **X:**132
   literature **IX:**194
   Murray, Pauli **IX:**227
   NOW **IX:**236; **X:**247
   Steinem, Gloria **X:**334
   women's status and rights **IX:**346, 347; **X:**371
Friedman, Lawrence **IV:**67
Friedman, Milton **X:**93
Friedman, William F. **VIII:**76
Friends (TV program) **X:**343
Friendship 7 (spacecraft) **IX:**296
Friends of the Land **VIII:**116
Friends school **II:**112
Fries, John **III:**86, 181
Fries's Rebellion **III:180–181,** 353, 464*c*
frigates **III:**464*c*
   Barbary Wars **III:**45, 46
   Constitution, USS **III:**107–108
   Continental navy **III:**117
   Quasi War **III:**353
Friml, Rudolph **VII:**218–219
Frobisher, Martin **I:***134,* **134–135,** 398*c;* **II:**177
   Company of Cathay **I:**87

   Drake, Sir Francis **I:**111
   Greenland **I:**144
   icebergs **I:**177
   Mandeville, Sir John **I:**228
   Northwest Passage **I:**273
   Settle, Dionyse **I:**331
Frobisher's Bay **I:**87, 134, 135
Frobisher's Strait **I:**134, 135
Froebel, Friedrich **VI:**207, 280
Frohman, Charles **VI:**355
Frohwerk v. United States **VII:**313
Froines, John **X:**73
From Here to Eternity (film) **VIII:**361
From Here to Eternity (Jones) **VIII:**219; **IX:**193
"From Me to You" (The Beatles) **IX:**37
From Puritan Days (MacDowell) **VI:**233
From the New World (Dvorák) **VI:**255
From the Virginia Plantation to the National Capitol (Langston) **VI:**219
frontier, the **II:**39; **III:181–182,** 459*c,* 461*c*
   Anglican Church **III:**20
   Armistead, Lewis A. **V:**17
   Blount, William **III:**53
   Blue Licks, Battle of **III:**54
   Boone, Daniel **III:**55–56
   Brackenridge, Hugh Henry **III:**60
   Brant, Joseph **III:**63
   Brown, Charles Brockden **III:**64
   Burgoyne, Sir John **III:**68
   California **III:**73
   Clark, George Rogers **III:**95
   Clark, William **III:**96
   Davis, Jefferson **V:**103
   Dragging Canoe **III:**139
   economy **III:**146
   fashion **V:**139
   Federalists **III:**165, 166
   Florida **III:**167
   Fort Stanwix, Treaty of **III:**170
   Franklin, William **III:**175
   Gallatin, Albert **III:**187
   Great Plains **III:**197
   Iroquois **III:**228
   Jay's Treaty **III:**231
   King's Mountain, Battle of **III:**247
   land riots **III:**254
   letters **V:**232
   Marshall, John **III:**289
   McCrea, Jane **III:**293
   Methodism **III:**296
   Native Americans **III:**312
   New Spain, northern frontier of **III:**317
   Pontiac's War **III:**340

   poverty **III:**344
   POWs **III:**345
   Proclamation of 1763 **III:**348
   Quakers **III:**351
   religion **III:**361–362
   rural life **III:**375
   St. Clair, Arthur **III:**378
   Scots-Irish **III:**385, 386
   slavery **III:**392
   South Carolina Regulation **III:**394–395
   Stuart, J. E. B. **V:**375
   Turner, Frederick Jackson **VI:**365–366
   Washington, George **III:**429
   Wayne, Anthony **III:**434
   Whiskey Rebellion **III:**439
   Wilderness Road **III:**442
   Wyoming Valley Massacre **III:**449
   Wyoming Valley Wars **III:**450
Front Royal, Virginia **V:**350
Frost, B. F. **VI:**37
Frost, Robert **VIII:**220
fruit **VIII:**322
Fruitlands (Harvard, Massachusetts) **IV:**379
Fruit of Islam **IX:**226
Fry, Joshua **V:**191
Frye, Marquette **IX:**339
FSA. *See* Farm Security Administration
FSA (Family Support Act) **X:128**
f.64 Group **VIII:**296
FSLN. *See* Sandinista Front of National Liberation
F Street Mess **V:**221
FTC. *See* Federal Trade Commission
FTP. *See* Federal Theatre Project
Fuca, Juan de **II:139**
Fuchs, Klaus **IX:**152, 280
Fuel Administration **VII:119,** 269, 393
fuel-efficient cars **X:**74
fuel oil **VIII:**322
fuel shortages **X:**109
fuel technology **X:**35
Fuerteventura **I:**57
Fugitive Blacksmith, The (Pennington) **V:**301, 362
Fugitive Days (Ayers) **X:**368
fugitive slave(s) **II:139–140;** **IV:**415*c*
   abolitionism **II:**2
   African Americans **II:**8
   emancipation **V:**128–129
   Emancipation Proclamation **V:**130
   Florida **II:**129, 130
   Fort Mose **II:**132
   slave resistance **II:**353
   Underground Railroad **V:**397

Fugitive Slave Act **IV:**415*c*, **447–449; V:**443*c*
  Brown, William Wells **V:**46
  Burns, Anthony **IV:**66
  Christiana, Pennsylvania, riot **V:**65
  Crittenden Compromise **V:**98
  Delany, Martin Robinson **V:**107
  Democratic Party **V:**109
  Douglas, Stephen A. **V:**114
  Fillmore, Millard **IV:**150
  Langston, John Mercer **VI:**218
  Mallory, Stephen R. **V:**247
  Mason-Dixon Line **V:**250
  personal liberty laws **IV:**299
  Pierce, Franklin **V:**307
  race and race relations **IV:**310
  Stowe, Harriet Beecher **V:**373
  Sumner, Charles **V:**377
  Taney, Roger B. **IV:**366
  Tappan, Arthur and Lewis **IV:**367
  Underground Railroad **V:**397
  Webster, Daniel **IV:**394
  Welles, Gideon **V:**428
fugitive slave clause **III:**107
Fugitive Slave Law of 1793 **IV:**168
fugitive slave laws **III:**463*c;* **IV:168–169**
  abolitionism **IV:**4
  African Americans **III:**9
  Compromise of 1850 **IV:**103, 104
  literature **IV:**229
  Missouri Compromise **IV:**257
  personal liberty laws **IV:**298–299
Fulani **I:135–136,** 199, 370
Fulbert of Chartres **I:**129
Fulbright, William **X:**28
Full Employment Bill **VIII:145**
  Economic Bill of Rights **VIII:**102
  Keynesianism **VIII:**201
  liberalism **VIII:**216
  postwar planning **VIII:**306
  Third New Deal **VIII:**393
  Wagner, Robert F. **VIII:**411
Fuller, Blind Boy **VII:**39
Fuller, Buckminster **VI:**31
Fuller, Margaret **IV:169**
  Brook Farm **IV:**65
  Emerson, Ralph Waldo **IV:**140
  Higginson, Thomas Wentworth **VI:**172
  journalism **IV:**208, 210
  literature **IV:**228
  transcendental movement **IV:**378, 379

Fuller, Melville W. **VI:**348
Fuller, Wayne **VI:**382
Fulton, Robert **III:***182,* **182–183,** 465*c*
  agriculture **IV:**12
  economy **IV:**130
  industrialization **IV:**200
  internal improvements **IV:**202
  Livingston, Robert R. **III:**270
  science and technology **III:**385; **IV:**333
  transportation **V:**390
Fulton, USS **IV:**298
Fulton Fish Market **VII:**326; **X:**97
Fundamental Constitution for the Government of Carolina **II:**209
Fundamental Constitutions of Carolina
  government, British American **II:**152
  Locke, John **II:**209
  North Carolina **II:**274
  proprietary colonies **II:**313, 314
  South Carolina **II:**369
fundamentalism
  Campbell, Thomas **IV:**78
  conservatism **VIII:**84
  religion **VII:**297–299; **VIII:**334, 335
fundamentalist Protestants **X:**4, 234
Fundamental Orders of Government **II:**76–77, 165
Fundamentals, The **VII:**298, 403*c*
Fundy, Bay of **II:**2
funerals **V:**273
Funny Face (Gershwin) **VII:**124
Funnyhouse of a Negro (Kennedy) **IX:**258
Furies, The **X:**133
Fur kingdom **I:**104
Furman Street Mission **VI:**327
Furman v. Georgia **X:**48, 66, 376*c*
Furnas, Charles **VII:**28
Furness, Frank **VI:**19
furniture **III:**334
fur trade **II:140–142,** *141;* **III:**183, 465*c;* **IV:169–172,** 170*m,* 411*c*
  agriculture **II:**9
  Alaska **III:**12, 13
  Alaska, Russia in **II:**14–15
  Aleut **II:**17
  Algonquin **II:**18
  American Fur Company **IV:**18–19
  animals **II:**22
  Armijo, Manuel **IV:**26
  Ashley, William Henry **IV:**31–33
  Astor, John Jacob **IV:**33–35
  Astoria **IV:**35–36

  Beaver Wars **II:**35
  Beckwourth, Jim **IV:**50
  Bent, Charles **IV:**51
  Bent, William **IV:**52
  Bent's Fort **IV:**54–55
  Bridger, James **IV:**64
  Canada **III:**77–79
  Choctaw **III:**89
  Chouteau family **IV:**87–88
  Delaware **II:**95
  environment **II:**119–120
  exploration **II:**123, 124; **IV:**144
  foreign policy **IV:**156–157
  Fort Laramie **IV:**156, 157
  Fort Vancouver **IV:**158, 159
  French colonies **II:**135, 137
  Great Plains **III:**197
  habitants **I:**149
  Hastings, Lansford W. **IV:**187
  Huron **II:**169
  Iberville, Pierre Le Moyne, sieur d' **II:**173
  Indian Affairs, Bureau of **IV:**196
  Indian Removal Act **IV:**197
  Iroquois **I:**187; **II:**179
  Jolliet, Louis **II:**189
  lead mines **IV:**223
  Livingston, Robert **II:**207
  Logan, James **II:**209
  McLoughlin, John **IV:**247–248
  métis **II:**232–233
  Missouri Fur Company **IV:**257–258
  Montagnais-Naskapi **I:**250
  Montreal **II:**242
  mountain men **IV:**266
  Native Americans **II:**251
  New York **II:**269–272
  Oneida **I:**280
  Onondaga **I:**280
  Oregon Trail **IV:**285
  Oregon Treaty of 1846 **IV:**287
  Pontiac's War **III:**339
  rendezvous **IV:**321–322
  Rocky Mountain Fur Company **IV:**324–325
  Russian settlements **II:**338
  St. Vrain, Céran **IV:**327–328
  Seneca **I:**329
  Smith, Jedediah Strong **IV:**350–351
  trade, domestic and foreign **II:**392
  Wyeth, Nathaniel J. **IV:**406
Fur Traders Descending the Missouri (Bingham) **IV:**29
Fusion Party **VIII:**209
Futurama exhibition (1939 New York World's Fair) **VIII:**29
FWP. *See* Federal Writers' Project

G

G-2 (War Department Military Intelligence Division) **VIII:**186
Gable, Clark **VIII:**446*c*
  Gone With the Wind **V:**169
  Monroe, Marilyn **IX:**223
  movies **VIII:**246
  recreation **VIII:**328
Gabon **I:**254–255; **X:**267
Gabriell (ship) **I:**134
Gabriel's Rebellion **III:185–186,** 204, 391, 464*c*
Gadsden, James **IV:**173
Gadsden Purchase **IV:173–174,** 174*m,* 415*c*
  economy **IV:**130
  exploration **IV:**146
  Guadalupe Hidalgo, Treaty of **IV:**181
  Pierce, Franklin **V:**307
  Santa Anna, Antonio López de **IV:**330
Gagarin, Yuri **IX:**355*c*
  NASA **IX:**231
  space exploration **IX:**296
  technology **IX:**312
Gage, Frances Dana **V:**393
Gage, Matilda Joslyn **V:**438; **VI:137,** 284
Gage, Thomas **III:***186,* **186–187**
  Burgoyne, Sir John **III:**67
  Church, Benjamin **III:**89
  Clinton, Sir Henry **III:**99
  Hancock, John **III:**209
  Lexington and Concord, Battles of **III:**264, 266
  Pontiac's War **III:**340
Gag Rule (1836)
  abolitionism **IV:**4
  Adams, John Quincy **IV:**6
  American Anti-Slavery Society **IV:**15
  Calhoun, John C. **IV:**69
Gaines, Edmund P.
  Black Hawk War **IV:**57
  Scott, Winfield **IV:**336
  Seminole **IV:**338
  Seminole War, First/Second **IV:**339
Gaines, William **IX:**314
Gaines's Mill
  Irish-American regiments **V:**205
  Peninsular campaign **V:**299
  Pickett, George Edward **V:**306
Gains v. Canada **IX:**227
Gaither Report **IX:**83
Galápagos Islands **VI:**122
Galawedos (emperor of Ethiopia) **I:**125
Galbraith, John Kenneth **IX:**13, 98, **129–130,** 354*c*
Gale, Leonard **IV:**264
Galen **II:**229

Galena, Illinois
    Grant, Julia Dent **V:**173
    Grant, Ulysses S. **V:**174
    lead mines **IV:**223, 224
Galena, USS **V:**207
Galena River **IV:**223
Galilee **IX:**160
Galileo (spacecraft) **X:**327
Gallatin, Albert **III:187–188;**
    IV:411*c*
    alcohol **III:**13
    Bank of the United States,
        First **III:**41
    citizenship **III:**94
    debt, national **III:**132
    Industrial Revolution
        III:226
    National Road **IV:**271
    Oregon Treaty of 1846
        IV:286
Gallatin, Missouri **VI:**376
Gallegos, Jose Manuel **IV:**222
Gallman, Robert E. **VI:**191
Galloway, Joseph **III:**113, 114,
    188–189, 324
Gallup, George Horace **VIII:**312,
    313; **IX:**130
Gallup Poll **IX:**18, **130–131,** 143
Galton, Francis
    eugenics **VII:**102
    intelligence tests **VII:**148
    Racial Integrity Act **VII:**284
Galveston, Battle of **V:163**
Galveston, Texas
    food riots **V:**148
    Lafitte, Jean **IV:**220
    urban reform **VII:**362
Galveston Bay **IV:**375, 379
Galveston flood **VI:137–138,** *138*
Galvéz, José de **III:**73
Galyan v. Press **IX:**337
Gama, Christovão da **I:**125
Gama, Vasco da **I:137,** 396*c*
    Cabral, Pedro Álvares **I:**46
    Dias, Bartholomeu **I:**106
    India **I:**181
    invention and technology
        I:184
    John III **I:**198
    Maravi **I:**231
    Portuguese seaborne empire
        I:299
Gambino crime family **X:**97
Gamble, James **IV:**131, 199
gambling
    horse racing **VI:**178
    popular culture **III:**341
    recreation **X:**304
    sports and recreation **V:**367
Gambling Outrages (Comstock)
    VI:79
Gandhi, Mohandas K. (Mahatma)
    Chávez, César Estrada
        IX:54
    civil disobedience **IX:**57, 58
    King, Martin Luther, Jr.
        IX:174

SNCC **IX:**302
    transcendental movement
        IV:379
gang violence. *See* youth gangs
GAO. *See* General Accounting
    Office; Government
    Accountability Office
Gao **I:137–138**
    Askia Muhammad I **I:**14
    Mansa Musa I **I:**228
    Songhai **I:**342
    Tuareg **I:**370
GAR. *See* Grand Army of the
    Republic
Garbo, Greta **VII:**214; **VIII:**245,
    246
Garden, Alexander **II:**413
Gardner, Alexander **V:**41,
    304–305
Gardoqui, Don Diego **III:**230
Garfield, Harry A. **VII:**119
Garfield, James Abram **VI:138–**
    139, *139,* 221, 235, 409*c*
    Arthur, Chester Alan
        VI:20–21
    Bayard, Thomas Francis
        VI:27
    Blaine, James Gillespie **VI:**41
    Chilean-American relations
        VI:67
    Civil Rights Act (1875) **V:**71
    civil service reform **VI:**73
    Conkling, Roscoe **VI:**81
    corruption, political **VI:**83
    Crédit Mobilier **V:**97
    Garnet, Henry Highland
        IV:175
    Hancock, Winfield Scott
        V:184
    Leslie, Frank and Miriam
        Florence Follin **VI:**221,
        221
    presidency **VI:**290
    presidential campaigns
        (1870–1899) **VI:**293
    Reid, Whitelaw **VI:**305
    Republican Party **VI:**311
    star route frauds **VI:**344
    Thirteenth Amendment
        V:388
Garfield, New Jersey **VII:**253
Garibaldi, Guiseppe **V:**441
Garland, Hamlin **VI:139–140**
    Crane, Stephen **VI:**85
    Howells, William Dean
        VI:180
    James, Henry **VI:**200
    literature **VI:**225, 226
Garland, Judy **VIII:**67
Garland Fund (American Fund
    for Public Service) **VII:**10
garment district (New York City)
    X:97
Garner, John Nance **VIII:147**
    Congress **VIII:**79
    Democratic Party **VIII:**92
    election of 1932 **VIII:**108

election of 1936 **VIII:**109
    Farley, James A. **VIII:**125
    Nye committee **VIII:**278
Garner et al. v. Louisiana **IX:**291,
    355*c*
Garner-Wagner relief bill
    VIII:331, 333
Garnet, Henry Highland **IV:174–**
    175
    African Americans **IV:**8
    54th Massachusetts
        Regiment **V:**142
    Negro Convention
        movement **IV:**279
Garnett, Richard B. **V:163–164**
Garrett, Bob **VI:**359
Garrett, John W. **IV:**44
Garrett, Pat **VI:**376
Garrett, Richard H. **V:**39
Garrison, Edward "Snapper"
    VI:178
Garrison, Lindley **VII:**227, 267
Garrison, Lucy McKim **VI:**255
Garrison, William Lloyd **IV:**412*c*,
    413*c*; **V:164–165,** *165*
    abolitionism **IV:**1–4; **V:**2–4
    ACS **IV:**17
    African Americans **IV:**9
    American Anti-Slavery
        Society **IV:**15
    Douglass, Frederick **V:**115,
        116
    female antislavery societies
        IV:147
    first *Liberator* editorial
        IV:428–429
    Foster, Abigail Kelley
        IV:161, 162
    Free-Soil Party **IV:**163
    Genius of Universal
        Emancipation **IV:**175
    Grimké, Angelina and Sarah
        IV:180
    Harper, Frances Ellen
        Watkins **VI:**159
    Higginson, Thomas
        Wentworth **VI:**171
    journalism **IV:**209
    Liberia **IV:**225
    Liberty Party **IV:**226
    Mott, Lucretia **IV:**265
    Paul, Nathaniel **IV:**295
    Phillips, Wendell **IV:**299
    race and race relations
        IV:311
    Seneca Falls convention
        IV:341
    Tappan, Arthur and Lewis
        IV:367
    Thirteenth Amendment
        V:388
    Truth, Sojourner **V:**393
    Weld, Theodore Dwight
        IV:396
Garvey, Marcus **VII:***121,* 121–
    122, 408*c*
    DuBois, W.E.B. **VII:**81

Harlem Renaissance **VII:**136
    Liberia **VI:**224
    Sweet trial **VII:**344
    UNIA **VII:**361
Gary, Elbert H.
    Industrial Revolution,
        Second **VI:**192
    open shop movement
        VII:247
    steel industry **VII:**336
    Steel Strike of 1919 **VII:**338
    U.S. Steel **VII:**365
    welfare capitalism **VII:**381
Gary, Indiana
    Foster, William Zebulon
        VII:117
    steel industry **VII:**337
    Steel Strike of 1919 **VII:**338
Gary, Joseph **VI:**12, 169
gas companies **X:**72
Gascoyne-Cecil, Robert Arthur
    Talbot (3d marquis of
    Salisbury) **VI:**373
gasoline
    black market **VIII:**46
    Energy, U.S. Department
        of **X:**122
    invention and technology
        VI:196
    Middle East **X:**227–228
    OPA **VIII:**282
    rationing **VIII:**322
gasoline rationing
    economy **X:**109
    energy **X:**119
    OPEC **X:**268
gasoline shortages **X:**122, 227–
    228, 376*c*
Gaspée affair **III:**101, **189,** 460*c*
Gastaldi, Giacomo **I:**274
Gastonia Strike **VII:122–123**
    Passaic Strike **VII:**253
    radical and labor press
        VII:286
    Vorse, Mary Heaton
        VII:375
Gaston v. United States **X:**48
Gates, Horatio **III:189–190,** *190*
    Arnold, Benedict **III:**31
    Camden, Battle of **III:**75–
        76
    Conway Cabal, the **III:**118
    Cornwallis, Charles, Lord
        III:120
    Kalb, Johann, baron de
        III:245
    Newburgh conspiracy
        III:316
    Saratoga, surrender at
        III:380, 382
    Wilkinson, James **III:**443
Gates, Sir Thomas **II:**89, **143–**
    144
Gates, William Henry "Bill," III
    X:87, *87,* **147–148**
Gateway Arch (St. Louis Missouri)
    IX:66

Gather Together in My Name
   (Angelou) **X**:26
Gatling, Richard **V**:341
Gatling guns **V**:237, 341
GATT. *See* General Agreement on
   Tariffs and Trade
Gauveau, Emile **VII**:160
gay and lesbian rights movement
   X:148–150, *149*, *214*, 375*c*,
   376*c*, 381*c*, 382*c*
   art and architecture **X**:31
   Brennan, William J., Jr.
      X:48
   Clinton, William J. **X**:80
   elections, presidential **X**:118
   feminism **X**:133, 134
   Libertarian Party **X**:209
   Moral Majority **X**:234
   NOW **X**:247–248
   political parties **X**:276
   Powell, Colin L. **X**:287
   sexual revolution **X**:322, 323
   Supreme Court **X**:339
Gaye, Marvin **X**:238
Gaylord, Frank **IX**:178
Gay Nineties **VI**:140
gays and lesbians **VIII**:147–148;
   IX:131–132
   Kinsey, Alfred C. **IX**:176
   Latino movement **IX**:186
   literature **IX**:194
   women's status and rights
      IX:347
   World War II **VIII**:427
   World War II home front
      VIII:433
Gaza Strip
   Camp David accords
      X:64–66
   Israel **IX**:160
   Middle East **X**:227, 229,
      230
   Rice, Condoleezza **X**:310
Gazette of the United States
   III:180, 240, 463*c*
GDP. *See* gross domestic product
GE. *See* General Electric
Gedi **I**:138
Gehrig, Lou **VIII**:303, 446*c*
Gehry, Frank **X**:32
Gell, Monday **IV**:388
Gemini program **IX**:285, 297
gender/gender roles **II**:144–145
   Algonquin **II**:18
   art **II**:26
   childhood **II**:67
   domesticity **II**:100
   ethnocentrism **II**:121
   feminism **X**:132
   labor/labor movements
      II:198–200
   Powhatan Confederacy
      II:307
   society, British American
      II:365
   Spanish colonies **II**:372
   theater **VI**:355

Ward, Nancy **II**:408
   women's status and rights
      II:422
gender discrimination/gender
   equality **X**:376*c*
   Brennan, William J., Jr. **X**:48
   education, higher **X**:112
   ERA **X**:124
   feminism **X**:132, 133
   gay and lesbian rights
      movement **X**:149
   Ginsburg, Ruth Bader
      X:152
   Grove City College v. Bell
      X:160
   labor/labor movements
      IX:182
   liberalism **X**:207
   NOW **IX**:236; **X**:247
   PCSW **IX**:262
   political correctness **X**:276
   Schlafly, Phyllis **X**:317
   Title IX **X**:386–387
   WEAL **IX**:345, 346
   women's status and rights
      IX:347; **X**:371
gender gap **X**:150, 378*c*
gender quotas **X**:48
gender ratios **X**:282
General Accounting Office (GAO)
   X:379*c*
   Budget and Accounting Act
      VII:44
   DHS **X**:168
   federalism **X**:131
   Gramm-Rudman-Hollings
      Act **X**:158
   House of Representatives
      X:170
General Agreement on Tariffs and
   Trade (GATT) **X**:150–151,
   380*c*
   Clinton, William J. **X**:82
   economy **X**:110
   foreign policy **X**:142
   WTO **X**:372
General Association of
   Massachusetts **III**:307
General Colored Association
   IV:389
General Education Board
   VII:329
General Electric (GE) **VI**:411*c*;
   VII:123, 403*c*; **IX**:132
   AEC **IX**:25
   banking, investment **VI**:24
   business **VIII**:57
   cities and urban life **VII**:54
   globalization **X**:153
   Industrial Revolution,
      Second **VI**:192
   invention and technology
      VI:196; **VII**:150, 151
   Morgan, John Pierpont
      VI:251
   New York World's Fair
      (1964) **IX**:246

popular culture **VII**:265
   radio **VII**:288, 289
   stock market crash
      VIII:376
   suburbanization/suburbs
      VIII:379–380
   technology **IX**:311
   Villard, Henry **VI**:375
General Electric Research
   Laboratory **VII**:313–314
General Federation of Women's
   Clubs (GFWC)
   ERA **X**:123
   mothers' pensions **VII**:214
   NACW **VI**:259–260
   New Woman **VII**:239
   Teapot Dome **VII**:351
   women's status and rights
      VII:387
General Foods Cooking School
   VII:5
General Foods Corporation
   VIII:19, 58
General Grant National Memorial
   V:268
General Historie of Virginia
   (Smith) **II**:362, 363
General History of the Pyrates
   (Johnson) **II**:385
General Jewish Council **VIII**:25
General Land Office (GLO)
   VI:141
General Leasing Act (1920)
   VII:351
General Maximum Price
   Regulation **VIII**:282, 409
General Mills **VIII**:58
General Motors (GM) **VIII**:445*c*;
   IX:132–133, 352*c*; **X**:384*c*
   American Liberty League
      VIII:19
   art and architecture
      VIII:28–29
   automobile industry **VII**:26,
      27; **VIII**:35; **IX**:25, 26;
      X:35, 37
   business **VIII**:57; **X**:58
   Chrysler Corporation Loan
      Guarantee Act **X**:74
   CIO **VIII**:82; **IX**:71
   COLA **IX**:76, 77
   dollar-a-year men **VIII**:96
   DuPont Corporation **IX**:91
   economy **VII**:84, 85
   Hillman, Sidney **VIII**:166
   labor/labor movements
      VIII:206
   literature **IX**:194
   military-industrial complex
      IX:216
   Nader, Ralph **X**:241
   New York World's Fair
      (1964) **IX**:246
   occupational health and
      safety **VII**:243
   Perot, H. Ross **X**:272
   Prohibition **VII**:274

Reuther, Walter **VIII**:339;
   IX:275
   steel industry **VIII**:373
   strikes **VIII**:377
   technology **IX**:313
General Motors Fisher Body Plant
   (Flint, Michigan) **VIII**:36
General Sherman Led by Victory
   (Saint-Gaudens) **VI**:321
General Survey Act **IV**:271
General Theological Seminary
   (Protestant Episcopal Church)
   VI:87
*General Theory of Employment,
   Interest and Money* (Keynes)
   VIII:445*c*
   CEA **IX**:77
   Great Society **IX**:139
   Keynesianism **VIII**:200
general track **VII**:88
General Trades Union **IV**:218,
   219
General Vigilance Committee
   IV:357
Genesee College **VI**:228
Geneseo **III**:359
Genêt, Edmond Charles **III**:190–
   191, 463*c*
   Democratic-Republican
      societies **III**:137
   foreign affairs **III**:168
   French Alliance **III**:178
   French Revolution **III**:178–
      179
   Neutrality Proclamation
      III:315
genetic engineering **X**:18–20, 224
genetics **VII**:102
Geneva, Switzerland **VIII**:443*c*
   Calvin, John **I**:53–54
   London Naval Conference
      VIII:222
   Naval Disarmament
      Conference **VII**:234,
      235
   Reformation **I**:316
   World Disarmament
      Conference **VIII**:426
Geneva Accords (1954)
   Dulles, John Foster **IX**:91
   SEATO **IX**:292
   Vietnam War **IX**:330
Geneva Conference (1962)
   IX:338
Geneva Conventions
   Barton, Clara **V**:29
   Hamdan v. Rumsfeld **X**:164
   POWs **VIII**:310, 311
   rules of war **V**:338
Geneva Medical College **IV**:250,
   415*c*
Geneva Naval Conference
   VII:164
Geneva Treaty **V**:29
Genevieve of New France **II**:386
Genghis Khan **I**:295
Genius, The (Dreiser) **VII**:285

Genius of Oblivion, The (Hale)
IV:183
Genius of Universal Emancipation
(periodical) IV:1–2, 147, **175**
Gennett Record Company
VII:97
Genoa I:84, 195
genocide
Africa X:17
Clinton, William J. X:81
defense policy X:102
UN X:357
genre painting
art IV:29; V:18
Eakins, Thomas VI:104
La Farge, John Frederick
Lewis Joseph VI:217
gens de couleur libre II:83;
III:203
genteel tradition VI:225
Genth, Frederick A. VI:144, 145
*Gentle Art of Making Enemies,
The* (Whistler) VI:390
Gentlemen Prefer Blondes (film)
IX:222, 225
Gentlemen's Agreement VII:**123–
124**, 404*c*
Great White Fleet VII:130
immigration restrictions
VI:187
nativism VII:234
race and race relations
VII:281
Roosevelt, Theodore
VII:304
Root-Takahira Agreement
VII:305
Geographical and Geological
Survey, U.S. VI:288
geography
Mercator, Gerhardus I:240
Mexico I:243
Morse, Jedidiah III:307
Peru I:289
Geography (Ptolemy) I:240, 313
Geography Made Easy (Morse)
III:307
Geological Society of America
VI:294
Geological Survey, U.S. (USGS)
VI:**140–142**, 409*c*
conservation/
environmentalism VI:81
environment VI:119
Hayden, Ferdinand
Vandeveer VI:165
King, Clarence VI:208
Marsh, Othniel Charles
VI:240
mining VI:246
Powell, John Wesley VI:288
science and technology
VI:325
Walcott, Charles Doolittle
VI:379, 380
Ward, Lester Frank VI:382
geological surveys VI:246

geology
Geological Survey, U.S.
VI:141
Hayden, Ferdinand
Vandeveer VI:164–165
King, Clarence VI:207–208
Powell, John Wesley VI:288
science and technology
III:384; VI:325;
VIII:352
Walcott, Charles Doolittle
VI:379–380
geophysics VIII:352
George, David VI:4
George, Henry VI:**142**, 409*c*
Anti-Imperialist League
VI:17
Johnson, Tom Loftin
VII:156
Sanger, Margaret VII:311–
312
Simpson, Jerry VI:330
George, Lake II:134
George, Milton VI:125
George, Walter F. VIII:326
George I (king of England)
II:240
George II (king of England)
II:240
George III (king of England)
III:*191*, 191–192, 459*c*–461*c*
art III:33
Brant, Joseph III:62
Bute, John Stuart, earl of
III:70–71
Catholics III:83
Cherokee II:65
Common Sense III:101
corporatism III:122
Crèvecoeur, J. Hector St.
John de III:127
Declaration of
Independence III:132,
133
Gage, Thomas III:187
Hancock, John III:208
immigration III:221
Johnson, Sir John III:237
liberty tree III:267
monarchy, British II:240–
241
Native Americans III:314
North, Frederick, Lord
III:320
Olive Branch Petition
III:324
Ostenaco II:280
Paris, Treaty of (1763)
III:331
Pitt, William III:337
Proclamation of 1763
III:348
resistance movement
III:366
West, Benjamin III:435,
436
writs of assistance III:448

George R. Smith College for
Negroes (Sedalia, Missouri)
VII:158
*George Washington Athenaeum
Portrait* III:400
George Washington Parke Custis,
USS V:25
George Washington University
VII:211; IX:168
George White's Scandals VII:124
Georgia I:360; II:**145–147**,
146*m*, 437*c*; IV:412*c*
abolitionism V:1
African Americans II:7;
III:9; IV:10
agriculture II:11; IV:10, 12
Andersonville Prison,
Georgia V:10–11
Anglican Church II:21
Bradley, Omar N. VIII:50
Briar's Creek, Battle of
III:63–64
Brown, Joseph Emerson
V:45
Carter, James Earl, Jr.
X:67–68
Cherokee IV:85
citizenship III:93
Cobb, Howell V:76
Constitution, ratification of
the III:104
constitutions, state III:110
cotton III:122, 123
Creek III:125, 126
disease/epidemics IV:123
Dow, Lorenzo IV:126
economy II:109
education, philanthropy and
VI:112
election of 1840 IV:138
environment III:155
Evans, Walker VIII:120
Federalists III:166
Florida II:129, 130
Frémont, John C. IV:166
Gastonia Strike VII:122
gold IV:176
governors V:172
habeas corpus, writ of
Portrait V:181
*Heart of Atlanta Motel v.
U.S.* IX:145–146
housing II:167
Indian Affairs, Bureau of
IV:197
Indian Removal Act IV:197,
198
Jackson, Andrew IV:205
Ku Klux Klan V:223;
VII:165
Ladies Memorial
Associations V:229
literature VI:226
McIntosh, William IV:247
migration IV:254
Native Americans IV:274,
275

Nullification Controversy
IV:282
Oglethorpe, James Edward
II:277–278
Pinckney, Charles
Cotesworth III:336
plantations V:308
proprietary colonies II:314
Pulaski, Casimir III:350
race and race relations
VIII:318
religion V:331
religion, Euro-American
II:329
Ridge, John IV:324
Ross, John IV:325
Savannah II:343
Savannah, Battle of III:382–
383
Savannah, siege of III:383
SCLC IX:292–293
Seminole IV:338
Seminole War, First/Second
IV:339
Sherman's March through
Georgia V:356–357
slavery III:390
slave trade III:393
SNCC IX:302
southern demagogues
VII:332
Sunbelt VIII:381
tactics and strategy V:382
Tomochichi II:392
Trail of Tears IV:378
Turner, Henry McNeal
VI:366
veterans V:416
violence and lawlessness
VI:375
Watson, Thomas Edward
VII:380
Georgia Expedition III:**192–193**
Georgia Mississippi Company
III:454
Georgian architecture III:27
Georgia plan II:277
Gephardt, Dick X:170, 171
Gerald of Wales I:248
Gericke, Wilhelm VI:28, 233
German American Bund
VIII:149
German-American regiments
V:**165–166**, 200
German Americans II:**147–148**,
437*c*; IV:*214*; VIII:**148–149**
anti-Catholic riots IV:23
canal era IV:79
cities and urban life V:66
civil liberties VIII:72
election of 1940 VIII:110
enemy aliens VIII:114–115
Executive Order 9066
VIII:121
Fries's Rebellion III:180
immigration IV:193–196;
V:199–201

isolationists **VIII:**189
Kaiser, Henry J. **VIII:**199
Kuhn, Justus Engelhardt
    II:196
labor/labor movements
    III:251
Lutherans **II:**212
Mittelberger, Gottlieb
    II:239
Muhlenberg, Henry
    Melchior **II:**246
news media **VIII:**271
New York **II:**271
North Carolina **II:**275
Philadelphia **II:**292
race and race relations
    VIII:318
religious liberty **III:**362
South Carolina **II:**370
Weiser, Johann Conrad
    II:409
Wistar, Caspar **II:**419
"German Belt" **IV:**195
German Democratic Republic
    (East Germany)
    Berlin blockade **IX:**38–39
    cold war, end of **X:**84
    Iron Curtain, collapse of
        X:189
    Soviet Union **IX:**295
German Diplomatic Corps
    VII:401
German Foreign Office,
    Switzerland **VIII:**285
German Historical School of
    economics **VI:**115, 120
German mercenaries. *See*
    Hessians
German Reformed Church
    II:148–149
German Socialist Party **VI:**213
German sympathizers **VIII:**384
Germantown, Battle of **III:**193*m,*
    193–194
    Cornwallis, Charles, Lord
        III:120
    Greene, Nathanael **III:**198
    Monroe, James **IV:**258
    Pinckney, Charles
        Cotesworth **III:**336
    Sullivan, John **III:**402
Germany **VII:**407*c;* **VIII:**443*c,*
    446*c*–448*c;* **X:**379*c*
    AEF **VII:**11
    aircraft industry **VIII:**13
    air power **VIII:**15
    amphibious warfare **VIII:**20
    Anglo-American relations
        VIII:21
    Army Air Forces, U.S.
        VIII:26
    Atlantic Charter **VIII:**34
    atomic bomb **VIII:**34
    automobile industry **X:**35
    Axis **VIII:**37–38
    Baldwin, Roger Nash
        VII:32

blitzkrieg **VIII:**47
Boas, Franz Uri **VII:**39
Bodmer, Karl **IV:**60
bombing **VIII:**47–48
Boxer Rebellion **VII:**40
Bradley, Omar N. **VIII:**51
Brandeis, Louis Dembitz
    VII:41
Britain, Battle of **VIII:**53–
    54
Bulge, Battle of the
    VIII:54–55
Casablanca Conference
    VIII:62
CDAAA **VIII:**77
chain stores **VI:**65
code breaking **VIII:**76
cold war **IX:**63
Committee for Public
    Information **VII:**60
conscription **VII:**63
Coolidge, Calvin John
    VII:65
Dawes Plan **VII:**72
demobilization (WWII)
    VIII:91
Democratic Party **VII:**74,
    75
education, higher **VI:**111
Ely, Richard Theodore
    VI:115
enemy aliens **VIII:**114
espionage **VIII:**117
Espionage Act **VII:**101
Europe **IX:**112
Executive Reorganization
    Act **VIII:**121
FCC **VIII:**131
Fordney-McCumber Tariff
    VII:112
foreign policy **VII:**113–116;
    VIII:140–142
German Americans
    VIII:148
Grand Alliance **VIII:**155–
    156
Great Depression **VIII:**157
Gutenberg, Johannes
    Gensfleisch zum **I:**148
Harding, Warren Gamaliel
    VII:135
Hiroshima and Nagasaki
    VIII:167
Holocaust **VIII:**169–170
Holy Roman Empire **I:**166
Hughes, Charles Evans
    VII:142
immigration **IV:**193; **VI:**184;
    VIII:184
intelligence **VIII:**187
investments, American,
    abroad **VI:**197
isolationists **VIII:**189–190
Italian Americans **VIII:**191
Italian campaign **VIII:**191
James, Henry **VI:**200
Jews **I:**194, 197; **VIII:**196

Johnson, Hiram Warren
    VII:154
Judaism **VI:**205
Kellogg-Briand Treaty
    VII:164
Kennedy, Joseph P.
    VIII:200
labor, radical **VI:**213
labor/labor movements
    X:202
League of Nations **VII:**175
Lend-Lease **VIII:**211, 212
liberalism **VIII:**216
Lodge, Henry Cabot
    VII:184
London Naval Conference
    VIII:222
Lusitania, RMS **VII:**187–
    188
Manchuria **VIII:**225
medicine **VII:**198
modernism **VII:**212
movies **VIII:**246
Munich Conference
    VIII:248
National Origins Act
    VII:227
Naval Disarmament
    Conference **VII:**235
Nazi-Soviet Pact **VIII:**266
neutrality **VII:**235–236
Neutrality Acts **VIII:**267
Non-Partisan League
    VII:241
North African campaign
    VIII:277
NWLB **VII:**229
Open Door Policy **VII:**246
OSS **VIII:**285
Owens, Jesse **VIII:**288, 289
peace movements **VII:**256
Potsdam Conference
    VIII:307
POWs **VIII:**310, 311
Preparedness **VII:**267
presidency **VII:**268
Prohibition **VII:**272
propaganda **VIII:**311
rationing **VIII:**323
Reformation **I:**315
refugees **VIII:**329, 330
Republican Party **VII:**300
Samoa **VI:**322, 323
Schenck v. U.S. **VII:**313
Seattle General Strike
    VII:317
second front **VIII:**355
Sedition Act **VII:**318
Selective Service Act
    VII:321
Siberian Expedition
    VII:324
Soviet-American relations
    VIII:368–369
Spanish civil war **VIII:**369
sports and recreation
    VIII:372

steel industry **IX:**301
Steel Strike of 1919
    VII:338
submarines **VIII:**378
tanks **VIII:**385–386
tariffs **VII:**350
Teheran Conference
    VIII:390, 391
trade, domestic and foreign
    VII:354
Trading with the Enemy Act
    VII:355
Truman, Harry S. **IX:**320
UN **VIII:**402; **X:**356
V-E Day **VIII:**405
Versailles, Treaty of
    VII:369–371
Villard, Henry **VI:**374
Wilson, Thomas Woodrow
    VII:383
witches/witchcraft **I:**384
World Disarmament
    Conference **VIII:**426
World War I **VII:**393
World War II **VIII:**427
World War II European
    theater **VIII:**429–431
Yalta Agreement **VIII:**467–
    468
Yalta Conference **VIII:**439,
    440
Zimmermann telegram
    VII:401
Zionism **VIII:**441
Germany, Federal Republic of
    (West Germany) **IX:**352*c*
    Berlin blockade **IX:**38
    cold war **IX:**63
    cold war, end of **X:**84
    Iron Curtain, collapse of
        X:189
    NATO **IX:**247
germ theory **V:**343
Gérôme, Jean-Léon **VI:**63
Geronimo **IV:**276; **VI:**17–18,
    142–143, *143,* 262, 263, 409*c,*
    410*c*
Gerry, Elbridge **III:194–195**
    Constitutional Convention
        III:108
    Pinckney Treaty **III:**336
    XYZ affair **III:**451
Gershon, Levi ben **I:**99
Gershwin, George **VII:***124,*
    124–125, 409*c*
    entertainment, popular
        VII:96
    jazz **VII:**153
    music **VII:**218–220;
        VIII:251, 252; **X:**238
    Tin Pan Alley **VII:**353
Gerth, Jeff **X:**380*c*
Gesell, Gerhard **X:**365
Gesner, Conrad von **I:**139
Gestapo **VIII:**187
"Get on the Water Wagon" sermon
    (Sunday) **VII:**342

Gettysburg, Battle of **V:166–168,** *167,* 445*c*
   Alexander, Edward P. **V:**8
   Armistead, Lewis A. **V:**17
   Brady, Mathew B. **V:**41
   brothers' war **V:**43
   Chamberlain, Joshua L. **V:**60
   Civil War **V:**74
   Comstock, Anthony **VI:**78–79
   Custer, George A. **V:**99
   desertion **V:**110
   Early, Jubal A. **V:**119
   elections **V:**126
   Ewell, Richard Stoddert **V:**135–136
   foreign policy **V:**151
   Garnett, Richard B. **V:**164
   Gordon, John B. **V:**170
   Hancock, Winfield Scott **V:**183–184
   Harvard Regiment **V:**187
   Hill, Ambrose P. **V:**190
   Hollywood Cemetery **V:**192
   Hood, John Bell **V:**196
   Hooker, Joseph **V:**197
   Howard, Oliver Otis **V:**197
   Lee, Robert E. **V:**231
   Longstreet, James **V:**242, 243
   McLaws, Lafayette **V:**253
   Meade, George Gordon **V:**254
   monuments **V:**268
   Oates, William C. **V:**287
   Philadelphia **V:**303–304
   photography **V:**304
   Pickett, George Edward **V:**305
   Reid, Whitelaw **VI:**304
   science and technology **V:**341
   Sickles, Daniel E. **V:**361
   Stuart, J. E. B. **V:**376
   tactics and strategy **V:**380
   veterans **V:**415, 416
   women soldiers **V:**435
   Zouaves **V:**442
Gettysburg Address **V:**129, **169,** 276, 445*c*, **461**
Gettysburg National Military Park **V:**276
Geyer, Enrique Bolanos **X:**255
GFWC. *See* General Federation of Women's Clubs
Ghana **I:139–140; II:**359
   Africa **IX:**3
   Akan **I:**5
   Asante **I:**13
   Dagomba **I:**103
   Fulani **I:**135
   Gao **I:**138
   gold **I:**141
   Guinea-Bissau **I:**148
   Mali **I:**225, 226
   Murray, Pauli **IX:**227

   Sahara **I:**324
   Sudan **I:**347
Ghent, Treaty of **IV:175–176,** 411*c*, **419–422**
   Adams, John Quincy **IV:**5
   American Fur Company **IV:**18
   Astor, John Jacob **IV:**34
   Astoria **IV:**36
   Canada **III:**79
   Clay, Henry **IV:**96
   Dartmoor Prison **IV:**114
   Decatur, Stephen **IV:**115
   economy **IV:**130
   Federalist Party **III:**165
   Florida **III:**167
   foreign affairs **III:**169
   foreign policy **IV:**154
   Free Trade and Sailor's Rights **IV:**165
   French Revolution **III:**179
   Hartford Convention **IV:**187
   Kearny, Stephen Watts **IV:**212
   Madison, James **III:**284
   New Orleans, Battle of **IV:**280
   War of 1812 **IV:**392
   Webster-Ashburton Treaty **IV:**394
ghettoes **I:**195; **X:**295
Ghorbanifar, Manucher **X:**183
Ghormley, Robert L. **VIII:**365
Ghost Dance movement **VI:**410*c*
   Geronimo **VI:**143
   Native Americans **VI:**262
   Red Cloud **VI:**303
   religion **VI:**309–310
   Sioux wars **VI:**331
   Sitting Bull **VI:**332
Ghost Dance War
   Apache War **VI:**17
   Indian Rights Association **VI:**190
   religion **VI:**310
Giant (film) **IX:**224
Gibbon, Edward **III:**365
Gibbon, John **V:**50–51
Gibbons v. Ogden **IV:**393, 412*c*
Gibbs, James **II:**25
Gibbs, Josiah Willard **VI:**2, **144,** 325, 408*c*
Gibbs, Wolcott **VI:144–145**
GI Bill of Rights **VIII:149–150,** 448*c*
   childhood **IX:**54
   Congress **VIII:**81
   consumerism **IX:**75
   demobilization (WWII) **VIII:**91
   Democratic Party **IX:**85
   economy **VIII:**104; **IX:**97
   education **VIII:**107; **IX:**99
   gays and lesbians **VIII:**148
   housing **VIII:**179
   Italian Americans **VIII:**191
   postwar planning **VIII:**306

   reconversion **VIII:**326
   religion **IX:**273
   suburbanization/suburbs **VIII:**380
   veterans **IX:**329
   WAC **VIII:**421
   World War II **VIII:**428
   World War II home front **VIII:**432
Gibraltar, Straits of **I:**314; **III:**45, 332
Gibson, Charles Dana **VI:**183, 236, 410*c*
Gibson, James (Paxton Boy) **II:**282
Gibson, James F. (photographer) **V:**304
Gibson, Josh **VII:**335; **VIII:**370
Gibson Girls **VI:**410*c*
   Gay Nineties **VI:**140
   illustration, photography, and graphic arts **VI:**183
   magazines **VI:**236
Gidden, George R. **IV:**311
Giddings, Joshua **IV:**4
Gideon, Clarence Earl **IX:**133–134; **X:**233
Gideon's Band **V:**312
Gideon v. Wainwright **IX:133–134,** 355*c*; **X:**233
Giffard, Henri **V:**341
Gifford, Walter S. **VIII:**310
GI Forum **IX:**185
G.I. Joe (action figure) **IX:**55
Gila Cliff Dwellings (New Mexico) **VII:**16
Gila River **II:**294; **IV:**173, 212
Gilbert, Sir Humphrey **I:140–141,** 398*c*
   Elizabeth I **I:**120
   Grenville, Sir Richard **I:**145
   monarchy, British **II:**240
   Newfoundland **II:**258
   Parmenius, Stephen **I:**286
   Peckham, Sir George **I:**288
Gilbert, Olive **V:**393
Gilbert, W. S. **VI:**257
Gilbert and Sullivan **VI:**257, 354
Gilbert Islands
   amphibious warfare **VIII:**20
   Halsey, William F. **VIII:**161
   Nimitz, Chester W. **VIII:**274
   Tarawa **VIII:**386
   World War II Pacific theater **VIII:**436
Gilded Age **V:**102, 275
Gilded Age, The: A Tale of Today (Twain and Warner) **VI:145–147,** 367
Gilder, Richard Watson **VI:147,** 319, 392
Gillepsie, Archibald **IV:**49
Gillespie, John Birks "Dizzy" **VIII:**195, 251, 448*c*
Gillette, King **VI:**196
Gillette, William **VI:**355

Gillette v. United States **X:**375*c*
Gillis House **IV:**242
Gillmore, Quincy A. **V:**342
Gilman, Charlotte Perkins **VII:125**
   literature **VI:**225
   politics (1900–1928) **VII:**261
   radicalism **VII:**288
   women's status and rights **VII:**388
Gilman, Daniel Coit **VI:148–149**
   education, higher **VI:**111
   Eliot, Charles William **VI:**114
   Ely, Richard Theodore **VI:**115
   Hall, Granville Stanley **VI:**157
   Peirce, Charles Sanders **VI:**281
   Royce, Josiah **VI:**318
   White, Andrew Dickson **VI:**391
Gilman, George F. **VI:**65
Gilmer, Thomas **IV:**383
Gilmore, James R. **V:**296
Gilmore, Patrick S. **VI:**170
Gilpin, Thomas **III:**17
Gimbel, Adam **VI:**96
Gingrich, Newton L. **X:151–152,** 381*c*
   Clinton, William J. **X:**82
   conservative movement **X:**94
   House of Representatives **X:**170
   UN **X:**357
   Wright, James C., Jr. **X:**372, 373
Ginsberg, Allen **IX:***78, 134,* **134–135,** 353*c*
   Beat Generation **IX:**36, 37
   counterculture **IX:**78
   gays and lesbians **IX:**132
   Kerouac, Jack **IX:**173
   Leary, Timothy **IX:**187
   literature **IX:**194, 195
   LSD **IX:**195
   music **IX:**229
   religion **IX:**272
Ginsberg, Naomi **IX:**134–135
Ginsburg, Ruth Bader **X:152–153**
   abortion **X:**4
   gun control **X:**162
   Hamdan v. Rumsfeld **X:**164
   Supreme Court **X:**339
   women's status and rights **X:**371
Giovanni, Nikki **VI:**102
Giovanni's Room (Baldwin) **IX:**34–35, 194
Giovannitti, Arturo **VII:**109, 173, 174
Girard, Stephen **III:**41, **195,** 414
Girard Bank **III:**195

Girard College **IV:**30; **V:**234

Girl Crazy (Gershwin) **VII:**124

Girl of the Streets, A (Crane)
VI:147

Girl Scouts **VIII:**67, 329

Gish, Lillian **VIII:**17

Gist, Christopher **II:**278; **III:**323

Gitlow, Benjamin **VII:**58, 343

Gitlow v. New York
censorship **VIII:**65
civil liberties **VII:**58
Schenck v. U.S. **VII:**313
Supreme Court **VII:**343

Giuliani, Rudolph **X:**97

Giustiniani, Tommaso **I:**98

Givenchy, Hubert de **IX:**116

Glackens, William **VII:**25

Gladden, Washington **VI:**149,
306, 335

"Gladiolus Rag" (Joplin) **VII:**219

Gladstein, Richard **IX:**86

Gladstone, W. D. **VI:**100

Gladwin, Henry **II:**132; **III:**340

Glaize, meeting at the **III:**54,
195, 359

Glarner, Fritz **VIII:**31

glasnost **X:153**
cold war, end of **X:**86
INF Treaty **X:**180
Soviet Union, breakup of
X:326

Glaspell, Susan **VII:**130–131, 375

Glass, Carter
Banking Act (1933) **VIII:**41
Banking Act (1935) **VIII:**41
Farley, James A. **VIII:**125

Glass, Hugh **IV:**64

Glass Ceiling Commission Report
X:381c

Glass-Steagall Act. *See* Banking
Act of 1933

Glazer, Nathan **X:**236

Glenn, John **IX:**355c
Operation Mongoose
IX:250
Senate, U.S. **X:**321
space exploration **IX:**296
technology **IX:**312

Glenn Canyon Dam **VII:**229

Glessner House (Chicago, Illinois)
VI:313

Glidden, Joseph F. **VI:**24

GLO (General Land Office)
VI:141

global interdependence **X:**205

globalization **X:153–155,** *154,*
380c
Clinton, William J. **X:**81
economy **X:**110
Nader, Ralph **X:**242
WTO **X:**372

Globalization Syndrome, The
(Mittelman) **X:**153

Global Military Force Policy
(1998) **X:**346

Global Positioning System (GPS)
X:320

global warming **IX:**356c; **X:155–
156,** *381c*
conservation/
environmentalism **X:**92
OPEC **X:**268
science and technology
IX:286

Globe (New York) **VI:**72

Globe Theatre **I:**334

Glorietta Pass **IV:**332

Glorious Revolution **II:149–150,**
436c
Andros, Sir Edmund **II:**20
citizenship **III:**92
commonwealthmen **III:**103
Leisler's Rebellion **II:**203
Massachusetts **II:**223
Mather, Cotton **II:**227
religious liberty **III:**362
republicanism **III:**364
Roman Catholicism **II:**336
Whigs **III:**439

Glover, Jose **II:**92

GM. *See* General Motors

GN. *See* Great Northern Railway
Company

Gnadenhutten Massacre **III:196,**
302

GNP. *See* gross national product

Go (Holmes) **IX:**36

Goa, India **I:**6

Goals 2000 **X:**115

God **I:**54

God and Man at Yale (Buckley)
IX:74; **X:**49

"God Bless America" **VIII:**252

Goddard, Henry **VII:**102

Goddard, Robert **VII:**178

Goddard, William **II:**304

Godey, Louis A. **IV:183–184,** 210

Godey's Lady's Book
fashion **V:**138
Hale, Sarah Josepha **IV:**184
journalism **IV:**208, 210
magazines **VI:**236
Stowe, Harriet Beecher
V:373

Godfrey, Thomas **II:150,** 288,
300

God in Christ (Bushnell) **IV:**319

Godkin, Edwin Lawrence
VI:149–150
Bryce, James **VI:**53
mugwumps **VI:**252
Nation, The **VI:**259
newspapers **VI:**265, 266
Villard, Henry **VI:**375

"God Save the South" **V:**274

gods/goddesses **II:**330
Cozumel **I:**99
Huitzilopochtli **I:**171
Huron **I:**171–172
Inca **I:**179
Massachusett **I:**233
Maya **I:**236
Niger River **I:**271
Quetzalcoatl **I:**309

God That Failed, The (Wright)
VIII:437

Godwin, E. W. **VI:**389

Goebbels, Joseph **VIII:**223, 311

Goethals, George **VII:**406c

Goethe, Johann Wolfgang von
VI:219

Go for Broke (film) **VIII:**194

Golan Heights **IX:**160; **X:**227

gold **I:141–143,** *142;* **IV:176–
179,** *177*
Akan **I:**5
Andes Mountains **I:**9
anti-Chinese agitation, rise
of **IV:**24
art and architecture **I:**13
Asante **I:**13
Atahualpa **I:**16
Aztecs **I:**22
Beckwourth, Jim **IV:**51
Cabot, Sebastian **I:**45
Castile **I:**66–67
Cherokee **IV:**85
Colorado gold rush **IV:**99
Columbian Exchange **I:**82
conquistadores **I:**88
Córdoba, Francisco
Hernández de **I:**90
Coronado, Francisco **I:**92
economy **V:**121
exploration **IV:**145–146
Florida **I:**131
Forty-niners **IV:**159–160
Frémont, John C. **IV:**167
Frobisher, Martin **I:**134,
135
Gao **I:**137
Ghana **I:**139–140
Gomes, Diogo **I:**143
Grenville, Sir Richard **I:**145
Guinea-Bissau **I:**148
Hastings, Lansford W.
IV:187
Henry the Navigator **I:**161
Hispaniola **I:**163
immigration **IV:**196
Larkin, Thomas Oliver
IV:223
Mali **I:**225–226
Mansa Musa I **I:**228
Maravi **I:**231
Mecca **I:**238
migration **IV:**255
mining **VI:**246
monetary policy **VIII:**243,
244
Native Americans **IV:**275
New Spain **I:**269
Niger River **I:**271
Nullification Controversy
IV:282
Oregon Trail **IV:**285
Oviedo y Valdés, Gonzalo
Fernández de **I:**281
Puerto Rico **I:**306
Sahara **I:**324
Santa Fe Trail **IV:**332

Senegambia **I:**330
Soto, Hernando de **I:**342
stock market crash **VIII:**376
Sudan **I:**347
Sutter, John **IV:**363
Timbuktu **I:**359
Velázquez, Diego de **I:**374

Gold, Harry **IX:**280

Gold, Michael **VII:**218

Gold Beach, Normandy, France
VIII:276

Goldberg, Arthur
Escobedo v. Illinois **IX:**111
UN **X:**357
Warren Court **IX:**337

Goldbergs, The (radio program)
VIII:301, 320

"Gold Bug, The" (Poe) **IV:**229

Gold Coast **I:143**
Africa **II:**4
Dias, Bartholomeu **I:**105
gold **I:**141
Royal African Company
II:337
slavery **I:**337
slave trade **I:**340

Gold Diggers of 1933 (film)
VIII:301

"Golden Age of Piracy" **II:**384

Golden Bowl, The (James) **VII:**179

Golden Era (newspaper) **VI:**162

Golden Gate Park, San Francisco
V:67

Golden Hill, Battle of **III:196,**
267, 413, 460c

Golden Hind (ship) **I:**111

Golden Horde **I:**295

*Golden Hour of the Little Flower,
The* (radio program) **VIII:**87

gold fever **IV:**159–160

Goldman, Emma **VII:125–126,**
126
birth control **VII:**36
Greenwich Village **VII:**131
labor, radical **VI:**213
public health **VII:**276
radical and labor press
VII:285
radicalism **VII:**288
women's status and rights
VII:388

Goldmark, Josephine Clara
VII:126–127, 199

Goldmark, Rubin **VII:**124

Gold Repeal Resolution
VIII:444c

Gold Reserve Act (1934)
VIII:150, 243

gold rush. *See specific gold rushes,
e.g.:* Black Hills gold rush

Gold Rush, The (film) **VIII:**216

gold standard **IV:**413c; **VI:**408c,
411c; **VIII:**150, 444c
bimetallism **VI:**38
Bland-Allison Act **VI:**41–42
Bretton Woods Conference
VIII:52

gold standard (*continued*)
    business cycles **VI:**59
    elections **VII:**89
    Emergency Banking Act of
        1933 **VIII:**113
    energy **X:**120
    Free-Silver Movement
        VI:135
    Great Depression
        VIII:157
    Harrison, Benjamin **VI:**161
    Hayes, Rutherford B.
        VI:168
    Liberal Republican Party
        VI:222
    London Economic
        Conference **VIII:**221
    McKinley, William **VI:**241
    monetary policy **VIII:**243
    Morgan, John Pierpont
        VI:251
    mugwumps **VI:**252
    Republican Party **VII:**299
    Sherman, John **VI:**329
    World Disarmament
        Conference **VIII:**426
Gold Standard Act
    bimetallism **VI:**38
    currency issue **VI:**90
    Free-Silver Movement
        VI:135
    McKinley, William **VI:**241
Goldwater, Barry **IX:135–136,**
    316, 354c, 356c
    advertising **IX:**3
    conservatism **VIII:**85;
        IX:74, 75
    conservative movement
        X:93
    elections **IX:**104
    Helms, Jesse A., Jr. **X:**165
    liberalism **IX:**191
    MFDP **IX:**220
    modern Republicanism
        IX:222
    Reagan, Ronald W. **X:**299
    Republican Party **IX:**274
    Schlafly, Phyllis **X:**317
    YAF **IX:**350
golf
    recreation **VII:**295;
        VIII:328; **X:**302–303
    sports and recreation
        VI:343; **VIII:**372; **X:**332
    television **X:**344
Golf Writers' Association of
    America (GWAA) **X:**332
Goliad **IV:**413c
    Alamo, The **IV:**14
    Houston, Sam **IV:**191
    Texas **IV:**372
    Texas Revolution **IV:**375
Golikov, Ivan **II:**338
Gomes, Diogo **I:143,** 337, 396c
Gomes, Fernão **I:**141
Gomes, Kiogo **I:**148
Gómez, Máximo **VI:**88

Gompers, Samuel **VI:***150*, **150–**
    151, 409c
    AFL **VI:**13; **VII:**11, 12;
        VIII:18; **IX:**11
    anticommunism **VIII:**22
    Buck's Stove **VII:**43
    Clayton Antitrust Act
        VII:59
    IWW **VII:**146
    labor, radical **VI:**213
    labor/labor movements
        VII:170, 172
    "Labor Movement Is a Fixed
        Fact, The" **VI:428–430**
    labor organizations **VI:**215
    NAM **VII:**226
    National Civic Federation
        VII:226
    New Unionism **VII:**237
    NWLB **VII:**229
    Shirtwaist Makers Strike
        VII:324
    Socialist Labor Party
        VI:336
    Steel Strike of 1919
        VII:338
    Teamsters Union **IX:**310
    Valesh, Eva McDonald
        VII:367
Gone With the Wind (film) **V:169–**
    170; VIII:245, 328, 446c
Gone with the Wind (Mitchell)
    Gone With the Wind **V:**169
    literature **V:**240; **VIII:**220
    lost cause, the **V:**245
Gonja **I:**103, **143–144**
gonorrhea **V:**316
Gonzales, Alberto **X:**322
Gonzáles, Rodolfo "Corky"
    IX:136–137, 183, 357c
Gonzales v. Carhart **X:**5
Gonzales v. Raich **X:**244
González, Elián **X:**194, 382c
"Goober Peas" **V:**273
Gooch, Daniel **V:**215
Gooch, William **II:**153
Good, Sarah **II:**276
Goodacre, Glenna **IX:**332
Goodale, Jim **IX:**272
"Goodbye to All That" (Morgan)
    IX:348
Good Friday Agreement (Ireland)
    X:83
Good Government League
    VII:181
Good Housekeeping **VII:**138
Goodman, Andrew **IX:**356c
    CORE **IX:**73
    MFDP **IX:**219
    race and race relations
        IX:270
Goodman, Benny **VIII:150–151,**
    444c, 446c
    big bands **VIII:**44
    Holiday, Billie **VIII:**169
    jazz **VII:**153; **VIII:**195
    music **VIII:**250

Good Neighbor policy **VIII:151–**
    152
    Army Act **VII:**22
    Berle, Adolf A., Jr. **VIII:**43
    Clark Memorandum
        VII:59
    foreign policy **IV:**155;
        VIII:140
    Hoover presidency
        VIII:174
    Hull, Cordell **VIII:**180
    Latin America **X:**206
    Welles, Sumner **VIII:**415
"Good Night Irene" **IX:**120, 229
"good war" **VIII:**427–429, 433
Goodyear, Charles
    economy **IV:**131
    industrialization **IV:**199
    science and technology
        IV:333
Goodyear Tire and Rubber
    CIO **VIII:**82
    cities and urban life **VII:**54
    labor/labor movements
        VIII:206
GOP. *See* Republican Party
Gorbachev, Mikhail **X:***85*, 180,
    378c
    arms race **IX:**17
    Bush, George H. W. **X:**52,
        53
    cold war, end of **X:**86
    defense policy **X:**101
    foreign policy **X:**142
    glasnost **X:**153
    INF Treaty **X:**179–181
    Iron Curtain, collapse of
        X:188
    Reagan, Ronald W. **X:**301
    Soviet Union, breakup of
        X:325–326
Gordon, Anna A. **VI:**394
Gordon, John B. **V:**16, 45,
    170–171
Gordon, Kermit **X:**349
Gordon, Thomas **III:**103
Gordon-Reed, Annette **III:**211
Gore, Albert, Jr. **X:***156*, **156–158,**
    383c
    Bush, George H. W. **X:**53
    Bush, George W. **X:**54, 55
    capital punishment **X:**66
    Clinton, William J. **X:**80, 83
    conservation/
        environmentalism **X:**92
    economy **X:**110
    elections, presidential
        X:116–118
    global warming **X:**156
    Green Party **X:**159
    Horton, Willie **X:**168
    House of Representatives
        X:169
    Internet **X:**182
    Jackson, Jesse, L. **X:**192
    Nader, Ralph **X:**242
    Persian Gulf War **X:**273

    political parties **X:**277
    Reno, Janet **X:**309
    Supreme Court **X:**339
Gore, Albert, Sr. **X:**156
Gorée Island **I:**144
Gorgas, Josiah **V:171**
    Confederate army **V:**81
    Peninsular campaign **V:**299
    Tredegar Iron Works **V:**392
Gorsuch, Edward **V:**65
Gorton, Samuel **II:150,** 333
Gosden, Freeman **VII:**290
Gosnold, Bartholomew **I:**233
"Gospel of Wealth, The" (Carnegie)
    VI:62, 410c, **423–426**
Gotcher, Emma **VII:**217
Go Tell It on the Mountain
    (Baldwin) **IX:**353c
    African Americans **IX:**5
    Baldwin, James **IX:**34–35
    literature **IX:**194
Gothic Line **VIII:**191, 431
Gothic Revival **IV:**30–31
Gotti, John **X:**97
Goulart, João **IX:**184
Gould, Jay **V:**446c; **VI:151**
    corruption, political **VI:**83
    Ingersoll, Robert Green
        VI:193
    Morgan, John Pierpont
        VI:251
    railroads **VI:**302
    Robber Barons, The **VI:**315
    Roosevelt, Theodore
        VII:303
Gould Library (New York City)
    VI:392
Gourges, Dominique de **I:**209
government **VIII:152–155,**
    153. See also business and
    government
government (state and local)
    IX:137–138
    Birmingham confrontation
        IX:39
    public housing **IX:**267
    service sector **IX:**289
    Submerged Lands Act
        (1953) **IX:**305
government, British American
    II:151–154, 436c
    banking **II:**33
    Burgesses, House of
        II:50–51
    Connecticut **II:**76
    Jamestown **II:**183
    Keith, William **II:**191
    Maryland **II:**221
    Mayflower Compact
        II:228–229
    Newfoundland **II:**258
    New Hampshire **II:**260
    New Jersey **II:**261–262
    New York **II:**271
    Pennsylvania **II:**286
    Philadelphia **II:**292
    Plymouth **II:**298

society, British American
II:365, 366
Virginia II:401
Government Accountability Office
(GAO) X:158, 168. *See also*
General Accounting Office
Government Building (Pan-
American Exposition) VII:252
government contractors X:9
*Government Information Manual
for the Motion Picture, The*
(BMP pamphlet) VIII:56
Government Performance and
Results Act (1993) X:266
governors (Civil War era) V:171–
173. *See also specific governors,
e.g.:* Brown, Joseph Emerson
amnesty, acts of V:9
civil liberties, Confederate
V:68
conscription V:91
habeas corpus, writ of V:181
impeachment of Andrew
Johnson V:203
Reconstruction V:325
states' rights V:370
strikes V:375
Union army V:400
volunteer army V:419
Governor's Island Accord X:81,
380c
Gowen, Franklin B. VI:248, 249
GPP (Prolonged Popular War)
movement X:254
GPS (Global Positioning System)
X:320
grace I:218
Graceland IX:263
Graduate, The (film) IX:226, 259
Graduation Act (1854) IV:13
Grady, Henry W. VI:265; VII:380
Graffenried, Christopher, baron
de II:154
Graham, Billy VIII:335, 448c;
IX:138, 271–272; X:125, 341
Graham, Franklin X:341
Graham, George Rex IV:210
Graham, Isabella III:344
Graham, Sylvester IV:122
Graham's Magazine IV:210
Gramm, Phil X:158
Gramm-Rudman-Hollings Act
(1985) X:158, 321, 378c
gramophone VII:96
Grän, Ahmad I:125
Granada
adelantado I:4
Columbus, Christopher I:84
Ferdinand and Isabella
I:128
Reconquista I:314
Gran Canaria I:57
Grand Alliance (Allies) VII:407c;
VIII:155–156, 447c, 448c
air power VIII:15
Anglo-American relations
VIII:21

anticommunism VIII:22
Army, U.S. VIII:25
Axis VIII:38
Bradley, Omar N. VIII:50–
51
Bulge, Battle of the
VIII:54–55
Casablanca Conference
VIII:62–63
code breaking VIII:76
espionage VIII:117–118
foreign policy VIII:142–143
Halsey, William F. VIII:161
Hopkins, Harry L. VIII:177
Italian campaign VIII:191
Lend-Lease VIII:211
Marshall, George C.
VIII:233
Nazi-Soviet Pact VIII:266
Normandy, invasion of
VIII:275
North African campaign
VIII:277–278
POWs VIII:311
propaganda VIII:311
reconversion VIII:326
Roosevelt, Franklin D.
VIII:346
second front VIII:355
Soviet-American relations
VIII:368
Teheran Conference
VIII:390
V-E Day VIII:405
War Manpower Commission
VIII:413
World War I VII:393
World War II VIII:427
World War II European
theater VIII:429–432
Yalta Conference VIII:439
Grand Army of the Republic
(GAR) V:446c; VI:151–152,
410c
Civil War V:75
Cleveland, Grover VI:74–75
common soldier V:79
54th Massachusetts
Regiment V:144
Ingersoll, Robert Green
VI:193
monuments V:267
Soldiers' Bonus VII:331
Taylor, Susie King V:385
Union army V:404
veterans V:415, 416;
VII:371
Grand Banks I:76–77; II:258;
III:332; IV:154
Grand Camp of Confederate
Veterans of Virginia V:415
Grand Canyon I:156–157;
VI:379; VII:16
Grand Coulee Dam VII:229;
VIII:199
Grand Depot Store VI:382
Grand Detour, Illinois IV:115

Grande Ronde River IV:285
grandfather clause VI:113, 152;
VII:56, 406c
Grand National Consolidated
Trades Union IV:292
Grand Ohio Company II:278
Grand Ole Opry VIII:250, 252
Grand-Staircase-Escalante
National Monument X:290
Grands Voyages I:38
Grand Treaty of 1701 II:180
Granganimeo II:417
Grange, Red VIII:328, 371
Granger, Gordon V:219
Granger, Lester IX:325, 326
Granger movement. *See* Patrons
of Husbandry
Granite Railway Company IV:200,
313, 314
Grant, Cary VIII:328; IX:224
Grant, James II:280
Grant, Julia Dent V:173, 174
Grant, Madison
anti-Semitism VII:17
eugenics VII:102
nativism VI:264
race and race relations
VII:281–282
Grant, Ulysses S. V:173–176,
175, 445c, 446c; VI:407c
Adams, Henry VI:1
Apache War VI:17
Appomattox campaign V:14
Appomattox Court House,
Virginia V:14–16
Atlanta campaign V:21
Blair, Francis Preston, Jr.
V:36
Bowles, Samuel VI:43
Canada VI:61
Chamberlain, Joshua L.
V:60
Chattanooga, Battle of V:63,
64
Civil Rights Act (1875) V:71
civil service reform VI:73
Civil War V:74
Cold Harbor, Battle of
V:76–77
Congress VI:79
Corinth, Battle of V:95
corruption, political VI:83
Dana, Charles A. V:102;
VI:91, 92
Dana, Richard Henry
IV:113
Democratic Party V:110
Douglass, Frederick V:116
education, philanthropy and
VI:112
elections V:127
Fifteenth Amendment
V:141
Five Forks, Battle of V:147
foreign policy V:151; VI:134
Grant, Julia Dent V:173
Greeley, Horace V:177

Greenback-Labor Party
VI:154
Halleck, Henry Wager
V:182
Hancock, Winfield Scott
V:184
Heroes of America V:188
homefront V:194
Howard, Oliver Otis V:197
Internal Revenue taxes
VI:194
Johnson, Andrew V:213
Johnston, Albert Sidney
V:214
Joint Committee on the
Conduct of the War
V:216
journalism V:218
Ku Klux Klan V:225
Ku Klux Klan Act V:225
Lee, Robert E. V:231, 232
Liberal Republican Party
VI:222
Lincoln, Abraham V:237
literature V:239
Lockwood, Belva Ann
Bennett McNall VI:229
Lookout Mountain, Battle of
V:243, 244
Meade, George Gordon
V:254
medicine V:257
Mexican-American War
IV:252
Milliken's Bend, Battle of
V:260
Mississippi River war V:264
Mobile campaign V:265
Mosby, John Singleton
V:271
Nast, Thomas V:275
Native Americans V:278,
279
Nez Perce War VI:267
Overland campaign V:290–
291
Parker, Ely Samuel V:295
Pemberton, John C. V:298
Petersburg campaign
V:301–303
presidency VI:290
presidential campaigns
(1870–1899) VI:291, 292
Radical Republicans V:321
Reconstruction V:326
Reconstruction Acts V:328
redemption V:328
Republican Party V:334;
VI:311
Santo Domingo, proposed
annexation of VI:323
scalawags V:340
Schurz, Carl VI:324
Shenandoah Valley:
Sheridan's campaign
V:351
Sheridan, Philip H. V:353

Grant, Ulysses S. *(continued)*
 Sherman, William T. **V:**354–355
 Shiloh, Battle of **V:**358–360
 Spotsylvania, Battles of **V:**367–368
 Sumner, Charles **V:**378
 tactics and strategy **V:**381–382
 Taft, William Howard **VII:**347
 Union army **V:**400, 403
 Van Lew, Elizabeth **V:**415
 Vicksburg campaign **V:**416–418
 Wallace, Lew **VI:**381
 Warmoth, Henry Clay **V:**424
 Washington, D.C. **V:**426
 Washington, Treaty of **VI:**385
 Whiskey Ring **V:**429, 430
 White, Andrew Dickson **VI:**391
 Wilderness, Battle of the **V:**432
 Wilson, Henry **V:**433
Grant, Ulysses S., III **IX:**61, 62
Grant Parish, Louisiana **V:**411–412
Grapes of Wrath, The (film) **VIII:**245, 301
Grapes of Wrath, The (Steinbeck) **VIII:**446c
 dust bowl **VIII:**98
 literature **VIII:**218, 219
 marriage and family **VIII:**230
 migration **VIII:**239
 Steinbeck, John **VIII:**374
graphic arts **VI:183–184**
Grasse, François-Joseph-Paul, comte de **III:197**
 Capes, Battle of the **III:**79, 80
 French Alliance **III:**178
 Rochambeau, Jean-Baptiste-Donatien de Vimeur, comte de **III:**372
 Saintes, Battle of the **III:**378
 Yorktown, surrender at **III:**455
Grateful Dead, the **IX:**280
Grattan, John L. **IV:**276
Gratz, Barnard **III:**236
Gratz, Michael **III:**236
Gratz v. Bollinger **X:**10, **158–159**
Gravano, Salvatore "Sammy the Bull" **X:**97
grave goods **I:**50, 254
Graves, Thomas
 Capes, Battle of the **III:**79, 80
 Grasse, François-Joseph-Paul, comte de **III:**197
 Yorktown, surrender at **III:**454

Graves, William S. **VII:**324–325
Gravesend Bay, Long Island **III:**271
gravity **VIII:**352
Gravity's Rainbow (Pynchon) **X:**211
Gray, Asa **VI:**122
Gray, Elisha **VI:**31
Gray, Robert **IV:**103
Gray, Victoria **IX:**219
Gray, William **X:**14
Grayson, Walter **VI:**128
Great American Desert **IV:**145, 275
Great Atlantic and Pacific Tea Company (A&P) **VI:**65
Great Awakening **II:154–157, 155,** 437c. *See also* First Great Awakening; Second Great Awakening
 Baptists **II:**33
 Chauncy, Charles **II:**64
 Congregationalists **II:**75
 Davenport, James **II:**91, 92
 education **II:**113
 Edwards, Jonathan **II:**114
 Edwards, Sarah Pierpont **II:**114
 Frelinghuysen, Theodorus Jacobus **II:**135
 German Reformed Church **II:**149
 New Jersey **II:**262
 Osborn, Sarah Haggar Wheaten **II:**279
 Presbyterians **II:**309
 Princeton College **II:**311
 Protestantism **II:**315
 religion, African-American **II:**328
 revitalization movements **II:**332
 Rhode Island **II:**334
 slavery **II:**357
 Tennent, Gilbert **II:**387, 388
 Tennent, William, Jr. **II:**388
 Virginia **II:**401–402
 Wheelock, Eleazar **II:**411
 Whitefield, George **II:**413, 414
 Wigglesworth, Edward **II:**414
Great Basin. *See* Great Salt Lake Valley
Great Bridge, Battle of **III:**143, 339
Great Britain **I:**292; **II:**437c; **III:**459c, 460c, 462c–465c; **IV:**411c, 414c; **VI:**407c; **VII:**407c, 408c; **VIII:**446c–448c; **IX:**352c–354c. *See also* England
 Acadians **II:**2
 Acts of Trade and Navigation **II:**3
 Adams, John **III:**5

Adams, John Quincy **IV:**5
Adams-Onís Treaty **IV:**6
Afghanistan War **X:**12
Africa **X:**16
agriculture **VIII:**11
aircraft industry **VIII:**13
air power **VIII:**16
America First Committee **VIII:**17
American Revolution **III:**18
Ames, Fisher **III:**19
amphibious warfare **VIII:**20
Angell, James Burrill **VI:**15
Anglo-American relations **VIII:**20–21
arms race **IX:**17
Astor, John Jacob **IV:**33
Astoria **IV:**35, 36
Atlantic Charter **VIII:**34
Audubon, John James **IV:**38
aviation **IX:**28
Axis **VIII:**37
Baltimore, Battle of **IV:**43
baseball **VII:**33
Bayard, Thomas Francis **VI:**27–28
Bering Sea dispute **VI:**34
Berlin blockade **IX:**38, 39
Berlin Decree **III:**49
Bernard, Sir Francis **III:**49
Big Stick diplomacy **VII:**34
Blackstone, Sir William **III:**52
Blatch, Harriot Eaton Stanton **VII:**38
Bonaparte, Napoleon **III:**55
Borah, William E. **VIII:**50
Boxer Rebellion **VII:**40
Brant, Joseph **III:**63
Britain, Battle of **VIII:**53–54
British Empire **II:**48
Bulge, Battle of the **VIII:**54
Cadore Letter **III:**73
Cairo Conference **VIII:**61
California missions **IV:**76
Canada **III:**78, 79; **VI:**61
Capes, Battle of the **III:**79–80
Carlisle commission **III:**81
Caroline affair **IV:**80–81
cash-and-carry **VIII:**63
CDAAA **VIII:**77
Chesapeake-Leopard affair **III:**88
Chilean-American relations **VI:**67
Choctaw **III:**89
citizenship **III:**92
Clayton-Bulwer Treaty **IV:**98–99
cold war **IX:**63
Columbia River **IV:**103
Committee for Public Information **VII:**59
committees of correspondence **III:**101

commonwealthmen **III:**103
Confederate States of America **V:**86
Continental Congress, First **III:**113–115
cotton **III:**123
Crummell, Alexander **VI:**87
Cuba **IV:**111, 112
Dartmoor Prison **IV:**113–114
Dawes Plan **VII:**72
debt, national **III:**129–130
Decatur, Stephen **IV:**115
Declaration of Independence **III:**132–133
Declaratory Act **III:**134
Democratic-Republican societies **III:**137
destroyers-for-bases deal **VIII:**94–95
disease/epidemics **IV:**121, 122
Dow, Lorenzo **IV:**126
Dragging Canoe **III:**139
dueling **III:**140
Eastman, George **VI:**105
emancipation **V:**130
embargo of 1807 **III:**151–152
espionage **VIII:**118
Essex, USS **IV:**143, 144
Essex decision **III:**157
Estaing, Charles-Henri Theodat, comte d' **III:**158
Ethiopia **VIII:**118–119
exploration **IV:**146
fashion **IX:**116–117
Florida **III:**166–167; **IV:**151–153
food riots **III:**167
foreign affairs **III:**168, 169
foreign policy **IV:**153–155; **V:**149–151; **VI:**133; **VII:**114, 116; **VIII:**141, 142
Fort Stanwix, Treaty of **III:**170
Fort Ticonderoga **III:**171
Franklin, Benjamin **III:**173–174
Franklin, William **III:**175–176
Free Trade and Sailor's Rights **IV:**165
French Alliance **III:**177
French Revolution **III:**178, 179
Fulton, Robert **III:**183
fur trade **IV:**170, 171
George III **III:**191–192
Ghent, Treaty of **IV:**175–176
gold standard **VIII:**150
Goodman, Benny **VIII:**151
Grand Alliance **VIII:**155

Haiti **III**:203
Harriman, W. Averell
    VIII:161–162
Hawaii **IV**:188
Hay, John Milton **VI**:164
Hillman, Sidney **VIII**:165
Hopkins, Harry L. **VIII**:177
immigration **IV**:193
industrialization **IV**:199
intelligence **VIII**:187
investments, foreign
    VII:151–152
investments, foreign, in the
    United States **VI**:197
Iraq War **X**:186, 187
Irish Americans **VIII**:188
Iron Acts **II**:177–178
Iroquois **III**:228
isolationists **VIII**:189–190
Israel **IX**:160
Jackson, Andrew **IV**:206
James, Henry **VI**:200
Jay, John **III**:229, 230
Jay's Treaty **III**:231
Jefferson, Joseph, III
    VI:202
Jefferson, Thomas **III**:233,
    234
jingoes **VI**:204
Kennedy, Joseph P.
    VIII:200
King, Rufus **III**:245
Knox, Frank **VIII**:202
labor/labor movements
    III:251, 252
Lafitte, Jean **IV**:220
Lake Erie, Battle of **IV**:220–
    221
League of Armed Neutrality
    III:257
League of Nations **VII**:175
Lend-Lease **VIII**:211
Liberal Republican Party
    VI:222
Limited Test Ban Treaty of
    1963 **IX**:192
Lincoln, Abraham **V**:236
literature **VI**:226
Little Belt incident **III**:269–
    270
London Economic
    Conference **VIII**:221
Loyalists **III**:275–276
Luce, Henry R. **VIII**:224
Lusitania, RMS **VII**:187
lynching **VI**:230
Macon's Bill No. 2 **III**:280
Madison, James **III**:284
Manhattan Project
    VIII:227
Manifest Destiny **IV**:234
Marshall Plan **IX**:204
McLoughlin, John **IV**:248
Mexican-American War
    IV:251
Mexican Revolution
    VII:204

Middle East **IX**:214; **X**:227
Milan Decree **III**:297
Monroe Doctrine **IV**:260
Monroe-Pinkney Treaty
    III:300, 301
mountain men **IV**:266
Munich Conference
    VIII:248
National Origins Act
    VII:227
Native Americans **III**:312,
    314; **IV**:273, 274
Native Americans in the War
    of 1812 **IV**:276, 277
Naval Disarmament
    Conference **VII**:234, 235
Nazi-Soviet Pact **VIII**:266
neutrality **VII**:235
Neutrality Acts **VIII**:268
Neutrality Proclamation
    III:315
New Orleans, Battle of
    IV:280–282
New Spain, northern
    frontier of **III**:317
Non-Intercourse Act
    III:319
North, Frederick, Lord
    III:320
NWTUL **VII**:230
Orders in Council **III**:325
Oregon Trail **IV**:285
Oregon Treaty of 1846
    IV:286–288
Owen, Robert **IV**:291, 292
Panama Canal **VII**:250
panic of 1837 **IV**:294–295
Paris, Treaty of (1763)
    III:331
Paris, Treaty of (1783)
    III:332
Paul, Alice **VII**:254
peace movements **VII**:256
Penobscot campaign
    III:334
Pinckney Treaty **III**:337
Pitt, William **III**:337
political parties **III**:338
Pontiac's War **III**:339
Potsdam Conference
    VIII:307–308
POWs **III**:345–346;
    VIII:310, 311
privateering **III**:347, 348
propaganda **VIII**:311–312
Quartering Act **III**:352
rationing **VIII**:323
religious liberty **III**:362
republicanism **III**:364, 365
resistance movement
    III:366
Revolutionary War **III**:368
riots **III**:371
Samoa **VI**:322, 323
SEATO **IX**:291, 292
second front **VIII**:355

Seward, William H. **V**:347,
    348
Soviet-American relations
    VIII:368
Spanish civil war **VIII**:369
Stamp Act **III**:395–396
submarines **VIII**:378
Suez crisis **IX**:306–307
Sugar Act **III**:401
Sumner, Charles **V**:378
Tea Act **III**:408–409
technology **IX**:312
Teheran Conference
    VIII:390
Thames, Battle of the
    IV:375
Townshend Duties **III**:412–
    413
trade, domestic and foreign
    III:413, 415; **VI**:360;
    VII:354
Truman, Harry S. **IX**:320
Truman Doctrine **IX**:321
UN **VIII**:402, 403; **X**:356
V-E Day **VIII**:405
Venezuela boundary dispute
    VI:373
Vergennes, Charles Gravier,
    comte de **III**:423
Versailles, Treaty of **VII**:369,
    371
Victorianism **VI**:374
V-J Day **VIII**:407
Walker, William **V**:423
War of 1812 **IV**:390–392
Washington, Treaty of
    VI:384–385
Washington Conference
    on Naval Disarmament
    VII:379
Webster-Ashburton Treaty
    IV:394–395
West Indies **III**:436
Whigs **III**:439; **IV**:396
Wilson, Thomas Woodrow
    VII:384
World Disarmament
    Conference **VIII**:426
World War I **VII**:393
World War II European
    theater **VIII**:429–431
World War II home front
    VIII:434
World War II Pacific theater
    VIII:435
Wright, Fanny **IV**:405
XYZ affair **III**:451
Zimmermann telegram
    VII:401
Great Chicago Fire. *See* Chicago
    Fire
*Great Christian Doctrine
    of Original Sin Defended*
    (Edwards) **II**:114
Great Comet (1843) **IV**:335
"Great Communicator, The"
    X:299

Great Compromise **III**:109, 283,
    463*c*
Great Cryptogram, The
    (Donnelly) **VI**:100
Great Depression **VIII**:**156–159**,
    158, 443*c*
    advertising **VIII**:1
    AFL **VIII**:18
    African Americans **VIII**:3
    Agricultural Adjustment Act
        VIII:5
    Agricultural Adjustment
        Administration **VIII**:7
    Agricultural Marketing Act
        VIII:8
    agriculture **VIII**:8, 9
    aircraft industry **VIII**:13
    Amalgamated Clothing
        Workers of America
        (ACW) **VIII**:16
    American Liberty League
        VIII:19
    Anglo-American relations
        VIII:21
    anticommunism **VIII**:22
    antimonopoly **VIII**:23
    anti-Semitism **VIII**:24–25
    art and architecture **VIII**:29,
        31
    Asian Americans **VIII**:32
    automobile industry
        VIII:35–36
    baby boom **IX**:31
    Bankhead-Jones Farm
        Tenant Act **VIII**:39
    banking **VIII**:39
    Banking Act (1933) **VIII**:40–
        41
    big bands **VIII**:44
    black market **VIII**:46
    blues **VII**:39
    Bonus Army **VIII**:48, 49
    Borah, William E. **VIII**:49
    Brain Trust **VIII**:51
    Bridges, Harry **VIII**:53
    Brotherhood of Sleeping Car
        Porters **VIII**:54
    business **VIII**:57–58
    Catholics **VIII**:63
    CCC **VIII**:70–71
    censorship **VIII**:65
    child labor **VII**:53
    children **VII**:400; **VIII**:66
    cities and urban life **VIII**:68,
        70
    civil liberties **VIII**:71
    Clark Memorandum
        VII:58
    coal industry **VIII**:74
    Communist Party **VII**:61
    Communists **VIII**:77
    Congress **VIII**:79
    conservatism **VIII**:83, 84
    conservative coalition
        VIII:85
    Coolidge, Calvin John
        VII:65

Great Depression *(continued)*
    Coughlin, Father Charles E.
        VIII:87–88
    criminal justice **VII:**67
    Democratic Party **VIII:**92
    department stores **VI:**96
    dust bowl **VIII:**98
    Eccles, Marriner S.
        VIII:101
    economy **VIII:**103–104;
        IX:96
    education **VIII:**105–106
    election of 1932 **VIII:**108
    election of 1936 **VIII:**109
    Ellington, Duke **VIII:**112
    Emergency Banking Act of
        1933 **VIII:**112–113
    ERAA **VIII:**113–114
    ethnic organizations
        VII:102
    Evans, Walker **VIII:**119–120
    FAP **VIII:**129
    FDIC **VIII:**132
    Federal Housing
        Administration **IX:**119
    Federal Housing
        Administration (FHA)
        VIII:133
    federalism **X:**130
    Federal National Mortgage
        Association **VIII:**135
    Federal Reserve Act
        VII:108
    FEPC **VIII:**123
    FERA **VIII:**132
    FHA **VIII:**126
    First New Deal **VIII:**138
    fiscal policy **VIII:**138–139
    FMP **VIII:**134
    Fordney-McCumber Tariff
        VII:112
    foreign policy **VII:**116;
        VIII:140
    FSA **VIII:**127
    Full Employment Bill
        VIII:145
    FWP **VIII:**136–137
    Garner, John Nance
        VIII:147
    German Americans
        VIII:148–149
    gold standard **VIII:**150
    government **VIII:**152,
        153–154
    Guthrie, Woody **VIII:**160
    Hawley-Smoot Tariff Act
        VIII:162–163
    Holocaust **VIII:**170
    Hoover, Herbert C.
        VIII:172
    Hoover presidency
        VIII:173, 175
    Ickes, Harold L. **VIII:**183
    ILGWU **VIII:**187
    immigration **VIII:**184
    Indian Reorganization Act
        VIII:185

    investments, foreign
        VII:152
    Irish Americans **VIII:**188
    Italian Americans **VIII:**190
    Jews **VIII:**195
    KKK **IX:**179
    labor/labor movements
        VIII:205
    La Follette, Robert M., Jr.
        VIII:208
    Lange, Dorothea **VIII:**210
    Levitt, William J. **IX:**188
    Lewis, John L. **VIII:**213
    liberalism **VIII:**215
    literature **VIII:**218
    London Economic
        Conference **VIII:**221
    London Naval Conference
        VIII:222
    Long, Huey P. **VIII:**222
    MacArthur, Douglas **IX:**197
    marriage and family
        VIII:230–231; **IX:**202
    McCarthy, Eugene **IX:**205
    McDonald's **IX:**208
    McPherson, Aimee Semple
        VII:197
    medicine **VIII:**235, 236
    Mellon, Andrew William
        VII:201
    Mexican Americans
        VIII:237
    Mexican immigration
        VII:203
    Mexican Repatriation
        Program **VIII:**238
    Middletown **VII:**206
    migration **VIII:**239
    military-industrial complex
        IX:216
    mobilization **VIII:**241
    monetary policy **VIII:**243
    movies **VIII:**245–246
    Murray, Pauli **IX:**227
    Murray, Philip **VIII:**249
    music **VII:**220; **VIII:**249,
        250
    NAACP **VIII:**255
    National Recovery
        Administration **VIII:**259
    Native Americans **VIII:**263
    New Deal **VIII:**268–269;
        IX:242
    news media **VIII:**271, 272
    NIRA **VIII:**256
    Norris–La Guardia Act
        VIII:277
    oil industry **VII:**245
    Patton, George S., Jr.
        VIII:291
    PECE **VIII:**309
    photography **VIII:**296
    Polish Americans **VIII:**297
    politics (Roosevelt era)
        VIII:298
    population trends **VII:**267;
        VIII:304–306; **IX:**260

    POUR **VIII:**309–310
    presidency **VII:**269;
        VIII:308, 309
    Prohibition **VII:**274
    public health **IX:**264–265
    public housing **IX:**266
    public opinion polls
        VIII:312
    PWA **VIII:**314
    race and race relations
        VIII:317
    radio **VIII:**319
    REA **VIII:**349
    Reciprocal Trade
        Agreements Act
        VIII:324–325
    recreation **VIII:**327–329
    refugees **VIII:**329
    relief **VIII:**330–333
    Relief and Reconstruction
        Act **VIII:**333
    religion **VIII:**334–336
    Republican Party **VIII:**336
    Reuther, Walter **VIII:**339
    RFC **VIII:**325
    Roosevelt, Franklin D.
        VIII:344, 345
    rural areas **VIII:**348
    Sanger, Margaret **VII:**313
    shipbuilding **VIII:**359
    Sinclair, Upton **VII:**326
    socialism **VII:**328
    socialists **VIII:**362
    Social Security Act
        VIII:363
    social work **VII:**330–331
    Soldiers' Bonus **VII:**331
    South **VIII:**366
    sports and recreation
        VIII:370
    steel industry **VIII:**373
    Steel Strike of 1919 **VII:**339
    Steinbeck, John **VIII:**374
    STFU **VIII:**367
    stock market crash **VIII:**376
    strikes **VIII:**377
    suburbanization/suburbs
        VIII:379
    Sunbelt **VIII:**380
    Supreme Court **VII:**343;
        VIII:381
    taxation **VIII:**387
    technology **VIII:**397
    Third New Deal **VIII:**393
    Thomas, Norman **VIII:**394
    TNEC **VIII:**391
    trade, domestic and foreign
        VII:355
    transportation **VIII:**395
    Tugwell, Rexford G.
        VIII:397
    UMWA **VIII:**360; **VIII:**401
    unemployment **VIII:**399,
        400
    vaudeville **VII:**369
    veterans **VII:**373
    Volstead Act **VII:**374

    Vorse, Mary Heaton
        VII:375
    Wagner, Robert F. **VIII:**410
    women's status and rights
        VIII:423
Great Duelist, The (Leavitt)
    IV:226
Greater Antilles **II:**59
    cacique **I:**49
    Jamaica **I:**191
    Taino **I:**352
    Velázquez, Diego de **I:**374
"greatest generation" **VIII:**427
"Greatest Show on Earth" **VI:**25,
    407*c*
Great Gatsby, The (Fitzgerald)
    VII:186
Great Lakes **I:**186; **IV:**411*c*
    American Fur Company
        IV:18
    Astor, John Jacob **IV:**35
    Audubon, John James **IV:**37
    Carnegie, Andrew **VI:**62
    cities and urban life **VI:**70
    ethnocentrism **II:**122
    exploration **II:**123
    foreign policy **IV:**154
    fur trade **II:**141; **IV:**170,
        171
    Ghent, Treaty of **IV:**176
    immigration **IV:**195
    industrialization **IV:**200
    internal improvements
        IV:202, 203
    Lake Erie, Battle of **IV:**221
    lumbering **IV:**231
    migration **IV:**254
    Native Americans **III:**311–
        312; **IV:**273, 274
    Native Americans in the War
        of 1812 **IV:**277
    Nicolet, Jean **II:**273
    Pontiac's War **III:**339, 340
    railroads **IV:**314
    science and technology
        IV:333
    steel industry **VII:**337–338
    Thames, Battle of the
        IV:375, 376
    Villard, Henry **VI:**375
Great Lakes Naval Training
    Station **VIII:**371
"Great Lawsuit, The: Man *versus*
    men. Woman *versus* Women"
    IV:169
Great *Mahele* (1848) **IV:**188
"Great Marianas Turkey Shoot"
    VIII:295
Great Migration (African
    American, early 20th century)
    VII:127–129, *128,* 406*c*
    African Americans **VIII:**2;
        IX:4
    art and architecture **VIII:**30
    blues **VII:**39
    cities and urban life **VII:**54,
        55

civil rights **VIII**:72
Harlem Renaissance **VII**:136
literature **VII**:181
Massachusetts **II**:222
migration **VII**:207
National Origins Act
  VII:227
popular culture **VII**:265
population trends **VII**:266
race and race relations
  VII:283
Rhinelander case **VII**:301
Great Migration (Irish
  immigration) **IV**:193, 195–196
Great Migration (Puritan)
  II:116–117
Great Migration (westward
  expansion) **IV**:253
"Great Nation of Futurity, The "
  (O'Sullivan) **IV**:234
Great Northern Railway Company
  (GN)
  banking, investment **VI**:23
  business and government
    VI:56
  Debs, Eugene Victor **VII**:72
  Hill, James J. **VI**:172, 173
  Morgan, John Pierpont
    VI:251
  Northern Securities Case
    VII:241
Great Peace **II**:93
Great Plains **III:197; VIII**:443c
  agriculture **VIII**:9
  animals **III**:22–23
  art and architecture **IV**:29
  buffalo **III**:64
  cattle kingdom **VI**:64
  foreign policy **IV**:156
  fur trade **III**:183
  Kearny, Stephen Watts
    IV:212
  literature **VI**:225
  migration **IV**:255
  Native Americans **III**:315;
    IV:276
  Native Americans in the War
    of 1812 **IV**:278
  New Spain, northern
    frontier of **III**:317
  Texas **IV**:370, 371
Great Plains Indians **II:157–158**
Great Platte River Road. *See*
  Oregon Trail
Great Powers **VII**:175
Great Pyramid (Mexico) **I**:74
Great Railroad Strike (1877)
  V:374, 392
Great Rebellion (Scotland) **II**:347
Great Reinforcement, The **IV**:224
Great Sabbath **VI**:93
Great Salt Lake
  art and architecture **X**:31
  Deseret, State of **IV**:119
  Donner party **IV**:125
  exploration **IV**:144, 145
  Frémont, John C. **IV**:166

migration **IV**:255
Mormon Church **VI**:251
religion **VI**:308
Smith, Jedediah Strong
  IV:350
Great Salt Lake Desert **IV**:125
Great Salt Lake Valley
  Deseret, State of **IV**:119–120
  exploration **IV**:144–145
  Mormon Church **IV**:90
  Mormon Trail **IV**:262
  Mormon War **IV**:263
  Young, Brigham **IV**:407, 408
Great Sedition Trial **VIII**:361
Great Sioux Reservation **VI**:408c
  Red Cloud **VI**:303
  Sioux wars **VI**:331
  Sitting Bull **VI**:332
"Great Skedaddle" **V**:50
Great Smoky Mountains **VIII**:392
Great Society **IX:138–139**, 356c,
  357c
  conservative movement
    X:93
  defense budget **IX**:84
  Democratic Party **IX**:85
  economy **IX**:98; **X**:108
  EEOC **IX**:110
  ESEA **IX**:106
  government, state/local
    IX:137
  Head Start **IX**:144
  Johnson, Lyndon B. **IX**:163
  liberalism **X**:208
  Medicaid **IX**:209
  Medicare **IX**:210
  Model Cities program
    IX:220
  NASA **IX**:231
  National Trails Act of 1968
    IX:239
  National Wilderness
    Preservation Act of 1964
    IX:240
  NEA **IX**:234
  New Deal **IX**:242
  New York World's Fair
    (1964) **IX**:246
  public housing **IX**:267
  Shriver, Robert Sargent, Jr.
    X:324
  VISTA **IX**:332
  War on Poverty **IX**:335
  Wild and Scenic Rivers Act
    of 1968 **IX**:343
Great Strike of 1877 **VI:152–154,**
  153, 408c
  Hay, John Milton **VI**:164
  Hayes, Rutherford B.
    VI:167–168
  labor organizations **VI**:215
  labor: strikes and violence
    VI:214
  Scott, Thomas Alexander
    VI:326
  violence and lawlessness
    VI:375

Great Swamp Fight **II**:333
Great Train Robbery (film)
  entertainment, popular
    VII:96
  movie industry **VII**:215
  popular culture **VII**:265
Great Tribulation **V**:125
Great Wagon Raid **V**:271
Great War. *See* World War I
Great White Fleet **VII:129–130,**
  405c
  foreign policy **VII**:113
  Gentlemen's Agreement
    VII:124
  presidency **VII**:268
  Roosevelt, Theodore
    VII:304
  Root-Takahira Agreement
    VII:306
  Russo-Japanese War
    VII:309
  trade, domestic and foreign
    VII:354
Great White Hope, The (play)
  X:280
Greece **II**:354
  astrolabe **I**:15
  cold war **IX**:63
  Crane, Stephen **VI**:85
  domino theory **IX**:89
  Europe **IX**:113
  history **VII**:139
  Leahy, William D. **VIII**:211
  Middle East **IX**:214
  National Origins Act
    VII:228
  printing press **I**:303
  republicanism **III**:365
  Truman Doctrine **IX**:321,
    322
Greek Revival **IV**:29–30
Greeley, Horace **V:176–177,**
  444c; **VI**:407c
  Bowles, Samuel **VI**:43
  Brook Farm **IV**:65
  civil liberties, Union **V**:70
  Cooper Union speech **V**:93,
    94
  Dana, Charles A. **V**:102;
    VI:91, 92
  Dickinson, Anna E. **V**:111
  Emancipation Proclamation
    V:131
  Fuller, Margaret **IV**:169
  Grant, Ulysses S. **V**:175
  Homestead Act **V**:194
  journalism **IV**:208
  Liberal Republican Party
    VI:222–223
  Lockwood, Belva Ann
    Bennett McNall **VI**:229
  Massachusetts Emigrant Aid
    Society **IV**:242
  McMaster, John Bach
    VI:242
  newspapers **VI**:265–266
  peace movements **V**:296

political parties, third
  VI:285–286
presidential campaigns
  (1870–1899) **VI**:291
public land policy **IV**:306
Pulitzer, Joseph **VI**:297
race and race relations
  V:319
Reid, Whitelaw **VI**:304, 305
religion **IV**:320; **VI**:309
Republican Party **V**:334
Schurz, Carl **VI**:324
Watterson, Henry **VI**:386
Green, Duff **IV**:136
Green, Edith **IX**:220
Green, Grafton **VII**:434–438
Green, William
  AFL **VII**:12; **VIII**:18
  CIO **IX**:72
  labor/labor movements
    VIII:205
Greenback-Labor Party **VI:154–**
  155
  currency issue **VI**:89
  Dana, Charles A. **VI**:92
  Internal Revenue taxes
    VI:194
  Lease, Mary Elizabeth
    Clyens **VI**:220
  political parties, third
    VI:286
  Powderly, Terence Vincent
    VI:287
Greenback Raid **V**:271
greenbacks **V:177–178; VI**:408c
  banking **V**:28
  Chase, Salmon P. **V**:63
  Congress **V**:89
  currency issue **VI**:88
  economy **V**:122
  farmers' alliances **VI**:125
  Greenback-Labor Party
    VI:154–155
  Sherman, John **VI**:329
Green Bay, Wisconsin **IV**:327
Greenbelt New Towns program
  VIII:339, 379
Greenberg, Clement **IX**:19
Green Corn Rebellion **VII**:327
Greene, Anne Terry **IV**:299
Greene, Christopher **III**:359
Greene, Graham **IX**:224
Greene, Nathanael **III**:*198*,
  198–199
  Brandywine, Battle of
    III:62
  Church, Benjamin **III**:89
  Cornwallis, Charles, Lord
    III:120
  Cowpens, Battle of **III**:124
  Delaware River forts
    III:135
  Eutaw Springs, Battle of
    III:159, 160
  Gates, Horatio **III**:190
  Guilford Courthouse, Battle
    of **III**:201, 202

Greene, Nathanael (*continued*)
  Hobkirk's Hill, Battle of
    III:213
  Kościuszko, Tadeusz
    III:248
  Long Island, Battle of
    III:271
  Revolutionary War **III:**368
  Wilkinson, James **III:**443
"Greenfield Hill" (Dwight) **III:**104
Greenglass, David and Ruth
  IX:280
Greenhill, James **II:**230
Green Hornet **VIII:**303
greenhouse gases **X:**381*c*, 383*c*
  Bush, George W. **X:**55, 56
  conservation/
    environmentalism **X:**92
  global warming **X:**155, 156
Greenhow, Rose O'Neal **V:**134,
  135, **178**
Greenland **I:144**, 395*c*
  Frobisher, Martin **I:**134,
    135
  icebergs **I:**177
  L'Anse aux Meadows **I:**204
  Norse **I:**272
Green Mountain Boys **III:199**,
  460*c*
  Allen, Ethan **III:**15
  Clinton, George **III:**98
  Fort Ticonderoga **III:**171
  land riots **III:**254
  Lyon, Matthew **III:**277
  Young, Thomas **III:**457
Green Party **X:159**
  conservation/
    environmentalism **X:**92
  elections, presidential
    X:117, 118
  Nader, Ralph **X:**242
Green River
  Ashley, William Henry
    IV:32
  Bridger, James **IV:**64
  Powell, John Wesley **VI:**288
  rendezvous **IV:**321
Green River Valley **IV:**31
Greenspan, Alan **X:**109, 110, 383*c*
Green Spring faction **II:**36
Greenville, Treaty of **III:199–
200**
  Blue Jacket **III:**54
  Fallen Timbers, Battle of
    III:162
  Jay's Treaty **III:**231
  Wayne, Anthony **III:**434
Green v. New Kent County **X:**48
Greenwich Village, New York City
  VII:130–131
  Beat Generation **IX:**36
  Dylan, Bob **IX:**92
  gays and lesbians **IX:**132
  Haywood, William Dudley
    VII:137
  literature **VII:**179
  The Masses **VII:**193

modernism **VII:**212
  radical and labor press
    VII:286
  Vorse, Mary Heaton
    VII:375
Greer, USS **VIII:**142
Gregg, David M. **V:**168
Gregg, Josiah **IV:**179
Gregg v. Georgia **X:**48, 66
Gregory VII (pope) **I:**166
Gregory XIII (pope) **I:**166
Grenada invasion (1983) **X:159–
160**, 378*c*
  cold war, end of **X:**85
  defense policy **X:**101
  Latin America **X:**206
  North, Oliver L. **X:**258
  Reagan, Ronald W. **X:**301
Grenville, George **III:200–201**,
  464*c*
  liberty tree **III:**267
  Stamp Act **III:**395, 396
  Sugar Act **III:**401
Grenville, Sir Richard **I:144–145**
  Lane, Ralph **I:**203
  North Carolina **II:**274
  Roanoke **I:**321
  Wingina **I:**417
Grenville, William **III:**231
Gresham, Newt **IX:**7
Gresham, Walter Q. **VI:**163
Grey, Charles **III:**20
Grey, Jane **I:**232
Greyhound **V:**7
Gridley, Richard **III:**65
Grierson, Benjamin H. **V:**417
Griffin, Michael **X:**289
Griffith, David Wark **VII:131–
132**, *132*, 406*c*
  Birth of a Nation, The
    VII:37
  entertainment, popular
    VII:96
  Ku Klux Klan **VII:**165
  movie industry **VII:**215, 216
  race and race relations
    VII:283
  Rhinelander case **VII:**301
Griffiths, Martha **X:**123
*Griggs et al. v. Duke Power
Company* **X:160**
  affirmative action **X:**9
  Brennan, William J., Jr.
    X:48
  Burger, Warren E. **X:**51
  race and race relations
    X:297
Grijalva, Juan de **I:145**
  Alvarado, Pedro de **I:**7
  Cozumel **I:**99
  Velázquez, Diego de **I:**374
Grimes, James W. **V:**255; **VI:**11
Grimké, Angelina and Sarah
  IV:179–180
  abolitionism **IV:**3
  American Anti-Slavery
    Society **IV:**15

"Appeal to the Christian
  Women of the South"
    IV:430–434
  Bloomer, Amelia **IV:**59–60
  female antislavery societies
    IV:147, 148
  Foster, Abigail Kelley
    IV:161
  Mott, Lucretia **IV:**265
  Seneca Falls convention
    IV:341
  Society of Friends **V:**364
  Weld, Theodore Dwight
    IV:396
  women's status and rights
    IV:404
Grimké, Charlotte Forten
  V:178–179
Grinnel College **VIII:**135
Griots **I:**350
Grisham, John **X:**212
Grissom, Virgil **IX:**231, 297
Griswold, Roger **III:**277
Griswold v. Connecticut
  birth control **X:**43
  Bork, Robert **X:**45
  Brennan, William J., Jr.
    X:48
  Roe v. Wade **X:**311
  sexual revolution **X:**322
  White, Byron R. **X:**369
Grito del Norte, El **IX:**186
Groce's Ferry **IV:**328
Grofé, Ferde **VII:**125
Grønlendiga Saga **I:**204
Gropius, Walter **IX:**20
Gross, Samuel **IV:**249; **VI:**104–
105
Gross Clinic, The (Eakins)
  VI:104–105
gross domestic product (GDP)
  X:110, 221
gross national product (GNP)
  business **IX:**46
  demobilization (WWII)
    IX:84
  economy **VII:**84; **IX:**96–98
  mobilization **VIII:**241, 242
  monetary policy **VIII:**243
  New Deal **VIII:**268
  rationing **VIII:**323
  recession of 1937–1938
    VIII:323–324
  service sector **IX:**289
  suburbanization/suburbs
    VIII:380
  World War II home front
    VIII:432
Gros Ventre Indians **IV:**276
Grotius, Hugo **I:145–146**
  Dutch East India Company
    I:115
  East India Company **I:**117
  Portuguese seaborne empire
    I:300
  Sequeira, Diogo Lopes de
    I:331

Groton, Connecticut **IV:**169
Group of Seventy-Seven **X:**355
Group of the Cross **I:**283
*Grove City College et al. v. Bell,
  Secretary of Education, et al.*
    X:160
Groves, Leslie Richard
  atomic bomb **VIII:**34
  Manhattan Project **VIII:**226,
    227
  Oppenheimer, J. Robert
    IX:251
Grow, Galusha **V:**195
Growing Up in New Guinea
  (Mead) **VII:**181, 197
Gruen, Victor **IX:**290
Gruening, Ernest **IX:**8
grunge music **X:**238
Grutter v. Bollinger **X:**10,
  158–159
Gua, Pierre du **II:**2, 136
Guadalajara **I:**267; **II:**158
Guadalcanal, Battle of **VIII:159–
160**, 447*c*, 448*c*
  Halsey, William F. **VIII:**161
  Hersey, John R. **VIII:**164
  literature **IX:**193
  Marines, U.S. **VIII:**230
  Solomon Islands **VIII:**365–
    366
  World War II Pacific theater
    VIII:435
Guadalquivir River **I:**332
Guadalupe Hidalgo, Treaty of
  IV:180–182, 414*c*, **440–441;**
  IX:357*c*
  Bent's Fort **IV:**55
  California **IV:**71
  Compromise of 1850
    IV:103
  exploration **IV:**146
  foreign policy **IV:**155
  Fort Laramie **IV:**157
  Forty-niners **IV:**160
  Gadsden Purchase **IV:**173
  immigration **IV:**193
  Lamy, Jean Baptiste **IV:**222
  Manifest Destiny **IV:**235
  Mexican-American War
    IV:253
  Polk, James K. **IV:**302
  San Jacinto, Battle of **IV:**328
  Santa Anna, Antonio López
    de **IV:**330
  Texas **IV:**372
Guale Indians **II:**429
Guam **I:**224
  Mariana Islands **VIII:**228,
    229
  Marines, U.S. **VIII:**230
  Philippine Sea, Battle of the
    VIII:295
  POWs **VIII:**311
  World War II Pacific theater
    VIII:436
Guamán Poma **I:**16, **146–147**,
  368, 369

Guanahatabey **I**:100; **II**:59

Guanches **I**:222

Guantánamo Bay Naval Base, Cuba
Army Act **VII**:22
Hamdan v. Rumsfeld **X**:164
Iraq War **X**:188

Guaranty Building (Buffalo, New York) **VI**:347

Guard of Honor (Cozzens) **VIII**:220

Guatavita, Lake **I**:118

Guatemala **IX**:353*c*
Alvarado, Pedro de **I**:7–8
CIA **IX**:52
cold war **IX**:64
Dulles, John Foster **IX**:91
Las Casas, Bartolomé de **I**:206
Latin America **IX**:184
military-industrial complex **IX**:216
Tlaxcala **I**:362

Guerrero, Gonzalo **I**:5, 90, **147–148**

Guerrero, Vicente **IV**:148

Guerrière, HMS
Constitution, USS **III**:108
Little Belt incident **III**:270
War of 1812 **IV**:391

guerrilla movements **X**:205, 206, 254

guerrilla warfare **V**:52

Guest of Honor, A (Joplin) **VII**:158

guest worker program **X**:176, 226–227

Guevara, Che **IX**:41

Guffey-Snyder Bituminous Coal Stabilization Act
coal industry **VIII**:75
Lewis, John L. **VIII**:213
Supreme Court **VIII**:382

Guggenheim, Peggy **IX**:19

Guggenheim, Simon **VII**:78

Guggenheim Brothers **VII**:85

Guggenheim family **VI**:247

Guggenheim Museum (New York City) **VII**:395

Guiana **I**:311, 312, 398*c*; **II**:391

Guide to Holiness (Palmer) **IV**:317

guilds **I**:29

Guilford Courthouse, Battle of **III**:201*m*, **201–202**, 462*c*
Cornwallis, Charles, Lord **III**:120
Greene, Nathanael **III**:199
Revolutionary War **III**:368
Tarleton, Banastre **III**:407

Guinea **IX**:3

Guinea-Bissau **I**:148, 199

Guinea islands **I**:129

Guinn, Joe **IX**:72

Guinn v. United States **VI**:152

Gulf Coast
slave trade, internal **IV**:348
South **VIII**:367

Sunbelt **VIII**:381
Texas **IV**:370, 371

Gulf of Guinea **I**:56, 271, 396*c*

Gulf of Mexico
Adams, John Quincy **IV**:5
Adams-Onís Treaty **IV**:6
Eads, James Buchanan **VI**:103
exploration **II**:123
foreign policy **VII**:114
Lafitte, Jean **IV**:220
oil industry **VII**:245
slave trade, internal **IV**:349
Texas **IV**:370

Gulf of Tonkin Resolution (1964) **IX**:356*c*
Johnson, Lyndon B. **IX**:163
McCarthy, Eugene **IX**:205
Vietnam War **IX**:330

Gulf Stream **IV**:335

Gulf War. *See* Persian Gulf War (1990–1991)

Gulick, Luther **VI**:343

Gullah **II**:158–159

gult **I**:124

Gumo, David **X**:289

gun(s). *See* firearms

gunboats
Navy, U.S. **VIII**:265
Shiloh, Battle of **V**:360
tactics and strategy **V**:381

Gunby, John **III**:213

gun control **X**:160–162, *162,* 380*c,* 381*c*
Clinton, William J. **X**:80
federalism **X**:131
Libertarian Party **X**:209
militia movement **X**:231
NRA **X**:249
Oklahoma City bombing **X**:267

Gun Control Act (1968) **X**:161

Gun Free School Zones Act (1990) **X**:161

gun manufacturers **X**:161–162

Gunning, Sarah Ogan **IX**:120, 121

gunpowder **V**:204

Gustav Line **VIII**:191, 431

Gutenberg, Johannes Gensfleisch zum **I**:148, 396*c*
invention and technology **I**:183
Mercator, Gerhardus **I**:240
paper **I**:285
printing press **I**:302, 303

Gutenberg Bible **I**:148

Guthrie, Woody **VIII**:160, *160,* 448*c*
Dylan, Bob **IX**:92
folk music revival **IX**:120
music **VIII**:250, 252; **IX**:229

Gutiérrez, José Ángel **IX**:183; **X**:166

Guy Fawkes Day **III**:341

Guyot, Arnold Henry **IV**:310

Guyot, Lawrence **IX**:219, 220

Guys and Dolls (musical) **IX**:258

Guzmán, Nuño de **II**:158

GWAA (Golf Writers' Association of America) **X**:332

H

habeas corpus, writ of **V**:181–182
Baltimore, Maryland, riots **V**:26
Bates, Edward **V**:31
civil liberties, Confederate **V**:68, 69
civil liberties, Union **V**:69, 70
Confederate States of America **V**:86
Congress **V**:90
Congress, Confederate **V**:88
Copperheads **V**:94–95
Davis, Jefferson **V**:104
Democratic Party **V**:109
elections **V**:126
Enforcement Acts **V**:133
Hamdan v. Rumsfeld **X**:164
Heroes of America **V**:188
Ku Klux Klan **V**:224, 225
Ku Klux Klan Act **V**:225
Ku Klux Klan cases **VI**:210
Letcher, John **V**:232
Lincoln, Abraham **V**:236
Stanton, Edwin M. **V**:369
Vance, Zebulon B. **V**:414
Wigfall, Louis T. **V**:431

Habeas Corpus Act (1863) **V**:445*c*

Habeas Corpus Indemnity Act **V**:182

Haber, Al **IX**:303

Habib, Philip C. **X**:163

habitants **I**:149; **II**:104; **III**:78

Habitat for Humanity **X**:70

Habsburg dynasty **II**:371–372

haciendas **I**:101, **149–150**; **II**:371

Hadden, Briton **VIII**:224

Hadia **II**:275

hadith **I**:188

Hadrian IV (pope) **I**:10

Hadrian's Wall **I**:292

Haeckel, Ernst **X**:90

Haener, Dorothy **IX**:236

Hague, Frank **VIII**:188

Hague Conventions **VIII**:310, 311

Hague Peace Conference, Second **VII**:235, 256

Hague Peace Palace (Netherlands) **VI**:63

Hahn, Jessica **X**:342

Haida **I**:150

Haig, Alexander M., Jr. **X**:163–164, 165

Haight-Ashbury, San Francisco **IX**:196, 229

Haile Selassie (emperor of Ethiopia) **VIII**:50, 118–119

Hailing the Ferry (Knight) **VI**:184

Hairy Ape, The (O'Neill) **VII**:179

Haiti **I**:163; **III**:203–204, 465*c*; **VII**:406*c,* 407*c*; **X**:164, 380*c*
abolitionism **III**:2; **IV**:4
Audubon, John James **IV**:37
Big Stick diplomacy **VII**:35
Bonaparte, Napoleon **III**:55
Clark Memorandum **VII**:58
Clinton, William J. **X**:81
Cuba **IV**:111
defense policy **X**:102
foreign affairs **III**:169
foreign policy **V**:151; **VII**:114
Free-Soil Party **IV**:164
Good Neighbor policy **VIII**:151
Grant, Ulysses S. **V**:175
Hall, Prince **III**:205
Hurston, Zora Neale **VIII**:181
Langston, John Mercer **VI**:219
Liberia **VI**:223
Louisiana Purchase **III**:273
Negro Convention movement **IV**:280
slavery **II**:354; **IV**:347
Spanish colonies **II**:372
U.S. intervention in 1993–1994 **X**:164
Vesey, Denmark **IV**:387
West Indies **III**:436
Wright, Fanny **IV**:405

Haitian Revolution **III**:203–205

hajj
Askia Muhammad I **I**:14
astrolabe **I**:15
Ibn Battuta **I**:175
Ibn Khaldûn, 'Abd-ar-Rahmân Abû Zayd ibn Muhammad ibn Muhammad **I**:176
Ignatius Loyola **I**:178
Islam **I**:188
Mansa Musa I **I**:228
Mecca **I**:238, 239

Hakim, Albert **X**:364

Hakluyt, Richard, the Elder **I**:150–151
Bristol **I**:37
Gilbert, Sir Humphrey **I**:141
Northwest Passage **I**:273

Hakluyt, Richard, the Younger **I**:151–153, 398*c*
Bristol **I**:37
Bry, Theodor de **I**:37
"Discourse Concerning Western Planting" **I**:423–425
East India Company **I**:117
Eden, Richard **I**:118
Elizabeth I **I**:121
French explorations of the Atlantic **I**:133

Hakluyt, Richard, the Younger
(*continued*)
Frobisher, Martin **I:**134,
135
Gilbert, Sir Humphrey
I:141
Grotius, Hugo **I:**146
Hakluyt, Richard, the Elder
I:151
Harriot, Thomas **I:**155
Hawkins, Sir John **I:**157
Henry the Navigator **I:**161
Ingram, David **I:**181, 182
Lane, Ralph **I:**203
Leo Africanus **I:**211
Linschoten, Jan Huygen van
I:215
London **I:**216
Mandeville, Sir John **I:**228
Mecca **I:**238
navigation technology **I:**262
New World **I:**270–271
Norumbega **I:**274
Purchas, Samuel **I:**306
Sequeira, Diogo Lopes de
I:331
Settle, Dionyse **I:**332
Spice Islands **I:**345
sugar **I:**349
travel narratives **I:**368
White, John **I:**383
*Hakluytus Posthumus or Purchas
his Pilgrimes* (Purchas) **I:**306
Hakodate, Japan **IV:**298
Halberg, Erik **VII:**345
Haldeman, H. R.
Haig, Alexander M., Jr.
X:163
Mitchell, John N. **X:**233
U.S. v. Nixon **X:**357
Watergate scandal **X:**366,
367
Hale, George Ellery **VI:**325;
VII:314, 315
Hale, John P. **IV:**164–165, 227
Hale, Nathan **III:204–205**
Hale, Sarah Josepha **IV:***183,*
183–184, 210, 229
Hale Telescope (California)
IX:296
Haley, Alex **IX:**6, 199, 356*c;*
X:*377c*
Haley, Bill, and the Comets
IX:229, 278, 353*c*
Half Breeds **V:**334; **VI:**311
half-freedom
New Netherland **II:**266
New York **II:**270
New York City **II:**272
Halfway Covenant **II:**436*c*
Mather, Cotton **II:**227
Mather, Increase **II:**228
Protestantism **II:**316
Puritans **II:**320
Halifax, Nova Scotia **III:**368
Hall, A. Oakey **VI:**369
Hall, Asaph **VI:**326

Hall, Bob **IX:**132
Hall, Granville Stanley **VI:157–
158**
Hall, James (paleontologist)
VI:164, 165, 379
Hall, James D. S. (missionary) **VI:**4
Hall, Prince **III:205**
African Americans **III:**9
antislavery **III:**26
Haiti **III:**204
Halleck, Fitz-Greene **IV:**228
Halleck, Henry Wager **V:182–
183**
Lieber, Francis **V:**234
Mason, Richard B. **IV:**241
McClellan, George Brinton
V:251
Murfreesboro/Stones River,
Battle of **V:**271
Sherman, William T. **V:**354
Shiloh, Battle of **V:**358
tactics and strategy **V:**381
Halliburton **X:**72
Hallidie, Andrew S. **IV:**105;
VI:360
Hallinan, Vincent **IX:**264
Hall of Fame for Great Americans
VI:103
Hallowell, Norwood **V:**142
hallucinogenic drugs **IX:**355*c*
Ginsberg, Allen **IX:**135
Leary, Timothy **IX:**187,
188
LSD **IX:**195–196
music **IX:**229
Hals, Frans **VI:**19
Halsey, William F., Jr. **VIII:161**
Arlington National Cemetery
V:17
Guadalcanal **VIII:**160
King, Ernest J. **VIII:**202
Leyte Gulf, Battle for
VIII:214
Nimitz, Chester W.
VIII:274
Solomon Islands **VIII:**366
World War II Pacific theater
VIII:435
Halstead, Murat **VI:**43
Halsted, William S. **VI:**244
Hamas **X:**229, 230
Hamburg riot (South Carolina)
VI:358, 375
Hamdan, Salim Ahmed **X:**164
Hamdan v. Rumsfeld **X:**164
Hamer, Fannie Lou **IX:141–142,**
219, 220
Hamill, Mark **X:**279
Hamilton, Alexander **II:**286;
III:205–208, *206,* 462*c,* 463*c,*
465*c*
Adams, John **III:**6
alcohol **III:**13
American System **IV:**19
Ames, Fisher **III:**19
Annapolis Convention
III:23

Bache, Benjamin Franklin
III:39
Bank of the United States,
First **III:**40
banks **III:**42
Burr, Aaron **III:**69, 70
Callender, James T. **III:**74
Constitutional Convention
III:108–109
Coxe, Tench **III:**125
debt, national **III:**129,
131–132
Democratic Party **IV:**116
Democratic-Republican
Party **III:**136
Democratic-Republican
societies **III:**137
dueling **III:**141
Duer, William **III:**141
economy **III:**146
election of 1800 **III:**150,
151
Federalist Papers **III:**162,
163
Federalist Party **III:**164
French Revolution **III:**179
Freneau, Philip **III:**180
Fries's Rebellion **III:**181
Gallatin, Albert **III:**188
Industrial Revolution
III:225
Jay's Treaty **III:**231
Jefferson, Thomas **III:**233
journalism **III:**240
King, Rufus **III:**246
Madison, James **III:**283
Neutrality Proclamation
III:315
panic of 1792 **III:**330
Pickering, Timothy **III:**335
Pinckney, Charles
Cotesworth **III:**336
political parties **III:**339
Schuyler, Philip John
III:384
secession **V:**344
states' rights **III:**397
Supreme Court **III:**403
tariffs **III:**406; **V:**383
Taylor, John, of Caroline
III:408
U.S. Military Academy at
West Point **V:**409
Washington, D.C. **III:**428
Whigs **IV:**396
Whiskey Rebellion **III:**439,
440
Yorktown, surrender at
III:457
Hamilton, Alice **VII:133,** 407*c*
environment **VII:**99
medicine **VII:**199
peace movements **VII:**256
Hamilton, Andrew **II:161**
Alexander, Mary Spratt
Provoost **II:**18
architecture **II:**25

postal service **II:**304
Zenger, John Peter **II:**433
Hamilton, Henry **III:**95, 96
Hamilton, James **III:**17
Hamilton, James, Jr. **IV:**282
Hamilton, William **III:**10, 26
Hamilton College **IV:**395
Hamilton-Gordon, George (4th
Earl Aberdeen) **IV:**287–288
Hamiltonian Program **III:**206–
207
Hamilton Street Baptist Church
IV:296
Hamlet (Shakespeare) **V:**387
Hamlin, Hannibal **IV:**323
Hammer v. Dagenhart **VII:**52–53,
163, 407*c*
Hammon, Briton **II:**206
Hammon, Jupiter **II:7, 161–162**
Hammond, James Henry **V:**419
Hammond, John **II:**173
Hammond, William A. **V:**257,
285
Hamor, Ralph (the Younger)
II:162
Hampton, Fred **IX:**41
Hampton, Lionel **VIII:**44
Hampton, Wade **V:**329; **VI:**358
Hampton Court Conference
I:192
Hampton Institute
Eastman, George **VI:**105
education, higher **VI:**111
education, philanthropy and
VI:112
Hampton Roads, Battle of
ironclads **V:**207
marine corps **V:**248
Monitor-Merrimack **V:**265–
266
science and technology
V:342
Union navy **V:**406
Hampton-Sidney College **IV:**184
Hanbury, John **III:**323
Hanbury, Thomas **III:**208
Hancock, Cornelia **V:**285
Hancock, John **II:**364; **III:***208,*
208–209, 460*c*
Adams, Samuel **III:**8
Boston Tea Party **III:**59
Constitution, ratification of
the **III:**105
Continental Congress,
Second **III:**115
Lexington and Concord,
Battles of **III:**264, 266
Liberty riot **III:**266
Warren, Joseph **III:**427
Hancock, John M. (1883–1956)
VIII:326
Hancock, Winfield Scott **V:***183,*
183–184; VI:*235,* 409*c*
Armistead, Lewis A.
V:17–18
Gettysburg, Battle of **V:**167
Howard, Oliver Otis **V:**197

Meade, George Gordon
V:254
presidential campaigns
(1870–1899) VI:293
Sickles, Daniel E. V:361
Spotsylvania, Battles of
V:368
Wilderness, Battle of the
V:432
Hancock County, Illinois IV:278
Hand, Learned IX:86
Handel and Haydn Society (Boston,
Massachusetts) VI:254
Handgun Control, Inc. X:161
handguns X:380c. See also Brady
Handgun Violence Prevention
Act
handicapped discrimination
X:379c
Handi-Wrap IX:90
Handler, Ruth IX:55
Handsome Lake III:209
alcohol III:13
Cornplanter III:118
Iroquois III:228
Native Americans III:314
Handy, W. C. VII:219; IX:125
Hanford, Washington VIII:227
Hanna, Marcus Alonzo VI:158
Anthracite Coal Strike
VII:15
Democratic Party VII:74
McKinley, William VI:240,
241
Mitchell, John VII:211
National Civic Federation
VII:226
Republican Party VII:299
Rhodes, James Ford VI:312
Hannegan, Robert VIII:139
Hanno the elephant I:153–154,
210
Hanover dynasty II:240–241
Hanover Presbytery II:92
Hansberry, Lorraine IX:354c
African Americans IX:5
literature IX:193
popular culture IX:258
Hansen, Alvin VIII:200
Hansen, Beck X:239
Hanson, Ole VII:318
Hanson, Roger W. V:288
Hapgood, Hutchins
Greenwich Village VII:131
modernism VII:212
Vorse, Mary Heaton
VII:375
haram I:238
harassment V:4
Hard Day's Night, A (film)
IX:225
Hardee, William J.
Bentonville, Battle of V:34
Cleburne, Patrick R. V:75
Confederate army V:79, 82
Sherman's March through
Georgia V:357

tactics and strategy V:379
uniforms V:399
Hardin, John III:96
Harding, Chester VI:280
Harding, Warren Gamaliel
VII:133–135, 134, 408c
AFL VII:12
Arlington National Cemetery
V:17
Baruch, Bernard M. VII:32
Budget and Accounting Act
VII:44
Capper-Volstead Act
VII:49
conservatism VIII:84
Coolidge, Calvin John
VII:63, 64
Democratic Party VII:75
elections VII:91, 92
environment VIII:115
Fordney-McCumber Tariff
VII:112
foreign policy VII:115
Hoover, Herbert C.
VIII:171
Hughes, Charles Evans
VII:142
labor/labor movements
VII:171
Mellon, Andrew William
VII:201
presidency VII:268, 269
public health VII:276
Railroad Shopmen's Strike
VII:291
Republican Party VII:301
Sheppard-Towner Act
VII:323
socialism VII:328
Soldiers' Bonus VII:331
Taft, William Howard
VII:348
tariffs VII:350
Teapot Dome VII:351
U.S. Shipping Board
VII:360
Veterans Bureau VII:373
Washington Conference
on Naval Disarmament
VII:379
Wheeler, Burton K.
VIII:416
Hardinge, Samuel Wylde, Jr. V:40
Hardtack and Coffee (Billings)
V:239
Hare, Robert III:384
Hargis, Billy James IX:272; X:93
Hargous, P.A. IV:173
Harkin, Tom X:24–25
Harkness, S. V. VII:335
Harlan, John Marshall VI:159,
411c
Baker v. Carr IX:33
Civil Rights Cases VI:72
Escobedo v. Illinois IX:111
Plessy v. Ferguson VI:284–
285, 434–438

Sherman Antitrust Act
VI:330
Supreme Court VI:348
Warren Court IX:337
Harlan County mine strike
VII:375
Harlem, New York
African Americans VIII:5;
IX:4, 6
Communist Party VII:61
Garvey, Marcus VII:121
Hurston, Zora Neale
VIII:181
jazz VII:153; VIII:195
Joplin, Scott VII:158
Malcolm X IX:198
Meredith, James IX:213
modernism VII:212
music VII:219, 220
race and race relations
VIII:318; X:295
UNIA VII:361
Harlem Globetrotters VIII:371
Harlem Heights, Battle of
III:172, 210; IV:258
Harlem Railroad IV:387
Harlem Renaissance VII:135–
137, 136, 408c
African Americans VIII:3
art VII:24; VIII:30
Baker, Ella Josephine
IX:32
Great Migration VII:129
Hurston, Zora Neale
VIII:181
jazz VII:153
literature VII:180–181
Locke, Alain LeRoy
VII:183
modernism VII:212
music VII:219
Harlem riots (1964) IX:6; X:295
Harlem Shadows (McKay)
VII:408c
Harley, Robert II:370
Harlow, Jean VIII:246, 328
Harmar, Josiah
Fallen Timbers, Battle of
III:161
Glaize, meeting at the
III:195
Native Americans III:314
Harmony Society IV:320
Harnack, Adolf von VI:335
Harnett, William Michael
VI:184
Harney, William S. IV:276
Harper, Frances Ellen Watkins
V:184–185; VI:159–160
Harper, William R. VI:66
Harper's Bazaar VI:410c
fashion VI:138
Hearst, William Randolph
VII:138
magazines VI:235
Harpers Ferry, Battle of
Antietam, Battle of V:12, 13

Harpers Ferry, West Virginia
V:186
Shenandoah Valley:
Jackson's campaign V:350
Harpers Ferry, West Virginia
V:185, 185–186, 443c
abolitionism V:4
Brown, John V:43–45
Civil War V:73
Higginson, Thomas
Wentworth V:189; VI:171
Langston, John Mercer
VI:218
Lee, Robert E. V:230
McClellan, George Brinton
V:251
Republican Party IV:323
Stuart, J. E. B. V:375
Harper's magazine
class consciousness VI:73
Dred Scott decision V:117
Howells, William Dean
VI:180
illustration, photography,
and graphic arts VI:183,
184
journalism V:218
Liberal Republican Party
VI:222–223
literature VI:225
Nast, Thomas V:275
Harriet Tubman, The Moses of
Her People (Bradford) V:395
Harriet Tubman Home for
Indigent Aged Negroes V:394
Harrigan, Edward "Ned" VI:257,
355
Harriman, Edward H.
banking, investment VI:23
Hill, James J. VI:172
Morgan, John Pierpont
VI:251
Harriman, W. Averell VIII:161–
162, 162
Harrington, James III:103
Harrington, Mark VI:387
Harrington, Michael IX:142–143,
355c
CAP IX:68
CORE IX:73
economy IX:98
Great Society IX:139
War on Poverty IX:335
Harriot, Thomas I:154–156, 155,
398c
Algonquian I:7
Battel, Andrew I:28
Bry, Theodor de I:37
Camden, William I:55
Hakluyt, Richard, the
Younger I:152
iron manufacturing II:178
Lane, Ralph I:203
literature II:206
Manteo I:229
Mantoac I:229
Monardes, Nicholas I:247

Harriot, Thomas *(continued)*
  Native American religion
    I:261
  Picts **I:**292
  population trends **I:**298
  Roanoke **I:**321
  Secotan **I:**329
  tobacco **I:**363
  travel narratives **I:**368, 369
  White, John **I:**383
Harris, Benjamin **II:162–163**
  New England Primer **II:**258
  newspapers **II:**268
  printing and publishing
    II:311
Harris, Charles K. **VII:**353
Harris, Eric **X:**382*c*
Harris, Isaac **VII:**356
Harris, Joel Chandler **VI:**226
Harris, John P. **VII:**96, 216, 404*c*
Harris, Roy **VIII:**134
Harris, Townsend **V:**443*c*
Harrisburg, Pennsylvania **IV:**316
Harrison, Benjamin **VI:160–162,**
  161, 410*c,* 411*c*
  Blaine, James Gillespie
    VI:41
  Chilean-American relations
    VI:67
  Cleveland, Grover **VI:**75
  conservation/
    environmentalism
    VI:81–82
  Constitution, ratification of
    the **III:**105
  corruption, political **VI:**83
  elections, presidential **X:**117
  Forest Reserve Act **VI:**134
  Geological Survey, U.S.
    VI:141
  Grand Army of the Republic
    VI:152
  Harlan, John Marshall
    VI:159
  Hawaii **VI:**163
  Mafia incident **VI:**234–235
  Morrill Land-Grant Act
    V:270
  Pan-American Union
    VI:276
  presidency **VI:**290
  presidential campaigns
    (1870–1899) **VI:**293
  Quay, Matthew Stanley
    VI:299
  Reid, Whitelaw **VI:**305
  Roosevelt, Theodore
    VII:303
  tariffs **VI:**352; **VII:**349
Harrison, Birge **VI:**275
Harrison, Francis Burton **VII:**157,
  221
Harrison, George **IX:**37–38
Harrison, James **V:**135
Harrison, Joseph **IV:**84
Harrison, Pat **VIII:**80
Harrison, Peter **II:**25, **163**

Harrison, Wallace **VIII:**28–29
Harrison, William Henry
  III:466*c;* **IV:184–186,** *185,*
  413*c,* 414*c*
  banking **IV:**47
  Bell, John **V:**32
  Black Hawk War **IV:**56–57
  Clay, Henry **IV:**97
  Democratic Party **IV:**118
  election of 1840 **IV:**139
  Ghent, Treaty of **IV:**176
  Harrison, Benjamin **VI:**160
  Lake Erie, Battle of **IV:**221
  Liberty Party **IV:**226
  Mexican-American War
    IV:251
  migration **IV:**253
  Native Americans **III:**314;
    IV:273
  Native Americans in the War
    of 1812 **IV:**276
  Prophet, the Shawnee
    III:349
  public land policy **IV:**305
  Tecumseh **III:**409
  Thames, Battle of the **IV:**375
  Tippecanoe, Battle of
    III:411, 412
  Tyler, John **IV:**382
  Van Buren, Martin **IV:**386
  War of 1812 **IV:**391
  Webster, Daniel **IV:**393
  Webster-Ashburton Treaty
    IV:394
  Whigs **IV:**397
Harrison Act. *See* Narcotics Act
Harris Treaty **V:**443*c*
Harris v. McRae **X:**3
Harry Potter books (Rowling)
  X:212
Hart, Frederick **IX:**332
Hart, Silas **III:**217
Hart, Tony **VI:**257
Harte, Bret **V:**240; **VI:162–163,**
  226, 305
Hartford, Connecticut **II:**435*c*
  Amistad incident **IV:**21
  Colt, Samuel **IV:**100, 101
  Easton, Hosea **IV:**129
  Hartford Convention
    IV:186
  industrialization **IV:**199
  Stewart, Maria **IV:**356
  Willard, Emma **IV:**400
Hartford, George Huntington
  VI:65
Hartford, Treaty of
  Native Americans **II:**252
  New Netherland **II:**265
  Pequot War **II:**290
Hartford, USS **V:**267
Hartford Convention **IV:186–**
187
  Democratic-Republican
    Party **III:**136
  Era of Good Feelings
    IV:141

  Federalist Party **III:**165
  Ghent, Treaty of **IV:**176
  Otis, Harrison Gray **III:**326
  states' rights **III:**397
  War of 1812 **IV:**390
Hartford Literary and Religious
  Institute **IV:**129
Hartsville, Tennessee **V:**269
Harvard, Massachusetts **IV:**5, 379
Harvard Business School **VIII:**43
Harvard Classics **VI:**114
Harvard College/University
  II:163
  Adams, John **III:**4
  Adams, John Quincy **IV:**5
  Baldwin, Roger Nash
    VII:31
  Berle, Adolf A., Jr. **VIII:**43
  Boston **II:**41
  Brandeis, Louis Dembitz
    VII:41
  Dana, Richard Henry
    IV:113
  education **IV:**134
  education, higher **VI:**111
  Eliot, Charles William
    VI:113
  evolution **VI:**122
  Fiske, John **VI:**128, 129
  football **VI:**130, 131
  Fuller, Margaret **IV:**169
  Hall, Granville Stanley
    VI:157
  Hearst, William Randolph
    VII:137
  history **VII:**139
  Holmes, Oliver Wendell
    VII:140
  James, Henry **VI:**200
  Kennedy, John F. **IX:**169
  Kennedy, Joseph P.
    VIII:199
  Kennedy, Robert F. **IX:**171
  King, Rufus **III:**246
  Ku Klux Klan **VII:**166
  Leverett, John **II:**204
  libraries, public **VI:**224
  literature **VI:**226
  Mather, Increase **II:**228
  medicine **VI:**244; **VII:**199
  Murray, Pauli **IX:**227
  Phillips, Wendell **IV:**299
  Pickering, Timothy **III:**334
  printing and publishing
    II:311
  Protestantism **II:**316
  science and technology
    II:345; **III:**384; **VI:**326;
    VIII:352
  social work **VII:**330
  Taylor, Frederick Winslow
    VII:350
  Thoreau, Henry David
    IV:376
  Trotter, William Monroe
    VII:357
  Tyler, Royall **III:**417

  Unitarianism **III:**419
  Wigglesworth, Edward
    II:414
  Willard, Samuel **II:**415
Harvard Divinity School **IV:**140,
  320
Harvard Law Review **VIII:**144
Harvard Law School
  Frankfurter, Felix **VIII:**144
  Lilienthal, David E.
    VIII:217
  Sacco and Vanzetti **VII:**311
  Taft, Robert A. **VIII:**385
Harvard Medical School **VII:**407*c*
  Delany, Martin Robinson
    V:107–108
  Hamilton, Alice **VII:**133
  James, William **VI:**200
Harvard Regiment **V:186–187**
Harvey, John **II:**183, 435*c*
Harvey, William H. **VI:**38, 90
Hasaw Chan K'awil **I:**359
Hasenfus, Eugene **X:**183
Hasidim **VIII:**334
Hassam, Childe **VI:**275; **VII:**24
Hastert, J. Dennis **X:**170
Hastie, William H. **VIII:**45, 445*c*
Hastings, Lansford W. **IV:**125,
  187
Hastings Cutoff **IV:**125
Hat Act (England) **II:**3, 214
Hatch, Orrin **X:**44
Hatch Act **VIII:**446*c*
  agriculture **VI:**8
  civil liberties **VIII:**71
  education, federal aid to
    VI:110
hate crimes **X:**97
hate speech **X:**316
Hatfield, Mark **X:**44
Hathaway, Anne **I:**333
Hatteras **V:**7
Haugen, Gilbert **VII:**195
Hauptmann, Bruno **IX:**149
Haury, Emil **I:**164
Hausa **I:**14, **156,** 370
Havana, Cuba **I:**101
  Carleton, Guy **III:**81
  Howe, Sir William **III:**215
  Johnson, Jack **VII:**155
  Maine, Remember the
    VI:237
  Montgomery, Richard
    III:301
  Putnam, Israel **III:**350
  sports and recreation
    VII:333
Havana Harbor **VI:**88
Havasupai **I:156–157**
Havel, Václav **X:**189
Havemeyer, Henry O. **VI:**228
Haverly, J. H. **VI:**116
Hawaii **III:210; IV:187–189;**
  VI:163, 411*c,* 412*c*
  abortion **X:**2
  Bayard, Thomas Francis
    VI:28

Bridges, Harry **VIII:**53
California gold rush **IV:**72
Cleveland, Grover **VI:**75
Executive Order 9066
    VIII:121
exploration **IV:**146
foreign policy **IV:**156; **V:**149,
    151–152; **VIII:**142
gay and lesbian rights
    movement **X:**149
Gentlemen's Agreement
    VII:123
Harrison, Benjamin **VI:**162
imperialism **VI:**187
Kamehameha I **IV:**211
Knox, Frank **VIII:**202
Mahan, Alfred Thayer
    VI:236
Manifest Destiny **IV:**236
marriage and family **X:**215
Mitchell, William (Billy)
    VII:212
Pearl Harbor **VIII:**291–
    293
population trends **X:**282
religion **IV:**317
segregation **VII:**319
statehood **IX:143**
tourism **IX:**319
WAVES **VIII:**418
Wilkes expedition **IV:**400
Hawaiians **X:**282
Hawaii Housing Authority v.
    Midkiff **X:**195
Hawikuh **I:**92, 393, 394
Hawker Hurricanes (RAF)
    VIII:53
Hawkins, Augustus **VII:**42
Hawkins, Benjamin **IV:**109, 247
Hawkins, Sir John **I:157**
    Drake, Sir Francis **I:**110,
        112
    Elizabeth I **I:**121
    Ingram, David **I:**181
    Lane, Ralph **I:**203
    slave trade **I:**339
    Spanish Armada **I:**344
    tobacco **I:**363
Hawkin's Zouaves **V:**441
Hawks, Howard **IX:**224
Hawley, Jesse **IV:**141
Hawley, Willis **VIII:**162
Hawley-Smoot Tariff Act
    VIII:162–163, 443*c*
    Anglo-American relations
        VIII:21
    censorship **VIII:**65
    Congress **VIII:**79
    Fordney-McCumber Tariff
        VII:112
    foreign policy **VII:**116;
        VIII:140
    Good Neighbor policy
        VIII:151
    Great Depression **VIII:**157
    Hoover presidency
        VIII:173, 174

London Economic
    Conference **VIII:**221
Reciprocal Trade
    Agreements Act
        VIII:324
Republican Party **VII:**300
tariffs **VII:**350
trade, domestic and foreign
    VII:355
Hawthorne, Charles **VII:**23
Hawthorne, Nathaniel **IV:**415*c*
    Brook Farm **IV:**65
    Emerson, Ralph Waldo
        IV:140
    Howells, William Dean
        VI:179
    James, Henry **VI:**199–200
    journalism **VI:**210
    literature **IV:**228; **V:**240
    Manifest Destiny **IV:**234
    Peabody, Elizabeth Palmer
        VI:279, 280
    transcendental movement
        IV:378, 379
Hay, Harry **IX:**131
Hay, John Milton **VI:164,** 412*c;*
    VII:404*c*
    Adams, Henry **VI:**1
    foreign policy **VII:**113
    Gilder, Richard Watson
        VI:147
    imperialism **VI:**188
    King, Clarence **VI:**208
    La Farge, John Frederick
        Lewis Joseph **VI:**217
    literature **VI:**225
    Mahan, Alfred Thayer
        VI:236
    McKinley, William **VI:**241
    Open Door Notes **VI:**272–
        273
    Open Door Policy **VII:**246
    Panama Canal **VII:**251
    Reid, Whitelaw **VI:**305
Hay-Bunau Varilla Treaty
    VII:251, 404*c;* **X:**270
Hayden, Carl **X:**123
Hayden, Casey **IX:**347
Hayden, Ferdinand Vandeveer
    VI:141, 164–165
Hayden, Palmer **VII:**136
Hayden, Sophia Gregoria **VI:165–
    166,** 402
Hayden, Tom **IX:143–144**
    "Chicago Eight" **X:**73
    New Left **IX:**243
    Port Huron Statement
        IX:260
    SDS **IX:**303, 304
Haydn, Franz **III:**309, 310
Hayek, Friedrich A. von
    conservatism **VII:**85
    conservative movement
        X:93
    Myrdal, Gunnar **VIII:**253
Hayer, Talmadge **IX:**23
Hayes, Lucy **VI:**37, 397

Hayes, Rutherford B. **VI:166–
    168,** *167,* 408*c*
    Adams, Henry **VI:**1
    African Americans **VI:**6
    Angell, James Burrill **VI:**15
    Bayard, Thomas Francis
        VI:27
    Bierstadt, Albert **VI:**37
    civil service reform **VI:**73
    communications **VI:**78
    Congress **VI:**80
    Conkling, Roscoe **VI:**81
    Democratic Party **V:**110
    education, philanthropy and
        VI:112
    elections **V:**127
    elections, presidential **X:**117
    Geological Survey, U.S.
        VI:140, 141
    Gilman, Daniel Coit **VI:**148
    Great Strike of 1877 **VI:**154
    Harlan, John Marshall
        VI:159
    Harte, Bret **VI:**162
    Hayden, Ferdinand
        Vandeveer **VI:**165
    Higginson, Thomas
        Wentworth **VI:**172
    immigration **VI:**68
    Ingersoll, Robert Green
        VI:193
    lobbying **VI:**228
    Marsh, George Perkins
        VI:239
    Mosby, John Singleton **V:**271
    presidency **VI:**290
    presidential campaigns
        (1870–1899) **VI:**291, 292
    Reconstruction **V:**326
    redemption **V:**329
    Reid, Whitelaw **VI:**305
    Republican Party **VI:**311
    Schurz, Carl **VI:**324
    Scott, Thomas Alexander
        VI:326
    Sherman, John **VI:**329
    star route frauds **VI:**343
    Tilden, Samuel Jones
        VI:357
    Van Lew, Elizabeth **V:**415
    Wallace, Lew **VI:**381
    Whiskey Ring **V:**430
    White, Andrew Dickson
        VI:391
    Winnemucca, Sarah **VI:**397
Haymarket riot **VI:168–169,**
    409*c*
    Altgeld, John Peter **VI:**12
    Anarchist Immigration Act
        VII:15
    Goldman, Emma **VII:**126
    Howells, William Dean
        VI:180
    labor, radical **VI:**213
    labor organizations **VI:**216
    Lloyd, Henry Demarest
        VI:227

Hayne, Robert Y. **IV:**412*c*
    Nullification Controversy
        IV:283
    Webster, Daniel **IV:**393
    Whigs **IV:**397
Haynes, John **II:**223
Hay-Pauncefote Treaties **VI:**241;
    VII:250, 403*c*
Hays, Arthur Garfield **VII:**344
Hays, Mary. *See* Molly Pitcher
Hays, William **III:**298
Hays Commission **VIII:**301
Hays's Big Fight **IV:**102
Haywood, William Dudley "Big
    Bill" **VII:137,** 405*c*
    Darrow, Clarence Seward
        VII:70
    Flynn, Elizabeth Gurley
        VII:109
    IWW **VII:**147
    labor/labor movements
        VII:170
    Lawrence Strike **VII:**174
    New Unionism **VII:**238
    Paterson Strike **VII:**253
    WFM **VII:**382
hazan **III:**236
Hazard, Rowland **VI:**14
Hazard of New Fortunes, A
    (Howells) **VI:**180, 226
hazardous waste **X:**91
Hazelwood, John **III:**135
Hazen, William B. **VI:**387
Hazleton, Pennsylvania **VI:**216–
    217
HBC. *See* Hudson's Bay Company
HBO. *See* Home Box Office
H. C. Frick Coke Company
    VI:135
H. D. (Hilda Doolittle) **VII:**179,
    212
HDI (human development
    indicators) **X:**155
Heade, Martin Johnson **V:**18;
    VI:275
Head of Coosa, Georgia **IV:**325
headright **I:158; II:**120
Head Start **IX:144–145,** 356*c*
    African Americans **X:**13
    Democratic Party **IX:**85
    Great Society **IX:**139
    Johnson, Lyndon B.
        IX:163
    Powell, Adam Clayton
        IX:261
    Shriver, Robert Sargent, Jr.
        X:324
    VISTA **IX:**333
    War on Poverty **IX:**335
Health, Education, and Welfare,
    U.S. Department of (HEW)
    IX:353*c*
    Economic Opportunity Act
        (1964) **IX:**95
    Medicaid **IX:**209
    Republican Party **IX:**274
    Richardson, Elliot L. **X:**310

Health and Body magazine
VII:160
Health and Human Services, U.S.
Department of **X:**17
health care
African Americans **X:**13
Clinton, Hillary Rodham
X:77
Clinton, William J. **X:**80
Great Society **IX:**139
House of Representatives
X:171
Kennedy, Edward M. **X:**197
liberalism **X:**208
Medicaid **IX:**209
technology **IX:**313, 314
War on Poverty **IX:**335
WEAL **IX:**345
health care industry **X:**109, 203
Health Care Security Act (1994)
X:380c
Health Committee of the League
of Nations **VII:**133
health insurance
Clinton, Hillary Rodham
X:77
Fair Deal **IX:**115
labor/labor movements
IX:182
Medicaid **IX:**209
Medicare **IX:**209–210
medicine **VIII:**235, 236;
IX:210; **X:**222
Native Americans **X:**251
public health **IX:**265–266
Health Maintenance Organization
Act (1973) **X:**196
Hearn, Lafcadio **VI:169–170**
Hearst, George **VI:**106
Hearst, William Randolph
VI:411c; **VII:137–138**, *138*
Bennett, James Gordon, Jr.
VI:33
de Lôme Letter **VI:**94
Hughes, Charles Evans
VII:142
journalism **VII:**159, 161
Knox, Frank **VIII:**202
news media **VIII:**271
newspapers **VI:**267
Pulitzer, Joseph **VI:**297
Remington, Frederic
VI:310
Republican Party **VIII:**337
Root-Takahira Agreement
VII:305
yellow journalism **VI:**405
heart, artificial **X:**224, 320
"Heartbreak Hotel" (Presley)
IX:263, 279
*Heart of Atlanta Motel, Inc. v.
United States* **IX:145–146**,
288, 356c
"hearts and minds" **IX:**255
Heath, William **III:**294
Heathcote, Caleb **II:163–164**
heating oil **X:**122

Heaven and Hell (Huxley)
IX:195
Heavenly Merchandise (Willard)
II:415
heavy metal **X:**238
Heberden, William **II:**361
Hebert, F. Edward **X:**169
Hebrew **I:**195
Hebrew Immigration Aid Society
VI:219
Hebrew Technical Institute for
Vocational Training **VI:**219
Hebrew Union College and
Seminary **VII:**298
Hecker, Friedrich **V:**165
Hecker, Isaac
Brook Farm **IV:**65
religion **III:**308
Roman Catholicism **VI:**316
Heckewelder equation **II:**96
Hecla Mining Company **VII:**209
Heidelberg Catechism **II:**149
Heinlein, Robert **IX:**287
Heisman Trophy **VIII:**371
Heister, Leopold Philip von
III:248
Helicon Home utopian
community (Englewood, New
Jersey) **VII:**326
helicopters **VIII:**14
Heller, Joseph **IX:**193
"Hell on the Rappahannock"
V:273
Hell's Angels **IX:**259
Hell's Kitchen (New York City)
VI:285; **VII:**293
Helms, Jesse A., Jr. **X:164–165**
abortion **X:**4
birth control **X:**44
Meredith, James **IX:**213
Reagan, Ronald W. **X:**300
Helms, Richard **VIII:**285
Help (film) **IX:**225
Help America Vote Act (2002)
X:171
Helsinki Accords **X:**100, 139
Helvering, et al. v. Davis
VIII:364
Hemings, Eston **III:**211
Hemings, Madison **III:**211
Hemings, Sally **III:210–211**
Callender, James T. **III:**74
election of 1800 **III:**150
Jefferson, Thomas **III:**233–
235
Hemingway, Ernest **VII:**409c
literature **VII:**180;
VIII:220; **IX:**192, 193
Lost Generation **VII:**185
Spanish civil war **VIII:**369
Hempstead Township, New York
IV:189
Henderson, Fletcher
Goodman, Benny **VIII:**151
jazz **VII:**153
music **VII:**220
Henderson, Kentucky **IV:**37

Henderson, Leon **VIII:163–164**
antimonopoly **VIII:**24
Keynesianism **VIII:**200
OPA **VIII:**282–283
OPM **VIII:**283
recession of 1937–1938
VIII:324
TNEC **VIII:**391
wage and price controls
VIII:409
Henderson, Richard **II:**280
Hendrick (Iroquois League
leader) **II:164**
Hendrick, Burton J. **IV:**387
Hendricks, Thomas **VI:**292
Hendrix, Jimi
folk music revival **IX:**121
music **IX:**230
popular culture **IX:**259
rock and roll **IX:**280
Hennessy, David C. **VI:**234
Henri, Robert **VII:**23, 26–27,
405c
Henrietta (yacht) **VI:**32
Henry, Aaron **IX:**219, 220, 302
Henry, Alice **VII:**231, 285
Henry, Andrew
Ashley, William Henry **IV:**31
Bridger, James **IV:**64
exploration **IV:**144
Rocky Mountain Fur
Company **IV:**324
Henry, Ashley **IV:**31
Henry, Carl F. H. **IX:**272
Henry, Joseph **IV:**334; **VI:**386–
387
Henry, O. (William Sydney Porter)
VI:236; **VII:**404c
Henry, Patrick **III:211–212**,
459c, 461c
anti-Federalists **III:**24
Clark, George Rogers
III:95
Constitution, ratification of
the **III:**105
Continental Congress,
Second **III:**115
Lee, Richard Henry **III:**260
Virginia Resolves **III:**425
Henry, William **III:**17; **IV:**387
Henry II (king of England and
Ireland) **I:**10
Henry II (king of France) **I:**371
Henry III (king of England) **I:**141
Henry III (king of France) **I:**158
Henry IV (Holy Roman Emperor)
I:166, 291
Henry IV (king of Castile) **I:**127
Henry IV (king of France) **I:**67,
158–159, 170
Henry VII (king of England) **I:**45,
159, **404–405**
Henry VIII (king of England)
I:159–160, *160*, 397c
Anglican Church **II:**21
Cabot, John **I:**43, 44
Cabot, Sebastian **I:**45

Church of England **I:**74, 75
Henry VII **I:**159
London **I:**216
Mary I **I:**232
monarchy, British **II:**240
Privy Council **I:**304
Protestantism **II:**315
Reformation **II:**316–317
religion, Euro-American
II:329
Henry Darnall III (Kuhn) **II:**196
Henry Ford Company **VII:**111
Henry's Fort. *See* Fort Henry
Henry Street Settlement House
(New York City)
Berle, Adolf A., Jr. **VIII:**43
Children's Bureau **VII:**53
settlement houses **VII:**328
Wald, Lillian **VII:**377
Henry the Navigator (prince of
Portugal) **I:160–161**, *161*,
395c
Cadamosto, Alvise de **I:**49
Canary Islands **I:**57
Gomes, Diogo **I:**143
slavery **I:**337–338
slave trade **I:**339
sugar **I:**348
Henry Ward Beecher (Ward)
VI:327
Henson, Josiah **V:**397
Hepburn, John **II:**1
Hepburn, Katharine **VIII:**246–
247; **IX:**147
Hepburn Act (1906) **VII:138–
139**, 404c
Allison, William Boyd **VI:**12
Cannon, Joseph Gurney
VII:48
Elkins Act **VII:**94
Mann-Elkins Act **VII:**190
muckrakers **VII:**217
politics (1900–1928)
VII:262
Roosevelt, Theodore
VII:304
Tillman, Benjamin Ryan
VI:358
Hepburn Bill (1902) **VII:**250
Hepburn v. Griswold **VI:**89
Herbert, Victor August **VI:170–
171**
entertainment, popular
VII:95
music **VI:**257; **VII:**219
theater **VI:**354
herbicides **VIII:**10
Herculaneum, Missouri **IV:**38
heredity **VIII:**352
Here Is Your War (Pyle) **VIII:**315
heresy
Church of England **I:**75
Ferdinand and Isabella
I:128
Luther, Martin **I:**218
witches/witchcraft **I:**384
Zumárraga, Juan de **I:**392

Heritage Foundation **X**:93, 349
Heritage USA (South Carolina) **X**:342
Herkimer, Nicholas **III**:63
Herland (Gilman) **VII**:125
Hernandez, Aileen **X**:247
Hernández, Francisco **I**:48
Herndon, Angelo **VIII**:317–318
Herndon, William H. **V**:187, 235
Herndon's Lincoln (Herndon) **V**:187
Hero and Leander (Herbert) **VI**:170
Herodotus **I**:348; **VII**:139
Heroes of America (HOA) **V**:187–188, 296
heroic medicine **IV**:248, 249
Heroic Slave, The (Douglass) **IV**:228
heroin **VII**:223; **X**:242–244
Herold, David E. **V**:19–21, 39
Herrán, Tomas **VII**:251
Herrman, Augustine **II**:164
Hersey, John R. **VIII**:164, 167
Hershey, Lewis B. **VIII**:164–165, 357, 413
Herskovits, Melville **VII**:181
Herter Brothers **VI**:3
Heschel, Abraham **VIII**:334
Hesselius, John **II**:164–165
Hessians **III**:212–213, 461*c*
    Brandywine, Battle of **III**:62
    Burgoyne, Sir John **III**:68
    Delaware River forts **III**:135
    Jersey, HMS **III**:235
    Jews **III**:236
    Knyphausen, Wilhelm, Baron von **III**:248
    music **III**:309
    POWs **III**:345
    Red Bank, Battle of **III**:359
    Riedesel, Frederica Charlotte, baroness von **III**:370
    Trenton and Princeton, Battles of **III**:416
    White Plains, Battle of **III**:440–441
Heston, Charlton **X**:248
Hetch Hetchy dam **VII**:98–99
Heterodoxy (feminist organization) **VII**:375
Heth, Henry **V**:166, 167, 192
Heth, Joice **VI**:25
HEW. *See* Health, Education, and Welfare, U.S. Department of
Hewlett-Packard **VIII**:58
Hexall, William **V**:191
Heylyn, Peter **I**:306
Heyward, DuBose **VII**:125
Hezbollah **X**:143, 229
Hezeta, Bruno de **IV**:103
Hiawatha **I**:161–162, 186, 280, 397*c*; **II**:93
"Hiawatha" (Longfellow) **VI**:49

Hickock, James "Wild Bill" **V**:297
Hicks, Elias **IV**:189
Hicks, Thomas H. **V**:172, 188, 426
Hicksites **IV**:189, 265
hidalgos **I**:332
Hidatsa Indians **I**:162; **IV**:413*c*
    Bodmer, Karl **IV**:60
    disease/epidemics **IV**:123
    Great Plains **III**:197
    Lewis and Clark Expedition **III**:263
    Sacagawea **III**:377
Hidden Persuaders, The (Packard) **IX**:354*c*
    consumerism **IX**:76
    literature **IX**:194
    Packard, Vance **IX**:253
hide and tallow trade
    Dana, Richard Henry **IV**:113
    Larkin, Thomas Oliver **IV**:222
    Stearns, Abel **IV**:356
Hieroglyphic Stairs **I**:90
Higgins, Andrew J. **VIII**:165, 359
Higgins, Eugene **VII**:26
Higgins, Incorporated **VIII**:165
Higgins boats **VIII**:20, 359
Higginson, Thomas Wentworth **V**:188–189; **VI**:171–172
    Dana, Charles A. **VI**:91
    Dickinson, Emily **VI**:97–98
    Jackson, Helen Hunt **VI**:199
    Massachusetts Emigrant Aid Society **IV**:242
Higham, John **VII**:233
High Bridge, Battle of **V**:14
higher criticism **VI**:307
higher education. *See* education, higher
Higher Education Act (1965) **IX**:99
Higher Life in Art, The (La Farge) **VI**:218
High Federalists **III**:335
Highland Park Ford Plant (Michigan)
    automobile industry **VII**:26–28
    Ford, Henry **VII**:111–112
    invention and technology **VII**:150
    mass production **VII**:195
    oil industry **VII**:245
High Noon (film) **IX**:65
High Performance Computing Act (1991) **X**:182
high school(s) **IV**:412*c*; **VII**:85–86, 88
high school dropout rates **X**:13
High Sierra (film) **VIII**:246
High Sierras **IV**:187
Highway Beautification Act (1965) **IX**:163

highways **IX**:354*c*
    automobile industry **IX**:26
    economy **VII**:84; **IX**:97
    Eisenhower, Dwight D. **IX**:101
    Interstate Highway Act of 1956 **IX**:158–159
    National Outdoor Recreation Review Commission **IX**:237
    recreation **IX**:271
    shopping centers **IX**:290
    Stevenson, Adali E. **IX**:302
    suburbanization/suburbs **IX**:306
    tourism **IX**:318
    urban redevelopment **IX**:326–327
Highway Safety Act (1966) **IX**:27
Highway Trust Fund **IX**:159
Hijar, José María **IV**:148–149
Hijaz **I**:238–239
hijrah **I**:238
hilalguía **I**:66
Hildreth, Richard **VI**:242
Hill, Ambrose P. **V**:189–190
    Antietam, Battle of **V**:13
    Banks, Nathaniel P. **V**:29
    Cedar Mountain, Battle of **V**:59
    Gettysburg, Battle of **V**:166, 167
    Longstreet, James **V**:242
    Peninsular campaign **V**:299
    Wilderness, Battle of the **V**:432
Hill, Anita Faye **X**:165–166, 321, 350, 380*c*
Hill, Daniel H. **V**:190
    Antietam, Battle of **V**:13
    Bentonville, Battle of **V**:34
    prisons **V**:313
    Toombs, Robert A. **V**:389
Hill, Faith **X**:240
Hill, Harry **VI**:44
Hill, James (Mississippi political leader) **V**:47
Hill, James J. (financier) **VI**:172, 172–173
    banking, investment **VI**:23
    business and government **VI**:56
    Morgan, John Pierpont **VI**:251
    Northern Securities Case **VII**:241
    Robber Barons, The **VI**:315
Hill, Joe **VII**:110, 147
Hill, Junius **VI**:28
Hill, Lauryn **X**:240
Hill, Nathaniel **IV**:100
Hill, T. Arnold **VIII**:227
Hill-Burton Act (1946) **IX**:211, 265
Hillman, Lewis **VIII**:195, 207
Hillman, Sidney **VIII**:165–166
    AFL **VIII**:18

    Amalgamated Clothing Workers of America (ACW) **VIII**:16
    CIO **VIII**:81, 82
    Dubinsky, David **VIII**:97
    labor/labor movements **VIII**:206
    Lewis, John L. **VIII**:213
    OPM **VIII**:283
    socialists **VIII**:362
Hillquit, Morris
    radicalism **VII**:287
    Socialist Labor Party **VI**:337
    Socialist Party **VI**:337
Hill's Business College (Dallas, Texas) **VIII**:197
Hill's Light Division **V**:190
Hill's saloon (New York City) **VI**:44
Hilton Head, South Carolina **V**:144
Himalayas **VIII**:27
Himes, Frank T. **VII**:374
Hinckley, John W.
    assassinations **X**:35
    Bush, George H. W. **X**:52
    gun control **X**:161
Hindenberg disaster **VIII**:271
Hinduism **X**:306
Hine, Lewis W. **VII**:258; **VIII**:296
hip-hop **X**:238
Hipparchus **I**:15
hippies. *See also* counterculture
    counterculture **IX**:78–79
    fashion **IX**:117
    New Left **IX**:244
    teenagers **IX**:315
Hippocrates **II**:229
Hippocratic oath **VII**:199
Hirabayashi v. United States **VIII**:203
Hirohito (emperor of Japan) **VIII**:437, 447*c*; **IX**:20
Hiroshima (Hersey) **VIII**:164, 167
Hiroshima and Nagasaki **VIII**:166–168, *167*, 449*c*
    AEC **IX**:25
    aircraft industry **VIII**:14
    air power **VIII**:16
    atomic bomb **VIII**:35
    Axis **VIII**:38
    bombing **VIII**:48
    Grand Alliance **VIII**:156
    Hersey, John R. **VIII**:164
    MacArthur, Douglas **IX**:198
    Manhattan Project **VIII**:226, 227
    Mariana Islands **VIII**:229
    Oppenheimer, J. Robert **IX**:251
    technology **IX**:311
    Truman, Harry S. **IX**:320
    Truman's Announcement of the Atomic Bombing of **VIII**:469–471

Hiroshima and Nagasaki
(*continued*)
V-J Day **VIII**:406
World War II **VIII**:427
World War II Pacific theater
VIII:437
Hirsch, Robert **X**:121
Hispanic Americans **X:166–167**
birthrates **X**:45
California **III**:73, 74
elections, presidential **X**:118
immigration **X**:176–177
multiculturalism **X**:236
New Spain, northern
frontier of **III**:318
population trends **X**:282
poverty **X**:285, 286
race and race relations
VII:282; **VIII**:319; **X**:295
Sunbelt **X**:338
Tijerina, Reies López
IX:317
Hispaniola **I:162–163**, 163*m*
adelantado **I**:4
Alvarado, Pedro de **I**:7
audiencia **I**:16
Balboa, Vasco Núñez de **I**:26
cacique **I**:49
Columbus, Bartholomew
I:83
Columbus, Christopher
I:85, 86
conquistadores **I**:88
Cortés, Hernán **I**:94
Dominicans **I**:110
Ferdinand and Isabella
I:128
gold **I**:142
horses **I**:168
Las Casas, Bartolomé de
I:205, 207–208
Ponce de León, Juan **I**:296
smallpox **I**:341
sugar **I**:349
Taino **I**:352
Hiss, Alger **IX:146–147**, 352*c*
anticommunism **IX**:15
Chambers, Whittaker **IX**:52,
53
communism **IX**:67
Dennis v. U.S. **IX**:86
Hoover, J. Edgar **IX**:149
HUAC **IX**:150
Nixon, Richard M. **X**:256
*Histoire d'un voyage faict en
la terre du Bresil autrement
dite Amerique* (Léry) **I**:213,
418–423
Histoire notable de la Floride, L'
(Laudonnière) **I**:208
Historia Animalium (Gesner)
I:139
*Historia General y Natural de las
Indias* (Oviedo y Valdés) **I**:281
*Historia naturael ende morael van
de Westersche Indien* (Acosta)
I:215

historians
Adams, Hannah **III**:4
Guamán Poma **I**:146–147
Leo Africanus **I**:210–211
historicism **VI**:18, 19
history **VII:139–140**
literature **VII**:180
movie industry **VII**:215
science and technology
VII:314
*History and Description of Africa
and the Notable Things Therein
Contained* (Leo Africanus)
I:210
*History of a Cosmopolite, or,
the Writings of the Rev.
Lorenzo Dow, Containing
his Experience and Travels in
Europe and America* (Dow)
IV:127
*History of a Voyage to the Land
of Brazil* (Léry). *See Histoire
d'un voyage faict en la terre du
Bresil autrement dite Amerique*
*History of England from the
Accession of James the Second*
(Macaulay) **II**:242
*History of Life in the Thirteen
Colonies, A* (Gilder) **VI**:147
History of New Hampshire
(Belknap) **III**:155
History of New York City
(Roosevelt) **VII**:304
History of Standard Oil, The
(Tarbell) **VII**:404*c*
muckrakers **VII**:217
oil industry **VII**:244
Standard Oil **VII**:336
Tarbell, Ida Minerva
VII:349
History of the American Indians
(Adair) **II**:4
*History of the Buyccaneers of
America* (Exquemelin) **II**:296
*History of the Conspiracy of
Pontiac, The* (Parkman)
VI:277–278
History of the Indies (Durán) **I**:4
History of the Indies (*Historia de
las Indias*) (Las Casas) **I**:207
*History of the Negro Race from
1619 to 1880* (Williams) **VI**:396
*History of the Negro Troops in the
War of Rebellion, A* (Williams)
VI:396
History of the New World
(Benzoni) **I**:32
*History of the People of the United
States* (McMaster) **VI**:242, 243
History of the United States
(Adams) **VI**:1
*History of the United States, or
Republic of America* (Willard)
IV:401
*History of the Warfare of Science
with Theology in Christendom,
A* (White) **VI**:391–392

History of Woman Suffrage
(Anthony, Stanton, and Gage)
VI:137; **VII**:38
Hitchcock, Alfred **IX**:224
Hitchcock, Ethan Allen **VII**:229
Hitchcok, George **VI**:275
Hitler, Adolf **VIII**:445*c*
Communists **VIII**:78
Coughlin, Father Charles E.
VIII:88
foreign policy **VIII**:141
Grand Alliance **VIII**:155
Hearst, William Randolph
VII:138
Holocaust **VIII**:169
isolationists **VIII**:189–190
Italian campaign **VIII**:191
Munich Conference
VIII:248
Nazi-Soviet Pact **VIII**:266
North African campaign
VIII:278
Owens, Jesse **VIII**:288
Sicily **VIII**:360
UN **VIII**:402
World Disarmament
Conference **VIII**:426
HIV **I**:108; **X**:6–7, 378*c*. *See also*
acquired immune deficiency
syndrome
Hiwassee **II**:280
H. L. Hunley, CSS **V**:83, **190–
191**, *191*, 342
H. L. v. Matheson **X**:20
H.M.S. Pinafore (Gilbert and
Sullivan) **VI**:257
HOA. *See* Heroes of America
Hoar, George F. **VI**:157, **173**, 229
Hobbes, Thomas
commonwealthmen **III**:103
Federalist Papers **III**:163
New Divinity **III**:316
Hobby, Oveta Culp **VIII**:419, 420
Hobkirk's Hill, Battle of **III**:159,
213–214
Hoboken Sicilian Cultural League
VIII:361
Hobson, J. A. **VIII**:51
Hoch Conservatory **VI**:233
Hochelaga **I**:61, 133, **163–164**
Ho Chi Minh
Asia **IX**:21
cold war **IX**:64
communism **IX**:68
SEATO **IX**:292
Soviet Union **IX**:295
Vietnam War **IX**:330
wars of national liberation
IX:339
Hockendauqua **II**:406
hockey **VII**:334–335; **VIII**:372–
373
Hodgers, Jennie **V**:435
Hodgkin, Henry **VII**:109
Hodgson v. Minnesota **X**:20–21
Hoey, Jane M. **VIII**:421
Hoff, Marcian E. **X**:86, 317

Hoffa, Jimmy **IX**:*310*, 356*c*
AFL **IX**:12
labor/labor movements
X:201
Teamsters Union **IX**:310,
311
union movement **IX**:323
Hoffman, Abbie **IX**:79; **X**:73
Hoffman, Dustin **IX**:226
Hoffman, Julius **X**:73
Hoffman, William **V**:314
Hoffmann, Albert **IX**:195
Hogan, James **VI**:131
Hoge, Jane C. **V**:228
Hohokam **I:164–165**
Hoke, Robert F. **V**:34
Holbrook, Josiah **IV**:231–232
Holbrooke, Richard **X**:357
HOLC. *See* Home Owners Loan
Corporation
Holden, William W. **V**:188, 223
Holden v. Hardy **VII**:182
holding companies
banking, investment **VI**:23
economy **VII**:85
Hill, James J. **VI**:172–173
PUHCA **VIII**:313
Rockefeller, John Davison
VII:302
Second New Deal **VIII**:356
trusts **VI**:364
Willkie, Wendell L.
VIII:417
Holiday, Billie **VIII:168–169**,
444*c*
big bands **VIII**:44
jazz **VIII**:195
music **VIII**:251
Holiday Inn **IX**:318
holidays **III**:341
Holiness movement **VII**:298
Holladay Overland Stage
Company **IV**:291
Holland. *See* Netherlands
Holland, Josiah **VI**:147
Holland-America (steamship line)
VI:186
Holland Land Company **III:214**
Holley, Alexander **VI**:34–35
Hollings, Ernest **X**:158
Holly, Buddy **IX**:37, 279, *279*,
280
Holly Springs, Mississippi **V**:417
Hollywood, California
Bureau of Motion Pictures
VIII:56
cosmetics and beauty
industry **VII**:65
Faulkner, William **VIII**:128
journalism **VII**:160
movies **VIII**:245–248;
X:234, 235
popular culture **VIII**:301
Hollywood Cemetery **V:191–192**,
267, 336
Hollywood Club (New York City)
VIII:112

Hollywood Production Code
X:235
Hollywood Ten **IX:**147–149, *148*,
351*c*
communism **IX:**67
HUAC **IX:**150
movies **IX:**223
Holmes, John **IV:**96
Holmes, John Clellon **IX:**36
Holmes, Oliver Wendell, Jr.
(Supreme Court justice)
VII:140–141, 403*c*
Brandeis, Louis Dembitz
VII:41
Buck v. Bell **VII:**43
civil liberties **VII:**58
Communist Party **VII:**61
Forbes, John Murray
VI:132
Harvard Regiment **V:**186
Lochner v. New York
VII:183
Peirce, Charles Sanders
VI:281
Roosevelt, Franklin D.
VIII:345
Schenck v. U.S. **VII:**313
Supreme Court **VII:**343
Holmes, Oliver Wendell, Sr.
(physician)
disease/epidemics **IV:**123
Holmes, Oliver Wendell
VII:140
lyceum movement **IV:**232
science and technology
IV:334
Holocaust, the **VIII:***169*, **169–
170**
anti-Semitism **VIII:**25
Axis **VIII:**38
Buck v. Bell **VII:**43
Hersey, John R. **VIII:**164
immigration **VIII:**184
Jews **VIII:**196
liberalism **VIII:**216
refugees **VIII:**329
religion **IX:**273
World War II **VIII:**427
Zionism **VIII:**441
Holt, Joseph **V:**315
Holty, Carl **VIII:**31
Holy Alliance **IV:**260
Holy Club **II:**413
Holy Land **VI:**227
Holy League **I:**159, **165–166**,
291
Holy Roman Empire **I:**70, **166–
167**, 384
Home, The (Gilman) **VII:**125
Home Administration Act
VIII:127
home appliances **X:**317–318
Home Box Office (HBO) **X:**280,
343, 344
Home Buildings (New York City)
VI:120, 408*c*
home economics **VI:**313, 400

homefront **V:192–194**
conscription **V:**91
economy **V:**123
employment **V:**132
habeas corpus, writ of
V:182
ladies aid societies **V:**227–
228
letters **V:**233
medicine **V:**257
race and race relations
V:319
science and technology
V:343
Stanton, Edwin M. **V:**369
taxation **V:**384
telegraph **V:**386
U.S. Sanitary Commission
V:410–411
volunteer army **V:**419, 420
women's status and rights
V:437
Home Insurance Building
(Chicago) **VI:**196
homeland security **X:**346
Homeland Security, U.S.
Department of (DHS) **X:167–
168**
defense policy **X:**103
House of Representatives
X:170
Hurricane Katrina **X:**174
Homeland Security Act (2002)
X:167
homelessness **VIII:**66
Home-Life in Germany (Brace)
VI:45
Home Owners Loan Corporation
(HOLC) **VIII:170–171**
Federal Housing
Administration (FHA)
VIII:133–134
housing **VIII:**177
marriage and family
VIII:231
New Deal **VIII:**269
RFC **VIII:**326
suburbanization/suburbs
VIII:379
USHA **VIII:**404
Home Owners Refinancing Act
VIII:170–171, 177
Homer, Winslow **VI:173–175**,
174
art **V:**18–19
Gilder, Richard Watson
VI:147
journalism **V:**218
magazines **VI:**235
homeschooling **X:112–113**
homespun **V:194**, 399
Homestead Act **V:194–195**, *195*,
444*c*, **457–458**
agriculture **IV:**13; **V:**6; **VI:**8
Congress **V:**89
homesteading **VI:**175
Lincoln, Abraham **V:**237

public land policy **IV:**306,
307
Republican Party **V:**333
Singleton, Benjamin **V:**361
Sooners **VI:**339
homesteading **VI:175**, 339
Homestead Strike **VI:175–176**,
411*c*
AFL **VI:**13
Carnegie, Andrew **VI:**62
Frick, Henry Clay **VI:**136
Goldman, Emma **VII:**126
labor, radical **VI:**213
labor/labor movements
VII:170
labor: strikes and violence
VI:213
labor trends **VI:**216
steel industry **VI:**337
U.S. Steel **VII:**365
homicide **X:**13
homosexuality. *See* gays and
lesbians
Honduras
filibustering **V:**145
foreign policy **IV:**156
Leslie, Frank and Miriam
Florence Follin **VI:**221
Manifest Destiny **IV:**235
Walker, William **V:**423
Honecker, Erich **X:**189
Honesdale, Pennsylvania **IV:**313
honeybees **II:**130
Honey Springs, Oklahoma **IV:**324
Hong import-export monopoly
III:88
Hong Kong **X:**203
honky-tonk music **VIII:**250
honor **II:**372
Hood, James **VI:**5
Hood, John Bell **V:195–196**
Antietam, Battle of **V:**13
Atlanta campaign **V:**22, 23
Confederate army **V:**82
Davis, Jefferson **V:**105
Forrest, Nathan Bedford
V:152
Johnston, Joseph E. **V:**215
Oates, William C. **V:**287
Sherman's March through
Georgia **V:**356
Hood, Raymond **VIII:**28
Hood, Samuel
Capes, Battle of the **III:**79
Grasse, François-Joseph-
Paul, comte de **III:**197
Yorktown, surrender at
III:454
Hooker, Isabella Beecher **VI:**176,
401
Hooker, John **VI:**176
Hooker, Joseph **V:196–197**, 445*c*
Antietam, Battle of **V:**13
Balloon Corps **V:**25
Chancellorsville, Battle of
V:60–62
Chattanooga, Battle of **V:**63

Gettysburg, Battle of **V:**166
Joint Committee on the
Conduct of the War
V:216
Lee, Robert E. **V:**231
Lincoln, Abraham **V:**237
Lookout Mountain, Battle of
V:243, 244
Meade, George Gordon
V:253–254
prostitution **V:**316
Hooker, Thomas **II:**165, 223,
435*c*
Hooks, Benjamin **X:**245
Hooper, Edward **VII:**26
Hoosac Tunnel **VI:176–177**
Hoover, Herbert C., and
administration **VII:**409*c;*
VIII:171–173, *172*, **173–176**,
175, 443*c*, 444*c*
AFL **VIII:**18
African Americans **VIII:**2
Agricultural Adjustment Act
VIII:5
Agricultural Marketing Act
VII:5–6; **VIII:**8
agriculture **VIII:**9
America First Committee
VIII:17
Anglo-American relations
VIII:21
antimonopoly **VIII:**23
banking **VIII:**39
Baruch, Bernard M.
VII:32
Bonus Army **VIII:**48–49
Borah, William E. **VIII:**49
Boxer Rebellion **VII:**40
Brain Trust **VIII:**51
civil liberties **VII:**58
Clark Memorandum **VII:**58
coal industry **VIII:**74, 75
Communists **VIII:**77
Congress **VIII:**78–79
conservatism **VIII:**84
Coolidge, Calvin John
VII:65
Coughlin, Father Charles E.
VIII:88
criminal justice **VII:**67
Democratic Party **VIII:**92–
93
election of 1932 **VIII:**108,
109
elections **VII:**92
Emergency Banking Act of
1933 **VIII:**113
environment **VIII:**115, 116
FCA **VIII:**125, 126
FCC **VIII:**131
FERA **VIII:**132
First New Deal **VIII:**138
fiscal policy **VIII:**138–139
foreign policy **VII:**116;
VIII:140
Garner, John Nance
VIII:147

Hoover, Herbert C., and
   administration (continued)
   German Americans
      VIII:148
   Good Neighbor policy
      VIII:151
   government VIII:152
   Great Depression VIII:157–
      158
   Hawley-Smoot Tariff Act
      VIII:162, 163
   HOLC VIII:170
   Hughes, Charles Evans
      VII:142
   immigration VIII:184
   Jones, Jesse H. VIII:197
   labor/labor movements
      VIII:205
   La Follette, Robert M., Jr.
      VIII:208
   Lewis, John L. VIII:212
   London Naval Conference
      VIII:222
   Long, Huey P. VIII:222
   Manchuria VIII:225
   McNary-Haugen Farm Bill
      VII:196
   Norris, George W. VIII:276
   Norris–La Guardia Act
      VIII:277
   PECE VIII:309
   politics (Roosevelt era)
      VIII:297–299
   POUR VIII:309–310
   presidency VII:269;
      VIII:173–176, 308
   Railroad Shopmen's Strike
      VII:291
   Recent Social Trends in the
      United States VIII:323
   recreation VIII:327
   refugees VIII:329
   relief VIII:330–332
   Relief and Reconstruction
      Act VIII:333
   Republican Party VII:301;
      VIII:336, 337
   RFC VIII:325
   Roosevelt, Franklin D.
      VIII:345
   SEC VIII:357
   Smith, Alfred E. VII:326–
      327
   Stimson, Henry L. VIII:375
   Supreme Court VIII:381
   tariffs VII:350
   taxation VIII:387
   Tennessee Valley Authority
      VIII:392
   Tugwell, Rexford G.
      VIII:397
   Wagner, Robert F. VIII:410
   World Disarmament
      Conference VIII:426
Hoover, J. Edgar VII:409c;
   IX:149, 149–150, 357c
   anticommunism VIII:22

Army-McCarthy hearings
      IX:18
   Black Panthers IX:41
   espionage VIII:118
   FBI VIII:130
   gays and lesbians IX:131
   Japanese Americans,
      relocation of VIII:193
   MFDP IX:220
   Palmer, Alexander Mitchell
      VII:249
   Rosenberg, Julius and Ethel
      IX:281
Hoover Commission report (1949)
   IX:238
Hoover Dam
   Johnson, Hiram Warren
      VII:154
   Kaiser, Henry J. VIII:199
   National Reclamation Act
      VII:229
Hoover Plan VIII:426
Hope, Bob VIII:245, 403
Hopewell, Treaty of II:408;
   III:87; IV:86
Hopewell culture I:167, 253–254,
   260, 395c
Hopi Indians I:167–168
   art and architecture I:13
   Coronado, Francisco I:92
   marriage and family IV:238
   Native American religion
      I:260
   Native Americans VII:233;
      VIII:264
   Pueblo I:305; II:317
   Pueblo Revolt II:318
Hopkey, Sophia II:410
Hopkins, Esek III:117
Hopkins, Harry L. VIII:176–177
   African Americans VIII:3
   Black Cabinet VIII:45
   CWA VIII:74
   ERAA VIII:114
   FAP VIII:128–129
   FERA VIII:132
   Flynn, Edward J. VIII:139
   FSA VIII:127
   FTP VIII:135
   FWP VIII:136
   Harriman, W. Averell
      VIII:161, 162
   Henderson, Leon VIII:163
   Ickes, Harold L. VIII:183
   Keynesianism VIII:200
   Lend-Lease VIII:211
   NYA VIII:262
   PWA VIII:314
   recession of 1937–1938
      VIII:324
   relief VIII:332
   Roosevelt, Eleanor
      VIII:343
   second front VIII:355
   Social Security Act
      VIII:363
   TNEC VIII:391

transportation VIII:395
   Wallace, Henry A. VIII:411
   WPA VIII:425, 426
Hopkins, Juliet Opie V:285
Hopkins, Lemuel III:104
Hopkins, Mark VI:180
Hopkins, Samuel II:279; III:316,
   317
Hopkins, Stephen II:333
Hopkins Medical School VI:148
Hopkinson, Francis III:17
Hopkinson, Joseph IV:245
Hopper, Dennis IX:225
Hopper, Edward VII:24, 405c;
   VIII:30, 31
Hoppus, Edward II:25
Horgan, Stephen VI:267
hormone therapy VIII:234
Hormuz, Strait of I:6
Horne, Lena IX:201
Hornet, USS (1805 brig) IV:144
Hornet, USS (aircraft carrier)
   VIII:238
Hornigold, Benjamin II:384–385
Horowitz, David X:94
horsecars VI:360
horse racing VI:177–178
   Comstock, Anthony VI:79
   recreation VIII:328
   sports and recreation V:367;
      VIII:373
horses I:168–170, 169; II:165–
   166
   animals II:22; III:23
   buffalo III:64–65
   Cabeza de Vaca, Álvar
      Núñez I:39
   Colombian Exchange I:81
   conquistadores I:88
   Flathead Indians II:127
   Great Plains III:197
   Great Plains Indians II:157
   Indians of the desert
      Southwest II:176
   Lewis and Clark Expedition
      III:263
   Native Americans III:315
   Oyo I:282
   travel II:394
   Valley Forge III:422
   war and warfare II:407
   Yoruba I:389
Horseshoe Bend, Battle of
   IV:189–190
   Cherokee III:87; IV:85
   Creek IV:109
   Crockett, Davy IV:110
   Native Americans IV:274
   Native Americans in the War
      of 1812 IV:277–278
   War of 1812 IV:391
Horsmanden, Daniel II:255
Hortalez and Cie III:48
horticulture. See agriculture and
   horticulture
Horton, Willie X:105, 168–169
Hosea I:23

Hosford, Mary III:277
Hoshour, Samuel K. VI:380
Hospers, John X:209
hospitals. See medicine, hospitals,
   and public health
Hospital Survey and Construction
   Act. See Hill-Burton Act
hostile takeovers X:57, 58
Hotchkiss, Jedediah V:57
hotels V:71
Hot Five and Hot Seven
   recordings (Armstrong)
   VII:153, 220, 409c
Hot Network X:283
Houdini, Harry VII:141, 141–
   142, 403c
"Hound Dog" (Presley) IX:229,
   263, 279
Hounsfield, Godfrey X:224
Hours at Home magazine VI:147
Housatonic, USS V:191, 342
House, Edward VII:175
House, Son VIII:250
House Committee on Un-
   American Activities. See
   House Un-American Activities
   Committee
"House Divided" Speech (Lincoln)
   V:443c, 447–450
House Ethics Committee X:152,
   373
House Foreign Affairs Committee
   VIII:441
House Foreign Relations
   Committee IV:68
household production III:224, 225
household work. See work,
   household
House Judiciary Committee
   ERA X:123
   impeachment of William J.
      Clinton X:178
   impeachment of Richard M.
      Nixon X:178
   women's status and rights
      V:438
   Woodhull, Victoria VI:401
House Made of Dawn (Momaday)
   X:210
House Majority Leader X:267
House Majority Whip
   Foley, Thomas S. X:137
   House of Representatives
      X:171
   O'Neill, Thomas "Tip" P., Jr.
      X:267
Houseman, John VIII:414
House Minority Leader X:271
House Minority Whip X:151, 271
House of Burgesses. See
   Burgesses, House of
House of Commons I:286
   Burgoyne, Sir John III:67
   Cornwallis, Charles, Lord
      III:119
   Franklin, Benjamin III:173
   Grenville, George III:200

impeachment **III:**222
Pitt, William **III:**337
republicanism **III:**364
Wilkes, John **III:**443
House of Delegates (Maryland)
V:188
House of Delegates (Virginia)
III:260, 408
House of Lords
Cornwallis, Charles, Lord
III:119
impeachment **III:**222
Pitt, William **III:**337
republicanism **III:**364
House of Mirth, The (Wharton)
VII:179
House of Representatives,
Massachusetts **VII:**184
House of Representatives, Ohio
VI:396
House of Representatives, U.S.
III:465c; **IV:**414c; **VII:**404c–
406c; **IX:**353c; **X:169–171,**
380c, 382c
Albert, Carl B. **X:**21–22
Amendment, Eleventh
III:16
Amendment, Twelfth **III:**16
Amendments to the U.S.
Constitution **X:**23
anti-Federalists **III:**24
Ashley, William Henry
IV:33
Baker v. Carr **IX:**34
Banks, Nathaniel P. **V:**28
Bonus Bill **IV:**62
Bush, George H. W. **X:**51
Cannon, Joseph Gurney
VII:48
Cheney, Richard B. **X:**72
Civil Rights Act (1957)
IX:58–59
Civil Rights Act (1960)
IX:60
Clay, Henry **IV:**96
Clinton, Hillary Rodham
X:77
Clinton, William J. **X:**82
Congress **VIII:**79–81
Congressional Budget and
Impoundment Control
Act **X:**89
Conkling, Roscoe **VI:**80
conservatism **VIII:**85
conservative coalition
VIII:86
Constitution, United States
III:106, 107
Constitutional Convention
III:109
Crockett, Davy **IV:**110–111
Davis, Jefferson **V:**103
Democratic Party **VII:**74,
75
Dickinson, Anna E. **V:**111
direct election of senators
VII:78

Dole, Robert **X:**104
Douglas, Stephen A. **V:**114
Drayton, William H. **IV:**127
election of 1800 **III:**150
elections **V:**126; **IX:**103, 104
ERA **X:**123
Federalist Papers **III:**163
Foley, Thomas S. **X:**137
foreign policy **X:**143
Garnet, Henry Highland
IV:174
gay and lesbian rights
movement **X:**149
Gerry, Elbridge **III:**194
Gingrich, Newton L. **X:**151,
152
Gore, Albert, Jr. **X:**157
Hearst, William Randolph
VII:138
Hull, Cordell **VIII:**180
Hurricane Katrina **X:**174
impeachment **III:**222
impeachment of William J.
Clinton **X:**178
impeachment of Andrew
Johnson **V:**203
impeachment of Richard M.
Nixon **X:**178
Interstate Highway Act of
1956 **IX:**159
Islam **X:**189
Johnson, Tom Loftin
VII:156
Kansas-Nebraska Act **V:**222
Kennedy, John F. **IX:**169
La Follette, Robert M.
VII:173
Lincoln, Abraham **V:**236
Lodge, Henry Cabot
VII:184
Macon, Nathaniel **III:**280
Madison, James **III:**283
Mann, Horace **IV:**237
Marshall, John **III:**290
McCarthy, Eugene **IX:**205
McGovern, George S. **X:**217
Medicare **IX:**210
NEA/NEH **X:**246
Nixon, Richard M. **X:**256
Norris, George W. **VIII:**276
nuclear freeze movement
X:261
O'Neill, Thomas "Tip" P., Jr.
X:267
Otis, Harrison Gray **III:**326
Palmer, Alexander Mitchell
VII:249
Pelosi, Nancy **X:**271
Pickering, Timothy **III:**334,
335
politics (1900–1928)
VII:261
politics (Roosevelt era)
VIII:298, 300
Polk, James K. **IV:**301
Rainey, Joseph H. **V:**323
Randolph, Edmund **III:**358

Rankin, Jeannette **VII:**292
reconversion **VIII:**326
Reed, Thomas Brackett
VI:304
republicanism **III:**365
Republican Party **VII:**300,
301
RFRA **X:**307
Rodney, Caesar Augustus
III:373
Rumsfeld, Donald **X:**312
Senate, U.S. **X:**321
Sickles, Daniel E. **V:**361
stem cell research **X:**336
Story, Joseph **III:**399
Tallmadge Amendment
IV:365
Tyler, John **IV:**382, 383
UN **X:**357
USA PATRIOT Act **X:**358,
359
Vallandigham, Clement L.
V:413
Washington, George **III:**429
Webster, Daniel **IV:**393
Wright, James C., Jr. **X:**372
Yancey, William Lowndes
V:439
House of the Seven Gables, The
(Hawthorne) **IV:**228–229, 379
House of Trade. *See* Casa de
Contratación
"House of Youth" **I:**21
Houser, George **IX:**72
House Rules Committee **VII:**48
House Select Committee on
Ethics **X:**152
House Subcommittee on
Appropriations **VIII:**426
House Un-American Activities
Committee (HUAC)
VIII:446c; **IX:150–151,** 351c,
356c
anticommunism **IX:**15
Chambers, Whittaker **IX:**52
civil liberties **VIII:**71
communism **IX:**67
Disney, Walt **IX:**88
Federal Employee Loyalty
Program **IX:**119
FTP **VIII:**136
FWP **VIII:**137
Hiss, Alger **IX:**146
Hollywood Ten **IX:**147–149
KKK **IX:**179–180
movies **IX:**223
Nixon, Richard M. **X:**256
Smith Act **VIII:**361–362
Supreme Court **VIII:**384
Warren, Earl **IX:**337
WPA **VIII:**426
House Ways and Means
Committee
Bush, George H. W. **X:**51
Polk, James K. **IV:**301
Randolph, John **III:**359
Stevens, Thaddeus **V:**372

housing **II:166–167; VI:***178,*
178–179, 408c; **VIII:177–179,**
178, 445c. *See also* public
housing
architecture **III:**27–28
business **VIII:**58; **X:**60
cities and urban life **III:**91;
IV:91–92; **VIII:**68–70
economy **X:**111
education **IX:**100
environment **II:**119
Ethical Culture movement
VI:121
Fair Deal **IX:**116
Federal Housing
Administration **IX:**119–
120
Federal Housing
Administration (FHA)
VIII:133–134
Flathead Indians **II:**127
GI Bill of Rights **VIII:**149–
150
Great Depression **VIII:**157
HOLC **VIII:**171
Levitt, William J. **IX:**188–
190
marriage and family **II:**219;
III:288
Massachusetts **II:**224
migration **VIII:**240; **IX:**215
Model Cities program
IX:221
progressivism **VI:**294
PWA **VIII:**314
race and race relations
VII:283
Resettlement Administration
VIII:338–339
RFC **VIII:**326
Riis, Jacob A. **VI:**314
rural life **III:**375
settlement houses **VI:**328
society, British American
II:367
sod houses **VI:**337–338
suburbanization/suburbs
VIII:379–380; **IX:**305
Taft, Robert A. **VIII:**385
urban redevelopment
IX:326
USHA **VIII:**404
Wagner, Robert F.
VIII:410
White, Alfred Tredway
VI:390
Housing Act (1937). *See* Wagner-
Steagall Housing Act
Housing Act (1949)
cities and urban life **IX:**56
New Deal **IX:**242
public housing **IX:**266
urban redevelopment
IX:326
USHA **VIII:**404
Housing Act (1959) **IX:**267
Housing Act (1968) **IX:**139

Housing and Urban Development, U.S. Department of (HUD)
Kemp, Jack F. **X:**196
liberalism **X:**208
Model Cities program **IX:**220, 221
USHA **VIII:**404
Housing and Urban Development Act (1965) **IX:**56, 267, 356*c*
housing-reform movement **VI:**120
Houston, Charles **VIII:**256
Houston, Sam **IV:***190*, **190–192**, 329, 413*c*
Alamo, The **IV:**14–15
Austin, Stephen F. **IV:**40, 41
Colt revolver **IV:**102
election of 1840 **IV:**138
foreign policy **IV:**155
Lamar, Mirabeau B. **IV:**221
Manifest Destiny **IV:**235
San Jacinto, Battle of **IV:**328
Santa Anna, Antonio López de **IV:***329*, 330
Texas **IV:**372, 373
Texas Revolution **IV:**374–375
Houston, Texas **IV:**222; **VIII:**197
Houston, Whitney **X:**238–239
Houston Grand Opera **VII:**158
Hovey, Frederick **VI:**342
Hovey, Richard **VI:**226
Howard, Frederick (earl of Carlisle) **III:**81, 82
Howard, Oliver Otis **V:197–198**
education, higher **VI:**111
Freedmen's Bureau **V:**160, 161
Gettysburg, Battle of **V:**166–167
Johnson, Andrew **V:**212
Meade, George Gordon **V:**254
Nez Perce War **VI:**268
Winnemucca, Sarah **VI:**397
Howard Johnson's **IX:**121, 318
Howard Medical School **VII:**200
Howard University
education, higher **VI:**111
education, philanthropy and **VI:**112
Howard, Oliver Otis **V:**197
Hurston, Zora Neale **VIII:**181
Langston, John Mercer **VI:**218
Howard University School of Law **IX:**202, 227
Howdy Doody **IX:**315
Howe, E. W. **VI:**226
Howe, George (Roanoke colonist) **I:**322
Howe, George Augustus, Viscount (British soldier) **II:167**
Howe, Julia Ward **V:198**
Jewett, Sarah Orne **VI:**202
music **V:**273
women's status and rights **V:**437

Howe, Louis M. **VIII:**139, **179**, 344
Howe, Richard, Lord **III:214–215**
Howe, Sir William **III:**215
Long Island, Battle of **III:**271
Sullivan, John **III:**402
Howe, Samuel **V:**198
Howe, Sir William **III:***215*, **215–216**, 461*c*
Brandywine, Battle of **III:**61–62
Bunker Hill, Battle of **III:**65, 67
Burgoyne, Sir John **III:**67, 68
Clinton, Sir Henry **III:**99
Cornwallis, Charles, Lord **III:**120
Dorchester Heights **III:**139
Fort Washington, capture of **III:**172
Franklin, Benjamin **III:**174
Gage, Thomas **III:**187
Galloway, Joseph **III:**189
Germantown, Battle of **III:**193
Hale, Nathan **III:**204
Howe, Richard, Lord **III:**214
Knox, Henry **III:**248
Long Island, Battle of **III:**271
Red Bank, Battle of **III:**359
Revolutionary War **III:**368
Saratoga, surrender at **III:**380
Trenton and Princeton, Battles of **III:**415–416
Washington, George **III:**430
Wayne, Anthony **III:**433
White Plains, Battle of **III:**440, 441
Howe Company **IV:**199
Howells, William Dean **VI:179–180**
Crane, Stephen **VI:**85
Dickinson, Emily **VI:**98
Dunbar, Paul Laurence **VI:**101, 102
Garland, Hamlin **VI:**140
Gilded Age, The: A Tale of Today **VI:**146
Harte, Bret **VI:**162
James, Henry **VI:**200
Jewett, Sarah Orne **VI:**202
La Farge, John Frederick Lewis Joseph **VI:**217
literature **VI:**225; **VII:**179
Philadelphia Centennial Exposition **VI:**284
theater **VI:**355
Twain, Mark **VI:**367
Howes, Edmund **I:**55

Howl and Other Poems (Ginsberg) **IX:**353*c*
Beat Generation **IX:**36, 37
counterculture **IX:**78
Ginsberg, Allen **IX:**134–135
literature **IX:**194
How the Other Half Lives (Riis) **VI:**410*c*, **426–427**
housing **VI:**179
illustration, photography, and graphic arts **VI:**183
progressivism **VII:**271
Riis, Jacob A. **VI:**314
White, Alfred Tredway **VI:**390
How the West Was Won (film) **IX:**223
How to Marry a Millionaire (film) **IX:**222
Hoxie, Herbert M. **V:**97
Hoyer, Steny **X:**171
Hoyt, Beatrix **VI:**343
Hoyt, William **VI:**359
HTML (Hyper Text Markup Language) **X:**319
HUAC. *See* House Un-American Activities Committee
Huang, John **X:**194
Huascar **I:**15–16
Huayna Capac (Inca emperor) **I:**15
Hubbard, Gardiner **VI:**31
Hubbard, John **IV:**234
Hubbardton, Battle of **III:**172, 380
Hubbell, Webster **X:**333
Hubble, Edwin **VIII:**352
Hubble Space Telescope **X:**327, 329, 379*c*
Huckleberry Finn (Twain) **VI:**203
HUD. *See* Housing and Urban Development, U.S. Department of
Hudson, Frederic **VI:**32
Hudson, Henry **II:167–168**, *168*
Delaware **II:**95
Dutch East India Company **I:**115
exploration **II:**124
Frobisher, Martin **I:**135
New Amsterdam **II:**256
New Netherland **II:**264
New York **II:**269
Northeast Passage **I:**273
Pennsylvania **II:**285
Purchas, Samuel **I:**307
Hudson Bay **II:**141, 189
Hudson Highlands campaign **III:**98, 99, **216**
Hudson River **II:**435*c*
agriculture **IV:**12
art and architecture **IV:**31
Audubon, John James **IV:**38
economy **IV:**131
Erie Canal **IV:**141
exploration **II:**124
Greenwich Village **VII:**130

Hudson, Henry **II:**168
Hudson Highlands campaign **III:**216
industrialization **IV:**200
Iroquois **II:**179
Long Island, Battle of **III:**271
migration **IV:**254
New York **II:**268
railroads **IV:**314
riots **III:**371
Saratoga, surrender at **III:**380, 382
science and technology **IV:**333
Stoney Point, Battle of **III:**399
Vanderbilt, Cornelius **IV:**386
West Point **III:**437
Hudson River Institute (Claverack, New York) **VI:**85
Hudson River Railroad **IV:**387
Hudson River School **IV:**28–29; **V:**18
Hudson River Valley
art and architecture **IV:**28
Kościuszko, Tadeusz **III:**248
land riots **II:**202; **III:**254
McDougall, Alexander **III:**294
tenants **II:**387
Hudson's Bay Company (HBC)
Applegate, Jesse **IV:**26
Ashley, William Henry **IV:**31–33
Astor, John Jacob **IV:**34, 35
Astoria **IV:**35, 36
Bent, Charles **IV:**51
Columbia River **IV:**103
exploration **II:**123
Fort Vancouver **IV:**158, 159
fur trade **III:**183; **IV:**170–171
Hastings, Lansford W. **IV:**187
Iberville, Pierre Le Moyne, sieur d' **II:**173
McLoughlin, John **IV:**247, 248
migration **IV:**255
Missouri Fur Company **IV:**258
mountain men **IV:**266, 267
Oregon Treaty of 1846 **IV:**287, 288
rendezvous **IV:**321
Rocky Mountain Fur Company **IV:**325
Smith, Jedediah Strong **IV:**350, 351
trade, domestic and foreign **II:**392
Wyeth, Nathaniel J. **IV:**406
Hudson Strait **I:**87
Huelga strike **X:**166

Huemac (Toltec ruler) **I:**364–365
Huerta, Dolores
Chávez, César Estrada **IX:**53
Latino movement **IX:**186
UFW **IX:**324, 325
Huerta, Victoriano **VII:**35, 204, 205
Huertgen Forest **VIII:**431
Huexotxingo **I:**19
Huggins, Charles B. **VIII:**234
Hughes, Charles (director) **X:**236
Hughes, Charles Evans (Supreme Court justice) **VII:142,** 406c
court-packing plan **VIII:**89
Democratic Party **VII:**74
elections **VII:**91
foreign policy **VII:**115
Ginsburg, Ruth Bader **X:**152
politics (1900–1928) **VII:**262
Progressive Party **VII:**270
Supreme Court **VIII:**381, 382
Washington Conference on Naval Disarmament **VII:**379
Hughes, Dorothy Pitman **X:**334
Hughes, John **III:**173; **IV:**24
Hughes, Langston
Freedom Train **IX:**125
Harlem Renaissance **VII:**136
Hurston, Zora Neale **VIII:**181
literature **VII:**181; **VIII:**219; **IX:**192
Hughes, Lloyd **VI:**177
Hughes, Sarah T. **IX:**164
Hugo, Victor **V:**46
Huguenots **I:170–171,** 397c
Caroline, Fort **I:**61
Drake Manuscript **I:**113
Florida **I:**131; **II:**128
French explorations of the Atlantic **I:**134
French immigrants **II:**139
Henry IV **I:**158
Laudonnière, René de **I:**208
Le Moyne, Jacques **I:**209
Léry, Jean de **I:**212
Philip II **I:**291
Ralegh, Sir Walter **I:**311
Walsingham, Sir Francis **I:**382
Huie, William Bradford **IX:**318
Huitzilopochtli **I:171; II:**330
Aztecs **I:**18, 19
Aztlán **I:**23
Florentine Codex **I:**130
Tenochtitlán **I:**354
Tezcatlipoca **I:**357
Huk rebellion **IX:**256
Hulbert, Edwin J. **VII:**209–210
Hulbert, William **VI:**26

Hull, Agrippa **III:216–217**
Hull, Cordell **VIII:179–180**
Bretton Woods Conference **VIII:**52
Ethiopia **VIII:**118
Good Neighbor policy **VIII:**151
London Economic Conference **VIII:**221
Manchuria **VIII:**225
Neutrality Acts **VIII:**267
Reciprocal Trade Agreements Act **VIII:**325
Roosevelt, Franklin D. **VIII:**346
Spanish civil war **VIII:**370
Welles, Sumner **VIII:**415
Hull, Isaac **IV:**192
Hull, Jane Dee **X:**371
Hull, William **III:**466c; **IV:**192
Cass, Lewis **IV:**83
Harrison, William Henry **IV:**185
Native Americans in the War of 1812 **IV:**277
War of 1812 **IV:**391
Hull-House **VI:**410c
Abbott, Grace **VII:**1
Addams, Jane **VII:**2–3
Americanization **VII:**13
Atkinson, Edward **VI:**22
criminal justice **VII:**66–67
Hamilton, Alice **VII:**133
immigration **VI:**186
Kelley, Florence **VII:**164
New Woman **VII:**240
progressivism **VI:**294
settlement houses **VI:**327, 328
social work **VII:**329, 330
urban reform **VII:**363
Hull-House Women's Labor Bureau **VII:**164
Humabon (Raja of Cebu Island) **I:**224
Humanae Vitae **X:**3, 43
human cloning **X:**172, 381c
human development indicators (HDI) **X:**155
human engineering **VI:**216
Human Genome Initiative **X:**172
Human Genome Project **X:171–172,** 221, 224, 225, 382c
humanism **I:**3
humanitarian aid
Afghanistan War **X:**11, 12
Africa **X:**16, 17
Bush, George W. **X:**56
defense policy **X:**102
UN **X:**355, 357
humanitarianism **III:217–218,** 352
Human Life Amendment **X:**44
Human Life Bill (1981) **X:**4, 44
human rights **X:**377c, 378c
Carter, James Earl, Jr. **X:**69
defense policy **X:**100, 102

foreign policy **X:**141
Latin America **X:**205
South Africa **X:**325
Human Rights **IV:**16
human sacrifice
Cozumel **I:**99
Durán, Diego **I:**114
Florentine Codex **I:**130
flowery wars **I:**131–132
Huitzilopochtli **I:**171
Human Work (Gilman) **VII:**125
Humboldt Bay **IV:**179
Humboldt Current **I:**289
Humboldt River **IV:**125
Hume, Sophia Wigington **II:168–169**
Humery, Conrad **I:**148
HUMINT (human intelligence) **IX:**52
humoral theory **II:**229; **III:**295, 296
Humphrey, Hubert H. **IX:151–152,** 357c
Agnew, Spiro T. **X:**18
Americans for Democratic Action **IX:**13, 14
antiwar movement, Vietnam **X:**29
"Chicago Eight" **X:**73
Democratic Party **IX:**85
elections **IX:**104
Kissinger, Henry A. **X:**198
McCarthy, Eugene **IX:**206
McGovern, George S. **X:**217
Mondale, Walter F. **X:**233
National Wilderness Preservation Act of 1964 **IX:**240
Nixon, Richard M. **X:**256
Republican Party **IX:**275
States' Rights Party **IX:**299
tobacco suits **X:**352
Humphreys, David **III:**45, 104
Humphreys, Joshua **III:**107
Hundred Days **VIII:**444c
CCC **VIII:**70
presidency **VIII:**309
Roosevelt, Franklin D. **VIII:**345
Hungary **I:**384, 385
Axis **VIII:**38
cold war **IX:**63
Europe **IX:**112, 113
Iron Curtain, collapse of **X:**189
Judaism **VI:**205
population trends **VII:**266
Seattle General Strike **VII:**317
Siberian Expedition **VII:**324
Soviet Union **IX:**295
World War I **VII:**393
Hungary in 1841 (Brace) **VI:**45
Hunkers **IV:**163
Hunley, Horace Lawson **V:**190, 191

Hunt, Edward Bissell **VI:**199
Hunt, E. Howard **X:**49, 366
Hunt, Henry J. **V:**168
Hunt, Jane **IV:**341; **V:**436
Hunt, Jim **X:**165
Hunt, Richard Morris **VI:**344
Hunt, Thomas **III:**376
Hunt, Walter **IV:**333
Hunt, Ward **VI:**16
Hunt, Washington **VI:**199
Hunt, William Morris **VI:**200, 217
Hunt, Wilson Price **IV:**36
Hunter, Alberta **VII:**219
Hunter, David **V:**144, 394
Hunter, HMS **III:**180
Hunter, Robert **II:**209; **V:**221
Hunter, William (postmaster) **II:**304
Hunter, William H. (chaplain) **VI:**4
Hunter College **IX:**227
hunter-gatherers **I:**2, 360
hunting
Aleut **II:**17
Algonquin **II:**18
animals **II:**22
Delaware **II:**94
food **II:**130
Iroquois **I:**185
Northwest Coast Indians **II:**275
Passamaquoddy **I:**287
recreation **VIII:**327
Huntington, Collis Potter **VI:180–181**
Huntington's chorea **VIII:**160
Huntley, Chet **IX:**315
Huntley-Brinkley Report, The **IX:**315
Huron, Lake **IV:**391
Huron Indians **I:171–173; II:169–170**
Aataentsic **I:**1
agriculture **II:**9
Algonquin **II:**18
architecture **II:**24
Beaver Wars **II:**35
Brébeuf, Jean de **II:**46
Brulé, Étienne **II:**49–50
fur trade **IV:**170
Iroquois **I:**187
Jesuits **II:**185
New Netherland **II:**265
religion **II:**330, 331
Hurricane Katrina **X:172–174,** 173, 384c
Bush, George W. **X:**56
cities and urban life **X:**76
DHS **X:**168
economy **X:**111
energy **X:**121
Gates, William Henry, III **X:**148
hurricanes **VI:**137–138
Hurston, Zora Neale **VIII:180–181,** 181
African Americans **VIII:**3
Boas, Franz Uri **VII:**39

Hurston, Zora Neale (continued)
Harlem Renaissance
VII:136
literature **VII:**181; **VIII:**219, 221
Hurt, Mississippi John **IX:**121
Hus, John (Jan) **I:**315; **III:**302
Husband, Herman **III:**218, 321
Husbands, Sam **VIII:**135
Huske, John **III:**267
Hussein (king of Jordan) **IX:**160
Hussein, Qusay **X:**186, 187
Hussein, Saddam **X:**383c, 384c
   Ali, Muhammad **IX:**10
   Bush, George H. W. **X:**53
   Bush, George W. **X:**56
   defense policy **X:**101
   foreign policy **X:**143
   Iraq War **X:**185–188
   Jackson, Jesse, L. **X:**192
   Middle East **IX:**214; **X:**229
   Persian Gulf War **X:**273–274
   Powell, Colin L. **X:**287
   Rice, Condoleezza **X:**309
   Rumsfeld, Donald **X:**313
   UN **X:**356
Hussein, Uday **X:**186, 187
Hussey, Obed **IV:**243
Huston, Felix **V:**213
Huston, John **IX:**148
Hutcheson, William L. "Big Bill"
   VIII:18, 213
Hutchinson, Anne Marbury
   II:170–171, 435c
   Coddington, William **II:**73
   Cotton, John **II:**82
   Dyer, Mary **II:**108
   Massachusetts **II:**223
   midwives **II:**234
   Rhode Island **II:**333
   Wheelwright, John **II:**412
   Winthrop, John **II:**418
   women's status and rights
   II:425
Hutchinson, John **II:**345
Hutchinson, Thomas **III:**218, 218–219
   Boston Massacre **III:**58
   Boston Tea Party **III:**59
   Franklin, Benjamin **III:**174
   MacIntosh, Ebenezer
   III:279
   Oliver, Andrew **III:**324, 325
   riots **III:**371
   Stamp Act **III:**396
   Warren, Mercy Otis **III:**427, 428
   Whately, Thomas **III:**437
   writs of assistance **III:**448–449
Hutchison Family Singers **IV:**269
Hutson, Don **VIII:**371
Hutton, Bobby **IX:**41
Hutton, Edward F. **VIII:**19
Hutus **X:**102
Huxley, Aldous **IX:**195

Huxley, Thomas Henry
   Gilman, Daniel Coit **VI:**148
   James, Henry **VI:**200
   Marsh, Othniel Charles
   VI:240
Hyde, Edward (viscount
   Cornbury). See Cornbury, Lord
Hyde, Henry **X:**317
Hyde Amendment **X:**3
hydraulic mining **VI:**246
hydroelectric power **VI:**411c
   electricity **VII:**92
   Norris, George W.
   VIII:276
   Tesla, Nikola **VI:**353
hydrofoil boats **VI:**31
hydrogen bomb **IX:**152–153, 153, 353c
   AEC **IX:**24
   arms race **IX:**17
   DuPont Corporation **IX:**91
   Oppenheimer, J. Robert
   IX:251
   science and technology
   IX:285
   technology **IX:**312
hygiene **V:**113
hymns **V:**255, 256
Hymns for Children: Selected and
   Altered (Dix) **IV:**124
Hypatica Society **VI:**220
hypertext **X:**182, 319
Hyper Text Markup Language
   (HTML) **X:**319

I

I, Robot (Asimov) **IX:**287
I, the Jury (Spillane) **IX:**195
Iacocca, Lee **X:**74
IAEA. See International Atomic
   Energy Agency
IAM (International Association of
   Machinists) **VII:**11
I Am a Fugitive from a Chain
   Gang (film) **VIII:**301
"I Am an American Day" **IX:**66
Ibadan University (Nigeria)
   IX:213
Ibadi Muslims **I:**324
Iberian Peninsula **I:**396c
   Bristol **I:**37
   Castile **I:**65–66
   Islam **I:**189
   Jews **I:**194
   Reconquista **I:**314
Iberville, Pierre Le Moyne, sieur
   d' **II:**37, 173
IBEW (International Brotherhood
   of Electrical Workers) **VII:**11
IBM (International Business
   Machines) **IX:**357c; **X:**378c
   business **VIII:**58
   computers **IX:**70, 71; **X:**87
   economy **VII:**85
   ENIAC **IX:**105

Gates, William Henry, III
   X:147
   Job Corps **IX:**161
   music **IX:**228
   science and technology
   X:318
   technology **IX:**311
Ibn al-Ahmar **I:**176
Ibn Battuta **I:**175
   Mali **I:**226
   Sufism **I:**348
   sugar **I:**348
   Timbuktu **I:**359
Ibn Khaldûn, 'Abd-ar-Rahmân
   Abû Zayd ibn Muhammad ibn
   Muhammad **I:**175–176
   Mali **I:**225
   Sufism **I:**348
   Sundiata Keita **I:**350
ibn Zargun, Mahmud **I:**360
Ibsen, Henrik **VI:**355
IBT. See International
   Brotherhood of Teamsters
IC4A (Intercollegiate Association
   of Amateur Athletes of
   America) **VI:**359
ICBMs. See intercontinental
   ballistic missiles
ICC. See Indian Claims
   Commission; Interstate
   Commerce Commission
icebergs **I:**176–177, 334
Iceland **I:**37, **177**, 272, 395c
Iceman Cometh, The (O'Neill)
   VIII:220
Ickes, Harold L. **VIII:**183–184, 185
   African Americans **VIII:**3
   Black Cabinet **VIII:**45, 46
   civil rights **VIII:**72
   coal industry **VIII:**76
   environment **VIII:**115
   ERAA **VIII:**114
   Federal Housing
   Administration (FHA)
   VIII:133
   Fortas, Abe **X:**145
   Hopkins, Harry L. **VIII:**176
   Indian Reorganization Act
   VIII:185, 186
   NAACP **VIII:**255
   Native Americans **VIII:**264
   NIRA **VIII:**257
   PWA **VIII:**314
   Roosevelt, Eleanor
   VIII:343
   Spanish civil war **VIII:**370
   transportation **VIII:**395
   USHA **VIII:**404
   Wallace, Henry A. **VIII:**411
   WPA **VIII:**425
ID (intelligent design) **X:**306–307
Idaho
   Applegate, Jesse **IV:**26
   Borah, William E. **VIII:**49
   Coeur d'Alene miners' strike
   VI:77

elections, conduct of
   VI:113
exploration **IV:**145
Haywood, William Dudley
   VII:137
Japanese Americans,
   relocation of **VIII:**194
Non-Partisan League
   VII:241
population trends **X:**282
Rocky Mountain Fur
   Company **IV:**324
woman suffrage **VII:**384
women's status and rights
   VI:399
Young, Brigham **IV:**408
Ide, William B. **IV:**49, 50
"ideal motherhood" **VI:**374
Idle Hours (Chase) **VI:**66
Idris Aloma (sultan of Bornu)
   I:324
IEDs (improvised explosive
   devices) **X:**188
IFOR. See Implementation Force
Igbo **I:**177–178
Ignatius Loyola **I:**178–179, 192–193
"I Goes to Fight Mitt Sigel" **V:**274
"I Got Rhythm" (Gershwin)
   VII:124
"I Have a Dream" Speech (King)
   IX:373–375
   King, Martin Luther, Jr.
   IX:174
   March on Washington
   (1963) **IX:**201
   SCLC **IX:**293
"I Heard the Bells on Christmas
   Day" **V:**274
I Know Why the Caged Bird Sings
   (Angelou) **X:**25, 26
ILA (Institute for Legislative
   Action) **X:**249
ILA (International
   Longshoremen's Association)
   VIII:53
ILD. See International Labor
   Defense
ILDF (International Labor
   Defense Fund) **VII:**61
Ile-Ife **I:**281, 389
ILGWU. See International Ladies'
   Garment Workers' Union
"I'll Be Seeing You" (Fain-Kahal)
   VIII:252
Illegal Fencing Act (1885) **VI:**24
illegal immigration **X:**226, 379c, 384c
   braceros **IX:**42, 43
   foreign policy **X:**144
   immigration **IX:**156;
   X:175–177
   IRCA **X:**177
   Latin America **X:**206
   Mexico **X:**226–227
   population trends **IX:**260
illicit drugs. See drugs, illicit

Illinois **I:**167; **IV:**413*c;* **VII:**405*c,* 407*c*
  abolitionism **IV:**3; **V:**1
  Agricultural Adjustment Act **VIII:**6
  agriculture **IV:**10, 11; **V:**6
  Altgeld, John Peter **VI:**12
  anti-Masonry **IV:**25
  Cannon, Joseph Gurney **VII:**48
  criminal justice **VII:**66–67
  Deere, John **IV:**115–116
  disease/epidemics **IV:**123
  Dred Scott decision **V:**116, 117
  economy **IV:**130
  exploration **IV:**145
  Harrison, William Henry **IV:**184
  industrialization **IV:**201
  Ingersoll, Robert Green **VI:**193
  internal improvements **IV:**203
  Kelley, Florence **VII:**164
  Keokuk **IV:**213
  lead mines **IV:**223
  Lewis, John L. **VIII:**212
  Liberty Party **IV:**226
  Lincoln, Abraham **V:**235
  Lovejoy, Elijah **IV:**230–231
  McCormick, Cyrus Hall **IV:**243
  migration **IV:**254
  Mormon Church **IV:**89
  Mormon Trail **IV:**261
  mothers' pensions **VII:**214
  Muller v. Oregon **VII:**217
  National Road **IV:**271
  Nauvoo **IV:**278–279
  New Madrid earthquake **IV:**280
  Obama, Barack Hussein **X:**263
  panic of 1819 **IV:**293
  Patrons of Husbandry **VI:**279
  polygamy **IV:**303
  railroads **IV:**314, 316
  religion **IV:**318
  Republican Party **IV:**321, 323
  rust belt **X:**314
  Sac and Fox **IV:**327
  Smith, Joseph, Jr. **IV:**353
  social work **VII:**330
  stem cell research **X:**335
  Taylor, Zachary **IV:**367
  urban reform **VII:**363
  Young, Brigham **IV:**407
Illinois Bureau of Labor Statistics **VII:**164
Illinois Central Railroad **V:**114, 250
"I'll Never Smile Again" (Lowe) **VIII:**361
illuminated manuscripts **I:**33

Illustrated London News **VI:**220
illustration, photography, and the graphic arts **VI:**183–184
"Illustrious Americans" (Brady) **V:**41
I Love Lucy **IX:**353*c*
  advertising **IX:**2
  cold war culture **IX:**65
  popular culture **IX:**259
Ilunga Kalala **I:**217
"I'm a Good Ole Rebel" **V:**274
IMF. *See* International Monetary Fund
Immigrants' Protection League **VII:**1
immigration **III:**221–222, 464*c;* **IV:**193–196, *194,* 195*t, 214;* **V:**199–201; **VI:**184–186, *185, 235,* 409*c,* 410*c;* **VII:***143,* 143–145, 403*c*–405*c,* 407*c,* 408*c;* **VIII:**184–185; **IX:**155–156, 353*c,* 357*c;* **X:**175–177, *176, 226,* 378*c,* 379*c,* 384*c. See also* illegal immigration; *specific immigrant groups, e.g.:* German Americans
  Abbott, Grace **VII:**1
  Addams, Jane **VII:**3
  AFL **VII:**12
  Alamo, The **IV:**14
  Alien and Sedition Acts **III:**14
  Amalgamated Clothing Workers of America (ACW) **VIII:**16
  Americanization **VII:**12
  American Protective Association **VI:**13, 14
  Anarchist Immigration Act **VII:**14–15
  Angell, James Burrill **VI:**15
  anti-Catholic riots **IV:**22–24
  anti-Chinese agitation, rise of **IV:**24
  anti-Semitism **VII:**16–17; **VIII:**25
  art and architecture **VI:**18
  Arthur, Chester Alan **VI:**21
  Asian-American movement **IX:**21
  Asian Americans **VIII:**31–32; **X:**32
  Audubon, John James **IV:**37
  Austin, Moses **IV:**39
  Austin, Stephen F. **IV:**39–40
  Baldwin, Roger Nash **VII:**31
  baseball **VIII:**32
  Beecher, Henry Ward **VI:**30
  braceros **IX:**42–43
  Cable Act **VII:**47
  California **IV:**71
  California gold rush **IV:**73, 75
  Canada **III:**78
  Catholics **III:**83; **VIII:**63

Chávez, César Estrada **IX:**54
children **VII:**399
Chinese Exclusion Act **VI:**68, **416–417**
cities and urban life **IV:**91; **V:**66; **VI:**70; **VII:**54; **IX:**56; **X:**75
citizenship **III:**93, 94; **VII:**56
class consciousness **VI:**73
Clinton, Hillary Rodham **X:**79
Colorado gold rush **IV:**99
Communist Party **VII:**61
Congress **VII:**61
conservatism **VIII:**83
Continental army **III:**111
contract labor **VI:**82
criminal justice **VII:**67
Democratic Party **IV:**118; **VIII:**92
Dillingham Commission **VII:**77–78
disease/epidemics **V:**113
dress **VII:**79
economy **IV:**130, 132
education **IV:**135; **VI:**107, 110
enemy aliens **VIII:**114
entertainment, popular **VI:**116
Erie Canal **IV:**142
Espionage Act **VII:**100–101
ethnic organizations **VII:**101–102
eugenics **VII:**102, 103
Fifteenth Amendment **V:**141
Foraker Act **VII:**110
foreign policy **IV:**155; **VI:**133; **X:**144
Gentlemen's Agreement **VII:**123–124
German Americans **VIII:**148
Goldman, Emma **VII:**126
Goldmark, Josephine Clara **VII:**127
Great Depression **VIII:**159
Great Migration **VII:**129
Hamilton, Alice **VII:**133
Holocaust **VIII:**170
Hoover presidency **VIII:**173
Houston, Sam **IV:**191
Immigration Act (1917) **VII:**145
immigration restrictions **VI:**186–187
industrialization **IV:**200
Industrial Revolution, Second **VI:**190–191
intelligence tests **VII:**148
Internal Security Act (1950) **IX:**158
IRCA **X:**177

Irish Americans **VIII:**188
Italian Americans **VIII:**190
Japanese Americans, relocation of **VIII:**193
Jews **VIII:**196
Jones Act (1917) **VII:**157
journalism **VII:**158–159
Journey to Pennsylvania (Mittelberger) **II:**444–445
Judaism **VI:**205
Kennedy, Edward M. **X:**196
Know-Nothing Party **IV:**214, 215
Ku Klux Klan **VII:**166
labor, child **VI:**212
labor/labor movements **III:**251; **IV:**219; **VIII:**205
labor trends **VI:**217
Latin America **X:**206
Lazarus, Emma **VI:**219
liberalism **VIII:**214
literature **VI:**225; **VIII:**218
Maine Law **IV:**233
Mann Act **VII:**189
marriage and family **VII:**191
McCarran-Walter Act **IX:**204–205
medicine **VII:**200
Mexican Americans **VIII:**237
Mexican immigration **VII:**202–203
Mexican Repatriation Program **VIII:**238
Mexican Revolution **VII:**205
Mexico **X:**226–227
migration **VII:**206
mining **VII:**210
movie industry **VII:**214
movies **VIII:**245
multiculturalism **X:**236
National Origins Act **VII:**227–228
National Reclamation Act **VII:**228
Native Americans **IV:**275
nativism **V:**280; **VI:**263–264; **VIII:**233–234
New Unionism **VII:**237
New Woman **VII:**239
New York City **V:**283
New York City draft riots **V:**285
photography **VII:**259
Polish Americans **VIII:**297
popular culture **VII:**263
population trends **III:**342; **V:**309, 310; **VI:**286; **VII:**266; **VIII:**304–306; **IX:**260
presidency **VII:**268
progressivism **VI:**294, 295; **VII:**271
Prohibition **VII:**272
Puerto Ricans **IX:**267

immigration *(continued)*
Quota Act **VII:**279
race and race relations **IV:**309, 312; **VII:**281–282
radicalism **VII:**286, 287
railroads **V:**322
refugees **VIII:**329–330
religion **IV:**316, 319; **VI:**307; **VII:**298; **VIII:**334
religious liberty **III:**362
Rhinelander case **VII:**301
Roman Catholicism **VI:**315, 316
Roosevelt, Franklin D. **VIII:**347
science and technology **VII:**314, 315
Scots-Irish **III:**385–386
Shirtwaist Makers Strike **VII:**324
socialism **VII:**327
social work **VII:**329
steel industry **VII:**337
Strauss, Levi **IV:**358
Sunbelt **X:**337–338
Texas **IV:**371
Texas Revolution **IV:**373
Trading with the Enemy Act **VII:**355
Triangle Shirtwaist Fire **VII:**356
UMWA **VII:**359
Valesh, Eva McDonald **VII:**367
vaudeville **VII:**368, 369
Victorianism **VI:**374
Villard, Henry **VI:**374–375
violence and lawlessness **VI:**375
welfare capitalism **VII:**381
Immigration, U.S. Bureau of immigration **VI:**184
Mexican immigration **VII:**203
Immigration Act (1917) (Alien Exclusion Act) **VII:145,** 407*c*
Cable Act **VII:**47
citizenship **VII:**56
Dillingham Commission **VII:**78
immigration **VII:**144
Mexican immigration **VII:**203
National Origins Act **VII:**227
nativism **VII:**234
population trends **VII:**266
progressivism **VII:**271
Quota Act **VII:**279
Trading with the Enemy Act **VII:**355
Immigration Act (1903). *See* Anarchist Immigration Act
Immigration Act (1924). *See* National Origins Act

Immigration Act (1965) **IX:156,** 357*c*
Asian Americans **X:**32
cities and urban life **IX:**56
Great Society **IX:**139
immigration **IX:**155; **X:**175
nativism **VII:**234
population trends **IX:**260
Immigration Act (1990) **X:**175, 379*c*
Immigration and Naturalization, U.S. Commission of **VII:**189
Immigration and Naturalization Act (1990) **X:**346
Immigration and Naturalization Service (INS)
DHS **X:**167
IRCA **X:**177
terrorism **X:**347
USA PATRIOT Act **X:**359
Immigration and Naturalization Service v. Chadha **X:**378*c*
Immigration Reform and Control Act (IRCA) **X:**175, **177,** 379*c*
Immigration Restriction League
citizenship **VII:**56
immigration **VII:**144
immigration restrictions **VI:**186
nativism **VI:**264
immigration restrictions **VI:186–187**
nativism **VI:**264
Omaha platform **VI:**272
Thomas, M. Carey **VI:**356
Immortal Mr. Teas, The (film) **IX:**226
impeachment (general) **III:222**
Abscam **X:**5, 6
Blount, William **III:**53
Chase, Samuel **III:**85, 86
Judiciary Act (1801) **III:**242
Rodney, Caesar Augustus **III:**373
Supreme Court **III:**403
impeachment of William J. Clinton **X:178,** 382*c*
Articles of Impeachment **X:409–411**
Clinton, William J. **X:**83
House of Representatives **X:**170
Senate, U.S. **X:**321
Starr, Kenneth **X:**333
impeachment of Andrew Johnson **V:201–203,** 202, 446*c*
Chase, Salmon P. **V:**63
Johnson, Andrew **V:**213
Reconstruction Acts **V:**328
Seward, William H. **V:**348
Sumner, Charles **V:**378
Wade, Benjamin Franklin **V:**421
impeachment of Richard M. Nixon **X:178,** 377*c*
Albert, Carl B. **X:**22

Clinton, Hillary Rodham **X:**77
Federal Information Act **X:**130
House of Representatives **X:**169
Nixon, Richard M. **X:**257
U.S. v. Nixon **X:**358
Watergate scandal **X:**366, 367
Imperato, Ferrante **I:**43
imperialism **VI:187–188**
Altgeld, John Peter **VI:**12
Atkinson, Edward **VI:**22
Bryan, William Jennings **VI:**52
Congress **VI:**79–80
foreign policy **VI:**133
Hay, John Milton **VI:**164
Hoar, George F. **VI:**173
jingoes **VI:**204
Lease, Mary Elizabeth Clyens **VI:**220
Liberal Republican Party **VI:**222
Mahan, Alfred Thayer **VI:**236
Social Darwinism **VI:**334
Social Gospel **VI:**335
Strong, Josiah **VI:**347
Tillman, Benjamin Ryan **VI:**358
Watterson, Henry **VI:**386
Imperial Japanese Navy **VIII:**214
Implementation Force (IFOR) **X:**99, 102
imports **III:**465*c*
Continental Congress, First **III:**114
economy **III:**146
embargo of 1807 **III:**152
energy **X:**120
industrialization **IV:**199–200
Madison, James **III:**282
merchant marine **VI:**245
Sugar Act **III:**401
trade, domestic and foreign **III:**414; **VI:**359, 360
impoundment of Congressional appropriations **X:**89
impressionism **VI:**63–64, 202
impressment **III:222–223;** **V:203–204**
Attucks, Crispus **III:**37
Chesapeake-Leopard affair **III:**88
citizenship **III:**94
civil liberties, Confederate **V:**68, 69
Confederate army **V:**81
Confederate States of America **V:**86
Congress, Confederate **V:**88
Davis, Jefferson **V:**104
elections **V:**126
foreign affairs **III:**168, 169

Free Trade and Sailor's Rights **IV:**165
French Revolution **III:**179
Jefferson, Thomas **III:**234
King, Rufus **III:**245
Letcher, John **V:**232
Liberty riot **III:**266
Little Belt incident **III:**269–270
Madison, James **III:**284
Monroe-Pinkney Treaty **III:**300
POWs **III:**346
slavery **V:**364
states' rights **V:**370
War of 1812 **IV:**390
Wigfall, Louis T. **V:**431
women's status and rights **V:**437
Improving America's Security Act **X:**171
improvised explosive devices (IEDs) **X:**188
Imuran **X:**224
Inaugural Addresses
Clinton, William Jefferson (Second Inaugural) **X:407–409**
Davis, Jefferson **V:454–456**
Lincoln, Abraham (First Inaugural) **V:**236, **450–454**
Lincoln, Abraham (Second Inaugural) **V:**72, 237, **346, 462–463**
Roosevelt, Franklin (First Inaugural) **VIII:451–453**
Inca **I:179–181,** 180, 397*c*; **II:**304
Acosta, José de **I:**3
Alvarado, Pedro de **I:**7
Andes Mountains **I:**9
Atahualpa **I:**15–16
Cieza de León, Pedro **I:**76
Cuzco **I:**101–102
El Dorado **I:**119
khipu **I:**200
Lima **I:**213
Machu Picchu **I:**221–222
Peru **I:**289
Pizarro, Francisco **I:**293
smallpox **I:**341
Soto, Hernando de **I:**342
incandescent light bulbs. *See* light bulbs, incandescent
Inchon, Korea **IX:**177, 198
Incidents of the Insurrection in Western Pennsylvania (Brackenridge) **III:**60
Incidents of Travel in Central America, Chiapas, and Yucatan (Stephens) **I:**90
In Cold Blood (Capote) **IX:**194, 357*c*
income
African Americans **X:**14
agriculture **IX:**7, 8
Asian Americans **X:**33

economy **IX:**97
labor/labor movements
X:203
Native Americans **VIII:**263–
264; **X:**251
New Deal **VIII:**268, 270
poverty **X:**285–286
recreation **X:**302
South **VIII:**366
wage and price controls
VIII:409
women's status and rights
X:370
World War II home front
VIII:432, 433
income tax, federal **VI:**411*c*;
VII:106–107; VIII:447*c*
Bryan, William Jennings
VI:51
Congress **V:**89
Democratic Party **VII:**74
economy **V:**121–122; **X:**109,
110
Hull, Cordell **VIII:**180
Internal Revenue taxes
VI:194
Laffer curve **X:**204
Libertarian Party **X:**209
Omaha platform **VI:**272
political parties, third
VI:286
presidency **VII:**269
Reagan, Ronald W. **X:**300
Republican Party **VII:**300
Revenue Act of 1942
VIII:340–341
Supreme Court **VI:**348
taxation **V:**384
Underwood-Simmons Tariff
VII:359
War Revenue Act **VII:**378,
379
World War II home front
VIII:433
Inconvenient Truth, An
(documentary film) **X:**92, 156
incunabula **I:**303
IND (Investigative New Drug)
X:222
In Dahomey (Cook) **VII:**219
In Demand (pay-per-view
distributor) **X:**283
indentured servitude **II:173–176,**
436*c*
abolitionism **III:**2
African Americans **II:**5–6
agriculture **II:**12
Burgesses, House of **II:**51
class **II:**70
Delaware **II:**96
Dunmore, John Murray, earl
of **III:**142
economy **II:**109
English immigrants **II:**117
environment **II:**120, 121
ethnocentrism **II:**122
Georgia **II:**146

German immigrants **II:**148
immigration **III:**221
Jamestown **II:**181
labor/labor movements
II:197, 198; **III:**251–252
marriage and family **III:**288
miscegenation **II:**237
Mittelberger, Gottlieb
II:239
Moraley, William **II:**242
mortality **II:**244
Philadelphia **II:**292
population trends **III:**343
redemptioners **II:**326–327
St. Mary's City **II:**342
Sampson, Deborah **III:**379
Scots immigrants **II:**346
Scots-Irish **II:**347
slavery **II:**354–355; **III:**390
suffrage **V:**380
tobacco **II:**390, 392
Virginia **II:**400
Virginia Company of
London **II:**402
women's status and rights
II:423
Independence, Kansas **VIII:**209
Independence, Missouri
Donner party **IV:**125
exploration **IV:**145
foreign policy **IV:**157
Forty-niners **IV:**160
Gregg, Josiah **IV:**179
Lee, Jason **IV:**224
Magoffin, James W. **IV:**233
Oregon Trail **IV:**285, 286
Santa Fe Trail **IV:**330, 331
Independence Hall (Philadelphia)
III:223–224, *224*
architecture **II:**25
commemoration **IX:**66
Constitutional Convention
III:109
Hamilton, Andrew **II:**161
Independence National Historical
Park **IX:**66
Independent Advertiser, The
II:192
independent candidates **X:**277,
278
independent counsel **X:179**
Clinton, William J. **X:**82
foreign policy **X:**142
Iran-contra affair **X:**184
Reno, Janet **X:**309
Scalia, Antonin **X:**316
Starr, Kenneth **X:**332–333
Walsh, Lawrence E. **X:**364
Independent Counsel Act (1978)
X:179
Independent Party **X:**117
Independent Treasury Act **IV:**47,
132, 414*c*
Independent Treasury System
IV:414*c*
banking **IV:**47
economy **IV:**132

panic of 1837 **IV:**295
Polk, James K. **IV:**302
Independent Voters' Association
VII:241
Index of American Composers
VIII:134, 250
Index of American Design
VIII:129
Index of Forbidden Books **I:**98
India **I:181,** 396*c*; **II:**48
Albuquerque, Alfonso de
I:6
Anglo-American relations
VIII:21
Army Air Forces, U.S.
VIII:27
Bourke-White, Margaret
VIII:50
Cabral, Pedro Álvares **I:**46
civil disobedience **IX:**57
disease/epidemics **IV:**121
foreign policy **IV:**156
Gama, Vasco da **I:**137
Ibn Battuta **I:**175
investments, foreign
VII:152
labor/labor movements
X:203
Lend-Lease **VIII:**212
Linschoten, Jan Huygen van
I:214
nuclear proliferation **X:**261
Prester John **I:**301
printing press **I:**303
Versailles, Treaty of **VII:**370
Indiana **III:**464*c*
abolitionism **V:**1
abortion **X:**2
agriculture **IV:**10; **V:**6
corruption, political **VI:**83
disease/epidemics **IV:**123
economy **IV:**130
education, federal aid to
VI:110
Foster, Abigail Kelley
IV:161
governors **V:**171
Greenville, Treaty of
III:200
Harrison, Benjamin **VI:**160–
161
Harrison, William Henry
IV:184
internal improvements
IV:202
Maine Law **IV:**234
marriage and family **IV:**240
migration **IV:**254
Morgan, John Hunt **V:**269
Morton, Oliver P. **V:**270
Native Americans in the War
of 1812 **IV:**276, 277
oil industry **VII:**245
panic of 1819 **IV:**293
personal liberty laws **IV:**298
politics (1900–1928)
VII:261

Prophet, the Shawnee
III:349
public health **VII:**275
railroads **IV:**314, 316
religion **IV:**318
rust belt **X:**314
Taylor, Zachary **IV:**367
Thames, Battle of the
IV:375
Tippecanoe, Battle of
III:411–412
Underground Railroad
V:397
Warren, Josiah **IV:**392
women's status and rights
IV:403
Indian Affairs, Bureau of (BIA)
IV:196–197, 412*c*; **IX:**353*c*;
X:376*c*
AIM **IX:**13
Burke Act **VII:**44
Indian Reorganization Act
VIII:186
Interior, Department of
IV:201
Native Americans **VII:**231,
233; **VIII:**263; **IX:**241;
X:250
Parker, Ely Samuel **V:**295
race and race relations
VIII:318
segregation **VII:**319
Teapot Dome **VII:**351
Indian Affairs, Office of **VI:188–**
190, *189*
Indian Rights Association
VI:190
Native Americans **VI:**263
Nez Perce War **VI:**267–268
Winnemucca, Sarah **VI:**397
Indiana Hospital **V:**423
Indian Americans **X:**33
Indiana National Guard **VIII:**164
Indianapolis, Indiana
currency issue **VI:**89
Johnson, Tom Loftin
VII:156
Kennedy, Robert F. **IX:**172
Ku Klux Klan **VII:**166
Indian Appropriation Act **VI:**407*c*
Indiana University **VII:**330;
IX:175–176
Indian boarding schools **VIII:**264
Indian Citizenship Act **VII:**233,
408*c*
Indian Civil Rights Act (1968)
IX:357*c*; **X:**250
Indian Claims Commission (ICC)
IX:156–157, 241, 319, 351*c*
Indian College **II:**163
Indian Education Act (1972)
X:250
Indian factory system
American Fur Company
IV:18
Astor, John Jacob **IV:**34
fur trade **IV:**171

Indian Gaming Regulatory Act (1988) **X**:251
"Indianist" movement **VI**:255
Indian King Tavern **II**:383
Indian Ocean **IV**:144
Indian Ocean tsunami (December 2004) **X**:384*c*
Indianola, Iowa **VI**:63
Indian Problem, The **VII**:233
Indian Removal Act **IV**:**197–199**, 412*c*, **427–428**
 Cherokee **IV**:85
 Creek **IV**:109
 Indian Affairs, Bureau of **IV**:197
 internal improvements **IV**:202
 Jackson, Andrew **IV**:207
 migration **IV**:253, 254
 Native Americans **IV**:273–275
 Osceola **IV**:289
 Permanent Indian Frontier **IV**:297
 race and race relations **IV**:312
 Seminole War, First/Second **IV**:339
 Trail of Tears **IV**:377
Indian Reorganization Act **VIII**:*185*, **185–186**, 444*c*
 ACLU **VIII**:17
 Native Americans **VIII**:264
 race and race relations **VIII**:319
Indian Rights Association **VI**:**190**, 262–263; **VII**:233, 351
Indians. *See* Native Americans; *specific tribes/nations*
Indian schools **VI**:263
Indian Self-Determination and Education Assistance Act (1975) **X**:250
Indian Sketches (MacDowell) **VI**:233
Indians of All Tribes **X**:375*c*
Indians of the desert Southwest **II**:**176**; **IV**:414*c*
Indian Springs, Treaty of **IV**:247
Indian Suite (MacDowell) **VI**:255
Indian Territory (Oklahoma) **IV**:413*c*; **V**:446*c*; **VI**:408*c*; **VII**:404*c*
 Boudinot, Elias **IV**:62
 Cherokee **IV**:85
 Chickasaw **IV**:86
 Choctaw **IV**:87
 cotton culture **IV**:108
 Creek **IV**:109
 Custer, George A. **V**:99
 Fort Laramie **IV**:157–158
 Houston, Sam **IV**:191
 Indian Affairs, Bureau of **IV**:197
 Jackson, Andrew **IV**:207
 Jackson, Helen Hunt **VI**:199

Lone Wolf v. Hitchcock **VII**:185
 Mason, Richard B. **IV**:241
 McIntosh, William **IV**:247
 migration **IV**:254
 Native Americans **IV**:274, 275; **V**:278; **VII**:232
 Nez Perce War **VI**:268
 Ridge, John **IV**:324
 Ross, John **IV**:325
 Sac and Fox **IV**:327
 Seminole **IV**:338
 Seminole War, First/Second **IV**:339
 Sequoyah **IV**:343
 slavery **IV**:346–347
 Sooners **VI**:339
 Trail of Tears **IV**:377–378
Indian Tract Manor **II**:406
Indian Trade, Office of **IV**:196
Indian wars **VI**:407*c*
 Native Americans **VI**:262–262
 Sioux wars **VI**:331
 Sitting Bull **VI**:332
Indies. *See* West Indies
Indies, Council of the **I**:71
indigo **I**:269; **II**:**176–177**, 437*c*
 agriculture **II**:11
 Continental Congress, First **III**:114
 economy **II**:109–110
 labor/labor movements **II**:199
 mercantilism **II**:231
 New Orleans **II**:267
 Pinckney, Elizabeth Lucas **II**:295; **III**:336
 plantations **II**:308
 plantation system **II**:297
 slavery **V**:363
 South Carolina **II**:370
individualism **X**:93
individual retirement accounts (IRAs) **X**:56, 135
Indochina
 antiwar movement, Vietnam **X**:29
 Dulles, John Foster **IX**:91
 WILPF **VII**:386
Indochina Peace Campaign (IPC) **IX**:144
Indo-China Refugee Act (1975) **X**:33
Indochina War, First **IX**:21
Indonesia **X**:267
In Dubious Battle (Steinbeck) **VIII**:374
indulgences **I**:217, 218
industrialization **IV**:**199–201**, *200*; **V**:**204–205**. *See also* factories
 agriculture **IV**:11
 architecture **VII**:19
 Brook Farm **IV**:65
 cities and urban life **IV**:91
 cotton culture **IV**:108–109

 economy **IV**:131–133; **V**:123; **VII**:83, 84
 environment **VII**:98
 Hepburn Act **VII**:138
 ILGWU **VII**:148–149
 immigration **IV**:193; **VII**:143, 144
 investments, foreign **VII**:152
 IWW **VII**:146–148
 journalism **IV**:210
 labor/labor movements **VII**:169
 literature **IV**:229
 McCormick, Cyrus Hall **IV**:243
 migration **IV**:255
 New York City **V**:283
 Nullification Controversy **IV**:282
 Owen, Robert **IV**:291–292
 Rauschenbusch, Walter **VII**:293
 religion **IV**:317
 science, invention, and technology **V**:340; **VII**:149, 150
 strikes **V**:374
 temperance movement **IV**:369
 women's status and rights **IV**:403
 workers' compensation **VII**:391
Industrial Poisons in the United States (Hamilton) **VII**:133
industrial production **VIII**:324
Industrial Relations Commission (USCIR) **VII**:**145–146**, 406*c*
 Adamson Act **VII**:2
 labor/labor movements **VII**:170, 172
 New Unionism **VII**:238
industrial research laboratories **VII**:150–151
Industrial Revolution **III**:**224–226**
 art and architecture **IV**:28, 30
 cities and urban life **V**:66, 67
 cotton **III**:123
 Fitzhugh, George **V**:147
 George III **III**:192
 industrialization **IV**:199
 Maine Law **IV**:233
 migration **IV**:255
 Owen, Robert **IV**:291
 penitentiary movement **IV**:296
 science and technology **III**:385
 Slater, Samuel **III**:389–390
 trade, domestic and foreign **III**:415
 Whitney, Eli **III**:442
Industrial Revolution, Second **VI**:**190–192**
 business cycles **VI**:57–58

 Congress **VI**:80
 education **VI**:108
 foreign policy **VII**:113
 global warming **X**:155
 immigration **VI**:185
 IWW **VII**:146
 New South **VI**:265
 newspapers **VI**:266
 Philadelphia Centennial Exposition **VI**:284
 religion **VI**:306
 Republican Party **VI**:311
 steel **VI**:345
 trusts **VI**:361–365
 utopianism **VI**:371
Industrial Toxicology (Hamilton) **VII**:133
Industrial Workers of the World (IWW) **VII**:**146–148**, *147*, 404*c*, 405*c*
 Baldwin, Roger Nash **VII**:31
 Bridges, Harry **VIII**:52–53
 Clayton Antitrust Act **VII**:59
 conscription **VII**:63
 Debs, Eugene Victor **VII**:73
 Espionage Act **VII**:101
 Flynn, Elizabeth Gurley **VII**:109, 110
 Foster, William Zebulon **VII**:116
 free speech fights **VII**:117–118
 Greenwich Village **VII**:130
 Haywood, William Dudley **VII**:137
 labor/labor movements **VII**:170–172
 Lawrence Strike **VII**:173, 174
 Ludlow Massacre **VII**:187
 Mitchell, John **VII**:211
 muckrakers **VII**:216
 NAM **VII**:225, 226
 National Civic Federation **VII**:226
 New Unionism **VII**:238
 Palmer, Alexander Mitchell **VII**:249
 Paterson Strike **VII**:253, 254
 Preamble to the Constitution of **VII**:**417**
 radical and labor press **VII**:284, 285
 radicalism **VII**:287, 288
 Red Scare **VII**:296
 Russian Revolution **VII**:308
 Sacco and Vanzetti **VII**:311
 Sanger, Margaret **VII**:312
 Seattle General Strike **VII**:317, 318
 Sedition Act **VII**:318–319
 socialism **VII**:327
 Trading with the Enemy Act **VII**:355–366

WFM **VII:**382
World War I **VII:**394
industry. *See* manufacturing and industry
infanticide **II:**218
infant mortality
    African Americans **X:**13
    children **VIII:**67
    medicine **X:**221
    Native Americans **VIII:**264
infantry
    Confederate army **V:**80
    Lee, Robert E. **V:**230
    tactics and strategy **V:**379–380
    uniforms **V:**399
    Union army **V:**401, 403
    U.S. Military Academy at West Point **V:**409
    Wilderness, Battle of the **V:**432
Infantry School (Fort Benning, Georgia) **VIII:**50
infections **VIII:**234
infectious diseases
    population trends **IX:**260
    public health **IX:**266
    technology **IX:**313
inflation **VI:**410*c;* **X:**376*c,* 378*c*
    Atkinson, Edward **VI:**22
    banking **V:**28
    COLA **IX:**76, 77
    Confederate States of America **V:**86
    debt, national **III:**130
    economy **V:**123; **IX:**97, 98; **X:**107–110
    elections **IX:**104
    employment **V:**132
    energy **X:**119
    farmers' alliances **VI:**125
    food riots **V:**148
    Ford, Gerald R. **X:**139
    Hayes, Rutherford B. **VI:**168
    homefront **V:**192
    OPEC **X:**268
    Reagan, Ronald W. **X:**300
    Reaganomics **X:**302
    recession of 1937–1938 **VIII:**324
    Richmond, Virginia **V:**335
    wage and price controls **VIII:**409, 410; **X:**363
    World War II home front **VIII:**432
Inflationary bill (1870) **VI:**290
Influence of Sea Power upon History, The (Mahan) **VI:**236; **VII:**113
influenza **IV:**123; **VII:**275–276, 407*c*
Information Processing Techniques Office (IPTO) **X:**181
informed consent **X:**172
Infortunate, The (Moraley) **II:**242, **443–444**

infrastructure. *See* internal improvements
INF Treaty. *See* Intermediate-Range and Shorter-Range Nuclear Forces Treaty
Ingersoll, Ebon Clark **VI:**193
Ingersoll, Jared **III:226–227**
Ingersoll, Robert Green **VI:192–194; VII:**311–312
Ingle, Richard **II:**220, 335
Ingle's Rebellion **II:**342–343
Ingram, David **I:181–182**
    Hakluyt, Richard, the Younger **I:**153
    Hawkins, Sir John **I:**157
    Purchas, Samuel **I:**307
inheritance
    gender **II:**144, 145
    marriage and family **III:**286, 288
    primogeniture and entail **II:**310
    Spanish colonies **II:**373
    women's status and rights **II:**423–424; **III:**445
injunctions, antistrike **VIII:**277, 444*c*
Inland Steel **IX:**300
in-migrants **VIII:**70
Inner Light **IV:**189
Inness, George **VI:**275
Innis, Roy **IX:**74
Innocents Abroad, The (Twain) **VI:**367
inns. *See* taverns and inns
Innu. *See* Montagnais-Naskapi
inoculation **II:**437*c;* **III:**464*c*
    Boylston, Zabdiel **II:**43
    disease/epidemics **II:**99; **III:**138
    Massachusetts **II:**225
    medicine **II:**230; **III:**295
    mortality **II:**244
    riots **III:**371
    smallpox **II:**361
    Valley Forge **III:**423
"Inquiry into the Effects of Spirituous Liquors" (Rush) **III:**410
Inquiry into the Principle and Policy of the United States Government, An (Taylor) **III:**408
Inquiry into the Rights of the British Colonies, An (Bland) **III:**53
inquisition **I:182–183**
    auto-da-fé **I:**17
    Dominicans **I:**110; **II:**101
    Ferdinand and Isabella **I:**128
    Jews **I:**194–196
    Zumárraga, Juan de **I:**392
INS. *See* Immigration and Naturalization Service
insanity
    medicine **III:**296

Rush, Benjamin **III:**376
    Valley Forge **III:**422
insider trading **X:**315
Inspection Act (Virginia) **II:**11
Instant Communication Relays (IRC) **X:**88
Instapundit **X:**183
Institute for Advanced Study (Princeton University) **VII:**313–314; **IX:**167, 168
Institute for International Economics **X:**350
Institute for Legislative Action (ILA) **X:**249
Institute for Sex Research **IX:**176
Institute for Social and Religious Research **VII:**205–206
Institute of Pacific Relations **VII:**115
Institutes of the Christian Religion (Calvin) **I:**53, 54
Institutionalists (economics) **IX:**129
Instructions of 1786 (Spain) **III:**317–318
Insular Cases **VII:**110
insulin **X:**224
insurance **III:**227. *See also specific types, e.g.:* health insurance
    cotton **III:**123
    journalism **VII:**159
    privateering **III:**348
    Progressive Party **VII:**270
    public health **VII:**275
    Quasi War **III:**352–353
    trade, domestic and foreign **III:**414
    veterans **VII:**371
Insurance Portability and Accountability Act (1997) **X:**197
insurgents
    contras **X:**94–95
    Iraq War **X:**185, 187, 188
    Middle East **X:**230
integrated circuits **IX:**354*c*
    computers **IX:**71; **X:**86, 87
    science and technology **IX:**285
    technology **IX:**313
integration. *See* desegregation/integration
intelligence **VIII:186–187,** 447*c*
    Berle, Adolf A., Jr. **VIII:**43
    Britain, Battle of **VIII:**53
    code breaking **VIII:**76
    Coral Sea, Battle of the **VIII:**87
    espionage **VIII:**116–118
    FBI **VIII:**130
    FCC **VIII:**131
    OSS **VIII:**284–285
    Pearl Harbor **VIII:**292
    photography **VIII:**296
    technology **VIII:**390
    WAVES **VIII:**418

intelligence gathering **X:**103, 359
intelligence tests **VII:**88, **148**
intelligent design (ID) **X:**306–307
Inter-Allied Declaration **VIII:**402
Inter-American Conference, First **VI:**276
Inter-American Development Bank **IX:**184
Inter-American Treaties **VIII:**443*c*
Inter-American Treaty of Reciprocal Assistance (1947, Brazil) **X:**204
Interboro Rapid Transit (IRT) **VI:**361
Inter Caetera (papal bull) **I:**367–368, 396*c*
Intercollegiate Association of Amateur Athletes of America (IC4A) **VI:**359
Intercollegiate Football Association **VI:**130
Intercollegiate Society of Individualists **X:**93
intercontinental ballistic missiles (ICBMs)
    arms race **IX:**17; **X:**29
    defense policy **X:**99–100
    science and technology **IX:**285
Interdenominational Congress **VI:**347
Interdepartmental Task Force **VIII:**43
interest **II:**33
interest groups. *See* lobbying
Interesting Narrative of the Life of Olaudah Equiano, The (Equiano) **III:**156, 463*c*
interest rates **X:**109–111, 383*c*
Intergovernmental Panel on Climate Change (IPCC) **X:**155
Interim Agreement on Strategic Offensive Arms **X:**103–104, 336
Interior, U.S. Department of the **IV:201–202**
    Black Cabinet **VIII:**45
    CCC **VIII:**71
    conservation/environmentalism **VI:**81
    education **VIII:**107
    Forest Reserve Act **VI:**134
    Geological Survey, U.S. **VI:**140–142
    Ickes, Harold L. **VIII:**183
    Indian Affairs, Bureau of **IV:**197
    Indian Affairs, Office of **VI:**188–189
    Jackson, Helen Hunt **VI:**199
    mining **VII:**209
    National Trails Act of 1968 **IX:**239
    Native Americans **VII:**232

Interior, U.S. Department of the
  (*continued*)
    occupational health and
      safety **VII**:243
    Powell, John Wesley **VI**:288
    Resettlement Administration
      VIII:338
    Teapot Dome **VII**:351
    Watt, James G. **X**:367
interior design **VI**:3, 276
intermarriage **VII**:408*c. See also*
  miscegenation
    casta paintings **I**:64
    ethnocentrism **II**:122
    eugenics **VII**:103
    fur trade **II**:140–142
    Jamestown **II**:181
    marriage and family **II**:218
    mestizaje **I**:241–242
    mestizo **I**:242
    Pocahontas **II**:300
    race and race relations
      VII:282
    Racial Integrity Act **VII**:284
    Rhinelander case **VII**:301
    slavery **II**:357
    zambo **I**:391
Intermediate-Range and Shorter-
  Range Nuclear Forces (INF)
  Treaty **X**:**179–181**, *180*, 379*c*
    cold war, end of **X**:86
    defense policy **X**:101
    Reagan, Ronald W. **X**:301
internal combustion engine
  VII:111
internal improvements **IV**:**202–
  203**
    American System **IV**:19–20
    Bank of the United States,
      Second **IV**:48
    Bonus Bill **IV**:62
    Democratic Party **IV**:118
    Erie Canal **IV**:141–143
    Morse, Samuel F. B. **IV**:264
    National Road **IV**:271
    Polk, James K. **IV**:302
    Whigs **IV**:396, 397
Internal Revenue, Bureau of
  V:384
Internal Revenue Act (1862)
  V:384
Internal Revenue Service (IRS)
  VI:396; **X**:178
Internal Revenue taxes **VI**:**194**
Internal Security Act (1950)
  IX:14–15, 67–68, **157–158,**
  352*c*
International Adult Literacy
  Survey (1997) **X**:210
International Association of
  Machinists (IAM) **VII**:11
International Atomic Energy
  Agency (IAEA) **X**:261, 262
International Bank for
  Reconstruction and
  Development **VIII**:52, 448*c*
International Brigades **VIII**:369

International Brotherhood of
  Electrical Workers (IBEW)
  VII:11
International Brotherhood of
  Teamsters (IBT) **IX**:310, 311
International Business Machines.
  See IBM
International Church of the Four-
  Square Gospel **VII**:196
International Compact for Iraq
  X:357
International Copyright Law
  (1891) **VI**:225, 411*c*
International Court of Justice
  (United Nations) **VIII**:402
International Criminal Tribunal
  X:382*c*
International Exhibition of
  Modern Art. *See* Armory Show
International Harvester
    cities and urban life **VII**:54
    Morgan, John Pierpont
      VI:251
    welfare capitalism **VII**:381
International Human Genome
  Sequencing Consortium **X**:172
internationalism
    Democratic Party **IX**:85
    Johnson, Hiram Warren
      VII:154
    LWV **IX**:186, 187
    modern Republicanism
      IX:221
International Labor Defense
  (ILD) **VIII**:255, 353
International Labor Defense
  Fund (ILDF) **VII**:61
International Labor Organization
  VII:408*c*
International Ladies' Garment
  Workers' Union (ILGWU)
  VII:**148–149; VIII**:**187–188**
    AFL **VII**:11
    Asian Americans **VIII**:32
    CIO **VIII**:82
    Dubinsky, David **VIII**:97
    ERA **VII**:100
    Hillman, Sidney **VIII**:165
    Jews **VIII**:195
    labor/labor movements
      VII:170; **VIII**:206
    Lewis, John L. **VIII**:213
    NWTUL **VII**:231
    Sacco and Vanzetti **VII**:311
    Shirtwaist Makers Strike
      VII:324
international law **VII**:49
International League for the
  Rights of Man **VII**:32
International Longshoremen's
  Association (ILA) **VIII**:53
International Migration Society
  VI:223–224
International Monetary Fund
  (IMF) **VIII**:448*c*
    Bretton Woods Conference
      VIII:52

business **IX**:46
Eccles, Marriner S.
  VIII:101
economy **VIII**:105
foreign policy **VIII**:142
globalization **X**:154
postwar planning **VIII**:307
International Opium Convention
  VII:222
International Peace Conference
  (1849) **V**:46
International Planned Parenthood
  Foundation **VII**:313
International Red Cross **V**:29;
  VIII:310
International Security Assistance
  Force (ISAF) **X**:12, 56
International Socialist Review
  VII:285, 356
International Space Station (ISS)
  X:56, 329
International Trade Union
  Educational League **VII**:117
International Typographical
  Union **IV**:217
International Union of Mine,
  Mill and Smelter Workers
  VII:382
International Women's Year (IWY)
  Conference **X**:134
International Workers Defense
  League **VII**:213
International Working People's
  Association **VI**:213
Internet **X**:**181–183**, 377*c*, 382*c*,
  384*c*
    business **X**:57, 59
    campaign finance **X**:64
    censorship **X**:71
    Christian Coalition **X**:73
    Clinton, Hillary Rodham
      X:78
    computers **X**:88
    DHS **X**:167
    economy **X**:110
    globalization **X**:153
    Gore, Albert, Jr. **X**:157
    literature **X**:212
    media **X**:217, 220
    music **X**:239–240
    popular culture **X**:278
    pornography **X**:283, 284
    recreation **X**:303, 304
    science and technology
      X:319
    sexual revolution **X**:323
    USA PATRIOT Act **X**:359
Internet Explorer **X**:381*c*
Internet service providers (ISPs)
  X:88
internment camps. *See* Japanese
  Americans, relocation of
internships **VIII**:262–263
Interoceanic Canal Commission
  V:151
interracial marriage. *See*
  intermarriage; miscegenation

interracial sexual relations
    mestizaje **I**:241–242
    mestizo **I**:242
    zambo **I**:391
interstate commerce **IV**:412*c*;
  VIII:351, 382, 446*c*; **X**:339,
  375*c*
Interstate Commerce Act (1887)
  VI:**420–423**
    Atkinson, Edward **VI**:22
    business and government
      VI:57
    Congress **VI**:80
    Elkins Act **VII**:94
    Hepburn Act **VII**:139
    Industrial Revolution,
      Second **VI**:192
    Mann-Elkins Act **VII**:190
    Patrons of Husbandry
      VI:279
    presidency **VI**:290
    railroads **VI**:303
Interstate Commerce Commission
  (ICC) **VI**:410*c*, 412*c*; **VII**:404*c*,
  405*c*
    business and government
      VI:57
    Elkins Act **VII**:94
    FCC **VIII**:131
    freedom rides **IX**:124
    Hepburn Act **VII**:138
    Mann-Elkins Act **VII**:190
    railroads **VI**:303
    Supreme Court **VI**:348
    transportation **VIII**:396
Interstate Highway Act of 1956
  IX:**158–159**, 354*c*
    agriculture **IX**:7
    automobile industry **IX**:26
    civil defense **IX**:57
    economy **IX**:97
    Eisenhower, Dwight D.
      IX:101
    GM **IX**:133
    government, state/local
      IX:137
    shopping centers **IX**:290
    suburbanization/suburbs
      IX:306
    tourism **IX**:318
    urban redevelopment
      IX:326–327
interstate highway system
    agriculture **X**:19
    commemoration **IX**:66
    modern Republicanism
      IX:221
interventionism
    destroyers-for-bases deal
      VIII:94
    Landon, Alfred M. **VIII**:209
    Roosevelt, Franklin D.
      VIII:346
"In the Good Old Summertime"
  VII:218, 353
"In the Shade of an Old Apple
  Tree" **VII**:353

Intolerable Acts **III:**173

Intolerance (film) **VII:**38, 132

Into the Valley (Hersey) **VIII:**164

intrastate commerce **VIII:**351, 382

Intrepid, USS **IV:**114

Intrepid plan **X:**199

Inuit **I:**144; **II:177**

  Aleut **II:**17

  ANSCA **X:**21

  Frobisher, Martin **I:**134, 135

  fur trade **II:**142

  Greenland **I:**144

  L'Anse aux Meadows **I:**204

  Settle, Dionyse **I:**331

Invasion from Mars, The (ORR survey) **VIII:**313

inventions **VIII:**283, 284

Investigation and Military Intelligence, Bureau of **VII:**268–269

Investigative New Drug (IND) **X:**222

Investiture Controversy **I:**166

investment **VIII:**356–357

investment banking. *See* banking, investment

investment firms **X:**57–58, 61

investments, foreign (American investment abroad) **VI:197; VII:151–152**

  Big Stick diplomacy **VII:**34–35

  economy **VII:**83

  Fordney-McCumber Tariff **VII:**112

  foreign policy **VII:**114, 116

  Mexican immigration **VII:**202

  tariffs **VII:**350

  trade, domestic and foreign **VII:**354, 355

investments, foreign, in the United States **VI:**197

"Invisible Empire" **IX:**179

Invisible Empire (Tourgée) **V:**389–390

Invisible Man (Ellison) **IX:**353*c*

  African Americans **IX:**5

  literature **IX:**194

  popular culture **IX:**258

involuntary servitude **VI:**284, 285

Iohn Huighen Van Linschoten his Discours of Voyages into ye Easte and West Indies (Linschoten) **I:**214

Iola Leroy; or, Shadows Lifted (Harper) **V:**184; **VI:**160

Iouskeha **I:**1

Iowa

  agriculture **IV:**10

  Allison, William Boyd **VI:**11

  Atkinson, Henry **IV:**36

  Catt, Carrie Lane Chapman **VII:**50

  currency issue **VI:**89

FHA **VIII:**126

Frémont, John C. **IV:**166

Keokuk **IV:**213

lead mines **IV:**223

Lewis, John L. **VIII:**212

Maine Law **IV:**234

marriage and family **IV:**216

migration **IV:**254

Mormon Trail **IV:**261, 262

Native Americans **IV:**274

Patrons of Husbandry **VI:**279

Sac and Fox **IV:**327

urban reform **VII:**362

Iowa Farmer's Union **VIII:**126

Iowa Indians **IV:**84

Iowa State University of Science and Technology **VI:**63

Iowa Woman Suffrage Association **VII:**50

IPC (Indochina Peace Campaign) **IX:**144

IPCC (Intergovernmental Panel on Climate Change) **X:**155

iPhone **X:**319

iPod **X:**240

IPTO (Information Processing Techniques Office) **X:**181

Ique **I:**29

IRA (Irish Republican Army) **X:**232

Iran **X:**377*c*, 383*c*

  Carter, James Earl, Jr. **X:**69

  CIA **IX:**52

  cold war **IX:**64

  Dulles, John Foster **IX:**91

  foreign policy **X:**143

  Leahy, William D. **VIII:**211

  Middle East **IX:**214; **X:**230

  military-industrial complex **IX:**216

  nuclear proliferation **X:**262

  OPEC **X:**267

  Perot, H. Ross **X:**272–273

  Rice, Condoleezza **X:**310

  Teheran Conference **VIII:**390

  terrorism **X:**345

Iran-contra affair **X:183–184,** 379*c*

  Boland Amendment **X:**45

  Bush, George H. W. **X:**52

  cold war, end of **X:**85

  contras **X:**95

  foreign policy **X:**142

  independent counsel **X:**179

  Mitchell, George **X:**231

  North, Oliver L. **X:**258

  Reagan, Ronald W. **X:**301

  terrorism **X:**346

  Tower Commission **X:**353

  Walsh, Lawrence E. **X:**364

Iran-contra hearings **X:**231, 232

Iranian hostage crisis **X:184–185,** 185, 377*c*, 378*c*

  Carter, James Earl, Jr. **X:**69

  economy **X:**109

foreign policy **X:**141

Middle East **X:**228

terrorism **X:**345

Iranian Revolution (1979)

  economy **X:**109

  energy **X:**120

  Middle East **IX:**214; **X:**228

Iraq **X:**379*c*, 383*c*

  Bush, George H. W. **X:**53

  Bush, George W. **X:**56

  Camp David accords **X:**65

  Cheney, Richard B. **X:**72

  Clinton, William J. **X:**81, 83

  defense policy **X:**101, 103

  Fellowship of Reconciliation **VII:**109

  foreign policy **X:**143

  Gore, Albert, Jr. **X:**157

  House of Representatives **X:**170

  Jackson, Jesse, L. **X:**192

  Middle East **X:**229

  NATO **X:**260

  nuclear proliferation **X:**262

  OPEC **X:**267

  Pelosi, Nancy **X:**271

  Persian Gulf War **X:**273–274

  Powell, Colin L. **X:**287

  Senate, U.S. **X:**321

  UN **X:**355, 357

Iraq Survey Group (ISG) **X:**356

Iraq War (2003–) **X:185–188,** 186, 218, 384*c*

  Africa **X:**16

  Bush, George W. **X:**56, 57

  Clinton, Hillary Rodham **X:**78, 79

  elections, presidential **X:**118

  House of Representatives **X:**171

  independent counsel **X:**179

  Middle East **X:**229–230

  neoconservatism **X:**252

  Rice, Condoleezza **X:**309

  Rumsfeld, Donald **X:**313

  Senate, U.S. **X:**322

  terrorism **X:**347

  UN **X:**356

IRAs. *See* individual retirement accounts

IRC (Instant Communication Relays) **X:**88

IRCA. *See* Immigration Reform and Control Act

Iredell, James **III:**403

Ireland **I:**395*c*, 397*c*

  Anglo-Normans **I:**10

  Bristol **I:**37

  Campbell, Thomas **IV:**78

  Carey, Mathew **III:**80

  Catholics **III:**83

  Charleston Expedition of 1776 **III:**83, 84

  class consciousness **VI:**73

  Clinton, William J. **X:**83

Continental Congress, First **III:**114

Elizabeth I **I:**120–121

ethnocentrism **II:**121

Gilbert, Sir Humphrey **I:**140, 141

Grenville, Sir Richard **I:**145

immigration **III:**221; **IV:**193; **VI:**184

Mitchell, George **X:**232

printing press **I:**303

Ralegh, Sir Walter **I:**311

religion **III:**362; **VI:**307

Roman Catholicism **VI:**315

Scots-Irish **III:**385

Washington, Treaty of **VI:**385

wolves **II:**421

Irish, Ned **VIII:**371

Irish-American regiments **V:**200, **205–206,** 206

Irish Americans **IV:**194, 214; **VIII:188–189**

  anti-Catholic riots **IV:**23

  canal era **IV:**79

  cities and urban life **V:**66

  Democratic Party **VIII:**92

  election of 1940 **VIII:**110

  Flynn, Edward J. **VIII:**139

  Forrestal, James V. **VIII:**143

  immigration **IV:**193–195; **V:**199–201

  isolationists **VIII:**189

  Kennedy, Joseph P. **VIII:**200

  Memphis riot (1866) **V:**259–260

  movies **VIII:**246

  Murray, Philip **VIII:**249

  New York City draft riots **V:**284–285

  Phillips, Wendell **IV:**299

  race and race relations **IV:**312; **VII:**281; **VIII:**318

  recreation **VIII:**328

Irish National League **VI:**220

Irish Republican Army (IRA) **X:**232

Iriye, Akira **VII:**246

iron

  Bessemer process **VI:**34–35

  industrialization **IV:**199–200

  Industrial Revolution **III:**224, 226

  Industrial Revolution, Second **VI:**192

  invention and technology **VI:**196

  mining **VI:**246

  New South **VI:**265

  scrap drives **VIII:**354

  trade, domestic and foreign **VI:**360

Iron Acts **II:177–178,** 178, 214

Iron and Steel Institute **VIII:**351

"Iron Brigade" **V:**51

ironclad oath **V:206–207**, 444*c*
  loyalty oaths **V:**246
  Reconstruction **V:**325
  Wade-Davis Bill **V:**421
ironclads **V:207–208**. *See also*
  Merrimack, CSS; Monitor,
  USS; Monitor-Merrimack
  Bulloch, James D. **V:**49
  Civil War **V:**74
  Confederate navy **V:**83
  Forbes, John Murray
    VI:132
  foreign policy **V:**150
  Mallory, Stephen R. **V:**247
  Mississippi River war **V:**263,
    264
  New Orleans, Battle of
    V:280
  science and technology
    V:342
  Tredegar Iron Works **V:**392
  Union navy **V:**406
  Welles, Gideon **V:**428
Iron Curtain, collapse of **X:188–**
  189. *See also* cold war, end of;
  Soviet Union, breakup of
Iron Heel, The (London) **VII:**179
iron lung **VIII:**234
iron manufacturing **I:**200; **II:**178
  industrial development
    V:204
  Maryland **II:**220
  technology **II:**385–386
  Tredegar Iron Works **V:**392
Iron Molders' International Union
  V:276; **VII:**43
Iron Moulders Lockout (1883)
  VI:213
Iroquois Indians (Five/Six Nations
  of the Iroquois Confederation)
  I:185–187, 397*c;* **II:178–180,**
  179*m,* 437*c;* **III:227–228**, 460*c,*
  461*c*
  agriculture **II:**9
  Albany Congress **II:**15
  Andros, Sir Edmund **II:**20
  art and architecture **I:**12;
    II:24, 26
  Beaver Wars **II:**35
  Brant, Joseph **III:**62, 63
  Canada **III:**78
  captivity **II:**58
  Cartier, Jacques **I:**61–62
  Cayuga **I:**69
  Cornplanter **III:**118, 119
  Dekanawideh **II:**93
  De Lancey, James **II:**93
  Fort Stanwix, Treaty of
    III:170–171
  French colonies **II:**136, 137
  fur trade **IV:**170
  Glaize, meeting at the
    III:195
  Handsome Lake **III:**209
  Hendrick **II:**164
  Hiawatha **I:**161–162
  Hochelaga **I:**164

Huron **I:**172, 173; **II:**169–
  170
Indian Removal Act **IV:**198
Iroquois **I:**185; **II:**178–180
  Mary Jemison's Account of
    Her Capture by **II:445–**
    446
  Johnson, Sir William
    II:187–188
  King William's War **II:**195
  Logan, James **II:**209
  marriage and family **II:**216
  Mohawk **I:**246–247
  Native Americans **II:**251,
    253; **III:**311–314
  Native Americans in the War
    of 1812 **IV:**276, 277
  New Netherland **II:**264,
    265
  New York **II:**269, 270
  Oneida **I:**280
  Onondaga **I:**280
  Parker, Ely Samuel **V:**295
  Pontiac's War **III:**340
  Red Jacket **III:**359–360
  religion **II:**330, 331
  Sac and Fox **IV:**327
  sachems **II:**341
  Seneca **I:**329
  shamans **II:**350
  smallpox **II:**360
  society, British American
    II:367
  Sullivan, John **III:**402
  Tuscarora **II:**394, 395
  Tuscarora War **II:**395
  Walking Purchase **II:**405
  Weiser, Johann Conrad
    II:409
  women's status and rights
    II:422, 426; **III:**446
irrigation **I:**164
  agriculture **II:**8, 11
  Indians of the desert
    Southwest **II:**176
  rice cultivation **II:**334
Irrigation Survey (IS) **VI:**141, 288
IRS. *See* Internal Revenue Service
IRT (Interboro Rapid Transit)
  VI:361
Irving, John **X:**370
Irving, Washington
  Jefferson, Joseph, III
    VI:202
  journalism **IV:**210
  literature **III:**268; **IV:**227,
    228
  population trends **III:**343
IS. *See* Irrigation Survey
Isabella I (queen of Castile). *See*
  Ferdinand and Isabella
ISAF. *See* International Security
  Assistance Force
ISG (Iraq Survey Group) **X:**356
Ishii, Kikujiro **VII:**407*c*
Ishmael **I:**238
Islamic fundamentalism **IX:**214

Islamic Jihad **X:**229
Islamic Revolution (Iran, 1979).
  See Iranian Revolution
Islamic Society of North America
  X:189
Islam/Muslims **I:188–189;**
  II:247–248; X:189–190. *See*
  also Nation of Islam
  Africa **II:**5
  Albuquerque, Alfonso de
    I:6
  Askia Muhammad I **I:**14
  astrolabe **I:**15
  auto-da-fé **I:**17
  Baba, Ahmad **I:**25
  Cameroon **I:**56
  Castile **I:**65–66
  Cayor **I:**69
  Dagomba **I:**103
  Darfur **I:**104
  defense policy **X:**102
  Dengel, Lebna **I:**105
  Djibouti **I:**109–110
  Ethiopia **I:**124, 125
  Ferdinand and Isabella
    I:128
  five pillars of **I:**188
  Fulani **I:**135–136
  Gama, Vasco da **I:**137
  Gao **I:**138
  Ghana **I:**140
  Gonja **I:**143
  Guinea-Bissau **I:**148
  Hausa **I:**156
  Holy League **I:**165
  Ibn Battuta **I:**175
  Ibn Khaldûn, 'Abd-ar-
    Rahmân Abû Zayd
    ibn Muhammad ibn
    Muhammad **I:**175
  inquisition **I:**182
  invention and technology
    I:185
  Leo Africanus **I:**210
  Lisbon **I:**215
  Madeira **I:**222
  Malcolm X **IX:**199
  Mali **I:**225, 226
  marabout **I:**230–231
  Mecca **I:**238
  Middle East **X:**230
  Mossi **I:**253
  Muhammad, Elijah **IX:**226–
    227
  Muslims **II:**248
  Niger River **I:**271
  Philip II **I:**291
  Reconquista **I:**314
  religion **IX:**273–274; **X:**306
  religion, African-American
    II:328
  Sahara **I:**324
  slavery **I:**337
  slave trade **I:**339
  Songhai **I:**342
  Sudan **I:**347
  Sufism **I:**347–348

Sundiata Keita **I:**350
Timbuktu **I:**360
Tuareg **I:**370
Island (Huxley) **IX:**195
Island Carib. *See* Carib
Island No. 10 **V:**263
isolationism/isolationists
  VIII:189–190
  aircraft industry **VIII:**13
  America First Committee
    VIII:17
  Atlantic Charter **VIII:**34
  Borah, William E. **VIII:**49
  Committee for Public
    Information **VII:**59
  Communists **VIII:**78
  Congress **VIII:**80
  destroyers-for-bases deal
    VIII:94
  election of 1940 **VIII:**110
  Ethiopia **VIII:**118
  Farewell Address of George
    Washington **III:**162
  foreign policy **VIII:**140
  Hearst, William Randolph
    VII:138
  Hoover, Herbert C.
    VIII:172–173
  Johnson, Hiram Warren
    VII:154
  Johnson, Hugh S. **VIII:**197
  Knox, Frank **VIII:**202
  labor/labor movements
    VIII:207
  La Follette, Robert M.
    VII:173
  La Follette, Robert M., Jr.
    VIII:208
  Landon, Alfred M.
    VIII:209
  Lend-Lease **VIII:**211
  Lewis, John L. **VIII:**213
  Luce, Henry R. **VIII:**224
  neutrality **VII:**236
  Neutrality Acts **VIII:**267
  Norris, George W. **VIII:**277
  Nye committee **VIII:**278
  Palmer, Alexander Mitchell
    VII:249
  peace movements **VII:**256
  Popular Front **VIII:**304
  Preparedness **VII:**267
  presidency **VII:**268, 269
  Republican Party **VIII:**337
  Roosevelt, Franklin D.
    VIII:346
  Selective Service Act
    VII:321
  socialists **VIII:**362
  Spanish civil war **VIII:**369
  Taft, Robert A. **VIII:**385
  Wheeler, Burton K.
    VIII:416
  World Disarmament
    Conference **VIII:**426
ISPs (Internet service providers)
  X:88

Israel **IX:160,** 352*c*, 354*c;* **X:**376*c*, 377*c*, 382*c*
Africa **X:**16
Bunche, Ralph **IX:**45
Bush, George W. **X:**56
Camp David accords **X:**64–66
Carter, James Earl, Jr. **X:**69
Clinton, William J. **X:**83
cold war, end of **X:**84
energy **X:**120
foreign policy **X:**141, 143
Iran-contra affair **X:**183
Jews and Judaism **X:**193
Middle East **IX:**214; **X:**227–230
Mitchell, George **X:**232
nuclear proliferation **X:**261, 262
OPEC **X:**268
religion **IX:**273
republicanism **III:**365
Rice, Condoleezza **X:**310
Suez crisis **IX:**307
Truman, Harry S. **IX:**320
UN **VIII:**403
Israeli-Egyptian Peace Treaty (1979) **X:**377*c*
Israeli settlements **X:**66
ISS. See International Space Station
Issei **VIII:**193
Isserman, Abraham **IX:**86
isthmian canal **IV:**98–99
It (film) **VII:**97
Italian Americans **VIII:190–191**
civil liberties **VIII:**72
DiMaggio, Joe **VIII:**95
election of 1940 **VIII:**110
enemy aliens **VIII:**114–115
Executive Order 9066 **VIII:**121
isolationists **VIII:**189
La Guardia, Fiorello **VIII:**209
news media **VIII:**271
World War II home front **VIII:**433
Italian campaign **VIII:191–192**
amphibious warfare **VIII:**20
Army, U.S. **VIII:**25
Axis **VIII:**38
North African campaign **VIII:**278
Sicily **VIII:**360
World War II European theater **VIII:**431
Italy **II:**354; **VII:**408*c;* **VIII:**447*c*, 448*c*
amphibious warfare **VIII:**20
Anglo-American relations **VIII:**21
arms race **IX:**17
Axis **VIII:**37–38
enemy aliens **VIII:**114
Ethiopia **VIII:**118, 119

foreign policy **VII:**113–115; **VIII:**141
Fuller, Margaret **IV:**169
Hersey, John R. **VIII:**164
Italian Americans **VIII:**191
Italian campaign **VIII:**191–192
Jews **I:**195, 196
League of Nations **VII:**175
Leo X **I:**210
Leonardo da Vinci **I:**211–212
London Naval Conference **VIII:**222
Mafia incident **VI:**234–235
Marsh, George Perkins **VI:**239
Michelangelo **I:**243
movie industry **VII:**216
Munich Conference **VIII:**248
National Origins Act **VII:**228
Naval Disarmament Conference **VII:**235
Neutrality Acts **VIII:**267
Open Door Policy **VII:**246
peace movements **VII:**256
population trends **VII:**266
POWs **VIII:**310, 311
Sacco and Vanzetti **VII:**311
Seton, Elizabeth Ann **IV:**344
Sicily **VIII:**360
Spanish civil war **VIII:**369
submarines **VIII:**378
Timbuktu **I:**360
Versailles, Treaty of **VII:**369
Washington Conference on Naval Disarmament **VII:**379
Wilson, Thomas Woodrow **VII:**384
World War I **VII:**393
World War II European theater **VIII:**429, 431, 432
Itasca, Lake **IV:**300
Itata (freighter) **VI:**67
It Can't Happen Here (Lewis) **VIII:**136
"It Don't Mean a Thing (If It Ain't Got That Swing)" (Ellington) **VIII:**112
It Happened One Night (film) **VIII:**62, 246
Itinerario, Voyage ofte Schipvaert Oost ofte Portugales Indien (Linschoten) **I:**181, 214, 215
Itinerary, An (Moryson) **I:**252
It's a Wonderful Life (film) **VIII:**62
It Takes a Village and Other Lessons Children Teach Us (Clinton) **X:**77–78
iTunes **X:**240, 384*c*
Iturbide, Agustín de **IV:**329

Itzá people **I:**72–73
Itzcóatl (Aztec leader) **I:**18, **189–190,** 361
Iuka, Battle of **V:**337
Ives, Charles **VII:**220; **X:**238
Ives v. South Buffalo Railway Company **VII:**392
Ivory Coast **II:**4
ivory trade **I:**231
Ivy League **VI:**131
I Was There (Leahy) **VIII:**211
"I Will Fight No More Forever" (Chief Joseph) **VI:413–414**
Iwo Jima **VIII:192,** *192,* 448*c*
amphibious warfare **VIII:**20
Forrestal, James V. **VIII:**143
Hiroshima and Nagasaki **VIII:**168
Marines, U.S. **VIII:**230
Navy, U.S. **VIII:**265
Nimitz, Chester W. **VIII:**274
photography **VIII:**296
World War II Pacific theater **VIII:**437
Iwo Jima Memorial, Virginia **IX:**66
IWW. *See* Industrial Workers of the World
IWY (International Women's Year) Conference **X:**134
Ix Chel **I:**99

J

Jack, Homer **IX:**72
Jack Benny Program, The **VII:**5; **VIII:**301
jackhammers **VI:**247
Jacks, James **VI:**259
Jackson, Andrew **IV:**45, **205–208,** *206,* 411*c*–413*c*
abolitionism **V:**3
Adams, John Quincy **IV:**5–6
Adams-Onís Treaty **IV:**6
American Revolution **III:**19
American System **IV:**20
Austin, Stephen F. **IV:**40
banking **IV:**46
Bank of the United States, Second **IV:**48
Bell, John **V:**32
Benton, Thomas Hart **IV:**53
Black Hawk War **IV:**56, 58
Bowie, James **IV:**62–63
Calhoun, John C. **IV:**69
Cass, Lewis **IV:**83
Cherokee **III:**87; **IV:**85
Chickasaw **IV:**86
Choctaw **IV:**86
civil service reform **VI:**72
Claiborne, William C. C. **IV:**94, 95
Clay, Henry **IV:**96, 97
Creek **IV:**109
Crockett, Davy **IV:**110

Democratic Party **IV:**117–118; **V:**108
Douglas, Stephen A. **V:**113
Drayton, William H. **IV:**127
dueling **III:**141
economy **IV:**130, 132
election of 1828 **IV:**135
election of 1840 **IV:**137–139
Federalist Party **III:**165
Florida **III:**167; **IV:**152
foreign policy **IV:**154, 155
Frémont, Jesse Benton **IV:**165
frontier, the **III:**182
Gadsden Purchase **IV:**173
Ghent, Treaty of **IV:**176
Harrison, William Henry **IV:**185
Horseshoe Bend, Battle of **IV:**190
Houston, Sam **IV:**190
immigration **IV:**195
Indian Affairs, Bureau of **IV:**197
Indian Removal Act **IV:**198–199
internal improvements **IV:**203
Johnson, Andrew **V:**212
Lafitte, Jean **IV:**220
McIntosh, William **IV:**247
Mexican-American War **IV:**251
migration **IV:**253
Native Americans **IV:**273–275
Native Americans in the War of 1812 **IV:**276–278
New Orleans, Battle of **IV:**280–281
Nullification Controversy **IV:**282, 283
panic of 1837 **IV:**294
Permanent Indian Frontier **IV:**297
Polk, James K. **IV:**301
Pushmataha **IV:**307
race and race relations **IV:**312
Ridge, John **IV:**324
Ross, John **IV:**325
Scott, Winfield **IV:**336
Seminole **IV:**338
Seminole War, First/Second **IV:**339
Sequoyah **IV:**342, 343
Story, Joseph **III:**399
Taney, Roger B. **IV:**365–366
Texas **IV:**372
Trail of Tears **IV:**377
Tyler, John **IV:**382
Van Buren, Martin **IV:**385–386
War of 1812 **IV:**391, 392
Webster, Daniel **IV:**393
Whigs **IV:**396
Jackson, Charles Thomas **IV:**264

Jackson, Claiborne F. **V:**172, **209**
Jackson, County, Alabama **IX:**276
Jackson, David
    Ashley, William Henry
        IV:32
    Rocky Mountain Fur
        Company **IV:**324
    Smith, Jedediah Strong
        IV:350
Jackson, Helen Hunt **VI:199**,
   409c
    Century of Dishonor
        VI:414–416
    Gilder, Richard Watson
        VI:147
    Higginson, Thomas
        Wentworth **VI:**171–172
    literature **VI:**225
    Winnemucca, Sarah **VI:**397–
        398
Jackson, Henry **X:**100
Jackson, Jesse L. **X:***191*, **191–192**,
   379c
    abortion **X:**3–4
    African Americans **X:**14, 15
    NAACP **X:**245
    SCLC **IX:**292
Jackson, Jimmy Lee **IX:**303
Jackson, Kate **VI:**393
Jackson, Michael **X:**238, 239, 279
Jackson, Mississippi
    freedom rides **IX:**124
    Meredith, James **IX:**213
    MFDP **IX:**219–220
Jackson, Rachel **IV:**205, 206
Jackson, Robert **VIII:**203
Jackson, Shoeless Joe **VII:**33
Jackson, Thomas J. "Stonewall"
   V:209–211, *210*, 444c, 445c
    Antietam, Battle of **V:**12, 13
    Baltimore & Ohio Railroad
        IV:44
    Banks, Nathaniel P.
        V:28–29
    Boyd, Belle **V:**40
    Bull Run/Manassas, First
        and Second Battles of
        V:50
    cartography **V:**57
    Cedar Mountain, Battle
        of **V:**59
    Chancellorsville, Battle of
        V:61, 62
    Ewell, Richard Stoddert
        V:135
    Fredericksburg, Battle of
        V:157–158
    Harpers Ferry, West Virginia
        V:186
    Hill, Ambrose P. **V:**189
    Hill, Daniel H. **V:**190
    homefront **V:**194
    Hood, John Bell **V:**196
    Howard, Oliver Otis **V:**197
    Ladies Memorial
        Associations **V:**229
    Lee, Robert E. **V:**230, 231

McClellan, George Brinton
   V:251–252
    monuments **V:**268
    Peninsular campaign **V:**299
    Shenandoah Valley:
        Jackson's campaign
        V:349–351
    volunteer army **V:**419
Jackson, Thomas Penfield **X:**148
Jackson, William Sharpless
   VI:199
Jackson Hole National Monument,
   Wyoming **VII:**16
Jacksonian Democracy
    anti-Masonry **IV:**25
    Jackson, Andrew **IV:**206
    literature **IV:**228
    medicine **IV:**248, 249
    penitentiary movement
        IV:296
    Polk, James K. **IV:**302
    race and race relations
        IV:312
Jackson State University
   (desegregation) **IX:**213
Jackson State University (Vietnam
   war protests) **IX:**332; **X:**192
Jacksonville Agreement **VIII:**74
Jacobellis v. Ohio **X:**71
Jacobins
    Democratic-Republican
        societies **III:**137
    French Revolution **III:**178,
        179
    Paine, Thomas **III:**329–330
Jacobites **II:**346
Jacobs, B. F. **VI:**306
Jacobs, Helen **VIII:**372
Jacobsen, David **X:**183
Jacob's Staff. *See* cross staff
Jacques, James F. **V:**296
Jailhouse Rock (film) **IX:**225, 263
jails **II:**83
Jaleo, El (Sargent) **VI:**324
Jaline, Paul de **I:**122
Jamaica **I:191**
    Columbus, Christopher **I:**86
    convict labor **II:**80
    Garnet, Henry Highland
        IV:174
    Garvey, Marcus **VII:**121, 122
    Hurston, Zora Neale
        VIII:181
    Saintes, Battle of the
        III:378, 379
    Taino **I:**352
    theater **II:**389
    UNIA **VII:**361, 362
    Virginius affair **VI:**377
    West Indies **III:**436
James, Frank **V:**446c
    entertainment, popular
        VI:118
    Quantrill, William Clarke
        V:317
    violence and lawlessness
        VI:376

James, Harry **VIII:**361
James, Henry **VI:199–200**
    Crane, Stephen **VI:**85
    Howells, William Dean
        VI:180
    James, William **VI:**200
    Jewett, Sarah Orne **VI:**203
    La Farge, John Frederick
        Lewis Joseph **VI:**217
    Lazarus, Emma **VI:**219
    literature **VI:**226; **VII:**179
    Peabody, Elizabeth Palmer
        VI:280
    Peirce, Charles Sanders
        VI:280
James, Jesse **V:**317, 446c; **VI:**375–
   376, *376*
James, Thomas L. **VI:**344
James, Wilkie **V:**142
James, William **VI:200–201**, *201*,
   410c
    Hall, Granville Stanley
        VI:157
    James, Henry **VI:**199
    La Farge, John Frederick
        Lewis Joseph **VI:**217
    Peirce, Charles Sanders
        VI:280, 281
    politics (1900–1928)
        VII:261
    pragmatism **VI:**289
    Royce, Josiah **VI:**318, 319
James I (king of England) **I:191–
   192**, 398c
    Acadia **I:**3
    Bermuda Company **I:**31
    Calvert, George **II:**56
    monarchy, British **II:**240
    Purchas, Samuel **I:**306
    Ralegh, Sir Walter **I:**312
    Rolfe, John **II:**335
    Sandys, Sir Edwin **I:**326
    Shakespeare, William **I:**334
    The Tempest **I:**353
    tobacco **I:**363
    Virginia **II:**398
James Anderson Library Institute
   (Allegheny City) **VI:**62
James B. Eads Bridge (St. Louis,
   Missouri). *See* Eads Bridge
James II (king of England,
   Scotland and Ireland)
    commonwealthmen **III:**103
    Delaware **II:**95
    Glorious Revolution **II:**149,
        150
    Massachusetts **II:**223
    monarchy, British **II:**240
    New York **II:**271
    Whigs **III:**439; **IV:**396
James River
    Lee, Robert E. **V:**231
    Monitor-Merrimack **V:**265,
        266
    Overland campaign **V:**291
    Peninsular campaign **V:**300
    Petersburg campaign **V:**301

James River Squadron **V:**346
Jamestown **I:**398c; **II:181–183**,
   182, 435c
    African Americans **II:**5
    agriculture **II:**10–11
    Bacon's Rebellion **II:**31–32
    Bermuda Company **I:**30
    Calvert, Leonard **II:**56
    Chesapeake Bay **II:**66
    De La Warr, Lord **I:**104–
        105
    disease/epidemics **I:**108;
        II:98
    English immigrants **II:**116
    Florida **II:**129
    Gates, Sir Thomas **II:**143–
        144
    Hakluyt, Richard, the
        Younger **I:**153
    Hamor, Ralph **II:**162
    indentured servitude **II:**174
    iron manufacturing **II:**178
    labor/labor movements
        II:197–198
    lotteries **II:**210
    miscegenation **II:**237
    Pocahontas **II:**299
    Powhatan **II:**305–306
    Powhatan Confederacy
        II:307
    Roanoke **I:**322
    Sandys, Sir Edwin **I:**326
    slave trade **II:**358
    Smith, John **II:**362
    tobacco **I:**363
    Virginia **II:**398, 399
    Virginia Company of
        London **II:**402
Jamestown, USS **VI:**132
J. and A. McLean publishers
   III:162
janjawid **X:**17
Japan **IV:**415c; **V:**443c; **VII:**404c,
   405c, 407c, 408c; **VIII:**443c,
   446c–449
    aircraft carriers **VIII:**12
    aircraft industry **VIII:**13
    air power **VIII:**15, 16
    amphibious warfare **VIII:**20
    Anglo-American relations
        VIII:21
    Army Air Forces, U.S.
        VIII:26
    Asia **IX:**20
    Asian Americans **VIII:**32
    atomic bomb **VIII:**34, 35
    automobile industry **X:**35
    Axis **VIII:**37–38
    Baldwin, Roger Nash
        VII:32
    Bataan Death March
        VIII:42
    bombing **VIII:**47
    Cairo Conference **VIII:**61
    Cassatt, Mary **VI:**64
    code breaking **VIII:**76
    cold war **IX:**63

Columbus, Christopher
I:84
Coral Sea, Battle of the
VIII:87
"Day of Infamy" speech
(Roosevelt) VIII:466
demobilization (WWII)
VIII:91
dollar diplomacy VII:79
enemy aliens VIII:114
espionage VIII:118
Fillmore, Millard IV:150
foreign policy IV:156;
VII:113; VIII:140–143
Gentlemen's Agreement
VII:123
Grand Alliance VIII:155,
156
Great White Fleet VII:130
Guadalcanal VIII:159–160
Hersey, John R. VIII:164
Hiroshima and Nagasaki
VIII:166–168
Hoover presidency
VIII:175
Hull, Cordell VIII:180
immigration restrictions
VI:187
intelligence VIII:187
investments, American,
abroad VI:197
Iwo Jima VIII:192
Johnson, Hiram Warren
VII:154
Kennan, George F. IX:167
Kennedy, John F. IX:169
Korean War IX:177
labor/labor movements
X:202
La Farge, John Frederick
Lewis Joseph VI:218
League of Nations VII:175,
176
Lend-Lease VIII:212
Leyte Gulf, Battle for
VIII:214
London Naval Conference
VIII:222
MacArthur, Douglas IX:197,
198
Manchuria VIII:225–226
Manifest Destiny IV:235
Mariana Islands VIII:228–
229
Middle East X:227
Midway, Battle of VIII:238
Munich Conference
VIII:248
National Origins Act
VII:228
nativism VII:234
Naval Disarmament
Conference VII:234, 235
Okinawa VIII:287–288
Open Door Policy VII:246
Pearl Harbor VIII:291,
292–293

Perry, Matthew Calbraith
IV:298
Philippine independence
IX:256
Philippines VIII:294
Potsdam Conference
VIII:307, 308
POWs VIII:310, 311
printing press I:303
propaganda VIII:311
Roosevelt, Theodore
VII:304
Root-Takahira Agreement
VII:305–306
Russo-Japanese War
VII:309
segregation VII:320
Siberian Expedition
VII:325
Solomon Islands VIII:365
Soviet-American relations
VIII:368, 369
steel industry VII:337;
IX:301
submarines VIII:378–379
Teheran Conference
VIII:390
terrorism X:346
Truman, Harry S. IX:320
V-E Day VIII:405
Versailles, Treaty of VII:370
V-J Day VIII:406–407
Washington Conference
on Naval Disarmament
VII:379
World Disarmament
Conference VIII:426
World War I VII:393
World War II VIII:427, 428
World War II European
theater VIII:429–430
World War II Pacific theater
VIII:434–435, 437
Yalta Conference VIII:440
Japanese American Citizens
League VIII:194
Japanese Americans X:379c
Asian Americans X:33
enemy aliens VIII:114–115
FCC VIII:131
Japanese Americans, relocation of
VIII:193, 193–194, 447c, 448c
ACLU VIII:17–18
Asian-American movement
IX:21, 22
Asian Americans VIII:32
Black, Hugo L. VIII:45
civil liberties VIII:72
civil rights VIII:73
Douglas, William O.
VIII:97
enemy aliens VIII:115
espionage VIII:117–118
Executive Order 9066
VIII:120–121, 466–467
Frankfurter, Felix VIII:144
FSA VIII:127

Internal Security Act (1950)
IX:157, 158
Italian Americans VIII:191
Korematsu v. U.S. VIII:203
Marshall, Thurgood IX:203
Morgenthau, Henry T., Jr.
VIII:244
race and race relations
VIII:319
Roosevelt, Eleanor
VIII:343
Roosevelt, Franklin D.
VIII:347
Stimson, Henry L. VIII:375
Supreme Court VIII:384
Thomas, Norman VIII:394
World War II VIII:427
World War II home front
VIII:433
Japanese Evacuation Claims Act
VIII:194
Japanese immigration
Gentlemen's Agreement
VII:123–124
Immigration Act (1917)
VII:145
nativism VII:234
Japanese Peace Treaty (1951)
IX:90, 352c
Japanese-Soviet neutrality pact
VIII:368
Jarvis, Frank VI:359
Java, HMS III:108; IV:391, 391
Javits Convention Center (New
York City) X:97
Jaworski, Leon X:192–193
Burger, Warren E. X:51
Nixon, Richard M. X:257
U.S. v. Nixon X:357
Watergate scandal X:366–
367
Jaws (film) X:279
Jay, John III:229–230, 230,
462c–464c
Adams, John III:5
constitutions, state III:110
Continental Congress, First
III:113, 114
dueling III:140
election of 1800 III:150
Federalist Papers III:162,
163
foreign affairs III:168
Franklin, Benjamin III:174
Jay-Gardoqui Treaty
III:230, 231
Jay's Treaty III:231–232
Madison, James III:283
Olive Branch Petition
III:324
Paris, Treaty of (1783)
III:331, 332
Supreme Court III:403
Trumbull, John III:416
Jaycees IX:66
Jay Cooke & Company VI:408c
business cycles VI:58

Cooke, Jay V:93
economy V:124
Jay-Gardoqui Treaty III:229,
230–231
jayhawkers V:211
Bleeding Kansas V:36–38
Cody, William Frederick
VI:75
Quantrill, William Clarke
V:317
slavery V:363
Jay's Treaty III:231–232, 464c
Ames, Fisher III:19
Astor, John Jacob IV:33
Bache, Benjamin Franklin
III:39
Canada III:79
Democratic Party IV:116
Federalist Party III:164
foreign affairs III:168
foreign policy IV:153
French Alliance III:178
French Revolution III:179
fur trade III:183
Greenville, Treaty of
III:200
Hamilton, Alexander
III:207
Jay, John III:229, 230
Monroe, James IV:259
Pickering, Timothy III:335
Pinckney Treaty III:337
Quasi War III:352
Supreme Court III:403
trade, domestic and foreign
III:415
XYZ affair III:451
Jay Street Baptist Church VI:4
jazz VII:153, 153–154;
VIII:194–195, 446c, 448c
African Americans VIII:3
art and architecture VIII:31
big bands VIII:44
cities and urban life VII:56
cosmetics and beauty
industry VII:66
Ellington, Duke VIII:111–
112
entertainment, popular
VII:97
FMP VIII:134
Gershwin, George VII:124,
125
Goodman, Benny VIII:150–
151
Harlem Renaissance
VII:136
Holiday, Billie VIII:168–
169
literature VIII:218
migration VII:207
music VI:256; VII:218–220;
VIII:249–251
popular culture VII:265
Sinatra, Frank VIII:361
work, household VII:390
zoot-suiters VIII:442

Jazz Singer, The (film) **VII:**97, 216

JCER (Joint Committee on Economic Recovery) **VIII:**255

J. Edgar Thompson Steel Works **VI:**73, 192

Jefferson, Blind Lemon **VII:**39, 220; **VIII:**250

Jefferson, Joseph, III **VI:201–202,** 355

Jefferson, Thomas **I:**50; **III:232–235,** *233,* 461*c,* 462*c,* 464*c,* 465*c*

  abolitionism **V:**1, 2
  Adams, Abigail **III:**3, 4
  Adams, John **III:**5, 6
  Adams, Samuel **III:**8
  African Americans **III:**9
  agriculture **III:**10
  alcohol **III:**13
  Alien and Sedition Acts **III:**14
  Amendment, Twelfth **III:**16
  American Revolution **III:**18–19
  American System **IV:**20
  Ames, Fisher **III:**19
  antislavery **III:**25
  architecture **III:**29
  artisans **III:**35
  Astor, John Jacob **IV:**33
  Austin, Moses **IV:**38
  Bache, Benjamin Franklin **III:**39
  banking **IV:**45
  Bank of the United States, First **III:**41
  Banneker, Benjamin **III:**43–44
  Barbary Wars **III:**45, 46
  Barlow, Joel **III:**46
  Berlin Decree **III:**49
  Blackstone, Sir William **III:**52
  Bland, Richard **III:**52
  Burr, Aaron **III:**70
  Callender, James T. **III:**74
  Carroll of Carrollton, Charles **III:**82
  Cass, Lewis **IV:**83
  Chase, Samuel **III:**86
  Chesapeake-Leopard affair **III:**88
  Chouteau family **IV:**87
  civil disobedience **IX:**57
  Claiborne, William C. C. **IV:**94
  commemoration **IX:**66
  Congressional Budget and Impoundment Control Act **X:**89
  Constitution, USS **III:**108
  constitutions, state **III:**110
  Continental Congress, Second **III:**115
  corporatism **III:**122
  debt, national **III:**132

  Declaration of Independence **III:**133
  deism **III:**134–135
  Democratic Party **IV:**116–117; **V:**108
  Democratic-Republican societies **III:**137
  economy **III:**147
  education **III:**147; **IV:**133
  election of 1800 **III:**149–151
  embargo of 1807 **III:**151, 152
  Enlightenment, American **II:**118
  environment **III:**155, 156
  Federalist Party **III:**164
  foreign affairs **III:**168, 169
  foreign policy **IV:**153
  Franklin, Benjamin **III:**174
  French Revolution **III:**179
  Freneau, Philip **III:**180
  Gallatin, Albert **III:**188
  Genêt, Edmond Charles **III:**191
  Haiti **III:**204
  Hamilton, Alexander **III:**207, 208
  Hemings, Sally **III:**210–211
  Hull, William **IV:**192
  humanitarianism **III:**217
  Industrial Revolution **III:**226
  internal improvements **IV:**202
  Jackson, Andrew **IV:**205
  Jay's Treaty **III:**231
  journalism **III:**240, 241
  Judiciary Act (1801) **III:**242
  Kościuszko, Tadeusz **III:**249
  Lafayette, marquis de **III:**254
  lawyers **III:**256
  Lee, Richard Henry **III:**260
  Lewis, Meriwether **III:**261, 262
  Lewis and Clark Expedition **III:**262
  libraries, public **VI:**224
  literature **III:**268
  Louisiana **II:**210
  Louisiana Purchase **III:**273
  Macon's Bill No. 2 **III:**280
  Madison, Dolley Payne Todd **III:**280–281
  Madison, James **III:**281–284
  Marbury v. Madison **III:**285
  Marshall, John **III:**290, 291
  Mason-Dixon Line **V:**250
  McIntosh, William **IV:**247
  medicine **IV:**248
  Monroe, James **IV:**258, 259
  Monroe-Pinkney Treaty **III:**300–301

  National Road **IV:**271
  Neutrality Proclamation **III:**315
  Non-Importation Act **III:**319
  Northwest Ordinances **III:**321
  Nullification Controversy **IV:**282
  Orders in Council **III:**325
  Oregon Trail **IV:**285
  Ostenaco **II:**280
  Paris, Treaty of (1783) **III:**331
  Permanent Indian Frontier **IV:**297
  Pickering, Timothy **III:**335
  Pike, Zebulon Montgomery **IV:**300
  political parties **III:**339
  race and race relations **III:**357; **IV:**310, 312
  Randolph, John **III:**358–359
  religion **III:**360
  religion, Euro-American **II:**330
  religious liberty **III:**363, 364
  Republican Party **IV:**322
  Rodney, Caesar Augustus **III:**373
  secession **V:**344
  slave trade **III:**393
  states' rights **III:**397
  Tammany Society **III:**405
  tariffs **III:**406
  Taylor, John, of Caroline **III:**408
  Trumbull, John **III:**416
  U.S. Army Corps of Engineers **V:**407
  U.S. Military Academy at West Point **V:**409
  Van Buren, Martin **IV:**385
  Virginia and Kentucky Resolutions **III:**424
  Virginia dynasty **III:**425
  War of 1812 **IV:**390
  Washington, D.C. **III:**428
  West Point **III:**437
  Wilkinson, James **III:**443, 444
  women's status and rights **III:**447
  Wright, Fanny **IV:**405
  Yorktown, surrender at **III:**454

Jefferson Airplane
  folk music revival **IX:**121
  music **IX:**230
  popular culture **IX:**259

Jefferson Barracks, Missouri **IV:**36

Jeffersonians. *See* Democratic-Republican Party

Jefferson in Paris (film) **III:**210

Jefferson Lecture **IX:**234

Jefferson Medical College (Philadelphia, Pennsylvania) **IV:**249; **VI:**103–104

Jefferson Park Presbyterian Church **VII:**342

Jeffersons, The **X:**343

Jeffords, James **X:**383*c*
  Bush, George W. **X:**55
  political parties **X:**277
  Senate, U.S. **X:**321

Jeffries, Jim **VII:**154, 155, 333

Jehovah's Witnesses
  conscientious objectors **VIII:**83
  Darwinism and religion **VI:**93
  religion **VI:**307; **X:**306
  Supreme Court **VIII:**384

Jemison, Mary **II:**58, **183–184, 445–446**

Jen, Gish **X:**211

Jenckes, Thomas A. **VI:**72–73

Jenco, Lawrence **X:**183

Jenkins, Charles Francis **IX:**315

Jenkins, Jerry **X:**212

Jenkins, Robert **II:**408

Jenkins, W. A., Jr. **IX:**39

Jenner, Edward **III:**138, 464*c*

Jennings, Elizabeth **VI:**20

Jennison, Charles "Doc" **V:**211

Jennison, Nathaniel **III:**355

Jenny, William Le Baron **VI:**18

Jenrette, John W. **X:**5

jeremiads **II:184,** 320

Jericho, New York **IV:**189

Jerome, Leonard **VI:**177

Jerome Park (Westchester County, New York) **VI:**177

Jerome Remick Company **VII:**124

Jersey, HMS **III:235–236**

Jersey City, New Jersey **VIII:**188

Jerusalem **X:**227

Jerusalem, Virginia **IV:**380, 381

Jervis, John **IV:**313

Jesuits **I:192–194; II:184–185**
  Acosta, José de **I:**3
  Azores **I:**18
  Brébeuf, Jean de **II:**46
  California **I:**51
  Calusa **I:**52
  Chesapeake Bay **II:**66
  Counterreformation **I:**98
  education **II:**111
  exploration **II:**124
  Florida **I:**131; **II:**129
  French colonies **II:**135–137
  Huron **II:**169
  Ignatius Loyola **I:**178–179
  Marquette, Jacques **II:**215
  mining **VII:**209
  missions **II:**238, 239
  Montagnais-Naskapi **I:**250
  Montreal **II:**242
  Native Americans **II:**253
  Pima revolt **II:**294

reducción **I**:314–315
religion, Native American
II:331
Ricci, Matteo **I**:319–320
Roman Catholicism **II**:336
White, Andrew **II**:412, 413
Jesup, Thomas S. **IV**:289, 339
Jesus Christ **I**:357; **X**:124, 125
jet airliners **IX**:28, 313, 353c
Jet magazine **X**:219
jewelry **VI**:3
Jewett, Frank **VIII**:283
Jewett, Sarah Orne **VI:202–203,**
226
Jewish Daily Forward **VII**:285
"Jewish Declaration of
Independence" **VI**:205
Jewish Enlightenment **VI**:205
Jewish Home for the Aged
VII:102
Jewish Institute of Religion
VII:298
Jews and Judaism **I:194–197,**
195, 396c; **II**:*185,* **185–186;**
III:236–237; V:445c; **VI**:205;
VII:406c; **VIII:195–196,** 448c;
X:193–194. *See also* anti-
Semitism
Alexander VI **I**:6
Amalgamated Clothing
Workers of America
(ACW) **VIII**:16
anti-Semitism **VIII**:24–25
auto-da-fé **I**:17
Benjamin, Judah P. **V**:33
citizenship **III**:92
class consciousness **VI**:73
Common Sense **III**:102
conservatism **VIII**:84
criminal justice **VII**:67
Democratic Party **VIII**:93
election of 1936 **VIII**:109
election of 1940 **VIII**:110
elections, presidential
X:118
ERA **X**:124
Ethical Culture movement
VI:120–121
Ferdinand and Isabella
I:128
Friedan, Betty **IX**:126
German Americans
VIII:148
Grant, Ulysses S. **V**:174
Hersey, John R. **VIII**:164
Holocaust **VIII**:169–170
immigration **III**:221; **V**:199;
VIII:184
inquisition **I**:182
Irish Americans **VIII**:188
Israel **IX**:160
KKK **IX**:179, 180
Ku Klux Klan **VII**:166
Lazarus, Emma **VI**:219–220
Leo Frank case **VII**:176
liberalism **VIII**:216
London **I**:216

Luther, Martin **I**:219
Madeira **I**:222
Morgenthau, Henry T., Jr.
VIII:244
nativism **VII**:234
neoconservatism **X**:252
New Deal **VIII**:270
news media **VIII**:271
Oglethorpe, James Edward
II:277
Owens, Jesse **VIII**:289
plague **I**:294
Polish Americans **VIII**:297
politics (Roosevelt era)
VIII:298
race and race relations
VIII:318
refugees **VIII**:329, 330
religion **IV**:319; **VI**:307,
308; **VII**:298, 299;
VIII:334–335; **IX**:273;
X:306, 307
religious liberty **III**:362
Roosevelt, Franklin D.
VIII:345, 347
São Tomé **I**:328
segregation **VII**:320
Spanish civil war **VIII**:369
Stuyvesant, Peter **II**:379
suburbanization/suburbs
VIII:380
suffrage **II**:380
Tanner, Benjamin Tucker
VI:351
Thomas, M. Carey **VI**:356
Zionism **VIII**:441
JFK (film) **X**:35
JFK International Airport **X**:97,
348, 384c
Jiang Jieshi. *See* Chiang Kai-shek
jihad
Fulani **I**:136
Ghana **I**:140
Islam **I**:188
Sufism **I**:348
Jim Crow laws **VI:203–204,** 409c
African Americans **VI**:6, 7;
VIII:2; **IX**:4
antilynching legislation
VIII:22
*Brown v. Board of
Education* **IX**:43, 44
civil rights **VIII**:72, 73
Civil Rights Cases **VI**:72
Civil War centennial **IX**:62
Johnson, Jack **VII**:155
Liberia **VI**:223
lost cause, the **V**:245
migration **VII**:207
Murray, Pauli **IX**:227
NAACP **IX**:232
Plessy v. Ferguson **VI**:285
race and race relations
VII:282, 283; **VIII**:318,
319
Red Scare **VII**:296
segregation **VII**:319

South **VIII**:366, 367
Washington, Booker T.
VI:384
Jim Crow minstrel acts **IV**:269,
412c
Jiménez de Cisneros, Francisco
I:205
Jiménez Moreno, Wigberto **I**:364
"Jingle Bells" **V**:274
jingoes **VI**:204
"J" machine (Japanese code
machine) **VIII**:76
JN-25 code (Japan) **VIII**:76
João (kings of Portugal). *See under*
John
Job Corps **IX:161–162,** 356c
Economic Opportunity Act
(1964) **IX**:95, 96
Great Society **IX**:139
Johnson, Lyndon B. **IX**:163
labor/labor movements
IX:182
VISTA **IX**:333
War on Poverty **IX**:335
Job Opportunities and Basic
Skills (JOBS) training program
X:128
Jobs, Steve **X**:87, 318
Job Training Partnership Act
(1982) **X**:293
Jocelyn, Simeon **V**:8
Jockey Hollow **III**:306
Jodrell Bank Observatory
(England) **IX**:296
Johannesburg, South Africa **IX**:4
John (João) I (king of Portugal)
I:160
John (João) II (king of Portugal)
I:137, 367, 368
John (João) III (king of Portugal)
I:35, 197–198
John XXIII (pope) **IX**:273
John Birch Society
AIP **X**:24
Buckley, William F., Jr. **X**:50
conservative movement
X:93
"John Brown's Body" **V**:273
John Crerar Library **VI**:224
John Deere Company **IV**:115
John Paul II (pope) **X**:67, 70
John Philoponos **I**:15
John Reed Club **VIII**:437
Johns, Jasper **IX**:19
Johns Hopkins Hospital **VI**:112
Johns Hopkins Medical School
VI:244; **VII**:133, 199
Johns Hopkins University
VI:408c
education, higher **VI**:111
education, philanthropy and
VI:112
Eliot, Charles William
VI:114
Ely, Richard Theodore
VI:115
Gilman, Daniel Coit **VI**:148

Hall, Granville Stanley
VI:157
history **VII**:139
science and technology
VI:326
Johnson, Albert **VII**:103, 227
Johnson, Andrew **V**:*211,* **211–
213,** 446c
Allison, William Boyd **VI**:11
amnesty, acts of **V**:8, 9
assassination of Abraham
Lincoln **V**:20, 21
Blair, Francis Preston, Jr.
V:36
Civil Rights Act (1866) **V**:70
Congress **V**:89, 90; **VI**:79
Democratic Party **V**:109
Freedmen's Bureau **V**:161
impeachment of. *See*
impeachment of Andrew
Johnson
Joint Committee on the
Conduct of the War
V:215
Memphis riot (1866) **V**:260
presidency **VI**:289, 290
Radical Republicans
V:320–321
Reconstruction **V**:325
Reconstruction Acts
V:327–328
Republican Party **V**:334
Sherman, William T. **V**:356
Stanton, Edwin M. **V**:369
Stevens, Thaddeus **V**:372–
373
Swing Around the Circle
V:378
Thirteenth Amendment
V:388
Tilden, Samuel Jones **VI**:357
Tredegar Iron Works **V**:392
Walker, Mary Edwards
V:423
Welles, Gideon **V**:428
Johnson, Anthony **II**:6, **186,** 187
Johnson, Ban **VII**:334
Johnson, Benjamin **III**:318
Johnson, Charles **II**:296, 385
Johnson, Guy **III**:62, 228
Johnson, Henry **III**:399
Johnson, Hiram Warren **VII:154**
Capper-Volstead Act **VII**:49
Congress **VII**:62
Progressive Party **VII**:270
progressivism **VII**:271
Republican Party **VII**:300
Taft, William Howard
VII:348
Johnson, Hugh S. **VIII:196–197**
America First Committee
VIII:17
Baruch, Bernard M. **VIII**:42
National Recovery
Administration **VIII**:259,
260
NIRA **VIII**:256

Johnson, Jack **VII:154–156**, *155*, 405*c*
  Dempsey, William Harrison "Jack" **VII:**76
  Mann Act **VII:**189–190
  sports and recreation **VII:**333
Johnson, James (Arkansas state senator) **IX:**118
Johnson, James Weldon
  antilynching legislation **VIII:**22
  NAACP **VII:**224; **VIII:**255; **IX:**232
  White, Walter **VIII:**416
Johnson, Sir John **III:237**
Johnson, Junior **X:**370
Johnson, Lady Bird **IX:**95, **162–163**, *164*
Johnson, Louis **IX:**248
Johnson, Lucy Baines **IX:**162
Johnson, Lynda Bird **IX:**162
Johnson, Lyndon B., and administration **IX:163–165**, *164*, *172*, *293*, 355*c*, 356*c*
  Acheson, Dean **IX:**2
  advertising **IX:**3
  affirmative action **X:**9
  Africa **IX:**4
  Amendments to the U.S. Constitution **X:**22
  antiwar movement, Vietnam **X:**28, 29
  assassinations **IX:**22, 23
  Baruch, Bernard M. **VIII:**42
  birth control **X:**43
  Bush, George H. W. **X:**51
  CAP **IX:**68
  cities and urban life **IX:**56
  Civil Rights Act (1957) **IX:**59
  Civil Rights Act (1964) **IX:**60
  conservatism **IX:**75
  conservative movement **X:**93
  CORE **IX:**73
  Cox, Archibald, Jr. **X:**95
  defense budget **IX:**84
  Democratic Party **IX:**85
  domino theory **IX:**89
  Economic Opportunity Act (1964) **IX:**95
  economy **IX:**98; **X:**108
  education **IX:**99
  elections **IX:**103, 104
  Ellington, Duke **VIII:**112
  ESEA **IX:**106
  Ford, Gerald R. **X:**138
  Fortas, Abe **X:**144, 145
  Galbraith, John Kenneth **IX:**129
  Goldwater, Barry **IX:**136
  government, state/local **IX:**137
  Graham, Billy **IX:**138

Great Society **IX:**138–139
Harriman, W. Averell **VIII:**162
Harrington, Michael **IX:**142
Head Start **IX:**144, 145
Hershey, Lewis B. **VIII:**164
Humphrey, Hubert H. **IX:**151
Immigration Act (1965) **IX:**156
Israel **IX:**160
Jaworski, Leon **X:**193
Job Corps **IX:**161, 162
Johnson, Lady Bird **IX:**162
Kennedy, John F. **IX:**169
King, Martin Luther, Jr. **IX:**174, 175
Kissinger, Henry A. **X:**198
labor/labor movements **IX:**182
Latin America **IX:**184; **X:**205
liberalism **X:**208
March on Washington (1963) **IX:**201
Marshall, Thurgood **IX:**203
McCarthy, Eugene **IX:**205
Medicaid **IX:**209
Medicare **IX:**209, 210
medicine **IX:**211
MFDP **IX:**220
Model Cities program **IX:**220, 221
modern Republicanism **IX:**222
Mondale, Walter F. **X:**233
National Traffic and Motor Vehicle Safety Act of 1966 **IX:**238
National Trails Act of 1968 **IX:**239
National Wilderness Preservation Act of 1964 **IX:**240
nativism **VII:**234
NEA **IX:**234
NEH **IX:**235
New Deal **IX:**242
O'Neill, Thomas "Tip" P., Jr. **X:**267
Oppenheimer, J. Robert **IX:**251
public health **IX:**265
public housing **IX:**267
race and race relations **IX:**271
recreation **IX:**271
SANE **IX:**284
SCLC **IX:**293
Stevenson, Adlai E. **IX:**302
television **IX:**316
Vietnam War **IX:**330–332
VISTA **IX:**332, 333
Voting Rights Act of 1965 **IX:**333
War on Poverty **IX:**335–336
Warren, Earl **IX:**337

Warren Court **IX:**337, 338
wars of national liberation **IX:**339
Wild and Scenic Rivers Act of 1968 **IX:**343, 344
Johnson, Malven **VII:**136
Johnson, Mary **II:**6, **186–187**; **V:**192
Johnson, Phillip E. **X:**306
Johnson, Richard M. **III:**409; **IV:**185
Johnson, Robert Underwood **VI:**253
Johnson, Samuel **II:187**
  Anglican Church **II:**21–22
  King's College **II:**194
  science and technology **II:**345
Johnson, Thomas **III:**403
Johnson, Thomas 15X **IX:**23
Johnson, Tom Loftin **VII:156**
  Pingree, Hazen S. **VII:**260
  politics (1900–1928) **VII:**261
  urban reform **VII:**362
Johnson, Sir William (1715–1774) **II:187—188**
  De Lancey, James **II:**93
  Fort Stanwix, Treaty of **III:**170
  Johnson, Sir John **III:**237
  Pontiac's War **III:**340
Johnson, William H. (1901–1970) **VII:**136
Johnson Company (Johnson Steel Street Rail Company) **VII:**156
Johnson Doctrine **IX:**184, 356*c*
Johnson Electric Company **VII:**156
Johnson-Reed Act. *See* National Origins Act
Johnson's Island **V:**315
Johnson's Ranch **IV:**126
Johnson Wax Company **VII:**395
Johnston, Albert Sidney **V:213–214**
  Beauregard, Pierre Gustave Toutant **V:**32
  Breckinridge, John C. **V:**42
  Bridger, James **IV:**64
  Confederate army **V:**82
  Shiloh, Battle of **V:**358–360
Johnston, Henrietta Deering **II:188**
Johnston, Joseph E. **V:214–215**, 444*c*
  Appomattox campaign **V:**14
  Appomattox Court House, Virginia **V:**15
  Atlanta campaign **V:**21–22
  Beauregard, Pierre Gustave Toutant **V:**32
  Bentonville, Battle of **V:**34
  Bull Run/Manassas, First and Second Battles of **V:**50
  Confederate army **V:**82

  Davis, Jefferson **V:**105
  Hill, Daniel H. **V:**190
  Hood, John Bell **V:**196
  Joint Committee on the Conduct of the War **V:**216
  Ladies Memorial Associations **V:**229
  Lee, Robert E. **V:**230, 232
  literature **V:**239
  McLaws, Lafayette **V:**253
  Meade, George Gordon **V:**253
  Mississippi River war **V:**264
  Peninsular campaign **V:**298, 299
  Sherman, William T. **V:**355, 356
  Vicksburg campaign **V:**417, 418
Johnston, Sarah Bush **V:**234
Johnston Act **III:**12
Johnstone, Anne Hartwell **IX:**187
Johnstone, George **III:**82
Johnstown flood **VI:204**
John Street Methodist Church (New York City) **VI:**5
John Street Theater (New York City) **III:**417
John Wanamaker & Co. **VI:**382
Joint Army and Navy Selective Service Committee **VIII:**164
Joint Chiefs of Staff **X:**379*c*
  Army, U.S. **VIII:**26
  Army Air Forces, U.S. **VIII:**26
  Arnold, Henry H. "Hap" **VIII:**28
  intelligence **VIII:**187
  Leahy, William D. **VIII:**211
  OSS **VIII:**284
  Powell, Colin L. **X:**286
Joint Commission on Mental Illness **IX:**236
Joint Committee on Economic Recovery (JCER) **VIII:**255
Joint Committee on Investment and Trade (U.S.-Mexico) **X:**226
Joint Committee on Reconstruction
  Radical Republicans **V:**321
  Reconstruction Acts **V:**327
  Stevens, Thaddeus **V:**373
Joint Committee on the Conduct of the War (CCW) **V:215–216**
  Congress **V:**89–90
  impeachment of Andrew Johnson **V:**202
  Julian, George Washington **V:**219
  Meade, George Gordon **V:**254
  Union army **V:**401
  Wade, Benjamin Franklin **V:**421

Joint Contract Termination Board **VIII:**326
Joliet, Illinois **V:**267
Jolliet, Louis **II:**123, **188–189,** 215
Jolson, Al
    entertainment, popular **VI:**116–117
    movie industry **VII:**216
    Rhinelander case **VII:**301
Jomini, Antoine-Henri, baron de **V:**182, **216–217,** 379
Jonah's Gourd Vine (Hurston) **VIII:**219
Jones, Absalom **II:**35; **III:**237–**238,** 464*c,* 465*c*
    abolitionism **V:**1
    African Americans **III:**9
    Allen, Richard **III:**16
    antislavery **III:**26–27
Jones, Alice Beatrice **VII:**301
Jones, Anson **IV:**372
Jones, Bobby **VIII:**372
Jones, Catesby **V:**266
Jones, David S. **I:**108
Jones, Earl **IX:**291
Jones, James **VIII:**219; **IX:**193
Jones, Jesse H. **VIII:197**
    Federal National Mortgage Association **VIII:**135
    RFC **VIII:**325, 326
    Wallace, Henry A. **VIII:**411
Jones, John Paul **III:**117, **238–239,** 239, 461*c*
Jones, Joseph **V:**258
Jones, Leroi. *See* Baraka, Amiri
Jones, Marvin **VIII:**39
Jones, Mary Harris "Mother" **VII:**147, 187
Jones, Paula Corbin **X:**381*c,* 382*c*
    Clinton, William J. **X:**82
    impeachment of William J. Clinton **X:**178
    Judicial Watch **X:**194
    Rehnquist, William H. **X:**305
    Starr, Kenneth **X:**333
Jones, Roger **V:**186
Jones, Samuel **VII:**156
Jones, Seaborn **V:**433
Jones, Walter (1776–1861) **IV:**245
Jones, Walter B. (1888–1963) **IX:**123
Jones, William (Bank of the United States president) **IV:**46, 48
Jones, William (steel works manager) **VI:**73
Jones, William Atkinson (congressman) **VII:**157
Jones Act (1916) **VII:156–157,** 406*c*
Jones Act (1917) **VII:**110, **157–158,** 407*c;* **IX:**267
Jonesborough, Tennessee **IV:**175
Jones & Laughlin **IX:**300

Jones Merchant Marine Act **VII:**360
Jones v. Flowers **X:**311
Jonson, Ben **I:**216
Joplin, Janis **IX:**79, 230
Joplin, Scott **VI:**140, 258, 412*c;* **VII:158,** 403*c*
Jordan
    Camp David accords **X:**65
    Israel **IX:**160
    Middle East **X:**227
Jordan, Barbara **X:**175, 377*c*
Jordan, Hamilton **X:**179
Jordan, Michael **X:**331, 331–332
Jordan, Thomas **V:**178
Jordan Commission **X:**175
Jorgensen, Jo **X:**209
Joseph (chief of the Nez Perce) **VI:**267, 408*c*
    Howard, Oliver Otis **V:**197–198
    "I Will Fight No More Forever" **VI:413–414**
    Native Americans **VI:**261
    Nez Perce War **VI:**267, 268
Josephson, Matthew **VI:**314–315
Joslyn Art Museum **IV:**61, 85
journalism **II:**189, 312; **III:**239–**241,** 241; **IV:208–210,** 413*c;* **V:217–219; VII:158–161; IX:**165, **165–166; X:**376*c. See also* media; newspapers; radical and labor press
    abolitionism **V:**2, 3
    Bache, Benjamin Franklin **III:**39
    Bloomer, Amelia **IV:**59
    Brackenridge, Hugh Henry **III:**60
    Burke, Edmund **III:**68
    Burr, Esther Edwards **II:**52
    business **VII:**46
    Callender, James T. **III:**74
    Carey, Mathew **III:**80
    Chambers, Whittaker **IX:**52–53
    Committee for Public Information **VII:**59
    Dana, Charles A. **V:**102; **VI:**91, 92
    Delany, Martin Robinson **V:**107
    Dickinson, John **III:**137
    Duane, William **III:**140
    Fitzhugh, George **V:**146–147
    Forten, James **III:**170
    Franklin, Benjamin **III:**173, 175
    Freneau, Philip **III:**179–180
    Gastonia Strike **VII:**122
    Gilman, Charlotte Perkins **VII:**125
    Godkin, Edwin Lawrence **VI:**149–150
    Greeley, Horace **V:**176–177

    Hale, Sarah Josepha **IV:**183–184
    Harte, Bret **VI:**162
    Hearn, Lafcadio **VI:**169
    Howells, William Dean **VI:**179, 180
    investments, foreign **VII:**152
journalism **III:**239–241
    Knight, Sarah Kemble **II:**195–196
    Letcher, John **V:**232
    literature **IV:**229
    Lyon, Matthew **III:**277
    Marx, Karl **V:**249
    The Masses **VII:**193
    Mencken, Henry Louis **VII:**201, 202
    Mooney-Billings case **VII:**213
    muckrakers **VII:**216–217
    Murray, Judith Sargent Stevens **III:**308
    Nast, Thomas **V:**275
    news media **VIII:**271, 272
    newspapers **VI:**267
    Niles, Hezekiah **III:**318–319
    Norton, Charles Eliot **VI:**269
    Olmsted, Frederick Law **V:**287
    Packard, Vance **IX:**253–254
    Paine, Thomas **III:**329–330
    popular culture **III:**341
    progressivism **VII:**271
    Pulitzer, Joseph **VI:**297
    Pyle, Ernie **VIII:**315
    Reed, Jack **VII:**296
    Reid, Whitelaw **VI:**304–305
    resistance movement **III:**365, 366
    Riis, Jacob A. **VI:**314
    Schurz, Carl **VI:**324, 325
    science and technology **V:**343
    Scopes Trial **VII:**317
    Seattle General Strike **VII:**318
    Sinclair, Upton **VII:**325–326
    Standard Oil **VII:**336
    Steffens, Lincoln **VII:**339
    Steinem, Gloria **X:**334
    Sweet trial **VII:**344
    Tarbell, Ida Minerva **VII:**349
    Trading with the Enemy Act **VII:**355
    Trotter, William Monroe **VII:**357
    Valesh, Eva McDonald **VII:**367
    Vorse, Mary Heaton **VII:**375
    Walker, William **V:**423
    War Revenue Act **VII:**378

    Watterson, Henry **VI:**385–386
    Webster, Noah **III:**434
    Welles, Gideon **V:**428
    Wells-Barnett, Ida Bell **VI:**387–388
    Whitman, Walt **V:**430
    Wilkes, John **III:**443
    Wolfe, Tom **X:**369–370
Journal of Christian Science
    Christian Science **VI:**69
    Eddy, Mary Baker **VI:**106
Journal of Commerce **IV:**218, 219
Journal of Hospital Life (Cumming) **V:**98
Journal of Negro History **VII:**140
Journal of the Franklin Institute **IV:**163
journeymen **II:190**
    artisans **II:**28; **III:**35
    Industrial Revolution **III:**225
    labor/labor movements **II:**200
Journey to Pennsylvania (Mittelberger) **II:**239, **444–445**
Joy, James F. **VI:**132
Joyce, James
    Baldwin, Roger Nash **VII:**31
    censorship **VIII:**65
    James, Henry **VI:**200
    radical and labor press **VII:**285
Joyfull Newes out of the Newe Founde Worlde (Monardes) **I:**247
J. P. Morgan & Company **VI:**23, 250, 251, 411*c*
J Typewriter (Japan) **VIII:**76
Juana (queen of Castile) **I:**128
Juan de Fuca, Straits of **IV:**146
Juárez, Benito **VI:**381
Judah, Theodore D.
    Huntington, Collis Potter **VI:**180
    lobbying **VI:**228
    Pacific Railroad Act **V:**293
Judaism. *See* Jews and Judaism
Judaism as a Civilization (Kaplan) **VIII:**335
Judd, Donald **X:**30
Judeo-Christian values **X:**93
Judge, William Quan **VI:**309
Judges v. Ashcroft, Governor of Missouri **X:**131
judicial activism
    Bork, Robert **X:**45
    Brennan, William J., Jr. **X:**47
    Burger, Warren E. **X:**51
judicial nationalism **IV:**361
Judicial Procedures Reform Bill **VIII:**89, 382–383
judicial restraint **X:**152

judicial review **III:**465*c*
  Marbury v. Madison
    III:285
  Supreme Court **III:**403;
    IV:361; **VIII:**382
  U.S. v. Nixon **X:**358
  Watergate scandal **X:**367
  Wilson, James **III:**445
  Yazoo claims **III:**454
Judicial Watch **X:194**
Judiciary Act of 1789 **III:**463*c*
  Judiciary Act (1801) **III:**242
  Marbury v. Madison
    III:285
  Marshall, John **III:**290, 291
  Supreme Court **III:**403,
    404
Judiciary Act of 1801 **III:241–**
  243, 465*c*
  Judiciary Act (1789) **III:**242
  Marbury v. Madison
    III:285
  Marshall, John **III:**290
  Supreme Court **III:**403–
    404
Judith of Bethulia (film) **VII:**131
Judson, Andrew T. **IV:**21–22
Judson, E. C. (Ned Buntline)
  Bridger, James **IV:**64–65
  Cody, William Frederick
    VI:76
  entertainment, popular
    VI:118
jukeboxes **VIII:**328
Julian, George Washington **V:219**
  Free-Soil Party **IV:**164–165
  impeachment of Andrew
    Johnson **V:**202
  Joint Committee on the
    Conduct of the War
    V:215
Juliana Library Company **III:**17
Julius II (pope) **I:**210, 244
July 4th **III:**133, 341
July Revolution (France) **IV:**67
Jumano Indians **IV:**371
"jumping the broom" **IV:**239
Juneteenth **V:219–220**
Juneteenth (Ellison) **V:**219–220
Jung, Carl **VI:**157
Jungle, The (Sinclair) **VII:**325,
  404*c*
  business **VII:**46
  Meat Inspection Act
    VII:198
  popular culture **VII:**265
  Pure Food and Drug Act
    VII:276–277
  Sinclair, Upton **VII:**325–
    326
junks (sailing vessels) **I:**225
Juno beach **VIII:**276
Junto
  American Philosophical
    Society **II:**20; **III:**17
  Bond, Thomas **II:**38
  Franklin, Benjamin **III:**173

Godfrey, Thomas **II:**150
  Pennsylvania **II:**288
Jupiter **X:**327
Jupiter, USS **VIII:**11
Jupiter missiles **IX:**81
Jurassic Park **X:**235
jury duty **VIII:**424
*Just Give Me a Cool Drink of Water
  'Fore I Die* (Angelou) **X:**26
Justice, Confederate Department
  of **V:**33
Justice, U.S. Department of
  (DOJ) **X:**381*c*
  Abscam **X:**5
  Bates, Edward **V:**31
  business **X:**58, 59
  civil liberties **VII:**58
  Civil Rights Act (1957)
    IX:58–59
  conscription **VII:**63
  crime and punishment **X:**97
  Executive Order 9066
    VIII:121
  FBI **VIII:**129
  Freedom Train **IX:**125
  Korematsu v. U.S. **VIII:**203
  Mann Act **VII:**190
  Meese, Edwin C., III **X:**225
  Mitchell, John N. **X:**233
  narcotics **X:**242, 243
  Northern Securities Case
    VII:242
  Palmer, Alexander Mitchell
    VII:249
  presidency **VII:**268
  Reno, Janet **X:**308–309
  Richardson, Elliot L. **X:**310
  RICO **X:**298
  Scalia, Antonin **X:**316
  Stanton, Edwin M. **V:**368
  Taft, William Howard
    VII:347
  Teapot Dome **VII:**351
  Veterans Bureau **VII:**373
Justice Department Antitrust
  Division **VIII:**24
justification by faith **I:**218
Juvenile Courts and Probation
  (Flexner and Nash) **VII:**31
juvenile delinquency
  children **VIII:**67
  cities and urban life **VIII:**70
  marriage and family
    VIII:232
  World War II **VIII:**427
  World War II home front
    VIII:433
Juvenile Miscellany **IV:**183
Juzgado de Indios **I:**17
J. Walter Thompson Company
  VII:4

K

Kaabu, kingdom of **I:199,** 330
Ka'ba **I:**188, 238

Kabul, Afghanistan **X:**12
Kachiquel kingdom **I:**235
Kaddish (Ginsberg) **IX:**135
Kaeo **IV:**211
Kahekili **IV:**211
Kahn, Albert **VII:**19, 111–112
Kahnawake **II:**386
Kaiser, David E. **VII:**311
Kaiser, Henry J. **VIII:199**
  aircraft industry **VIII:**14
  medicine **VIII:**236
  mobilization **VIII:**242
  shipbuilding **VIII:**359
Kaiser Foundation **IX:**188
Kaiser Permanente **VIII:**199, 236
Kaiser Shipbuilding **VIII:**199
Kalakmul empire **I:**235–236, 359
Kalaniopuu **IV:**211
Kalb, Johann, baron de **III:245**
Kallen, Horace **VII:**181, 233–234
Kalm, Peter **II:191**
Kamehameha I (king of Hawaii)
  III:210; **IV:**188, **211–212**
Kamehameha III (king of Hawaii)
  IV:188
Kamehameha IV (king of Hawaii)
  V:149
kamikaze
  Leyte Gulf, Battle for
    VIII:214
  Okinawa **VIII:**288
  World War II Pacific theater
    VIII:437
Kaminaljuyu **I:**356
Kampelman, Max **X:**70
Kanagawa, Treaty of
  foreign policy **IV:**156
  Manifest Destiny **IV:**235
  Perry, Matthew Calbraith
    IV:298
Kanawha Salt Company **VI:**362
Kandahar, Afghanistan **X:**12, 143
"Kandy-Kolored Tangerine-Flake
  Streamline Baby, The" (Wolfe)
  X:370
Kangaba kingdom **I:**225–226, 350
Kansas **IV:**415*c*; **V:**443*c*, 444*c*
  Armijo, Manuel **IV:**26
  Atkinson, Henry **IV:**36
  Bleeding Kansas **V:**36–38
  Brown, John **V:**44
  *Brown v. Board of
    Education* **IX:**43–44
  Buchanan, James **V:**48
  cattle kingdom **VI:**64
  Cody, William Frederick
    VI:76
  Douglas, Stephen A. **V:**114
  dust bowl **VIII:**97
  Exodusters **VI:**122, 123
  exploration **IV:**145
  foreign policy **IV:**158
  Fort Leavenworth **IV:**158
  fugitive slave laws **IV:**169
  Hoar, George F. **VI:**173
  Kansas-Nebraska Act **V:**221,
    222

Keokuk **IV:**213
Landon, Alfred M. **VIII:**209
Lease, Mary Elizabeth
  Clyens **VI:**220
Massachusetts Emigrant Aid
  Society **IV:**241, 242
migration **IV:**254
Native Americans **V:**278
popular sovereignty **IV:**304
public health **VII:**275
religion **X:**307
Republican Party **IV:**321,
  323
Rocky Mountain Fur
  Company **IV:**325
Simpson, Jerry **VI:**330
Singleton, Benjamin **V:**361
socialism **VII:**327
sod houses **VI:**337
Stuart, J. E. B. **V:**375
Kansas City, Kansas **IV:**242
Kansas City, Missouri
  Civil Rights Cases **VI:**72
  Irish Americans **VIII:**188
  jazz **VIII:**195
  Meat Inspection Act
    VII:198
  mothers' pensions **VII:**214
Kansas City jazz **VIII:**195, 250
Kansas Emigrant Aid Society of
  Northern Ohio **IV:**242
Kansas Freedmen's Aid
  Association **VI:**123
Kansas-Nebraska Act **IV:**415*c*;
  V:221–222, 443*c*
  abolitionism **V:**3
  Bell, John **V:**32
  Benton, Thomas Hart **IV:**54
  Bleeding Kansas **V:**37
  Bowles, Samuel **VI:**42
  Civil War **V:**73
  Davis, Jefferson **V:**104
  Democratic Party **IV:**118;
    V:109
  Douglas, Stephen A. **V:**114,
    115
  Forbes, John Murray
    VI:132
  Fort Laramie **IV:**158
  Greeley, Horace **V:**177
  Higginson, Thomas
    Wentworth **VI:**171
  jayhawkers **V:**211
  Massachusetts Emigrant Aid
    Society **IV:**241
  Missouri Compromise
    IV:257
  Pierce, Franklin **V:**307
  popular sovereignty **IV:**304
  Republican Party **IV:**321,
    322; **V:**332
  slavery **IV:**346
  Stephens, Alexander
    Hamilton **V:**371
  Sumner, Charles **V:**377
  Wade, Benjamin Franklin
    V:421

Kansas & Pacific Railroad **VI:**64, 76

Kansas Regulars **V:**44

Kansas State Board of Charities **VI:**220

Kansas v. Hendricks **X:**381*c*

Kant, Immanuel **II:**117; **VI:**120

Kaplan, Mordecai **VIII:**334–335

Karankawa Indians **I:**39

Karlsefni, Thorfinn Thordsson **I:**378, 395*c*

Karo, Joseph **I:**196, 197

Karzai, Hamid **X:**12

Kasavubu, Joseph **IX:**339

Käsebier, Gertrude **VII:***191*, 258

Kasserine Pass **VIII:**278, 431

Katipunan **IX:**256

Katzew, Ilona **I:**64

Kaufman, Arnold **IX:**260

Kaufman, George S. **VII:**124

Kaufman, Irving R. **IX:**280

KCIA (South Korean Central Intelligence Agency) **X:**199

KDKA radio (Pittsburgh, Pennsylvania) **VII:**408*c*

  entertainment, popular **VII:**97

  journalism **VII:**160

  popular culture **VII:**265

  radio **VII:**289

Keane, Thomas **II:**389

Kearns, Jack "Doc" **VII:**75

Kearny, Stephen Watts **IV:212**, *212*

  Armijo, Manuel **IV:**26

  Bent, Charles **IV:**52

  Bent, William **IV:**52

  Bent's Fort **IV:**55

  California **IV:**71

  Carson, Kit **IV:**82

  Fort Leavenworth **IV:**158

  Frémont, John C. **IV:**167

  Magoffin, James W. **IV:**233

  Mason, Richard B. **IV:**241

  Mexican-American War **IV:**252

  Santa Fe Trail **IV:**332

Kearny, USS **VIII:**142

Kearsarge, USS **V:**7

Keating, Charles **X:**321

Keating Five **X:**321

Keating-Owen Act **VII:163**, 406*c*, 407*c*

  Abbott, Grace **VII:**1

  child labor **VII:**52–53

  Democratic Party **VII:**74

  elections **VII:**91

  muckrakers **VII:**217

  New Freedom **VII:**236

  Wilson, Thomas Woodrow **VII:**384

Keaton, Buster **VII:**97

Keats, John **IX:**189

Keayne, Thomas **II:**405

keelboats **V:**262

Keeler, James E. **VI:**326

Keely, Michael **VI:**24

Keenan, Henry F. **VI:**225

Keene, Laura **V:**387

Keepler, Joseph **VI:**235

Kefauver, Estes **IX:**218

Kefauver-Harris Amendments (1962) **IX:**76

Kehew, Mary Morton **VII:**230

Kehoe, John **V:**248

Keira sultanate **I:**104

Keith, B. F. **VI:**117

Keith, William **II:191**

Keithean schism **II:**322

Kelley, Abigail. *See* Foster, Abigail Kelley

Kelley, Florence **VII:163–164**

  Addams, Jane **VII:**3

  Children's Bureau **VII:**53

  ERA **X:**123

  Goldmark, Josephine Clara **VII:**127

  Hamilton, Alice **VII:**133

  peace movements **VII:**256

  radicalism **VII:**288

  urban reform **VII:**363

Kelley, Oliver H. **VI:**278

Kelley, William D. **V:222–223**

Kellogg, Frank B.

  Carnegie Endowment for International Peace **VII:**49, 50

  foreign policy **VII:**114–115

  Kellogg-Briand Treaty **VII:**164

  peace movements **VII:**257

Kellogg, John Harvey **VI:**307

Kellogg, Paul **VII:**259

Kellogg, William P. **V:**412

Kellogg-Briand Treaty **VII:164–165**

  Carnegie Endowment for International Peace **VII:**49, 50

  Coolidge, Calvin John **VII:**65

  foreign policy **VII:**115, 116

  peace movements **VII:**257

  presidency **VII:**269

  WILPF **VII:**386

Kellor, Frances **VII:**13

Kelly, Clyde **VII:**165

Kelly, George "Machine Gun" **VIII:**130

Kelly, King **VI:**26

Kelly, Richard **X:**5

Kelly, William **VI:**34

Kelly Air Mail Act **VII:**28, 29, **165**, 409*c*

Kelo, Susette **X:**195

Kelo v. City of New London **X:195**

Kemal, Mustafa **VII:**370

Kemble, Fanny **VI:**132

Kemp, Jack F. **X:195–196**

Kemp, Robert **IV:**269

Kempei **VIII:**187

Kendall, Josias **II:**220

Kendall, Willmoore **IX:**74; **X:**49

Kendell, N. E. **VII:**103

Kendrick, Francis **IV:**23

Kennan, Georgĕ (1845–1924) **VI:**147

Kennan, George F. (1904–2005) **IX:167–168**, 351*c*

  Acheson, Dean **IX:**2

  cold war **IX:**63

  communism **IX:**68

  Europe **IX:**113

  "Sources of Soviet Conduct" **IX:363–366**

  White Paper **IX:**343

Kennebec River **II:**213

Kennedy, Adrienne **IX:**258

Kennedy, Anthony

  gun control **X:**162

  Hamdan v. Rumsfeld **X:**164

  Reagan, Ronald W. **X:**300

  Souter, David **X:**324

  Supreme Court **X:**339

Kennedy, Arabella **IX:**168

Kennedy, Caroline Bouvier **IX:**168, 171

Kennedy, Edward M. **X:196–197**

  Carter, James Earl, Jr. **X:**69

  immigration **X:**177

  Quayle, J. Danforth **X:**293

Kennedy, Ethel **IX:**172

Kennedy, Eunice **X:**323

Kennedy, Jacqueline **IX:***164, 168*, **168–169**

  assassinations **IX:**22

  fashion **IX:**117

  food **IX:**122

  Kennedy, John F. **IX:**171

Kennedy, John F., and administration **IX:***23, 112*, **169–171**, *170*, 354*c*–356*c*

  ABM Treaty **X:**26

  Acheson, Dean **IX:**2

  Africa **IX:**3–4

  Alliance for Progress **IX:**10, 11

  Arlington National Cemetery **V:**17

  arms race **IX:**17

  assassinations **IX:**22; **X:**34, 35

  Baruch, Bernard M. **VIII:**42

  Bay of Pigs **IX:**35, 36

  Berle, Adolf A., Jr. **VIII:**43

  Birmingham confrontation **IX:**40

  CAP **IX:**68

  CIA **IX:**52

  civil defense **IX:**57

  Civil Rights Act (1964) **IX:**60

  Civil War centennial **IX:**62

  cold war **IX:**64

  Cox, Archibald, Jr. **X:**95

  Cuban missile crisis **IX:**80–81

  defense budget **IX:**83–84

  Democratic Party **IX:**85

  domino theory **IX:**89

  economy **IX:**98

  education **IX:**99

  elections **IX:**103, 104

  elections, presidential **X:**116

  Engel v. Vitale **IX:**108

  ESEA **IX:**105–106

  Federal Housing Administration **IX:**120

  feminism **X:**132

  freedom rides **IX:**123, 124

  Galbraith, John Kenneth **IX:**129

  Goldwater, Barry **IX:**135

  Gonzáles, Rodolfo "Corky" **IX:**136

  government, state/local **IX:**137

  Graham, Billy **IX:**138

  Great Society **IX:**138, 139

  Harriman, W. Averell **VIII:**162

  Harrington, Michael **IX:**142

  Hershey, Lewis B. **VIII:**164

  Immigration Act (1965) **IX:**156

  Johnson, Lady Bird **IX:**162

  Johnson, Lyndon B. **IX:**163

  journalism **IX:**165

  Kennedy, Jacqueline **IX:**168–169

  Kennedy, Robert F. **IX:**171

  King, Martin Luther, Jr. **IX:**174

  Kissinger, Henry A. **X:**198

  Latin America **X:**205

  Lewis, John **IX:**190

  Limited Test Ban Treaty of 1963 **IX:**192

  Luce, Henry R. **VIII:**224

  March on Washington (1963) **IX:**201

  McGovern, George S. **X:**217

  Meredith, James **IX:**213

  Mitchell, John N. **X:**233

  Murray, Pauli **IX:**227

  NASA **IX:**231

  National Wilderness Preservation Act of 1964 **IX:**240

  NEA **IX:**234

  NEH **IX:**235

  New Deal **IX:**242

  New Frontier **IX:**242–243

  Nixon, Richard M. **X:**256

  NOW **IX:**236; **X:**247

  O'Neill, Thomas "Tip" P., Jr. **X:**267

  Operation Mongoose **IX:**250

  Oswald, Lee Harvey **IX:**252

  PCSW **IX:**262

  Peace Corps **IX:**255

  Powell, Adam Clayton **IX:**261

  race and race relations **IX:**269

Kennedy, John F., and
    administration (continued)
    religion **IX:**273
    Republican Party **IX:**274
    Roosevelt, Eleanor
        VIII:344
    SANE **IX:**283
    science and technology
        IX:285
    Shriver, Robert Sargent, Jr.
        X:323
    sit-ins **IX:**291
    Soviet Union **IX:**295
    space exploration **IX:**297
    Stevenson, Adali E. **IX:**302
    technology **IX:**312–313
    television **IX:**315, 316
    Vietnam War **IX:**330
    VISTA **IX:**332
    War on Poverty **IX:**335
    Warren, Earl **IX:**337
    Warren Court **IX:**337
    wars of national liberation
        IX:338, 339
    White, Byron R. **X:**369
    women's status and rights
        IX:346
Kennedy, John F., Jr. **IX:**168, 171
Kennedy, Joseph P., II **IX:**172
Kennedy, Joseph P., Sr. **VIII:199–
    200**
    Catholics **VIII:**63
    Irish Americans **VIII:**188
    Kennedy, John F. **IX:**169
    SEC **VIII:**357
Kennedy, Patrick Bouvier **IX:**168
Kennedy, Robert F. **IX:171–173,
    172**, 293, 354c, 357c
    assassinations **IX:**23; **X:**34
    Democratic Party **IX:**85
    elections **IX:**104
    freedom rides **IX:**124
    gun control **X:**161
    Kennedy, Jacqueline **IX:**168
    Kennedy, John F. **IX:**170
    King, Martin Luther, Jr.
        IX:174
    McCarthy, Eugene **IX:**206
    Model Cities program
        IX:221
    Operation Mongoose
        IX:250
    race and race relations
        X:295
    Teamsters Union **IX:**310
    union movement **IX:**323
    VISTA **IX:**332
    Weathermen/Weather
        Underground **IX:**341
    White, Byron R. **X:**369
Kennedy, Robert F., Jr. **IX:**172
Kennesaw Mountain, Battle of
    Atlanta campaign **V:**22
    Sherman, William T. **V:**355
    Thomas, George H. **V:**389
Kensett, John F. **VI:**275
Kensington, Pennsylvania **IV:**23

Kent, James **IV:**412c
Kent State University protests
    IX:332; **X:**28, **197**, 375c
Kentucky **II:**124; **III:**459c, 460c
    African Americans **III:**9
    agriculture **IV:**10; **V:**6
    Alamo, The **IV:**14
    American System **IV:**20
    Appalachia **IX:**15
    Blue Licks, Battle of **III:**54
    Boone, Daniel **III:**55–56
    Cherokee **III:**87
    Civil Rights Cases **VI:**72
    Clark, George Rogers
        III:95
    Clay, Henry **IV:**96
    Corinth, Battle of **V:**95
    Dragging Canoe **III:**139,
        140
    Fort Stanwix, Treaty of
        III:170
    Forty-niners **IV:**160
    governors **V:**172
    Harlan, John Marshall
        VI:159
    horse racing **VI:**178
    Know-Nothing Party **IV:**215
    Lovejoy, Elijah **IV:**230
    *McCreary County v. ACLU/
        Van Orden v. Perry*
        X:216
    McGuffey, William Holmes
        IV:246
    migration **IV:**253, 254
    Morgan, John Hunt **V:**268,
        269
    New Orleans, Battle of
        IV:280–281
    Nullification Controversy
        IV:282
    Orphan Brigade **V:**288
    panic of 1819 **IV:**293
    population trends **III:**343
    railroads **IV:**314
    religion **III:**362; **IV:**317
    Second Great Awakening
        IV:337
    Sherman, William T. **V:**354
    slave trade, internal **IV:**349
    suffrage **III:**401
    Taylor, Zachary **IV:**367
    temperance movement
        IV:369
    violence and lawlessness
        VI:375
    Wilderness Road **III:**442
Kentucky Derby **VI:**177
Kentucky Fried Chicken **IX:**98
Kentucky Resolutions. *See*
    Virginia and Kentucky
    Resolutions
Kentucky State Guard **V:**81
Kenya **I:**138, 217
Kenya embassy bombings. *See*
    embassy bombings
Keokuk **IV:**57, 58, **213**, *213*, 327
Keoua **IV:**211

Kepler, Johannes **I:**156
Kerik, Bernard **X:**168
Kern, Jerome **VII:**96, 219
Kerner, Otto **IX:**271
Kern-McGillicuddy Workmen's
    Compensation Act. *See*
    Workmen's Compensation Act
Kernstown, First Battle of **V:**163,
    350
Kernstown, Second Battle of
    V:351
kerosene **VI:**191, 271
Kerouac, Jack **IX:173**, 354c
    Beat Generation **IX:**36, 37
    counterculture **IX:**78
    Ginsberg, Allen **IX:**134
    Leary, Timothy **IX:**187
    literature **IX:**194
    religion **IX:**272
Kerr, Clark **IX:**126, 284
Kerr-Mills Act (1960) **IX:**209
Kerry, John **X:**384c
    Bush, George W. **X:**56
    campaign finance **X:**64
    elections, presidential **X:**118
Kesey, Ken
    Beat Generation **IX:**37
    literature **IX:**194
    LSD **IX:**196
Kesselring, Albert **VIII:**191, 360
Kettle Hill **VI:**412c
    Roosevelt, Theodore
        VII:304
    Rough Riders **VI:**317, 318
    Spanish-American War
        VI:341
Kevlar **IX:**91
Key, Francis Scott **IV:**43, 176,
    213–214
Keyes, Alan **X:**263
*Key into the Language of America,
    A* (Williams) **II:**417
keyless automobile entry **X:**320
Keynes, John Maynard **VIII:**445c
    CEA **IX:**77
    economy **IX:**96, 98
    fiscal policy **VIII:**139
    Great Society **IX:**139
    Keynesianism **VIII:**200
    Versailles, Treaty of **VII:**370
Keynesianism **VIII:200–201**
    antimonopoly **VIII:**24
    Democratic Party **VIII:**94
    Eccles, Marriner S.
        VIII:101
    economy **VIII:**104
    fiscal policy **VIII:**139
    Full Employment Bill
        VIII:145
    government **VIII:**154
    Great Depression **VIII:**159
    Henderson, Leon **VIII:**163
    Hopkins, Harry L. **VIII:**176
    liberalism **VIII:**215–216
    mobilization **VIII:**242
    Morgenthau, Henry T., Jr.
        VIII:244

New Deal **VIII:**269, 270
NRPB **VIII:**261
postwar planning **VIII:**306
PWA **VIII:**314
recession of 1937–1938
    VIII:324
taxation **VIII:**386–388
Third New Deal **VIII:**393
TNEC **VIII:**391
unemployment **VIII:**400
World War II **VIII:**428
World War II home front
    VIII:434
Keys, Donald **IX:**283
Keystone Bridge Company **VI:**62
Keystone Kops **VII:**96
Key to Uncle Tom's Cabin, A
    (Stowe) **V:**239, 374
Key West, Florida **V:**247
Key West Tales (Hersey)
    VIII:164
KFSG radio (Los Angeles,
    California) **VII:**197
KGB
    CIA **IX:**52
    espionage **VIII:**118
    intelligence **VIII:**186
Khalizad, Zalmay **X:**357
Khan, Abdul Q. **X:**262
khipu **I:**76, 179, **199–200**
Khmer Rouge **X:**141, 260, 377c
Khobar Towers, Saudi Arabia
    X:346
Khomeini, Ayatollah Ruhollah
    Carter, James Earl, Jr. **X:**69
    Iranian hostage crisis **X:**184,
        185
    Middle East **X:**228
Khrushchev, Nikita **IX:**355c
    Bay of Pigs **IX:**35
    cold war culture **IX:**65
    consumerism **IX:**75
    Cuban missile crisis **IX:**80,
        81
    Europe **IX:**113
    Kennedy, John F. **IX:**171
    Limited Test Ban Treaty of
        1963 **IX:**192
    Nixon, Richard M. **X:**256
    Soviet Union **IX:**295
    television **IX:**316
    wars of national liberation
        IX:338
Khubilai Khan **I:**294, 295
Kickapoo Indians
    Greenville, Treaty of
        III:200
    Native Americans **IV:**273
    Sac and Fox **IV:**327
Kid, The (film) **VII:**216
Kidd, William **II:**296, 312
Kieft, Willem
    Dutch-Indian Wars **II:**105
    New Netherland **II:**265
    New York **II:**270
Kifayat al-Muktaj (Baba) **I:**25
Kilby, Jack **X:**86, 317

Kildeer Mountain, Battle of **VI**:332

Kilkenny Statutes **I**:10

Killer Angels, The (Shaara) **V**:240

Kilrain, Jake **VI**:44

kilts **V**:399

Kimball, Heber C. **IV**:352

Kim Dong-Jo **X**:199

Kim Il Sung **X**:177

Kimmel, Husband E.
    King, Ernest J. **VIII**:202
    Navy, U.S. **VIII**:265
    Pearl Harbor **VIII**:292

Kincaid, Thomas C.
    King, Ernest J. **VIII**:202
    Leyte Gulf, Battle for **VIII**:214
    Nimitz, Chester W. **VIII**:274

kindergarten **VI**:207
    Peabody, Elizabeth Palmer **VI**:279, 280
    settlement houses **VI**:327
    White, Alfred Tredway **VI**:390
    Willard, Frances **VI**:394

Kindergarten Chats (Sullivan) **VI**:347

Kindred Spirits (Durand) **IV**:*28*, 29

Kinetoscope **VII**:214

King, Billie Jean **X**:302, 303

King, Clarence **VI**:**207–208**
    Adams, Henry **VI**:1
    Bierstadt, Albert **VI**:37
    Geological Survey, U.S. **VI**:141
    Hayden, Ferdinand Vandeveer **VI**:165
    La Farge, John Frederick Lewis Joseph **VI**:217
    Powell, John Wesley **VI**:288
    science and technology **VI**:325

King, Coretta Scott
    elections **IX**:103
    King, Martin Luther, Jr. **IX**:175
    March on Washington (1963) **IX**:201

King, David **X**:106

King, Dexter **IX**:175

King, Edward **V**:385; **VI**:327

King, Edwin **IX**:220, 302

King, Ernest J. **VIII**:*201*, **201– 202**
    Knox, Frank **VIII**:202
    Navy, U.S. **VIII**:265
    Solomon Islands **VIII**:365
    WAVES **VIII**:418

King, John **III**:295

King, MacKenzie. *See* King, W. L. MacKenzie

King, Martin Luther, Jr. **IX**:**173– 175**, *174*, 293, 353*c*–357*c*; **X**:378*c*
    African Americans **IX**:5
    Angelou, Maya **X**:26

assassinations **IX**:22, 23; **X**:34, 35
    Baker, Ella Josephine **IX**:33
    Birmingham confrontation **IX**:39
    Chávez, César Estrada **IX**:54
    civil disobedience **IX**:58
    Democratic Party **IX**:85
    elections **IX**:103, 104
    Fellowship of Reconciliation **VII**:109
    freedom rides **IX**:123
    gun control **X**:161
    Helms, Jesse A., Jr. **X**:165
    Hoover, J. Edgar **IX**:149– 150
    "I Have a Dream" Speech **IX**:**373–375**
    Jackson, Jesse, L. **X**:191
    Kennedy, Robert F. **IX**:172
    "Letter from Birmingham Jail" **IX**:**366–373**
    Lewis, John **IX**:190
    Malcolm X **IX**:199
    March on Washington (1963) **IX**:200, 201
    Meredith, James **IX**:213
    MFDP **IX**:222
    Muhammad, Elijah **IX**:227
    Parks, Rosa **IX**:254
    race and race relations **IX**:270; **X**:295
    Randolph, A. Philip **VIII**:321
    religion **IX**:272
    Robinson, Jackie **IX**:278
    SANE **IX**:283
    SCLC **IX**:292–294
    segregation **IX**:288
    sit-ins **IX**:291
    SNCC **IX**:303
    transcendental movement **IV**:379
    Voting Rights Act of 1965 **IX**:333

King, Mary **IX**:347

King, Rodney **X**:296, 380*c*

King, Rufus **III**:108, **245–246**; **IV**:411*c*

King, Stephen **X**:212

King, Thomas Starr **VI**:162

King, W. L. MacKenzie **VII**:14; **VIII**:446*c*

King Center (Atlanta, Georgia) **IX**:175

King Coal (Sinclair) **VII**:326

"King Cotton" **V**:308, 363

King Creole (film) **IX**:263

"Kingdom Coming" **V**:274

Kingdom of Matthias **V**:393

King Features Syndicate **VII**:138

King George's War **II**:**192**, 437*c*
    Franklin, William **III**:175
    Hutchinson, Thomas **III**:218
    Johnson, Sir William **II**:188

Massachusetts **II**:224
    New Hampshire **II**:260
    New York **II**:272
    privateering **II**:313

King Philip. *See* Metacom

King Philip's War **II**:**193**, 436*c*
    Massachusetts **II**:223
    Metacom **II**:232
    Native Americans **II**:253
    Pequot **II**:289
    Plymouth **II**:298
    Rhode Island **II**:332
    Rowlandson, Mary White **II**:337
    Wetamo **II**:411

King's Bridge, New York **III**:123

King's Chapel (Boston) **II**:163

King's College (Columbia University) **II**:**193–195**, *194*
    Anglican Church **II**:22; **III**:20
    De Lancey, James **II**:94
    Dutch Reformed Church **II**:107
    Hamilton, Alexander **III**:205
    Livingston, William **III**:271
    medicine **III**:295

King's Ferry, New York **III**:399

kingship **I**:234

Kingsley, Charles **VI**:335

King's Men **I**:334

King's Mountain, Battle of **III**:246*m*, **246–247**
    Cornwallis, Charles, Lord **III**:120
    Revolutionary War **III**:368
    Tarleton, Banastre **III**:407

Kingston, Jamaica **VII**:361

Kingston, Maxine Hong **X**:211

Kingston Trio **IX**:121, 259

King Street, Boston **III**:56

King William's War **II**:**195**, 436*c*
    monarchy, British **II**:240
    New Hampshire **II**:260
    New York **II**:272

Kinkel, Gottfried **VI**:324

Kinney, Abbot **VI**:199

Kino, Eusebio **II**:294; **IV**:75

Kinsey, Alfred C. **IX**:131, **175– 176**, *176*, 352*c*

kinship groups **II**:422

Kinyoun, Joseph J. **IX**:235

Kiowa Indians **VII**:404*c*
    Bent, Charles **IV**:51
    Bent's Fort **IV**:55
    Chouteau family **IV**:88
    Cody, William Frederick **VI**:75–76
    Lone Wolf v. Hitchcock **VII**:185
    Santa Fe Trail **IV**:330

Kirby-Smith, Edmund **V**:48

Kircher, Henry **V**:166

Kirchner, Christina Fernández de **X**:206

Kirchner, Nestor **X**:206

Kirina, battle of **I**:350

Kirk, George W. **V**:223

Kirk, Russell **X**:93

Kirkland, John T. **VI**:279

Kirkland, Lane **X**:201

Kirkpatrick, Evron **X**:252

Kirkpatrick, Jeane **X**:196, 357

Kirkuk, Iraq **X**:187

Kirtland, Jared Potter **VI**:164

Kirtland, Ohio
    Mormon Church **IV**:88, 89
    Mormon War **IV**:263
    Smith, Joseph, Jr. **IV**:352

Kirtland Anti-Banking Society Bank **IV**:88, 352

Kisale, Lake **I**:217

Kissinger, Henry A. **X**:**197–198**, *198*
    cold war, end of **X**:84
    defense policy **X**:100
    détente **X**:103
    Ford, Gerald R. **X**:138
    foreign policy **X**:140
    Haig, Alexander M., Jr. **X**:163
    Latin America **X**:206
    Middle East **X**:227, 228
    Nixon, Richard M. **X**:257
    SALT I/SALT II **X**:336
    Vietnam War **IX**:332
    Vietnam War, end of U.S. involvement **X**:361, 362

Kissinger Commission Report, The **X**:206

Kit Carson National Forest **IX**:317, 357*c*

"kitchen debate"
    cold war culture **IX**:65
    food **IX**:121
    Nixon, Richard M. **X**:256
    television **IX**:316

Kitt Chappell, Sally A. **I**:50

Kitty Hawk, North Carolina **VII**:28, 404*c*

Kitzmiller v. Dover Area School District **X**:307

kivas **I**:264; **II**:176

Kiwalo (Hawaiian ruler) **IV**:211

KKK. *See* Ku Klux Klan

KLA (Kosovo Liberation Army) **X**:199

Klamath Indians **IX**:241

Klaw, Mark **VI**:355

Klayman, Larry **X**:194

Klebold, Dylan **X**:382*c*

Kleindienst, Richard **X**:305

Klepp, Susan E. **II**:7

Klinghoffer, Leon **X**:345

Klinkenborg, Verlyn **I**:113

Klondike gold rush **VI**:**208–209**, *209*, 411*c*

Knapp, Louisa **VI**:235

Knickerbocker Club **VI**:219

Knickerbocker Magazine **IV**:210

Knickerbocker School **IV**:228

Knies, Karl **VI**:115

Knife River **I**:162

Knight, Daniel Ridgway **VI:**184
Knight, Sarah Kemble **II:195–196**, 225, 394
Knight, Tobias **II:**385
Knight Company **VI:**330
Knights of Labor **VI:209–210**, 408c, 409c
   AFL **VI:**13; **VII:**11
   class consciousness **VI:**73
   contract labor **VI:**82
   farmers' alliances **VI:**125
   immigration **V:**201
   immigration restrictions **VI:**187
   Internal Revenue taxes **VI:**194
   labor, radical **VI:**213
   labor, woman **VI:**215
   labor/labor movements **IV:**219
   labor organizations **VI:**215
   Lease, Mary Elizabeth Clyens **VI:**220
   Mitchell, John **VII:**211
   People's Party **VI:**282
   Powderly, Terence Vincent **VI:**287
   radicalism **VII:**286, 287
   Socialist Labor Party **VI:**337
   Socialist Party **VI:**337
   Willard, Frances **VI:**394
Knights of Saint Crispin **VI:**215
Knights of the Golden Circle
   Booth, John Wilkes **V:**38
   espionage **V:**135
   peace movements **V:**295
Knights of the Holy Cross **III:**349
Knolle, Henry **VII:**351
Knollys, Francis **I:**111
Knopf, Alfred **VII:**179
Knot, Richard **II:**384
Knowlton, Thomas **III:**204, 210
Know-Nothing Party **IV:**214, **214–215; V:**443c
   anti-Catholic riots **IV:**24
   Banks, Nathaniel P. **V:**28
   Democratic Party **IV:**118
   Fillmore, Millard **IV:**150
   Harlan, John Marshall **VI:**159
   Hicks, Thomas H. **V:**188
   Houston, Sam **IV:**192
   immigration **IV:**196
   nativism **V:**280; **VI:**263
   religion **IV:**319
   Republican Party **IV:**322; **V:**332
   Roman Catholicism **VI:**315
   Whigs **IV:**398
Knox, Frank **VIII:202–203**
   election of 1936 **VIII:**109
   Forrestal, James V. **VIII:**143
   Navy, U.S. **VIII:**265
   Republican Party **VIII:**337, 338

Knox, Henry **III:**247, **247–248**, 461c
   Cincinnati, Order of **III:**90
   Pickering, Timothy **III:**335
   U.S. Military Academy at West Point **V:**408
Knox, John **I:**54
Knox, Philander C. **VII:**79, 114
Knox, William Franklin **IX:**302
Knoxville, Tennessee **VIII:**392
Knoxville, Tennessee campaign **V:**253
Knoxville Whig **V:**68
Knox v. Lee **VI:**89
Knudsen, William S.
   dollar-a-year men **VIII:**96
   Hillman, Sidney **VIII:**166
   OPM **VIII:**283
Knyphausen, Wilhelm, Baron von **III:**62, **248**
Kodak **VI:**105, 410c; **VII:**258
Kodak box cameras **VI:**196
Kodak Brownie cameras **VI:**105; **VII:**258
Kodiak Island **II:**338; **III:**12
Kommandatura (Germany) **IX:**38
Kongo **I:200**, 337, 353
Konkomba **I:**103
Konoye, Fumimaro **VIII:**226
Konstam, Angus **I:**6, 277
Kopechne, Mary Jo **X:**196
Koran. *See* Qur'an
Korea **VII:**309, 320
Korea, Democratic People's Republic of (North Korea) **X:**380c, 383c
   Asia **IX:**21
   Clinton, William J. **X:**81
   cold war **IX:**63, 64
   communism **IX:**68
   foreign policy **X:**144
   Korean War **IX:**177, 178
   NATO **IX:**247
   nuclear proliferation **X:**262
   Rice, Condoleezza **X:**310
   Soviet Union **IX:**295
Korea, Republic of (South Korea) **X:**380c
   Asia **IX:**21
   Clinton, William J. **X:**81
   cold war **IX:**63, 64
   communism **IX:**68
   Habib, Philip C. **X:**163
   Koreagate **X:**199
   Korean War **IX:**177, 178
   NATO **IX:**247
   Soviet Union **IX:**295
   Truman, Harry S. **IX:**320
Koreagate **X:**193, **199**
Korean Americans **X:**33
Korean People's Army (North Korea) **IX:**177
Korean War **IX:177–179**, *178*, 352c, 353c
   Acheson, Dean **IX:**2
   aircraft industry **VIII:**14
   anticommunism **IX:**14

Arlington National Cemetery **V:**17
Asia **IX:**21
Asian-American movement **IX:**22
   aviation **IX:**29
   Bourke-White, Margaret **VIII:**50
   CIO **IX:**72
   cold war **IX:**63
   communism **IX:**68
   conscription, end of **X:**89
   defense budget **IX:**83
   demobilization (WWII) **VIII:**92
   Dennis v. U.S. **IX:**86
   Eisenhower, Dwight D. **IX:**100
   elections **IX:**103
   Goldwater, Barry **IX:**135
   Hershey, Lewis B. **VIII:**164
   MacArthur, Douglas **IX:**197, 198
   medicine **IX:**210, 211
   migration **IX:**215
   military-industrial complex **IX:**216
   Monroe, Marilyn **IX:222–223**
   NATO **IX:**247
   Progressive Party **IX:**264
   Rosenberg, Julius and Ethel **IX:**280
   science and technology **IX:**285
   SEATO **IX:**292
   Soviet Union **IX:**295
   Taft, Robert A. **VIII:**385
   technology **IX:**311
   Truman, Harry S. **IX:**320
   Truman Doctrine **IX:**322
   UMWA **VIII:**402
   UN **VIII:**403
   veterans **IX:**329
   White Paper **IX:**343
Korean War memorial **IX:**178–179, 330
Korematsu, Fred **VIII:**203
Korematsu v. United States **VIII:203**, 448c
   Asian Americans **VIII:**32
   Black, Hugo L. **VIII:**45
   civil liberties **VIII:**72
   Executive Order 9066 **VIII:**121
   Frankfurter, Felix **VIII:**144
   Japanese Americans, relocation of **VIII:**194
   Supreme Court **VIII:**384
Koresh, David **X:**46, 231
Kornfeld, Artie **X:**371
Kościuszko, Tadeusz **III:**217, **248–249**, *249*, 437, 461c
Kosovo **X:199–200**, 382c
   Clinton, William J. **X:**83
   Dayton accords **X:**99

   defense policy **X:**102
   House of Representatives **X:**170
Kosovo Liberation Army (KLA) **X:**199
Kossi (king of Songhai) **I:**342
Kotoko **I:200–201**
Koumbi-Saleh, Ghana **I:**140
Koyukon people **I:**260
Kraenzlein, Alfred **VI:**359
Kramer, Jack **VIII:**372
Krasner, Lee **IX:**19
Kremlin **IX:**248
Krimmel, John Lewis **IV:**29
Kristallnacht **VIII:**169
Kristol, Irving **X:**252
Kroc, Ray **IX:**122, 208
Kropotkin, Peter **VII:**287
KTBC radio (Austin, Texas) **IX:**162
Kuapoge pueblo **I:**326
Kubrick, Stanley
   movies **IX:**224
   popular culture **X:**279
   science fiction **IX:**287
Kuhn, Adam **II:**287
Kuhn, Justus Engelhardt **II:196**
Kuhn, Loeb, & Company **VI:**23, 251
Ku Klux Klan (KKK) **V:223–225**, *224*, 446c; **VII:165–167**, *166*, 406c; **VIII:**445c; **IX:**179, **179–180**, 356c
   anti-Semitism **VII:**17
   Birth of a Nation, The **VII:**37
   Black, Hugo L. **VIII:**45
   Byrnes, James F. **VIII:**60
   Communist Party **VII:**61
   Democratic Party **V:**110; **VII:**75
   elections **VII:**91
   Forrest, Nathan Bedford **V:**152, 153
   Garvey, Marcus **VII:**122
   Griffith, David Wark **VII:**131, 132
   Ku Klux Klan Act **V:**225
   lobbying **VII:**181
   lost cause, the **V:**245
   lynching **VI:**229
   Malcolm X **IX:**198
   movie industry **VII:**215
   nativism **VI:**264; **VII:**234
   race and race relations **IX:**269, 270; **X:**297
   Reconstruction **V:**326
   religion **VII:**299
   Republican Party **V:**334
   Rhinelander case **VII:**301
   sharecropping **V:**349
   Southern Manifesto **IX:**294
   Sweet trial **VII:**344
   Tarbell, Ida Minerva **VII:**349
   Tourgée, Albion W. **V:**389
   UNIA **VII:**361

Union League **V:**404
U.S. v. Cruikshank **V:**412
White Citizens' Councils
  IX:342
Ku Klux Klan Act (1871) **V:225;**
  VI:407*c*
    Elliot, Robert Brown **V:**127
    Enforcement Acts **V:**133
    Ku Klux Klan **V:**224–225
    redemption **V:**328
Ku Klux Klan cases **VI:210,** 222
Kukulcán **I:**236, 364
Kupperman, Karen Ordahl **I:**329
Kurile Islands **VIII:**440
Kurita, Takeo **VIII:**161, 214
Kursk, Soviet Union **VIII:**431
Kurtzman, Harvey **IX:**314
Kuwait **X:**379*c*
    Bush, George H. W. **X:**53
    Camp David accords **X:**65
    Cheney, Richard B. **X:**72
    Clinton, William J. **X:**81
    defense policy **X:**101
    Middle East **IX:**214; **X:**229
    NATO **X:**260
    OPEC **X:**267
    Persian Gulf War **X:**273
    UN **X:**355
Kwantung Army **VIII:**225
Kweskin, Jim **IX:**121
Kyoto Protocol **X:**383*c*
    Bush, George W. **X:**55
    global warming **X:**156
    Gore, Albert, Jr. **X:**157
    OPEC **X:**268
Kyoto Summit **X:**381*c*

L

Labbadie, Sylvestre **IV:**258
Labor (journal) **VII:**285
Labor, Bureau of **VII:**243
labor, child. *See* child labor
labor, contract. *See* contract labor
labor, free. *See* free labor
labor, radical **VI:***212,* **212–213.**
    See also labor: strikes and
    violence
Labor, U.S. Department of
  VIII:444*c*
    Adamson Act **VII:**2
    CCC **VIII:**71
    Children's Bureau **VII:**53
    Fair Labor Standards Act
      VIII:124
    Perkins, Frances **VIII:**293
    Pure Food and Drug Act
      VII:277
    Social Security Act
      VIII:364
    women's network **VIII:**421
    women's status and rights
      VIII:422
labor, woman **VI:214–215,** 217
Labor Advisory Board **VIII:**97,
  165

labor and labor movements
  II:197–200, *200;* **III:***251,* **251–**
  253; IV:217–220; VI:215–216,
  408*c;* **VII:169–172,** *170, 171,*
  406*c;* **VIII:205–208,** *206,* 445*c,*
  447*c;* **IX:181–183; X:201–204,**
  202, 203*t,* 381*c. See also* labor
  unions
    abolitionism **II:**1
    AFL **VI:**13; **VII:**11–12;
      VIII:18
    African Americans **II:**6–7;
      IV:8; **VIII:**3
    agriculture **II:**12–13; **VII:**8
    Algonquin **II:**18
    Amalgamated Clothing
      Workers of America
      (ACW) **VIII:**16
    America First Committee
      VIII:17
    American Plan **VII:**14
    anticommunism **VIII:**22
    antilynching legislation
      VIII:23
    antimonopoly **VIII:**23
    artisans **III:**35–36
    Asian Americans **VIII:**32
    Atkinson, Edward **VI:**22
    automobile industry **VII:**27;
      VIII:36
    baby boomers **X:**39
    Baldwin, Roger Nash
      VII:31
    braceros **IX:**42–43
    Brandeis, Louis Dembitz
      VII:41
    Bridges, Harry **VIII:**53
    Brotherhood of Sleeping Car
      Porters **VIII:**54
    Buck's Stove **VII:**42–43
    business **VIII:**57–59
    Byrnes, James F. **VIII:**60
    camp followers **III:**77
    Caribbean **II:**59
    Carnegie, Andrew **VI:**62
    Chesapeake Bay **II:**66
    childhood **II:**66
    child labor **VII:**51–53
    children **VIII:**67
    CIO **IX:**71, 72
    cities and urban life **III:**92;
      VIII:68
    civil liberties **VII:**58;
      VIII:71
    class **II:**70
    class consciousness **VI:**73–
      74
    Clayton Antitrust Act
      VII:59
    Cleveland, Grover **VI:**75
    Clinton, William J. **X:**81
    Coeur d'Alene miners' strike
      VI:77
    Committee for Public
      Information **VII:**60
    Communist Party **VII:**61
    Congress **VIII:**80

    conservatism **VIII:**83
    convict labor **II:**79–80
    Coolidge, Calvin John
      VII:64
    cotton **III:**122–123
    crowd actions **II:**86
    Dale, Sir Thomas **II:**89
    Danbury Hatters **VII:**69
    Debs, Eugene Victor
      VII:73
    Democratic Party **VII:**75;
      VIII:93
    domesticity **II:**100
    Dubinsky, David **VIII:**97
    Economic Opportunity Act
      (1964) **IX:**95
    economy **II:**109, 110;
      IV:131, 132; **VIII:**104
    election of 1936 **VIII:**109,
      110
    election of 1944 **VIII:**111
    ERA **X:**123
    Fair Labor Standards Act
      VIII:124
    FAP **VIII:**129
    FBI **VIII:**130
    Federal Farm Loan Act
      VII:106
    Fellowship of Reconciliation
      VII:109
    Flynn, Elizabeth Gurley
      VII:109–110
    Ford, Henry **VII:**112
    Foster, William Zebulon
      VII:116–117
    free speech fights **VII:**117–
      118
    Free Trade and Sailor's
      Rights **IV:**165
    Frick, Henry Clay **VI:**135,
      136
    FSA **VIII:**127
    Fuel Administration
      VII:119
    Full Employment Bill
      VIII:145
    Garner, John Nance
      VIII:147
    Gastonia Strike **VII:**122
    gender **II:**144
    Gompers, Samuel **VI:**150–
      151
    Great Depression **VIII:**157
    Great Strike of 1877
      VI:152–154
    Greenwich Village **VII:**130,
      131
    Griffith, David Wark
      VII:132
    Guthrie, Woody **VIII:**160
    Haymarket riot **VI:**168–169
    Haywood, William Dudley
      VII:137
    Hearst, William Randolph
      VII:138
    Higgins, Andrew J.
      VIII:165

    Hillman, Sidney **VIII:**165–
      166
    Homestead Strike **VI:**175–
      176
    Hoover, Herbert C.
      VIII:172
    Hoover presidency
      VIII:174
    Ickes, Harold L. **VIII:**183
    ILGWU **VII:**148–149
    immigration **VI:**186;
      VIII:184
    immigration restrictions
      VI:187
    indentured servitude
      II:173–175
    industrialization **IV:**201
    Industrial Relations
      Commission **VII:**145–
      146
    Industrial Revolution,
      Second **VI:**190–192
    Irish Americans **VIII:**188,
      189
    iron manufacturing **II:**178
    Italian Americans **VIII:**190
    IWW **VII:**146–147, 417
    Jews **VIII:**195
    Johnson, Hiram Warren
      VII:154
    Johnson, Hugh S. **VIII:**196
    journalism **VII:**160
    Kaiser, Henry J. **VIII:**199
    Keating-Owen Act **VII:**163
    Kelley, Florence **VII:**164
    Knights of Labor **VI:**209–
      210
    labor, radical **VI:**213
    labor, woman **VI:**215
    "Labor Movement Is a
      Fixed Fact" (Gompers)
      VI:428–430
    La Follette, Robert M., Jr.
      VIII:208
    La Guardia, Fiorello
      VIII:209
    Lawrence Strike **VII:**173–
      174
    Lewis, John L. **VIII:**212–
      213
    liberalism **VIII:**215; **IX:**191
    literature **VIII:**218
    Lloyd, Henry Demarest
      VI:227
    Locke, John **II:**208–209
    manufacturing and industry
      II:214
    Mexican immigration
      VII:202–203
    Mexican Revolution
      VII:204, 205
    migration **VII:**206;
      VIII:240; **IX:**215
    mining **VII:**208–210
    Mitchell, John **VII:**211
    mobilization **VIII:**242
    Mondale, Walter F. **X:**233

labor and labor movements
(*continued*)
    Mooney-Billings case
        VII:213
    Murray, Philip **VIII:**248–
        249
    NAM **VII:**225–226
    National Civic Federation
        VII:226
    National Recovery
        Administration **VIII:**259
    nativism **VII:**234
    New Deal **VIII:**268–270
    New Unionism **VII:**237–
        238
    New Woman **VII:**240
    New York **II:**270
    NIRA **VIII:**256–257
    NLRA **VIII:**257–258
    NLRB **VIII:**258–259
    Norris, George W. **VIII:**276
    Norris–La Guardia Act
        VIII:277
    NWLB **VII:**229–230;
        VIII:261–262
    NWTUL **VII:**230, 231
    Omaha platform **VI:**272
    open shop movement
        VII:247
    OPM **VIII:**283
    Owen, Robert **IV:**291
    OWMR **VIII:**287
    Palmer, Alexander Mitchell
        VII:249
    panic of 1837 **IV:**295
    Passaic Strike **VII:**252–253
    Paterson Strike **VII:**253–
        254
    PCSW **IX:**262
    Perkins, Frances **VIII:**293
    Philadelphia **II:**292
    Phillips, Wendell **IV:**299
    plantation system **II:**297–
        298
    politics (1900–1928)
        VII:262
    politics (Roosevelt era)
        VIII:300
    popular culture **III:**340–341
    Powderly, Terence Vincent
        VI:287
    presidency **VII:**268
    prisons **III:**347
    professional organizations,
        rise of **VI:**293
    Progressive Party **VII:**270
    Protestant work ethic
        II:316–317
    Pure Food and Drug Act
        VII:277
    radical and labor press
        VII:284–286
    radicalism **VII:**287–288
    Railroad Shopmen's Strike
        VII:291–292
    Randolph, A. Philip
        VIII:321

    recession of 1937–1938
        VIII:324
    reconversion **VIII:**326
    redemptioners **II:**327
    Red Scare **VII:**296
    religion **VIII:**334
    Republican Party **VIII:**337
    Reuther, Walter **VIII:**339
    Rodney, Caesar Augustus
        III:373
    Roosevelt, Franklin D.
        VIII:345
    Sacco and Vanzetti **VII:**311
    Sanger, Margaret **VII:**312
    scientific management
        VII:316
    Seattle General Strike
        VII:105, 317–318
    service sector **IX:**288–289
    shipbuilding **VIII:**359
    Shirtwaist Makers Strike
        VII:324
    Sinclair, Upton **VII:**325
    slavery **II:**354
    socialism **VI:**336; **VII:**327
    Socialist Labor Party
        VI:336–337
    socialists **VIII:**362
    society, British American
        II:365, 366
    Spanish colonies **II:**371
    Standard Oil **VII:**336
    steel industry **VII:**337;
        VIII:373, 374
    Steel Strike of 1919
        VII:338–339
    strikes **VIII:**377, 378
    Sumner, William Graham
        VI:349
    Sunday, William Ashley, Jr.
        VII:342
    Supreme Court **VII:**343
    Taft, William Howard
        VII:347
    technology **II:**385
    temperance movement
        III:410
    Third New Deal **VIII:**393
    Thomas, Norman **VIII:**394
    Townsend, Francis E.
        VIII:394
    Triangle Shirtwaist Fire
        VII:356–357
    Tugwell, Rexford G.
        VIII:397
    UMWA **VII:**359–360;
        VIII:401–402
    U.S. Steel **VII:**365–366
    Valesh, Eva McDonald
        VII:367
    veterans **VII:**373
    Vorse, Mary Heaton
        VII:375
    wage and price controls
        II:405; **VIII:**409
    Wagner, Robert F. **VIII:**410
    Wald, Lillian **VII:**377

    War Manpower Commission
        VIII:413
    War Production Board
        VIII:414
    welfare capitalism **VII:**380–
        381
    WFM **VII:**381–382
    women's status and rights
        VII:387
    Woodhull, Victoria **VI:**401
    workers' compensation
        VII:391–392
    Workmen's Compensation
        Act **VII:**392
    World War II **VIII:**428
    World War II home front
        VIII:432
labor contracts **V:**35, 349
Labor Day **VII:**217
Labor Management Relations Act
    of 1947. *See* Taft-Hartley Act
Labor Movement in America (Ely)
    VI:115
"Labor Movement Is a Fixed Fact,
    The" (Gompers) **VI:428–430**
labor organizations. *See* labor
    unions
labor press. *See* radical and labor
    press
Labor Reform Party **VI:**215
labor shortages **VIII:**447*c*
Labor's New Millions (Vorse)
    VII:375
Labor's Non-Partisan League
    VII:241
    CIO **VIII:**82
    Farmer-Labor Party
        VII:105
    Hillman, Sidney **VIII:**166
    labor/labor movements
        VIII:207
    Lewis, John L. **VIII:**213
    politics (1900–1928)
        VII:262
    socialism **VII:**327
Labor Standards, U.S. Division of
    VII:133
Labor Statistics, Bureau of (BLS)
    IX:76, 77
labor: strikes and violence **V:374–
    375; VI:213–214,** *214,* 408*c,*
    411*c;* **VII:**405*c,* 407*c*–409*c;*
    VIII:377, **377, 377–378,** 444*c,* 445*c,*
    448*c;* **IX:**352*c. See also specific
    strikes, e.g.:* Anthracite Coal
    Strike
    AFL **VI:**13; **VII:**11, 12
    Amalgamated Clothing
        Workers of America
        (ACW) **VIII:**16
    automobile industry
        VIII:36
    Chávez, César Estrada
        IX:53, 54
    CIO **VIII:**82; **IX:**71, 72
    coal industry **VIII:**75, 76
    Congress **VIII:**80

    conservatism **VIII:**85
    conservative coalition
        VIII:86
    Debs, Eugene Victor
        VII:72–73
    Democratic Party **VII:**75
    Dubinsky, David **VIII:**97
    employment **V:**132, 133
    Free Trade and Sailor's
        Rights **IV:**165
    Frick, Henry Clay **VI:**135–
        136
    Gompers, Samuel **VI:**150–
        151
    Great Strike of 1877
        VI:152–154
    Greeley, Horace **V:**176
    Haymarket riot **VI:**168–169
    Hispanic Americans **X:**166
    Homestead Strike **VI:**175–
        176
    ILGWU **VII:**149; **VIII:**187
    Industrial Relations
        Commission **VII:**145,
        146
    IWW **VII:**146, 147
    King, Martin Luther, Jr.
        IX:175
    Knights of Labor **VI:**209–
        210
    labor/labor movements
        III:252; **VII:**169–172;
        VIII:205, 207; **X:**201, 202
    Lewis, John L. **VIII:**213
    Ludlow Massacre **VII:**186–
        187
    Murray, Philip **VIII:**249
    NLRB **VIII:**259
    Norris–La Guardia Act
        VIII:277
    NWLB **VIII:**261, 262
    Powderly, Terence Vincent
        VI:287
    Pullman Strike **VI:**297–298
    radicalism **VII:**287
    railroads **VI:**301
    Red Scare **VII:**296
    Reuther, Walter **VIII:**339;
        IX:275
    Scott, Thomas Alexander
        VI:326
    socialists **VIII:**362
    steel industry **VIII:**373;
        IX:300
    Taft-Hartley Act **IX:**309
    Teamsters Union **IX:**310
    UFW **IX:**324, 325
    UMWA **VIII:**402
    union movement **IX:**323
    War Manpower Commission
        VIII:413
    WFM **VII:**381, 382
Labor Temple, New York City
    VII:297
labor trends **VI:216–217**
labor unions **VI:215–216;**
    VII:404*c,* 406*c,* 407*c,* 409*c;*

VIII:445c; **IX:323–324,**
351c. *See also* labor and labor
movements
Adamson Act **VII:**1–2
AFL **VII:**11–12; **IX:**11–12
agriculture **X:**19–20
American Plan **VII:**14
Anthracite Coal Strike
VII:15
automobile industry **IX:**26
business **IX:**47
campaign finance **X:**63
Chávez, César Estrada
IX:53–54
CIO **VIII:**81–82; **IX:**71–72
cities and urban life **VIII:**68
class consciousness **VI:**73–
74
Cleveland, Grover **VI:**75
coal industry **VIII:**75–76
Colored National Labor
Union **V:**77
Communists **VIII:**78
crime and punishment **X:**97
Danbury Hatters **VII:**69
Democratic Party **VII:**74
economy **X:**108
employment **V:**133
Employment Act of 1946
IX:107
ERA **VII:**100
immigration **V:**201; **X:**176
Industrial Relations
Commission **VII:**145–146
labor, radical **VI:**213
labor, woman **VI:**215
labor/labor movements
IX:182; **X:**201–204
lobbying **VII:**181
Murray, Philip **VIII:**249
NAFTA **X:**259
National Labor Union
V:276
NLRA **VIII:**257, 258
NLRB **VIII:**258–259
Norris–La Guardia Act
VIII:277
NWLB **VIII:**261–262
Operation Dixie **IX:**249–
250
PACs **X:**275
Perkins, Frances **VIII:**293
Polish Americans **VIII:**297
Progressive Party **IX:**264
radicalism **VII:**287
Randolph, A. Philip
VIII:321
Red Scare **VII:**296
Reuther, Walter **VIII:**339;
IX:275
Rosie the Riveter **VIII:**347
service sector **IX:**289
Stanton, Elizabeth Cady
V:370
steel industry **VIII:**373, 374;
IX:300
strikes **V:**374, 375; **VIII:**377

Taft-Hartley Act **IX:**309
Teamsters Union **IX:**310
UFW **IX:**324–325
Wagner, Robert F. **VIII:**410
women's status and rights
IX:347
World War II **VIII:**428
World War II home front
VIII:434
Labrador **I:**77
Lackawanna Coal and Iron
Company **VI:**214
Laclède, Pierre **IV:**87
Ladder, The (journal) **IX:**131
La Demoiselle (Miami leader)
II:201
ladies aid societies **V:227–228,** 411
Ladies Aid Society of Philadelphia
V:228
Ladies' Album **IV:**183
Ladies' Garment Worker **VII:**149
Ladies' Home Journal
advertising **VI:**2
illustration, photography, and
graphic arts **VI:**183, 184
journalism **VII:**159
magazines **VI:**235, 236
suburbanization/suburbs
VIII:380
Ladies' Magazine **IV:**183
Ladies Memorial Associations
V:229
Hollywood Cemetery **V:**192
lost cause, the **V:**244
Ladies Professional Golf
Association (LPGA) **X:**303
"Ladies Repository" (Chandler)
IV:147
LaDuke, Winona **X:**159
Lady, Be Good (Gershwin) **VII:**124
Lady at a Tea Table (Cassatt)
VI:64
Lady Chatterley's Lover
(Lawrence) **VIII:**65
*Ladye Annabel, The; or, The
Doom of the Poisoner* (Lippard)
IV:227
Lady's Book **IV:**184
LaFarge, John (Jesuit priest)
VIII:64
La Farge, John Frederick Lewis
Joseph (artist and writer)
VI:217–218
Adams, Henry **VI:**1
Aesthetic movement **VI:**3
painting **VI:**275
Richardson, Henry Hobson
VI:313
Lafayette, Marie-Joseph-Paul-
Yves-Roch-Gilbert de Motier,
marquis de **III:**253, **253–254,**
462c
Barry, John **III:**47
Carey, Mathew **III:**80
French Revolution **III:**178
Kalb, Johann, baron de
III:245

Monmouth, Battle of
III:299–300
Pushmataha **IV:**308
Washington, George
III:432
Wright, Fanny **IV:**405
Yorktown, surrender at
III:454
Lafayette College (Pennsylvania)
VI:85
Lafayette Square (Washington,
D.C.) **VI:**193
Laffer, Arthur Betz **X:**204
Laffer curve **X:204**
Lafitte, Jean **IV:**63, **220,** 281
La Flesche, Susette. *See* Bright
Eyes
La Follette, Philip **VIII:**217
La Follette, Robert M. **VII:172–
173,** 408c
Congress **VII:**62
Coolidge, Calvin John
VII:64
Democratic Party **VII:**74
elections **VII:**91, 92
elections, presidential **X:**116
Ely, Richard Theodore
VI:115
politics (1900–1928)
VII:261, 262
Progressive Party **VII:**269,
270
progressivism **VII:**271
Republican Party **VII:**300
Seattle General Strike
VII:105
Taft, William Howard
VII:347–348
La Follette, Robert M., Jr.
VIII:208
America First Committee
VIII:17
Congress **VIII:**79
isolationists **VIII:**189
McCarthy, Joseph R. **IX:**206
relief **VIII:**331
Republican Party **VIII:**336
Wheeler, Burton K.
VIII:416
La Follette, Suzanne **VII:**388
La Guardia, Fiorello **VIII:208–
209,** 444c
antimonopoly **VIII:**23
Berle, Adolf A., Jr. **VIII:**43
Italian Americans **VIII:**190
March on Washington
Movement **VIII:**228
Norris–La Guardia Act
VIII:277
OCD **VIII:**281
taxation **VIII:**387
Tugwell, Rexford G.
VIII:398
La Guardia Airport (New York)
VIII:314, 395
LaHaye, Tim **X:**212
Laird, Melvin **X:**89

Laird & Sons **V:**7
laissez-faire economics
business and government
VI:56
Field, Stephen Johnson
VI:126, 127
Lochner v. New York
VII:182
Ward, Lester Frank **VI:**382,
383
Lake Lucerne (Bierstadt) **VI:**37
Lake of the Woods **IV:**286, 394
Lake Plains **IV:**254
Lake Shore Drive (Chicago,
Illinois) **VIII:**395
Lakota Indians **II:**166; **IV:**276;
VI:86
L.A. Law **X:**343
Laman, Gary **X:**320
Lamar, Mirabeau B. **IV:**191,
221–222, 372
Lamarck, Jean-Baptiste **IV:**37;
VI:122
Lamb, William **VI:**125
Lamon, Ward Hill **V:**20
LaMountain, John **V:**25
L'Amour, Louis **X:**212
Lamy, Jean Baptiste **IV:222**
Lancaster, Burt **IX:**193
Lancaster, Pennsylvania **III:**413;
VI:65
Lancaster State Industrial
School for Girls (Lancaster,
Massachusetts) **VIII:**95
land **II:201–202; IV:**412c
agriculture **II:**12
Dawes Severalty Act
VI:93–94
Florida **III:**167
Fort Stanwix, Treaty of
III:170
Franklin, state of **III:**175
Native Americans **II:**252;
VI:261–263
New Netherland **II:**264
New York **II:**270
Nez Perce War **VI:**267
Ohio Company of Virginia
III:323
plantation system **II:**297
society, British American
II:367
tenants **II:**386–387
Yazoo claims **III:**454
Landa, Diego de **I:**390
Land Act (1796) **IV:**304–305
Land Act (1800) **IV:**184, 305
Land Act (1820) **IV:**305, 412c
Land Act (1841) **IV:**414c
Land Act (1851) **IV:**306
land allotment **VII:**185; **VIII:**263,
264
land banks
banking **II:**33
Massachusetts **II:**224
Wigglesworth, Edward
II:414

Lander, Frederick West **VI**:37
land-grant colleges
  agriculture **V**:6
  Congress **V**:89
  education **V**:125
  education, federal aid to
    VI:110
  education, higher **VI**:111
  education, philanthropy and
    VI:112
  Morrill Land-Grant Act
    V:269–270
land grants **V**:444c
  Bosomworth, Mary
    Musgrove **II**:40–41
  Brent, Margaret Reed **II**:47
  business and government
    VI:56
  carpetbaggers **V**:56
  Freedmen's Bureau **V**:161
  French colonies **II**:136
  hacienda **I**:149
  headright **I**:158
  land **II**:201
  Montreal **II**:242
  Rensselaerswyck **II**:331
  Special Field Order No. 15
    V:365–366
  Van Rensselaer, Maria Van
    Cortlandt **II**:397
  veterans **V**:416
Landis, James M. **VIII**:357
Landis, John **VIII**:281–282
Landis, Kenesaw Mountain
  VII:33, 334
Land Law. *See* Land Act
Land League **V**:201
Land Management, Bureau of
  IX:239
land mines **V**:341, 380
Landon, Alfred M. **VIII:209**,
  445c
  American Liberty League
    VIII:19
  Borah, William E. **VIII**:50
  conservatism **VIII**:84
  election of 1936 **VIII**:109
  Farley, James A. **VIII**:125
  Gallup Poll **IX**:130
  Hoover, Herbert C.
    VIII:172
  Knox, Frank **VIII**:202
  politics (Roosevelt era)
    VIII:298, 299
  Republican Party **VIII**:337
  Townsend, Francis E.
    VIII:395
  Willkie, Wendell L.
    VIII:417
Land Ordinance. *See* Ordinance
  of 1785
land redistribution **V**:160, 161,
  312
land reform **VII**:261
land rights claims **X**:21, 250
land riots **II:202**; **III:254–255**
  riots **III**:371

Shays's Rebellion **III**:388
Wyoming Valley Wars
  III:450
Landrum, Phil **IX**:95
Landrum-Griffin Act
  labor/labor movements
    IX:182
  NLRB **VIII**:259
  union movement **IX**:323
land rushes **VI**:410c
landscape architecture **V**:288
landscape painting **V**:18
land speculation
  Altgeld, John Peter **VI**:12
  banks **III**:42
  Bingham, William **III**:51
  Boone, Daniel **III**:56
  Canada **III**:77
  frontier, the **III**:182
  Gallatin, Albert **III**:187
  Homestead Act **V**:195
  homesteading **VI**:175
  Morris, Robert **III**:306
  Ohio Company of Associates
    III:323
Lane, Fitz Hugh **VI**:275
Lane, Franklin **VII**:228
Lane, Henry S. **V**:270
Lane, James Henry **V**:4, 211
Lane, Ralph **I:203**; **II**:417
  Drake, Sir Francis **I**:112
  Grenville, Sir Richard **I**:145
  Roanoke **I**:321
Lane Theological Seminary
  (Cincinnati, Ohio) **IV**:15, 396
Lang, Michael **X**:371
Langdon, F. W. **VI**:248
Lange, Dorothea **VIII:209–210**,
  210, 445c
  art and architecture **VIII**:30
  dust bowl **VIII**:98
  photography **VII**:258;
    VIII:296
Langley, Samuel P. **VI**:326
Langley, USS **VIII**:11
Langley Act (1921) **VII**:276
Langmuir, Irving **VII**:123
Langston, John Mercer **V**:142;
  VI:218–219
Lanham, Fritz G. **VIII**:179
Lanham Defense Housing Act
  VIII:179
Lanier, Sydney **VI**:226
Lansdale, Edward G. **IX**:250
L'Anse aux Meadows **I:203–204**,
  395c
Lansing, Robert **VII**:407c
Lansing-Ishii Agreement
  VII:407c
Laos **X**:377c
  Asian Americans **X**:33
  cold war, end of **X**:84
  SEATO **IX**:291
  Vietnam War, end of U.S.
    involvement **X**:361
  wars of national liberation
    IX:338–339

Laotians **X**:33
La Petite Democrate **III**:191
Lapham, Increase A. **IV**:335;
  VI:387
Lapowinsa **II**:406
Lapu Lapu (king of Mactan
  Island) **I**:224
Laramie River **IV**:156
La Raza Unida **IX:183**, 186;
  X:166
Lardner, Ring, Jr. **IX**:147, *148*
Laredo, Texas **IV**:371
Largent, Steve **X**:215
Larkin, Thomas Oliver **IV**:49, 71,
  222–223
La Roche, Mesgouez de **II**:135
Larry King Live **X**:273
Larsen, Nella **VII**:136, 181
Larson, Jonathan **X**:281
Lasalle, Ferdinand **VI**:212
La Salle, René-Robert Cavelier,
  sieur de **II:202–203**, 436c
  exploration **II**:123
  French colonies **II**:137
  Louisiana **II**:210
  Texas **IV**:371
*La Salle and the Discovery of the
  Great West* (Parkman) **VI**:242
Las Casas, Bartolomé de **I:204–
  208**, 397c; **X**:101
  black legend **I**:31–32
  Canary Islands **I**:57
  Charles V **I**:70
  Cuba **I**:101
  Dominicans **I**:110
  Ferdinand and Isabella **I**:128
  Requerimiento **I**:319
  Sepúlveda, Juan Ginés de
    I:330, 331
  smallpox **I**:341
  Vitoria, Francisco de **I**:379
Las Casas, Pedro **I**:205
lasers **X**:28, 317
Las Gorras Blancas **VI**:376
Las Guasimas, Battle of **VI**:317
Lasker, Albert **VII**:4, 360–361
Lassalleans
  socialism **VI**:336
  Socialist Labor Party **VI**:336
  Socialist Party **VI**:337
"Last Fight of the Revenge, The"
  (Tennyson) **I**:145
Last of the Mohicans, The
  (Cooper) **IV**:228, 412c
*Last Rambles Amongst the Indians
  of the Rocky Mountains and the
  Andes* **IV**:85
Last Valley, The - Paradise Rocks
  (La Farge) **VI**:217
Las Vegas, Nevada **IV**:120; **IX**:319
"latch-key" children **VIII**:231
latent classicism **X**:31
Lateran Council, Fifth **I**:98
Lathrop, Julia
  Abbott, Grace **VII**:1
  Children's Bureau **VII**:53, 54
  social work **VII**:330

Latin America **II**:374; **VII**:404c,
  409c; **VIII**:443c; **IX:183–184**,
  354c; **X:204–207**, *205*
  Alliance for Progress **IX**:10,
    11
  Berle, Adolf A., Jr. **VIII**:43
  Big Stick diplomacy
    VII:35–36
  Blaine, James Gillespie
    VI:41
  Bush, George W. **X**:56
  castas **I**:64–65
  Clark Memorandum
    VII:58–59
  dollar diplomacy **VII**:79
  FCC **VIII**:131
  foreign policy **V**:149;
    VII:113, 114, 116;
    VIII:140–141; **X**:144
  Good Neighbor policy
    VIII:151–152
  hacienda **I**:149
  Hoover presidency
    VIII:174
  Hull, Cordell **VIII**:180
  immigration **IX**:155
  Immigration Act (1965)
    IX:156
  investments, foreign
    VII:151
  Kennedy, John F. **IX**:170
  Leahy, William D. **VIII**:210
  Lindbergh, Charles
    Augustus **VII**:178
  mestizaje **I**:241
  mining **VII**:210
  nativism **VII**:233
  Nicaragua **X**:254
  Ostend Manifesto **V**:289
  Pan-American Union
    VI:276
  Peace Corps **IX**:255
  Point Four Program
    IX:257
  population trends **IX**:260
  presidency **VII**:268
  Puerto Ricans **IX**:267
  religion **IX**:272
  trade, domestic and foreign
    VII:354
  wars of national liberation
    IX:338, 339
  Welles, Sumner **VIII**:415
Latino movement **IX**:110, **185–
  186**, 350
Latinos
  suburbanization/suburbs
    IX:305
  veterans **IX**:329
  Vietnam War **IX**:331
latitude **I**:15
Latrobe, Benjamin Henry **III**:29,
  280–281
Lattimer massacre **VI**:73, 214
Latvia **X**:384c
  cold war **IX**:63
  Europe **IX**:112

Teheran Conference **VIII:**390

Versailles, Treaty of **VII:**370

Laudonnière, René de **I:208–209**

Caroline, Fort **I:**61

Le Moyne, Jacques **I:**209

Thevet, André **I:**358

Timucua **I:**360

Laughlin, Harry **VII:**43, 102

Laughlin, Ledlie **II:**291

laundresses **V:**285, 286, 374, 375

Lauren, John **III:**141

Laurence, E. O. **VIII:**352

Laurens, Henry **II:**231; **III:255–256**

dueling **III:**140

Franklin, Benjamin **III:**174

Jay, John **III:**229

Paris, Treaty of (1783) **III:**331, 332

Lausanne (vessel) **IV:**224

Lauste, Eugene **VII:**214

Lau v. Nichols **X:**42

La Vengeance **III:**353

La Venta **I:**278, 279

La Vérendrye, Pierre de **II:**123

Lavoisier, Antoine Laurent **III:**17

Law, Richard **III:**2

"law and order" **IX:**79

Lawrence, Amos A. **IV:**242

Lawrence, Charles **II:**2

Lawrence, D. H.

censorship **VIII:**65

James, Henry **VI:**200

literature **IX:**195

Lawrence, Jacob **VIII:**30

Lawrence, James **IV:**165

Lawrence, Kansas **V:**445*c*

Bleeding Kansas **V:**37

Massachusetts Emigrant Aid Society **IV:**243

Quantrill, William Clarke **V:**317

Lawrence, USS **IV:**221

Lawrence Scientific School (Harvard College)

education, higher **VI:**111

Eliot, Charles William **VI:**114

James, William **VI:**200

Lawrence Strike **VII:173–175, 174, 405c**

Fellowship of Reconciliation **VII:**109

Flynn, Elizabeth Gurley **VII:**109

Greenwich Village **VII:**130

Haywood, William Dudley **VII:**137

IWW **VII:**147

New Unionism **VII:**238

Passaic Strike **VII:**253

Paterson Strike **VII:**253

radicalism **VII:**287

Sanger, Margaret **VII:**312

Vorse, Mary Heaton **VII:**375

Laws and Liberties of 1648, The **II:**223

Laws of Burgos (Spain) **I:**122

Lawson, Ernest **VII:**25

Lawson, James **VII:**109

Lawson, John (British trader) **II:**395

Lawson, John Howard (screenwriter) **IX:**147, 148

lawyers **III:256–257; VI:**409*c*

Adams, John **III:**4

Allison, William Boyd **VI:**11

Blackstone, Sir William **III:**52

Brackenridge, Hugh Henry **III:**60

Burr, Aaron **III:**70

Chase, Samuel **III:**85

cities and urban life **III:**90

Deane, Silas **III:**129

education **III:**147

Galloway, Joseph **III:**188–189

Hamilton, Alexander **III:**206

Ingersoll, Jared **III:**226–227

Judiciary Act (1789) **III:**242

Martin, Luther **III:**291

Otis, James, Jr. **III:**326–327

Pinckney, Charles Cotesworth **III:**336

professional organizations, rise of **VI:**294

Quincy, Josiah **III:**354

Rodney, Caesar **III:**373

Rodney, Caesar Augustus **III:**373–374

Tyler, Royall **III:**417

Wilson, James **III:**444

women's status and rights **VI:**400

Lay, Benjamin **II:**1, **203**

Lay, Kenneth **X:**59

Lazarsfeld, Paul **VIII:**313

Lazarus, Emma **VI:219–220, 345**

Lazio, Rick **X:**78

Leadbelly (Huddie Ledbetter) **VIII:**250; **IX:**229

lead mines **IV:223–224**

Austin, Moses **IV:**38

Austin, Stephen F. **IV:**39

Beckwourth, Jim **IV:**50

lead poisoning **VII:**243

Leadville Strike **VI:**214

League for Progressive Political Action **VII:**271

League for Social Service **VI:**347

League of American Wheelmen **VI:**35–36

League of Armed Neutrality **III:257**

League of Conservation Voters **X:**275

League of Nations **VII:175–176, 407c, 408c; VIII:443c**

Borah, William E. **VIII:**49

Carnegie Endowment for International Peace **VII:**49

Coolidge, Calvin John **VII:**65

Dawes, Charles Gates **VII:**71

Democratic Party **VII:**75

Ethiopia **VIII:**118–119

foreign policy **VII:**115; **VIII:**140

Hamilton, Alice **VII:**133

Harding, Warren Gamaliel **VII:**134

Hughes, Charles Evans **VII:**142

Hull, Cordell **VIII:**180

Johnson, Hiram Warren **VII:**154

Lodge, Henry Cabot **VII:**184

Manchuria **VIII:**225

Naval Disarmament Conference **VII:**235

Paul, Alice **VII:**254

peace movements **VII:**256–257

presidency **VII:**269

Republican Party **VII:**300

Taft, William Howard **VII:**348

UN **VIII:**402

Versailles, Treaty of **VII:369–371**

WILPF **VII:**386

Wilson, Thomas Woodrow **VII:**384

World Disarmament Conference **VIII:**426

World War I **VII:**394

League of Nations Health Committee **VII:**133

League of Nations Non-Partisan Association (LNNPA) **VII:**49, 115

League of Nations Society (Great Britain) **VII:**175

League of Women Voters (LWV) **IX:186–187**

Catt, Carrie Lane Chapman **VII:**50

ERA **X:**123

lobbying **VII:**181

politics (1900–1928) **VII:**261

women's status and rights **VII:**388

League to Enforce Peace **VII:**267

Leahy, William D. **VIII:210–211, 439**

Leale, Charles **V:**21

Lear, William **X:**320

Lear Jet Aviation Company **X:**320

learning disabilities **X:**116

Leary, Timothy **IX:**78, **187–188,** 355*c*

Beat Generation **IX:**37

counterculture **IX:**78

Ginsberg, Allen **IX:**135

LSD **IX:**195, 196

music **IX:**230

narcotics **X:**242

sexual revolution **X:**322

Lease, Mary Elizabeth Clyens **VI:220**

Leatherstocking Club. *See* Junto

Leather-stocking Tales (Cooper) **IV:**228; **VI:**98

Leave It to Beaver

advertising **IX:**2

suburbanization/suburbs **IX:**306

television **IX:**315

Leavenworth, Henry **IV:**36, 158

Leavenworth, Kansas **VII:**156

Leaves of Grass (Whitman) **IV:**229, 415*c*; **V:**430, 431

Leavitt, Joshua **IV:**226

Lebanese civil war **X:**163

Lebanon **X:**378*c*

foreign policy **X:**143

Iran-contra affair **X:**183

Middle East **X:**229

Reagan, Ronald W. **X:**301

Lebna Dengel. *See* Dengel, Lebna

Lebrón, Lolita **IX:**185

LeCler, Chrestien **II:**440–441

Leclerc, Victor-Emmanuel **III:**55, 203–204

Le Compte, Joseph **V:**258

Lecompton Constitution **V:**443*c*

Bleeding Kansas **V:**38

Buchanan, James **V:**48

Douglas, Stephen A. **V:**114

LeConte, Joseph **VI:**318

Lectures on Revivals of Religion (Finney) **IV:**151

Lederer, John **II:**124

Lederer, Raymond F. **X:**5

Le Duc Tho **X:**140, 361, 362

Lee, Ang **X:**279

Lee, Ann **III:257,** 387, 460*c*

Lee, Arthur **III:257–258**

African Americans **III:**8

Deane, Silas **III:**129

Olive Branch Petition **III:**324

Lee, Charles **III:258–259**

Charleston Expedition of 1776 **III:**84

dueling **III:**141

Federalists **III:**165

Lafayette, marquis de **III:**253

Monmouth, Battle of **III:**299–300

Lee, Fitzhugh

Appomattox campaign **V:**14

Five Forks, Battle of **V:**147

Hollywood Cemetery **V:**192

Maine, Remember the **VI:**237

Lee, Harper **IX:**194

Lee, Henry "Light-Horse Harry"
  Federalists **III:**165
  Hobkirk's Hill, Battle of
    III:213
  Lee, Robert E. **V:**229
Lee, Henry "Light-Horse Harry"
  III:259, **259–260**
Lee, Jason **IV:224–225**
  Fort Vancouver **IV:**159
  McLoughlin, John **IV:**248
  Wyeth, Nathaniel J. **IV:**406
Lee, John D. **IV:**90
Lee, Richard Henry **III:260**
  Constitution, ratification of
    the **III:**105
  Continental Congress, First
    III:113
  Declaration of
    Independence **III:**133
  Lee, Arthur **III:**258
Lee, Robert E. **V:229–232,** *230,*
  443c–446c
  Alexander, Edward P. **V:**8
  Antietam, Battle of **V:**12, 13
  Appomattox campaign **V:**14
  Appomattox Court House,
    Virginia **V:**14–16
  Arlington National Cemetery
    V:16, 17
  Beauregard, Pierre Gustave
    Toutant **V:**32
  Brown, John **V:**44–45
  Bull Run/Manassas, First
    and Second Battles of
    V:50, 51
  Burnside, Ambrose E. **V:**52
  Cedar Mountain, Battle
    of **V:**59
  Chancellorsville, Battle of
    V:60–62
  Civil War **V:**74
  Cold Harbor, Battle of
    V:76–77
  Confederate army **V:**82
  Confederate States of
    America **V:**87
  Congress, Confederate **V:**88
  Davis, Jefferson **V:**104, 105
  desertion **V:**110
  Early, Jubal A. **V:**119
  Farewell to His Troops
    V:463
  fire-eaters **V:**146
  Five Forks, Battle of **V:**147
  foraging **V:**149
  Fredericksburg, Battle of
    V:157–159
  Gettysburg, Battle of
    V:166–168
  Gordon, John B. **V:**170
  Grant, Ulysses S. **V:**174
  Halleck, Henry Wager
    V:182
  Hancock, Winfield Scott
    V:183
  Harpers Ferry, West Virginia
    V:186

  Hill, Ambrose P. **V:**190
  Hill, Daniel H. **V:**190
  Hood, John Bell **V:**195, 196
  Hooker, Joseph **V:**197
  Jackson, Thomas J.
    "Stonewall" **V:**210, 211
  Johnston, Joseph E. **V:**214
  Lee, Henry **III:**260
  literature **V:**239
  Longstreet, James **V:**241–
    242
  lost cause, the **V:**244
  McClellan, George Brinton
    V:251, 252
  McLaws, Lafayette **V:**253
  Meade, George Gordon
    V:253, 254
  medicine **V:**257
  Mexican-American War
    IV:252
  monuments **V:**268
  music **V:**272
  Overland campaign **V:**290–
    291
  Peninsular campaign **V:**299,
    300
  Petersburg campaign
    V:301–303
  Pickett, George Edward
    V:306
  Rhodes, James Ford
    VI:312
  Richmond, Virginia **V:**336,
    337
  Shenandoah Valley:
    Jackson's campaign
    V:349–351
  Shenandoah Valley:
    Sheridan's campaign
    V:351, 352
  Spotsylvania, Battles of
    V:367–368
  tactics and strategy **V:**380,
    382
  U.S. Army Corps of
    Engineers **V:**407
  U.S. Military Academy at
    West Point **V:**409
  Washington, D.C. **V:**426
  Wheeler, Joseph **V:**428
  Wigfall, Louis T. **V:**431
  Wilderness, Battle of the
    V:432
  Zouaves **V:**441
Lee, Spike **X:**236
Lee, Stephen D. **V:**190
Lee, Thomas **III:**323
Lee, William Raymond **V:**186
Lee Camp **V:**416
Lees, Edith **VII:**95
Lee's Legion **III:**259
Leete, William **II:**175
Lee v. Weisman **X:**324
Leeward Islands **I:**262–263
LeFeber, Walter **VII:**34
Lefebre, E. A. **VI:**339
Left Behind (Jenkins) **X:**212

Legal Defense Fund of the
  NAACP **VIII:**72
Le Gallienne, Eva **VII:**95
Legal News **VI:**46
Legal Tender Act **V:**444*c*
  banking **V:**28
  Conkling, Roscoe **VI:**81
  currency issue **VII:**88
  economy **V:**122
  greenbacks **V:**177–178
  Sherman, John **VI:**329
Legal Tender cases **VI:**89, 127
"Legend of Sleepy Hollow, The"
  (Irving) **IV:**228
legends. *See* myths and legends
Legion of Honor **IV:**245
Legislative Reorganization Act
  (1970) **X:**169
Lehár, Franz **VII:**95, 218
Lehigh Canal **IV:**79
Lehman Brothers **X:**61
Leibowitz, Samuel S. **VIII:**317,
  353
Leif Eriksson **I:**395*c*
  Cabot, John **I:**44
  Greenland **I:**144
  Norse **I:**272
  Vinland **I:**378
Leigh, Vivien **V:**169; **VIII:**446*c*
Leigh-Mallory, Trafford
  VIII:275
Leiper, Thomas **IV:**313
Leiserson Shirtwaist Company
  VII:324
Leisler, Jacob **II:**437*c*
  crowd actions **II:**86
  Dominion of New England
    II:102
  Dudley, Joseph **II:**103
  Glorious Revolution **II:**150
  Leisler's Rebellion **II:**203
  New York **II:**271
  Roman Catholicism **II:**336
Leisler, Peter **II:**107
Leisler's Rebellion **II:**86, **203–
  204,** 271, 436*c*
Le Jeune, Paul **II:**137
Leland, John **III:**44
LeMay, Curtis E.
  AIP **X:**24
  bombing **VIII:**48
  Wallace, George C. **X:**364
Lemhi, Idaho **IV:**120, 408
Lemke, William "Liberty Bill"
  Coughlin, Father Charles E.
    VIII:88
  election of 1936 **VIII:**109
  Long, Huey P. **VIII:**223
  Union Party **VIII:**401
Lemlich, Clara **VII:**324
Lemmon Slave case **VI:**20
Le Moyne, Jacques **I:***209,*
  209–210
  Bry, Theodor de **I:**37–38
  Laudonnière, René de
    I:208
  Timucua **I:**360

Lend-Lease **VIII:211–212,**
  447*c*
  agriculture **VIII:**11
  America First Committee
    VIII:17
  Anglo-American relations
    VIII:21
  Arnold, Henry H. "Hap"
    VIII:28
  Atlantic, Battle of the
    VIII:33
  Atlantic Charter **VIII:**34
  Axis **VIII:**38
  Cairo Conference **VIII:**61
  Casablanca Conference
    VIII:62
  cash-and-carry **VIII:**63
  CDAAA **VIII:**77
  Congress **VIII:**80
  destroyers-for-bases deal
    VIII:95
  foreign policy **VIII:**142
  Four Freedoms **VIII:**143
  Grand Alliance **VIII:**155
  Harriman, W. Averell
    VIII:161, 162
  Hopkins, Harry L. **VIII:**177
  isolationists **VIII:**190
  Knox, Frank **VIII:**202
  La Follette, Robert M., Jr.
    VIII:208
  mobilization **VIII:**241
  Morgenthau, Henry T., Jr.
    VIII:244
  Neutrality Acts **VIII:**268
  Polish Americans **VIII:**297
  rationing **VIII:**322
  Roosevelt, Franklin D.
    VIII:346
  second front **VIII:**355
  Soviet-American relations
    VIII:368
  Taft, Robert A. **VIII:**385
  Wheeler, Burton K.
    VIII:416
  Willkie, Wendell L.
    VIII:417
  World War II European
    theater **VIII:**429
L'Enfant, Pierre-Charles **III:260–
  261,** 428–429, 463*c*; **VI:**55
Lenin, Vladimir Ilych
  art and architecture **VIII:**31
  communism **IX:**67
  Popular Front **VIII:**304
  Reed, Jack **VII:**296, 297
  Russian Revolution **VII:**308
  Siberian Expedition
    VII:324
Leningrad, Soviet Union
  VIII:142, 431
Lenni Lenape. *See* Delaware
  Indians
Lennon, John
  assassinations **X:**35
  Beatles **IX:**37–38
  popular culture **X:**279

Lennox, Charlotte Ramsay **II:204**
Lennox, David **III:**440
Lennox Research Library **VI:**224
Lenroot, Katharine **VIII:**421
Leo X (pope) **I:210**
    cabinet of curiosities **I:**43
    Franciscans **I:**133
    Hanno the elephant **I:**153
    Leo Africanus **I:**210
    Luther, Martin **I:**218
    Reformation **I:**315
Leo XIII (pope) **VI:**308, 316;
    VII:297–298
Leo Africanus **I:210–211**
    Djenne-Djeno **I:**109
    Gao **I:**138
    Leo X **I:**210
    Mali **I:**226
    Ramusio, Giovanni Battista
      I:313
    Timbuktu **I:**360
    travel narratives **I:**368
Leo Frank case **VII:**176
Leonardo da Vinci **I:211–212**
    art and architecture **I:**13
    Eads, James Buchanan
      VI:103
    Mandeville, Sir John **I:**228
Leonardson, Samuel **II:**105
Leopard, HMS **III:**88, 465*c*
Leopard's Spots, The (Dixon)
    VII:37
Leopold, Aldo **IX:**108, 240
Leopold, Nathan. *See* Leopold
    and Loeb
Leopold II (king of Belgium)
    VI:396
Leopold and Loeb **VII:**10, 70,
    176–177, 409*c*
Lepanto, Battle of **I:**165
Le Populaire **IV:**67
Léry, Jean de **I:212–213**
    cannibalism **I:**59
    French explorations of the
      Atlantic **I:**134
    Histoire d'un voyage faict
      en la terre du Bresil
      autrement dite Amerique
      I:418–423
    Linschoten, Jan Huygen van
      I:214
    Thevet, André **I:**358
    tobacco **I:**363
    travel narratives **I:**368
    Tupinambá **I:**371
lesbians **VIII:**418, 420. *See also*
    gays and lesbians
Leslie, Frank, and Miriam
    Florence Follin **VI:220–222,**
    221
    journalism **IV:**210
    Liberal Republican Party
      VI:222
    NAWSA **VII:**223
Leslie Fund **VII:**223
Leslie's Weekly **VI:**183
Lesseps, Ferdinand de **VI:**103

Lesser Antilles
    Carib **I:**60
    Martinique **I:**232
    Montserrat **I:**251
    Nevis **I:**262–263
    Taino **I:**352
Letang, Eugene **VI:**165
Letcher, John **V:**148, 172, **232**
lethal injection **X:**67
"Letter from Birmingham Jail"
    (King) **IX:**355*c*, **366–373**
    Birmingham confrontation
      IX:39
    civil disobedience **IX:**58
    King, Martin Luther, Jr.
      IX:174
Letterman, Jonathon **V:**257
letters **V:232–233**
    common soldier **V:**77, 78
    desertion **V:**110
    Fifteenth Amendment
      V:141
    German-American
      regiments **V:**166
    Greenhow, Rose O'Neal
      V:178
    journalism **V:**218
    nurses **V:**285
    prisons **V:**315
    U.S. Christian Commission
      V:408
    U.S. Sanitary Commission
      V:411
    Wakeman, Sarah Rosetta
      V:422
Letters from a Farmer in
    Pennsylvania (Dickinson)
    III:137, 412, 459*c*
Letters from an American Farmer
    (Crèvecoeur) **III:**126, 127,
    268, 462*c*
Letters of a Federal Farmer
    III:25
Letters on the Equality of the
    Sexes and the Condition of
    Women (Grimké) **IV:**180
Letters to Catharine Beecher
    (Grimké) **IV:**180
Letter to the Reverend Mr. George
    Whitefield, A (Wigglesworth)
    II:414
Let Us Now Praise Famous Men
    (Agee) **VIII:**120
Leutze, Emanuel **VI:**36, 37
levadas **I:**222
Levant **I:**357
Levant, HMS **III:**108
Levant Company **I:213**
Levasseur, Pierre-Noël **II:**27
'Leven More Poems (Riley)
    VI:227
Leverett, John **II:204**
Lever Food and Fuel Act
    VII:119
Levine, Jack **VIII:**31
Levison, Stanley **IX:**32
Levitt, Alfred **IX:**188, 190

Levitt, William J. **IX:188–190,**
    189, 351*c*
    McDonald's **IX:**208
    migration **IX:**215
    suburbanization/suburbs
      IX:305
Levitt and Sons **IX:**188
Levittown, New York **IX:**215
Levittowns/Levittown homes
    IX:351*c*
    cold war culture **IX:**65
    housing **VIII:**179
    Levitt, William J. **IX:**188–
      190
    migration **IX:**215
    suburbanization/suburbs
      VIII:379; **IX:**305, 306
Lewinsky, Monica **X:**382*c*
    Clinton, Hillary Rodham
      X:78
    Clinton, William J. **X:**82–83
    impeachment of William J.
      Clinton **X:**178
    Starr, Kenneth **X:**333
Lewis, Andrew **IV:**258
Lewis, John (civil rights leader)
    IX:190–191
    Carmichael, Stokely **IX:**49
    freedom rides **IX:**123
    March on Washington
      (1963) **IX:**201
    race and race relations
      IX:270
    sit-ins **IX:**291
    SNCC **IX:**302, 303
Lewis, John L.(labor leader)
    VIII:212–213, *213,* 445*c,* 446*c*
    AFL **VIII:**18
    Amalgamated Clothing
      Workers of America
      (ACW) **VIII:**16
    America First Committee
      VIII:17
    CIO **VIII:**81, 82
    coal industry **VIII:**74–76
    Communists **VIII:**78
    conservatism **VIII:**85
    Dubinsky, David **VIII:**97
    Hillman, Sidney **VIII:**165–
      166
    labor/labor movements
      VIII:205–207
    Murray, Philip **VIII:**249
    NWLB **VIII:**262
    steel industry **VIII:**373
    strikes **VIII:**377, 378
    UMWA **VII:**360; **VIII:**401
Lewis, Meriwether **III:261–262,**
    465*c*
    American Philosophical
      Society **III:**18
    Astor, John Jacob **IV:**33
    Astoria **IV:**35
    Chouteau family **IV:**88
    Clark, William **III:**96, 97
    Columbia River **IV:**103
    exploration **IV:**144

Kearny, Stephen Watts
    IV:212
Lewis and Clark Expedition
    III:262–264
    Native Americans **IV:**273
    Oregon Trail **IV:**285
    race and race relations
      IV:311
    Sacagawea **III:**377
Lewis, Oliver **VI:**177
Lewis, Sinclair **VII:***180;*
    VIII:443*c*
    FTP **VIII:**136
    Hersey, John R. **VIII:**164
    literature **VII:**180; **VIII:**218,
      220
Lewis and Clark Expedition
    II:124; **III:262–264,** *263,* 465*c*
    Astor, John Jacob **IV:**33
    Astoria **IV:**35
    Bent, Charles **IV:**51
    Bodmer, Karl **IV:**60
    Clark, George Rogers **III:**95
    Clark, William **III:**96
    Columbia River **IV:**103
    exploration **IV:**144, 145
    fur trade **III:**183; **IV:**171
    Great Plains **III:**197
    Jefferson, Thomas **III:**234
    Lewis, Meriwether **III:**261
    Missouri Fur Company
      IV:257
    mountain men **IV:**266
    Native Americans **IV:**273
    Oregon Trail **IV:**285
    Oregon Treaty of 1846
      IV:287
    race and race relations
      IV:311
    Sacagawea **III:**377
Lewis's Farm **V:**14
Lewis v. United States **X:**161
Lexington, Tennessee **VI:**193
Lexington, USS (aircraft carrier)
    aircraft carriers **VIII:**11
    Coral Sea, Battle of the
      VIII:87
    King, Ernest J. **VIII:**201
Lexington, USS (brigantine)
    III:47, 461*c*
Lexington, USS (Civil War
    gunboat) **V:**260
Lexington and Concord, Battles of
    III:264–266, 265*m,* 461*c*
    Burgoyne, Sir John **III:**67
    Declaration of
      Independence **III:**133
    Earle, Ralph **III:**145
    foreign affairs **III:**168
    French Alliance **III:**177
    Gage, Thomas **III:**187
    minutemen **III:**298
    resistance movement
      III:366
    Revere, Paul **III:**367
    Revolutionary War **III:**367
    Washington, George **III:**430

Lexington Rifles **V:**268
Lexow Committee (New York City) **VI:**121
Leyden Jar **II:**345
Leyland, Frederick R. **VI:**390
Leyte Gulf, Battle for **VIII:**214
    Halsey, William F. **VIII:**161
    Iwo Jima **VIII:**192
    Navy, U.S. **VIII:**265
    Nimitz, Chester W. **VIII:**274
    Philippines **VIII:**295
    World War II Pacific theater **VIII:**437
Leyte Island, Philippines **VIII:**214
Libby, Irving Lewis "Scooter" **X:**179
Libby Prison
    Andersonville Prison, Georgia **V:**10
    prisons **V:**314, 315
    Van Lew, Elizabeth **V:**414, 415
libel **II:**437*c*
    Brennan, William J., Jr. **X:**47
    Duane, James **III:**140
    Hamilton, Andrew **II:**161
    journalism **III:**240
    newspapers **II:**268
    New York **II:**271
    Paine, Thomas **III:**329
    Wilkes, John **III:**443
    Zenger, John Peter **II:**433–434
liberal arts colleges **VI:**111
liberalism **VIII:214–217; IX:191–192; X:207–209**
    African Americans **X:**14
    Americans for Democratic Action **IX:**13
    antimonopoly **VIII:**23
    Buckley, William F., Jr. **X:**49–50
    Burger, Warren E. **X:**50–51
    capital punishment **X:**66
    Carter, James Earl, Jr. **X:**68
    Catholics **VIII:**64
    Chambers, Whittaker **IX:**53
    Congress **VIII:**80
    conservatism **VIII:**83, 84; **IX:**74
    conservative coalition **VIII:**86
    court-packing plan **VIII:**89
    Democratic Party **VIII:**94; **IX:**85
    Eagleton, Thomas F. **X:**107
    Economic Bill of Rights **VIII:**102
    education **VIII:**105
    election of 1936 **VIII:**110
    feminism **X:**133
    fiscal policy **VIII:**139
    Frankfurter, Felix **VIII:**144
    FSA **VIII:**127

Full Employment Bill **VIII:**145
Hiss, Alger **IX:**147
House of Representatives **X:**169
Howe, Louis M. **VIII:**179
Keynesianism **VIII:**200
La Follette, Robert M., Jr. **VIII:**208
McCarthy, Eugene **IX:**205–206
Murray, Philip **VIII:**249
NAACP **VIII:**255
New Deal **VIII:**268, 270
NRPB **VIII:**261
Obama, Barack Hussein **X:**264
OWMR **VIII:**287
Pelosi, Nancy **X:**271
political correctness **X:**276
politics (Roosevelt era) **VIII:**300
popular culture **VIII:**301
pornography **X:**284
postwar planning **VIII:**306
race and race relations **VIII:**319
recession of 1937–1938 **VIII:**324
reconversion **VIII:**326
religion **VII:**297; **VIII:**336
Roosevelt, Franklin D. **VIII:**347
SDS **IX:**304
South **VIII:**367
Supreme Court **VIII:**382
televangelism **X:**341
Third New Deal **VIII:**393
TNEC **VIII:**391
Wagner, Robert F. **VIII:**410
Wallace, Henry A. **VIII:**411, 412
World War II home front **VIII:**434
Liberal Party (Mexico) **IV:**330
Liberal Republican Party **VI:222–223**
    Adams, Henry **VI:**1
    Bowles, Samuel **VI:**43
    Donnelly, Ignatius Loyola **VI:**100
    Grant, Ulysses S. **V:**175
    Lockwood, Belva Ann Bennett McNall **VI:**229
    political parties, third **VI:**285–286
    presidential campaigns (1870–1899) **VI:**291
    Pulitzer, Joseph **VI:**297
    Reid, Whitelaw **VI:**305
    Republican Party **VI:**311
    Schurz, Carl **VI:**324
    Watterson, Henry **VI:**386
Liberals (theology) **III:**316
Liberation Theology **IX:**272
Liberator, The (1920s radical journal) **VII:**286

Liberator, The (abolitionist journal) **IV:**412*c*
    abolitionism **IV:**3
    ACS **IV:**17
    American Anti-Slavery Society **IV:**15
    Douglass, Frederick **V:**115
    Editorial, First Issue **IV:428–429**
    female antislavery societies **IV:**147
    Foster, Abigail Kelley **IV:**161
    Garrison, William Lloyd **V:**164, 165
    Grimké, Angelina and Sarah **IV:**180
    journalism **IV:**209
Liberia **IV:225–226; VI:223–224**
    abolitionism **IV:**3
    ACS **IV:**17
    Crummell, Alexander **VI:**87
    economy **VII:**85
    Exodusters **VI:**123
    Garnet, Henry Highland **IV:**175
    Turner, Henry McNeal **VI:**366
    Turner, Nat **IV:**380
Liberian Exodus Joint Stock Steamship Company **VI:**223
Libertarian National Committee **X:**209
Libertarian Party **X:209–210**
    conservative movement **X:**93
    elections, presidential **X:**118
    pornography **X:**284
    property rights **X:**290
    Scalia, Antonin **X:**316
Liberty Bonds **VII:**32
Liberty Enlightening the World (Lazarus) **VI:**219–220
Liberty League **VI:**17
Liberty Loans **VII:**378; **VIII:**310
Liberty Men **III:**255
liberty of contract **VI:**127; **VII:**182
Liberty Party **IV:226–227,** 413*c*
    abolitionism **V:**3
    Chase, Salmon P. **V:**62
    Free-Soil Party **IV:**163
    Garrison, William Lloyd **V:**165
    Polk, James K. **IV:**302
    Republican Party **IV:**322
    Whigs **IV:**397
Liberty riot **III:**209, **266,** 412, 460*c*
liberty ships
    race and race relations **VIII:**318
    shipbuilding **VIII:**359
    steel industry **VIII:**374
Liberty Street Presbyterian Church **IV:**174

liberty tree **III:**267, **267–268**
    Fries's Rebellion **III:**180
    Golden Hill, Battle of **III:**196
    McDougall, Alexander **III:**294
    Oliver, Andrew **III:**324
    taverns and inns **III:**407
libraries **II:**288; **III:**173; **VI:**224
Library of Congress
    FMP **VIII:**134
    libraries, public **VI:**224
    music **VIII:**250
Library of Congress, Joint Committee of the **VI:**239
Libya **X:**378*c*, 383*c*
    Africa **X:**15, 16
    Barbary Wars **III:**46
    defense policy **X:**101
    foreign policy **X:**142
    nuclear proliferation **X:**262
    OPEC **X:**267
    terrorism **X:**346, 347
Lichtenstein, Roy **IX:**19, 20; **X:**30
Liddy, G. Gordon **X:**366
Lie, Jonas **VII:**24
Lieb, Hermann **V:**260, 313
Lieber, Francis **V:234,** 338
Lieber Code
    prisons **V:**313
    rules of war **V:**338
    volunteer army **V:**420
Lieberman, Joseph I. **X:**156
    conservation/environmentalism **X:**92
    global warming **X:**156
    Gore, Albert, Jr. **X:**157
    Jews and Judaism **X:**194
Life among the Paiutes: Their Wrongs and Claims (Winnemucca) **VI:**398
Life and Adventures of James P. Beckwourth, Mountaineer, Scout, Pioneer and Chief of the Crow Nation (Bonner) **IV:**51
"Life and Death of Lincoln, The" (Brooks) **VI:**50
Life and Labor (journal) **VII:**231, 285
Life and Times of Harriot Stuart, The (Lennox) **II:**204
life expectancy
    medicine **VIII:**234; **X:**221, 222
    population trends **VIII:**305–306; **IX:**260
    public health **IX:**264, 266
    technology **IX:**314
    women's status and rights **X:**370
Life in America series **VIII:**137
life insurance **III:**227
Life magazine **VIII:**217, 445*c*
    art and architecture **VIII:**30
    Bourke-White, Margaret **VIII:**50
    Hersey, John R. **VIII:**164

illustration, photography, and graphic arts **VI:**183
Luce, Henry R. **VIII:**224
magazines **VI:**235, 236
news media **VIII:**272
photography **VIII:**296
recreation **VIII:**329
Life of an American Fireman (film) **VII:**96, 215
Life of Olaudah Equiano, or Gustavus Vassa the African Written by Himself **II:**446–448
Life of Washington (Irving) **IV:**228
Life Studies (Lowell) **IX:**195
Liggett, Hunter **VII:**11
Liggett Group **X:**351, 352
light bulbs, incandescent **VI:**409*c*; **VII:**123, 403*c*
Light Horse (Cherokee police force) **III:**87
Light in August (Faulkner) **VIII:**220
lighting
    Edison, Thomas Alva **VI:**107
    Industrial Revolution, Second **VI:**191
    invention and technology **VI:**194–195
lightning rod **II:**385
Lilienthal, David E. **VIII:**217–218, 392; **IX:**24, 25
Liliuokalani (queen of Hawaii) **IV:**189; **VI:**163, 411*c*; **IX:**143
Lily, The (magazine) **IV:**59, 60, 404, 414*c*
Lily of the Mohawks **II:**386
Lima, Peru **I:**213
    Andes Mountains **I:**9
    Peru **I:**289
    Wilkes expedition **IV:**400
Limbaugh, Rush **X:**220
limited liability **III:**121
Limited Test Ban Treaty of 1963 **IX:**192, 355*c*
    arms race **IX:**17
    civil defense **IX:**57
    Humphrey, Hubert H. **IX:**151
    hydrogen bomb **IX:**153
    SANE **IX:**283
    Soviet Union **IX:**295
Limits to Growth, The **X:**90
limners **II:**205
limpieza de sangre **I:**64, **214**; **II:**372
Lin, Maya **IX:**332
Lincoln, Abraham **V:234–238,** 235, 443*c*–445*c*
    abolitionism **IV:**4; **V:**4
    African-American regiments **V:**4
    amnesty, acts of **V:**8, 9
    Anderson, Robert **V:**10
    Antietam, Battle of **V:**13

Applegate, Jesse **IV:**26
Appomattox Court House, Virginia **V:**16
assassination of. *See* assassination of Abraham Lincoln
Balloon Corps **V:**25
Baltimore, Maryland, riots **V:**26
Barton, Clara **V:**29
Bates, Edward **V:**30–31
Bell, John **V:**32, 33
Bennett, James Gordon, Jr. **VI:**32
Birth of a Nation, The **VII:**37
Black Hawk War **IV:**57
Blair, Francis Preston, Jr. **V:**36
Booth, John Wilkes **V:**38–39
bounty system **V:**39
Bowles, Samuel **VI:**42
Brady, Mathew B. **V:**41
brothers' war **V:**43
Buchanan, James **V:**48
Bull Run/Manassas, First and Second Battles of **V:**50
Chancellorsville, Battle of **V:**62
Chase, Salmon P. **V:**63
civil liberties, Union **V:**69, 70
Civil War **V:**72–74
Civil War centennial **IX:**62
common soldier **V:**77
Confederate States of America **V:**84
Confiscation Acts **V:**87
Congress **V:**89; **VI:**79
conscription **V:**90, 91
Cooper Union speech **V:**93, 94
Copperheads **V:**95
Crittenden Compromise **V:**98
Dahlgren, John A. B. **V:**101
Daly, Maria Lydig **V:**102
Dana, Charles A. **V:**102
Davis, Jefferson **V:**104
Democratic Party **IV:**119
Dickinson, Anna E. **V:**111
Douglas, Stephen A. **V:**113, 114
Douglass, Frederick **V:**116
education, federal aid to **VI:**110
elections **V:**125, 126
emancipation **V:**128
Emancipation Proclamation **V:**130–131, 460
Emerson, Ralph Waldo **IV:**140
employment **V:**132
espionage **V:**134, 135
54th Massachusetts Regiment **V:**142, 144

Fillmore, Millard **IV:**150
Finney, Charles Grandison **IV:**151
fire-eaters **V:**146
First Inaugural Address **V:450–454**
Fort Pillow **V:**153–154
Fort Sumter **V:**154–155
Fredericksburg, Battle of **V:**157, 159
Frémont, Jesse Benton **IV:**166
Frémont, John C. **IV:**167
fugitive slave laws **IV:**169
Garrison, William Lloyd **V:**165
Gettysburg, Battle of **V:**166
Gettysburg Address **V:**169, 461
governors **V:**172
Grant, Ulysses S. **V:**174
Greeley, Horace **V:**177
habeas corpus, writ of **V:**181, 182
Hale, Sarah Josepha **IV:**184
Halleck, Henry Wager **V:**182
Harpers Ferry, West Virginia **V:**186
Hay, John Milton **VI:**164
Herndon, William H. **V:**187
Heroes of America **V:**188
Hicks, Thomas H. **V:**188
homefront **V:**193
Homestead Act **V:**195
Hooker, Joseph **V:**196–197
"House Divided" speech **V:447–450**
Howard, Oliver Otis **V:**197
Howe, Julia Ward **V:**198
Howells, William Dean **VI:**179
Huntington, Collis Potter **VI:**180
immigration **IV:**195
Johnson, Andrew **V:**212
Joint Committee on the Conduct of the War **V:**215, 216
journalism **V:**218
Juneteenth **V:**219
Kansas-Nebraska Act **V:**221, 222
ladies aid societies **V:**228
Leslie, Frank and Miriam Florence Follin **VI:**221
Lieber, Francis **V:**234
Lincoln, Mary Todd **V:**238
literature **V:**239
loyalty oaths **V:**246
Manifest Destiny **IV:**235
March on Washington (1963) **IX:**201
Marx, Karl **V:**249, 250
McClellan, George Brinton **V:**250–252

Meade, George Gordon **V:**254
Medal of Honor **V:**255
Mexican-American War **IV:**251
Morrill Land-Grant Act **V:**269
Morton, Oliver P. **V:**270
Murfreesboro/Stones River, Battle of **V:**271
music **V:**273
Nast, Thomas **V:**275
Pacific Railroad Act **V:**293
peace movements **V:**296
Peninsular campaign **V:**298
Popular Front **VIII:**304
presidency **VI:**290
prisons **V:**313–315
Proclamation of Amnesty and Reconstruction **V:461–462**
public land policy **IV:**307
race and race relations **IV:**311; **V:**319–320
Reconstruction **V:**324–325
Republican Party **IV:**323; **V:**333, 334
Rhodes, James Ford **VI:**312
secession **V:**344–345
Second Inaugural Address **V:**346, 462–463
Seward, William H. **V:**347
Seymour, Horatio **V:**348
Shenandoah Valley: Jackson's campaign **V:**350
Shenandoah Valley: Sheridan's campaign **V:**351
slavery **IV:**346; **V:**363
Stanton, Edwin M. **V:**368, 369
Stephens, Alexander Hamilton **V:**371
Stevens, Thaddeus **V:**372
Stowe, Harriet Beecher **V:**374
Sumner, Charles **V:**377
tactics and strategy **V:**381
tariffs **VII:**349
Thirteenth Amendment **V:**387–388
Truth, Sojourner **V:**393
Tyler, John **IV:**383
Union army **V:**400, 401, 403
Union League **V:**404
Union navy **V:**405
Vallandigham, Clement L. **V:**414
Vicksburg campaign **V:**416–418
volunteer army **V:**419
Wade-Davis Bill **V:**421
Wallace, Lew **VI:**381
war contracting **V:**424
Washington, D.C. **V:**425–427
Watterson, Henry **VI:**386

Lincoln, Abraham *(continued)*
  Welles, Gideon **V:**428
  Whigs **IV:**396, 398
  Whitman, Walt **V:**431
Lincoln, Benjamin
  Briar's Creek, Battle of
    III:64
  Charleston, siege of
    III:84–85
  Savannah, siege of **III:**383
  Shays's Rebellion **III:**388
Lincoln, Edward Dickinson
  V:235
Lincoln, Mary Todd **V:238**
  assassination of Abraham
    Lincoln **V:**20
  brothers' war **V:**43
  Daly, Maria Lydig **V:**102
  Herndon, William H. **V:**187
  Lincoln, Abraham **V:**235,
    236
  religion **VI:**309
  Sumner, Charles **V:**377
Lincoln, Nancy Hanks **V:**187, 234
Lincoln, Robert Todd **V:**235, 238
Lincoln, Thomas "Tad" **V:**234,
  235, 238
Lincoln, William Wallace "Willie"
  Lincoln, Abraham **V:**235
  Lincoln, Mary Todd **V:**238
  Washington, D.C. **V:**425
Lincoln County War **VI:**376, 381
Lincoln-Douglas debates **V:**114,
  236
Lincoln Memorial (Washington,
  D.C.) **VIII:**446c
  African Americans **VIII:**3
  Lincoln, Abraham **V:**234
  March on Washington
    (1963) **IX:**201
  sculpture **VI:**327
Lincoln Memorial University
  V:197, 268
Lind, Jenny
  Barnum, Phineas T. **VI:**25
  cities and urban life **IV:**92
  music **IV:**269
Lindbergh, Anne Morrow
  VII:178
Lindbergh, Charles Augustus
  VII:177–179, *178,* 409c
  America First Committee
    VIII:17
  aviation **VII:**29
  Ford Motor Corporation
    IX:122
  Hoover, J. Edgar **IX:**149
  Kelly Air Mail Act **VII:**165
  Lend-Lease **VIII:**211
  technology **VIII:**389
Lindbergh Boom **VIII:**13
Linder, Max **VII:**216
Linderfelt, Karl **VII:**187
Lindsay, John **X:**253
Lindy Hop (dance) **VII:**265
Lingg, Louis **VI:**169
Lining, John **II:**205

Linnaeus, Carolus **I:**139
  American Philosophical
    Society **III:**17
  Kalm, Peter **II:**191
  science and technology
    II:345
Linné, Carl von **I:**41
linotype **VI:**267
Linowitz Commission Report
  X:205
Linschoten, Jan Huygen van
  I:214–215
  Dutch East India Company
    I:115
  India **I:**181
  travel narratives **I:**368
L'Insurgente **III:**353
Lion King, The (film) **X:**279
Lions Clubs **IX:**66
Lippard, George **IV:**227–228
Lippmann, Walter **VII:**135; **IX:**62
Liri Valley, Italy **VIII:**191
Lisa, Manuel
  Chouteau family **IV:**87
  fur trade **IV:**171
  Missouri Fur Company
    IV:257
  mountain men **IV:**266
Lisbon **I:215**
  Drake, Sir Francis **I:**112
  Linschoten, Jan Huygen van
    I:214
  Stade, Hans **I:**346, 347
Li Shih-chen **I:**348
Lister, Joseph **V:**112, 256, 258;
  VI:244
Listerine **X:**7
Liston, Sonny **IX:**5, 9
Liszt, Franz **VI:**233
Litchfield, Connecticut **IV:**84
literacy **X:210**
  African Americans **II:**7
  carpetbaggers **V:**56
  common soldier **V:**77
  education **II:**111, 112;
    III:147
  Massachusetts **II:**225
  New England Primer **II:**258
  newspapers **VI:**265
  popular culture **III:**341
  slavery **V:**364
literacy tests
  Civil Rights Act (1964) **IX:**60
  Immigration Act (1917)
    VII:145
  Latino movement **IX:**185
  Voting Rights Act of 1965
    IX:333, 334
Literary Digest **VIII:**312
literature **II:205–206; III:268–**
  269; IV:227–229, *229,* 415c;
  V:238–240; VI:224–227;
  VII:179–181, *180;* **VIII:218–**
  221, *220,* 443c, 445c–447c;
  IX:192–195, *193;* **X:210–212,**
  211
  Adams, Hannah **III:**4

African Americans **III:**8;
  VIII:3; **IX:**5
African Methodist Episcopal
  Church **V:**5
Alcott, Louisa May **VI:**10
Alger, Horatio **VI:**10–11
Angelou, Maya **X:**25–26
Baldwin, James **IX:**34–35
Banneker, Benjamin **III:**43
Barlow, Joel **III:**46
Bland, Richard **III:**53
Brackenridge, Hugh Henry
  III:60–61
Brown, Charles Brockden
  III:64
Carson, Rachel **IX:**50
Cary, Mary Ann Shadd
  V:58
Connecticut Wits **III:**104
counterculture **IX:**78
Crane, Stephen **VI:**84–85
Crèvecoeur, J. Hector St.
  John de **III:**127
currency issue **VI:**90
De Forest, John William
  V:107
Delany, Martin Robinson
  V:108
DHS **X:**167–168
dime novels **VI:**98–99
dust bowl **VIII:**98
Dwight, Timothy **III:**143
Emerson, Ralph Waldo
  IV:140
Faulkner, William **VIII:**127–
  128
Franklin, Benjamin **III:**175
Fuller, Margaret **IV:**169
FWP **VIII:**136–137
Garland, Hamlin **VI:**140
Gastonia Strike **VII:**122
gays and lesbians **IX:**131–
  132
*Gilded Age, The: A Tale of
  Today* **VI:**145–146
Great Depression **VIII:**159
Great Migration **VII:**129
Greenwich Village **VII:**131
Hale, Sarah Josepha
  IV:183–184
Hall, Prince **III:**205
Harlem Renaissance
  VII:135–136
Harper, Frances Ellen
  Watkins **V:**184
Harrington, Michael **IX:**142
Harte, Bret **VI:**162–163
Hay, John Milton **VI:**164
Hearn, Lafcadio **VI:**169–
  170
Hersey, John R. **VIII:**164
Howells, William Dean
  VI:179–180
Hurston, Zora Neale
  VIII:181
Hutchinson, Thomas
  III:219

Internal Security Act (1950)
  IX:158
Irish Americans **VIII:**189
Jackson, Helen Hunt
  VI:199
James, Henry **VI:**200
Jewett, Sarah Orne **VI:**202–
  203
journalism **II:**189; **III:**240;
  VII:158–161
La Farge, John Frederick
  Lewis Joseph **VI:**217
Lazarus, Emma **VI:**219–
  220
Lost Generation **VII:**185–
  186
marriage and family
  III:286–287
Massachusetts **II:**225
McGuffey, William Holmes
  IV:246–247
Mead, Margaret **VII:**197
Mencken, Henry Louis
  VII:201
modernism **VII:**212
Murray, Judith Sargent
  Stevens **III:**308
Murray, Pauli **IX:**227
NEA **IX:**234
Packard, Vance **IX:**253–254
political parties **III:**338
popular culture **III:**341;
  VII:263, 265; **IX:**258
recreation **VIII:**327,
  328–329
Robber Barons, The **VI:**314–
  315
Rowson, Susanna Haswell
  III:374
Sanger, Margaret **VII:**312
science fiction **IX:**287
Selective Service Act
  VII:321
sexuality **VII:**322
sexual revolution **X:**323
Sinclair, Upton **VII:**325–
  326
Steinbeck, John **VIII:**374–
  375
Stowe, Harriet Beecher
  V:373–374
Taylor, John, of Caroline
  III:408
Tourgée, Albion W. **V:**389–
  390
Tyler, Royall **III:**417
Updike, John **X:**358
Victorianism **VI:**374
Warren, Mercy Otis
  III:427–428
Webster, Noah **III:**434
Weems, "Parson" Mason
  Locke **III:**435
Wheatley, Phillis **III:**438–
  439
Wilder, Laura Ingalls
  VI:392–393

women's status and rights **III**:446–447
Wright, Richard **VIII**:437
Yep, Laurence **IX**:349
Lithuania **X**:384*c*
cold war **IX**:63
Europe **IX**:112
foreign policy **X**:142
Teheran Conference **VIII**:390
Versailles, Treaty of **VII**:370
Little, Earl **IX**:198
Little Belt incident **III:269–270**
Little Bighorn, Battle of **V:240–241; VI**:408*c*
Black Hills gold rush **VI**:39
Cody, William Frederick **VI**:77
Crazy Horse **VI**:85
Custer, George A. **V**:99
Native Americans **VI**:261
Red Cloud **VI**:303
Sheridan, Philip H. **V**:353
Sioux wars **VI**:331
Sitting Bull **VI**:332
"Little Boy" (atomic bomb) **VIII**:166, 227
Little Caesar (film) **VIII**:245, 301
Little Carpenter **II**:28
Little Crow **V**:444*c*
Little Egg Harbor, New Jersey **III**:350
Little Egypt **VI**:117
Little Falls, Minnesota **IV**:300
Little House in the Big Woods (Wilder) **VI**:393
Little House on the Prairie (Wilder) **VI**:393
Little Ice Age **I**:144
Little Italies **VIII**:190
Little League Baseball **VIII**:328
"Little Major, The" **V**:273
Little Men (Alcott) **VI**:10
"Little Old Log Cabin in the Lane" **VII**:97
Little Review, The (literary journal)
Greenwich Village **VII**:131
literature **VII**:179
modernism **VII**:212
radical and labor press **VII**:285
Little Richard **IX**:278
Little Rock, Arkansas school desegregation **IX**:354*c*
Brown v. Board of Education **IX**:44
Eisenhower, Dwight D. **IX**:101
Faubus, Orval **IX**:117, 118
modern Republicanism **IX**:221
race and race relations **X**:297
Southern Manifesto **IX**:294
Little Rock & Fort Smith Railroad **VI**:83

Little Round Top
Chamberlain, Joshua L. **V**:60
Gettysburg, Battle of **V**:167
Lee, Robert E. **V**:231
Meade, George Gordon **V**:254
Oates, William C. **V**:287
Little Sarah affair **III**:191
"Little Steel"
CIO **VIII**:82
Murray, Philip **VIII**:249
steel industry **VIII**:373, 374; **IX**:300
Little Steel formula **VIII**:262, 409
Little Steel strike **VII**:375
Little Turtle **VI**:463*c*
Fallen Timbers, Battle of **III**:161
Greenville, Treaty of **III**:200
Harrison, William Henry **IV**:184
Native Americans **IV**:273
Sac and Fox **IV**:327
Wayne, Anthony **III**:434
Little Women (Alcott) **V**:446*c*; **VI**:10
Litton Industries **IX**:161
Litz wire **VI**:354
Live Poultry Code **VIII**:351
Liveright, Horace **VII**:179
Livermore, Mary A. **V**:228
Liverpool, England **IX**:37
livestock. *See* animals
Living My Life (Goldman) **VII**:126
Living Newspapers **VIII**:136
Living of Charlotte Perkins Gilman, The (Gilman) **VII**:125
Livingston, Philip **II:206–207**
Livingston, Robert (1654–1728) **II:207**
Livingston, Robert R. (1718–1775) **II:207**
Livingston, Robert R. (1746–1813) **III:270**, 461*c*
Florida **III**:167
Fulton, Robert **III**:183
Louisiana Purchase **III**:273
Yates, Abraham **III**:453
Livingston, William **II**:194–195; **III**:141, **270–271**
Livingstone, David **VI**:33, 266
Living Wage, A (Ryan) **VII**:298
Lloyd, David **II:207–208**, 286
Lloyd, Edward **I**:80
Lloyd, Harold **VII**:97
Lloyd, Henry Demarest **VI:227–228**, 364, 409*c*; **VII**:303
Lloyd, James **III**:427
Lloyd George, David **VII**:175, 369, 370
Lloyd's of London **I**:80; **III**:227
Lloyd Webber, Andrew **X**:281

LNNPA. *See* League of Nations Non-Partisan Association
Loan, Benjamin F. **V**:215
loans
farmers' alliances **VI**:125–126
Relief and Reconstruction Act **VIII**:333
RFC **VIII**:325, 326
lobbies and pressure groups **VI:228; VII:181–182**
American Legion **VII**:13
Catt, Carrie Lane Chapman **VII**:50
Children's Bureau **VII**:53
economy **VII**:85
elections **VII**:89
Kelley, Florence **VII**:164
McNary-Haugen Farm Bill **VII**:195
National Park Service **VII**:228
Native Americans **VII**:233
New Freedom **VII**:236
Niagara Movement **VII**:240
NWP **VII**:230
NWTUL **VII**:231
politics (1900–1928) **VII**:261
Pure Food and Drug Act **VII**:277
science and technology **VII**:315
Soldiers' Bonus **VII**:331
suburbanization/suburbs **VII**:340
urban transportation **VII**:364–365
veterans **VII**:373
lobbying
Christian Coalition **X**:74
elderly **VIII**:108
GI Bill of Rights **VIII**:149
Hawley-Smoot Tariff Act **VIII**:163
Nader, Ralph **X**:241
NRA **X**:249
Townsend, Francis E. **VIII**:394–395
Zionism **VIII**:441
Lochner, Joseph **VII**:182
Lochner, Louis **VII**:286
Lochner v. New York **VII:182–183**, 217, 218, 343, 404*c*
Locke, Alain LeRoy **VII:183**
Boas, Franz Uri **VII**:40
Harlem Renaissance **VII**:136
literature **VII**:181
Locke, John **II:208–209**
Calhoun, John C. **IV**:68
civil disobedience **IX**:57
Common Sense **III**:102
commonwealthmen **III**:103
constitutions, state **III**:110
Declaration of Independence **III**:133

deism **III**:134
government, British American **II**:151, 152
kindergarten **VI**:207
King George's War **II**:192
North Carolina **II**:274
race and race relations **IV**:309
science and technology **II**:345
Yates, Abraham **III**:453
Lockerbie bombing. *See* Pan Am flight 103
Lockhart, Robert **VI**:343
Lockheed Aircraft **IX**:27, 28
Lockheed C-69 Constellation **VIII**:397
Lockheed P-80 Shooting Star **VIII**:14
Lockport, New York **VI**:228
Lockwood, Belva Ann Bennett McNall **VI**:228, **228–229**, 400, 409*c*
Lockwood, In re **VI**:400
Lodge, George Cabot **VI**:226
Lodge, Henry Cabot **VII:184,** *184*, 407*c*
Bunche, Ralph **IX**:45
Democratic Party **VII**:75
elections **IX**:103
Enforcement Acts **V**:133
foreign policy **VII**:115
Goldwater, Barry **IX**:136
League of Nations **VII**:175
Mahan, Alfred Thayer **VI**:236
National Defense Act **VII**:227
Republican Party **VII**:300
Versailles, Treaty of **VII**:370
World War I **VII**:394
LodgeNet **X**:283
Lodi, New Jersey **VII**:253
Loeb, Richard. *See* Leopold and Loeb
Loeffler, Charles Martin **VI**:255
Loewe, E. W. **VII**:69
Loewe v. Lawlor. See Danbury Hatters case
lo-fi **X**:239
Logan, Adele Hunt **VII**:225
Logan, James **II:209**
Pennsylvania **II**:287
science and technology **II**:345
Walking Purchase **II**:405–406
Logan, John **V**:401
"Log College"
Tennent, Gilbert **II**:388
Tennent, William, Jr. **II**:388
Tennent, William, Sr. **II**:389
Lok, Michael **I**:134, 274; **II**:139
Lolita (Nabokov) **IX**:194
Lomax, John and Alan **VIII**:250
Lomax, Lunsford L. **V**:352

London, England **I:215–217,**
334
  bombing **VIII:**47
  Bridges, Harry **VIII:**52
  Britain, Battle of **VIII:**53–
54
  Eastman, George **VI:**105
  education, philanthropy and
VI:112
  Ethical Culture movement
VI:121
  fashion **IX:**116
  Harriman, W. Averell
VIII:161–162
  James, Henry **VI:**200
  Jefferson, Joseph, III
VI:202
  Leslie, Frank and Miriam
Florence Follin **VI:**222
  London Economic
Conference **VIII:**221
  London Naval Conference
VIII:222
  Open Door Notes **VI:**272–
273
  Pingree, Hazen S. **VII:**261
  UN **VIII:**403
London, Jack **VII:**155, 179, 404c
London Bridge **I:**216
London Daily Mirror **VII:**160
London Economic Conference
VIII:221
  Anglo-American relations
VIII:21
  foreign policy **VIII:**140
  Hull, Cordell **VIII:**180
  Moley, Raymond C.
VIII:243
  Reciprocal Trade
Agreements Act **VIII:**325
  Stimson, Henry L. **VIII:**375
  World Disarmament
Conference **VIII:**426
London Metropolitan Model **V:**67
London Naval Conference
VIII:222
  Anglo-American relations
VIII:21
  foreign policy **VIII:**140
  Hoover presidency
VIII:174
  World Disarmament
Conference **VIII:**426
London Society for the
Suppression of Vice **VI:**79
London Stock Exchange **VIII:**376
London subway bombings (2006)
X:347
London Yearly Meeting **II:**2
Lone Wolf v. Hitchcock **VII:**184–
185, 233
Long, Breckinridge **VIII:**170, 330
Long, George Washington **VI:**33
Long, Huey P. **VIII:222–223,**
445c
  literature **IX:**194
  New Deal **VIII:**270

Revenue Act of 1935
VIII:340
  Second New Deal **VIII:**356
  southern demagogues
VII:332
  taxation **VIII:**387
  Townsend, Francis E.
VIII:395
  Union Party **VIII:**401
Long, John **VII:**304
Long, Maxey **VI:**359
Long, Stephen Harriman **IV:**36,
145
Long Beach, California **VIII:**394
Long Beach Press–Telegraph
VIII:394
Long Day's Journey into Night, A
(O'Neill) **VIII:**220
Longfellow, Henry Wadsworth
IV:414c
  Alden, John **II:**16
  Alden, Priscilla **II:**17
  Bright Eyes **VI:**49
  Jewett, Sarah Orne **VI:**203
  journalism **IV:**210
  literature **IV:**229
  music **V:**274
  Remington, Frederic
VI:310
  Revere, Paul **III:**366
  Standish, Myles **II:**376
Longhouse Religion **III:**209
longhouses
  art and architecture **I:**12;
II:24, 25
  Huron **I:**171; **II:**169
  Iroquois **I:**186–187
  Secotan **I:**329
Longinqua Oceani **VI:**308, 316
Long Island, Battle of **III:271–
272,** 272m, 461c
  Barlow, Joel **III:**46
  Clinton, Sir Henry **III:**99
  Cornwallis, Charles, Lord
III:120
  Hale, Nathan **III:**204
  Hamilton, Alexander
III:205
  Howe, Richard, Lord
III:214
  Howe, Sir William **III:**215
  Putnam, Israel **III:**350
  Revolutionary War **III:**368
  Sullivan, John **III:**402
Long Island, New York
  Amistad incident **IV:**21
  Chase, William Merritt
VI:66
  espionage **VIII:**117
  Hicks, Elias **IV:**189
  Levitt, William J. **IX:**188
  sports and recreation
VI:343
  wampum **II:**406
  Warren, Josiah **IV:**392–393
  Youngs, John **II:**431
Long Island, Treaty of **III:**87

Long Island Motor Parkway
VII:365
Longley, James B. **X:**232
Long Parliament **II:**116
"Long Roll, The" **V:**273
longshoremen **VIII:**377
Longshoremen's Strike (New York,
1887) **VI:**213
Longstreet, James **V:241–243,**
444c
  Alexander, Edward P. **V:**8
  Antietam, Battle of **V:**12
  Armistead, Lewis A. **V:**17
  Bull Run/Manassas, First and
Second Battles of **V:**51
  Chancellorsville, Battle of
V:60
  Chattanooga, Battle of **V:**63
  Chickamauga, Battle of
V:65
  Fredericksburg, Battle of
V:157, 158
  Gettysburg, Battle of
V:166–168
  Hood, John Bell **V:**196
  Lee, Robert E. **V:**230, 231
  literature **V:**239
  McLaws, Lafayette **V:**253
  Oates, William C. **V:**287
  Pickett, George Edward
V:306
  scalawags **V:**339–340
  Sickles, Daniel E. **V:**361
  Wilderness, Battle of the
V:432
"Long Telegram" **IX:**113, 167,
351c
Long Wharf **II:**41, 224
Longworth, Alice Roosevelt
VIII:17
Look Homeward, Angel (Wolfe)
VIII:219, 443c
Looking Backward (Bellamy)
  Bellamy, Edward **VI:**32
  business cycles **VI:**58
  Higginson, Thomas
Wentworth **VI:**172
  literature **VI:**226
  socialism **VI:**336
  Socialist Party **VI:**337
  utopianism **VI:**371
Looking Glass **VI:**268
Look magazine
  news media **VIII:**272
  photography **VIII:**296
  Till, Emmett Louis **IX:**318
Lookout Mountain, Battle of
V:243, **243–244**
  Chattanooga, Battle of **V:**63
  Hooker, Joseph **V:**197
  Longstreet, James **V:**242
  Warmoth, Henry Clay **V:**424
Loomis, Francis B. **VII:**251
Lopez, Nancy **X:**303
Lòpez, Narciso **IV:**111–112
Lopez family (Newport
merchants) **III:**236

Loranbec **I:**113
Loray Mill (Gastonia, North
Carolina) **VII:**122
Lord, Miles **X:**233
Lord, Nancy **X:**209
Lord and Thomas **VII:**4
Lord Chamberlin's Men **I:**333
Lord Weary's Castle (Lowell)
IX:195
"Lorena" **V:**273
Lorentz, Pare **VIII:**303
Lorenzo the Magnificent. *See*
Medici, Lorenzo de'
Lorimer, Peter **IV:**224
Lorimer, William **VII:**78
Loring, Ellis Gray **IV:**367
Lorraine, France **VII:**370
Lorraine Hotel (Memphis,
Tennessee) **IX:**23, 175
Los Alamos, New Mexico
VIII:447c
  atomic bomb **VIII:**34
  Manhattan Project **VIII:**227
  Oppenheimer, J. Robert
IX:250, 251
  Sunbelt **VIII:**381
Los Angeles, California
VIII:448c; **IX:**356c; **X:**380c
  Catholics **VIII:**64
  cities and urban life
VIII:68; **IX:**56; **X:**75
  exploration **IV:**145
  Frémont, John C. **IV:**167
  FTP **VIII:**136
  gays and lesbians **VIII:**147;
IX:131–132
  Gentlemen's Agreement
VII:123
  Griffith, David Wark
VII:131, 132
  Kearny, Stephen Watts
IV:212
  Kennedy, Robert F. **IX:**172
  McPherson, Aimee Semple
VII:196
  Mexican Americans
VIII:237
  Mexican Repatriation
Program **VIII:**238
  migration **VIII:**240
  movie industry **VII:**216
  music **VII:**218
  overland mail **IV:**290
  popular sovereignty **IV:**306
  race and race relations
VIII:319; **IX:**270; **X:**295,
296
  riots (1965) **X:**295
  riots (1992) **X:**296, 380c
  Stearns, Abel **IV:**356
  Stockton, Robert Field
IV:358
  Taylor, Zachary **IV:**368
  V-J Day **VIII:**407
  Watts uprising **IX:**339–340
  zoot-suiters **VIII:**442
Los Angeles Examiner **VII:**138

Los Angeles riots (1965) **X**:295
Los Angeles riots (1992) **X**:296, 380c
Los Angeles Times bombing **VII**:145
"Lost Arts, The" (Phillips) **IV**:299
lost cause, the **V**:244–245
   Civil War **V**:75
   Early, Jubal A. **V**:119, 120
   Ladies Memorial Associations **V**:229
   literature **V**:239
   New South **VI**:265
   religion **V**:332
   Richmond, Virginia **V**:337
   United Daughters of the Confederacy **V**:407
Lost Cause, The (Pollard) **V**:244
Lost Generation **VII**:136, 180, **185–186**, *186*
Lott, Eric **VI**:116
Lott, Trent **X**:321
Lott Carey Baptist Foreign Mission Convention **VI**:4
lotteries **II:210**
Louima, Abner **X**:382c
Louis, Joe *VIII*:223, **223–224**, 446c
   African Americans **IX**:5
   popular culture **VIII**:303
   recreation **VIII**:328
   sports and recreation **VIII**:371
Louis XII (king of France) **I**:211
Louis XIV (king of France) **II**:137
Louis XVI (king of France)
   French Revolution **III**:178
   Jefferson, Thomas **III**:233
   Lafayette, Marie-Joseph-Paul-Yves-Roch-Gilbert de Motier, marquis de **III**:253
   Morris, Gouverneur **III**:304
   Rochambeau, Jean-Baptiste-Donatien de Vimeur, comte de **III**:372
   Vergennes, Charles Gravier, comte de **III**:423
Louisbourg, Cape Breton Island **II**:192, 241, 438c
Louisbourg, siege of
   Gage, Thomas **III**:186
   Howe, Sir William **III**:215
   Montgomery, Richard **III**:301
Louisiana **II:210–211**, 211m, 436c, 437c. *See also* New Orleans, Louisiana
   Acadians **II**:2
   African Americans **III**:9
   Agricultural Adjustment Act **VIII**:6
   agriculture **IV**:10; **V**:6
   amnesty, acts of **V**:9
   art **II**:27
   Ashley, William Henry **IV**:31
   Astor, John Jacob **IV**:33

Bienville, Jean-Baptiste Le Moyne, sieur de **II**:37
Black Codes **V**:35
Blount, William **III**:53
Bonaparte, Napoleon **III**:55
Butler, Benjamin Franklin **V**:53
Chouteau family **IV**:87
Claiborne, William C. C. **IV**:94–95
Creole **II**:82–83
disease/epidemics **IV**:123
elections, conduct of **VI**:113
Exodusters **VI**:122
exploration **II**:123; **IV**:144
Florida **IV**:151, 152
Freedmen's Bureau **V**:161
grandfather clause **VI**:152
Hurricane Katrina **X**:173–174
Jefferson, Joseph, III **VI**:202
Jim Crow laws **VI**:203, 204
Ku Klux Klan **V**:223
La Salle, René-Robert Cavelier, sieur de **II**:202
lead mines **IV**:223
Liberia **VI**:223
marriage and family **IV**:239
migration **II**:254
miscegenation **II**:238
Mississippi River **V**:262
music **VIII**:250
Native Americans **II**:253, 254
New Orleans **II**:266–267
New Orleans, Battle of **IV**:280
New Orleans riot **V**:281–282
New Spain, northern frontier of **III**:317
Oregon Trail **IV**:285
Paris, Treaty of (1763) **III**:331
Pinckney Treaty **III**:337
Plessy v. Ferguson **VI**:284, 285, **433–438**
popular sovereignty **IV**:304, 305
railroads **IV**:314, 316
religion **III**:317; **X**:306
Sheridan, Philip H. **V**:354
slavery **IV**:346, 347
slave trade, internal **IV**:348, 349
southern demagogues **VII**:332
suffrage **III**:401
Taylor, Zachary **IV**:367
Texas **IV**:370, 371
Texas Revolution **IV**:373
U.S. v. Cruikshank **V**:411–412
veterans **V**:416
Warmoth, Henry Clay **V**:425
White Citizens' Councils **IX**:342

Louisiana Electoral Commission **VI**:159
Louisiana Native Guard **V**:53
Louisiana Purchase **III:272–275**, 274m, 465c; **IV**:411c
   Adams-Onís Treaty **IV**:6
   African Americans **III**:9
   agriculture **III**:11
   Ashley, William Henry **IV**:31
   Astoria **IV**:35
   Austin, Moses **IV**:38, 39
   Bent, Charles **IV**:51
   Bent, William **IV**:52
   Bingham, William **III**:51
   Bowie, James **IV**:62
   Catholics **III**:83
   Choctaw **IV**:86
   Chouteau family **IV**:87
   citizenship **III**:94
   Clay, Henry **IV**:96
   Compromise of 1850 **IV**:103
   economy **IV**:130
   exploration **IV**:144
   Florida **III**:167; **IV**:152
   foreign affairs **III**:169
   foreign policy **IV**:153, 154
   fur trade **III**:183
   Jefferson, Thomas **III**:234
   Kearny, Stephen Watts **IV**:212
   lead mines **IV**:223
   Lewis and Clark Expedition **III**:262
   Livingston, Robert R. **III**:270
   migration **IV**:253
   Missouri Compromise **IV**:257
   Monroe, James **IV**:259
   Native Americans **IV**:273
   New Spain, northern frontier of **III**:317
   Oregon Treaty of 1846 **IV**:286
   Pickering, Timothy **III**:335
   Pike, Zebulon Montgomery **IV**:299, 300
   Randolph, John **III**:359
   slavery **IV**:346
   slave trade, internal **IV**:348
   states' rights **III**:397
   Talleyrand-Périgord, Charles-Maurice de **III**:405
   Tallmadge Amendment **IV**:365
   Texas **IV**:371
   Wilkinson, James **III**:443–444
Louisiana Railroad Commission **VIII**:222
Louisiana Territory
   African Americans **III**:9
   foreign affairs **III**:169
   Lewis, Meriwether **III**:261, 262
   Wilkinson, James **III**:443–444

Louisiana Tigers **V:245**, 441, 442
Louis-Philippe (king of France) **IV**:67
Louisville, Cincinnati and Charleston Railroad **IV**:173
Louisville, Kentucky
   anti-Catholic riots **IV**:24
   Audubon, John James **IV**:37
   Johnson, Tom Loftin **VII**:156
   slave trade, internal **IV**:350
Louisville *Courier-Journal* **VI**:386
Louvain, University of **I**:240–241
Louverture, Toussaint **III**:203, 204; **IV**:153
Louvre Museum (Paris, France) **VI**:217
Love, Nancy Harkness **VIII**:419
Love Canal, New York **X**:91
Lovejoy, Elijah P. **IV**:*230*, **230–231**, 413c
   abolitionism **IV**:3; **V**:3
   American Anti-Slavery Society **IV**:15
   Forbes, John Murray **VI**:132
   Garrison, William Lloyd **V**:164
   Phillips, Wendell **IV**:299
Lovelace, Francis **II**:304
Lovell, Bernard, Sir **IX**:296
Lovell, Solomon **III**:333, 334
Love Medicine (Erdrich) **X**:210–211
"Love Me Do" (The Beatles) **IX**:229
Love Me Tender (film) **IX**:263
Lovett, Robert A. **VIII**:25, 375
Loving v. Alabama **V**:261
Loving v. Virginia **X**:213
Loving You (film) **IX**:263
Low, Seth **VII**:226
Low, Will **VI**:276
Low Countries **I**:70, 71. *See also* Belgium; Netherlands
   blitzkrieg **VIII**:47
   Britain, Battle of **VIII**:53
   isolationists **VIII**:189–190
Lowe, Thaddeus **V**:25, 341
Lowell, Amy **VII**:179
Lowell, Esther **VII**:286
Lowell, Francis Cabot
   economy **IV**:131
   industrialization **IV**:199, 200
   Industrial Revolution **III**:226
   Slater, Samuel **III**:390
Lowell, James Russell
   Howells, William Dean **VI**:179
   Jewett, Sarah Orne **VI**:203
   journalism **IV**:210
   literature **IV**:229
   Norton, Charles Eliot **VI**:269

Lowell, Massachusetts
  economy **IV:**131
  industrialization **IV:**199
  Industrial Revolution
    III:226
  Kerouac, Jack **IX:**173
  labor/labor movements
    IV:218
  railroads **IV:**314
Lowell, Robert **IX:**195
Lowell Mills **IV:**201
Lower South **II:**366, 368
Lowland Scots **II:**346
Low Level Radioactive Waste
  Policy Amendments Act (1985)
  X:131
Lowndes, Sara **IX:**92
Lowndes County Freedom
  Organization **IX:**49
Lowndes County Freedom Party
  IX:40
Lowry, Robert **VI:**257
Loyalists **II:**94; **III:275–276,**
  462*c*
  American Philosophical
    Society **III:**17
  André, John **III:**20
  Anglican Church **III:**21
  art **III:**32–33
  Asbury, Francis **III:**36
  Boucher, Jonathan **III:**59
  Brant, Joseph **III:**62
  Briar's Creek, Battle of
    III:63
  Canada **III:**77, 78
  Charleston Expedition of
    1776 **III:**83–84
  Church, Benjamin **III:**89
  cities and urban life **III:**90
  citizenship **III:**93
  Clinton, George **III:**98
  Continental Congress, First
    III:114
  Copley, John Singleton
    III:118
  Cornwallis, Charles, Lord
    III:120
  Cowboys and Skinners
    III:123
  Cowpens, Battle of **III:**124
  Crèvecoeur, J. Hector St.
    John de **III:**127
  economy **III:**146
  Florida **III:**167
  food riots **III:**167
  Franklin, Benjamin **III:**174
  Franklin, William **III:**175–
    76, 176
  freemasonry **III:**176
  Galloway, Joseph **III:**188–
    189
  Hamilton, Alexander
    III:206
  Hutchinson, Thomas
    III:218–219
  immigration **III:**221
  Ingersoll, Jared **III:**226–227

Jews **III:**236
Johnson, Sir John **III:**237
King's Mountain, Battle of
  III:246–247
Moore's Creek Bridge,
  Battle of **III:**301, 302
North, Frederick, Lord
  III:320
Oliver, Andrew **III:**324–325
Paris, Treaty of (1783)
  III:332
Penobscot campaign
  III:333, 334
population trends **III:**342
privateering **III:**347
Quakers **III:**351
Revolutionary War **III:**369
Rodney, Caesar **III:**373
Seabury, Samuel **III:**386–
  387
West Indies **III:**436
women's status and rights
  III:445, 446
Wyoming Valley Massacre
  III:449
Loyal Nine **III:276,** 459*c*
  Adams, Samuel **III:**7
  MacIntosh, Ebenezer
    III:279
  Sons of Liberty **III:**394
  Stamp Act **III:**396
Loyal Publication Society **V:**234
loyalty oaths **V:**9, **245–246,** 324,
  325
Loyalty Review Board **IX:**119
LPC (likely to become a public
  charge) clause **VIII:**184
LPGA (Ladies Professional Golf
  Association) **X:**303
LSD (lysergic acid diethylamide)
  IX:195–196
  counterculture **IX:**78
  Leary, Timothy **IX:**187, 188
  medicine **X:**222
  music **IX:**229
  narcotics **X:**242
LTVs (vans) **X:**36
Luba **I:217**
Lublin, Poland **VIII:**439
Lublin Poles **IX:**63, 112
Lucas, Charles **IV:**53
Lucas, George **X:**235, 279, 377*c*
*Lucas v. South Carolina Coast
  Council* **X:**316
Luce, Clare Boothe **IX:***101,* 212,
  257
Luce, Henry R. **VIII:224**
  Asian Americans **VIII:**32
  Bourke-White, Margaret
    VIII:50
  Hersey, John R. **VIII:**164
  Life magazine **VIII:**217
  news media **VIII:**272
  Republican Party **VIII:**338
  Willkie, Wendell L.
    VIII:417
Luciano, Charles "Lucky" **IX:**87

Lucite **IX:**91
"Luck of Roaring Camp, The"
  (Harte) **VI:**162
Ludlow, Fitz Hugh **VI:**37
Ludlow Amendment **VIII:**189
Ludlow Massacre **VII:186–187,**
  406*c*
  Industrial Relations
    Commission **VII:**146
  mining **VII:**209
  UMWA **VII:**360
Ludwell, Philip **II:**183
Luftwaffe
  air power **VIII:**15
  Arnold, Henry H. "Hap"
    VIII:28
  Britain, Battle of **VIII:**53–
    54
  Normandy, invasion of
    VIII:276
Luhya **I:217**
Luís, Alfonso **I:**79
Luisetti, Hank **VIII:**371
Luker, Kristin **X:**214
Luks, George
  Ashcan School **VII:**25
  Hearst, William Randolph
    VII:138
  yellow journalism **VI:**405
Lula da Silva, Luiz Inácio **X:**206
Lull, Ramon **I:**348
Lumbee Indians **V:**278
lumbering **II:211–212,** 259;
  IV:231
  Aroostook War **IV:**27
  business and government
    VI:56
  conservation/
    environmentalism **VI:**81
  environment **VI:**119
  Forest Reserve Act **VI:**134
  Indian Removal Act **IV:**197
  invention and technology
    VI:196
  Muir, John **VI:**254
  Webster-Ashburton Treaty
    IV:394
lumber mills **III:**224
luminism **V:**18; **VI:**275
Lumpkin, Grace **VIII:**218
Lumumba, Patrice **IX:**339
Luna, Tristán de **I:**89
Luna 1 (spacecraft) **IX:**296
Luna 9 (spacecraft) **IX:**296
Luna Park (Coney Island, New
  York) **VII:**263
Lundu kingdom **I:**231
Lundy, Benjamin
  abolitionism **IV:**1–2
  female antislavery societies
    IV:147
  *Genius of Universal
    Emancipation* **IV:**175
Lundy's Lane, Battle of **IV:**336,
  392
lung cancer **X:**351
Luque, Hernando de **I:**292

Lusitania, RMS **VII:187–188,**
  406*c*
  foreign policy **VII:**115
  National Defense Act
    VII:227
  Preparedness **VII:**267
  World War I **VII:**393
  Zimmermann telegram
    VII:401
Luther, Martin **I:217–219,** *218,*
  397*c*
  Calvin, John **I:**53
  Charles V **I:**70
  Church of England **I:**74
  German Reformed Church
    II:148
  Hanno the elephant **I:**154
  Huguenots **I:**170
  Jews **I:**196–197
  Leo X **I:**210
  Lutherans **II:**212
  printing press **I:**303
  Protestantism **II:**315–316
  Reformation **I:**315–316
  religion, Euro-American
    II:329
  Trent, Council of **I:**369–370
Lutherans/Lutheranism **II:212**
  Charles V **I:**70
  Dürer, Albrecht **I:**114
  isolationists **VIII:**189
  Moravians **III:**302
  Muhlenberg, Henry
    Melchior **II:**245–246
  Protestantism **II:**315–316
  Reformation **I:**315
  religion **VI:**307, 308;
    VIII:334
  religion, Euro-American
    II:329
  religious liberty **III:**362
  Weiser, Johann Conrad
    II:409
Luttwak, Edward **X:**121
Luxembourg **VIII:**47
Luzon, Philippines
  amphibious warfare **VIII:**20
  Bataan Death March
    VIII:42
  Philippines **VIII:**294, 295
LWV. *See* League of Women Voters
lyceum movement **IV:231–232**
  education **IV:**135
  Ingersoll, Robert Green
    VI:193
  literature **IV:**229
Lycra **IX:**91
Lyell, Sir Charles **VI:**122, 306
Lynch, James **VI:**4, 5
Lynch, John R. **V:**47
Lynch, Michael **X:**121
Lynchburg Baptist College **X:**234
lynching **VI:229–231,** *230,* 409*c,*
  411*c;* **VII:**408*c*
  African Americans **VI:**7;
    VIII:3; **IX:**4
  civil rights **VIII:**72

Leo Frank case **VII**:176
lobbying **VII**:182
Mafia incident **VI**:234
Muhammad, Elijah **IX**:226
NAACP **VII**:224
NACW **VI**:259
race and race relations **VII**:283; **VIII**:317
Red Scare **VII**:296
segregation **VII**:320
South **VIII**:367
Tarbell, Ida Minerva **VII**:349
Till, Emmett Louis **IX**:318
Tillman, Benjamin Ryan **VI**:358
violence and lawlessness **VI**:375
Wells-Barnett, Ida Bell **VI**:388
Lynch v. Donnelly **X**:378*c*
Lynd, Helen Merrell **VII**:205–206
Lynd, Robert **VII**:205–206
Lynd, Staughton **IX**:219
Lyndhurst Villa **IV**:31
Lynn, Massachusetts **IV**:161; **V**:374
Lynn Female Anti-Slavery Society **IV**:161
Lynn Female Peach Society **IV**:161
Lyon, Matthew **III**:14, **277**
Lyon, Nathaniel
  Jackson, Claiborne F. **V**:209
  Price, Sterling **V**:313
  Quantrill, William Clarke **V**:317
Lyon, Phyllis **IX**:131
Lyrics of Lowly Life (Dunbar) **VI**:101, 102

M

Mabila **I:221**
Macao **I**:68, 319–320
MacArthur, Arthur **VI**:128
MacArthur, Douglas, II **X**:184
MacArthur, Douglas A. **VIII:***294,* 447*c*; **IX:***197,* **197–198**, 352*c*
  amphibious warfare **VIII**:20
  Asia **IX**:21
  Bonus Army **VIII**:49
  cold war **IX**:63
  Eisenhower, Dwight D. **IX**:100
  Korean War **IX**:177
  Leyte Gulf, Battle for **VIII**:214
  Nimitz, Chester W. **VIII**:274
  OSS **VIII**:284
  Philippine independence **IX**:256
  Philippines **VIII**:294, 295

Solomon Islands **VIII**:365, 366
  Tarawa **VIII**:386
  World War II Pacific theater **VIII**:435, 437
Macaulay, Thomas Babington **VI**:242
Macbeth (Shakespeare) **V**:387; **VIII**:136
Macbeth Gallery **VII**:23, 26, 405*c*
Macdonald, Charles **VI**:343
Macdonough, Thomas **IV**:392
MacDowell, Edward Alexander **VI:233**, 255, 409*c*
MacDowell Colony **VI**:233
Macedonian, HMS **IV**:115, 391
macehualtin **I**:20
Macfadden, Bernarr **VII**:160
MacFarlane, Robert **X**:45
MacGahan, Aloysius **VI**:33
MacGregor, Gordon **VII**:152
machine age **VII**:24
machine guns **V**:380
machine politics **VI:234**
  Plunkitt, George Washington **VI**:285
  presidential campaigns (1870–1899) **VI**:293
  Quay, Matthew Stanley **VI**:299–300
  Tweed Ring **VI**:368–369
Machinery and Transportation Building (Pan-American Exposition) **VII**:252
Machinery Hall (Philadelphia Centennial Exposition) **VI**:284
Machinists and Blacksmiths International Union **VI**:287
Machu Picchu **I:***180,* **221–222**
MacIntosh, Ebenezer **III:276, 279**
Mackall, William W. **V**:263
Mackenzie, Alexander **IV**:35
MacKenzie, William Lyon **IV**:81
Mackinac, Strait of **II**:273
MacLaury, Bruce **X**:349
MacLeish, Archibald **VIII**:137
MacMonnies, Frederick **VI**:327
Macomb, Alexander **III**:330; **IV**:336
Macon, Nathaniel **III:279–280,** 280
Macon's Bill No. 2 **III:280,** 465*c*
  Bonaparte, Napoleon **III**:55
  foreign affairs **III**:169
  Macon, Nathaniel **III**:280
  Non-Intercourse Act **III**:320
  War of 1812 **IV**:390
Mac/OS operating system **X**:147
MacReynolds, James **VIII**:382
Macune, Charles W. **VI**:125
Macy, William **IV**:137
Macy's **VI**:96
MAD. *See* mutually assured destruction
Madame X (Sargent) **VI**:324

Maddox, Lester **X**:24, 68
Madeira Islands **I:222**, 348, 395*c*
Madeira wine
  alcohol **III**:13
  Madeira Islands **I**:222
  Sugar Act **III**:401
Madero, Francisco **VII**:204, 405*c*
Madison, Dolley Payne Todd **III:280–281,** *281,* 283–284; **IV**:84
Madison, James **II**:330; **III:281–284,** *283,* 461*c,* 463*c,* 465*c,* 466*c;* **IV**:411*c*
  ACS **IV**:17
  Adams, John **III**:6
  Alien and Sedition Acts **III**:14
  Amendments to the U.S. Constitution **X**:23
  American System **IV**:20
  Austin, Moses **IV**:38
  Bank of the United States, First **III**:41
  Bank of the United States, Second **IV**:48
  banks **III**:43
  Bill of Rights **III**:50
  Bonaparte, Napoleon **III**:55
  Bonus Bill **IV**:62
  Brackenridge, Hugh Henry **III**:60
  Cadore Letter **III**:73
  Clinton, George **III**:99
  Constitution, ratification of the **III**:105
  Constitutional Convention **III**:108, 109
  Continental Congress, Second **III**:115
  Democratic Party **IV**:116; **V**:108
  Democratic-Republican Party **III**:136
  Democratic-Republican societies **III**:137
  embargo of 1807 **III**:152–153
  Erie Canal **IV**:141
  Federalist Papers **III**:162, 163
  Federalist Party **III**:164
  Federalists **III**:165, 166
  Florida **III**:167
  foreign affairs **III**:169
  foreign policy **IV**:154
  Freneau, Philip **III**:179, 180
  Ghent, Treaty of **IV**:175
  Hamilton, Alexander **III**:207
  Hartford Convention **IV**:187
  Hull, William **IV**:192
  journalism **III**:240
  Lafitte, Jean **IV**:220
  Liberia **IV**:225
  Madison, Dolley Payne Todd **III**:280, 281

Marbury v. Madison **III**:285
Marshall, John **III**:290
Monroe, James **IV**:259
Monroe Doctrine **IV**:260
Morris, Gouverneur **III**:304
National Road **IV**:271
Native Americans in the War of 1812 **IV**:276
Neutrality Proclamation **III**:315
Nullification Controversy **IV**:282
political parties **III**:338
Randolph, John **III**:359
Rodney, Caesar Augustus **III**:373
states' rights **III**:397
tariffs **III**:406
transportation **V**:390
U.S. Military Academy at West Point **V**:409
Virginia and Kentucky Resolutions **III**:424
Virginia dynasty **III**:425
War Message (1812) **IV:417–419**
War of 1812 **IV**:390
Washington, D.C. **III**:428
Madison Guaranty Savings & Loan **X**:82
Madison Square Garden (New York City)
  anti-Semitism **VIII**:25
  entertainment, popular **VI**:118
  Garvey, Marcus **VII**:121
  Paterson Strike **VII**:254
  sports and recreation **VIII**:371
  UNIA **VII**:361
  White, Stanford **VI**:392
Mad Magazine **IX**:314
Madonna **X**:238–240, 279
Madrid, Spain **I**:332; **VI**:377
Madrid, Treaty of **II**:372
Madrid codex **I**:47
Madrid train bombings (2004) **X**:347
Maennerchor **IV**:195
Mafia **IX**:149
Mafia incident (New Orleans, Louisiana) **VI**:162, **234–235**
magazines **VI**:235, **235–236**. *See also specific magazines*
  advertising **VI**:2; **VII**:5; **X**:7
  Gilder, Richard Watson **VI**:147
  illustration, photography, and graphic arts **VI**:183
  journalism **IV**:209–210
  literature **VI**:224; **X**:211
  media **X**:219
  neoconservatism **X**:252
  news media **VIII**:271, 272
  popular culture **VIII**:301
  recreation **VIII**:329

Magee, Matthew M. **IV**:36
Magellan, Ferdinand **I**:223,
   223–225, 397*c*
   Cabot, Sebastian **I**:45
   caravel **I**:59–60
   Drake, Sir Francis **I**:111
   Pigafetta, Antonio **I**:292
   Sequeira, Diogo Lopes de
      I:331
Magellan, Strait of
   Drake, Sir Francis **I**:111
   Forty-niners **IV**:159
   Magellan, Ferdinand **I**:224
Maggie: A Girl of the Streets
   (Crane) **VI**:85, 226
Magha **I**:139
Maghreb
   Islam **I**:189
   marabout **I**:231
   Sufism **I**:348
magic **I**:384, 385; **III**:341
Magical Mystery Tour (film)
   IX:38
Magician among the Spirits, A
   (Houdini) **VII**:142
Magic intelligence (code) **VIII**:76,
   238
Magnalia Christi Americana
   (Mather) **II**:227
magnetic resonance imaging
   (MRI) **X**:224
Magnetic Telegraph Company
   IV:265
magnetism **VIII**:352
Magoffin, Beriah **V**:172
Magoffin, James W. **IV**:26, **233**
Magoffinville, Texas **IV**:233
Magruder, Jeb **X**:366
Magruder, John B.
   Cobb, Howell **V**:76
   Galveston, Battle of **V**:163
   Hill, Daniel H. **V**:190
   Peninsular campaign **V**:299
Mahan, Alfred Thayer **VI**:236
   foreign policy **VII**:113
   Hawaii **VI**:163
   Lodge, Henry Cabot
      VII:184
Mahan, Asa **IV**:161
Mahan, Frank **VI**:343
Mahar, William L. **VI**:116
Maharishi Mahesh Yogi **IX**:38
Mahayana Buddhism **IX**:272
Maher v. Roe **X**:3, 288
Mahfuz (emir of Adal) **I**:124–
   125
Mahican Indians **II**:45, 179
mah-jongg **VII**:295
Mahmout, Yarrow **II**:248
Mahmud al-Kati **I**:360
Mahone, William **VI**:219
Mahoney, William **VII**:291
Ma Huan **I**:225, 238, 368
Mahwood, Charles **III**:416
mail, U.S. *See* overland mail;
   postal service; Post Office
   Department

Mailer, Norman **IX**:352*c*
   Beat Generation **IX**:37
   literature **VIII**:219; **IX**:193,
      194
   popular culture **IX**:258
   Wolfe, Tom **X**:370
mail-order houses **VI**:236–237
Maiman, Theodore H. **X**:317
Maine **II**:213; **IV**:395*m*
   Abenaki **I**:1
   Aroostook War **IV**:27
   art and architecture **IV**:30
   Blaine, James Gillespie
      VI:40
   Chamberlain, Joshua L.
      V:60
   crowd actions **II**:86
   Eliot, Charles William
      VI:114
   espionage **VIII**:117
   foreign policy **IV**:154
   fur trade **II**:140
   Ghent, Treaty of **IV**:176
   immigration **V**:200
   Jewett, Sarah Orne **VI**:202
   King William's War **II**:195
   land riots **III**:254–255
   literature **VI**:226
   lumbering **II**:211
   Maine Law **IV**:234
   Maliseet **I**:227
   Massachusetts **II**:223
   mass production **VII**:195
   Missouri Compromise
      IV:257
   Mitchell, George **X**:231,
      232
   Penobscot campaign
      III:333–334
   population trends **X**:282
   Reed, Thomas Brackett
      VI:304
   slavery **IV**:346
   Tallmadge Amendment
      IV:365
   War of 1812 **IV**:392
   Webster-Ashburton Treaty
      IV:394
Maine, Remember the **VI**:237–
   238
Maine, USS **VI**:238, 412*c*
   Arlington National Cemetery
      V:17
   Cuba **VI**:88
   Maine, Remember the
      VI:237, 238
   Roosevelt, Theodore
      VII:304
   Spanish-American War
      VI:340
Maine Indian Settlement Act
   (1980) **X**:250
Maine Law **IV**:233–234, 370
Maine Temperance Union **IV**:233,
   234
Maine Woods, The (Thoreau)
   IV:377

Main Line canal system **VI**:204
Main Street (Lewis) **VII**:180
Main-Travelled Roads (Garland)
   VI:140
Mainz, Germany **I**:148
Mair, John **I**:379
maize. *See* corn
Majority Whip. *See* House
   Majority Whip
Major League Baseball **VII**:33;
   X:329–330, 380*c*
Majors and Minors (Dunbar)
   VI:101
Makataimeshiekiakiak. *See* Black
   Hawk
Makemiek, Francis **II**:309
"Make the World Safe for
   Democracy" speech (Wilson)
   VII:424–427
Makin, Gilbert Islands **VIII**:386
Making of an American, The (Riis)
   VI:314
Malacca, Strait of **I**:6, 345
*Malaeska, the Indian Wife of
   the White Hunter* (Stephens)
   VI:98
"Malaise" Speech (Carter) **X**:393–
   396
malaria **I**:107; **II**:213–214
   Bataan Death March
      VIII:42
   disease/epidemics **II**:98;
      III:138; **IV**:123; **V**:112
   medicine **VIII**:234
   Mississippi River war **V**:264
   mortality **II**:243
   science and technology
      VII:314
Malawi **I**:231
Malay **I**:115, 224
Malcolm X **IX**:198–199, *199,*
   352*c*, 356*c*
   African Americans **IX**:6
   assassinations **IX**:22–23;
      X:34
   Black Panthers **IX**:40, 41
   Farrakhan, Louis A. **X**:129
   King, Martin Luther, Jr.
      IX:174
   Louis, Joe **VIII**:223–224
   Muhammad, Elijah **IX**:226,
      227
   Nation of Islam **X**:249
   race and race relations
      IX:271
   religion **IX**:273
   Robinson, Jackie **IX**:278
Male and Female (Mead) **VII**:197
Mali **I**:225–226
   Askia Muhammad I **I**:14
   Gao **I**:137, 138
   Ghana **I**:139, 140
   gold **I**:141
   Gonja **I**:143
   Guinea-Bissau **I**:148
   Henry the Navigator **I**:161
   Ibn Battuta **I**:175

Kaabu, kingdom of **I**:199
Kongo **I**:200
Mansa Musa I **I**:228–229
Niger River **I**:271
Senegambia **I**:330
Songhai **I**:342
Sudan **I**:347
Sundiata Keita **I**:350
Timbuktu **I**:359
Maliki, Nuri al- **X**:188
Malinche **I**:226–227
   Aguilar, Gerónimo de **I**:5
   Aztecs **I**:21
   castas **I**:65
   Cortés, Hernán **I**:95
   Tabasco **I**:351
Maliseet Indians **I**:227
   Acadia **I**:2
   Canada **III**:77
   Passamaquoddy **I**:287
Mall, The (Washington, D.C.)
   VI:55–56
Mallory, Stephen R. **V**:247–248
   Bulloch, James D. **V**:49
   Confederate navy **V**:83
   Confederate States of
      America **V**:85
   Monitor-Merrimack **V**:265
malnutrition
   Dartmoor Prison **IV**:113
   Permanent Indian Frontier
      IV:297–298
   Trail of Tears **IV**:377
Malocello, Lancelotto **I**:57
Malone, Annie Turnbo **VII**:66
Malone, Dumas **III**:233
Malone, Michael P. **VI**:315
Malta **VIII**:118
Maltese Falcon, The (film)
   VIII:246
Malthusian population control
   VII:102
Maltz, Albert **IX**:147, *148*
Malvern Hill, Battle of **V**:444*c*
   Armistead, Lewis A. **V**:17
   Early, Jubal A. **V**:119
   Hill, Daniel H. **V**:190
   Irish-American regiments
      V:205
   Peninsular campaign **V**:300
Mamprussi **I**:252
Manabe, Syukuro **IX**:286, 356*c*
Manabi **I**:392
Man and Nature (Marsh) **VI**:239
Man at the Crossroads (Rivera)
   VIII:31
Manchester *Leader* **VIII**:202
Manchukuo **VIII**:38
Manchuria **VIII**:225–226, 443*c*
   Anglo-American relations
      VIII:21
   dollar diplomacy **VII**:79
   foreign policy **VIII**:140
   Hoover presidency
      VIII:175
   League of Nations **VII**:176
   MacArthur, Douglas **IX**:198

Open Door Notes **VI**:273
Open Door Policy **VII**:246
POWs **VIII**:311
Root-Takahira Agreement **VII**:305
Russo-Japanese War **VII**:309
World War II Pacific theater **VIII**:434
Yalta Conference **VIII**:440
Manco Capac **I**:101
Manco Inca **I**:16, 180
Mandan Indians **I**:162; **IV**:413*c*
  Bodmer, Karl **IV**:60, 61
  Catlin, George **IV**:84, 85
  disease/epidemics **IV**:123
  Great Plains **III**:197
  Lewis and Clark Expedition **III**:263
  Native Americans **IV**:275
Mandela, Nelson **X**:16, 325
Mandelbaum, Seymour J. **VI**:369
Mande people **I**:350
Mandeville, Sir John **I:227–228**
  Hakluyt, Richard, the Younger **I**:153
  monsters **I**:248
  Prester John **I**:301
Mandinka **I**:225–226
Manhattan, New York
  art and architecture **VIII**:28–29
  Dutch-Indian Wars **II**:106
  Greenwich Village **VII**:130
  Harlem Heights, Battle of **III**:210
  immigration **IV**:194; **VI**:184
  migration **IX**:215
  Minuit, Peter **II**:236
  New Amsterdam **II**:256
  New Netherland **II**:264, 265
  New York City **V**:282
  Stuyvesant, Peter **II**:379
  Vanderbilt, Cornelius **IV**:386
  White Plains, Battle of **III**:440, 441
Manhattan Project **VIII**:*226*, **226–227**
  AEC **IX**:24
  atomic bomb **VIII**:34
  business **VIII**:59
  Communists **VIII**:78
  espionage **VIII**:118
  Grand Alliance **VIII**:155
  Hiroshima and Nagasaki **VIII**:166, 167
  intelligence **VIII**:187
  Lilienthal, David E. **VIII**:217
  Oppenheimer, J. Robert **IX**:251
  OSRD **VIII**:283
  Roosevelt, Franklin D. **VIII**:346

Rosenberg, Julius and Ethel **IX**:280
  Sunbelt **VIII**:381
  Tennessee Valley Authority **VIII**:393
Manhattan Railway Company **VII**:303
Manhattan State Hospital **VII**:158
Manifest Destiny **IV:234–236**, *235*, 236*m*
  Alamo, The **IV**:14
  art **IV**:27; **V**:18
  Bent, William **IV**:52
  Bierstadt, Albert **VI**:37
  Colt revolver **IV**:102
  Cuba **IV**:111, 112
  Douglas, Stephen A. **V**:114
  filibustering **V**:144, 145
  foreign policy **IV**:155, 156; **VI**:133
  Forty-niners **IV**:160
  imperialism **VI**:188
  Mexican-American War **IV**:251
  migration **IV**:255
  Native Americans **IV**:276
  Oregon Treaty of 1846 **IV**:287
  race and race relations **IV**:312
  Reid, Whitelaw **VI**:305
  religion **V**:331
  Texas **IV**:372
Manifesto to the Mexican Republic, The **IV**:149
Manila, Philippines
  demobilization (WWII) **VIII**:91
  imperialism **VI**:188
  MacArthur, Douglas **IX**:198
  Philippines **VIII**:294, 295
Manila Bay, Battle of **VI**:*341*
  Dewey, George **VI**:97
  Filipino insurrection **VI**:127
  Spanish-American War **VI**:341
Manila Bay, Philippines **VIII**:42–43
Man in Full, A (Wolfe) **X**:370
manioc **I**:9
Mankiller (Ostenaco) **II:280**
Mann, Horace **IV:236–238**, *237*, 413*c*
  cities and urban life **IV**:93
  education **IV**:133, 135; **V**:124
  Peabody, Elizabeth Palmer **VI**:279
Mann, James Robert **VII**:189, 222
Mann, J. M. **VI**:359
Mann, Mary Peabody **VI**:397, 398
Mann, Woodrow **IX**:118
Mann Act **VII:189–190**, 405*c*
  criminal justice **VII**:67
  Johnson, Jack **VII**:155
  Narcotics Act **VII**:222

Mann-Elkins Act **VII:190**, 262, 347, 405*c*
Man Nobody Knows, The (Barton) **VII**:5
manorial system **II**:387
Mansa Musa I (emperor of Mali) **I:228–229**
  Gao **I**:138
  Mali **I**:225
  Mecca **I**:238
  Songhai **I**:342
  Timbuktu **I**:359
Mansa Sulayman (emperor of Mali) **I**:175
Mansa Uli Keita (emperor of Mali) **I**:225
Mansfield, Joseph **V**:13, 426
Mansfield, Mike
  ERA **X**:123
  Ford, Gerald R. **X**:138
  Senate, U.S. **X**:320
Manship, Paul **VII**:24
Manson, Charles **X**:35
Mansur. *See* Ahmad I al-Mansur
Manteo **I**:229, 398*c*; **II**:274
  Barlowe, Arthur **I**:28
  Roanoke **I**:321, 322
  Wanchese **I**:382
  White, John **I**:383
Mantoac **I**:229, 261
Mantux **I**:392
Manual of Military Surgery for the Use of Surgeons in the Confederate States Army **V**:258
Manuel I (king of Portugal) **I**:396*c*
  Albuquerque, Alfonso de **I**:6
  Cabral, Pedro Álvares **I**:46
  Hanno the elephant **I**:153–154
  Leo X **I**:210
  Magellan, Ferdinand **I**:223
manufacturing and industry **II:214**, 287
  business **IX**:46
  cities and urban life **IX**:55
  computers **X**:87
  Coxe, Tench **III**:125
  economy **III**:146
  Hamilton, Alexander **III**:207
  industrial development **V**:204–205
  Industrial Revolution **III**:224–226
  investments, foreign **VII**:152
  labor/labor movements **IX**:181; **X**:202–203
  Mexican Americans **VIII**:237
  service sector **IX**:288–289
  trade, domestic and foreign **III**:415
  union movement **IX**:324
  Whitney, Eli **III**:442

manumission
  abolitionism **II**:1; **IV**:1
  ACS **IV**:17
  African Americans **III**:9
  Creole **II**:83
  miscegenation **II**:238
  slavery **III**:390
  Spanish colonies **II**:374
  Wheatley, Phillis **III**:438
  women's status and rights **III**:447
manuscripts
  Codex Mendoza **I**:77–78
  illuminated **I**:33
  scribal publication **I**:328
Manuzio, Aldo **I**:195
Manzanar internment camp **VIII**:319
Mao Zedong **IX**:352*c*
  Asia **IX**:20, 21
  Black Panthers **IX**:40
  cold war **IX**:63
  Korean War **IX**:177
  Luce, Henry R. **VIII**:224
  NSC-68 **IX**:247
  Soviet Union **IX**:295
  Truman Doctrine **IX**:322
  White Paper **IX**:343
"Maple Leaf Rag" (Joplin) **VI**:412*c*
  Gay Nineties **VI**:140
  Joplin, Scott **VII**:158
  music **VI**:258; **VII**:219
Map of Virginia, A (Smith) **II**:363
mappae mundi **I**:30, **229–230**, 230
Mapplethorpe, Robert **X**:31, 245
maps. *See* cartography
Maqeda (queen of Sheba) **I**:124
maquiladoras **X**:259
marabout **I**:69, **230–231**, 348
Maracaibo, Lake **I**:277
maranos **I**:194–196; **II**:185
Maravi **I**:231
Marble, Alice **VIII**:372
Marble Faun, The (Faulkner) **VIII**:128
Marblehead, Massachusetts **III**:194, 371
Marble Palace **VI**:96
Marburg, Germany **VI**:113
Marbury, William **III**:285, 290
Marbury v. Madison **III:285**, 465*c*
  Federalist Party **III**:164
  Marshall, John **III**:290, 291
  Supreme Court **III**:403
  U.S. v. Nixon **X**:358
  Watergate scandal **X**:367
"Marching Song of the First Arkansas" **V**:274
"Marching Through Georgia" **V**:273
March of Dimes **IX**:265
March of Time (newsreels) **VIII**:303

March on Washington (1963)
IX:199–201, *200*, 355*c*
  African Americans **IX**:5
  CORE **IX**:73
  "I Have a Dream" Speech
    (King) **IX:373–375**
  King, Martin Luther, Jr.
    IX:174
  NAACP **IX**:232
  Randolph, A. Philip
    VIII:321
  SCLC **IX**:293
  SNCC **IX**:303
  Wilkins, Roy **IX**:344
March on Washington (1968). *See*
  Poor People's Campaign and
  March on Washington
March on Washington Committee
  (MOWC) **VIII**:228
March on Washington Movement
  (MOWM) **VIII:227–228**,
  447*c*
  African Americans **VIII**:4
  Brotherhood of Sleeping Car
    Porters **VIII**:54
  civil rights **VIII**:72–73
  enemy aliens **VIII**:114–115
  Executive Order 8802
    VIII:120
  FEPC **VIII**:123
  NAACP **VIII**:256
  race and race relations
    VIII:319
  Randolph, A. Philip
    VIII:321
March to the Sea. *See* Sherman's
  March through Georgia
Marconi, Guglielmo **VII**:151,
  288
Marcos, Ferdinand E. **X**:163
Marcy, William **IV**:112; **V**:290
Mardi (Melville) **IV**:229
Mardian, Robert **X**:357, 367
Mare liberum (Grotius)
  Dutch East India Company
    I:115
  East India Company **I**:117
  Grotius, Hugo **I**:145–146
  Sequeira, Diogo Lopes de
    I:331
Mareth line **VIII**:278
Margarita Island **I**:119
Mariana Griswold Van Rensselaer
  (Saint-Gaudens) **VI**:321
Mariana Islands **VIII:228–229**
  air power **VIII**:16
  amphibious warfare **VIII**:20
  Army Air Forces, U.S.
    VIII:27
  bombing **VIII**:48
  Iwo Jima **VIII**:192
  Leyte Gulf, Battle for
    VIII:214
  Marines, U.S. **VIII**:230
  Navy, U.S. **VIII**:265
  Nimitz, Chester W.
    VIII:274

Philippine Sea, Battle of the
    VIII:295
  Tarawa **VIII**:386
  World War II Pacific theater
    VIII:436, 437
Marian devotions **VIII**:64
Marias River **IV**:18
Mariel boatlift **X**:378*c*
marijuana
  Leary, Timothy **IX**:187
  Mexico **X**:226
  music **IX**:229
  narcotics **X**:242, 244
  Narcotics Act **VII**:223
Marin, John **VII**:25
Marine, James E. **VII**:37–38
Marine Committee **III**:116
Marine Corps, U.S. **V:248**
  conscription **VII**:63
  foreign policy **VII**:114
  Harpers Ferry, West Virginia
    V:186
  McCarthy, Joseph R.
    IX:206
  Oswald, Lee Harvey **IX**:251
  Siberian Expedition
    VII:325
marine insurance **III**:227
Marine Park (Brooklyn, New
  York) **VI**:391
Mariner 2 (spacecraft) **IX**:296
mariners **II:214–215**
  class **II**:70
  Jews **II**:185
  King George's War **II**:192
  Newport, Christopher
    II:267
  Philadelphia **II**:292
  piracy **II**:296–297
  slave resistance **II**:353
  taverns and inns **II**:384
Mariner space program **X**:327
Marines, U.S. *VIII*:229, **229**, **229–230**,
  448*c*
  Afghanistan War **X**:12
  amphibious warfare
    VIII:19–20
  Army, U.S. **VIII**:25
  demobilization (WWII)
    VIII:91
  Guadalcanal **VIII**:159
  Haiti **X**:164
  Higgins, Andrew J.
    VIII:165
  Iwo Jima **VIII**:192
  King, Ernest J. **VIII**:202
  March on Washington
    Movement **VIII**:227
  Mariana Islands **VIII**:228
  Nimitz, Chester W.
    VIII:274
  Okinawa **VIII**:287
  photography **VIII**:296
  Solomon Islands **VIII**:365
  Tarawa **VIII**:386
  World War II Pacific theater
    VIII:436

Marion, Francis **III:285–286**
  Hobkirk's Hill, Battle of
    III:213
  Tarleton, Banastre **III**:407
  Weems, "Parson" Mason
    Locke **III**:435
Marion *Democratic Mirror*
  VII:134
Marion *Star* **VII**:134
Maritime Commission, U.S.
  VIII:200
Mark I computer **IX**:311
Mark V Panther tank **VIII**:386
Mark VI Tiger **VIII**:386
Markham, William **II**:296
Markoe, William **VIII**:64
Marne, Second Battle of the
  VII:407*c*
Marot, Helen **VII**:231
Marquette, Jacques **II:215–216**,
  216
  exploration **II**:123
  Jolliet, Louis **II**:188, 189
  Roman Catholicism **II**:336
Marrant, John **II**:156
marriage and family life **II:216–**
  219, *217*; **III:286–289**, *287*;
  IV:238–241; **V:248–249**;
  VII:190–193, *191*, 408*c*;
  VIII:230–232; **IX:201–202**;
  X:127–128, **213–216**, *214*
  African Americans **II**:7;
    III:10; **IV**:7, 8
  Asian Americans **X**:33
  Aztecs **I**:20–21
  baby boom **IX**:31
  baby boomers **X**:39
  birth control **VII**:36–37
  Cable Act **VII**:47
  childhood **II**:66–67;
    IX:54–55
  children **VIII**:66
  Civil War **V**:75
  cold war culture **IX**:64–65
  cosmetics and beauty
    industry **VII**:65–66
  Delaware Indians **II**:96–97
  economy **IX**:97
  education **III**:147
  election of 1828 **IV**:137
  emancipation **V**:129–130
  Expatriation Act **VII**:103–
    104
  family life **X**:127
  feminism **X**:134
  food **IX**:122
  Franklin, Deborah Read
    II:134
  Friedan, Betty **IX**:126–127
  gay and lesbian rights
    movement **X**:149, 150
  George III **III**:192
  Great Depression **VIII**:159
  Huron **II**:169
  Iroquois **I**:186
  Jackson, Andrew **IV**:205,
    206

Johnson, Jack **VII**:155
  labor/labor movements
    III:252
  Lee, Ann **III**:257
  Mead, Margaret **VII**:197
  New Woman **VII**:238–239
  North Carolina **II**:273–274
  "The Pill" **IX**:257
  polygamy **IV**:303
  popular culture **III**:341
  population trends **III**:342–
    343; **VII**:266; **VIII**:304–
    305; **IX**:260
  pornography **X**:284
  poverty **III**:344
  race and race relations
    VII:282
  rural life **III**:374–375;
    VII:306
  Seneca Falls convention
    IV:340, 341
  Seton, Elizabeth Ann
    IV:343–344
  slave trade, internal **IV**:348
  society, British American
    II:366
  spiritualism **IV**:355
  suburbanization/suburbs
    VIII:380
  television **IX**:315
  temperance movement
    III:410
  Willard, Emma **IV**:400
  women's status and rights
    III:445–446, 448; **IV**:403;
    VI:399; **VII**:387, 389;
    VIII:422–424; **X**:370, 371
  World War II **VIII**:427
  World War II home front
    VIII:433
  Wright, Fanny **IV**:405
Marriage of Figaro
  (Beaumarchais) **III**:48
Married Women's Independent
  Citizenship Act. *See* Cable Act
Marriott Hotels **X**:283
Mars **X**:327, 381*c*
Mars Global Surveyor mission
  X:329
Marsh, George Perkins **VI:238–**
  239, 294; **VII**:98
Marsh, Othniel Charles **VI:239–**
  240
  Cody, William Frederick
    VI:76–77
  Hayden, Ferdinand
    Vandeveer **VI**:165
  King, Clarence **VI**:208
  science and technology
    VI:325
Marshall, A. D. **X**:349
Marshall, Burke **IX**:269
Marshall, Charles **V**:15
Marshall, George C. *VIII*:232,
  232–233
  Acheson, Dean **IX**:1
  Army, U.S. **VIII**:26

atomic bomb **VIII**:35
Bradley, Omar N. **VIII**:50
Hopkins, Harry L. **VIII**:177
Marshall Plan **IX**:204,
    361–363
McCarthy, Joseph R. **IX**:207
military-industrial complex
    IX:216
Roosevelt, Franklin D.
    VIII:346
second front **VIII**:355
Stimson, Henry L.
    VIII:375
Marshall, James W. **IV**:*177*, 414*c*
California **IV**:71
California gold rush **IV**:72
Forty-niners **IV**:159
gold **IV**:176
McCulloch v. Maryland
    IV:246
panic of 1819 **IV**:293
Marshall, John **III**:**289–291,** *290,*
    464*c*
Bank of the United States,
    Second **IV**:48
Cherokee **IV**:85
Dartmouth College case
    IV:114
Federalist Party **III**:165
Indian Reorganization Act
    VIII:186
Jackson, Andrew **IV**:207
Judiciary Act (1801) **III**:242,
    243
lawyers **III**:256
Marbury v. Madison
    III:285
Native Americans **IV**:275
Nullification Controversy
    IV:282
Pinckney Treaty **III**:336
Story, Joseph **III**:399
Supreme Court **III**:403;
    IV:362
Taney, Roger B. **IV**:366
XYZ affair **III**:451
Yazoo claims **III**:454
Marshall, Lenore **IX**:283
Marshall, Martha Stearns **II**:33
Marshall, Thomas **III**:289
Marshall, Thurgood **IX**:**202–203,**
    203, 357*c*
*Brown v. Board of
    Education* **IX**:44
Kennedy, John F. **IX**:170
Murray, Pauli **IX**:227
NAACP **VIII**:256; **IX**:232
Warren Court **IX**:338
Wilkins, Roy **IX**:344
Marshall, William Edgar **VI**:319
Marshall Court **III**:403, 404
Marshall Field Wholesale Store
    (Chicago, Illinois) **VI**:96, 313
Marshall Islands
amphibious warfare **VIII**:20
Halsey, William F. **VIII**:161
Marines, U.S. **VIII**:230

Nimitz, Chester W.
    VIII:274
World War II Pacific theater
    VIII:436
Marshall Plan **IX**:**203–204,** 351*c,*
    361–363
Alliance for Progress **IX**:10,
    11
business **IX**:46
cold war **IX**:63
demobilization (WWII)
    IX:84
Europe **IX**:113
Harriman, W. Averell
    VIII:162
LWV **IX**:187
Marshall, George C.
    VIII:233
military-industrial complex
    IX:216
Native Americans **IX**:241
NATO **IX**:247
Progressive Party **IX**:264
Soviet Union **IX**:295
Truman, Harry S. **IX**:320
Truman Doctrine **IX**:321
White Paper **IX**:343
Marshalltown Fire Brigade
    VII:341
Mars Pathfinder **X**:329
Martha's Vineyard **II**:308
Martha Washington societies
    IV:369
martial law **V**:444*c*
Baltimore, Maryland, riots
    V:26
civil liberties, Confederate
    V:68, 69
elections **V**:126
governors **V**:172
habeas corpus, writ of **V**:181
Ku Klux Klan **V**:223
Martian Chronicles, The
    (Bradbury) **IX**:195
Martin, Albro **VI**:315
Martin, Del **IX**:131
Martin, Josiah **III**:301
Martin, Luther **III**:**291–292**
antislavery **III**:26
Constitution, ratification of
    the **III**:105
McCulloch v. Maryland
    IV:245
Martin, Thomas **III**:281
Martin Eden (London) **VII**:179
Martinez, Elizabeth "Betita"
    IX:186
Martinez, Jose Antonio **IV**:222
Martinique **I**:**232**
Martin Luther King, Jr. Award
    IX:255
Martin Luther King, Jr. Day
    IX:175
Martin v. Hunter's Lessee **III**:291,
    399; **IV**:411*c*
Martin v. Wilks **X**:77
Martyr, Peter **I**:118

martyrdom **II**:46
"Martyr of Alabama, The" (Harper)
    VI:160
Marx, Groucho **VIII**:443*c*
Marx, Karl **V**:**249–250**
communism **IX**:67
Debs, Eugene Victor **VII**:73
journalism **IV**:208
Kelley, Florence **VII**:164
labor, radical **VI**:212
politics (1900–1928)
    VII:261
Popular Front **VIII**:304
socialism **VI**:335
Socialist Party **VI**:337
Woodhull, Victoria **VI**:401
Marx Brothers **VIII**:245
Marxism
Africa **X**:15–16
Communists **VIII**:77
DuBois, W.E.B. **VII**:81
labor, radical **VI**:212–213
The Masses **VII**:193
Mills, C. Wright **IX**:217
socialism **VI**:336
Socialist Labor Party **VI**:336
Weathermen/Weather
    Underground **IX**:341
Marxists, The (Mills) **IX**:217
Marxist Workingmen's Association
    VI:336, 401
Mary (queen of Hungary) **I**:240
Mary I Tudor (queen of England)
    I:**232–233; II**:315
Church of England **I**:75
Puritans **I**:307
Spanish Armada **I**:344
Mary II (queen of England)
    II:150
Mary Chesnut's Civil War
    (Chesnut) **V**:64, 239
Marye's Heights
Fredericksburg, Battle of
    V:158
Irish-American regiments
    V:205–206
Longstreet, James **V**:242
Meade, George Gordon
    V:253
Quay, Matthew Stanley
    VI:299
Maryland **II**:**219–222,** 435*c;*
    III:463*c;* **IV**:411*c*
abolitionism **IV**:1; **V**:1
agriculture **V**:6
Annapolis Convention
    III:23
antislavery **III**:26
Articles of Confederation
    III:34
Baltimore, Maryland, riots
    V:26
Calvert, George **II**:56
Calvert, Leonard **II**:56–57
Carroll of Carrollton,
    Charles **III**:82
Chase, Samuel **III**:85

citizenship **III**:93
civil liberties, Union **V**:69
Compromise of 1850 **IV**:104
Constitution, ratification of
    the **III**:105
constitutions, state **III**:110
Continental army **III**:111
Continental Congress, First
    III:114
convict labor **II**:80
cotton culture **IV**:107, 108
economy **II**:109
Gettysburg, Battle of **V**:166
Glorious Revolution
    II:149–150
government, British
    American **II**:151
governors **V**:172
habeas corpus, writ of **V**:181
Hamilton, Andrew **II**:161
Herrman, Augustine **II**:164
Hicks, Thomas H. **V**:188
housing **II**:166–167
internal improvements
    IV:202
Jesuits **II**:185
Jim Crow laws **VI**:204
Know-Nothing Party **IV**:215
lead mines **IV**:223
Madison, James **III**:282
Marshall, John **III**:291
Martin, Luther **III**:291–292
Mason-Dixon Line **V**:250
McCulloch v. Maryland
    IV:245–246
migration **IV**:254
miscegenation **V**:261
mulattoes **II**:246
National Road **IV**:271
proprietary colonies **II**:313
Protestantism **II**:314
religion, Euro-American
    II:329
riots **III**:371
Roman Catholicism **II**:335–
    336
St. Mary's City **II**:342–343
Scots immigrants **II**:346
Seton, Elizabeth Ann **IV**:344
slavery **III**:390, 392
slave trade, internal **IV**:349
society, British American
    II:365
stem cell research **X**:335
suffrage **III**:401
Susquehannock War **II**:380
Taney, Roger B. **IV**:365
tenants **II**:387
tobacco **II**:391
Warren, Mary Cole **II**:409
Washington, D.C. **V**:425,
    426
White, Andrew **II**:413
women's status and rights
    II:423, 424
Workmen's Compensation
    Act **VII**:392

Maryland Gazette **II**:189
"Mary's Lamb" (Hale) **IV**:183–184
Mary Stuart (queen of Scotland)
　Drake, Sir Francis **I**:112
　Elizabeth I **I**:121
　James I **I**:191
Mashpee Indians **III**:37; **IV**:227
Mason, Charles **V**:250
Mason, George **III**:105, **292;**
　IV:241
Mason, James
　foreign policy **V**:150
　Kansas-Nebraska Act **V**:221
　Morrill Land-Grant Act
　　V:269
Mason, John **II:222**
　Account of the Puritan-
　　Pequot War **II:439–440**
　New Hampshire **II**:259, 260
　Ostend Manifesto **V**:290
Mason, Joseph **IV**:37
Mason, Lowell **IV**:268
Mason, Richard B. **IV:241**
Mason, Robert Tufton **II**:326
Mason, William **VI**:254
Mason City, Iowa **VII**:50
Mason-Dixon Line **V**:73, **250**
Masonic Temple (Chicago,
　Illinois) **VI**:333
Masons. *See* freemasonry
Massachusett Indians **I:233–234**
Massachusetts **II:222–225,** 436*c;*
　III:461*c,* 462*c*
　abolitionism **III**:1; **IV**:3, 4
　Adams, John Quincy **IV**:5
　Adams, Samuel **III:**7–8
　African Americans **IV**:9
　agriculture **II**:13
　American Anti-Slavery
　　Society **IV**:15
　anti-Catholic riots **IV**:23
　antislavery **III**:25
　Aroostook War **IV**:27
　Baptists **III**:44
　Bernard, Sir Francis **III**:49
　Bradstreet, Anne Dudley
　　II:45
　Catholics **III**:83
　conservation/
　　environmentalism **VI**:82
　Constitution, ratification of
　　the **III**:105
　constitutions, state **III**:110,
　　111
　Continental Congress, First
　　III:113–114
　Continental Congress,
　　Second **III**:115
　Cooke, Elisha, Jr. **II**:80
　Coolidge, Calvin John
　　VII:63–64
　Dana, Richard Henry
　　IV:113
　Day, Stephen **II**:92
　debt, national **III**:130
　disease/epidemics **II**:100;
　　IV:123

Dix, Dorothea **IV**:124–125
Dominion of New England
　II:102
Dudley, Joseph **II**:103
Dukakis, Michael S. **X**:105,
　106
Duston, Hannah Emerson
　II:105
Dyer, Mary **II**:108
economy **IV**:132
education **IV**:133, 135
education, philanthropy and
　VI:112
Eliot, John **II**:115
Ely, Samuel Cullick **III**:151
Emerson, Ralph Waldo
　IV:140
fairs, agricultural **III**:161
Federalist Party **III**:165
female antislavery societies
　IV:148
54th Massachusetts
　Regiment **V**:142–144
Foster, Abigail Kelley
　IV:161
Freeman, Elizabeth **III**:176
fugitive slave laws **IV**:168
Gage, Thomas **III**:187
gay and lesbian rights
　movement **X**:150
Gorton, Samuel **II**:150
government, British
　American **II**:153
Grimké, Angelina and Sarah
　IV:180
Hall, Prince **III**:205
Hancock, John **III**:209
Hartford Convention
　IV:186
Harvard Regiment **V**:186–
　187
Holmes, Oliver Wendell
　VII:140
Horton, Willie **X**:168
Hull, William **IV**:192
Hutchinson, Thomas
　III:218–219
Industrial Revolution
　III:226
iron manufacturing **II**:178
Jackson, Helen Hunt
　VI:199
Jefferson, Joseph, III
　VI:202
Kennedy, Edward M. **X**:196
King, Rufus **III**:246
King George's War **II**:192
King William's War **II**:195
Know-Nothing Party **IV**:214
Lawrence Strike **VII**:173
lead mines **IV**:223
Lee, Arthur **III**:258
Lee, Jason **IV**:224
Lexington and Concord,
　Battles of **III**:264–266
literature **IV**:227
lotteries **II**:210

lyceum movement **IV**:231
Mann, Horace **IV**:237
marriage and family **X**:216
Mason, John **II**:222
Massachusetts Emigrant Aid
　Society **IV**:242
Mather, Cotton **II**:227
Mather, Increase **II**:227–
　228
Mexican-American War
　IV:251–252
minutemen **III**:298
Morton, Thomas **II**:244
Native Americans **II**:252;
　III:312
New Hampshire **II**:260
New Netherland **II**:265
Oliver, Andrew **III**:324, 325
Parris, Samuel **II**:281
Penobscot campaign
　III:333, 334
personal liberty laws **IV**:299
Pickering, Timothy **III**:334
postal service **II**:304
printing and publishing
　II:311
Prohibition **VII**:273
Quakers **II**:322
Queen Anne's War **II**:323,
　324
Quok Walker Case **III**:354–
　355
race and race relations
　IV:311
railroads **IV**:313
Randolph, Edward **II**:326
Red Jacket **III**:359
religion, Euro-American
　II:329
religious liberty **III**:363,
　364
Republican Party **IV**:321
Revere, Paul **III**:366–367
Revolutionary War **III**:367
Riedesel, Frederica
　Charlotte, baroness von
　III:370
riots **III**:371
Rowlandson, Mary White
　II:336
Seven Years' War **II**:348
Sewall, Samuel **II**:350
Shays's Rebellion **III**:388
shipbuilding **II**:351
slavery **III**:390
Suffolk Resolves **III**:400
Tallmadge Amendment
　IV:365
Taney, Roger B. **IV**:366
tariffs **III**:406
taverns and inns **II**:383–384
Thoreau, Henry David
　IV:376–377
Townshend Duties **III**:412
transcendental movement
　IV:378–379
travel **II**:393

Unitarianism **III**:419
violence and lawlessness
　VI:375
Webster-Ashburton Treaty
　IV:394
Weld, Theodore Dwight
　IV:396
Wetamo **II**:411
Wheelwright, John **II**:412
witches/witchcraft **II**:419
women's status and rights
　II:424; **IV**:404
writs of assistance **III**:448
Massachusetts Anti-Slavery
　Society **IV**:413*c;* **V**:46, 115
Massachusetts Assembly **III**:174
Massachusetts Bay Colony **II**:435*c*
　Boston **II**:41–43
　Coddington, William **II**:73
　Congregationalists **II**:75
　Dudley, Thomas **II**:103
　education **II**:111
　Endecott, John **II**:115–116
　government, British
　　American **II**:151
　Hutchinson, Anne Marbury
　　II:170–171
　land **II**:201
　Pequot **II**:289
　Pequot War **II**:289
　Puritans **II**:320
　society, British American
　　II:365
　taverns and inns **II**:384
　women's status and rights
　　II:426
　Wood, William **II**:426
Massachusetts Bay Company
　II:225–226
　Massachusetts **II**:222
　Williams, Roger **II**:415–416
　Winthrop, John **II**:417–418
　wolves **II**:421
Massachusetts Board of Education
　IV:133, 237, 413*c*
Massachusetts Circular Letter
　III:412
Massachusetts Commission on the
　Minimum Wage **VIII**:95
Massachusetts Emigrant Aid
　Society **IV:241–243**
Massachusetts General Court
　Coercive Acts **III**:100
　Oliver, Andrew **III**:324
　Otis, James, Jr. **III**:326
Massachusetts General Hospital
　V:257
Massachusetts Government Act
　III:100, 113, 460*c*
Massachusetts High School Law
　IV:412*c*
Massachusetts Institute of
　Technology (MIT)
　Bush, Vannevar **VIII**:56
　Eastman, George **VI**:105
　Eliot, Charles William
　　VI:113

ENIAC **IX:**105
GE **VII:**123
Hayden, Sophia Gregoria
  VI:165
Richards, Ellen Henrietta
  Swallow **VI:**312–313
technology **IX:**311
women's status and rights
  VI:400
World's Columbian
  Exposition **VI:**402
Massachusetts Kansas Aid Society
  VI:171
Massachusetts Metaphysical
  College **VI:**69, 106
Massachusetts School Act **II:226**
Massachusetts Society for the
  Suppression of Intemperance
  (MSSI) **IV:**369
Massachusetts State House
  III:65, 367
Massasoit **II:226, 294, 376**
Massengil Company **VIII:**140
Masses, The **VII:193**
  Greenwich Village **VII:**130,
    131
  radical and labor press
    VII:285, 286
  Reed, Jack **VII:**296, 297
  Trading with the Enemy Act
    VII:356
  Vorse, Mary Heaton
    VII:375
Massillon, Ohio **VI:**84
Massillon Tigers **VII:**333
mass media **VIII:**273
mass production **III:**465c;
  VII:194–195
  automobile industry
    VII:26–28
  economy **VII:**84
  Ford, Henry **VII:**111–112
  Ford Motor Corporation
    IX:122
  immigration **VII:**144
  industrialization **IV:**199
  Industrial Revolution
    III:226
  invention and technology
    VII:149
  labor/labor movements
    VII:169
  marriage and family
    VII:192
  McCormick, Cyrus Hall
    IV:243
  McDonald's **IX:**208
  Meat Inspection Act
    VII:198
  migration **VII:**206; **IX:**215
  New Unionism **VII:**237
  oil industry **VII:**245
  scientific management
    VII:315–316
  Seattle General Strike
    VII:105
  socialism **VII:**327

Steel Strike of 1919 **VII:**338
  Whitney, Eli **III:**442
Master Card **IX:**79
master craftsmen **III:**35
Masters and Servants Act **IV:**188
Mast Free Riot **II:**259
Matagorda Bay **IV:**233, 371
Matamba kingdom **I:**274
Maternity and Infancy Act. *See*
  Sheppard-Towner Act
Matewan, West Virginia **VII:**360
mathematics **I:**212; **VI:**281, 325
Mather, Cotton **II:227**
  Boylston, Zabdiel **II:**43
  disease/epidemics **II:**99
  Duston, Hannah Emerson
    II:105
  Enlightenment, American
    II:118
  Massachusetts **II:**223
  medicine **II:**230
  printing and publishing
    II:312
  smallpox **II:**361
  witches/witchcraft **II:**419
  wolves **II:**422
  Yale College **II:**429
Mather, Increase **II:**227, **227–
228**
  Boston Philosophical Society
    II:43
  Leverett, John **II:**204
  Massachusetts **II:**223, 225
  printing and publishing
    II:312
  Walter, Thomas **II:**406
  witches/witchcraft **II:**420
Mather, Richard **II:**115
Mather, Stephen **VII:**228
Mathew, Thomas **II:**31
Mathews, Dean Shailer **VI:**131
Mathews, Henry M. **VI:**154
Mathias, Charles **X:**29
Matisse, Henri **VIII:**30
matrilineal succession
  Delaware Indians **II:**96
  Huron **II:**169
  Iroquois **I:**186
  Kaabu, kingdom of **I:**199
  Mali **I:**226
  Mbundu **I:**237
  women's status and rights
    II:422, 426
Matta, Manuel Antonio **VI:**67
Mattachine Review (journal)
  IX:131
Mattachine Society **IX:**131;
  X:322
Mattaponi **II:**308
Mattel **IX:**55
Matthews, Robert **V:**393
Matthews, Stanley **VI:**386
Mattson, Ingrid **X:**189
Mauchly, John W. **IX:**69, 70, 105
Mauldin, Bill **VIII:233–234**
Maumee River, Ohio **IV:**185
Maury, Dabney Herndon **V:**265

Maury, James **III:**232
Maury, Matthew (minister)
  III:261
Maury, Matthew Fontaine
  (oceanographer/Confederate
  officer) **IV:**335; **V:**83
Maximilian II (Holy Roman
  emperor) **I:**144–145
Maximilian von Wied, Alexander
  Philipp **IV:**60–61, 413c
Maximum Freight Rate case
  VI:57, 303
Maxixcatzin **I:**362
Max Schmitt in a Single Scull
  (Eakins) **VI:**104
Maxtla (lord of Tepaneca) **I:**189
Maxwell, James Clerk **VI:**144
Maxwell Motor Company **VII:**84
May, Henry **V:**30
May 2nd Movement **IX:**340–341
Maya **I:234–237, 235**
  Aguilar, Gerónimo de **I:**5
  Alvarado, Pedro de **I:**7
  art and architecture **I:**13
  Aztecs **I:**21
  cacao **I:**47, 48
  Chichén Itzá **I:**71–73
  Cholula **I:**74
  Copán **I:**89–90
  Córdoba, Francisco
    Hernández de **I:**90–91
  Cozumel **I:**99
  Grijalva, Juan de **I:**145
  Guerrero, Gonzalo **I:**147
  khipu **I:**199
  Native American religion
    I:260
  New Spain **I:**267
  Olmecs **I:**278, 279
  Palenque **I:**283
  Tabasco **I:**351
  Tikal **I:**358–359
  Toltecs **I:**364
  Yucatán Peninsula **I:**390
Mayan language **I:**5
Mayapan **I:**73
"May Day" mail bombing (1919)
  VII:61
mayeque **I:**20
Mayer, Louis B. **IX:**147
Mayflower (ship)
  Alden, John **II:**16
  Alden, Priscilla **II:**17
  Bradford, William **II:**44
  Mayflower Compact **II:**228
  Pilgrims **II:**294
  Plymouth **II:**298
Mayflower Compact **II:228–229,
229, 435c**
  Alden, John **II:**16
  Bradford, William **II:**44
  Pilgrims **II:**294
  Plymouth **II:**298
  Standish, Myles **II:**376
Mayhew, Jonathan **II:**22; **III:293**
Mayhew, Thomas **II:**253, 308–309
Maynard, Robert **II:**385

Mayo, Henry T. **VIII:**201
Mayo Clinic **VIII:**177
Mayo Indians **IV:**267
Mays, Willie **IX:**5
Maysville Road Bill **IV:**20, 301,
  302
Mazey, Emil **IX:**12
Mazzoli, Romano **X:**177
Mbundu **I:237–238**
MC (Michigan Central Railroad)
  VI:132
McAdoo, William
  elections **VII:**91
  Railroad Administration
    VII:291
  War Revenue Act **VII:**378
McAfee, Mildred **VIII:**418
McAlister, Lyle N. **I:**368
McAuliffe, Anthony **VIII:**54–55
McAuliffe, Sharon Christa **X:**327
McCabe, Charles **V:**198
McCain, John S., III **X:119, 384c**
  campaign finance **X:**63, 64
  conservation/
    environmentalism **X:**92
  conservative movement
    X:94
  elections, presidential **X:**118
  global warming **X:**156
  immigration **X:**177
  Obama, Barack Hussein
    X:264
  PACs **X:**275
  Senate, U.S. **X:**321
McCain, John S., Sr. **VIII:**274
McCall's magazine **IX:**127
McCann, William **VIII:**64
McCardell, Claire **IX:**116
McCarran, Patrick J. **IX:**157–158,
  204
McCarran Act (1950). *See* Internal
  Security Act
McCarran-Walter Act (1952)
  IX:155, **204–205**, 353c
McCarthy, Eugene **IX:205–206**
  Clinton, Hillary Rodham
    X:77
  Democratic Party **IX:**85
  elections **IX:**104
  Galbraith, John Kenneth
    IX:129
  SANE **IX:**284
McCarthy, Joseph R. **IX:206–
208, 207, 352c, 353c**
  Americans for Democratic
    Action **IX:**14
  anticommunism **IX:**15
  Army-McCarthy hearings
    IX:18
  Buckley, William F., Jr. **X:**50
  cold war culture **IX:**64
  communism **IX:**67
  Eisenhower, Dwight D.
    IX:101
  Gallup Poll **IX:**131
  gays and lesbians **IX:**131
  Hoover, J. Edgar **IX:**149

McCarthy, Joseph R. *(continued)*
HUAC **IX:**150
journalism **IX:**165
Kennedy, Robert F. **IX:**171
La Follette, Robert M., Jr.
VIII:208
literature **IX:**193
Oppenheimer, J. Robert
IX:251
television **IX:**316
McCarthy and His Enemies
(Buckley) **X:**50
McCarthyism
Army-McCarthy hearings
IX:18
communism **IX:**67
conservatism **IX:**74
McCarthy, Joseph R.
IX:206–207
McCartney, Paul **IX:**37–38
McClean, John **V:**117
McClellan, George Brinton
V:250–252, *251*, *444c*
Antietam, Battle of **V:**12,
13
Balloon Corps **V:**25
Buell, Don C. **V:**48
Bull Run/Manassas, First
and Second Battles of
V:50, 51
Burnside, Ambrose E.
V:52
cartography **V:**57
Cedar Mountain, Battle
of **V:**59
Copperheads **V:**95
Daly, Maria Lydig **V:**102
Democratic Party **V:**109
elections **V:**126
espionage **V:**134
foreign policy **V:**150
governors **V:**171
Hancock, Winfield Scott
V:183
Harlan, John Marshall
VI:159
Hill, Ambrose P. **V:**189
homefront **V:**193
Howard, Oliver Otis **V:**197
Irish-American regiments
V:205
Johnston, Joseph E. **V:**214
Joint Committee on the
Conduct of the War
V:215, 216
Jomini, Antoine-Henri,
baron de **V:**217
Lee, Robert E. **V:**230, 231
Lincoln, Abraham **V:**237
McDowell, Irvin **V:**252
medicine **V:**257
Mexican-American War
IV:252
peace movements **V:**296
Peninsular campaign
V:298–300
Scott, Winfield **IV:**336

Shenandoah Valley: Jackson's
campaign **V:**349, 350
Stanton, Edwin M. **V:**368
Stuart, J. E. B. **V:**375, 376
tactics and strategy **V:**381
Union army **V:**400
U.S. Army Corps of
Engineers **V:**407
Vallandigham, Clement L.
V:414
Washington, D.C. **V:**426
Zouaves **V:**441
McClellan Committee **IX:**310–
311, *354c*
McClellan's Own Story
(McClellan) **V:**252
McClernand, John A. **V:**424
McClintock, Ann **IV:**341
McClintock, Mary **V:**436
McCloy, John J.
Army, U.S. **VIII:**25
Japanese Americans,
relocation of **VIII:**193
Stimson, Henry L. **VIII:**375
McClure, Michael **IX:**78
McClure, S. S. **VII:**349
McClure, William **III:**156
McClure's Magazine **VII:**403c
journalism **VII:**159
literature **VII:**179
The Masses **VII:**193
Meat Inspection Act
VII:198
muckrakers **VII:**217
oil industry **VII:**244
Rockefeller, John Davison
VII:303
Standard Oil **VII:**336
Steffens, Lincoln **VII:**339
Tarbell, Ida Minerva
VII:349
McCone, John **IX:**36
McConnell, Mitch **X:**64, 275
McConnell v. FEC **X:**64
McCord, James **X:**366
McCormack, John D. **X:**169
McCormick, Anne O'Hare
VIII:173
McCormick, Cyrus Hall **IV:**243–
245, *244*, *412c*
agriculture **IV:**11
economy **IV:**131
industrialization **IV:**200
science and technology
IV:333
McCormick, Katherine Dexter
IX:211–212, 257
McCormick Harvesting Machine
Company **VI:**168–169
McCormick Theological Seminary
of Chicago **IV:**245
McCorvey, Norma **X:**311
McCosh, James **VI:**111, 242
McCown, John P. **V:**263
McCrea, Jane **III:**293–294
*McCreary County, Kentucky v.
ACLU of Kentucky* **X:**216

McCrummell, James C. **IV:**15
McCulloch, Ben **V:**296, 317
McCulloch, Henry **V:**260
McCulloch, Hugh **V:**246
McCulloch, James **IV:**48, 245, 246
McCulloch v. Maryland **IV:**245–
246, *411c*
banking **IV:**46
Bank of the United States,
Second **IV:**48
Marshall, John **III:**291
Martin, Luther **III:**291
Supreme Court **III:**403
Webster, Daniel **IV:**393
McCusker, John J. **II:**230
McDaniel, David **IV:**66
McDermott, John **VI:**343
McDonald, Donald **III:**301–302
McDonald, John D. **V:**429
McDonald, Richard and Maurice
IX:122, 208
McDonald's **IX:**98, 122, **208–209,**
352c
McDougal, James **X:**82
McDougall, Alexander **III:**98,
196, **294**
McDougall, Duncan **IV:**34, 36
McDowell, Ephraim **III:**295
McDowell, Irvin **V:**252–253
Balloon Corps **V:**25
Bull Run/Manassas, First
and Second Battles of
V:49, 50
Lincoln, Abraham **V:**237
McClellan, George Brinton
V:250
Peninsular campaign **V:**298
Shenandoah Valley:
Jackson's campaign **V:**349,
350
tactics and strategy **V:**381
Union army **V:**400
McDowell, Virginia **V:**350, 351
McDuffie, George **IV:**413c
McFarland, Ernest W. **IX:**135
McFarland, James **III:**440
McFarlane, Robert **X:**28
McFate, Yale **IX:**219
McGillicuddy, Valentine T.
VI:303
McGillivray, Alexander **III:**126,
294–295; IV:109
McGill University **VI:**130
McGovern, George S. **X:**216–
217, *376c*
Clinton, William J. **X:**79
Eagleton, Thomas F. **X:**107
Galbraith, John Kenneth
IX:129
Mondale, Walter F. **X:**233
McGraw-Hill Building (New York
City) **VII:**28
McGready, James **IV:**317
McGuffey, Alexander Hamilton
IV:246
McGuffey, William Holmes
IV:134, 183, **246–247**

McGuire, Peter J. **VI:**213; **VII:**11
McGwire, Mark **X:**330
McHenry, Donald **X:**357
McHenry, James **III:**150, 207
McHenry, John **V:**412
McIlvaine v. Coxe **III:**93
McIntire, Carl **IX:**272
McIntire, Rufus **IV:**27
McIntosh, William (Creek chief)
IV:109, **247**
McKay, Alexander **IV:**35
McKay, Claude **VII:**136, 181,
408c
McKay, James C. **X:**225
McKean, Thomas **III:**373
McKeen, James **VI:**157
McKees Rocks Strike **VII:**287
McKenney, Thomas L. **IV:**196–
197, *412c*
McKenzie, Kenneth **IV:**18
McKiddy, Cecil **VIII:**374
McKim, Charles Follen **VI:**409c
art and architecture **VI:**18
Burnham, Daniel Hudson
VI:55
Richardson, Henry Hobson
VI:313
White, Stanford **VI:**392
McKim, Mead & White **VI:**392
McKim, Randolph **VI:**268
McKinley, William **VI:**240–242,
241, *411c,* *412c;* **VII:**403c
Aguinaldo, Emilio **VII:**9
Anarchist Immigration Act
VII:15
Angell, James Burrill **VI:**15
Arlington National Cemetery
V:17
armed forces **VII:**20
Army Act **VII:**22
Atkinson, Edward **VI:**22
Big Stick diplomacy **VII:**34
Bryan, William Jennings
VI:52
Congress **VI:**80
Cuba **VI:**88
Currency Act **VII:**68
currency issue **VI:**90
de Lôme Letter **VI:**94
Democratic Party **VII:**74
elections **VI:**90
foreign policy **VI:**133, 134;
VII:113
Free-Silver Movement
VI:135
Hanna, Marcus Alonzo
VI:158
Hawaii **IV:**187; **VI:**163
Hay, John Milton **VI:**164
imperialism **VI:**188
Lease, Mary Elizabeth
Clyens **VI:**220
Maine, Remember the
VI:237–238
Manifest Destiny **IV:**236
movie industry **VII:**214
Open Door Policy **VII:**246

Panama Canal **VII:**250
Pan-American Exposition **VII:**252
People's Party **VI:**282
Philippine independence **IX:**256
Pinchot, Gifford **VII:**260
presidency **VI:**290; **VII:**268
presidential campaigns (1870–1899) **VI:**293
Republican Party **VI:**311; **VII:**299
Roosevelt, Theodore **VII:**304
Schurz, Carl **VI:**325
Sherman, John **VI:**329
Spanish-American War **VI:**340
Taft, William Howard **VII:**347
tariffs **VI:**352, 353
veterans **V:**416
Watson, Thomas Edward **VII:**380
McKinley Tariff **VI:**410c
Allison, William Boyd **VI:**12
business and government **VI:**56
Congress **VI:**80
Harrison, Benjamin **VI:**161, 162
Hawaii **VI:**163
McKinley, William **VI:**240
presidency **VI:**290
tariffs **VI:**352; **VII:**349
McKinney, Cynthia **X:**118
McKinney, J. **VII:**440
McKissick, Floyd **IX:**74
McLachlan, Sarah **X:**240
McLane, Louis **IV:**44
McLane, Robert M. **VI:**27
McLaughlin, M. Louise **VI:**3
McLaughlin, Patrick **IV:**105
McLaurin, Charles **IX:**220
McLaurin v. Oklahoma State Regents **IX:**203
McLaws, Lafayette **V:**76, 186, **253**
McLean, J. and A. **III:**162
McLean, Wilmer **V:**15, 16, 232
McLeod, Alexander **IV:**81
McLeod, Donald **III:**302
McLoughlin, John **IV:247–248**
Fort Vancouver **IV:**159
Oregon Trail **IV:**286
Smith, Jedediah Strong **IV:**351
McLuhan, Marshall **X:**153
McMardle, ex parte **VI:**127
McMaster, John Bach **VI:242–243**
McNair, Lesley J. **VIII:**25, 233
McNamara, Frank **IX:**79, 352c
McNamara, Robert S.
ABM Treaty **X:**26–27
antiwar movement, Vietnam **X:**29

Ford Motor Corporation **IX:**123
Pentagon Papers **X:**271
Vietnam War **IX:**330
McNary, Charles
election of 1940 **VIII:**110
McNary-Haugen Farm Bill **VII:**195
Republican Party **VIII:**337
McNary-Haugen Farm Bill **VII:195–196**
agriculture **VII:**8; **VIII:**9
Johnson, Hiram Warren **VII:**154
lobbying **VII:**182
McNider, Hanford **VII:**373
McNutt, Paul V. **VIII:**413
McParlan, James **VI:**248–249
McPherson, Aimee Semple **VII:***196*, **196–197**, 299
McPherson's Ridge **V:**167
MCRA (Medical Care Recovery Act) **X:**353
McReynolds, James C. **VIII:**89
McTeague (Norris) **VI:**226; **VII:**179
McVeigh, Timothy **X:**381c
militia movement **X:**231
Oklahoma City bombing **X:**267
terrorism **X:**346
McVey, Sam **VII:**154
Mead, George Herbert **VII:**180
Mead, Lake **VIII:**327
Mead, Margaret **VII:197–198**, 409c
Boas, Franz Uri **VII:**39
literature **VII:**181
race and race relations **VII:**282
women's status and rights **VII:**389
Mead, William R. **VI:**392, 409c
Meade, George Gordon **V:253–254**, 445c
Fredericksburg, Battle of **V:**158
Gettysburg, Battle of **V:**166–168
Hancock, Winfield Scott **V:**183, 184
Hooker, Joseph **V:**197
Joint Committee on the Conduct of the War **V:**216
Longstreet, James **V:**242
Petersburg campaign **V:**301
Sickles, Daniel E. **V:**361
Meade, Richard Worsam **V:**253
Meagher, Thomas Francis **IV:**196; **V:**205
Means, Gardiner C. **VIII:**43
Meany, George
AFL **IX:**11–12
CIO **IX:**72
Irish Americans **VIII:**189

labor/labor movements **X:**201
Reuther, Walter **VIII:**340; **IX:**275
measles **II:**100
fur trade **IV:**171
medicine **X:**222
population trends **VII:**266
Whitman, Marcus **IV:**398
Whitman, Narcissa **IV:**398, 399
measles vaccine **IX:**211, 212, 313
meat
black market **VIII:**46
OPA **VIII:**282
rationing **VIII:**322, 323
Meat Inspection Act **VII:198**, 404c
Cannon, Joseph Gurney **VII:**48
muckrakers **VII:**217
Pure Food and Drug Act **VII:**277
Republican Party **VII:**300
Roosevelt, Theodore **VII:**304
Sinclair, Upton **VII:**325
"Meat Out of the Easter" (Wigglesworth) **II:**415
meatpacking **VI:243**; **VII:**404c
agriculture **X:**20
cattle kingdom **VI:**64
Sherman Antitrust Act **VI:**330
Mecca **I:238–239**
astrolabe **I:**15
Ibn Battuta **I:**175
Ibn Khaldûn, 'Abd-ar-Rahmân Abû Zayd ibn Muhammad ibn Muhammad **I:**176
Islam **I:**188
Leo Africanus **I:**210
Malcolm X **IX:**199
Mali **I:**225
Mansa Musa I **I:**228
MEChA (Movimiento Estudiantil Chicano de Aztlán) **X:**166
mechanical reaper. *See* reaper, mechanical
Mechanics' Union of Trade Associations **IV:**217, 218
Mechanicsville, Battle of **V:**299
mechanization
agriculture **VI:**8; **VII:**6–8
Industrial Revolution **III:**224
labor trends **VI:**216
South **VIII:**367
Medal of Freedom. *See* Presidential Medal of Freedom
Medal of Honor **V:254–255**; **X:**381c
African-American regiments **V:**5
Andrews's Raid **V:**11

Carney, William Harvey **V:**55
Chamberlain, Joshua L. **V:**60
Cody, William Frederick **VI:**76
54th Massachusetts Regiment **V:**143
Howard, Oliver Otis **V:**197
Lindbergh, Charles Augustus **VII:**178
Quay, Matthew Stanley **VI:**299
Walker, Mary Edwards **V:**423
"Me Decade and the Third Great Awakening" (Wolfe) **X:**370
Medfield, Massachusetts **IV:**123
media **X:217–220**, *218*, 376c, 381c
advertising **X:**7, 8
censorship **X:**71
Christian Coalition **X:**73
gun control **X:**161
Internet **X:**183
literature **X:**210
movies **X:**234–236
political parties **X:**278
religion **X:**306
median age
Asian Americans **X:**33
Hispanic Americans **X:**167
Native Americans **X:**250
population trends **X:**283
median income
African Americans **X:**14
Asian Americans **X:**33
labor/labor movements **X:**203
Native Americans **X:**251
poverty **X:**286
recreation **X:**302
women's status and rights **X:**370
Medicaid **IX:**209, 356c
African Americans **X:**13
Great Society **IX:**139
Johnson, Lyndon B. **IX:**163
liberalism **X:**208
Medicare **IX:**210
medicine **IX:**211
New Deal **IX:**242
Powell, Adam Clayton **IX:**261
public health **IX:**265
Social Security Act **VIII:**365
medical bankruptcy **X:**379c
Medical Care Recovery Act (MCRA) **X:**353
Medical College of Ohio **IV:**249
medical insurance. *See* health insurance
Medicare **IX:209–210**, 356c
abortion **X:**4
African Americans **X:**13
Great Society **IX:**139
Harrington, Michael **IX:**142

Medicare (continued)
House of Representatives **X:**171
Humphrey, Hubert H. **IX:**151
Johnson, Lyndon B. **IX:**163
liberalism **X:**208
Medicaid **IX:**209
medicine **IX:**211; **X:**222
New Deal **IX:**242
Powell, Adam Clayton **IX:**261
public health **IX:**265
Senate, U.S. **X:**321
Social Security Act **VIII:**365
Medicare Catastrophic Coverage Act (1988) **X:**379c
Medicare Prescription Drug, Improvement, and Modernization Act (2003) **X:**171
Medicare Secondary Payer provisions of Social Security Act **X:**353
Medici, Catherine de' **I:**358
Medici, Giovanni de'. See Leo X (pope)
Medici, Lorenzo de' (the Magnificent) **I:**211, 243, 244
Medici family **I:**210, 243
medicine, hospitals, and public health **II:**229–230; **III:**295–296; **IV:**248–250, 250, 415c; **V:**255–259, 256, 258; **VI:**243–245, 244; **VII:**198–200, 199, 274–276, 275, 403c; **VIII:**234–236, 235; **IX:**210–213, 212; **X:**221–225, 221t, 223
Abbott, Grace **VII:**1
agriculture **VIII:**10
alcohol **III:**13
Aleut **II:**17
birth control **VII:**36–37
Blackwell, Elizabeth **VI:**40
Bond, Thomas **II:**38
Boylston, Zabdiel **II:**43
Children's Bureau **VII:**53–54
cities and urban life **VI:**71; **VII:**55
Colden, Cadwallader **II:**73
disease/epidemics **III:**138; **V:**112
elderly **VIII:**107
FSA **VIII:**127
Gilman, Daniel Coit **VI:**148
Goldmark, Josephine Clara **VII:**127
immigration **VI:**184, 185
journalism **VII:**159
ladies aid societies **V:**228
Lining, John **II:**205
marriage and family **II:**218
McLoughlin, John **IV:**247
Meat Inspection Act **VII:**198
medicine **VII:**198–200

midwives **II:**234
miracle drugs **IX:**217–218
Narcotics Act **VII:**221
Native Americans **VII:**233
NIH **IX:**235–236
nurses **V:**285–286
OSRD **VIII:**284
Pember, Phoebe Yates Levy **V:**297
Philadelphia **II:**293
population trends **VII:**266
Pott, John **II:**305
professional organizations, rise of **VI:**293
public health **VII:**274; **IX:**264–266, 265
Pure Food and Drug Act **VII:**277
refugees **V:**330
Richmond, Virginia **V:**336
Rockefeller, John Davison **VII:**303
Rush, Benjamin **III:**375–376
Sanger, Margaret **VII:**312–313
science and technology **IV:**333; **V:**343; **VII:**314; **VIII:**351; **X:**320
service sector **IX:**289
Sheppard-Towner Act **VII:**323
Shippen, William, Jr. **II:**351
smallpox **II:**361
social work **VII:**329, 330
technology **IX:**313, 314
temperance movement **IV:**369
urban reform **VII:**362
Valley Forge **III:**422
veterans **V:**415
Wald, Lillian **VII:**377
Walker, Mary Edwards **V:**422–423
Warren, Joseph **III:**427
Washington, D.C. **V:**426–427
women's status and rights **V:**437; **VI:**400; **VIII:**424
Medicine Lodge, Treaty of **VII:**185
medicine wagons **V:**257
Medina **I:**238
Medina, J. H. **IX:**86
Meditations for Private Hours (Dix) **IV:**124
Mediterranean Sea **I:**77; **III:**462c
Barbary Wars **III:**45, 46
Chauncey, Isaac **III:**86
Constitution, USS **III:**108
Decatur, Stephen **IV:**115
Ethiopia **VIII:**118
mediums **IV:**355
Meehan, Marty **X:**63
Meek, Fielding Branford **VI:**164, 165
Meek, Joe **IV:**324, 398–399

Meese, Edwin C., III **X:**163, **225**, 300
Meet Me in St. Louis (film) **VIII:**246
"Meet Me in St. Louis, Louis" **VII:**218
Meet the Press (TV program) **IX:**52, 146
megamergers **X:**58, 59
al-Megrahi, Abdel Baset Ali Mohmed **X:**383c
Meharry Medical School **VII:**200
Meier, Johann Jakob **IV:**60
Meigs, John Rodgers **V:**17
Meigs, Montgomery C.
Arlington National Cemetery **V:**17
Lookout Mountain, Battle of **V:**244
Union army **V:**402
Melanchthon, Philipp **I:**219
Melbourne, Australia **VIII:**52
Melchers, Gari **VI:**275
Mellen, James **IX:**341
Mellett, Lowell **VIII:**56
Mellon, Andrew William **VII:**200–201**
Coolidge, Calvin John **VII:**65
Fordney-McCumber Tariff **VII:**112
Soldiers' Bonus **VII:**331
tariffs **VII:**350
Mellon and Sons **VII:**201
Mellon Institute for Industrial Research **VII:**201
Mellon National Bank **VII:**201
melodrama **VI:**354–355
Melville, Herman **IV:**228; **VI:**226, 227
Member of the Third House, A (Garland) **VI:**140
Memminger, Christopher G. **V:**259
banking **V:**27
Confederate States of America **V:**85
Congress, Confederate **V:**88
economy **V:**122
memoirs **III:**463c
Alexander, Edward P. **V:**8
Boyd, Belle **V:**40
Equiano, Olaudah **III:**156–157
Grant, Ulysses S. **V:**176
Jersey, HMS **III:**235–236
literature **V:**239–240
Riedesel, Frederica Charlotte, baroness von **III:**370
Memoirs (Finney) **IV:**151
Memoirs (Sherman) **V:**356
Memoirs of the Campaign of the Northwestern Army of the United States: A. D. 1812 (Hull) **IV:**192
Memoirs v. Massachusetts **X:**284

Memorial Ampitheater (Arlington National Cemetery) **V:**17
Memorial Day
Arlington National Cemetery **V:**17
Grand Army of the Republic **VI:**152
United Daughters of the Confederacy **V:**407
veterans **V:**416
Memorial Day, Confederate **V:**192, 229
Memorial Day Massacre
censorship **VIII:**65
Murray, Philip **VIII:**249
Vorse, Mary Heaton **VII:**375
Memorial Hall (Philadelphia Centennial Exposition) **VI:**284
Memphis, Tennessee
blues **VII:**39
cities and urban life **VI:**71
King, Martin Luther, Jr. **IX:**175
lynching **VI:**230
Mississippi River war **V:**263
music **VII:**218, 219
New Madrid earthquake **IV:**280
overland mail **IV:**290
prostitution **V:**316
race and race relations **X:**296
riot (1866) **V:**259–260
Taylor, Zachary **IV:**367
Terrell, Mary Eliza Church **VII:**352
Memphis Board of Censors **VIII:**65
Memphis Slim **VIII:**250
Menard, Pierre **IV:**257
Menard, Russell **II:**230
Men at Work (Hine) **VII:**259
Menawa **IV:**190, 247
Mencken, Henry Louis **VII:**201–202**
conservatism **VIII:**84
Harding, Warren Gamaliel **VII:**134
literature **VII:**179, 180; **VIII:**218
Scopes Trial **VII:**317
Mendel, Gregor **VII:**102
Mendians **IV:**21, 367
Mendoza, Antonio de **I:**239–240**
Alvarado, Pedro de **I:**7
New Spain **I:**268
Peru **I:**289
Zumárraga, Juan de **I:**392
Mendoza, Luis de **I:**223
Menendez de Aviles, Pedro **I:**208, 209
Men in Black (film) **IX:**246
Menlo Park, New Jersey **VI:**195; **VII:**123
Mennonites **II:**147; **V:**295; **VIII:**164

Men of Zeal: A Candid Inside Story of the Iran-Contra Hearings (Mitchell and Cohen) **X:**232
Menominee Indians **IX:**241
mental health **X:**222–223
mental health reform **IV:**124–125, 414*c*
mental illness **X:**107. *See also* insanity
mentally handicapped **X:**67
Men without Women (Davis) **VIII:**31
mercantilism **I:**269–270; **II:230–231**
    Acts of Trade and Navigation **II:**3
    Alexander, Mary Spratt Provoost **II:**17–18
    banks **III:**42
    British Empire **II:**48
    Declaratory Act **III:**134
    Duer, William **III:**141
    economy **II:**109
    Forbes, John Murray **VI:**131, 132
    Iron Acts **II:**178
    Jews **III:**236
    Massachusetts **II:**224
    Morris, Robert **III:**305
    Philadelphia **II:**292
    Sugar Act **III:**402
    Tea Act **III:**409
    trade, domestic and foreign **III:**413–415
    wage and price controls **II:**405
    writs of assistance **III:**448
Mercator, Gerhardus **I:***240,* **240–241,** 382
Mercer, George **III:**323
Mercer, Hugh **IV:**258
Mercer, Jesse **V:**331
Mercer, John Francis **III:**105
Mercer, Lucy **VIII:**342, 344
merchant marine **VI:245**
    armed forces **VII:**21
    business and government **VI:**56
    impressment **III:**223
    Jay's Treaty **III:**231
    Mahan, Alfred Thayer **VI:**236
Merchant Marine Act
    business and government **VI:**56
    merchant marine **VI:**245
    U.S. Shipping Board **VII:**361
merchants **II:231,** 436*c*
    Astor, John Jacob **IV:**33–35
    banking **II:**32
    Boston **II:**41
    China trade **III:**88
    cities and urban life **III:**90
    class **II:**70
    clothing **II:**72

    crime and punishment **II:**83
    Duer, William **III:**141
    Essex decision **III:**157
    Georgia **II:**147
    government, British American **II:**153
    indentured servitude **II:**175
    Jamestown **II:**181
    Jews **III:**236
    Larkin, Thomas Oliver **IV:**222
    Morris, Robert **III:**305
    New Netherland **II:**264
    New York City **II:**272
    Philadelphia **II:**292
    rationing **VIII:**322
    rum trade **II:**338
    St. Vrain, Céran **IV:**327–328
    Seven Years' War **II:**348, 349
    smuggling **II:**364
    society, British American **II:**365
    Spanish colonies **II:**373
    SPG **II:**368
    Stearns, Abel **IV:**356
    Sublette, William **IV:**359
    Sugar Act **III:**402
    Theus, Jeremiah **II:**390
    Wyeth, Nathaniel J. **IV:**406
merchant ships **VIII:**359
Merck & Co. **VIII:**57
MERCOSUR (Mercado Comun del Sur tariff union) **X:**206
Mercury space program
    NASA **IX:**231
    Operation Mongoose **IX:**250
    science and technology **IX:**285
Mercury Theater of the Air **VIII:**414–415
Meredith, James **IX:**49, **213,** *213,* 303, 355*c,* 357*c*
mergers **VI:**412*c*
    business **X:**57–59
    business and government **VI:**57; **X:**57–59
    literature **X:**212
    trusts **VI:**365
Meridian, Mississippi **IX:**219
merit system **VI:**73, 74
Merkel, Angela **X:**143
Merlin **III:**135
Merrell, James **I:**225
Merriam Report on the Problem of Indian Administration **VII:**233
Merrill, William E. **V:**57
Merrill Lynch **X:**61
Merrimack, CSS **V:**207. *See also Monitor-Merrimack*
Merritt, Ezekiel **IV:**49
Merritt, Wesley **V:**352
Merryman, ex parte **V:**69, 181
Merryman, John **V:**69, 181
Merry Mount **II:**244, 245, 376

Merry Widow, The (Lehár) **VII:**95, 218
Mesabi Iron Range **VII:**109, 238
Mesabi region **IV:**394–395
Mescalero Apache Indians **V:**444*c;* **VI:**376
Mesoamerica
    Chichén Itzá **I:**71
    Maya **I:**234–237
    Mexico **I:**242–243
    Monte Albán **I:**250–251
    Nahua **I:**257
    Nahuatl **I:**258
    Olmecs **I:**277–279
    Quetzalcoatl **I:**309
    Tabasco **I:**351
    Teotihuacán **I:**356
    Toltecs **I:**364–367
Messenger (Brotherhood of Sleeping Car Porters journal) **VII:**136
Messiah **X:**125
Messina, Straits of **VIII:**191, 360
mestizaje **I:241–242**
    castas **I:**64
    New Spain **I:**269
    zambo **I:**391
mestizos **I:242**
    casta paintings **I:**64
    castas **I:**64, 65
    ethnocentrism **II:**122
    limpieza de sangre **I:**214
    miscegenation **II:**237
    New Spain **I:**269
    São Tomé **I:**328
    Spanish colonies **II:**373
    Spanish immigration **II:**375
Metacom **II:**193, 223, **231–232,** 232
Metacom's War. *See* King Philip's War
metal industry **VII:**408*c*
Metalious, Grace **IX:**195
metalwork **VI:**3
Metcalfe, Ralph **VIII:**372
meteorology **VI:**386–387
methamphetamine **X:**244
Methodism/Methodists **III:296–297**
    abolitionism **V:**1
    African-American churches, growth of **VI:**4–5
    African Americans **VI:**7; **X:**14
    African Methodist Episcopal Church **V:**5
    Allen, Richard **III:**15–16
    antislavery **III:**26
    Asbury, Francis **III:**36
    camp meetings **III:**77
    Chautauqua Institute **VI:**66
    Dix, Dorothea **IV:**124
    Dow, Lorenzo **III:**139; **IV:**126–127
    evangelical Christians **X:**125
    Great Awakening **II:**156

    Lee, Jason **IV:**224
    literature **IV:**227
    McLoughlin, John **IV:**248
    Negro Convention movement **IV:**279
    religion **III:**361, 362; **IV:**317–319; **V:**331, 332; **VII:**298; **VIII:**335
    religious liberty **III:**363, 364
    Second Great Awakening **IV:**337
    Virginia **II:**402
    Wesley, John **II:**410
    Young, Brigham **IV:**407
Methodist Board of Overseers **IV:**224
Methodist Episcopal Church **IV:**227
Methodist Episcopal Zion Church **IV:**129
Methodist Society **IV:**227
methylphenidate **X:**223
métis **II:**104, 122, **232–233**
Metro Broadcasting v. Federal Communications Commission **X:**9
Metro-Goldwyn-Mayer (MGM) **V:**169; **VII:**216
Metropolis, The (Sinclair) **VII:**326
Metropolitan Magazine **VII:**296
Metropolitan Museum of Art (New York City)
    art **V:**19
    La Farge, John Frederick Lewis Joseph **VI:**218
    Marsh, George Perkins **VI:**239
    Morgan, John Pierpont **VI:**251
    New York City **V:**282
Metropolitan Opera Company **VIII:**251; **IX:**228
Metropolitan Opera House (New York City) **VII:**356
Metzner, Ralph **IX:**78
Meuse River **VIII:**55
Mexica. *See* Aztecs
Mexican-American civil rights movement **X:**166
Mexican Americans **VIII:237,** 443*c,* 448*c;* **IX:**357*c*
    Asian Americans **VIII:**32
    braceros **IX:**42–43
    Catholics **VIII:**64
    Chávez, César Estrada **IX:**53–54
    children **VIII:**67
    cities and urban life **VIII:**70; **IX:**56
    civil liberties **VIII:**71
    civil rights **VIII:**72, 73
    FMP **VIII:**134
    Gonzáles, Rodolfo "Corky" **IX:**136–137
    Great Depression **VIII:**159

Mexican Americans (*continued*)
Hispanic Americans **X:**166, 167
immigration **VIII:**184
La Raza Unida **IX:**183
Latino movement **IX:**185, 186
literature **X:**211
Mexican Repatriation Program **VIII:**238
migration **VIII:**240
population trends **V:**311
race and race relations **VIII:**319
suburbanization/suburbs **VIII:**380
Tijerina, Reies López **IX:**317–318
UFW **IX:**324–325
unemployment **VIII:**399
women's status and rights **IX:**348
World War II **VIII:**427
World War II home front **VIII:**433
Young Chicanos for Community Action **IX:**350
zoot-suiters **VIII:**441, 442
Mexican-American War **IV:250–253,** *252,* **414***c*
abolitionism **V:**3
Anderson, Robert **V:**9
Armijo, Manuel **IV:**26
Armistead, Lewis A. **V:**17
Beauregard, Pierre Gustave Toutant **V:**32
Bent, Charles **IV:**52
Bent, William **IV:**52
Bent's Fort **IV:**55
Bidwell, John **IV:**56
Bragg, Braxton **V:**42
Buell, Don C. **V:**48
Burnside, Ambrose E. **V:**51
Calhoun, John C. **IV:**69
California **IV:**71
California Trail **IV:**77
Cass, Lewis **IV:**83
citizen-soldier **V:**68
Clay, Henry **IV:**97
Clayton-Bulwer Treaty **IV:**98
Colt revolver **IV:**102
Compromise of 1850 **IV:**103
conscription **V:**90
Davis, Jefferson **V:**103
Democratic Party **IV:**118; **V:**109
Deseret, State of **IV:**120
disease/epidemics **IV:**123
exploration **IV:**145, 146
Farragut, David Glasgow **V:**137
foreign policy **IV:**155
Fort Leavenworth **IV:**158
Gadsden Purchase **IV:**173

Gorgas, Josiah **V:**171
Grant, Ulysses S. **V:**173
Gregg, Josiah **IV:**179
Guadalupe Hidalgo, Treaty of **IV:**180–181, **440–441**
Halleck, Henry Wager **V:**182
Hancock, Winfield Scott **V:**183
Hastings, Lansford W. **IV:**187
Hill, Ambrose P. **V:**189
Hill, Daniel H. **V:**190
Hooker, Joseph **V:**196
immigration **IV:**193
Johnston, Albert Sidney **V:**213
Johnston, Joseph E. **V:**214
journalism **IV:**209; **V:**217
Kearny, Stephen Watts **IV:**212
Know-Nothing Party **IV:**214
Lamar, Mirabeau B. **IV:**222
Lamy, Jean Baptiste **IV:**222
Larkin, Thomas Oliver **IV:**223
Lincoln, Abraham **V:**236
Longstreet, James **V:**241
Magoffin, James W. **IV:**233
Manifest Destiny **IV:**235
McClellan, George Brinton **V:**250
McDowell, Irvin **V:**252
McLaws, Lafayette **V:**253
Meade, George Gordon **V:**253
Monroe Doctrine **IV:**261
Mormon Trail **IV:**262
overland mail **IV:**289
Pemberton, John C. **V:**298
Perry, Matthew Calbraith **IV:**298
Pickett, George Edward **V:**306
Pierce, Franklin **V:**307
Polk, James K. **IV:**302
popular sovereignty **IV:**304
race and race relations **IV:**312
Rosecrans, William S. **V:**337
St. Vrain, Céran **IV:**328
Santa Anna, Antonio López de **IV:**330
Santa Fe Trail **IV:**332
Scott, Winfield **IV:**335, 336
tactics and strategy **V:**379, 380
Taylor, Zachary **IV:**368
Texas **IV:**372
Thomas, George H. **V:**388
U.S. Military Academy at West Point **V:**409
Vallandigham, Clement L. **V:**413
Wallace, Lew **VI:**381
Webster, Daniel **IV:**394
Whigs **IV:**397

Wilmot Proviso **V:**432
Zimmermann telegram **VII:**401
Mexican Constitution **IV:**191
Mexican immigration **VII:202–203,** 266, 320
Mexican Invasion **VII:203–204,** 406*c*
Big Stick diplomacy **VII:**35
foreign policy **VII:**114
Pershing, John Joseph **VII:**258
Zimmermann telegram **VII:**401
Mexican Labor Program **IX:**43, 352*c*
Mexican Plateau **I:**13, 243
Mexican Repatriation Program **VIII:238,** 443*c*
civil liberties **VIII:**71
immigration **VIII:**184
Mexican Americans **VIII:**237
race and race relations **VIII:**319
Mexican Revolution **VII:204–205,** *205,* 405*c,* 406*c*
investments, American, abroad **VI:**197
MacArthur, Douglas **IX:**197
Mexican immigration **VII:**203
Mexican Invasion **VII:**203
Reed, Jack **VII:**296
Texas Revolution **IV:**373
Mexico **I:242–243,** 395*c;* **IV:**414*c,* 415*c;* **VII:**406*c,* 407*c;* **VIII:**443*c,* 447*c;* **X:225–227,** 380*c. See also* Mexican-American War
Aguilar, Francisco de **I:**4
Aguilar, Gerónimo de **I:**5
Alvarado, Pedro de **I:**7–8
Armijo, Manuel **IV:**26–27
art and architecture **I:**12, 13
Austin, Stephen F. **IV:**39–41
Aztecs **I:**18–22
Aztlán **I:**23
Bear Flag Revolt **IV:**49–50
Big Stick diplomacy **VII:**35–36
black legend **I:**31
Bush, George W. **X:**56
cabildo **I:**41
Calhoun, John C. **IV:**69
California **I:**52; **III:**73; **IV:**70, 71
California missions **IV:**76–77
Cholula **I:**74
Córdoba, Francisco Hernández de **I:**90
corn **I:**91
Cortés, Hernán **I:**94
Crane, Stephen **VI:**85
Cuba **IV:**111

Díaz del Castillo, Bernal **I:**106
economy **X:**110
Escalante, Juan de **I:**123
Figueroa, José **IV:**148–149
filibustering **V:**145
Florentine Codex **I:**130
Florida **IV:**153
foreign policy **IV:**155, 156; **V:**151; **VII:**114, 115; **X:**142, 144
Gadsden Purchase **IV:**173–174
Good Neighbor policy **VIII:**151
Gregg, Josiah **IV:**179
Grijalva, Juan de **I:**145
Guadalajara **II:**158
Guadalupe Hidalgo, Treaty of **IV:**180–182
Hearst, William Randolph **VII:**138
Hershey, Lewis B. **VIII:**164
horses **I:**168
House of Representatives **X:**171
immigration **VII:**144; **VIII:**184; **IX:**156; **X:**177
imperialism **VI:**188
investments, American, abroad **VI:**197
IRCA **X:**177
Jefferson, Joseph, III **VI:**202
Kearny, Stephen Watts **IV:**212
labor/labor movements **X:**203
Lamar, Mirabeau B. **IV:**221
Larkin, Thomas Oliver **IV:**223
Latin America **X:**206
Lee, Robert E. **V:**230
Magoffin, James W. **IV:**233
Manifest Destiny **IV:234–235**
Mendoza, Antonio de **I:**239
Mexican immigration **VII:**202–203
Mexican Invasion **VII:**203–204
Mexican Revolution **VII:**204–205
migration **IV:**255; **VII:**207
Monroe Doctrine **IV:**259
Monte Albán **I:**250–251
Murrieta, Joaquín **IV:**267–268
NAFTA **X:**259
Nahua **I:**257–258
Nahuatl **I:**258
neutrality **VII:**236
New Spain **I:**266–270
New Spain, northern frontier of **III:**317–318
Olmecs **I:**277
Palenque **I:**283

Pershing, John Joseph
VII:258
Polk, James K. IV:302
population trends I:297;
VII:266; IX:260
printing press I:303
Pueblo I:305
Purchas, Samuel I:307
religion IV:319
Sahagún, Bernardino de
I:323
St. Vrain, Céran IV:327–328
Sandoval, Gonzalo de I:325
Santa Anna, Antonio López
de IV:328–330
Santa Fe Trail IV:330, 332
Sequoyah IV:343
silver I:336
Spanish colonies II:371,
373, 374
Tabasco I:351
Tacuba I:352
Tarascan I:353
Taylor, Zachary IV:368
Tenochtitlán I:354–356
Teotihuacán I:356
Texas IV:371
Texas Revolution IV:373–
375
Tezcatlipoca I:357
Tlaxcala I:361–363
Toltecs I:364
Travis, William Barret
IV:379–380
Veracruz I:376
Walker, William V:423
Wallace, Lew VI:381
Williams, George
Washington VI:395
Wilmot Proviso V:432
Wilson, Thomas Woodrow
VII:383
Yucatán Peninsula I:390
Zacatecas I:391
Zimmermann telegram
VII:401
Mexico, Republic of
Alamo, The IV:14
Figueroa, José IV:149
Houston, Sam IV:191
Lamy, Jean Baptiste IV:222
Santa Anna, Antonio López
de IV:328–329
Santa Fe Trail IV:330
Texas IV:371–372
Mexico City, Mexico IV:414c
Alamo, The IV:14
Armijo, Manuel IV:26
Austin, Stephen F. IV:39, 40
foreign policy IV:155
Guadalupe Hidalgo, Treaty
of IV:181
Hill, Ambrose P. V:189
Houston, Sam IV:191
Kearny, Stephen Watts
IV:212
Manifest Destiny IV:235

Mexican-American War
IV:252
Mexican immigration
VII:202
Mexican Revolution
VII:205
Mexico I:243
New Spain I:267–269
Santa Anna, Antonio López
de IV:329
Scott, Winfield IV:336
Spanish colonies II:372
Texas IV:371, 372
Texas Revolution IV:373,
374
Travis, William Barret
IV:379
Zimmermann telegram
VII:401
Mexico City Policy X:4
Meyer, Frank IX:74
Meyer, Grant E. IX:286
Meyer, Russ IX:226
mezzotint II:283
MFDP. *See* Mississippi Freedom
Democratic Party
Mfume, Kweisi X:245
MGM. *See* Metro-Goldwyn-
Mayer
MGM Studios VIII:128
MI-5/MI-6 (Great Britain)
VIII:76, 187
MIA. *See* Montgomery
Improvement Association
Miami, Florida X:295, 308
Miami Indians II:201
Cherokee III:87
Clark, George Rogers
III:95
Dragging Canoe III:139,
140
Fallen Timbers, Battle of
III:161
Greenville, Treaty of
III:200
Native Americans III:311,
312, 314; IV:273
Red Jacket III:359–360
Sac and Fox IV:327
Miami University (Oxford, Ohio)
IV:246; IX:219
Miantonomo II:233, 249, 417
Michaelius, Jonas II:106
Michaell (ship) I:134
Michelangelo I:243–244
art and architecture I:13
Leonardo da Vinci I:211
New York World's Fair
(1964) IX:246
Michelson, Albert VII:314
Micheltorena, Manuel IV:56
Michener, James X:212
Michigan
abolitionism V:1
abortion X:2
agriculture IV:10
disease/epidemics IV:123

economy IV:130
education, federal aid to
VI:110
Foster, Abigail Kelley
IV:161
Harrison, William Henry
IV:184
Hull, William IV:192
internal improvements
IV:202
invention and technology
VII:150
Liberty Party IV:226
lumbering IV:231
Maine Law IV:234
mass production VII:195
migration IV:254
mining VII:210
Native Americans in the War
of 1812 IV:277
New Unionism VII:238
Pike, Zebulon Montgomery
IV:300
Pingree, Hazen S. VII:260–
261
race and race relations
VIII:318
railroads IV:316
Republican Party IV:321
rust belt X:314
Sac and Fox IV:327
Siberian Expedition
VII:325
Sweet trial VII:344
Thames, Battle of the
IV:375
Weld, Theodore Dwight
IV:396
WFM VII:382
Michigan, Lake II:273; IV:391;
VI:71
Michigan Central Railroad (MC)
VI:132
Michigan Civil Rights Initiative
X:10
Michilimackinac
French colonies II:137
fur trade II:142
Jolliet, Louis II:189
Michilimackinac Company IV:18
Mickey Mouse IX:88
Mickey Mouse Club, The (TV
program) IX:88–89, 315
"Micmac Indian Responds to the
French, A" (LeCler) II:440–
441
Micmac Indians
Acadia I:2
Canada III:77
Cartier, Jacques I:61
Native American religion
I:260
Micro Instrumentation Telemetry
Systems (MITS) X:86, 147
microprocessors X:86, 317, 318,
320, 376c
microscopes V:258; X:320

Microsoft Corporation X:381c–
383c. *See also* Windows
operating system
business X:59
computers X:87
economy X:109
Gates, William Henry, III
X:147–148
globalization X:153
microwave ovens X:317–318
Middle Ages I:215
Middle Atlantic states
cities and urban life VI:69
internal improvements
IV:202
railroads IV:316
Middle Border VI:226
Middlebury, Vermont IV:400
Middlebury College IV:400
Middlebury Female Academy
IV:401
middle class II:71
advertising VI:2
economy IX:98
marriage and family III:288
Mills, C. Wright IX:217
shopping centers IX:289,
290
Middle Colonies
agriculture II:12, 14
economy II:109
education III:147
English immigrants II:117
Franklin, Deborah Read
II:134
gender II:145
labor/labor movements
II:199
Logan, James II:209
marriage and family II:217;
III:286, 287
mortality II:244
population trends II:302
religion III:360
religion, Euro-American
II:329
religious liberty III:362
slavery III:390
society, British American
II:366
tenants II:387
Tennent, Gilbert II:388
Middle East IX:214–215, 354c;
X:227–230, 228
Africa X:15
Bunche, Ralph IX:45
Bush, George W. X:56
Camp David accords
X:65–66
Clinton, William J. X:83
cold war IX:63
cold war, end of X:84
Dulles, John Foster IX:91
elections IX:103
energy X:120, 121
foreign policy X:140, 143
Habib, Philip C. X:163

Middle East *(continued)*
Israel **IX:**160
labor/labor movements
X:202
Mitchell, George **X:**232
OPEC **X:**268
Powell, Colin L. **X:**287
Reagan, Ronald W. **X:**301
Rice, Condoleezza **X:**310
Suez crisis **IX:**306–307
terrorism **X:**348
middle passage **I:244,** 339
Equiano, Olaudah **III:**156–
157
slave resistance **II:**352–353
slave trade **II:**359
Middle Temple (London)
Hakluyt, Richard, the Elder
I:150, 151
Hakluyt, Richard, the
Younger **I:**152
Ralegh, Sir Walter **I:**311
Middleton, Arthur **II:233–234**
Middleton, Christopher **I:**273
*Middletown: A Study in Modern
American Culture* (Lynd and
Lynd) **VII:**191, 205, **205–206**
Middletown in Transition (Lynd
and Lynd) **VII:**206
"Midnight Special, The" **IX:**120
Midvale Steel Company
labor trends **VI:**216
steel industry **VII:**337
Taylor, Frederick Winslow
VII:350
Midway, Battle of **VIII:238–239,**
447*c*
aircraft carriers **VIII:**12
code breaking **VIII:**76
Guadalcanal **VIII:**159
Navy, U.S. **VIII:**265
Nimitz, Chester W. **VIII:**274
Solomon Islands **VIII:**365
World War II Pacific theater
VIII:436
Midway Plaisance (World's
Columbian Exposition) **VI:**403
midwestern United States
agriculture **V:**6; **VIII:**9
cattle kingdom **VI:**64
cities and urban life **VI:**69,
71; **IX:**55; **X:**75
Copperheads **V:**95
Deere, John **IV:**115
Democratic Party **VIII:**92
disease/epidemics **IV:**123
dust bowl **VIII:**98
economy **IV:**130
education **IV:**133–134
FHA **VIII:**126
fugitive slave laws **IV:**168–
169
governors **V:**171
Ickes, Harold L. **VIII:**183
immigration **V:**200; **VI:**184
Indian Removal Act **IV:**197
industrialization **IV:**201

Irish Americans **VIII:**188
isolationists **VIII:**189
jazz **VIII:**195
lead mines **IV:**224
McCormick, Cyrus Hall
IV:243, 245
migration **IV:**255; **VIII:**239,
240
mining **VII:**207, 209
Non-Partisan League
VII:241
Omaha platform **VI:**272
population trends **VII:**266,
267; **VIII:**305; **X:**281
poverty **X:**286
Progressive Party **VII:**269
property rights **X:**290
railroads **IV:**314
religion **IV:**318
science and technology
IV:335
sports and recreation
VII:333, 335
Sunbelt **VIII:**381
Tappan, Arthur and Lewis
IV:366
technology **VIII:**397
UMWA **VIII:**401
Union League **V:**404
Villard, Henry **IV:**374
violence and lawlessness
VI:375
World War II **VIII:**428
midwives **II:234**
alcohol **II:**16
fertility **II:**126
medicine **II:**230; **III:**295
Shippen, William, Jr. **II:**351
women's status and rights
II:425
Miers, Harriet **X:**265, 339
Mies van der Rohe, Ludwig **IX:**20
Mifflin, Thomas **III:**182
migrant labor
agriculture **X:**19–20
braceros **IX:**42, 43
Chávez, César Estrada
IX:53–54
FSA **VIII:**127
Hispanic Americans **X:**166
immigration **VIII:**184
IWW **VII:**147
Lange, Dorothea **VIII:**210
Resettlement Administration
VIII:338
UFW **IX:**324
unemployment **VIII:**399
World War II home front
VIII:432, 433
"Migrant Mother" (Lange)
VIII:210
migration **IV:253–255,** 254*m;*
VII:206–207; VIII:239–240
African Americans **VIII:**2;
X:13, 14
agriculture **IV:**10, 12;
VIII:9

American System **IV:**19
Applegate, Jesse **IV:**26
Bantu **I:**26–27
Becknell, William **IV:**50
Bidwell, John **IV:**56
California gold rush **IV:**73,
75
California Trail **IV:**77–78
Choctaw **IV:**86
cities and urban life **VII:**54,
55; **VIII:**70
claim clubs **IV:**95–96
class consciousness **VI:**73
consumption **II:**79
cotton culture **IV:**107
Delaware Indians **II:**97
Deseret, State of **IV:**119–
120
Donner party **IV:**125–126
dust bowl **VIII:**98
economy **VIII:**132
exploration **IV:**145–146
FEPC **VIII:**123
foreign policy **IV:**157
Forty-niners **IV:**159–160
Foster, William Zebulon
.**VII:**116
Fulani **I:**135–136
gays and lesbians **VIII:**147
gold **IV:**179
Great Depression **VIII:**159
Gregg, Josiah **IV:**179
Hastings, Lansford W.
IV:187
Houston, Sam **IV:**190
Jews **I:**195
labor trends **VI:**216–217
marriage and family
VIII:231
Mason, Richard B. **IV:**241
Mexican Americans
VIII:237
mobilization **VIII:**241
Mormon Trail **IV:**261
Mormon War **IV:**262–263
National Origins Act
VII:227
National Reclamation Act
VII:228
Native Americans **IV:**275
Nauvoo **IV:**279
Oregon Trail **IV:**285–286
"Pike's Peak or Bust" **IV:**300
popular sovereignty **IV:**305
population trends **V:**310;
VII:267; **VIII:**305
race and race relations
VIII:319
railroads **IV:**313–316
Santa Fe Trail **IV:**332
Singleton, Benjamin **V:**361
slavery **IV:**347
slave trade, internal **IV:**348–
349
Smith, Jedediah Strong
IV:350
South **VIII:**367

South Pass **IV:**354
Sunbelt **VIII:**380, 381;
X:337
technology **VIII:**397
Travis, William Barret
IV:379
World War II **VIII:**428
World War II home front
VIII:432, 433
YMCA/YWCA **VII:**397
Young, Brigham **IV:**407
migration chains **VI:**185
Migration Series (Lawrence)
VIII:30
migration trends **IX:215,** 305
Mikan, George **VIII:**371
Milam, J. W. **IX:**318
Milan, Italy **I:**211
Milan Decree **III:297–298**
Berlin Decree **III:**49
Bonaparte, Napoleon
III:55
Cadore Letter **III:**73
embargo of 1807 **III:**152
foreign affairs **III:**169
Orders in Council **III:**325
Miles, Manly **VI:**8
Miles, Nelson A. **VI:**268, 331
military, U.S. **VIII:**446*c,* 447*c.*
See also specific branches, e.g.:
Army, U.S.
children **VIII:**67
civil rights **VIII:**73
computers **IX:**69, 70
conscientious objectors
VIII:83
economy **IX:**98
Eisenhower, Dwight D.
IX:100
gays and lesbians **IX:**131
March on Washington
Movement **VIII:**227, 228
mobilization **VIII:**241
NASA **IX:**231
National Security Act of
1947 **IX:**237
Native Americans **VIII:**264
OWMR **VIII:**287
Progressive Party **IX:**264
reconversion **VIII:**326, 327
recreation **VIII:**329
scrap drives **VIII:**354
Selective Service **VIII:**357–
358
War Manpower Commission
VIII:413
WAVES **VIII:**418
women's status and rights
VIII:424
military academies. *See* United
States Military Academy at
West Point; United States
Naval Academy at Annapolis
Military Affairs Committee
VII:291
military aid **X:**29
military bases **VIII:**381

military budget. *See* defense budget
Military Commissions Act **X**:164, 171
Military Court of Inquiry **VII**:42
Military Department of the Missouri **V**:184
military detainees **X**:164
military districts **V**:325, 328
Military Division of Mississippi **V**:418
military-industrial complex **IX**:216, 354*c*
  arms race **IX**:17
  defense budget **IX**:83
  DuPont Corporation **IX**:91
  economy **IX**:98
  government **VIII**:154
  Korean War **IX**:178
  Mills, C. Wright **IX**:217
  Port Huron Statement **IX**:260
  World War II home front **VIII**:434
military-industrial-university complex
  business **VIII**:59
  dollar-a-year men **VIII**:96
  economy **VIII**:104
Military Intelligence Service **VIII**:194
Military Intelligence Service, Special Intelligence Branch **VIII**:76
Military Order of the Loyal Legion of the United States (MOLLUS) **V**:415
military pensions. *See* pensions
military service **VII**:407*c*; **X**:123, 124
Military Training Camps Association **VIII**:357
military transport **VI**:326
military tribunals **V**:70, 413, 414
Militia Act
  conscription **V**:90
  contrabands **V**:92
  emancipation **V**:129
  Emancipation Proclamation **V**:130
  Roman Catholicism **II**:336
militia movement **X**:230–231, 267
militias
  armed forces **VII**:21
  Blue Licks, Battle of **III**:54
  Booth, John Wilkes **V**:38
  Camden, Battle of **III**:76
  citizen-soldier **V**:68
  Clark, George Rogers **III**:95–96
  Confederate army **V**:81
  Continental army **III**:111
  Fort Mose **II**:132
  Gnadenhutten Massacre **III**:196
  Great Strike of 1877 **VI**:154

Green Mountain Boys **III**:199
Guilford Courthouse, Battle of **III**:201–202
  Hamilton, Alexander **III**:205
  Henry, Patrick **III**:212
  Jews **III**:236
  King's Mountain, Battle of **III**:247
  Livingston, William **III**:271
  Lyon, Matthew **III**:277
  Marion, Francis **III**:285–286
  minutemen **III**:298
  Moore's Creek Bridge, Battle of **III**:301
  Morgan, John Hunt **V**:268
  music **V**:273
  Peale, Charles Willson **III**:332–333
  Revere, Paul **III**:367
  Revolutionary War **III**:367, 369
  Rhode Island, Battle of **III**:370
  Rodney, Caesar **III**:373
  Sullivan, John **III**:402
  taverns and inns **II**:383
  Union army **V**:400
  Vallandigham, Clement L. **V**:413
  Washington, George **III**:430
Milken, Michael **X**:57–59
Mill, John Stuart **VI**:176; **VII**:148
Millbury, Massachusetts **IV**:231
millennialism
  Columbus, Christopher **I**:85
  Darwinism and religion **VI**:93
  Husband, Herman **III**:218
  religion **III**:362; **VI**:307
  Shakers **III**:387
Miller, Arthur **IX**:193, 352*c*
  cold war culture **IX**:64
  literature **IX**:193
  Monroe, Marilyn **IX**:223
  popular culture **IX**:258
Miller, Elizabeth Smith **IV**:60
Miller, Francis Trevelyan **V**:305
Miller, Glenn
  big bands **VIII**:44
  jazz **VIII**:195
  music **VIII**:250, 252
Miller, Henry **VIII**:65
Miller, Joaquin **VI**:226
Miller, John **VI**:68
Miller, Lewis **VI**:66
Miller, Nathan **VIII**:19
Miller, Phineas **III**:442
Miller, Polk **V**:192
Miller, William **IV**:319–320; **VI**:5, 307
Miller Brothers 101 Ranch Wild West Show **VI**:118

Millerites **IV**:320
Miller-Tydings Act **VIII**:24
Miller v. California **X**:284
Millet, Francis Davis **VI**:275
Millet, Jean-François **IV**:61
Millet, Kate **X**:371, 375*c*
Mill Grove, Pennsylvania **IV**:37
Milliken's Bend, Battle of **V**:4, **260–261**
"Million Man March" (1995) **X**:129, 249, 381*c*
"Mill Mother's Lament" (Wiggins) **VII**:122
mills **II**:234–235, 235
  Heathcote, Caleb **II**:164
  Industrial Revolution **II**:224
  Iron Acts **II**:177
  lumbering **II**:211–212
  manufacturing and industry **II**:214
  technology **II**:385
Mills, C. Wright **IX**:216–217, 353*c*
  business **IX**:47
  Hayden, Tom **IX**:144
  New Left **IX**:243
Mills, Marcus **VI**:128
Mills, Robert **III**:29
Mills, Wilbur **IX**:210
Mills Bill **VI**:80
Mills College **VI**:109
MILNET **X**:181
Milošević, Slobodan **X**:382*c*
  Clinton, William J. **X**:83
  Dayton accords **X**:99
  defense policy **X**:102
  Jackson, Jesse, L. **X**:192
  Kosovo **X**:199–200
Milroy, Robert H **V**:350
Milton, Tommy **IX**:90
Milton Berle Show, The **IX**:263
Milward, Alan M. **VIII**:105
Milwaukee, Wisconsin
  cities and urban life **VI**:70
  immigration **VI**:184; **VII**:144
  socialism **VII**:327
  vaudeville **VII**:368
Milwaukee Leader **VII**:285, 356
Mimbres ware **I**:263
Mind (journal) **VI**:157
Mind of Primitive Man, The (Boas) **VII**:39, 405*c*
Mine á Breton **IV**:223
Mine La Motte **IV**:223
Mine Owners Protective Association **VI**:77
Mineral Point, Wisconsin **IV**:223
miners **VII**:146
mines **V**:247, 445*c*
Mines, Bureau of
  mining **VII**:209
  occupational health and safety **VII**:243
  Walcott, Charles Doolittle **VI**:380

Ming dynasty
  Cathay **I**:68
  Ricci, Matteo **I**:319
  silver **I**:335
Mingo Creek Church **III**:440
miniature golf **VIII**:328
Minié, Claude **V**:340
Minié ball **V**:340, 341
Minikus, Lee **IX**:339
minimalism **X**:30, 211
minimum wage **VII**:408*c*; **VIII**:446*c*; **IX**:357*c*
  Adkins v. Children's Hospital **VII**:3
  agriculture **IX**:8
  Clinton, William J. **X**:82
  ERA **VII**:100
  Fair Deal **IX**:115, 116
  House of Representatives **X**:171
  labor/labor movements **IX**:182
  liberalism **X**:207
  Libertarian Party **X**:209
  modern Republicanism **IX**:221
  New Frontier **IX**:243
  news media **VIII**:271
  Powell, Adam Clayton **IX**:261
  Progressive Party **IX**:264
  Senate, U.S. **X**:322
  Supreme Court **VIII**:382
  Wagner, Robert F. **VIII**:410
  women's status and rights **VIII**:423
mining **VI**:246, **246–247**; **VII**:207–210, 208, 403*c*, 404*c*. *See also* gold
  Anthracite Coal Strike **VII**:15
  Appalachia **IX**:15, 16
  business **IX**:46
  child labor **VII**:51
  coal industry **VIII**:74–76
  Coeur d'Alene miners' strike **VI**:77
  conservatism **VIII**:85
  Darrow, Clarence Seward **VII**:70
  economy **VIII**:85
  Hearst, William Randolph **VII**:138
  Industrial Revolution, Second **VI**:191
  invention and technology **VI**:196
  labor, child **VI**:211
  labor/labor movements **VII**:170
  labor: strikes and violence **VI**:214
  literature **VI**:226
  Ludlow Massacre **VII**:186–187
  Mitchell, John **VII**:211
  Murray, Philip **VIII**:249

mining *(continued)*
New Jersey **II:**262
New Spain **I:**269
New Unionism **VII:**237
Peru **I:**289
Potosí **I:**300
Spanish colonies **II:**370, 371
strikes **VIII:**378
Venezuela boundary dispute **VI:**373
WFM **VII:**381–382
workers' compensation **VII:**391, 392
Mining Law (1872) **IV:**179
ministers
crime and punishment **II:**83
Quakers **II:**322
women's status and rights **II:**423
Ministry of Information (Great Britain) **VIII:**311–312
Minkins, Shadrach **IV:**113, 168
Minneapolis, Minnesota
flour milling **VI:**129–130
Hamilton, Alice **VII:**133
Mann Act **VII:**189–190
music **VII:**219
social work **VII:**329
strikes **VIII:**377
Minnesota **IV:**415c
abolitionism **V:**1
agriculture **IV:**10
economy **IV:**130
Farmer-Labor Party **VII:**105
Ghent, Treaty of **IV:**176
immigration **IV:**195; **VI:**184
lumbering **IV:**231
Maine Law **IV:**234
McCarthy, Eugene **IX:**205
migration **IV:**254
Mondale, Walter F. **X:**233
New Unionism **VII:**238
Non-Partisan League **VII:**241
Omaha platform **VI:**272
Oregon Treaty of 1846 **IV:**286
socialism **VII:**327
Taylor, Zachary **IV:**367
tobacco suits **X:**352
Minnesota, USS **V:**207, 266
Minnesota Farmer-Labor Party **VII:**105
Minnesota Farmers' Alliance **VI:**100
Minnesota River **IV:**36
Minnesota State Capitol **VI:**217
Minnesota Union Advocate **VII:**291
Minor, D. Kimball **IV:**44
Minorca **III:**332
minorities **X:**381c. *See also specific minorities, e.g.:* African Americans
affirmative action **X:**9
art and architecture **X:**31

Asian Americans **X:**32–34
Bakke case **X:**40–41
Carter, James Earl, Jr. **X:**68
Clinton, William J. **X:**80
education, higher **X:**112
liberalism **X:**208
Libertarian Party **X:**209
NWLB **VIII:**262
Minor v. Happersett **VI:**16, 399, 408c
minstrelsy **IV:**412c
entertainment, popular **VI:**116
Foster, Stephen C. **V:**156
Jefferson, Joseph, III **VI:**202
music **IV:**269; **VI:**257
Mint, U.S. **V:**255; **VIII:**422
Minton's Playhouse (Harlem, New York City) **VIII:**442
Minuit, Peter **II:235–237,** *236,* 435c, 436c
New Amsterdam **II:**257
New Netherland **II:**264
New York City **II:**272
Swedish colonies **II:**381
Minutemen (20th century militia group) **X:**230
minutemen (Revolutionary War) **III:**187, 264–266, **298,** 461c
miracle drugs **IX:217–218,** 260, 313
Miracle Mongers and Their Methods (Houdini) **VII:**142
Miranda, Ernesto **IX:**218–219
Miranda v. Arizona **IX:218–219,** 357c
Escobedo v. Illinois **IX:**111
Marshall, Thurgood **IX:**203
Rehnquist, William H. **X:**305
Warren, Earl **IX:**337
Warren Court **IX:**338
Mirror of Liberty (magazine) **IV:**413c
MIRV (multiple independently targeted reentry vehicle) **X:**99–100
miscegenation **II:237–238; V:261.** *See also* intermarriage
Creole **II:**83
marriage and family **X:**213
métis **II:**232–233
mulattoes **II:**246
"misery index" **X:**109
Misfits, The (film) **IX:**223
Miss America Pageant (1968) **IX:**348
Miss English's Female Seminary (Washington, D.C.) **IV:**165
Misses Patten's school (Hartford, Connecticut) **IV:**400
Misses Prescott's school (Groton, Connecticut) **IV:**169
missile(s). *See* ballistic missiles; intercontinental ballistic missiles

missile defense
ABM Treaty **X:**26–28
cold war, end of **X:**84
foreign policy **X:**144
INF Treaty **X:**179–181
SDI **X:**337
missile gap
ABM Treaty **X:**26
cold war **IX:**84
Democratic Party **IX:**85
elections **IX:**103
missionaries
Acosta, José de **I:**3
African-American churches, growth of **VI:**4, 5
Anglican Church **II:**21, 22
art **II:**27
Asbury, Francis **III:**36
Brainerd, David **II:**45–46
Brébeuf, Jean de **II:**46
California **I:**51, 52; **III:**73, 74
Dartmouth College **II:**91
Dominicans **I:**110
Dyer, Mary **II:**108
Eliot, John **II:**115
Ethiopia **I:**125
Florida **I:**131; **II:**129
Franciscans **I:**133
French colonies **II:**136–137
Gnadenhutten Massacre **III:**196
Hawaii **III:**210
Iroquois **II:**180
Jesuits **I:**193
Léry, Jean de **I:**212–213
Marquette, Jacques **II:**215
Mormon Church **IV:**90
Native American religion **I:**262
Native Americans **II:**253
New Mexico **I:**266; **II:**263
Pima revolt **II:**294
Priber, Christian Gottlieb **II:**309–310
Protestantism **II:**314–315
Pueblo **I:**305
Quakers **III:**352
reducción **I:**314
religion **I:**362
Ricci, Matteo **I:**319–320
Santa Fe **I:**327
Serra, Junípero **II:**347
SPG **II:**368
Timucua **I:**360
Wesley, John **II:**410
Wheelock, Eleazar **II:**411, 412
White, Andrew **II:**412–413
Yucatán Peninsula **I:**390
Zeisberger, David **II:**433
Missionary Ridge, Battle of
Bragg, Braxton **V:**42
Chattanooga, Battle of **V:**63
Cleburne, Patrick R. **V:**75
Sheridan, Philip H. **V:**353
mission churches **III:**29

Mission Indians (California) **VI:**199
missions **II:238–239,** 437c, 438c
Apalachee **I:**11
architecture **III:**29
British Empire **II:**49
California **III:**73, 74; **IV:75–77**
California Indians **II:**55
Dominicans **II:**101
exploration **II:**124
Figueroa, José **IV:**148–149
Florida **I:**131; **II:**129
French colonies **II:**137
gold **IV:**178
Larkin, Thomas Oliver **IV:**222
Native Americans **III:**315
New Mexico **II:**263
New Spain, northern frontier of **III:**318
religion, Native American **II:**331
Mississippi **V:**446c
agriculture **IV:**10; **V:**6
art and architecture **IV:**30
Black Codes **V:**35
Bruce, Blanche Kelso **V:**46–47
Carmichael, Stokely **IX:**49
Chickasaw **II:**66; **IV:**86
Choctaw **II:**67; **III:**89; **IV:**87
Claiborne, William C. C. **IV:**94
corruption, political **VI:**83
Creek **III:**126
economy **IV:**130
Evans, Walker **VIII:**120
Exodusters **VI:**122
Fillmore, Millard **IV:**150
Florida **IV:**151, 152
foraging **V:**149
Forrest, Nathan Bedford **V:**152, 153
Forty-niners **IV:**160
Freedmen's Bureau **V:**161
Hurricane Katrina **X:**173
Indian Removal Act **IV:**197
Jim Crow laws **VI:**204
Johnston, Joseph E. **V:**214
Ku Klux Klan **V:**225; **VII:**166
literature **VIII:**220
medicine **VII:**200
Meredith, James **IX:**213
migration **IV:**254
Native Americans **IV:**275
Native Americans in the War of 1812 **IV:**277
panic of 1819 **IV:**293
popular sovereignty **IV:**305, 307
race and race relations **IV:**312; **VII:**283
railroads **IV:**314
REA **VIII:**349

Revels, Hiram R. **V:**335
slave trade, internal **IV:**348, 349
SNCC **IX:**302
southern demagogues **VII:**332
States' Rights Party **IX:**299
Taylor, Zachary **IV:**367, 368
Thames, Battle of the **IV:**375
Till, Emmett Louis **IX:**318
tobacco suits **X:**352
Trail of Tears **IV:**378
Van Buren, Martin **IV:**386
Voting Rights Act of 1965 **IX:**334
White Citizens' Councils **IX:**342
women's status and rights **IV:**404
workers' compensation **VII:**392
Yazoo claims **III:**454
Mississippian **I:244–245**
Cahokia **I:**50–51
Cofitachequi **I:**80
Coosa **I:**89
Florida **I:**131
Mabila **I:**221
Natchez **I:**259
Native American religion **I:**260
Mississippi Delta **VII:**39
Mississippi Democratic Party **IX:**219, 220
Mississippi Freedom Democratic Party (MFDP) **IX:219–220,** 356c
Baker, Ella Josephine **IX:**32, 33
CORE **IX:**73
Hamer, Fannie Lou **IX:**141
Mondale, Walter F. **X:**233
SNCC **IX:**303
Mississippi Freedom Summer Project **IX:**356c
Hamer, Fannie Lou **IX:**141
MFDP **IX:**219
race and race relations **IX:**270
SNCC **IX:**302–303
Voting Rights Act of 1965 **IX:**333
Mississippi River **II:**436c; **III:**462c, 464c; **V:261–262,** 262, 445c
abolitionism **IV:**3
Adams-Onís Treaty **IV:**6
agriculture **IV:**12
art and architecture **IV:**29
Astor, John Jacob **IV:**35
Audubon, John James **IV:**37
Austin, Moses **IV:**38
Bates, Edward **V:**31
Bruce, Blanche Kelso **V:**47
Cahokia **I:**50
Carnegie, Andrew **VI:**62

Chouteau family **IV:**88
Civil War **V:**74
Confederate navy **V:**83
contrabands **V:**92
Copperheads **V:**95
Deere, John **IV:**115
Democratic Party **IV:**118
Eads, James Buchanan **VI:**103
economy **IV:**130
entertainment, popular **VI:**117
Exodusters **VI:**123
exploration **IV:**144
Farragut, David Glasgow **V:**137
Florida **IV:**151
foreign policy **IV:**153, 158
Frémont, John C. **IV:**166
Fuel Administration **VII:**119
immigration **IV:**194
Indian Affairs, Bureau of **IV:**197
Indian Removal Act **IV:**197
industrialization **IV:**200
internal improvements **IV:**202, 203
Jackson, Andrew **IV:**207
Jay, John **III:**229
Jay-Gardoqui Treaty **III:**230–231
Jolliet, Louis **II:**188, 189
Kearny, Stephen Watts **IV:**212
Keokuk **IV:**213
La Salle, René-Robert Cavelier, sieur de **II:**202, 203
lead mines **IV:**223, 224
Lewis and Clark Expedition **III:**262
literature **VI:**226
Louisiana Purchase **III:**272–273
Lovejoy, Elijah **IV:**230
Marquette, Jacques **II:**215
McIntosh, William **IV:**247
migration **IV:**253–255
Mississippi River war **V:**263–264
Mormon Trail **IV:**261
music **IV:**268
National Road **IV:**271
Native Americans **IV:**273
Native Americans in the War of 1812 **IV:**276
Nauvoo **IV:**278
New Madrid earthquake **IV:**280
New Orleans, Battle of **IV:**282; **V:**280
New Spain, northern frontier of **III:**317
Nullification Controversy **IV:**282
Osceola **IV:**289

Permanent Indian Frontier **IV:**297
Pike, Zebulon Montgomery **IV:**300
Pinckney Treaty **III:**336–337
politics (1900–1928) **VII:**262
popular sovereignty **IV:**306–308
Porter, David Dixon **V:**311
race and race relations **III:**357
railroads **IV:**314
Ross, John **IV:**325
Sac and Fox **IV:**327
Scott, Winfield **IV:**336
Seminole **IV:**338
Seminole War, First/Second **IV:**339
Shiloh, Battle of **V:**358
Soto, Hernando de **I:**343
tactics and strategy **V:**381
Texas **IV:**371
trade, domestic and foreign **III:**413, 415
Trail of Tears **IV:**377
transportation **V:**390
Vicksburg campaign **V:**416, 417
Mississippi River Valley
American System **IV:**19
Atkinson, Henry **IV:**36
disease/epidemics **IV:**122–123
Eaton, John, Jr. **V:**120
Houston, Sam **IV:**191
Joplin, Scott **VII:**158
lead mines **IV:**223
New Orleans, Battle of **IV:**280
Pike, Zebulon Montgomery **IV:**300
popular sovereignty **IV:**307
Texas Revolution **IV:**373
Mississippi River war **V:263–264**
Mississippi v. Johnson **V:**446c
Missoula, Montana **VII:**109, 117
Missouri **V:**444c; **V:**405c
abolitionism **IV:**3; **V:**2
agriculture **V:**6
American System **IV:**19
anti-Masonry **IV:**25
Applegate, Jesse **IV:**26
Ashley, William Henry **IV:**31
Austin, Moses **IV:**38
Austin, Stephen F. **IV:**39
Bates, Edward **V:**31
Blair, Francis Preston, Jr. **V:**36
Boone, Daniel **III:**56
Carver, George Washington **VI:**63
Civil Rights Cases **VI:**72
Clark, William **III:**96
Cody, William Frederick **VI:**76

Deseret, State of **IV:**119
Exodusters **VI:**123
exploration **IV:**145
federalism **X:**131
foreign policy **IV:**156
Forty-niners **IV:**160
Frémont, Jesse Benton **IV:**166
Frémont, John C. **IV:**167
governors **V:**172
Gregg, Josiah **IV:**179
immigration **IV:**194
industrialization **IV:**201
Jackson, Claiborne F. **V:**209
jayhawkers **V:**211
Joplin, Scott **VII:**158
lead mines **IV:**223
Liberal Republican Party **VI:**222
Lovejoy, Elijah **IV:**230
Massachusetts Emigrant Aid Society **IV:**242
migration **IV:**254
Mississippi River **V:**262
Missouri Compromise **IV:**255–257
Missouri Fur Company **IV:**257–258
Mormon Church **IV:**88–89
Mormon War **IV:**263
mothers' pensions **VII:**214
National Road **IV:**271
Nauvoo **IV:**278
New Madrid earthquake **IV:**280
overland mail **IV:**290
panic of 1819 **IV:**293, 294
Pea Ridge/Elkhorn Tavern, Battle of **V:**296
Pike, Zebulon Montgomery **IV:**300
popular sovereignty **IV:**306
race and race relations **VII:**283; **VIII:**318
railroads **IV:**314
Resolution for the Admission of Missouri **IV:**425
Rocky Mountain Fur Company **IV:**325
slavery **IV:**346
Smith, Joseph, Jr. **IV:**352–353
social work **VII:**330
Sublette, William **IV:**359
Tallmadge Amendment **IV:**365
Taylor, Zachary **IV:**367
violence and lawlessness **VI:**375–376
Webster v. Reproductive Health Services **X:**368
Young, Brigham **IV:**407
Missouri, Department of the **IV:**158
Missouri, USS **VIII:**407, 437
Missouria Indians **IV:**84

Missouri Compromise **IV:255–**
257, 256*m*, 411*c*–412*c*, 415*c*,
423–425
  abolitionism **V:**3
  Act Abolishing the Slave
    Trade in the District of
    Columbia **IV:449**
  Benton, Thomas Hart **IV:**54
  Bleeding Kansas **V:**37
  Civil War **V:**73
  Clay, Henry **IV:**96, 97
  Compromise of 1850
    IV:103
  Constitution of Missouri
    IV:424–425
  Crittenden Compromise
    V:98
  Davis, Jefferson **V:**103
  Democratic Party **IV:**118–
    119
  Douglas, Stephen A. **V:**114
  Dred Scott decision **V:**117
  Genius of Universal
    Emancipation **IV:**175.
  Kansas-Nebraska Act **V:**221
  King, Rufus **III:**246
  Know-Nothing Party **IV:**215
  Mason-Dixon Line **V:**250
  Missouri Enabling Act
    IV:424
  Monroe, James **IV:**259
  popular sovereignty **IV:**304
  Republican Party **IV:**322,
    323
  Resolution for the
    Admission of Missouri
    IV:425
  slavery **IV:**346
  Tallmadge Amendment
    IV:256–257, **365**, 423
  Taney, Roger B. **IV:**366
  Taylor, Zachary **IV:**368
  Taylor Amendment **IV:423–**
    424
  Thomas Amendment
    IV:424
  Tyler, John **IV:**382
  Vesey, Denmark **IV:**388
Missouri Enabling Act **IV:**257,
  424
Missouri ex rel. Gaines v. Canada
  VIII:256, 446*c*
Missouri Fur Company **IV:257–**
258
  American Fur Company
    IV:18
  Bent, Charles **IV:**51
  Bent's Fort **IV:**54
  Chouteau family **IV:**87, 88
Missouri Gazette **IV:**31
Missouri River
  American Fur Company
    IV:18
  art and architecture **IV:**29
  Ashley, William Henry **IV:**31
  Astor, John Jacob **IV:**35
  Atkinson, Henry **IV:**36

  Cahokia **I:**50
  Chouteau family **IV:**88
  disease/epidemics **IV:**123
  exploration **IV:**146
  Frémont, John C. **IV:**166
  fur trade **III:**183
  Hidatsa **I:**162
  Lewis and Clark Expedition
    III:262–264
  migration **IV:**255
  Mormon Trail **IV:**261
  rendezvous **IV:**321
  Smith, Jedediah Strong
    IV:350
  transportation **V:**390
Missouri River Basin Project
  VIII:448*c*
Missouri State Guard **V:**317
Missouri Territorial Legislature
  IV:39
Miss Ravenel's Conversion from
  Secession to Loyalty (De
  Forest) **V:**107, 240
Mr. Deeds Goes to Town (film)
  VIII:62
Mr. Smith Goes to Washington
  (film) **VIII:**62, 246
MIT. *See* Massachusetts Institute
  of Technology
mita **I:**3, 336
Mitchell, Arthur W. **VIII:**2–3
Mitchell, Charley **VI:**44
Mitchell, George **IX:**357*c;*
  X:231–232
  AIM **IX:**12
  Clinton, William J. **X:**83
  Senate, U.S. **X:**321
Mitchell, John (labor leader)
  VII:210–211
  Anthracite Coal Strike
    VII:15
  Buck's Stove **VII:**43
  class consciousness **VI:**74
  labor/labor movements
    VII:170
  mining **VII:**208–209
  National Civic Federation
    VII:226
  New Unionism **VII:**237
  UMWA **VII:**360
Mitchell, John N. (attorney
  general) **X:232–233**
  Nixon, Richard M. **X:**257
  U.S. v. Nixon **X:**357
  Watergate scandal **X:**365–
    367
Mitchell, Margaret **V:**169–170,
  240; **VIII:**220
Mitchell, Maria **IV:**335; **VI:247–**
  248, 312, 325
Mitchell, Wesley C. **VI:**59;
  IX:129
Mitchell, William "Billy" **VII:**21,
  28, **211–212**, 409*c*
Mitchell Report **X:**384*c*
Mithridates: De differentis linguis
  (Gesner) **I:**139

MITS. *See* Micro Instrumentation
  Telemetry Systems
Mitscher, Marc **VIII:**265, 274
Mittelberger, Gottlieb **II:239,**
  286, **444–445**
Mittelman, James H. **X:**153
Miwok Indians **IV:**70
Mixtec Indians **I:**101, 250–251
MK-ULTRA program **IX:**195
Moab, Utah **IV:**120
Mobe, the. *See* National
  Mobilization to End the War in
  Vietnam
Mobile, Alabama
  agriculture **IV:**12
  Confederate navy **V:**83
  food riots **V:**148
  race and race relations
    VIII:318
  segregation **VII:**320
  slave trade, internal
    IV:350
  Texas **IV:**371
Mobile Army Division **VII:**20
Mobile Bay **IV:**6, 278
Mobile Bay, Battle of **V:**445*c*
  elections **V:**126
  Farragut, David Glasgow
    V:137
  marine corps **V:**248
  Mobile campaign **V:**265
Mobile campaign **V:264–265**
mobile homes **VIII:**328
Mobile Indians **I:**343
mobility **III:**342–343
mobilization **VIII:240–243**, *241*
  advertising **VIII:**1
  African Americans **VIII:**3
  antimonopoly **VIII:**24
  automobile industry
    VIII:35–36
  Bush, Vannevar **VIII:**56
  business **VIII:**57
  cities and urban life **VIII:**70
  Congress **VIII:**81
  conservatism **VIII:**85
  demobilization (WWII)
    VIII:92
  dollar-a-year men **VIII:**96
  economy **VIII:**102, 104
  education **VIII:**106
  Executive Order 8802
    VIII:120
  FEPC **VIII:**123
  Forrestal, James V.
    VIII:143
  Full Employment Bill
    VIII:145
  gays and lesbians **VIII:**147
  government **VIII:**154
  housing **VIII:**179
  Ickes, Harold L. **VIII:**183
  Irish Americans **VIII:**189
  Kaiser, Henry J. **VIII:**199
  Kennedy, Joseph P.
    VIII:200
  Keynesianism **VIII:**201

  labor/labor movements
    VIII:207
  liberalism **VIII:**216
  March on Washington
    Movement **VIII:**227
  Mexican Americans
    VIII:237
  migration **VIII:**239
  Morgenthau, Henry T., Jr.
    VIII:244
  Nelson, Donald M.
    VIII:266, 267
  New Deal **VIII:**269
  NWLB **VIII:**261
  OPA **VIII:**282
  OPM **VIII:**283
  OSRD **VIII:**283
  OWI **VIII:**286
  OWM **VIII:**286–287
  OWMR **VIII:**287
  popular culture **VIII:**303
  presidency **VIII:**309
  rationing **VIII:**322
  reconversion **VIII:**326
  Revenue Act of 1942
    VIII:341
  RFC **VIII:**325, 326
  Roosevelt, Franklin D.
    VIII:346
  steel industry **VIII:**373
  strikes **VIII:**378
  Sunbelt **VIII:**381
  tanks **VIII:**386
  taxation **VIII:**386, 388
  technology **VIII:**390
  Third New Deal **VIII:**393
  TNEC **VIII:**391
  unemployment **VIII:**400
  wage and price controls
    VIII:409
  Wallace, Henry A.
    VIII:411
  War Manpower Commission
    VIII:413
  War Production Board
    VIII:414
  White, Walter **VIII:**417
  World War II home front
    VIII:432, 433
  zoot-suiters **VIII:**442
Mobilizing Woman Power (Blatch)
  VII:38
Moby-Dick; or The Whale
  (Melville) **IV:**229
Mocenigo, Alvise **I:**312
Moctezuma I Ilhuicamina (Aztec
  leader)
  Aztecs **I:**18
  Aztlán **I:**23
  Tlacacla **I:**361
Moctezuma II Xocoyotzin (Aztec
  leader) **I:245–246**, 397*c*
  Aguilar, Francisco de **I:**4
  Aztecs **I:**19–22
  Cacamatzin **I:**47
  Codex Aubin **I:**410
  Cortés, Hernán **I:**96

Cuauhtémoc **I:**100
Cuitláhuac **I:**101
Díaz del Castillo, Bernal **I:**106
Escalante, Juan de **I:**124
Florentine Codex **I:**130
flowery wars **I:**131, 132
Malinche **I:**227
Quetzalcoatl **I:**309
Sahagún, Bernardino de **I:**323
Tabasco **I:**351
Tacuba **I:**352
Tlacacla **I:**361
Model A Ford **VII:**111
Model Cities program **IX:**56, **220–221**
model homes **VIII:**379
"Model of Christian Charity" (Winthrop) **II:**184, 418, **439**
Model T Ford **VII:**405c
  automobile industry **VII:**26–27
  Ford, Henry **VII:**111
  Ford Motor Corporation **IX:**122
  invention and technology **VII:**150
  mass production **VII:**195
  rural life **VII:**306
  urban transportation **VII:**364
Model Treaty of 1776 **III:**257
moderates
  Ford, Gerald R. **X:**137
  immigration **X:**177
  Souter, David **X:**324
  Supreme Court **X:**339
  White, Byron R. **X:**369
Modern Chivalry (Brackenridge) **III:**60–61, 269
Modern Corporation and Private Property, The (Berle and Means) **VIII:**43
Modern Devotion movement **I:**315
Modern Instance, A (Howells) **VI:**179, 225–226
modernism **VII:212–213**
  art and architecture **VII:**23, 24; **X:**31, 32
  conservative movement **X:**94
  Greenwich Village **VII:**130, 131
  Harlem Renaissance **VII:**136
  literature **VII:**179–181
  Lost Generation **VII:**185
  music **VII:**220
  religion **VI:**308; **VII:**297, 298; **VIII:**334, 335
  Roman Catholicism **VI:**316
modernization **VII:**169
modern liberalism **X:**208
Modern Mephistopheles (Alcott) **VI:**10

Modern Quarterly **VII:**286
modern Republicanism **IX:221–222**
Moderns **III:**176
Modern Times (film) **VIII:**301
Modern Times anarchist colony (Long Island, New York) **IV:**392–393
Modern Woman (Cassatt) **VI:**64
Modoc Indians **IV:**70
Mod Squad, The **X:**343
Moffett, Thomas **I:**130
Mogadishu, Somalia **X:**16, 81, 380c
mogho naaba **I:**252
Mogollon Culture **I:**263–264
Mohammad Reza Pahlavi (shah of Iran) **X:**228
Mohammed. *See* Muhammad
Mohawk & Hudson Railroad **IV:**202, 314
Mohawk Indians **I:**185–187, **246–247,** 398c
  Algonquin **II:**18
  Beaver Wars **II:**35
  Brant, Joseph **III:**62
  Dutch-Indian Wars **II:**105, 106
  Dutch Reformed Church **II:**107
  Hendrick **II:**164
  Iroquois **II:**179, 180
  Johnson, Sir William **II:**187, 188
  King Philip's War **II:**193
  Native Americans **III:**313
  Native Americans in the War of 1812 **IV:**277
  SPG **II:**368
  Wheelock, Eleazar **II:**412
Mohawk River valley **I:**280; **III:**237
Mohegan Indians
  Mason, John **II:**222
  Miantonomo **II:**233
  Pequot War **II:**289, 290
  Wheelock, Eleazar **II:**412
Mohican Indians **III:**311
Mojave Desert
  Deseret, State of **IV:**119
  exploration **IV:**144
  Smith, Jedediah Strong **IV:**350
Mojave Indians **IV:**70, 350
molasses **III:**401, 402; **V:**383
Molasses Act **II:**437c
  Acts of Trade and Navigation **II:**3
  smuggling **II:**364
  Sugar Act **III:**401
  tariffs **III:**406
Molesworth, Robert **III:**103
Moley, Raymond C. **VIII:243**
  Berle, Adolf A., Jr. **VIII:**43
  Brain Trust **VIII:**51
  Emergency Banking Act of 1933 **VIII:**113

London Economic Conference **VIII:**221
  monetary policy **VIII:**243
  Tugwell, Rexford G. **VIII:**397
Moline, Illinois **IV:**115
Moline Plow Company **VIII:**196
molinillo **I:**48
Mollin, Jean **I:**248
MOLLUS (Military Order of the Loyal Legion of the United States) **V:**415
Molly Maguires **V:**201; **VI:248–249**
Molly Pitcher **III:298,** 298, 300, 461c
Molotov, Vyacheslav M. *VIII:162,* 355; **IX:**204
Moltmann, Jurgen **IX:**272
Momaday, N. Scott **X:**210
Mona Lisa (Leonardo da Vinci) **I:**211–212
monarchy **II:240–241**
  Anglican Church **II:**21
  British Empire **II:**48
  Common Sense **III:**102
  corporatism **III:**122
  Dominion of New England **II:**101–102
  English Civil War **II:**116
  George III **III:**191–192
  Glorious Revolution **II:**149
  Ohio Company of Virginia **II:**278
  republicanism **III:**364
  royal colonies **II:**337–338
Monardes, Nicholas **I:**247, 363
monasteries **I:**75
Monck's Corner, Battle of **III:**84, 407
Monckton, Robert **II:**241; **III:**189
Moncure, Henry **III:**284
Mondale, Walter F. **X:233–234,** 378c
  Albright, Madeleine K. **X:**22
  Carter, James Earl, Jr. **X:**67, 68
  Dole, Robert **X:**105
  Ferraro, Geraldine A. **X:**135
  Reagan, Ronald W. **X:**300
Monday Club (Boston, Massachusetts) **VII:**329
Monday Night Football **X:**344
"Mondo Nuovo" letter of 1504 (Vespucci) **I:405–409**
Mondrian, Piet **VIII:**31
monetary policy **VIII:243–244**
  banking **VIII:**39–40
  Banking Act (1935) **VIII:**41
  Eccles, Marriner S. **VIII:**101
  economy **VIII:**104; **X:**109
  Keynesianism **VIII:**200
  Morgenthau, Henry T., Jr. **VIII:**244
  New Deal **VIII:**269

recession of 1937–1938 **VIII:**324
  Villard, Henry **VI:**375
money. *See* currency
money laundering **X:**358, 359
"'Mong Girls Who Toil" (Valesh) **VII:**367
Mongol dynasty **I:**67–68, 294–296
Mongolia **VIII:**440
Mongrel Tariff **VI:**21, 80
monism **VI:**319
Monitor, USS
  ironclads **V:**207
  Lincoln, Abraham **V:**237
  Monitor-Merrimack **V:**265–266
  Peninsular campaign **V:**299
  science and technology **V:**342
  Union navy **V:**406
Monitor-Merrimack **V:265–266,** 266m, 267, 444c
Monks Mound **I:**50
Monmouth, Battle of **III:298–300,** 299m, 461c
  Clinton, Sir Henry **III:**99
  Cornwallis, Charles, Lord **III:**120
  dueling **III:**141
  Greene, Nathanael **III:**198
  Lafayette, marquis de **III:**253
  Lee, Charles **III:**258, 259
  Molly Pitcher **III:**298
  Washington, George **III:**431
Monmouth Courthouse, Battle of **IV:**258
Monocacy, Battle of the **V:**120
monoclonal antibodies **X:**222
Monongah coal mine disaster **VII:**209, 243
Monongahela River **IV:**271; **VI:**119
monopolies **VI:**411c; **VII:**404c, 406c; **X:**381c
  banking, investment **VI:**23
  business and government **VI:**57
  computers **X:**87
  Elkins Act **VII:**94
  Lloyd, Henry Demarest **VI:**227
  Patrons of Husbandry **VI:**278
  railroads **VI:**302, 303
  Republican Party **VII:**300
  Rockefeller, John Davison **VII:**302
  Roosevelt, Theodore **VII:**304
  Sherman Antitrust Act **VI:**330
  Supreme Court **VI:**348
  trusts **VI:**363–364
Monopolist, the **VI:**278
monopoly **I:**269
Monopoly (game) **VIII:**328

monotheism **VIII:**336
Monro, George **II:**134
Monroe, Bill, and the Blue Grass Boys **VIII:**250
Monroe, Harriet
  literature **VII:**179
  modernism **VII:**212
  radical and labor press **VII:**285
Monroe, James **IV:258–259,** 259, 411*c*, 412*c*
  Adams, John Quincy **IV:**5
  American System **IV:**19, 20
  anti-Federalists **III:**24
  architecture **III:**29
  Calhoun, John C. **IV:**69
  Democratic Party **IV:**117
  Drayton, William H. **IV:**127
  election of 1828 **IV:**135
  Era of Good Feelings **IV:**141
  Essex decision **III:**157–158
  Florida **III:**167; **IV:**152
  foreign policy **IV:**154–155
  Gabriel's Rebellion **III:**185–186
  Hamilton, Alexander **III:**207
  Hollywood Cemetery **V:**192
  industrialization **IV:**199
  King, Rufus **III:**246
  Latin America **X:**204
  Liberia **IV:**225
  Louisiana Purchase **III:**273
  Monroe Doctrine **IV:**259–261
  Monroe-Pinkney Treaty **III:**300, 301
  panic of 1819 **IV:**293–294
  Permanent Indian Frontier **IV:**297
  political parties **III:**339
  Pushmataha **IV:**308
  Randolph, John **III:**359
  Roosevelt Corollary **VII:**305
  Virginia dynasty **III:**425
Monroe, Marilyn **IX:**222, **222–223,** 352*c*
  DiMaggio, Joe **VIII:**96
  fashion **IX:**117
  movies **IX:**224–225
  popular culture **IX:**259
Monroe Doctrine **IV:259–261,** 412*c*, **425–427; VII:**404*c*, 409*c*; **VIII:**448*c*
  Adams, John Quincy **IV:**5
  Clark Memorandum **VII:**58
  Cleveland, Grover **VI:**75
  foreign affairs **III:**169
  foreign policy **IV:**154–155; **VII:**113
  Good Neighbor policy **VIII:**151
  Kellogg-Briand Treaty **VII:**164
  Latin America **X:**204
  Mahan, Alfred Thayer **VI:**236

Monroe, James **IV:**259
  presidency **VII:**268
  Roosevelt, Theodore **VII:**304
  Roosevelt Corollary **VII:**304–305
  Seward, William H. **V:**347, 348
Monroe Doctrine and Cuba Libra, The (film) **VII:**215
Monroe-Pinkney Treaty **III:300–301**
Monrovia, Liberia **IV:**225; **VI:**223–224
Monster and Other Stores, The (Crane) **VI:**85
monsters **I:247–249,** 248
  art and architecture **I:**13
  Mandeville, Sir John **I:**228
  mappae mundi **I:**230
  Monsters et Prodiges (excerpt) **I:412–413**
  Settle, Dionyse **I:**331
Monstres et Prodigies, Des (Paré) **I:412–413**
Montagnais-Naskapi **I:249–250**
  Champlain, Samuel de **II:**62
  French colonies **II:**136, 137
  fur trade **II:**140
Montagne's Tavern **III:**407
Montagu, John (fourth earl of Sandwich) **IV:**188
Montaigne, Michel de
  Brazil **I:**34
  cannibalism **I:**58
  Monardes, Nicholas **I:**247
Montana **IV:**410*c*
  abortion **X:**2
  Bourke-White, Margaret **VIII:**50
  cattle kingdom **VI:**64
  Crow **II:**85
  exploration **IV:**144
  Flathead Indians **II:**127
  free speech fights **VII:**117
  Little Bighorn, Battle of **V:**240
  mining **VII:**209, 210
  Native Americans **IV:**275
  Non-Partisan League **VII:**241
  Wheeler, Burton K. **VIII:**416
Montana Freemen **X:**346
Montana State College **VIII:**5
Montauk, New York **IV:**21
Montauk Building (Chicago, Illinois) **VI:**55, 196
Montcalm, Louis Joseph **II:**349
  Fort Ticonderoga **III:**171
  Fort William Henry Massacre **II:**134
  French colonies **II:**139
  Native Americans **III:**312
  Seven Years' War **II:**349
  Wolfe, James **II:**421

Montcalm and Wolfe (Parkman) **VI:**278
Monte Albán **I:250–251**
Monte Cassino, Italy **VIII:**191
Montejo, Francisco de
  Guerrero, Gonzalo **I:**147
  Maya **I:**235
  Yucatán Peninsula **I:**390
Montenegro **VII:**370
Monterey, California
  California **III:**73, 74
  Larkin, Thomas Oliver **IV:**222
  Stearns, Abel **IV:**356
  Stockton, Robert Field **IV:**358
Monterrey, Mexico **IV:**252
Montes, Pedro **IV:**21
Montesinos, Anton de **I:**110, 379
Montesquieu, Charles-Louis, Baron **III:**24, 154
Montessori, Maria **VII:**193
Monte Verde **I:**251
Montevideo, Uruguay **VIII:**151, 180
Montez, Lola **VI:**221
Montgomery, Alabama **IX:**353*c*
  African Americans **IX:**5
  freedom rides **IX:**123–124
  King, Martin Luther, Jr. **IX:**173–174
  Parks, Rosa **IX:**254
Montgomery, Archibald **II:**280
Montgomery, Benjamin **V:**106, 107
Montgomery, Bernard L.
  Normandy, invasion of **VIII:**275
  North African campaign **VIII:**278
  Sicily **VIII:**360
Montgomery, James E. **V:**263
Montgomery, Little Brother **VIII:**250
Montgomery, Richard **III:301,** 461*c*
  Allen, Ethan **III:**15
  Canada **III:**78
  Carleton, Guy **III:**81
  Quebec, Battle of **III:**353
  Schuyler, Philip John **III:**384
Montgomery bus boycott **IX:**353*c*
  African Americans **IX:**5
  Civil Rights Act (1957) **IX:**58
  freedom rides **IX:**123
  King, Martin Luther, Jr. **IX:**173–174
  NAACP **IX:**232
  Parks, Rosa **IX:**254
  religion **IX:**272
Montgomery Charter **II:**94
Montgomery County, Virginia **V:**188
Montgomery Improvement Association (MIA) **IX:**174, 254

Montgomery Ward & Company **VI:**410*c*
  American Liberty League **VIII:**19
  business **VII:**46
  mail-order houses **VI:**237
Monthly Consular and Trade Reports **VII:**152
Monthly Magazine and American Review, The **IV:**209
Monticello plantation **III:**232, 233, 235
Montour, Andrew **II:**241
Montour, Madame **II:241–242**
Montpelier plantation **III:**280, 281, 283, 284
Montreal, Quebec **I:**163; **II:242; III:**461*c*
  Allen, Ethan **III:**15
  Carleton, Guy **III:**81
  French colonies **II:**136
  fur trade **IV:**170
  Howe, Sir William **III:**215
  Iberville, Pierre Le Moyne, sieur d' **II:**173
  Montgomery, Richard **III:**301
  Putnam, Israel **III:**350
  Revolutionary War **III:**368
  sports and recreation **VII:**334–335
Mont-Saint-Michel and Chartres (Adams) **VI:**1
Montserrat **I:**251
Montt, Pedro **VI:**67
monuments **I:**278; **V:267–268**
  Civil War **V:**75
  Gettysburg, Battle of **V:**168
  Lincoln, Abraham **V:**234
  national military parks **V:**276
  Richmond, Virginia **V:**337
  Saint-Gaudens, Augustus **VI:**321
  veterans **V:**416
"Mood Indigo" (Ellington) **VIII:**112
Moods (Alcott) **VI:**10
Moody, Dwight Lyman **VI:249,** **249–250,** 306, 307, 382
Moody, Helen Wills **VIII:**372
Moody, John **II:**389
Moody, William Vaughn **VI:**226
Moody Bible Institute (Chicago, Illinois) **VIII:**44; **IX:**272
Moon **IX:**285, 296, 297
Mooney, Tom **VII:**213
Mooney-Billings case **VII:213**
Moon Is Down, The (Steinbeck) **VIII:**374
Moon landing **X:**326, 375*c*
Moor, Joshua **II:**91
Moor, William **I:**273
Moore, Alfred **III:**403
Moore, Alvin **IX:**219
Moore, Charles **X:**31
Moore, Gordon **X:**88

Moore, James, Jr. **II**:395
Moore, Lorrie **X**:211
Moore, Mike **X**:352
Moore, Samuel Preston **V**:256, 257
Moore School of Electrical Engineering (University of Pennsylvania) **X**:86
Moore's Creek Bridge, Battle of **III**:84, **301–302**
Moore's Law **X**:88
Moors **I**:396*c*
Moor's Indian Charity School **II**:91, 412
Moosic, Pennsylvania **VI**:211
Moral and Literary Society of the Cherokee Nation **IV**:324
Moral Culture of Infancy and Kindergarten Guide (Peabody and Mann) **VI**:280
morale
　OSS **VIII**:285
　propaganda **VIII**:312
　public opinion polls **VIII**:313
　Roosevelt, Franklin D. **VIII**:346
moral economy doctrine **II**:405
moral embargo **VIII**:267
Morales, Evo **X**:206, 207
Moraley, William **II**:174, **242–243, 443–444**
morality
　abortion **X**:1–5
　censorship **X**:71
　dress **VII**:79, 80
Moral Majority **X**:234
　abortion **X**:4
　conservative movement **X**:94
　evangelical Christians **X**:125
　feminism **X**:134
　televangelism **X**:342
Moravians **III**:302
　Fries's Rebellion **III**:180
　Gnadenhutten Massacre **III**:196
　music **II**:247
　Zeisberger, David **II**:433
More, Paul Elmer **VIII**:84
More, Sir Thomas **I**:74–75
Morehouse College **IX**:173
Moresby, Port **VIII**:87, 435
Morgan, Arthur E. **VIII**:217, 392, 393
Morgan, Daniel **III**:303, *303,* 462*c*
　Cornwallis, Charles, Lord **III**:120
　Cowpens, Battle of **III**:124
　Greene, Nathanael **III**:199
　Saratoga, surrender at **III**:380
Morgan, Edmund **I**:307
Morgan, Edwin D. **VI**:20
Morgan, Frederic **VIII**:275
Morgan, Garrett **VII**:149

Morgan, Harcourt **VIII**:217, 392
Morgan, Sir Henry **II**:296
Morgan, James D. **V**:34, 42
Morgan, John (physician) **III**:295–296
Morgan, John Hunt **V**:268–269
　Burnside, Ambrose E. **V**:52
　bushwhackers **V**:52
　Confederate army **V**:81
Morgan, John Pierpont **VI**:250, **250–251; VII**:403*c*
　banking, investment **VI**:23, 24
　Comstock, Anthony **VI**:79
　GE **VII**:123
　Hill, James J. **VI**:172
　Industrial Revolution, Second **VI**:192
　labor/labor movements **VII**:169
　mining **VII**:209
　National Civic Federation **VII**:226
　Northern Securities Case **VII**:241
　railroads **VI**:302
　Robber Barons, The **VI**:315
　steel industry **VII**:336
　trusts **VI**:364–365
　U.S. Steel **VII**:365
　Villard, Henry **VI**:375
Morgan, J. P., Jr. **VIII**:279
Morgan, Robin **IX**:348
Morgan, Thomas Hunt **VII**:314
Morgan, William **III**:177; **IV**:25
Morganfield, McKinley (Muddy Waters) **VIII**:250
Morgenthau, Henry T., Jr. **VIII**:244–245
　Bretton Woods Conference **VIII**:52
　Eccles, Marriner S. **VIII**:101
　FCA **VIII**:126
　Holocaust **VIII**:170
　immigration **VIII**:184
　Jews **VIII**:196
　Keynesianism **VIII**:200
　monetary policy **VIII**:243
　recession of 1937–1938 **VIII**:324
　refugees **VIII**:330
　religion **VIII**:335
　Revenue Act of 1935 **VIII**:340
　Social Security Act **VIII**:363
　taxation **VIII**:387, 388
　TNEC **VIII**:391
　war bonds **VIII**:412
　Zionism **VIII**:441
Morgenthau Plan **VIII**:244
Moriscos **I**:165
Morison, Samuel Eliot **I**:224
Morisot, Berthe **VI**:64
Mormon Battalion **IV**:262

Mormon Church. *See* Church of Jesus Christ of Latter-day Saints
Mormons **VIII**:101
Mormon Trail **IV**:145, **261–262,** 262*m*
Mormon War **IV**:262–264
　Bridger, James **IV**:64
　Smith, Joseph, Jr. **IV**:353
　Young, Brigham **IV**:408
morning-after pill **X**:43
Morocco
　Barbary Wars **III**:45–46
　Coelho, Jorge d'Albuquerque **I**:79
　Jay, John **III**:229
　North African campaign **VIII**:277
　Patton, George S., Jr. **VIII**:291
　Sahara **I**:324
　Timbuktu **I**:360
　World War II European theater **VIII**:431
Moro Insurrection **VII**:22, 258
Moroni (angel) **IV**:88, 352
morphine **V**:112
Morrill, Justin **V**:269; **VI**:110
Morrill Act (1890) **VI**:110; **VIII**:107
Morrill Act (1935) **VIII**:107
Morrill Land-Grant Act (1862) **V**:269–270, 444*c*
　agriculture **VI**:8
　Congress **V**:89
　education **V**:125
　education, federal aid to **VI**:110
　education, higher **VI**:111
　education, philanthropy and **VI**:112
　Republican Party **V**:333
　White, Andrew Dickson **VI**:391
　women's colleges **VI**:398
Morrill Tariff Act (1861) **V**:444*c*
　business and government **VI**:56
　economy **V**:121
　tariffs **V**:383
Morris, Gouverneur **III**:108, **303–305,** 330
Morris, Lewis **II**:243, 262, 433
Morris, Robert **III**:305–306, 462*c*
　Articles of Confederation **III**:34
　Bank of North America **III**:40
　banks **III**:42
　Barry, John **III**:47
　Carlisle commission **III**:82
　Continental Congress, Second **III**:116
　Continental navy **III**:117
　debt, national **III**:130
　economy **III**:146

Federalists **III**:165
Holland Land Company **III**:214
insurance **III**:227
Jews **III**:236
Madison, James **III**:282
Morris, Gouverneur **III**:304
Newburgh conspiracy **III**:316
Ross, Betsy **III**:374
Morris, Thomas **IV**:226
Morris, William (designer/art critic)
　Aesthetic movement **VI**:3
　Lazarus, Emma **VI**:219
　Richardson, Henry Hobson **VI**:313
Morris, William S. (president of southern telegraph companies) **V**:386
Morris County, Missouri **VI**:123
Morrison, Frank **VII**:43
Morrison, Toni **X**:210, *211*
Morrison, William **IV**:257
Morrison v. Olson **X**:316
Morris Park **VI**:177
Morrissey, John **V**:367; **VI**:177
Morristown, New Jersey, encampment of **III**:306–307
　Continental army, mutinies of **III**:113
　Greene, Nathanael **III**:198
　Washington, George **III**:431
Morrow, Anne (Lindbergh, Anne Morrow) **VII**:178
Morrow, Dwight **VII**:29, 165
Morse, Jedidiah **III**:4, **307–308,** 419
Morse, Samuel F. B. **IV**:264, **264–265,** 413*c*
　art and architecture **IV**:28
　Brady, Mathew B. **V**:41
　code breaking **VIII**:76
　Colt, Samuel **IV**:101
　economy **IV**:131
　immigration **IV**:195
　industrialization **IV**:200
　nativism **V**:280
　science and technology **IV**:333
　telegraph **V**:385
Morse, Wayne **IX**:107
Morse Code **IV**:264; **V**:385
mortality **II**:243, **243–244**
　African Americans **X**:13
　childhood **II**:66
　disease/epidemics **II**:97
　indentured servitude **II**:175
　Jamestown **II**:181
　labor/labor movements **II**:198
　Maryland **II**:221
　miracle drugs **IX**:218
　population trends **II**:302; **IX**:260
　public health **IX**:266

mortality (*continued*)
  slave trade **II**:359
  society, British American **II**:365
  Virginia **II**:400
mortgage-backed securities **X**:61
mortgage crisis **X**:61
mortgage lenders **X**:60
mortgages
  Agricultural Adjustment Act **VIII**:5, 6
  agriculture **VIII**:9
  FCA **VIII**:126
  FDIC **VIII**:132
  Federal Housing Administration (FHA) **VIII**:133–134
  Federal National Mortgage Association **VIII**:135
  FHA **VIII**:126
  HOLC **VIII**:170–171
  housing **VI**:179; **VIII**:177–178
  USHA **VIII**:404
Mortimer, Elias H. **VII**:373
Morton, Charles **II**:345
Morton, Ferdinand "Jelly Roll"
  entertainment, popular **VII**:97
  jazz **VII**:153
  music **VII**:219
Morton, Oliver P. **V**:171, 172, **270**; **VI**:160
Morton, Samuel George **IV**:311
Morton, Thomas **II**:116, **244–245**, 376
Morton, William Thomas **IV**:333; **V**:257
Moryson, Fynes **I**:**252**
Mosaic (Web browser) **X**:319
Mosby, John Singleton **V**:**270–271**
  bushwhackers **V**:52
  Confederate army **V**:81
  espionage **V**:135
Mosby's rangers **V**:270, 271, 317
Moscow, Russia **VI**:272–273; **VII**:117
Moscow, Soviet Union
  Bourke-White, Margaret **VIII**:50
  Harriman, W. Averell **VIII**:162
  Hull, Cordell **VIII**:180
  literature **VIII**:218
  Popular Front **VIII**:303, 304
  World War II European theater **VIII**:431
Moscow Conference Declarations **VIII**:448c
Moscow Summit **VIII**:212
Moselle River **VIII**:55
Moses, Bob (civil rights activist) **IX**:219
Moses, Robert (urban planner) **IX**:244, 246

mosques **I**:138; **X**:189
Mosquito Coast **IV**:98, 99; **V**:423
mosquitoes **I**:107; **II**:98, 100, 431
Mossadegh, Mohammad
  cold war **IX**:64
  Dulles, John Foster **IX**:91
  Iranian hostage crisis **X**:184
  Middle East **IX**:214
Mossi **I**:14, **252–253**
Most, Johann **VI**:213; **VII**:126
most-favored-nation status
  foreign policy **VI**:133
  Quasi War **III**:352
  Reciprocal Trade Agreements Act **VIII**:325
  trade, domestic and foreign **III**:413, 415
Most Valuable Player Award **IX**:298
Mosul, Iraq **X**:187
Motecuhzoma. *See* Moctezuma II Xocoyotzin
Mother and the Law, The (film) **VII**:132
Mother Earth (radical journal)
  Goldman, Emma **VII**:126
  Greenwich Village **VII**:131
  radical and labor press **VII**:285
Mother Earth News **IX**:110
motherhood **VI**:374
Mother Jones. *See* Jones, Mary Harris "Mother"
"Mother's Letters to a Daughter on Woman's Suffrage, A" (Hooker) **VI**:176
mothers' pensions **VII**:**213–214**
  Children's Bureau **VII**:53–54
  citizenship **VII**:57
  marriage and family **VII**:192
  progressivism **VII**:271
  public health **VII**:276
  social work **VII**:330
  women's network **VIII**:421
Motion Picture Association of America **VIII**:65
Motion Picture Production Code **X**:235
Motion Picture Rating System (MPRS) **X**:235
motion pictures **VI**:411c
  Griffith, David Wark **VII**:131
  Houdini, Harry **VII**:141
  invention and technology **VI**:196
  Middletown **VII**:206
  movie industry **VII**:214
  music **VII**:220
  popular culture **VII**:263–265
  race and race relations **VII**:283

recreation **VII**:294–295
  Tin Pan Alley **VII**:353
  urban transportation **VII**:363
Motor Carrier Act **VIII**:395–396
motors, electric **VII**:93
Motor Vehicle Air Pollution Control Act (1965) **IX**:109, 357c
Motown Records **IX**:229; **X**:238
Mott, Lucretia **IV**:**265–266**, 414c
  abolitionism **V**:3
  African Americans **IV**:9
  American Anti-Slavery Society **IV**:16
  Bloomer, Amelia **IV**:59–60
  female antislavery societies **IV**:147, 148
  Foster, Abigail Kelley **IV**:161
  Seneca Falls convention **IV**:341
  Society of Friends **V**:364
  women's status and rights **IV**:404; **V**:436
Moulton, Forest R. **VI**:325
Moulton, Frank **VI**:30
Moultrie, William **III**:84, 259
Moultrie Creek, Treaty of **IV**:338
mound builders **I**:**253–254**, *254*, 395c
  Cahokia **I**:50
  Calusa **I**:52
  Hohokam **I**:165
  Mississippian **I**:245
  Native American religion **I**:260
Mound City **V**:263
Mount, William Sidney **V**:18
Mountaineering in the Sierra Nevada (King) **VI**:208
Mountain Meadows Massacre **IV**:90, 121
mountain men **IV**:**266–267**, *267*
  Ashley, William Henry **IV**:31
  Beckwourth, Jim **IV**:50
  Bent, Charles **IV**:51
  Bent, William **IV**:52
  Bidwell, John **IV**:56
  Bridger, James **IV**:64
  Deseret, State of **IV**:119
  exploration **IV**:144
  Fort Vancouver **IV**:159
  Oregon Trail **IV**:285
  rendezvous **IV**:322
  Rocky Mountain Fur Company **IV**:324
Mountbatten, Louis, Lord **VIII**:435
Mount Dexter, Treaty of **IV**:307
Mounted Rifles **IV**:375
Mount Pleasant Ohio **IV**:175
Mount Rainier National Park **VI**:82, 119–120
Mount Suribachi, Iwo Jima **VIII**:192
Mount Vernon **II**:245; **III**:462c
  Washington, D.C. **III**:428

Washington, George **III**:430, 431
  Washington, Martha **III**:432
mourning wars **I**:186; **II**:58, 253
Moussaoui, Zacarias **X**:348
moveable type
  Mercator, Gerhardus **I**:240
  paper **I**:285
  printing press **I**:302–303
MoveOn.org **X**:275
movie industry **VII**:**214–216**, *215*, 404c, 406c, 407c
  Birth of a Nation, The **VII**:**37–38**
  Committee for Public Information **VII**:60
  entertainment, popular **VII**:96, 97
  Gone With the Wind **V**:**169–170**
  invention and technology **VII**:151
  journalism **VII**:160
  music **VII**:218
  popular culture **VII**:264–265
  vaudeville **VII**:368, 369
movies **VIII**:**245–248**, *247*, 447c; **IX**:**223–226**, *225*, 351c, 352c; **X**:**234–236**, *235*
  Beatles **IX**:38
  Bureau of Motion Pictures **VIII**:56
  business **VIII**:58
  Capra, Frank **VIII**:61–62
  censorship **VIII**:65
  children **VIII**:67
  cities and urban life **VIII**:70
  cold war culture **IX**:65
  Disney, Walt **IX**:88
  fashion **IX**:117
  Faulkner, William **VIII**:128
  FMP **VIII**:134
  Great Depression **VIII**:159
  Hersey, John R. **VIII**:164
  Jews **VIII**:195
  Kennedy, Joseph P. **VIII**:199
  media **X**:220
  Monroe, Marilyn **IX**:222–223
  music **IX**:228
  news media **VIII**:271
  New York World's Fair (1964) **IX**:246
  OWI **VIII**:285, 286
  popular culture **VIII**:301, 302; **IX**:259; **X**:278–279
  pornography **X**:283
  Presley, Elvis **IX**:263
  recreation **VII**:327–328; **IX**:271; **X**:303
  Robeson, Paul **VIII**:341, 342
  science and technology **IX**:286
  science fiction **IX**:287

sexual revolution **X:**323
Sinatra, Frank **VIII:**361
technology **VIII:**389
television **X:**344
Welles, Orson **VIII:**414, 415
World War II home front
VIII:433
Movimiento Estudiantil Chicano
de Aztlán (MEChA) **X:**166
MOWC (March on Washington
Committee) **VIII:**228
Mower, Joseph A. **V:**34
MOWM. *See* March on
Washington Movement
Moynihan, Daniel Patrick
family life **X:**127
neoconservatism **X:**252
UN **X:**357
Moytoy **II:**280
Mozambique **I:**231
Mozart, Wolfgang Amadeus
III:48, 309, 310
MP3 technology **X:**239–240
MPLA. *See* Popular Movement
for the Liberation of Angola
Mpongwe **I:254–255**
MPRS (Motion Picture Rating
System) **X:**235
MRI (magnetic resonance
imaging) **X:**224
Mrs. Warren's Profession (Shaw)
VI:79
MS-DOS (Microsoft Disk
Operating System) **X:**147
Ms. magazine
media **X:**219
Steinem, Gloria **X:**334
women's status and rights
IX:348
MSNBC (Microsoft National
Broadcasting Corporation)
X:217, 344
MSSI (Massachusetts Society
for the Suppression of
Intemperance) **IV:**369
M Street School (Washington,
D.C.) **VII:**352
MTV (Music Television) **X:**239,
279, 378*c*
muckrakers **VII:216–217**, 403*c*,
404*c*
business **VII:**46
journalism **VII:**159
The Masses **VII:**193
oil industry **VII:**244
politics (1900–1928)
VII:262
progressivism **VII:**271
Pure Food and Drug Act
VII:276
radical and labor press
VII:285
Sinclair, Upton **VII:**325–
326
Standard Oil **VII:**336
Steffens, Lincoln **VII:**339
Tarbell, Ida Minerva **VII:**349

Mudd, Samuel **V:**39
Mudge, Rose, Guthrie, Alexander,
and Mitchell **X:**233
Mud Island, Delaware **III:**135
Muenster, Sebastien **I:**118
Mugabe, Robert **X:**16
Mughal Empire **I:**181
mugwumps **VI:252**
Atkinson, Edward **VI:**22
Beecher, Henry Ward
VI:30
Higginson, Thomas
Wentworth **VI:**172
presidential campaigns
(1870–1899) **VI:**293
Republican Party **VI:**311
Schurz, Carl **VI:**325
Muhammad (prophet of Islam)
coffee **I:**79
Islam **I:**188
Mecca **I:**238
Sufism **I:**347
Muhammad, Elijah **IX:226–227**,
352*c*
African Americans **IX:**6
Ali, Muhammad **IX:**9
Farrakhan, Louis A. **X:**129
Malcolm X **IX:**198, 199
Nation of Islam **X:**249
religion **IX:**273
Muhammad, Wallace Dean
X:129, 249
Muhammad I Askia (Songhai
emperor). *See* Askia
Muhammad I
Muhlenberg, Henry Melchior
II:245–246
Lutherans **II:**212
Moravians **III:**302
Protestantism **II:**316
Muir, John **VI:252–254**, *253*,
410*c*
conservation/
environmentalism **VI:**81,
82
environment **VII:**98, 99;
IX:108
Pinchot, Gifford **VII:**260
Mujeres Pro-Raza Unida **IX:**183
mulattoes **II:246**
Bruce, Blanche Kelso
V:46–47
casta paintings **I:**64
castas **I:**65
Corps d'Afrique **V:**96
limpieza de sangre **I:**214
miscegenation **II:**237, 238
New Spain **I:**269
race and race relations
VII:283
slavery **II:**357
Spanish colonies **II:**373,
374
Spanish immigration **II:**375
Muldoon, William **VI:**44
Mule Bone (Hughes and Hurston)
VIII:181

Mules and Men (Hurston)
VIII:181
"Mule Shoe"
Gordon, John B. **V:**170
Overland campaign **V:**291
Spotsylvania, Battles of
V:368
Muller, Curt **VII:**217
Muller v. Oregon **VII:217–218**,
405*c*, **417–420**
Adkins v. Children's Hospital
VII:3
Brandeis, Louis Dembitz
VII:41
Goldmark, Josephine Clara
VII:127
Kelley, Florence **VII:**164
Supreme Court **VII:**343
Mulligan Guard Ball, The
(Harrigan and Hart) **VI:**257
Mullins, Priscilla. *See* Alden,
Priscilla
multiculturalism **VI:**169; **X:236–
237**, 240
multiple independently targeted
reentry vehicle (MIRV)
X:99–100
multiplicity **VI:**3
Mumbet (Freeman, Elizabeth)
III:176
mumps **X:**222
Muncie, Indiana **VII:**205
Munich Conference **VIII:248**
Anglo-American relations
VIII:21
foreign policy **VIII:**141
isolationists **VIII:**189
radio **VIII:**320
Munitions Board **IX:**238
munitions control board
VIII:267
Munn, Daniel W. **VI:**193
Munn v. Illinois **VI:**408*c*
business and government
VI:57
due process clause **VI:**101
Field, Stephen Johnson
VI:127
Patrons of Husbandry
VI:279
railroads **VI:**303
Supreme Court **VI:**348
Munsee **II:**97
Munsey's Magazine **VI:**236
Münster, Sebastian **I:**58
Muqaddimah (Ibn Khaldûn)
I:176
Mural (Pollock) **VIII:**31
murals **VI:**276
murder **X:**66, 96–97
"Murders in the Rue Morgue, The"
(Poe) **IV:**229, 414*c*
Murdoch, Rupert **X:**283
Murfreesboro/Stones River, Battle
of **V:271–272**, *272*
Bragg, Braxton **V:**42
Cleburne, Patrick R. **V:**75

music **V:**274
Rosecrans, William S. **V:**337
Sheridan, Philip H. **V:**353
Murphy, Charles **VI:**35; **VII:**356
Murphy, Frank
automobile industry
VIII:36
cities and urban life **VIII:**69
Korematsu v. U.S. **VIII:**203
Sweet trial **VII:**344
Murphy, Isaac **VI:**177, 178
Murphy, John Francis **VI:**275
Murphy, John M. **IX:**206; **X:**5
Murphy, Thomas **VI:**20
Murphy Brown **X:**293
Murray, Donald **VIII:**256
Murray, James **IX:**106, 107
Murray, John. *See* Dunmore, John
Murray, earl of
Murray, Judith Sargent Stevens
III:308
Murray, Pauli **IX:227–228**, 236,
262
Murray, Philip **VIII:248–249**
AFL **IX:**11
CIO **VIII:**82; **IX:**72
Irish Americans **VIII:**189
labor/labor movements
VIII:206, 207
steel industry **VIII:**373
Murray, Walter **II:**389
Murrieta, Joaquín **IV:267–268**
Murrow, Edward R. **VIII:**272;
IX:165, *165*
Musashi (Japanese
superbattleship) **VIII:**214
Muscle Shoals, Alabama **VIII:**392
Muscovy Company **II:**167
Cabot, Sebastian **I:**45
Company of Cathay **I:**87
Frobisher, Martin **I:**134
Museum of Modern Art (New
York City)
art and architecture **VIII:**29
Evans, Walker **VIII:**119
Lange, Dorothea **VIII:**210
Life magazine **VIII:**217
Museum of Television and Radio
IX:316
Musharraf, Pervez **X:**10–11, 287
music **II:247**; **III:308–310**;
IV:268–269; **V:272–274**;
VI:254–258, *256*; **VII:218–
220**, *219*, 409*c*; **VIII:249–252**,
251, 444*c*, 446*c*, 448*c*; **IX:**228,
228–230, *229*, 353*c*, 355*c*;
X:237–240, *239*
African Americans **VI:**7;
VIII:3
art **II:**26
Baltimore, Battle of **IV:**43
Beach, Amy Marcy Cheney
VI:28–29
Beatles **IX:**37–38
big bands **VIII:**44
Billings, William **III:**50
blues **VII:**39

music (*continued*)
computers **X:**88
counterculture **IX:**79
Dylan, Bob **IX:**92–93
Ellington, Duke **VIII:**111–112
entertainment, popular **VII:**96–97
FMP **VIII:**134–135
folk music revival **IX:**120–121
Foster, Stephen C. **V:**156
Gay Nineties **VI:**140
Gershwin, George **VII:**124–125
Goodman, Benny **VIII:**150–151
Great Migration **VII:**129
Guthrie, Woody **VIII:**160
Harlem Renaissance **VII:**135–136
Herbert, Victor August **VI:**170–171
Holiday, Billie **VIII:**168–169
Howe, Julia Ward **V:**198
illustration, photography, and graphic arts **VI:**183
immigration **IV:**195
jazz **VII:**153; **VIII:**194–195
Joplin, Scott **VII:**158
MacDowell, Edward Alexander **VI:**233
marriage and family **IX:**202
Massachusetts **II:**225
media **X:**219–220
migration **VII:**207
movies **IX:**225
NEA **IX:**234
Pelham, Peter **II:**283
popular culture **III:**341; **VII:**263; **VIII:**301; **IX:**259; **X:**278–280
Presley, Elvis **IX:**262–263
radio **VII:**290; **VIII:**320
recreation **VIII:**327, 328
rock and roll **IX:**278–280
Sinatra, Frank **VIII:**361
slavery **V:**362
Sousa, John Philip **VI:**339–340
teenagers **IX:**314
theater **VI:**354
Tin Pan Alley **VII:**353
Walter, Thomas **II:**406
Woodstock festival **X:**371–372
World War II home front **VIII:**433
"Yankee Doodle" **III:**453
zoot-suiters **VIII:**442
musical revues **VII:**95–96, 405c
musical theater
entertainment, popular **VI:**116
Herbert, Victor August **VI:**170

music **VI:**257; **X:**238
popular culture **X:**280–281
Music for the Theatre (Copland) **VII:**220
Music Is My Mistress (Ellington) **VIII:**112
music publishing **VI:**257–258
Music Television (MTV) **X:**239, 279, 378c
music videos **X:**239
muskets
Civil War **V:**74
Confederate army **V:**81
science and technology **V:**340
Shiloh, Battle of **V:**358
Muskie, Edmund S.
Albright, Madeleine K. **X:**22
Humphrey, Hubert H. **IX:**151
Mitchell, George **X:**231, 232
Tower Commission **X:**353
Muslim Mosque, Inc. **IX:**199
Muslims. *See* Islam/Muslims
Muslim Student Association **X:**189
Mussolini, Benito
Coughlin, Father Charles E. **VIII:**88
Ethiopia **VIII:**118
Hearst, William Randolph **VII:**138
Italian Americans **VIII:**190
Italian campaign **VIII:**191
Munich Conference **VIII:**248
Sicily **VIII:**360
World War II European theater **VIII:**431
Mutual Film Corporation **VII:**131
mutually assured destruction (MAD)
ABM Treaty **X:**26
cold war, end of **X:**85
defense policy **X:**99
détente **X:**104
Muybridge, Eadweard
Bierstadt, Albert **VI:**37
Eakins, Thomas **VI:**104
illustration, photography, and graphic arts **VI:**183–184
Muzorewa, Abel **X:**16
MX missile **X:**100, 101
My American Journey (Powell) **X:**287
My Ántonia (Cather) **VII:**179
My Bondage and My Freedom (Douglass) **V:**115
Myer, Albert J. **VI:**387
Myers, Abraham C. **V:**203, 204
Myers, Isaac **V:**77
Myers, Jerome **VII:**26
Myers, Michael O. **X:**5
Myers v. NBC **X:**5

My Fair Lady (musical) **IX:**258
My First Days in the White House (Long) **VIII:**223
Mylar **IX:**91
Myrdal, Alva **VIII:**253
Myrdal, Gunnar **VIII:**252–253, 448c
African Americans **VIII:**5
Bunche, Ralph **IX:**44–45
civil rights **VIII:**73
liberalism **VIII:**216
race and race relations **VIII:**317, 319
My Son John (film) **IX:**65
Mystic Fort **II:**222, 289, 290
mysticism **X:**253
myths and legends **II:**93
Brendan the Navigator, Saint **I:**36
Prester John **I:**301
Sundiata Keita **I:**350
Venice **I:**374

N

NA. *See* National Association of Professional Base Ball Players
NAACP. *See* National Association for the Advancement of Colored People
NAB. *See* National Association of Broadcasters
NAB (National Association of Base Ball Clubs) **VI:**25
Nabaga (Gonja ruler) **I:**143
Nabokov, Vladimir **IX:**194
NACC (North Atlantic Cooperation Council) **X:**260
Nacogdoches, Battle of **IV:**63
NACW. *See* National Association of Colored Women
Nader, Ralph **IX:**357c; **X:**241–242
Abscam **X:**5
automobile industry **IX:**27; **X:**35
business **IX:**47
consumerism **IX:**76
elections, presidential **X:**117, 118
GM **IX:**133
Green Party **X:**159
literature **IX:**194
National Traffic and Motor Vehicle Safety Act of 1966 **IX:**238
political parties **X:**277
"Nader's Raiders" **X:**241
NAFTA. *See* North American Free Trade Agreement
Nagasaki, Japan **IV:**298. *See also* Hiroshima and Nagasaki
Na Gbewa **I:**252
Nagin, Ray **X:**173
Nagumo, Chuichi **VIII:**292
Nahua Indians **I:**257–258, 258, 361; **II:**158

Nahuatl **I:**258
Aguilar, Gerónimo de **I:**5
Aztlán **I:**23
Chimalpahin, Domingo Francisco de San Antón Muñón **I:**73
Cortés, Hernán **I:**95
Durán, Diego **I:**114
Nahua **I:**257
Sahagún, Bernardino de **I:**323
Tlaxcala **I:**361
Toltecs **I:**364
Nairobi, Kenya, embassy bombing. *See* embassy bombings
Naismith, James **VI:**343; **VII:**334
Naked and the Dead, The (Mailer) **VIII:**219; **IX:**193, 258, 352c
Naked Lunch (Burroughs) **IX:**36–37, 194
Naked Society, The (Packard) **IX:**253
NAM. *See* National Association of Manufacturers
Namiba **IX:**4
Namozine Church **V:**14
nanotechnology **X:**320
Nantes, Edict of
French immigrants **II:**139
Henry IV **I:**158
Huguenots **I:**170–171
Nanticoke **II:**95; **III:**311
Nanumba **I:**252
NAOWS (National Association Opposed to Woman Suffrage) **VII:**18
Naples **III:**257
Napoleon I Bonaparte (emperor of the French) **III:**210
Florida **IV:**152
Ghent, Treaty of **IV:**176
New Orleans, Battle of **IV:**280
Texas **IV:**371
War of 1812 **IV:**390–392
Napoleon III (emperor of the French)
Bulloch, James D. **V:**49
foreign policy **V:**151
Seward, William H. **V:**348
Napoleonic Wars
Adams, John Quincy **IV:**5
agriculture **III:**11
foreign policy **IV:**154
Free Trade and Sailor's Rights **IV:**165
immigration **VI:**184
Monroe Doctrine **IV:**261
neutrality **VII:**235
panic of 1819 **IV:**293
Napolitano, Janet **X:**168
Napster **X:**88, 240, 382c
NARAL. *See* National Abortion Rights Action League
NARAL (National Association for the Repeal of Abortion Laws) **X:**289

narcotics **X:**242–244, *243*, 369.
See also drugs, illicit
Narcotics Act **VII:221–223,** *222,*
406*c*
Narcotics and Dangerous Drugs,
Bureau of **X:**242
Narragansett Bay **II:**333
Narragansett Indians **II:249**
  Canonchet **II:**57
  Canonicus **II:**57
  Miantonomo **II:**233
  Pequot War **II:**289, 290
  Rhode Island **II:**332, 333
  Rowlandson, Mary White
    II:337
  Wetamo **II:**411
  Williams, Roger **II:**416, 417
*Narrative of Arthur Gordon Pym,
  The* (Poe) **IV:**229
*Narrative of Col. Ethan Allen's
  Captivity* (Allen) **III:**15
Narrative of Sojourner Truth, The
  (Gilbert) **V:**393
*Narrative of the Colored People
  during the Late Yellow Fever
  Epidemic* (Allen and Jones)
  III:26
*Narrative of the Life of David
  Crockett...Written by Himself*
  (Crockett) **IV:**111
*Narrative of the Life of Frederick
  Douglass, An American Slave,
  Written by Himself*
    African Americans **IV:**9
    Douglass, Frederick **V:**115
    literature **IV:**228; **V:**239
    slavery **V:**362
*Narrative of the Life of Mrs. Mary
  Jemison* (Seaver) **II:445–446**
*Narrative of the United States
  Exploring Expedition* (Wilkes)
  IV:146
*Narrative of William W. Brown,
  an American Slave* (Brown)
  V:362
*Narrative relating to Francisco
  Coronado's explorations of
  the Southwest, 1540–1542*
  I:410–412
Narváez, Pánfilo de **I:258–259**
  Apalachee **I:**11
  Cabeza de Vaca, Álvar
    Núñez **I:**39
  Cuba **I:**100
  Sandoval, Gonzalo de **I:**325
  Texas **IV:**371
  Tezcatlipoca **I:**357
  Timucua **I:**360
NAS. *See* National Academy of
  Sciences
NASA. *See* National Aeronautics
  and Space Administration
NASCAR (National Association
  for Stock Car Auto Racing)
  X:331, 332
NASDAQ index **X:**59
Nash, C. C. **V:**412

Nash, Diane **IX:**123
Nash, Gary B. **X:**237
Nashoba community, Tennessee
  IV:405
Nashville, Battle of **V:**389
Nashville, Tennessee
  education, higher **VI:**111
  education, philanthropy and
    VI:112
  Exodusters **VI:**123
  Fellowship of Reconciliation
    VII:109
  Fillmore, Millard **IV:**150
  freedom rides **IX:**123
  Jackson, Andrew **IV:**205
  prostitution **V:**316
  sit-ins **IX:**291
  Vanderbilt, Cornelius
    IV:387
Nashville, USS **VII:**251
Nashville Pike **V:**271
Nasi, Gracia **I:**195, 196
Naskapi. *See* Montagnais-
  Naskapi
Nassau Hall (Princeton
  University) **III:**205
Nasser, Gamal Abdel
  anticommunism **IX:**14
  Dulles, John Foster **IX:**91
  Israel **IX:**160
  Middle East **IX:**214; **X:**227
  Suez crisis **IX:**306, 307
Nast, Thomas **V:275–276;**
  VI:407*c*
  class consciousness **VI:**73
  journalism **V:**218, 219
  Liberal Republican Party
    VI:222–223
  magazines **VI:**235
  Tweed Ring **VI:**369
Natchez, Mississippi **III:**10, 391
Natchez Indians **I:259–260**
  Louisiana **II:**210
  Natchez Revolt **II:**249–250
  population trends **I:**298
Natchez Revolt **II:249–250**
  Bienville, Jean-Baptiste Le
    Moyne, sieur de **II:**38
  Choctaw **II:**68
  Louisiana **II:**211
Natchez Trace **IV:**86
Natchitoches, Louisiana **IV:**300
Nathan, George Jean **VII:**201
Nathan, Tony **X:**209
Nation, Carry **VI:**295
Nation, The **VI:259**
  Atkinson, Edward **VI:**21
  Ely, Richard Theodore
    VI:115
  Forbes, John Murray
    VI:132
  Godkin, Edwin Lawrence
    VI:149
  Jackson, Helen Hunt
    VI:199
  magazines **VI:**235
  The Masses **VII:**193

Norton, Charles Eliot
    VI:269
  Thomas, Norman **VIII:**394
  Villard, Henry **VI:**375
National Abortion Rights Action
  League (NARAL) **X:**4, 134
National Academy of Arts
  VIII:164
National Academy of Design
  art and architecture **IV:**28;
    VII:23
  Catlin, George **IV:**84
  Chase, William Merritt
    VI:66
  Jefferson, Joseph, III
    VI:202
  Morse, Samuel F. B. **IV:**264
  painting **VI:**276
  Ryder, Albert Pinkham
    VI:319
National Academy of Sciences
  (NAS)
  King, Clarence **VI:**208
  science and technology
    VII:315
  Walcott, Charles Doolittle
    VI:380
National Advertising Review
  Board **X:**8
National Advisory Committee for
  Aeronautics
  aircraft industry **VIII:**13
  Bush, Vannevar **VIII:**56
  invention and technology
    VII:150
  technology **VIII:**389
National Aeronautics and Space
  Administration (NASA)
  IX:231–232, 354*c;* **X:**381*c*
  arms race **IX:**17
  aviation **IX:**29
  computers **IX:**70
  Eisenhower, Dwight D.
    IX:101
  Humphrey, Hubert H.
    IX:151
  science and technology
    IX:285
  space exploration **IX:**296
  space policy **X:**326, 327,
    329
  technology **IX:**312, 313
National Air Quality Control Act.
  See Clean Air Act
National Air Transport **VII:**28,
  165
National Americanization Day
  VII:13
National American Lyceum
  IV:231–232
National American Woman
  Suffrage Association (NAWSA)
  VI:410*c;* **VII:223–224,** 403*c*
  Anthony, Susan B. **VI:**16
  Blatch, Harriot Eaton
    Stanton **VII:**38
  Brown, Olympia **VI:**51

Catt, Carrie Lane Chapman
    VII:50
  NWP **VII:**230
  Paul, Alice **VII:**254
  Rankin, Jeannette **VII:**292
  Shaw, Anna Howard **VI:**329
  Terrell, Mary Eliza Church
    VII:352
  Wells-Barnett, Ida Bell
    VI:388
  woman suffrage **VII:**384,
    385
  women's status and rights
    VI:399
National Archives **III:**134;
  IX:125
National Association for the
  Advancement of Colored
  People (NAACP) **VII:224–
  225,** 405*c;* **VIII:255–256,**
  443*c,* 449*c;* **IX:232–234,** *233;*
  X:244–245
  African Americans **VI:**7–8;
    VIII:2, 4; **IX:**4, 5; **X:**14
  antilynching legislation
    VIII:22
  Baker, Ella Josephine **IX:**32
  *Brown v. Board of
    Education* **IX:**43, 44
  civil rights **VIII:**72, 73
  DuBois, W.E.B. **VII:**80–81
  Economic Opportunity Act
    (1964) **IX:**95, 96
  Farmer, James L. **X:**129
  Faubus, Orval **IX:**118
  FEPC **VIII:**123
  Freedom Train **IX:**125
  gun control **X:**161
  Harlem Renaissance
    VII:136
  Howells, William Dean
    VI:180
  lobbying **VII:**182
  March on Washington
    Movement **VIII:**227
  Marshall, Thurgood **IX:**202–
    203
  Niagara Movement **VII:**240
  NWTUL **VII:**231
  Parks, Rosa **IX:**254, 255
  race and race relations
    VIII:317, 319; **IX:**269
  Robinson, Jackie **IX:**278
  Scottsboro Boys **VIII:**353
  sit-ins **IX:**291
  Sweet trial **VII:**344
  Till, Emmett Louis **IX:**318
  Trotter, William Monroe
    VII:357
  Wald, Lillian **VII:**377
  Washington, Booker T.
    VI:384
  White, Walter **VIII:**416,
    417
  Wilkins, Roy **IX:**344–345
  Williams, Fannie Barrier
    VI:395

National Association for the
Repeal of Abortion Laws
(NARAL) **X**:289
National Association of Base Ball
Clubs (NAB) **VI**:25
National Association of
Broadcasters (NAB) **VIII**:272;
X:343
National Association of Colored
Women (NACW) **VI**:259–260;
VII:225
    African Americans **VI**:7
    Harper, Frances Ellen
        Watkins **V**:184; **VI**:160
    Terrell, Mary Eliza Church
        VII:352
    Williams, Fannie Barrier
        VI:395
    women's status and rights
        VII:389
National Association of
Evangelicals **X**:125
National Association of
Manufacturers (NAM)
VII:225–226
    Buck's Stove **VII**:42
    coal industry **VIII**:75
    Danbury Hatters **VII**:69
    Economic Opportunity Act
        (1964) **IX**:95
    Employment Act of 1946
        IX:106
    labor/labor movements
        VII:169
    National Civic Federation
        VII:226
    open shop movement
        VII:247
    professional organizations,
        rise of **VI**:293
National Association of
Professional Base Ball Players
(NA) **V**:367; **VI**:25–26; **VII**:334
National Association of Real
Estate Boards **VIII**:178
National Association of Women
Lawyers **X**:123
National Association Opposed to
Woman Suffrage (NAOWS)
VII:18
National Bank Act (1864) **IV**:47,
132
National Banking Act (1863)
V:445c
    banking **V**:28
    currency issue **VI**:88
    economy **V**:122
national banking system **VI**:260–
261
    business and government
        VI:57
    Democratic Party **VI**:96
    farmers' alliances **VI**:125
    Omaha platform **VI**:272
    political parties, third **VI**:286
National Baptist Convention
(NBC) **VI**:4

National Baptist Convention,
U.S.A. **X**:14
National Baptist Convention of
America **X**:14
National Barn Dance **VIII**:250
National Baseball Commission
VII:32–33, 334
National Baseball Hall of Fame
and Museum (Cooperstown,
New York) **VIII**:370, 445c
National Basketball Association
(NBA) **VII**:334; **X**:331, 332
National Basketball League
VII:334
National Birth Control League
VII:37, 407c
National Black Feminist
Organization **IX**:348
National Board of Health **VII**:275
National Book Award for Fiction
VIII:128
National Broadcasting
Corporation (NBC)
    cold war culture **IX**:65
    entertainment, popular
        VII:97
    GE **IX**:132
    journalism **VII**:161; **IX**:165
    music **VII**:220
    popular culture **VII**:265
    radio **VII**:290
    television **IX**:315; **X**:344
National Bureau of Economic
Research **X**:111
National Bureau of Standards
VII:151
National Cancer Institute
VIII:235, 236; **IX**:235
National Catholic Community
Services **VIII**:403
National Catholic Welfare Council
VIII:64; **IX**:106
National Cemetery, Gettysburg
V:169
National Child Labor Committee
    Ethical Culture movement
        VI:121
    Kelley, Florence **VII**:164
    photography **VII**:259
National Citizens Rights
Association **V**:390
National Civic Federation
    Clayton Antitrust Act
        VII:59
    Mitchell, John **VII**:211
    New Unionism **VII**:237
    Valesh, Eva McDonald
        VII:367
National Civil Liberties Bureau
(NCLB) **VII**:9, 31
National Colored Colonization
Society **VI**:123
National Colored Convention
IV:129
National Commission on
Excellence in Education
X:113–115

National Commission on Law
Observance and Enforcement
VII:67
National Committee for
Organizing Iron and Steel
Workers **VII**:117, 247
National Committee of
Autonomous State Parties
X:24
National Committee on the Cause
and Cure of War (NCCCW)
VII:49
National Conference of Catholic
Charities **VII**:298
National Conference of Charities
and Corrections **VII**:328
National Conference of
Commissions on the Status of
Women, Third **X**:247
National Conference of Social
Work **VII**:329
National Congress of American
Indians (NCAI) **VIII**:264;
IX:240, 319
National Congress of Mothers
VII:214
National Conservation
Commission **VII**:315
National Conservatory of Music
VI:170, 255
National Consumers League
(NCL)
    Children's Bureau **VII**:53
    Dewson, Mary **VIII**:95
    Goldmark, Josephine Clara
        VII:127
    Hamilton, Alice **VII**:133
    Kelley, Florence **VII**:164
    Muller v. Oregon **VII**:218
National Council for the
Prevention of War (NCPW)
VII:49
National Council of Catholic
Bishops **X**:3, 4, 70
National Council of Catholic
Women **X**:124
National Council of Negro
Women **VIII**:3, 44
National Council of Women
VIII:44
National Council on Disability
X:24–25
National Council on Limitation of
Armaments **VII**:257
National Council on the Arts
IX:234
National Council on the
Humanities **IX**:234, 235
National Counterterrorism Center
(NCTC) **X**:347
National Credit Corporation
(NCC) **VIII**:174, 325
National Currency Act (1863)
IV:47, 132
National Day of Mourning **IX**:22
national debt. *See* debt, national;
deficit, federal

National Defense Act **VII**:227
    armed forces **VII**:20
    education **IX**:99
    Preparedness **VII**:267–268
National Defense Act
    amendments **VII**:21
National Defense Advisory
Commission (NDAC)
    dollar-a-year men **VIII**:96
    Hillman, Sidney **VIII**:166
    Nelson, Donald M.
        VIII:266
    OPM **VIII**:283
National Defense Appropriations
Act **VIII**:80, 241, 446c
National Defense Day **VIII**:227
National Defense Education Act
(1958) **IX**:99, 312, 354c
National Defense Garden
Conference **VIII**:405
National Defense Mediation
Board **VIII**:261
National Defense Production
Board (NDPB) **VIII**:378
National Defense Research
Committee (NDRC) **VIII**:56,
283
National Democratic Institute for
International Affairs **X**:234
National Dress Reform
Association (NDRA) **V**:139
National Education Association
    education **VIII**:106
    education, primary/
        secondary **X**:114, 115
    ERA **X**:123
    ESEA **IX**:106
    professional organizations,
        rise of **VI**:294
National Encampment **VI**:151–
152
National Endowment for the Arts
(NEA) **IX**:234, 356c; **X**:245–
246, 382c
    Great Society **IX**:139
    music **IX**:228
    NEH **IX**:234
*National Endowment for the Arts
v. Finley* **X**:382c
National Endowment for the
    Humanities (NEH) **IX**:234–
235, 356c; **X**:245–246
    Bennett, William J. **X**:41
    Great Society **IX**:139
    NEA **IX**:234
National Energy Policy
Development Group (NEPDG)
X:72
National Enforcement Plan
IX:110
National Enquirer **X**:219
National Environmental Policy
Act (NEPA) **X**:246, 375c
    conservation/
        environmentalism **X**:90
    environment **IX**:109
    property rights **X**:290

National Equal Rights League **VII:**357

National Era **V:**239

National Farmers' Alliance and Industrial Union **VI:**125, 410c

National Farmers Organization (NFO) **IX:**7, 353c

National Farmers Union **IX:**7

National Farm Workers Association (NFWA)
  braceros **IX:**43
  Chávez, César Estrada **IX:**53
  Latino movement **IX:**186
  UFW **IX:**324

National Federation of African American Women **VII:**225

National Federation of Business and Professional Women **X:**123

National Female Anti-Slavery Society **IV:**148

National Firearms Act (1934) **X:**160–161, 249

National Flag Conference **X:**135

National Football League (NFL) **VII:**333; **VIII:**371; **X:**302, 330, 331

National Forest Commission **VII:**260

National Forest Reserve program **VI:**81, 119

National Foundation on the Arts and Humanities Act (1965) **IX:**356c
  Great Society **IX:**139
  NEA **IX:**235
  NEA/NEH **X:**245
  NEH **IX:**234

National Freedmen's Relief Association **V:**393

National Gazette **III:**180

National Guard **IX:**354c, 355c
  AEF **VII:**10
  armed forces **VII:**20, 21
  Army, U.S. **VIII:**26
  Birmingham confrontation **IX:**40
  Faubus, Orval **IX:**118
  foreign policy **VII:**113
  Gastonia Strike **VII:**122
  Hershey, Lewis B. **VIII:**164
  Homestead Strike **VI:**176
  Hurricane Katrina **X:**173
  Industrial Relations Commission **VII:**146
  Kent State protests **X:**197
  Ludlow Massacre **VII:**187
  MacArthur, Douglas **IX:**197
  National Defense Act **VII:**227
  Preparedness **VII:**268
  Southern Manifesto **IX:**294
  Stevenson, Adali E. **IX:**302
  strikes **V:**375

national health insurance **VIII:**236, 363

National Heart Institute **VIII:**236

National Historic Sites **IX:**263

National Hockey League (NHL) **VII:**334–335; **VIII:**372, 373; **IX:**299

National Housing Act (1934) **VIII:**445c
  Federal Housing Administration **IX:**119
  Federal Housing Administration (FHA) **VIII:**133
  Federal National Mortgage Association **VIII:**135
  housing **VIII:**177

National Housing Act (1949) **IX:**116

National Human Genome Research Institute (NHGRI) **X:**171, 172

National Humanities Medal **IX:**234

National Hurricane Center (NHC) **X:**173

National Independent Party. *See* Greenback-Labor Party

National Indian Youth Council (NIYC) **IX:**241, 242, 319; **X:**250

National Industrial Recovery Act (NIRA) **VIII:256–257,** 444c, 445c
  AFL **VIII:**18
  antimonopoly **VIII:**23
  Brain Trust **VIII:**51
  Bridges, Harry **VIII:**53
  Byrnes, James F. **VIII:**60
  Communists **VIII:**77
  Congress **VIII:**79
  conservatism **VIII:**84
  Dubinsky, David **VIII:**97
  economy **VIII:**104
  First New Deal **VIII:**138
  Ickes, Harold L. **VIII:**183
  Johnson, Hugh S. **VIII:**196
  labor/labor movements **VIII:**205–206
  Lewis, John L. **VIII:**213
  liberalism **VIII:**215
  Long, Huey P. **VIII:**222
  National Recovery Administration **VIII:**259, 260
  New Deal **VIII:**269
  NLRA **VIII:**257
  NLRB **VIII:**258–259
  Perkins, Frances **VIII:**293
  PWA **VIII:**314
  Schechter Poultry Corporation v. U.S. **VIII:**351
  socialists **VIII:**362
  strikes **VIII:**377
  Supreme Court **VIII:**382
  taxation **VIII:**387
  Tugwell, Rexford G. **VIII:**397–398

UMWA **VIII:**401
  Wagner, Robert F. **VIII:**410

National Institute for Occupational Safety and Health (NIOSH) **X:**264

National Institute of Mental Health (NIMH) **IX:**235, 236

National Institutes of Health (NIH) **IX:235–236**
  Human Genome Project **X:**171, 172
  medicine **VIII:**235, 236; **IX:**210; **X:**225
  public health **IX:**265
  stem cell research **X:**335

National Institutes of Health Revitalization Act (1994) **X:**5, 289

National Intelligencer **IV:**163

National Invitation Tournament (NIT) **VIII:**371

nationalism
  African Americans **X:**14, 15
  Confederate States of America **V:**87
  Republican Party **V:**334

Nationalist Clubs **VI:**172

Nationalist Party (Spain) **VIII:**303

Nationalists **III:**108, 109, 116

National Jewish Welfare Board **VIII:**403

National Kansas Committee **IV:**242

National Labor Relations Act (NLRA) **VIII:257–258,** 445c
  AFL **VIII:**18
  automobile industry **VIII:**36
  business **VIII:**59
  Byrnes, James F. **VIII:**60
  civil liberties **VIII:**71
  coal industry **VIII:**75
  Communists **VIII:**77
  Congress **VIII:**79
  conservatism **VIII:**84
  court-packing plan **VIII:**89
  government **VIII:**152
  Hughes, Charles Evans **VII:**142
  labor/labor movements **VIII:**206
  Lewis, John L. **VIII:**213
  liberalism **VIII:**215
  New Deal **VIII:**269, 270
  NLRB **VIII:**258
  Perkins, Frances **VIII:**293
  Roosevelt, Franklin D. **VIII:**345
  Second New Deal **VIII:**356
  socialists **VIII:**362
  steel industry **VIII:**373
  strikes **VIII:**377
  Supreme Court **VIII:**382
  Taft, Robert A. **VIII:**385
  Taft-Hartley Act **IX:**309

UFW **IX:**324
  Wagner, Robert F. **VIII:**410
  women's status and rights **VIII:**423

National Labor Relations Board (NLRB) *VIII:258,* **258–259**
  FCC **VIII:**131
  labor/labor movements **VIII:**206; **X:**203
  NLRA **VIII:**257
  NWLB **VIII:**261
  Wagner, Robert F. **VIII:**410

National Labor Relations Board v. Jones and Laughlin Steel Corporation **VIII:**258

National Labor Union (NLU) **V:276**
  Colored National Labor Union **V:**77
  contract labor **VI:**82
  employment **V:**133
  labor organizations **VI:**215
  strikes **V:**375

National Lawyers Guild **IX:**86

National League **VIII:**370

National League of Colored Women **VI:**395; **VII:**225

National League of Professional Base Ball Clubs (NL) **VI:**26, 27; **VII:**32–33, 334

National Liberation Front (NLF) **IX:**330, 332, 339

National Library of Medicine **IX:**236

National Mall, Washington, D.C. **IX:**329, 330

National Manpower Council **IX:**346

National Mental Health Act (1946) **IX:**235

National Military Cemetery, Vicksburg **V:**277

National Military Establishment (NME) **IX:**238, 351c

national military parks **V:276–277**

National Mobilization to End the War in Vietnam (the Mobe) **X:**28, 73

national monuments **VII:**16, 404c; **VIII:**327, 328

National Mothers' Congress **VII:**181, 261

National Museum of the American Indian Act (1989) **X:**250

National Negro Business League **VI:**384

National Negro Congress **VIII:**54, 318

National Negro Convention **IV:**174

National Negro Labor Convention **V:**323

National Organization for Public Health **VII:**377

National Organization for the Reform of Marijuana Laws (NORML) **X**:244

National Organization for Women (NOW) **IX**:236, 357*c*; **X**:247–248
  abortion **X**:4
  ERA **X**:123, 124
  feminism **X**:132–134
  Friedan, Betty **IX**:127
  Murray, Pauli **IX**:227
  pro-life/pro-choice movements **X**:289
  Roe v. Wade **X**:312
  Steinem, Gloria **X**:334
  WEAL **IX**:345
  women's status and rights **IX**:347; **X**:371

National Origins Act (Johnson-Reed Act, 1924) **VII**:227–228, 408*c*; **IX**:353*c*
  AFL **VII**:12
  anti-Semitism **VII**:17
  Asian Americans **VIII**:32
  Cable Act **VII**:47
  citizenship **VII**:56
  conservatism **VIII**:83
  Coolidge, Calvin John **VII**:65
  Dillingham Commission **VII**:78
  immigration **VII**:144; **IX**:155
  Immigration Act (1965) **IX**:156
  McCarran-Walter Act **IX**:204
  Mexican immigration **VII**:203
  nativism **VII**:234
  population trends **VII**:266
  progressivism **VII**:271
  race and race relations **VII**:282

national origins standard **X**:175

National Outdoor Recreation Review Commission **IX**:237, 354*c*

National Packing Company **VI**:243

national parks
  Antiquities Act **VII**:16
  Independence Hall **III**:224
  recreation **VIII**:327, 328

National Park Service (NPS) **VII**:228, 406*c*
  commemoration **IX**:66
  monuments **V**:268
  national military parks **V**:276, 277
  recreation **VIII**:327
  Roosevelt, Theodore **VII**:304
  science and technology **VII**:315

National Park System **IX**:240

National Progressive Republican League
  Congress **VII**:62
  elections **VII**:91
  Johnson, Hiram Warren **VII**:154
  Progressive Party **VII**:270
  Republican Party **VII**:300
  Taft, William Howard **VII**:348

National Pro-Life Alliance **X**:289

National Public Radio (NPR) **X**:220

National Rainbow Coalition **X**:191, 192

National Reclamation Act **VII**:228–229, 304, 315

National Recovery Act **VII**:42

National Recovery Administration (NRA) **VIII**:259–260, *260*
  advertising **VIII**:1
  African Americans **VIII**:3
  Agricultural Adjustment Act **VIII**:5
  antimonopoly **VIII**:23–24
  automobile industry **VIII**:36
  Baruch, Bernard M. **VIII**:42
  Brain Trust **VIII**:51
  children **VIII**:67
  coal industry **VIII**:75
  Dubinsky, David **VIII**:97
  Fair Labor Standards Act **VIII**:124
  First New Deal **VIII**:138
  Food, Drug, and Cosmetic Act **VIII**:139
  Harriman, W. Averell **VIII**:161
  Henderson, Leon **VIII**:163
  Hillman, Sidney **VIII**:165
  Hughes, Charles Evans **VII**:142
  ILGWU **VIII**:187
  Johnson, Hugh S. **VIII**:196
  labor/labor movements **VIII**:206
  Lewis, John L. **VIII**:213
  New Deal **VIII**:269
  news media **VIII**:271
  NIRA **VIII**:256
  PWA **VIII**:314
  Schechter Poultry Corporation v. U.S. **VIII**:351
  South **VIII**:366
  Supreme Court **VIII**:382

National Recreation Association **VIII**:327

National Reform Party **IV**:163

National Register of Historic Places **IX**:118

National Republican Party
  anti-Masonry **IV**:25
  Clay, Henry **IV**:97
  Jackson, Andrew **IV**:206

Van Buren, Martin **IV**:385–386
  Webster, Daniel **IV**:393
  Whigs **IV**:396

National Research and Education Network (NREN) **X**:182

National Research Council **VII**:315

National Resources Planning Board (NRPB) **VIII**:260–261
  CEA **IX**:77
  Congress **VIII**:81
  Economic Bill of Rights **VIII**:102
  Executive Reorganization Act **VIII**:121
  Full Employment Bill **VIII**:145
  GI Bill of Rights **VIII**:149
  government **VIII**:153
  Keynesianism **VIII**:201
  liberalism **VIII**:216
  postwar planning **VIII**:306
  Third New Deal **VIII**:393

National Review **IX**:52; **X**:49, 50

National Rifle Association (NRA) **X**:248, 248–249
  campaign finance **X**:64
  gun control **X**:161
  PACs **X**:275

National Right to Life Organization **X**:134, 289

National Rip Saw **VII**:285

National Road **III**:466*c*; **IV**:271–273, 272*m*
  agriculture **IV**:12
  American System **IV**:20
  Baltimore & Ohio Railroad **IV**:43
  Bonus Bill **IV**:62
  economy **IV**:130
  internal improvements **IV**:202
  migration **IV**:254
  transportation **V**:390

National Safety Council **VII**:243, 392

National School Lunch Act (1946) **IX**:8

National Science Foundation (NSF) **IX**:352*c*
  Bush, Vannevar **VIII**:56, 57
  Internet **X**:181
  medicine **IX**:210
  science and technology **IX**:286
  technology **IX**:311

National Sculpture Society **VI**:18

national security **X**:376*c*
  civil liberties **VIII**:71
  elections, presidential **X**:118
  Gingrich, Newton L. **X**:152
  immigration **X**:177
  Pentagon Papers **X**:272
  USA PATRIOT Act **X**:358

National Security Act (1947) **IX**:237–238, 351*c*
  CIA **IX**:51
  Forrestal, James V. **VIII**:143
  OSS **VIII**:285
  Progressive Party **IX**:264
  Truman, Harry S. **IX**:320

National Security Act (1949) **IX**:238, 352*c*

National Security Advisor **X**:198, 309

National Security Council (NSC) **IX**:351*c*, 352*c*
  Albright, Madeleine K. **X**:22
  Boland Amendment **X**:45
  defense budget **IX**:83
  National Security Act of 1947 **IX**:237, 238
  North, Oliver L. **X**:258
  NSC-68 **X**:247
  Tower Commission **X**:353
  Truman, Harry S. **IX**:320

National Security Council Document 68. *See* NSC-68

National Security Decision Directive 13 (NSDD–13) **X**:30

National Security League **VII**:227, 267

National Security Political Action Committee **X**:168

National Security Resources Board **IX**:237

National Service Board for Religious Objectors (NSBRO) **VIII**:83

National Service Corps (NSC) **IX**:332–333

National Space Act (1958) **X**:326

National Spiritualism Association **VI**:309

National Style **IV**:29–30

National System of Interstate and Defense Highways **IX**:159, 354*c*

National Textile Workers Union **VII**:122

National Trades Union **IV**:218

National Traffic and Motor Vehicle Safety Act (1966) **IX**:238, 357*c*
  automobile industry **IX**:27
  business **IX**:47
  consumerism **IX**:76
  literature **IX**:194
  Nader, Ralph **X**:241

National Trails Act (1968) **IX**:237, **239**, *239*, 271, 357*c*

National Trails System **IX**:239, 357*c*

National Trails System Act (1983) **X**:290

National Travelers Aid Organization **VIII**:403

National Tube **VII**:336

National Union for Social Justice (NUSJ) **VIII**:88

National Union for the Total
Independence of Angola
(UNITA) **X**:85
National Unity Party **X**:25
National University Law School
VI:229
National Urban League (NUL)
African Americans **VI**:7–8;
X:14
March on Washington
Movement **VIII**:227
race and race relations
VIII:317
National War Labor Board
(NWLB) **VII:229–230**, 407*c*;
VIII:261–262
AFL **VII**:12
coal industry **VIII**:75
Fuel Administration **VII**:119
labor/labor movements
VII:170–172; **VIII**:207
mobilization **VIII**:242
NLRB **VIII**:259
OPA **VIII**:282
steel industry **VIII**:374
Steel Strike of 1919
VII:338–339
strikes **VIII**:378
Taft, William Howard
VII:348
wage and price controls
VIII:409
War Manpower Commission
VIII:412
World War I **VII**:393
National Wilderness Preservation
Act of 1964 **IX**:240, 356*c*
conservation/
environmentalism **X**:90
environment **IX**:108, 109
National Outdoor
Recreation Review
Commission **IX**:237
Wild and Scenic Rivers Act
of 1968 **IX**:344
National Wildlife Federation
VIII:116; **IX**:108
National Wildlife Refuge System
IX:240
National Woman's Christian
Temperance Union (WCTU)
V:184. *See also* Women's
Christian Temperance Union
National Woman's Party (NWP)
VII:230, 406*c*
Blatch, Harriot Eaton
Stanton **VII**:38
Cable Act **VII**:47
Catt, Carrie Lane Chapman
VII:50
ERA **VII**:100
Paul, Alice **VII**:254
Terrell, Mary Eliza Church
VII:353
woman suffrage **VII**:385
women's status and rights
VII:388

National Woman Suffrage
Association (NWSA) **V:277**,
446*c*; **VI**:408*c*
Anthony, Susan B. **VI**:16
Brown, Olympia **VI**:51
Cary, Mary Ann Shadd **V**:58
Gage, Matilda Joslyn **VI**:137
Hooker, Isabella Beecher
VI:176
Lockwood, Belva Ann
Bennett McNall **VI**:229
NAWSA **VII**:223
Ray, Charlotte **V**:323
Shaw, Anna Howard **VI**:329
Stanton, Elizabeth Cady
V:370
Stone, Lucy **VI**:346
women's status and rights
V:437, 438; **VI**:399
National Women's Law Center
X:350
National Women's Political
Caucus (NWPC)
feminism **X**:133, 134
NOW **X**:247
Steinem, Gloria **X**:334
National Women's Rights
Convention **V**:437; **VI**:39
National Women's Trade Union
League (NWTUL) **VII:230–
231**
Blatch, Harriot Eaton
Stanton **VII**:38
Hamilton, Alice **VII**:133
New Woman **VII**:240
radical and labor press
VII:285
Shirtwaist Makers Strike
VII:324
Wald, Lillian **VII**:377
women's status and rights
VII:387
National World War II Memorial
IX:330
National Youth Administration
(NYA) **VIII:262–263**
African Americans **VIII**:3
Bethune, Mary McLeod
VIII:44
Black Cabinet **VIII**:45, 46
children **VIII**:66
education **VIII**:106
ERAA **VIII**:114
HOLC **VIII**:171
Johnson, Lyndon B. **IX**:163
marriage and family
VIII:231
recreation **VIII**:327
relief **VIII**:332
Roosevelt, Eleanor
VIII:343
WPA **VIII**:425
National Zeitung **V**:70
Nation at Risk, A (National
Commission on Excellence in
Education report) **X**:113–115
nation-building **X**:22

Nation of Islam **VIII**:443*c*;
IX:352*c*; **X:249–250**
African Americans **IX**:5;
X:14
Ali, Muhammad **IX**:9
assassinations **IX**:22
Farrakhan, Louis A. **X**:129
Hurricane Katrina **X**:174
Jackson, Jesse, L. **X**:192
Malcolm X **IX**:198–199
Muhammad, Elijah **IX**:226–
227
race and race relations
X:297
religion **IX**:273
Nation of Strangers, A (Packard)
IX:253
Native American Association
IV:23, 196
Native American Democratic
Association **V**:280
Native American Grave Protection
and Repatriation Act (1990)
X:250
Native American language groups
I:6–7
Native American Mound Builders
IV:335
Native American Party **IV**:196
Native American religion **I**:1,
260–262, 261*m*
Native Americans **II:250–254**,
251, 435*c*; **III:311–315**, 313*m*,
460*c*, 464*c–466c*; **IV:273–276**,
412*c*, 413*c*; **V:277–279**, 279*m*,
443*c*, 444*c*, 446*c*; **VI:261–263**,
262, 407*c*, 409*c–411c*;
VII:231–233, *232*, 404*c*, 408*c*;
VIII:263–265, *264*, 444*c*,
448*c*; **IX:240–242**, 353*c*, 357*c*;
X:375*c*. *See also* Alaska Natives
Abenaki **I**:1–2
abolitionism **II**:1
Adair, James **II**:4
agriculture **II**:8–10, 14
AIM **IX**:12–13
Alaska **III**:12
alcohol **III**:13
Algonquian **I**:6–7
Algonquin **II**:18
American Fur Company
IV:18
Anglican Church **II**:21, 22
animals **II**:22–23; **III**:22–23
Apache War **VI**:17–18
Apalachee **I**:11
art and architecture **II**:24–
26; **III**:28, 29; **IV**:28, 29;
V:18
Astor, John Jacob **IV**:33–35
Astoria **IV**:35
Atkinson, Henry **IV**:36
Attakullakulla **II**:28–29
Attucks, Crispus **III**:37
Bacon's Rebellion **II**:31–32
banks **III**:42
Baptists **II**:33

Beckwourth, Jim **IV**:51
Bent, William **IV**:52–53
Bidwell, John **IV**:56
Bilingual Education Act
X:42
Black Hawk War **IV**:56
Blount, William **III**:53
Blue Jacket **III**:54
Blue Licks, Battle of **III**:54
Boas, Franz Uri **VII**:39
Bodmer, Karl **IV**:60–61
Boone, Daniel **III**:56
borderlands **II**:39–40
Bosomworth, Mary
Musgrove **II**:40
Bowles, Samuel **VI**:43
Brainerd, David **II**:45
Brant, Joseph **III**:62–63
Bright Eyes **VI**:48–49
Brims **II**:47
British Empire **II**:49
Brown, Charles Brockden
III:64
Bry, Theodor de **I**:38
buffalo **III**:64
buffalo, extermination of
VI:53
Burgoyne, Sir John **III**:68
Burke Act **VII**:44
Cahokia **I**:50–51
California **I**:52; **III**:74;
IV:70, 72
California gold rush **IV**:75
California missions **IV**:76
Calusa **I**:52–53
Canada **III**:77–79
captivity **II**:57–58
Carson, Kit **IV**:82
Cartier, Jacques **I**:61–62
Cass, Lewis **IV**:83
Catawba **II**:61
Catlin, George **IV**:84
cattle kingdom **VI**:64
Cayuga **I**:69
Champlain, Samuel de
II:62
Cherokee **II**:64–65;
III:86–87
Chesapeake Bay **II**:65–66
Chickasaw **IV**:86
childhood **II**:67
Choctaw **III**:89; **IV**:86
citizenship **III**:92
Clark, George Rogers
III:95, 96
Clark, William **III**:96, 97
clothing **II**:71, 72
Cody, William Frederick
VI:76
Coercive Acts **III**:100
College of William and Mary
II:74
Colorado gold rush **IV**:99–
100
Columbian Exchange
I:81–82
Connecticut **II**:75–77

Native Americans (*continued*)
consumption **II**:79
corn **I**:91–92; **II**:80–81
Cornplanter **III**:118–119
cotton culture **IV**:106, 107
crafts **II**:82
Creek **III**:125–126; **IV**:109
Crow **II**:85
crowd actions **II**:87
Custer, George A. **V**:99
dance **II**:90
Dartmouth College **II**:91
Dawes Severalty Act **VI**:93–
94, **418–420**
Delaware **II**:94–96
Delaware Indians **II**:96–98
Democratic Party **IV**:118
Deseret, State of **IV**:119–
121
dime novels **VI**:98
disease/epidemics **II**:97–98;
IV:123
Dragging Canoe **III**:139–
140
Dunmore, John Murray, earl
of **III**:142
Duston, Hannah Emerson
II:105
Dutch Reformed Church
II:107
Easton, Hosea **IV**:129
Eaton, John, Jr. **V**:120
economy **IV**:129
education **II**:111; **VI**:108–
109
EEOC **IX**:110
election of 1828 **IV**:136–137
Eliot, John **II**:115
Enlightenment, American
II:119
entertainment, popular
VI:118, 119
environment **II**:119; **III**:153
ethnocentrism **II**:121–123
exploration **IV**:144, 145
Fallen Timbers, Battle of
III:161–162
Federalists **III**:165
fertility **II**:125–126
fishing **II**:126
Flathead Indians **II**:127–
128
Florida **III**:167; **IV**:153
FMP **VIII**:134
food **II**:130
foreign affairs **III**:168
foreign policy **IV**:154
forests **II**:131
Fort Laramie **IV**:156–158
forts **II**:133
Fort Stanwix, Treaty of
III:170–171
Fort William Henry
Massacre **II**:134
Franklin, state of **III**:175
French colonies **II**:135, 136
frontier, the **III**:181–182

fur trade **II**:140–142;
IV:170, 171
Gates, Sir Thomas **II**:143–
144
gender **II**:145
Ghent, Treaty of **IV**:175
Glaize, meeting at the
III:195
Gnadenhutten Massacre
III:196
gold **IV**:178, 179
Great Plains **III**:197
Great Plains Indians
II:157–158
Greenville, Treaty of
III:199, 200
Guadalajara **II**:158
Handsome Lake **III**:209
Harrison, William Henry
IV:184
horses **II**:165, 166
housing **II**:166
Howard, Oliver Otis
V:197–198
Hudson's Bay Company
II:168
Hull, William **IV**:192
imperialism **VI**:188
Indian Affairs, Bureau of
IV:196
Indian Affairs, Office of
VI:188–190
Indian Claims Commission
IX:156–157
Indian Removal Act
IV:197, **197–199**, 412c,
427–428
Indian Reorganization Act
VIII:185–186
Indian Rights Association
VI:190
iron manufacturing **II**:178
Iroquois **II**:178–180;
III:227–228
Jackson, Andrew **IV**:205
Jackson, Helen Hunt
VI:199
Japanese Americans,
relocation of **VIII**:194
Jay's Treaty **III**:231
Jesuits **II**:185
Johnson, Sir John **III**:237
Keokuk **IV**:213
Kieft, Willem **II**:192
King Philip's War **II**:193
King William's War **II**:195
Knox, Henry **III**:248
labor/labor movements
II:198
Lamy, Jean Baptiste **IV**:222
land **II**:201
lead mines **IV**:223
Lee, Jason **IV**:224
Lewis, Meriwether **III**:261
Lewis and Clark Expedition
III:262, 263
Libertarian Party **X**:209

literature **II**:205; **IV**:227;
VI:225; **X**:210–211
Little Bighorn, Battle of
V:240–241
Locke, John **II**:208–209
Lone Wolf v. Hitchcock
VII:184–185
Louisiana **II**:210
Louisiana Purchase **III**:272
mariners **II**:215
marriage and family **II**:216–
218; **III**:289; **IV**:238
Mason, John **II**:222
Massachusetts **II**:222
McCrea, Jane **III**:293
McGillivray, Alexander
III:294–295
medicine **II**:230; **III**:296
Metacom **II**:231–232
métis **II**:232–233
Miantonomo **II**:233
migration **IV**:253, 254
miscegenation **II**:237
missions **II**:238–239
Missouri Fur Company
IV:258
Montour, Andrew **II**:241
Montour, Madame **II**:241–
242
Moravians **III**:302
Mormon Church **IV**:90
mortality **II**:244
mountain men **IV**:267
movies **IX**:224
music **VI**:255
Narragansett **II**:249
Natchez Revolt **II**:249–250
Native Americans in the War
of 1812 **IV**:276
Navajo **II**:254–255
Neolin **II**:255–256
New Hampshire **II**:259,
260
New Jersey **II**:261
New Mexico **II**:263–264
New Netherland **II**:265
New Orleans, Battle of
IV:280
New Spain, northern
frontier of **III**:317–318
New York **II**:269
Nez Perce War **VI**:267–268
North Carolina **II**:273–274
Northwest Coast Indians
II:275
Northwest Ordinances
III:322
Oglethorpe, James Edward
II:277
Oregon Trail **IV**:285, 286
Osceola **IV**:289
Pan-American Exposition
VII:252
Paris, Treaty of (1763)
III:331
Paris, Treaty of (1783)
III:332

Parker, Ely Samuel **V**:294–
295
Parkman, Francis **VI**:277–
278
Passamaquoddy **I**:287
Paxton Boys **II**:282
Peabody, Elizabeth Palmer
VI:280
Pennsylvania **II**:284–285,
287
Pequot **II**:289
Permanent Indian Frontier
IV:297, 298
Pickering, Timothy **III**:335
Pima revolt **II**:294
Plymouth **II**:298
polygamy **IV**:303
Pontiac's War **III**:339–340
population trends **II**:302;
V:310–311; **VII**:266
Powhatan **II**:305–307
Powhatan Confederacy
II:307–308
POWs **III**:345
praying towns **II**:308–309
Proclamation of 1763
III:348
Prophet, the Shawnee
III:348–349
public land policy **IV**:306
Pushmataha **IV**:307–308
Quakers **III**:351, 352
race and race relations
II:325–326; **III**:357;
IV:310, 312; **VII**:281,
282; **VIII**:318–319
Racial Integrity Act **VII**:284
Red Cloud **VI**:303
Red Jacket **III**:359–360
religion **II**:330–331; **VI**:307,
309–310
revitalization movements
II:332
RFRA **X**:307
Rhode Island **II**:332
Roanoke **I**:321–322
Ross, John **IV**:325
rural life **III**:375
Sacagawea **III**:377
sachems **II**:341
St. Clair, Arthur **III**:378
scalping **II**:343–344
Schurz, Carl **VI**:325
Scots-Irish **III**:386
segregation **VII**:319
Sequoyah **IV**:342–343
Seven Years' War **II**:348,
349
shamans **II**:350–351
Sheridan, Philip H. **V**:353
Sherman, William T. **V**:356
slave resistance **II**:353
slavery **II**:355; **IV**:346
slave trade, internal **IV**:348
smallpox **II**:360
Smith, Jedediah Strong
IV:350

socialism **VI**:335

society, British American **II**:365, 367

Sooners **VI**:339

South Carolina **II**:368–369

Spanish colonies **II**:373

SPG **II**:368

sports and recreation **VII**:335

Squanto **II**:376

Stuart, John **II**:378

suffrage **II**:380

Supreme Court **IV**:362

Susquehannock War **II**:380

taverns and inns **II**:384

Teapot Dome **VII**:351

technology **II**:385

Tecumseh **III**:409

Teedyuscung **II**:386

Tekakwitha, Kateri **II**:386

Texas **IV**:371, 372

Thames, Battle of the **IV**:375–376

theater **II**:389

Thoreau, Henry David **IV**:377

Tippecanoe, Battle of **III**:411, 412

tobacco **II**:390

Tomochichi **II**:392

trade, domestic and foreign **II**:392

Trail of Tears **IV**:377

treaty rights **IX**:319–320

Tuscarora **II**:394–395

Van Buren, Martin **IV**:386

Vargas, Diego de **II**:397–398

violence and lawlessness **VI**:375

Virginia **II**:398, 399

Walking Purchase **II**:405–406

war and warfare **II**:407

Ward, Nancy **II**:408

War Hawks **IV**:390

War of 1812 **IV**:390

in the War of 1812 **IV**:276–278

Washington, George **III**:429, 431

Watie, Stand **V**:427

Wayne, Anthony **III**:434

Weiser, Johann Conrad **II**:409

Westo **II**:410–411

Wetamo **II**:411

Wheelock, Eleazar **II**:411, 412

White, Andrew **II**:413

Whitman, Narcissa **IV**:399

Wilderness Road **III**:442

Wilkes expedition **IV**:400

Williams, Roger **II**:417

Winnemucca, Sarah **VI**:397–398

wolves **II**:421–422

women's status and rights **II**:422–424, 426; **III**:446; **IV**:404, 405

Woolman, John **II**:427

World War II **VIII**:427

Wyoming Valley Massacre **III**:449

Yamasee **II**:429–430

Native Americans (Caribbean)

audiencia **I**:17

cannibalism **I**:57

Charles V **I**:70–71

Columbus, Christopher **I**:85–87

Cuba **I**:100–101

Dominicans **I**:110

encomienda **I**:122

population trends **I**:298

smallpox **I**:341

Taino **I**:352–353

Vitoria, Francisco de **I**:379

Native Americans (Central America)

Aztecs **I**:18–23

Cabeza de Vaca, Álvar Núñez **I**:39–40

casta paintings **I**:64

Cortés, Hernán **I**:94–96

encomienda **I**:122

Franciscans **I**:133

Maya **I**:234–237

New Spain **I**:269

Oñate, Juan de **I**:279–280

Panama **I**:284

population trends **I**:297

Pueblo **I**:304–305

repartimiento **I**:318

Requerimiento **I**:318–319

Sepúlveda, Juan Ginés de **I**:330–331

slavery **I**:338

Soto, Hernando de **I**:342, 343

Native Americans (South America)

Brazil **I**:34

corn **I**:91–92

Coronado, Francisco **I**:92–93

disease/epidemics **I**:107–109

encomienda **I**:122

Harriot, Thomas **I**:154, 155

Hiawatha **I**:161

Hidatsa **I**:162

Hochelaga **I**:164

Hohokam **I**:164–165

Hopewell culture **I**:167

Hopi **I**:167

horses **I**:168

Inca **I**:179–181

Iroquois **I**:185–187

Mabila **I**:221

Maliseet **I**:227

Manteo **I**:229

Mantoac **I**:229

Massachusett **I**:233–234

Mohawk **I**:246–247

monsters **I**:249

Natchez **I**:259–260

Passamaquoddy **I**:287

population trends **I**:297, 298

Powhatan **I**:300–301

Pueblo **I**:304–305

reducción **I**:314–315

repartimiento **I**:318

Requerimiento **I**:318–319

Santa Fe **I**:327

Secotan **I**:329

Sepúlveda, Juan Ginés de **I**:330–331

silver **I**:336

Soto, Hernando de **I**:343

Wanchese **I**:382

werowance **I**:383

White, John **I**:383

Native Son (Wright) **VIII**:447*c*

African Americans **VIII**:3; **IX**:5

literature **VIII**:219; **IX**:194

Wright, Richard **VIII**:437

Native Sons and Daughters of the Golden West **VIII**:32

nativism **V**:280; **VI**:263–264, 410*c*; **VII**:233–234

American Protective Association **VI**:13–14

Catholics **VIII**:63

Great White Fleet **VII**:130

immigration **V**:200; **VI**:186; **VII**:144

Immigration Act (1917) **VII**:145

immigration restrictions **VI**:186

New Woman **VII**:239

religion **VI**:308

Republican Party **V**:332

Rhinelander case **VII**:301

Roman Catholicism **VI**:315

NATO. *See* North Atlantic Treaty Organization

natural gas **X**:120

Natural History (Catesby) **II**:62

naturalism

literature **VI**:226

Pan-American Exposition **VII**:252

Victorianism **VI**:374

naturalists **III**:47–48

naturalization

citizenship **III**:93, 94

immigration **III**:221

nativism **V**:280

Naturalization Act (1790) **III**:221; **IV**:309

Naturalization Act (1795) **III**:464*c*

Naturalization Act (1798) **III**:14, 464*c*

Naturalization Act (1855) **VII**:103

natural resources **II**:119–120, 259

natural theology **II**:118, 344

Nature (Emerson) **IV**:413*c*

Emerson, Ralph Waldo **IV**:140

literature **IV**:228

transcendental movement **IV**:379

Nature, Certainty, and Evidence of True Christianity, The (Osborn) **II**:279

Nature's Divine Revelations (Davis) **IV**:320

Naughty Marietta (Herbert) **VII**:95, 219

Nauman, Bruce **X**:31

Nautilus (1800s submarine) **III**:182–183

Nautilus, USS (nuclear submarine) **IX**:24

Nauvoo **IV**:278–279, 279

Cabet, Étienne **IV**:67

Deseret, State of **IV**:119

Mormon Church **IV**:89

Mormon Trail **IV**:261

Mormon War **IV**:263

Young, Brigham **IV**:407

Nauvoo Charter **IV**:353

Nauvoo Expositor **IV**:278–279

Nauvoo Legion **IV**:278, 353

Navajo code talkers **VIII**:264, 264

Navajo Community College **IX**:242

Navajo Indians **II**:176, **254–255**; **IV**:414*c*; **V**:444*c*

Carson, Kit **IV**:82

Indian Reorganization Act **VIII**:186

Native Americans **VII**:233; **VIII**:264; **IX**:242; **X**:250

New Mexico **I**:264

Santa Fe **I**:327

Navajo reservation **VIII**:186

Naval Academy, U.S. *See* United States Naval Academy at Annapolis

Naval Affairs Committee **V**:247

naval disarmament **VII**:50

Naval Disarmament Conference **VII:234–235**

Naval School. *See* United States Naval Academy at Annapolis

Naval Stores Act (England) **II**:275

Naval War College **VIII**:201–202

navigation

Mississippi River **V**:261

Northwest Ordinances **III**:322

WAVES **VIII**:418

Navigation, Bureau of **VIII**:274

Navigation Acts. *See* Acts of Trade and Navigation

Navigationi e Viaggi (Ramusio)

Cabral, Pedro Álvares **I**:47

corn **I**:92

Oviedo y Valdés, Gonzalo Fernández de **I**:281

Ramusio, Giovanni Battista **I**:313

navigation technology **I:262**
　astrolabe **I:**15
　cross staff **I:**99
　Henry the Navigator **I:**161
　icebergs **I:**177
Navigatio of Saint Brendan
　I:35–36
Navragrio (Coelho) **I:**334
Navy, Japanese
　air power **VIII:**15
　Coral Sea, Battle of the
　　VIII:87
　Guadalcanal **VIII:**160
　Halsey, William F. **VIII:**161
　Leyte Gulf, Battle for
　　VIII:214
　Philippines **VIII:**295
　Philippine Sea, Battle of the
　　VIII:295
　Solomon Islands **VIII:**366
　World War II Pacific theater
　　VIII:436–437
Navy, U.S. **IV:**415*c;* **VII:**409*c;*
　VIII:265–266, 446*c,* 448*c;*
　IX:351*c*
　African Americans **VIII:**3
　aircraft carriers **VIII:**11–13
　amphibious warfare
　　VIII:20
　armed forces **VII:**20–21
　Army, U.S. **VIII:**25
　Atlantic, Battle of the
　　VIII:33–34
　Axis **VIII:**38
　Barbary Wars **III:**45, 46
　Barry, John **III:**47
　Carter, James Earl, Jr. **X:**67
　Casablanca Conference
　　VIII:62
　censorship **VIII:**65
　Chauncey, Isaac **III:**86
　Chesapeake-Leopard affair
　　III:88
　Colt, Samuel **IV:**101
　conscription **VII:**63
　convoys **VIII:**87
　Coral Sea, Battle of the
　　VIII:87
　Decatur, Stephen **IV:**114
　demobilization (WWII)
　　VIII:91
　Dewey, George **VI:**97
　espionage **VIII:**117
　Essex, USS **IV:**143–144
　foreign policy **IV:**154;
　　VI:133
　Forrestal, James V. **VIII:**143
　Fulton, Robert **III:**183
　gays and lesbians **VIII:**148
　Guadalcanal **VIII:**159
　Halsey, William F. **VIII:**161
　Hersey, John R. **VIII:**164
　Higgins, Andrew J.
　　VIII:165
　Hiroshima and Nagasaki
　　VIII:167
　Kerouac, Jack **IX:**173

King, Ernest J. **VIII:**201–
　202
Knox, Frank **VIII:**202
Knox, Henry **III:**248
Lafitte, Jean **IV:**220
Lake Erie, Battle of **IV:**220–
　221
Leahy, William D. **VIII:**211
Levitt, William J. **IX:**188
Leyte Gulf, Battle for
　VIII:214
March on Washington
　Movement **VIII:**227
Mariana Islands **VIII:**228
Marines, U.S. **VIII:**229
Mitchell, William (Billy)
　VII:212
mobilization **VIII:**241
Nimitz, Chester W.
　VIII:274
Okinawa **VIII:**287–288
Pearl Harbor **VIII:**291
Perry, Matthew Calbraith
　IV:298
Philippine Sea, Battle of the
　VIII:295
Porter, David Dixon **V:**311
race and race relations
　VIII:318
radio **VII:**288
science and technology
　IX:285
shipbuilding **VIII:**359
Siberian Expedition
　VII:325
Sicily **VIII:**360
Solomon Islands **VIII:**365,
　366
steel industry **VIII:**373–374
Stockton, Robert Field
　IV:357–358
submarines **VIII:**378
Tarawa **VIII:**386
trade, domestic and foreign
　VII:354
War of 1812 **IV:**391
War Production Board
　VIII:414
WAVES **VIII:**418
Welles, Gideon **V:**427, 428
Wilkes expedition **IV:**399
World War II Pacific theater
　VIII:435, 436
Navy, U.S. Department of the
　Farragut, David Glasgow
　　V:137
　Forbes, John Murray
　　VI:132
　National Security Act of
　　1947 **IX:**237, 238
　Roosevelt, Theodore
　　VII:304
　Washington, D.C. **V:**425
Navy and Marine Corps Medal
　IX:169
Navy Communications Security
　Unit, U.S. **VIII:**76

Navy Department, Confederate
　V:247
Navy Nurse Corps **VII:**63
Navy Operations Division, U.S.
　(N-2) **VIII:**76
Navy Relief Society **VIII:**223
NAWSA. *See* National American
　Woman Suffrage Association
Nayler, James **II:**321
Nazi Germany **VIII:**446*c,* 448*c*
　aircraft industry **VIII:**13
　Anglo-American relations
　　VIII:21
　Army Air Forces, U.S.
　　VIII:26
　blitzkrieg **VIII:**47
　bombing **VIII:**47
　Bulge, Battle of the **VIII:**55
　CDAAA **VIII:**77
　cold war **IX:**63
　movies **VIII:**246
　Nazi-Soviet Pact **VIII:**266
　Owens, Jesse **VIII:**288, 289
　propaganda **VIII:**311
　refugees **VIII:**329, 330
　Soviet-American relations
　　VIII:368–369
　Spanish civil war **VIII:**369
　sports and recreation
　　VIII:372
　World War II **VIII:**427
　World War II European
　　theater **VIII:**429
　Zionism **VIII:**441
Nazi Ministry of Propaganda
　and Popular Enlightenment
　VIII:311
Nazi-Soviet Pact **VIII:266**
　anticommunism **VIII:**22
　Axis **VIII:**37
　Baldwin, Roger Nash
　　VII:31
　Communists **VIII:**78
　foreign policy **VIII:**141
　Robeson, Paul **VIII:**342
　Soviet-American relations
　　VIII:368
　Teheran Conference
　　VIII:390
Nazi sympathizers **VIII:**71, 85
NBA. *See* National Basketball
　Association
NBC. *See* National Broadcasting
　Corporation
NBC (National Baptist
　Convention) **VI:**4
NBC Blue/Red **VIII:**321
NCAA Tournament **VIII:**371
NCAI. *See* National Congress of
　American Indians
NCC. *See* National Credit
　Corporation
NCCCW (National Committee
　on the Cause and Cure of War)
　VII:49
NCL. *See* National Consumers
　League

NCLB. *See* National Civil
　Liberties Bureau
NCPW (National Council for the
　Prevention of War) **VII:**49
NCTC (National Counterterrorism
　Center) **X:**347
NDAC. *See* National Defense
　Advisory Commission
NDPB (National Defense
　Production Board) **VIII:**378
NDRA (National Dress Reform
　Association) **V:**139
NDRC. *See* National Defense
　Research Committee
NEA. *See* National Endowment
　for the Arts
Neal, Claude **VIII:**317
Neale, John **II:**186
Neamathla (Seminole chief)
　IV:339
Near East **IX:**255
Near v. Minnesota ex rel. Olson
　VII:313; **VIII:**65, 443*c*
Neau, Elias **II:**7
Nebraska
　Ashley, William Henry **IV:**31
　Bleeding Kansas **V:**36, 37
　Cody, William Frederick
　　VI:76
　Douglas, Stephen A. **V:**114
　exploration **IV:**145, 146
　foreign policy **IV:**158
　fugitive slave laws **IV:**169
　immigration **VI:**184
　Kansas-Nebraska Act **V:**221
　Maine Law **IV:**234
　Massachusetts Emigrant Aid
　　Society **IV:**241
　Mormon Trail **IV:**261
　Native Americans **IV:**276
　Pike, Zebulon Montgomery
　　IV:300
　Republican Party **IV:**321
　Young, Brigham **IV:**407
Nebraska Geological Survey
　VI:165
Neff, Mary **II:**105
Negev (desert) **IX:**160
Negro Air Corps **VIII:4**
Negro American Labor Council
　VIII:321
Negro American League **IX:**277,
　298, 299
Negro Convention movement
　IV:174, **279–280**
Negro Eastern League **VII:**335
Negro Fellowship League **VI:**388
Negro Leagues
　Aaron, Henry L. "Hank" **X:**1
　recreation **VIII:**328
　sports and recreation
　　VIII:370
Negro National League **VII:**34,
　335

Negro National News **IX**:32
Negro Plot (1741) **II:255**
  African Americans **II**:8
  New York **II**:271
  slave resistance **II**:353
Negroponte, John D. **X**:357
Negro Seaman's Act **IV**:388
Negro World **VII**:121, 361
NEH. *See* National Endowment
  for the Humanities
Nehru, Jawaharlal **IX**:58
Neighborhood Guild (New York)
  VI:121
Neihardt, John G. **VI**:49
Neill, Robert **VI**:45
Neill-Reynolds report **VII**:198
Neisse River **VIII**:439
Nell, William C. **IV**:415*c*
Nelson, Byron **VIII**:372; **X**:332
Nelson, Donald M. **VIII:266–267**
  dollar-a-year men **VIII**:96
  mobilization **VIII**:241
  OPM **VIII**:283
  OWM **VIII**:286–287
  War Production Board
    VIII:414
Nelson, Gaylord **X**:90
Nelson, George "Baby Face"
  IX:149
Nelson, Jordan **VI**:246
Nelson, Ted **X**:182
Nelson, Willie **X**:20
Nemattanew **II**:279
neoclassicism
  architecture **III**:27
  art **VII**:23
  Bulfinch, Charles **III**:65
  Hayden, Sophia Gregoria
    VI:165–166
neoconservatism **X**:70, 94, *251*,
  251–252
neoexpressionism **X**:31
neofascists **VIII**:85
Neolin **II:255–256**, 332; **III**:13,
  340
NEPA. *See* National
  Environmental Policy Act
NEPDG (National Energy Policy
  Development Group) **X**:72
Neponset River **IV**:200
Nesbit, Evelyn **VI**:392
Netherlands **I**:214–215; **VII**:408*c*
  blitzkrieg **VIII**:47
  debt, national **III**:130, 131
  fur trade **IV**:170
  League of Armed Neutrality
    III:257
  Paris, Treaty of (1783)
    III:332
  Perry, Matthew Calbraith
    IV:298
  Washington Conference
    on Naval Disarmament
    VII:379
  World War II Pacific theater
    VIII:435
Netscape Navigator **X**:319

NetValue **X**:283
Neumann, John von **VIII**:389;
  IX:69
neutrality **III**:465*c*; **VII:235–236**,
  406*c*; **VIII**:446*c*
  Adams, John Quincy **IV**:5
  Borah, William E. **VIII**:50
  China trade **III**:88
  Committee for Public
    Information **VII**:59
  Democratic Party **VII**:74
  foreign affairs **III**:169
  foreign policy **IV**:153; **V**:150,
    151; **VII**:114
  Free Trade and Sailor's
    Rights **IV**:165
  French Revolution **III**:179
  Jay's Treaty **III**:231
  Jefferson, Thomas **III**:233
  League of Armed Neutrality
    III:257
  The Masses **VII**:193
  Milan Decree **III**:297–298
  Native Americans **V**:278
  peace movements **VII**:256
  Preparedness **VII**:267
  Quakers **III**:352
  Spanish civil war **VIII**:370
  trade, domestic and foreign
    III:415; **VII**:354
  Washington, George **III**:431
  West Indies **III**:436–437
  Wilson, Thomas Woodrow
    VII:383
  XYZ affair **III**:451
  Zimmermann telegram
    VII:401
Neutrality Act of 1818 **IV**:81
Neutrality Acts (1935–1941)
  VIII:267–268, 446*c*, **457–460**
  aircraft industry **VIII**:13
  America First Committee
    VIII:17
  Anglo-American relations
    VIII:21
  Borah, William E. **VIII**:50
  cash-and-carry **VIII**:63
  Congress **VIII**:80
  destroyers-for-bases deal
    VIII:95
  Ethiopia **VIII**:118
  foreign policy **VIII**:141
  isolationists **VIII**:189, 190
  La Follette, Robert M., Jr.
    VIII:208
  Lend-Lease **VIII**:211
  Neutrality Act of 1937
    VIII:457–460
  Nye committee **VIII**:278
  Roosevelt, Franklin D.
    VIII:346
  Spanish civil war **VIII**:370
Neutrality Proclamation **III:315–
  316**, 463*c*
  foreign affairs **III**:168
  Genêt, Edmond Charles
    III:191

Neutrality Treaty **X**:271
neutral rights
  War Hawks **IV**:390
  War of 1812 **IV**:390
neutron bomb **X**:100
Nevada **IV**:414*c*
  Applegate, Jesse **IV**:26
  Comstock Lode **IV**:104–106
  Crime of '73 **VI**:86
  currency issue **IV**:89
  Deseret, State of **IV**:120
  exploration **IV**:145
  Frémont, John C. **IV**:166
  gold **IV**:179
  immigration **IV**:193
  National Reclamation Act
    VII:229
  Native Americans **IV**:275
  population trends **X**:282
  Young, Brigham **IV**:408
Nevada Test Site **IX**:25
Neville, John **III**:440
Nevins, Allan **VI**:315; **IX**:62
Nevis **I:262–263**
New Age movement **X:252–253**
New Amsterdam **II:256–258**,
  257, 435*c*
  Dutch-Indian Wars **II**:105
  Dutch Reformed Church
    II:106
  Jews **II**:185
  New Netherland **II**:264
  New York City **II**:272
New Archangel **II**:338, 339; **III**:12
Newark, New Jersey
  Edison, Thomas Alva
    VI:107
  Triangle Shirtwaist Fire
    VII:356–357
  Villard, Henry **VI**:375
Newberry, John Strong **VI**:164,
  165
Newberry Library **VI**:224
New Brunswick, Canada
  Aroostook War **IV**:27
  Canada **III**:77–79
  foreign policy **IV**:154
  Loyalists **III**:276
  Maliseet **I**:227
New Brunswick, New Jersey
  IV:386
New Brunswick Presbytery
  II:388
Newburgh conspiracy **III:316**
New Canaan, Connecticut **VI**:78
New Castle **II**:95, 96
New Christian Right **X**:94
"New Colossus, The" (Lazarus)
  VI:219
Newcomb, Simon **VI**:115
Newcombe, Don **IX**:277
New Deal **VIII:268–271**, 445*c*,
  446*c*; **IX:242**. *See also* First
  New Deal; Second New Deal;
  Third New Deal
  AFL **VIII**:18
  African Americans **VIII**:3

Agricultural Adjustment Act
  VIII:5, 6
agriculture **VIII**:9; **IX**:7
American Liberty League
  VIII:19
Americans for Democratic
  Action **IX**:13
anticommunism **VIII**:22
antilynching legislation
  VIII:23
antimonopoly **VIII**:23
anti-Semitism **VIII**:24
Asian Americans **VIII**:32
automobile industry
  VIII:36
Baldwin, Roger Nash
  VII:31
Bankhead-Jones Farm
  Tenant Act **VIII**:39
banking **VIII**:40
Banking Act (1933) **VIII**:40
Banking Act (1935)
  VIII:41
Baruch, Bernard M. **VII**:32;
  VIII:42
Bethune, Mary McLeod
  VIII:44
Black, Hugo L. **VIII**:45
Black Cabinet **VIII**:45
Borah, William E. **VIII**:49
Brain Trust **VIII**:51
Brandeis, Louis Dembitz
  VII:41, 42
Bridges, Harry **VIII**:53
Brotherhood of Sleeping Car
  Porters **VIII**:54
business **VIII**:58–59
Byrnes, James F. **VIII**:60
Catholics **VIII**:63, 64
CCC **VIII**:70–71
children **VIII**:66–67
cities and urban life
  VIII:68–70
civil rights **VIII**:72
Communists **VIII**:77
Congress **VIII**:78–81
conservatism **VIII**:83–85;
  IX:74
conservative coalition
  VIII:85–86
Coughlin, Father Charles E.
  VIII:88
court-packing plan **VIII**:89
criminal justice **VII**:67
CWA **VIII**:74
Democratic Party **VIII**:93,
  94; **IX**:85
dollar-a-year men **VIII**:96
Douglas, William O.
  VIII:97
dust bowl **VIII**:98
Eccles, Marriner S.
  VIII:101
economy **VIII**:102, 103–
  104; **IX**:96
education **VIII**:105,
  106–107

New Deal (continued)
Eisenhower, Dwight D.
IX:101
elderly VIII:107
election of 1932 VIII:108
election of 1936 VIII:109,
110
election of 1944 VIII:111
elections IX:102
Emergency Banking Act of
1933 VIII:112–113
Employment Act of 1946
IX:106
environment VIII:116;
IX:108
ERAA VIII:113–114
Evans, Walker VIII:119–
120
Executive Reorganization
Act VIII:121
Fair Deal IX:115
FAP VIII:128–129
FBI VIII:129
FCC VIII:130, 131
FDIC VIII:132
Federal Housing
Administration (FHA)
VIII:133
FERA VIII:132
FHA VIII:126
fireside chats VIII:138
First New Deal VIII:138
fiscal policy VIII:139
FMP VIII:134
folk music revival IX:120
Food, Drug, and Cosmetic
Act VIII:139
Fortas, Abe X:144–145
Four Freedoms VIII:144
FSA VIII:127
FTP VIII:135
Full Employment Bill
VIII:145
FWP VIII:136
Garner, John Nance
VIII:147
German Americans
VIII:148–149
Goldwater, Barry IX:135
government VIII:152,
153–154
government, state/local
IX:137
Great Depression VIII:159
Hawley-Smoot Tariff Act
VIII:163
Hearst, William Randolph
VII:138
Hillman, Sidney VIII:165
HOLC VIII:170
Hoover, Herbert C.
VIII:172
Hoover presidency
VIII:173, 176
Hopkins, Harry L. VIII:176
housing VIII:177–178
Howe, Louis M. VIII:179

HUAC IX:150
Hughes, Charles Evans
VII:142
Humphrey, Hubert H.
IX:151
Ickes, Harold L. VIII:183
ILGWU VIII:187
Indian Reorganization Act
VIII:185
Irish Americans VIII:188
isolationists VIII:189
Italian Americans VIII:190
Jews VIII:195–196
Johnson, Hiram Warren
VII:154
Johnson, Hugh S. VIII:196
Johnson, Lyndon B. IX:163
Jones, Jesse H. VIII:197
Kennedy, Joseph P.
VIII:199–200
Keynesianism VIII:200
Knox, Frank VIII:202
labor/labor movements
VIII:205
La Follette, Robert M., Jr.
VIII:208
La Guardia, Fiorello
VIII:209
Landon, Alfred M. VIII:209
Lewis, John L. VIII:213
liberalism VIII:214; IX:191
Lilienthal, David E.
VIII:217
literature VIII:219
London Economic
Conference VIII:221
Long, Huey P. VIII:222
marriage and family
VIII:231
Medicaid IX:209
Mexican Repatriation
Program VIII:238
modern Republicanism
IX:221
Moley, Raymond C.
VIII:243
Morgenthau, Henry T., Jr.
VIII:244
mothers' pensions VII:213
Murray, Pauli IX:227
Murray, Philip VIII:249
NAACP VIII:255
National Recovery
Administration VIII:259
Native Americans VIII:264
news media VIII:271, 272
NIRA VIII:257
Norris, George W. VIII:276
NYA VIII:262, 263
OWI VIII:286
Perkins, Frances VIII:293
Polish Americans VIII:297
political parties X:276
politics (Roosevelt era)
VIII:298, 300
popular culture VIII:301
presidency VIII:309

progressivism VII:272
public health IX:265
PUHCA VIII:313
PWA VIII:314
REA VIII:349–350
recession of 1937–1938
VIII:323, 324
Reciprocal Trade
Agreements Act VIII:324
recreation VIII:327
relief VIII:330, 332, 333
religion VIII:334
Republican Party VIII:336–
338; IX:274
Resettlement Administration
VIII:338
Reuther, Walter VIII:339
Revenue Act of 1935
VIII:340
RFC VIII:325
Roosevelt, Franklin D.
VIII:344–346
rural areas VIII:349
Schechter Poultry
Corporation v. U.S.
VIII:351
SEC VIII:356–357
Second New Deal VIII:356
Smith, Alfred E. VII:327
socialists VIII:362
Social Security Act
VIII:362, 363, 453–457
South VIII:366
Stevenson, Adali E. IX:301
stock market crash VIII:376
strikes VIII:377
suburbanization/suburbs
VIII:379
Supreme Court VIII:381–
382
Taft, Robert A. VIII:385
Taft-Hartley Act IX:309
taxation VIII:386–388
technology VIII:390
Tennessee Valley Authority
VIII:392
Thomas, Norman VIII:394
transportation VIII:395
unemployment VIII:399,
400
Union Party VIII:401
USHA VIII:404
Wagner, Robert F. VIII:410
Wallace, Henry A. VIII:411
Ward, Lester Frank VI:382
Wheeler, Burton K.
VIII:416
Willkie, Wendell L.
VIII:417
women's network VIII:421
women's status and rights
VIII:422, 423
WPA VIII:425–426
New Democracy VII:41
New Divinity III:316–317
New Echota, Treaty of IV:413c
Boudinot, Elias IV:62

Cherokee IV:85
Ridge, John IV:324
Ross, John IV:325
Trail of Tears IV:378
Watie, Stand V:427
New Economic Policy X:108, 363
"New Education, The: Its
Organization" (Eliot) VI:113–
114
Newell, Robert IV:324
New England II:435c, 436c
Abenaki I:1–2
ACS IV:17
African Americans II:7
agriculture II:13, 14; IV:10;
V:6
Anglican Church II:21–22;
III:21
anti-Masonry IV:25
architecture II:24, 25;
III:28–29
banks III:42
Baptists II:33
Birth of a Nation, The
VII:37
Burgoyne, Sir John III:67
Calhoun, John C. IV:68
Catholics III:82–83
Christian Science VI:69
class II:69
cod I:77
committees of
correspondence III:101
Comstock, Anthony VI:79
Congregationalists II:75
Constitution, ratification of
the III:105
Continental army III:111
Crummell, Alexander VI:87
debt, national III:130
Deere, John IV:115
Democratic-Republican
Party III:136
Dewson, Mary VIII:95
disease/epidemics II:98,
100
domesticity II:101
Dominion of New England
II:101–103
Dudley, Joseph II:103
Dummer, Jeremiah II:103
Easton, Hosea IV:129
economy II:109; IV:131,
133
education II:111; III:147;
IV:133–134; V:124
Emerson, Ralph Waldo
IV:140
English Civil War II:116
English immigrants II:117
environment II:119;
III:155
ethnocentrism II:122, 123
Evans, Walker VIII:119
exploration II:124
Federalist Party III:164–
165

female antislavery societies
IV:148
fishing **II:**126, 127
foreign policy **IV:**154
Foster, Abigail Kelley
IV:161
fugitive slave laws **IV:**168–
169
Fuller, Margaret **IV:**169
gender **II:**145
*Genius of Universal
Emancipation* **IV:**175
Ghent, Treaty of **IV:**176
government, British
American **II:**151
Hamilton, Alexander
III:208
Hartford Convention
IV:186–187
housing **II:**166
immigration restrictions
VI:187
indentured servitude **II:**175
industrialization **IV:**199, 201
internal improvements
IV:202
iron manufacturing **II:**178
jazz **VIII:**194
Jewett, Sarah Orne **VI:**202
King Philip's War **II:**193
labor/labor movements
II:199
Larkin, Thomas Oliver
IV:222
Liberty Party **IV:**226
literature **IV:**228
Louisiana Purchase **III:**273
Lovejoy, Elijah **IV:**230
lumbering **II:**211; **IV:**231
lyceum movement **IV:**231
Maine Law **IV:**234
marriage and family **II:**217;
III:286, 287
Massachusetts Emigrant Aid
Society **IV:**242
McCormick, Cyrus Hall
IV:243
mortality **II:**243, 244
music **IV:**268; **VI:**254
Native Americans **II:**251
New Divinity **III:**316
panic of 1819 **IV:**293
Perry, Matthew Calbraith
IV:298
popular culture **III:**341
population trends **II:**302
praying towns **II:**308
primogeniture and entail
II:310
proprietary colonies **II:**314
Protestantism **II:**316
Puritans **I:**307; **II:**319–320
railroads **IV:**316
religion **III:**360–362;
IV:318
religion, Euro-American
II:329

religious liberty **III:**362–
364
Republican Party **IV:**321
Rhode Island, Battle of
III:369
rum trade **II:**338
Slater, Samuel **III:**389
slave trade **III:**393
society, British American
II:365–366
spinsters **II:**375
Squanto **II:**376
states' rights **III:**397
temperance movement
III:410; **IV:**370
Thoreau, Henry David
IV:376
transcendental movement
IV:378
Van Buren, Martin **IV:**386
wampum **II:**406
War Hawks **IV:**389–390
War of 1812 **IV:**390
Warren, Josiah **IV:**392
Whigs **IV:**397
women's status and rights
III:445, 446
World War II **VIII:**428
New England Anti-Slavery Society
abolitionism **IV:**3
African Americans **IV:**9
Foster, Abigail Kelley
IV:162
New England Association **IV:**217
New England Confederation
II:102, 223
New England Conservatory
VI:254
New England Courant **II:**268,
312
New England Emigrant Aid
Company **IV:**242; **V:**37
New England Farmhouse style
IV:30
New England Female Medical
College **VI:**400
New England Loyal Publication
Society **VI:**132, 269
New England Mississippi Land
Company **III:**454
New England Non-Resistant
Society **IV:**161
New England Primer **II:**162, **258**
New England Psalm Singer, The
(Billings) **III:**50, 308
New England Renaissance
IV:228–229
New England school
(composition) **VI:**254–255
New England's Prospect (Wood)
II:426
New England Tract Society
III:307–308
New England Woman Suffrage
Association **VI:**176
New England Women's Aid
Association **V:**228

New England Yearly Meeting
II:2
New English Canaan (Morton)
II:245
New Era **VI:**385
Newfoundland **I:**395*c*, 398*c*;
II:258–259, 313; **III:**462*c*
Atlantic Charter **VIII:**34
Cabot, John **I:**43, 44
cod **I:**77
destroyers-for-bases deal
VIII:95
Gilbert, Sir Humphrey
I:141
icebergs **I:**177
L'Anse aux Meadows
I:203–204
Paris, Treaty of (1783)
III:332
Peckham, Sir George **I:**288
New Fourteenth Street Theater
VI:257
New France **I:**149, 397*c*
British Empire **II:**49
Canada **III:**77
Champlain, Samuel de
II:62
French colonies **II:**136
Quebec City **II:**323
theater **II:**389
New Freedom **VII:236**
agriculture **VII:**8
elections **VII:**91
Federal Farm Loan Act
VII:106
Federal Trade Commission
Act **VII:**108
New Nationalism **VII:**237
progressivism **VII:**271
rural life **VII:**306
Wilson, Thomas Woodrow
VII:383
New Frontier **IX:242–243,** 243
arms race **IX:**17
Democratic Party **IX:**85
economy **IX:**98
government, state/local
IX:137
Kennedy, John F. **IX:**169
New Deal **IX:**242
Peace Corps **IX:**255
New Frontier Media **X:**283
New Georgia **VIII:**366
New Granada **II:**372; **IV:**414*c*
New Guinea
amphibious warfare **VIII:**20
MacArthur, Douglas **IX:**197
Mead, Margaret **VII:**197
Solomon Islands **VIII:**365
World War II Pacific theater
VIII:435
New Hampshire **I:**2; **II:259–261**
abolitionism **III:**1–2
Allen, Ethan **III:**14
Baptists **III:**44
Constitution, ratification of
the **III:**105, 106

constitutions, state **III:**111
Dartmouth College **II:**91
Dartmouth College case
IV:114
disease/epidemics **II:**100
Dominion of New England
II:102
Garnet, Henry Highland
IV:174
gay and lesbian rights
movement **X:**149
Hartford Convention
IV:186
Jews **III:**237
Know-Nothing Party
IV:214
Knox, Frank **VIII:**202
land riots **III:**254
lumbering **II:**211
Marshall, John **III:**291
Prohibition **VII:**273
religious liberty **III:**363
Shays's Rebellion **III:**388
Souter, David **X:**324
Vermont **II:**398
Volstead Act **VII:**374
Webster, Daniel **IV:**393
Wheelock, Eleazar **II:**412
Wheelwright, John **II:**412
New Hampshire, USS **VIII:**201
New Hampshire primary (March
1968) **IX:**206
New Harmony, Indiana
Bodmer, Karl **IV:**60
Owen, Robert **IV:**291
religion **IV:**320
Warren, Josiah **IV:**392
Wright, Fanny **IV:**405
New Harmony *Gazette* **IV:**405
New Haven, Connecticut
Amistad incident **IV:**21
Evans, Walker **VIII:**120
industrialization **IV:**199
Ingersoll, Jared **III:**226
Sherman, Roger **III:**389
New Haven colony **II:**223
New Helvetia, California **IV:**363,
364
New Hope Church, Battle of
V:22
New Icaria **IV:**67
New Immigration **VI:**185
New Ironsides, USS **V:**207
New Jersey **II:261–263,** 436*c*
abolitionism **III:**2, 3
African Americans **III:**9
architecture **II:**25
Carteret, Philip **II:**61
cities and urban life **VI:**69
Constitution, ratification of
the **III:**104
Continental Congress,
Second **III:**116
Delaware Indians **II:**97
entertainment, popular
VI:117
Federalists **III:**166

New Jersey *(continued)*
　Fort Washington, capture of
　　III:172
　Franklin, William **III:**175,
　　176
　gay and lesbian rights
　　movement **X:**149
　government, British
　　American **II:**152
　Great Awakening **II:**155
　Hyde, Edward, Viscount
　　Cornbury **II:**171
　Knyphausen, Wilhelm,
　　Baron von **III:**248
　Lafayette, Marie-Joseph-
　　Paul-Yves-Roch-Gilbert
　　de Motier, marquis de
　　III:253
　land riots **II:**202
　Liberty Party **IV:**226
　Livingston, William **III:**270,
　　271
　Louisiana Purchase **III:**273
　Morris, Lewis **II:**243
　Morristown encampment
　　III:306–307
　Northern Securities Case
　　VII:241
　Passaic Strike **VII:**253
　Paterson Strike **VII:**253
　Penn, William **II:**284
　Princeton College **II:**311
　Prohibition **VII:**273
　Quakers **II:**322
　railroads **IV:**313, 316
　Red Bank, Battle of **III:**359
　religious liberty **III:**362
　riots **III:**371
　Scots immigrants **II:**346
　stem cell research **X:**335
　suffrage **III:**401; **IV:**360
　Trenton and Princeton,
　　Battles of **III:**416
　trusts **VI:**364
　Vanderbilt, Cornelius
　　IV:386
　Villard, Henry **VI:**375
　Weld, Theodore Dwight
　　IV:396
　women's status and rights
　　II:423
New Jersey Plan **III:**109, 463*c*
New Journalism **IX:**166; **X:**369,
　370
New Lanark, Scotland **IV:**291
Newlands, Francis G. **VII:**229
Newlands Act. *See* National
　Reclamation Act
Newlands Project **VII:**229
New Laws of 1542 **I:**122, 206
New Lebanon, New York **III:**387
New Left **IX:243–244,** 355*c*
　Hayden, Tom **IX:**143–144
　Mills, C. Wright **IX:**217
　neoconservatism **X:**252
　Port Huron Statement
　　IX:260

SANE **IX:**283
SDS **IX:**304
women's status and rights
　IX:347
"New Lights"
　Brainerd, David **II:**45
　Connecticut **II:**78
　Great Awakening **II:**156
　Presbyterians **II:**309
　Princeton College **II:**311
　religion **III:**360
　Tennent, Gilbert **II:**388
　Tennent, William, Jr. **II:**388
New Lives for Old (Mead)
　VII:197
New London, Connecticut
　VIII:201; **X:195**
New Look, The (fashion) **IX:**116
New Look policy (foreign
　relations) **IX:**83, 90, 91
New Lost City Ramblers **IX:**121
New Madrid, Missouri **IV:**280;
　V:263
New Madrid earthquake **IV:280**
Newman, Charles **X:**211
New Men of Power, The (Mills)
　IX:217
New Mexico **I:263–266,** *264,*
　398*c;* **II:**263, **263–264,** 436*c;*
　IV:414*c;* **V:**444*c;* **VII:**406*c*
　agriculture **V:**6
　Alvarado, Pedro de **I:**7
　Armijo, Manuel **IV:**26, 27
　art **II:**27
　Compromise of 1850
　　IV:103, 104
　Deseret, State of **IV:**120
　dust bowl **VIII:**97
　exploration **IV:**144, 145
　Fillmore, Millard **IV:**150
　foreign policy **IV:**155
　Fort Leavenworth **IV:**158
　Great Plains Indians **II:**157
　Gregg, Josiah **IV:**179
　Guadalupe Hidalgo, Treaty
　　of **IV:**180–181
　Hastings, Lansford W.
　　IV:187
　Hiroshima and Nagasaki
　　VIII:166
　Hopi **I:**168
　immigration **IV:**193
　Indians of the desert
　　Southwest **II:**176
　Kearny, Stephen Watts
　　IV:212
　Lamy, Jean Baptiste **IV:**222
　Latino movement **IX:**186
　Manifest Destiny **IV:**235
　Mexican-American War
　　IV:251–253
　Mexican Invasion **VII:**203
　Native Americans **II:**253;
　　X:250, 251
　New Spain, northern
　　frontier of **III:**317
　Oñate, Juan de **I:**279–280

Polk, James K. **IV:**302
popular sovereignty **IV:**304
Pueblo **I:**305; **II:**317
Pueblo Revolt **II:**318
St. Vrain, Céran **IV:**328
Santa Fe **I:**326
Santa Fe Trail **IV:**330
Sunbelt **VIII:**381
Taylor, Zachary **IV:**368
Texas **IV:**372
Vargas, Diego de **II:**397–
　398
violence and lawlessness
　VI:376
Wallace, Lew **VI:**381
Zuni **I:**393–394
New Nationalism **VII:236–237**
　elections **VII:**91
　Federal Reserve Act
　　VII:108
　Federal Trade Commission
　　Act **VII:**108
　Progressive Party **VII:**270
　progressivism **VII:**271
　Roosevelt, Theodore
　　VII:304
　Taft, William Howard
　　VII:348
New Negro, The (Locke)
　Harlem Renaissance
　　VII:136
　literature **VII:**181
　Locke, Alain LeRoy
　　VII:183
New Netherland **II:264–266,**
　436*c*
　British Empire **II:**48
　Delaware **II:**95
　Dutch-Indian Wars **II:**105–
　　106
　government, British
　　American **II:**152
　Kieft, Willem **II:**192
　Minuit, Peter **II:**235–236
　New Amsterdam **II:**256
　New York **II:**269, 270
　Stuyvesant, Peter **II:**379
　Youngs, John **II:**431
New Netherland Company **II:**264
New Orleans, Battle of **IV:280–**
　282, 281*m,* 411*c;* **V:280–281,**
　281, 444*c*
　Bowie, James **IV:**62–63
　Canada **III:**79
　Choctaw **IV:**86
　Democratic Party **IV:**117
　Era of Good Feelings
　　IV:141
　Farragut, David Glasgow
　　V:137
　Federalist Party **III:**165
　foreign policy **IV:**154
　Ghent, Treaty of **IV:**176
　Jackson, Andrew **IV:**206
　Lafitte, Jean **IV:**220
　marine corps **V:**248
　Mississippi River war **V:**263

Native Americans **IV:**275
panic of 1819 **IV:**294
Porter, David Dixon **V:**311
Union navy **V:**405
War of 1812 **IV:**392
New Orleans, Louisiana **II:266–**
　267, 437*c;* **III:**464*c;* **X:**384*c*
　agriculture **III:**11; **IV:**12
　Alamo, The **IV:**14
　architecture **II:**25
　Austin, Stephen F. **IV:**39
　Benjamin, Judah P. **V:**33
　Bienville, Jean-Baptiste Le
　　Moyne, sieur de **II:**37
　Bridges, Harry **VIII:**52–53
　cities and urban life
　　X:75–76
　Claiborne, William C. C.
　　IV:94–95
　Corps d'Afrique **V:**96
　Dewey, George **VI:**97
　disease/epidemics **IV:**123
　economy **IV:**130
　entertainment, popular
　　VI:117
　Florida **IV:**151
　foreign policy **IV:**153
　freedom rides **IX:**123
　French colonies **II:**137
　gun control **X:**161
　Hearn, Lafcadio **VI:**169
　Higgins, Andrew J.
　　VIII:165
　Hurricane Katrina **X:**173–
　　174
　immigration **VI:**184
　Jackson, Andrew **IV:**205–
　　206
　jazz **VII:**153; **VIII:**194
　Lafitte, Jean **IV:**220
　lead mines **IV:**224
　literature **VI:**226
　Long, Huey P. **VIII:**222
　Louisiana **IV:**210
　Louisiana Purchase **III:**273
　Mafia incident **VI:**234
　Marquette, Jacques **II:**215
　Mississippi River **V:**261, 262
　Mississippi River war **V:**263,
　　264
　music **VII:**218, 219
　New Orleans, Battle of
　　IV:280, 281
　Paris, Treaty of (1763)
　　III:331
　Pinckney Treaty **III:**337
　race and race relations
　　VII:283
　railroads **IV:**314
　riot (1866) **V:281–282**
　slave trade, internal **IV:**350
　Texas **IV:**371, 372
　theater **V:**387
New Orleans Superdome **X:**173,
　384*c*
New Panama Canal Company
　VII:250, 251

Newport, Christopher **II:267–268**

Newport, New Hampshire **IV:**183

Newport, Rhode Island **II:267**
architecture **II:**25
cities and urban life **III:**90
Coddington, William **II:**73
Dyer, Mary **II:**108
Estaing, Charles-Henri
Theodat, comte d'
III:158
French Alliance **III:**178
Greene, Nathanael **III:**198
Harrison, Peter **II:**163
Howe, Richard, Lord
III:214–215
Kennedy, Jacqueline **IX:**168
La Farge, John Frederick
Lewis Joseph **VI:**217
Lazarus, Emma **VI:**219
Osborn, Sarah Haggar
Wheaten **II:**279
privateering **II:**313
Rhode Island **II:**333
Rhode Island, Battle of
III:369, 370
Rochambeau, Jean-Baptiste-
Donatien de Vimeur,
comte de **III:**372
Sullivan, John **III:**402
U.S. Naval Academy at
Annapolis **V:**410
Williams, Roger **II:**416

Newport Casino (Newport, Rhode
Island) **VI:**392

Newport Folk Festival (1965)
IX:92, 259

Newport Jazz Festival (1956)
VIII:112

new Republicanism (modern
Republicanism) **IX:221–222**

New Review **VII:**296

New Right
conservative movement **X:**94
Helms, Jesse A., Jr. **X:**165
modern Republicanism
IX:222
think tanks **X:**349

News and Courier (Charleston)
VI:203

news media **VIII:271–272**, 443*c*,
445*c*
advertising **VIII:**1
art and architecture **VIII:**30
Congress **VIII:**81
FBI **VIII:**130
fireside chats **VIII:**138
government **VIII:**153
Hersey, John R. **VIII:**164
Life magazine **VIII:**217
presidency **VIII:**309
propaganda **VIII:**311
Pyle, Ernie **VIII:**314–315
radio **VIII:**320
technology **VIII:**389
World War II **VIII:**427–428
zoot-suiters **VIII:**442

New South **VI:**95, *264*, **264–265**

New Spain **I:266–270; II:**370–
373. *See also* Mexico
Aguilar, Francisco de **I:**4
cacao **I:**48
California **III:**73–74
casta paintings **I:**64
Cortés, Hernán **I:**96–97
Mendoza, Antonio de **I:**239
mestizo **I:**242, 243
Mexico **I:**242
Native Americans **III:**315
Santa Fe **I:**326–327
silver **I:**335–336
slavery **I:**338
Veracruz **I:**376
Zacatecas **I:**391
Zumárraga, Juan de **I:**392

New Spain, northern frontier of
III:317–318

Newspaper Enterprise Association
VII:159

newspapers **II:268**, 437*c*;
VI:265–267, 411*c*. *See also*
journalism
Adams, John Quincy **IV:**5
advertising **VI:**2; **X:**7
Alamo, The **IV:**14
Amistad incident **IV:**21
Angell, James Burrill **VI:**14
anti-Semitism **VII:**17
Bennett, James Gordon, Jr.
VI:32–34
Bloomer, Amelia **IV:**59
Bowles, Samuel **VI:**42–43
Brannan, Samuel **IV:**64
cities and urban life **IV:**92
civil liberties, Confederate
V:68
civil liberties, Union **V:**70
communications **VI:**78
Copperheads **V:**94
Crane, Stephen **VI:**85
Crummell, Alexander **VI:**86
education **IV:**135
election of 1828 **IV:**136
Garrison, William Lloyd
V:164
George, Henry **VI:**142
Greeley, Horace **V:**176–177
Harris, Benjamin **II:**163
illustration, photography,
and graphic arts **VI:**183
Ingersoll, Robert Green
VI:193
journalism **II:**189
labor, child **VI:**211–212
Leslie, Frank and Miriam
Florence Follin **VI:**221–
222
literature **IV:**229
Lovejoy, Elijah **IV:**230–231
Massachusetts Emigrant Aid
Society **IV:**242
media **X:**219
neoconservatism **X:**252
Newport **II:**267

news media **VIII:**271, 272
New York City **V:**282
printing and publishing
II:311–312
Pulitzer, Joseph **VI:**297
radio **VII:**290
Reid, Whitelaw **VI:**304–305
Walker, David **IV:**389
War Revenue Act **VII:**378
Williams, George
Washington **VI:**396

New Sweden **II:**436*c*
Lutherans **II:**212
Protestantism **II:**316
Swedish colonies **II:**381

Newsweek magazine **VIII:**272

Newton, Huey P. **IX:**6, 40, 41,
357*c*

Newton, Isaac **II:**345

Newton, John **II:**247

New Unionism **VII:237–238**
Adamson Act **VII:**2
AFL **VII:**11
Flynn, Elizabeth Gurley
VII:109
Haywood, William Dudley
VII:137
IWW **VII:**146–148
labor/labor movements
VII:170, 172
Lawrence Strike **VII:**173,
174
National Civic Federation
VII:226
UMWA **VII:**359–360

New View of Society, A (Owen)
IV:291

New Woman **VII:**131, **238–240**,
239, 390

New World **I:270–271**

New Year's Day **III:**341

New York, New Haven &
Hartford Railroad **IV:**313, 316

New York, Port of **VI:**20

New York, Synod of **II:**388

New York, Treaty of **III:**293–295;
IV:109

New York Anti-Slavery Society
V:46

New York Associated Press **VI:**78,
80

New York Athletic Club **VI:**44

New York Bay **IV:**386

New York Board of Regents
IX:107

New York Call **VII:**285

New York Central Railroad (NYC)
Baltimore & Ohio Railroad
IV:44
banking, investment **VI:**23
economy **IV:**131
industrialization **IV:**200
internal improvements
IV:203
Morgan, John Pierpont
VI:250
oil **VI:**271

transportation **VIII:**396
Vanderbilt, Cornelius
IV:387

*New York Central Railroad
Company v. White* **VII:**392

New York Charity Organization
Society **VII:**330

New York Church of the Messiah
VI:87

New York City **II:272–273**, 437*c*;
III:461*c*, 462*c*; **IV:**92; **V:282–
283; VI:**70, 407*c*; **VII:**405*c*,
406*c*; **VIII:**444*c*, 448*c*; **X:**377*c*.
See also Manhattan, New York
draft riots (Civil War). *See*
New York City draft riots
Dubinsky, David **VIII:**97
Eakins, Thomas **VI:**104
economy **IV:**131
Edison, Thomas Alva
VI:107
education **IV:**135
Ellington, Duke **VIII:**112
entertainment, popular
VI:116–118; **VII:**95
environment **VI:**119
Erie Canal **IV:**141–143
espionage **V:**135
Ethical Culture movement
VI:121
Evans, Walker **VIII:**119
FAP **VIII:**129
Federalist Papers **III:**162–
163
Federalists **III:**165, 166
Finney, Charles Grandison
IV:151
fire (1776) **III:318**
Flynn, Elizabeth Gurley
VII:110
Fort Washington, capture of
III:172
Free Trade and Sailor's
Rights **IV:**165
FTP **VIII:**136
Fuller, Margaret **IV:**169
Garnet, Henry Highland
IV:174
Garvey, Marcus **VII:**121,
122
gays and lesbians **VIII:**147
Gershwin, George **VII:**124
Golden Hill, Battle of
III:196
Greenwich Village **VII:**130
Griffith, David Wark
VII:131, 132
Guthrie, Woody **VIII:**160
Hancock, Winfield Scott
V:184
Harlem Heights, Battle of
III:210
Harlem Renaissance
VII:135–136
Hearst, William Randolph
VII:137, 138
Heathcote, Caleb **II:**164

New York City (*continued*)
Hillman, Sidney **VIII**:165
Holiday, Billie **VIII**:169
homefront **V**:193
Hopkins, Harry L. **VIII**:176
housing **VI**:179
How the Other Half Lives
(Riis) **VI**:426–427
Hudson Highlands
campaign **III**:216
Hughes, Charles Evans
VII:142
Hurston, Zora Neale
VIII:181
ILGWU **VII**:148–149
immigration **IV**:193–194;
VI:184, 186; **VII**:144
internal improvements
IV:203
invention and technology
VI:194–196
Irish Americans **VIII**:188
Iroquois **III**:227, 228
Jackson, Helen Hunt
VI:199
James, Henry **VI**:199, 200
James, William **VI**:200
Japanese Americans,
relocation of **VIII**:194
jazz **VII**:153
Jefferson, Joseph, III
VI:202
Jews **II**:185–186; **III**:236;
VIII:195
Johnson, Hugh S. **VIII**:196
Joplin, Scott **VII**:158
journalism **V**:217; **VII**:160
Kelley, Florence **VII**:164
Kennedy, Jacqueline **IX**:169
Kerouac, Jack **IX**:173
King's College **II**:193, 194
KKK **IX**:180
Knox, Henry **III**:248
Knyphausen, Wilhelm,
Baron von **III**:248
labor/labor movements
IV:217–218
labor: strikes and violence
VI:213–214
ladies aid societies **V**:227,
228
La Farge, John Frederick
Lewis Joseph **VI**:217
La Guardia, Fiorello
VIII:208
Latino movement **IX**:185
Lazarus, Emma **VI**:219
Leisler's Rebellion **II**:203–
204
L'Enfant, Pierre-Charles
III:261
liberty tree **III**:267
Lincoln, Abraham **V**:236
Livingston, Robert R.
III:270
Long Island, Battle of
III:271–272

lynching **VI**:230
machine politics **VI**:234
McDougall, Alexander
III:294
mining **VII**:209
monuments **V**:268
Mooney-Billings case
VII:213
Morris, Gouverneur **III**:304
Morris, Lewis **II**:243
Morse, Samuel F. B. **IV**:264
Murray, Pauli **IX**:227
music **VI**:257–258; **VII**:218;
IX:228
Native Americans **III**:314
nativism **V**:280
Negro Plot of 1741 **II**:255
newspapers **VI**:265
nurses **V**:285
NWTUL **VII**:230, 231
Olmsted, Frederick Law
V:287–288
panic of 1792 **III**:330
panic of 1857 **V**:294
Paterson Strike **VII**:254
photography **VII**:258–259
Plunkitt, George
Washington **VI**:285
popular culture **III**:341;
VII:263
population trends **III**:343;
V:309; **VI**:286
poverty **III**:344
POWs **III**:345
printing and publishing
II:311
prisons **III**:347
progressivism **VII**:271
prostitution **V**:315, 316
Quartering Act **III**:352
race and race relations
VII:283; **VIII**:318
railroads **IV**:314, 316
Rauschenbusch, Walter
VII:293
religion **IV**:321; **VI**:309
religious liberty **III**:362
Revolutionary War **III**:367–
368
riots **III**:371
Sacco and Vanzetti **VII**:311
Sanger, Margaret **VII**:312
Saratoga, surrender at
III:380
Seton, Elizabeth Ann
IV:343, 344
settlement houses **VI**:327,
328
Shirtwaist Makers Strike
VII:324
skyscrapers **VI**:333
slave resistance **II**:352–353
Smith, Alfred E. **VII**:326
socialism **VII**:327
social work **VII**:329
society, British American
II:366

Sons of Liberty **III**:394
spiritualism **IV**:355
sports and recreation
VII:334
Stamp Act Congress **III**:396
Stewart, Maria **IV**:357
strikes **V**:374, 375
suffrage **III**:401
Tammany Society **III**:405
technology **VIII**:389
temperance movement
IV:370
theater **III**:410–411; **V**:387
Thomas, Norman **VIII**:394
Tin Pan Alley **VII**:353
tourism **IX**:319
transportation **V**:390
transportation, urban
VI:360, 361
Triangle Shirtwaist Fire
VII:356
Tweed Ring **VI**:368–369
Tyler, Royall **III**:417
UN **VIII**:403
UNIA **VII**:361
urban reform **VII**:363
urban transportation
VII:363, 364
Valesh, Eva McDonald
VII:367
Vanderbilt, Cornelius
IV:386
vaudeville **VII**:368, 369
V-J Day **VIII**:407
Vorse, Mary Heaton
VII:375
Wald, Lillian **VII**:377
Walsh, Lawrence E. **X**:364
Washington, George
III:430, 431
Williams, Peter, Jr. **IV**:402
women's status and rights
VII:388
Yates, Abraham **III**:453–
454
yellow fever **II**:431
Zionism **VIII**:441
zoot-suiters **VIII**:442
Zouaves **V**:441
New York City bailout (1974)
X:253–254
New York City draft riots **V**:283,
283–285, 445c
conscription **V**:91
employment **V**:133
homefront **V**:193
immigration **V**:200
New York City **V**:283
race and race relations
V:320
Union army **V**:401
Women's National Loyal
League **V**:435
women's status and rights
V:437
New York City Planning
Commission **VIII**:398

New York City Police Department
VI:121
New York Civil Service Reform
Association **VI**:80
New York Crystal Palace
Exhibition **IV**:93–94
New York Customs House **IV**:31;
VI:84
New York *Daily Commercial
Advertiser* **IV**:85
New York *Daily Graphic*
VII:160
New York *Daily Mirror* **VII**:160
New York Daily News **VII**:160
New Yorker, The **VIII**:164, 167
New York Evening Post
Godkin, Edwin Lawrence
VI:149
Jackson, Helen Hunt
VI:199
newspapers **VI**:266
Schurz, Carl **VI**:325
Villard, Henry **VI**:375
New York *Evening Transcript*
IV:208
New York Giants **VII**:334
New York *Herald*
Bennett, James Gordon, Jr.
VI:32–34
cities and urban life **IV**:92
Crane, Stephen **VI**:85
Howe, Louis M. **VIII**:179
journalism **IV**:208; **V**:217,
218
newspapers **VI**:266
Villard, Henry **VI**:374
New York Illustrated News **V**:275
New York *Independent Journal*
III:162
New York Journal **VI**:411c
Cuba **V**:88
de Lôme Letter **VI**:94
journalism **IV**:208, 210
labor, child **VI**:211
Pulitzer, Joseph **VI**:297
Valesh, Eva McDonald
VII:367
yellow journalism **VI**:405
New York Journal American
VII:159
New York Journal of Commerce
IV:366, 367
New York Kansas League **IV**:242
New York Land League **VI**:396
New York Ledger **VI**:98
New York magazine **X**:276
New York Manumission Society
III:25, 462c; **IV**:17
New York Married Women's
Property Act **IV**:414c
New York Morning Journal
VI:405; **VII**:137
New York Packet **III**:162
New York Philharmonic Orchestra
VIII:448c
New York Philharmonic Society
IV:195; **VI**:254

New York Police Department **VII:**304

New York Press **VI:**405

New York Protestant Association **V:**280

New York Public Library **VI:**224

New York Redstockings **IX:**348

New York School of Social Work **VII:**254, 330

New York Society for the Suppression of Vice **VI:**79, 251

New York State **II:268–272,** *269,* 436*c;* **IV:**411*c;* **VII:**406*c*

   abortion **X:**2

   African Americans **III:**9

   agriculture **IV:**10

   American System **IV:**20

   Andros, Sir Edmund **II:**20

   anti-Masonry **IV:**25

   architecture **II:**25

   Articles of Confederation **III:**34

   artisans **III:**35

   Astor, John Jacob **IV:**33

   baseball **VII:**33

   Blatch, Harriot Eaton Stanton **VII:**38

   Burgoyne, Sir John **III:**67–68

   Burr, Aaron **III:**70

   canal era **IV:**79

   citizenship **III:**93

   Cleveland, Grover **VI:**74

   Clinton, DeWitt **III:**97

   Clinton, George **III:**98–99

   Conkling, Roscoe **VI:**80

   conservation/ environmentalism **VI:**81

   Constitution, ratification of the **III:**105, 106

   constitutions, state **III:**110

   Continental Congress, First **III:**114

   Continental Congress, Second **III:**116

   corruption, political **VI:**83, 84

   Crèvecoeur, J. Hector St. John de **III:**127

   Crummell, Alexander **VI:**86

   Declaration of Independence **III:**133

   Democratic Party **VIII:**92

   Democratic-Republican Party **III:**136

   Deseret, State of **IV:**119

   Dewey, Thomas E. **IX:**87, 88

   Dewson, Mary **VIII:**95

   disease/epidemics **IV:**122, 123

   Dow, Lorenzo **IV:**126

   economy **IV:**131

   education, philanthropy and **VI:**112

   election of 1828 **IV:**137

   Ely, Richard Theodore **VI:**114, 116

   entertainment, popular **VI:**117

   Erie Canal **IV:**141–143

   Farley, James A. **VIII:**125

   FBI **VIII:**130

   Federalist Papers **III:**163

   female antislavery societies **IV:**148

   Fifteenth Amendment **V:**141

   Fillmore, Millard **IV:**149

   Finney, Charles Grandison **IV:**150–151

   Flynn, Edward J. **VIII:**139

   Flynn, Elizabeth Gurley **VII:**109

   Fort Stanwix, Treaty of **III:**170

   Foster, Abigail Kelley **IV:**161

   Franklin, William **III:**176

   Free-Soil Party **IV:**163

   Garnet, Henry Highland **IV:**174

   GE **VII:**123

   Ghent, Treaty of **IV:**176

   Goldman, Emma **VII:**126

   government, British American **II:**152, 153

   Hamilton, Alexander **III:**208

   Harriman, W. Averell **VIII:**162

   Heathcote, Caleb **II:**163–164

   Hicks, Elias **IV:**189

   Holland Land Company **III:**214

   Hughes, Charles Evans **VII:**142

   Hyde, Edward, Viscount Cornbury **II:**171

   industrialization **IV:**199–201

   Ingersoll, Robert Green **VI:**193

   internal improvements **IV:**202

   Iroquois **III:**227

   Jay, John **III:**229, 230

   Kennedy, Robert F. **IX:**171

   King, Rufus **III:**246

   King William's War **II:**195

   Know-Nothing Party **IV:**214

   Ku Klux Klan **VII:**166

   labor, radical **VI:**213

   labor/labor movements **II:**199

   land riots **III:**254

   lead mines **IV:**223

   Lease, Mary Elizabeth Clyens **VI:**220

   Liberty Party **IV:**226

   Livingston, Philip **II:**206, 207

   Livingston, Robert **II:**207

   Livingston, Robert R. **III:**270

   Louisiana Purchase **III:**273

   lumbering **IV:**231

   Maine Law **IV:**234

   marriage and family **IV:**240

   Marshall, John **III:**291

   McCormick, Cyrus Hall **IV:**243

   medicine **IV:**250

   Missouri Compromise **IV:**256

   Morris, Gouverneur **III:**303–304

   mothers' pensions **VII:**213

   Mott, Lucretia **IV:**265

   Native Americans **III:**314

   Nauvoo **IV:**278

   NRA **X:**249

   penitentiary movement **IV:**296

   politics (1900–1928) **VII:**261

   population trends **III:**343; **X:**283

   postal service **II:**304

   Presbyterians **II:**309

   primogeniture and entail **II:**310

   prisons **III:**347

   privateering **II:**313

   Prohibition **VII:**273

   public health **VII:**275

   railroads **IV:**313

   Red Jacket **III:**359, 360

   religion **III:**361; **IV:**317; **VI:**309

   religious liberty **III:**362

   Roman Catholicism **II:**336

   Roosevelt, Eleanor **VIII:**343

   Roosevelt, Franklin D. **VIII:**344, 345

   Roosevelt, Theodore **VII:**304

   Schuyler, Philip John **III:**384

   Second Great Awakening **IV:**337

   Seneca Falls convention **IV:**341

   Seymour, Horatio **V:**348

   slave resistance **II:**353

   Smith, Alfred E. **VII:**326

   Smith, Joseph, Jr. **IV:**352

   spiritualism **IV:**354–355

   sports and recreation **VII:**334–335

   suffrage **III:**401

   Supreme Court **VII:**343

   Tappan, Arthur and Lewis **IV:**366

   temperance movement **IV:**370

   Tilden, Samuel Jones **VI:**357

   Van Buren, Martin **IV:**385

   Vanderbilt, Cornelius **IV:**386

   Van Rensselaer, Maria Van Cortlandt **II:**397

   Vermont **II:**398

   Villard, Henry **VI:**375

   Weiser, Johann Conrad **II:**409

   Weld, Theodore Dwight **IV:**395, 396

   Wilkes expedition **IV:**400

   Willard, Emma **IV:**401

   women's status and rights **II:**424

   Woodstock festival **X:**371–372

   Yates, Abraham **III:**453–454

   Young, Brigham **IV:**407

   Youngs, John **II:**431

New York State Association of NAWSA **VII:**50

New York State Reservation (Niagara Falls) **VI:**81

New York State Tenement House Commission **VI:**179, 390

New York Stock Exchange

   Baruch, Bernard M. **VII:**32

   economy **VII:**103

   Great Depression **VIII:**158

   McDonald's **IX:**208

   SEC **VIII:**357

   stock market crash **VIII:**376

New York Suffrage Society **V:**437

New York Sun

   cities and urban life **IV:**92

   Dana, Charles A. **V:**102; **VI:**92

   journalism **IV:**208, 209; **VII:**160

   newspapers **VI:**266

New York Suspending Act **III:**352

New York Tenement House Law (1901) **VI:**179

New York Times, The

   Bennett, James Gordon, Jr. **VI:**33

   ENIAC **IX:**105

   evolution **VI:**122

   Great Strike of 1877 **VI:**154

   journalism **V:**218; **VII:**159, 160

   KKK **IX:**180

   McCarran-Walter Act **IX:**205

   Model Cities program **IX:**221

   newspapers **VI:**267

   Pentagon Papers **X:**271, 272

   SANE **IX:**283

   Valesh, Eva McDonald **VII:**367

   Washington, Booker T. **VI:**384

New York Times v. Sullivan **X:**47

New York Times v. U.S. **X:**272, 376*c*. See also Pentagon Papers

New York Training School for
    Teachers **VIII**:209–210
New York Transcript **IV**:209
New York Tribune **V**:444*c*
    Crane, Stephen **VI**:85
    Dana, Charles A. **V**:102;
        VI:91
    Fuller, Margaret **IV**:169
    Greeley, Horace **V**:176, 177
    illustration, photography,
        and graphic arts **VI**:183
    journalism **IV**:208, 209; **V**:218
    Liberal Republican Party
        VI:222
    newspapers **VI**:266
    public land policy **IV**:306
    Reid, Whitelaw **VI**:304–305
    Villard, Henry **VI**:374
New York University
    Hughes, Charles Evans
        VII:142
    Morse, Samuel F. B. **IV**:264
    White, Stanford **VI**:392
New York v. United States **X**:131
New York Weekly **VI**:98
New York World **VI**:411*c*
    Bennett, James Gordon, Jr.
        VI:33
    boxing **VI**:44
    civil liberties, Union **V**:70
    Dana, Charles A. **VI**:92
    Hearst, William Randolph
        VII:137–138
    journalism **VII**:158–159
    labor, child **VI**:211
    Lease, Mary Elizabeth
        Clyens **VI**:220
    Pulitzer, Joseph **VI**:297
    yellow journalism **VI**:405
New York World's Fair (1939–
    1940) **VIII**:**272–274**, *273*, 446*c*
    advertising **VIII**:1
    art and architecture
        VIII:28–29
    FAP **VIII**:129
    New York World's Fair
        (1964) **IX**:246
    suburbanization/suburbs
        VIII:380
    technology **VIII**:389
    television **IX**:315
New York World's Fair (1964)
    IX:73, 123, **244–246**, *245*
New York Yankees **VII**:334;
    VIII:95, 370
New Zealand **IX**:353*c*
    investments, foreign
        VII:152
    SEATO **IX**:291, 292
    Wilkes expedition **IV**:400
Nezahuacóyotl (king of Texcoco)
    I:258
Nez Perce Indians
    Howard, Oliver Otis **V**:198
    "I Will Fight No More
        Forever" (Chief Joseph)
        VI:**413–414**

Lewis and Clark Expedition
    III:263
    Whitman, Marcus **IV**:398
Nez Perce War **VI**:261, *267*,
    267–268, 408*c*
NFL. *See* National Football
    League
NFO. *See* National Farmers
    Organization
NFWA. *See* National Farm
    Workers Association
Ngbanya **I**:143
NGOs. *See* nongovernmental
    organizations
NHC (National Hurricane
    Center) **X**:173
NHGRI. *See* National Human
    Genome Research Institute
NHL. *See* National Hockey
    League
Niagara, USS **IV**:221
Niagara Bible Conference **VI**:93,
    307
Niagara campaign **IV**:391, 392
Niagara Falls **VI**:411*c*
    Caroline affair **IV**:80–81
    conservation/
        environmentalism **VI**:81
    foreign policy **IV**:154
    invention and technology
        VI:196
    Niagara Movement **VII**:240
    Tesla, Nikola **VI**:353
Niagara Frontier **IV**:336
Niagara Movement **VII**:**240**,
    404*c*
    Declaration of Principles
        VII:**415–417**
    DuBois, W.E.B. **VII**:80
    NAACP **VII**:224
    Trotter, William Monroe
        VII:357
Niagara River **IV**:25, 391, 392
Niani **I**:226
Niantic Indians **II**:332
Nicaragua **IV**:415*c*; **V**:443*c*;
    VII:405*c*; **X**:**254–255**, 377*c*,
    378*c*
    Alliance for Progress **IX**:11
    Big Stick diplomacy
        VII:34–35
    Boland Amendment **X**:45
    Clayton-Bulwer Treaty
        IV:98
    cold war, end of **X**:85, 86
    contras **X**:94–95
    dollar diplomacy **VII**:79
    filibustering **V**:145
    foreign policy **IV**:156; **V**:149,
        151; **VII**:114; **X**:142
    Good Neighbor policy
        VIII:151
    Iran-contra affair **X**:183
    Latin America **X**:205, 206
    Manifest Destiny **IV**:235
    Mexico **X**:226
    North, Oliver L. **X**:258

Panama Canal **VII**:250
    Reagan, Ronald W. **X**:301
    Stimson, Henry L. **VIII**:375
    Vanderbilt, Cornelius
        IV:387
    Walker, William **V**:423
    WILPF **VII**:386
Nicholas II (czar of Russia)
    VII:175, 305
Nicholette, Charles **II**:220
Nicholls, Richard
    government, British
        American **II**:152
    New Netherland **II**:266
    New York **II**:270
Nichols, Mike **IX**:226
Nichols, Terry
    militia movement **X**:231
    Oklahoma City bombing
        X:267
    terrorism **X**:346
Nickelodeon (TV channel) **X**:344
nickelodeons **VII**:404*c*
    entertainment, popular
        VII:96
    movie industry **VII**:216
    popular culture **VII**:264
Nicklaus, Jack **X**:332
Nickles, Don **X**:215
Nicodemus, Kansas **V**:361
Nicolay, John G. **VI**:147, 164
Nicolet, Jean **II**:123, **273**
Nicollet, Joseph **IV**:166
Nicuesa, Diego de **I**:284
Niebuhr, H. Richard **VIII**:335
Niebuhr, Joseph **IX**:13, 14
Niebuhr, Reinhold **VIII**:335–336
Niger Bend **I**:253
Nigeri **IX**:213
Nigeria **II**:4
    Calabar **I**:51
    energy **X**:121
    Hausa **I**:156
    Igbo **I**:177–178
    OPEC **X**:267
    Oyo **I**:281
Niger River **I**:**271**
    Askia Muhammad I **I**:14
    Djenne-Djeno **I**:109
    Gao **I**:137
    Igbo **I**:178
    Leo Africanus **I**:211
    Mali **I**:226
    Sudan **I**:347
"Night and Day" (Porter) **VIII**:361
Nighthawks (Hopper) **VIII**:*30*, 31
Nightingale, Florence **V**:257
Nightingale, Taylor **VI**:388
NIH. *See* National Institutes of
    Health
Nike X system **X**:27
Nike Zeus project **X**:26, 27
Niles, Hezekiah **III**:**318–319**
Niles' Weekly Register **III**:318,
    319; **IV**:210
NIMH. *See* National Institute of
    Mental Health

Nimitz, Chester W. **VIII**:**274**,
    447*c*
    Coral Sea, Battle of the
        VIII:87
    King, Ernest J. **VIII**:202
    Knox, Frank **VIII**:202
    Marines, U.S. **VIII**:230
    Midway, Battle of **VIII**:238
    World War II Pacific theater
        VIII:435
Nine-Power Pact **VII**:379, 408*c*
1919 (Dos Passos) **VIII**:219
Nineteenth Amendment **VII**:408*c*
    Blackwell, Antoinette Brown
        VI:39
    Blatch, Harriot Eaton
        Stanton **VII**:38
    Cable Act **VII**:47
    Catt, Carrie Lane Chapman
        VII:50
    citizenship **VII**:57
    Coolidge, Calvin John
        VII:63–64
    elections **VII**:89
    feminism **X**:131–132
    Friedan, Betty **IX**:127
    LWV **IX**:186
    marriage and family **VII**:191
    NAWSA **VII**:223
    NWP **VII**:230
    Paul, Alice **VII**:254
    politics (1900–1928)
        VII:262
    Supreme Court **VII**:343
    woman suffrage **VII**:385
    women's status and rights
        VII:388
    World War I **VII**:394
95 Theses **I**:218
99th Pursuit Squadron, Tuskegee
    Airmen **VIII**:27
Ninety-Six, Battle of **III**:319
Ninth Air Force, U.S. **VIII**:27
Ninth Amendment **III**:50
Ninth Army, U.S. **VIII**:50–51
Ninth Kansas Cavalry **VI**:75–76
Niobara River **IV**:146
Niobe (British warship) **VI**:377
NIOSH (National Institute
    for Occupational Safety and
    Health) **X**:264
Nipmuc **I**:332
NIRA. *See* National Industrial
    Recovery Act
Nirenberg, Marshall W. **IX**:286
Nirvana (band) **X**:238
Nisei **VIII**:193, 194
Nissan **IX**:27; **X**:35
NIT (National Invitation
    Tournament) **VIII**:371
Nitze, Paul H. **IX**:247
Nixon, Richard M., and
    administration **IX**:353*c*,
    354*c*, 357*c*; **X**:255, **255–258**,
    375*c*–377*c*
    ABM Treaty **X**:26, 27
    affirmative action **X**:9

Agnew, Spiro T. **X:**18
Albert, Carl B. **X:**21
ANSCA **X:**21
antiwar movement, Vietnam
    X:29
arms race **IX:**17
birth control **X:**43
Bork, Robert **X:**45
Buchanan, Patrick J. **X:**49
Burger, Warren E. **X:**50, 51
Bush, George H. W. **X:**51
Chambers, Whittaker **IX:**52
Cheney, Richard B. **X:**71,
    72
"Chicago Eight" **X:**73
Clinton, Hillary Rodham
    X:77
cold war, end of **X:**84
cold war culture **IX:**65
Congressional Budget and
    Impoundment Control
    Act **X:**88–89
conscription, end of **X:**89
conservation/
    environmentalism **X:**90
conservatism **IX:**75
conservative movement
    X:93
consumerism **IX:**75
counterculture **IX:**79
Cox, Archibald, Jr. **X:**95
Democratic Party **IX:**85
détente **X:**103, 104
Dewey, Thomas E. **IX:**88
Dole, Robert **X:**105
economy **X:**108, 109
Eisenhower, Dwight D.
    IX:100
elections **IX:**103, 104
elections, presidential **X:**116
Ellington, Duke **VIII:**112
energy **X:**120
Energy, U.S. Department
    of **X:**122
federalism **X:**130
food **IX:**121
Ford, Gerald R. **X:**137, 138
foreign policy **X:**140
Goldwater, Barry **IX:**135,
    136
Graham, Billy **IX:**138
Helms, Jesse A., Jr. **X:**165
Hershey, Lewis B.
    VIII:164–165
Hiss, Alger **IX:**146, 147
Hoover, J. Edgar **IX:**149,
    150
HUAC **IX:**150
Humphrey, Hubert H.
    IX:151
impeachment **X:**178
Jaworski, Leon **X:**193
Job Corps **IX:**162
journalism **IX:**165
Kennedy, Edward M. **X:**196
Kennedy, John F. **IX:**169
Kent State protests **X:**197

King, Martin Luther, Jr.
    IX:174
Koreagate **X:**199
labor/labor movements
    X:201
Latin America **IX:**184;
    X:205
Leary, Timothy **IX:**187
Lend-Lease **VIII:**212
liberalism **IX:**191; **X:**208
McCarthy, Eugene **IX:**206
McGovern, George S. **X:**217
Mexico **X:**226
Mitchell, John N. **X:**232,
    233
neoconservatism **X:**252
NEPA **X:**246
New Left **IX:**244
Occupational Safety and
    Health Act **X:**264
OMB **X:**266
Pentagon Papers **X:**272
political parties **X:**276
Powell, Lewis **X:**288
property rights **X:**290
race and race relations
    X:297
Reagan, Ronald W. **X:**299–
    300
Republican Party **IX:**274–
    275
Resignation Speech **X:390–
    392**
Richardson, Elliot L.
    X:310–311
Robinson, Jackie **IX:**278
Ruckelshaus, William D.
    X:312
Rumsfeld, Donald **X:**312
SALT I/SALT II **X:**336
shopping centers **IX:**290
"Silent Majority" Speech
    X:385–386
South Africa **X:**325
space policy **X:**327
Supreme Court **X:**338
Teamsters Union **X:**311
television **IX:**316
Thurmond, James Strom
    X:351
U.S. v. Nixon **X:**357–358
veto (presidential) **X:**361
Vietnam War **IX:**332
Vietnam War, end of U.S.
    involvement **X:**361, 362
VISTA **IX:**333
wage and price controls
    X:363
Wallace, George C. **X:**364
Watergate scandal **X:**365–
    367
Nixon Doctrine
    defense policy **X:**99
    foreign policy **X:**140
    Latin America **X:**205
NIYC. *See* National Indian Youth
    Council

Niza, Marcos de
    Coronado, Francisco **I:**92
    New Mexico **I:**265
    Pueblo **I:**305
Nkomo, Joshua **X:**16
Nkongolo dynasty **I:**217
Nkrumah, Kwame **IX:**45
NKVD (People's Commissariat for
    Internal Affairs) **VIII:**118, 187
NL. *See* National League of
    Professional Base Ball Clubs
nleke **I:**337
NLF. *See* National Liberation
    Front
NLRA. *See* National Labor
    Relations Act
NLRB. *See* National Labor
    Relations Board
NLU. *See* National Labor Union
NME. *See* National Military
    Establishment
Noad (emperor of Ethiopia)
    I:124–125
Nobel Peace Prize **IX:**352*c*
    Addams, Jane **VII:**3
    Bunche, Ralph **IX:**44, 45
    Carter, James Earl, Jr. **X:**70
    conservation/
        environmentalism **X:**92
    Dawes, Charles Gates
        VII:71
    global warming **X:**156
    Hull, Cordell **VIII:**180
    Kissinger, Henry A. **X:**198
    Lockwood, Belva Ann
        Bennett McNall **VI:**229
    Marshall, George C.
        VIII:232
    Middle East **X:**228, 229
    Roosevelt, Theodore
        VII:304
Nobel Prize (economics) **X:**93
Nobel Prize (literature) **VIII:**443*c*,
    445*c*, 446*c*; **IX:**352*c*
    Faulkner, William **VIII:**128
    Irish Americans **VIII:**189
    literature **VIII:**220; **IX:**193
    Myrdal, Gunnar **VIII:**253
    Steinbeck, John **VIII:**374,
        375
no-bid contracts **X:**72
nobles **I:**19–20, 332
Nobody Knows My Name
    (Baldwin) **IX:**35
Noche Triste
    Alvarado, Pedro de **I:**7
    Aztecs **I:**22
    Cacamatzin **I:**47
    Cuauhtémoc **I:**100
No Child Left Behind Act (2002)
    Bush, George W. **X:**56
    education, primary/
        secondary **X:**115
    House of Representatives
        X:170
Nock, Albert Jay **VIII:**84
no-fault divorce **X:**213, 216, 375*c*

Noli, Antonio de **I:**148
no-lockout pledge **VIII:**261
Nomex **IX:**91
"no new taxes" **X:**110
nongovernmental organizations
    (NGOs) **X:**17, 90
Non-Importation Act **III:**152,
    280, **319,** 465*c*
Non-Intercourse Act **III:319–
    320,** 465*c*
    Bonaparte, Napoleon **III:**55
    Cadore Letter **III:**73
    foreign affairs **III:**169
Non-Partisan Committee for
    Peace through Revision of the
    Neutrality Act **VIII:**76–77
Non-Partisan League. *See* Labor's
    Non-Partisan League
nonrecognition **VIII:**225
nonviolence **IX:**354*c*–356*c*
    Chávez, César Estrada
        IX:54
    civil disobedience **IX:**57–58
    CORE **IX:**72, 74
    King, Martin Luther, Jr.
        IX:174, 175
    Lewis, John **IX:**190
    race and race relations
        IX:269
    religion **IX:**272
    SCLC **IX:**292–293
    SDS **IX:**304
    sit-ins **IX:**290–291
    SNCC **IX:**302
Nookta **II:**275
Norcross, Gerald **V:**192
Norfolk, Connecticut **IV:**161
Norfolk, Virginia
    Chesapeake-Leopard affair
        III:88
    disease/epidemics **IV:**122–
        123
    habeas corpus, writ of **V:**181
    slave trade, internal **IV:**350
    Wilkes expedition **IV:**399
Norfolk *Daily Southern Argus*
    IV:123
Norfolk Navy Yard **V:**265
Noriega, Manuel **X:**270, 379*c*
    Bush, George H. W. **X:**52
    defense policy **X:**101
    Panama invasion (1989–
        1990) **X:**269
    Powell, Colin L. **X:**286
Norman Conquest **I:**215
Normandy, Allied invasion of
    VIII:275, **275–276,** 448*c*
    air power **VIII:**15
    amphibious warfare **VIII:**20
    Army, U.S. **VIII:**25
    Bradley, Omar N. **VIII:**50–
        51
    Bulge, Battle of the **VIII:**54
    Eisenhower, Dwight D.
        IX:100
    Higgins, Andrew J.
        VIII:165

Normandy, Allied invasion of
(*continued*)
  Italian campaign **VIII**:191–
    192
  King, Ernest J. **VIII**:202
  Navy, U.S. **VIII**:265
  Patton, George S., Jr.
    VIII:291
  photography **VIII**:296
  second front **VIII**:355
  shipbuilding **VIII**:359
  Soviet-American relations
    VIII:368
  tanks **VIII**:386
  Teheran Conference
    VIII:391
  World War II European
    theater **VIII**:431
Normans. *See* Anglo-Normans
Norman v. Reed **X**:324
Norplant birth control device **X**:43
Norris, Frank
  business **VII**:46
  dime novels **VI**:99
  literature **VI**:226; **VII**:179
Norris, George W. **VIII**:**276–277**
  antimonopoly **VIII**:23
  Cannon, Joseph Gurney
    VII:48
  Capper-Volstead Act **VII**:49
  Congress **VII**:62; **VIII**:79
  isolationists **VIII**:189
  Norris–La Guardia Act
    VIII:277
  Republican Party **VIII**:336
  Tennessee Valley Authority
    VIII:392
Norris, John **I**:112
Norris, William **IV**:333
Norris–La Guardia Act **VIII**:**277**,
  444*c*
  antimonopoly **VIII**:23
  Hoover presidency
    VIII:174
  labor/labor movements
    VIII:205
  La Guardia, Fiorello
    VIII:209
  Norris, George W. **VIII**:276
  strikes **VIII**:377
Norristown, Pennsylvania **IV**:37
Norse **I**:**271–272**, 395*c*
  Cabot, John **I**:44
  cod **I**:77
  Greenland **I**:144
  Iceland **I**:177
  L'Anse aux Meadows
    I:203–204
  Montagnais-Naskapi **I**:250
  navigation technology **I**:262
  Vinland **I**:378
North, Frederick, Lord **III**:**320**
  Carlisle commission **III**:81
  Coercive Acts **III**:100
  Franklin, Benjamin **III**:174
  Suffolk Resolves **III**:400
  Townshend Duties **III**:413

North, Oliver L. **X**:**258–259**
  Boland Amendment **X**:45
  foreign policy **X**:142
  Iran-contra affair **X**:183,
    184
  Mitchell, George **X**:231,
    232
  Walsh, Lawrence E. **X**:364,
    365
North Africa **VIII**:448*c*
  Albuquerque, Alfonso de
    I:6
  Barbary Wars **III**:45
  Islam **I**:189
  Middle East **IX**:214
North African campaign
  VIII:**277–278**, 447*c*
  amphibious warfare **VIII**:20
  Army, U.S. **VIII**:25
  Atlantic Charter **VIII**:34
  Axis **VIII**:38
  Bradley, Omar N. **VIII**:50
  Casablanca Conference
    VIII:62
  Hersey, John R. **VIII**:164
  Italian campaign **VIII**:191
  Patton, George S., Jr.
    VIII:291
  second front **VIII**:355
  submarines **VIII**:378
  tanks **VIII**:385–386
  World War II European
    theater **VIII**:431
North American Free Trade
  Agreement (NAFTA) **X**:**259**,
  380*c*
  Bush, George H. W. **X**:53
  Clinton, William J. **X**:81–82
  economy **X**:110
  foreign policy **X**:142
  globalization **X**:154
  labor/labor movements
    X:203
  Latin America **X**:206
  Mexico **X**:226
North American Land Company
  III:306
North American Review
  journalism **IV**:209–210
  literature **VI**:225
  Norton, Charles Eliot
    VI:269
Northampton Church **II**:114, 115
North Anna, Battle of **V**:190
North Atlantic Cooperation
  Council (NACC) **X**:260
North Atlantic Ocean
  icebergs **I**:176–177
  Iceland **I**:177
  Norse **I**:272
North Atlantic Treaty
  Organization (NATO) **IX**:**246–
  247**, 352*c*; **X**:**259–260**, 379*c*,
  384*c*
  Acheson, Dean **IX**:1
  Afghanistan War **X**:11, 12
  Africa **IX**:3

  arms race **IX**:17
  Bush, George W. **X**:56
  Clinton, William J. **X**:81, 83
  cold war **IX**:63, 64
  defense policy **X**:100, 102
  Dulles, John Foster **IX**:91
  Eisenhower, Dwight D.
    IX:100
  Europe **IX**:113
  foreign policy **X**:143
  Haig, Alexander M., Jr.
    X:163, 164
  INF Treaty **X**:180
  Iron Curtain, collapse of
    X:188
  Kosovo **X**:199
  Marshall, George C.
    VIII:233
  McCarran-Walter Act
    IX:205
  militia movement **X**:231
  NSC-68 **IX**:247
  Soviet Union **IX**:295
  Truman, Harry S. **IX**:320
  Truman Doctrine **IX**:322
North Bend, Ohio **IV**:186
North Carolina **I**:28; **II**:273–275;
  IV:412*c*
  agriculture **V**:6
  Appalachia **IX**:15
  Blount, William **III**:53
  Burger, Warren E. **X**:51
  cities and urban life **X**:75
  citizenship **III**:93
  Constitution, ratification of
    the **III**:105, 106
  constitutions, state **III**:110
  disease/epidemics **IV**:123
  Dow, Lorenzo **IV**:126
  environment **III**:155
  Franklin, state of **III**:175
  Gastonia Strike **VII**:122
  gold **IV**:176
  governors **V**:172
  Guilford Courthouse, Battle
    of **III**:201–202
  habeas corpus, writ of **V**:181
  Heroes of America **V**:187,
    188
  Hill, Daniel H. **V**:190
  invention and technology
    VII:150
  Jackson, Andrew **IV**:205
  Jews **III**:237
  Jim Crow laws **VI**:204
  King's Mountain, Battle of
    III:246
  Ku Klux Klan **V**:223, 225
  labor/labor movements
    IV:219
  lead mines **IV**:223
  lumbering **II**:212
  lynching **VI**:230
  Moore's Creek Bridge,
    Battle of **III**:301–302
  mulattoes **II**:246
  Native Americans **IV**:275

  Ostenaco **II**:280
  peace movements **V**:296
  Polk, James K. **IV**:301
  race and race relations
    VIII:318
  religion, Euro-American
    II:329
  Revolutionary War **III**:368
  segregation **VII**:320
  slavery **III**:390
  slave trade, internal **IV**:349
  SNCC **IX**:302
  South Carolina **II**:369
  taverns and inns **II**:383, 384
  Teach, Edward **II**:385
  Tuscarora **II**:394–395
  Tuscarora War **II**:395
  Vance, Zebulon B. **V**:414
  violence and lawlessness
    VI:375
  Wingina **II**:417
  Yorktown, surrender at
    III:454
North Carolina Regulation
  III:**320–321**, 460*c*
  Alamance, Battle of **III**:12
  Husband, Herman **III**:218
North Carolina Society of Ex-
  Sailors and Soldiers **V**:415
North Dakota **I**:162; **VI**:410*c*
  cattle kingdom **VI**:64
  exploration **IV**:146
  Farmer-Labor Party
    VII:105
  immigration **VI**:184
  Lewis and Clark Expedition
    III:263
  Native Americans **IV**:275
  Non-Partisan League
    VII:241
  population trends **X**:282
  socialism **VII**:327
northeastern United States
  agriculture **IV**:12, 13
  art and architecture **IV**:30
  chain stores **VI**:65
  cities and urban life **VI**:69;
    IX:55
  Democratic Party **IV**:118
  economy **IV**:130
  Finney, Charles Grandison
    IV:151
  fur trade **IV**:170
  ILGWU **VIII**:187
  immigration **VI**:184
  industrialization **IV**:201
  Irish Americans **VIII**:188
  Jackson, Andrew **IV**:207
  Massachusetts Emigrant Aid
    Society **IV**:241
  Mexican-American War
    IV:251–252
  migration **IV**:253, 254
  mining **VII**:209
  panic of 1837 **IV**:294
  Passaic Strike **VII**:253
  population trends **X**:281

poverty **X**:286
Seneca Falls convention
IV:341
Seton, Elizabeth Ann
IV:344
Tappan, Arthur and Lewis
IV:366
technology **VIII**:397
violence and lawlessness
VI:375
Webster-Ashburton Treaty
IV:394
Northeast Passage **I**:115, 214,
272–273
North Elba, New York **V**:44
North End Caucus **III**:366
Northern Alliance **X**:11–12, 143
Northern Command, U.S. **X**:173
Northern Ireland **X**:232
Northern Natural Gas Company
IV:61
Northern Pacific Railroad (NP)
banking, investment **VI**:23
Cooke, Jay **V**:93
Donnelly, Ignatius Loyola
VI:100
environment **VI**:119–120
Hill, James J. **VI**:172, 173
Morgan, John Pierpont
VI:251
Northern Securities Case
VII:241
Villard, Henry **VI**:375
Northern Securities Case
VII:**241–242**, 404*c*
business **VII**:46
New Nationalism **VII**:237
railroads **VI**:302
Roosevelt, Theodore
VII:304
Northern Securities Company
banking, investment **VI**:23
Hill, James J. **VI**:172–173
Morgan, John Pierpont
VI:251
railroads **VI**:302
Northern Star, The (Douglass)
IV:228
northern United States
abolitionism **IV**:1, 3; **V**:3
African Americans **III**:9, 10;
IV:7–9; **IX**:4
agriculture **IV**:10–13; **V**:6
American Anti-Slavery
Society **IV**:15
American Fur Company
IV:18
anti-Masonry **IV**:25
antislavery **III**:26
banking **V**:27–28
Civil War **V**:73–75
conservative coalition
VIII:86
cotton **III**:123
Deere, John **IV**:116
Democratic Party **IV**:116,
118; **VIII**:92

economy **IV**:130, 132–133;
V:121–124
employment **V**:132
Frémont, John C. **IV**:167
governors **V**:172
Great Migration **VII**:127
homefront **V**:192–193
industrial development
IV:201; **V**:204–205
jazz **VII**:153; **VIII**:195
labor/labor movements
IV:217–219
ladies aid societies **V**:227,
228
literature **V**:239
lost cause, the **V**:245
lynching **VI**:230–231
Massachusetts Emigrant Aid
Society **IV**:242
McCormick, Cyrus Hall
IV:245
migration **VIII**:239; **IX**:215
Native Americans in the War
of 1812 **IV**:277
nurses **V**:286
peace movements **V**:295
popular culture **VII**:265
population trends **III**:343;
V:310; **VII**:266
Progressive Party **VII**:269
race and race relations
VII:283
redemption **V**:328
refugees **V**:330
religion **V**:331–332
Republican Party **IV**:321,
323
rural life **III**:375
secession **V**:344
segregation **IX**:288
slavery **III**:391; **IV**:344;
V:362, 364
slave trade **III**:393
Society of Friends **V**:365
tariffs **V**:383
Union League **V**:404–405
Webster, Daniel **IV**:393
Northfield, Minnesota **VI**:376
Northgate shopping center
(Seattle) **IX**:290
North Korea. *See* Korea,
Democratic People's Republic of
North Market Sabbath School
VI:249
North Platte, Nebraska **VI**:118
North Pole **VII**:405*c*, 409*c*
Northrup, Lucius B. **V**:203
North Salem, New York **IV**:199
North Star, The **IV**:16
North Vietnam **IX**:356*c*; **X**:**260–
261**, 377*c*
Asia **IX**:21
cold war, end of **X**:84
foreign policy **X**:140, 141
Hayden, Tom **IX**:144
Soviet Union **IX**:295
Vietnam War **IX**:330, 332

Vietnam War, end of U.S.
involvement **X**:361, 362
wars of national liberation
IX:339
Weathermen/Weather
Underground **X**:367
Northwest Coast Indians **II**:**275**
North West Company
American Fur Company
IV:18
Astor, John Jacob **IV**:33–35
Astoria **IV**:35, 36
Columbia River **IV**:103
fur trade **IV**:171
McLoughlin, John **IV**:247–
248
mountain men **IV**:266
Oregon Treaty of 1846
IV:287
rendezvous **IV**:321
Northwestern Farmers' Alliance
VI:125, 126, 281, 282
Northwestern Sanitary
Commission **V**:228
northwestern United States
VI:271; **VII**:238
Northwestern University
Ely, Richard Theodore
VI:116
Hamilton, Alice **VII**:133
medicine **VI**:244
Sunday, William Ashley, Jr.
VII:342
Willard, Frances **VI**:393
Northwest Ordinances **III**:**321–
322**, 462*c*
abolitionism **III**:3; **IV**:1; **V**:1
African Americans **III**:9
Articles of Confederation
III:34
Continental Congress,
Second **III**:116
education **III**:147
Jefferson, Thomas **III**:233
Missouri Compromise
IV:257
Mormon War **IV**:263
slavery **IV**:344
Tallmadge Amendment
IV:365
Northwest Passage **I**:**273–274**,
396*c*, 398*c*
Cabot, Sebastian **I**:45
Cartier, Jacques **I**:61
Cathay **I**:68
Company of Cathay **I**:87
exploration **II**:124
Frobisher, Martin **I**:134
Fuca, Juan de **II**:139
Gilbert, Sir Humphrey
I:140
Greenland **I**:144
Grenville, Sir Richard **I**:145
Hawaii **IV**:188
Hudson, Henry **II**:167
icebergs **I**:177
Norumbega **I**:274

Northwest Territory **III**:462*c*–
464*c*
Adams-Onís Treaty **IV**:6
Astor, John Jacob **IV**:33
Cass, Lewis **IV**:82
Cooper Union speech **V**:94
economy **IV**:130
Erie Canal **IV**:141
foreign policy **IV**:153, 154
Free-Soil Party **IV**:164
Harrison, William Henry
IV:184
internal improvements
IV:202
Native Americans **IV**:273,
274
Northwest Ordinances
III:321–322
popular sovereignty **IV**:305
St. Clair, Arthur **III**:377,
378
Tallmadge Amendment
IV:365
War of 1812 **IV**:392
Whigs **IV**:397
Wilkes expedition **IV**:400
*Northwood: A Tale of New
England* (Hale) **IV**:183
Norton, Charles Eliot **VI**:**268–
269**
art and architecture **VI**:19
Jewett, Sarah Orne **VI**:203
professional organizations,
rise of **VI**:294
Norton, Ken **IX**:10
Norumbega **I**:**274**, 377
Norway
Atlantic, Battle of the
VIII:33
blitzkrieg **VIII**:47
Britain, Battle of **VIII**:53
Norwich, Connecticut **IV**:314
no-strike pledge **VIII**:261, 262
Notes of a Native Son (Baldwin)
IX:35, 194
"Notes of Eight Years Travel
Amongst the North American
Indians" (Catlin) **IV**:85
"Notes on Coinage" (Jefferson)
III:233
Notes on the State of Virginia
(Jefferson)
abolitionism **V**:2
Banneker, Benjamin **III**:43
environment **III**:155
Jefferson, Thomas **III**:232
literature **III**:268
race and race relations
IV:310
Notman, John **V**:191–192
Notorious (film) **IX**:224
Notre Dame football **VIII**:328,
371
Nott, Josiah Clark **IV**:311
Not Without Laughter (Hughes)
VII:136, 181
Novak, Kim **IX**:224

Novak, Robert **X:**165
Nova Scotia **I:**3; **II:**437*c;* **III:**462*c*
  Canada **III:**77–79
  Loyalists **III:**275, 276
  Monckton, Robert **II:**241
  Paris, Treaty of (1783)
    III:332
  Queen Anne's War **II:**323
  Revolutionary War **III:**368
  Seabury, Samuel **III:**387
  Seven Years' War **II:**348
Nova Zembla **I:**272, 273
novels
  Alcott, Louisa May **VI:**10
  Alger, Horatio **VI:**11
  dime novels **VI:**98–99
  literature **V:**239, 240
NOW. *See* National Organization
  for Women
NOW v. Scheidler **X:**248
Noyce, Robert **X:**86
Noyes Academy (New
  Hampshire) **IV:**174; **VI:**86
NP. *See* Northern Pacific Railroad
NPR (National Public Radio)
  X:220
NPS. *See* National Park Service
NPT. *See* Nuclear Non-
  proliferation Treaty
NRA. *See* National Recovery
  Administration; National Rifle
  Association
NRC (Nuclear Regulatory
  Commission) **IX:**25
NREN (National Research and
  Education Network) **X:**182
NRPB. *See* National Resources
  Planning Board
NSBRO (National Service Board
  for Religious Objectors)
  VIII:83
NSC. *See* National Security
  Council
NSC (National Service Corps)
  IX:332–333
NSC-68 **IX:247–248,** 352*c*
  Acheson, Dean **IX:**1–2
  defense budget **IX:**83
  military-industrial complex
    IX:216
NSDD–13 (National Security
  Decision Directive 13) **X:**30
NSF. *See* National Science
  Foundation
NSFNET (Internet service
  provider) **X:**182
Ntine Wene **I:**200
nuclear family **X:**127, 128, 134
nuclear freeze movement
  VII:109; **X:**70, **261**
Nuclear Incident Response Team
  X:167
Nuclear Non-proliferation Treaty
  (NPT) **IX:**357*c*
  arms race **X:**30
  hydrogen bomb **IX:**153
  nuclear proliferation **X:**261

nuclear power **IX:**24, 25, 311,
  312, 351*c*, 353*c*
nuclear proliferation **X:261–262**
nuclear reactors
  AEC **IX:**25
  Oppenheimer, J. Robert
    IX:251
  technology **IX:**311
Nuclear Regulatory Commission
  (NRC) **IX:**25
nuclear submarines. *See*
  submarines, nuclear-powered
Nuclear Test Ban Treaty
  VIII:162
nuclear testing
  AEC **IX:**24–25
  environment **IX:**108
  Humphrey, Hubert H.
    IX:151
  Limited Test Ban Treaty of
    1963 **IX:**192
  SANE **IX:**283
nuclear weapons **IX:**355*c;* **X:**377*c,*
  379*c. See also* atomic bomb;
  hydrogen bomb
  arms race **IX:**17; **X:**29
  Clinton, William J. **X:**81
  cold war **IX:**64
  Cuban missile crisis
    IX:80–81
  defense policy **X:**99
  DuPont Corporation **IX:**91
  hydrogen bomb **IX:**152–
    153
  nuclear proliferation **X:**262
  Oppenheimer, J. Robert
    IX:251
  Rosenberg, Julius and Ethel
    IX:280
  SALT I/SALT II **X:**336
  SANE **IX:**283
  science and technology
    IX:285
*Nuclear Weapons and Foreign
  Policy* (Kissinger) **X:**198
nudity **X:**323, 343
Nueces River
  Guadalupe Hidalgo, Treaty
    of **IV:**181
  Mexican-American War
    IV:251
  Taylor, Zachary **IV:**368
NUL. *See* National Urban League
nullification **IV:**412*c,* 413*c*
  American System **IV:**20
  Clay, Henry **IV:**96
  Democratic Party **V:**109
  Drayton, William H. **IV:**127
  Fillmore, Millard **IV:**149
  Jackson, Andrew **IV:**207,
    208
  Memminger, Christopher
    G. **V:**259
  Nullification Controversy
    IV:282–283
  secession **V:**344
  Vesey, Denmark **IV:**388

  Virginia and Kentucky
    Resolutions **III:**424
  Webster, Daniel **IV:**393
  Whigs **IV:**397
Nullification Controversy **IV:282–
  283,** 413*c*
  Clay, Henry **IV:**96
  Drayton, William H. **IV:**127
  election of 1840 **IV:**137
  Jackson, Andrew **IV:**208
  Webster, Daniel **IV:**393
Nullification Crisis (1832–1833)
  V:343
Nullifiers **III:**291
Nunez, Jacob **II:**277
Nunn, Sam **X:**164
Nupe **I:**281
Nuremberg Laws **VIII:**169
Nuremberg Trials **VII:**165
Nurenberg Chronicle (Schedel)
  I:248
Nurse, Rebecca **II:275–276**
Nurse and Spy in the Union Army
  (Edmonds) **V:**134, 239
Nurse Corps, Army **VIII:**419
Nurse Corps, Navy **VIII:**418
nursery schools **VIII:**67
nurses **V:285–286**
  Bickerdyke, Mary Ann **V:**34
  Civil War **V:**74
  Cumming, Kate **V:**98
  disease/epidemics **V:**112
  homefront **V:**193
  ladies aid societies **V:**227,
    228
  medicine **V:**257, 258
  Tubman, Harriet **V:**394
  women's status and rights
    V:437
*Nursing and Nursing Education in
  the United States* (Goldmark)
  VII:127, 199
Nusbaum, Aaron **VI:**237
NUSJ (National Union for Social
  Justice) **VIII:**88
Nutimus **II:**405, 406
Nuttall, Thomas **III:**385
NWLB. *See* National War Labor
  Board
NWP. *See* National Woman's
  Party
NWPC. *See* National Women's
  Political Caucus
NWSA. *See* National Woman
  Suffrage Association
NWTUL. *See* National Women's
  Trade Union League
N. W. Ayer and Son **VII:**4
NYA. *See* National Youth
  Administration
NYC. *See* New York Central
  Railroad
Nye, Gerald P.
  America First Committee
    VIII:17
  antimonopoly **VIII:**23–24
  Neutrality Acts **VIII:**267

  Nye committee **VIII:**278,
    279
  Spanish civil war **VIII:**370
Nye, Russel B. **VI:**116
Nye committee **VIII:278–279**
  America First Committee
    VIII:17
  Congress **VIII:**80
  isolationists **VIII:**189
  Neutrality Acts **VIII:**267
NYPD Blue **X:**323, 343
nzimbu **I:**200
Nzinga (queen of Angola) **I:**237,
  274–275

O

"O, Tannenbaum" **V:**274
OAA. *See* Old-Age Assistance
Oacpicagigua, Luis **II:**294
OAI. *See* Old-Age Insurance
Oakes Ames Memorial Hall
  (North Easton, Massachusetts)
  VI:313
Oak Hall clothing store
  (Philadelphia, Pennsylvania)
  VI:381–382
Oakley, Annie
  Cody, William Frederick
    VI:77
  entertainment, popular
    VI:118
  Native Americans **VI:**263
  Sitting Bull **VI:**332
Oak Ridge, Tennessee
  Lilienthal, David E.
    VIII:217
  Manhattan Project **VIII:**227
  Oppenheimer, J. Robert
    IX:251
  Sunbelt **VIII:**381
  Tennessee Valley Authority
    VIII:393
Oak Ridge Cemetery (Springfield,
  Illinois) **V:**21
OAPEC (Organization of
  Arab Petroleum Exporting
  Countries) **X:**227
OAS. *See* Organization of
  American States
OASI (Old-Age and Survivors
  Insurance) **VIII:**365
Oates, William C. **V:287**
Oath of a Free-Man, The **II:**92,
  311
oath of fealty **I:**129
Oath of Office remarks (Ford)
  X:392–393
Oaxaca, Valley of **I:**250–251
oba **I:**29
Oba Ewuare (king of Benin) **I:**29
Obama, Barack Hussein **X:**263,
  263–264, 384*c*
  ABM Treaty **X:**28
  Afghanistan War **X:**12
  African Americans **X:**15

Biden, Joseph **X:**42
business **X:**61
campaign finance **X:**64
Clinton, Hillary Rodham
    X:79
conservation/
    environmentalism **X:**92
elections, presidential **X:**118
foreign policy **X:**144
global warming **X:**156
Internet **X:**183
Middle East **X:**230
Mitchell, George **X:**232
NAFTA **X:**259
race and race relations
    X:298
Senate, U.S. **X:**322
stem cell research **X:**336
Supreme Court **X:**339
Oberlin College
    Burns, Anthony **IV:**66
    education, higher **VI:**111
    Finney, Charles Grandison
        IV:151
    Foster, Abigail Kelley
        IV:161–162
    Langston, John Mercer
        VI:218
    Tappan, Arthur and Lewis
        IV:366
    Weld, Theodore Dwight
        IV:396
    women's colleges **VI:**398
obiter dictum **V:**117
"Objections to the Federal
    Constitution" (Mason) **III:**292
obscenity
    Brennan, William J., Jr. **X:**47
    censorship **X:**71
    pornography **X:**283, 284
    Supreme Court **X:**338
    television **X:**343
    White, Byron R. **X:**369
Observants **I:**133
*Observations of the Act of
    Parliament* (Quincy) **III:**354
obsidian **I:**365
obstruction of justice **X:**178
Ocala, Florida **VI:**272
OCCA. *See* Organized Crime
    Control Act
Occom, Samson **II:**412
occupational diseases **X:**264
occupational health and safety
    VII:243–244
    child labor **VII:**51–52
    Hamilton, Alice **VII:**133
    medicine **VII:**199
    mining **VII:**209
    public health **VII:**275
    steel industry **VII:**337
    Triangle Shirtwaist Fire
        VII:356–357
    workers' compensation
        VII:391–392
    Workmen's Compensation
        Act **VII:**392

Occupational Safety and Health
    Act (1970) **X:264,** 375*c*
Occupational Safety and Health
    Administration (OSHA) **X:**264
Occupational Safety and Health
    Review Commission (OSHRC)
    X:264
occupied territories **X:**227
OCD. *See* Office of Civil Defense;
    Office of Civilian Defense
oceanography **IV:**335; **VIII:**352
Ocean Parkway, Brooklyn, New
    York **VI:**120
Ochs, Adolph
    Bennett, James Gordon, Jr.
        VI:33
    journalism **VII:**159
    newspapers **VI:**267
Ockenga, Harold John **IX:**272;
    X:125
"O Come, All Ye Faithful" **V:**274
O'Connor, Harvey **VII:**286
O'Connor, Jessie **VII:**286
O'Connor, Sandra Day **X:264–
    265,** 265, 378*c*
    Kelo v. City of New London
        X:195
    Reagan, Ronald W. **X:**300
    Rehnquist, William H.
        X:305
    Roberts, John G. **X:**311
    Souter, David **X:**324
    Supreme Court **X:**339
    *Webster v. Reproductive
        Health Services* **X:**368
O'Connor, William **V:**431
Ocotelolco **I:**362
OCR (Office for Civil Rights) **X:**17
October Revolution **VII:**115, 308
October War (1973). *See* Arab-
    Israeli War (1973)
Octopus, The (Norris) **VII:**46, 179
Octoroon, The (Boucicault) **V:**387
Odd Fellows **VI:**333
Odell, Moses **V:**215
Oder River **VIII:**432, 439
Odets, Clifford **VIII:**218
Oduduwa **I:**281
OEO. *See* Office of Economic
    Opportunity
Of Cabbages and Kings (Henry)
    VII:404*c*
"Of Cannibals" (Montaigne)
    Brazil **I:**34
    cannibalism **I:**58
    Monardes, Nicholas **I:**247
Offenbach, Jacques **VI:**354
offensive-defensive warfare **V:**74,
    380, 381
Office for Civil Rights (OCR)
    X:17
Office of Bilingual and Minority
    Language Affairs **X:**42
Office of Censorship **VIII:**65,
    66, 286
Office of Civil Defense (OCD)
    IX:56, 57, 355*c*

Office of Civilian Defense (OCD)
    VIII:209, *281,* **281–282**
Office of Defense Mobilization
    IX:57
Office of Defense Transportation
    VIII:396
Office of Economic Opportunity
    (OEO)
    CAP **IX:**68
    Economic Opportunity Act
        (1964) **IX:**95
    Head Start **IX:**144
    Native Americans **IX:**242
    Rumsfeld, Donald **X:**312
    VISTA **IX:**333
    War on Poverty **IX:**335
Office of Economic Stabilization
    Byrnes, James F. **VIII:**60
    government **VIII:**154
    OPA **VIII:**282
    wage and price controls
        VIII:409
Office of Education **VIII:**107
Office of Emergency Planning
    IX:57
Office of Federal Contract
    Compliance **X:**9
Office of Government Ethics
    X:225
Office of Health and
    Environmental Research
    X:171
Office of Homeland Security
    (OHS) **X:**55, 167
Office of Information and
    Regulatory Affairs **X:**266
Office of Intergovernmental
    Affairs **X:**18
Office of Management and
    Budget (OMB) **X:**158, **266**
Office of National Drug Control
    Policy **X:**41, 244
Office of Naval Intelligence, U.S.
    (ONI)
    intelligence **VIII:**186
    Japanese Americans,
        relocation of **VIII:**193
    OSS **VIII:**284
Office of Price Administration
    (OPA) **VIII:282–283,** 447*c*
    black market **VIII:**46
    Congress **VIII:**81
    consumerism **IX:**76
    government **VIII:**154
    Henderson, Leon **VIII:**163–
        164
    labor/labor movements
        VIII:207
    mobilization **VIII:**242
    NWLB **VIII:**262
    rationing **VIII:**322
    wage and price controls
        VIII:409
    War Production Board
        VIII:414
    women's status and rights
        VIII:424

Office of Price Administration and
    Civilian Supply (OPACS)
    OPA **VIII:**282
    OPM **VIII:**283
    wage and price controls
        VIII:409
Office of Production Management
    (OPM) **VIII:283**
    Harriman, W. Averell
        VIII:161
    Hillman, Sidney **VIII:**166
    labor/labor movements
        VIII:207
    mobilization **VIII:**241
    Nelson, Donald M.
        VIII:266–267
Office of Public Opinion Research
    (Princeton University)
    VIII:313
Office of Radio Research (ORR)
    VIII:313
Office of Scientific Research
    and Development (OSRD)
    VIII:283–284
    atomic bomb **VIII:**34
    Bush, Vannevar **VIII:**56–57
    government **VIII:**154
    Manhattan Project
        VIII:226
    mobilization **VIII:**242
    World War II home front
        VIII:434
Office of Selective Service
    Records **VIII:**164
Office of Strategic Services (OSS)
    VIII:284–285, 285, 447*c*
    CIA **IX:**51
    espionage **VIII:**118
    intelligence **VIII:**187
Office of War Information (OWI)
    VIII:285–286, 447*c*
    advertising **VIII:**1
    art and architecture
        VIII:30
    Bureau of Motion Pictures
        VIII:55–56
    censorship **VIII:**66
    Four Freedoms **VIII:**144
    Lange, Dorothea **VIII:**210
    movies **VIII:**246
    news media **VIII:**272
    photography **VIII:**296
    popular culture **VIII:**303
    propaganda **VIII:**312
    public opinion polls
        VIII:313
Office of War Mobilization
    (OWM) **VIII:286–287**
    Byrnes, James F. **VIII:**60
    Congress **VIII:**81
    government **VIII:**154
    mobilization **VIII:**241, 242
    reconversion **VIII:**326
    War Manpower Commission
        VIII:413
    War Production Board
        VIII:414

Office of War Mobilization
and Reconversion (OWMR)
VIII:287
   mobilization **VIII:**242
   reconversion **VIII:**327
   War Manpower Commission
      VIII:413
Of Human Bondage (film)
   VIII:246
Of Mice and Men (Steinbeck)
   VIII:219, 374
Of Thee I Sing (Gershwin and
   Kaufman) **VII:**124; **VIII:**252
oga **I:**255
Ogburn, William Fielding
   VIII:323
Ogden Mills **VI:**21
Ogdensburg Declaration
   VIII:446*c*
Oglala Sioux Indians
   Black Hills gold rush **VI:**39
   Crazy Horse **VI:**85
   Red Cloud **VI:**303
   treaty rights **IX:**319
Oglethorpe, James Edward
   II:277, **277–278**
   Bosomworth, Mary
      Musgrove **II:**40
   Georgia **II:**145
   Tomochichi **II:**392
   War of Jenkins' Ear **II:**408–
      409
Oglethorpe Light Infantry **V:**81
Ogooue River **I:**255
Oh, Kay! (Gershwin) **VII:**124
O'Hair, Madalyn Murray **IX:**273
O'Hara, John **VIII:**189
Ohio **I:**167; **III:**460*c*, 464*c*
   abolitionism **IV:**4; **V:**1
   agriculture **IV:**10–12
   *Akron v. Akron Center for
      Reproductive Health*
      X:20–21
   anti-Masonry **IV:**25
   Appalachia **IX:**15
   Cass, Lewis **IV:**82–83
   Deseret, State of **IV:**119
   economy **IV:**130
   Fallen Timbers, Battle of
      III:161–162
   Finney, Charles Grandison
      IV:151
   Forty-niners **IV:**160
   Foster, Abigail Kelley **IV:**161
   fugitive slave laws **IV:**168
   governors **V:**171
   Greenville, Treaty of
      III:199–200
   Hanna, Marcus Alonzo
      VI:158
   Harrison, William Henry
      IV:185, 186
   Hayes, Rutherford B.
      VI:166, 168
   industrialization **IV:**201
   internal improvements
      IV:202

Johnson, Tom Loftin
   VII:156
Kent State protests **X:**197
Langston, John Mercer
   VI:218
Liberty Party **IV:**226
Mann, Horace **IV:**237
McCormick, Cyrus Hall
   IV:243
McGuffey, William Holmes
   IV:246
migration **IV:**254
Morgan, John Hunt **V:**269
National Road **IV:**271
Native Americans **IV:**273,
   274
Native Americans in the War
   of 1812 **IV:**276
oil **VI:**271
politics (1900–1928)
   VII:261
population trends **III:**343
railroads **IV:**314, 316
religion **IV:**318
rust belt **X:**314
St. Clair, Arthur **III:**378
slavery **IV:**344
Smith, Joseph, Jr. **IV:**352
sports and recreation
   VII:333
strikes **VIII:**377
Taft, Robert A. **VIII:**385
Underground Railroad
   V:397
Vallandigham, Clement L.
   V:413, 414
volunteer army **V:**419
WEAL **IX:**345
Weld, Theodore Dwight
   IV:396
Ohio Anti-Slavery Society **IV:**3
Ohio Central College **VII:**133
Ohio Company of Associates
   III:323
Ohio Company of Virginia
   II:278; **III:**292, **323**
Ohio Indians **II:**85
Ohio Life Insurance Company of
   Cincinnati **V:**121
Ohio River
   agriculture **IV:**12
   American Fur Company
      IV:19
   Astor, John Jacob **IV:**35
   Audubon, John James
      IV:37
   Fallen Timbers, Battle of
      III:161
   Fort Stanwix, Treaty of
      III:170
   Lovejoy, Elijah **IV:**230
   migration **IV:**253
   Missouri Compromise
      IV:257
   Ohio Company of Virginia
      III:323
   popular sovereignty **IV:**305

railroads **IV:**314
Tennessee Valley Authority
   VIII:392
transportation **V:**390
Ohio River Valley
   agriculture **IV:**12, 13
   American System **IV:**19
   banks **III:**42
   Blue Jacket **III:**54
   Blue Licks, Battle of **III:**54
   economy **IV:**130
   forts **II:**133
   Fort Stanwix, Treaty of
      III:170–171
   Franklin, William **III:**175
   fur trade **II:**141
   immigration **IV:**194–195
   Indian Removal Act **IV:**197,
      198
   migration **IV:**253
   National Road **IV:**271
   Native Americans **III:**312,
      314; **IV:**273
   Native Americans in the War
      of 1812 **IV:**277
   Paris, Treaty of (1763)
      III:331
   Pontiac's War **III:**339
   religion **III:**361
   Wayne, Anthony **III:**434
Ohio State Anti-Slavery Society
   VI:218
Ohio State University **VII:**330
Ohio University **IV:**246
*Ohio v.. Akron Center for
   Reproductive Health* **X:**20–21
Ohke Pueblo **I:**266, 327
Ohrlin, Glenn **IX:**121
OHS. *See* Office of Homeland
   Security
oil **X:**376*c*. *See also* gasoline
   business **X:**57–58
   conservation/
      environmentalism **X:**92
   energy **X:**120–121
   Energy, U.S. Department
      of **X:**122
   labor/labor movements
      X:202
   Middle East **IX:**214
   OPEC **X:**268
   Submerged Lands Act
      (1953) **IX:**305
   Sunbelt **X:**338
Oil! (Sinclair) **VII:**326
oil embargo (1973) **X:**376*c*
   automobile industry **X:**35
   economy **X:**109
   energy **X:**118–120
   Middle East **X:**227–228
   OPEC **X:**268
   wage and price controls
      X:363
oil industry **VI:271–272**, 272,
   407*c*; **VII:244–245**, *245*, 403*c*
   business **VIII:**58
   Cheney, Richard B. **X:**72

economy **VII:**85
   Fuel Administration
      VII:119
   Industrial Revolution,
      Second **VI:**191, 192
   New Unionism **VII:**237
   OPEC **X:**267–268
   Persian Gulf War **X:**273
   Rockefeller, John Davison
      VII:302–303
   Sherman Antitrust Act
      VI:330
   Standard Oil **VII:**335–336
   trusts **VI:**362
Ojeda, Alonso de **I:**277, 284
Ojibwa Indians **IV:**273; **V:**261,
   278
Ojo Caliente Reservation **VI:**17,
   143
Okeechobee, Lake, Battle of
   IV:339, 367–368
O'Keefe, Georgia **VI:**66; **VII:**25
Okeh Records **VII:**220
oki **I:**171
Okinawa **VIII:287–288**, 448*c*
   amphibious warfare **VIII:**20
   Eisenhower, Dwight D.
      IX:100
   Hiroshima and Nagasaki
      VIII:168
   Iwo Jima **VIII:**192
   Leyte Gulf, Battle for
      VIII:214
   Marines, U.S. **VIII:**230
   Navy, U.S. **VIII:**265
   Nimitz, Chester W.
      VIII:274
   Pyle, Ernie **VIII:**315
   tanks **VIII:**386
   World War II Pacific theater
      VIII:437
Oklahoma **VI:**410*c*; **VII:**404*c*. *See
   also* Indian Territory
   dust bowl **VIII:**97
   grandfather clause **VI:**152
   Guthrie, Woody **VIII:**160
   Jim Crow laws **VI:**204
   literature **VIII:**218
   Lone Wolf v. Hitchcock
      VII:185
   migration **IV:**254; **VIII:**239
   Native Americans **X:**250,
      251
   race and race relations
      VII:283
   socialism **VII:**327
   Sooners **VI:**339
   Taylor, Zachary **IV:**367
Oklahoma! (Rodgers and
   Hammerstein) **VIII:**252;
   IX:228
Oklahoma City bombing **X:**231,
   266, **266–267**, 346, 381*c*
Oklahoma City National
   Memorial **X:**267
O'Laughlin, Michael **V:**19
Olcott, Henry Steel **VI:**309

Old-Age, Survivors, and Disability Insurance (OASDI) **VIII:**365
Old-Age and Survivors Insurance (OASI) **VIII:**365
Old-Age Assistance (OAA) **VIII:**108, 363, 364, 453–454
Old-Age Insurance (OAI) **VIII:**445c
  elderly **VIII:**107–108
  New Deal **VIII:**269
  Perkins, Frances **VIII:**293
  Social Security Act **VIII:**364, 365
Old-Age Revolving Pensions, Ltd. **VIII:**394
"Old Briton" (La Demoiselle) **II:201**
Old Calvinism **III:**316, 317
Old Deluder Satan Act (Massachusetts School Act) **II:226**
Old-Fashioned Girl, An (Alcott) **VI:**10
Old Guard Republicans
  Cannon, Joseph Gurney **VII:**48
  elections **VII:**90, 91
  Republican Party **VII:**300
"old guard" socialists **VIII:**362
"Old Hundredth" **V:**273
Old Immigration **VI:**184
"Old Ironsides" **III:**108
"Old Lights"
  Connecticut **II:**78
  Great Awakening **II:**156
  Presbyterians **II:**309
  religion **III:**360
  Tennent, Gilbert **II:**388
Old North Church (Boston) **II:**25; **III:**264
Old Northwest. *See also* Great Lakes; Northwest Territory
  economy **IV:**130
  Free-Soil Party **IV:**164
  Ghent, Treaty of **IV:**175
  Harrison, William Henry **IV:**184–185
  Hull, William **IV:**192
  Liberty Party **IV:**226
  migration **IV:**253, 254
  Pike, Zebulon Montgomery **IV:**300
  Polk, James K. **IV:**302
  popular sovereignty **IV:**305
  Sac and Fox **IV:**327
  slavery **IV:**344
  Webster-Ashburton Treaty **IV:**394–395
Olds, Ransom E. **VII:**26
Old Settlers **IV:**85–86
Oldsmobile **VII:**26
Olds Motor Vehicle Company **IX:**132
Old South Church (Boston) **III:323–324**, 457
Old Southwest **IV:**1, 348
Old Spanish Trail **IV:**145

Old Stone Academy **IV:**246
Old Swimmin' Hole, The (Riley) **VI:**227
Old-Time Gospel Hour **X:**234, 342
Old Violin, The (Harnett) **VI:**184
Old West **VI:**376
Old World
  disease/epidemics **I:**107–109
  entertainment, popular **VI:**118
  James, Henry **VI:**200
  population trends **I:**297
"O Little Town of Bethlehem" (Brooks) **VI:**50
Olive Branch Petition **III:**189, **324**
Oliver, Andrew **III:324–325**
  liberty tree **III:**267
  Loyal Nine **III:**276
  MacIntosh, Ebenezer **III:**279
  Stamp Act **III:**396
Oliver, James **VI:**8
Oliver, Joe "King" **VII:**153, 219
Oliver, Robert **III:**414
Oliver Baptist Church **VIII:**335
Olivi, Giovanni Battista **I:**43
Olmecs **I:277–279, 278, 395c**
  art and architecture **I:**13
  Aztecs **I:**21
  cacao **I:**47
  Tabasco **I:**351
  Veracruz **I:**376
Olmstead v. United States **VII:**58, 409c
Olmsted, Frederick Law **V:287–288**
  art and architecture **IV:**31
  Brace, Charles Loring **VI:**45
  cities and urban life **V:**67
  conservation/environmentalism **VI:**81
  cotton culture **IV:**108
  environment **VI:**120
  U.S. Sanitary Commission **V:**411
  World's Columbian Exposition **VI:**402
Olmsted, John **VI:**45
Olney, Richard
  Bayard, Thomas Francis **VI:**28
  Debs, Eugene Victor **VII:**73
  Pullman Strike **VI:**297
  Venezuela boundary dispute **VI:**373
Olson, Culbert L. **VII:**213
Olustee, Battle of **V:**144
Olympic National Park (Washington State) **VIII:**115
Olympic Peninsula **IV:**146
Olympics (Athens, 1896) **VI:**359
Olympics (Atlanta, 1996) **IX:**10; **X:**346
Olympics (Beijing, 2008) **X:**384c

Olympics (Berlin, 1936) **VIII:**288–289, 303, 445c
Olympics (Los Angeles, 1932) **VIII:**372
Olympics (Los Angeles, 1984) **X:**69
Olympics (Mexico City, 1968) **IX:**42
Olympics (Moscow, 1980) **X:**69, 229, 378c
Olympics (Paris, 1900) **VI:**359
Olympics (Rome, 1960) **IX:**5, 9
Olympics (Seoul, 1988) **IX:**178
Omaha Beach **VIII:**276, 386
Omaha Indians **IV:**84; **VI:**199
Omaha platform **VI:272**
  Donnelly, Ignatius Loyola **VI:**100
  farmers' alliances **VI:**126
  People's Party **VI:**282
O'Mahoney, Joseph C. **VIII:**391
O'Malley, Walter **IX:**298, 354c
Omar, Mullah Muhammed **X:**10, 12, 383c
OMB. *See* Office of Management and Budget
omnibus **V:**66
Omnibus Act (1950) **IX:**210
Omnibus Crime Control and Safe Streets Act (1994) **X:**97
Omnibus Trade and Competitiveness Act (1988) **X:**140
Omni Hotel **X:**283
Omoo (Melville) **IV:**229
Onassis, Aristotle **IX:**169
Oñate, Juan de **I:**265–266, **279–280**, 327, 398c; **II:**263
"On Being Brought from Africa to America" (Wheatley) **III:**439
"On Cannibals" (Montaigne) **I:**247
"On Civil Liberty, Passive Obedience, and Nonresistance" (Boucher) **III:**59–60
"one-drop" standard **VII:**282, 301
100th Infantry Battalion (U.S. Army) **VIII:**194
114 Songs (Ives) **VII:**220
Oneida, New York **IV:**320
Oneida Indians **I:**280, 398c
  Iroquois **I:**185, 186
  Native Americans **III:**312–313
  Weiser, Johann Conrad **II:**409
Oneida Institute (Whitesboro, New York) **IV:**395; **VI:**87
Oneida Perfectionist Community **VI:**371
O'Neill, Eugene **VII:**408c; **VIII:**220, 445c
  entertainment, popular **VII:**95
  Greenwich Village **VII:**130–131
  Irish Americans **VIII:**189

  literature **VII:**179; **VIII:**220, 220; **IX:**193
  modernism **VII:**212
  Robeson, Paul **VIII:**341
  Vorse, Mary Heaton **VII:**375
O'Neill, Thomas "Tip" P., Jr. **X:**169, 170, 199, **267**, 377c
ONE magazine **IX:**131, 132
"one person, one vote" **IX:**34; **X:**48
One World (Willkie) **VIII:**417
ONI. *See* Office of Naval Intelligence, U.S.
Onís, Luis de **IV:**6
Only Method of Attracting Everyone to the True Religion (Del único modo de atraer a todos los pueblos a la verdader religión) (Las Casas) **I:**206
Onondaga **I:**185, 186, **280–281**, 398c; **II:**180
OnStar system **X:**320
Ontario
  Canada **III:**79
  Loyalists **III:**276
  Native Americans **IV:**274
Ontario, Lake **I:**185
  Canada **III:**77
  Chauncey, Isaac **III:**86
  Clinton, George **III:**98
  Lake Erie, Battle of **IV:**220
  War of 1812 **IV:**391
"On the Compromise of 1850" (Clay) **IV:446**
"On the Constitution" (Franklin) **III:**463c
"On the Equilibrium of Heterogeneous Substances" (Gibbs) **VI:**144, 325
On the Geology and Natural History of the Upper Missouri (Hayden) **VI:**164
"On the Jews and Their Lies" (Luther) **I:**219
On the Origin of Species (Darwin)
  Darwinism and religion **VI:**92
  evolution **VI:**122
  race and race relations **IV:**311
  religion **VI:**306
  Social Darwinism **VI:**334
"On the Question of Slavery" (McDuffie) **IV:**413c
On the Road (Kerouac) **IX:**354c
  Beat Generation **IX:**36, 37
  counterculture **IX:**78
  Kerouac, Jack **IX:**173
  literature **IX:**194
On the Waterfront (film)
  cold war culture **IX:**65
  movies **IX:**224
  union movement **IX:**323
On Wings of Eagles (Follett) **X:**273
OPA. *See* Office of Price Administration

OPACS. *See* Office of Price
Administration and Civilian
Supply
Opana Mobile Radar Unit, Hawaii
VIII:292
op art **X:**30
OPEC. *See* Organization of
Petroleum Exporting Countries
Opechancanough **II:278–279,**
435c, 436c
ethnocentrism **II:**122
Native Americans **II:**252
Powhatan Confederacy
II:307, 308
Virginia **II:**399, 400
Open Door notes **VI:272–273,**
412c
foreign policy **VII:**113
Hay, John Milton **VI:**164
imperialism **VI:**188
Mahan, Alfred Thayer
VI:236
McKinley, William **VI:**241
Open Door Policy **VII:**246
Open Door Policy **VII:245–246,**
403c, 405c, 408c
Boxer Rebellion **VII:**40, 41
foreign policy **VII:**113
Great White Fleet **VII:**130
Hughes, Charles Evans
VII:142
Root-Takahira Agreement
VII:305
trade, domestic and foreign
VII:354
Washington Conference
on Naval Disarmament
VII:379
open-heart surgery **VIII:**234
open-pit mining **VI:**246
open shop movement **VII:247**
American Plan **VII:**14
Farmer-Labor Party
VII:105
labor/labor movements
VII:170–171
NAM **VII:**226
NWLB **VII:**229
Seattle General Strike
VII:317
opera **VIII:**251; **X:**238
operating systems **X:**87,
147–148
Operation Barbarossa **VIII:**431
Operation Bingo **IX:**250
Operation Bolero **VIII:**355
Operation Bootstrap **IX:**185, 267,
351c
Operation Breadbasket (Chicago)
X:191
Operation Cooperation **X:**226
Operation Desert Shield **X:**273
Operation Desert Storm
Bush, George H. W. **X:**53
Persian Gulf War **X:**273
Powell, Colin L. **X:**286
Operation Dirty Trick **IX:**250

Operation Dixie **IX:249–250,**
351c
Operation Enduring Freedom
X:10, 11
Operation Good Times **IX:**250
Operation Husky **VIII:**360
Operation Intercept **X:**226
Operation Iraqi Freedom **X:**187,
188
Operation Just Cause. *See*
Panama, U.S. invasion of
Operation Midnight Climax
IX:195
Operation Mongoose **IX:**36, 80,
81, **250**
Operation Musketeer Revise
IX:307
Operation Neptune **VIII:**276
Operation Overlord
Eisenhower, Dwight D.
IX:100
Higgins, Andrew J.
VIII:165
Normandy, invasion of
VIII:275
second front **VIII:**355
Teheran Conference
VIII:390, 391
Operation PUSH (People United
to Serve Humanity) **X:**191,
192
Operation Rescue **X:**289
Operation Roundup **VIII:**355
Operation Sledgehammer
VIII:355
Operation Torch
Eisenhower, Dwight D.
IX:100
North African campaign
VIII:277
World War II European
theater **VIII:**431
Operation Zapata **IX:**36
operettas
entertainment, popular
VII:95
music **VI:**257
Sousa, John Philip **VI:**340
theater **VI:**354
O Pioneers! (Cather) **VII:**179
opium
Afghanistan War **X:**12
narcotics **X:**242
Narcotics Act **VII:**221, 222
OPM. *See* Office of Production
Management
Oppenheimer, J. Robert
VIII:447c; **IX:250–251**
atomic bomb **VIII:**34
Hiroshima and Nagasaki
VIII:166
hydrogen bomb **IX:**152
Manhattan Project *VIII:*226,
227
Opportunity (journal) **VII:**136
opportunity liberalism **X:**208
oral contraception. *See* "The Pill"

Oral Roberts Evangelical
Association **X:**342
oral tradition
Crow **II:**85
Cuzco **I:**101
Dagomba **I:**103
Iroquois **I:**186
literature **II:**205–206
Mbundu **I:**237
Mossi **I:**252–253
Native American religion
I:261
Oyo **I:**281
Yoruba **I:**389
Oran, Algeria **VIII:**431
Orange Bowl **VIII:**371
Orange County, New York
III:127
Orange County, North Carolina
III:321
Orange Plank Road **V:**432
Oranyan **I:**281
*Oration on the Abolition of the
Slave Trade, An* (Williams)
IV:402
Orchard Knob **V:**63
Orchestra Hall (Chicago, Illinois)
VII:219
orchestras **VI:**254
Ord, Edward O. C. **V:**14
Order of Cincinnati **III:**248,
260–261
order of extermination **IV:**353
Orders in Council **III:325–326**
Berlin Decree **III:**49
Bonaparte, Napoleon **III:**55
embargo of 1807 **III:**152
foreign affairs **III:**169
Free Trade and Sailor's
Rights **IV:**165
Milan Decree **III:**297
Ordinance of 1784 **III:**233, 321
Ordinance of 1785 **III:**462c
education, federal aid to
VI:110
Northwest Ordinances
III:321–322
popular sovereignty **IV:**306
public land policy **IV:**304,
307
Ordinance of 1787 **III:**321, 322
Ordinance of Nullification **IV:**388
Ordinance of Secession (Alabama)
V:146
Ordinance of Secession (South
Carolina) **V:**146
Ordinances of Discovery and
Settlement of 1573 **I:**207
Ordnance, Bureau of **V:**101
Oregon **IV:**411c
Adams, John Quincy **IV:**5
Adams-Onís Treaty **IV:**6
Applegate, Jesse **IV:**26
Ashley, William Henry **IV:**31
Astoria **IV:**35
Bates, Edward **V:**30
Deseret, State of **IV:**120

disease/epidemics **IV:**123
economy **IV:**132
exploration **IV:**144, 145
foreign policy **IV:**154, 155
Fort Vancouver **IV:**158–
159
Frémont, John C. **IV:**166
fur trade **IV:**171
Hastings, Lansford W.
IV:187
Japanese Americans,
relocation of **VIII:**193
Kelley, Florence **VII:**164
Lee, Jason **IV:**224
Manifest Destiny **IV:**234
Massachusetts Emigrant Aid
Society **IV:**242–243
McLoughlin, John **IV:**248
migration **IV:**254, 255
Monroe Doctrine **IV:**261
Muller v. Oregon **VII:**217,
218
Native Americans **IV:**275
Oregon Boundary Treaty
IV:439–440
Oregon Trail **IV:**285
Oregon Treaty of 1846
IV:286
Polk, James K. **IV:**302
Rocky Mountain Fur
Company **IV:**325
Smith, Jedediah Strong
IV:351
Supreme Court **VII:**343
Villard, Henry **VI:**375
Webster-Ashburton Treaty
IV:394
Whitman, Marcus **IV:**398,
399
Whitman, Narcissa **IV:**398
Wilkes expedition **IV:**400
Wyeth, Nathaniel J. **IV:**406
Oregon, USS **VIII:**210
Oregon Boundary Treaty **IV:439–
440**
Oregon & California Railroad
VI:375
Oregon City, Oregon **IV:**187, 285
Oregon Joint Occupation Treaty
IV:248
Oregon Steam and Navigation
Company **VI:**375
Oregon Steamship Company
VI:375
Oregon Trail **IV:285–286,** 414c
California **IV:**71
California Trail **IV:**77
Columbia River **IV:**103
exploration **IV:**145
Fort Laramie **IV:**156–157
Fort Leavenworth **IV:**158
Forty-niners **IV:**159
Frémont, John C. **IV:**166
Lee, Jason **IV:**224–225
McLoughlin, John **IV:**248
migration **IV:**254–255
Mormon Trail **IV:**261, 262

mountain men **IV**:267
Native Americans **IV**:275
Smith, Jedediah Strong
IV:350
Oregon Trail, The (Parkman)
VI:277
Oregon Treaty (1846) **IV**:286–
288, 288*m*, 414*c*
Adams-Onís Treaty **IV**:6
Clayton-Bulwer Treaty **IV**:98
economy **IV**:130
exploration **IV**:146
foreign policy **IV**:155
Fort Laramie **IV**:157
Fort Vancouver **IV**:159
Manifest Destiny **IV**:234
Polk, James K. **IV**:302
Washington, Treaty of
VI:385
Oregon v. Mitchell **X**:23
O'Reilly, Bill **X**:220
O'Reilly, Leonora **VII**:231
Orellana, Francisco de **I**:9, 34
Organic Act (1884) **IX**:8
Organic Act (1897) **VI**:82
Organic Act, Second (1912) **IX**:8
Organization of American States
(OAS) **VI**:276; **IX**:184, 352*c*;
X:204–206
Organization of Arab Petroleum
Exporting Countries (OAPEC)
X:227
Organization of Petroleum
Exporting Countries (OPEC)
X:267–268, 376*c*
automobile industry **X**:35
economy **X**:109
energy **X**:118, 120, 121
labor/labor movements
X:202
Middle East **X**:227
wage and price controls
X:363
organized crime **X**:96, 97, 298–
299, 375*c*
Organized Crime Control Act
(OCCA) **X**:97, 298, 375*c*
organized labor. *See* labor and
labor movements; labor unions
organs, artificial **X**:224, 320
organ transplants **X**:224
Original Dixieland Jazz Band
VII:219
Origin of Species (Darwin). *See*
On the Origin of Species
O'Riley, Peter **IV**:105
Orinoco River
Carib **I**:60
Columbus, Christopher
I:86
Venezuela boundary dispute
VI:373
Oriskany, Battle of **III**:63, 237
Orlando, Vittorio **VII**:369
Orleans Territory **IV**:94, 305
Orlon **IX**:91
Ormiston, Kenneth **VII**:197

Ormond (Brown) **III**:64
Ornithological Biography, The
(Audubon) **IV**:38
ornithology **IV**:335
Ornitz, Samuel **IX**:147, *148*
Orphan Brigade **V**:42, **288**
Orphans of the Storm (film)
VII:132
"orphan trains" **VI**:45–46
Orpheum Circuit **VI**:117
Orphir mine **IV**:105
ORR (Office of Radio Research)
VIII:313
Ortega, Daniel **X**:255
Orteig, Raymond **VII**:177
Orthodox Judaism **VI**:308;
VII:298; **VIII**:334; **X**:193, 307
OS/2 operating system **X**:147
Osage Indians **IV**:87, 88, 300
Osage Mission, Kansas **VI**:220
Osawatomie, Kansas **VII**:237
Osbon, B. S. **V**:217
Osborn, Alex **VII**:5
Osborn, Fairfield **IX**:108
Osborn, Henry F. **VI**:242
Osborn, Sarah Haggar Wheaten
II:279
Osborne, Sir Edward **I**:213
Osceola (Seminole chief) **IV**:289,
289, 413*c*
Native Americans **IV**:274
Seminole **IV**:338
Seminole War, First/Second
IV:339
Van Buren, Martin **IV**:386
Osceola Consolidated Mining
Company **VII**:210
Osei Tutu (Asante king) **I**:13–14
OSHA (Occupational Safety and
Health Administration) **X**:264
OSHRC (Occupational Safety and
Health Review Commission)
X:264
Osler, William, Sir **VI**:148
Osmond, Henry **IX**:195
OSRD. *See* Office of Scientific
Research and Development
OSS. *See* Office of Strategic
Services
Ossali, Giovanni Angelo **IV**:169
Ostenaco **II**:280
Ostend Manifesto **V**:289, **289–290**
Buchanan, James **V**:47, 48
Cuba **IV**:112
foreign policy **V**:149
Osterhaus, Peter **V**:166
Ostfriesland (German battleship)
VII:212
O'Sullivan, John **IV**:155, 234–236
O'Sullivan, Mary Kenney **VII**:230
O'Sullivan, Timothy H. **V**:41, 304
Oswald, Lee Harvey **IX**:251–252,
252, 356*c*
assassinations **IX**:22
journalism **IX**:165
Kennedy, John F. **IX**:171
Warren, Earl **IX**:337

Otermín, Antonio de **II**:318
Othello (Shakespeare) **VIII**:341,
342, 448*c*
Other America, The (Harrington)
IX:355*c*
CAP **IX**:68
economy **IX**:98
Great Society **IX**:139
Harrington, Michael **IX**:142
War on Poverty **IX**:335
Other People's Money (Brandeis)
VII:41
Other Voices, Other Rooms
(Capote) **IX**:194
Otis, Elisha **IV**:91, 333; **VI**:196,
410*c*
Otis, Harrison Gray **III**:221, **326**
Otis, James, Jr. **II**:224; **III**:326–
327, 459*c*
antislavery **III**:25–26
Hutchinson, Thomas
III:219
Otis, Harrison Gray **III**:326
Revere, Paul **III**:366
Warren, Mercy Otis **III**:427
writs of assistance **III**:448–
449
Otis, James, Sr. **III**:219
Otoe Indians **IV**:84
Ottawa Indians **II**:35; **IV**:192,
273; **V**:278
Otto, Bodo **III**:17
Ottoman Empire
foreign policy **VII**:114–115
Jews **I**:196
Middle East **IX**:214
Suleiman I **I**:349–350
Ouagadougou **I**:252, 253
Ould, Robert **V**:314
Our American Cousin (Taylor)
VI:202
*Our Country: Its Possible Future
and Its Present Crisis* (Strong)
VI:409*c*
imperialism **VI**:188
Social Gospel **VI**:335
Strong, Josiah **VI**:346–347
Our Land and Land Policy
(George) **VI**:142
Our Plundered Planet (Osborn)
IX:108
"Outcasts of Poker Flat" (Harte)
VI:162
Outcault, Richard **VI**:405;
VII:138
Outdoor Resources Review
Commission **IX**:344
Outerbridge, Mary **VI**:342
Outlines of Cosmic Philosophy
(Fiske) **VI**:408*c*
Darwinism and religion
VI:93
Fiske, John **VI**:129
religion **VI**:306
out-migration **VI**:216–217
out-of-wedlock births **X**:214

ouvidor **I**:35
Oval Office tapes. *See* White
House tapes
Ovando, Nicolás de **I**:86
Overhill family **II**:28–29
Overland campaign **V**:290–291
Cold Harbor, Battle of
V:76–77
Ewell, Richard Stoddert
V:136
Gordon, John B. **V**:170
Grant, Ulysses S. **V**:174
Harvard Regiment **V**:187
homefront **V**:193
Lee, Robert E. **V**:231
Lincoln, Abraham **V**:237
Spotsylvania, Battles of
V:367–368
Stuart, J. E. B. **V**:376
Union army **V**:403
Wilderness, Battle of the
V:432
overland mail **IV**:158, **289–291**,
290
Overland Mail Company **IV**:290–
291
Overland Monthly **VI**:162
Overland Trail **IV**:144
overpopulation **X**:1, 43
overproduction **X**:9–10
over-the-counter medicines **X**:244
Overton Act **VII**:291
Oviedo y Valdés, Gonzalo
Fernández de **I**:281
Bermuda **I**:30
Linschoten, Jan Huygen van
I:214
pearl diving **I**:287–288
Ramusio, Giovanni Battista
I:313
Ovington, Mary White **VI**:384·
Owen, Chandler **VIII**:321
Owen, Robert **IV**:291–292
industrialization **IV**:201
religion **IV**:320
Warren, Josiah **IV**:392
Wright, Fanny **IV**:405
Owen, Ruth Bryan **VIII**:421, 422
Owens, Jesse **VIII**:288, **288–289**,
445*c*
African Americans **IX**:5
popular culture **VIII**:303
sports and recreation
VIII:372
OWI. *See* Office of War
Information
OWM. *See* Office of War
Mobilization
OWMR. *See* Office of War
Mobilization and Reconversion
Ox-Bow Trail **IV**:145
Oxenham, John **I**:285
Oxford, Mississippi **VIII**:128
Oxford, Ohio **IV**:246
Oxford University **VIII**:224
Oxley, Michael G. **X**:315
Oya (goddess) **I**:271

Oyo kingdom **I:**125, **281–282,** 389
Ozawa, Jisaburo **VIII:**295
Ozma, Agnes **VII:**298
Ozment, Steven **I:**218
Ozzie and Harriet Show, The
   cold war culture **IX:**65
   marriage and family **IX:**202
   popular culture **IX:**259

P

P-47 Thunderbolt bomber **VIII:**16
P-51 Mustang escort fighters **VIII:**16, 47–48
PA (Palestinian Authority) **X:**230
Pabst, Daniel **VI:**19
PAC (Presidential Advisory Committee) **VIII:**330
Paca, William **III:**105
Pace v. Alabama **V:**261
Pachacuti (Inca emperor) **I:**179, 221–222
Pacific Coast
   Adams, John Quincy **IV:**5
   American Fur Company **IV:**18
   Astor, John Jacob **IV:**33, 34
   Astoria **IV:**35
   cities and urban life **VIII:**68
   exploration **IV:**146
   foreign policy **IV:**153
   Forty-niners **IV:**159
   fur trade **IV:**171
   migration **IV:**254; **VIII:**239, 240
   Native Americans **IV:**273
   overland mail **IV:**289–290
   Perry, Matthew Calbraith **IV:**298
   popular sovereignty **IV:**307
   population trends **VIII:**305
   technology **VIII:**397
   Wilkes expedition **IV:**400
Pacific Coast Defense League **VII:**213
Pacific Coast League **VIII:**95
Pacific Crest Trail **IX:**239
Pacific Fleet, U.S. **VIII:**447*c*
   Navy, U.S. **VIII:**265
   Nimitz, Chester W. **VIII:**274
   World War II Pacific theater **VIII:**435
Pacific Fur Company
   American Fur Company **IV:**18
   Astor, John Jacob **IV:**34
   Astoria **IV:**35
   Columbia River **IV:**102
   fur trade **III:**183
Pacific Grove Mission **VII:**342
Pacific Islanders **X:**33, 282
Pacific Islands **VI:**122

Pacific Northwest **IV:**414*c*
   Adams-Onís Treaty **IV:**6
   American Fur Company **IV:**18
   Astor, John Jacob **IV:**34, 35
   Astoria **IV:**35, 36
   Boas, Franz Uri **VII:**39
   Canada **VI:**61
   Democratic Party **IV:**118
   exploration **IV:**146
   Fort Vancouver **IV:**158, 159
   fur trade **IV:**170
   Kaiser, Henry J. **VIII:**199
   McLoughlin, John **IV:**247, 248
   Monroe Doctrine **IV:**260
   Northern Securities Case **VII:**241
   Oregon Treaty of 1846 **IV:**286
   Villard, Henry **VI:**375
   Whitman, Marcus **IV:**398
Pacific Ocean **VII:**408*c*
   Adams-Onís Treaty **IV:**6
   Balboa, Vasco Núñez de **I:**26
   Clark, William **III:**96
   Eads, James Buchanan **VI:**103
   Essex, USS **IV:**143
   evolution **VI:**122
   exploration **IV:**146
   imperialism **VI:**187
   King, Ernest J. **VIII:**202
   Lewis, Meriwether **III:**262
   Lewis and Clark Expedition **III:**262, 263
   Leyte Gulf, Battle for **VIII:**214
   Magellan, Ferdinand **I:**223, 224
   Mariana Islands **VIII:**228
   Midway, Battle of **VIII:**238
   Oregon Treaty of 1846 **IV:**286
   Panama **I:**284
   Panama Canal **VII:**250
   Wilkes expedition **IV:**400
Pacific Railroad Act (1862) **V:**293–294, 444*c*, **458–460**
   Congress **V:**89
   Crédit Mobilier **V:**96
   economy **V:**123
   Republican Party **V:**333
Pacific Railroad Company **IV:**131, 200
Pacific Railroad of Missouri **V:**293, 294
Pacific Railway Act **VI:**180, 228
pacifism
   Baldwin, Roger Nash **VII:**31
   Lee, Ann **III:**257
   Moravians **III:**302
   peace movements **V:**295
   Quakers **III:**351
   Society of Friends **V:**364–365

Packard, Vance **IX:**253–254, 354*c*
   business **IX:**47
   consumerism **IX:**76
   literature **IX:**194
Packwood, Bab **X:**321
PACs. *See* political action committees
Pact of Paris **VII:**409*c*
Padilla, Juan de **I:**168
Padres, José María **IV:**148–149
Paducah, Kentucky **VIII:**392
Page, Thomas Nelson **V:**245
Page, William **V:**40
Paige, Satchel **VII:**335; **VIII:**370
Paik, Nam June **X:**31
Paine, H. E. **VI:**387
Paine, John Knowles **VI:**254
Paine, Lewis **V:**19–21, 348
Paine, Thomas **II:**240–241; **III:329–330,** *330,* 461*c*
   antislavery **III:**26
   artisans **III:**35
   Barlow, Joel **III:**46
   Burke, Edmund **III:**69
   Common Sense **III:**101–103
   corporatism **III:**122
   deism **III:**135
   Franklin, Benjamin **III:**174
   literature **III:**268
   Morse, Jedidiah **III:**307
   republicanism **III:**365
   resistance movement **III:**366
painting **III:**462*c*; **VI:275–276,** 409*c*
   art **II:**26, 27; **III:**32; **VI:**18–19
   Ashcan School **VII:**26
   Bierstadt, Albert **VI:**36–38
   Copley, John Singleton **III:**118
   Eakins, Thomas **VI:**103–105
   Feke, Robert **II:**125
   Homer, Winslow **VI:**173–175
   Peale, Charles Willson **III:**332–333
   Remington, Frederic **VI:**310
   Ryder, Albert Pinkham **VI:**319–320
   Sargent, John Singer **VI:**323–324
   Stuart, Gilbert **III:**399–400
   Theus, Jeremiah **II:**389–390
   Tiffany, Louis Comfort **VI:**356
   Trumbull, John **III:**416–417
   West, Benjamin **III:**435–436
   Whistler, James Abbott McNeill **VI:**388–390
Paiute Indians **VI:**410*c*
   Donner party **IV:**125
   Mormon Church **VI:**252
   Winnemucca, Sarah **VI:**397, 398

Pakenham, Edward **IV:**281
Pakistan **IX:**353*c*
   Afghanistan War **X:**10–11
   Bourke-White, Margaret **VIII:**50
   nuclear proliferation **X:**261
   Powell, Colin L. **X:**287
   SEATO **IX:**291, 292
   UN **VIII:**403
Palace of the Sun **I:**101–102
Palace of Versailles (Paris, France) **VII:**369
Palace Theater (New York City) **VI:**117
Palacios Rubios, Juan López de **I:**318, 379, **409–410**
Palaus Islands **VIII:**274
palazzi **I:**375
Palenque (Mayan city-state) **I:283,** 359
palenques (escaped slave communities) **II:**374
Paleo-Indians **I:**395*c*; **II:**17, 269
paleontology
   Marsh, Othniel Charles **VI:**239, 240
   science and technology **VI:**325
   Walcott, Charles Doolittle **VI:**379
Paleontology of the Eureka District (Walcott) **VI:**379
Palermo, Sicily **VIII:**360
Palestine **I:**303; **IX:**352*c*; **X:**382*c*
   Bunche, Ralph **IX:**45
   Bush, George W. **X:**56
   Clinton, William J. **X:**83
   Israel **IX:**160
   Jews **VIII:**195
   Lazarus, Emma **VI:**219
   Middle East **IX:**214; **X:**227–230
   Mitchell, George **X:**232
   Zionism **VIII:**441
Palestine Implementation Commission **IX:**45
Palestine Liberation Organization (PLO)
   Camp David accords **X:**66
   Habib, Philip C. **X:**163
   Middle East **X:**229, 230
   terrorism **X:**346
Palestinian Authority (PA) **X:**230
Paley Center for Media **IX:**316
Palfrey, John **IV:**210
Palfrey, Sarah **VIII:**372
Palin, Sarah **X:***119,* 384*c*
Palladio, Andrea **II:**25
Palmeiro, Rafael **X:**330
Palmer, Alexander Mitchell **VII:249,** 408*c*
   anticommunism **VIII:**22
   civil liberties **VII:**58
   Communist Party **VII:**61
   Coolidge, Calvin John **VII:**64
   Democratic Party **VII:**75

elections **VII**:91
Fuel Administration **VII**:119
labor/labor movements **VII**:171
New Unionism **VII**:238
radicalism **VII**:288
Red Scare **VII**:296
Russian Revolution **VII**:308
socialism **VII**:328
Trading with the Enemy Act **VII**:355
women's status and rights **VII**:389
Palmer, Arnold **X**:332
Palmer, Bertha **VI**:165, 166
Palmer, John M. **V**:317; **VI**:193
Palmer, Nathaniel Brown **IV**:146, 411*c*
Palmer, Phoebe **IV**:317
Palmer Raids **VII**:308
Palmetto State **V**:344, 345
Palomar Observatory (California) **IX**:296
Pamunkey Indians
Native Americans **V**:278
Opechancanough **II**:278, 279
Powhatan Confederacy **II**:308
Pan-Africanism **VI**:87; **VII**:81
Panama **I**:283–285; **IV**:414*c*; **VII**:404*c*, 406*c*
Balboa, Vasco Núñez de **I**:26
Columbus, Christopher **I**:86
disease/epidemics **IV**:122
Drake, Sir Francis **I**:111, 112
foreign policy **VII**:114
Forty-niners **IV**:159, 160
Grijalva, Juan de **I**:145
Latin America **IX**:184
Panama Canal **VII**:250
Pizarro, Francisco **I**:292
presidency **VII**:268
smallpox **I**:341
Panama, U.S. invasion of (1989–1990) **X**:269–270, 270, 379*c*
Bush, George H. W. **X**:52
defense policy **X**:101
Latin America **X**:205
Powell, Colin L. **X**:286
Panama Canal **VII**:250, **250–251**, 403*c*, 404*c*, 406*c*; **VIII**:446*c*
Big Stick diplomacy **VII**:34
Eads, James Buchanan **VI**:103
foreign policy **V**:151; **VII**:114
Hay, John Milton **VI**:164
NAM **VII**:225
Roosevelt, Theodore **VII**:304

Panama Canal, U.S. turnover of **X**:139, 141, **270–271**, 377*c*, 382*c*
Panama Canal Treaty **X**:69, 271
Panama Canal Zone
Good Neighbor policy **VIII**:151
Latin America **IX**:184; **X**:205
Panama Canal turnover **X**:270–271
Panama invasion (1989–1990) **X**:269
Panama Defense Forces (PDF) **X**:269
Pan-American Conference (1889) **VI**:161; **X**:204
Pan-American Conference (1933) **VIII**:151, 180
Pan-American Exposition **VII**:**251–252**, 252, 403*c*
Pan-Americanism **VI**:41
Pan American Petroleum and Transportation Company **VII**:351
Pan-American Union **VI**:**276–277**
Pan-American Union Building (Washington, D.C.) **VI**:62
Pan American World Airways **VII**:179; **IX**:319
Pan Am flight 103 (Lockerbie bombing) **X**:16, 345, 379*c*, 383*c*
Panay, USS **VIII**:141, 225
Pancoast, Henry S. **VI**:190
panic of 1792 **III**:**330–331**, 463*c*
panic of 1819 **IV**:**293–294**
agriculture **IV**:13
Alamo, The **IV**:14
American System **IV**:19
Ashley, William Henry **IV**:31
Audubon, John James **IV**:37
Austin, Moses **IV**:39
banking **IV**:46
Bank of the United States, Second **IV**:48
Benton, Thomas Hart **IV**:53
business cycles **VI**:58
economy **IV**:132
Era of Good Feelings **IV**:141
industrialization **IV**:200
labor/labor movements **IV**:217, 219
migration **IV**:254
popular sovereignty **IV**:305
public land policy **IV**:305
Texas **IV**:371
Travis, William Barret **IV**:379
Turner, Nat **IV**:380
panic of 1837 **IV**:**294–295**
banking **IV**:46
Bank of the United States, Second **IV**:48
Brown, John **V**:43

business cycles **VI**:58
Caroline affair **IV**:81
Deere, John **IV**:115
economy **IV**:132
election of 1840 **IV**:138
Florida **IV**:153
Harrison, William Henry **IV**:186
industrialization **IV**:200
internal improvements **IV**:202
labor/labor movements **IV**:218, 219
marriage and family **IV**:240
McCormick, Cyrus Hall **IV**:243
Tappan, Arthur and Lewis **IV**:366
Van Buren, Martin **IV**:386
Whigs **IV**:397
Yancey, William Lowndes **V**:439
panic of 1857 **V**:294
Cooke, Jay **V**:93
economy **IV**:132; **V**:121
employment **V**:132
Republican Party **IV**:323
panic of 1869 **V**:446*c*
panic of 1873 **VI**:407*c*–408*c*, 411*c*
business cycles **VI**:58
Cooke, Jay **V**:93
Crazy Horse **VI**:85
economy **V**:124
entertainment, popular **VI**:116
Grant, Ulysses S. **V**:175
Leslie, Frank and Miriam Florence Follin **VI**:221
National Labor Union **V**:276
Reconstruction **V**:326
Villard, Henry **VI**:375
panic of 1884 **VI**:58
panic of 1893
business cycles **VI**:58, 59
Coxey's Army **VI**:84
currency issue **VI**:89
Democratic Party **VI**:95; **VII**:74
presidential campaigns (1870–1899) **VI**:293
Republican Party **VI**:311
tariffs **VI**:353
Villard, Henry **VI**:375
World's Columbian Exposition **VI**:403
panic of 1907 **VI**:251; **VII**:107
pan-Indian movement
Greenville, Treaty of **III**:200
Native Americans **III**:312
Tecumseh **III**:409
Tippecanoe, Battle of **III**:411
Wayne, Anthony **III**:434
Pankhurst, Emmeline **VII**:385
Panoplist, The **III**:307

Panzer divisions **VIII**:385–386
Paoli, Battle of **III**:433
papacy **I**:379
Papago **II**:176
papal bull(s) **I**:367–368
Papal Bull Inter Caetera of 1493 **I**:**400–402**
paper **I**:**285–286**
book, the **I**:33
Codex Mendoza **I**:77
printing press **I**:302
Papua New Guinea **VIII**:365, 435
Paracelsus **II**:229
Paradise Valley (Detroit, Michigan) **VII**:344
Paradise Valley (New England Pasture Land) (La Farge) **VI**:217
Paraguay **II**:238; **X**:206
Paramount Pictures **IX**:223
Paramount Records **VII**:39
Paramount Theater, New York City **VIII**:361
Parchman Penitentiary **IX**:49
Pardo, Juan **I**:80, 89
pardons, presidential **X**:377*c*
Ford, Gerald R. **X**:138–139
impeachment of Richard M. Nixon **X**:178
Reconstruction **V**:325
Paré, Ambroise
cabinet of curiosities **I**:43
monsters **I**:248–249
Monstres et Prodigies (excerpt) **I**:**412–413**
Paredes, Mariano **IV**:252
parental consent **X**:3, 4, 20–21
parental guidelines **X**:280
Parham, Charles **VII**:298
Paris, France **I**:80; **VII**:448*c*
Bodmer, Karl **IV**:61
Cassatt, Mary **VI**:63
demobilization (WWII) **VIII**:91
Eakins, Thomas **VI**:104
Eliot, Charles William **VI**:113
Evans, Walker **VIII**:119
Johnson, Jack **VII**:155
Kellogg-Briand Treaty **VII**:164
medicine **IV**:249
Open Door Notes **VI**:272–273
Tarbell, Ida Minerva **VII**:349
Versailles, Treaty of **VII**:370
Vorse, Mary Heaton **VII**:375
Paris, Treaty of (1763) **II**:438*c*; **III**:**331**, 459*c*
Acadians **II**:2
British Empire **II**:48
Canada **III**:78
Florida **II**:130; **III**:166
French colonies **II**:139
Louisiana **II**:210

Paris, Treaty of (1763) *(continued)*
neutrality **VII:**235
Pitt, William **III:**337
Seven Years' War **II:**349
Paris, Treaty of (1783) **III:331–332,** 462*c*
Adams-Onís Treaty **IV:**6
Aroostook War **IV:**27
Astor, John Jacob **IV:**33–35
Canada **III:**79
Florida **III:**166; **IV:**152
Franklin, Benjamin **III:**174
frontier, the **III:**181
Iroquois **III:**228
Jay, John **III:**229
journalism **III:**240
Louisiana Purchase **III:**272–273
Loyalists **III:**276
Native Americans **III:**314
Penobscot campaign **III:**334
Texas **IV:**371
Washington, George **III:**431
Webster-Ashburton Treaty **IV:**394
Paris, Treaty of (1856) **V:**84; **VII:**235
Paris, Treaty of (1898) **VI:**412*c*
Army Act **VII:**22
Bryan, William Jennings **VI:**52
Cuba **VI:**88
Paris Agreements (1954) **IX:**247
Paris Conservatory **VI:**233
Paris Exposition (1867) **VI:**374
Parish, David **III:**195
Paris Peace Accords (1973) **X:**376*c*
détente **X:**104
Nixon, Richard M. **X:**257
Vietnam War **IX:**332
Paris Peace Conference (1919)
Democratic Party **VII:**74
League of Nations **VII:**175
Versailles, Treaty of **VII:**369
Paris Salon **VI:**63
Park, Mungo **I:**211
Park, Robert **VII:**282
Park Chung Hee **X:**199
Parker, Alton B. **VII:**91, 226, 404*c*
Parker, Charlie **VIII:**195, 251, 448*c*
Parker, Dorothy **VII:**180
Parker, Edie **IX:**173
Parker, Ely Samuel **V:**16, 278, 279, **294–295**
Parker, Horatio **VI:**255; **VII:**219
Parker, John (Minuteman captain) **II:**234; **III:**265–266
Parker, John H. (Abraham Lincoln's bodyguard) **V:**20
Parker, John J. (Supreme Court nominee) **VIII:**443*c*
African Americans **VIII:**2
civil rights **VIII:**72

NAACP **VIII:**255; **IX:**232
Supreme Court **VIII:**381
White, Walter **VIII:**416
Parker, Sir Peter **III:**83, 84
Parker, Robert **II:**186
Parker, Samuel **IV:**398
Parker, Theodore **IV:**318
Parker, William **V:**65
Parker's Ferry, Battle of **III:**286
Parkinson, Kenneth W. **X:**357, 367
Parkinson's disease **VIII:**50; **IX:**10
Parkman, Francis **VI:277–278**
Dana, Richard Henry **IV:**113
journalism **IV:**210
McMaster, John Bach **VI:**242
Norton, Charles Eliot **VI:**268
Parks, Rosa **IX:**254, **254–255,** 353*c*
African Americans **IX:**5
freedom rides **IX:**123
King, Martin Luther, Jr. **IX:**173
segregation **IX:**288
Park Street Church (Boston) **III:**307
Park Theater (New York City) **III:**411
Park Tong Sun **X:**199
Parliament **I:**286; **II:**435*c*; **III:**459*c*
Acts of Trade and Navigation **II:**3
banks **III:**42
Bernard, Sir Francis **III:**49
Blackstone, Sir William **III:**52
Burke, Edmund **III:**68–69
Church of England **I:**75
Coercive Acts **III:**100
Currency Act **III:**128
Declaratory Act **III:**134
Drake, Sir Francis **I:**111
Elizabeth I **I:**120
Hawkins, Sir John **I:**157
Henry VIII **I:**160
Iron Acts **II:**177–178
Mary I **I:**232, 233
North, Frederick, Lord **III:**320
Oglethorpe, James Edward **II:**277, 278
Otis, James, Jr. **III:**326–327
Privy Council **I:**304
Quartering Act **III:**352
Reformation **I:**317
Stamp Act Congress **III:**397
Townshend Duties **III:**412–413
Wilkes, John **III:**443
Wilson, James **III:**444
Parmenius, Stephen **I:**141, **286–287,** 398*c*

parochial schools **VI:**109–110, 409*c*
Parrington, Vernon **VII:**139–140, 180
Parris, Alexander **III:**29
Parris, Samuel **II:**281, 390, 419
Parrish, Samuel B. **VI:**397
Parrott, Robert **V:**342
Parrott, Russell **III:**10
Parsons, August **VI:**168, 169
Parsons, Charles **VI:**184
Parsons, Lucy **VII:**147
Parsons, Theophilus **IV:**5
Parsons' Cause **II:281–282**
Anglican Church **III:**21
Bland, Richard **III:**53
Henry, Patrick **III:**211
partial birth abortion **X:**5, 324, 382*c*
Partial-Birth Abortion Ban Act (2003) **X:**5, 171
Partial Test Ban Treaty **IX:**171
Partisan Rangers. *See* Mosby's rangers
partisanship
House of Representatives **X:**170, 171
political parties **X:**277
Senate, U.S. **X:**321, 322
Partnership for a New Generation of Vehicles (PNGV) **X:**35
Partnership for Peace (PFP) **X:**260
Pascendi Gregis **VII:**298
Pasiphae (Pollock) **VIII:**31
Paspiheigh Indians **II:**181
Passaic Strike **VII:252–253,** 409*c*
Passamaquoddy Bay **I:**227
Passamaquoddy Indians **I:287**
Passing (Larsen) **VII:**136, 181
Passing of the Great Race (Grant)
anti-Semitism **VII:**17
eugenics **VII:**102
race and race relations **VII:**281–282
Passionate Pilgrim, The (James) **VI:**200
Passion Flowers (Howe) **V:**198
Pasteur, Louis **V:**112
Pastor, Tony **VI:**117, 257
Patagonia **I:**223, 224
PATCO. *See* Professional Air Traffic Controllers Association
Patent Act (1790) **III:**225
Patent Granted by King Henry VII to John Cabot and his Sons (March 1496) **I:404–405**
Patent Office, U.S. **IV:**12
patents **VII:**150
paternalism **III:**122; **VI:**297
Paterson, New Jersey **IV:**101, 102
Paterson, William
Constitutional Convention **III:**109
Judiciary Act (1789) **III:**242
Supreme Court **III:**403
Paterson Plan **III:**109

Paterson Strike **VII:253–254**
free speech fights **VII:**118
Greenwich Village **VII:**130
Haywood, William Dudley **VII:**137
IWW **VII:**147
Pathfinder (spacecraft) **X:**381*c*
Pathfinder, The (Cooper) **IV:**228
Path of the Law, The (Holmes) **VII:**344
Patman, Wright **X:**169
Patman Bonus Bill **VIII:**48
Patowmack Company **IV:**79
patriarchal system
banking **II:**33
domesticity **II:**100, 101
gender **II:**144
society, British American **II:**365
patrilineal descent **I:**135, 389
patriotism
common soldier **V:**78
loyalty oaths **V:**246
popular culture **VIII:**301, 303
Patriot movement **X:**267
Patriot War (1837–1838) **IV:**154
patronage **V:**202
patronato real **I:**270
Patrons of Husbandry (Granger movement) **VI:**278, **278–279,** 408*c*, 410*c*
business and government **VI:**57
farmers' alliances **VI:**125
Field, Stephen Johnson **VI:**127
mail-order houses **VI:**237
railroads **VI:**303
patroons
labor/labor movements **II:**199
New Netherland **II:**265
New York **II:**269, 270
Rensselaerswyck **II:**331
Van Rensselaer, Maria Van Cortlandt **II:**397
Patterson, John **IX:**123, 124
Patterson, Robert (Union general) **V:**50
Patterson, Robert B. (White Citizens' Council leader) **IX:**342
Patterson, Robert P. (Under Secretary of War) **VIII:**25, 375
Patterson v. McLean Credit Union **X:**77
Pattie, James Ohio **IV:**145
Pattison, Robert **VI:**176
Patton, Charley **VII:**39; **VIII:**250
Patton, George S., Jr. **VIII:**62, **291,** 447*c*
AEF **VII:**11
African Americans **VIII:**3–4
Bulge, Battle of the **VIII:**55

Mauldin, Bill **VIII:**233
Mitchell, William (Billy) **VII:**211
North African campaign **VIII:**277, 278
Sicily **VIII:**360
tanks **VIII:**385
Patuxet Indians **II:**376
Paul, Alice **VII:**254–255, 406c, 408c
  Amendments to the U.S. Constitution **X:**23
  ERA **VII:**100; **X:**123
  NAWSA **VII:**223
  NWP **VII:**230
  woman suffrage **VII:**385
  women's status and rights **VII:**388
Paul, Nathaniel **III:**10; **IV:**295–296
Paul, William **IV:**388
Paul III (pope)
  Jesuits **I:**193
  Luther, Martin **I:**219
  Michelangelo **I:**244
  Trent, Council of **I:**369
Paul IV (pope) **I:**196
Paul VI (pope) **X:**3, 43
Paulding, James Kirke **IV:**228
Pauling, Linus **IX:**283
"Paul Revere's Ride" (Longfellow) **III:**366
Paulson, Henry **X:**61, 111
Paulus Hook, Battle of **III:**259
Pawnee Bill's Show **VI:**118
Pawnee Indians **IV:**84, 300
Pawnshop, The (film) **VII:**216, 407c
Paxton Boys **II:**282; **III:**302
Payne, Daniel A. **VI:**351
Payne, David L. **VI:**339
Payne, Francis **II:**282–283
Payne-Aldrich Tariff Act **VII:**255, 405c
  business and government **VI:**56
  Congress **VII:**62
  Progressive Party **VII:**269–270
  Republican Party **VII:**300
  Taft, William Howard **VII:**347–348
  tariffs **VII:**349
Payne's Landing, Treaty of (Seminole Treaty) **IV:**289, 338, 413c
pay-per-view television **X:**283
payroll deductions **VIII:**447c
  recession of 1937–1938 **VIII:**324
  Revenue Act of 1942 **VIII:**341
  Social Security Act **VIII:**364
  World War II home front **VIII:**433
payroll taxes **VIII:**324

PBS. *See* Public Broadcasting Service
PCs. *See* personal computers
PCSW. *See* President's Commission on the Status of Women
PDF (Panama Defense Forces) **X:**269
Peabody, Elizabeth Palmer **IV:**169; **VI:**279–280, 397, 398
Peabody, Francis Greenwood **VI:**335
Peabody, George
  education, philanthropy and **VI:**112
  investments, foreign, in the United States **VI:**197
  Marsh, Othniel Charles **VI:**240
Peabody, Mary **VI:**279, 280
Peabody Education Fund **VI:**112
Peabody Museum **VI:**240
Peabody School **VI:**398
peace activism **X:**261
Peace Convention (Washington, D.C., 1861) **VI:**132
Peace Corps **IX:**255–256, 355c
  Kennedy, John F. **IX:**170
  New Frontier **IX:**243
  Shriver, Robert Sargent, Jr. **X:**324
Peace Democrats. *See* Copperheads
peacekeeping operations/troops
  Africa **X:**16
  Dayton accords **X:**99
  Kosovo **X:**199
  UN **X:**355, 357
peace movements (Civil War) **V:**188, 295–296
peace movements (Progressive Era) **VII:**255–257
  ACLU **VII:**9
  Carnegie Endowment for International Peace **VII:**49–50
  Fellowship of Reconciliation **VII:**108–109
  foreign policy **VII:**115–116
  Hamilton, Alice **VII:**133
  Kellogg-Briand Treaty **VII:**164
  Vorse, Mary Heaton **VII:**375
Peace of Amiens **III:**415
Peace of Paris (1783). *See* Paris, Treaty of
Peace Parties **V:**193
Peace! Peace! (Spring) **V:**295
peace pipes. *See* calumet
Peach Orchard **V:**167, 231
Peachtree Creek **V:**389
Peach Tree War **II:**105, 106
Peacock, USS **IV:**400
"peacock revolution" **IX:**117
Peacock Room (Whistler) **VI:**3, 390

Peale, Charles Willson **III:**332–333
  art **III:**32, 33
  Catlin, George **IV:**84
  Enlightenment, American **II:**118
  Muslims **II:**248
  Washington, George **III:**430
  West, Benjamin **III:**436
Peale, Samuel Seymour **IV:**145
Peale, Titian **IV:**145, 400
Pearce, Charles Sprague **VI:**19
Pea Ridge/Elkhorn Tavern, Battle of **V:**278, 296–297
pearl diving **I:**287–288
Pearl Harbor, Hawaii **V:**151–152
Pearl Harbor invasion **VIII:**291–293, 292, 447c
  advertising **VIII:**1
  aircraft carriers **VIII:**12
  aircraft industry **VIII:**13
  air power **VIII:**15
  America First Committee **VIII:**16–17
  Anglo-American relations **VIII:**21
  Asian Americans **VIII:**32
  automobile industry **VIII:**37
  Axis **VIII:**38
  Bataan Death March **VIII:**42
  CDAAA **VIII:**77
  Communists **VIII:**78
  "Day of Infamy" speech (Roosevelt) **VIII:**466
  enemy aliens **VIII:**115
  espionage **VIII:**117
  Executive Order 9066 **VIII:**121
  fireside chats **VIII:**138
  foreign policy **VIII:**142
  Halsey, William F. **VIII:**161
  Hersey, John R. **VIII:**164
  Hillman, Sidney **VIII:**166
  Hiroshima and Nagasaki **VIII:**167
  Hull, Cordell **VIII:**180
  intelligence **VIII:**186
  isolationists **VIII:**190
  Italian Americans **VIII:**191
  Japanese Americans, relocation of **VIII:**193
  Johnson, Hugh S. **VIII:**197
  King, Ernest J. **VIII:**202
  Knox, Frank **VIII:**202
  labor/labor movements **VIII:**207
  La Follette, Robert M., Jr. **VIII:**208
  Manchuria **VIII:**226
  Navy, U.S. **VIII:**265
  news media **VIII:**272
  OCD **VIII:**281
  radio **VIII:**320
  Republican Party **VIII:**338

Roosevelt, Franklin D. **VIII:**346
Soviet-American relations **VIII:**368
Thomas, Norman **VIII:**394
World War II **VIII:**427
World War II Pacific theater **VIII:**435
Pearl of Orr's Island (Stowe) **VI:**202
Pearl River **IV:**152
Pearl Street, New York City **VI:**191
Peary, Robert E. **VII:**405c
peasants **I:**149, 332–333
Peasants' Rebellion **I:**315
Pease Creek **IV:**339
PECE. *See* President's Emergency Committee for Employment
Peck, Clara S. **I:**113
Peck, Gregory **IX:**194
Peck, Jim **IX:**123
Peckham, Sir George **I:**288; **II:**174
Peckham, Rufus **VII:**183
Pecora, Ferdinand **VIII:**356
Pecos Indians **I:**92–93
Pecos River **IV:**331
Pedagogical Seminary (journal) **VI:**158
Pedro the Cruel (king of Castile) **I:**176
Peek, George N.
  Agricultural Adjustment Act **VIII:**6
  America First Committee **VIII:**17
  Baruch, Bernard M. **VIII:**42
Peekskill, New York **III:**216
Peel, Robert **IV:**287–288
Pegg, Thomas **V:**278
Pei, I. M. **IX:**280
Peirce, Charles Sanders **VI:**280–281
  pragmatism **VI:**289
  professional organizations, rise of **VI:**294
  Royce, Josiah **VI:**318
Peleliu **VIII:**20, 230
Pelham, Peter **II:**205, 225, **283**
Pelham-Holles, Thomas (first Duke of Newcastle) **III:**337
Pelosi, Nancy **X:**271, 384c
  global warming **X:**156
  House of Representatives **X:**171
  women's status and rights **X:**371
pelt trade. *See* fur trade
Pember, Phoebe Yates Levy **V:**297
Pemberton, John C. **V:**297–298
  Confederate army **V:**82
  Johnston, Joseph E. **V:**214
  Milliken's Bend, Battle of **V:**260

Pemberton, John C. *(continued)*
 Mississippi River war **V:**264
 Vicksburg campaign **V:**417, 418
Pemisapan. *See* Wingina
Pend d'Oreille Indians **II:**127
Pender, William Dorsey **V:**166, 167
Pendergast, Thomas **VIII:**188
Pendleton, Edmund **III:**115
Pendleton, George Hunt **VI:**27
Pendleton Civil Service Reform Act (1883) **VI:**409*c*
 Arthur, Chester Alan **VI:**21
 Bayard, Thomas Francis **VI:**27
 civil service reform **VI:**73
 Congress **VI:**80
 corruption, political **VI:**84
 Garfield, James Abram **VI:**139
 Hanna, Marcus Alonzo **VI:**158
 Hayes, Rutherford B. **VI:**167
 Hoar, George F. **VI:**173
penicillin
 agriculture **VIII:**10
 business **VIII:**59
 medicine **VIII:**234, 236; **X:**222
 miracle drugs **IX:**218
 Point Four Program **IX:**258
 population trends **IX:**260
 public health **IX:**264
 technology **IX:**313
Peninsular campaign **V:**298, **298–300,** 444*c*
 Balloon Corps **V:**25–26
 cartography **V:**57
 Cedar Mountain, Battle of **V:**59
 Custer, George A. **V:**99
 Gordon, John B. **V:**170
 Harvard Regiment **V:**186
 Hill, Ambrose P. **V:**190
 Hill, Daniel H. **V:**190
 Hooker, Joseph **V:**196
 Howard, Oliver Otis **V:**197
 Irish-American regiments **V:**205
 McClellan, George Brinton **V:**251
 McLaws, Lafayette **V:**253
 Meade, George Gordon **V:**253
 medicine **V:**257
 Mosby, John Singleton **V:**271
 Sickles, Daniel E. **V:**361
 tactics and strategy **V:**381
 Toombs, Robert A. **V:**389
 Union army **V:**403
peninsulares **I:**268; **II:**372, 375
penitentiary movement **IV:**124–125, 169, **296–297,** 297
Penn, Arthur **IX:**226

Penn, John **II:**405, 406; **III:**17, 377
Penn, Richard **III:**324
Penn, Thomas **II:**405, 406
Penn, William **II:283–284,** 436*c*
 Conestoga **II:**75
 Delaware **II:**95, 96
 Delaware Indians **II:**96
 education **II:**111–112
 Enlightenment, American **II:**118
 French immigrants **II:**139
 gender **II:**144
 government, British American **II:**152
 land **II:**201
 Lloyd, David **II:**208
 Logan, James **II:**209
 monarchy, British **II:**240
 New Jersey **II:**261
 Pennsylvania **II:**285–288
 Philadelphia **II:**291; **V:**303
 potato **II:**305
 proprietary colonies **II:**313, 314
 Protestantism **II:**316
 Quakers **II:**321, 322
 religion, Euro-American **II:**330
 religious liberty **III:**362
 Roman Catholicism **II:**336
 Swedish colonies **II:**381
 Weems, "Parson" Mason Locke **III:**435
Penn Central Transportation v. New York City **X:**290
Penn family **V:**250
Penniman, Richard (Little Richard) **IX:**278
Pennington, James William Charles **V:300–301,** 362
Pennington Academy (New Jersey) **VI:**85
Pennsylvania **II:284–288,** 285, 436*c,* 437*c;* **III:**462*c*
 abolitionism **II:**1; **III:**2; **V:**1
 ACS **IV:**17
 African Americans **III:**9
 Agricultural Adjustment Act **VIII:**6
 agriculture **IV:**10, 12
 Akron v. Akron Center for Reproductive Health **X:**21
 Albany Congress **II:**15
 Anthracite Coal Strike **VII:**15
 anti-Masonry **IV:**25
 antislavery **III:**25
 Appalachia **IX:**15
 architecture **III:**24
 artisans **III:**35
 Bank of North America **III:**40
 banks **III:**42
 Brackenridge, Hugh Henry **III:**60

Brandywine, Battle of **III:**61–62
Campbell, Thomas **IV:**78
citizenship **III:**93
class consciousness **VI:**73
College of Philadelphia **II:**74
Conestoga **II:**74–75
conscription **VII:**62
Constitution, ratification of the **III:**105
constitutions, state **III:**110, 111
Continental army **III:**111
Continental army, mutinies of **III:**113
Continental Congress, First **III:**114
Continental Congress, Second **III:**116
corruption, political **VI:**83
Croghan, George **II:**84–85
Delaware **II:**95, 96
education **II:**111–112
English immigrants **II:**117
foraging **V:**149
Forten, James **III:**170
Fort Stanwix, Treaty of **III:**170
Foster, Abigail Kelley **IV:**161
Franklin, Benjamin **III:**173, 174
Fries's Rebellion **III:**180–181
fugitive slave laws **IV:**168
Fulton, Robert **III:**182
Gallatin, Albert **III:**187–188
gender **II:**144
German immigrants **II:**147, 148
Gettysburg, Battle of **V:**166–168
government, British American **II:**153
Haiti **III:**204
ILGWU **VIII:**187
immigration **VI:**184
indentured servitude **II:**175
industrialization **IV:**199, 201
iron manufacturing **II:**178
Iroquois **II:**179
Jews **III:**237
Johnstown flood **VI:**204
Keating-Owen Act **VII:**163
Keith, William **II:**191
Know-Nothing Party **IV:**215
labor/labor movements **II:**199; **VIII:**206
labor: strikes and violence **VI:**214
land **II:**201
lead mines **IV:**223
Liberty Party **IV:**226
Lloyd, David **II:**207–208
Logan, James **II:**209
lumbering **IV:**231

Lutherans **II:**212
machine politics **VI:**234
Mason-Dixon Line **V:**250
migration **VIII:**239
mining **VII:**207, 209
Molly Maguires **VI:**248
Monroe, James **IV:**258
Moravians **III:**302
National Road **IV:**271
New Unionism **VII:**238
oil **VI:**271
Paxton Boys **II:**282
penitentiary movement **IV:**296
Penn, William **II:**283–284
Pinchot, Gifford **VII:**260
population trends **II:**302–303; **X:**282
prisons **III:**347
proprietary colonies **II:**314
Protestantism **II:**314–316
Quakers **II:**322, 323; **III:**351, 352
Quay, Matthew Stanley **VI:**299–300
railroads **IV:**313, 314, 316
religion **X:**307
religion, Euro-American **II:**329, 330
religious liberty **III:**362
Rittenhouse, David **III:**372
Roman Catholicism **II:**336
rum trade **II:**338
rust belt **X:**314
St. Clair, Arthur **III:**378
Scots immigrants **II:**346
Scots-Irish **II:**347
Seven Years' War **II:**348
slavery **III:**390, 391
slave trade **II:**360; **III:**393
Stevens, Thaddeus **V:**372
strikes **V:**374
suffrage **III:**400
tariffs **III:**406
taverns and inns **II:**384
temperance movement **IV:**369
Tennent, William, Sr. **II:**389
transportation **VIII:**395
Underground Railroad **V:**397
Walking Purchase **II:**405
Weiser, Johann Conrad **II:**409
Weld, Theodore Dwight **IV:**396
Whiskey Rebellion **III:**439–440
Wistar, Caspar **II:**419
women's status and rights **II:**423
Wyoming Valley Massacre **III:**449
Wyoming Valley Wars **III:**450
Young, Thomas **III:**457
Zouaves **V:**442

Pennsylvania, Commonwealth of
III:174
Pennsylvania, USS VIII:11
Pennsylvania Abolition Society
III:460*c*
ACS IV:17
antislavery III:25
Coxe, Tench III:125
Cuffe, Paul III:127
Pennsylvania Academy of Fine
Arts
art and architecture IV:29
Cassatt, Mary VI:63
Catlin, George IV:84
Chase, William Merritt
VI:66
Eakins, Thomas VI:103–104
Jefferson, Joseph, III
VI:202
painting VI:276
Pennsylvania Anti-Slavery Society
III:174
Pennsylvania Factory Inspection
Act (1899) VI:215
Pennsylvania Gazette
Franklin, Benjamin III:173
fugitive slaves II:140
journalism II:189
newspapers II:268
Pennsylvania Hospital II:293
Pennsylvania Main Line Canal
IV:79
Pennsylvania National Guard
VI:176
Pennsylvania Railroad (PRR)
Baltimore & Ohio Railroad
IV:44
banking, investment VI:23
Carnegie, Andrew VI:62
Cassatt, Mary VI:64
corruption, political VI:83
economy IV:131
Great Strike of 1877 VI:154
industrialization IV:200
Johnstown flood VI:204
Lloyd, Henry Demarest
VI:227
Morgan, John Pierpont
VI:250
National Road IV:273
newspapers VI:267
oil VI:271
railroads IV:316
Scott, Thomas Alexander
VI:326
steel industry VII:336
Pennsylvania State Assembly V:47
Pennsylvania State Constabulary
VII:337
Pennsylvania State House III:223
Pennsylvania Station (New York
City) VI:392
Pennsylvania Turnpike VIII:395
Pennsylvania University VI:131
penny papers
advertising VI:2
Alamo, The IV:14

cities and urban life IV:92
journalism IV:206, 208, 209
Penobscot campaign III:333–
334, 367
Pensacola, Florida
disease/epidemics IV:123
Florida II:129; IV:151–152
Native Americans in the War
of 1812 IV:278
Pension Arrears Act VI:152
pensions
Grand Army of the Republic
VI:152
Harrison, Benjamin VI:161
Hull, Agrippa III:217
Newburgh conspiracy
III:316
nurses V:286
Sampson, Deborah III:380
veterans V:415, 416
Pentagon VIII:25
Pentagon attacks (September
11, 2001) X:143, 347, 383*c.*
See also September 11, 2001,
terrorist attacks
Pentagon Operations and Plans
Division VIII:26
Pentagon Papers X:271–272
Brennan, William J., Jr.
X:47–48
censorship X:71
Watergate scandal X:365
Pentecostal Church IX:263
Pentecostalism
African Americans X:14
Christian Science VI:69
McPherson, Aimee Semple
VII:196
migration VII:207
religion VII:298, 299;
VIII:334; IX:272–273;
X:306
Peonage Abolition Act (1867)
V:446*c*
People of the Long House II:180
People's Convention of Friends of
Free Territory IV:163
People Shapers, The (Packard)
IX:253
People's Party (1970s) IX:298
People's Party (Populist Party,
1892–1908) VI:281–283, 411*c*
bimetallism VI:38
Bryan, William Jennings
VI:51, 52
Butler, Benjamin Franklin
V:53
Coxey's Army VI:84
currency issue VI:90
Democratic Party VI:96
Donnelly, Ignatius Loyola
VI:100
farmers' alliances VI:126
Free-Silver Movement
VI:135
Internal Revenue taxes
VI:194

Lease, Mary Elizabeth
Clyens VI:220
Lloyd, Henry Demarest
VI:227–228
Morton, Oliver P. V:270
national banking system
VI:261
Omaha platform VI:272
party platform (1892)
VI:430–432
political parties, third VI:286
Powderly, Terence Vincent
VI:287
Simpson, Jerry VI:330
Watson, Thomas Edward
VII:380
Willard, Frances VI:394
People v. Hall IV:312
Peoria, Illinois VI:193
Pepperell, Sir William II:224
Pequot Indians II:289, 436*c*
Connecticut II:76
Endecott, John II:116
forts II:133
land II:201
Miantonomo II:233
Narragansett II:249
Native Americans II:252
Pequot War II:289–291, 290
Canonicus II:57
Connecticut II:76
Endecott, John II:116
Mason, John II:222,
439–440
Massachusetts II:223
Narragansett II:249
Pequot II:289
Peralta, Don Pedro de I:327
Percy, George
Gates, Sir Thomas II:143
Jamestown II:181
Sandys, Sir Edwin I:326
Percy, Hugh, Lord III:266
Perdido River IV:151, 152
Peress, Irving IX:18
Perestrello, Rafael I:68
perestroika
cold war, end of X:86
Soviet Union, breakup of
X:326
Perez, Albino IV:26
performance art X:31
perjury IX:352*c*
Chambers, Whittaker IX:52,
53
Hiss, Alger IX:146, 147
HUAC IX:150
impeachment of William J.
Clinton X:178
Perkins, Carl IX:37
Perkins, Edward X:357
Perkins, Frances VIII:293–294,
444*c*
Democratic Party VIII:93
Dewson, Mary VIII:95
Fair Labor Standards Act
VIII:124

labor/labor movements
VIII:206
New Deal VIII:270
Smith, Alfred E. VII:326
Social Security Act
VIII:363
women's network VIII:421
women's status and rights
VIII:422
Perkins, Jacob IV:333
Perkins, Williams II:81, 82
Perle, Richard X:252
Permanent Court of Arbitration
VII:175
Permanent Indian Frontier
IV:157–158, 254, 255, 297–298
Permanent Joint Board of
Defense VIII:446*c*
Pernambuco II:107
Perot, H. Ross X:272–273, 380*c,*
381*c*
Bush, George H. W. X:53
Clinton, William J. X:80
elections, presidential
X:116, 117
political parties X:277, 278
Reform Party X:304
Perry, Benjamin F. V:439
Perry, Matthew Calbraith IV:298,
415*c*
Fillmore, Millard IV:150
foreign policy IV:156
Manifest Destiny IV:235
Perry, Oliver Hazard
Harrison, William Henry
IV:185
Lake Erie, Battle of IV:220–
221
Perry, Matthew Calbraith
IV:298
War of 1812 IV:391
Perry, William X:102, 206
Perry Mason X:343
Perryville, Battle of V:48, 74
Pershing, John Joseph VII:257,
257–258, 406*c*, 407*c*
AEF VII:10, 11
Arlington National Cemetery
V:17
armed forces VII:21
conscription VII:62
Dawes, Charles Gates
VII:71
foreign policy VII:113
Hershey, Lewis B. VIII:164
Johnson, Hugh S. VIII:196
Marshall, George C.
VIII:233
Mexican Invasion VII:203,
204
Mitchell, William (Billy)
VII:211
Selective Service Act VII:321
Wilson, Thomas Woodrow
VII:383
Zimmermann telegram
VII:401

Pershing II missiles **X:**100
Persian Empire **IX:**214
Persian Gulf War (1990–1991)
    X:273–274, *274,* 379*c*
        Bush, George H. W. **X:**51, 53
        Cheney, Richard B. **X:**72
        Clinton, William J. **X:**81
        defense policy **X:**101
        foreign policy **X:**142
        Gore, Albert, Jr. **X:**157
        Iraq War **X:**186
        Mauldin, Bill **VIII:**234
        Middle East **IX:**214; **X:**229
        nuclear proliferation **X:**262
        Powell, Colin L. **X:**286
        UN **X:**355
personal computers (PCs) **X:**378*c*
        computers **X:**86–88
        Gates, William Henry, III
            X:147
        science and technology
            X:318, 319
personal liberty laws **IV:**66, 168,
    298–299
Personal Memoirs (Grant)
        Grant, Julia Dent **V:**173
        Grant, Ulysses S. **V:**176
        literature **V:**239
Personal Responsibility and Work
    Opportunity Reconciliation Act
    (1996) **X:**131
Peru **I:289,** 395*c,* 397*c;* **II:**370
        Acosta, José de **I:**3
        Andes Mountains **I:**9
        Bush, George H. W. **X:**52
        Chilean-American relations
            VI:67
        Cieza de León, Pedro **I:**76
        corn **I:**91
        Guamán Poma **I:**146–147
        horses **I:**168
        Lima **I:**213
        Mendoza, Antonio de **I:**239
        Monroe Doctrine **IV:**259
        Pizarro, Francisco **I:**292–293
        printing press **I:**303
        slavery **I:**338
        smallpox **I:**341
        Soto, Hernando de **I:**342
        Valdivia, Pedro de **I:**373
        Wilkes expedition **IV:**400
Peruschi, Mario de **I:**154
pesquisa **I:**128
Pestalozzi, Johann **VI:**207
pesticides
        agriculture **X:**20
        Carson, Rachel **IX:**50, 51
        Chávez, César Estrada
            IX:54
        consumerism **IX:**76
        environment **IX:**109
Peter, Paul, and Mary **IX:**121, 201
Peter Martyr **I:290,** 397*c*
        Ramusio, Giovanni Battista
            I:313
        sugar **I:**349
        The Tempest **I:**353

Petersburg, siege of **V:**445*c;*
    VI:395
Petersburg, Virginia **V:**14, 15
Petersburg campaign **V:301–303,**
    302, 303*m*
        Burnside, Ambrose E. **V:**52
        Chamberlain, Joshua L.
            V:60
        field fortifications **V:**141
        Hancock, Winfield Scott
            V:184
        Harvard Regiment **V:**187
        Hill, Ambrose P. **V:**190
        homefront **V:**194
        Lee, Robert E. **V:**231
        Meade, George Gordon
            V:254
        Union army **V:**403
Peterson, Douglas B. **X:**261
Peterson, Esther
        NOW **IX:**236
        PCSW **IX:**262
        women's status and rights
            IX:346
Peterson, Scott C. **X:**283
*Peterson's Ladies' National
    Magazine* **IV:**210
Peterson v. City of Greenville
    IX:291
Peter the Great (czar of Russia)
    II:36
Petits Voyages **I:**38
Petraeus, David **X:**384*c*
Petrarch **I:**375
petroglyphs **II:**26
petroleum. *See* oil
Pettigrew, James J.
        Fort Sumter **V:**154
        Gettysburg, Battle of **V:**168
        Pickett, George Edward
            V:306
        volunteer army **V:**419
Pettus Bridge (Alabama) **IX:**303
pewter **II:291**
peyote **X:**307
Peyton Place (Metalious) **IX:**195
Pfizer Inc. **VIII:**234
PFP (Partnership for Peace)
    X:260
PGA. *See* Professional Golfers
    Association
Phagan, Mary **VII:**176
Phair, Liz **X:**239
Phelps, Amos **IV:**147
Phelps, Charlotte **IV:**147
Phelps, Elizabeth Stuart **VI:**225
Phelps, Michael **X:**384*c*
Philadelphia, Pennsylvania
    II:291–293, 437*c;* **V:303–304**
        ACS **IV:**17
        African Americans **II:**7;
            III:9; **IV:**10
        agriculture **II:**14
        Alice **II:**19
        Allen, Richard **III:**15–16
        American Anti-Slavery
            Society **IV:**15

American Philosophical
    Society **II:**20; **III:**17
André, John **III:**20
anti-Catholic riots **IV:**23–24
antislavery **III:**26–27
Arnold, Benedict **III:**31
art and architecture
    IV:29–30
artisans **III:**35
Audubon, John James **IV:**38
Austin, Moses **IV:**38
Bank of North America
    III:40
banks **III:**42
Carey, Mathew **III:**80
Catholics **III:**83
Catlin, George **IV:**84
Catto, Octavius V. **V:**58–59
cities and urban life **II:**68,
    69; **V:**67; **VI:**70
Continental army, mutinies
    of **III:**113
Continental Congress, First
    III:113
Continental Congress,
    Second **III:**115, 116
corruption, political **VI:**83
Crummell, Alexander **VI:**87
Decatur, Stephen **III:**114
disease/epidemics **II:**100;
    III:138; **IV:**122, 123
Drayton, William H. **IV:**127
Eakins, Thomas **VI:**103
Easton, Hosea **IV:**129
economy **II:**110
female antislavery societies
    IV:148
Finney, Charles Grandison
    IV:151
Forten, James **III:**169–170
Foster, Abigail Kelley
    IV:161
Franklin, Benjamin **III:**172–
    175
Franklin Institute **IV:**162–
    163
Freedom Train **IX:**125
Grimké, Angelina and Sarah
    IV:180
Hale, Sarah Josepha **IV:**184
Howe, Richard, Lord
    III:214
Howe, Sir William **III:**215
ILGWU **VIII:**187
immigration **IV:**194, 196;
    VI:184, 186
Indian Rights Association
    VI:190
industrialization **IV:**199, 200
invention and technology
    VI:194
Irish Americans **VIII:**188
Jefferson, Joseph, III **VI:**202
journalism **V:**217
Kelley, Florence **VII:**164
labor/labor movements
    IV:217–219

libraries, public **VI:**224
literature **IV:**227
lotteries **II:**210
medicine **IV:**249
mining **VII:**209
Mott, Lucretia **IV:**265
Muhlenberg, Henry
    Melchior **II:**245–246
music **VII:**219
oil industry **VII:**244
Paine, Thomas **III:**329
panic of 1819 **IV:**293
Peale, Charles Willson
    III:332–333
penitentiary movement
    IV:296
Pennsylvania **II:**286–288
population trends **III:**343
postal service **II:**304
Presbyterians **II:**309
printing and publishing
    II:311
prisons **III:**347
prostitution **V:**316
railroads **IV:**313, 314, 316
redemptioners **II:**327
religion **IV:**318, 320
Revolutionary War **III:**368
riots (1726) **II:**437*c*
Rittenhouse, David **III:**372
Saratoga, surrender at
    III:380
settlement houses **VI:**327
shipbuilding **II:**351
Smith, Robert **II:**363
society, British American
    II:366
spiritualism **IV:**355
Still, William **IV:**357
Sunday, William Ashley, Jr.
    VII:342
taverns and inns **II:**383, 384
Tennent, William, Jr. **II:**388
Tennent, William, Sr. **II:**389
theater **II:**389
urban redevelopment **IX:**326
urban transportation
    VII:363, 364
Washington, George **III:**431
Weld, Theodore Dwight
    IV:396
Wistar, Caspar **II:**419
witches/witchcraft **II:**420
yellow fever **II:**431
Young, Thomas **III:**457
Philadelphia, USS **III:**465*c*
        Barbary Wars **III:**46
        Decatur, Stephen **IV:**114
        POWs **III:**346
Philadelphia and Reading
    Company **VII:**208–209
Philadelphia Anti-Slavery Society
        African Americans **IV:**9
        female antislavery societies
            IV:147
        Society of Friends **V:**364
Philadelphia Association **II:**33

Philadelphia Athletics **VII**:334
Philadelphia Baptist Association **III**:44
Philadelphia Bible Society **IV**:320
Philadelphia Brigade **V**:303–304
Philadelphia Centennial Exposition **VI**:*283*, **283–284**, 408*c*
   Anthony, Susan B. **VI**:16
   Bell, Alexander Graham **VI**:31
   communications **VI**:78
   department stores **VI**:96
   Gage, Matilda Joslyn **VI**:137
   painting **VI**:276
   Pan-American Exposition **VII**:251
   Sousa, John Philip **VI**:339
   Wanamaker, John **VI**:382
Philadelphia Charter **II**:292
Philadelphia City Hall **VI**:327
Philadelphia Eagles **VIII**:371
Philadelphia Evening Journal **V**:70
Philadelphia Female Anti-Slavery Society **IV**:180
Philadelphia Hospital **III**:296
Philadelphia Mechanics' Union **IV**:217–218
Philadelphia Museum of Art **V**:19
Philadelphia Negro Convention (1832) **V**:301
Philadelphia Plan **X**:9, 375*c*
Philadelphia Public Ledger **IV**:208, 209
Philadelphia & Reading Railroad **IV**:316
Philadelphia School of Design for Women **IV**:184
Philadelphia Society for the Abolition of Slavery **V**:1
Philadelphia Story, The (film) **VIII**:247
Philadelphia Woman's Club **VII**:164
Philadelphia Yearly Meeting
   abolitionism **II**:1–2
   Benezet, Anthony **II**:35–36
   Quakers **III**:351
   Woolman, John **II**:426–427
Philanthropist **IV**:175
philanthropy
   and education **VI**:**112–113**
   Gates, William Henry, III **X**:148
   Rockefeller, John Davison **VII**:303
Philip II (king of Spain) **I**:**290–292**
   Acosta, José de **I**:3
   cabildo **I**:41
   Casa de Contratación **I**:63
   Castile **I**:66, 67
   Charles V **I**:71
   Drake, Sir Francis **I**:112
   Elizabeth I **I**:121
   Holy League **I**:165

   Las Casas, Bartolomé de **I**:207
   Lisbon **I**:215
   Mary I **I**:232
   Spanish Armada **I**:344, 345
Philip III (king of Spain) **I**:16, 146, 147
Philip IV (king of Spain) **I**:333
Philippine independence **IX**:**256–257**
Philippine Insurrection
   foreign policy **VII**:113
   Jones Act (1916) **VII**:156
   Mitchell, William (Billy) **VII**:211
Philippine Organic Act (1902) **VII**:156–157
Philippines **I**:224, 397*c*; **VI**:412*c*; **VII**:403*c*; *VIII*:*294*, **294–295**, 444*c*, 447*c*, 448*c*
   amphibious warfare **VIII**:20
   Anti-Imperialist League **VI**:17
   Army, U.S. **VIII**:25
   Army Act **VII**:22
   Asian Americans **VIII**:32
   Atkinson, Edward **VI**:22
   Bataan Death March **VIII**:42–43
   Bryan, William Jennings **VI**:52
   Filipino insurrection **VI**:127
   foreign policy **VI**:134; **VII**:113
   Habib, Philip C. **X**:163
   Halsey, William F. **VIII**:161
   Hay, John Milton **VI**:164
   Hoar, George F. **VI**:173
   immigration **VIII**:184
   imperialism **VI**:188
   intelligence **VIII**:186
   Johnson, Hugh S. **VIII**:196
   Jones Act (1916) **VII**:156–157
   Leyte Gulf, Battle for **VIII**:214
   MacArthur, Douglas **IX**:197
   Mahan, Alfred Thayer **VI**:236
   Manifest Destiny **IV**:236
   McKinley, William **VI**:241
   Narcotics Act **VII**:221
   Navy, U.S. **VIII**:265
   Nimitz, Chester W. **VIII**:274
   Open Door Policy **VII**:246
   peace movements **VII**:255
   Pershing, John Joseph **VII**:258
   POWs **VIII**:311
   presidency **VII**:268
   segregation **VII**:319
   Siberian Expedition **VII**:324
   southern demagogues **VII**:332

   Spanish-American War **VI**:341
   Stimson, Henry L. **VIII**:375
   Taft, William Howard **VII**:347
   Tarawa **VIII**:386
   World War II Pacific theater **VIII**:435–437
Philippines, Commonwealth of the **IX**:353*c*
   MacArthur, Douglas **IX**:197, 198
   Philippine independence **IX**:256
   SEATO **IX**:291, 292
Philippines Department **IX**:197
Philippine Sea, Battle of the **VIII**:**295**
   air power **VIII**:15
   Leyte Gulf, Battle for **VIII**:214
   Navy, U.S. **VIII**:265
   Nimitz, Chester W. **VIII**:274
   World War II Pacific theater **VIII**:436
Philipse, Frederick **II**:364
Phillips, David Graham **VII**:78, 217
Phillips, Howard **X**:24
Phillips, Sam **IX**:263
Phillips, Wendell **IV**:**299**
   American Anti-Slavery Society **IV**:15
   Burns, Anthony **IV**:66
   Douglass, Frederick **V**:115
   Fifteenth Amendment **V**:141
   Forbes, John Murray **VI**:132
Phillips Exeter Academy **VII**:350
Philosophical Society of Texas **IV**:221
philosophy
   Boston Philosophical Society **II**:43
   Enlightenment, American **II**:118
   Peirce, Charles Sanders **VI**:280, 281
   Royce, Josiah **VI**:318–319
   science and technology **II**:345
Phips, William
   King William's War **II**:195
   Massachusetts **II**:223–224
   Mather, Cotton **II**:227
   Mather, Increase **II**:228
   piracy **II**:296
   witches/witchcraft **II**:420
Phiri clan **I**:231
Phoebe, HMS **IV**:143
Phoenix Society **IV**:402
phonographs/phonograph records **VI**:408*c*
   Bell, Alexander Graham **VI**:31
   Edison, Thomas Alva **VI**:107

   entertainment, popular **VII**:96, 97
   FMP **VIII**:134
   invention and technology **VI**:196
   music **VI**:258; **VII**:219; **VIII**:249, 250
Photographic History of the Civil War **V**:305
Photographic Sketchbook of the War **V**:305
Photographic Views of Sherman's Campaign **V**:305
photography **V**:**304–305**, *305*; **VI**:410*c*; **VII**:**258–259**, *259*, 404*c*; **VIII**:*296*, 445*c*
   art and architecture **VII**:24; **VIII**:30; **X**:31
   Bourke-White, Margaret **VIII**:50
   Brady, Mathew B. **V**:40–41
   Eastman, George **VI**:105
   Evans, Walker **VIII**:119–120
   illustration, photography, and graphic arts **VI**:183
   Iwo Jima **VIII**:192
   journalism **V**:218
   Lange, Dorothea **VIII**:210
   Life magazine **VIII**:217
   news media **VIII**:272
   newspapers **VI**:267
   popular culture **VIII**:303
   Resettlement Administration **VIII**:339
   Riis, Jacob A. **VI**:314
   science, invention, and technology **VII**:151, 315
   World War II **VIII**:428
photojournalism **VIII**:296
photorealism **X**:31
Photo Secession **VII**:258–259
Phyfe, Duncan **III**:35, **334**
Physical Culture magazine **VII**:160
Physical Geography of the Sea (Maury) **IV**:335
physics **I**:139; **VI**:144, 325, 408*c*; **VIII**:352
Piano Concerto (Copland) **VII**:220
Piazza d'Italia (New Orleans) **X**:31
Pickawillany **II**:201
Pickens, Francis **V**:154, 155
Pickering, John
   election of 1800 **III**:150
   impeachment **III**:222
   Rodney, Caesar **III**:373
   Rodney, Caesar Augustus **III**:373
Pickering, Thomas **X**:357
Pickering, Timothy **III**:**334–335**
Pickering Treaty (1794) **IX**:241, 319
picketing **VIII**:277, 444*c*

Pickett, George Edward **V:305–306**

Five Forks, Battle of **V:147**
Garnett, Richard B. **V:163, 164**
Gettysburg, Battle of **V:168**
Harvard Regiment **V:187**
Hill, Ambrose P. **V:189**
Hollywood Cemetery **V:192**
tactics and strategy **V:380**

Pickett's Charge

Alexander, Edward P. **V:8**
Garnett, Richard B. **V:164**
Gettysburg, Battle of **V:168**
Hancock, Winfield Scott **V:184**
Lee, Robert E. **V:231**
Longstreet, James **V:242**
Pickett, George Edward **V:306**
tactics and strategy **V:380**

Pickford, Mary **VII:60, 265**
Picknell, William Lamb **VI:275**
Pico, Pío **IV:49**
pictographs **II:26**
Picts **I:155, 292**
piecework **VI:191**
Piedmont region

Catawba **II:61**
Gastonia Strike **VII:122**
North Carolina Regulation **III:320–321**
southern demagogues **VII:332**
Tuscarora **II:394**
Tuscarora War **II:395**
Virginia **II:401**

Pierce, Edward **V:312**
Pierce, Franklin **IV:415c; V:306–307**

Bleeding Kansas **V:37–38**
Buchanan, James **V:47**
Clayton-Bulwer Treaty **IV:98**
Cuba **IV:112**
Davis, Jefferson **V:104**
Democratic Party **IV:118**
Dix, Dorothea **IV:125**
foreign policy **IV:155; V:150**
Gadsden Purchase **IV:173**
Kansas-Nebraska Act **V:222**
Manifest Destiny **IV:235**
Ostend Manifesto **V:290**
Republican Party **IV:322**
Scott, Winfield **IV:336**

Pierce, Joseph **III:247**
Pierce Patent **II:298**
Pierce v. Society of the Sisters **VII:409c**
Pierre's Hole, Wyoming **IV:406**
Pierson, Abraham **II:429**
Pierson, Elijah **V:393**
Pierson, Sarah **V:393**
Pietà (Michelangelo) **IX:246**
pietism **II:135; III:360**
Pigafetta, Antonio **I:223, 224, 292**

Pigot, John **III:370**
pigs **I:81**

animals **II:23**
environment **III:153**
food **II:130**

Pike, Zebulon Montgomery **IV:299–300**

exploration **IV:144**
Great Plains **III:197**
"Pike's Peak or Bust" **IV:300**
Wilkinson, James **III:444**

Pike County Ballads and Other Pieces (Hay) **VI:164**
Pike's Peak

Atkinson, Henry **IV:36**
exploration **IV:144**
Pike, Zebulon Montgomery **IV:300**
"Pike's Peak or Bust" **IV:300–301**

Pike's Peak gold rush **V:443c**

Cody, William Frederick **VI:75**
Colorado gold rush **IV:99**
"Pike's Peak or Bust" **IV:300–301**
Villard, Henry **VI:374**

"Pike's Peak or Bust" **IV:300–301**
Pilcher, Joshua **IV:258**
Pilgrim (vessel) **IV:113**
pilgrimage. *See* hajj
Pilgrim Baptist Church **VIII:335**
Pilgrims **II:293–294, 435c**

agriculture **II:13**
Alden, John **II:16**
Alden, Priscilla **II:17**
Bradford, William **II:44**
Congregationalists **II:75**
Finney, Charles Grandison **IV:150**
literature **II:206**
Massachusetts **II:222**
Massasoit **II:226**
Mayflower Compact **II:228**
music **II:247**
Pilgrims **II:293**
Plymouth **II:298**
Puritans **II:319**
Squanto **II:376**
Standish, Myles **II:376**
Williams, Roger **II:415**

"The Pill" (birth control pill) **IX:257, 354c**

birth control **X:43**
medicine **IX:211–212**
science and technology **IX:286**
sexual revolution **X:322**
technology **IX:314**

Pillsbury brothers **VI:129**
Pilot's Knob **V:313**
Piloty, Karl von **VI:66**
Pima Indians **II:176**
Pima revolt **II:294**
Pinchback, Pinckney B. S. **V:307; VI:5**
Pinchot, Amos **VII:118**

Pinchot, Gifford **VII:259–260**

conservation/environmentalism **VI:82**
environment **VII:98, 99**
Progressive Party **VII:270**
Republican Party **VII:300**
Taft, William Howard **VII:348**

Pinckney, Charles Cotesworth **III:335, 335–336, 465c**

election of 1800 **III:150**
Pinckney, Elizabeth Lucas **III:336**
XYZ affair **III:451**

Pinckney, Elizabeth Lucas **II:144, 177, 294–295; III:336**
Pinckney, Thomas

Hamilton, Alexander **III:207**
Pinckney, Elizabeth Lucas **III:336**
Pinckney Treaty **III:336, 337**

Pinckney Treaty **III:336–337, 464c**

Amistad incident **IV:22**
Chickasaw **IV:86**
Florida **IV:152**
foreign affairs **III:169**
foreign policy **IV:153**
Jay's Treaty **III:231**
Louisiana Purchase **III:273**
Native Americans **III:314**
trade, domestic and foreign **III:415**

pineapples **VIII:53**
Pine Ridge Agency

Red Cloud **VI:303**
religion **VI:310**
Sioux wars **VI:331**

Pine Ridge Reservation **VI:262**
Pine Ridge Sioux reservation **X:250**
ping-pong **VII:295**
Pingree, Hazen S. **VII:156, 260–261, 362**
Pingree and Smith Shoe Company **VII:260**
Pinkerton, Allan **V:134, 135; VI:213**
Pinkerton, James **X:168**
Pinkerton Detective Agency (Pinkertons)

Coeur d'Alene miners' strike **VI:77**
Homestead Strike **VI:175–176**
labor: strikes and violence **VI:213**
Molly Maguires **VI:248**
U.S. Steel **VI:365**

Pinkham, Lydia E. **VI:2**
Pinkney, William **III:300; IV:245**
Pinocchio (film) **IX:88**
Pinochet, Augusto **X:377c**
Pinzón, Vicente Yáñez **I:9**
Pioneer Band **IV:261**

Pioneers, The (Cooper) **IV:228**
Pioneer space program **X:327**
Pioneer X **X:327**
pipes **II:56**
pipiltin **I:20**
piracy **I:36; II:295, 295–297**

Barbary Wars **III:45–46**
Bonnet, Stede **II:38–39**
Confederate navy **V:84**
mariners **II:215**
privateering **II:312–313; III:347**
Spanish colonies **II:372**
Teach, Edward **II:384–385**

PIRGs. *See* public interest research groups
Piscataway Indians

Calvert, Leonard **II:56**
St. Mary's City **II:342**
Susquehannock War **II:380**

Pistole Fee controversy **III:53**
"Pit and the Pendulum, The" (Poe) **IV:229**
Pitcairn, John **III:265–266**
Pitcher, Molly. *See* Molly Pitcher
Pitchlynn, John **IV:307**
pithouses **I:263**
Pitt, William **III:337**

Bute, John Stuart, earl of **III:71**
Mayhew, Jonathan **III:293**
Paris, Treaty of (1763) **III:331**
Seven Years' War **II:348**
Townshend Duties **III:412**
Wilkes, John **III:442**
Wolfe, James **II:421**

Pitts, John and Hiram **IV:333**
Pittsburg, USS **V:263**
Pittsburgh, Pennsylvania

Carnegie, Andrew **VI:62, 63**
Deere, John **IV:115**
environment **VI:119**
Free-Soil Party **IV:164**
Great Migration **VII:129**
Johnstown flood **VI:204**
Judaism **VI:205**
labor, radical **VI:213**
labor organizations **VI:215–216**
Mellon, Andrew William **VII:201**
movie industry **VII:216**
music **VII:219**
National Road **IV:271**
oil industry **VII:244**
popular culture **VII:265**
popular sovereignty **IV:305**
railroads **IV:316**
Republican Party **IV:321**
steel industry **VII:336**
Steel Strike of 1919 **VII:338**
unemployment **VIII:399**
violence and lawlessness **VI:375**

Pittsburgh Manifesto **VI:213**

Pittsburgh Pirates **VII**:341–342;
IX:277
Pittsburgh Steelers **VIII**:371
Pittsburgh Survey **VII**:259
Pittsburgh Symphony Orchestra
VI:170
Pittsburg Landing, Tennessee
V:358–360
Pius V (pope) **I**:120, 165
Pius IX (pope) **IV**:23
Dix, Dorothea **IV**:125
religion **IV**:319
Roman Catholicism **VI**:315,
316
Pius X (pope) **VII**:298
Pius XI (pope) **VIII**:64
Pius XII (pope) **VIII**:50, 64
Pizarro, Francisco **I**:**292–293**,
293, *397c*
Andes Mountains **I**:9
Atahualpa **I**:15, 16
Balboa, Vasco Núñez de
I:26
Cuzco **I**:102
El Dorado **I**:118–119
gold **I**:142
Inca **I**:180
Lima **I**:213
Panama **I**:285
Peru **I**:289
Soto, Hernando de **I**:342
Spanish colonies **II**:374
Valdivia, Pedro de **I**:373
Pizarro, Gonzalo **I**:119
Pizza Connection **X**:97
PL. *See* Progressive Labor Party
PL (Players League) **VI**:26
Placentia Bay, Newfoundland
VIII:34
placer gold **IV**:99
placer mining **IV**:99, 100; **VI**:246
Placerville, California **IV**:73
plague **I**:**293–294**; **II**:98
Cholula **I**:74
Colombian Exchange **I**:81,
82
disease/epidemics **I**:107
Gesner, Conrad von **I**:139
Iceland **I**:177
Léry, Jean de **I**:213
population trends **I**:298
Shakespeare, William **I**:333
smallpox **I**:340
Tlaxcala **I**:362
Plain Dealer (Detroit) **VI**:72
*Plain Instructions for Inoculation
in the Small-Pox* (Heberden)
II:361
"Plain Language from Truthful
James" (Harte) **VI**:162
Plains Cree Indians **IV**:84
Plains Indians **II**:56; **IV**:*413c*
animals **III**:22–23
buffalo, extermination of
VI:53
Custer, George A. **V**:99
Great Plains **III**:197

Little Bighorn, Battle of
V:240
music **VI**:255
Native Americans **VI**:261,
263
Plains of Abraham **III**:168
Plame, Valerie. *See* Wilson,
Valerie Plame
Plan 9 from Outer Space (film)
IX:224
Planck, Max **IV**:163; **VII**:314
*Plan for Improving Female
Education* (Willard) **IV**:401
Planned Parenthood **VII**:*407c*
birth control **VII**:37
medicine **IX**:212
"The Pill" **IX**:257
pro-life/pro-choice
movements **X**:289
public health **VII**:276
*Planned Parenthood of Central
Missouri v. Danforth* **X**:3,
20–21
*Planned Parenthood of
Southeastern Pennsylvania v.
Casey*
*Akron v. Akron Center for
Reproductive Health*
X:21
Rehnquist, William H.
X:305
Souter, David **X**:324
*Webster v. Reproductive
Health Services* **X**:368
White, Byron R. **X**:369
"Plan of the Barrio" **IX**:136
Plan of Union **II**:15, *437c*
Planston, Anthony **IV**:333
Plantagenet family **I**:161
Plantation Act (Great Britain)
III:92, 221
Plantation Club (Harlem, New
York) **VII**:220
plantations/plantation system
II:**297–298**; **V**:**307–309**, *308*
African Americans **VI**:6, 7
agriculture **II**:13; **V**:6
Black Codes **V**:35
Caribbean **II**:59
cities and urban life **II**:68
class **II**:70–71
Davis Bend, Mississippi,
freedmen's colony **V**:106
economy **II**:109
education **II**:112; **V**:124
environment **III**:155
food **II**:131
Freedmen's Bureau **V**:161
Gone With the Wind **V**:170
Haiti **III**:203
Harpers Ferry, West Virginia
V:185
homefront **V**:193
indentured servitude **II**:175
marriage and family **II**:218;
III:288, 289
Mississippi River **V**:262

New Orleans **II**:267
Ostend Manifesto **V**:289
Pinckney, Elizabeth Lucas
II:295
Port Royal Experiment
V:312
primogeniture and entail
II:310
race and race relations
V:319
Red River campaign **V**:329
religion **V**:331
rum trade **II**:338
sharecropping **V**:349
Sherman's March through
Georgia **V**:357
slavery **II**:354; **III**:390;
V:363
slave trade **I**:340
society, British American
II:365
Spanish colonies **II**:371,
374
Underground Railroad
V:397
Virginia Company of
London **II**:402
women's status and rights
II:423; **V**:437
Yancey, William Lowndes
V:439
plastics
DuPont Corporation **IX**:91
GE **IX**:132
technology **IX**:313
platform mounds **I**:244, 245
Platform of the American Anti-
Imperialist League (1899)
VI:**441–442**
Platt, Charles Adams **VI**:19
Platt, Orville **VI**:12; **VII**:22
Platt, Thomas C.
Reid, Whitelaw **VI**:305
Republican Party **VII**:299
Roosevelt, Theodore
VII:304
Platt Amendment **VII**:*403c*
Army Act **VII**:22
Big Stick diplomacy **VII**:34
Cuba **VI**:88
foreign policy **VII**:113–114
Good Neighbor policy
VIII:151
imperialism **VI**:188
Platte River
Colorado gold rush **IV**:99
Donner party **IV**:125
exploration **IV**:145, 146
foreign policy **IV**:156
gold **IV**:179
Mormon Trail **IV**:261–262
Oregon Trail **IV**:285
Smith, Jedediah Strong
IV:350
Plattsburgh, Battle of **IV**:392
Plattsburgh, New York **IV**:392;
VII:267

Plattsburgh idea **VII**:20
Playboy magazine **X**:219
Players Club **VI**:202
Players League (PL) **VI**:26
PLC (Public Lands Commission)
VI:141
"Plea for Captain Brown, A"
(Thoreau) **IV**:376
Plecker, Walter Ashby **VII**:284
Pledge of Allegiance **IX**:66, 272
Plessy, Homer J. **V**:390; **VI**:284
Plessy v. Ferguson **VI**:**284–285**,
411c, **433–438**
abortion **X**:4
African Americans **VI**:7;
VIII:5
*Brown v. Board of
Education* **IX**:43, 44
civil rights **VIII**:72
Civil Rights Cases **VI**:72
due process clause **VI**:101
education **VI**:108
Fourteenth Amendment
V:157
Harlan, John Marshall
VI:159
Jim Crow laws **VI**:203
Marshall, Thurgood **IX**:202,
203
NAACP **VIII**:256; **IX**:232
segregation **VII**:319; **IX**:288
Southern Manifesto **IX**:294
Supreme Court **VI**:348
Tourgée, Albion W. **V**:390
Pliny the Elder **I**:247
PLO. *See* Palestine Liberation
Organization
Ploscowe, Morris **VII**:67
plows **VI**:8
Plow That Broke the Plains, The
(film) **VIII**:303
"plumbers" (White House
plumbers) **X**:272, 365, 366
Plum Run Bend, Tennessee
V:263
Plunkitt, George Washington
VI:83–84, 234, **285**
Plunkitt of Tammany Hall
(Plunkitt) **VI**:285
pluralism **VI**:319
plutonium **VIII**:227; **X**:261, 262
Plymouth, Massachusetts **II**:**298–
299**, *435c*
agriculture **II**:13
alcohol **II**:15–16
Alden, John **II**:16
Alden, Priscilla **II**:17
Congregationalists **II**:75
Dominion of New England
II:102
Massachusetts **II**:222, 223
Massasoit **II**:226
Mayflower Compact **II**:228
Metacom **II**:232
Pilgrims **II**:293, 294
Standish, Myles **II**:376
Plymouth, Vermont **VII**:63

Plymouth Church (Brooklyn, New York) **IV:**414c
pneumoconiosis **VII:**209
pneumonia **II:**100
    disease/epidemics **IV:**123; **V:**112
    Emerson, Ralph Waldo **IV:**140
    Harrison, William Henry **IV:**186
    Mitchell, John **VII:**211
    public health **VII:**275–276
PNGV (Partnership for a New Generation of Vehicles) **X:**35
Poage, W. R. **X:**169
Pocahontas **II:**299, **299–300,** 435c
    captivity **II:**58
    Dale, Sir Thomas **II:**89
    Gates, Sir Thomas **II:**144
    Hamor, Ralph **II:**162
    Native Americans **II:**252
    Powhatan **II:**306, 307
    Powhatan Confederacy **II:**308
    race and race relations **VII:**282
    Racial Integrity Act **VII:**284
    Rolfe, John **II:**334, 335
    Smith, John **II:**363
pochteca **I:**20
pocket veto
    Reconstruction **V:**325
    veto (presidential) **X:**361
    Wade-Davis Bill **V:**421
Podhoretz, Norman **X:**252
Poe, Edgar Allan **IV:**414c
    journalism **IV:**210
    literature **IV:**227, 229
    Manifest Destiny **IV:**234
    U.S. Military Academy at West Point **V:**409
Poems (Emerson) **IV:**228
Poems and Translations Written between the Ages of Fourteen and Sixteen (Lazarus) **VI:**219
Poems for our Children (Hale) **IV:**183
Poems on Miscellaneous Subjects (Harper) **VI:**159
Poems on Various Subjects, Religious and Moral (Wheatley) **III:**438
poetry **VII:**408c
    African Americans **II:**7; **III:**8; **VI:**7
    Angelou, Maya **X:**26
    Barlow, Joel **III:**46
    Beat Generation **IX:**36, 37
    Bradstreet, Anne Dudley **II:**45
    Dickinson, Emily **VI:**97–98
    Dunbar, Paul Laurence **VI:**101–102
    Freneau, Philip **III:**179–180
    Ginsberg, Allen **IX:**134–135

Gonzáles, Rodolfo "Corky" **IX:**136
Hammon, Jupiter **II:**161, 162
Harper, Frances Ellen Watkins **V:**184; **VI:**159
Harte, Bret **VI:**162
Lazarus, Emma **VI:**219–220
literature **VI:**226–227; **VII:**179; **IX:**195; **X:**211
Murray, Judith Sargent Stevens **III:**308
Prince, Lucy Terry **II:**311
Rowson, Susanna Haswell **III:**374
Wheatley, Phillis **III:**438–439
Whitman, Walt **V:**430, 431
Wigglesworth, Michael **II:**414–415
Poetry: A Magazine of Verse
    literature **VII:**179
    modernism **VII:**212
    radical and labor press **VII:**285
Poindexter, John
    Boland Amendment **X:**45
    Iran-contra affair **X:**183, 184
    Walsh, Lawrence E. **X:**364, 365
Poinsett, Joel R. **IV:**127
Point Four Program **IX:**257–258
    business **IX:**46
    Marshall Plan **IX:**204
    Native Americans **IX:**241
Point Pleasant, Battle of **II:**81; **III:**312
Poland **I:**385; **VIII:**446c
    air power **VIII:**15
    blitzkrieg **VIII:**47
    cold war **IX:**63
    Dubinsky, David **VIII:**97
    espionage **VIII:**117
    Europe **IX:**112, 113
    foreign policy **VIII:**141, 142
    Grand Alliance **VIII:**156
    Holocaust **VIII:**169
    Hoover, Herbert C. **VIII:**173
    Iron Curtain, collapse of **X:**188
    isolationists **VIII:**189–190
    Judaism **VI:**205
    Kościuszko, Tadeusz **III:**248–249
    Munich Conference **VIII:**248
    National Origins Act **VII:**228
    Nazi-Soviet Pact **VIII:**266
    Polish Americans **VIII:**297
    Potsdam Conference **VIII:**307
    Pulaski, Casimir **III:**349–350
    SDI **X:**337

Soviet-American relations **VIII:**368
Soviet Union **IX:**295
Teheran Conference **VIII:**390, 391
Versailles, Treaty of **VII:**370, 371
World War II European theater **VIII:**432
Yalta Agreement **VIII:**468–469
Yalta Conference **VIII:**439, 440
Polaroid Corporation **VIII:**58
Polaroid Land Camera **VIII:**120
Polemical Works (Dow) **IV:**127
police **III:**91; **V:**67
"police action" **IX:**177
Police Firearms Instructor certification program **X:**249
polio
    Douglas, William O. **VIII:**96
    medicine **VIII:**234
    Roosevelt, Eleanor **VIII:**342
    Roosevelt, Franklin D. **VIII:**344
Poliomyelitis Surveillance Unit **IX:**212
polio vaccine **IX:**212, 353c
    medicine **IX:**212
    population trends **IX:**260
    public health **IX:**265
    technology **IX:**313
Polish Americans **VIII:**110, 271, **297**
Polish Relief Commission **VIII:**173
Polish Welfare Association **VII:**102
political action committees (PACs) **X:**63, 152, **274–275**
political advertising **X:**8–9
political cartoons **V:**275
political correctness **X:**275–276
    censorship **X:**71
    conservative movement **X:**94
    multiculturalism **X:**237
political corruption **VI:82–84,** 83, 407c
    Budget and Accounting Act **VII:**44
    business **VII:**46
    direct election of senators **VII:**78
    Ethical Culture movement **VI:**121
    Gilded Age, The: A Tale of Today **VI:**145–146
    Harding, Warren Gamaliel **VII:**135
    Hepburn Act **VII:**138
    Johnson, Hiram Warren **VII:**154
    journalism **VII:**159

    muckrakers **VII:**216
    Native Americans **VII:**232
    New Nationalism **VII:**237
    occupational health and safety **VII:**243
    Pingree, Hazen S. **VII:**260
    politics (1900–1928) **VII:**262
    Steffens, Lincoln **VII:**339
    Taft, William Howard **VII:**347
    Tarbell, Ida Minerva **VII:**349
    Teapot Dome **VII:**351–352
    urban reform **VII:**362
    veterans **VII:**371
    Veterans Bureau **VII:**373
political dissent **VIII:**361
political parties **VII:337–339; VI:285–286; X:276–278.**
    See also specific parties, e.g. Democratic Party
political parties, third **VI:285–286**
    elections **VII:**90
    People's Party **VI:**281–283
    Prohibition Party **VI:**295–296
political science **V:**234
Political Warfare Executive (Great Britain) **VIII:**312
Political Wire (blog) **X:**183
politics (1900–1928) **VII:261–263**
    Congress **VII:**61–62
    direct election of senators **VII:**78
    elections **VII:**89–92
    lobbying **VII:**181—182
    movie industry **VII:**215
    presidency **VII:**268–269
    southern demagogues **VII:**332
    urban reform **VII:**362
politics in the Roosevelt era **VIII:297–300,** 299
    Brain Trust **VIII:**51
    cities and urban life **VIII:**69
    Communists **VIII:**77–78
    election of 1932 **VIII:**108–109
    election of 1936 **VIII:**109–110
    election of 1940 **VIII:**110–111
    election of 1944 **VIII:**111
    Full Employment Bill **VIII:**145
    Good Neighbor policy **VIII:**151–152
    government **VIII:**154
    Great Depression **VIII:**159
    Jews **VIII:**195–196
    New Deal **VIII:**268
    Roosevelt, Franklin D. **VIII:**344
    World War II **VIII:**428
    World War II home front **VIII:**434

Polk, James K. **IV:***301*, **301–303**, 414*c*
   Bear Flag Revolt **IV:**49
   Bell, John **V:**32
   Buchanan, James **V:**47
   Carson, Kit **IV:**82
   Clay, Henry **IV:**97
   Clayton-Bulwer Treaty **IV:**98
   Colt revolver **IV:**102
   Democratic Party **IV:**118; **V:**109
   exploration **IV:**146
   foreign policy **IV:**155
   Fort Vancouver **IV:**159
   Forty-niners **IV:**159
   Free-Soil Party **IV:**163
   Frémont, John C. **IV:**166–167
   Guadalupe Hidalgo, Treaty of **IV:**181
   Houston, Sam **IV:**191
   Larkin, Thomas Oliver **IV:**223
   Liberty Party **IV:**226–227
   Manifest Destiny **IV:**234–235
   Mexican-American War **IV:**251, 252
   Monroe Doctrine **IV:**261
   Oregon Treaty of 1846 **IV:**287, 288
   Ostend Manifesto **V:**290
   Taylor, Zachary **IV:**368
   Tyler, John **IV:**383
   Whigs **IV:**397
   Wilmot Proviso **V:**432, 433
Polk, Leonidas L.
   Chickamauga, Battle of **V:**65
   Confederate army **V:**82
   People's Party **VI:**282
Pollack, Ben **VIII:**150
Pollard, Edward A. **V:**244
Pollard, Joy **VII:**382
Pollock, Jackson **VIII:**30, 31, 129; **IX:**19
Pollock v. Farmers' Loan and Trust Company
   federal income tax **VII:**106
   Internal Revenue taxes **VI:**194
   Supreme Court **VI:**348
poll tax **IX:**356*c*
   Carroll of Carrollton, Charles **III:**82
   Rainey, Joseph H. **V:**323
   Voting Rights Act of 1965 **IX:**333, 334
pollution **X:**375*c*, 376*c*, 379*c*
   automobile industry **X:**35
   conservation/ environmentalism **X:**91
   environment **VII:**98, 99
   property rights **X:**290
Polo, Don José **VI:**377
Polo, Maffeo **I:**295

Polo, Marco **I:294–296**
   Cathay **I:**67–69
   Columbus, Christopher **I:**84
   Ramusio, Giovanni Battista **I:**313
   Silk Road **I:**335
   sugar **I:**348
Polo, Niccolò **I:**294, 295
Polyanna (Porter) **VII:**265
polygamy **IV:303**
   Bowles, Samuel **VI:**43
   Deseret, State of **IV:**119–121
   immigration **VI:**184
   marriage and family **IV:**240
   Mormon Church **IV:**88–90; **VI:**251, 252
   Mormon War **IV:**263, 264
   religion **IV:**319; **VI:**308, 309
   Young, Brigham **IV:**407, 408
polygyny **I:**60
Polynesians
   Hawaii **III:**210
   Magellan, Ferdinand **I:**224
   navigation technology **I:**262
Pomeroy, Samuel C. **IV:**242; **VI:**146
Ponca Indians **VI:**199
Ponce de León, Juan **I:296–297**, 396*c*
   adelantado **I:**4
   Calusa **I:**52
   conquistadores **I:**88
   Florida **I:**131; **II:**128
   horses **II:**165
Pontiac (Indian leader) **III:**459*c*
   Fort Detroit **II:**132
   Neolin **II:**256
   Pontiac's War **III:**340
   revitalization movements **II:**332
Pontiac Bonneville **IX:**133
Pontiac Motor Company **VII:**26
Pontiac's War **III:339–340**
   Gage, Thomas **III:**186
   Native Americans **III:**312
   Ohio Company of Virginia **II:**278
   Paris, Treaty of (1763) **III:**331
   Putnam, Israel **III:**350
   Seven Years' War **II:**349
pontoons **V:**157, 158, 301
Pontotoc Creek, Treaty of **IV:**86
Pony Express **V:**443*c*
   Cody, William Frederick **VI:**75
   entertainment, popular **VI:**118
   foreign policy **IV:**158
   overland mail **IV:**290
Poole, Frederick C. **VII:**325
Poole, William F. **VI:**224
pools (trusts) **VI:**362

poorhouses. *See* almshouses
Poor People's Campaign and March on Washington (1968)
   Gonzáles, Rodolfo "Corky" **IX:**136
   Juneteenth **V:**219
   King, Martin Luther, Jr. **IX:**175
   SCLC **IX:**294
   Tijerina, Reies López **IX:**317
Poor Richard's Almanack **II:300–301**, 317, 437*c*; **III:**173
Poor Sarah; or, The Indian Woman (Boudinot) **IV:**61
pop art **X:**30, 31
Popé **II:301–302**
   Indians of the desert Southwest **II:**176
   Native Americans **II:**252
   Pueblo **II:**317
   Pueblo Revolt **II:**318
Pope, Alexander **VI:**193
Pope, John **V:**444*c*
   Bull Run/Manassas, First and Second Battles of **V:**50, 51
   Cedar Mountain, Battle of **V:**59
   Jackson, Thomas J. "Stonewall" **V:**210
   Lee, Robert E. **V:**230, 231
   McClellan, George Brinton **V:**251
   McDowell, Irvin **V:**252
   Mississippi River war **V:**263
Pope County, Arkansas **IV:**343
Pope Day **III:**82, 279
Popenoe, David **X:**214
Popol Vuh **I:**47, 236
popular culture **III:340–342**, *342*; **VII:263–266**, *264*; **VIII:300–303**, *302*; **IX:258–259**; **X:278–281**, *279*
   advertising **VIII:**1
   atomic bomb **VIII:**35
   baseball **VII:**33
   Beatles **IX:**37–38
   business **VIII:**58
   children **VIII:**67
   cities and urban life **VII:**56
   FMP **VIII:**134
   Great Depression **VIII:**159
   Jews **VIII:**195
   Life magazine **VIII:**217
   literature **IX:**195
   McDonald's **IX:**208
   movie industry **VII:**215
   movies **VII:**245–248; **IX:**223–226; **X:**234–236
   music **III:**308–310; **VII:**218; **VIII:**249–252
   news media **VIII:**271–272
   New York World's Fair (1939–1940) **VIII:**272–274

radio **VIII:**321
   recreation **VIII:**327–329
   Sinatra, Frank **VIII:**361
   sports and recreation **VIII:**370
   teenagers **IX:**314
   Tin Pan Alley **VII:**353
   women's status and rights **IX:**346
   World War II home front **VIII:**433
popular entertainment. *See* entertainment, popular
Popular Front **VIII:303–304**
   anticommunism **VIII:**22
   Communists **VIII:**77, 78
   literature **VIII:**218
   Nazi-Soviet Pact **VIII:**266
Popular Mechanics magazine **VII:**314–315
Popular Movement for the Liberation of Angola (MPLA) **X:**15, 85
popular music **VI:**256–258; **X:**237–240
Popular Party **II:**208
Popular Science
   children **VIII:**67
   illustration, photography, and graphic arts **VI:**183
   science and technology **VII:**314–315
   teenagers **IX:**314
popular sovereignty **IV:303–304**, 415*c*
   Bleeding Kansas **V:**37
   Buchanan, James **V:**48
   Cass, Lewis **IV:**83
   Clay, Henry **IV:**97
   Davis, Jefferson **V:**104
   Democratic Party **IV:**119
   Douglas, Stephen A. **V:**114
   Dred Scott decision **V:**117
   Greeley, Horace **V:**177
   Guadalupe Hidalgo, Treaty of **IV:**181–182
   jayhawkers **V:**211
   Kansas-Nebraska Act **V:**221, 222
   Massachusetts Emigrant Aid Society **IV:**241
   Republican Party **IV:**322
   Taylor, Zachary **IV:**368
popular vote **X:**116–118
population trends **I:297–299**; **II:302–303**, *303*; **III:342–344**; **V:309–311**, *310m*; **VI:286–287**; **VII:266–267**; **VIII:304–306**; **IX:259–260**; **X:281–283**, *282*. *See also* census, U.S.
   agriculture **VIII:**9, 10
   Asian Americans **X:**32–33
   blues **VII:**39
   California **III:**74
   Catholics **III:**83
   children **VIII:**66

population trends (*continued*)
cities and urban life **II:**69;
III:90; **VII:**54; **VIII:**68;
IX:55–56; **X:**75–76
Connecticut **II:**77
environment **III:**155;
VII:98
Federal Housing
Administration (FHA)
VIII:134
Great Depression **VIII:**159
Hispanic Americans **X:**166,
167
immigration **V:**199; **VII:**143
Islam **X:**189
Loyalists **III:**275
Maryland **II:**221
Mexican Americans
VIII:237
Mexican Repatriation
Program **VIII:**238
migration **VII:**206–207;
VIII:239–240
National Reclamation Act
VII:228
Native Americans **II:**250–
251; **X:**250
New Mexico **II:**264
New Netherland **II:**266
popular culture **VII:**263
poverty **III:**344
Scots-Irish **III:**386
slavery **III:**391
Spanish colonies **II:**372,
373
suburbanization/suburbs
VII:339–341
Sunbelt **X:**338
technology **VIII:**397
trade, domestic and foreign
III:414–415
urban redevelopment
IX:326
urban transportation
VII:363–365
Virginia **II:**401
World War II **VIII:**428
World War II home front
VIII:432–433
Populist Movement
anti-Semitism **VII:**16, 17
Farmer-Labor Party
VII:105
radicalism **VII:**287
segregation **VII:**319
Populist Party. *See* People's Party
(1892–1908)
Populist Party Platform (1892)
VI:430–432
Porcher, Francis P. **V:**258
Porgy and Bess (Gershwin and
Heyward) **VII:**124, 125, 220;
VIII:251
pornography **X:283–284**
censorship **X:**71
Christian Coalition **X:**73
computers **X:**88

Internet **X:**182
sexual revolution **X:**323
television **X:**342
porphyria **III:**192
Porras, Francisco **I:**168
Porres, St. Martín de **I:299**
Port Arthur, Manchuria **VII:**246,
309
Port Chicago, California **VIII:**318
Porter, Cole **VII:**124, 219;
VIII:252
Porter, David Dixon **V:311**
Essex, USS **IV:**144
Free Trade and Sailor's
Rights **IV:**165
Milliken's Bend, Battle of
V:260
Mississippi River war **V:**264
Union navy **V:**405
U.S. Naval Academy at
Annapolis **V:**410
Vicksburg campaign **V:**417
Welles, Gideon **V:**428
Porter, Edwin Stratton
entertainment, popular
VII:96
Griffith, David Wark
VII:131
movie industry **VII:**215
Porter, Eleanor H. **VII:**265
Porter, Fitz-John
Antietam, Battle of **V:**13
Balloon Corps **V:**25
Bull Run/Manassas, First
and Second Battles of
V:51
Peninsular campaign **V:**299
Porter, Henry **IV:**381
Porter, Horace **V:**291
Porter, Noah **VI:**111, 148
Porter, Paul **X:**145
Porter, William David **V:**43
Porter, William Sydney (O.
Henry) **VI:**236
Porterfield, E. E. **VII:**214
Port Folio, The **IV:**209
Port Hudson, Louisiana **V:**4, 418
Port Hudson, siege of
Banks, Nathaniel P. **V:**29
De Forest, John William
V:107
Mississippi River war **V:**264
Port Huron Statement **IX:260–
261,** 355c
childhood **IX:**55
Hayden, Tom **IX:**143–144
New Left **IX:**243
SDS **IX:**303
Portland, Maine **IV:**233, 234
Portland, Oregon **VII:**110
Portland Rum Riot **IV:**234
Portolá, Gaspar de **IV:**76
Porto Santo **I:**222
Portrait of a Lady, The (James)
VI:226
Portrait of Myself (Bourke-White)
VIII:50

Portrait of the Assassin (Ford and
Stiles) **X:**138
portraits **V:**18
Port Republic, Battle of **V:**210,
350, 351
Port Royal, Nova Scotia
French colonies **II:**136
King William's War **II:**195
Queen Anne's War **II:**323
Port Royal, South Carolina,
Experiment **V:**129, **311–312**
Portsmouth, New Hampshire
IV:393
Portsmouth, Ohio **IV:**202
Portsmouth, Rhode Island **II:**73
Portsmouth, Treaty of
foreign policy **VII:**113
Root-Takahira Agreement
VII:305
Russo-Japanese War **VII:**309
Portsmouth, Virginia **V:**181
Portugal **VII:**408c
Barbary Wars **III:**45
Dominicans **II:**101
League of Armed Neutrality
III:257
slavery **II:**354
slave trade **II:**358
Washington Conference
on Naval Disarmament
VII:379
Portuguese seaborne empire
I:299–300, 395c, 396c
Akan **I:**5
Albuquerque, Alfonso de
I:6
Amazon River **I:**9
Azores **I:**17–18
Bahía **I:**25–26
Brazil **I:**33–35
Cabot, Sebastian **I:**45
Cabral, Pedro Álvares **I:**46
Cameroon **I:**56
Cathay **I:**68
Dutch East India Company
I:115
East India Company **I:**117
Ethiopia **I:**125
Fernando Póo **I:**129
Gama, Vasco da **I:**137
gold **I:**141
Gold Coast **I:**143
Gomes, Diogo **I:**143
Gorée Island **I:**144
Grotius, Hugo **I:**146
Guinea-Bissau **I:**148
Hanno the elephant
I:153–154
invention and technology
I:184
Jews **I:**195
John III **I:**197–198
Kongo **I:**200
Lisbon **I:**215
Madeira **I:**222
Magellan, Ferdinand **I:**223
Mbundu **I:**237

Northeast Passage **I:**272
Nzinga **I:**274–275
Philip II **I:**291
Príncipe **I:**302
Ricci, Matteo **I:**319–320
São Tomé **I:**328
Sequeira, Diogo Lopes de
I:331
shipwreck narratives **I:**334
slavery **I:**337–338
slave trade **I:**339
smallpox **I:**341
Spice Islands **I:**345
sugar **I:**348–349
Tordesillas, Treaty of **I:**367,
368
Pory, John **I:**211
*Posados de Puerto Rico v. Tourism
Co.* **X:**7
Posen, Poland **VII:**370
posses **VI:**230
Post, Amy and Isaac **IV:**354–355
postal service **II:303–304;**
VI:407c, 409c, 411c. *See also*
Post Office Department
Cleveland, Grover **VI:**75
communications **VI:**78
corruption, political **VI:**84
illustration, photography,
and graphic arts **VI:**183
overland mail **IV:289–291**
star route frauds **VI:**343
Postclassic period (Mesoamerica)
I:235
postmillennialism **X:**125
postmodernism **X:**31–32
*Postmortem: New Evidence in
the Case of Sacco and Vanzetti*
(Kaiser and William) **VII:**311
Post Office Department **II:**304;
VII:409c
Arthur, Chester Alan **VI:**21
aviation **VII:**28, 29
FCC **VIII:**131
Kelly Air Mail Act **VII:**165
radical and labor press
VII:285
star route frauds **VI:**343
Wanamaker, John **VI:**382
World War I **VII:**394
Postwar Economic Policy and
Planning **VIII:**326
Post-War Plan and Program
(NRPB report)
Economic Bill of Rights
VIII:102
Keynesianism **VIII:**201
NRPB **VIII:**261
postwar planning (WWII)
VIII:306–307
Full Employment Bill
VIII:145
NRPB **VIII:**261
reconversion **VIII:**326
unemployment **VIII:**401
World War II home front
VIII:434

potato **II:304–305**
Potawatomi Indians **II:**104;
 III:200; **IV:**192
potlatch **II:**275
Potomac River **II:**245
 Annapolis Convention
  III:23
 Antietam, Battle of **V:**12, 13
 Gettysburg, Battle of **V:**168
 Lee, Robert E. **V:**231
 Madison, James **III:**282
 Washington, D.C. **V:**425,
  426
Potosí **I:**300; **II:**370, 371
 Andes Mountains **I:**9
 Peru **I:**289
 silver **I:**336
 slavery **I:**338
 Zacatecas **I:**391
Potrerillos, Chile **VII:**210
Potsdam Conference *VIII:307,*
 307–308, 448c
 Anglo-American relations
  VIII:21
 Arnold, Henry H. "Hap"
  VIII:28
 atomic bomb **VIII:**34
 foreign policy **VIII:**142
 Forrestal, James V. **VIII:**143
 Grand Alliance **VIII:**156
 Hiroshima and Nagasaki
  VIII:166, 168
 Leahy, William D. **VIII:**211
 Soviet-American relations
  VIII:369
 Soviet Union **IX:**295
 Truman, Harry S. **IX:**320
 V-J Day **VIII:**406–407
Potsdam Declaration
 atomic bomb **VIII:**34–35
 Grand Alliance **VIII:**156
 Hiroshima and Nagasaki
  VIII:166
Pott, John **II:305**
Pottawatomie Creek **V:**37, 44
Pottawatomie Rifles **V:**44
Potter, John **V:**246
Potter Committee **VI:**304
pottery **II:**26
 Aesthetic movement **VI:**3
 art and architecture **I:**13
 Iroquois **I:**185
 New Mexico **I:**263
Potts, Isaac **III:**421
Poughkeepsie, New York **IV:**265
Poughkeepsie Bridge **VI:**47
poultry **II:**23
Pound, Ezra **VII:**179, 212
Pound, Roscoe **VII:**140
POUR. *See* President's
 Organization on
 Unemployment Relief
poverty **III:**344; **VI:**410c;
 IX:355c; **X:**285, **285, 285–286,** 285t,
 286, 378c
 agriculture **VIII:**11
 almshouses **II:**19

Appalachia **IX:**16
apprentices **II:**23
art and architecture **VIII:**30
Asian Americans **X:**33, 34
banking **V:**28
birth control **X:**43
CAP **IX:**68–69
cities and urban life **III:**91;
 VIII:70; **IX:**56
Democratic Party **VIII:**94
Economic Opportunity Act
 (1964) **IX:**96
economy **IX:**98
elderly **VIII:**107
Evans, Walker **VIII:**119–
 120
FERA **VIII:**133
FSA **VIII:**127
Georgia **II:**147
government **VIII:**152
Great Depression **VIII:**159
Great Society **IX:**139
Harrington, Michael
 IX:142
Head Start **IX:**144–145
Holiday, Billie **VIII:**169
How the Other Half Lives
 (Riis) **VI:426–427**
humanitarianism **III:**217
King, Martin Luther, Jr.
 IX:175
Lange, Dorothea **VIII:**210
liberalism **X:**207
literature **VIII:**219
marriage and family **IX:**202;
 X:214, 215
Medicaid **IX:**209
medicine **VIII:**235–236
Native Americans **VIII:**264;
 X:251
New York City **V:**282
Norton, Charles Eliot
 VI:268, 269
Philadelphia **II:**292–293
race and race relations
 IX:269, 270
relief **VIII:**332
religion **VIII:**336
rural areas **VIII:**348
SCLC **IX:**294
Scots-Irish **III:**386
settlement houses **VI:**327
Sunbelt **VIII:**380
Tennessee Valley Authority
 VIII:392
Thomas, Norman **VIII:**394
unemployment **VIII:**400
VISTA **IX:**332–333
Wald, Lillian **VII:**377
War on Poverty **IX:**335–336
Willard, Frances **VI:**394
women's status and rights
 III:448
"poverty gap" **X:**285
Poverty Point **I:**253
Powderly, Terence Vincent
 VI:287

Knights of Labor **VI:**209,
 210
Socialist Labor Party
 VI:336–337
Powell, Adam Clayton **IX:**213,
 261
Powell, Bud **VIII:**195
Powell, Colin L. **X:286–288,** 287,
 356, 379c, 383c
 defense policy **X:**101
 Haiti **X:**164
 Iraq War **X:**187
 Kennan, George F. **IX:**168
Powell, John Wesley **VI:287–288**
 Geological Survey, U.S.
  VI:141
 Hayden, Ferdinand
  Vandeveer **VI:**165
 King, Clarence **VI:**208
 science and technology
  VI:325
 Walcott, Charles Doolittle
  VI:379
Powell, Lewis **X:**288
 assassination of Abraham
  Lincoln **V:**19
 Bakke case **X:**40
 Rehnquist, William H.
  X:305
 Supreme Court **X:**339
Powell v. Alabama **VIII:**444c
Powel's Tavern (Halifax, North
 Carolina) **II:**383
Power Elite, The (Mills) **IX:**217,
 353c
Powhatan **I:300–301; II:305–
 307,** 306m, 435c
 Dale, Sir Thomas **II:**89
 Gates, Sir Thomas **II:**143–
  144
 literature **II:**205
 Opechancanough **II:**278,
  279
 Pocahontas **II:**299, 300
 Roanoke **I:**322
 Rolfe, John **II:**335
 Smith, John **II:**362–363
 Virginia **II:**398
 werowance **I:**383
Powhatan, USS **V:**155
Powhatan Confederacy **II:307–
 308**
 Bacon's Rebellion **II:**31
 Jamestown **II:**181
 Native Americans **II:**251,
  252
 Virginia **II:**398–400
POWs. *See* prisoners of war
POWs for Truth **X:**118
powwows **I:**233
Poyas, Peter **IV:**388
Poynter, Nelson **VIII:**56
pragmatism **VI:**201, 281, **288–
 289**
*Pragmatism: A New Name for
 Old Ways of Thinking* (James)
 VI:201

Prague Spring movement **IX:**113
Prairie, The (Cooper) **IV:**228
Prairie du Chien, Wisconsin
 IV:300
Prairie Farmer **IV:**116
Prairie School **VII:**395
Praise the Lord (PTL) Club
 X:342
Pratt, Charles **VI:**35
Pratte, Chouteau and Company
 IV:18, 19
Pratz, Simon le Page du **I:**259
prayer (in schools) **IX:**355c
 Brennan, William J., Jr.
  X:48
 Engel v. Vitale **IX:**107–108
 Equal Access Act **X:**122
 religion **IX:**273, 274
 Warren, Earl **IX:**337, 338
"Prayer of Twenty Millions"
 V:444c
Praying Indians **II:**115, 223
praying towns **II:308–309**
 ethnocentrism **II:**123
 Native Americans **II:**253
 religion, Native American
  II:331
Preakness Stakes **VI:**177
Preamble to the Constitution of
 the Industrial Workers of the
 World **VII:417**
Preble, Edward **IV:**144
Preclassic period (Mesoamerica)
 I:234
Predergast, Maurice **VII:**25
predestination **II:**329
 Calvin, John **I:**54, 55
 James I **I:**192
 New Divinity **III:**316, 317
 religion **III:**362
preemption **IV:**203, 305, 306,
 414c
Preemption Act (1830) **IV:**13
Preemption Act (1841)
 agriculture **IV:**13
 claim clubs **IV:**95
 public land policy **IV:**306
pregnancy
 abortion **X:**1–5
 African Americans **X:**13
 AIDS **X:**6
 birth control **X:**42–44
 pro-life/pro-choice
  movements **X:**288–289
Preliminary Emancipation
 Proclamation (1862) **V:**193
premillennialism **X:**125
Prenatal Care (Children's Bureau)
 VII:53
preparationism **II:**165
Preparedness Day **VII:**213, 267
Preparedness movement
 VII:267–268
 Americanization **VII:**13
 Jones Act (1917) **VII:**157
 Lodge, Henry Cabot
  VII:184

Preparedness movement
(*continued*)
Mooney-Billings case
VII:213
National Defense Act
VII:227
peace movements **VII:**256
Selective Service Act
VII:321
veterans **VII:**373
Pre-Raphaelites **VI:**389
Presbyterians/Presbyterianism
II:309
Carver, George Washington
VI:63
Davenport, James **II:**91–92
Davies, Samuel **II:**92
education **IV:**134
Ely, Richard Theodore
VI:114, 115
Finney, Charles Grandison
IV:150
Garnet, Henry Highland
IV:174
Great Awakening **II:**156
Ingersoll, Robert Green
VI:192
Liberty Party . **IV:**226
Lovejoy, Elijah **IV:**230
McCormick, Cyrus Hall
IV:243, 245
McGuffey, William Holmes
IV:246
Native Americans **III:**313
New Jersey **II:**262
Polk, James K. **IV:**301
religion **III:**360–362;
IV:317, 318; **V:**331;
VI:307; **VII:**298;
VIII:335
religious liberty **III:**363
Scots immigrants **II:**346
Scots-Irish **II:**346, 347;
III:385, 386
temperance movement
III:410
Tennent, Gilbert **II:**388
Tennent, William, Jr. **II:**388
Tennent, William, Sr.
II:388–389
Whitman, Marcus **IV:**398
Whitman, Narcissa **IV:**398
Witherspoon, John **III:**445
Prescott, William Hickling **III:**65,
67; **VI:**381
prescription drugs **X:**222
preservationists **VII:**98
presidency, the **VI:289–290;**
VII:268–269; VIII:308,
308–309. *See also specific*
presidents, e.g.: Arthur, Chester
Alan
Congress **VIII:**78
Constitution, United States
III:107
Constitutional Convention
III:109

elections **VII:**90–92
Executive Reorganization
Act **VIII:**121
Federalist Papers **III:**163
foreign policy **VI:**133, 134
government **VIII:**153
New Deal **VIII:**269
NRPB **VIII:**261
OWMR **VIII:**287
presidential campaigns
(1870–1899) **VI:**290–292
Republican Party **VII:**300
Woodhull, Victoria **VI:**400–
401
World War II **VIII:**428
President, USS
Chauncey, Isaac **III:**86
Decatur, Stephen **IV:**115
Little Belt incident **III:**269,
270
Presidential Address to a Joint
Session of Congress and the
American People (George W.
Bush, 2001) **X:411–414**
Presidential Advisory Committee
(PAC) **VIII:**330
presidential campaigns (1872–
1900) **VI:290–293,** 291*t*, 292
presidential debate (1960) **IX:**169,
354*c*
Presidential Library Act (1955)
IX:321
Presidential Medal of Freedom
Ali, Muhammad **IX:**10
Chávez, César Estrada
IX:54
Ellington, Duke **VIII:**112
Farmer, James L. **X:**129
Ford, Gerald R. **X:**139
Galbraith, John Kenneth
IX:130
Korematsu v. U.S. **VIII:**203
Mitchell, George **X:**232
Owens, Jesse **VIII:**289
Parks, Rosa **IX:**255
presidential pardons. *See* pardons,
presidential
presidential powers **VIII:**81
presidential Reconstruction
V:325, 327
President Pro Tempore **III:**280
President's Commission on the
Status of Women (PCSW)
IX:261–262
Murray, Pauli **IX:**227
NOW **IX:**236
Roosevelt, Eleanor
VIII:344
women's status and rights
IX:346
President's Committee on
Administrative Management
VIII:121
President's Committee on Civil
Rights **IX:**351*c*
President's Committee on
Economic Security **VIII:**107

President's Emergency
Committee for Employment
(PECE) **VIII:309**
Hoover presidency
VIII:174
POUR **VIII:**310
relief **VIII:**331
President's Gold Medal **VIII:**112
President's Organization on
Unemployment Relief (POUR)
VIII:174, **309–310,** 331
President's Research Committee
on Social Trends **VIII:**323, 327
presidios **I:**131
Presley, Elvis **IX:262–263,** 353*c*
movies **IX:**225
music **IX:**229
popular culture **IX:**259
rock and roll **IX:**279, 280
teenagers **IX:**314, 315
television **IX:**315
Presley, Lisa Marie **IX:**263
Press Association of the Southern
States **V:**218
pressure groups. *See* lobbies and
pressure groups
Prester John **I:**301
Dias, Bartholomeu **I:**105
Henry the Navigator **I:**161
mappae mundi **I:**230
Preston, John S. **V:**111
Preston, Thomas **III:**57–58
Prevost, Augustine **III:**63, 383
Prevost, Mark **III:**63
Priber, Christian Gottlieb **II:309–**
310
Price, Byron **VIII:**65, 66, 286
Price, Sterling **V:312–313**
Corinth, Battle of **V:**95
Pea Ridge/Elkhorn Tavern,
Battle of **V:**296, 297
Quantrill, William Clarke
V:317
Price-Anderson Act (1957) **IX:**25
price controls. *See* wage and price
controls
price fixing **VI:**243
price supports **VII:**48
price wars **VI:**362
Priestley, Joseph **III:345**
Prigg v. Pennsylvania **IV:**298
primary education. *See* education,
primary and secondary
Primitive Methodism **IV:**126
Primo de Rivera, Miguel **VI:**127
primogeniture and entail **I:123;**
II:310–311
agriculture **II:**12
Spanish immigration **II:**375
women's status and rights
II:423
Primrose and West **VI:**116
Prince, Lucy Terry **II:**7, **311**
Prince, Sally **II:**52
Prince Hall Masonry **IV:**389
Princeton, Battle of (1777)
IV:192

Princeton, USS (aircraft carrier)
VIII:214
Princeton, USS (steam sloop)
IV:383
Princeton College/University
II:311
Davies, Samuel **II:**92
education, higher **VI:**111
football **VI:**130, 131
Forrestal, James V. **VIII:**143
Kennedy, John F. **IX:**169
McMaster, John Bach
VI:242
New Jersey **II:**262
Presbyterians **II:**309
public opinion polls
VIII:313
science and technology
IV:334
Tennent, Gilbert **II:**388
Thomas, Norman **VIII:**394
track and field **VI:**359
Witherspoon, John **III:**445
Princeton Radio Research Project
VIII:313
Princeton Theological Seminary
IV:3, 230
Princeton University Institute for
Advanced Study **IX:**167, 168
Principal Navigations (Hakluyt)
I:152, 153, 157
Príncipe **I:302**
Principles of Geology (Lyell)
VI:306
Principles of Psychology (James)
VI:200–201, 410*c*
Principles of Scientific
Management, The (Taylor)
VII:45, 405*c*
Pring, Martin **I:**233; **II:**259
Prinstein, Meyer **VI:**359
printing and publishing **II:311–**
312. *See also* journalism
Bradford, Cornelia Smith
II:44
Carey, Mathew **III:**80
cities and urban life **II:**68
Day, Stephen **II:**92
Franklin, Ann Smith **II:**134
Harris, Benjamin **II:**162–
163
literature **X:**212
Massachusetts **II:**223
media **X:**218–219
newspapers **II:**268
Poor Richard's Almanack
II:300–301
Zenger, John Peter **II:**433–
434
printing press **I:**302, **302–304**
art and architecture **I:**13
book, the **I:**33
Bry, Theodor de **I:**37
Gutenberg, Johannes
Gensfleisch zum **I:**148
invention and technology
I:183–184

London **I:**216
Mercator, Gerhardus **I:**240
Oviedo y Valdés, Gonzalo
Fernández de **I:**281
paper **I:**285
scribal publication **I:**328
travel narratives **I:**368
Printz, John **II:**381
Printz v. United States **X:**131, 161,
381*c*
Prioleau, John **IV:**388
prison **VIII:**83
prisoner exchanges
assassination of Abraham
Lincoln **V:**19–21
Greenhow, Rose O'Neal
V:178
prisons **V:**313–315
Prisoners from the Front (Homer)
VI:174
prisoners of war (POWs) **III:345–
346; VIII:310–311,** 447*c*
Allen, Ethan **III:**15
Andersonville Prison,
Georgia **V:**10–11
Bataan Death March
VIII:42–43
Davis, Jefferson **V:**105
foreign affairs **III:**169
Hayden, Tom **IX:**144
ironclad oath **V:**206
Jersey, HMS **III:**235–236
Joint Committee on the
Conduct of the War
V:216
Korean War **IX:**178
Laurens, Henry **III:**255
Perot, H. Ross **X:**272
Pinckney, Charles
Cotesworth **III:**336
prisons **V:**313–315
Prison Number 4 **IV:**113
prison reform. *See* penitentiary
movement
prisons **III:346–347; V:313–315**
Andersonville Prison,
Georgia **V:**10
crime and punishment **X:**96
habeas corpus, writ of **V:**181
Quakers **III:**352
Richmond, Virginia **V:**335
Rush, Benjamin **III:**376
Van Lew, Elizabeth **V:**414
Walker, Mary Edwards
V:423
Pritchard, Gullah Jack **IV:**388
Privacy Act. *See* Federal
Information Act
privacy rights **X:**2, 4, 172
privateering **II:312–313;
III:347–348**
African Americans **III:**9
Bingham, William **III:**51
Clinton, George **III:**98
Continental navy **III:**117
Drake, Sir Francis **I:**110–
111

Dutch West India Company
II:107
economy **III:**145
foreign affairs **III:**168
Forten, James **III:**169
French Alliance **III:**177
Frobisher, Martin **I:**134
Genêt, Edmond Charles
III:191
Industrial Revolution
III:224
Jersey, HMS **III:**235
mariners **II:**214
Newport, Christopher **II:**267
New York City **II:**272
Paine, Thomas **III:**329
Penobscot campaign
III:333
piracy **II:**295
POWs **III:**346
Quasi War **III:**352, 353
Revolutionary War **III:**368,
369
Seward, William H. **V:**348
Stuart, John **II:**378
trade, domestic and foreign
III:413
privatization **X:**221–222
*Privileges and Prerogatives
Granted by Their Catholic
Majesties to Christopher
Columbus<\#209>1492*
I:399–400
Privy Council **I:**104, 286, **304;
II:**48, 49
prize fighting. *See* boxing
"Problem, The" (Emerson) **IV:**140
Problem of Christianity, The
(Royce) **VI:**319
*Problem of Civilization Solved,
The* (Lease) **VI:**220
*Problems of Indian Administration,
The* (Brookings Institution)
VIII:263
Proclamation of 1763 **II:**438*c;*
III:348, 459*c*
Canada **III:**78
Coercive Acts **III:**100
Fort Stanwix, Treaty of
III:170
frontier, the **III:**181
Iroquois **III:**227
Ohio Company of Virginia
II:278; **III:**323
Pontiac's War **III:**340
Scots-Irish **III:**386
slavery **II:**357–358
Proclamation of Amnesty (1865)
amnesty, acts of **V:**9
Freedmen's Bureau **V:**161
impeachment of Andrew
Johnson **V:**202
Port Royal Experiment
V:312
Proclamation of Amnesty and
Reconstruction (1863) **V:**8–9,
324, 445*c,* **461–462**

"Proclamation to the People of
South Carolina" (Jackson)
IV:283
Procter, Henry
Harrison, William Henry
IV:185
Native Americans **IV:**274
Thames, Battle of the
IV:375
Procter, William **IV:**131, 199
Procter & Gamble **VIII:**57
produce loan **V:**122
Producers, The (musical) **X:**281
Production Code **X:**278
Production Code Administration
VIII:65
Professional Air Traffic
Controllers Association
(PATCO) **X:**202, 203
Professional Golfers Association
(PGA) **VIII:**372; **X:**332
professional organizations, rise of
VI:293–294
Profiles in Courage (Kennedy)
IX:169
Profintern (Red International of
Labor Unions) **VII:**117
Program for Economic Recovery
X:302
Progress and Poverty (George)
VI:142, 409*c;* **VII:**156
Progressive Baptist Convention
X:14
Progressive Era **X:**208
Progressive Labor Party (PL)
IX:340, 341; **X:**367
Progressive Party **VII:269–270,**
405*c;* **IX:263–264,** 352*c*
Americans for Democratic
Action **IX:**14
Children's Bureau **VII:**53
Coolidge, Calvin John
VII:64
Democratic Party **VII:**74;
IX:85
elections **VII:**90–92; **IX:**102
Federal Trade Commission
Act **VII:**108
Johnson, Hiram Warren
VII:154
La Follette, Robert M.
VII:172, 173
La Follette, Robert M., Jr.
VIII:208
muckrakers **VII:**216
New Freedom **VII:**236
New Nationalism **VII:**237
Payne-Aldrich Tariff Act
VII:255
politics (1900–1928)
VII:262
progressivism **VII:**271
Republican Party **VII:**300
Roosevelt, Theodore
VII:304
Taft, William Howard
VII:348

tariffs **VII:**349
Wallace, Henry A. **VIII:**411,
412
Wheeler, Burton K.
VIII:416
progressivism (1890s) **VI:294–
295**
civil service reform **VI:**73
Comstock, Anthony **VI:**79
Ely, Richard Theodore
VI:115
Gladden, Washington
VI:149
Internal Revenue taxes
VI:194
Social Gospel **VI:**335
progressivism (early 20th century)
VII:270–272
Adamson Act **VII:**1–2
Addams, Jane **VII:**2–3
Adkins v. Children's Hospital
VII:3
AFL **VII:**11
Antiquities Act **VII:**16
anti-Semitism **VII:**17–18
Baldwin, Roger Nash
VII:31–32
Buck v. Bell **VII:**43
Budget and Accounting Act
VII:44
business **VII:**46
Cannon, Joseph Gurney
VII:48
Catt, Carrie Lane Chapman
VII:50
child labor **VII:**52
Children's Bureau **VII:**53
Committee for Public
Information **VII:**59
Congress **VII:**62
criminal justice **VII:**66
Democratic Party **VII:**74
Dewey, John **VII:**77
Dillingham Commission
VII:77
direct election of senators
VII:78
Elkins Act **VII:**94
eugenics **VII:**103
Farmer-Labor Party
VII:105
Federal Trade Commission
Act **VII:**108
free speech fights **VII:**117–
118
Gilman, Charlotte Perkins
VII:125
Goldmark, Josephine Clara
VII:127
Harding, Warren Gamaliel
VII:134
Hearst, William Randolph
VII:138
Hepburn Act **VII:**138–139
history **VII:**139
Johnson, Hiram Warren
VII:154

progressivism (early 20th century)
(continued)
  journalism **VII**:159, 160
  La Follette, Robert M.
    VII:172–173
  Mann-Elkins Act **VII**:190
  marriage and family
    VII:191
  mothers' pensions **VII**:213–
    214
  muckrakers **VII**:216–217
  Muller v. Oregon **VII**:217–
    218, **417–420**
  New Freedom **VII**:236
  New Nationalism **VII**:237
  New Unionism **VII**:238
  Non-Partisan League
    VII:241
  NWLB **VII**:229
  oil industry **VII**:244
  Palmer, Alexander Mitchell
    VII:249
  Pan-American Exposition
    VII:252
  Paul, Alice **VII**:254
  Payne-Aldrich Tariff Act
    VII:255
  peace movements **VII**:255
  Pinchot, Gifford **VII**:260
  Pingree, Hazen S. **VII**:260
  politics (1900–1928)
    VII:261–262
  Progressive Party **VII**:269–
    270
  Prohibition **VII**:272–274
  Pure Food and Drug Act
    VII:277
  radicalism **VII**:288
  Rauschenbusch, Walter
    VII:293
  science and technology
    VII:314
  Sinclair, Upton **VII**:325
  social work **VII**:330
  Supreme Court **VII**:342–
    343
  Taft, William Howard
    VII:347, 348
  tariffs **VII**:349
  Triangle Shirtwaist Fire
    VII:356–357
  Underwood-Simmons Tariff
    VII:359
  U.S. Steel **VII**:365
  veterans **VII**:371
  Vorse, Mary Heaton
    VII:375
  Wald, Lillian **VII**:377
  WILPF **VII**:386
  workers' compensation
    VII:391
"Progress of Colored Women, The"
  (Terrell) **VII**:352
Prohibition **VII**:**272–274**, *273*;
  VIII:444*c*
  agriculture **VII**:8
  conservatism **VIII**:83–84

criminal justice **VII**:67
Democratic Party **VII**:75;
  VIII:92, 93
election of 1932 **VIII**:108
elections **VII**:90
FMP **VIII**:134
jazz **VIII**:195
liberalism **VIII**:214
Maine Law **IV**:233–234
Mencken, Henry Louis
  VII:202
New Woman **VII**:240
presidency **VII**:269
progressivism **VI**:294;
  VII:270–272
radicalism **VII**:287
recreation **VIII**:328
religion **VII**:298
Smith, Alfred E. **VII**:326,
  327
taxation **VIII**:387
Volstead Act **VII**:374
Prohibition Amendment. *See*
  Eighteenth Amendment
Prohibition Bureau **VII**:135
Prohibition Party **VI**:**295–296**,
  296; **VII**:405*c*
  elections **VII**:90
  political parties, third
    VI:286
  Willard, Frances **VI**:394
Project Mercury. *See* Mercury
  space program
Proletarios **X**:254
Pro-Life Action League **X**:289
pro-life/pro-choice movements
  X:**288–289**
  birth control **X**:43
  Roberts, John G. **X**:311
  Roe v. Wade **X**:312
  Webster v. Reproductive
    Health Services **X**:369
Prolonged Popular War (GPP)
  movement **X**:254
Promise of American Life, The
  (Croly) **VII**:237
Promontory Point, Utah
  Mormon Church **IV**:90
  Pacific Railroad Act **V**:294
  Young, Brigham **IV**:408
propaganda **VII**:407*c*; **VIII**:**311–**
312
  advertising **VIII**:1
  Bureau of Motion Pictures
    VIII:55
  Capra, Frank **VIII**:62
  censorship **VIII**:65
  news media **VIII**:272
  OSS **VIII**:285
  OWI **VIII**:286
  war bonds **VIII**:412
  World War I **VII**:394
Propaganda and Popular
  Enlightenment, Nazi Ministry
  of **VIII**:311
Propaganda Movement
  (Philippines) **IX**:256

property forfeiture **X**:298
property rights **X**:**290–291**
  Brent, Margaret Reed **II**:47
  computers **X**:88
  conservation/
    environmentalism **X**:92
  Field, Stephen Johnson
    VI:126, 127
  Human Genome Project
    X:172
  Kelo v. City of New London
    X:195
  Locke, John **II**:208–209
  Scalia, Antonin **X**:316
  suffrage **II**:380; **III**:400–401
  women's status and rights
    II:424; **VI**:399
property taxes
  cities and urban life
    VIII:69
  education, primary/
    secondary **X**:113
  Supreme Court **X**:338
  taxation **V**:384
Prophecy Conferences **VI**:93
Prophet, the Shawnee
  (Tenskwatawa) **III**:**348–349**,
  465*c*, 466*c*
  alcohol **III**:13
  Catlin, George **IV**:84
  Harrison, William Henry
    IV:185
  Native Americans **III**:314,
    315; **IV**:274
  Native Americans in the War
    of 1812 **IV**:276, 277
  Tecumseh **III**:409
  Tippecanoe, Battle of
    III:411, 412
Prophetstown **III**:465*c*
  Harrison, William Henry
    IV:185
  Native Americans **III**:314;
    IV:274
  Native Americans in the War
    of 1812 **IV**:276
  Prophet, the Shawnee
    III:349
  Tecumseh **III**:409
  Tippecanoe, Battle of
    III:411
Proposition 8 **X**:150, 216
Proposition 22 **X**:149
Proposition 187 **X**:176
Proposition 209 **X**:10, 297, 381*c*
proprietary colonies **II**:**313–314**
  Lloyd, David **II**:208
  Maryland **II**:219–222
  Morris, Lewis **II**:243
Prospect before Us, The
  (Callender) **III**:74
Prospect Park (Brooklyn, New
  York) **VI**:120
Prosser, Gabriel **III**:10; **V**:362
Prosser, Thomas **III**:185
Prosser Slave Rebellion **IV**:344–
345

prostitution **V**:**315–316**
  Bowles, Samuel **VI**:43
  Greeley, Horace **V**:176
  progressivism **VI**:294
  Richmond, Virginia **V**:336
protectionism
  Harrison, Benjamin **VI**:161
  McKinley, William **VI**:240,
    241
  presidential campaigns
    (1870–1899) **VI**:293
  tariffs **VI**:352
Protestant, The **V**:280
Protestant Association **II**:220
Protestantism/Protestants **I**:397*c*;
  II:**314–316**; **III**:465*c*. *See also*
  specific Protestant faiths, e.g.:
  Baptists
  abortion **X**:4
  African-American churches,
    growth of **VI**:3–5
  African Americans **IV**:8;
    X:14
  Alamo, The **IV**:14
  anti-Catholic riots **IV**:22–24
  Austin, Stephen F. **IV**:40
  black legend **I**:31–32
  Bradford, William **II**:44
  Bradstreet, Anne Dudley
    II:45
  Calvin, John **I**:53–55
  Canada **III**:78
  Castile **I**:67
  Catholics **III**:82–83
  Chautauqua Institute **VI**:66
  Church of England **I**:74
  citizenship **III**:92
  Civil War **V**:73
  Congregationalists **II**:75
  Counterreformation **I**:98
  criminal justice **VII**:67
  Darwinism and religion
    VI:93
  deism **III**:134
  Democratic Party **IV**:118;
    VIII:92
  Dutch West India Company
    II:107
  education **II**:111; **VI**:110
  election of 1932 **VIII**:108
  elections, presidential **X**:118
  Elizabeth I **I**:120–121
  evangelical Christians
    X:124–125
  Finney, Charles Grandison
    IV:151
  Florida **II**:128
  Foxe's Book of Martyrs
    I:132
  Frémont, John C. **IV**:166
  French immigrants **II**:139
  German immigrants **II**:148
  German Reformed Church
    II:148–149
  government, British
    American **II**:151, 152
  Graham, Billy **IX**:138

Great Awakening **II**:154–157
Henry IV **I**:158
Henry VIII **I**:160
Huguenots **I**:170–171
Ignatius Loyola **I**:178–179
immigration **IV**:195; **V**:200;
  VI:186
imperialism **VI**:188
Indian Rights Association
  VI:190
James I **I**:192
Jesuits **I**:193
Know-Nothing Party **IV**:214
Léry, Jean de **I**:212–213
Luther, Martin **I**:217–219
Mary I **I**:232, 233
Massachusetts **II**:222
Mayhew, Jonathan **III**:293
Middletown **VII**:205
migration **IV**:255
monarchy, British **II**:240
Moody, Dwight Lyman
  VI:249–250
Native Americans **II**:253
nativism **VII**:234
neoconservatism **X**:252
Oregon Trail **IV**:285, 286
Philip II **I**:291
popular culture **III**:341
praying towns **II**:308
Presbyterians **II**:309
Prohibition Party **VI**:295–
  296
Puritans **I**:307–308;
  II:318–320
race and race relations
  IV:312
Ralegh, Sir Walter **I**:311
Reformation **I**:315, 317–318
religion **III**:360–362;
  IV:319, 321; **V**:331;
  VI:306–307; **VII**:297–
  299; **VIII**:334–336;
  IX:272; **X**:306, 307
religion, Euro-American
  II:328–329
religion, Native American
  II:331
religious liberty **III**:362
Republican Party **IV**:321
Roman Catholicism **II**:335;
  VI:315
St. Mary's City **II**:342–343
Seton, Elizabeth Ann
  IV:343
slavery **II**:357
Smith, John **II**:362
Social Gospel **VI**:334–335
Spanish Armada **I**:344
Spanish civil war **VIII**:369
spiritualism **IV**:355
Strong, Josiah **VI**:347
Sumner, William Graham
  VI:347
televangelism **X**:341–342
Texas Revolution **IV**:373
Trent, Council of **I**:369–370

Unitarianism **III**:419
Victorianism **VI**:374
Virginia **II**:402
YMCA/YWCA **VII**:397
Protestant work ethic **II**:**316–317**
"Prove It on Me Blues" (Waters)
  VII:220
Providence, Rhode Island **II**:435*c*
  Crummell, Alexander **VI**:87
  Easton, Hosea **IV**:129
  Fuller, Margaret **IV**:169
  Gilman, Charlotte Perkins
    VII:125
  lobbying **VI**:228
  railroads **IV**:314
  Rhode Island **II**:333
  Williams, Roger **II**:416
Providence Island (Bahamas)
  II:384, 385
Providence Journal **VI**:14
Provident, Lake **V**:260
Provident Hospital (Chicago,
  Illinois) **VI**:395
Provincetown, Massachusetts
  VII:179
Provincetown Players **VII**:130–
  131, 375
Provisional Army **V**:79, 80
Provisional Junta of National
  Reconstruction (Nicaragua)
  X:254
Provo, Utah **IV**:408
Prozac **X**:223
PRR. *See* Pennsylvania Railroad
Pruili, Antonio **I**:281
Prussia **IV**:260; **VII**:370
Pryor, Arthur **VI**:339, 340
Pryor, Ralph **IX**:179–180
pseudoephedrine **X**:244
PSLs (personal seat licenses)
  X:331
psychedelic drugs **IX**:355*c*
  Ginsberg, Allen **IX**:135
  Leary, Timothy **IX**:187, 188
  LSD **IX**:195–196
  music **IX**:229
psychiatry **III**:376
psychological warfare **VIII**:311,
  312
psychology **VI**:157–158
Psychology of Sex (Havelock)
  VII:118–119
"psycholytic" therapy **IX**:195
psychotropic drugs **X**:223–224
PT-109 **IX**:169
PT boats **VIII**:265, 359; **IX**:169
PTL (Praise the Lord) Club **X**:342
Ptolemy
  astrolabe **I**:15
  Mercator, Gerhardus **I**:240
  Ramusio, Giovanni Battista
    I:313
public assistance
  ethnic organizations **VII**:102
  poverty **III**:344
  Social Security Act
    VIII:363–365

Public Assistance, Bureau of
  VIII:421
Public Broadcasting Service (PBS)
  X:217, 344
Public Citizen **X**:241
Public Company Accounting
  Oversight Board **X**:171, 315
Public Company Accounting
  Reform and Investor Protection
  Act. *See* Sarbanes-Oxley Act
public education. *See* Mann,
  Horace
Public Enemy, The (film)
  VIII:245, 246
public health **III**:295; **VIII**:366;
  IX:**264–266**, 265. *See also*
  medicine, hospitals, and public
  health
Public Health Service, U.S.
  (USPHS) **VII**:403*c*; **VIII**:444*c*
  Children's Bureau **VII**:54
  medicine **VIII**:236; **IX**:210
  occupational health and
    safety **VII**:243
  public health **VII**:275, 276
  Sheppard-Towner Act
    VII:323
  Social Security Act
    VIII:364
  veterans **VII**:372
  Veterans Bureau **VII**:373
Public Health Service Act (1944)
  VIII:236; **IX**:265
public house. *See* taverns and inns
public housing **VIII**:445*c*;
  IX:**266–267**, 356*c*; **X**:379*c*
  cities and urban life **IX**:56
  Fair Deal **IX**:116
  liberalism **X**:208
  PWA **VIII**:314
  urban redevelopment
    IX:326
  Wagner, Robert F.
    VIII:410
Public Housing Act. *See* Wagner-
  Steagall Housing Act
public interest research groups
  (PIRGs) **X**:90, 241
*Publick Occurences Both Foreign
  and Domestick* **II**:163, 311
Public Land Act (1800) **IV**:293
public land policy **IV**:**304–307,**
  306*t*
  agriculture **IV**:13
  Cabet, Étienne **IV**:67
  claim clubs **IV**:95
  economy **IV**:130
  election of 1828 **IV**:136–137
  Harrison, William Henry
    IV:184
  lead mines **IV**:224
  migration **IV**:253, 255
  New Madrid earthquake
    IV:280
  panic of 1819 **IV**:293
Public Lands Commission (PLC)
  VI:141

Public Law 280 **IX**:241
Public Law 689 **VIII**:418
Public Law 733 **IX**:119
Public Opinion (Cantril)
  VIII:313
public opinion polls **VIII**:**312–
  313,** 445*c*
  advertising **VIII**:1
  election of 1940 **VIII**:110
  election of 1944 **VIII**:111
  Farley, James A. **VIII**:125
  Full Employment Bill
    VIII:145
  Italian Americans **VIII**:190
  Jews **VIII**:196
  liberalism **VIII**:216
  Munich Conference
    VIII:248
  popular culture **VIII**:303
  refugees **VIII**:330
  World War II home front
    VIII:434
public services **VI**:71
public transportation. *See* urban
  transportation
Public Utility Holding Company
  Act (PUHCA) **VIII**:**313–314**
  antimonopoly **VIII**:24
  Black, Hugo L. **VIII**:45
  Second New Deal **VIII**:356
  Willkie, Wendell L.
    VIII:417
public utility industry **VIII**:313
Public Works Administration
  (PWA) **VIII**:314
  Black Cabinet **VIII**:45, 46
  CWA **VIII**:74
  environment **VIII**:116
  ERAA **VIII**:114
  Federal Housing
    Administration (FHA)
    VIII:133
  Hopkins, Harry L. **VIII**:176
  Ickes, Harold L. **VIII**:183
  National Recovery
    Administration **VIII**:260
  Native Americans **VIII**:264
  NIRA **VIII**:257
  race and race relations
    VIII:319
  Social Security Act
    VIII:363
  transportation **VIII**:395
  USHA **VIII**:404
Public Works of Art Project
  (PWAP) **VIII**:29
publishing. *See* printing and
  publishing
Puck magazine **VI**:235, *235*
pueblo (structure)
  Indians of the desert
    Southwest **II**:176
  New Mexico **I**:264, 266
  Santa Fe **I**:326–327
Pueblo Bonito **I**:264
Pueblo Indian reservation
  VIII:186

Pueblo Indians **I:**_304_, **304–305;**
II:317–318
  art and architecture **I:**12
  Carson, Kit **IV:**82
  gender **II:**144
  Great Plains Indians **II:**157
  Hopi **I:**167
  Indian Reorganization Act
    VIII:186
  Indians of the desert
    Southwest **II:**176
  missions **II:**238
  Native Americans **II:**252;
    VII:233
  New Mexico **II:**263, 264
  Pueblo Revolt **II:**318
  religion **II:**330, 331
  Santa Fe **I:**326
  Vargas, Diego de **II:**397–
    398
Pueblo Lands Act **VII:**233
Pueblo Revolt **II:318,** 436_c_
  agriculture **II:**10
  Hopi **I:**168
  Indians of the desert
    Southwest **II:**176
  missions **II:**239
  Native Americans **II:**252
  Navajo **II:**254
  New Mexico **I:**266; **II:**263
  Popé **II:**301
  Pueblo **I:**305; **II:**317
puerpal fever **IV:**123
Puerto Rican nationalists
    IX:353_c_
Puerto Ricans **IX:267–268**
  cities and urban life **IX:**56
  Hispanic Americans **X:**166,
    167
  Latino movement **IX:**185
Puerto Rico **I:305–306; VI:**412_c_;
    VII:403_c_, 407_c_, 408_c_; **IX:**351_c_.
    See also Operation Bootstrap
  advertising **X:**7
  Columbus, Christopher
    I:85
  Foraker Act **VII:**110
  foreign policy **VI:**134;
    VII:113
  Jones Act (1917) **VII:**157
  Leahy, William D. **VIII:**211
  McKinley, William **VI:**241
  Ponce de León, Juan **I:**296
  presidency **VII:**268
  Taino **I:**352
  Tugwell, Rexford G.
    VIII:398
Puget Sound
  exploration **IV:**146
  Oregon Treaty of 1846
    IV:286, 287
  Wilkes expedition **IV:**400
PUHCA. _See_ Public Utility
    Holding Company Act
Pulaski, Casimir **III:**_349_, **349–**
    350, 383
Pulaski's Legion **III:**349, 350

Pulitzer, Joseph **VI:296–297,**
    411_c_
  Bennett, James Gordon, Jr.
    VI:33
  boxing **VI:**44
  Dana, Charles A. **VI:**92
  Hearst, William Randolph
    VII:137–138
  journalism **VII:**159
  newspapers **VI:**266, 267
  Statue of Liberty **VI:**344
  Watterson, Henry **VI:**386
  yellow journalism **VI:**405
Pulitzer Prize **VIII:**446_c_
  Faulkner, William **VIII:**128
  Garland, Hamlin **VI:**140
  Gershwin, George **VII:**124
  Hersey, John R. **VIII:**164
  literature **IX:**193, 194
  Mauldin, Bill **VIII:**233,
    234
  music **VII:**220; **VIII:**252
  photography **VIII:**296
  Pyle, Ernie **VIII:**314, 315
  Sinclair, Upton **VII:**326
Pullman, George M. **VI:**297;
    VII:73
Pullman Company
  Brotherhood of Sleeping Car
    Porters **VIII:**54
  cities and urban life **VII:**54
  Cleveland, Grover **VI:**75
  invention and technology
    VI:196
  Randolph, A. Philip
    VIII:321
Pullman Strike **VI:297–298,**
    411_c_
  Altgeld, John Peter **VI:**12
  Cleveland, Grover **VI:**75
  Darrow, Clarence Seward
    VII:70
  Debs, Eugene Victor
    VII:72–73
  Great Strike of 1877 **VI:**154
  Howells, William Dean
    VI:180
  labor/labor movements
    VII:170
  labor: strikes and violence
    VI:214
  Lloyd, Henry Demarest
    VI:227
  National Civic Federation
    VII:226
  World's Columbian
    Exposition **VI:**403
pulp fiction **VII:**265
Pulp Fiction (film) **X:**279
"pumpkin papers" **IX:**53, 146–147
punishment. _See_ crime and
    punishment
"punitive expedition." _See_ Mexican
    Invasion
Purchas, Samuel **I:306–307**
  art and architecture **I:**13
  Battel, Andrew **I:**28

  Henry the Navigator **I:**161
  London **I:**216
  Spice Islands **I:**345
Purchas his Pilgrimage (Purchas)
    I:306
Pure Food and Drug Act
    VII:276–277, 404_c_
  business **VII:**46
  Cannon, Joseph Gurney
    VII:48
  Meat Inspection Act **VII:**198
  muckrakers **VII:**217
  Narcotics Act **VII:**221
  Republican Party **VII:**300
  Roosevelt, Theodore
    VII:304
  Sinclair, Upton **VII:**325
Puritan-Pequot War. _See_ Pequot
  War
Puritans **I:307–308,** _308;_ **II:318–**
    320, _319,_ 435_c_, 436_c_
  alcohol **II:**16
  Anglican Church **II:**21
  Bermuda Company **I:**31
  black legend **I:**32
  Boston **II:**41
  Calvin, John **I:**55
  childhood **II:**67
  Church of England **I:**76
  Connecticut **II:**78
  Cotton, John **II:**81–82
  domesticity **II:**100, 101
  Dudley, Thomas **II:**103
  education **II:**111
  Eliot, John **II:**115
  Elizabeth I **I:**121
  Endecott, John **II:**116
  English Civil War **II:**116
  English immigrants **II:**117
  environment **II:**119
  government, British
    American **II:**151–153
  Harvard College **II:**163
  Hooker, Thomas **II:**165
  Jackson, Helen Hunt
    VI:199
  jeremiads **II:**184
  labor/labor movements
    II:200
  literature **II:**206
  Mann, Horace **IV:**237
  marriage and family **III:**288
  Maryland **II:**220
  Massachusetts **II:**222–224
  Massachusetts Bay Company
    II:225–226
  Mather, Cotton **II:**227
  Mather, Increase **II:**227–228
  Middletown **VII:**206
  monarchy, British **II:**240
  Morton, Thomas **II:**245
  music **II:**247
  New England Primer **II:**258
  New Hampshire **II:**260
  New Jersey **II:**261
  New York **II:**270
  Pequot War **II:**289

  praying towns **II:**308–309
  Presbyterians **II:**309
  Protestantism **II:**314, 316
  Protestant work ethic
    II:316–317
  religion **IV:**318
  religion, Euro-American
    II:329
  Sewall, Samuel **II:**350
  society, British American
    II:365
  transcendental movement
    IV:379
  Wheelwright, John **II:**412
  Wigglesworth, Michael
    II:414, 415
  Willard, Samuel **II:**415
  Winthrop, John **II:**417–418
  women's status and rights
    II:424–425
Purple code (Japan) **VIII:**76
Purple Heart **V:**255
Purviance, Edna **VII:**_215_
Purvis, Robert
  American Anti-Slavery
    Society **IV:**15
  54th Massachusetts
    Regiment **V:**142
  Underground Railroad
    V:397
Pusan, South Korea **IX:**177
Pushmataha **IV:307–308**
  Choctaw **IV:**86
  New Orleans, Battle of
    IV:281
  popular sovereignty **IV:**307
Putin, Vladimir **X:**143
Putnam, Ann **II:**275
Putnam, Israel **III:350**
  Bunker Hill, Battle of
    III:65
  Hudson Highlands
    campaign **III:**216
  Long Island, Battle of
    III:271
Putnam, James **III:**4
Putnam, Rufus **III:**323
Putnam, William L. **VI:**15
Putney, Vermont **VII:**320
Putún Maya **I:**351
PWA. _See_ Public Works
  Administration
PWAP (Public Works of Art
  Project) **VIII:**29
Pyequick **IX:**121
Pygmies **I:**56
Pyle, Ernie **VIII:314–315**
  Bradley, Omar N. **VIII:**50
  Mauldin, Bill **VIII:**233
  news media **VIII:**272
Pyle, Howard **VI:**183
Pynchon, Thomas **X:**211
Pyongyang, North Korea **IX:**177
pyramids
  Cholula **I:**74
  Palenque **I:**283
  Tikal **I:**359

Q

Qaddafi, Muammar al- **X**:16
al-Qaeda **X**:383c
  Afghanistan War **X**:10, 12
  Bush, George W. **X**:56
  foreign policy **X**:143
  Iraq War **X**:187
  Middle East **X**:229
  terrorism **X**:347, 348
Qaramanli, Yusuf **III**:46
Qatar **X**:267
Qing dynasty **VII**:40
Quadragesimo Anno **VIII**:64
Quaker City, The; or, The Monks
  of Monk-Hall (Lippard)
  IV:227–228
Quakers (Society of Friends)
  II:321–323, *322*, 436c;
  III:351–352, 460c; **V**:364–365
  abolitionism **II**:1–2; **III**:2;
    V:1
  African Americans **III**:8;
    IV:9
  American Anti-Slavery
    Society **IV**:15
  antislavery **III**:25
  Bartram, John **II**:34
  Benezet, Anthony **II**:35–36
  Bradford, William **II**:45
  citizenship **III**:92
  conscientious objectors
    VIII:83
  Cuffe, Paul **III**:127
  Dyer, Mary **II**:108
  education **II**:111–112
  Endecott, John **II**:116
  English immigrants **II**:117
  Enlightenment, American
    II:118
  Fellowship of Reconciliation
    VII:109
  female antislavery societies
    IV:147
  Foster, Abigail Kelley
    IV:161
  Franklin, Benjamin **III**:173,
    174
  Fries's Rebellion **III**:180
  gender **II**:145
  Genius of Universal
    Emancipation **IV**:175
  government, British
    American **II**:152, 153
  Great Awakening **II**:156
  Grimké, Angelina and Sarah
    IV:180
  Hicks, Elias **IV**:189
  Hoover, Herbert C.
    VIII:171
  Hume, Sophia Wigington
    II:169
  Husband, Herman **III**:218
  immigration **III**:221
  indentured servitude **II**:175
  Kalm, Peter **II**:191
  Lay, Benjamin **II**:203

  Lee, Ann **III**:257
  Liberty Party **IV**:226
  Lloyd, David **II**:208
  marriage and family **III**:288
  Mott, Lucretia **IV**:265, 266
  New Jersey **II**:261, 262
  Niles, Hezekiah **III**:318
  North Carolina Regulation
    III:321
  Palmer, Alexander Mitchell
    VII:249
  Paul, Alice **VII**:254
  Paxton Boys **II**:282
  peace movements **V**:295
  Penn, William **II**:283–284
  Pennsylvania **II**:284–286
  Philadelphia **II**:291
  Protestantism **II**:316
  religion **III**:360; **IV**:317;
    VI:309
  religion, Euro-American
    II:329
  religious liberty **III**:362
  Roman Catholicism **II**:336
  Ross, Betsy **III**:374
  Seneca Falls convention
    IV:340–341
  Shakers **III**:387
  slavery **III**:390, 391
  society, British American
    II:366
  Starbuck, Mary Coffin
    II:377
  Stuyvesant, Peter **II**:379
  Underground Railroad
    V:397
  Willard, Samuel **II**:415
  Wistar, Caspar **II**:419
  women's status and rights
    II:425
  Woolman, John **II**:426–427
Quant, Mary **IX**:116
Quanta Cura **VI**:315
Quantrill, William Clarke **V**:52,
  317–318, 445c
Quantrill's Raiders **V**:317
quantum computing **X**:88
quantum physics **VIII**:352
quarantine **III**:295
"quarantine speech" (Roosevelt)
  VIII:189
Quarry, Robert **II**:208
Quartering Act **III**:100, **352**,
  459c, 460c
Quarterly Anti-Slavery Magazine
  IV:16
Quartermaster Department
  V:401, 402
quartz mining **IV**:100
Quasi-War **III**:352–353, 464c
  Adams, Abigail **III**:3
  Adams, John **III**:6
  agriculture **III**:11
  Alien and Sedition Acts
    III:14
  Bache, Benjamin Franklin
    III:39

  Chauncey, Isaac **III**:86
  Democratic-Republican
    Party **III**:136
  Duane, James **III**:140
  Federalist Party **III**:164
  foreign affairs **III**:168, 169
  French Alliance **III**:178
  French Revolution **III**:179
  Fries's Rebellion **III**:180
  Hamilton, Alexander **III**:207
  Morse, Jedidiah **III**:307
  privateering **III**:348
  Talleyrand-Périgord, Charles-
    Maurice de **III**:405
  trade, domestic and foreign
    III:415
  XYZ affair **III**:451
Quay, Matthew Stanley **VI**:83,
  299–300, 382
Quayle, J. Danforth **X**:52,
  293–294
  Bush, George H. W. **X**:52
  Dukakis, Michael S. **X**:105
  neoconservatism **X**:252
Quebec **I**:186, 187; **II**:435c, 438c
  Canada **III**:78, 79
  Carleton, Guy **III**:81
  Champlain, Samuel de
    II:62, 63
  French colonies **II**:136
  Howe, Sir William **III**:215
  Jesuits **II**:185
  Loyalists **III**:276
  theater **II**:389
Quebec, Battle of **III**:353, *354*
  Arnold, Benedict **III**:31
  Burr, Aaron **III**:69
  Canada **III**:78
  Crèvecoeur, J. Hector St.
    John de **III**:127
  Montgomery, Richard
    III:301
  Morgan, Daniel **III**:303
  Revolutionary War **III**:368
  Schuyler, Philip John
    III:384
Quebec Act **II**:185; **III**:460c
  Canada **III**:77–79
  Carleton, Guy **III**:81
  Catholics **III**:83
  Coercive Acts **III**:100
  frontier, the **III**:181
  Proclamation of 1763
    III:348
Quebec City **II**:323
  King William's War **II**:195
  Queen Anne's War **II**:324
  Seven Years' War **II**:348–
    349
  Wolfe, James **II**:421
Quebec Conference **VIII**:275,
  431
Queen Anne's War **II**:323–324,
  437c
  Deerfield Massacre
    II:92–93
  Massachusetts **II**:224

  New York **II**:272
  privateering **II**:313
Queens, New York City **VIII**:273
Queensberry Rules **VI**:44
Queens College (Cambridge
  University) **VI**:87
Queen's College (Rutgers
  University) **II**:107
Queenston Heights, Battle of
  Canada **III**:79
  Scott, Winfield **IV**:336
  War of 1812 **IV**:391
Quelch, John **II**:296
Queries of Highest Consideration
  (Williams) **II**:416
Querini, Vincenzo **I**:98
Quesada, Gaspar de **I**:223
Quest for Common Learning,
  The (Carnegie Foundation)
  X:113
Questions of the Soul (Hecker)
  VI:316
Quetzalcoatl **I**:309
  Aztecs **I**:21
  Cholula **I**:74
  Cortés, Hernán **I**:96
  Durán, Diego **I**:114
  Maya **I**:236
  Moctezuma II Xocoyotzin
    I:246
  Sahagún, Bernardino de
    I:323
  Toltecs **I**:364
Quezon, Manuel **IX**:256
quibla **I**:138
Quiché kingdom **I**:235
Quids **III**:280
quilombos **II**:374
Quilting Frolic (Krimmel) **IV**:29
Quimby, Phineas Parkhurst **VI**:69,
  106
Quincy, Hannah Sturgis **III**:354
Quincy, Josiah **III**:354, 460c
  Adams, John **III**:5
  Boston Massacre **III**:58
  Boston Tea Party **III**:59
Quincy Mining Company **VII**:210
Quincy River **IV**:200
Quinn, Paul **VI**:4
quipu. *See* khipu
Quitman, John A. **IV**:112
quitrent
    land **II**:201
    land riots **II**:202
    Penn, William **II**:284
Quivira **I**:93
quiz shows **X**:344
Quok Walker Case **III**:354–355
  abolitionism **III**:1
  antislavery **III**:25
  Freeman, Elizabeth
    III:176
Quorum of the Twelve Apostles
  Deseret, State of **IV**:119
  Mormon Church **IV**:90
  Nauvoo **IV**:279
  Young, Brigham **IV**:407

Quota Act **VII:279,** 408*c*
  AFL **VII:**12
  anti-Semitism **VII:**17
  citizenship **VII:**56
  Coolidge, Calvin John **VII:**65
  immigration **VII:**144
  Mexican immigration
    VII:203
  National Origins Act
    VII:227
  nativism **VII:**234
  population trends **VII:**266
  progressivism **VII:**271
  race and race relations
    VII:282
quotas **VIII:**330
quota system **IX:**353*c*; **X:**376*c*,
  377*c*
  agriculture **IX:**7, 8
  Asian Americans **X:**32
  Gramm-Rudman-Hollings
    Act **X:**158–159
  Great Society **IX:**139
  immigration **IX:**155; **X:**175
  Immigration Act (1965)
    IX:156
  McCarran-Walter Act
    IX:204, 205
  population trends **IX:**260
Qur'an
  Islam **I:**188
  slave trade **I:**339
  Sufism **I:**347
Quraysh **I:**238

R

RA. *See* Resettlement
  Administration
Rabaul, Solomon Islands
  MacArthur, Douglas
    IX:197–198
  Solomon Islands **VIII:**366
  World War II Pacific theater
    VIII:435
Rabb, Maxwell **IX:**45
Rabbit, Run (Updike) **X:**358
rabies **VII:**198
Rabin, Yitzhak **X:**229
Raccoon Roughs **V:**170
race and race relations **IV:309–**
  313
race and racial conflict **II:325–**
  326, 436*c*; **III:357–358;**
  V:319–320; VII:281–284,
  407*c*; **VIII:317–319,** 443*c*,
  447*c*, 448*c*; **IX:269–271,** 270*;*
  X:295–298, 296, 381*c*
  abolitionism **V:**1–4
  ACLU **VIII:**17–18
  AFL **VIII:**18
  Africa **IX:**4
  African Americans **III:**9–10;
    VIII:2–5; **IX:**4
  antilynching legislation
    VIII:22

anti-Semitism **VII:**16–18
Baldwin, James **IX:**35
Baptists **II:**33; **III:**44–45
Bethune, Mary McLeod
  VIII:44
big bands **VIII:**44
Birmingham confrontation
  IX:39–40
Birth of a Nation, The
  VII:37
Black Panthers **IX:**40–41
Boas, Franz Uri **VII:**39–40
Brownsville Riot **VII:**42
Buffalo Soldiers **VI:**54
Burger, Warren E. **X:**51
Burke Act **VII:**44
Catto, Octavius V. **V:**59
censorship **VII:**65
children **VIII:**67
cities and urban life **V:**67;
  VIII:70; **IX:**56
citizenship **VII:**57
civil rights **VIII:**72–73
cosmetics and beauty
  industry **VII:**66
DuBois, W.E.B. **VII:**81
Easton, Hosea **IV:**130
EEOC **IX:**110
environment **III:**155–156
ethnocentrism **II:**122, 123
Executive Order 8802
  VIII:120, 465–466
Executive Order 9066
  VIII:120–121, 466–467
Faulkner, William **VIII:**128
FEPC **VIII:**123
FERA **VIII:**133
Foraker Act **VII:**110
Forten, James **III:**170
government **VIII:**154
Graham, Billy **IX:**138
Great Migration **VII:**129
Great Society **IX:**139
Haiti **III:**204
Hall, Prince **III:**205
Hamer, Fannie Lou **IX:**141
Harlem Renaissance
  VII:136
Higginson, Thomas
  Wentworth **V:**189
immigration **III:**221
intelligence tests **VII:**148
jazz **VIII:**195
Jefferson, Thomas **III:**234,
  235
Johnson, Andrew **V:**213
Johnson, Hiram Warren
  VII:154
Johnson, Jack **VII:**154–155
Jones Act (1917) **VII:**157
Joplin, Scott **VII:**158
Ku Klux Klan **VII:**165
liberalism **VIII:**215, 216
Locke, Alain LeRoy
  VII:183
lost cause, the **V:**245
Louis, Joe **VIII:**223

Mead, Margaret **VII:**197
Memphis riot (1866)
  V:259–260
Methodism **III:**297
Mexican Americans
  VIII:237
migration **VII:**207;
  VIII:240
mothers' pensions **VII:**214
music **VII:**220
Myrdal, Gunnar **VIII:**252–
  253
NAACP **VII:**224
NACW **VII:**225
Navy, U.S. **VIII:**265
Negro Convention
  movement **IV:**279–280
New York City draft riots
  V:284
Niagara Movement **VII:**240
Owens, Jesse **VIII:**289
Pan-American Exposition
  VII:252
Parks, Rosa **IX:**254
postwar planning **VIII:**306
praying towns **II:**309
Red Scare **VII:**296
Rhinelander case **VII:**301
riots **II:**372
Robinson, Jackie **IX:**277–
  278
scalawags **V:**339, 340
science and technology
  VII:315
Scottsboro Boys **VIII:**353–
  354
segregation **VII:**319–321
Selective Service **VIII:**358
sharecropping **V:**349
Singleton, Benjamin **V:**361
slave resistance **II:**352–353
slavery **II:**356; **III:**391;
  V:364
South **VIII:**367
southern demagogues
  VII:332
sports and recreation
  VII:335
Sweet trial **VII:**344–345
Tarbell, Ida Minerva
  VII:349
Terrell, Mary Eliza Church
  VII:352
Thomas, Norman **VIII:**394
Till, Emmett Louis **IX:**318
Trotter, William Monroe
  VII:357
Turner, Henry McNeal
  VI:366
UFW **IX:**324
UNIA **VIII:**361–362
White, Walter **VIII:**416
women's status and rights
  IX:348
World War II **VIII:**427
zoot-suiters **VIII:**441–442
Race Track, The (Ryder) **VI:**320

racial discrimination/racism
  IX:355*c*, 356*c*
  affirmative action **X:**10
  African Americans **IX:**4, 5;
    X:14–15
  Asian-American movement
    IX:21
  Black Power **IX:**41
  Burger, Warren E. **X:**51
  Civil Rights Act (1964)
    IX:60–61
  Civil Rights Act (1991) **X:**77
  education, higher **X:**112
  Great Society **IX:**139
  *Heart of Atlanta Motel v.
    U.S.* **IX:**145–146
  Horton, Willie **X:**168
  Jackson State protests **X:**192
  labor/labor movements
    IX:182
  Levitt, William J. **IX:**189
  liberalism **X:**208
  marriage and family **IX:**202
  McCarran-Walter Act
    IX:204, 205
  militia movement **X:**231
  Native Americans **IX:**241
  PCSW **IX:**262
  political correctness **X:**276
  Rickey, Branch **IX:**277
  SNCC **IX:**302–303
  Urban League **IX:**325
  Voting Rights Act of 1965
    IX:333–334
  Warren Court **IX:**338
  Wilkins, Roy **IX:**345
racial harassment **X:**77
Racial Integrity Act **VII:284,** 301,
  408*c*
racial quotas **X:**376*c*
Racine College **VII:**211
racing **VIII:**328
racism. *See* racial discrimination/
  racism
Racketeer Influenced and Corrupt
  Organizations Act (RICO)
  X:298–299, 375*c*
  abortion **X:**4–5
  crime and punishment **X:**97
  pro-life/pro-choice
    movements **X:**289
  tobacco suits **X:**353
Rackham, Calico Jack **II:**296
radar
  aviation **IX:**27
  GE **IX:**132
  technology **IX:**311
Radcliffe College **VI:**109
radical and labor press **VII:284–**
  286
  birth control **VII:**36
  Buck's Stove **VII:**42–43
  Flynn, Elizabeth Gurley
    VII:109
  ILGWU **VII:**149
  literature **VII:**179
  The Masses **VII:**193

muckrakers **VII:**216
NWTUL **VII:**231
occupational health and
    safety **VII:**243
Sanger, Margaret **VII:**312
Seattle General Strike
    VII:318
socialism **VII:**327
Supreme Court **VII:**343
Tarbell, Ida Minerva
    VII:349
Trading with the Enemy Act
    VII:355–366
Valesh, Eva McDonald
    VII:367
Vorse, Mary Heaton
    VII:375
"Radical Chic" (Wolfe) **X:**370
radicalism **VII:286–288**
    American Legion **VII:**13–14
    Anarchist Immigration Act
        VII:14–15
    civil liberties **VIII:**71
    feminism **X:**133, 134
    labor/labor movements
        VII:171
    neoconservatism **X:**252
    radical and labor press
        VII:285, 286
    Red Scare **VII:**296
    Russian Revolution **VII:**308
radical labor **VI:**212, **212–213.**
    See also labor: strikes and
    violence
Radical Reconstruction
    Exodusters **VI:**122
    Freedmen's Bureau **V:**161
    Garrison, William Lloyd
        V:165
    Harper, Frances Ellen
        Watkins **VI:**160
    Hayes, Rutherford B.
        VI:166
    Liberia **VI:**223
    Mallory, Stephen R. **V:**248
    race and race relations
        V:320
    veterans **V:**415
Radical Republicans **V:320–321,**
    446c
    Allison, William Boyd **VI:**11
    amnesty, acts of **V:**9
    assassination of Abraham
        Lincoln **V:**21
    Black Codes **V:**35
    Blair, Francis Preston, Jr.
        V:36
    Butler, Benjamin Franklin
        V:53
    Civil Rights Act (1866) **V:**70
    Civil War **V:**74
    Congress **V:**89–90
    Copperheads **V:**94
    Democratic Party **V:**109
    Dickinson, Anna E. **V:**111
    impeachment of Andrew
        Johnson **V:**201–203

Ingersoll, Robert Green
    VI:193
Johnson, Andrew **V:**212, 213
Joint Committee on the
    Conduct of the War
    V:215, 216
journalism **V:**219
Julian, George Washington
    V:219
Lincoln, Abraham **V:**236
loyalty oaths **V:**246
Morton, Oliver P. **V:**270
Reconstruction **V:**324–325
Reconstruction Acts **V:**327,
    328
Sheridan, Philip H. **V:**353
Sickles, Daniel E. **V:**361
slavery **V:**364
Stevens, Thaddeus **V:**372,
    373
Thirteenth Amendment
    V:388
U.S. Military Academy at
    West Point **V:**409
violence and lawlessness
    VI:376
Wade, Benjamin Franklin
    V:421
Wade-Davis Bill **V:**421
Watterson, Henry **VI:**386
Wilson, Henry **V:**433
women's status and rights
    VI:399
radio **VII:288–290,** *289, 408c,*
    409c; **VIII:319–321,** *320, 443c*
    advertising **VII:**4, 5; **VIII:**1;
        X:7
    affirmative action **X:**9
    anti-Semitism **VIII:**25
    big bands **VIII:**44
    business **VIII:**58
    Catholics **VIII:**64
    censorship **VIII:**65
    Congress **VIII:**81
    Coughlin, Father Charles E.
        VIII:87–88
    electricity **VII:**93
    Ellington, Duke **VIII:**112
    entertainment, popular
        VII:95, 97
    FCC **VIII:**130–131
    fireside chats **VIII:**137–138
    FMP **VIII:**134
    GE **VII:**123; **IX:**132
    Goodman, Benny **VIII:**150
    government **VIII:**153
    Graham, Billy **IX:**138
    Great Migration **VII:**129
    Guthrie, Woody **VIII:**160
    invention and technology
        VII:151
    Irish Americans **VIII:**188
    Jews **VIII:**195
    journalism **VII:**160–161
    Long, Huey P. **VIII:**223
    marriage and family
        VIII:230

McPherson, Aimee Semple
    VII:197
media **X:**219–220
mining **VII:**210
Muhammad, Elijah **IX:**226
music **VII:**220; **VIII:**249–
    251
news media **VIII:**271–272
OWI **VIII:**285–286
popular culture **VII:**263,
    265; **VIII:**301–303
propaganda **VIII:**311, 312
public opinion polls
    VIII:312, 313
race and race relations
    VIII:317
recreation **VIII:**327, 329
religion **VIII:**334; **IX:**271
rock and roll **IX:**278–279
Roosevelt, Franklin D.
    VIII:345
sports and recreation **IX:**298
technology **VIII:**389
Tin Pan Alley **VII:**353
vaudeville **VII:**369
Welles, Orson **VIII:**414, 415
White Citizens' Councils
    IX:342
World War II home front
    VIII:433
Radio Act (1912) **VII:**151
Radio Act (1927)
    FCC **VIII:**130
    invention and technology
        VII:151
    journalism **VII:**161
Radio City Music Hall (New York
    City) **VIII:**28
Radio Corporation of America
    (RCA) **VII:**97, 288
Radio Free Europe **VIII:**43
Radio Security Service (MI-6)
    VIII:187
radio telescope **VIII:**352
RAF. *See* Royal Air Force
Raff, Joachim **VI:**233
raffia **I:**200
Ragged Dick (Alger) **VI:**11
Ragnarok: The Age of Fire
    (Donnelly) **VI:**100
ragtime
    jazz **VII:**153
    Joplin, Scott **VII:**158
    music **VI:**258; **VII:**219, 220
Ragtime Dance, The (Joplin)
    VII:158
Railroad Administration **VII:**12,
    290–291
Railroad Retirement **IX:**210
Railroad Retirement Act
    VIII:382
railroads **IV:313–316,** *314,*
    315m, 415c; **V:321–322,** *322,*
    446c; **VI:301–303,** *302, 408c;*
    VII:404c, 407c, 408c
    Adamson Act **VII:**1, 2
    AFL **VII:**12

agriculture **IV:**12; **VI:**8
Allison, William Boyd **VI:**11,
    12
Andrews's Raid **V:**11
anti-Chinese agitation, rise
    of **IV:**24
Atkinson, Edward **VI:**21
banking, investment **VI:**23
Boxer Rebellion **VII:**40
Bruce, Blanche Kelso **V:**47
business and government
    VI:56, 57; **VII:**46
business cycles **VI:**58
California Trail **IV:**78
canal era **IV:**80
Carnegie, Andrew **VI:**62
carpetbaggers **V:**56
cattle kingdom **VI:**64
Chinese Exclusion Act
    VI:68
cities and urban life **IV:**91;
    V:66; **VI:**70
Civil War **V:**74
Coeur d'Alene miners' strike
    VI:77
communications **VI:**77, 78
Comstock Lode **IV:**105–106
Copperheads **V:**95
corruption, political **VI:**83
Crédit Mobilier **VI:**96–97
Democratic Party **VI:**95
Deseret, State of **IV:**120
dollar diplomacy **VII:**79
Donnelly, Ignatius Loyola
    VI:99, 100
Douglas, Stephen A. **V:**114
economy **IV:**131; **V:**121, 124
Edison, Thomas Alva
    VI:106–107
Elkins Act **VI:**94
Ely, Richard Theodore
    VI:115
entertainment, popular
    VI:118
Erie Canal **IV:**143
Exodusters **VI:**123
exploration **IV:**146
farmers' alliances **VI:**125
filibustering **V:**145
flour milling **VI:**129–130
Forbes, John Murray
    VI:132
foreign policy **IV:**158
Gadsden Purchase **IV:**173–
    174
Gould, Jay **VI:**151
Great Strike of 1877 **VI:**154
Greeley, Horace **V:**176
Hayes, Rutherford B.
    VI:167–168
Hill, James J. **VI:**172–173
homesteading **VI:**175
Hoosac Tunnel **VI:**176–177
Huntington, Collis Potter
    VI:180–181
illustration, photography,
    and graphic arts **VI:**183

railroads (continued)
immigration **V:**200, 201;
VI:185–186
industrial development
IV:200; **V:**204–205
Industrial Revolution,
Second **VI:**190, 192
Ingersoll, Robert Green
VI:193
internal improvements
IV:202–203
Interstate Commerce Act
VI:420–423
investments, foreign, in the
United States **VI:**197
Jim Crow laws **VI:**203, 204
Johnson, Hiram Warren
VII:154
journalism **IV:**209
Knights of Labor **VI:**209,
210
Lease, Mary Elizabeth
Clyens **VI:**220
Lincoln, Abraham **V:**237
lobbying **VI:**228
Longstreet, James **V:**242
lumbering **IV:**231
Mann-Elkins Act **VII:**190
Marsh, George Perkins
VI:239
McClellan, George Brinton
V:250
Meat Inspection Act
VII:198
meatpacking **VI:**243
Mexican-American War
IV:252–253
Mexican immigration
VII:202
Mexican Revolution
VII:204
migration **IV:**255
mining **VII:**208, 210
Mitchell, John **VII:**211
Morgan, John Pierpont
VI:250–251
Mormon Church **IV:**90
Mormon Trail **IV:**262
Morse, Samuel F. B. **IV:**264
National Road **IV:**273
Native Americans **VII:**232
New Freedom **VII:**236
New South **VI:**265
New York City **V:**282
Northern Securities Case
VII:241
occupational health and
safety **VII:**243
oil **VI:**271
oil industry **VII:**244
Omaha platform **VI:**272
Open Door Policy **VII:**246
Oregon Trail **IV:**286
overland mail **IV:**291
Pacific Railroad Act **V:**293–
294, **458–460**
panic of 1857 **V:**294

Patrons of Husbandry
VI:278, 279
photography **V:**304
Plessy v. Ferguson **VI:**284
political parties, third
VI:286
Pullman Strike **VI:**297–298
Railroad Administration
VII:290–291
Republican Party **V:**333
Santa Fe Trail **IV:**332
science, invention, and
technology **IV:**333;
V:342–343; **VI:**196
Scott, Thomas Alexander
VI:326
Sherman Antitrust Act
VI:330
Shiloh, Battle of **V:**358
Standard Oil **VII:**335
steel industry **VII:**336
Stevens, Thaddeus **V:**372
strikes **V:**374
suburbanization/suburbs
VII:340
Supreme Court **VI:**348
tactics and strategy **V:**380
Taft, William Howard
VII:347
trade, domestic and foreign
VI:359
transportation **V:**390–392
trusts **VI:**361–362
Vanderbilt, Cornelius
IV:387
Vicksburg campaign **V:**416,
417
Villard, Henry **VI:**375
violence and lawlessness
VI:376
Washington, D.C. **V:**426
Wells-Barnett, Ida Bell
VI:387
Whigs **IV:**396
Young, Brigham **IV:**408
Railroad Shopmen's Strike
VII:291–292, 408*c*
Adamson Act **VII:**2
Harding, Warren Gamaliel
VII:135
labor/labor movements
VII:171
presidency **VII:**269
Railway Labor Act (1934) **VIII:**54
Rainbow City **VII:**251
Rainbow People, The (Laurence)
IX:349
Rainey, Gertrude "Ma" **VII:**219,
220
Rainey, Joseph H. **V:322–323**
Rains, Claude *VIII:*247
Rains, Joseph **V:**341
Raisin in the Sun, A (Hansberry)
IX:354*c*
African Americans **IX:**5
literature **IX:**193
popular culture **IX:**258

Rajai, Ali **X:**185
Ralegh, Sir Walter **I:311–312,**
312, 398*c*
Barlowe, Arthur **I:**28
El Dorado **I:**119
Elizabeth I **I:**121
Gilbert, Sir Humphrey
I:140
Grenville, Sir Richard
I:145
Harriot, Thomas **I:**154, 156
horses **II:**166
Lane, Ralph **I:**203
Manteo **I:**229
monarchy, British **II:**240
monsters **I:**249
North Carolina **II:**274
Requerimiento **I:**319
Roanoke **I:**320, 322
Spanish Armada **I:**345
Thevet, André **I:**357
Wanchese **I:**382
White, John **I:**383
Raleigh **III:**47
Ramirez, Manny **X:**330
Ramona (Jackson) **VI:**199
Ramsay, Bertram **VIII:**275
Ramsey, Alexander **VI:**99
Ramusio, Giovanni Battista
I:312–313
Cabral, Pedro Álvares **I:**47
corn **I:**92
French explorations of the
Atlantic **I:**133
Hakluyt, Richard, the
Younger **I:**152
khipu **I:**199
Leo Africanus **I:**210
Oviedo y Valdés, Gonzalo
Fernández de **I:**281
Peter Martyr **I:**290
Timbuktu **I:**360
Venice **I:**376
rancheros **IV:**356
Ranch Life and the Hunting Trail
(Roosevelt) **VI:**310
rancho system
California **IV:**70–71
California missions **IV:**77
Dana, Richard Henry
IV:113
Larkin, Thomas Oliver
IV:222
public land policy **IV:**306
Rand, Ayn **X:**93
Randall, Samuel J. **VI:**292
Rand Corporation **X:**349
Randolph, A. Philip **VIII:321–
322,** 447*c*
African Americans **VIII:**4
Brotherhood of Sleeping Car
Porters **VIII:**54
civil rights **VIII:**72
Executive Order 8802
VIII:120
FEPC **VIII:**123
Garvey, Marcus **VII:**122

March on Washington
(1963) **VIII:**227–228
NAACP **VIII:**256
race and race relations
VIII:318, 319
White, Walter **VIII:**416
Randolph, Edmund **III:358,**
463*c*
Constitutional Convention
III:109
Madison, James **III:**282
Neutrality Proclamation
III:315
Pickering, Timothy **III:**335
Wilkinson, James **III:**443
Randolph, Edward **II:326**
Dominion of New England
II:102
Dudley, Joseph **II:**103
smuggling **II:**364
Randolph, George Wythe **V:**73,
85
Randolph, John **III:358–359**
Non-Importation Act
III:319
Non-Intercourse Act
III:319
Randolph, Edmund **III:**358
War Hawks **IV:**389
Randolph, Peyton **III:**115
Randsell Act (1930) **IX:**235
Ranger, USS **III:**239
Range wars **VI:**376
Ranke, Leopold von **VII:**139
Rankin, Jeannette **VII:292,** 406*c*
Hamilton, Alice **VII:**133
isolationists **VIII:**190
peace movements **VII:**256
Rankin, John **IX:**147, 150
Rankin, Thomas **III:**36
rape
capital punishment **X:**66
marriage and family **II:**218
women's status and rights
II:426
rape crisis hotlines **X:**133
Rapidan River
Chancellorsville, Battle of
V:61
Overland campaign **V:**290
Wilderness, Battle of the
V:432
Rapid City, South Dakota **VI:**85
Rapier, James T. **V:323**
rap music **X:**238, 279
Rapp, George **IV:**320
Rappahannock River
Chancellorsville, Battle of
V:61, 62
Fredericksburg, Battle of
V:157
Harvard Regiment **V:**186
Lee, Robert E. **V:**231
Peninsular campaign **V:**298
"rapture" **X:**125
Raritan, New Jersey **IV:**396
Raritan Indians **II:**192

Raskob, John J. **VIII**:19
Rathbone, Henry Reed **V**:20–21, 39
rationality **X**:207
rationing *VIII:322*, **322–323**, 447c
black market **VIII**:46
Henderson, Leon **VIII**:163
Hoover, Herbert C. **VIII**:171
marriage and family **VIII**:232
mobilization **VIII**:242
OPA **VIII**:282
OWMR **VIII**:287
reconversion **VIII**:326
recreation **VIII**:328
rubber **VIII**:348
scrap drives **VIII**:354
transportation **VIII**:396
wage and price controls **VIII**:409
women's status and rights **VIII**:424
World War II **VIII**:427
World War II home front **VIII**:432, 433
Raton Mountains **IV**:330
Raton Pass **IV**:330, 332
rats **I**:81
Rauh, Ida **VII**:375
Rauh, Joseph **IX**:13, 14, 220
Raulston, John T. **VII**:317
Rauschenberg, Robert **IX**:19
Rauschenbusch, Walter **VII**:292–293
radicalism **VII**:288
religion **VII**:297
Social Gospel **VI**:335
Rauwolf, Leonhard **I**:79
"Raven, The" (Poe) **IV**:229
Ravitch, Diane **X**:237
R.A.V. v. City of St. Paul **X**:316
Rawdon, Francis
Charleston, siege of **III**:84
Eutaw Springs, Battle of **III**:159
Hobkirk's Hill, Battle of **III**:213, 214
Rawlins, John A. **V**:267
Raw People **I**:393
Ray, Charlotte **V**:323–324
Ray, James Earl **IX**:23; **X**:34
Rayburn, Sam **VIII**:313
Raymond, Henry J. **V**:446c
Raynal, Abbé **III**:127
Raynolds, William **IV**:64
Raytheon Corporation **IX**:286
RCA (Radio Corporation of America)
business **VIII**:57
computers **IX**:71
invention and technology **VII**:151
Job Corps **IX**:161
radio **VII**:289, 290
stock market crash **VIII**:376

RCA building (New York City) **VIII**:28
RCA Victor Records
entertainment, popular **VII**:97
music **VII**:220
Presley, Elvis **IX**:263
REA. *See* Rural Electrification Administration
Read, Deborah **III**:173, 175
Read, George **III**:373
Read, Mary **II**:296
Ready.gov **X**:167
Reagan, John H. **V**:85, 247
Reagan, Ronald W., and administration **X**:*34, 85, 180, 299*, **299–302**, 378c, 379c
ABM Treaty **X**:27, 28
abortion **X**:4
Africa **X**:15, 16
Americans for Democratic Action **IX**:13
Anderson, John B. **X**:25
arms race **IX**:17; **X**:30
assassinations **X**:35
Bennett, William J. **X**:41
Boland Amendment **X**:45
Bork, Robert **X**:45
Brandenburg Gate Remarks **X**:396–399
Buchanan, Patrick J. **X**:49
Buckley, William F., Jr. **X**:49, 50
Bush, George H. W. **X**:52
business **X**:57
campaign finance **X**:63
Carter, James Earl, Jr. **X**:67, 69
Catholic Bishops' Letter **X**:70
cold war, end of **X**:85
conservatism **IX**:75
conservative movement **X**:92–94
contras **X**:95
defense policy **X**:100
détente **X**:104
Dole, Robert **X**:105
economy **X**:109, 110
education, primary/secondary **X**:113
elections, presidential **X**:116
federalism **X**:130–131
feminism **X**:134
Ford, Gerald R. **X**:139
foreign policy **X**:142
Free Speech Movement **IX**:126
Goldwater, Barry **IX**:136
Grenada, invasion of **X**:160
gun control **X**:161
Habib, Philip C. **X**:163
Haig, Alexander M., Jr. **X**:163, 164
Helms, Jesse A., Jr. **X**:165
House of Representatives **X**:169

INF Treaty **X**:179–181
Iran-contra affair **X**:183–184
Iranian hostage crisis **X**:185
Kemp, Jack F. **X**:196
labor/labor movements **X**:202
Laffer curve **X**:204
Latin America **X**:206
Meese, Edwin C., III **X**:225
Middle East **X**:228, 229
military-industrial complex **IX**:216
Mitchell, George **X**:232
Mondale, Walter F. **X**:234
Moral Majority **X**:234
NEA/NEH **X**:245
neoconservatism **X**:252
NEPA **X**:246
Nicaragua **X**:254
North, Oliver L. **X**:258
O'Connor, Sandra Day **X**:265
OMB **X**:266
O'Neill, Thomas "Tip" P., Jr. **X**:267
political parties **X**:276, 277
pro-life/pro-choice movements **X**:289
property rights **X**:290
Reaganomics **X**:302
Rehnquist, William H. **X**:305
Republican Party **IX**:275
SALT I/SALT II **X**:337
Scalia, Antonin **X**:316
SDI **X**:337
Senate, U.S. **X**:320
South Africa **X**:325
Soviet Union, breakup of **X**:326
Supreme Court **X**:338–339
terrorism **X**:346
Thurmond, James Strom **X**:351
Tower Commission **X**:353
veto (presidential) **X**:361
Watt, James G. **X**:367
Reagan Doctrine **X**:301
Reaganomics **X**:109, **302**
realism
art **VII**:24
Carnegie, Andrew **VI**:62
Crane, Stephen **VI**:84–85
Eakins, Thomas **VI**:104
Howells, William Dean **VI**:179–180
Jewett, Sarah Orne **VI**:202–203
La Farge, John Frederick Lewis Joseph **VI**:217
literature **VI**:225–226
theater **VI**:355
Victorianism **VI**:374
reality TV **X**:280, 343
reaper, mechanical **IV**:*244*, 412c
agriculture **IV**:11
economy **IV**:131

industrialization **IV**:200
McCormick, Cyrus Hall **IV**:243–245
science and technology **IV**:333
reapportionment **X**:48, 380c
Reason the Only Oracle of God (Allen) **III**:15
Rebecca of Sunnybrook Farm (Wiggin) **VII**:265
"Rebel Girl" (Hill) **VII**:110
Rebel Private: Front and Rear (Fletcher) **V**:239
Rebel without a Cause (film)
fashion **IX**:117
movies **IX**:224
popular culture **IX**:259
Recco, Niccoloso de **I**:57
Recent Social Trends in the United States **VIII**:**323**
recession (1764) **III**:145
recession (1833–1834) **IV**:207, 396
recession (1920–1921)
Garvey, Marcus **VII**:122
Passaic Strike **VII**:252
UNIA **VII**:361
recession (1937–1938) **VIII**:**323–324**, 446c
antimonopoly **VIII**:24
automobile industry **VIII**:37
CIO **VIII**:82
Congress **VIII**:80
conservative coalition **VIII**:86
Democratic Party **VIII**:94
Eccles, Marriner S. **VIII**:101
economy **VIII**:104
fiscal policy **VIII**:139
Full Employment Bill **VIII**:145
Henderson, Leon **VIII**:163
HOLC **VIII**:171
Hopkins, Harry L. **VIII**:176
Johnson, Hugh S. **VIII**:196–197
Keynesianism **VIII**:200–201
labor/labor movements **VIII**:207
liberalism **VIII**:215
monetary policy **VIII**:244
New Deal **VIII**:269
politics (Roosevelt era) **VIII**:300
Roosevelt, Franklin D. **VIII**:346
steel industry **VIII**:373
taxation **VIII**:388
Third New Deal **VIII**:393
TNEC **VIII**:391
unemployment **VIII**:400
WPA **VIII**:425
recession (1970s-early 1980s) **X**:108–110, 314, 376c
recession (2001–2003) **X**:110–111, 383c

Reciprocal Trade Agreements Act
  VIII:324–325, 444*c*
    Good Neighbor policy
      VIII:151
    Hawley-Smoot Tariff Act
      VIII:163
    Hull, Cordell **VIII:**180
    London Economic
      Conference **VIII:**221
reciprocity **VIII:**325
Reclamation, Bureau of **VII:**229;
  VIII:115, 116
Recohockrians **II:**411
reconcentrado **VI:**88
reconciliationist movement **V:**75
Reconquista **I:314,** 396*c*
  adelantado **I:**3–4
  Castile **I:**65–67
  Ferdinand and Isabella
    I:128
  inquisition **I:**182
  Jews **I:**194
  Leo Africanus **I:**210
Reconstruction **V:324–327,** 445*c,*
  446*c;* **VI:**408*c*
    abolitionism **IV:**4; **V:**4
    African Americans **IV:**7;
      VI:5, 6
    African Methodist Episcopal
      Church **V:**5
    amnesty, acts of **V:8, 8–9,** 9
    assassination of Abraham
      Lincoln **V:**21
    banking **V:**28
    Bennett, James Gordon, Jr.
      VI:33
    Birth of a Nation, The
      VII:37
    Black Codes **V:**34
    Blair, Francis Preston, Jr.
      V:36
    Brown, Joseph Emerson
      V:45
    Butler, Benjamin Franklin
      V:53
    carpetbaggers **V:**55–56
    Civil Rights Act (1875) **V:**71
    Congress **V:**89; **VI:**79
    Davis Bend, Mississippi,
      freedmen's colony **V:**107
    Democratic Party **V:**109–
      110; **VI:**95
    education **V:**124
    education, philanthropy and
      VI:112
    elections **V:**126, 127
    Elliot, Robert Brown **V:**127
    emancipation **V:**130
    Exodusters **VI:**122
    Fifteenth Amendment
      V:141
    foreign policy **V:**151
    Garnet, Henry Highland
      IV:174
    Grant, Ulysses S. **V:**175
    Great Migration **VII:**128
    Greeley, Horace **V:**177

Griffith, David Wark
  VII:131
Grimké, Charlotte Forten
  V:178
Hancock, Winfield Scott
  V:184
Harper, Frances Ellen
  Watkins **VI:**160
Hayes, Rutherford B.
  VI:166, 167
impeachment of Andrew
  Johnson **V:**201–203
industrial development
  V:205
Ingersoll, Robert Green
  VI:193
Johnson, Andrew **V:**212, 213
Joint Committee on the
  Conduct of the War
  V:216
journalism **V:**219
Julian, George Washington
  V:219
Kelley, William D. **V:**222
Ku Klux Klan **V:**223;
  VII:165
Ladies Memorial
  Associations **V:**229
Langston, John Mercer
  VI:218
Liberia **VI:**223
Lincoln, Abraham **V:**237
literature **V:**240
Longstreet, James **V:**242
loyalty oaths **V:**246
lynching **VI:**229–230
Memphis riot (1866) **V:**259,
  260
miscegenation **V:**261
Morton, Oliver P. **V:**270
movie industry **VII:**215
Native Americans **V:**279
Negro Convention
  movement **IV:**280
Proclamation of Amnesty
  and Reconstruction
  V:461–462
Radical Republicans
  V:320–321
Rapier, James T. **V:**323
redemption **V:**328
Republican Party **V:**334
Rhodes, James Ford **VI:**312
scalawags **V:**339–340
Sheridan, Philip H. **V:**353
Sickles, Daniel E. **V:**361
slavery **IV:**344; **V:**364
Society of Friends **V:**365
Stanton, Edwin M. **V:**369
Stevens, Thaddeus **V:**372,
  373
Sumner, Charles **V:**378
Swing Around the Circle
  V:378
Thirteenth Amendment
  V:388
Tourgée, Albion W. **V:**389

Union League **V:**404
United Daughters of the
  Confederacy **V:**407
U.S. v. Cruikshank **V:**412
violence and lawlessness
  VI:375–376
Wade, Benjamin Franklin
  V:421
Wade-Davis Bill **V:**421
Warmoth, Henry Clay
  V:424
Watterson, Henry **VI:**386
Welles, Gideon **V:**428
Wilson, Henry **V:**433
women's status and rights
  V:438
Reconstruction, Second **IX:**232
Reconstruction Acts **V:**327, **327–
  328,** 446*c*
    amnesty, acts of **V:**9
    Freedmen's Bureau **V:**161
    impeachment of Andrew
      Johnson **V:**203
    Radical Republicans **V:**321
    Turner, Henry McNeal
      VI:366
Reconstruction Finance
  Corporation (RFC) **VIII:325–
  326,** 443*c*
    banking **VIII:**39–40
    Congress **VIII:**79
    Emergency Banking Act of
      1933 **VIII:**113
    FCA **VIII:**125
    Federal National Mortgage
      Association **VIII:**135
    Hoover, Herbert C.
      VIII:172
    Hoover presidency
      VIII:174
    Jones, Jesse H. **VIII:**197
    mobilization **VIII:**242
    relief **VIII:**331
    Relief and Reconstruction
      Act **VIII:**333
    transportation **VIII:**396
    Wagner, Robert F.
      VIII:410
reconversion **VIII:326–327**
    aircraft industry **VIII:**15
    automobile industry
      VIII:37
    Baruch, Bernard M.
      VIII:42
    Congress **VIII:**81
    demobilization (WWII)
      VIII:91
    labor/labor movements
      VIII:207
    mobilization **VIII:**242
    Nelson, Donald M.
      VIII:267
    OSRD **VIII:**284
    OWMR **VIII:**287
    postwar planning **VIII:**306
    steel industry **VIII:**374
    V-J Day **VIII:**407

War Production Board
  VIII:414
World War II home front
  VIII:434
Recording Industry Association of
  America (RIAA) **X:**382*c*
records. *See* phonographs/
  phonograph records
recreation *VIII:*327, **327–329;**
  IX:271, 354*c;* **X:302–304,** 303.
  See also sports and recreation
    advertising **IX:**2
    cities and urban life **VIII:**70
    Great Depression **VIII:**159
    Japanese Americans,
      relocation of **VIII:**194
    marriage and family **VIII:**230
    movies **VIII:**247
    National Outdoor
      Recreation Review
      Commission **IX:**237
    National Trails Act of 1968
      IX:239
    sports and recreation **X:**332
    theme parks **IX:**317
    USO **VIII:**403
    World War II home front
      VIII:433
Recreational Demonstration
  Areas **VIII:**327
recruitment **V:**80, 171, 172
Rector, Henry **V:**172
Red Army (Soviet Union)
    Potsdam Conference
      VIII:307
    POWs **VIII:**310
    second front **VIII:**355
    World War II European
      theater **VIII:**430–432
    Yalta Conference **VIII:**439
Red Army GRU (Soviet Union)
  VIII:118, 187
Red Badge of Courage, The
  (Crane) **V:**240; **VI:**85, 226
Red Bank, Battle of **III:**135, **359**
Redburn (Melville) **IV:**229
Red Cloud (Oglala Sioux leader)
  V:446*c;* **VI:303–304**
    Crazy Horse **VI:**85
    Native Americans **VI:**261,
      263
    Sioux wars **VI:**331
    Sitting Bull **VI:**332
Red Cross. *See also* American Red
  Cross; International Red Cross
    Barton, Clara **V:**29
    Johnstown flood **VI:**204
    POWs **VIII:**310
    Selective Service Act
      VII:321
    women's status and rights
      VIII:424
*Redeemed Captive Returning to
  Zion, The* (Williams) **II:**93
redemption **V:328–329**
    African Americans **VI:**5
    carpetbaggers **V:**56

Fifteenth Amendment
V:142
Reconstruction V:326–327
Republican Party V:334
Society of Friends V:365
Tillman, Benjamin Ryan
VI:358
Union League V:404
U.S. v. Cruikshank V:412
redemptioners II:326–327
indentured servitude
II:174
labor/labor movements
III:251, 252
Roman Catholicism II:336
Redemptorists VI:316
Red International of Labor
Unions (Profintern) VII:117
Red Jacket III:119, 195, 359–
360, *360;* IV:411*c*
Red-Light Abatement Movement
VII:67
Red Mill, The (operetta) VII:219
Red Orchestra VIII:118
Red Power IX:241, 242
Red River IV:19, 370
Red River campaign V:329–330
Banks, Nathaniel P. V:29
Porter, David Dixon V:311
Wakeman, Sarah Rosetta
V:422
women soldiers V:435
Red Scare (1919–1920) VII:295–
296, 408*c*
Baldwin, Roger Nash
VII:31
citizenship VII:57
civil liberties VII:58
Committee for Public
Information VII:60
Communist Party VII:61
Democratic Party VII:75
Gilman, Charlotte Perkins
VII:125
Goldman, Emma VII:126
National Civic Federation
VII:226
nativism VII:234
New Unionism VII:238
Palmer, Alexander Mitchell
VII:249
Passaic Strike VII:252
politics (1900–1928)
VII:262
population trends VII:266
radical and labor press
VII:285
radicalism VII:286, 288
Russian Revolution VII:308
Sacco and Vanzetti VII:311
Seattle General Strike
VII:318
socialism VII:328
WILPF VII:386
women's status and rights
VII:389
World War I VII:394

Red Scare (1950s)
Americans for Democratic
Action IX:14
anticommunism IX:14
Buckley, William F., Jr. X:50
CIO IX:72
communism IX:67
hydrogen bomb IX:152
McCarthy, Joseph R.
IX:206–207
movies IX:223
Nixon, Richard M. X:256
Red Shoes II:327
Red Stick War IV:189, 190
Red Summer VII:407*c*
reducción I:3, 314–315
Reduce, Reuse, and Recycle
campaign X:91
Reed, James IV:125, 126
Reed, John VII:296–297
Greenwich Village VII:130,
131
Haywood, William Dudley
VII:137
The Masses VII:193
modernism VII:212
radical and labor press
VII:285
Vorse, Mary Heaton
VII:375
Reed, Joseph III:82
Reed, Ralph X:73, 94
Reed, Stanley IX:336
Reed, Thomas Brackett VI:304
Congress VI:80
Republican Party VII:299
tariffs VI:352
Reed rules VI:304
Reese, Jack IV:381
Reese, Pee Wee IX:278
Reeve, Tapping
Calhoun, John C. IV:68
Catlin, George IV:84
Freeman, Elizabeth III:176
lawyers III:256
Mann, Horace IV:237
*Reflections on the Revolution in
France* (Burke) III:69, 329
reforestation VIII:71
Reformation I:315–318, *316,*
397*c*
Anglican Church II:21
art and architecture I:12
Calvin, John I:53
Church of England I:74, 75
Counterreformation I:98
Dominicans I:110
Foxe's *Book of Martyrs*
I:132
German Reformed Church
II:148
Jesuits I:193
Jews I:196
Leo X I:210
Léry, Jean de I:212
London I:216
Luther, Martin I:217

Protestantism II:315
Puritans I:307
religion, Euro-American
II:328–329
Trent, Council of I:369, 370
Reformed churches I:55,
315–316
Reforming Synod II:320
Reform Judaism
Jews and Judaism X:193
Judaism VI:205
religion VI:308; VII:298;
VIII:334; X:307
reform novels IV:229
Reform Party X:304
Buchanan, Patrick J. X:49
elections, presidential X:117
Perot, H. Ross X:273
refrigerator cars VI:243
refrigerators VII:123
Refugee Act (1980) X:33
Refugee Home Society V:58
refugees V:330; VIII:329–330;
X:377*c*
Africa X:17
anti-Semitism VIII:25
Asian Americans X:33
Cary, Mary Ann Shadd V:58
Civil War V:74
contrabands V:92–93
elections V:127
food riots V:148
Freedmen's Bureau V:160
German Americans
VIII:148
Holocaust VIII:170
immigration VIII:184;
IX:155; X:177
Israel IX:160
Jews VIII:196
Kennedy, Edward M. X:196
Native Americans V:278
Reconstruction V:324
Roosevelt, Franklin D.
VIII:347
Special Field Order No. 15
V:366
Vietnam War IX:332
Zionism VIII:441
Refugees, Freedmen and
Abandoned Lands, Bureau of.
See Freedmen's Bureau
Regan, Donald X:184
regattas VI:359
Regensburg, Germany VIII:47
*Regents of the University of
California v. Allan Bakke. See
Bakke* case
Reggio, Italy VIII:191
regidores I:41
regionalism VIII:31
regulation
advertising X:7–9
agriculture X:20
aviation VII:29
business and government
VI:57

railroads VI:302, 303
Roosevelt, Theodore
VII:304
*Regulations for the Army of the
Confederate States* V:399
*Regulations for the Order and
Discipline of the Troops of the
United States* III:398
*Regulations for the Uniform and
Dress of the Army of the United
States* V:399
*Regulations Lately Made
concerning the Colonies*
(Whately) III:437
Regulations of 1772 (Spain)
III:317
Regulators III:459*c,* 460*c*
Alamance, Battle of III:12
North Carolina Regulation
III:321
riots III:371
South Carolina Regulation
III:395
violence and lawlessness
VI:376
rehabilitation VIII:234
Rehabilitation Act (1973) IX:110;
X:24–25
Rehnquist, William H. X:304–
306, 379*c*
Burger, Warren E. X:51
Mitchell, George X:232
Reagan, Ronald W. X:300
Roberts, John G. X:311
Roe v. Wade X:311
Scalia, Antonin X:316
Supreme Court X:339
*Webster v. Reproductive
Health Services* X:368
Reich, Robert X:74
Reid, Harry X:271
Reid, John VI:343
Reid, Richard X:348
Reid, Robert VII:102
Reid, Thomas IV:78
Reid, Whitelaw V:94; VI:265–266,
304–305
Reign of Terror
Democratic-Republican
societies III:137
French Revolution III:178
Paine, Thomas III:330
Rochambeau, Jean-Baptiste-
Donatien de Vimeur,
comte de III:373
Reiter, Thomas X:329
relação I:35
relief VIII:330–333, *331,* 445*c*
African Americans VIII:3
art and architecture VIII:29
Asian Americans VIII:32
Bonus Army VIII:48
Bridges, Harry VIII:53
CCC VIII:70–71
children VIII:66
cities and urban life VIII:68
Communists VIII:77

relief *(continued)*
    Congress **VIII**:79
    conservatism **VIII**:85
    CWA **VIII**:74
    Democratic Party **VIII**:93
    economy **VIII**:103–104
    ERAA **VIII**:113
    FAP **VIII**:128
    FERA **VIII**:132
    fiscal policy **VIII**:139
    FMP **VIII**:134
    FTP **VIII**:135
    FWP **VIII**:136
    government **VIII**:152
    Great Depression **VIII**:159
    HOLC **VIII**:171
    Hoover, Herbert C.
        VIII:172
    Hoover presidency
        VIII:174
    Ickes, Harold L. **VIII**:183
    immigration **VIII**:184
    Keynesianism **VIII**:200
    liberalism **VIII**:215
    medicine **VIII**:235
    Mexican Repatriation
        Program **VIII**:238
    Native Americans **VIII**:264
    New Deal **VIII**:268, 269
    NRPB **VIII**:261
    NYA **VIII**:262
    PECE **VIII**:309
    Perkins, Frances **VIII**:293
    POUR **VIII**:310
    PWA **VIII**:314
    recession of 1937–1938
        VIII:324
    recreation **VIII**:327
    RFC **VIII**:325
    Second New Deal **VIII**:356
    Social Security Act
        VIII:363
    South **VIII**:366
    Thomas, Norman **VIII**:394
    unemployment **VIII**:400
    Wagner, Robert F. **VIII**:410
    Wallace, Henry A. **VIII**:411
    women's status and rights
        VIII:423
    WPA **VIII**:425–426
Relief and Reconstruction Act
    VIII:333, 443*c*
    Congress **VIII**:79
    FERA **VIII**:132
    Hoover presidency
        VIII:174
    relief **VIII**:331
    RFC **VIII**:325
    Wagner, Robert F. **VIII**:410
religion **III**:360–362, *361;*
    IV:316–321, *318;* **V**:331–332;
    VI:305–310, *309;* **VII**:297–
    299; **VIII**:333–336, 446*c*,
    448*c*; **IX**:271–274; **X**:306–307.
    See also Darwinism and
    religion; *specific religions, e.g.:*
    Protestantism

religion, African-American
    II:327–328
    Africa **II**:5
    African Americans **II**:8
    slavery **II**:357
religion, Euro-American **II**:328–
    330, *329. See also specific
    religions, e.g.:* Protestantism
    Congregationalists **II**:75
    Connecticut **II**:77–78
    crime and punishment **II**:83
    education **II**:111, 112
    Gorton, Samuel **II**:150
    Great Awakening **II**:154–
        157
    Hutchinson, Anne Marbury
        II:170
    King's College **II**:194
    marriage and family **II**:218
    Maryland **II**:219–220
    New York **II**:270
    Pennsylvania **II**:286
    Philadelphia **II**:293
    Protestantism **II**:314–316
    Puritans **II**:318–320
    Virginia **II**:401
    women's status and rights
        II:424–425
religion, Native American
    II:330–331
    Huron **II**:169
    Powhatan Confederacy
        II:307
    women's status and rights
        II:424
Religion, Wars of **I**:170, 171
*Religious Aspect of Philosophy,
    The* (Royce) **VI**:319
religious displays **X**:216, 378*c*
religious freedom
    Baptists **II**:33
    Penn, William **II**:284
    Philadelphia **II**:293
    Roman Catholicism **II**:335–
        336
    Williams, Roger **II**:416–417
Religious Freedom Restoration
    Act (RFRA) **X**:307–308
Religious Land Use and
    Institutionalized Persons Act
    (2000) **X**:307–308
religious liberty **III**:362–364,
    363, 462*c*
    Backus, Isaac **III**:39–40
    Catholics **III**:83
    Jews **III**:236
    Madison, James **III**:282
    Methodism **III**:297
    religion **III**:360, 361
    Taylor, John, of Caroline
        III:408
Religious Right **X**:341
Religious Rights Watch **X**:74
religious tolerance
    government, British
        American **II**:152
    New York **II**:270

Pennsylvania **II**:286
    proprietary colonies **II**:313
    religion, Euro-American
        II:330
    Rhode Island **II**:333
Remarks at the Brandenburg Gate
    (Reagan) **X**:396–399
*Remarks on Prisons and Prison
    Discipline in the United States*
    (Dix) **IV**:125
Remarks on Taking the Oath of
    Office (Ford) **X**:392–393
Remarks to the Fourth World
    Conference on Women:
    Madeleine K. Albright, U.S.
    Permanent Representative to
    the United Nations **X**:405–
    407
Remington, Frederic **VI**:310,
    410*c*
    art **V**:18
    illustration, photography,
        and graphic arts **VI**:183
    sculpture **VI**:327
Reminiscences of the South Seas
    (La Farge) **VI**:218
Remmel, Pratt **IX**:117
Remond, Charles Lenox **IV**:413*c*
Remus, George **VII**:273
Renaissance, American. *See*
    American Renaissance
Renaissance, the
    art and architecture **I**:12,
        13; **VI**:19
    citizenship **III**:92
    Leonardo da Vinci **I**:211–
        212
    Venice **I**:374, 375
Renaut, Philippe **IV**:223
rendezvous **IV**:321–322
    Ashley, William Henry
        IV:31, 32
    Beckwourth, Jim **IV**:50
    Bent, Charles **IV**:51
    exploration **IV**:144
    Fort Laramie **IV**:156
    McLoughlin, John **IV**:248
    Missouri Fur Company
        IV:258
    mountain men **IV**:266
    Rocky Mountain Fur
        Company **IV**:324
    Smith, Jedediah Strong
        IV:350, 351
Rendova Island **VIII**:366
renegados **I**:238
Rennell's Island, Battle of
    VIII:366
Reno, Janet **X**:*308,* 308–309,
    380*c*
    Branch Davidians **X**:46
    Clinton, Hillary Rodham
        X:77
    Clinton, William J. **X**:82
    feminism **X**:134
    independent counsel **X**:179
    Judicial Watch **X**:194

Reno, Marcus **V**:241
Reno, Milo **VIII**:126
Renoir, Auguste **VI**:64
Reno v. ACLU **X**:381*c*
    censorship **X**:71
    Internet **X**:182
    pornography **X**:284
Rensselaer Polytechnic Institute
    IX:311
Rensselaerswyck **II**:331–332
    New Netherland **II**:265
    New York **II**:269
    Van Rensselaer, Maria Van
        Cortlandt **II**:397
rent control **VIII**:282, 409
Renwick, James **IV**:30, 31
reparations **X**:379*c*
    Dawes Plan **VII**:72
    Potsdam Conference
        VIII:307
    race and race relations
        X:296–297
Reparations Commission **VII**:72,
    354–355
repartimiento **I**:289, **318,** 336;
    II:373
repatriation **VIII**:238
repeaters (voting) **VI**:83
repeating rifles **V**:341
*Report of the Exploring
    Expedition to Oregon and
    California, A* (Frémont)
    IV:166
*Report on Economic Conditions in
    the South* (National Emergency
    Council) **VIII**:367
Report on Manufactures
    (Hamilton) **V**:383
Report on Organization (White)
    VI:391
Report on Public Credit
    (Hamilton) **III**:131
"Report on the Subject of
    Manufactures" (Hamilton)
    III:125, 225
Representation of Facts, A
    (Laurens) **III**:255
reproductive rights **X**:382*c*
    abortion **X**:1, 2
    birth control **X**:43
    NOW **X**:247, 248
republicanism **III**:364–365
    American Revolution **III**:18
    anti-Federalists **III**:24
    art **III**:33
    Association, the **III**:37
    Boston Tea Party **III**:58
    Brackenridge, Hugh Henry
        III:60
    Cincinnati, Order of **III**:90
    commonwealthmen **III**:103
    Connecticut Wits **III**:104
    Continental Congress, First
        III:114
    corporatism **III**:122
    Federalist Party **III**:164–
        165

Federalists **III:**165
freemasonry **III:**177
French Revolution **III:**178
immigration **III:**221
Kościuszko, Tadeusz
 III:248
labor/labor movements
 III:252
Livingston, William **III:**271
marriage and family
 III:287–288
Murray, Judith Sargent
 Stevens **III:**308
Paine, Thomas **III:**329
political parties **III:**338
theater **III:**411
Witherspoon, John **III:**445
women's status and rights
 III:446, 448
Republican Motherhood **IV:**340–
342, 404
Republican National Committee
 X:105, 275
Republican National Convention
 (1860) **VI:**374
Republican National Convention
 (1876) **VI:**159, 193
Republican Party **IV:**322–323,
415*c;* **V:**332–335, *333;* **VI:**311;
VII:299–301; **VIII:**336–338;
IX:274–275; **X:**380*c*
abolitionism **V:**3, 4
abortion **X:**4
African Americans **VIII:**2
Amendments to the U.S.
 Constitution **X:**23
America First Committee
 VIII:17
American System **IV:**19, 20
amnesty, acts of **V:**9
Anderson, John B. **X:**25
Anthony, Susan B. **VI:**16
anticommunism **VIII:**22
Army-McCarthy hearings
 IX:18
Arthur, Chester Alan **VI:**20
Banks, Nathaniel P. **V:**28
Blaine, James Gillespie
 VI:40–41
Blair, Francis Preston, Jr.
 V:36
Borah, William E. **VIII:**49
Bruce, Blanche Kelso **V:**47
Bush, George H. W.
 X:51–53
Calhoun, John C. **IV:**68
Cannon, Joseph Gurney
 VII:48
carpetbaggers **V:**55, 56
Christian Coalition **X:**74
cities and urban life **X:**75,
76
Civil Rights Act (1957)
 IX:58
Civil War **V:**73
Clinton, William J. **X:**82
common soldier **V:**79

Congress **V:**89; **VI:**80;
 VII:62; **VIII:**78–81
conservatism **VIII:**83, 85;
 IX:74, 75
conservative coalition
 VIII:85–86
conservative movement
 X:93
Coolidge, Calvin John
 VII:65
Cooper Union speech **V:**94
corruption, political **VI:**83
Currency Act **VII:**68
Davis, Jefferson **V:**104
Davis, Varina Howell **V:**106
defense policy **X:**100
Democratic Party **IV:**116–
 117, 119; **V:**109, 110;
 VII:74, 75; **VIII:**92–93
Dewey, Thomas E. **IX:**87
Dole, Robert **X:**104–105
Douglas, Stephen A. **V:**114
Douglass, Frederick **V:**116
Dred Scott decision **V:**117
election of 1932 **VIII:**108,
 109
election of 1936 **VIII:**109
election of 1940 **VIII:**110
election of 1944 **VIII:**111
elections **V:**125, 126;
 VII:89–92; **IX:**102–104
elections, presidential **X:**118
Elliot, Robert Brown **V:**127
employment **V:**132, 133
ERA **X:**123, 124
feminism **X:**134
Fifteenth Amendment
 V:141
Fillmore, Millard **IV:**150
Ford, Gerald R. **X:**138, 139
Foster, Abigail Kelley
 IV:162
Free-Soil Party **IV:**165
Frémont, Jesse Benton
 IV:165
Frémont, John C. **IV:**166,
 167
fugitive slave laws **IV:**168
German Americans
 VIII:148
Gingrich, Newton L.
 X:151–152
global warming **X:**156
Goldwater, Barry **IX:**135
governors **V:**172
Grant, Ulysses S. **V:**174–176
Great Depression **VIII:**159
Greeley, Horace **V:**177
Harding, Warren Gamaliel
 VII:134, 135
Harlan, John Marshall
 VI:159
Harrison, Benjamin **VI:**160,
 161
Hawaii statehood **IX:**143
Hawley-Smoot Tariff Act
 VIII:163

Hay, John Milton **VI:**164
Hayes, Rutherford B.
 VI:166–168
Helms, Jesse A., Jr. **X:**165
Herndon, William H. **V:**187
Hillman, Sidney **VIII:**166
Hoar, George F. **VI:**173
homefront **V:**193
Hoover, Herbert C.
 VIII:171
Hoover presidency
 VIII:173
House of Representatives
 X:169–171
Howard, Oliver Otis **V:**198
HUAC **IX:**150
Huntington, Collis Potter
 VI:180
immigration **X:**176, 177
impeachment of Andrew
 Johnson **V:**201–203
independent counsel **X:**179
Internal Security Act (1950)
 IX:157
isolationists **VIII:**189
Johnson, Andrew **V:**213
Johnson, Hiram Warren
 VII:154
Julian, George Washington
 V:219
Kansas-Nebraska Act **V:**221
Kelley, William D. **V:**222
Kemp, Jack F. **X:**196
Know-Nothing Party **IV:**215
Knox, Frank **VIII:**202
Ku Klux Klan **V:**223
labor/labor movements
 VIII:205, 207
La Follette, Robert M., Jr.
 VIII:208
La Guardia, Fiorello
 VIII:208
Landon, Alfred M. **VIII:**209
Langston, John Mercer
 VI:218
liberalism **IX:**191; **X:**208
Liberty Party **IV:**226
Lincoln, Abraham **V:**234,
 236
lobbying **VII:**182
Luce, Henry R. **VIII:**224
machine politics **VI:**234
marriage and family **X:**214
Marx, Karl **V:**249
McCarthy, Joseph R.
 IX:206, 207
Meredith, James **IX:**213
miscegenation **V:**261
Mitchell, John **VII:**211
modern Republicanism
 IX:221, 222
Mormon War **IV:**263
Morrill Land-Grant Act
 V:269
Morton, Oliver P. **V:**270
mugwumps **VI:**252
NAACP **VIII:**255

Nast, Thomas **V:**275
New Deal **IX:**242
New Freedom **VII:**236
Nicaragua **X:**254
Nixon, Richard M. **X:**256
Norris, George W. **VIII:**276
panic of 1819 **IV:**294
Payne-Aldrich Tariff Act
 VII:255
political parties **X:**276–278
political parties, third
 VI:286
politics (1900–1928)
 VII:261
politics (Roosevelt era)
 VIII:297–300
presidential campaigns
 (1870–1899) **VI:**290–293
Prohibition Party **VI:**296
pro-life/pro-choice
 movements **X:**289
public land policy **IV:**307
public opinion polls
 VIII:312
Radical Republicans
 V:320–321
Rainey, Joseph H. **V:**323
Reagan, Ronald W. **X:**299–
300
Reconstruction **V:**325, 326
redemption **V:**328, 329
Reed, Thomas Brackett
 VI:304
Reid, Whitelaw **VI:**304–305
Roosevelt, Franklin D.
 VIII:346
Roosevelt, Theodore
 VII:303
scalawags **V:**339–340
Schlafly, Phyllis **X:**317
Schurz, Carl **VI:**324
SEATO **IX:**292
Senate, U.S. **X:**320–322
Seward, William H. **V:**346–
347
Sherman, John **VI:**329
slavery **V:**364
Stanton, Elizabeth Cady
 V:369
Stevens, Thaddeus **V:**372
Sunbelt **X:**338
Sunday, William Ashley, Jr.
 VII:342
Taft, Robert A. **VIII:**385
Taft, William Howard
 VII:347
tariffs **VI:**352, 353; **VII:**349
Teapot Dome **VII:**352
Thirteenth Amendment
 V:388
Tourgée, Albion W. **V:**389
Townsend, Francis E.
 VIII:395
Union League **V:**404
U.S. v. Cruikshank **V:**412
veterans **VII:**371
Veterans Bureau **VII:**373

Republican Party (*continued*)
  volunteer army **V:**420
  Wade, Benjamin Franklin
    V:421
  Warmoth, Henry Clay **V:**425
  Welles, Gideon **V:**428
  Whigs **IV:**398
  Willkie, Wendell L.
    VIII:417
  World War II home front
    VIII:434
  Wright, James C., Jr. **X:**373
Republican Reconstruction
  VI:167
Republic of Lower California
  V:145
Republic Steel **VII:**337; **IX:**300
Republic Steel Company
  VIII:249, 373. *See also*
  Memorial Day Massacre
Requerimiento **I:**318–319, 398*c*
  Coronado, Francisco **I:**92
  Cortés, Hernán **I:**95
  Inca **I:**180
  New Spain **I:**270
Requerimiento (The
  Requirement) **I:**409–410
Rerum Novarum **VI:**316;
  VII:297–298
Resaca, Battle of **V:**22
Rescued from an Eagle's Nest
  (film) **VII:**131, 215
research **IX:**352*c*
  LSD **IX:**195, 196
  medicine **IX:**210
  NIH **IX:**235, 236
  science and technology
    VIII:352; **IX:**286
  technology **IX:**311
Research and Development Board
  IX:238
research laboratories **VII:**150–
  151
reservations **IV:**297–298;
  VIII:263, 264, 448*c*; **X:**250. *See
  also* Dawes Severalty Act
Reserve Officers Training Corps
  (ROTC)
  armed forces **VII:**20
  education **IX:**99
  Morrill Land-Grant Act
    V:269
Resettlement Administration (RA)
  VIII:338–339, 445*c*
  agriculture **VIII:**10
  dust bowl **VIII:**99
  ERAA **VIII:**114
  Evans, Walker **VIII:**119–
    120
  FSA **VIII:**127
  housing **VIII:**177
  Lange, Dorothea **VIII:**210
  medicine **VIII:**235
  suburbanization/suburbs
    VIII:379
  Tugwell, Rexford G.
    VIII:397

residencia
  corregidor **I:**93
  Ferdinand and Isabella
    I:128
  New Spain **I:**268
residency requirements **III:**93,
  94, 221, 464*c*
resident aliens **VIII:**65, 71–72,
  446*c*
Resident Commission of Puerto
  Rico **VII:**110
resident status **X:**177
Resignation Speech (Nixon)
  X:390–392
resistance movement **III:365–
  366**
  Adams, John **III:**5
  Adams, Samuel **III:**7
  African Americans **III:**9
  American Revolution **III:**18
  Anglican Church **III:**21
  artisans **III:**35
  Attucks, Crispus **III:**37
  Beaumarchais, Pierre-
    Auguste Caron de **III:**48
  Bland, Richard **III:**53
  Boston Tea Party **III:**58–59
  Chase, Samuel **III:**85
  cities and urban life **III:**90
  citizenship **III:**92
  committees of
    correspondence **III:**101
  Deane, Silas **III:**129
  Dickinson, John **III:**137
  Dragging Canoe **III:**139–140
  Dulany, Daniel **III:**142
  Dunmore, John Murray, earl
    of **III:**142
  economy **III:**145
  foreign affairs **III:**168
  Gage, Thomas **III:**186–187
  Golden Hill, Battle of
    III:196
  Grenville, George **III:**200
  Hancock, John **III:**209
  Jews **III:**236
  journalism **III:**240
  Laurens, Henry **III:**255
  Liberty riot **III:**266
  liberty tree **III:**267–268
  literature **III:**268
  Loyal Nine **III:**276
  MacIntosh, Ebenezer
    III:279
  Marion, Francis **III:**286
  music **III:**309
  Old South Church **III:**323
  Paris, Treaty of (1763)
    III:331
  Pontiac's War **III:**340
  popular culture **III:**341
  Quakers **III:**351
  Quartering Act **III:**352
  riots **III:**371
  Rodney, Caesar **III:**373
  Shays's Rebellion **III:**388
  Stamp Act **III:**395

suffrage **III:**400
taverns and inns **III:**407
Townshend Duties **III:**412
Virginia Resolves **III:**425
Warren, Joseph **III:**427
Washington, George
  III:430
Whiskey Rebellion **III:**339–
  440
women's status and rights
  III:446
Young, Thomas **III:**457
"Resistance to Civil Government"
  (Thoreau). *See* "Civil
  Disobedience"
Resolution, HMS **IV:**188
Resolution for the Admission of
  Missouri **IV:425**
Resor, Helen Lansdowne **VII:**4
Resource Conservation and
  Recovery Act (1976) **X:**91
Restoration Movement **IV:**78,
  319
Resumption Act **VI:**329
Retraining and Reemployment
  Administration **VIII:**326
Return of Lanny Budd, The
  (Sinclair) **VII:**326
"Reuben James" (Guthrie)
  VIII:160
Reuther, Valentine **IX:**275
Reuther, Walter P. **VIII:339–
  340; IX:275**, 353*c*
  AFL **IX:**11–12
  Americans for Democratic
    Action **IX:**13, 14
  labor/labor movements
    VIII:206; **X:**201
  socialists **VIII:**362
Revels, Hiram R. **V:335; VI:**5,
  407*c*
Revenue Act (1663) **II:**3
Revenue Act (1916) **VII:**378
Revenue Act (1918) **VII:**378
Revenue Act (1921) **VII:**201
Revenue Act (1932) **VIII:**387
Revenue Act (1934) **VIII:**387
Revenue Act (1935) **VIII:340**
  antimonopoly **VIII:**24
  Congress **VIII:**79
  conservatism **VIII:**84
  New Deal **VIII:**269
  Roosevelt, Franklin D.
    VIII:345
  Second New Deal **VIII:**356
  taxation **VIII:**387
  Union Party **VIII:**401
Revenue Act (1936) **VIII:**388
Revenue Act (1937) **VIII:**388
Revenue Act (1938) **VIII:**388
Revenue Act (1939) **VIII:**388
Revenue Act (1942) **VIII:340–
  341,** 447*c*
  Keynesianism **VIII:**201
  taxation **VIII:**388
  World War II home front
    VIII:433

Revere, Paul **III:366–367,** 367,
  461*c*
  Boston Massacre **III:**58
  Hancock, John **III:**209
  Industrial Revolution
    III:226
  Lexington and Concord,
    Battles of **III:**264–265
  Massachusetts **II:**225
  Warren, Joseph **III:**427
Revere, Paul, Jr. **V:**186, 415
reverse discrimination **X:**112, 297
revitalization movements **II:**256,
  332
revivals/revivalism **III:**465*c;*
  VIII:448*c. See also* Second
  Great Awakening
  African Americans **IV:**8
  camp meetings **III:**77
  Dow, Lorenzo **IV:**126
  Finney, Charles Grandison
    IV:150–151
  Great Awakening **II:**155
  humanitarianism **III:**217
  medicine **IV:**249
  Moody, Dwight Lyman
    VI:249–250
  music **VI:**257
  recreation **VII:**295
  religion **III:**360, 362;
    IV:316–317; **VI:**306;
    VII:298
  temperance movement
    IV:369
  Tennent, William, Jr. **II:**388
  Virginia **II:**402
Revolutionary War **III:367–369,**
  461*c,* 462*c. See also* American
  Revolution; *specific battles, e.g.:*
  Alamance, Battle of
  abolitionism **III:**2; **IV:**1
  Adams, Samuel **III:**7
  African Americans **III:**8–9
  agriculture **III:**11
  Allen, Ethan **III:**14
  American Revolution **III:**18
  Ames, Fisher **III:**19
  Anglican Church **III:**21
  anti-Masonry **IV:**25
  antislavery **III:**25
  Arnold, Benedict **III:**30–31
  Aroostook War **IV:**27
  art **III:**32–33
  Articles of Confederation
    III:33
  Asbury, Francis **III:**36
  Baptists **III:**44
  Barlow, Joel **III:**46
  Barry, John **III:**47
  Beaumarchais, Pierre-
    Auguste Caron de **III:**48
  Boone, Daniel **III:**56
  Brackenridge, Hugh Henry
    III:60
  Brant, Joseph **III:**62
  Burgoyne, Sir John **III:**67–
    68

Burr, Aaron **III:**69
camp followers **III:**76–77
Carleton, Guy **III:**81
Charleston Expedition of 1776 **III:**83–84
Cherokee **III:**86, 87
Choctaw **III:**89
Church, Benjamin **III:**89
cities and urban life **III:**90
citizenship **III:**92, 93
citizen-soldier **V:**68
Clark, George Rogers **III:**95–96
Clinton, Sir Henry **III:**99
Confederate States of America **V:**86
conscription **V:**90
Continental army, mutinies of **III:**112–113
Continental Congress, Second **III:**115
Continental navy **III:**117
Cornplanter **III:**119
Cornwallis, Charles, Lord **III:**119–121
cotton **III:**122, 123
Cowboys and Skinners **III:**123
Coxe, Tench **III:**125
Creek **III:**126
Crèvecoeur, J. Hector St. John de **III:**127
Deane, Silas **III:**129
debt, national **III:**129, 130, 132
Declaration of Independence **III:**132–134
Dragging Canoe **III:**139
dueling **III:**140
economy **III:**145–146
education **IV:**134
Estaing, Charles-Henri Theodat, comte d' **III:**158
Federalists **III:**166
Florida **III:**167; **IV:**152
food riots **III:**167
Forten, James **III:**169
Fort Ticonderoga **III:**171–172
Franklin, William **III:**176
freemasonry **III:**176–177
French Alliance **III:**177–178
French Revolution **III:**178
Freneau, Philip **III:**179
fur trade **IV:**171
Gage, Thomas **III:**186–187
Galloway, Joseph **III:**188
Gates, Horatio **III:**189–190
George III **III:**191
Girard, Stephen **III:**195
Gnadenhutten Massacre **III:**196
Grasse, François-Joseph-Paul, comte de **III:**197

Greene, Nathanael **III:**198–199
Green Mountain Boys **III:**199
Hale, Nathan **III:**204
Hamilton, Alexander **III:**204
Hessians **III:**212–213
Howe, Richard, Lord **III:**214, 215
Howe, Sir William **III:**215–216
Hull, William **IV:**192
impressment **III:**223
Independence Hall **III:**223
Industrial Revolution **III:**224–225
insurance **III:**227
Iroquois **III:**228
Jefferson, Thomas **III:**232
Jersey, HMS **III:**235
Jews **III:**236
Johnson, Sir John **III:**237
journalism **III:**240
Kalb, Johann, baron de **III:**245
Knox, Henry **III:**247
Knyphausen, Wilhelm, Baron von **III:**248
Lafayette, marquis de **III:**253–254
lead mines **IV:**223
Lee, Ann **III:**257
Lexington and Concord, Battles of **III:**264
literature **III:**268, 269; **IV:**227
Livingston, Robert R. **III:**270
Loyalists **III:**275
Marion, Francis **III:**286
Medal of Honor **V:**255
medicine **III:**295
Monroe, James **IV:**258
Morris, Robert **III:**305
Morristown encampment **III:**306–307
music **III:**309
Native Americans **III:**311, 312, 314; **IV:**273
Native Americans in the War of 1812 **IV:**276
Newburgh conspiracy **III:**316
New Spain, northern frontier of **III:**317
North, Frederick, Lord **III:**320
North Carolina Regulation **III:**321
Ohio Company of Associates **III:**323
Ohio Company of Virginia **III:**323
Paine, Thomas **III:**329
Paris, Treaty of (1763) **III:**331

Paris, Treaty of (1783) **III:**331
Peale, Charles Willson **III:**333
Penobscot campaign **III:**333–334
Pickering, Timothy **III:**334
Pinckney, Charles Cotesworth **III:**335, 336
political parties **III:**338
popular culture **III:**341
POWs **III:**345
privateering **III:**347, 348
Pulaski, Casimir **III:**350
Putnam, Israel **III:**350
Quakers **III:**351, 352
railroads **IV:**313
Randolph, Edmund **III:**358
Red Jacket **III:**359
religion **III:**361
religious liberty **III:**362, 363
Riedesel, Frederica Charlotte, baroness von **III:**370
riots **III:**371
Rittenhouse, David **III:**372
Rochambeau, Jean-Baptiste-Donatien de Vimeur, comte de **III:**372–373
Rodney, Caesar **III:**373
Ross, Betsy **III:**374
rules of war **V:**338
rural life **III:**375
Rush, Benjamin **III:**376
St. Clair, Arthur **III:**377–378
Sampson, Deborah **III:**379
Saratoga, surrender at **III:**380
Scots-Irish **III:**386
Seminole War, First/Second **IV:**339
Seneca Falls convention **IV:**340
slavery **IV:**344
Sullivan, John **III:**402
tactics and strategy **V:**380
Tarleton, Banastre **III:**406–407
Taylor, John, of Caroline **III:**408
theater **III:**411
trade, domestic and foreign **III:**413
Trenton and Princeton, Battles of **III:**415–416
Trumbull, John **III:**416
U.S. Army Corps of Engineers **V:**407
U.S. Military Academy at West Point **V:**408
Valley Forge **III:**421–423
Vergennes, Charles Gravier, comte de **III:**423
Warren, Joseph **III:**427
Washington, George **III:**430–431

Webster-Ashburton Treaty **IV:**394
West Indies **III:**436
Whigs **III:**439
Wilkes, John **III:**443
Wilkinson, James **III:**443
women's status and rights **III:**446, 447; **IV:**403
"Yankee Doodle" **III:**453
Yorktown, surrender at **III:**454–457
Young, Thomas **III:**457
Revolutionary Youth Movement (RYM) **X:**367
"Revolving Door" campaign ad **X:**168
Reykjavik, Iceland **I:**177, 272
Reynolds, Debbie **IX:**117
Reynolds, John (Illinois governor) **IV:**57, 58
Reynolds, John (Royal governor of Georgia) **II:**147
Reynolds, John F. (Union general)
　Bull Run/Manassas, First and Second Battles of **V:**51
　Gettysburg, Battle of **V:**166–167
　Hancock, Winfield Scott **V:**183
　Howard, Oliver Otis **V:**197
　Meade, George Gordon **V:**253, 254
Reynolds, Malvina **IX:**305
Reynolds, Maria **III:**74, 207
Reynolds v. Sims **IX:**34, **276**, 337, 338, 357*c*
Rezanov, Nikilay Petrovich **II:**338; **III:**12
Reza Shah Pahlavi (shah of Iran) **X:**377*c*
　Carter, James Earl, Jr. **X:**69
　Iranian hostage crisis **X:**184, 185
　Middle East **X:**228
　terrorism **X:**345
RFC. *See* Reconstruction Finance Corporation
RFRA (Religious Freedom Restoration Act) **X:307–308**
Rhapsody in Blue (Gershwin) **VII:**124, 125, 220, 409*c*
Rhee, Syngman **IX:**177, 178
Rheet, Robert Barnwell **IV:**282
Rheinberger, Josef **VI:**254
Rhett, Robert B. **V:**146, 345
Rhett, William **II:**39
rheumatoid arthritis **VI:**202
Rhinelander, Kip **VII:**160
Rhinelander case **VII:**160, **301–302**
Rhine River **VIII:**431, 432
Rhode Island **II:332–334**, 435*c*; **III:**463*c*; **IV:**414*c*
　abolitionism **III:**2
　abortion **X:**2
　African Americans **III:**9

Rhode Island *(continued)*
  agriculture **II:**14
  architecture **II:**25
  Articles of Confederation **III:**34
  Baptists **II:**33; **III:**44
  Coddington, William **II:**73
  Constitution, ratification of the **III:**105, 106
  Continental Congress, Second **III:**116
  Dominion of New England **II:**102
  Easton, Hosea **IV:**129
  Federalists **III:**165
  fugitive slave laws **IV:**168
  Gaspée affair **III:**189
  Gorton, Samuel **II:**150
  Greene, Nathanael **III:**198
  Hartford Convention **IV:**186
  industrialization **IV:**199
  Jews **III:**237
  Know-Nothing Party **IV:**214
  La Farge, John Frederick Lewis Joseph **VI:**217
  Miantonomo **II:**233
  Narragansett **II:**249
  Newport **II:**267
  Osborn, Sarah Haggar Wheaten **II:**279
  piracy **II:**296
  primogeniture and entail **II:**310
  Protestantism **II:**315
  Quakers **II:**321–322
  railroads **IV:**314
  religion, Euro-American **II:**329, 330
  Rochambeau, Jean-Baptiste-Donatien de Vimeur, comte de **III:**372
  suffrage **III:**401
  trade, domestic and foreign **II:**393
  Tyler, John **IV:**383
  Williams, Roger **II:**415–417
  wolves **II:**422
Rhode Island, Battle of **III:369–370**
  Estaing, Charles-Henri Theodat, comte d' **III:**158
  French Alliance **III:**178
  Greene, Nathanael **III:**198
  Howe, Richard, Lord **III:**215
  Lafayette, marquis de **III:**253
  Sullivan, John **III:**402
Rhode Island Army of Observation **III:**198
Rhode Island General Assembly **II:**134
Rhode Island School of Design **VII:**125
Rhodes, James A. **X:**197

Rhodes, James Ford **VI:311–312**
rhythm and blues (R&B) **VIII:**252
RIAA (Recording Industry Association of America) **X:**382c
ribat **I:**348
Ribault, Jean **I:**61, 208; **II:**128
Ribicoff, Abraham **IX:**238
Ricci, Matteo **I:**193, *319*, **319–320**, 369
rice **II:334**
  agriculture **II:**11, 13
  Continental Congress, First **III:**114
  economy **II:**109–110
  labor/labor movements **II:**198–199
  Middleton, Arthur **II:**234
  plantations **V:**308
  plantation system **II:**297
  slavery **III:**390, 392; **IV:**347; **V:**363
  South Carolina **II:**369–370
  Stono Rebellion **II:**378
  Sudan **I:**347
Rice, Condoleezza **X:309–310**, *310*
  Powell, Colin L. **X:**287
  SDI **X:**337
  women's status and rights **X:**371
Rice, Dan **IV:**412c
Rice, Edwin **VII:**123
Rich, Robert **II:**402
Richard III (king of England) **I:**159
Richard M. Nixon Library and Birthplace **X:**257–258
Richards, Ann **X:**54
Richards, Ellen Henrietta Swallow **VI:312–313**
  Atkinson, Edward **VI:**22
  Mitchell, Maria **VI:**248
  women's status and rights **VI:**400
Richards, Theodore **VII:**314
Richardson, Bill **X:**357
Richardson, Elliot L. **X:310–311**, 376c
  Cox, Archibald, Jr. **X:**95
  Nixon, Richard M. **X:**257
  Ruckelshaus, William D. **X:**312
  Watergate scandal **X:**366
Richardson, Henry Hobson **VI:313–314**
  art and architecture **VI:**18
  La Farge, John Frederick Lewis Joseph **VI:**217
  White, Stanford **VI:**392
Richardson, Israel **V:**13
Richardson, William A. **V:**94
"Richardson Romanesque" **VI:**18, 313
Richmond, Mary **VII:**330
Richmond, Texas **IV:**222

Richmond, Virginia **V:335–337**, *336*
  Appomattox campaign **V:**14
  Appomattox Court House, Virginia **V:**15
  Austin, Moses **IV:**38
  Beauregard, Pierre Gustave Toutant **V:**32
  Bull Run/Manassas, First and Second Battles of **V:**49–50
  Confederate army **V:**82
  Confederate navy **V:**83
  Confederate States of America **V:**85
  economy **V:**123
  Ewell, Richard Stoddert **V:**136
  food riots **V:**148
  habeas corpus, writ of **V:**181
  Hollywood Cemetery **V:**191–192
  invention and technology **VI:**195–196
  Johnston, Joseph E. **V:**214
  Lee, Robert E. **V:**230
  McClellan, George Brinton **V:**251
  medicine **V:**257
  monuments **V:**267
  nurses **V:**285
  Pember, Phoebe Yates Levy **V:**297
  Peninsular campaign **V:**298, 299
  Shenandoah Valley: Jackson's campaign **V:**349, 350
  slavery **IV:**344–345
  slave trade, internal **IV:**350
  tactics and strategy **V:**381, 382
  Tredegar Iron Works **V:**392
  Vance, Zebulon B. **V:**414
  Van Lew, Elizabeth **V:**414, 415
Richmond Grays **V:**38
Richmond Penitentiary **III:**347
Richmond Theater **III:**411
Rickenbacker, Eddie **VIII:**17
Rickey, Branch **IX:276–277**
  African Americans **IX:**5
  Robinson, Jackie **IX:**277
  sports and recreation **IX:**298
Rickover, Hyman G.
  AEC **IX:**25
  Arlington National Cemetery **V:**17
  Carter, James Earl, Jr. **X:**67
  Maine, Remember the **VI:**238
RICO. *See* Racketeer Influenced and Corrupt Organizations Act
Ride, Sally **X:**378c
Ride Through Kanzas, A (Higginson) **VI:**171

Ridge, John **IV:323–324**, *324*
  Boudinot, Elias **IV:**62
  Cherokee **IV:**85
  Ross, John **IV:**325
  Trail of Tears **IV:**378
Ridge, Tom **X:**167, 168
Ridgway, Matthew **IX:**177
Riedesel, Adolph, baron von **III:**380
Riedesel, Frederica Charlotte, baroness von **III:**370, **370–371**
Riedesel, Friederich, baron von **III:**370
Rieger, Wallingford **VII:**124
Riegle, Donald **X:**321
Riesener, Jean-Henri **VI:**19
Riesman, David **IX:**47
Rieve, Emil **IX:**11
Rifle and Light Infantry Tactics (Hardee) **V:**79, 379
rifled muskets
  Civil War **V:**74
  Confederate army **V:**81
  science and technology **V:**340
riflemen **III:**111
rifles **V:**341, 379
Rigdon, Sidney **IV:**352
Riggs, Bobby **VIII:**372
"Rights and Wrongs of Women, The" (Dickinson) **V:**111
Rights of All, The (newspaper) **IV:**209, 295
Rights of Man, The (Paine) **III:**69, 329
Rights of the British Colonies (Otis) **III:**25–26, 459c
"rights revolution" **X:**208–209
Right Stuff, The (Wolfe) **X:**370
right to bear arms **III:**51
right to counsel **IX:**355c, 356c
  Escobedo v. Illinois **IX:**111
  Gideon v. Wainwright **IX:**133–134
  Miranda v. Arizona **IX:**218–219
Right to Life Amendment **X:**289
right-to-life movement **X:**322
right to privacy **X:**376c, 379c
  abortion **X:**2, 4
  birth control **X:**43, 44
  Bork, Robert **X:**45
  Brennan, William J., Jr. **X:**48
  computers **X:**87–88
  Human Genome Project **X:**172
  Roe v. Wade **X:**311
  White, Byron R. **X:**369
Right to Privacy, The (Brandeis) **VII:**58
"Right to Work, The" (Baker) **VII:**217
right-wing extremism **X:**230
Riis, Jacob A. **VI:**314, *314*, 410c
  housing **VI:**179
  How the Other Half Lives **VI:426–427**

illustration, photography,
and graphic arts **VI**:183
photography **VIII**:296
progressivism **VI**:294;
VII:271
White, Alfred Tredway
VI:390
Riley, Bennett **IV**:241
Riley, James Whitcomb **VI**:227
Riley, William Bell **VII**:298
Rinehart, William **VI**:397
Ring Dance **II**:90
Ringgold, Georgia **V**:75
Ringling Bros. Circus **VI**:118
Rio de Janeiro Conference (1942)
VIII:131, 152
Rio de la Plata
Cabeza de Vaca, Álvar
Núñez **I**:40
Cabot, Sebastian **I**:45
Magellan, Ferdinand **I**:223
Rio de Minas **I**:181
Rio Grande
Adams-Onís Treaty **IV**:6
cattle kingdom **VI**:64
Florida **IV**:153
foreign policy **IV**:155
Guadalupe Hidalgo, Treaty
of **IV**:181
Houston, Sam **IV**:191
Magoffin, James W. **IV**:233
Mexican-American War
IV:251, 253
New Mexico **I**:264, 265
Pike, Zebulon Montgomery
IV:300
Pueblo **II**:317
San Jacinto, Battle of
IV:328
Santa Anna, Antonio López
de **IV**:330
Taylor, Zachary **IV**:368
Texas **IV**:370–372
Rio Pact (1947) **IX**:184, 351*c*
Riordon, William L. **VI**:285
riots **III**:371–372, 460*c;* **VI**:409*c;*
VIII:448*c;* **IX**:356*c;* **X**:377*c,*
382*c. See also specific riots,*
e.g.: New York City draft riots
African Americans **IX**:6
Alamance, Battle of **III**:12
assassinations **IX**:23
Attucks, Crispus **III**:37–38
Baltimore, Maryland, riots
V:26
Boston Massacre **III**:56–58
"Chicago Eight" **X**:73
cities and urban life **III**:91;
IX:56
civil rights **VIII**:73
conscription **V**:91
conservative movement
X:93
counterculture **IX**:79
economy **V**:123
food riots **III**:167–168
gays and lesbians **IX**:132

Golden Hill, Battle of
III:196
homefront **V**:193
impressment **III**:223
journalism **III**:241
land riots **III**:254–255
Lee, Henry **III**:260
Liberty riot **III**:266
Louisiana Tigers **V**:245
MacIntosh, Ebenezer
III:279
Memphis riot (1866)
V:259–260
Meredith, James **IX**:213
New Orleans riot **V**:281–282
North Carolina Regulation
III:321
race and race relations
III:358; **V**:320; **VII**:283;
VIII:317–319; **IX**:270;
X:295
resistance movement
III:366
Shays's Rebellion **III**:388
Sons of Liberty **III**:394
South **VIII**:367
Stamp Act **III**:395–396
Tillman, Benjamin Ryan
VI:358
Townshend Duties **III**:412
Watts uprising **IX**:339–340
Weathermen/Weather
Underground **IX**:341;
X:367–368
Wells-Barnett, Ida Bell
VI:388
Wilson, James **III**:444
World War II home front
VIII:433
Wyoming Valley Wars
III:450
Ripken, Cal, Jr. **X**:330
Ripley, Emerson **IV**:169
Ripley, George
Brook Farm **IV**:65
Dana, Charles A. **VI**:91
Fuller, Margaret **IV**:169
literature **IV**:228
Rip Van Winkle (Irving) **IV**:228;
VI:202
Risalah **I**:188
"Rise and Fall of Free Speech
in America, The" (Griffith)
VII:38, 132
*Rise and Fall of the Confederate
Government, The* (Davis)
V:105, 239
Rise of Silas Lapham, The
(Howells) **VI**:180, 226
"Rising Glory of America, The"
(Brackenridge and Freneau)
III:60, 179
Ritalin **X**:223
Ritchie, Thomas **IV**:117
Ritchie v. People **VII**:217
rites of passage **I**:21
Ritschl, Albrecht **VI**:335

Rittenhouse, David **II**:288; **III**:17,
372, 384, *385*
Rivals, The (Sheridan) **VI**:202
River, The (film) **VIII**:303
Rivera, Diego **VIII**:31
River and Harbor Act **VI**:21
River Rouge automobile plant
(Dearborn, Michigan)
automobile industry **VII**:28
cities and urban life **VII**:54
invention and technology
VII:150
Rivers, Larry **IX**:19
Riverside Buildings (Brooklyn,
New York) **VI**:120
Riyadh, Saudi Arabia **X**:346
Rizal, Jose **IX**:256
roads **III**:466*c*
Cherokee **III**:87
Choctaw **III**:89
Creek **III**:126
Holland Land Company
III:214
trade, domestic and foreign
III:415
Wilderness Road **III**:442
Road to Serfdom, The (Hayek)
VIII:85; **X**:93
Roanoke **I**:320–322, *321*, 398*c*
Algonquian **I**:7
Barlowe, Arthur **I**:28
Bry, Theodor de **I**:37
Dare, Virginia **II**:90–91
Elizabeth I **I**:121
Grenville, Sir Richard **I**:144,
145
Harriot, Thomas **I**:154–156
Lane, Ralph **I**:203
Manteo **I**:229
Mantoac **I**:229
monarchy, British **II**:240
North Carolina **II**:274
population trends **I**:298
Ralegh, Sir Walter **I**:311
White, John **I**:383
Wingina **II**:417
Roanoke Indians **II**:417
Roanoke Island **V**:33
Robb, Charles **X**:258
Robber Barons **VI**:181, 365
Robber Barons, The (Josephson)
VI:314–315
Robbins, Harold **X**:212
Robert-Houdin, Jean-Eugène
VII:142
Roberto, Holden **IX**:3
Roberts, Buckshot **VI**:376
Roberts, John (music promoter)
X:371
Roberts, John G. (Supreme Court
justice) **X**:311
Clinton, Hillary Rodham
X:78
gun control **X**:162
O'Connor, Sandra Day
X:265
Supreme Court **X**:339

Roberts, Lawrence G. **X**:181
Roberts, Oral **X**:342
Roberts, Owen J.
court-packing plan **VIII**:89
Korematsu v. U.S. **VIII**:203
Supreme Court **VIII**:381–
383
Robertson, Donald **III**:281
Robertson, Edward V. **IX**:237
Robertson, Marion Gordon "Pat"
Christian Coalition **X**:73, 74
conservative movement
X:94
evangelical Christians **X**:125
televangelism **X**:341, 342
Robertson Aircraft Corporation
VII:28, 165
Robeson, Paul **VII**:408*c;*
VIII:*341,* **341–342**, 448*c;*
IX:223
Robespierre, Maximilian
French Revolution **III**:179
Paine, Thomas **III**:330
Rochambeau, Jean-Baptiste-
Donatien de Vimeur,
comte de **III**:373
Robins, Mary Dreier **VII**:231
Robinson, Bill "Bojangles" **VII**:96
Robinson, Charles **IV**:242
Robinson, Jackie **IX**:277, **277–
278**, 351*c*
African Americans **IX**:5
March on Washington
(1963) **IX**:201
Rickey, Branch **IX**:276, 277
sports and recreation
VIII:370; **IX**:298
Robinson, James R. **IX**:72
Robinson, John **II**:75, 293
Robinson, Mack **VIII**:372
Robinson, Theodore **VI**:275
Robinson-Patman Act **VIII**:24
Robinson v. California **X**:369
Robot (Asimov) **IX**:287
Rochambeau, Jean-Baptiste-
Donatien de Vimeur, comte de
III:372–373
Capes, Battle of the **III**:79
French Alliance **III**:178
Yorktown, surrender at
III:455
Rochefort, Joseph P., Jr. **VIII**:76
Rochester, New York
Eastman, George **VI**:105
Finney, Charles Grandison
IV:151
Islam **X**:189
spiritualism **IV**:355
suffrage **IV**:360
rock and roll **IX**:**278–280,** *279,*
353*c*
Beatles **IX**:37–38
counterculture **IX**:79
movies **IX**:225
music **IX**:229; **X**:238
popular culture **IX**:259
Presley, Elvis **IX**:262–263

rock and roll *(continued)*
  teenagers **IX**:314
  Woodstock festival **X**:371–
    372
Rock and Roll Hall of Fame
  Beatles **IX**:38
  Guthrie, Woody **VIII**:160
  rock and roll **IX**:280
"Rock around the Clock" (Bill
  Haley and the Comets) **IX**:278,
  353*c*
Rockbridge County, Virginia
  IV:243
Rockefeller, David **X**:148
Rockefeller, John Davison
  VI:407*c*, 409*c*; **VII**:302, 302–
  303, 404*c*, 407*c*
  business **VII**:45
  education, philanthropy and
    VI:112–113
  Industrial Revolution,
    Second **VI**:191, 192
  labor/labor movements
    VII:169
  Ludlow Massacre **VII**:186,
    187
  Middletown **VII**:205–206
  muckrakers **VII**:217
  oil **VI**:271
  oil industry **VII**:244
  Republican Party **VII**:300
  Robber Barons, The
    VI:315
  science and technology
    VIII:352
  Standard Oil **VII**:335
  steel industry **VII**:336
  Sunday, William Ashley, Jr.
    VII:342
  Tarbell, Ida Minerva
    VII:349
  trusts **VI**:362–363
  U.S. Steel **VII**:365
  Washington, Booker T.
    VI:384
Rockefeller, John Davison, Jr.
  American Plan **VII**:14
  Industrial Relations
    Commission **VII**:146
  open shop movement
    VII:247
Rockefeller, Nelson **IX**:*316*
  Ford, Gerald R. **X**:138
  Goldwater, Barry **IX**:136
  Kissinger, Henry A. **X**:198
  Latin America **X**:205
  modern Republicanism
    IX:221, 222
  New York City bailout
    X:253
  Republican Party **IX**:275
Rockefeller, William **VII**:335
Rockefeller Center (New York
  City) **VIII**:28, 31
Rockefeller Foundation
  Goldmark, Josephine Clara
    VII:127

Rockefeller, John Davison
  VII:303
  science and technology
    VII:313–314
Rockefeller Foundation
  Committee for the Study of
    Nursing Education **VII**:127
Rockefeller Institute for Medical
  Research **VII**:303
*Rockefeller Report on the
  Americas* **X**:205
Rock Hill, South Carolina **IX**:123
Rockingham, Charles, Lord
  III:68, 69, 396
Rock Island, Illinois. *See*
  Saukenuk, Illinois
Rock Island prison **V**:314
Rockne, Knute **VII**:160; **VIII**:371
"Rock of Ages" **V**:273
Rock Springs, Wyoming **VI**:214
Rock Springs Seminary (Illinois)
  IV:26
Rockwell, Norman
  art and architecture **VIII**:31
  Four Freedoms **VIII**:144
  Rosie the Riveter **VIII**:347
Rocky Mountain Fur Company
  IV:324–325
  Ashley, William Henry
    IV:32
  Astor, John Jacob **IV**:35
  Beckwourth, Jim **IV**:50
  Bridger, James **IV**:64
  Wyeth, Nathaniel J. **IV**:406
Rocky Mountain News **IV**:100;
  IX:136
Rocky Mountains **IV**:412*c*
  Adams, John Quincy **IV**:5
  American Fur Company
    IV:18
  Ashley, William Henry
    IV:31, 32
  Atkinson, Henry **IV**:36
  Beckwourth, Jim **IV**:50
  Bridger, James **IV**:64
  Clark, William **III**:96
  Coeur d'Alene miners' strike
    VI:77
  Deseret, State of **IV**:119
  disease/epidemics **IV**:122
  exploration **IV**:144–146
  foreign policy **IV**:154, 156
  Frémont, John C. **IV**:167
  fur trade **III**:183; **IV**:170,
    171
  gold **IV**:179
  Jackson, Helen Hunt
    VI:199
  Lewis and Clark Expedition
    III:263, 264
  Louisiana Purchase **III**:272
  migration **IV**:255
  Missouri Fur Company
    IV:257
  mountain men **IV**:267
  Oregon Treaty of 1846
    IV:286

Pacific Railroad Act **V**:293
Pike, Zebulon Montgomery
  IV:300
"Pike's Peak or Bust" **IV**:301
Powell, John Wesley **VI**:288
rendezvous **IV**:321–322
Rocky Mountain Fur
  Company **IV**:325
Smith, Jedediah Strong
  IV:350
Texas **IV**:371
Webster-Ashburton Treaty
  IV:394
Whitman, Marcus **IV**:398
Whitman, Narcissa **IV**:399
Rocky Mountains, The (Bierstadt)
  VI:37
Roddenberry, Gene **IX**:287
Roden, Ben **X**:46
Rodeo (Copland) **VIII**:251
Roderick Hudson (James) **VI**:200,
  226
Rodgers, Jimmie **VIII**:250
Rodgers, John **III**:46
Rodgers, Richard **VIII**:252
Rodham, Hugh **X**:77
Rodman, Isaac **V**:13
Rodman, Thomas **V**:342
Rodney, Caesar **III**:373
Rodney, Caesar Augustus
  III:373–374
Rodney, Sir George **III**:378, 379
Rodriguez, Alex **X**:330
Rodríguez, Augustín **I**:265
Roebling, John Augustus **IV**:333;
  VI:47
Roebling, Washington **VI**:47
Roebuck, Alvah Curtis **VI**:237
Roethke, Theodore **IX**:195
Roe v. Wade **X**:311–312, 376*c*,
  387–390
  abortion **X**:2–5
  birth control **X**:43, 44
  Bork, Robert **X**:45
  Brennan, William J., Jr.
    X:48
  Burger, Warren E. **X**:51
  Clinton, Hillary Rodham
    X:79
  conservative movement
    X:93
  feminism **X**:132, 133
  Ginsburg, Ruth Bader
    X:152–153
  Powell, Lewis **X**:288
  pro-life/pro-choice
    movements **X**:289
  Reagan, Ronald W. **X**:300
  Rehnquist, William H.
    X:305
  Supreme Court **X**:339
  *Webster v. Reproductive
    Health Services* **X**:368
  White, Byron R. **X**:369
  women's status and rights
    X:371
Rogers, Edith **VIII**:419

Rogers, Ginger **VII**:124
Rogers, John **III**:269
Rogers, Robert **IV**:103
Rogers, Roy **VIII**:246, 250
Rogers, Will **VIII**:92, 246
Rogue River Valley **IV**:325
ROK. *See* Korea, Republic of
Roldán, Francisco **I**:83, 86
Rolfe, John **I**:334–335, 435*c*
  agriculture **II**:11
  Dale, Sir Thomas **II**:89
  Gates, Sir Thomas **II**:144
  Hamor, Ralph **II**:162
  Jamestown **II**:182
  Pocahontas **II**:300
  Powhatan Confederacy
    II:308
  race and race relations
    VII:282
  Virginia **II**:399
roller-skating **V**:367
rolling blackouts **X**:383*c*
Rolling Stone, The (weekly paper,
  1894–1895) **VI**:236
Rolling Stones, the
  music **IX**:230; **X**:238
  popular culture **IX**:259
  rock and roll **IX**:279
  teenagers **IX**:314
Roma (Gypsies) **VIII**:169–170
Roman Catholic Church/Catholics
  I:397*c*; **II**:335–336; **III**:82–
  83; **VI**:315–316; **VIII**:63–65.
  See also anti-Catholicism
  abortion **X**:3, 4
  Alamo, The **IV**:14
  Alexander VI **I**:6
  American Protective
    Association **VI**:13–14
  anti-Catholic riots **IV**:22–24
  anticommunism **VIII**:22
  anti-Semitism **VII**:17;
    VIII:25
  Austin, Stephen F. **IV**:40
  auto-da-fé **I**:17
  birth control **X**:43
  black legend **I**:31, 32
  California missions **IV**:75–
    77
  Calvin, John **I**:53
  Canada **III**:78
  capital punishment **X**:66–67
  Carroll of Carrollton,
    Charles **III**:82
  Castile **I**:67
  Catholic Bishops' Letter
    X:70
  censorship **X**:71
  Christian Coalition **X**:73
  Church of England **I**:74, 75
  class consciousness **VI**:73
  cod **I**:77
  Coercive Acts **III**:100
  conservative movement
    X:93
  Coughlin, Father Charles E.
    VIII:88

Counterreformation **I**:98
criminal justice **VII**:67
Democratic Party **VIII**:92
Dominicans **I**:110
Dow, Lorenzo **IV**:126
Durán, Diego **I**:114
Dürer, Albrecht **I**:114
education **VI**:109–110
election of 1936 **VIII**:109
elections, presidential **X**:118
Elizabeth I **I**:120, 121
encomienda **I**:122
entertainment, popular
    VI:117
ERA **X**:124
ESEA **IX**:106
Ethiopia **I**:125
Ferdinand and Isabella
    I:128
Florida **II**:128–129
foreign policy **IV**:155
Franciscans **I**:133
French Alliance **III**:177
French colonies **II**:136–137
French immigrants **II**:139
Glorious Revolution
    II:149–150
government, British
    American **II**:151
Henry IV **I**:158
Henry VIII **I**:160
Holy League **I**:165
Huguenots **I**:170
Human Genome Project
    X:172
immigration **III**:221;
    IV:195; **V**:200
immigration restrictions
    VI:187
Indians of the desert
    Southwest **II**:176
inquisition **I**:182
Irish Americans **VIII**:188
Iroquois **II**:180
isolationists **VIII**:189
Italian Americans **VIII**:190
James I **I**:192
Jesuits **I**:192–194; **II**:184–
    185
Jews **VIII**:195–196
Kennedy, John F. **IX**:169
KKK **IX**:179
Know-Nothing Party **IV**:214
Kongo **I**:200
Ku Klux Klan **VII**:166
Lamy, Jean Baptiste **IV**:222
Lease, Mary Elizabeth
    Clyens **VI**:220
Leo X **I**:210
Luther, Martin **I**:218, 219
Lutherans **II**:212
Mary I **I**:232, 233
Maryland **II**:219–220
Mexican Americans
    VIII:237
missions **II**:238–239
nativism **V**:280; **VII**:234

neoconservatism **X**:252
New Deal **VIII**:270
New Spain **I**:270
Philip II **I**:291
politics (Roosevelt era)
    VIII:298
Porres, St. Martín de **I**:299
Protestantism **II**:314–315
Puritans **I**:307
race and race relations
    IV:312
Reformation **I**:315–317
religion **III**:362; **IV**:316,
    318–320; **VI**:307–308;
    VII:297–299; **VIII**:334;
    IX:272, 273; **X**:306, 307
religion, Euro-American
    II:328–329
religion, Native American
    II:331
religious liberty **III**:362
Republican Party **IV**:321
Requerimiento **I**:318–319,
    409–410
Roosevelt, Franklin D.
    VIII:345
St. Mary's City **II**:342, 343
Santa Anna, Antonio López
    de **IV**:329
Schlafly, Phyllis **X**:316
Scots-Irish **III**:385
Seton, Elizabeth Ann **IV**:343
slavery **II**:357
Smith, Alfred E. **VII**:326
Spanish Armada **I**:344
Spanish civil war **VIII**:369,
    370
Spanish colonies **II**:372
suffrage **II**:380
Tekakwitha, Kateri **II**:386
Texas Revolution **IV**:373
Thevet, André **I**:357, 358
Tordesillas, Treaty of **I**:367
Trent, Council of **I**:369–370
Union Party **VIII**:401
Vitoria, Francisco de **I**:379
Walsingham, Sir Francis
    I:382
Zumárraga, Juan de **I**:392
Roman Catholic Legion of
    Decency **VIII**:65
Roman Empire **II**:354
    astrolabe **I**:15
    London **I**:215, 216
    republicanism **III**:365
Romanesque Revival **IV**:30, 31
Romania **X**:384c
    Axis **VIII**:38
    cold war **IX**:63
    Europe **IX**:112
    Iron Curtain, collapse of
        X:189
Roman law **I**:337
romanticism
    art and architecture
        IV:27–28
    medicine **IV**:248–249

religion **IV**:320
transcendental movement
    IV:379
Rome, Georgia **IV**:325
Rome, Italy **VIII**:448c
    Fuller, Margaret **IV**:169
    Italian campaign **VIII**:191
    Open Door Notes **VI**:272–
        273
    World War II European
        theater **VIII**:431
Rome, New York **IV**:151
Romeo and Juliet (Shakespeare)
    I:333
Romer v. Evans **X**:153, 381c
Rommel, Erwin
    Normandy, invasion of
        VIII:276
    North African campaign
        VIII:278
    tanks **VIII**:385–386
Romney, HMS **III**:266
Ronald McDonald **IX**:208
Rondout, New York **IV**:313
Rookwood Pottery **VI**:3
Room in New York (Hopper)
    VIII:31
Rooney, John **IX**:108
Rooney, Mickey **VIII**:67, 246
Roosevelt, Eleanor **VIII:342–
    344**, *343*, 449c
    African Americans **VIII**:3
    Americans for Democratic
        Action **IX**:13, 14
    antilynching legislation
        VIII:23
    Baruch, Bernard M. **VIII**:42
    Bethune, Mary McLeod
        VIII:44
    Black Cabinet **VIII**:45
    Bonus Army **VIII**:49
    civil rights **VIII**:72
    Democratic Party **VIII**:93
    Dewson, Mary **VIII**:95
    FBI **VIII**:130
    feminism **X**:132
    Howe, Louis M. **VIII**:179
    Lange, Dorothea **VIII**:210
    March on Washington
        Movement **VIII**:228
    NAACP **VIII**:255
    NYA **VIII**:262
    OCD **VIII**:282
    PCSW **IX**:261
    Perkins, Frances **VIII**:293
    Roosevelt, Franklin D.
        VIII:344
    SANE **IX**:283
    Wallace, Henry A. **VIII**:411
    WAVES **VIII**:418
    women's status and rights
        VIII:422; **IX**:346
Roosevelt, Franklin Delano, and
    administration *VIII:62*, **344–
    347**, *346, 358, 440, 444c–448c*
    Acheson, Dean **IX**:1
    AFL **VIII**:18; **IX**:11

African Americans **VIII**:3, 4
Agricultural Adjustment Act
    VIII:5
Agricultural Adjustment
    Administration **VIII**:7
Agricultural Marketing Act
    VIII:8
agriculture **VIII**:9
aircraft industry **VIII**:13
Amalgamated Clothing
    Workers of America
    (ACW) **VIII**:16
America First Committee
    VIII:16–17
American Liberty League
    VIII:19
Anglo-American relations
    VIII:21
antilynching legislation
    VIII:23
antimonopoly **VIII**:23
Antiquities Act **VII**:16
anti-Semitism **VIII**:24
Army, U.S. **VIII**:25
Army Act **VII**:22
Arnold, Henry H. "Hap"
    VIII:28
Asian Americans **VIII**:32
Atlantic Charter **VIII**:34,
    461
atomic bomb **VIII**:34
automobile industry
    VIII:36
Bankhead-Jones Farm
    Tenant Act **VIII**:39
banking **VIII**:40
Banking Act (1933) **VIII**:40,
    41
Banking Act (1935) **VIII**:41
Baruch, Bernard M. **VII**:32;
    VIII:41
Berle, Adolf A., Jr. **VIII**:43
Bethune, Mary McLeod
    VIII:44
Black, Hugo L. **VIII**:45
Black Cabinet **VIII**:45, 46
bombing **VIII**:48
Bonus Army **VIII**:49
Borah, William E. **VIII**:49
Bourke-White, Margaret
    VIII:50
Brain Trust **VIII**:51
Brotherhood of Sleeping Car
    Porters **VIII**:54
Bureau of Motion Pictures
    VIII:55–56
Bush, Vannevar **VIII**:56
Byrnes, James F. **VIII**:60
Cairo Conference **VIII**:61
Casablanca Conference
    VIII:62
cash-and-carry **VIII**:63
Catholics **VIII**:63, 64
CCC **VIII**:70
CDAAA **VIII**:77
censorship **VIII**:65, 66
CIO **VIII**:82

Roosevelt, Franklin Delano, and
   administration (*continued*)
   cities and urban life **VIII**:69
   civil defense **IX**:56
   civil rights **VIII**:72, 73
   Clark Memorandum **VII**:59
   coal industry **VIII**:75–76
   communism **IX**:67
   Communists **VIII**:77
   Congress **VIII**:79–81
   conscientious objectors
      VIII:83
   conservatism **VIII**:83–85
   conservative coalition
      VIII:85, 86
   Coughlin, Father Charles E.
      VIII:87, 88
   court-packing plan **VIII**:88–
      89
   CWA **VIII**:74
   "Day of Infamy" speech
      VIII:**466**
   Democratic Party **VIII**:92,
      94
   destroyers-for-bases deal
      VIII:94
   Dewson, Mary **VIII**:95
   direct election of senators
      VII:78
   dollar-a-year men **VIII**:96
   Douglas, William O.
      VIII:96–97
   Dubinsky, David **VIII**:97
   dust bowl **VIII**:99
   Eccles, Marriner S.
      VIII:101
   Economic Bill of Rights
      VIII:102
   economy **VIII**:102, 103–
      104; **IX**:96
   education **VIII**:106
   elderly **VIII**:107
   election of 1932 **VIII**:108–
      109
   election of 1936 **VIII**:109–
      110
   election of 1940 **VIII**:110–
      111
   election of 1944 **VIII**:111
   Emergency Banking Act of
      1933 **VIII**:112–113
   Employment Act of 1946
      IX:106, 107
   enemy aliens **VIII**:114–115
   environment **VIII**:115, 116
   ERAA **VIII**:113, 114
   espionage **VIII**:117
   Ethiopia **VIII**:118
   Executive Order 8802
      VIII:120, **465–466**
   Executive Order 9066
      VIII:120–121, **466–467**
   Executive Reorganization
      Act **VIII**:121–122
   Fair Labor Standards Act
      VIII:124
   FAP **VIII**:128

Farley, James A. **VIII**:125
FBI **VIII**:130
FCC **VIII**:131
FDIC **VIII**:132
Federal National Mortgage
   Association **VIII**:135
FEPC **VIII**:123
FERA **VIII**:132
FHA **VIII**:126
fireside chats **VIII**:137–138
First New Deal **VIII**:138
fiscal policy **VIII**:138–139
Flynn, Edward J. **VIII**:139
foreign policy **VII**:116;
   VIII:140, 141
Forrestal, James V.
   VIII:143
Four Freedoms **VIII**:143
"Four Freedoms" speech
   VIII:**461–465**
Frankfurter, Felix **VIII**:144
FSA **VIII**:127
Full Employment Bill
   VIII:145
Gallup Poll **IX**:130
Garner, John Nance
   VIII:147
German Americans
   VIII:148–149
GI Bill of Rights **VIII**:149
gold standard **VIII**:150
Good Neighbor policy
   VIII:151–152
government **VIII**:152
government, state/local
   IX:137
Grand Alliance **VIII**:155–
   156
Great Depression **VIII**:159
Harriman, W. Averell
   VIII:161, 162
Henderson, Leon **VIII**:163
Hershey, Lewis B. **VIII**:164
Higgins, Andrew J.
   VIII:165
Hillman, Sidney **VIII**:165
Hiroshima and Nagasaki
   VIII:167
HOLC **VIII**:170–171
Holocaust **VIII**:170
Hoover, Herbert C.
   VIII:172, 173
Hoover presidency
   VIII:173
Hopkins, Harry L.
   VIII:176–177
housing **VIII**:177
Howe, Louis M. **VIII**:179
Hughes, Charles Evans
   VII:142
Hull, Cordell **VIII**:180
ILGWU **VIII**:187
immigration **VIII**:184
Inaugural Address, First
   VIII:**451–453**
Indian Reorganization Act
   VIII:186

Irish Americans **VIII**:188,
   189
isolationists **VIII**:189, 190
Italian Americans **VIII**:190
Japanese Americans,
   relocation of **VIII**:193
Jews **VIII**:195–196
Johnson, Hugh S. **VIII**:196
Jones, Jesse H. **VIII**:197
Kennedy, Joseph P.
   VIII:199
Keynesianism **VIII**:200
King, Ernest J. **VIII**:202
Knox, Frank **VIII**:202
labor/labor movements
   VIII:205–207
La Follette, Robert M., Jr.
   VIII:208
La Guardia, Fiorello
   VIII:209
Landon, Alfred M. **VIII**:209
Leahy, William D. **VIII**:210,
   211
Lend-Lease **VIII**:211
letter from Einstein (1939)
   VIII:**460–461**
Lewis, John L. **VIII**:213
liberalism **VIII**:215
Lilienthal, David E.
   VIII:217
Lindbergh, Charles
   Augustus **VII**:178
London Economic
   Conference **VIII**:221
Long, Huey P. **VIII**:222,
   223
MacArthur, Douglas **IX**:197
Manchuria **VIII**:225
Manhattan Project **VIII**:226
March on Washington
   Movement **VIII**:227–228
Marshall, George C.
   VIII:233
medicine **VIII**:234, 236
Mellon, Andrew William
   VII:201
mobilization **VIII**:241
Moley, Raymond C.
   VIII:243
monetary policy **VIII**:243,
   244
Morgenthau, Henry T., Jr.
   VIII:244
movies **VIII**:247
Munich Conference
   VIII:248
Murray, Philip **VIII**:249
NAACP **VIII**:255, 256
Neutrality Acts **VIII**:267,
   268, 457–460
New Deal **VIII**:268–271;
   IX:242
news media **VIII**:272
NIRA **VIII**:256
NLRA **VIII**:257–258
NLRB **VIII**:259
Norris, George W. **VIII**:276

North African campaign
   VIII:277
NRPB **VIII**:260–261
NWLB **VIII**:261
NYA **VIII**:262
Nye committee **VIII**:278
OPM **VIII**:283
Oppenheimer, J. Robert
   IX:250
OSS **VIII**:284
OWI **VIII**:285, 286
OWM **VIII**:286
Pearl Harbor **VIII**:292
Perkins, Frances **VIII**:293
Philippines **VIII**:294
Polish Americans **VIII**:297
politics (Roosevelt era)
   VIII:298–300
popular culture **VIII**:301–
   302
Popular Front **VIII**:303,
   304
presidency **VIII**:308–309
public health **IX**:265
public opinion polls
   VIII:312
PUHCA **VIII**:313
PWA **VIII**:314
race and race relations
   VIII:317, 319
radio **VIII**:320
Randolph, A. Philip
   VIII:321
recession of 1937–1938
   VIII:323, 324
Reciprocal Trade
   Agreements Act
   VIII:324–325
reconversion **VIII**:326
recreation **VIII**:327
refugees **VIII**:329–330
relief **VIII**:330–333
religion **VIII**:334, 335
Republican Party **VIII**:336–
   338
Resettlement Administration
   VIII:338
Reuther, Walter **VIII**:339
Revenue Act of 1935
   VIII:340
Revenue Act of 1942
   VIII:341
RFC **VIII**:325, 326
Roosevelt, Eleanor
   VIII:342, 343
rubber **VIII**:348
rural areas **VIII**:348
*Schechter Poultry
   Corporation v. U.S.*
   VIII:351
scrap drives **VIII**:354
SEC **VIII**:356, 357
second front **VIII**:355
Second New Deal **VIII**:356
Selective Service **VIII**:357–
   358
Smith, Alfred E. **VII**:326

socialists **VIII**:362
Social Security Act
  VIII:364
South **VIII**:366, 367
Soviet-American relations
  VIII:368, 369
Spanish civil war **VIII**:370
sports and recreation
  VIII:370–371
Stimson, Henry L. **VIII**:375
strikes **VIII**:377, 378
Supreme Court **VIII**:381,
  382–383
Taft, Robert A. **VIII**:385
taxation **VIII**:386–388
technology **VIII**:389
Teheran Conference
  VIII:390
television **IX**:315
Tennessee Valley Authority
  VIII:392
Third New Deal **VIII**:393
Thomas, Norman **VIII**:394
TNEC **VIII**:391
Townsend, Francis E.
  VIII:395
transportation **VIII**:396
Truman, Harry S. **IX**:320
Tugwell, Rexford G.
  VIII:397–398
UN **VIII**:402
Union Party **VIII**:401
USHA **VIII**:404
USO **VIII**:403
wage and price controls
  VIII:409
Wagner, Robert F. **VIII**:410
Wallace, Henry A. **VIII**:411
war bonds **VIII**:412
War Manpower Commission
  VIII:412–413
War Production Board
  VIII:413, 414
WAVES **VIII**:418
Welles, Sumner **VIII**:415
Willkie, Wendell L.
  VIII:417
women's network **VIII**:421
World Disarmament
  Conference **VIII**:426
World War II **VIII**:427
World War II European
  theater **VIII**:430
World War II home front
  VIII:434
Yalta Agreement **VIII**:467–
  469
Yalta Conference **VIII**:439,
  440
Zionism **VIII**:441
Roosevelt, Theodore **VI**:*317*,
  412*c*; **VII**:*303*, **303–304**,
  403*c*–405*c*
  Anarchist Immigration Act
    VII:15
  Anthracite Coal Strike
    VII:15

Antiquities Act **VII**:16
Big Stick diplomacy **VII**:34
Brownsville Riot **VII**:42
business **VII**:46
Cannon, Joseph Gurney
  VII:48
Children's Bureau **VII**:53
Congress **VI**:80; **VII**:61
Coolidge, Calvin John **VII**:64
Democratic Party **VII**:74
Dewey, George **VI**:97
dollar diplomacy **VII**:79
elections **VII**:90–91
Elkins Act **VII**:94
environment **VII**:98, 99
Federal Reserve Act
  VII:108
Federal Trade Commission
  Act **VII**:108
foreign policy **VII**:113, 114
Gentlemen's Agreement
  VII:124
Great White Fleet **VII**:129
Harrison, Benjamin **VI**:161
Hay, John Milton **VI**:164
Hearst, William Randolph
  VII:138
Hepburn Act **VII**:138–139
Holmes, Oliver Wendell
  VII:141
Hughes, Charles Evans
  VII:142
Ickes, Harold L. **VIII**:183
investments, foreign
  VII:152
Johnson, Hiram Warren
  VII:154
Knox, Frank **VIII**:202
Lease, Mary Elizabeth
  Clyens **VI**:220
Lodge, Henry Cabot
  VII:184
MacArthur, Douglas **IX**:197
Mahan, Alfred Thayer
  VI:236
Mann-Elkins Act **VII**:190
Meat Inspection Act
  VII:198
mining **VII**:208–209
Mitchell, John **VII**:211
Morgan, John Pierpont
  VI:251
muckrakers **VII**:216
Narcotics Act **VII**:222
Nast, Thomas **V**:276
National Defense Act
  VII:227
National Park Service
  VII:228
National Reclamation Act
  VII:229
New Freedom **VII**:236
New Nationalism **VII**:236–
  237
Northern Securities Case
  VII:242
oil industry **VII**:244

Open Door Policy **VII**:246
Panama Canal **VII**:250, 251
Payne-Aldrich Tariff Act
  VII:255
peace movements **VII**:255–
  256
Pinchot, Gifford **VII**:259–
  260
Pingree, Hazen S. **VII**:261
politics (1900–1928) **VII**:262
Preparedness **VII**:267
presidency **VII**:268
Progressive Party **VII**:269,
  270
progressivism **VII**:271
Pure Food and Drug Act
  VII:277
Reid, Whitelaw **VI**:305
Remington, Frederic
  VI:310
Republican Party **VII**:300
Riis, Jacob A. **VI**:314
Roosevelt, Eleanor
  VIII:342
Roosevelt, Franklin D.
  VIII:344
Roosevelt Corollary **VII**:305
Root-Takahira Agreement
  VII:305
Rough Riders **VI**:317, 318
Russo-Japanese War
  VII:309
science and technology
  VII:315
Sinclair, Upton **VII**:325
Spanish-American War
  VI:341
Standard Oil **VII**:336
"Strenuous Life" Speech
  VII:411–415
Taft, William Howard
  VII:347
trade, domestic and foreign
  VII:354
UMWA **VII**:360
veterans **VII**:371
Washington, Booker T.
  VI:384
White, Alfred Tredway
  VI:390
workers' compensation
  VII:391
Roosevelt Coalition
  African Americans **VIII**:2
  Democratic Party **VIII**:93–
    94
  election of 1932 **VIII**:108
  election of 1936 **VIII**:109
  election of 1940 **VIII**:111
  election of 1944 **VIII**:111
  labor/labor movements
    VIII:205
Roosevelt Corollary **VII**:304–
  305, 404*c*
  Clark Memorandum **VII**:58
  foreign policy **IV**:155;
    VII:113

Good Neighbor policy
  VIII:151
Roosevelt, Theodore
  VII:304
Roosevelt Library **IX**:66
Roosevelt Recession. *See*
  recession (1937–1938)
Root, Elihu
  armed forces **VII**:20
  Army Act **VII**:22
  foreign policy **VII**:113
  investments, foreign
    VII:152
  mining **VII**:209
  peace movements **VII**:255
Root, George F. **V**:273
Root, John Wellborn **VI**:54–55
Roots (Haley) **X**:377*c*
Roots (TV miniseries) **X**:280
Root-Takahira Agreement
  VII:**305–306**, 405*c*
  foreign policy **VII**:113
  Roosevelt, Theodore
    VII:304
  Russo-Japanese War
    VII:309
Roper, Elmo **VIII**:312, 313
Roper v. Simmons **X**:67
Rosa Parks Freedom Award
  IX:255
Rose, A (Anshutz) **VII**:23
Rose, Ernestine **V**:434, 437
Rose Bowl **VIII**:371
Rosebud Creek, Battle of **VI**:408*c*
  Black Hills gold rush **VI**:39
  Crazy Horse **VI**:86
  Sioux wars **VI**:331
  Sitting Bull **VI**:332
Rosecrans, William S. **V**:**337**
  Buell, Don C. **V**:49
  Chattanooga, Battle of **V**:63
  Chickamauga, Battle of
    V:64, 65
  Corinth, Battle of **V**:95–96
  Lookout Mountain, Battle
    of **V**:243
  Murfreesboro/Stones River,
    Battle of **V**:271, 272
  Thomas, George H. **V**:389
Roseland Ballroom (New York
  City) **VII**:220
Rosemarie (operetta) **VII**:218–
  219
Rosenberg, Harold **IX**:19
Rosenberg, Julius and Ethel
  IX:**280–281**, 352*c*
  anticommunism **IX**:15
  communism **IX**:67
  espionage **VIII**:118
  Hoover, J. Edgar **IX**:149
  hydrogen bomb **IX**:152
Rosenman, Joel **X**:371
Rosenthal, Joe
  commemoration **IX**:66
  Iwo Jima **VIII**:192
  photography **VIII**:296
Rosenwald, Julius **VI**:237

Roses, Wars of the **I**:159
Rosie the Riveter **VIII:347–348**
   aircraft industry **VIII**:15
   shipbuilding **VIII**:359
   women's status and rights
      VIII:423
   World War II **VIII**:428
   World War II home front
      VIII:433
Ross, Alexander **IV**:102
Ross, Betsy **III:374**
Ross, Diana **IX**:229
Ross, George **III**:374
Ross, John **IV:325–326**
   Boudinot, Elias **IV**:61
   Cherokee **IV**:85
   Ridge, John **IV**:324
   Trail of Tears **IV**:378
   Watie, Stand **V**:427
Ross, Nellie Tayloe **VIII**:422
Ross, Robert **IV**:43
Rosselli, Johnny **IX**:250
Rossetti, William Michael **V**:431
Rossiter, Thomas L. **V**:352
Ross's Landing, Tennessee **IV**:325
Rostenkowski, Dan **X**:170
Rota, Mariana Islands **VIII**:228,
   295
Rota Island **I**:224
rotary press **V**:343
ROTC. *See* Reserve Officers
   Training Corps
Rothafel, Samuel Lionel "Roxy"
   VIII:28
Rothko, Mark **VIII**:31; **IX**:19
Roth v. United States
   Brennan, William J., Jr. **X**:47
   censorship **X**:71
   pornography **X**:283.284
Rouen **I**:371
Rough Riders **VI**:*317*, **317, 317–318,**
   412c
   Knox, Frank **VIII**:202
   Roosevelt, Theodore
      VII:304
   Spanish-American War
      VI:341
   Wheeler, Joseph **V**:429
Rough Rock Demonstration
   School **IX**:242
Rousseau, Jean-Jacques
   Franklin, Benjamin **III**:174
   Gallatin, Albert **III**:187
   kindergarten **VI**:207
Rousseau, Théodore **IV**:37, 61
Route 66 **VIII**:396
Rovaag, Karl F. **X**:233
Rowell, George P. **VI**:2
rowhouses **VI**:178
Rowland, Henry **VI**:144
Rowlandson, Mary White **II**:58,
   206, **336–337**
Rowling, J. K. **X**:212
Rowson, Susanna Haswell
   III:269, 341, **374**
Royal Academy (London) **III**:145,
   435

Royal Academy (Munich) **VI**:66
Royal African Company **II**:209,
   337, 437*c*
Royal Air Force (RAF)
   air power **VIII**:15
   bombing **VIII**:47
   Britain, Battle of **VIII**:53
   Normandy, invasion of
      VIII:275
Royal Air Force (RAF) Fighter
   Command **VIII**:53
Royal American Regiment
   III:175
Royal Blue (train) **VIII**:396
Royal Canadian Air Force
   VIII:128
royal charters **II**:436*c*
   Calvert, George **II**:56
   College of William and Mary
      II:74
   Connecticut **II**:77
   Maryland **II**:219
   Massachusetts Bay Company
      II:225, 226
   monarchy, British **II**:240
   proprietary colonies **II**:313
   Virginia Company of
      London **II**:402
   Williams, Roger **II**:416
royal colonies **II:337–338**
Royal Greens **III**:237
Royal Navy
   aircraft carriers **VIII**:11
   CDAAA **VIII**:77
   convoys **VIII**:86–87
   destroyers-for-bases deal
      VIII:95
   Lafitte, Jean **IV**:220
   mariners **II**:215
   Navy, U.S. **VIII**:265
   Normandy, invasion of
      VIII:275
   Teach, Edward **II**:385
royal patents **I**:152
Royal Philosophical Society
   III:173
Royal Society
   Audubon, John James **IV**:38
   Rittenhouse, David **III**:372
   science and technology
      III:384
Royal Spanish Infantry **IV**:328
Royce, Josiah **VI**:148, 281,
   318–319
Rozelle, Pete **X**:330
Rozier, Ferdinand **IV**:37
RU-486 (abortion drug) **X**:4, 43,
   382*c*
rubber **VIII:348,** 447*c*
   Baruch, Bernard M.
      VIII:42
   business **VIII**:58
   CIO **VIII**:82
   economy **VIII**:104
   labor/labor movements
      VIII:206
   rationing **VIII**:322

RFC **VIII**:326
   science and technology
      IV:333
   scrap drives **VIII**:354
   strikes **VIII**:377
   Sunbelt **VIII**:381
   UMWA **VIII**:401
rubber companies **VII**:85
Rubber Reserve Corporation
   VIII:354
Rubenstein, Arthur **VIII**:252
Rubin, Jerry **IX**:79; **X**:73
Rubinstein, Helena **VII**:65
Ruby, Jack **IX**:252
   assassinations **IX**:22
   Oswald, Lee Harvey **IX**:252
   Warren, Earl **IX**:337
Ruby Ridge, Idaho **X**:231
Ruckelshaus, William D. **X:312,**
   376*c*
   Cox, Archibald, Jr. **X**:95
   Nixon, Richard M. **X**:257
   Watergate scandal **X**:366
Rudd, Mark **IX**:341; **X**:367
Rudman, Warren **X**:158
Ruef, Abraham **VII**:154
Ruffin, Edmund
   fire-eaters **V**:146
   homespun **V**:194
   secession **V**:386
Ruffin, Josephine St. Pierre **VI**:7,
   259–260; **VII**:225
rugby **VI**:130, 131
Ruggieri, Michele **I**:320
Ruggles, David **IV**:413*c*
Rugova, Ibrahim **X**:199
Ruhr Valley **VIII**:432
Ruiz, José **IV**:21
Rule of 1756 (Great Britain)
   III:415
"Rule of Phase" **VI**:2
rules of war **V:337–338**
   foraging **V**:149
   Lieber, Francis **V**:234
   volunteer army **V**:420
rum
   alcohol **III**:13
   animals **III**:22
   Sugar Act **III**:401
Ruml, Beardsley **VIII**:341
Rumsfeld, Donald **X**:56–57, 72,
   312–313
Rumsfeld Doctrine **X**:313
rum trade **II**:214, **338**
"Runaway Scrape" **IV**:328
Runyon v. McCrary et al. **X**:377*c*
rural areas **VIII:348–349**
   African Americans **VIII**:4
   agriculture **VIII**:10
   art and architecture **VIII**:31
   banking **VIII**:39
   Evans, Walker **VIII**:120
   FCA **VIII**:125
   FMP **VIII**:134
   FSA **VIII**:127
   German Americans
      VIII:148

   isolationists **VIII**:189
   Lange, Dorothea **VIII**:210
   medicine **VIII**:235–236
   migration **VIII**:239, 240
   population trends **VIII**:305
   PUHCA **VIII**:313
   REA **VIII**:349–350
   *Recent Social Trends in the
      United States* **VIII**:323
   Resettlement Administration
      VIII:338–339
   South **VIII**:366, 367
   technology **VIII**:389, 397
   World War II home front
      VIII:432
   zoot-suiters **VIII**:442
Rural Electrification
   Administration (REA)
   VIII:349–350
   agriculture **VIII**:10
   ERAA **VIII**:114
   PUHCA **VIII**:313
   RFC **VIII**:325
   rural areas **VIII**:349
rural life **III:374–375,** 466*c*;
   VII:306–307, *307*
   Agricultural Marketing Act
      VII:5–6
   education **V**:124; **VI**:109
   electricity **III**:94
   fairs, agricultural **III**:161
   fashion **V**:139
   Federalists **III**:166
   labor/labor movements
      III:252
   mail-order houses **VI**:236–
      237
   marriage and family **III**:288
   population trends **III**:343;
      VI:286
Rush, Benjamin **III:375–376,**
   376, 460*c,* 463*c*
   Adams, John **III**:6
   Allen, Richard **III**:16
   antislavery **III**:26
   medicine **III**:296
   penitentiary movement
      IV:296
   prisons **III**:347
   slave trade **III**:393
   temperance movement
      III:410
Rush, Howard **VIII**:234
Rush, Richard **IV**:286
Rush-Bagot Treaty **IV**:154, 411*c*
Rusher, William **X**:24, 50
Ruskin, John
   settlement houses **VI**:327
   Social Gospel **VI**:335
   Whistler, James Abbott
      McNeill **VI**:389
Russel, Cabot **V**:142
Russell, Almira **V**:183
Russell, Andrew J. **V**:304
Russell, Bill **X**:331
Russell, Charles Taze **VI**:307
Russell, Henry **IV**:269

Russell, Howard **VII**:272
Russell, Lillian **VI**:117
Russell, William Green **IV**:99, 100
Russell, William H. **IV**:125
Russell & Company **VI**:131
Russell Sage Foundation **VIII**:163
Russia. *See also* Soviet Union
  Afghanistan War **X**:10
  Alaska **III**:12–13
  Bonaparte, Napoleon **III**:54
  Boxer Rebellion **VII**:40
  Cabot, Sebastian **I**:45, 46
  disease/epidemics **IV**:121
  foreign policy **VII**:113, 114; **X**:143
  fur trade **IV**:170
  Goldman, Emma **VII**:125–126
  Great White Fleet **VII**:130
  Hearst, William Randolph **VII**:138
  Hillman, Sidney **VIII**:165
  jingoes **VI**:204
  Judaism **VI**:205
  League of Nations **VII**:175
  Monroe Doctrine **IV**:260, 261
  Northeast Passage **I**:272, 273
  Open Door Policy **VII**:246
  peace movements **VII**:256
  population trends **VII**:266
  printing press **I**:303
  Root-Takahira Agreement **VII**:305
  Russian Revolution **VII**:308
  Russo-Japanese War **VII**:309
  Seattle General Strike **VII**:317
  Siberian Expedition **VII**:324
  space policy **X**:329
  UN **X**:356
  World War I **VII**:393
  World War II European theater **VIII**:432
  WTO **X**:372
Russian-American Company
  Alaska **III**:12
  California missions **IV**:76
  Monroe Doctrine **IV**:260
Russian Civil War **VII**:324–325
"Russian Hymn" **V**:274
Russian Revolution **VII**:308–309, 407*c*
  anticommunism **VIII**:22
  Baldwin, Roger Nash **VII**:31
  civil liberties **VII**:58
  Committee for Public Information **VII**:60
  communism **IX**:67
  Communist Party **VII**:61
  foreign policy **VII**:115

Hearst, William Randolph **VII**:138
  Jews **VIII**:195
  liberalism **VIII**:215
  The Masses **VII**:193
  nativism **VII**:234
  New Unionism **VII**:238
  Palmer, Alexander Mitchell **VII**:249
  public health **VII**:275
  radical and labor press **VII**:286
  Red Scare **VII**:296
  Reed, Jack **VII**:296, 297
  Sacco and Vanzetti **VII**:311
  Schenck v. U.S. **VII**:313
  Siberian Expedition **VII**:324
  socialism **VII**:328
  Supreme Court **VII**:342
Russian settlements **II**:338–339
  Alaska, Russia in **II**:14–15
  Aleut **II**:17
  exploration **II**:124
  Inuit **II**:177
Russo-Japanese War **VII**:309, 404*c*
  code breaking **VIII**:76
  foreign policy **VII**:113
  Great White Fleet **VII**:130
  intelligence **VIII**:187
  Open Door Policy **VII**:246
  peace movements **VII**:256
  presidency **VII**:268
  Roosevelt, Theodore **VII**:304
  Yalta Conference **VIII**:440
Russwurm, John B. **IV**:17, 209, 412*c*
Rust, William P. **VI**:379
rust belt **IX**:55; **X**:75, 76, *313*, 313–314, 337, 338
Rusticherllo of Pisa **I**:295
Rustin, Bayard **IX**:32, 73
Rust v. Sullivan **X**:368
Rutgers University **II**:107; **VI**:130
Rutgers v. Waddington **III**:206
Ruth, Babe **VII**:*33*, 409*c*
  Aaron, Henry L. "Hank" **X**:1
  baseball **VII**:33
  journalism **VII**:160
  popular culture **VIII**:303
  recreation **VIII**:328
  sports and recreation **VII**:334, 335; **VIII**:370
Rutherford, Joseph Franklin **VI**:307
Rutledge, Ann **V**:187, 235
Rutledge, John **III**:403
Rwanda
  Africa **X**:17
  Clinton, William J. **X**:81
  defense policy **X**:102
Ryan, George H. **X**:67
Ryan, Monsignor John A.
  Catholics **VIII**:64
  Irish Americans **VIII**:188
  religion **VII**:298

Ryan, Paddy **VI**:44
Ryder, Albert Pinkham **VI**:275, **319–320**
Ryder, Charles W. **VIII**:277
Ryder Truck **VIII**:58
RYM (Revolutionary Youth Movement) **X**:367
Ryswick, Treaty of **II**:372

S

Saarinen, Eero **IX**:20
Saarland, Germany **VII**:370
Sabin, Albert B. **IX**:212
Sabin, Pauline **VII**:274
Sabine Crossroads, Battle of **V**:29, 329
Sabine River **IV**:6, 370, 371
Sacagawea **III**:263, **377**
Sac and Fox Indians **IV**:327
  Black Hawk War **IV**:56, 57
  Catlin, George **IV**:84
  Keokuk **IV**:212
  lead mines **IV**:223
  Native Americans **IV**:274
Sacco and Vanzetti **VII**:311, 409*c*
  Baldwin, Roger Nash **VII**:31
  Communist Party **VII**:61
  radical and labor press **VII**:286
SACEUR (Supreme Allied Commander Europe) **X**:163
sachems **II**:341
  Aleut **II**:17
  Canonchet **II**:57
  Canonicus **II**:57
  Iroquois **I**:186; **II**:180
  Massachuset **I**:233
  Miantonomo **II**:233
  Narragansett **II**:249
  wampum **II**:406
  Wetamo **II**:411
  Wingina **II**:417
  women's status and rights **II**:422
Sacher, Harry **IX**:86
Sack Dress **IX**:116
Sackett's Harbor **III**:86
Sackville, George, Lord Germain **III**:81
Sacramento, California
  corruption, political **VI**:83
  Hastings, Lansford W. **IV**:187
  Sutter, John **IV**:363
  Wilkes expedition **IV**:400
Sacramento River **IV**:400
Sacramento River Valley **IV**:145, 363
sacred sites **I**:250–251
sacrifices **I**:18–19, *19*, 357
Sacsahuaman **I**:101, 102
Sadat, Anwar el- **X**:64, *65*, 66, 69
Sa'di, 'Abd al-Rahman ibn' Abd Allah ibn 'Imran al- **I**:360

"Safe Car You Can't Buy, The" (*Nation* article) **X**:241
Safe Drinking Water Act (1974) **X**:290
Safeguard program **X**:27
Saffir-Simpson Hurricane Scale **X**:173
Safford, Laurence F. **VIII**:76
SAG (Screen Actors Guild) **X**:299
Sagard, Gabriel **II**:50
Saginaw River **IV**:327
Sagoyewatha. *See* Red Jacket
Sahagún, Bernardino de **I**:130, **323**
Sahara **I**:323–324
  Cameroon **I**:56
  Gao **I**:137
  Ghana **I**:139
  Gold Coast **I**:143
  Mossi **I**:252
  Songhai **I**:342
  Tuareg **I**:370
Sahel **I**:252, 370
Saigon, South Vietnam **IX**:332
sailing vessels
  brigantine **I**:36
  caravel **I**:59–60
  merchant marine **VI**:245
St. Augustine, Florida **I**:397*c*; **II**:341–342, *342*
  Florida **I**:131; **II**:128, 130; **III**:167
  Fort Mose **II**:132
  Laudonnière, René de **I**:208
  Oglethorpe, James Edward **II**:278
  Queen Anne's War **II**:323
  Stono Rebellion **II**:377
  War of Jenkins' Ear **II**:408–409
St. Bartholomew's Day Massacre **I**:170, 382
St. Clair, Arthur **III**:377–378, 463*c*
  Blue Jacket **III**:54
  Fallen Timbers, Battle of **III**:161
  Fort Ticonderoga **III**:172
  Glaize, meeting at the **III**:195
  Harrison, William Henry **IV**:184
  Native Americans **III**:314
St. Clair, James **X**:357, 367
St. Clair County, Missouri **IV**:26
St. Croix River **I**:227; **IV**:27
Saint Domingue **II**:354, 372. *See also* Haiti
St. Elizabeth's Academy (Allegheny, New York) **VI**:220
Saintes, Battle of the **III**:197, **378–379**, 436
St. Eustatuis **III**:197
St. Francis County, Louisiana **IV**:223

Saint-Gaudens, Augustus **VI:321,** 322
  Burnham, Daniel Hudson **VI:**55
  54th Massachusetts Regiment **V:**142
  sculpture **VI:**327
  White, Stanford **VI:**392
St. George, California **IV:**408
Saint-Germain-des-Prés, Edict of **I:**170
St. John, John P. **VI:**123, 296
St. John River **I:**227; **IV:**27, 394
St. John's College (Fordham University) **VI:**217
St. Joseph, Missouri **IV:**160, 285
St. Kitts **III:**197
St. Lawrence expedition **IV:**336
St. Lawrence River
  agriculture **II:**9
  Canada **VI:**61
  Cartier, Jacques **I:**61–62
  French colonies **II:**136
  French explorations of the Atlantic **I:**133
  fur trade **II:**141; **III:**183
  Hochelaga **I:**164
  Iroquois **II:**178–179
  Quebec, Battle of **III:**353
  Quebec City **II:**323
  Webster-Ashburton Treaty **IV:**394
St. Lawrence Seaway **VI:**15
St. Leger, Abastenia **VII:**24
St. Leger, Barry
  Brant, Joseph **III:**63
  Burgoyne, Sir John **III:**67, 68
  Johnson, Sir John **III:**237
  Saratoga, surrender at **III:**380
St. Louis, Missouri
  abolitionism **IV:**3
  American Fur Company **IV:**18
  Ashley, William Henry **IV:**32–33
  Astor, John Jacob **IV:**33, 35
  Astoria **IV:**36
  Atkinson, Henry **IV:**36
  Austin, Moses **IV:**39
  Baldwin, Roger Nash **VII:**31
  blues **VII:**39
  Buck's Stove **VII:**43
  Carnegie, Andrew **VI:**62
  chain stores **VI:**65
  Chouteau family **IV:**87–88
  Clark, William **III:**96, 97
  corruption, political **VI:**84
  Eads, James Buchanan **VI:**103
  Exodusters **VI:**123
  Frémont, John C. **IV:**167
  fur trade **IV:**171
  Great Migration **VII:**129
  immigration **VI:**184

industrialization **IV:**201
Joplin, Scott **VII:**158
labor, radical **VI:**213
lead mines **IV:**223
libraries, public **VI:**224
Lovejoy, Elijah **IV:**230
Missouri Fur Company **IV:**257–258
overland mail **IV:**290
Pike, Zebulon Montgomery **IV:**300
public housing **IX:**266
Pulitzer, Joseph **VI:**297
race and race relations **VII:**283
Rocky Mountain Fur Company **IV:**324
Smith, Jedediah Strong **IV:**350
Sweet trial **VII:**344
"St. Louis Blues" (Handy) **VII:**219
St. Louis Cardinals **IX:**277
St. Louis Chronicle **VII:**159–160
St. Louis Gazette **IV:**266, 350
St. Louis Observer **IV:**3, 230
St. Louis *Voice of the People* **VI:**213
St. Mary's City **II:342–343**
  Calvert, Leonard **II:**57
  Chesapeake Bay **II:**66
  Maryland **II:**220, 221
  Roman Catholicism **II:**335
St. Mary's College (Emmitsburg, Maryland) **VI:**217
St. Matthews Episcopal church (Detroit, Michigan) **VII:**344
St. Mihiel, France **VII:**211
St. Patrick's Church (New York City) **IV:**30
St. Paul, Minnesota **VI:**65
St. Paul Globe **VII:**367
St. Paul & Pacific Railroad **VI:**172
St. Phillips Episcopal Church **IV:**402
St. Thomas' African Episcopal Church **III:**238
St. Vrain, Céran de Hault de Lassus de **IV:327–328**
  Bent, Charles **IV:**51
  Bent, William **IV:**52
  Bent's Fort **IV:**54
Saipan
  Mariana Islands **VIII:**228, 229
  Marines, U.S. **VIII:**230
  Philippine Sea, Battle of the **VIII:**295
  World War II Pacific theater **VIII:**436
Sakhalin Island **VIII:**440
Salary Grab Act (1873) **VI:**173
Salazar y Mendoza, José Francisco Xavier **II:**27
Salem, Massachusetts
  African Americans **IV:**9
  Essex, USS **IV:**143

female antislavery societies **IV:**147
  Pickering, Timothy **III:**334
Salem, Oregon **IV:**224
Salem witchcraft trials **II:**437c
  Brattle, Thomas **II:**46
  crime and punishment **II:**83
  Massachusetts **II:**223–224
  Nurse, Rebecca **II:**275–276
  Parris, Samuel **II:**281
  Sewall, Samuel **II:**350
  Tituba **II:**390
  Willard, Samuel **II:**415
  witches/witchcraft **II:**419–421
  women's status and rights **II:**425
Salerno, Italy **VIII:**20
sales tax **V:**384
Salinas de Gortari, Carlos **X:**226
Salinger, J. D.
  literature **IX:**194
  popular culture **IX:**258
  teenagers **IX:**314
Salisbury, Lord Robert Arthur **VI:**373
Salisbury Prison **V:**314
Salish Indians **II:**127, 128
Salk, Jonas **IX:**353c
  medicine **IX:**212
  public health **IX:**265
  technology **IX:**313
Salk polio vaccine **IX:**212
Salle, David **X:**31
Sally Hemings (Chase-Riboud) **III:**210
Salmagundi **X:**211
Salmon, Lucy Maynard
  history **VII:**140
  literature **VII:**180
Salomon, Haym **III:**236
Salt Creek, Oregon **IV:**26
Salt Creek, Wyoming **VII:**351
Salt Desert **IV:**187
Saltillo, Mexico **IV:**179, 233
SALT I/SALT II. *See* Strategic Arms Limitation Treaties
Salt Lake City, Utah
  California Trail **IV:**78
  cities and urban life **X:**76
  Deseret, State of **IV:**120
  Eccles, Marriner S. **VIII:**101
  Haywood, William Dudley **VII:**137
  Mormon Trail **IV:**262
  Mormon War **IV:**263
  South Pass **IV:**354
  V-J Day **VIII:**407
Salt of the Earth (film) **IX:**65
Saltonstall, Dudley **III:**333, 334
Salt River **I:**164, 165
Salt River Dam **VII:**229
Salt River Valley **II:**8–10, 176
salt trade **I:324–325**
  Ghana **I:**139, 140
  Sahara **I:**324
  Sudan **I:**347

salvation **I:**218, 369–370
Salvation Army
  McPherson, Aimee Semple **VII:**196
  Social Gospel **VI:**335
  USO **VIII:**403
Salzburger family **II:**148
Salzman, Jack **VI:**98–99
same-sex marriage **X:**150, 215–216. *See also* civil unions
Samoa **VI:322–323**
  Harrison, Benjamin **VI:**161
  public health **VII:**275
  Wilkes expedition **IV:**400
Samoset **II:**294
Sampson, Deborah **III:**379, **379–380**
Samsah Bay, China **VI:**273
San Antonio (ship) **I:**223, 224
San Antonio, Texas
  Alamo, The **IV:**13–15
  Austin, Moses **IV:**39
  Gregg, Josiah **IV:**179
  Magoffin, James W. **IV:**233
  Santa Anna, Antonio López de **IV:**330
  Texas **IV:**370–372
  Texas Revolution **IV:**375
  Travis, William Barret **IV:**380
San Bernardino, California
  Deseret, State of **IV:**120
  McDonald's **IX:**208
  Young, Brigham **IV:**408
San Bernardino Strait **VIII:**161, 214
San Carlos Reservation **VI:**17–18, 143, 409c
Sánchez, David **IX:**350
sanctions
  Africa **X:**16
  Iraq War **X:**186, 187
  South Africa **X:**325
Sandburg, Carl **VIII:**220
Sand County Almanac, A (Leopold) **IX:**108
Sand Creek Massacre **IV:**52–53, 100; **V:**445c
Sandford, John F. A. **IV:**362; **V:**116–117
San Diego, California
  Chilean-American relations **VI:**67
  free speech fights **VII:**118
  Kearny, Stephen Watts **IV:**212
Sandinista Front of National Liberation (FSLN) **X:**377c, 378c
  contras **X:**94–95
  foreign policy **X:**142
  Iran-contra affair **X:**183
  Latin America **X:**205, 206
  Mexico **X:**226
  Nicaragua **X:**254
Sandino, Augusto César **X:**254
Sandler, Bernice **X:**133

Sandoval, Gonzalo de **I:325–326**
Sandow the Strong Man **VI:**117
Sandoz Pharmaceuticals **IX:**195
Sandusky, Battle of **III:**314
Sandy Creek Association **III:**321
Sandy Hook, New York **IV:**115
Sandys, Sir Edwin **I:326; II:**151, 402
Sandys, George **II:343**
SANE (National Committee for a Sane Nuclear Policy) **IX:**153, **283–284,** 297
San Felipe, Mexico **IV:**379, 380
San Francisco, California
    anti-Chinese agitation, rise of **IV:**24
    Asian Americans **VIII:**32
    Bridges, Harry **VIII:**53
    California **III:**73; **IV:**72
    cities and urban life **V:**67; **VI:**70
    Civil Rights Cases **VI:**72
    communications **VI:**78
    counterculture **IX:**78
    disease/epidemics **IV:**122
    Donner party **IV:**126
    Forty-niners **IV:**159
    Frémont, Jesse Benton **IV:**165
    gays and lesbians **IX:**131
    Gentlemen's Agreement **VII:**123, 124
    gold **IV:**178
    Great White Fleet **VII:**130
    Greenwich Village **VII:**131
    Harte, Bret **VI:**162
    Hearst, William Randolph **VII:**137, 138
    immigration **V:**200; **VI:**184
    invention and technology **VI:**194
    Irish Americans **VIII:**188
    Johnson, Hiram Warren **VII:**154
    Lange, Dorothea **VIII:**210
    LSD **IX:**196
    Mitchell, William (Billy) **VII:**212
    Monroe Doctrine **IV:**260
    Mooney-Billings case **VII:**213
    music **IX:**229
    overland mail **IV:**290
    social work **VII:**329
    Steffens, Lincoln **VII:**339
    Strauss, Levi **IV:**358, 359
    strikes **VIII:**377
    Sutter, John **IV:**363
    transportation, urban **VI:**360
    UN **VIII:**402
    Vanderbilt, Cornelius **IV:**387
San Francisco, USS **VIII:**201
San Francisco Board of Education **VII:**320
San Francisco Chronicle **VII:**158–159

San Francisco *Evening Journal* **VI:**142
San Francisco *Examiner* **VII:**137
San Francisco–Oakland Bay Bridge **VIII:**314
San Francisco Seals **VIII:**95
San Francisco Stock Exchange **IV:**105–106
San Francisco World's Fair (1939) **VIII:**129
San Gabriel, California **IV:**144
San Gabriel de Yungue-Ouinge, New Mexico **I:**327
San Gabriel Mission **IV:**350–351
Sangamon County, Illinois **IV:**125
Sanger, Margaret **VII:311–313,** *312, 406c, 407c*
    birth control **VII:**36, 37; **X:**43
    "Children's Era" Speech **VII:432–434**
    Ellis, Henry Havelock **VII:**95
    eugenics **VII:**103
    Flynn, Elizabeth Gurley **VII:**109
    Greenwich Village **VII:**131
    medicine **IX:**211–212
    "The Pill" **IX:**257
    public health **VII:**276
    radical and labor press **VII:**284
    women's status and rights **VII:**388
Sanger, William **V:**315
Sangre de Cristo range **IV:**300
San Ildefonso, Treaty of **III:**273
Sanitary Fairs
    homefront **V:**193
    ladies aid societies **V:**228
    Philadelphia **V:**303
    U.S. Sanitary Commission **V:**411
sanitation **III:**138; **IV:**122; **V:**112; **VI:**407*c;* **VIII:**234
San Jacinto, Battle of **IV:328,** *413c*
    Alamo, The **IV:**14–15
    Austin, Stephen F. **IV:**41
    foreign policy **IV:**155
    Houston, Sam **IV:**191
    Lamar, Mirabeau B. **IV:**221
    Santa Anna, Antonio López de **IV:**330
    Texas **IV:**372
San Jacinto, USS **V:**150, 405
San Jacinto River **IV:**328
San Joaquin Valley
    exploration **IV:**144
    Murrieta, Joaquín **IV:**268
    Smith, Jedediah Strong **IV:**350
San Juan, Puerto Rico **I:**305
San Juan de los Caballeros, New Mexico **I:**279
San Juan de Ulúa, Mexico **I:**96, 110–111

San Juan Hill, Battle of **VI:***317,* 412*c*
    Pershing, John Joseph **VII:**258
    Roosevelt, Theodore **VII:**304
    Rough Riders **VI:**318
    Spanish-American War **VI:**341
    Wheeler, Joseph **V:**429
San Juan Islands **VI:**61, 385
San Julián, Patagonia **I:**223, 224
Sankey, Ira **VI:**249, 257
San Lorenzo, Mexico **I:**277–278
San Lorenzo, Treaty of. *See* Pinckney Treaty
San Marco, Church of **I:**375
San Miguel **IV:**331
San Pasqual, Battle of **IV:**82, 212
San Patricio battalion **IV:**252
San Salvador **I:**83, 85
San Simeon, California **VII:**138
Santa Anna, Antonio López de **IV:328–330,** 329
    Alamo, The **IV:**14
    Austin, Stephen F. **IV:**40
    Bowie, James **IV:**63
    Crockett, Davy **IV:**111
    Figueroa, José **IV:**149
    foreign policy **IV:**155
    Gadsden Purchase **IV:**173
    Guadalupe Hidalgo, Treaty of **IV:**181
    Houston, Sam **IV:**191
    Manifest Destiny **IV:**235
    Mexican-American War **IV:**252
    San Jacinto, Battle of **IV:**328
    Scott, Winfield **IV:**336
    Taylor, Zachary **IV:**368
    Texas **IV:**372
    Texas Revolution **IV:**374, 375
    Travis, William Barret **IV:**379–380
    Wilmot Proviso **V:**432
Santa Barbara, California **III:**73
Santa Clara County v. Southern Pacific Railroad Company **VI:**101, 127, 410*c*
Santa Cruz Islands, Battle of the **VIII:**366
Santa Fe, New Mexico **I:**263, 266, **326–327; II:**397
    California **III:**73
    Chouteau family **IV:**88
    exploration **IV:**145
    Gregg, Josiah **IV:**179
    Kearny, Stephen Watts **IV:**212
    Lamy, Jean Baptiste **IV:**222
    Magoffin, James W. **IV:**233
    Mexican-American War **IV:**252
    Pike, Zebulon Montgomery **IV:**300

St. Vrain, Céran **IV:**327–328
Santa Fe Trail **IV:**330
    Smith, Jedediah Strong **IV:**351
    Teapot Dome **VII:**351
    Texas **IV:**371, 372
Santa Fe Trail **IV:330–332,** 331*m*
    Armijo, Manuel **IV:**26
    Becknell, William **IV:**50
    Bent's Fort **IV:**54, 55
    Carson, Kit **IV:**81
    exploration **IV:**145
    Fort Leavenworth **IV:**158
    Gregg, Josiah **IV:**179
    Magoffin, James W. **IV:**233
Santayana, George **VI:**226; **VIII:**84
Santee Sioux **IV:**415*c;* **V:**444*c*
Santiago (ship) **I:**223, 224
Santiago, Battle of **VIII:**210
Santiago, Cuba **VI:**377
Santiago, Guatemala **I:**7, 8
Santiago campaign **VI:**317
Santo Domingo
    audiencia **I:**16
    Columbus, Bartholomew **I:**83
    foreign policy **VI:**133, 134
    Hispaniola **I:**162, 163
    Liberal Republican Party **VI:**222
    Oñate, Juan de **I:**279
    proposed annexation of **VI:323**
    Schurz, Carl **VI:**324
    wars of national liberation **IX:**339
    White, Andrew Dickson **VI:**391
Sanudo, Marin **I:**375
São Francisco River **I:**33
Sao kingdom **I:**56
São Tomé **I:328**
Sapir, Edward **VII:**181
Sapiro, Aaron **VII:**17
Sarajevo **X:**102
Saran Wrap **IX:**90
Saratoga, surrender at **III:380–382,** 381*m,* 461*c*
    Beaumarchais, Pierre-Auguste Caron de **III:**48
    Burgoyne, Sir John **III:**68
    Clinton, George **III:**98
    Clinton, Sir Henry **III:**99
    Conway Cabal, the **III:**118
    Fort Ticonderoga **III:**172
    French Alliance **III:**177
    Gates, Horatio **III:**190
    Kościuszko, Tadeusz **III:**248
    POWs **III:**346
    Revolutionary War **III:**368, 369
Saratoga, USS (aircraft carrier) **VIII:**11
Saratoga, USS (sloop-of-war) **V:**137

Saratoga Springs, New York
VI:177
Saratoga *Sun* **VIII:**179
Sarbanes-Oxley Act (2002) **X:**59, 170, **315**
Sargent, Aaron A. **VI:**229
Sargent, John Singer **V:**19; **VI:**275, **323–324; VII:**23
Sargent, Winthrop **IV:**94
Sarin nerve gas **X:**346
Sarter, Caesar **III:**8
Sartoris (Faulkner) **VIII:**443*c*
Sassacus **II:**222, 291
Sassamon, John **II:**193, 232
SAT (Scholastic Aptitude Test) **X:**113
satellite(s) **IX:**354*c*
  arms race **IX:**17
  aviation **IX:**29
  NASA **IX:**231
  space exploration **IX:**296
  technology **IX:**312
satellite communications **X:**153, 181
satellite radio **X:**220
satire **III:**179
Saturday Bulletin **IV:**210
Saturday Evening Post
  journalism **IV:**210
  Rosie the Riveter **VIII:**347
  science fiction **IX:**287
"Saturday Night Massacre" **X:**376*c*
  Cox, Archibald, Jr. **X:**95
  independent counsel **X:**179
  Jaworski, Leon **X:**193
  Ruckelshaus, William D. **X:**312
  Watergate scandal **X:**366
Saturiba (Timucua chief) **I:**208
Saudi Arabia
  Camp David accords **X:**65
  Middle East **IX:**214; **X:**229
  OPEC **X:**267, 268
  Persian Gulf War **X:**273
  terrorism **X:**346
  Zionism **VIII:**441
Saukenuk, Illinois **IV:**213, 327
Sauk Indians **IV:**36
Saunders, Barry **VI:**210
Saunders, Roger **II:**140
Savage, Augusta **VII:**136
Savage's Station **V:**205
Savannah, Battle of **III:**87, 368, **382–383**
Savannah, Georgia **II:343**
  Confederate navy **V:**83
  Dahlgren, John A. B. **V:**101
  disease/epidemics **IV:**122, 123
  Georgia **II:**145
  marine corps **V:**248
  Oglethorpe, James Edward **II:**277
  Sherman's March through Georgia **V:**357–358
  Special Field Order No. 15 **V:**365–366

Tomochichi **II:**392
Wesley, John **II:**410
Whitefield, George **II:**413
Savannah, siege of **III:**158, 178, **383**
Savannah, USS **IV:**333
savings and loan crisis **X:**53, 58
Savio, Mario **IX:**58, 126, **284**
Savo Island, Battle of **VIII:**159, 366
Saw Mill Flat **IV:**267
Sawyer, Philetus **VII:**173
Saxton, Rufus **V:**366
Saybrook, Connecticut **II:**116
Sayler's Creek, Battle of
  Appomattox campaign **V:**14
  Appomattox Court House, Virginia **V:**15
  Gordon, John B. **V:**170
  marine corps **V:**248
Sayles, John **X:**236
Sayre, John Nevin **VII:**109
scalawags **V:339–340**
  carpetbaggers **V:**55, 56
  Longstreet, James **V:**242
  Reconstruction **V:**324
Scali, John **X:**357
Scalia, Antonin **X:315–316**
  Ginsburg, Ruth Bader **X:**152
  gun control **X:**162
  independent counsel **X:**179
  Reagan, Ronald W. **X:**300
  Rehnquist, William H. **X:**305
  Supreme Court **X:**339
  Thomas, Clarence **X:**350
scalping **II:**282, **343–344,** *344*
scandals **VII:**407*c*, 408*c. See also* corruption; political corruption
  business **X:**59
  Clinton, Hillary Rodham **X:**78
  Clinton, William J. **X:**82
  Crédit Mobilier **V:**97
  Ferraro, Geraldine A. **X:**135
  Ford, Gerald R. **X:**138
  House of Representatives **X:**170, 171
  Iraq War **X:**188
  Koreagate **X:**199
  religion **X:**306
  Rhinelander case **VII:**301
  Sarbanes-Oxley Act **X:**315
  Senate, U.S. **X:**321
  Stevens, Thaddeus **V:**372
  televangelism **X:**342
  Watergate scandal **X:**365–367
Scandinavia **I:**271–272
  blitzkrieg **VIII:**47
  immigration **VI:**185
  isolationists **VIII:**189–190
  National Origins Act **VII:**227
Scandinavian Americans **VIII:**189

scanners **X:**319
Scarface (film) **VIII:**245
Scarlet Letter, The (Hawthorne) **IV:**415*c*
  Jewett, Sarah Orne **VI:**203
  literature **IV:**228
  transcendental movement **IV:**379
S. C. Johnson Company **IX:**246
Schapiro, Meyer **IX:**19
Schechter Poultry Corporation v. United States **VIII:351,** 445*c*
  antimonopoly **VIII:**24
  Fair Labor Standards Act **VIII:**124
  First New Deal **VIII:**138
  National Recovery Administration **VIII:**260
  NIRA **VIII:**257
  Supreme Court **VIII:**382
Schedel, Hartmann **I:**248
Scheele, Leonard **IX:**265
Schenck, Charles **VII:**58, 343
Schenck v. United States **VII:313**
  civil liberties **VII:**58
  Committee for Public Information **VII:**60
  Holmes, Oliver Wendell **VII:**141
  Supreme Court **VII:**343
Schenectady, New York
  cities and urban life **VII:**54
  GE **VII:**123
  Villard, Henry **VI:**375
schepens **II:**266
Schiavo, Terry **X:**322
Schiff, Jacob H.
  banking, investment **VI:**23
  Morgan, John Pierpont **VI:**251
  Wald, Lillian **VII:**377
Schillinger, Joseph **VII:**124
Schine, David **IX:**18
Schivelbusch, Wolfgang **I:**48
Schlafly, Fred **X:**93, 300
Schlafly, Phyllis **X:316–317**
  ABM Treaty **X:**27
  Amendments to the U.S. Constitution **X:**23
  Christian Coalition **X:**74
  conservative movement **X:**93, 94
  ERA **X:**124
  feminism **X:**133.134
  Helms, Jesse A., Jr. **X:**165
  Panama Canal turnover **X:**271
  women's status and rights **X:**371
Schlatter, Michael **II:**149
Schlesinger, Arthur M., Jr.
  Americans for Democratic Action **IX:**13, 14
  multiculturalism **X:**237
  presidency **VII:**268
Schlesinger, Benjamin **VII:**149

Schlesinger, James R.
  defense policy **X:**100
  energy **X:**120
  Energy, U.S. Department of **X:**122
Schlesinger and Mayer Company Store (Chicago) **VI:**347
Schleswig, Germany **VII:**370
Schmalkaldic League **I:**219
Schmeling, Max **VIII:**223, 371, 446*c*
Schmidt, Harry **VIII:**230
Schneiderman, Rose **VII:**231
Schoenberg, Arnold **VII:**220; **VIII:**252
Schofield, John M. **V:**356
scholarship **I:**357–358
scholastic achievement **X:**113–115
Scholastic Aptitude Test (SAT) **X:**113
Schomburgk, Robert **VI:**373
school(s) **V:**71
School and Society, The (Dewey) **VII:**76
school busing **X:**377*c*
  Brennan, William J., Jr. **X:**48
  Kennedy, Edward M. **X:**197
  race and race relations **X:**297
school desegregation **X:**375*c*
  race and race relations **X:**297
  Supreme Court **X:**338
  Thurmond, James Strom **X:**351
school enrollment **X:**115
School for Scandal, The (Sheridan) **III:**417
School of Mines (Columbia University) **VI:**247
school prayer. *See* prayer (in schools)
school shootings **X:**161
school vouchers **X:**115
schout **II:**266
Schreiner, Olive **VII:**95
Schubert, Franz **III:**309; **VI:**257
Schultz, George **X:**165
Schumer, Charles **X:**78
Schurz, Carl **VI:324–325**
  environment **VI:**119
  Forest Reserve Act **VI:**134
  Grant, Ulysses S. **V:**175
  Hayes, Rutherford B. **VI:**167
  immigration **IV:**196
  Liberal Republican Party **VI:**222
  mugwumps **VI:**252
  Nez Perce War **VI:**268
  Pulitzer, Joseph **VI:**297
  Republican Party **V:**334
  Villard, Henry **VI:**375
  Winnemucca, Sarah **VI:**397
Schurz, Margarethe **VI:**207, 280

Schuurman, Jacobus **II:**135
Schuykill County, Pennsylvania **VI:**248
Schuykill River **III:**135
Schuyler, George **IX:**32
Schuyler, Louisa Lee **V:**285
Schuyler, Philip John **III:**383–384
   Gates, Horatio **III:**190
   Johnson, Sir John **III:**237
   Montgomery, Richard **III:**301
   Saratoga, surrender at **III:**380
Schwab, Charles M. **VII:**336, 365
Schwab, Eugene **VI:**169
Schwartz, Fred C. **IX:**272
Schwartzchild & Sulzberger **VI:**243
Schwarz, Charles **X:**382*c*
Schwarz, Fred **X:**93
Schwarzkopf, Norman
   Middle East **X:**229
   Persian Gulf War **X:**273
   Powell, Colin L. **X:**286
Schweinfurt, Germany **VIII:**47
Schwerner, Michael **IX:**356*c*
   CORE **IX:**73
   MFDP **IX:**219
   race and race relations **IX:**270
Schwieger, Walter **VII:**188
science, invention and technology
   I:*183*, 183–185, 285; **II:**344–346, 345, **385–386; III:**384–385, *385;* **IV:**332–335, *334;* **V:**340–343, *341*, 446*c;* **VI:**194–197, *195*, 325–326; **VII:**149, 149–151, *150*, 313–315, *314*, 315, 403*c;* **VIII:**351–353, **389–390; IX:**284–287, 285, 311–314, *312;* **X:**317–320, *318*, 382*c*
   ABM Treaty **X:**28
   advertising **VIII:**1; **X:**9
   agriculture **II:**9; **IV:**10–11, 13; **VII:**6; **VIII:**10; **IX:**6–7; **X:**18–20
   aircraft industry **VIII:**14
   American Philosophical Society **III:**17–18
   art and architecture **IV:**29; **VII:**19, 24
   atomic bomb **VIII:**35
   aviation **IX:**28–29
   barbed wire **VI:**24
   Bartram, John **II:**34
   Bartram, William **III:**47–48
   Bell, Alexander Graham **VI:**31
   Boas, Franz Uri **VII:**39–40
   bombing **VIII:**48
   Brattle, Thomas **II:**46
   Britain, Battle of **VIII:**53
   Bush, Vannevar **VIII:**56–57
   business **VII:**45; **VIII:**57–59; **X:**57, 59

Carnegie, Andrew **VI:**62
Carson, Rachel **IX:**50
child labor **VII:**53
cities and urban life **VII:**55
Civil War **V:**74
Clinton, Hillary Rodham **X:**78
Coeur d'Alene miners' strike **VI:**77
Colden, Cadwallader **II:**73
Colden, Jane **II:**73–74
computers **IX:**69–71; **X:**86–88
conservation/environmentalism **X:**90
Darwinism and religion **VI:**92–93
Dow Chemical Corporation **IX:**89–90
dust bowl **VIII:**97–98
Eads, James Buchanan **VI:**103
Eastman, George **VI:**105
economy **IV:**131; **VII:**84; **VIII:**104; **IX:**97; **X:**110
Edison, Thomas Alva **VI:**106–107
education **III:**148; **IX:**99
electricity **VI:**92–94
ENIAC **IX:**104–105
Enlightenment, American **II:**118
entertainment, popular **VII:**96–97
environment **III:**153, 156
eugenics **VII:**102
evolution **VI:**122
flour milling **VI:**129
FMP **VIII:**134
Ford, Henry **VII:**111
Fordney-McCumber Tariff **VII:**112
Franklin, Benjamin **III:**173, 174
Franklin Institute **IV:**163
Fulton, Robert **III:**182–183
GE **VII:**123; **IX:**132
George III **III:**192
Gesner, Conrad von **I:**139
Gibbs, Josiah Willard **VI:**144
globalization **X:**153
global warming **X:**155–156
GM **IX:**133
Godfrey, Thomas **II:**150
gold **IV:**178, 179
Great Plains Indians **II:**157
Human Genome Project **X:**171–172
hydrogen bomb **IX:**152
illustration, photography, and graphic arts **VI:**183, 188
immigration **VI:**185–186
industrialization **IV:**199
Industrial Revolution, Second **VI:**191

Internet **X:**181–183
Jefferson, Thomas **III:**232
Johnson, Tom Loftin **VII:**156
journalism **IV:**209; **V:**217, 218
Kalm, Peter **II:**191
King, Clarence **VI:**208
Kinsey, Alfred C. **IX:**175–176
Ku Klux Klan **VII:**166
labor, child **VI:**212
lead mines **IV:**224
Leonardo da Vinci **I:**212
Lewis and Clark Expedition **III:**262–264
Life magazine **VIII:**217
Lincoln, Abraham **V:**237
literature **X:**212
lumbering **IV:**231
Manhattan Project **VIII:**227
Mather, Cotton **II:**227
McCormick, Cyrus Hall **IV:**243–245
Mead, Margaret **VII:**197
meatpacking **VI:**243
medicine **VII:**198; **VIII:**234–236
Middletown **VII:**206
military-industrial complex **IX:**216
mobilization **VIII:**242
Monitor-Merrimack **V:**265
movie industry **VII:**214
movies **IX:**224
Muir, John **VI:**252
music **VI:**258; **VII:**218; **VIII:**249
NASA **IX:**231–232
newspapers **VI:**266–267
New York World's Fair (1939–1940) **VIII:**274
NIH **IX:**235
oil industry **VII:**245
OSRD **VIII:**283–284
Paine, Thomas **III:**329
Pan-American Exposition **VII:**251–252
Peirce, Charles Sanders **VI:**280, 281
Pennsylvania **II:**287–288
Philadelphia Centennial Exposition **VI:**284
photography **VII:**258
popular culture **X:**278
Priestley, Joseph **III:**345
public health **IX:**264
race and race relations **III:**357; **IV:**310–311
radio **VII:**288–290
recreation **X:**303
religion **VI:**306; **VII:**297, 298; **VIII:**335
Rittenhouse, David **III:**372
Rush, Benjamin **III:**375
rust belt **X:**314
SDI **X:**337
social work **VII:**330

space exploration **IX:**296–297
space policy **X:**326–329
steel industry **VII:**336, 337
stem cell research **X:**335–336
suburbanization/suburbs **VIII:**379
Sumner, William Graham **VI:**347
tanks **VIII:**385–386
tariffs **VII:**350
Taylor, Frederick Winslow **VII:**351
Teamsters Union **IX:**310
technology **VIII:**389; **IX:**311
television **IX:**315–316
Tesla, Nikola **VI:**353–354
Unitarianism **III:**419
urban transportation **VII:**363
U.S. Steel **VII:**365
Ward, Lester Frank **VI:**382
Webster, Noah **III:**434
women's status and rights **VI:**400; **VIII:**424
work, household **VII:**389–390
World War II **VIII:**428
World War II home front **VIII:**433–434
Science and Health (Eddy) **VI:**69, 106, 408*c*
science fiction **IX:**195, 224, **287**
Science in World War II series (Atlantic Monthly Press) **VIII:**283
Science News Service **VII:**314–315
Science of Cooking and Cleaning, The (Richards) **VI:**313
Science Service Syndicate **VII:**159
Science: The Endless Frontier (Bush) **VIII:**56, 57, 283
Scientific American **VII:**314–315
scientific management **VII:315–316,** 405*c*
   armed forces **VII:**20
   automobile industry **VII:**27
   business **VII:**45–46
   Ford, Henry **VII:**111
   Industrial Revolution, Second **VI:**191
   IWW **VII:**146
   labor/labor movements **VII:**169
   mass production **VII:**194–195
   New Unionism **VII:**237
   progressivism **VII:**271
   science, invention, and technology **VII:**150, 314, 315
   steel industry **VII:**337
   Taylor, Frederick Winslow **VII:**350
   technology **VIII:**390

Sciopodes **I**:248
SCLC. *See* Southern Christian Leadership Conference
Sclopis, Federico **VI**:385
Scofield, Cyrus Ingerson **VI**:93, 307
Scofield Reference Bible **VI**:93, 307
Scopes, John Thomas **VI**:52; **VII**:317
Scopes Trial (*Scopes v. The State of Tennessee*) **VII**:*316*, 316–317, 409*c*, 434–440
  ACLU **VII**:10
  Baldwin, Roger Nash **VII**:31
  conservatism **VIII**:84
  Darrow, Clarence Seward **VII**:70
  Mencken, Henry Louis **VII**:202
  religion **VII**:299
  science and technology **VII**:314
Scorpion, HMS **III**:180
Scorsese, Martin **X**:279
Scotch hearth **IV**:224
Scotia Seminary (North Carolina) **VIII**:44
Scotland **I**:10, 395*c*
  English Civil War **II**:116
  ethnocentrism **II**:121
  Gage, Thomas **III**:186
  investments, American, abroad **VI**:197
  Owen, Robert **IV**:291
  Whigs **IV**:396
  wolves **II**:421
  Wright, Fanny **IV**:405
Scots immigrants **II**:145–146, 261, 262, **346**
Scots-Irish **II**:346–347, 437*c*; **III**:385–386
  immigration **III**:221
  North Carolina **II**:275
  Paxton Boys **II**:282
  Presbyterians **II**:309
  South Carolina **II**:370
Scott, Adrian **IX**:147
Scott, Dred. *See also Dred Scott* decision
  Missouri Compromise **IV**:257
  Republican Party **IV**:323
  Supreme Court **IV**:362
Scott, Hugh **X**:320
Scott, Isaac E. **VI**:19
Scott, Thomas Alexander **VI**:326
  Carnegie, Andrew **VI**:62
  Great Strike of 1877 **VI**:154
  Hayes, Rutherford B. **VI**:167–168
  Huntington, Collis Potter **VI**:181
  oil **VI**:271

Scott, Winfield **IV**:*335*, **335–336**, 413*c*–415*c*
  Aroostook War **IV**:27
  Black Hawk War **IV**:58
  Civil War **V**:73
  disease/epidemics **IV**:122
  Fort Sumter **V**:154
  Guadalupe Hidalgo, Treaty of **IV**:181
  habeas corpus, writ of **V**:181
  Hill, Daniel H. **V**:190
  Jackson, Thomas J. "Stonewall" **V**:209
  Lee, Robert E. **V**:230
  Lincoln, Abraham **V**:237
  McClellan, George Brinton **V**:250
  McDowell, Irvin **V**:252
  Medal of Honor **V**:255
  Mexican-American War **IV**:252
  monuments **V**:267
  Pemberton, John C. **V**:298
  Polk, James K. **IV**:302
  Santa Anna, Antonio López de **IV**:330
  Seminole War, First/Second **IV**:339
  tactics and strategy **V**:380, 381
  Webster-Ashburton Treaty **IV**:394
  Whigs **IV**:398
Scott-Brown, Denise **IX**:20
Scottsboro Boys **VIII**:*353*, 353–354, 443*c*, 444*c*
  African Americans **VIII**:3
  Baldwin, Roger Nash **VII**:31
  Bethune, Mary McLeod **VIII**:44
  civil rights **VIII**:72
  Communists **VIII**:77
  NAACP **VIII**:255
  race and race relations **VIII**:317
scouting **VI**:76
Scouts of the Prairies (Buntline) **VI**:76
Scowcroft, Brent **X**:353
Scranton, Pennsylvania **VI**:214; **VIII**:187
Scranton, William **X**:357
scrap drives **VIII**:**354,** 447*c*
  children **VIII**:67
  women's status and rights **VIII**:424
  World War II home front **VIII**:433
Screen Actors Guild (SAG) **X**:299
screwball comedy **VIII**:246
screw propeller **V**:342
scribal publication **I**:**328–329**
  book, the **I**:33
  Drake Manuscript **I**:113
  Florentine Codex **I**:130

  Mandeville, Sir John **I**:228
  printing press **I**:303
  travel narratives **I**:368
Scribner, Charles **VI**:147
Scribner's Monthly Magazine **VI**:147, 183
Scripps, Edward W.
  journalism **VII**:159
  newspapers **VI**:267
  science and technology **VII**:314–315
Scripps-Howard **VIII**:196
scriptoria **I**:303
Scruggs, William L. **VI**:373
Scudder, Vida **VI**:327
Scudder's American Museum **VI**:25
Scull, Nicholas **II**:288
Scully, Vincent **I**:12
sculpture **VI**:**326–327**
  art and architecture **VI**:18; **X**:30–31
  Michelangelo **I**:243–244
  Olmecs **I**:278
  Remington, Frederic **VI**:310
  Saint-Gaudens, Augustus **VI**:321
scurvy **I**:107; **II**:98; **IV**:123; **V**:112, 257
SD (Sicherheitsdienst) **VIII**:187
SDA (Students for Democratic Action) **X**:233
SDI. *See* Strategic Defense Initiative
SDP. *See* Social Democratic Party
SDS. *See* Students for a Democratic Society
Sea Around Us, The (Carson) **IX**:51
Seabiscuit (racehorse) **VIII**:373
Seabury, Samuel **III**:21, **386–387**
"Sea Dogs" **II**:295
Sea Islands **V**:312; **VI**:21
Sea Islands Mission **V**:178
Seale, Bobby **IX**:357*c*
  African Americans **IX**:6
  Black Panthers **IX**:40
  "Chicago Eight" **X**:73
seal hunting **VI**:27–28, 34
seances **VI**:309
seaports
  Charleston **II**:63–64
  class **II**:70
  Newport **II**:267
  New York City **II**:272
  Philadelphia **II**:292
  trade, domestic and foreign **II**:393
search and seizure **III**:51
search and surveillance powers **X**:358, 359
Searchers, The (film) **IX**:224
search warrants **III**:448; **X**:359
Searles, John E., Jr. **VI**:228
Sears, Richard Warren **VI**:237, 342

Sears, Roebuck and Company
  America First Committee **VIII**:17
  business **VII**:46
  dollar-a-year men **VIII**:96
  mail-order houses **VI**:237
  Nelson, Donald M. **VIII**:266
  shopping centers **IX**:290
  stock market crash **VIII**:376
Seated Figure (de Kooning) **VIII**:31
SEATO. *See* Southeast Asia Treaty Organization
Seattle, Washington **VI**:209
Seattle Computer Products **X**:147
Seattle General Strike **VII**:**317–318,** 407*c*
  Coolidge, Calvin John **VII**:64
  Red Scare **VII**:296
  Russian Revolution **VII**:308
Seattle Metal Trades Council **VII**:317
Seaver, James Everett **II**:184
Sebold, William G. **VIII**:117
SEC. *See* Securities and Exchange Commission
secession **V**:**343–346,** *344*, 443*c*–444*c*
  abolitionism **V**:4
  Booth, John Wilkes **V**:38
  Brown, Joseph Emerson **V**:45
  Buchanan, James **V**:48
  Civil War **V**:73
  Confederate States of America **V**:84
  Congress **V**:89
  Copperheads **V**:94
  Crittenden Compromise **V**:97
  Davis, Jefferson **V**:104
  Early, Jubal A. **V**:119
  Fillmore, Millard **IV**:149–150
  fire-eaters **V**:145, 146
  Greeley, Horace **V**:177
  habeas corpus, writ of **V**:181
  Hicks, Thomas H. **V**:188
  ironclad oath **V**:206
  Jackson, Claiborne F. **V**:209
  Jackson, Thomas J. "Stonewall" **V**:210
  Johnson, Andrew **V**:212
  Letcher, John **V**:232
  Longstreet, James **V**:241
  Mallory, Stephen R. **V**:247
  Medal of Honor **V**:255
  Nullification Controversy **IV**:283
  Price, Sterling **V**:313
  Reconstruction **V**:324
  Seward, William H. **V**:347
  states' rights **V**:370
  Stephens, Alexander Hamilton **V**:371, 372

United Daughters of the
Confederacy **V:**407
Vance, Zebulon B. **V:**414
Wigfall, Louis T. **V:**431
Wise, Henry A. **V:**434
Yancey, William Lowndes
V:439
2nd Infantry Regiment **IV:**212
2nd Marines **VIII:**386
Second Amendment
Bill of Rights **III:**51
citizen-soldier **V:**68
gun control **X:**161, 162
militia movement **X:**230
secondary education. *See*
education, primary and
secondary
Second Cello Concerto (Herbert)
VI:170
Second Church of Boston **IV:**140
Second Coming
Darwinism and religion
VI:93
religion **VI:**307
Tanner, Benjamin Tucker
VI:351
second front **VIII:355,** 447*c,* 448*c*
Anglo-American relations
VIII:21
Casablanca Conference
VIII:62
foreign policy **VIII:**142
Grand Alliance **VIII:**155
Hopkins, Harry L. **VIII:**177
Italian campaign **VIII:**191
Lend-Lease **VIII:**212
Marshall, George C.
VIII:233
Normandy, invasion of
VIII:275–276
Teheran Conference
VIII:390
World War II European
theater **VIII:**430, 431
Second Great Awakening **IV:336–
338,** 337, 337*t*
abolitionism **V:**2
anti-Catholic riots **IV:**22–24
anti-Masonry **IV:**25
Finney, Charles Grandison
IV:150–151
humanitarianism **III:**217
Maine Law **IV:**233
Moravians **III:**302
religion **III:**362; **IV:**316–
317, 320, 321; **V:**331
Republican Party **IV:**322
temperance movement
IV:369
Second Hague Peace Conference.
See Hague Peace Conference,
Second
Second Industrial Revolution. *See*
Industrial Revolution, Second
Second New Deal **VIII:355–356**
antimonopoly **VIII:**24
Banking Act (1935) **VIII:**41

Byrnes, James F. **VIII:**60
Congress **VIII:**79
conservatism **VIII:**84
Executive Reorganization
Act **VIII:**121
FERA **VIII:**133
liberalism **VIII:**215
Long, Huey P. **VIII:**223
New Deal **VIII:**269, 270
NLRB **VIII:**258
NYA **VIII:**262
PUHCA **VIII:**313
relief **VIII:**332
Republican Party **VIII:**337
Revenue Act of 1935
VIII:340
Roosevelt, Franklin D.
VIII:345
Social Security Act
VIII:363
Union Party **VIII:**401
Second Presbyterian Church
IV:388
Second Seminole War **IV:**289
Second Stage, The (Friedan)
IX:127
Secord, Richard **X:**364
Secotan **I:**329
Secretariat of the United Nations
VIII:402
Secretary of Foreign Affairs
III:270
secret ballot
citizenship **VII:**56
elections, conduct of **VI:**113
House of Representatives
X:169
Omaha platform **VI:**272
progressivism **VII:**270
Secret Committee **III:**116
*Secret Diary of Harold L. Ickes,
The* (Ickes) **VIII:**184
Secret Service
assassinations **IX:**23
DHS **X:**167
impeachment of Richard M.
Nixon **X:**178
secret service (England) **I:**382
"Secret Six" **VI:**171
sectionalism **VI:**365
secularism **VIII:**334, 335
Secularization Law (1833) **IV:**149
Secure America and Orderly
Immigration Act (2005) **X:**177
Secure Borders, Economic
Opportunity and Immigration
Act (2007) **X:**79
Secure Fence Act (2006) **X:**177
Securities Act (1933) **VIII:**356,
444*c*
Securities and Exchange Act
(1934) **VIII:**357, 444*c*
Securities and Exchange
Commission (SEC) **VIII:356–
357,** 444*c*
business **X:**58, 59
Catholics **VIII:**63

Douglas, William O.
VIII:96–97
FCC **VIII:**131
Henderson, Leon **VIII:**163
Kennedy, Joseph P.
VIII:199–200
New Deal **VIII:**269
PUHCA **VIII:**313
RICO **X:**299
Second New Deal **VIII:**356
stock market crash **VIII:**376
securities industry **X:**57
Security, Work, and Relief Policies
(NRPB report) **VIII:**261
Sedalia, Missouri **VII:**158
Seddon, James A. **V:**85
Sedgwick, Catharine Maria
IV:229
Sedgwick, John
Antietam, Battle of **V:**13
Chancellorsville, Battle of
V:61, 62
Harvard Regiment **V:**186
Sedgwick family **III:**176
Sedima, S.P.R.L. v. Imrex Co.
X:299
sedition **III:**14, 277
Sedition Act **I:**464*c;* **VII:318–
319,** 407*c*
ACLU **VII:**9
Alien and Sedition Acts
III:14
Anarchist Immigration Act
VII:15
Bache, Benjamin Franklin
III:39
Callender, James T. **III:**74
censorship **VIII:**65
Committee for Public
Information **VII:**60
conscription **VII:**63
Duane, James **III:**140
Fuel Administration
VII:119
journalism **III:**241
Palmer, Alexander Mitchell
VII:249
Schenck v. U.S. **VII:**313
socialism **VII:**328
World War I **VII:**394
Seeger, Pete **IX:***120*
cold war culture **IX:**64
folk music revival **IX:**120,
121
Guthrie, Woody **VIII:**160
music **IX:**229
popular culture **IX:**259
Segal, George **X:**30
segregation **VI:**411*c;* **VII:319–
321,** *320;* **VIII:**447*c;* **IX:287–
288**
ACLU **VIII:**17–18
African Americans **VI:**7;
VIII:2; **IX:**4, 5
African Methodist Episcopal
Church **V:**5
Baker, Ella Josephine **IX:**33

Baker v. Carr **IX:**33–34
baseball **VII:**34
big bands **VIII:**44
Black Codes **V:**35
Brotherhood of Sleeping Car
Porters **VIII:**54
*Brown v. Board of
Education* **IX:**43–44
Carmichael, Stokely **IX:**49
Carter, James Earl, Jr. **X:**67
children **VIII:**67
cities and urban life **VII:**55;
IX:56
citizenship **VII:**56
civil rights **VIII:**72, 73
Civil Rights Act (1957)
IX:59
Civil Rights Cases **VI:**72
conservatism **IX:**75
CORE **IX:**72–73
DuBois, W.E.B. **VII:**80, 81
education **VI:**108
education, philanthropy and
VI:112
EEOC **IX:**110
Eisenhower, Dwight D.
IX:101
entertainment, popular
VI:117
ESEA **IX:**106
ethnocentrism **II:**123
Fair Deal **IX:**115
Faubus, Orval **IX:**117–118
Federal Housing
Administration **IX:**120
FEPC **VIII:**123
Fort Mose **II:**132
Fourteenth Amendment
V:157
Freedom Train **IX:**125
Gentlemen's Agreement
VII:123
Goldwater, Barry **IX:**136
Graham, Billy **IX:**138
Great Migration **VII:**127,
128
Great White Fleet **VII:**130
Hamer, Fannie Lou **IX:**141
Helms, Jesse A., Jr. **X:**165
Japanese Americans,
relocation of **VIII:**194
Jim Crow laws **VI:**203–204
Johnson, Jack **VII:**155
Kelley, William D. **V:**222
King, Martin Luther, Jr.
IX:174
KKK **IX:**179
Latino movement **IX:**185
Lewis, John **IX:**190
lynching **VI:**230
Malcolm X **IX:**199
March on Washington
(1963) **IX:**200, 201
Marshall, Thurgood **IX:**203
medicine **VII:**200
migration **IX:**215
Murray, Pauli **IX:**227

segregation (continued)
  NAACP **VII:**224; **VIII:**256; **IX:**232
  nativism **VII:**234
  Operation Dixie **IX:**249
  Parks, Rosa **IX:**254
  Plessy v. Ferguson **VI:**284–285, **433–438**
  Progressive Party **IX:**264
  race and race relations **VII:**282; **VIII:**318; **IX:**269; **X:**297
  Racial Integrity Act **VII:**284
  Randolph, A. Philip **VIII:**321
  religion **IX:**272
  SCLC **IX:**292–294
  sit-ins **IX:**290
  South Africa **X:**324
  southern demagogues **VII:**332
  Southern Manifesto **IX:**294
  sports and recreation **VII:**335
  States' Rights Party **IX:**300
  Supreme Court **VIII:**383
  Sweet trial **VII:**344
  Tanner, Benjamin Tucker **VI:**351
  Terrell, Mary Eliza Church **VII:**352, 353
  Thurmond, James Strom **X:**351
  Tourgée, Albion W. **V:**390
  Trotter, William Monroe **VII:**357
  UFW **IX:**324
  UNIA **VII:**362
  urban redevelopment **IX:**326
  Wallace, George C. **X:**364
  Warren, Earl **IX:**337
  Warren Court **IX:**338
  White Citizens' Councils **IX:**341–342
  Wilkins, Roy **IX:**344, 345
Seifritz, Max **VI:**170
Seigenthaler, John **IX:**123
seigneurs **I:**149; **III:**78
Seinfeld **X:**343
seismology **VIII:**352
SEIU (Service Employees International Union) **X:**203
Selden, George Baldwin **VI:**196; **VII:**111
Select Bipartisan Committee to Investigate the Preparation and Response to Hurricane Katrina **X:**174
selective serotonin uptake reinhibitors (SSRIs) **X:**223
Selective Service **VIII:357–359,** 358. *See also* conscription
  ACLU **VIII:**18
  Army, U.S. **VIII:**26
  Atlantic Charter **VIII:**34
  conscientious objectors **VIII:**83

foreign policy **VIII:**141
government **VIII:**154
Hershey, Lewis B. **VIII:**164
Johnson, Hugh S. **VIII:**196
mobilization **VIII:**241
Roosevelt, Franklin D. **VIII:**346
Selective Service **VIII:**357
Taft, Robert A. **VIII:**385
War Manpower Commission **VIII:**413
Selective Service Act (1917) **VII:**321, 407c
  ACLU **VII:**9
  AEF **VII:**10
  armed forces **VII:**20
  Baldwin, Roger Nash **VII:**31
  citizenship **VII:**57
  conscription **VII:**62
  National Defense Act **VII:**227
  Preparedness **VII:**268
  World War I **VII:**393
Selective Service System **VII:**268
Selective Training and Service Act (1940) **VIII:**447c
  civil liberties **VIII:**72
  Congress **VIII:**80
  demobilization (WWII) **VIII:**91
  La Follette, Robert M., Jr. **VIII:**208
  Norris, George W. **VIII:**277
  Selective Service **VIII:**357–359
  Stimson, Henry L. **VIII:**375
  Wheeler, Burton K. **VIII:**416
  Willkie, Wendell L. **VIII:**417
"Self-Reliance" (Emerson) **IV:**379
Selma-to-Montgomery marches (1965) **IX:**356c
  King, Martin Luther, Jr. **IX:**174
  SCLC **IX:**293–294
  SNCC **IX:**303
  Voting Rights Act of 1965 **IX:**333
Selznick, David O. **V:**169
seminaries **VI:**4
Seminary Ridge **V:**167
Seminole Indians **IV:338,** 411c, 413c. *See also* Five Civilized Tribes
  Adams-Onís Treaty **IV:**6
  Beckwourth, Jim **IV:**51
  Florida **III:**167
  foreign policy **IV:**154
  Hill, Ambrose P. **V:**189
  Horseshoe Bend, Battle of **IV:**190
  Indian Removal Act **IV:**197
  Jackson, Andrew **IV:**206
  Native Americans **IV:**274; **VII:**233

Native Americans in the War of 1812 **IV:**278
New Orleans, Battle of **IV:**280
Osceola **IV:**289
Pushmataha **IV:**307
race and race relations **IV:**312
Scott, Winfield **IV:**336
Taylor, Zachary **IV:**367
Van Buren, Martin **IV:**386
Seminole Treaty (Treaty of Payne's Landing) **IV:**338, 413c
Seminole War, First and Second **IV:339–340,** 411c, 413c
  Anderson, Robert **V:**9
  Beckwourth, Jim **IV:**51
  Black Hawk War **IV:**56
  Bragg, Braxton **V:**42
  Buell, Don C. **V:**48
  Colt, Samuel **IV:**101
  election of 1840 **IV:**138
  Florida **IV:**153
  Gadsden Purchase **IV:**173
  Garnett, Richard B. **V:**163
  Horseshoe Bend, Battle of **IV:**190
  Johnston, Joseph E. **V:**214
  McIntosh, William **IV:**247
  Meade, George Gordon **V:**253
  Native Americans **IV:**274
  Osceola **IV:**289
  Pemberton, John C. **V:**297
  Scott, Winfield **IV:**336
  Seminole **IV:**338
  Sherman, William T. **V:**354
  Taylor, Zachary **IV:**367–368
Seminole War, Third **IV:**338, 339
Semmelweis, Ignaz, P. **IV:**123, 334
Semmes, Raphael **V:**7, 83, **346**
senado da câmara **I:**35
Senate, Arizona **X:**265
Senate, U.S. **IX:**353c; **X:320–322,** 376c, 378c, 379c, 381c, 383c
  Amendment, Twelfth **III:**16–17
  Amendments to the U.S. Constitution **X:**23
  anti-Federalists **III:**24
  Army Act **VII:**22
  Army-McCarthy hearings **IX:**18
  Baker v. Carr **IX:**34
  Bell, John **V:**32
  Birth of a Nation, The **VII:**37–38
  Borah, William E. **VIII:**49
  Bruce, Blanche Kelso **V:**47
  Byrd, Robert **X:**61
  Carroll of Carrollton, Charles **III:**82
  Chase, Salmon P. **V:**62
  Civil Rights Act (1957) **IX:**59

Clay, Henry **IV:**96
Clinton, DeWitt **III:**97
Clinton, Hillary Rodham **X:**78, 79
Clinton, William J. **X:**82
Congress **VIII:**79–81
Congressional Budget and Impoundment Control Act **X:**89
Conkling, Roscoe **VI:**80–81
conservative coalition **VIII:**86
Constitution, United States **III:**106, 107
Constitutional Convention **III:**109
Davis, Jefferson **V:**104
Democratic Party **VII:**75
direct election of senators **VII:**78
Dole, Robert **X:**104, 105
Douglas, Stephen A. **V:**114
Eagleton, Thomas F. **X:**107
elections **IX:**103, 104
ERA **X:**123, 124
Federalist Papers **III:**163
Federalists **III:**166
foreign policy **X:**143
Gadsden Purchase **IV:**173
Gallatin, Albert **III:**188
gay and lesbian rights movement **X:**150
global warming **X:**156
Gore, Albert, Jr. **X:**157
Helms, Jesse A., Jr. **X:**164, 165
Hoar, George F. **VI:**173
House of Representatives **X:**169
Houston, Sam **IV:**191
Hull, Cordell **VIII:**179–180
Hull, William **IV:**192
Humphrey, Hubert H. **IX:**151
impeachment **III:**222
impeachment of William J. Clinton **X:**178
impeachment of Richard M. Nixon **X:**
Interstate Highway Act of 1956 **IX:**159
Jackson, Andrew **IV:**205
Johnson, Hiram Warren **VII:**154
Johnson, Lyndon B. **IX:**163
Kansas-Nebraska Act **V:**222
Kennedy, Edward M. **X:**196
Kennedy, John F. **IX:**169
Kennedy, Robert F. **IX:**171
King, Rufus **III:**245
La Follette, Robert M. **VII:**173
La Follette, Robert M., Jr. **VIII:**208
Macon, Nathaniel **III:**280
Madison, James **III:**283
Mallory, Stephen R. **V:**247

McCarthy, Eugene **IX:**205–206

McCarthy, Joseph R. **IX:**206, 207

McCulloch v. Maryland **IV:**246

McGovern, George S. **X:**216–217

Medicare **IX:**210

Mitchell, George **X:**231, 232

Mondale, Walter F. **X:**233

NEA/NEH **X:**246

Nixon, Richard M. **X:**256

Norris, George W. **VIII:**276

Obama, Barack Hussein **X:**263–264

Otis, Harrison Gray **III:**326

Pickering, Timothy **III:**334, 335

Pinchback, P. B. S. **V:**307

Pingree, Hazen S. **VII:**261

politics (1900–1928) **VII:**262

politics (Roosevelt era) **VIII:**298, 300

Quay, Matthew Stanley **VI:**299

Quayle, J. Danforth **X:**293

Randolph, Edmund **III:**358

reconversion **VIII:**326

republicanism **III:**365

Republican Party **VII:**300, 301

Revels, Hiram R. **V:**335

Rodney, Caesar Augustus **III:**374

Seward, William H. **V:**347

stem cell research **X:**336

Stockton, Robert Field **IV:**358

Sumner, Charles **V:**377–378

Taylor, John, of Caroline **III:**408

Thurmond, James Strom **X:**350–351

Truman, Harry S. **IX:**320

Tyler, John **IV:**383

USA PATRIOT Act **X:**358, 359

Vance, Zebulon B. **V:**414

Wade, Benjamin Franklin **V:**421

Wagner, Robert F. **VIII:**410

Webster, Daniel **IV:**393

Wilson, Thomas Woodrow **VII:**384

Senate Armed Services Committee **X:**78

Senate Committee on Education and Labor **VIII:**208

Senate Committee on Improper Activities in the Labor Field. *See* McClellan Committee

Senate Committee on Public Lands **VII:**351

Senate Finance Committee
Dole, Robert **X:**105
Payne-Aldrich Tariff Act **VII:**255

Senate Foreign Relations Committee
Borah, William E. **VIII:**49
Canada **VI:**61
Helms, Jesse A., Jr. **X:**165
Lodge, Henry Cabot **VII:**184
Santo Domingo, proposed annexation of **VI:**323
Washington, Treaty of **VI:**385

Senate Judiciary Committee **X:**197

Senate Majority Leader **X:**61, 231

Senate Minority Leader **X:**61

Senate Naval Affairs Committee **V:**83, 255

Senate Permanent Subcommittee on Investigations **IX:**18, 64

senatorial courtesy **VI:**167

Seneca Falls convention **IV:**340–342, 414c
Bloomer, Amelia **IV:**59
female antislavery societies **IV:**148
Fuller, Margaret **IV:**169
Gage, Matilda Joslyn **VI:**137
marriage and family **IV:**240
Mott, Lucretia **IV:**266
NWSA **V:**277
Seneca Falls convention **IV:**341
Stanton, Elizabeth Cady **V:**369
women's status and rights **IV:**404; **V:**436, 438

Seneca Indians **I:**329–330, 397c; **IV:**411c
Beaver Wars **II:**35
Brulé, Étienne **II:**50
Cornplanter **III:**118
Handsome Lake **III:**209
Iroquois **I:**186; **II:**179, 180
Jemison, Mary **II:**184
Native Americans **III:**313; **V:**278; **VII:**233; **IX:**241
Native Americans in the War of 1812 **IV:**277
Parker, Ely Samuel **V:**294–295
Pickering, Timothy **III:**335
Pontiac's War **III:**340
Quakers **III:**352
treaty rights **IX:**319
Wyoming Valley Massacre **III:**449

Senegal **I:**199

Senegal River
Cadamosto, Alvise de **I:**49
Fulani **I:**135
Senegambia **I:**330

Senegambia **I:**330, 339, 340; **II:**4, 248

Sennett, Mack **VII:**96, 215–216

Sense of Wonder, The (Carson) **IX:**51

Sentinel Defense System (Nike X) **X:**27

Seoul, South Korea **IX:**198

Separate Baptists **III:**44

"separate but equal" doctrine
Brown v. Board of Education **IX:**43, 44
Murray, Pauli **IX:**227
NAACP **IX:**232
segregation **IX:**288
Southern Manifesto **IX:**294

separation of powers **X:**357, 367

Separatists **I:**307. *See also* Pilgrims

Sephardic Jews/Judaism **I:**194, 196; **II:**185–186; **VI:**219–220

September 11, 2001, terrorist attacks **X:**383c
Afghanistan War **X:**10
Bush, George W. **X:**53–55
Cheney, Richard B. **X:**72
Clinton, Hillary Rodham **X:**78
defense policy **X:**102
DHS **X:**167
economy **X:**110
foreign policy **X:**143
immigration **X:**177
Iraq War **X:**187
Mexico **X:**226
Middle East **X:**229
Mitchell, George **X:**232
Powell, Colin L. **X:**287
Presidential Address to a Joint Session of Congress and the American People **X:**411–414
Rice, Condoleezza **X:**309
Rumsfeld, Donald **X:**313
Senate, U.S. **X:**321
terrorism **X:**345, 347, 348
UN **X:**355
USA PATRIOT Act **X:**358

Sepúlveda, Juan Ginés de **I:**206–207, **330–331**

Sequeira, Diogo Lopes de **I:**299, **331**, 345

sequels **X:**235

Sequel to Drum Taps (Whitman) **V:**431

Sequera manuscript. *See* Florentine Codex

sequestration **X:**158

Sequoia National Park **VI:**82

Sequoyah **IV:**342, **342, 342–343**, 412c
Boudinot, Elias **IV:**61
Cherokee **IV:**85
Native Americans **IV:**275

Serapis, HMS **III:**117, 239

Serbia **X:**381c, 382c
Albright, Madeleine K. **X:**22
Dayton accords **X:**99
Kosovo **X:**199, 200
Versailles, Treaty of **VII:**370
World War I **VII:**393

Serbs **X:**99, 102

seriatim **III:**290, 403

Series E bonds **VIII:**412

"Series of Letters by a Man of Colour" (Forten) **III:**170

sermons **II:**184

Serra, Junípero **II:**347; **IV:**70, 76

Serra, Richard **X:**31

Serrano, Andres **X:**245

servants **II:**384

Servetus, Michael **I:**54

Service Employees International Union (SEIU) **X:**203

Serviceman's Readjustment Act (1944) **IX:**99

service sector **IX:**288–289
business **IX:**46
cities and urban life **IX:**55
economy **IX:**97; **X:**108
labor/labor movements **IX:**181; **X:**203
women's status and rights **X:**371

Services of Colored Americans in the Wars of 1776 and 1812 (Nell) **IV:**415c

Services of Supply (U.S. Army) **VIII:**25

Seton, Elizabeth Ann **IV:**343, **343–344**

Seton, William Magee **IV:**343

Settle, Dionyse **I:**331–332

settlement houses **VI:**327–328, 410c
Addams, Jane **VII:**2
Aesthetic movement **VI:**3
Americanization **VII:**13
Children's Bureau **VII:**53
criminal justice **VII:**66
education **VI:**110
Ethical Culture movement **VI:**121
housing **VI:**179
immigration **VI:**186
mothers' pensions **VII:**214
nativism **VII:**234
New Woman **VII:**239, 240
Perkins, Frances **VIII:**293
progressivism **VI:**294–295; **VII:**271
religion **VII:**297
Riis, Jacob A. **VI:**314
social work **VII:**329, 330
Wald, Lillian **VII:**377
Williams, Fannie Barrier **VI:**395

settlements (frontier)
frontier, the **III:**181
population trends **III:**343
Proclamation of 1763 **III:**348

settlements (Israeli) **X:**66

settlers. *See also* frontier, the
Cherokee **III:**87
Creek **III:**126

settlers *(continued)*
 Native Americans **III:**312, 314
 Wyoming Valley Wars **III:**450
SEUM. *See* Society for the Encouragement for Useful Manufactures
Seven Arts **VII:**131, 285
Seven Cities of Cíbola **I:**394
Seven Days' Battle
 Balloon Corps **V:**26
 Cobb, Howell **V:**76
 Hill, Daniel H. **V:**190
 homefront **V:**194
 Jackson, Thomas J. "Stonewall" **V:**210
 Lee, Robert E. **V:**230
 Longstreet, James **V:**241–242
 McClellan, George Brinton **V:**251
 Peninsular campaign **V:**300
Seven Great Statesmen in the Warfare of Humanity with Unreason (White) **VI:**392
Seven Pines, Battle of
 Armistead, Lewis A. **V:**17
 Balloon Corps **V:**25
 Johnston, Joseph E. **V:**214
 Longstreet, James **V:**241
 McClellan, George Brinton **V:**251
 Peninsular campaign **V:**299
 Pickett, George Edward **V:**306
Seven Sisters (colleges) **VI:**398
Seven Sisters (oil companies) **VII:**245, 336
17th Connecticut Volunteer Infantry **VI:**79
Seventeenth Amendment **VII:**405c
 direct election of senators **VII:**78
 New Freedom **VII:**236
 politics (1900–1928) **VII:**262
 Wilson, Thomas Woodrow **VII:**384
7th cavalry **V:**99, 240, 241
Seventh Amendment **III:**51
Seventh-Day Adventist Church
 Branch Davidians **X:**46
 Darwinism and religion **VI:**93
 religion **IV:**320; **VI:**307
Seventh Fleet (U.S. Navy)
 Halsey, William F. **VIII:**161
 King, Ernest J. **VIII:**202
 Leyte Gulf, Battle for **VIII:**214
Seventh Kansas Cavalry **VI:**76
Seventh New York Regiment **V:**426
75th Division, U.S. **VIII:**55
Seven Year Itch, The (film) **IX:**222

Seven Years' War. *See* French and Indian War
Severn, Battle of the **II:**220
Sevier, John **II:**408; **III:**175
Seville **I:**332–333; **II:**375
 Casa de Contratación **I:**63
 Council of the Indies **I:**97
 Las Casas, Bartolomé de **I:**205
 Linschoten, Jan Huygen van **I:**214
Sewall, Arthur M. **VI:**282
Sewall, Samuel **II:**1, **350**
Seward, William H. **V:346–348,** 347, 444c, 446c
 abolitionism **V:**4
 assassination of Abraham Lincoln **V:**20
 Compromise of 1850 **IV:**104
 Cooper Union speech **V:**93
 Crittenden Compromise **V:**98
 Dred Scott decision **V:**117
 employment **V:**132
 Fillmore, Millard **IV:**149–150
 foreign policy **V:**150, 151
 Fort Sumter **V:**154
 Greeley, Horace **V:**176, 177
 Republican Party **V:**333
 slavery **V:**363
 Taylor, Zachary **IV:**368
 Whigs **IV:**397
sewer systems **VI:**245
sewing machines
 fashion **V:**139
 industrial development **V:**205
 science and technology **V:**343
Sex and Temperament in Three Cultures (Mead) **VII:**197
sex discrimination. *See* gender discrimination/gender equality
sex offenders **X:**381c
Sexton, Anne **IX:**195
sexual abuse **X:**306
sexual activity among adolescents **X:**214
Sexual Behavior in the Human Male (Kinsey) **IX:**176, 352c
sexual harassment **X:**380c, 381c
 Clinton, William J. **X:**82
 Hill, Anita Faye **X:**166
 impeachment of William J. Clinton **X:**178
 Judicial Watch **X:**194
 Rehnquist, William H. **X:**305
 Starr, Kenneth **X:**333
 Thomas, Clarence **X:**350
Sexual Inversion (Ellis) **VII:**95
sexuality **VII:321–323**
 birth control **VII:**36–37
 cosmetics and beauty industry **VII:**65–66

Ellis, Henry Havelock **VII:**94–95
Freud, Sigmund **VII:**118–119
Gilman, Charlotte Perkins **VII:**125
journalism **VII:**160
Kinsey, Alfred C. **IX:**175–176
literature **IX:**194
marriage and family **VII:**192–193
The Masses **VII:**193
medicine **IX:**212
Monroe, Marilyn **IX:**222
population trends **VII:**266
Presley, Elvis **IX:**263
public health **VII:**275
rock and roll **IX:**279
Sanger, Margaret **VII:**312–313
sexually transmitted diseases **X:**6, 13
Sexual Politics (Millet) **X:**371, 375c
sexual promiscuity **VIII:**418, 419
sexual revolution **X:322–323**
 birth control **X:**43
 censorship **X:**71
 gay and lesbian rights movement **X:**148
 marriage and family **X:**213
Seymour, Horatio **V:348–349,** 446c
 Blair, Francis Preston, Jr. **V:**36
 conscription **V:**91
 Johnson, Andrew **V:**213
 Tilden, Samuel Jones **VI:**357
Seymour, Jane **I:**75
Seymour, Thomas Hart **VI:**148
Seymour, William **VII:**298
Sforza, Lodovico **I:**211
Shaara, Michael **V:**240
Shadow, The (radio show) **VIII:**414
Shadows of Our Social System (Blackwell) **VI:**39
Shaheen, Jeanne **X:**371
Shahn, Ben **VIII:**31
Shakers **III:**387, 460c
 Lee, Ann **III:**257
 migration **IV:**253
 religion **IV:**320
Shakespeare, John **I:**333
Shakespeare, William **I:333–334; VIII:**448c
 assassination of Abraham Lincoln **V:**19
 Donnelly, Ignatius Loyola **VI:**100
 Eden, Richard **I:**118
 London **I:**216
 Robeson, Paul **VIII:**341, 342
 The Tempest **I:**353–354
 theater **V:**387; **VI:**354

shamans **II:350–351**
 Abenaki **I:**2
 Brazil **I:**34
 medicine **II:**230
 midwives **II:**234
 religion, Native American **II:**330
 women's status and rights **II:**424
Shame of the Cities, The (Steffens)
 Johnson, Tom Loftin **VII:**156
 muckrakers **VII:**217
 Steffens, Lincoln **VII:**339
Shannon, HMS **IV:**165, 391
Shannon, James A. **IX:**235
sharecropping **V:349; VIII:**445c
 agriculture **V:**6
 banking **V:**28
 Black Codes **V:**35
 carpetbaggers **V:**56
 Communists **VIII:**78
 employment **V:**133
 Freedmen's Bureau **V:**161
 Ku Klux Klan **V:**223
 marriage and family **VIII:**230
 plantations **V:**309
 race and race relations **VIII:**318
 radicalism **VII:**287
 Reconstruction **VII:**326
 rural areas **VIII:**348
 Singleton, Benjamin **V:**361
 slavery **V:**364
 South **VIII:**366, 367
 STFU **VIII:**367–368
Share Our Wealth movement **VIII:**445c
 Long, Huey P. **VIII:**223
 Revenue Act of 1935 **VIII:**340
 Second New Deal **VIII:**356
 Union Party **VIII:**401
Sharon, Ariel **X:**56
Sharon Statement **IX:**350
Sharpe, George H. **V:**134
Sharpsburg, Battle of. *See* Antietam/Sharpsburg, Battle of
Sharpton, Al **X:**14
Shasta Indians **IV:**70
Shaw, Anna Howard **VI:**328, **328–329; VII:**50, 223
Shaw, Artie
 big bands **VIII:**44
 Holiday, Billie **VIII:**169
 jazz **VII:**153
Shaw, George Bernard **VI:**79, 355
Shaw, Josephine **V:**227
Shaw, Lemuel **IV:**218–219
Shaw, Quincy A. **VII:**209–210
Shaw, Robert Gould
 African-American regiments **V:**4
 Carney, William Harvey **V:**55

54th Massachusetts Regiment **V:**142, 144
ladies aid societies **V:**227
Saint-Gaudens, Augustus **VI:**321
Washington, D.C. **V:**426
Shaw Memorial (Saint-Gaudens) **VI:**321
Shawnee Indians **III:**460*c*
  Black Hawk War **IV:**56
  Blue Jacket **III:**54
  Boone, Daniel **III:**56
  Clark, George Rogers **III:**95
  Cornstalk **II:**81
  Creek **IV:**109
  Dragging Canoe **III:**139
  Dunmore, John Murray, earl of **III:**142
  Fallen Timbers, Battle of **III:**161
  foreign policy **IV:**154
  Glaize, meeting at the **III:**195
  Greenville, Treaty of **III:**200
  Harrison, William Henry **IV:**184, 185
  Hull, William **IV:**192
  McIntosh, William **IV:**247
  Native Americans **III:**311, 312, 314; **IV:**273, 274
  Native Americans in the War of 1812 **IV:**276
  New Orleans, Battle of **IV:**281
  Ostenaco **II:**280
  Pennsylvania **II:**284
  Prophet, the Shawnee **III:**348–349
  Pushmataha **IV:**307
  Sac and Fox **IV:**327
  Tecumseh **III:**409
  Van Buren, Martin **IV:**386
  Wilderness Road **III:**442
Shawnee Prophet, the. *See* Prophet, the Shawnee
Shawneetown, Illinois **VI:**193
Shaw v. Hunt **X:**381*c*
Shaw v. Reno **X:**380*c*
shaykh **I:**348
Shays, Christopher **X:**63, 64, 275
Shays, Daniel **III:**388
Shays's Rebellion **III:388,** 462*c*
  Connecticut Wits **III:**104
  economy **III:**146
  Federalists **III:**165
  Hull, William **IV:**192
  Penobscot campaign **III:**334
  riots **III:**371
  Tyler, Royall **III:**417
Shearer, William K. **X:**24
Sheeler, Charles **VI:**66
Sheen, Fulton J. **VIII:**64; **IX:**273
sheep herding **I:**66
Sheffield Scientific School (Yale College) **VI:**111, 148

Sheftall, Mordecai **III:**236
Sheik, The (film) **VII:**97
Shelby, Isaac **III:**139
Sheldon, Ronald **VI:**359
Shelikhov, Grigory Ivanovich **II:**338; **III:**12
Shelley, Mary Wollstonecraft **IX:**287
Shelley v. Kraemer **IX:**43
Shell Oil Company
  business **VIII:**57
  oil industry **VII:**245
  Standard Oil **VII:**336
"She Loves You" (The Beatles) **IX:**37
Shelton, Robert M., Jr. **IX:**179, *179,* 180
Shenandoah (dirigible) **VII:**212
Shenandoah, CSS **V:**84
Shenandoah, Pennsylvania **VI:**214
Shenandoah National Park (Virginia) **VIII:**115
Shenandoah River **V:**185
Shenandoah Valley **II:**12, 124
Shenandoah Valley: Jackson's campaign **V:349–351**
  Banks, Nathaniel P. **V:**28–29
  Boyd, Belle **V:**40
  cartography **V:**57
  Gordon, John B. **V:**170
  Harpers Ferry, West Virginia **V:**186
  Jackson, Thomas J. "Stonewall" **V:**210
  Peninsular campaign **V:**299
Shenandoah Valley: Sheridan's campaign **V:351–352**
  Early, Jubal A. **V:**120
  elections **V:**126
  Mosby, John Singleton **V:**270, 271
  Petersburg campaign **V:**302
  Sheridan, Philip H. **V:**353
  tactics and strategy **V:**382
Shepard, Alan B. **IX:**296, 355*c*
  NASA **IX:**231
  space exploration **IX:**296
  technology **IX:**312
Shepard, Jeremiah **II:**424
Shepard, Sam **X:**281
Shepard, William **III:**388
Sheppard, Morris **VII:**53, 274
Sheppard-Towner Act **VII:**323
  Abbott, Grace **VII:**1
  Kelley, Florence **VII:**164
  medicine **VIII:**235
  public health **VII:**276
  Social Security Act **VIII:**364
  women's status and rights **VII:**388–389
Sherbert v. Verner **X:**307
Sheridan, Philip H. **V:352–354**
  Appomattox campaign **V:**14
  Appomattox Court House, Virginia **V:**15

Arlington National Cemetery **V:**17
Custer, George A. **V:**99
elections **V:**126
entertainment, popular **VI:**118
Five Forks, Battle of **V:**147
Grant, Ulysses S. **V:**174
immigration **V:**196
Lincoln, Abraham **V:**237
McMaster, John Bach **VI:**242
monuments **V:**268
Mosby, John Singleton **V:**271
Nez Perce War **VI:**268
Petersburg campaign **V:**303
Shenandoah Valley: Sheridan's campaign **V:**351–352
tactics and strategy **V:**382
Wilderness, Battle of the **V:**432
Sheridan, Richard Brinsley **III:**417; **VI:**202
Sherman, Cindy **X:**31
Sherman, John (senator) **VI:329**
  presidential campaigns (1870–1899) **VI:**293
  Radical Republicans **V:**320
  Sherman Antitrust Act **VI:**330
Sherman, John B. (stockyard magnate) **VI:**54
Sherman, Roger **III:389,** 461*c,* 463*c*
  abolitionism **III:**2
  Continental Congress, First **III:**113
  Madison, James **III:**283
Sherman, William T. **V:354–356,** 355
  Anderson, Robert **V:**10
  Andersonville Prison, Georgia **V:**11
  Atlanta campaign **V:**21–23
  Bentonville, Battle of **V:**34
  Buffalo Soldiers **VI:**54
  Chattanooga, Battle of **V:**63
  Civil War **V:**74
  Copperheads **V:**95
  Dahlgren, John A. B. **V:**101
  elections **V:**126
  emancipation **V:**129
  foraging **V:**149
  Forrest, Nathan Bedford **V:**152
  Freedmen's Bureau **V:**160
  Grant, Ulysses S. **V:**174
  homefront **V:**193, 194
  Hood, John Bell **V:**196
  Howard, Oliver Otis **V:**197
  Johnston, Joseph E. **V:**215
  Joint Committee on the Conduct of the War **V:**216
  journalism **V:**218

Lincoln, Abraham **V:**237
Lookout Mountain, Battle of **V:**243
Nez Perce War **VI:**268
Overland campaign **V:**290
photography **V:**304
Sherman's March through Georgia **V:**356–358
Shiloh, Battle of **V:**358–360
Special Field Order No. 15 **V:**365
tactics and strategy **V:**381
Thomas, George H. **V:**389
Union army **V:**400, 403
Vicksburg campaign **V:**417, 418
Wheeler, Joseph **V:**428
Sherman Antitrust Act **VI:329–330,** 410*c,* 411*c,* **427–428;** **VII:**404*c,* 406*c*
  Buck's Stove **VII:**42, 43
  business and government **VI:**57; **VII:**46
  Capper-Volstead Act **VII:**49
  Clayton Antitrust Act **VII:**59
  Danbury Hatters **VII:**69
  Debs, Eugene Victor **VII:**73
  Harlan, John Marshall **VI:**159
  Harrison, Benjamin **VI:**161
  Hill, James J. **VI:**173
  Hoar, George F. **VI:**173
  labor/labor movements **VII:**170
  Northern Securities Case **VII:**241, 242
  oil industry **VII:**244
  presidency **VI:**290
  progressivism **VII:**271
  Pullman Strike **VI:**297
  railroads **VI:**302
  Sherman, John **VI:**329
  Standard Oil **VII:**335–336
  Supreme Court **VI:**348
  trusts **VI:**364
  U.S. Steel **VII:**365
Sherman House (William Watts Sherman House, Newport, Rhode Island) **VI:***19*
Sherman Silver Purchase Act **VI:**410*c,* 411*c*
  bimetallism **VI:**38
  Bryan, William Jennings **VI:**51
  Cleveland, Grover **VI:**75
  Crime of '73 **VI:**86
  currency issue **VI:**89, 90
  Free-Silver movement **VI:**135
  Harrison, Benjamin **VI:**161
  presidency **VI:**290
Sherman's March through Georgia **V:356–358,** 357*m,* 445*c*
  Blair, Francis Preston, Jr. **V:**36
  cartography **V:**57

Sherman's March through
Georgia *(continued)*
 foraging **V:**149
 Hood, John Bell **V:**196
 Orphan Brigade **V:**288
 plantations **V:**309
 rules of war **V:**338
 Sherman, William T. **V:**354–356
 tactics and strategy **V:**382
Sherman tanks **VIII:**385–386
Sherrill, Charles **VI:**359
Sherwood, Robert **VIII:**137
Shia Muslims **I:**188; **X:**186–188
Shields, Art **VII:**286
Shields, James **V:**210, 350
Shikellamy **II:**409
Shiloh (Foote) **V:**240
Shiloh, Battle of **V:358–360**, 359, 444c
 Beauregard, Pierre Gustave Toutant **V:**32
 Bickerdyke, Mary Ann **V:**34
 Bragg, Braxton **V:**42
 Breckinridge, John C. **V:**42
 Buell, Don C. **V:**48
 Cleburne, Patrick R. **V:**75
 common soldier **V:**78
 Confederate army **V:**82
 Cumming, Kate **V:**98
 Forrest, Nathan Bedford **V:**152
 Grant, Ulysses S. **V:**174
 homefront **V:**194
 Ingersoll, Robert Green **VI:**193
 Johnston, Albert Sidney **V:**214
 Morgan, John Hunt **V:**268
 Reid, Whitelaw **VI:**304
 Sherman, William T. **V:**355
 Wallace, Lew **VI:**381
Shiloh National Military Park **V:**267, 276
Shimoda, Japan **IV:**298
Shin, Yi Sun **V:**207
Shinn, Everett **VII:**25
Shinnecock Hills Golf Club (Long Island, New York) **VI:**343
Shinnecock School of Art **VI:**66
shipbuilding **II:**351; **VIII:359–360**
 Atlantic, Battle of the **VIII:**33
 Boston **II:**41
 CIO **VIII:**82
 environment **II:**119
 Higgins, Andrew J. **VIII:**165
 Industrial Revolution **III:**224
 Kaiser, Henry J. **VIII:**199
 Kennedy, Joseph P. **VIII:**199
 labor/labor movements **VIII:**207
 manufacturing and industry **II:**214

Maryland **II:**221
Massachusetts **II:**224
medicine **VIII:**236
mobilization **VIII:**242
Navy, U.S. **VIII:**265
Newport **II:**267
South **II:**367
steel industry **VIII:**373
Sunbelt **VIII:**381
trade, domestic and foreign **II:**393
Shippen, William, Jr. **II:351;** **III:**296, 376
Shipping Act (1916) **VII:**360
shipping technology **I:**59, 184
ships **VIII:**354
shipwreck narratives **I:**78, 79, 300, **334–335**
Shipwreck Suffered (Coelho) **I:**79
Shirley, William
 De Lancey, James **II:**94
 Hutchinson, Thomas **III:**218
 King George's War **II:**192
 Massachusetts **II:**224
Shirtwaist Makers Strike **VII:324,** 405c
 ILGWU **VII:**149
 New Unionism **VII:**238
 NWTUL **VII:**231
 Wald, Lillian **VII:**377
Shock, Albert **VI:**35
Shockley, William B. **IX:**70, 352c; **X:**86
shock therapy **X:**223
shoemakers/shoemaking **III:**225; **V:**374
shoes
 black market **VIII:**46
 OPA **VIII:**282
 rationing **VIII:**322
Shokaku (Japanese sip) **VIII:**87
shopping centers **IX:**65, **289–290,** 306
Short, Walter **VIII:**292
Short Account of the Destruction of the Indies (Las Casas) **I:**397c
short mortgages **VI:**179
short sword **I:**365
Shoshone Indians
 Bridger, James **IV:**64
 Lewis and Clark Expedition **III:**263
 Sacagawea **III:**377
Shotts, John **VI:**343
Shotwell, James T.
 Carnegie Endowment for International Peace **VII:**49
 foreign policy **VII:**116
 Kellogg-Briand Treaty **VII:**164
Shoulder Arms (film) **VII:**216
Shouse, Jouett **VIII:**19
Show Boat (Ferber) **VII:**180
Show Indians **VI:**119

Shreve, Henry Miller **V:**262
Shreve, Lamb, and Harmon, Architects **VIII:**28
Shreveport, Louisiana **VI:**123
Shriver, Robert Sargent, Jr. **X:**107, 217, **323–324**
Shriver, Sargent **IX:**144, 255
Shuffle Along (musical) **VII:**96
Shulhan Arukh (Karo) **I:**196, 197
Shuttlesworth, Fred **IX:**39, 200
Shy, John **III:**367, 368
Sibbes, Richard **II:**81, 82
Siberia **VIII:**97
Siberia and the Exile System (Kennan) **VI:**147
Siberian Expedition **VII:**308, **324–325**
Sibley, H. H. **V:**82, 444c
Sicherheitsdienst (SD) **VIII:**187
Sicily **I:**70; **VIII:360–361,** 447c, 448c
 amphibious warfare **VIII:**20
 Army, U.S. **VIII:**25
 Bradley, Omar N. **VIII:**50
 Casablanca Conference **VIII:**62
 Italian campaign **VIII:**191
 Patton, George S., Jr. **VIII:**291
 second front **VIII:**355
 World War II European theater **VIII:**431
sickle-cell anemia **II:**98, 213
Sickles, Daniel E. **V:360–361**
 Gettysburg, Battle of **V:**167
 Meade, George Gordon **V:**254
 monuments **V:**268
 presidential campaigns (1870–1899) **VI:**291
 prostitution **V:**316
Sidney, Sir Henry **I:**140
siege cannon **V:**140–141
Siegfried line **VIII:**431
Siemens-Martin steelmaking process **VI:**35, 345
Sierra Club
 conservation/environmentalism **VI:**82
 environment **VII:**98; **VIII:**116; **IX:**108
 Muir, John **VI:**254
 National Wilderness Preservation Act of 1964 **IX:**240
Sierra Leone **II:**4
 African Americans **III:**9
 Amistad incident **IV:**22
 Cuffe, Paul **III:**127, 128
 gold **I:**141
 slave trade **I:**340
Sierra Nevada
 Deseret, State of **IV:**119
 Donner party **IV:**125–126
 exploration **IV:**144, 145
 Forty-niners **IV:**160
 Frémont, John C. **IV:**166

gold **IV:**178
Hastings, Lansford W. **IV:**187
Murrieta, Joaquín **IV:**267
Native Americans **IV:**275
Smith, Jedediah Strong **IV:**350
Sigel, Franz
 Breckinridge, John C. **V:**42
 German-American regiments **V:**165–166
 Pea Ridge/Elkhorn Tavern, Battle of **V:**297
Signal Corps
 La Guardia, Fiorello **VIII:**208
 Mitchell, William (Billy) **VII:**211
 WAC **VIII:**420
Significance of the Sections in American History (Turner) **VI:**365
Sigourney, Lydia **IV:**183
Sigsbee, Charles D. **VI:**237
Sikorsky R-4 Hoverfly **VIII:**14
"silent majority"
 New Left **IX:**244
 Nixon speech that introduced term **X:375c,** **385–386**
 Republican Party **IX:**275
Silent Sentinels **VII:**254, 385
Silent Spring (Carson) **IX:355c**
 Carson, Rachel **IX:**50, 51
 conservation/environmentalism **X:**89, 90
 consumerism **IX:**76
 environment **IX:**108–109
 literature **IX:**194
 NEPA **X:**246
 science and technology **IX:**286
silk **III:**88, 89
Silko, Leslie Marmon **X:**210
Silk Road **I:335**
Sill, Edward Rowland **VI:**318
Sillery mission **II:**137
Silliman, Benjamin **IV:**334
silos **VI:**8
silver **I:335–336**
 Aesthetic movement **VI:**3
 Andes Mountains **I:**9
 Atahualpa **I:**16
 Cabot, Sebastian **I:**45
 Casa de Contratación **I:**63
 Castile **I:**66–67
 China trade **III:**88
 Columbian Exchange **I:**82
 Comstock Lode **IV:**104–106
 Djibouti **I:**109
 Las Casas, Bartolomé de **I:**207
 Mexico **I:**243
 mining **VI:**246
 New Spain **I:**269
 Panama **I:**285

Peru **I:**289
Potosí **I:**300
slavery **I:**338
Spanish colonies **II:**370, 371
Zacatecas **I:**391
Silver, Gray **VII:**49
Silver Bank **II:**224
silver coinage/silver standard
 VI:408c, 410c
 Allison, William Boyd **VI:**12
 bimetallism **VI:**38
 Bland-Allison Act **VI:**41, 42
 Bryan, William Jennings
  VI:51–52
 business cycles **VI:**59
 "Cross of Gold" Speech
  (Bryan) **VI:438–441**
 Free-Silver movement
  VI:135
 Harrison, Benjamin **VI:**161
 Hayes, Rutherford B.
  VI:168
 Republican Party **VII:**299
Silverman, Harriet **VII:**244
Silver Shirt League **VIII:**25
Silvester, Peter **III:**453
Simmons, Robert J. **V:**143
Simmons, William J. **VI:**388
Simmons College **VII:**330
Simms, Willie **VI:**177
Simon, Neil **X:**281
Simon, William **X:**122, 138
Simons, Arthur D. **X:**272
Simons, Elwin L. **IX:**286
Simpson, Alan **X:**177
Simpson, George **IV:**248
Simpson, Howard N. **IV:**123
Simpson, Jerry **VI:330–331**
Simpson, O. J. **X:**71, 297, 381c
Simpson College (Iowa) **VI:**63
Sims, M. O. **IX:**276
sin **I:**218
Sinai Peninsula **IX:**354c
 Camp David accords
  X:64–66
 Israel **IX:**160
 Middle East **X:**227, 228
Sinaloa, Mexico **IV:**148
Sinatra, Frank **VIII:361**
 Americans for Democratic
  Action **IX:**13
 Goodman, Benny **VIII:**151
 literature **IX:**193
 music **VIII:**251, 252;
  IX:228
 popular culture **IX:**259
Sinclair, Harry **VII:**135, 351
Sinclair, Upton **VII:**325, **325–
 326,** 404c
 business **VII:**46
 environment **VII:**99
 journalism **VII:**159
 literature **VII:**179
 The Masses **VII:**193
 Meat Inspection Act
  VII:198
 muckrakers **VII:**217

progressivism **VII:**271
Pure Food and Drug Act
 VII:276
Steffens, Lincoln **VII:**339
Tarbell, Ida Minerva
 VII:349
Singer Manufacturing Company
 VI:197
singing **II:**247
Singing Master's Assistant, The
 (Billings) **III:**50, 309
Singin' in the Rain (film) **IX:**225
"single tax" **VI:**409c
 Anti-Imperialist League
  VI:17
 George, Henry **VI:**142
 Simpson, Jerry **VI:**330
Singleton, Benjamin **V:361–362;**
 VI:123, 409c
Singleton, John **X:**236
Singleton Colony **VI:**123
*Singularitez de la France
 antarctique, Les* (Thevet)
 I:357–358
"Sinners in the Hands of an Angry
 God" (Edwards) **II:**114, 206,
 442–443
Sino-Japanese War **VIII:**141, 187
Sioux City, Iowa **VIII:**126
Sioux Indians **II:**157–158;
 IV:415c; **V:**446c; **VI:**408c,
 410c–411c
 Black Hawk War **IV:**58
 buffalo, extermination of
  VI:53
 Catlin, George **IV:**84
 Cody, William Frederick
  VI:77
 Crazy Horse **VI:**85
 entertainment, popular
  VI:118
 foreign policy **IV:**156
 Great Plains **III:**197
 Indian Rights Association
  VI:190
 Keokuk **IV:**213
 Lewis and Clark Expedition
  III:263
 Little Bighorn, Battle of
  V:240–241
 Native Americans **IV:**276;
  X:250
 Parkman, Francis **VI:**277
 Pershing, John Joseph
  VII:258
 Pike, Zebulon Montgomery
  IV:300
 Sac and Fox **IV:**327
 Sioux wars **VI:**331
 Sitting Bull **VI:**332
Sioux wars **VI:331**
 Black Hills gold rush
  VI:38–39
 buffalo, extermination of
  VI:54
 Crazy Horse **VI:**85–86
 Fort Laramie **IV:**158

Native Americans **VI:**261–
 263
 Red Cloud **VI:**303
 Sitting Bull **VI:**332
Sirhan, Sirhan Bishara **IX:**23,
 172; **X:**34
Sirica, John
 Nixon, Richard M. **X:**257
 U.S. v. Nixon **X:**357
 Watergate scandal **X:**366,
  367
Sissle, Noble **VII:**96
Sister Carrie (Dreiser) **VI:**226;
 VII:179
Sisters of Charity **IV:**343
Sistine Chapel **I:**244
sit-down strikes **VIII:**377
Sit-In Movement Inc. **IX:**291
sit-ins **IX:290–291,** 354c, 355c
 African Americans **IX:**5
 Baker, Ella Josephine
  IX:33
 Birmingham confrontation
  IX:39
 Carmichael, Stokely **IX:**49
 civil disobedience **IX:**58
 CORE **IX:**72, 73
 education **IX:**100
 Free Speech Movement
  IX:126
 King, Martin Luther, Jr.
  IX:174
 Lewis, John **IX:**190
 NAACP **IX:**232
 race and race relations
  IX:269
 Savio, Mario **IX:**284
 SDS **IX:**304
 segregation **IX:**288
 SNCC **IX:**302
Sitting Bull **VI:**332, *332,* 408c
 Black Hills gold rush **VI:**39
 Buffalo Soldiers **VI:**54
 Cody, William Frederick
  VI:77
 entertainment, popular
  VI:118
 Native Americans **VI:**261–
  263
 religion **VI:**310
 Sioux wars **VI:**331
Six Companies, Inc. **VIII:**199
Six-Day War. *See* Arab-Israeli War
 (1967)
Six Flags theme parks **IX:**317
Six Nations of the Iroquois
 Albany Congress **II:**15
 Brant, Joseph **III:**63
 Cornplanter **III:**119
 Dekanawideh **II:**93
 Fort Stanwix, Treaty of
  III:170–171
 Glaize, meeting at the
  III:195
 Iroquois **III:**227
 Johnson, Sir William **II:**187,
  188

New York **II:**272
Parker, Ely Samuel **V:**295
Red Jacket **III:**359
Tuscarora **II:**395
Sixteenth Amendment **VII:**405c,
 406c
 federal income tax **VII:**107
 Internal Revenue taxes
  VI:194
 Republican Party **VII:**300
 taxation **VIII:**387
 Underwood-Simmons Tariff
  VII:359
 War Revenue Act **VII:**378
6th Infantry Regiment **IV:**36
6th Massachusetts Infantry
 Hicks, Thomas H. **V:**188
 Washington, D.C. **V:**426
 Williams, George
  Washington **VI:**395
6th Wisconsin Infantry **V:**273
Sixth Amendment
 Bill of Rights **III:**51
 Escobedo v. Illinois **IX:**111
 Gideon v. Wainwright
  IX:133, 134
 Warren Court **IX:**338
Sixth Military Department
 IV:212
Sixth World Congress of the
 Communist International
 VII:61
Skenesboro, Battle of **III:**172
Sketch Book (Irving) **IV:**228
Sketches of American Character
 (Hale) **IV:**183
*Sketches of Eighteenth-Century
 America* (Crèvecoeur) **III:**127
Skidmore, Thomas **IV:**218
skiing **VII:**295; **X:**302
Skilling, Jeffrey **X:**59
Skinners, Cowboys and **III:123–
 124**
Skinner v. the State of Oklahoma
 VII:43–44
skirmishing **V:**380
Skraelings **I:**204
Skylab (space station) **IX:**232;
 X:327
Skylark of Space, The (Smith)
 IX:287
Skyline Drive (Virginia) **VIII:**314
skyscrapers **VI:333,** *333;*
 VIII:443c
 art and architecture **VI:**18;
  VII:19
 Bessemer process **VI:**35
 Burnham, Daniel Hudson
  VI:54, 55
 chain stores **VI:**65
 invention and technology
  VI:196
 Sullivan, Louis H. **VI:**347
Slany, John **II:**376
slash-and-burn agriculture
 Amazon River **I:**9
 Arawak **I:**11

slash-and-burn agriculture
  (continued)
    Huron I:172
    Maya I:234
    Taino I:352
Slater, John VI:112
Slater, Samuel III:389–390,
    463c
  economy III:146; IV:131
  industrialization IV:199
  Industrial Revolution
    III:225
  science and technology
    III:385
Slater Fund VI:112
Slaughterhouse Cases
  civil liberties VII:57
  due process clause VI:101
  Field, Stephen Johnson
    VI:127
  Fourteenth Amendment
    V:157
  Supreme Court VI:348
"Slave Auction, The" (Harper)
  VI:160
slave codes II:352, 437c
  African Americans II:6
  Caribbean II:59
  New York City II:272–273
  slave resistance II:353
  slavery II:354
  society, British American
    II:365, 366
  Stono Rebellion II:378
slave resistance/rebellions II:352–
  354, 437c; IV:381, 412c, 413c
  abolitionism V:2
  African Americans II:8;
    III:10
  agriculture II:13
  Brown, John V:44
  Calhoun, John C. IV:69
  Civil War V:73
  crowd actions II:87
  foreign policy IV:153
  Gabriel's Rebellion III:185–
    186
  Garnet, Henry Highland
    IV:174
  Haiti III:203, 204
  Higginson, Thomas
    Wentworth VI:171
  labor/labor movements
    IV:219
  New Spain I:269
  New York II:271
  religion IV:318
  slavery III:391; IV:347–348;
    V:362
  society, British American
    II:366
  Stono Rebellion II:377–378
  Turner, Nat IV:380–382
  Vesey, Denmark IV:388–
    389
  Walker, David IV:389
  West Indies III:436

slavery I:336–339; II:354–358,
  355, 436c; III:390–392, 391;
  IV:344–348, 345, 346m,
  413c–415c; V:362–364, 363,
  443c–445c
  abolitionism. See abolition/
    abolitionism
  ACS IV:16–17
  Act Abolishing the Slave
    Trade in the District of
    Columbia IV:449
  Adams, John Quincy IV:6
  Africa II:4, 5
  African-American churches,
    growth of VI:4
  African Americans II:5–8;
    III:8–10; IV:7–10
  agriculture II:12–14; III:11;
    IV:11
  Alamo, The IV:14
  alcohol III:13
  Alice II:19
  Allen, Richard III:15, 16
  American Revolution
    III:19
  American System IV:19, 20
  Amistad incident IV:21–22,
    434–438
  animals II:23
  antislavery. See abolition/
    abolitionism
  Applegate, Jesse IV:26
  Arthur, Chester Alan VI:20
  Austin, Stephen F. IV:40
  Aztecs I:20
  Bahía I:26
  Baptists III:45
  Barbados I:27
  Bates, Edward V:30
  Bell, John V:32–33
  Benezet, Anthony II:35–36
  Benton, Thomas Hart IV:53,
    54
  Bermuda Company I:31
  Bienville, Jean-Baptiste Le
    Moyne, sieur de II:38
  Booth, John Wilkes V:38
  Bowles, Samuel VI:42
  Brooks, Phillips VI:50
  Brown, Joseph Emerson
    V:45
  Brown, William Wells V:46
  Buchanan, James V:48
  Burns, Anthony IV:65–66
  Byrd, William, II II:53
  Calhoun, John C. IV:69
  camp followers III:77
  Carib I:60
  Caribbean II:59, 60
  Cass, Lewis IV:83
  childhood II:67
  cities and urban life II:68
  civil rights VIII:72
  Civil War V:71–75
  class II:70–71
  Clay, Henry IV:96, 97
  clothing II:73

Columbus, Christopher
  I:85, 86
common soldier V:77
Compromise of 1850
  IV:103
Confederate States of
  America V:85
Confiscation Acts V:87⁻88
Congress V:89
Congress, Confederate V:88
Connecticut II:77
Constitutional Convention
  III:109
contrabands V:93
cotton III:122, 123
cotton culture IV:107, 108
crime and punishment
  II:83, 84
Crittenden Compromise
  V:98
Cuba IV:111
Cuffe, Paul III:128
dance II:90
Davis, Jefferson V:103, 104
Davis, Varina Howell V:106
Declaration of
  Independence III:133
Delaware II:96
Democratic Party IV:117–
  119; V:108, 109
disease/epidemics II:98;
  IV:123
Djibouti I:109
Douglas, Stephen A. V:114
Douglass, Frederick V:115,
  116
Dred Scott decision V:116–
  118
Dunmore, John Murray, earl
  of III:142
Dutch Reformed Church
  II:107
economy II:110; III:146;
  IV:133
election of 1828 IV:137
election of 1840 IV:139
elections V:125
emancipation V:127–130
Emancipation Proclamation
  V:130–132, 445c, 460
Emerson, Ralph Waldo
  IV:140
employment V:132
encomienda I:122
environment II:120
Equiano, Olaudah III:156–
  157
Era of Good Feelings
  IV:141
female antislavery societies
  IV:147–148
fertility II:125
filibustering V:145
Fillmore, Millard IV:149–
  150
Finney, Charles Grandison
  IV:151

fire-eaters V:145, 146
Fitzhugh, George V:146–
  147
Florida III:166, 167
food II:131
foreign policy IV:155; V:149,
  151
Fort Mose II:132
Franklin, Benjamin III:174
Freeman, Elizabeth III:176
Free-Soil Party IV:163
Fugitive Slave Act IV:447–
  449
fugitive slave laws IV:168–
  169
fugitive slaves II:139–140
Gabriel's Rebellion III:185–
  186
Gadsden Purchase IV:173
Garrison, William Lloyd
  V:164
gender II:145
Genius of Universal
  Emancipation IV:175
Georgia II:145–147
gold I:141
Gold Coast I:143
Gomes, Diogo I:143
Greeley, Horace V:176, 177
Grimké, Angelina and Sarah
  IV:180
Guadalupe Hidalgo, Treaty
  of IV:181–182
Guerrero, Gonzalo I:147
Guinea-Bissau I:148
hacienda I:149
Haiti III:203
Hammon, Jupiter II:161–
  162
Harpers Ferry, West Virginia
  V:185
Hispaniola I:163
homefront V:193
"House Divided" Speech
  (Lincoln) V:447–450
housing II:167
Houston, Sam IV:191
indentured servitude
  II:175
Indian Removal Act IV:198
Islam I:189
Jackson, Andrew IV:205
Jackson, Claiborne F. V:209
Jamestown II:182
jayhawkers V:211
Jefferson, Thomas III:232
Johnson, Andrew V:212
Johnson, Mary II:187
Jones, Absalom III:238
Juneteenth V:219
Kansas-Nebraska Act V:221
King, Rufus III:246
King Philip's War II:193
Know-Nothing Party IV:214,
  215
Kościuszko, Tadeusz
  III:249

labor/labor movements
    II:197–199; **III:**251;
    IV:219
Lamar, Mirabeau B. **IV:**221
Las Casas, Bartolomé de
    I:205, 206
Lay, Benjamin **II:**203
lead mines **IV:**223
Liberia **IV:**225
Liberty Party **IV:**226
Life of Olaudah Equiano
    (excerpt) **II:446–448**
Lincoln, Abraham **V:**234,
    236
literature **IV:**228, 229;
    V:239
Locke, John **II:**209
Louisiana **II:**210
Louisiana Purchase **III:**273
Lovejoy, Elijah **IV:**230
Madeira **I:**222
Madison, James **III:**283
Mali **I:**225, 226
Mallory, Stephen R. **V:**247
Manifest Destiny **IV:**235
manufacturing and industry
    II:214
marriage and family **II:**219;
    III:288–289; **IV:**238–239
Martinique **I:**232
Maryland **II:**221
Mason, George **III:**292
Mason-Dixon Line **V:**250
Massachusetts **II:**223
Massachusetts Emigrant Aid
    Society **IV:**241–242
McClellan, George Brinton
    V:251
Mexican-American War
    IV:251
middle passage **I:**244
Middleton, Arthur **II:**234
migration **IV:**254, 255
miscegenation **II:**237–238
Missouri Compromise
    IV:255–257
Monroe, James **IV:**259
Montserrat **I:**251
Mormon War **IV:**263
Morris, Gouverneur **III:**304
mortality **II:**244
Mott, Lucretia **IV:**266
Mount Vernon **II:**245
music **II:**247; **VI:**255
Muslims **II:**247–248
Native Americans **IV:**274,
    275
New Jersey **II:**262
New Orleans **II:**267
New York **II:**270
New York City **II:**272
Northwest Ordinances
    III:322
nurses **V:**285
Oglethorpe, James Edward
    II:277–278
Ostend Manifesto **V:**289

Panama **I:**284–285
panic of 1837 **IV:**295
Paul, Nathaniel **IV:**295
Penn, William **II:**284
Philadelphia **II:**292
Phillips, Wendell **IV:**299
Pickering, Timothy **III:**335
Pinckney, Charles
    Cotesworth **III:**336
plague **I:**294
plantations **V:**308–309
plantation system **II:**297–
    298
Polk, James K. **IV:**301
polygamy **IV:**303
popular sovereignty **IV:**303–
    304
population trends **II:**303;
    III:343
POWs **III:**346
public land policy **IV:**305
Quakers **II:**323
Quok Walker Case **III:**354–
    355
race and race relations
    III:357–358; **IV:**309–312;
    V:319–320
Reconstruction **V:**324
religion **III:**362; **IV:**317–
    318; **V:**331
religion, African-American
    II:328
Republican Party **IV:**321–
    323; **V:**332–336
Rhode Island **II:**333
Rhodes, James Ford **VI:**312
rice cultivation **II:**334
rum trade **II:**338
rural life **III:**375
Rush, Benjamin **III:**376
St. Augustine **II:**341–342
St. Mary's City **II:**342
salt trade **I:**324
secession **V:**344–345
Second Great Awakening
    IV:337
Seminole **IV:**338
Seminole War, First/Second
    IV:339
Seneca Falls convention
    IV:341
Seville **I:**333
Sewall, Samuel **II:**350
Sherman's March through
    Georgia **V:**357
Singleton, Benjamin
    V:361–362
slave codes **II:**352
slave resistance **II:**352–353
slave trade **I:**339–340
slave trade, internal **IV:**348–
    350
Smith, Venture **II:**363–364
society, British American
    II:366–367
Society of Friends **V:**364
South Carolina **II:**369–370

South Carolina Regulation
    III:394
Spanish colonies **II:**374
SPG **II:**368
states' rights **V:**370
Stephens, Alexander
    Hamilton **V:**371
Stono Rebellion **II:**377–
    378
Story, Joseph **III:**399
Sudan **I:**347
sugar **I:**349
Supreme Court **IV:**362
Tallmadge Amendment
    IV:365, 423
Taney, Roger B. **IV:**366
Tappan, Arthur and Lewis
    IV:366
tariffs **V:**383
taverns and inns **II:**384
Taylor, Zachary **IV:**367, 368
Taylor Amendment **IV:423–
    424**
Texas **IV:**372
theater **V:**387
Thirteenth Amendment
    V:387–388
Thoreau, Henry David
    IV:376
tobacco **II:**390, 392
Tuareg **I:**370
Turner, Nat **IV:**380
Underground Railroad
    V:397
United Daughters of the
    Confederacy **V:**407
Vesey, Denmark **IV:**387–
    388
Virginia **II:**400
Walker, David **IV:**389
War of Jenkins' Ear **II:**408
Washington, George
    III:432
Webster, Daniel **IV:**394
Weld, Theodore Dwight
    IV:396
West Indies **III:**436
Whigs **IV:**397
Whitney, Eli **III:**442
Wigfall, Louis T. **V:**431
Williams, Peter, Jr. **IV:**402
Wilmot Proviso **V:**432, 433
Wilson, Henry **V:**433
Wise, Henry A. **V:**433
Women's National Loyal
    League **V:**434
women's status and rights
    II:423, 426; **III:**446, 447;
    IV:402
Woolman, John **II:**426, 427
Wright, Fanny **IV:**405
Yeardley, Sir George **II:**430
Young, Brigham **IV:**408
zambo **I:**391–392
"Slavery in Massachusetts"
    (Thoreau) **IV:**376
Slave's Friend **IV:**16

Slave Songs of the United States
    (Allen, Ware and Garrison)
    VI:255
slave trade **I:339–340**, 396c;
    II:358–360, 359, 360, 435c–
    437c; **III:393**, 393, 464c, 465c
    abolitionism **III:**2; **V:**1
    African Americans **II:**6, 7;
        III:10
    Akan **I:**5
    antislavery **III:**25–26
    Brazil **I:**35
    British Empire **II:**48
    Calabar **I:**51
    Cameroon **I:**56
    Canary Islands **I:**57
    Cayor **I:**69
    Charleston **II:**64
    Columbian Exchange **I:**81
    Constitution, United States
        III:106
    Constitutional Convention
        III:109
    Cuba **I:**101
    Dahomey **I:**103
    Dutch West India Company
        II:107
    economy **II:**109
    Enlightenment, American
        II:118
    Equiano, Olaudah **III:**156
    Fang **I:**127
    Florida **I:**131
    Forrest, Nathan Bedford
        V:152
    Forten, James **III:**170
    Gao **I:**137
    Ghana **I:**139, 140
    gold **I:**141
    Gorée Island **I:**144
    Guinea-Bissau **I:**148
    Hawkins, Sir John **I:**157
    Igbo **I:**178
    Kaabu, kingdom of **I:**199
    Kongo **I:**200
    labor/labor movements
        II:199
    Laurens, Henry **III:**255
    Locke, John **II:**209
    Luba **I:**217
    mariners **II:**214
    Martinique **I:**232
    Mbundu **I:**237–238
    merchants **II:**231
    middle passage **I:**244
    Mpongwe **I:**254, 255
    New Netherland **II:**266
    Newport **II:**267
    Nzinga **I:**274
    Oyo **I:**282
    Pinckney, Charles
        Cotesworth **III:**336
    population trends **I:**298–
        299; **III:**343
    Príncipe **I:**302
    race and race relations
        II:325; **III:**357

slave trade *(continued)*
  Royal African Company
    II:337
  Sahara **I:**324
  São Tomé **I:**328
  Senegambia **I:**330
  slavery **I:**336–338; **II:**354;
    III:390, 392
  smallpox **I:**341
  sugar **I:**349
  Téké **I:**353
  Timbuktu **I:**359
  trade, domestic and foreign
    II:392, 393; **III:**413
  Tuareg **I:**370
  Woolman, John **II:**426
slave trade, internal **IV:348–350**
  abolitionism **IV:**1
  Act Abolishing the Slave
    Trade in the District of
    Columbia **IV:449**
  African Americans **IV:**7
  cotton culture **IV:**108
  Liberty Party **IV:**227
  slavery **IV:**347
Slave Trade Abolition Act
  III:465*c*
SLBMs (submarine-launched
  ballistic missiles) **X:**99–101
Slidell, John **V:**149, 150, 269
Sloan, Alfred P.
  American Liberty League
    VIII:19
  automobile industry **VII:**26
  GM **IX:**133
Sloan, John
  art **VII:**23, 24
  Ashcan School **VII:**25
  Greenwich Village **VII:**130
Sloane, William Milligan **VI:**359
Slocum, Henry W. **V:**34, 168
Sloo, A. G. **IV:**173
Slovakia **VIII:**38; **X:**384*c*
Slovenia **X:**384*c*
SLP. *See* Socialist Labor Party
slum(s) **VIII:**70
slum clearance **VIII:**314
Small, Albion W. **VI:**335
smallpox **I:340–341; II:360–361,**
  437*c*; **III:**464*c*; **IV:**413*c*
  Atahualpa **I:**15
  Aztecs **I:**22
  Boylston, Zabdiel **II:**43
  cities and urban life **III:**91
  Cuitláhuac **I:**101
  disease/epidemics **I:**107–
    108; **II:**98, 99; **III:**138;
    IV:123
  Flathead Indians **II:**127
  fur trade **IV:**171
  Iceland **I:**177
  Iroquois **I:**187
  Massachusetts **II:**225
  medicine **III:**295
  mortality **II:**244
  Native Americans **II:**252
  Pizarro, Francisco **I:**293

Pontiac's War **III:**340
riots **III:**371
Soto, Hernando de **I:**343
South Carolina **II:**369
Tenochtitlán **I:**356
Valley Forge **III:**422–423
Walter, Thomas **II:**406
"smart phones" **X:**319
Smart Set, The **VII:**180, 201
Smeal, Eleanor **X:**124
Smibert, John **II:**283, **361**
Smith, Adam **II:**230; **IV:**130
Smith, Alfred E. **VII:326–327,**
  409*c*
  American Liberty League
    VIII:19
  conservatism **VIII:**84
  Democratic Party **VII:**75;
    VIII:92
  Dewson, Mary **VIII:**95
  elections **VII:**91, 92
  Irish Americans **VIII:**188
  Italian Americans **VIII:**190
  Perkins, Frances **VIII:**293
  politics (Roosevelt era)
    VIII:297, 298
  Roosevelt, Franklin D.
    VIII:345
  Triangle Shirtwaist Fire
    VII:356
  Wagner, Robert F.
    VIII:410
Smith, Bessie
  entertainment, popular
    VII:97
  Holiday, Billie **VIII:**169
  music **VII:**219, 220
Smith, David **IX:**19
Smith, Edmund Kirby
  Confederate army **V:**82
  Corinth, Battle of **V:**95
  Milliken's Bend, Battle of
    V:260
  Red River campaign **V:**329
Smith, E. E. Doc **IX:**287
Smith, Ellison D. "Cotton Ed"
  VIII:60
Smith, Francis **III:**264, 266
Smith, Gerald L. K.
  conservatism **VIII:**84
  Coughlin, Father Charles E.
    VIII:88
  Long, Huey P. **VIII:**223
  Union Party **VIII:**401
Smith, Gerard **X:**336
Smith, Gerrit
  Free-Soil Party **IV:**163
  Liberty Party **IV:**226
  Massachusetts Emigrant Aid
    Society **IV:**242
Smith, Gustavus W. **V:**357
Smith, Harry **VI:**7
Smith, Hoke **VI:**141
Smith, Holland M. "Howling Mad"
  VIII:228, 230
Smith, Howard W. **VIII:**361
Smith, Hyrum **IV:**279, 353

Smith, Jedediah Strong **IV:350–**
  352, 351*m*
  Ashley, William Henry **IV:**31
  Beckwourth, Jim **IV:**50
  Bridger, James **IV:**64
  California Trail **IV:**77
  exploration **IV:**144
  Fort Vancouver **IV:**159
  McLoughlin, John **IV:**248
  mountain men **IV:**266
  Rocky Mountain Fur
    Company **IV:**324, 325
Smith, John (explorer and colonist)
  I:233, 398*c*; **II:**362, **362–363**
  agriculture **II:**9
  captivity **II:**58
  Jamestown **II:**181
  literature **II:**205
  New Hampshire **II:**259
  Opechancanough **II:**278–
    279
  Pennsylvania **II:**285
  Pocahontas **II:**299, 300
  Powhatan **II:**305–307
  Powhatan Confederacy
    II:307
Smith, John G. (presidential
  candidate) **X:**24
Smith, Joseph **VI:**251, 308
Smith, Joseph (Union Navy
  captain) **V:**266
Smith, Joseph, Jr. **IV:**352, **352–**
  354, 412*c*
  Brannan, Samuel **IV:**63
  Deseret, State of **IV:**119
  Mormon Church **IV:**88
  Mormon War **IV:**263
  Nauvoo **IV:**278
  polygamy **IV:**303
  religion **IV:**319
  Young, Brigham **IV:**407
Smith, Julian **VIII:**386
Smith, Kate **VIII:**252
Smith, Lydia H. **V:**372
Smith, Mamie **VII:**219
Smith, Matthew **II:**282
Smith, Melancton **III:**24, 106
Smith, Nathan (paleontologist)
  IV:335
Smith, Nathan Davis (physician)
  IV:250
Smith, Robert **II:363**
Smith, Ruby Doris **IX:**124
Smith, Theobald **VI:**244
Smith, Thomas **II:**402
Smith, Thomas J. S. **V:**413
Smith, Tommie **IX:**42
Smith, Venture **II:363–364**
Smith, W. Eugene **VIII:**217, 296
Smith, Will **IX:**10
Smith, William
  American Philosophical
    Society **III:**17
  College of Philadelphia **II:**74
  West, Benjamin **III:**435
Smith, William "Extra Billy"
  V:172

Smith, William French **X:**300, 311
Smith Act (1940) **VIII:361–362,**
  446*c*; **IX:**352*c*–353*c*
  ACLU **VIII:**18
  censorship **VIII:**65, 66
  civil liberties **VIII:**71–72
  Dennis v. U.S. **IX:**86
  enemy aliens **VIII:**114
  espionage **VIII:**117
  Flynn, Elizabeth Gurley
    VII:110
  Warren, Earl **IX:**337
Smith and Wesson **X:**162
Smith College
  education **VI:**109
  Friedan, Betty **IX:**126
  social work **VII:**330
Smith College School of
  Psychiatric Social Work
  VII:330
Smith-Connally War Labor
  Disputes Act **VIII:**448*c*
  coal industry **VIII:**76
  conservatism **VIII:**85
  labor/labor movements
    VIII:207
  Lewis, John L. **VIII:**213
  NWLB **VIII:**262
  strikes **VIII:**378
Smithson, Robert **X:**31
Smithsonian Institution
  art and architecture **IV:**31
  Catlin, George **IV:**85
  commemoration **IX:**66
  Geological Survey, U.S.
    VI:141
  Hiroshima and Nagasaki
    VIII:166
  Marsh, George Perkins
    VI:239
  music **VIII:**250
  Walcott, Charles Doolittle
    VI:380
  Washington, D.C. **V:**425
  Weather Bureau, U.S.
    VI:386
  Wilkes expedition **IV:**400
Smith v. Allwright **VIII:**448*c*
  civil rights **VIII:**72
  NAACP **VIII:**256
  Supreme Court **VIII:**383
smog **X:**155
smoke detectors **X:**318
"Smoking and Health" (Surgeon
  General's Report) **X:**351
Smoky Mountains **VIII:**392
Smoot, Reed **VIII:**162
Smoot-Hawley Tariff Act. *See*
  Hawley-Smoot Tariff
smoothbore muskets **V:**81, 340
smuggling **II:**333, **364**
  assassination of Abraham
    Lincoln **V:**19
  Gaspée affair **III:**189
  Sugar Act **III:**401, 402
  Tea Act **III:**409
Smythe, Thomas **I:**117

Snake River
   exploration **IV**:146
   migration **IV**:255
   Oregon Trail **IV**:285
   Rocky Mountain Fur
      Company **IV**:325
   Smith, Jedediah Strong
      IV:350
   Wilkes expedition **IV**:400
   Wyeth, Nathaniel J. **IV**:406
Snap the Whip (Homer) **VI**:174
SNCC. *See* Student Nonviolent
   Coordinating Committee
Snead, Sam **VIII**:372
Snell, Bertrand **VIII**:337
Snow, John **IV**:122
Snowden, George **VI**:176
*Snow White and the Seven
   Dwarfs* (film) **VIII**:247, 446c
Snyder, Gary
   Beat Generation **IX**:36
   counterculture **IX**:78
   religion **IX**:272
soap operas **X**:280
soccer **X**:331
social conservatism **X**:214–215
Social Darwinism **VI**:334
   Adams, Henry **VI**:1–2
   Boas, Franz Uri **VII**:39
   conservatism **VIII**:84
   eugenics **VII**:103
   evolution **VI**:122
   Gilman, Charlotte Perkins
      VII:125
   immigration restrictions
      VI:187
   imperialism **VI**:188
   Rauschenbusch, Walter
      VII:293
   Sumner, William Graham
      VI:347–348
Social Democratic Party (SDP)
   Debs, Eugene Victor **VII**:73
   radicalism **VII**:287
   socialism **VII**:327
   Socialist Party **VI**:337
*Social Destiny of Man, The: Or,
   Theory of the Four Movements*
   (Fourier) **IV**:162
Social Diagnosis (Richmond)
   VII:330
social engineering **VII**:141, 284
Social Gospel **VI**:334–335
   Beecher, Henry Ward **VI**:30
   Berle, Adolf A., Jr. **VIII**:43
   Ely, Richard Theodore
      VI:115
   Gladden, Washington **VI**:149
   Middletown **VII**:205
   Rauschenbusch, Walter
      VII:293
   religion **VI**:306, 307;
      VII:297
   Strong, Josiah **VI**:346
   Sunday, William Ashley, Jr.
      VII:342
   Thomas, Norman **VIII**:394

Social History of Missouri
   (Benton) **VIII**:31
socialism **VI**:335–336, 407c;
   VII:327–328, 407c. *See also*
   socialists
   Baldwin, Roger Nash
      VII:31
   Bellamy, Edward **VI**:32
   Blatch, Harriot Eaton
      Stanton **VII**:38
   business **VII**:46
   Communist Party **VII**:61
   Debs, Eugene Victor
      VII:72–73
   DuBois, W.E.B. **VII**:81
   Ely, Richard Theodore
      VI:115
   Flynn, Elizabeth Gurley
      VII:109
   Foster, William Zebulon
      VII:116
   Fourier, Charles **IV**:162
   Gilman, Charlotte Perkins
      VII:125
   Haywood, William Dudley
      VII:137
   ILGWU **VII**:149
   IWW **VII**:147
   Kelley, Florence **VII**:164
   labor, radical **VI**:212–213
   Lease, Mary Elizabeth
      Clyens **VI**:220
   liberalism **X**:207
   Marx, Karl **V**:249
   The Masses **VII**:193
   New Unionism **VII**:238
   Non-Partisan League
      VII:241
   NWTUL **VII**:230
   Palmer, Alexander Mitchell
      VII:249
   politics (1900–1928)
      VII:261
   progressivism **VII**:271
   radical and labor press
      VII:284
   radicalism **VII**:287, 288
   Reagan, Ronald W. **X**:299
   Russian Revolution **VII**:308
   Sinclair, Upton **VII**:325
   Socialist Party **VI**:337
   Trading with the Enemy Act
      VII:355–356
   utopianism **VI**:371
   Willard, Frances **VI**:394
   Woodhull, Victoria **VI**:400,
      401
socialist feminism **X**:133
Socialist Labor Party (SLP)
   VI:336–337
   labor, radical **VI**:213
   political parties, third
      VI:286
   Powderly, Terence Vincent
      VI:287
   radicalism **VII**:287
   socialism **VI**:336; **VII**:327

Socialist Party **VI**:337; **VII**:405c
   Communist Party **VII**:61
   Debs, Eugene Victor **VII**:73
   Espionage Act **VII**:101
   Foster, William Zebulon
      VII:116
   free speech fights **VII**:118
   labor, radical **VI**:213
   labor/labor movements
      VII:172
   muckrakers **VII**:216
   Non-Partisan League
      VII:241
   Randolph, A. Philip
      VIII:321
   Red Scare **VII**:296
   Russian Revolution **VII**:308
   Schenck v. U. S. **VII**:313
   Seattle General Strike
      VII:105
   Sedition Act **VII**:318–319
   Shirtwaist Makers Strike
      VII:324
   Sinclair, Upton **VII**:326
   socialists **VIII**:362
   Trading with the Enemy Act
      VII:355–366
Socialist Party of America (SPA)
   VII:403c
   Debs, Eugene Victor **VII**:73
   IWW **VII**:147
   National Civic Federation
      VII:226
   radicalism **VII**:287
   socialism **VII**:327, 328
socialists **VIII**:362. *See also*
   socialism
   Agricultural Adjustment Act
      VIII:6
   America First Committee
      VIII:17
   anticommunism **VIII**:22
   Communists **VIII**:78
   Dubinsky, David **VIII**:97
   election of 1932 **VIII**:109
   Hillman, Sidney **VIII**:166
   Jews **VIII**:195–196
   liberalism **VIII**:215
   literature **VIII**:218
   Popular Front **VIII**:303
   Robeson, Paul **VIII**:342
   Thomas, Norman **VIII**:394
Socialist Trade and Labor Alliance
   VI:213
Socialist Workers Party **VIII**:361
Social Justice (magazine) **VIII**:88
"Social Principle Among A People;
   and Its Bearing on Their
   Progress and Development"
   (Crummel) **VI**:87
social realism **VIII**:31
social reform
   Abbott, Grace **VII**:1
   Addams, Jane **VII**:2–3
   art **VII**:24
   Brace, Charles Loring
      VI:45–46

Comstock, Anthony **VI**:79
Knights of Labor **VI**:210
labor, child **VI**:212
labor, woman **VI**:215
Langston, John Mercer
   VI:218–219
Lease, Mary Elizabeth
   Clyens **VI**:220
liberalism **X**:207
Liberal Republican Party
   VI:222
Lloyd, Henry Demarest
   VI:227–228
pragmatism **VI**:288–289
progressivism **VI**:294–295
settlement houses **VI**:327–
   328
Social Gospel **VI**:335
Villard, Henry **VI**:375
Wald, Lillian **VI**:377
Ward, Lester Frank **VI**:383
White, Alfred Tredway
   VI:390–391
Willard, Frances **VI**:393–
   394
Wilson, Thomas Woodrow
   VII:383
Social Register **VII**:301
Social Revolutionary Party **VI**:213
social science **VII**:180
Social Science Research Council
   VII:115
Social Security
   Fair Deal **IX**:116
   Great Society **IX**:139
   liberalism **X**:207, 208
   Medicare **IX**:210
   modern Republicanism
      IX:221
   New Deal **IX**:242
   poverty **X**:286
   War on Poverty **IX**:335
Social Security Act (1935)
   VIII:362–365, 363, 445c,
   453–457
   advertising **VIII**:1
   African Americans **X**:13
   business **VIII**:58
   children **VIII**:67
   Congress **VIII**:79
   conservatism **VIII**:84
   elderly **VIII**:107–108
   election of 1936 **VIII**:109
   Ely, Richard Theodore
      VI:115
   ERAA **VIII**:114
   FERA **VIII**:133
   government **VIII**:152
   Hughes, Charles Evans
      VII:142
   liberalism **VIII**:215
   marriage and family
      VIII:231
   Medicaid **IX**:209
   Medicare **IX**:210
   medicine **VIII**:235
   New Deal **VIII**:269

Social Security Act (1935)
(*continued*)
  Perkins, Frances **VIII:**293
  recession of 1937–1938
   VIII:324
  relief **VIII:**332
  Roosevelt, Franklin D.
   VIII:345
  Second New Deal **VIII:**356
  Supreme Court **VIII:**382
  taxation **VIII:**387
  Townsend, Francis E.
   VIII:395
  Tugwell, Rexford G.
   VIII:398
  Union Party **VIII:**401
  women's network **VIII:**421
  women's status and rights
   VIII:423
  WPA **VIII:**425
Social Security Act (1950)
 IX:116
Social Security Administration
 VIII:364; **X:**56
Social Security Amendments
 (1965) **IX:**356*c*
Social Security Board **VIII:**95,
 364
Social Security reform **X:**111
social services **V:**407–408; **X:**109
social structure
 Aztecs **I:**19–20
 Haida **I:**150
 Havasupai **I:**157
 Hopewell culture **I:**167
 horses **I:**170
 Mossi **I:**253
social work **VII:328–331,** 329
 Abbott, Grace **VII:**1
 Addams, Jane **VII:**2–3
 Baldwin, Roger Nash
  VII:31
 Children's Bureau **VII:**53–
  54
 criminal justice **VII:**66
 Goldmark, Josephine Clara
  VII:126–127
 mothers' pensions **VII:**213
 progressivism **VII:**271
 science and technology
  VII:314, 315
 Wald, Lillian **VII:**377
Société Français des Peintres-
 Graveurs **VI:**63–64
Society for Ethical Culture
 VI:121; **VII:**127
Society for the Encouragement
 for Useful Manufactures
 (SEUM)
 Duer, William **III:**141
 Hamilton, Alexander
  III:207
 Industrial Revolution
  III:225, 226
Society for the Improvement and
 Colonization of East European
 Jews **VI:**219

Society for the Promotion of
 Temperance **IV:**317
Society for the Propagation of the
 Gospel in Foreign Parts (SPG)
 II:368
 African Americans **II:**7
 Anglican Church **II:**21;
  III:20, 21
 Morse, Jedidiah **III:**308
Society for the Relief of Poor
 Widows with Small Children
 III:344
Society for the Suppression of
 Vice
 journalism **VII:**160
 sexuality **VII:**322
 Whitman, Walt **V:**431
Society of American Artists
 art **VII:**23
 Chase, William Merritt
  VI:66
 Ryder, Albert Pinkham
  VI:319
Society of American Indians
 VII:233
Society of Faces **I:**185
Society of Friends. *See* Quakers
Society of Missionary Priests of St.
 Paul the Apostle **VI:**316
Society of Righteous and
 Harmonious Fists **VII:**40
Society of the Army of the James
 V:415
Sociological Department (Ford
 Motor Company) **VII:**112
sociology **VI:**382–383
Sociology for the South (Fitzhugh)
 Fitzhugh, George **V:**146, 147
 literature **V:**239
 slavery **V:**362
sod houses **VI:337–338,** 338
sodomy **X:**379*c*, 382*c*
SOE. *See* Special Operations
 Executive
softball **VIII:**328
soft money **X:**63, 64, 275
software **X:**87, 181
Soil Conservation and Domestic
 Allotment Act **VIII:**445*c*
 Agricultural Adjustment Act
  VIII:6
 Agricultural Adjustment
  Administration **VIII:**7
 agriculture **VIII:**9–10
Soil Conservation Service
 VIII:98–99, 115
Sojourner (spacecraft) **X:**329
Sokoloff, Nikolai **VIII:**134
sola fide **I:**218
Solar America Initiative **X:**32
Soldiers' Aid Society of Northern
 Ohio **V:**228
Soldiers' Bonus **VII:331,** 409*c*
 citizenship **VII:**57
 politics (1900–1928) **VII:**262
 veterans **VII:**372–373
 Veterans Bureau **VII:**374

soldiers' homes **V:**416
Soldiers' Pay (Faulkner) **VII:**180;
 VIII:128
Solidarity (IWW journal) **VII:**284,
 285
Solid South **VI:**95, **338–339;**
 VIII:298
Solinus **I:**247
Solomon (king of Israel) **I:**124
Solomon Islands **VIII:365–366,**
 447*c*
 Coral Sea, Battle of the
  VIII:87
 Guadalcanal **VIII:**159
 Halsey, William F.
  VIII:161
 MacArthur, Douglas
  IX:197–198
 Marines, U.S. **VIII:**230
 World War II Pacific theater
  VIII:435
Solzhenitsyn, Alexander **X:**165
Somalia **X:**380*c*
 Africa **X:**15, 16
 Clinton, William J. **X:**81
 cold war, end of **X:**85
 defense policy **X:**102
Some Chinese Ghosts (Hearn)
 VI:169
*Some Considerations on the
 Keeping of Negroes* (Woolman)
 II:426
Some Like It Hot (film) **IX:**223,
 225
"Someone to Watch Over Me"
 (Gershwin) **VII:**124
Somers, George **I:**30
Somerset, Isabel **VI:**394
Somers Island Company. *See*
 Bermuda Company
Somervell, Brehon B. **VIII:**25,
 233
Something's Got to Give (film)
 IX:223
Somoza, Anastasio **X:**377*c*
 contras **X:**94
 Latin America **X:**205, 206
 Mexico **X:**226
 Nicaragua **X:**254
Somoza family (Nicaragua) **IX:**11
Sondheim, Stephen **X:**281
Songhai **I:341–342**
 Askia Muhammad I **I:**14
 Gao **I:**137, 138
 Mali **I:**226
 Mansa Musa I **I:**228
 Mossi **I:**252–253
 Sahara **I:**324
 Sudan **I:**347
 Timbuktu **I:**359–360
Song of Hiawatha (Longfellow)
 VI:310
Song of the Sierras (Miller)
 VI:226
Songs of a Semite (Lazarus)
 VI:219
Soninke people **I:**139

Sonni Ali Ber (Songhai ruler)
 I:14, 226
Sonni Bakari Da'o (Songhai ruler)
 I:14
Sonni dynasty **I:**14
*Son of the Forest, A: The
 Experience of William Apess,
 a Native of the Forest* (Apess)
 IV:227
Son of the Middle Border, A
 (Garland) **VI:**140
Sonora, Mexico
 Figueroa, José **IV:**148
 Mexican immigration
  VII:202
 Murrieta, Joaquín **IV:**267
Sons of Dan **IV:**89
Sons of Liberty **III:394**
 Adams, Samuel **III:**7
 artisans **III:**35
 Boston Tea Party **III:**59
 citizenship **III:**93
 Golden Hill, Battle of
  III:196
 Hancock, John **III:**209
 liberty tree **III:**267
 Loyal Nine **III:**276
 McDougall, Alexander
  III:294
 peace movements **V:**295
 Putnam, Israel **III:**350
 resistance movement
  III:365–366
 Revere, Paul **III:**366
 Stamp Act **III:**396
 taverns and inns **III:**407
 Vallandigham, Clement L.
  V:413
Sons of Temperance **IV:**369
Sons of the Confederate Veterans
 V:244, 415
Sonthonax, Léger Félicté **III:**203
Sony v. Universal **X:**317, 378*c*
Sooners **VI:**339
"Sophisticated Lady" (Ellington)
 VIII:112
Sorbonne, the **IX:**168
Sorge, Richard **VIII:**118
Soros, George **X:**64
Sorrell, Herbert K. **IX:**88
Sosso **I:**350
Soto, Hernando de **I:342–343,**
 343, **397***c*
 animals **II:**23
 Apalachee **I:**11
 Choctaw **IV:**86
 Cofitachequi **I:**80
 Coosa **I:**89
 Hakluyt, Richard, the
  Younger **I:**153
 horses **II:**165
 Mabila **I:**221
 Natchez **I:**259
 Timucua **I:**360
Sotomayor, Sonia **X:**339, 371
Sotteville-les-Rouen, France
 VIII:47

Soule, Pierre **V:**290
soul music **X:**238
Souls of Black Folk, The (Du Bois)
    VII:404*c*
        DuBois, W.E.B. **VII:**80
        Rhinelander case **VII:**301
        Washington, Booker T.
            VI:384
Soul Train **X:**239
Sound and the Fury, The
    (Faulkner) **V:**240; **VIII:**128,
    220, 443*c*; **IX:**193
Sound of Music, The (film)
    IX:225
sound recordings. *See* compact
    discs; phonographs/phonograph
    records
"Sources of Soviet Conduct"
    (Kennan) **IX:**167, **363–366**
Sousa, John Philip **VI:**140, 257,
    258, **339–340,** 411*c*
Sousa, Tomé de **I:**35
Souter, David **X:**162, 164, **324,**
    339, 384*c*
South Africa **X:324–325,** 379*c*
        Africa **IX:**4; **X:**16
        Bourke-White, Margaret
            VIII:50
        cold war, end of **X:**85
        investments, foreign
            VII:152
        UN **X:**355
South African National Party
    X:324
South America
        Acadians **II:**2
        Amazon River **I:**8–9
        Andes Mountains **I:**9
        Arawak **I:**11
        Brazil **I:**33–35
        cold war **IX:**63
        evolution **VI:**122
        foreign policy **IV:**155
        Lange, Dorothea **VIII:**210
        Monroe Doctrine **IV:**259–
            261
        Peru **I:**289
        slavery **II:**354
South Americans **X:**167
Southampton County, Virginia
    IV:412*c*
        religion **IV:**318
        slavery **IV:**348
        Turner, Nat **IV:**380, 381
South Asian tsunami (December
    2004) **X:**384*c*
South Carolina **II:368–370,**
    436*c*–438*c*; **III:**462*c*; **V:**443*c*–
    444*c*
        abolitionism **IV:**1
        African Americans **II:**7, 8;
            III:9
        agriculture **II:**11, 13; **III:**11;
            IV:10, 12
        American System **IV:**20
        Anderson, Robert **V:**9–10
        Black Codes **V:**35

Byrnes, James F. **VIII:**60
Calhoun, John C. **IV:**68–70
Camden, Battle of **III:**74–
    76
Charleston **II:**63–64
Charleston, siege of
    III:84–85
Cherokee **II:**64–65
citizenship **III:**93
class **II:**70–71
Confederate States of
    America **V:**84
Constitution, ratification of
    the **III:**105
Continental Congress, First
    III:114
cotton **III:**122, 123
Cowpens, Battle of **III:**124–
    125
Democratic Party **V:**108–
    109
Dow, Lorenzo **IV:**126
Drayton, William H.
    IV:127
economy **II:**109
elections, conduct of **VI:**113
Elliot, Robert Brown **V:**127
environment **III:**155
Eutaw Springs, Battle of
    III:159–160
Exodusters **VI:**122
Fillmore, Millard **IV:**149
fire-eaters **V:**146
foraging **V:**149
foreign policy **IV:**156
Fort Sumter **V:**154–155
freedom rides **IX:**123
Free-Soil Party **IV:**164
Gastonia Strike **VII:**122
Georgia **II:**146
government, British
    American **II:**153
grandfather clause **VI:**152
Gullah **II:**158
Haiti **III:**204
Hume, Sophia Wigington
    II:168–169
indigo **II:**177
Jackson, Andrew **IV:**205
Jim Crow laws **VI:**203–204
Johnston, Henrietta Deering
    II:188
King's Mountain, Battle of
    III:246
Ku Klux Klan **V:**223–225
Ku Klux Klan Act **V:**225
labor/labor movements
    II:198–199
land **II:**201
Liberia **VI:**223
manufacturing and industry
    II:214
Marion, Francis **III:**285–
    286
marriage and family **IV:**240;
    VII:192
merchants **II:**231

Mexican-American War
    IV:251
Middleton, Arthur **II:**233–
    234
miscegenation **II:**238
mulattoes **II:**246
Ninety-Six, Battle of
    III:319
Nullification Controversy
    IV:282–283
Osceola **IV:**289
Ostenaco **II:**280
Pinckney, Charles
    Cotesworth **III:**335, 336
Pinckney, Elizabeth Lucas
    II:294–295; **III:**336
plantations **V:**308
population trends **II:**303
Queen Anne's War **II:**323
race and race relations
    VII:282
Rainey, Joseph H. **V:**322–
    323
redemption **V:**328, 329
rice cultivation **II:**334
Scots immigrants **II:**346
secession **V:**344, 345
Sherman, William T. **V:**355
shipbuilding **II:**351
sit-ins **IX:**291
slave codes **II:**352
slave resistance **II:**353
slavery **III:**390, 392; **IV:**346–
    348; **V:**363
slave trade **III:**393
society, British American
    II:366
South Carolina Regulation
    III:394–395
southern demagogues
    VII:332
Stono Rebellion **II:**377–378
tariffs **V:**383
Teach, Edward **II:**385
Tillman, Benjamin Ryan
    VI:358
Tuscarora War **II:**395
Tyler, John **IV:**382
Van Buren, Martin **IV:**386
Vesey, Denmark **IV:**387–
    388
veterans **V:**416
War of Jenkins' Ear **II:**408
White Citizens' Councils
    IX:342
workers' compensation
    VII:392
Yamasee **II:**429–430
South Carolina Exposition
    IV:412*c*
South Carolina Railroad **IV:**173,
    314, 316
South Carolina Regulation
    III:394–395
South Carolina Sea Islands **V:**160,
    161; **VI:**21
South Carolina Society **II:**390

South Dakota **VI:**410*c*
        cattle kingdom **VI:**64
        Crazy Horse **VI:**85
        exploration **IV:**145, 146
        immigration **VI:**184
        McGovern, George S.
            X:216–217
        Native Americans **X:**251
        Red Cloud **VI:**303
Southeast Asia **IX:**156. *See also*
    specific countries, e.g.: Vietnam
        Asian Americans **X:**33
        cold war **IX:**63
        cold war, end of **X:**84
        domino theory **IX:**89
        foreign policy **X:**141
        immigration **IX:**155
        journalism **IX:**166
        OSS **VIII:**285
        SEATO **IX:**291–292
        wars of national liberation
            IX:338
Southeast Asia Treaty
    Organization (SEATO)
    IX:291–292, 353*c*
        Dulles, John Foster **IX:**91
        Eisenhower, Dwight D.
            IX:101
        wars of national liberation
            IX:339
Southeastern Ceremonial
    Complex **I:**245
southeastern European
    immigration
        Amalgamated Clothing
            Workers of America
            (ACW) **VIII:**16
        immigration **VIII:**184
        Irish Americans **VIII:**188
        Italian Americans **VIII:**190
        Jews **VIII:**195
        labor/labor movements
            VIII:205
southeastern United States
        fur trade **IV:**170
        Indian Removal Act **IV:**198
        migration **IV:**254
        New Orleans, Battle of
            IV:280
        panic of 1819 **IV:**293
        Trail of Tears **IV:**377, 378
Southeby, William **II:**1
Southern Baptist Convention
    IV:317; **VIII:**334, 335; **IX:**272,
    342
Southern Christian Leadership
    Conference (SCLC) **IX:292–**
    294, 293, 354*c*, 355*c*
        African Americans **IX:**5
        Baker, Ella Josephine **IX:**32,
            33
        Birmingham confrontation
            IX:39
        civil disobedience **IX:**58
        Jackson, Jesse, L. **X:**191
        King, Martin Luther, Jr.
            IX:174–175

Southern Christian Leadership
Conference (*continued*)
  March on Washington
    (1963) **IX:**200
  Parks, Rosa **IX:**254, 255
  race and race relations
    IX:269, 270
  religion **IX:**272
  sit-ins **IX:**291
  Voting Rights Act of 1965
    IX:333
Southern Colonial style **IV:**30
Southern Conference Education
  Fund **IX:**33
Southern Conference for Human
  Rights **VIII:**319
Southern Conference for Human
  Welfare **VIII:**366
Southern Cotton Manufacturers
  VII:163
"Southern Cross" **V:**31
southern demagogues **VII:332**
Southern European immigrants
  cities and urban life **VII:**54
  immigration **VII:**144
  Immigration Act (1917)
    VII:145
  IWW **VII:**146
  Mann Act **VII:**189
  marriage and family
    VII:191
  National Origins Act
    VII:227–228
  nativism **VII:**233, 234
  New Unionism **VII:**237
  population trends **VII:**266
  progressivism **VII:**271
  Quota Act **VII:**279
Southern Farmers' Alliance
  farmers' alliances **VI:**125,
    126
  People's Party **VI:**281, 282
  Powderly, Terence Vincent
    VI:287
Southern Historical Society **V:**244
*Southern Historical Society
  Papers* (Early) **V:**243
Southern Homestead Act (1966)
  V:161
Southern Literary Messenger
  IV:210
Southern Manifesto **IX:294–295,**
  353*c*
  Faubus, Orval **IX:**118
  NAACP **IX:**232
  race and race relations
    IX:269
  Thurmond, James Strom
    X:351
  Wigfall, Louis T. **V:**431
Southern Pacific Railroad (SP)
  business **VII:**46
  corruption, political **VI:**83
  Gadsden Purchase **IV:**174
  Huntington, Collis Potter
    VI:181
  Santa Fe Trail **IV:**332

Southern Quarterly Review **IV:**210
Southern Regional Council
  VIII:306
Southern Review, The **IV:**210
Southern States Industrial
  Council **IX:**249
Southern Tenant Farmers Union
  (STFU) **VIII:367–368**
  Agricultural Adjustment Act
    VIII:6
  Bethune, Mary McLeod
    VIII:44
  race and race relations
    VIII:318
  socialists **VIII:**362
  South **VIII:**366
  Thomas, Norman **VIII:**394
southern United States **VIII:366–**
  367. *See also* Sunbelt
  abolitionism **IV:**1, 4; **V:**1–3
  African Americans **III:**9–10;
    IV:7; **VIII:**2–4; **IX:**4
  agriculture **III:**10–11;
    IV:10–13; **V:**5–6
  Alamo, The **IV:**14
  America First Committee
    VIII:17
  amnesty, acts of **V:**9
  antilynching legislation
    VIII:22
  anti-Masonry **IV:**25
  antislavery **III:**26
  art and architecture **IV:**30
  Bankhead-Jones Farm
    Tenant Act **VIII:**39
  banking **V:**27
  Bethune, Mary McLeod
    VIII:44
  Birth of a Nation, The
    VII:37
  Black Codes **V:**34–35
  blues **VII:**39
  CIO **IX:**72
  cities and urban life **VI:**69;
    VII:54; **VIII:**68; **IX:**55
  citizenship **VII:**56
  civil rights **VIII:**72, 73
  Civil Rights Act (1957)
    IX:58, 59
  Civil War **V:**73–75
  Civil War centennial **IX:**62
  Clinton, Sir Henry **III:**99
  Communist Party **VII:**61
  Communists **VIII:**78
  Comstock, Anthony **VI:**79
  Congress **VII:**62
  conservative coalition
    VIII:86
  currency issue **VI:**88
  Davis, Jefferson **V:**104
  Democratic Party **IV:**116–
    118; **VIII:**92
  disease/epidemics **III:**138;
    IV:122
  Dow, Lorenzo **IV:**126
  economy **IV:**130–133;
    V:121–123; **VIII:**104

  education **V:**124; **VI:**108;
    VIII:105, 106
  education, federal aid to
    VI:110
  education, philanthropy and
    VI:112
  election of 1840 **IV:**138
  election of 1936 **VIII:**109
  election of 1940 **VIII:**111
  election of 1944 **VIII:**111
  elections **IX:**104
  elections, conduct of
    VI:113
  employment **V:**132
  environment **III:**155
  Evans, Walker **VIII:**120
  Exodusters **VI:**122
  Fair Labor Standards Act
    VIII:124
  Faulkner, William **VIII:**128
  federal income tax **VII:**106
  FEPC **VIII:**123
  fire-eaters **V:**145–146
  foreign policy **IV:**154
  freedom rides **IX:**123–124
  Freedom Train **IX:**125
  government **VIII:**154
  governors **V:**171–172
  Great Migration **VII:**127,
    129
  Griffith, David Wark
    VII:131, 132
  Hartford Convention **IV:**187
  Hastings, Lansford W.
    IV:187
  Hayes, Rutherford B.
    VI:167
  Higgins, Andrew J.
    VIII:165
  Hillman, Sidney **VIII:**166
  homefront **V:**192–193
  Houston, Sam **IV:**190
  Hurston, Zora Neale
    VIII:181
  Indian Removal Act **IV:**197–
    198
  industrial development
    IV:201; **V:**205
  internal improvements
    IV:202
  ironclad oath **V:**206–207
  isolationists **VIII:**189
  jazz **VIII:**195
  Jefferson, Joseph, III
    VI:202
  Jim Crow laws **VI:**203–204
  Keating-Owen Act **VII:**163
  Kennedy, John F. **IX:**169,
    170
  KKK **IX:**179–180
  Ku Klux Klan **VII:**165
  labor/labor movements
    IV:219
  ladies aid societies **V:**227
  Ladies Memorial
    Associations **V:**229
  Lange, Dorothea **VIII:**210

  Langston, John Mercer
    VI:218
  Lease, Mary Elizabeth
    Clyens **VI:**220
  liberalism **IX:**191
  Liberal Republican Party
    VI:222
  Liberia **VI:**223
  literature **V:**239; **VIII:**219
  lost cause, the **V:**244–245
  loyalty oaths **V:**246
  lynching **VI:**229–231
  marriage and family **III:**287,
    288
  McCormick, Cyrus Hall
    IV:245
  medicine **VIII:**235
  Methodism **III:**297
  Mexican-American War
    IV:252
  Middletown **VII:**206
  migration **IV:**253; **VII:**207;
    VIII:239, 240; **IX:**215
  mining **VII:**207
  miscegenation **V:**261
  Missouri Compromise
    IV:255–257
  mothers' pensions **VII:**214
  music **IV:**269; **VIII:**250
  NAACP **VII:**224; **VIII:**255
  Native Americans in the War
    of 1812 **IV:**276, 277
  New South **VI:**263–265
  Nullification Controversy
    IV:282
  nurses **V:**286
  Omaha platform **VI:**272
  Operation Dixie **IX:**249–
    250
  panic of 1819 **IV:**293, 294
  panic of 1837 **IV:**294, 295
  Passaic Strike **VII:**253
  peace movements **V:**296
  Phillips, Wendell **IV:**299
  politics (Roosevelt era)
    VIII:298
  popular culture **VII:**265
  popular sovereignty **IV:**305
  population trends **III:**343;
    V:310; **VII:**266, 267;
    VIII:305; **X:**281
  postwar planning **VIII:**306
  poverty **X:**285, 286
  POWs **III:**346
  race and race relations
    VII:282, 283; **VIII:**317–
    319; **IX:**269
  Reconstruction **V:**324
  redemption **V:**328–329
  refugees **V:**330
  religion **III:**360, 361; **V:**331–
    332; **VI:**306; **VIII:**334,
    335
  religious liberty **III:**362
  Republican Party **IV:**321,
    323
  rock and roll **IX:**278

Roosevelt, Franklin D.
VIII:345
rural life III:375
scalawags V:339–340
Scottsboro Boys VIII:353–354
secession V:344–345
segregation IX:287–288
shipbuilding VIII:360
slavery III:390, 391; IV:344–347; V:362–364
slave trade, internal IV:348–350
socialists VIII:362
Society of Friends V:365
Solid South VI:338
southern demagogues VII:332
Southern Manifesto IX:294
states' rights V:370
States' Rights Party IX:299–300
STFU VIII:367–368
Sunbelt VIII:380, 381
tariffs V:383
technology VIII:397
Texas IV:372
UMWA VIII:401
Union League V:404
USHA VIII:404
Van Buren, Martin IV:386
violence and lawlessness VI:375
Voting Rights Act of 1965 IX:333–334
War Hawks IV:389–390
Warren Court IX:338
Whigs IV:397
White Citizens' Councils IX:341–342
women's status and rights III:448; IV:404
World War II VIII:428
World War II home front VIII:433
zoot-suiters VIII:442
Southern Woman's Story, A (Pember) V:297
South Fork Dam (Pennsylvania) VI:204
South Fork Fishing and Hunting Club VI:204
South Improvement Company Industrial Revolution, Second VI:192
oil VI:271
South Korea. See Korea, Republic of
South Korean Central Intelligence Agency (KCIA) X:199
South Mountain, Battle of
Cobb, Howell V:76
Garnett, Richard B. V:164
Gordon, John B. V:170
Meade, George Gordon V:253
South Orkney Islands IV:146

South Pacific
Mead, Margaret VII:197
Pan-American Exposition VII:252
Samoa VI:322–323
Wilkes expedition IV:399
South Pacific VIII:252
South Pass IV:354
Ashley, William Henry IV:31
California Trail IV:77
Carson, Kit IV:81
exploration IV:144
Forty-niners IV:159
Oregon Trail IV:285
Smith, Jedediah Strong IV:350
South Sea Company II:370
South Sea islands VI:218
Southside Railroad V:14
South Vietnam IX:353c, 355c, 357c; X:377c
antiwar movement, Vietnam X:29
Asia IX:21
cold war IX:64
cold war, end of X:84
communism IX:68
Dulles, John Foster IX:91
foreign policy X:140, 141
SEATO IX:291
Soviet Union IX:295
Vietnam War IX:330–332
Vietnam War, end of U.S. involvement X:361, 362
wars of national liberation IX:339
Southwestern Indians. See Indians of the desert Southwest
southwestern United States
agriculture VIII:9
Catholics VIII:64
economy IV:130
environment VIII:115
exploration IV:144, 146
foreign policy VII:115
Ickes, Harold L. VIII:183
immigration IV:193
Kearny, Stephen Watts IV:212
Lamy, Jean Baptiste IV:222
Mexican immigration VII:203
migration IV:255; VIII:239, 240
popular sovereignty IV:305
religion IV:319
Rocky Mountain Fur Company IV:325
Santa Fe Trail IV:332
segregation VII:320
Smith, Jedediah Strong IV:351
Sunbelt VIII:380, 381
technology VIII:397
Van Buren, Martin IV:386

violence and lawlessness VI:375
Webster-Ashburton Treaty IV:394
Southwest Fur Company IV:18
Southworth, Mrs. E. D. E. N. IV:229
Sovereign, James P. VI:213
sovereignty, Native American X:250
sovereignty, state. See state sovereignty
Sovereignty & Goodness of God, The (Rowlandson) II:337
Soviet-American relations VIII:368–369
Anglo-American relations VIII:21
atomic bomb VIII:35
Bretton Woods Conference VIII:52
foreign policy VIII:140–143
Grand Alliance VIII:155
Hiroshima and Nagasaki VIII:168
isolationists VIII:190
Lend-Lease VIII:212
liberalism VIII:216
Nazi-Soviet Pact VIII:266
Potsdam Conference VIII:307, 308
Teheran Conference VIII:391
UN VIII:402
V-J Day VIII:407
World War II VIII:427
Yalta Conference VIII:439
Soviet Union (USSR) VIII:444c, 446c–448c; IX:295–296, 351c–355c; X:378c, 379c. See also Russia
ABM Treaty X:26–28
Acheson, Dean IX:1, 2
Africa IX:3
air power VIII:16
Americans for Democratic Action IX:14
Anglo-American relations VIII:21
anticommunism VIII:22; IX:14
antiwar movement, Vietnam X:29
arms race IX:17; X:29–30
Asia IX:20, 21
Atlantic, Battle of the VIII:33
Atlantic Charter VIII:34
aviation IX:29
Axis VIII:37, 38
Baldwin, Roger Nash VII:31
Bay of Pigs IX:35, 36
Berlin blockade IX:38–39
blitzkrieg VIII:47
Bourke-White, Margaret VIII:50

Bretton Woods Conference VIII:52
Cairo Conference VIII:61
Carter, James Earl, Jr. X:69
Casablanca Conference VIII:62
Catholic Bishops' Letter X:70
Catholics VIII:64
CDAAA VIII:77
CIA IX:52
Clinton, William J. X:81
cold war IX:62–64
cold war, end of X:84–86
communism IX:67
Communists VIII:78
conservative movement X:93–94
Cuban missile crisis IX:80–81
defense policy X:99–101
demobilization (WWII) VIII:92; IX:84
Dennis v. U.S. IX:86
détente X:103–104
domino theory IX:89
Dulles, John Foster IX:90–91
education IX:99
espionage VIII:118
Europe IX:112–113
Ford, Gerald R. X:139
foreign policy VIII:140–143; X:140–142
Forrestal, James V. VIII:143
Gastonia Strike VII:122
glasnost X:153
Goldman, Emma VII:126
Haig, Alexander M., Jr. X:164
Harriman, W. Averell VIII:161
Haywood, William Dudley VII:137
Helms, Jesse A., Jr. X:165
Hersey, John R. VIII:164
Hiroshima and Nagasaki VIII:166, 168
Holocaust VIII:169
Hopkins, Harry L. VIII:177
Hull, Cordell VIII:180
hydrogen bomb IX:152
INF Treaty X:179–181
intelligence VIII:186, 187
Internet X:181
Iron Curtain, collapse of X:188
Israel IX:160
Kennan, George F. IX:167, 168
Kennedy, John F. IX:171
Korean War IX:177
Latin America IX:184
League of Nations VII:175
Lend-Lease VIII:212
liberalism VIII:215

Soviet Union (*continued*)
  Limited Test Ban Treaty of
    1963 **IX:**192
  literature **VIII:**218
  Manhattan Project **VIII:**227
  Marshall Plan **IX:**204
  Middle East **IX:**214;
    X:227–229
  military-industrial complex
    IX:216
  modern Republicanism
    IX:221
  NASA **IX:**231
  NATO **IX:**247; **X:**259
  Nazi-Soviet Pact **VIII:**266
  New Frontier **IX:**243
  Nicaragua **X:**254
  Nixon, Richard M. **X:**257
  NSC-68 **IX:**247, 248
  nuclear freeze movement
    X:261
  Oswald, Lee Harvey
    IX:251–252
  Peace Corps **IX:**255, 256
  Potsdam Conference
    VIII:307–308
  POWs **VIII:**310
  Progressive Party **IX:**263,
    264
  propaganda **VIII:**311
  radical and labor press
    VII:286
  Reagan, Ronald W. **X:**299,
    301
  Reuther, Walter **IX:**275
  Rice, Condoleezza **X:**309
  Robeson, Paul **VIII:**342
  Rosenberg, Julius and Ethel
    IX:280
  Russian Revolution **VII:**308
  SALT I/SALT II **X:**336–337
  SANE **IX:**283
  science and technology
    IX:285
  science fiction **IX:**287
  second front **VIII:**355
  Siberian Expedition
    VII:325
  socialism **VII:**328
  socialists **VIII:**362
  "Sources of Soviet Conduct"
    (Kennan) **IX:363–366**
  Soviet-American relations
    VIII:368–369
  space exploration **IX:**296,
    297
  Spanish civil war **VIII:**369
  Steffens, Lincoln **VII:**339
  submarines **VIII:**379
  Suez crisis **IX:**307
  technology **IX:**311–312
  Teheran Conference
    VIII:390
  Truman, Harry S. **IX:**320
  Truman Doctrine **IX:**321,
    322
  UN **VIII:**402, 403; **X:**355

V-E Day **VIII:**405
Versailles, Treaty of **VII:**369
V-J Day **VIII:**406, 407
Wallace, Henry A. **VIII:**411,
  412
wars of national liberation
  IX:338, 339
White Paper **IX:**343
World War II **VIII:**428
World War II European
  theater **VIII:**429, 431
Yalta Conference **VIII:**439
Soviet Union, breakup of **X:325–
326,** 380c
  arms race **X:**30
  Bush, George H. W. **X:**52,
    53
  Clinton, William J. **X:**83
  cold war, end of **X:**86
  détente **X:**104
  INF Treaty **X:**181
  Iron Curtain, collapse of
    X:189
SP. *See* Southern Pacific Railroad
SPA. *See* Socialist Party of
  America
Spaatz, Carl **VIII:**47–48
SPAB. *See* Supply Priorities and
  Allocation Board
Space Advisory Committee **X:**18
Space Age **IX:**244
space exploration *IX:296,* **296–
  297,** 354c, 355c
  aviation **IX:**29
  Kennedy, John F. **IX:**170
  NASA **IX:**231–232
  science and technology
    IX:285
  science fiction **IX:**287
  technology **IX:**312, 313
space policy **X:326–329,** 328
space shuttle **X:**327
space station **X:**327
Spain **III:**462c, 464c; **IV:**411c;
  VI:407c, 412c
  Adams-Onís Treaty **IV:**6
  Aguinaldo, Emilio **VII:**8–9
  Alamo, The **IV:**13–14
  Amistad incident **IV:**21, 22
  architecture **III:**29
  Austin, Moses **IV:**39
  California **III:**73–74; **IV:**70
  California missions **IV:**76
  Caribbean **II:**59
  Choctaw **III:**89; **IV:**86
  Chouteau family **IV:**88
  Columbia River **IV:**103
  Creek **III:**126
  Cuba **IV:**111, 112; **VI:**88
  de Lôme Letter **VI:**94
  Dutch West India Company
    II:107
  Essex decision **III:**157
  exploration **II:**124
  Florida **III:**166, 167;
    IV:151–153
  foreign affairs **III:**168, 169

foreign policy **V:**149, 151;
  VII:113; **VIII:**141
fur trade **IV:**170
Haiti **III:**203
Jackson, Andrew **IV:**206
Jay, John **III:**229
Jay-Gardoqui Treaty
  III:230–231
Jay's Treaty **III:**231
Jones Act (1917) **VII:**157
land **II:**201
League of Armed Neutrality
  III:257
Louisiana Purchase **III:**273
McGillivray, Alexander
  III:294
Monroe Doctrine **IV:**260,
  261
Native Americans **III:**314
New Spain, northern
  frontier of **III:**317–318
Open Door Policy **VII:**246
Ostend Manifesto **V:**289–
  290
Panama Canal **VII:**250
Pan-American Exposition
  VII:252
Paris, Treaty of (1763)
  III:331
Paris, Treaty of (1783)
  III:332
peace movements **VII:**255
Pinckney Treaty **III:**336–
  337
Popular Front **VIII:**303
privateering **II:**312
Queen Anne's War **II:**323–
  324
St. Augustine **II:**341–342
Santa Fe Trail **IV:**330
Seminole **IV:**338
slavery **II:**354
slave trade **II:**358
Spanish-American War
  VI:340–341
Spanish civil war **VIII:**369–
  370
trade, domestic and foreign
  III:413, 415
Vergennes, Charles Gravier,
  comte de **III:**423
Virginius affair **VI:**377
War of Jenkins' Ear **II:**408–
  409
Wilkinson, James **III:**443,
  444
Spalding, Lyman **IV:**123
Spam **IX:**121
Spanish-American War **VI:***317,*
  340–342, *341,* 412c
  American Anti-Imperialist
    League Platform (1899)
    VI:441–442
  Anti-Imperialist League
    VI:16–17, **441–442**
  Army Act **VII:**22
  Balloon Corps **V:**26

Barton, Clara **V:**30
Big Stick diplomacy **VII:**34
Bryan, William Jennings
  VI:52
Crane, Stephen **VI:**85
Cuba **VI:**87
Dewey, George **VI:**97
Filipino insurrection
  VI:127
Foraker Act **VII:**110
foreign policy **IV:**156;
  V:151; **VII:**113
Hanna, Marcus Alonzo
  VI:158
Hawaii **VI:**163
Hay, John Milton **VI:**164
Hearst, William Randolph
  VII:137
Hull, Cordell **VIII:**180
imperialism **VI:**188
investments, American,
  abroad **VI:**197
Jones Act (1916) **VII:**156
Jones Act (1917) **VII:**157
King, Ernest J. **VIII:**201
Knox, Frank **VIII:**202
Leahy, William D. **VIII:**210
Maine, Remember the
  VI:237
Manifest Destiny **IV:**236
McKinley, William **IV:**241
Mitchell, William (Billy)
  VII:211
Panama Canal **VII:**250
Pan-American Exposition
  VII:252
Pershing, John Joseph
  VII:258
Philippine independence
  IX:256
presidency **VII:**268
Puerto Ricans **IX:**267
Reid, Whitelaw **VI:**305
Roosevelt, Theodore
  VII:304
Rough Riders **VI:**317
southern demagogues
  VII:332
veterans **VII:**371
Watterson, Henry **VI:**386
Wheeler, Joseph **V:**429
Spanish Armada **I:344–345,** 398c
  Castile **I:**67
  Drake, Sir Francis **I:**112
  Elizabeth I **I:**121
  Frobisher, Martin **I:**135
  Grenville, Sir Richard **I:**145
  Hawkins, Sir John **I:**157
  Philip II **I:**291
  Walsingham, Sir Francis
    I:382
Spanish civil war **VIII:369–370**
  anticommunism **VIII:**22
  foreign policy **VIII:**141
  Neutrality Acts **VIII:**267
  Popular Front **VIII:**303,
    304

Spanish colonies **II:370–374**
  agriculture **II:**10
  art **II:**27
  Dominicans **II:**101
  Florida **II:**128–130
  Fort Mose **II:**132
  Indians of the desert
    Southwest **II:**176
  miscegenation **II:**237
  missions **II:**238–239
  mulattoes **II:**246
  Native Americans **II:**252
  Navajo **II:**254
  New Mexico **II:**263
  Popé **II:**301
  printing and publishing
    II:311
  Pueblo **II:**317
  Pueblo Revolt **II:**318
  Roman Catholicism **II:**336
  slave trade **II:**358
  theater **II:**389
  Vargas, Diego de **II:**397–
    398
  Westo **II:**411
Spanish exploration and
  colonization **I:**396*c*, 398*c*
  Acosta, José de **I:**3
  adelantado **I:**4
  Alvarado, Pedro de **I:**7
  Apalachee **I:**11
  audiencia **I:**16–17
  auto-da-fé **I:**17
  Aztecs **I:**21–22
  Barbados **I:**27
  black legend **I:**31–32
  cabildo **I:**40–41
  Cabot, Sebastian **I:**45
  cacique **I:**49
  California **I:**51, 52
  Canary Islands **I:**57
  Casa de Contratación **I:**63
  Castile **I:**65–67
  conquistadores **I:**87–89
  corregidor **I:**93
  Cozumel **I:**99
  Drake, Sir Francis **I:**110–
    112
  Dutch East India Company
    I:115
  El Dorado **I:**119
  encomienda **I:**122–123
  entail **I:**123
  Ferdinand and Isabella
    I:127–128
  Florida **I:**130–131; **II:**128
  Ghana **I:**139–140
  gold **I:**142
  Grijalva, Juan de **I:**145
  Guamán Poma **I:**147
  Guerrero, Gonzalo **I:**147
  hacienda **I:**149–150
  Hispaniola **I:**162–163
  Holy League **I:**165
  Ibn Battuta **I:**175
  Indians of the desert
    Southwest **II:**176
  inquisition **I:**182–183
  invention and technology
    I:184
  Islam **I:**189
  Jamaica **I:**191
  Jews **I:**194–195
  Las Casas, Bartolomé de
    I:204–208
  Lima **I:**213
  limpieza de sangre **I:**214
  Linschoten, Jan Huygen van
    I:214
  Machu Picchu **I:**221
  Magellan, Ferdinand **I:**223,
    224
  Mary I **I:**232, 233
  Maya **I:**235
  mestizaje **I:**241
  mestizo **I:**242
  Nahua **I:**257
  Nahuatl **I:**258
  New Mexico **I:**265–266
  New Spain **I:**266–270
  Northwest Passage **I:**274
  Panama **I:**284
  Peru **I:**289
  Philip II **I:**290–292
  Potosí **I:**300
  Protestantism **II:**314–315
  Pueblo **I:**305
  Puerto Rico **I:**305–306
  Ralegh, Sir Walter **I:**312
  reducción **I:**314–315
  Requerimiento **I:**318–319,
    409–410
  Sepúlveda, Juan Ginés de
    I:330–331
  Seville **I:**332–333
  silver **I:**335–336
  slavery **I:**338
  Spanish Armada **I:**344–345
  Tabasco **I:**351
  Taino **I:**352
  Tenochtitlán **I:**354, 356
  Tlaxcala **I:**361–363
  Tordesillas, Treaty of
    I:367–368
  Vitoria, Francisco de **I:**379
  zambo **I:**391–392
Spanish Flu Epidemic (1918–
  1919) **VII:**275–276
Spanish immigration **II:**372,
  374–375
Spanish missions **IV:**339
Spanish Viceroyalty of Peru **I:**213
Sparkman, John **IX:**103
SPARS (United States Coast
  Guard Women's Reserve)
  VIII:424
Spartan missile **X:**27
Spaulding, Elbridge G. **V:**177
Spaulding, Eliza **IV:**399
Spaulding, Henry H. **IV:**398
speakeasies
  music **VII:**220
  Prohibition **VII:**273–274
  sexuality **VII:**322
Speaker of the House
  Albert, Carl B. **X:**21–22
  Cannon, Joseph Gurney
    VII:48
  Foley, Thomas S. **X:**137
  Gingrich, Newton L. **X:**151
  House of Representatives
    X:170, 171
  Macon, Nathaniel **III:**280
  O'Neill, Thomas "Tip" P., Jr.
    X:267
  Pelosi, Nancy **X:**271
  Wright, James C., Jr. **X:**372
Spears, Britney **X:**238
Special and Secret Service Bureau
  V:134
Special Field Order No. 15
  V:365–366
    Freedmen's Bureau **V:**160
    Port Royal Experiment
      V:312
    Sherman, William T. **V:**356
    Sherman's March through
      Georgia **V:**358
Special Field Order No. 67
  V:356
Special Forces, U.S. **X:**11, 12
Special Intelligence Branch of the
  Military Intelligence Service
  VIII:76
specialization **VII:**169
Special Operations Executive
  (SOE) **VIII:**118, 284
Special Order No. 191
  (Confederate) **V:**12
Special Service Organizations
  (Japan) **VIII:**117
Special Verification Commission
  (SVC) **X:**180
specie **IV:**413*c*
  banking **V:**27
  Bank of the United States,
    First **III:**41
  banks **III:**42, 43
  Chase, Salmon P. **V:**63
  economy **V:**122
  greenbacks **V:**177
Specie Circular **IV:**413*c*
  banking **IV:**46–47
  economy **IV:**132
  panic of 1819 **IV:**293
  panic of 1837 **IV:**294
specie payments **VI:**168
Specie Resumption Act **VI:**408*c*
  currency issue **VI:**89
  Grant, Ulysses S. **V:**176
  Greenback-Labor Party
    VI:154–155
Specter, Arlen **IX:**22
speculation
  Altgeld, John Peter **VI:**12
  Homestead Act **V:**195
  homesteading **VI:**175
  panic of 1792 **III:**330
  SEC **VIII:**357
speedometers **X:**320
Spellman, Francis Joseph **VIII:**64
Spencer, Herbert
  Darwinism and religion
    VI:93
  evolution **VI:**122
  Fiske, John **VI:**128, 129
  James, Henry **VI:**200
  James, William **VI:**200
  literature **VI:**226
  Lochner v. New York
    VII:183
  pragmatism **VI:**289
  religion **VI:**306–307
  Social Darwinism **VI:**334
  Sumner, William Graham
    VI:347
Spencer, Lilly Martin **V:**18
Spencer, Percy **X:**317
Spence v. Washington **X:**135
Spewack, Sam **VIII:**56
SPG. *See* Society for the
  Propagation of the Gospel in
  Foreign Parts
sphere of influence
  Boxer Rebellion **VII:**41
  foreign policy **VII:**113, 116
  Open Door Policy **VII:**246
  presidency **VII:**268
"Sphinx, The" (Emerson) **IV:**140
Spice Girls, the **X:**238
Spice Islands **I:345–346**
  art and architecture **I:**13
  Cabral, Pedro Álvares **I:**46
  Grotius, Hugo **I:**146
  Magellan, Ferdinand **I:**223
  Portuguese seaborne empire
    I:299, 300
  Sequeira, Diogo Lopes de
    I:331
Spielberg, Steven **X:**235, *235*, 279
spies. *See* espionage
Spies, August **VI:**168, 169
Spillane, Mickey **IX:**195
Spindletop Strike **VI:**271
Spingarn Medal **IX:**255
Spinks, Leon **IX:**10
spinsters **II:375–376**
Spiral Jetty (Smithson) **X:**31
"Spirit of 1776" **IX:**125
Spirit of St. Louis **VII:**29, 177,
  178
Spirit of the Laws (Montesquieu)
  III:154
Spirit of the Times, The (Lippard)
  IV:227
Spiritual Exercises (Ignatius
  Loyola) **I:**178, 193
spiritualism **IV:354–356**
  Hooker, Isabella Beecher
    VI:176
  New Age movement
    X:252–253
  Owen, Robert **IV:**292
  religion **IV:**320; **VI:**309
  socialism **VI:**336
  Woodhull, Victoria **VI:**400,
    401
spirituals **VI:**255

Spock, Benjamin **IX:297–298,** 351*c*
　baby boomers **X:**39
　childhood **IX:**55
　SANE **IX:**283
Spoil of Office, A (Garland) **VI:**140
"Spoils Conference" **VII:**29
spoils system
　civil service reform **VI:**72, 73
　Cleveland, Grover **VI:**74
　Congress **VI:**80
　Conkling, Roscoe **VI:**80–81
　Democratic Party **IV:**118
　election of 1828 **IV:**137
　Jackson, Andrew **IV:**205, 206
　Liberal Republican Party **VI:**222
　suffrage **IV:**360
　Taylor, Zachary **IV:**368
　White, Andrew Dickson **VI:**391
Spokane, Washington
　Flynn, Elizabeth Gurley **VII:**109
　Foster, William Zebulon **VII:**116
　free speech fights **VII:**117
Spokane Indians **I:**261
Spooner, John **V:**12
Spooner Act (1902) **VII:**22, 251, 403*c*
Sporting News and Sporting Life, The **VI:**26
Sport of the Gods, The (Dunbar) **VI:**102
sports and recreation **V:366–367,** *367;* **VI:***342,* **342–343,** 409*c;* **VII:293–295,** *294,* **332–335,** *333;* **VIII:370–373,** *372;* **IX:298–299,** *299;* **X:329–332,** *331,* 384*c. See also* recreation
　Aaron, Henry L. "Hank" **X:**1
　African Americans **IX:**5
　Ali, Muhammad **IX:**9–10
　baseball **VII:**32–34
　bicycling **VI:**35–36
　Black Power **IX:**42
　boxing **VI:**43–45
　cities and urban life **VII:**56; **VIII:**70
　Dempsey, William Harrison "Jack" **VII:**75–76
　DiMaggio, Joe **VIII:**95–96
　education, higher **X:**112
　football **VI:**130–131
　Gay Nineties **VI:**140
　Great Depression **VIII:**159
　Johnson, Jack **VII:**154–156
　literature **VIII:**218
　Louis, Joe **VIII:**223–224
　Luce, Henry R. **VIII:**224
　National Park Service **VII:**228
　Owens, Jesse **VIII:**288–289

popular culture **VII:**263; **VIII:**301, 303; **X:**280
　radio **VIII:**320
　recreation **VII:**295; **VIII:**327; **IX:**271
　Rickey, Branch **IX:**276–277
　Robinson, Jackie **IX:**277–278
　sexuality **VII:**322
　social work **VII:**329
　sports and recreation **VII:**332–335
　television **X:**344
　track and field **VI:**359
　women's status and rights **X:**371
　work, household **VII:**390
　World War II home front **VIII:**433
　YMCA/YWCA **VII:**397–398
Sports Illustrated **VIII:**224; **X:**219
sport utility vehicles (SUVs) **X:**36
Spot Resolution **V:**236
Spotswood, Alexander
　exploration **II:**124
　postal service **II:**304
　Teach, Edward **II:**385
Spotsylvania, Battles of **V:367–368,** 445*c*
　Burnside, Ambrose E. **V:**52
　Early, Jubal A. **V:**119
　field fortifications **V:**141
　Gordon, John B. **V:**170
　Grant, Ulysses S. **V:**174
　Hancock, Winfield Scott **V:**184
　homefront **V:**193
　Lee, Robert E. **V:**231
　Louisiana Tigers **V:**245
　Meade, George Gordon **V:**254
　Overland campaign **V:**291
spotted fever **IV:**123
spousal consent **X:**3, 4, 20–21
Sprague, Frank J. **VI:**195
Spring, Lindley **V:**295
Springfield, Battle of **III:**248
Springfield, Illinois **IV:**125
Springsteen, Bruce **X:**239, *239*
Spring Wells Treaty **IV:**185
Sprint missiles **X:**27
Spruance, Raymond A.
　King, Ernest J. **VIII:**202
　Nimitz, Chester W. **VIII:**274
　Philippine Sea, Battle of the **VIII:**295
　Tarawa **VIII:**386
Sputnik satellite **IX:**354*c*
　arms race **IX:**17
　aviation **IX:**29
　defense budget **IX:**83
　education **IX:**99
　Ford Motor Corporation **IX:**123
　Internet **X:**181

NASA **IX:**231
　science and technology **IX:**285
　space exploration **IX:**296
　technology **IX:**312
Spy, The (Cooper) **III:**123
spy planes **X:**383*c*
Squanto **I:**294; **II:376**
　Bradford, William **II:**44
　captivity **II:**57–58
　Pilgrims **II:**294
Square Deal **VII:**94, 190
squatters **II:**12, 202
Squibb Pharmaceutical company **VIII:**234
Squier, Ephraim George **IV:**335; **VI:**221
SR-71 Blackbird spy plane **IX:**29
SS (Schutzstaffel) **VIII:**187
SSI. *See* Supplemental Security Income
SSRIs (selective serotonin uptake reinhibitors) **X:**223
Staats-Zeitung, New York **VI:**374
Stack, Carol **X:**127
Stackpole, Peter **VIII:**217
Stadacona **I:**61–62, 133
Stade, Hans **I:**58, **346–347,** 371
Stagecoach (film) **VIII:**301
Stager, Anson **V:**385
"stagflation" **X:**109
stained glass **VI:**3, 356–357
"stainless banner" **V:**31
Stalin, Joseph **VIII:**307, 440, 448*c*
　Anglo-American relations **VIII:**21
　anticommunism **VIII:**22
　Army, U.S. **VIII:**25
　Asia **IX:**21
　atomic bomb **VIII:**35
　Bourke-White, Margaret **VIII:**50
　Cairo Conference **VIII:**61
　Casablanca Conference **VIII:**62
　CDAAA **VIII:**77
　cold war **IX:**62, 63
　communism **IX:**67
　Communists **VIII:**77
　Europe **IX:**112, 113
　foreign policy **VIII:**140
　Grand Alliance **VIII:**155–156
　Harriman, W. Averell **VIII:**162
　Hopkins, Harry L. **VIII:**177
　Italian campaign **VIII:**191
　Korean War **IX:**177
　Nazi-Soviet Pact **VIII:**266
　Potsdam Conference **VIII:**307–308
　propaganda **VIII:**311
　Roosevelt, Franklin D. **VIII:**346
　Russian Revolution **VII:**308
　second front **VIII:**355

Soviet-American relations **VIII:**368, 369
Soviet Union **IX:**295
Teheran Conference **VIII:**390
Truman Doctrine **IX:**322
UN **VIII:**402
V-E Day **VIII:**405
Wallace, Henry A. **VIII:**412
White Paper **IX:**343
World War II European theater **VIII:**430, 431
Yalta Agreement **VIII:**467–469
Yalta Conference **VIII:**439–440
Stalingrad, Battle of
　foreign policy **VIII:**142
　second front **VIII:**355
　World War II European theater **VIII:**431
Stalinist purges **IX:**167
"Stalking the Billion-Footed Beast" (Wolfe) **X:**370
Stalwarts
　Arthur, Chester Alan **VI:**20, 21
　Conkling, Roscoe **VI:**81
　Republican Party **VI:**311
Stamp Act **III:395–396,** *396,* 459*c*
　Adams, John **III:**4
　American Revolution **III:**18
　Attucks, Crispus **III:**37
　Bernard, Sir Francis **III:**49
　Bland, Richard **III:**53
　Burke, Edmund **III:**68
　cities and urban life **III:**90
　Dulany, Daniel **III:**142
　economy **III:**145
　Franklin, Benjamin **III:**173
　Franklin, William **III:**175
　Golden Hill, Battle of **III:**196
　Grenville, George **III:**200
　Hancock, John **III:**209
　Henry, Patrick **III:**211
　Hutchinson, Thomas **III:**219
　Ingersoll, Jared **III:**226
　Jews **III:**236
　journalism **III:**240
　Lee, Richard Henry **III:**260
　liberty tree **III:**267
　Livingston, Robert R. **II:**207
　Loyal Nine **III:**276
　MacIntosh, Ebenezer **III:**279
　Mason, George **III:**292
　Mayhew, Jonathan **III:**293
　Oliver, Andrew **III:**324, 325
　Pitt, William **III:**337
　resistance movement **III:**365–366
　Revere, Paul **III:**366
　riots **III:**371

Seven Years' War **II:**349–350

Sons of Liberty **III:**394

Stamp Act Congress **III:**396–397

theater **III:**410

Townshend Duties **III:**412

Virginia Resolves **III:**425

Whately, Thomas **III:**437

Stamp Act Congress **II:**206; **III:**396–397, 459c

Dickinson, John **III:**137

Hancock, John **III:**209

resistance movement **III:**366

Stamp Act **III:**395

standardized testing **X:**13, 114, 115

Standard Oil **VI:**407c, 409c; **VII:**335–336, 336, 404c, 405c

business **VII:**45; **VIII:**57

Industrial Revolution, Second **VI:**192

Lloyd, Henry Demarest **VI:**227

muckrakers **VII:**217

New Nationalism **VII:**237

Northern Securities Case **VII:**241

oil **VI:**271

oil industry **VII:**244

Prohibition **VII:**274

railroads **VI:**302

Rockefeller, John Davison **VII:**302

Roosevelt, Theodore **VII:**304

Steffens, Lincoln **VII:**339

Tarbell, Ida Minerva **VII:**349

trusts **VI:**362–364

U.S. Steel **VII:**365

Standard Oil Company of New Jersey et al. v. United States **VII:**405c

Standard Oil Trust Agreement **VI:**363–364

Standards, Bureau of **VII:**151

Standing Bear (Ponca chief) **VI:**48, 49, 199

Standing Bear v. George Crook **VI:**49

standing committees **III:**116

Standish, Myles **II:**376

Alden, John **II:**16

Alden, Priscilla **II:**17

Morton, Thomas **II:**245

Stanford, Leland **VI:**112

Stanford University **VI:**112; **VIII:**171

Stanislaw II (king of Poland) **III:**350

Stanley, Henry M. **VI:**33, 266

Stanley Cup **VII:**334

Stanley-Smith, James, Lord Strange **III:**67

Stanleyville airlift **IX:**4

Stanton, Edwin M. **V:**368–369, 446c

Andrews's Raid **V:**11

Appomattox Court House, Virginia **V:**16

Arlington National Cemetery **V:**17

assassination of Abraham Lincoln **V:**21

Dana, Charles A. **V:**102; **VI:**91, 92

governors **V:**172

impeachment of Andrew Johnson **V:**201, 203

Johnson, Andrew **V:**213

Medal of Honor **V:**255

Reconstruction Acts **V:**328

Sherman, William T. **V:**356

Special Field Order No. 15 **V:**365

telegraph **V:**385

Union army **V:**402

war contracting **V:**424

Washington, D.C. **V:**426

Stanton, Elizabeth Cady **IV:**414c; **V:**369, 369–370, 446c

abolitionism **V:**3

American Anti-Slavery Society **IV:**16

Anthony, Susan B. **VI:**15–16

Blackwell, Antoinette Brown **VI:**39

Blatch, Harriot Eaton Stanton **VII:**38

Bloomer, Amelia **IV:**59

Brown, Olympia **VI:**51

female antislavery societies **IV:**148

Fourteenth Amendment **V:**157

Gage, Matilda Joslyn **VI:**137

Hooker, Isabella Beecher **VI:**176

marriage and family **IV:**240

Mott, Lucretia **IV:**266

NAWSA **VII:**223

NWSA **V:**277

Seneca Falls convention **IV:**341

Stone, Lucy **VI:**346

temperance movement **IV:**370

woman suffrage **VII:**384, 385

women's colleges **VI:**398

Women's National Loyal League **V:**434

women's status and rights **IV:**404; **V:**436, 437; **VI:**399

Woodhull, Victoria **VI:**401

World's Columbian Exposition **VI:**402

Stanton, Henry B. **IV:**396

Staper, Richard **I:**213

Staples Act **II:**3

Starbuck, Mary Coffin **II:**377

Stark, Harold R. **VIII:**265

Stark, John **VII:**158

Star of the West **V:**154

Starr, Ellen Gates

Addams, Jane **VII:**2

immigration **VI:**186

progressivism **VI:**294

settlement houses **VI:**327

Starr, Kenneth **X:**332–333, 380c, 382c

Clinton, Hillary Rodham **X:**77

Clinton, William J. **X:**82, 83

independent counsel **X:**179

Reno, Janet **X:**309

Starr, Ringo **IX:**37–38

star route frauds **VI:**343–344

Arthur, Chester Alan **VI:**21

corruption, political **VI:**84

Ingersoll, Robert Green **VI:**193

"Stars and Bars" **V:**31

"Stars and Stripes" **V:**31

Stars and Stripes (newspaper) **VIII:**233

Starship Troopers (Heinlein) **IX:**287

"Star Spangled Banner" (Francis Scott Key) **IV:**176, 213

"Star Spangled Banner" (Jimi Hendrix rendition) **IX:**230, 259

Star Spangled Banner, Order of the **IV:**214

START. *See* Strategic Arms Reduction Treaty

Star Trek (TV series) **IX:**287

starvation **V:**11, 148

Star Wars (film) **X:**235, 279, 377c

"Star Wars" program. *See* Strategic Defense Initiative

Stassen, Harold **X:**50

State, U.S. Department of

Albright, Madeleine K. **X:**22

Clinton, Hillary Rodham **X:**79

Haig, Alexander M., Jr. **X:**163

Hiss, Alger **IX:**146, 147

Kennan, George F. **IX:**167

Kissinger, Henry A. **IX:**198

McCarthy, Joseph R. **IX:**206

military-industrial complex **IX:**216

Powell, Colin L. **X:**286, 287

Rice, Condoleezza **X:**309–310

State Board of Charities (Kansas) **VI:**220

state college system **V:**269

State Department, Confederate **V:**33

State Department, U.S.

anti-Semitism **VIII:**25

Berle, Adolf A., Jr. **VIII:**43

Buchanan, James **V:**47

FCC **VIII:**131

foreign policy **VI:**133

Holocaust **VIII:**170

immigration **VIII:**184

Interior, Department of **IV:**201

investments, foreign **VII:**152

Jefferson, Thomas **III:**233

Jews **VIII:**196

Lilienthal, David E. **VIII:**217

Madison, James **III:**284

Marshall, John **III:**290

Randolph, Edmund **III:**358

Washington, D.C. **V:**425

Zimmermann telegram **VII:**401

Zionism **VIII:**441

state governors

Bush, George W. **X:**54

Carter, James Earl, Jr. **X:**68

Clinton, William J. **X:**79–80

Dukakis, Michael S. **X:**105

Reagan, Ronald W. **X:**299

women's status and rights **X:**371

statehood **VI:**410c

Amendments to the U.S. Constitution **X:**23

Blount, William **III:**53

Constitution, United States **III:**107

Northwest Ordinances **III:**321–322

state/local government. *See* government (state and local)

"Statement of a Proper Military Policy for the United States"

armed forces **VII:**20

National Defense Act **VII:**227

Preparedness **VII:**267

Statement on Fundamentals of American Foreign Policy **VIII:**449c

Staten Island **II:**264

Greene, Nathanael **III:**198

Long Island, Battle of **III:**271

Morristown encampment **III:**307

Sullivan, John **III:**402

State of the Union Address (Ford, 1975) **X:**104

State of the Union Address (G. W. Bush, 2002) **X:**56

State of the Union Address (G. W. Bush, 2004) **X:**56

State of the Union address (Truman, 1949) **IX:**115

state sovereignty

Bill of Rights **III:**50–51

Constitutional Convention **III:**109

federalism **X:**130–131

Federalist Papers **III:**163

Jay, John **III:**230

states' rights **III:397–398**, 463c;
  IV:412c, 413c; **V:370–371;**
  IX:353c. See also nullification;
  Nullification Controversy
    anti-Federalists **III:**23–24
    Aroostook War **IV:**27
    Baker v. Carr **IX:**33
    Bank of the United States,
      First **III:**41
    Brown, Joseph Emerson
      V:45
    Calhoun, John C. **IV:**69, 70
    civil liberties, Confederate
      V:68
    Civil Rights Act (1964)
      IX:61
    Civil War **V:**72
    common soldier **V:**77
    Compromise of 1850
      IV:103, 104
    Confederate States of
      America **V:**85–87
    Congress, Confederate **V:**88
    conscription **V:**91
    Davis, Jefferson **V:**103
    Democratic Party **IV:**117,
      119; **V:**108
    education, federal aid to
      VI:110
    election of 1828 **IV:**137
    election of 1840 **IV:**137
    elections **V:**126, 127
    Federalist Papers **III:**163
    fire-eaters **V:**145, 146
    Gadsden Purchase **IV:**173
    governors **V:**172
    Hancock, Winfield Scott
      V:183
    Harlan, John Marshall
      VI:159
    Hartford Convention
      IV:186
    Henry, Patrick **III:**211
    impeachment of Andrew
      Johnson **V:**202
    Jackson, Andrew **IV:**206
    Johnson, Andrew **V:**212
    Lamar, Mirabeau B. **IV:**221
    Letcher, John **V:**232
    lost cause, the **V:**244, 245
    Madison, James **III:**284
    Marshall, John **III:**291
    Martin, Luther **III:**291
    McCulloch v. Maryland
      IV:246
    Memminger, Christopher
      G. **V:**259
    modern Republicanism
      IX:221
    Otis, Harrison Gray **III:**326
    peace movements **V:**296
    personal liberty laws **IV:**299
    Pickering, Timothy **III:**334
    Pierce, Franklin **V:**307
    polygamy **IV:**303
    Randolph, John **III:**358–
      359

Reconstruction Acts **V:**328
secession **V:**344
slavery **IV:**345, 346
Stephens, Alexander
  Hamilton **V:**371
Submerged Lands Act
  (1953) **IX:**305
Supreme Court **VIII:**382
Taney, Roger B. **IV:**366
Taylor, John, of Caroline
  III:408
Toombs, Robert A. **V:**389
Tyler, John **IV:**382, 383
Vallandigham, Clement L.
  V:413
Van Buren, Martin **IV:**385
Virginia and Kentucky
  Resolutions **III:**424
Webster, Daniel **IV:**393
Welles, Gideon **V:**428
Whigs **IV:**397
Wigfall, Louis T. **V:**431
Wise, Henry A. **V:**434
State's Rights Party (Dixiecrats)
  IX:299–300, 352c
    Americans for Democratic
      Action **IX:**14
    Democratic Party **IX:**85
    elections **IX:**102
    liberalism **IX:**191
    Thurmond, James Strom
      X:351
Statue of Liberty **VI:**344, **344–
  345**, 410c
    Lazarus, Emma **VI:**219–220
    newspapers **VI:**266
    yellow journalism **VI:**405
Status Seekers, The (Packard)
  IX:253
"Statute of Religious Freedom"
  (Jefferson) **III:**363
Steagall, Henry **VIII:**41
stealth aircraft **X:**101
steamboat(s) **III:**465c
    agriculture **IV:**12
    Eads, James Buchanan
      VI:103
    economy **IV:**130
    Exodusters **VI:**123
    Fulton, Robert **III:**182, 183
    immigration **IV:**194;
      VI:185–186
    industrialization **IV:**200
    internal improvements
      IV:202
    merchant marine **VI:**245
    Mexican-American War
      IV:252–253
    migration **IV:**254
    Mississippi River **V:**262
    National Road **IV:**271
    science and technology
      III:385; **IV:**333; **V:**342
    transportation **V:**390
    Vanderbilt, Cornelius
      IV:386–387
Steamboat Act **V:**390

Steamboat Willie (film) **IX:**88
steam locomotives **IV:**333
steam power/steam engine
    Carnegie, Andrew **VI:**62
    Coeur d'Alene miners' strike
      VI:77
    science, invention and
      technology **IV:**333;
      VI:195–196
Stearns, Abel **IV:356**
Stearns, George L. **V:**142
steel **VI:345**
    Bessemer process **VI:**34–
      35
    bridges **VI:**47, 48
    foreign policy **VI:**133
    Frick, Henry Clay **VI:**135,
      136
    industrialization **IV:**199–200
    Industrial Revolution,
      Second **VI:**191, 192
    invention and technology
      VI:196
    merchant marine **VI:**245
    Morgan, John Pierpont
      VI:251
    New South **VI:**265
    Robber Barons, The **VI:**315
    skyscrapers **VI:**333
    trade, domestic and foreign
      VI:360
    trusts **VI:**365
Steel, Danielle **X:**212
Steele, Frederick **V:**265
Steele, Valerie **IX:**116
steel-frame construction **VII:**19
steel industry **VII:336–338**, 403c,
  407c; **VIII:373–374**, 445c;
  IX:300–301, 352c
    automobile industry **VIII:**37
    business **VIII:**45; **VIII:**57
    CIO **VIII:**82; **IX:**72
    Communists **VIII:**78
    economy **VIII:**104
    Great Migration **VII:**129
    labor/labor movements
      VIII:206, 207
    Lewis, John L. **VIII:**213
    mobilization **VIII:**241
    Murray, Philip **VIII:**249
    New Unionism **VII:**237
    recession of 1937–1938
      VIII:324
    scrap drives **VIII:**354
    Sunbelt **VIII:**381
    War Production Board
      VIII:414
    welfare capitalism **VII:**381
    workers' compensation
      VII:391
Steel Strike of 1919 **VII:**338,
  338–339
    AFL **VII:**12
    Committee for Public
      Information **VII:**60
    Coolidge, Calvin John
      VII:64

Foster, William Zebulon
  VII:117
labor/labor movements
  VII:171
New Unionism **VII:**238
open shop movement
  VII:247
steel industry **VII:**337
U.S. Steel **VII:**366
Vorse, Mary Heaton
  VII:375
Steel Workers Organizing
  Committee (SWOC)
    CIO **VIII:**82
    labor/labor movements
      VIII:206
    Murray, Philip **VIII:**249
    steel industry **VIII:**373,
      374
    strikes **VIII:**377
    U.S. Steel **VII:**366
Steffens, Lincoln **VII:339**, 403c
    Johnson, Tom Loftin
      VII:156
    journalism **VII:**159
    muckrakers **VII:**217
    NAACP **VII:**224
    progressivism **VII:**271
    Tarbell, Ida Minerva
      VII:349
Steichen, Edward **VII:**258;
  VIII:296
Stein, Gertrude
    literature **VII:**179; **IX:**192
    Lost Generation **VII:**185
    modernism **VII:**212
Steinbeck, John **VIII:374–375**,
  446c
    dust bowl **VIII:**98
    literature **VIII:**218, 219;
      IX:192
    marriage and family
      VIII:230
    migration **VIII:**239
    movies **VIII:**245
    popular culture **VIII:**301
Steinem, Gloria **X:333–335**
    Friedan, Betty **IX:**127
    NOW **X:**247
    women's status and rights
      IX:348
Steinfels, Peter **X:**251
Steinmetz, Charles **VII:**123
stelae **I:**278
stem cell research **X:335–336**,
  383c
    Bush, George W. **X:**56
    Clinton, William J. **X:**80
    Human Genome Project
      X:172
    medicine **X:**224
Stenberg v. Carhart **X:**382c
    Ginsburg, Ruth Bader
      X:152
    Rehnquist, William H.
      X:305
    Souter, David **X:**324

Stengstacke, John **IX:**13
Stennis, John **IX:**219; **X:**95
Stephens, Alexander Hamilton **V:371–372**
    civil liberties, Confederate **V:**69
    Civil War **V:**73
    Confederate States of America **V:**84–86
    Congress, Confederate **V:**88
    Davis, Jefferson **V:**104
    elections **V:**127
    homespun **V:**194
    Johnson, Andrew **V:**212
    Kansas-Nebraska Act **V:**222
    Watson, Thomas Edward **VII:**380
Stephens, Ann Sophia **VI:**98
Stephens, George E. **V:**143
Stephens, John Lloyd
    Copán **I:**90
    exploration **IV:**146
    Maya **I:**234
Stephens, John W. **V:**223
Stephens, Thomas **II:**146
Stephens, Uriah **VI:**209, 287
Stephens, William (colonial governor of Georgia) **II:**278
Stephens, William D. (governor of California) **VII:**213
Stephenson, Benjamin F. **VI:**151
Stephenson, David **VII:**166–167
Stepto, Robert **X:**26
Steptoe, E. W. **IX:**220
stereotypes
    Banneker, Benjamin **III:**43
    dime novels **VI:**98
    Loyalists **III:**275
    NACW **VI:**259
    popular culture **VIII:**302
sterilization **VII:**409c
    disease/epidemics **V:**112
    eugenics **VII:**103
    medicine **V:**256
Sterilization Act **VII:**284
steroids **X:**330, 384c
Stettheimer, Florine **VII:**24
Stettinus, Edward, Jr. **VIII:**211; **IX:**302
Stetzle, Charles **VII:**297
Steuben, Frederick, baron von **III:398, 398–399,** 461c
    Continental army **III:**111
    Lafayette, marquis de **III:**253
    Valley Forge **III:**423
Steunenberg, Frank **VII:**70, 137
Stevens, Alzina P. **VI:**12
Stevens, David **VI:**4
Stevens, Edwin A. **IV:**316
Stevens, John (railway engineer) **IV:**313
Stevens, John L. (minister to Hawaiian Islands) **IV:**187; **VI:**163

Stevens, John Paul (Supreme Court justice)
    gun control **X:**162
    Hamdan v. Rumsfeld **X:**164
    Kelo v. City of New London **X:**195
    Supreme Court **X:**338
Stevens, Nettie **VII:**314
Stevens, Robert (anthrax victim) **X:**383c
Stevens, Robert Livingston **IV:**316, 333
Stevens, Thaddeus **V:372–373,** 446c
    impeachment of Andrew Johnson **V:**201
    Radical Republicans **V:**320
    Reconstruction **V:**324
    Republican Party **V:**334
    Sumner, Charles **V:**377
    Whigs **V:**397
Stevens, Thomas **VI:**35
Stevens Institute of Technology **VII:**350
Stevenson, Adlai E., II *IX:301,* **301–302,** 353c, 354c
    computers **IX:**70
    Democratic Party **IX:**85
    Eisenhower, Dwight D. **IX:**100
    elections **IX:**103
    Free Speech Movement **IX:**125
    Hersey, John R. **VIII:**164
    Nixon, Richard M. **X:**256
    Republican Party **IX:**274
    Roosevelt, Eleanor **VIII:**344
Stevenson, Adlai E., III **X:**29
Stevenson, Carter L. **V:**63, 243
Steward, Theophilus G. **VI:**351
Steward v. Davis **VIII:**364
Stewart, Alexander (British military officer) **III:**159, 160
Stewart, Alexander H. (department store merchant) **VI:**96
Stewart, Alexander P. (Confederate general) **V:**34
Stewart, James W. **IV:**356
Stewart, Jimmy **VIII:**246, *247;* **IX:**224
Stewart, Maria **IV:356–357**
Stewart, Potter
    Baker v. Carr **IX:**33
    Engel v. Vitale **IX:**108
    Escobedo v. Illinois **IX:**111
    Warren Court **IX:**337
Stewart, William **VI:**146
STFU. *See* Southern Tenant Farmers Union
Stickney, Trumbull **VI:**226
Stieglitz, Alfred **VII:**404c
    art **VII:**24, 25; **VIII:**30
    literature **VII:**179
    photography **VII:**258–259; **VIII:**296

Stiles, John R. **X:**138
Still, William **IV:357; V:**397; **VI:**159
Stilwell, Joseph W. **VIII:**435
Stimson, Henry Lewis *VIII:358,* **375**
    armed forces **VII:**20
    Army, U.S. **VIII:**25
    Executive Order 9066 **VIII:**121
    foreign policy **VIII:**140
    Hoover presidency **VIII:**175
    Manchuria **VIII:**225
    Marshall, George C. **VIII:**233
    National Defense Act **VII:**227
    Reciprocal Trade Agreements Act **VIII:**325
    Republican Party **VIII:**338
    Zimmermann telegram **VII:**401
Stimson Doctrine **VIII:**140, 225, 443c
stockades **V:**141
Stockbridge Indians **III:**312–313
stock car racing **X:**331, 332
stock market **II:**379
    business **X:**58, 59
    Douglas, William O. **VIII:**96
    Duer, William **III:**141
    economy **X:**109–111
    elections, presidential **X:**118
    Forrestal, James V. **VIII:**143
    SEC **VIII:**356–357
stock market crash (1929) **VIII:376–377,** 443c
    African Americans **VIII:**3
    Banking Act (1933) **VIII:**40
    economy **VIII:**103
    FCA **VIII:**125
    foreign policy **VIII:**140
    Great Depression **VIII:**156–158
    Hoover, Herbert C. **VIII:**172
    investments, foreign **VII:**152
    literature **VIII:**218
    movies **VIII:**245
    politics (Roosevelt era) **VIII:**298
    popular culture **VIII:**301
    SEC **VIII:**356
stock market manipulation **X:**58–59
stocks
    Comstock Lode **IV:**105–106
    Crédit Mobilier **V:**97
    gold **IV:**178
Stockton, California **IV:**267
Stockton, Robert Field **IV:357–358**
    Bidwell, John **IV:**56
    California **IV:**71

Frémont, John C. **IV:**167
    Kearny, Stephen Watts **IV:**212
Stockyards Labor Council **VII:**117
Stoddard, Richard Henry **VI:**225
Stoddard, Solomon **II:**228, 320
Stoddert, Benjamin **III:**353
Stokes, Carl **X:**296
Stokowski, Leopold **VI:**96
Stone, Barton Warren **IV:**78, 319
Stone, Charles P. **V:**215, 426
Stone, Harlan Fiske **VIII:**447c
    court-packing plan **VIII:**89
    Hughes, Charles Evans **VII:**142
    Supreme Court **VIII:**382, 383
Stone, Kate **V:**319, 330
Stone, Lucy **IV:**414c; **VI:345–346**
    Anthony, Susan B. **VI:**16
    Blackwell, Antoinette Brown **VI:**39
    Brown, Olympia **VI:**51
    Harper, Frances Ellen Watkins **VI:**160
    Higginson, Thomas Wentworth **VI:**171, 172
    Mitchell, Maria **VI:**248
    NAWSA **VII:**223
    NWSA **V:**277
    woman suffrage **VII:**384
    Women's National Loyal League **V:**434
    women's status and rights **V:**437; **VI:**399
    World's Columbian Exposition **VI:**402
Stone, Oliver **X:**35
Stone, William **II:**220
stone carving **I:**89, 90
Stone City, Iowa (Wood) **VIII:**31
Stoneites **IV:**319
Stoneman, George **V:**61, 76
Stone Mountain, Georgia
    KKK **IX:**179
    Ku Klux Klan **VII:**165
    monuments **V:**268
Stonewall, CSS **V:**49, 207
Stonewall Riot **X:**148, 322, 375c
Stoney Point, Battle of **III:399,** 433
Stono Rebellion **II:377–378,** 437c
    African Americans **II:**8
    agriculture **II:**13
    crowd actions **II:**87
    Fort Mose **II:**132
    slave resistance **II:**353
    slavery **II:**357
    South Carolina **II:**370
STOP ERA movement
    conservative movement **X:**93
    ERA **X:**124
    feminism **X:**133–134
    Schlafly, Phyllis **X:**317

Storm in the Rocky Mountains, Mt. Rosalie (Bierstadt) **VI**:37
Story, Joseph **III:399**
    Marshall, John **III**:291
    Phillips, Wendell **IV**:299
    U.S. v. Libellants and Claimants of the Schooner Amistad **IV:434–438**
    Yazoo claims **III**:454
"Story of a Great Monopoly, The" (Lloyd) **VI**:227, 409*c*
Stoughton, Edwin H. **V**:271
Stover, Charles B. **VI**:327
stoves **VII**:123
Stowe, Harriet Beecher **IV**:415*c;* **V:373, 373–374**
    abolitionism **V**:3
    American Anti-Slavery Society **IV**:15–16
    Civil War **V**:73
    Hooker, Isabella Beecher **VI**:176
    Jackson, Helen Hunt **VI**:199
    Jewett, Sarah Orne **VI**:202
    literature **IV**:228, 229; **V**:239
    race and race relations **IV**:311
    religion **IV**:317
    theater **V**:387; **VI**:355
    Truth, Sojourner **V**:393
    Weld, Theodore Dwight **IV**:396
Stowe, John **I**:55
Strachan, Gordon **X**:357
Strachey, William **II**:143, 299
Straits of... *See under location, e.g.: Messina, Straits of*
Strang, James Jesse **IV:358**
"Strange Fruit" (Holiday) **VIII**:169
Strangites **IV**:358
Strasberg, Lee **IX**:222
Strasser, Adolph **VI**:150; **VII**:11
Strategic Arms Limitation Treaties (SALT I; SALT II) **X:336–337,** 376*c,* 377*c*
    ABM Treaty **X**:26, 27
    arms race **IX**:17; **X**:29, 30
    Carter, James Earl, Jr. **X**:69
    cold war, end of **X**:84, 85
    defense policy **X**:99, 100
    détente **X**:103–104
    foreign policy **X**:140–142
    Helms, Jesse A., Jr. **X**:165
    Moral Majority **X**:234
    Nixon, Richard M. **X**:257
Strategic Arms Reduction Treaty (START)
    cold war, end of **X**:86
    INF Treaty **X**:180, 181
    Reagan, Ronald W. **X**:301
Strategic Defense Initiative (SDI) **X:337**
    ABM Treaty **X**:28
    cold war, end of **X**:85

defense policy **X**:101
    Reagan, Ronald W. **X**:301
strategy. *See* tactics and strategy
Stratemeyer, Edward **IX**:195
Stratford-upon-Avon **I**:333
Strathmore-at-Manhasset **VIII**:379
stratigraphy **VI**:379
Straus, Nathan **VI**:96
Strauss, Eduard **VI**:170
Strauss, Leo **X**:93, 252
Strauss, Levi **IV:358–359,** 359
Stravinsky, Igor **VII**:220; **VIII**:252
Strawberry Banke **II**:259, 260
"straw vote" survey **VIII**:312
Strayhorn, Billy **VIII**:112
Stray Leaves from Strange Literature (Hearn, ed.) **VI**:169
Streetcar Named Desire, A (Williams) **IX**:193, 351*c*
streetcars
    cities and urban life **VI**:71; **VII**:54–55
    electricity **VII**:92
    invention and technology **VI**:195; **VII**:149
    Jim Crow laws **VI**:203, 204
    Johnson, Tom Loftin **VII**:156
    socialism **VII**:327
    suburbanization/suburbs **VII**:340, 341
    transportation **V**:392
    transportation, urban **VI**:360
    urban reform **VII**:362–363
    urban transportation **VII**:363–364
Street v. New York **X**:135
"Strenuous Life" Speech (Roosevelt) **VII:411–415**
streptomycin
    medicine **IX**:211
    miracle drugs **IX**:218
    population trends **IX**:260
Stricker, John **IV**:43
Strickland, William **III**:29; **IV**:29–30
strict scrutiny **X**:159
Strike! (Vorse) **VII**:122
strikebreaking **VIII**:257; **X**:202, 378*c*
strikes. *See* labor: strikes and violence
Strike Up the Band (Gershwin) **VII**:124
Strong, Anna Louise **VII**:286
Strong, Caleb **III**:242
Strong, George **VIII**:283
Strong, George Templeton **V**:403, 411
Strong, Josiah **VI:346–347,** 347, 409*c*
    Darwinism and religion **VI**:93
    imperialism **VI**:188

religion **VI**:306, 307
    Social Darwinism **VI**:334
    Social Gospel **VI**:335
Strong, Theodore **III**:384
Strong, William L. **VII**:304
Strongbow, Richard **I**:10
Struggles of the Two Natures in Man (Barnard) **VI**:327
Strutt, Jedediah **III**:389
Stryker, Roy **VIII**:296
Stuart, Charles **IV**:395
Stuart, George H. **V**:408
Stuart, Gilbert **III**:32, **399–400,** 436, 464*c*
Stuart, Henry **I**:191
Stuart, J. E. B. **V:375–376,** 444*c*
    Antietam, Battle of **V**:13
    Chancellorsville, Battle of **V**:62
    Confederate army **V**:81
    Custer, George A. **V**:99
    Gettysburg, Battle of **V**:166, 168
    Hollywood Cemetery **V**:192
    Mosby, John Singleton **V**:270–271
    Sheridan, Philip H. **V**:353
Stuart, John (colonial Indian superintendent) **II:378–379;** **III**:126, 314
Stuart, John Todd (lawyer) **V**:235
Stuart, R. Douglas **VIII**:17
Stuart, Robert **IV**:18, 144
Stuart & Company **IV**:199
Stuart dynasty **II**:48, 240
student activism **IX**:125–126, 143–144, 356*c*
Student Nonviolent Coordinating Committee (SNCC) **IX:302– 303,** 354*c*–357*c*
    African Americans **IX**:5, 6
    Baker, Ella Josephine **IX**:32, 33
    Black Panthers **IX**:41
    Black Power **IX**:41
    Carmichael, Stokely **IX**:49, 50
    CORE **IX**:73, 74
    freedom rides **IX**:123, 124
    Hamer, Fannie Lou **IX**:141
    Hayden, Tom **IX**:143
    Lewis, John **IX**:190
    March on Washington (1963) **IX**:201
    Meredith, James **IX**:213
    MFDP **IX**:219
    NAACP **IX**:232
    race and race relations **IX**:270
    sit-ins **IX**:290, 291
    teenagers **IX**:315
    Voting Rights Act of 1965 **IX**:333
    women's status and rights **IX**:347
students **IX**:356*c*

Economic Opportunity Act (1964) **IX**:95
    education, higher **X**:111
    Jackson State protests **X**:192
    narcotics **X**:244
    New Left **IX**:243–244
    sit-ins **IX**:290–291
    USA PATRIOT Act **X**:359
Students for a Democratic Society (SDS) **IX:303–304,** 304, 355*c*
    "Chicago Eight" **X**:73
    counterculture **IX**:78
    Hayden, Tom **IX**:143, 144
    Mills, C. Wright **IX**:217
    New Left **IX**:243
    Port Huron Statement **IX**:260
    SANE **IX**:283
    Weathermen/Weather Underground **IX**:340, 341; **X**:367
    women's status and rights **IX**:347
Students for Democratic Action (SDA) **X**:233
Student War Loans Program **VIII**:107
Studies in the Psychology of Sex (Ellis) **VII**:95
Studs Lonigan (Farrell) **VIII**:188, 219
Sturges v. Crowninshield **III**:291
Sturgis, Samuel **V**:13
Stuyvesant, Peter **II**:379, **379– 380**
    Dutch-Indian Wars **II**:106
    New Amsterdam **II**:257, 258
    New Netherland **II**:265, 266
    New York **II**:270
    Pennsylvania **II**:285
Sublette, Andrew **IV**:35, 51
Sublette, Milton **IV**:266, 324
Sublette, William **IV:359**
    American Fur Company **IV**:18
    Astor, John Jacob **IV**:35
    Bridger, James **IV**:64
    Fort Laramie **IV**:156
    mountain men **IV**:266
    Rocky Mountain Fur Company **IV**:324
    Smith, Jedediah Strong **IV**:350
submarine(s) **VII**:406*c;* **VIII:378– 379,** 447*c;* **IX**:25, 353*c. See also* U-boats
    AEC **IX**:25
    Atlantic, Battle of the **VIII**:33
    Carter, James Earl, Jr. **X**:67
    convoys **VIII**:87
    foreign policy **VII**:115
    Fulton, Robert **III**:182, 183
    H.L. Hunley, CSS **V**:190–191

Mitchell, William (Billy)
VII:211
National Defense Act
VII:227
Navy, U.S. VIII:265
neutrality VII:236
OCD VIII:281
Pearl Harbor VIII:292
Philippine Sea, Battle of the
VIII:295
population trends VII:266
Preparedness VII:267
science and technology
V:342; VII:315
Selective Service Act
VII:321
technology IX:311
trade, domestic and foreign
VII:354
World War I VII:393
World War II Pacific theater
VIII:437
Zimmermann telegram
VII:401
Submarine Division 11 VIII:201
Submarine Division Three
VIII:201
submarine-launched ballistic
missiles (SLBMs) X:99–101
Submerged Lands Act (1953)
IX:305, 353c
subprime mortgages X:60, 111
subscription libraries II:288
subsidies VI:56–57
Subsistence Homestead Division,
Department of the Interior
VIII:338
subsistence systems I:186, 245
substitutes V:284, 401
"Subterranean Homesick Blues"
(Dylan) IX:341
subtreasury system VI:125–126
suburbanization IX:305–306,
306
automobile industry IX:26
cold war culture IX:64, 65
economy IX:97
Federal Housing
Administration IX:120
government, state/local
IX:137
marriage and family
IX:202
McDonald's IX:208
migration IX:215
National Outdoor
Recreation Review
Commission IX:237
shopping centers IX:290
theme parks IX:317
urban redevelopment
IX:326, 327
suburbs VII:339–341; VIII:379–
380
cities and urban life VII:55;
VIII:68
environment VIII:116

Federal Housing
Administration (FHA)
VIII:134
GI Bill of Rights VIII:150
housing VIII:177–178
migration VIII:239
population trends VIII:305
urban transportation
VII:364
World War II VIII:428
Subversive Activities Control
Board IX:158
subways VI:361; VII:363
Sudan I:347; X:382c, 383c
Africa X:15–17
Bush, George W. X:56
Darfur I:104
Islam I:189
Leo Africanus I:210
Timbuktu I:360
Sudentenland VIII:248
Suez Canal VIII:118
Suez crisis IX:306–307, 354c
Dulles, John Foster IX:91
elections IX:103
Israel IX:160
Middle East X:227
Soviet Union IX:295
Suffolk Resolves III:400, 460c
Continental Congress, First
III:113
Gage, Thomas III:187
Warren, Joseph III:427
suffrage II:380; III:400–401;
IV:359–360, 412c. See also
African-American suffrage;
woman suffrage
American Anti-Slavery
Society IV:16
Anthony, Susan B. VI:16
artisans III:35
Boston II:41
Chase, Samuel III:86
Chautauqua Institute VI:66
citizenship III:94, 95
class consciousness VI:74
Democratic Party IV:117
Deseret, State of IV:121
elections, conduct of
VI:113
Harper, Frances Ellen
Watkins VI:160
Hayes, Rutherford B.
VI:168
Hoar, George F. VI:173
Lease, Mary Elizabeth
Clyens VI:220
Leslie, Frank and Miriam
Florence Follin VI:222
Liberia VI:223
Lockwood, Belva Ann
Bennett McNall VI:229
Massachusetts II:223
New Hampshire II:260
New Netherland II:266
Seneca Falls convention
IV:342

tenants II:387
Virginia II:401
women's status and rights
III:447–448
Sufism I:136, 189, 347–348
sugar I:348–349
agriculture II:12; III:11
Bahía I:25, 26
black market VIII:46
Brazil I:35
Bridges, Harry VIII:53
Caribbean II:59
Hawaii VI:163
indentured servitude II:175
Jamaica I:191
Madeira I:222
Martinique I:232
mercantilism II:231
Montserrat I:251
Nevis I:263
New Spain I:269
OPA VIII:282
Ostend Manifesto V:289
plantations V:308, 309
Príncipe I:302
Puerto Rico I:306
rationing VIII:322
rum trade II:338
São Tomé I:328
Sherman Antitrust Act
VI:330
slavery I:338
Spanish colonies II:371
trade, domestic and foreign
VI:360
Sugar Act III:401–402, 459c
alcohol III:13
Bernard, Sir Francis III:49
Grenville, George III:200
Stamp Act III:395
Stamp Act Congress III:397
tariffs III:406
Vice-Admiralty Courts
III:424
West Indies III:436
Whately, Thomas III:437
Sugar Bowl VIII:371
sugarcane IV:111, 188–189
Sugar Trust VI:159, 364
suicide VIII:288
Suleiman I (Ottoman sultan)
I:349–350
Sullivan, Arthur VI:257
Sullivan, Ed IX:38; X:239
Sullivan, John (Continental Army
officer) III:461c
Brandywine, Battle of
III:62
Brant, Joseph III:63
Estaing, Charles-Henri
Theodat, comte d'
III:158
French Alliance III:178
Howe, Richard, Lord
III:214–215
Iroquois III:228
King, Rufus III:246

Red Jacket III:359
Rhode Island, Battle of
III:370
Sullivan, John (Continental army
officer) III:402
Sullivan, John L. (boxer) VI:44
boxing VI:44, 45
Johnson, Jack VII:154
Lloyd, Henry Demarest
VI:409c
Sullivan, Leonor K. X:123
Sullivan, Louis H. VI:347–348
art and architecture VI:18;
VII:19
Burnham, Daniel Hudson
VI:55
Eads, James Buchanan
VI:103
World's Columbian
Exposition VI:402
Sullivan Island, South Carolina
III:84
Sully, Thomas V:18
Sulsey, Joseph V:143
Sultana (vessel) IV:406
Sumanguru (West African ruler)
I:140, 350
"Summary View of the Rights of
British America, A" (Jefferson)
III:232
"Summer of Love" IX:78
Summer Olympics. See Olympics
Summer on the Lakes IV:169
"Summertime" (Gershwin) VII:125
Summit of the Americas X:206
Sumner, Charles V:376–378, 377,
443c
abolitionism V:4
amnesty, acts of V:9
Bierstadt, Albert VI:37
Bleeding Kansas V:37
Canada VI:61
Civil Rights Act (1875) V:71
Emancipation Proclamation
V:131
foreign policy V:151
Free-Soil Party IV:164
impeachment of Andrew
Johnson V:201
Langston, John Mercer
VI:219
presidency VI:290
Radical Republicans V:320
Reconstruction V:324
Republican Party V:334
Santo Domingo, proposed
annexation of VI:323
slavery V:363
Stevens, Thaddeus V:372
Turner, Henry McNeal
VI:366
Wade, Benjamin Franklin
V:421
Washington, Treaty of VI:385
Wilson, Henry V:433
Women's National Loyal
League V:435

Sumner, Edwin V. **V:**13
Sumner, William Graham
VI:348–349
James, William **VI:**200
literature **VII:**180
pragmatism **VI:**289
Social Darwinism **VI:**334
Sumpter Banner **IV:**109
sumptuary laws **II:**71, 72
Sumter, Thomas **III:**213
Sun, Temple of the **I:**283
Sun Also Rises, The (Hemingway)
VII:180, 185, 409*c*
Sunbelt **VIII:380–381; X:337–
338**
aircraft industry **VIII:**14
business **IX:**46
cities and urban life
VIII:68, 70; **IX:**55; **X:**75
economy **VIII:**104
migration **VIII:**240;
IX:215
mobilization **VIII:**241
population trends **VIII:**305
shipbuilding **VIII:**359
union movement **IX:**324
World War II **VIII:**428
World War II home front
VIII:432
Sunday, William Ashley, Jr. "Billy"
VII:299, *341*, **341–342**
*Sunday, Women Drying Their
Hair* (Sloan) **VII:**24
Sunday Morning in Virginia
(Homer) **VI:**174
Sunday School Magazine **IV:**321
Sunday school movement **IV:**321;
VI:327
Sundiata Keita (king of Mali)
I:350
Ghana **I:**140
Mali **I:**225, 226
Mansa Musa I **I:**228
sunnah **I:**188
Sunni Ali Ber (king of Songhai)
I:109, 342
Sunni Islam/Sunni Muslims
I:188; **X:**186–188, 249
Sun Records **IX:**263
sunset clause **X:**358, 359
"sunshine" rules **X:**169
Super Bowl **X:**344
supercomputers **X:**87
Superdome (New Orleans,
Louisiana) **X:**173, 384*c*
Superfund **X:**91
superheroes **VIII:**303
Superior, Lake
mining **VII:**209, 210
War of 1812 **IV:**391
Webster-Ashburton Treaty
IV:394
WFM **VII:**382
Superman **VIII:**303
Supermarine Spitfires (RAF)
VIII:53
superstitions **III:**341

Supplemental Security Income
(SSI) **VIII:**363, 365
Supplementum chronicarum
I:375
Supply Priorities and Allocation
Board (SPAB) **VIII:**267, 283
supply-side economics
Kemp, Jack F. **X:**196
Laffer curve **X:**204
Reaganomics **X:**302
Supremacy Clause **X:**130, 131
Supreme Allied Commander
Europe (SACEUR) **X:**163
Supreme Court, California **X:**158,
216
Supreme Court, Connecticut
X:195
Supreme Court, Delaware
III:373
Supreme Court, Florida **X:**117
Supreme Court, Massachusetts
marriage and family **X:**216
Story, Joseph **III:**399
writs of assistance **III:**448,
449
Supreme Court, New York
III:256
Supreme Court, Pennsylvania
III:60
Supreme Court, Tennessee (*John
Thomas Scopes v. The State*)
VII:434–440
Supreme Court, U.S. **III:402–
404,** 464*c*, 465*c*; **IV:360–363,**
411*c*–413*c*; **VI:349,** 408*c*–410*c*;
VII:342–344, 403*c*–409*c*;
VIII:381–384, *382*, *383*,
443*c*–446*c*, 448*c*; **IX:352*c*,**
353*c*, 355*c*–357*c*; **X:338–339,**
375*c*–382*c*
abortion **X:**2, 3, 5
Abscam **X:**5
advertising **X:**7
affirmative action **X:**9, 10
African Americans **VI:**7;
VIII:2, 3
Agricultural Adjustment Act
VIII:6
Agricultural Adjustment
Administration **VIII:**7
agriculture **VIII:**9; **IX:**7–8
*Akron v. Akron Center for
Reproductive Health*
X:20–21
Amendment, Eleventh
III:16
Amendments to the U.S.
Constitution **X:**23
Amistad incident **IV:**22,
434–438
antimonopoly **VIII:**24
Asian Americans **VIII:**32
Baker v. Carr **IX:**33–34
Bakke case **X:**40–41
Bilingual Education Act
X:42
Bill of Rights **III:**51

birth control **X:**43
Black, Hugo L. **VIII:**45
Bork, Robert **X:**45
Brandeis, Louis Dembitz
VII:41–42
Brennan, William J., Jr. **X:**47
Breyer, Stephen **X:**48
*Brown v. Board of
Education* **IX:**43–44
Buck's Stove **VII:**42–43
Buck v. Bell **VII:**43
Burger, Warren E. **X:**50
Bush, George W. **X:**55
Byrnes, James F. **VIII:**60
campaign finance **X:**63, 64
capital punishment **X:**66, 67
censorship **VIII:**65; **X:**71
Chase, Samuel **III:**85
child labor **VII:**52–53
citizenship **III:**93
civil liberties **III:**57
Civil Rights Act (1991) **X:**77
Civil Rights Cases **VI:**72
Clinton, William J. **X:**82
coal industry **VIII:**75
Compromise of 1850
IV:103
Congress **VI:**79, 80
Conkling, Roscoe **VI:**81
conservatism **VIII:**84
Constitution, United States
III:107
corporations **III:**121
court-packing plan **VIII:**89
currency issue **VI:**89
Danbury Hatters **VII:**69
Dartmouth College case
IV:114
Dennis v. U.S. **IX:**86
Douglas, William O.
VIII:96–97
Dred Scott decision **V:**116–
118
due process clause **VI:**100–
101
education **VI:**108
EEOC **IX:**110
Eisenhower, Dwight D.
IX:101
elections, presidential
X:117–118
Engel v. Vitale **IX:**107–108
Equal Access Act **X:**122
ERA **X:**124
Escobedo v. Illinois **IX:**111
Executive Order 9066
VIII:121
Fair Labor Standards Act
VIII:124
Faubus, Orval **IX:**117–118
Federal Employee Loyalty
Program **IX:**119
federal income tax **VII:**106
federalism **X:**131
Federalist Papers **III:**163
Federalist Party **III:**164,
165

birth control **X:**43
feminism **X:**132, 133
Field, Stephen Johnson
VI:126
flag burning **X:**135, 136
Food, Drug, and Cosmetic
Act **VIII:**140
Foraker Act **VII:**110
Fortas, Abe **X:**145
Fourteenth Amendment
V:157
Frankfurter, Felix **VIII:**144
freedom rides **IX:**123
fugitive slave laws **IV:**168
gay and lesbian rights
movement **X:**149
gays and lesbians **IX:**131
Gideon v. Wainwright
IX:133–134
Ginsburg, Ruth Bader
X:152–153
government **VIII:**152, 154
Gramm-Rudman-Hollings
Act **X:**158–159
grandfather clause **VI:**152
*Gratz v. Bollinger/Grutter v.
Bollinger* **X:**158
*Griggs v. Duke Power
Company* **X:**160
Grove City College v. Bell
X:160
gun control **X:**161, 162
Hamdan v. Rumsfeld **X:**164
Harlan, John Marshall
VI:159
*Heart of Atlanta Motel v.
U.S.* **IX:**145–146
Henderson, Leon **VIII:**163
Hill, Anita Faye **X:**166
Hill, James J. **VI:**173
Holmes, Oliver Wendell
VII:140–141
Hughes, Charles Evans
VII:142
independent counsel
X:179
Internal Revenue taxes
VI:194
Internet **X:**182
Irish Americans **VIII:**188
Jay, John **III:**229–230
Jim Crow laws **VI:**203
Judiciary Act (1789)
III:242
Judiciary Act (1801)
III:242–243
Keating-Owen Act **VII:**163
Kelo v. City of New London
X:195
Korematsu v. U.S. **VIII:**203
Ku Klux Klan cases **VI:**210
labor/labor movements
VII:172; **VIII:**206
Lochner v. New York
VII:182–183
Lockwood, Belva Ann
Bennett McNall **VI:**228,
229

Lone Wolf v. Hitchcock
  VII:185
Mann Act **VII:**189
Marbury v. Madison
  III:285
marriage and family **X:**213
Marshall, John **III:**290, 291
Marshall, Thurgood **IX:**203
McCreary County v. ACLU/
  Van Orden v. Perry
  X:216
McCulloch v. Maryland
  IV:245
Meese, Edwin C., III **X:**225
Miranda v. Arizona **IX:**218–
  219
miscegenation **V:**261
Missouri Compromise
  IV:257
Mitchell, George **X:**232
Mitchell, John N. **X:**233
Mondale, Walter F. **X:**233
Muller v. Oregon **VII:**217–
  218, **417–420**
Murray, Pauli **IX:**227
NAACP **VIII:**256; **IX:**232;
  X:245
narcotics **X:**244
Native Americans **X:**250
NIRA **VIII:**257
Nixon, Richard M. **X:**257
NLRA **VIII:**257–258
Northern Securities Case
  VII:241, 242
O'Connor, Sandra Day
  X:264, 265
oil industry **VII:**244
PACs **X:**275
panic of 1819 **IV:**293
Patrons of Husbandry
  VI:279
Pentagon Papers **X:**272
Plessy v. Ferguson **VI:**284–
  285, **433–438**
political correctness **X:**275
politics (1900–1928)
  VII:261
pornography **X:**283, 284
Powell, Lewis **X:**288
presidency **VII:**268;
  VIII:308–309
Prohibition **VII:**273
pro-life/pro-choice
  movements **X:**289
property rights **X:**290
Pullman Strike **VI:**298
race and race relations
  IV:310; **X:**297
Reagan, Ronald W. **X:**300
Rehnquist, William H.
  X:304, 305
religion **IX:**273, 274; **X:**306,
  307
Republican Party **VII:**300
Reynolds v. Sims **IX:**276
RFRA **X:**307
RICO **X:**298, 299

Roberts, John G. **X:**311
Roe v. Wade **X:**311–312,
  387–390
Scalia, Antonin **X:**316
Schechter Poultry
  Corporation v. U.S.
  VIII:351
Schenck v. U.S. **VII:**313
science and technology
  X:317
Scopes Trial **VII:**317
Scottsboro Boys **VIII:**353
Sedition Act **VII:**319
segregation **VII:**319;
  IX:288
sexual revolution **X:**322
Sherman Antitrust Act
  VI:330
sit-ins **IX:**291
slavery **IV:**346
Smith Act **VIII:**362
Social Security Act
  VIII:364
Souter, David **X:**324
Southern Manifesto **IX:**294
Standard Oil **VII:**336
Story, Joseph **III:**399
Submerged Lands Act
  (1953) **IX:**305
Taft, Robert A. **VIII:**385
Taft, William Howard
  VII:347, 348
Taney, Roger B. **IV:**365, 366
Tarbell, Ida Minerva
  VII:349
taxation **VIII:**387–388
Tennessee Valley Authority
  VIII:392–393
Thomas, Clarence **X:**350
Trail of Tears **IV:**378
Twenty-sixth Amendment
  X:354
USA PATRIOT Act **X:**359
U.S. v. Cruikshank **V:**411
U.S. v. Nixon **X:**357–358
Warren, Earl **IX:**336–337
Warren Court **IX:**337–338
Washington, D.C. **III:**429
Watergate scandal **X:**367
Webster v. Reproductive
  Health Services **X:**368
White, Byron R. **X:**369
Wilson, James **III:**444–445
women's status and rights
  VI:399, 400; **X:**371
Yazoo claims **III:**454
Supreme Court, Vermont
  X:215–216
Supremes, the **IX:**229
Surgeon General **IX:**210; **X:**351
surgery **IV:**249; **V:**257; **VIII:**352;
  X:320
Suribachi, Mount (Iwo Jima)
  VIII:296
Surigao Strait **VIII:**214
Surplus Property Administration
  VIII:327

Surplus War Property
  Administration **VIII:**326
Surratt, John **V:**19
Surratt, Mary **V:**21
surveillance, electronic
  impeachment of Richard M.
    Nixon **X:**178
  Supreme Court **X:**338
  terrorism **X:**347
  USA PATRIOT Act **X:**359
surveillance powers **X:**358, 359
Susann, Jacqueline **X:**212
Susquehanna Coal Company
  VI:247
Susquehannah Company **III:**450
Susquehanna River **II:**332;
  III:311
Susquehannock Indians
  Conestoga **II:**74
  Iroquois **II:**178, 179
  Pennsylvania **II:**284
  Virginia **II:**400
Susquehannock War **II:**380
Sutherland, George **VIII:**89, 382
Sutro, Adolph **IV:**106
Sutter, John **IV:**363, **363–364**
  Bidwell, John **IV:**56
  California **IV:**71
  California gold rush **IV:**72
  California Trail **IV:**77
  Forty-niners **IV:**159
  gold **IV:**176, 178
  Hastings, Lansford W.
    IV:187
SUVs (sport utility vehicles) **X:**36
SVC (Special Verification
  Commission) **X:**180
Swaggart, Jimmy Lee **X:**234, 342
swamp fever **X:**405
Swan, Abraham **II:**25
"Swanee" (Gershwin) **VII:**124
Swank, James M. **VI:**228
Swann, Thomas **IV:**44
Swann v. Charlotte-Mecklenburg
  Board of Education **X:**51, 297,
  375c
Swanson, Gloria **VII:**97
Swanson and Sons **IX:**122
Swanson's TV dinners **IX:**122
Swarthmore College
  Henderson, Leon **VIII:**163
  Palmer, Alexander Mitchell
    VII:249
  Paul, Alice **VII:**254
Sweatt v. Painter **IX:**43, 203
Sweden **III:**257
Swedenborgians **VI:**309
Swedish colonies **II:**95, 212, **381**,
  381
Sweeney, John **X:**203, 204, 381c
Sweeny, Peter B. **VI:**369
Sweet, Ossian **VII:**344, 409c
Sweet Act **VII:**373
"Sweet Adeline" **VII:**218, 353
"Sweet By and By" (Webster and
  Bennett) **VI:**257
Sweet trial **VII:**70, **344–345**

Sweetwater (Laurence) **IX:**349
Sweetwater River
  Oregon Trail **IV:**285
  Smith, Jedediah Strong
    IV:350
  South Pass **IV:**354
Sweetwater Saber Club **VI:**358
Swift, Charles **X:**164
Swift, Gustavus F. **VI:**243; **VII:**45
Swift Boat Veterans for Truth
  campaign finance **X:**64
  elections, presidential **X:**118
  PACs **X:**275
Swift & Company **VII:**198
Swimming Hole, The (Eakins)
  VI:105
Swing Around the Circle **V:**213,
  328, **378**
Swing Era
  African Americans **VIII:**3
  big bands **VIII:**44
  Goodman, Benny **VIII:**151
  jazz **VIII:**195
  music **VIII:**250
  zoot-suiters **VIII:**442
Swing Landscape (Davis) **VIII:**31
Swiss immigrants **II:**154, 370
Switzerland
  Bodmer, Karl **IV:**60
  espionage **VIII:**118
  investments, American,
    abroad **VI:**197
  James, Henry **VI:**200
  OSS **VIII:**285
  V-J Day **VIII:**406
SWOC. *See* Steel Workers
  Organizing Committee
"'S Wonderful" (Gershwin)
  VII:124
Sword beach **VIII:**276
Sybil, HMS **III:**47
Sybil, The: A Review of the Tastes,
  Errors and Fashions of Society
  V:139
Sycamore Shoals, Treaty of **III:**87
Sydney, Australia **VII:**154, 333
Sykes, George **V:**51, 167
Syllabus of a Course of Lectures in
  Chemistry (Rush) **III:**375–376,
  460c
Syllabus of Errors (Pius IX) **IV:**319
Sylvis, William **V:**77, 276
Symphony Hall (Boston,
  Massachusetts) **VII:**219
Symphony No. 9 (*From the New*
  World) (Dvořák) **VI:**255
symphony orchestras **X:**238
synagogues **III:**236; **VI:**308
synchronicity **VI:**3
syndicalism **VII:**287
Synopsis of Birds of North
  America (Audubon) **IV:**38
syphilis **II:**97; **VIII:**444c; **X:**381c
  Columbian Exchange **I:**82
  disease/epidemics **I:**107
  Food, Drug, and Cosmetic
    Act **VIII:**140

syphilis *(continued)*
medicine **VIII:**236
prostitution **V:**316
public health **VII:**275
Syracuse, New York **IV:**163
Syracuse University **VI:**85, 244
Syria **X:**383*c*
Camp David accords **X:**65
cold war, end of **X:**84
Israel **IX:**160
Jackson, Jesse, L. **X:**192
Middle East **X:**227
Systematic Treatise on the Principal Diseases of the Interior Valley of North America (Drake) **IV:**249
Systemic Geology (King) **VI:**208
System of Doctrines (Hopkins) **III:**317
System of Surgery: Pathological, Diagnostic, Therapeutic, and Operative (Gross) **IV:**249
System of Universal History in Perspective, A (Willard) **IV:**401
System of World Geography, A (Willard) **IV:**401
Szilard, Leo **VIII:**226; **IX:**250

T

Tabascan Indians **I:**95
Tabasco **I:351**
Aguilar, Gerónimo de **I:**5
Grijalva, Juan de **I:**145
Malinche **I:**226
Olmecs **I:**277
tabloid TV **X:**343
tabula rasa **III:**110
tactics and strategy **V:379–382,** 380
Cairo Conference **VIII:**61
Civil War **V:**74
Dahlgren, John A. B. **V:**101
Jackson, Thomas J. "Stonewall" **V:**209
Jomini, Antoine-Henri, baron de **V:**216–217
Lincoln, Abraham **V:**236, 237
Longstreet, James **V:**242
Mallory, Stephen R. **V:**247
Marshall, George C. **VIII:**233
McClellan, George Brinton **V:**251
Richmond, Virginia **V:**336
science and technology **V:**340
Union army **V:**403
Union navy **V:**405
Vicksburg campaign **V:**416, 417
Tacuba **I:**22, 190, **352**
Tadadaho **I:**186

Tadoussac **I:**287; **II:**135–136, 140
Taft, Alfonso **VI:**396
Taft, Robert A. **VIII:385**
Burger, Warren E. **X:**50
conservatism **VIII:**85
Dewey, Thomas E. **IX:**87
election of 1940 **VIII:**110
Employment Act of 1946 **IX:**106, 107
ERA **X:**123
liberalism **IX:**191
Republican Party **VIII:**337; **IX:**274
Taft, William Howard **VII:347–348,** *348*, 405*c*
Army Act **VII:**22
Big Stick diplomacy **VII:**34–35
Budget and Accounting Act **VII:**44
business **VII:**46
Cannon, Joseph Gurney **VII:**48
Children's Bureau **VII:**53
Congress **VII:**62
criminal justice **VII:**67
Democratic Party **VII:**74
dollar diplomacy **VII:**79
elections **VII:**91
Federal Trade Commission Act **VII:**108
foreign policy **VII:**114
Hughes, Charles Evans **VII:**142
Industrial Relations Commission **VII:**145
labor/labor movements **VII:**172
Mann-Elkins Act **VII:**190
New Freedom **VII:**236
NWLB **VII:**229
Payne-Aldrich Tariff Act **VII:**255
Philippine independence **IX:**256
Pinchot, Gifford **VII:**260
presidency **VII:**268
Progressive Party **VII:**269–270
progressivism **VII:**271
radicalism **VII:**288
Republican Party **VII:**300
Roosevelt, Theodore **VII:**304
Stimson, Henry L. **VIII:**375
tariffs **VII:**349
Taft-Hartley Act (1947) **IX:309,** 351*c*
AFL **IX:**11
CIO **IX:**72
Fair Deal **IX:**115
Gallup Poll **IX:**130
labor/labor movements **VIII:**207, 208; **IX:**182
Lewis, John L. **VIII:**213
NLRB **VIII:**259

Progressive Party **IX:**264
strikes **VIII:**378
Taft, Robert A. **VIII:**385
Teamsters Union **IX:**310
UMWA **VIII:**402
union movement **IX:**323
Tahiti **IV:**400
ta'ifa **I:**348
Tailoresses' Society **IV:**218
tailors **V:**374
Taino **I:352–353; II:**58
Arawak **I:**11
cacique **I:**49
Carib **I:**60
Cuba **I:**100
Hispaniola **I:**162–163
Jamaica **I:**191
Nevis **I:**263
Puerto Rico **I:**305
smallpox **I:**341
Taiwan. *See* China, Republic of
"Take the A Train" (Strayhorn) **VIII:**112
Talbot v. Seeman **III:**290
Talcott Street Congregational Church **IV:**129
Talese, Gay **IX:**166
Taliaferro, Lawrence **V:**116
Taliaferro, William **V:**51
Taliban **X:**383*c*
Afghanistan War **X:**10–12
Bush, George W. **X:**55, 56
foreign policy **X:**143
Middle East **X:**229
terrorism **X:**347
Taliwa, Battle of **II:**408
talk radio **X:**220
talk shows (TV) **X:**343
Talks to Teachers on Psychology (James) **VI:**200–201
Tallapoosa River **IV:**190
Talleyrand-Périgord, Charles-Maurice de, prince de Bénévent **III:**194, **405,** 451
Tallmadge, James **IV:**256, 365
Tallmadge Amendment **IV:**256–257, **365, 423**
Talmadge, Eugene **VII:**332
Talmud **I:**195
Tamaulipas, Mexico **IV:**343
Tammany Hall
Cleveland, Grover **VI:**74
corruption, political **VI:**83–84
Democratic Party **VI:**95
Ethical Culture movement **VI:**121
Farley, James A. **VIII:**125
immigration **V:**200; **VI:**186
La Guardia, Fiorello **VIII:**208
machine politics **VI:**234
Plunkitt, George Washington **VI:**285
Sickles, Daniel E. **V:**360
Smith, Alfred E. **VII:**326, 327

Triangle Shirtwaist Fire **VII:**356
Tweed Ring **VI:**369
Wagner, Robert F. **VIII:**410
Tammany Society **III:405–406,** 462*c*
Tampico, Mexico **IV:**233; **VII:**114
Tan, Amy **X:**211
Tandy Corporation **X:**87
Taney, Roger Brooke **IV:365–366,** 413*c*
Amistad incident **IV:**22
banking **IV:**46
civil liberties, Union **V:**69
Cooper Union speech **V:**94
Dred Scott decision **V:**117
Field, Stephen Johnson **VI:**126
Lincoln, Abraham **V:**236
Republican Party **IV:**323
Supreme Court **IV:**361, 362
TANF (Temporary Aid to Needy Families) **VIII:**365
Tanger **I:**160
Tanguay, Eva **VI:**117
tanks **VIII:385–386**
Army, U.S. **VIII:**26
automobile industry **VIII:**37
blitzkrieg **VIII:**47
Higgins, Andrew J. **VIII:**165
Lend-Lease **VIII:**212
scrap drives **VIII:**354
Tanner, Benjamin Tucker **VI:**223, **351–352,** 366
Tanner, Henry O. **VI:**7, 275
Tanner, James **VI:**161
Tanzania embassy bombings. *See* embassy bombings
Taoism **IV:**319
Taos, New Mexico
counterculture **IX:**79
exploration **IV:**144
Greenwich Village **VII:**131
St. Vrain, Céran **IV:**327–328
Taos Indians **IV:**52, 55
Tappan, Arthur and Lewis **IV:366–367**
abolitionism **IV:**3; **V:**3
American Anti-Slavery Society **IV:**15
American Missionary Association **V:**8
Amistad incident **IV:**21
Weld, Theodore Dwight **IV:**395
Tappan, Henry **VI:**391
"Taps" **V:**273
tar **II:**212
Tarantino, Quentin **X:**279
Taranto, Italy **VIII:**191
Tarascan **I:**267, **353**
Tarawa **VIII:386**
amphibious warfare **VIII:**20
Marines, U.S. **VIII:**230
World War II Pacific theater **VIII:**436

Tarbell, Ida Minerva **VII:349,**
404*c*
environment **VII:**99
journalism **VII:**159
muckrakers **VII:**217
oil industry **VII:**244
progressivism **VII:**271
Rockefeller, John Davison
VII:303
Steffens, Lincoln **VII:**339
tariff(s) **III:406,** *406;* **IV:**414*c;*
V:382–383, 444*c;* **VI:352–353,**
410*c*–412*c;* **VII:349–350,** 405*c,*
406*c*
American System **IV:**19–20
Arthur, Chester Alan **VI:**21
Atkinson, Edward **VI:**22
Bryan, William Jennings
VI:51
business and government
VI:56
Calhoun, John C. **IV:**68, 69
Carey, Mathew **III:**80
Chautauqua Institute **VI:**66
class consciousness **VI:**74
Clay, Henry **IV:**96, 97
Cleveland, Grover **VI:**74,
75
Congress **VI:**80; **VII:**62
Congress, Confederate
V:88
corruption, political **VI:**83
Democratic Party **IV:**118;
V:108–109; **VI:**95
Drayton, William H. **IV:**127
economy **IV:**132; **V:**121,
122; **VII:**83, 85
election of 1828 **IV:**137
elections **VII:**91
foreign policy **VII:**116
Grant, Ulysses S. **V:**175
Greeley, Horace **V:**176
Hanna, Marcus Alonzo
VI:158
Harding, Warren Gamaliel
VII:134
Hawaii **VI:**163
industrialization **IV:**200
Industrial Revolution
III:225
Industrial Revolution,
Second **VI:**190–191
investments, American,
abroad **VI:**197
investments, foreign
VII:152
Jackson, Andrew **IV:**206
Liberal Republican Party
VI:222
lobbying **VI:**228
McKinley, William **VI:**240,
241
mugwumps **VI:**252
New Freedom **VII:**236
Nullification Controversy
IV:282–283
Omaha platform **VI:**272

Open Door Policy **VII:**246
Oregon Treaty of 1846
IV:287
panic of 1819 **IV:**294
Payne-Aldrich Tariff Act
VII:255
Polk, James K. **IV:**302
presidential campaigns
(1870–1899) **VI:**293
Progressive Party **VII:**269–
270
Republican Party **V:**333;
VI:311; **VII:**299, 300
secession **V:**344
Sedition Act **VII:**318
Stevens, Thaddeus **V:**372
taxation **V:**383–384
Taylor, Zachary **IV:**368
Tyler, John **V:**382, 383
Underwood-Simmons Tariff
VII:359
veterans **VII:**371
Watterson, Henry **VI:**386
Webster, Daniel **IV:**393
Wilson, Thomas Woodrow
VII:383
Tariff Act (1828) (Tariff of
Abominations) **IV:**412*c*
American System **IV:**20
Calhoun, John C. **IV:**69
Democratic Party **V:**108
election of 1828 **IV:**137
Nullification Controversy
IV:282
tariffs **V:**383
Tariff Act (1833) (Compromise
Tariff) **IV:**413*c*
American System **IV:**20
Clay, Henry **IV:**96
Drayton, William H. **IV:**127
Fillmore, Millard **IV:**149
Jackson, Andrew **IV:**207
Nullification Controversy
IV:283
tariffs **V:**383
Whigs **IV:**397
Tariff Act (1789) **III:**406
Tariff Act (1824) **IV:**294, 412*c*
Tariff Act (1832) **IV:**282, 413*c*
Tariff Act (1842) **IV:**149
Tariff Act (1857) **V:**294
Tariff Act (1930). *See* Hawley-
Smoot Tariff
tariffs **VIII:**443*c,* 444*c;* **X:**377*c,*
379*c*
Agricultural Adjustment Act
VIII:5
Bretton Woods Conference
VIII:52
Congress **VIII:**79
economy **X:**110
GATT **X:**150–151
Good Neighbor policy
VIII:151
Great Depression **VIII:**157
Hawley-Smoot Tariff Act
VIII:162–163

Hoover presidency
VIII:173
Hull, Cordell **VIII:**180
London Economic
Conference **VIII:**221
Mexico **X:**226
Reciprocal Trade
Agreements Act
VIII:324, 325
Ta'rikh al-Sudan (al-Sa'di) **I:**360
Tarleton, Banastre **III:406–407,**
462*c*
Charleston, siege of **III:**84
Cornwallis, Charles, Lord
III:120
Cowpens, Battle of **III:**124
Greene, Nathanael **III:**199
Jefferson, Thomas **III:**232
Morgan, Daniel **III:**303
Revolutionary War **III:**368
TARP (Troubled Assets Relief
Program) **X:**37
Tarrentines **II:**140
tarring and feathering **III:**371,
440
Tascaluza **I:**221
Task Force on National Health
Care Reform **X:**77
Taskigi, Tennessee **IV:**342
task system (slavery) **II:**13, 333
Tassafaronga, Battle of **VIII:**366
taverns and inns **II:383–384;**
III:407–408
alcohol **III:**13
cities and urban life **III:**91
journalism **III:**240
music **III:**309
popular culture **II:**341
postal service **II:**304
recreation **VIII:**328
travel **II:**393, 394
Tawiscaron **I:**1
taxation **III:**459*c,* 464*c;* **V:383–
384; VI:**409*c,* 411*c;* **VIII:386–
389,** 447*c. See also* income tax,
federal
Acts of Trade and Navigation
II:3
Adams, Samuel **III:**7
Anti-Imperialist League
VI:17
antimonopoly **VIII:**24
Articles of Confederation
III:34
banking **V:**27
Baptists **III:**44
Bernard, Sir Francis **III:**49
Bryan, William Jennings
VI:51
Carroll of Carrollton,
Charles **III:**82
Confederate States of
America **V:**86
Congress **V:**89; **VIII:**79
Congress, Confederate
V:88
conservatism **VIII:**84

Continental Congress, First
III:115
corruption, political **VI:**84
Cuffe, Paul **III:**127
debt, national **III:**131–132
Declaratory Act **III:**134
Democratic-Republican
Party **III:**136
Dulany, Daniel **III:**142
economy **V:**121–123;
VIII:104; **X:**109, 110
education **V:**124
education, primary/
secondary **X:**113
elections **V:**126
federalism **X:**131
Federalists **III:**165
Frankfurter, Felix **VIII:**144
Fries's Rebellion **III:**180
George, Henry **VI:**142
government **VIII:**154
Grenville, George **III:**200–
201
Hamilton, Alexander
III:206–207
Hull, Cordell **VIII:**180
Internal Revenue taxes
VI:194
Keynesianism **VIII:**201
Kieft, Willem **II:**192
Laffer curve **X:**204
Libertarian Party **X:**209
Mason, George **III:**292
mobilization **VIII:**242
New Deal **VIII:**269
NIRA **VIII:**257
Omaha platform **VI:**272
Parsons' Cause **II:**281–282
political parties, third
VI:286
Quasi War **III:**353
Reagan, Ronald W. **X:**300
recession of 1937–1938
VIII:324
Revenue Act of 1935
VIII:340
Revenue Act of 1942
VIII:340–341
Shays's Rebellion **III:**388
Simpson, Jerry **VI:**330
Social Security Act
VIII:456
Spanish colonies **II:**373
Stamp Act **III:**395–396
Stamp Act Congress **III:**397
states' rights **III:**397; **V:**370
Sugar Act **III:**401–402
Supreme Court **VI:**348
tariffs **III:**406; **V:**382
Townshend Duties **III:**412–
413
Virginia Resolves **III:**425
Wallace, Henry A. **VIII:**411
Whately, Thomas **III:**437
Whiskey Rebellion **III:**439–
440
Whiskey Ring **V:**429

taxation (*continued*)
Williams, George
Washington **VI:**396
World War II home front
VIII:433, 434
Taxation: The People's Business
(Mellon) **VII:**201
tax cuts
Bush, George W. **X:**56
Clinton, Hillary Rodham
X:78
economy **X:**109, 110
Laffer curve **X:**204
tax-in-kind **V:**122, 384
tax reform **X:**196
Tax Reform Act (1986) **X:**232,
379*c*
Tayasal kingdom **I:**235
Taylor, Bayard **VI:**284
Taylor, Charles H. J. **VI:**223
Taylor, Fiddlin' Bob **VII:**332
Taylor, Frederick Winslow
VII:350–351, 405*c*
business **VII:**45–46
economy **VII:**84
Ford, Henry **VII:**111
Industrial Revolution,
Second **VI:**191
invention and technology
VII:150
IWW **VII:**146
labor trends **VI:**216
mass production **VII:**194
scientific management
VII:315–316
steel industry **VII:**337
Taylor, Glen **IX:**263
Taylor, Graham **VII:**330
Taylor, John, of Caroline **III:**282,
339, **408**
Taylor, Major **VI:**35
Taylor, Nathaniel W. **III:**362;
IV:318
Taylor, Paul S. **VIII:**296
Taylor, Richard
Banks, Nathaniel P. **V:**29
cartography **V:**57
Milliken's Bend, Battle of
V:260
Red River campaign **V:**329
Taylor, Sarah Knox **V:**103
Taylor, Susie King **V:**285, **384–
385**
Taylor, Tom **VI:**202
Taylor, Zachary **IV:**367, **367–368,**
414*c*, 415*c*
Bowles, Samuel **VI:**42
Buell, Don C. **V:**48
Cass, Lewis **IV:**83
Clayton-Bulwer Treaty **IV:**98
Colt, Samuel **IV:**101
Compromise of 1850
IV:104
Davis, Jefferson **V:**103
Deseret, State of **IV:**120
Fillmore, Millard **IV:**149,
150

Free-Soil Party **IV:**163
Guadalupe Hidalgo, Treaty
of **IV:**181
immigration **IV:**196
Lamar, Mirabeau B. **IV:**222
Marsh, George Perkins
VI:239
Mexican-American War
IV:251, 252
Native Americans in the War
of 1812 **IV:**276
Pemberton, John C. **V:**297
Red River campaign **V:**329
Santa Anna, Antonio López
de **IV:**330
Scott, Winfield **IV:**336
Seminole War, First/Second
IV:339
Whigs **IV:**397
Taylor Amendment **IV:423–424**
Taylorism **IV:**318–319
tea **II:**79
alcohol **III:**13
China trade **III:**88, 89
Coercive Acts **III:**100
Tea Act **III:408–409,** 460*c*
American Revolution **III:**18
Boston Tea Party **III:**58
Burke, Edmund **III:**69
cities and urban life **III:**90
Coercive Acts **III:**100
committees of
correspondence **III:**101
Franklin, Benjamin **III:**173
North, Frederick, Lord
III:320
Old South Church **III:**324
resistance movement
III:365, 366
Teach, Edward **II:**39, 296,
384–385
teachers **X:**114
Team Drivers International Union
IX:310
teamsters **VIII:**377
Teamsters National Union **IX:**310
Teamsters Union **IX:***310*, **310–
311,** 354*c*, 356*c*
AFL **IX:**12
labor/labor movements
X:201, 203
Reuther, Walter **IX:**275
UFW **IX:**325
union movement **IX:**323
Teapot Dome **VII:351–352,**
408*c*
Harding, Warren Gamaliel
VII:135
Native Americans **VII:**233
Supreme Court **VIII:**381
Veterans Bureau **VII:**373
"tear down this wall" speech
(Remarks at the Brandenburg
Gate) (Reagan) **X:396–399**
Tebbell, John **X:**219
technical schools **X:**111
technical workers **X:**203

technology. *See* science, invention
and technology
technology transfer **X:**301
Tecumseh **III:409–410,** 465*c*,
466*c*; **IV:**411*c*
Black Hawk War **IV:**56
Cherokee **III:**87
Choctaw **IV:**86
Creek **III:**126; **IV:**109
Dragging Canoe **III:**140
foreign policy **IV:**154
Ghent, Treaty of **IV:**176
Greenville, Treaty of
III:199
Harrison, William Henry
IV:185
Hull, William **IV:**192
McIntosh, William **IV:**247
migration **IV:**253
Native Americans **III:**314,
315; **IV:**273, 274
Native Americans in the War
of 1812 **IV:**276, 277
Prophet, the Shawnee
III:348, 349
Pushmataha **IV:**307
Sac and Fox **IV:**327
Thames, Battle of the
IV:375
Tippecanoe, Battle of
III:411, 412
War of 1812 **IV:**390
Tedder, Arthur **VIII:**360
Teedyuscung **II:386**
teenagers **IX:314–315**
birthrates **X:**44
children **VIII:**67
fashion **IX:**116–117
Job Corps **IX:**161
marriage and family
VIII:231, 232
recreation **VIII:**329
rock and roll **IX:**278–279
tobacco suits **X:**352, 353
teen pregnancy **X:**13
teetotal movement **IV:**370
Teflon **IX:**91
Teheran, Iran **VIII:**390, 402
Teheran Conference **VIII:390–
391,** 448*c*
Anglo-American relations
VIII:21
Cairo Conference **VIII:**61
foreign policy **VIII:**142
Grand Alliance **VIII:**155
Harriman, W. Averell
VIII:162
Hopkins, Harry L.
VIII:177
Leahy, William D. **VIII:**211
Normandy, invasion of
VIII:275
Roosevelt, Franklin D.
VIII:346
second front **VIII:**355
Soviet-American relations
VIII:368

Soviet Union **IX:**295
World War II European
theater **VIII:**431
Yalta Conference **VIII:**439
Tehuantepec, Isthmus of **VI:**103
Tekakwitha, Kateri **II:**331, **386**
Téké **I:353**
Telecommunications Act (1996)
X:284, 319, 381*c*
telecommunications industry
VII:149, 405*c*
Telegraph Plateau **IV:**335
telegraphs **IV:**413*c*; **V:385–386,**
386, 443*c*
Balloon Corps **V:**25
Boxer Rebellion **VII:**40
business cycles **VI:**58
Carnegie, Andrew **VI:**62
Civil War **V:**74
communications **VI:**77, 78
economy **IV:**131
Edison, Thomas Alva
VI:107
foreign policy **IV:**158
immigration **VI:**185–186
industrialization **IV:**200
Industrial Revolution,
Second **VI:**191, 192
invention and technology
VII:151
journalism **IV:**209; **V:**217,
218
labor, woman **VI:**214
Lincoln, Abraham **V:**237
Mann-Elkins Act **VII:**190
Morse, Samuel F. B. **IV:**264–
265
Mosby, John Singleton
V:271
newspapers **VI:**267
New York City **V:**282
Preparedness **VII:**267
science and technology
IV:333; **V:**342, 343
tactics and strategy **V:**380
Washington, D.C. **V:**426
Telenet **X:**181
telephones **VI:**408*c*
Bell, Alexander Graham
VI:31
business cycles **VI:**58
communications **VI:**78
Edison, Thomas Alva
VI:107
FCC **VIII:**130, 131
Industrial Revolution,
Second **VI:**191
labor, woman **VI:**214
Mann-Elkins Act **VII:**190
newspapers **VI:**266–267
Philadelphia Centennial
Exposition **VI:**284
science, invention and
technology **VI:**196;
X:319
technology **VIII:**389
telegraph **V:**386

telescopes **VIII**:352
teleuhctin **I**:19
televangelism **X**:*341*, **341–342**
  conservative movement
    X:94
  media **X**:219
  Moral Majority **X**:234
  movies **X**:236
  religion **X**:306
television **IX**:315–317, *316*, 353c,
  355c; **X**:342–345, 343
  advertising **IX**:2; **X**:7
  affirmative action **X**:9
  Army-McCarthy hearings
    IX:18
  assassinations **IX**:22
  Beatles **IX**:37
  Buchanan, Patrick J. **X**:49
  censorship **X**:71
  childhood **IX**:55
  Christian Coalition **X**:73
  cities and urban life **IX**:56
  civil defense **IX**:56
  Clinton, William J. **X**:80
  cold war culture **IX**:64, 65
  computers **IX**:70
  conservation/
    environmentalism **X**:91
  consumerism **IX**:75
  credit cards **IX**:79
  Cuban missile crisis **IX**:81
  Disney, Walt **IX**:88
  Dow Chemical Corporation
    IX:90
  economy **IX**:97
  elections **IX**:103
  FCC **VIII**:131
  food **IX**:122
  Ford Motor Corporation
    IX:123
  GE **IX**:132
  GM **IX**:133
  Goldwater, Barry **IX**:136
  Graham, Billy **IX**:138
  gun control **X**:161
  Horton, Willie **X**:168
  House of Representatives
    X:169
  Internal Security Act (1950)
    IX:158
  Iraq War **X**:188
  Johnson, Lady Bird **IX**:162
  journalism **IX**:165
  Kennedy, John F. **IX**:169–
    171
  Life magazine **VIII**:217
  Malcolm X **IX**:199
  marriage and family **IX**:202
  McCarthy, Eugene **IX**:206
  McDonald's **IX**:208
  media **X**:217–218
  MFDP **IX**:220
  movies **IX**:223
  music **X**:239
  political parties **X**:278
  popular culture **IX**:258–
    259; **X**:278, 280

pornography **X**:283
Presley, Elvis **IX**:263
race and race relations
  X:297
recreation **IX**:271; **X**:302,
  303
religion **IX**:271, 273
Republican Party **IX**:274
science, invention and
  technology **VII**:151;
  IX:286; **X**:320
science fiction **IX**:287
SCLC **IX**:293
sexual revolution **X**:323
shopping centers **IX**:289–
  290
SNCC **IX**:302
sports and recreation
  IX:298; **X**:329, 330
suburbanization/suburbs
  IX:306
technology **IX**:313
teenagers **IX**:314
Vietnam War **IX**:331
Weathermen/Weather
  Underground **IX**:341
White Citizens' Councils
  IX:342
Teller, Edward
  hydrogen bomb **IX**:152
  Manhattan Project **VIII**:226
  SDI **X**:337
Teller Amendment (1898) **VI**:88
Tellico **II**:280
Tell My Horse (Hurston) **VIII**:181
"Tell-Tale Heart, The" (Poe)
  IV:229
temperance movement **III**:**410,**
  465c; **IV**:369–370
  anti-Masonry **IV**:25
  Bloomer, Amelia **IV**:59
  Brown, William Wells **V**:46
  Democratic Party **IV**:118
  entertainment, popular
    VI:116, 117
  Finney, Charles Grandison
    IV:151
  Harper, Frances Ellen
    Watkins **VI**:160
  Herndon, William H. **V**:187
  Higginson, Thomas
    Wentworth **VI**:171
  Johnson, Hiram Warren
    VII:154
  Langston, John Mercer
    VI:218
  Lovejoy, Elijah **IV**:230
  Maine Law **IV**:233–234
  Mann, Horace **IV**:237
  Mott, Lucretia **IV**:265
  Owen, Robert **IV**:291
  progressivism **VI**:294
  Prohibition Party **VI**:295–
    296
  religion **IV**:317
  Weems, "Parson" Mason
    Locke **III**:435

Willard, Frances **VI**:393–
  394
women's status and rights
  IV:404; **V**:436
Tempest, The **I**:353–354
Temple, Shirley **VIII**:67, 245,
  444c
Temple of Music (Pan-American
  exhibition, Buffalo, New York)
  VII:252
Temple School (Boston) **IV**:169;
  VI:279
Temporary Aid to Needy Families
  (TANF) **VIII**:365
Temporary Emergency Relief
  Administration **VIII**:133, 176
Temporary National Economic
  Committee (TNEC) **VIII**:391–
  392
  antimonopoly **VIII**:24
  Henderson, Leon **VIII**:163
  New Deal **VIII**:270
  recession of 1937–1938
    VIII:324
Temptations, the **IX**:229
tenant farmers **VIII**:445c
  Communists **VIII**:78
  marriage and family
    VIII:230
  South **VIII**:366, 367
  STFU **VIII**:367–368
tenants **II**:**386–387**
  crowd actions **II**:86
  Rensselaerswyck **II**:331
  society, British American
    II:366
  Virginia Company of
    London **II**:402, 403
Ten Articles of Faith **I**:75
Ten Commandments, public
  display of **X**:216
Ten Days That Shook the World
  (Reed) **VII**:296, 297
Tender Land, The (Copland)
  IX:228
Tenement House Commission
  VI:121
Tenement House Law (1901)
  VI:121
tenements **VI**:294, 390
Tennent, Gilbert **II**:387, **387–
  388**
  Frelinghuysen, Theodorus
    Jacobus **II**:135
  Osborn, Sarah Haggar
    Wheaten **II**:279
  religion **III**:360
Tennent, William, Jr. **II**:388
Tennent, William, Sr. **II**:155,
  388–389; III:386
Tennessee **II**:66; **V**:445c
  African Americans **III**:9
  agriculture **V**:6
  Alamo, The **IV**:14
  Appalachia **IX**:15
  Blount, William **III**:53
  Chickasaw **IV**:86

Civil Rights Cases **VI**:72
Claiborne, William C. C.
  IV:94
Cody, William Frederick
  VI:76
Confederate army **V**:82
Corinth, Battle of **V**:95
Crockett, Davy **IV**:110–111
Dow, Lorenzo **IV**:126
Dragging Canoe **III**:140
education, higher **VI**:111
Exodusters **VI**:123
Forrest, Nathan Bedford
  V:152
Fort Stanwix, Treaty of
  III:170
Franklin, state of **III**:175
Houston, Sam **IV**:190
Jackson, Andrew **IV**:205
Jim Crow laws **VI**:204
Johnson, Andrew **V**:212
Johnston, Joseph E. **V**:214
KKK **IX**:179
Ku Klux Klan **V**:223
Lookout Mountain, Battle
  of **V**:243
Mexican-American War
  IV:251
migration **IV**:253, 254
Morgan, John Hunt **V**:268
Native Americans **III**:314
Native Americans in the War
  of 1812 **IV**:277
New Orleans, Battle of
  IV:280–281
panic of 1819 **IV**:293
Polk, James K. **IV**:301
railroads **IV**:314
Scopes Trial **VII**:316–317
Second Great Awakening
  IV:337
Shiloh, Battle of **V**:358–360
Singleton, Benjamin **V**:361
sit-ins **IX**:291
slave trade, internal **IV**:349
southern demagogues
  VII:332
Sunbelt **VIII**:381
tactics and strategy **V**:381
temperance movement
  IV:369
United Daughters of the
  Confederacy **V**:407
Vanderbilt, Cornelius
  IV:387
violence and lawlessness
  VI:375
Wright, Fanny **IV**:405
Tennessee Coal, Iron, & Railroad
  Company **VI**:251
Tennessee River Valley **VIII**:10,
  392–393
Tennessee Valley Authority (TVA)
  VIII:*392,* **392–393,** 444c
  agriculture **VIII**:10
  Black, Hugo L. **VIII**:45
  conservatism **VIII**:84

Tennessee Valley Authority
(*continued*)
    environment **VIII**:116
    Fair Deal **IX**:115
    Hull, Cordell **VIII**:180
    Lilienthal, David E.
        VIII:217
    New Deal **VIII**:270
    Norris, George W. **VIII**:276
    REA **VIII**:349–350
    South **VIII**:366
    Willkie, Wendell L.
        VIII:417
tennis **VI**:342; **VII**:295; **VIII**:372;
    X:302
Tennyson, Alfred, Lord **I**:145;
    VI:203
Tenochtitlán **I**:354–356, 355*m*,
    397*c*
    Alvarado, Pedro de **I**:7
    Aztecs **I**:18, 19, 21, 22
    Aztlán **I**:23
    chinampas **I**:73
    Codex Aubin **I**:410
    Codex Mendoza **I**:77
    Columbian Exchange **I**:82
    Cortés, Hernán **I**:96
    Cuitláhuac **I**:101
    Huitzilopochtli **I**:171
    Mexico **I**:242
    New Spain **I**:267
    Quetzalcoatl **I**:309
    Sandoval, Gonzalo de **I**:325
    Tacuba **I**:352
    Tezcatlipoca **I**:357
    Tlacacla **I**:361
    Tláloc **I**:361
    Tlaxcala **I**:362
Ten Percent Plan **V**:9, 324, 325
Tensaw, Alabama **IV**:126
Tenskwatawa. *See* Prophet, the
    Shawnee
10th Air Force, U.S. **VIII**:27
Tenth Amendment
    Agricultural Adjustment
        Administration **VIII**:7
    anti-Federalists **III**:24
    Bill of Rights **III**:50–51
    federalism **X**:130
    gun control **X**:161
    Supreme Court **VIII**:382
"Tenting Tonight on the Old
    Campground" **V**:274
Tenure of Office Act **V**:446*c*
    impeachment of Andrew
        Johnson **V**:203
    Johnson, Andrew **V**:213
    Radical Republicans **V**:321
    Stanton, Edwin M. **V**:369
Ten Years' War **VI**:87–88
Teotihuacán **I**:356–357
    Aztecs **I**:21
    Maya **I**:234
    Monte Albán **I**:250
    Quetzalcoatl **I**:309
    Tikal **I**:358–359
    Tláloc **I**:361

Tepaneca **I**:189, 352
Terceristas **X**:254
Teresa of Ávila, Saint **I**:98
Tereshkova, Valentina **IX**:297
Termination policy **IX**:157, 240,
    241, 353*c*
term limits **X**:137, 381*c*
terms of office **VIII**:444*c*
Terrell, Mary Eliza Church **VI**:7;
    VII:225, 352, **352–353**
Terrill, Edwin **V**:317
Terrill, James **V**:43
Terrill, William **V**:43
terrorism **X**:345–349, 347, 348,
    379*c*, 383*c*
    Afghanistan War **X**:10
    Africa **X**:16
    Bush, George W. **X**:55, 56
    Clinton, William J. **X**:81,
        83
    defense policy **X**:101
    economy **X**:110
    foreign policy **X**:142, 143
    Hamdan v. Rumsfeld
        X:164
    House of Representatives
        X:170
    immigration **X**:177
    Iran-contra affair **X**:183
    Iraq War **X**:187
    Middle East **X**:229
    Oklahoma City bombing
        X:266–267
    Powell, Colin L. **X**:287
    Rice, Condoleezza **X**:309
    UN **X**:355–356
    USA PATRIOT Act **X**:358,
        359
    Weathermen/Weather
        Underground **X**:367–
        368
Terry, Alfred H.
    Custer, George A. **V**:99
    Little Bighorn, Battle of
        V:241
    Porter, David Dixon **V**:311
Terry, John **III**:385
Terry, Lucy **II**:206
Terry, Luther **IX**:266, 355*c*
Terry, USS **VIII**:201
Tertium Quid **III**:408
Tesla, Nikola **VI**:191, 194, 196,
    353, **353–354**, 410*c*, 411*c*
Tesla Electric Company **VI**:353
Testem Benevolentiae **VI**:316;
    VII:298
test pilots **VIII**:419
test scores. *See* standardized
    testing
teteuhctin **I**:19–20
Tet Offensive (1968) **IX**:164, 332,
    357*c*
Tetzel, Johann **I**:218; **II**:101
Tew, Thomas **II**:296
Tewa Pueblo **I**:305
Tewksbury, John Walter **VI**:359
Texaco **VII**:245, 336

Texas **II**:61, 437*c*; **IV**:370–373,
    373, 413*c*, 414*c*; **VII**:403*c*,
    404*c*; **VIII**:448*c*
    Adams, John Quincy **IV**:6
    Adams-Onís Treaty **IV**:6,
        411*c*, **422–423**
    agriculture **IV**:10; **V**:6
    annexation of **IV**:438–439
    Armijo, Manuel **IV**:26
    Austin, Moses **IV**:38–39
    Austin, Stephen F. **IV**:39–41
    Bear Flag Revolt **IV**:49
    blues **VII**:39
    Bowie, James **IV**:62
    Branch Davidians **X**:46
    Brownsville Riot **VII**:42
    Bush, George W. **X**:54
    Cabet, Étienne **IV**:67
    Calhoun, John C. **IV**:69
    California Trail **IV**:77
    cattle kingdom **VI**:64
    cities and urban life **X**:75
    Clay, Henry **IV**:97
    Colt revolver **IV**:102
    Compromise of 1850
        IV:103
    cotton culture **IV**:106
    Crockett, Davy **IV**:110
    Democratic Party **IV**:118;
        V:109
    dust bowl **VIII**:97
    economy **IV**:130, 132
    election of 1840 **IV**:138
    farmers' alliances **VI**:125
    Fillmore, Millard **IV**:150
    foreign policy **IV**:154, 155;
        VII:115
    Free-Soil Party **IV**:163
    Galveston, Battle of **IV**:163
    Galveston flood **VI**:137–138
    Hispanic Americans **X**:167
    Houston, Sam **IV**:190–192
    immigration **IV**:193, 195
    IRCA **X**:177
    Johnson, Hugh S. **VIII**:196
    Johnson, Lady Bird **IX**:163
    Johnston, Albert Sidney
        V:213
    Jones, Jesse H. **VIII**:197
    Juneteenth **V**:219
    Ku Klux Klan **V**:223
    Lamar, Mirabeau B. **IV**:221
    La Raza Unida **IX**:183
    Latino movement **IX**:186
    Magoffin, James W. **IV**:233
    McCreary County v. ACLU/
        Van Orden v. Perry
        X:216
    medicine **X**:223
    Mexican-American War
        IV:251, 252
    Mexican immigration
        VII:203
    migration **IV**:254
    Mitchell, William (Billy)
        VII:212
    music **VIII**:250

New Spain, northern
    frontier of **III**:317, 318
oil **VI**:271
oil industry **VII**:245
Oregon Treaty of 1846
    IV:286
overland mail **IV**:290
Polk, James K. **IV**:301, 302
population trends **X**:283
race and race relations
    VIII:318
railroads **IV**:316
San Jacinto, Battle of
    IV:328
Santa Anna, Antonio López
    de **IV**:329
Santa Fe Trail **IV**:330
slave trade, internal **IV**:348,
    349
Submerged Lands Act
    (1953) **IX**:305
Sunbelt **VIII**:381
Taylor, Zachary **IV**:368
Texas Declaration of
    Independence **IV**:429–
    430
Travis, William Barret
    IV:379–380
Tyler, John **IV**:383
urban reform **VII**:362
veterans **V**:416
violence and lawlessness
    VI:376
Webster, Daniel **IV**:394
Whigs **IV**:397
Wigfall, Louis T. **V**:431
Zimmermann telegram
    VII:401
Texas, Republic of **IV**:413*c*
    Alamo, The **IV**:14
    Armijo, Manuel **IV**:26
    Austin, Stephen F. **IV**:40–
        41
    Florida **IV**:153
    foreign policy **IV**:155
    Houston, Sam **IV**:190
    Lamar, Mirabeau B. **IV**:221
    Larkin, Thomas Oliver
        IV:223
    Manifest Destiny **IV**:234
    Mexican-American War
        IV:251
    Polk, James K. **IV**:301
    San Jacinto, Battle of
        IV:328
    Santa Fe Trail **IV**:332
    Taylor, Zachary **IV**:368
    Texas **IV**:372
    Texas Revolution **IV**:375
    Tyler, John **IV**:383
Texas and New Mexico Act
    IV:446–447
Texas Brigade **V**:196
Texas Declaration of
    Independence **IV**:429–430
Texas Instruments **VIII**:58;
    IX:71

Texas & Pacific Railroad (T&P)
    Huntington, Collis Potter
        VI:181
    lobbying **VI:**228
    Scott, Thomas Alexander
        VI:326
Texas Rangers **IV:**102, 413*c;* **X:**54
Texas Revolution **IV:**329, **373–375**
    Austin, Stephen F. **IV:**40–41
    Bent's Fort **IV:**55
    Bowie, James **IV:**63
    California Trail **IV:**77
    election of 1840 **IV:**138
    foreign policy **IV:**155
    Houston, Sam **IV:**190
    Magoffin, James W. **IV:**233
    San Jacinto, Battle of
        IV:328
    Santa Anna, Antonio López
        de **IV:**330
    Santa Fe Trail **IV:**332
    Texas **IV:**372
    Travis, William Barret
        IV:380
Texas School Book Depository
    (Dallas) **IX:**22, 252
Texas v. Johnson **X:**379*c*
    Brennan, William J., Jr.
        X:48
    flag burning **X:**135–136
    Scalia, Antonin **X:**316
    White, Byron R. **X:**369
Texas Volunteers **IV:**222
Texcoco
    Aztecs **I:**18
    Cacamatzin **I:**47
    Itzcóatl **I:**190
    Tacuba **I:**352
    Tlaxcala **I:**362
Texcoco, Lake **I:**357
*Textbook of the Origin and
    History of Colored People*
    (Pennington) **V:**300
textbooks **X:**237
textile industry **III:**463*c;* **IV:***200;*
    VII:405*c,* 409*c*
    architecture **III:**29–30
    economy **III:**146
    fashion **V:**139
    indigo **II:**177
    industrialization **IV:**199
    Industrial Revolution
        III:225
    IWW **VII:**147
    Kongo **I:**200
    labor/labor movements
        II:199–200
    New South **VI:**265
    science and technology
        III:385
    Slater, Samuel **III:**389–390
    South **VIII:**366
    strikes **VIII:**377
    Sugar Act **III:**401
Textile Workers Organizing
    Committee **VIII:**166

Tezcatlipoca **I:357**
    Quetzalcoatl **I:**309
    Tláloc **I:**361
    Toltecs **I:**364
Tezozomoc **I:**18
Thadadaho **I:**162
Thailand **VIII:**435; **IX:**291, 292,
    353*c*
thalidomide **X:**222
Thames, Battle of the **IV:375–376**
    Cass, Lewis **IV:**83
    Ghent, Treaty of **IV:**176
    Harrison, William Henry
        IV:185
    Native Americans **IV:**274
    Native Americans in the War
        of 1812 **IV:**277
    Prophet, the Shawnee
        III:349
    Tecumseh **III:**409
    War of 1812 **IV:**391
Thanksgiving **IV:**184
"Thanksgiving Day Address"
    (Hosea) **IV:**129
Thanksgiving Day championship
    VI:131
Thatcher, Margaret **X:**301, 302
Thaw, Harry **VI:**392
Thayer, Abbott Handerson **VI:**19;
    VII:23
Thayer, Eli **IV:**241
Thayer, Martin **VI:**131
Thayer, Sylvanus **V:**409
Thea Nectar **VI:**65
theater **I:**333; **II:**389; **III:410–
    411,** *411,* 462*c;* **V:386–387;**
    VI:354–355, *355;* **VII:**408*c*
    African Americans **IX:**6
    Beaumarchais, Pierre-
        Auguste Caron de **III:**48
    cities and urban life **III:**91
    Civil Rights Act (1875)
        V:71
    Dunlap, William **III:**142
    entertainment, popular
        VI:116; **VII:**95–96
    Foster, Stephen C. **V:**156
    Gay Nineties **V:**140
    Gershwin, George **VII:**124
    Jefferson, Joseph, III
        VI:201–202
    music **III:**309–310; **V:**273;
        VI:257; **VII:**218–220;
        VIII:252
    NEA **IX:**234
    New York City **V:**282
    popular culture **III:**341;
        VII:263, 264; **IX:**258;
        X:278, 280–281
    recreation **VIII:**327
    Rowson, Susanna Haswell
        III:374
    sexual revolution **X:**322
    Sousa, John Philip **VI:**340
    Tin Pan Alley **VII:**353
    Tyler, Royall **III:**417

urban transportation
    VII:363
    vaudeville **VII:**368–369
    Victorianism **VI:**374
    Welles, Orson **VIII:**414
Theatre Owners Booking
    Association **VI:**117
theft **II:**84
Their Eyes Were Watching God
    (Hurston)
    African Americans **VIII:**3
    Hurston, Zora Neale
        VIII:181
    literature **VIII:**219
theme parks **IX:**88, 89, **317,** 319
Theobroma cacao **I:**47
theology **III:316–317**
Theology for the Social Gospel, A
    (Rauschenbusch) **VII:**293
*Theory and Practice of Landscape
    Gardening, The* (Downing)
    IV:31
Theosophical Society **VI:**309
Theosophy **VI:**309
Thermidorian reaction **III:**179
thermodynamics **VI:**144
thermonuclear bomb. *See*
    hydrogen bomb
These Are Our Lives (FWP)
    VIII:137
Theus, Jeremiah **II:389–390**
Thevet, André **I:357–358**
    Atahualpa **I:**16
    *Cosmographie Universelle,
        La* **I:413–418**
    French explorations of the
        Atlantic **I:**134
    tobacco **I:**363
    travel narratives **I:**369
    Tupinambá **I:**371
Thief of Bagdad, The (film)
    VII:97
Thieu, Nguyen Van **IX:**330
*Thinker, The: Portrait of Louis N.
    Kenton* (Eakins) **VII:**23
think tanks **X:349–350**
Thin Red Line, The (Jones)
    IX:193
3rd Infantry Regiment **IV:**36
3rd Virginia Infantry Regiment
    IV:258
Third Amendment **III:**51
Third Army, U.S. **VIII:**50–51, 55
Third Communist International
    VII:61, 407*c*
Third Fleet (U.S. Navy)
    Halsey, William F. **VIII:**161
    King, Ernest J. **VIII:**202
    Leyte Gulf, Battle for
        VIII:214
Third Man, The (film) **IX:**224
Third New Deal **VIII:393–394**
    Executive Reorganization
        Act **VIII:**121
    Full Employment Bill
        VIII:145
    liberalism **VIII:**215

New Deal **VIII:**270
    recession of 1937–1938
        VIII:324
    Second New Deal **VIII:**356
    TNEC **VIII:**391
third parties. *See* political parties,
    third
third-party candidates
    Buchanan, Patrick J. **X:**49
    elections, presidential
        X:116, 117
    Green Party **X:**159
    Libertarian Party **X:**209
    Nader, Ralph **X:**242
    Perot, H. Ross **X:**273
    political parties **X:**277, 278
    Reform Party **X:**304
    Wallace, George C. **X:**364
Third Provincial Council of Lima
    I:3
Third World
    CIA **IX:**52
    Kennan, George F. **IX:**167
    Weathermen/Weather
        Underground **IX:**341
13th Infantry Regiment **IV:**212
Thirteenth Amendment **V:387–
    388,** 445*c*
    abolitionism **IV:**4; **V:**4
    Civil Rights Act (1866) **V:**70
    Civil Rights Cases **VI:**72
    Civil War **V:**74
    Confiscation Acts **V:**88
    Constitution, United States
        III:106
    Douglass, Frederick **V:**116
    emancipation **V:**128, 129
    Fourteenth Amendment
        V:157
    Garrison, William Lloyd
        V:165
    Harlan, John Marshall
        VI:159
    *Heart of Atlanta Motel v.
        U.S.* **IX:**145, 146
    Johnson, Andrew **V:**212
    Lincoln, Abraham **V:**237
    Plessy v. Ferguson **VI:**284,
        285
    race and race relations
        V:320
    Reconstruction **V:**325
    Republican Party **V:**334
    slavery **V:**364
    women's status and rights
        VI:399
38th parallel
    Asia **IX:**21
    cold war **IX:**64
    communism **IX:**68
    Korean War **IX:**177
    MacArthur, Douglas
        IX:198
31st Infantry **VII:**324
Thirty-Nine Articles (England)
    I:120
33rd U.S. Colored Troops **V:**189

Thirty Years of Lynching in the United States (NAACP report) **VII**:224; **VIII**:22
Thirty Years View (Benton) **IV**:54
This Is the Army (musical) **VIII**:252
"This Land Is Your Land" (Guthrie) **VIII**:160, 252
Thom, Mel **IX**:241
Thomas, Augustus **VI**:355
Thomas, Cal **X**:74
Thomas, Clarence **X**:**350**, 380c
  African Americans **X**:14, 15
  gun control **X**:162
  Hill, Anita Faye **X**:166
  NAACP **X**:245
  Senate, U.S. **X**:321
  Supreme Court **X**:339
Thomas, Elman **VIII**:6
Thomas, Ernest **IX**:74
Thomas, George H. **V**:**388–389**
  Chattanooga, Battle of **V**:63
  Chickamauga, Battle of **V**:64, 65
  Hood, John Bell **V**:196
  Lookout Mountain, Battle of **V**:243
  Sherman's March through Georgia **V**:356
Thomas, Henry **IX**:123
Thomas, J. B. **IV**:257
Thomas, John **IV**:320, 365
Thomas, J. Parnell **IX**:147, 148, 150
Thomas, Lorenzo **V**:203
Thomas, M. Carey **VI**:**356**, 398
Thomas, Norman **VIII**:**394**
  Agricultural Adjustment Act **VIII**:6
  America First Committee **VIII**:17
  election of 1932 **VIII**:109
  election of 1936 **VIII**:109
  politics (Roosevelt era) **VIII**:298
  Reuther, Walter **VIII**:339
  socialists **VIII**:362
Thomas, Philip E. **IV**:44
Thomas, Theodore
  Beach, Amy Marcy Cheney **VI**:28
  MacDowell, Edward Alexander **VI**:233
  music **VI**:254
Thomas, Vivien **VIII**:234
Thomas Amendment **IV**:257, 365, **424**
Thomas Aquinas (saint)
  civil disobedience **IX**:57
  Dominicans **I**:110
  Jesuits **I**:193
Thomas Edison Laboratories **VII**:214
Thomas-Houston Electric Company **VI**:194, 196
Thomas Mellon and Sons **VII**:201
Thomas Proviso **IV**:257

Thomas Road Baptist Church, Lynchburg, Virginia **X**:234
Thompson, Benjamin **III**:384
Thompson, David **II**:259; **IV**:103
Thompson, Sir Eric **I**:351
Thompson, Frank **X**:5
Thompson, Jacob **V**:135
Thompson, James **IX**:111
Thompson, J. W. (construction contractor) **VII**:373
Thompson, J. Walter (advertising) **VI**:2; **VII**:4
Thompson, Tommy **X**:356
Thompson, Wiley **IV**:289
Thomson, Charles **III**:17
Thomson, Elihu **VI**:194
Thomson-Houston Electric Company **VI**:123
Thomson-Urrutia Treaty **VII**:406c
Thoreau, Henry David **IV**:376, **376–377**, 414c
  Alcott, Louisa May **VI**:10
  art and architecture **IV**:28
  civil disobedience **IX**:57
  "Civil Disobedience" **IV**:**443–446**
  environment **VI**:120; **VII**:98
  literature **IV**:228
  lyceum movement **IV**:232
  Peabody, Elizabeth Palmer **VI**:280
  religion **IV**:320
  transcendental movement **IV**:378
  Warren, Josiah **IV**:392
Thorn, Jonathan **IV**:35
Thornton, John **I**:337
Thorpe, Jim **VII**:333, 335
"Thoughts on African colonization" (Garrison) **IV**:17
Thoughts on Art (Emerson) **IV**:28–29
Thoughts on Government (Adams) **III**:5
"Thousand Points of Light" Speech (Bush) **X**:**399–403**
three-fifths clause
  antislavery **III**:26
  citizenship **III**:95
  Constitutional Convention **III**:109
  Fourteenth Amendment **V**:157
  Pickering, Timothy **III**:335
Three Henries, War of the **I**:158
332nd Fighter Group **VIII**:3–4
Three Little Pigs, The (film) **VIII**:247
Three Mile Island nuclear power plant **X**:377c
Three Soldiers (Dos Passos) **VII**:179, 180
"three strikes" policy **X**:97
Throckmorton, Elizabeth **I**:311
Thucydides **VII**:139
Thurman, A. G. **VI**:95

Thurmond, James Strom **IX**:352c; **X**:**350–351**
  Americans for Democratic Action **IX**:13, 14
  Democratic Party **IX**:85
  Dewey, Thomas E. **IX**:87
  elections **IX**:102, 103
  liberalism **IX**:191
  Republican Party **IX**:274
  States' Rights Party **IX**:299, 300
  White Citizens' Councils **IX**:342
Tianjin, China **VII**:40
Tibbles, Thomas Henry **VI**:48–49
Tidewater region
  plantation system **II**:297
  primogeniture and entail **II**:310
  slavery **II**:354, 355, 357–358
  Virginia **II**:401
Tiffany, Louis Comfort **VI**:**356–357**
  Aesthetic movement **VI**:3
  La Farge, John Frederick Lewis Joseph **VI**:218
  painting **VI**:276
Tiffany and Company
  Aesthetic movement **VI**:3
  art and architecture **VI**:19
  department stores **VI**:96
  Tiffany, Louis Comfort **VI**:356
Tiffany Foundation **VI**:357
Tiffany Studios **VI**:356, 357
Tiger Rifles **V**:245
Tiguex **I**:93
Tijerina, Reies López **IX**:136, 186, **317–318**
Tikal **I**:**358–359**
  Maya **I**:235–236
  Native American religion **I**:260
  Teotihuacán **I**:356
Tikas, Louis **VII**:187
Tikrit, Iraq **X**:187
Tilden, Samuel Jones **VI**:**357–358**, 408c
  Dana, Charles A. **VI**:92
  Democratic Party **V**:110; **VI**:95
  Hayes, Rutherford B. **VI**:167
  libraries, public **VI**:224
  presidential campaigns (1870–1899) **VI**:291
  Reconstruction **V**:326
  Reid, Whitelaw **VI**:305
  Tweed Ring **VI**:369
  Watterson, Henry **VI**:386
Till, Emmett Louis **IX**:166, 269, **318**
Tillman, Benjamin Ryan "Pitchfork Ben" **VI**:**358**; **VII**:332
Tilted Arc (Serra) **X**:31
Tilton, Elizabeth **VI**:30, 176

Tilton, Theodore
  Beecher, Henry Ward **VI**:30
  Beecher-Tilton scandal **VI**:30
  Woodhull, Victoria **VI**:401
timber
  National Park Service **VII**:228
  Native Americans **VII**:232
  Pinchot, Gifford **VII**:260
Timber and Stone Act **VI**:56, 119
Timber Culture Act **VI**:407c
Timberlake, Henry **II**:280
Timbuktu **I**:**359–360**
  Askia Muhammad I **I**:14
  Baba, Ahmad **I**:25
  Djenne-Djeno **I**:109
  Leo Africanus **I**:210
  Songhai **I**:342
  Tuareg **I**:370
time-and-motion studies **VII**:84.
  See also scientific management
Time Inc. **VIII**:217, 224
Time Machine, The (Wells) **IX**:287
Time magazine
  Chambers, Whittaker **IX**:52
  Evans, Walker **VIII**:120
  food **IX**:122
  Hersey, John R. **VIII**:164
  Levitt, William J. **IX**:190
  Luce, Henry R. **VIII**:224
  Malcolm X **IX**:199
  news media **VIII**:272
  Parks, Rosa **IX**:255
Times-Democrat, New Orleans **VI**:169
"Times They Are A-Changin'" (Dylan)
  Dylan, Bob **IX**:92
  music **IX**:229
  teenagers **IX**:314
Timucua Indians **I**:209, **360**
  Florida **II**:128
  Laudonnière, René de **I**:208
  Le Moyne, Jacques **I**:209–210
tin **VIII**:354
tindamba **I**:103
Tin Goose (Ford Trimotor) **VII**:29
Tinian
  Mariana Islands **VIII**:228, 229
  Marines, U.S. **VIII**:230
  Philippine Sea, Battle of the **VIII**:295
  World War II Pacific theater **VIII**:436
Tin Pan Alley **VII**:**353**
  entertainment, popular **VII**:95
  Gershwin, George **VII**:124
  Herbert, Victor August **VI**:170
  jazz **VII**:153
  music **VI**:257–258; **VII**:218, 220

Tintoretto, Jacobo **I:**313
Tipaldo case **VIII:**382
Tippecanoe, Battle of **III:411–412,** 466*c*
  frontier, the **III:**181, 182
  Harrison, William Henry **IV:**185
  Native Americans **III:**315; **IV:**274
  Native Americans in the War of 1812 **IV:**276, 277
  Prophet, the Shawnee **III:**349
  Tecumseh **III:**409
  Van Buren, Martin **IV:**386
  War of 1812 **IV:**390
"Tippecanoe and Tyler, Too" **IV:**186
Tippit, J. D. **IX:**252
Tip-Toes (Gershwin) **VII:**124
Tiran, Strait of **IX:**160
tires
  automobile industry **X:**37
  black market **VIII:**46
  OPA **VIII:**282
  rationing **VIII:**322
  rubber **VIII:**348
Titanic (film) **X:**279
Titanic, RMS **VII:**405*c*
Title V program **VIII:**67
Title VII (Civil Rights Act of 1964) **X:**9
Title VII (Education Amendments of 1972) **X:**112
Title IX (Education Amendments of 1972) **X:386–387**
  education, higher **X:**112
  Grove City College v. Bell **X:**160
  women's status and rights **X:**371
Title XVIII (Social Security Act) **IX:**210; **X:**222
Tito, Marshal (Josip Broz)
  Europe **IX:**113
  Kosovo **X:**199
  Soviet Union **IX:**295
  Truman Doctrine **IX:**321
Tituba **II:**281, **390,** 419
Titusville, Pennsylvania
  Industrial Revolution, Second **VI:**191
  oil **VI:**271
  oil industry **VII:**244
  Standard Oil **VII:**335
Tlacacla **I:361**
  Aztecs **I:**18
  flowery wars **I:**132
  Itzcóatl **I:**190
tlacohtin **I:**20
Tlacopan **I:**18
Tláloc **I:**171, 354, **361**
tlamacazcalli **I:**20
Tlatelolco **I:**18
Tlaxcala **I:361–363**
  Aztecs **I:**19
  Cholula **I:**74

Nahua **I:**257
Sandoval, Gonzalo de **I:**325
Xicotencatl the Elder **I:**387
tlepochcalli **I:**20
Tlingit
  Alaska **III:**12
  Northwest Coast Indians **II:**275
  Russian settlements **II:**339
TNCs. *See* transnational corporations
TNEC. *See* Temporary National Economic Committee
tobacco **I:**363, **363–364,** 397*c;* **II:390–392,** *391,* 435*c,* 436*c*
  Acts of Trade and Navigation **II:**3
  African Americans **VI:**7
  agriculture **II:**9, 11–13; **III:**10–11; **V:**6; **VI:**9
  Bermuda Company **I:**31
  Caribbean **II:**59
  Carter, Robert "King" **II:**60–61
  Chesapeake Bay **II:**66
  cotton culture **IV:**107
  Crow **II:**85
  crowd actions **II:**86
  Delaware **II:**96
  Drake, Sir Francis **I:**112
  Drake Manuscript **I:**113
  economy **II:**109
  environment **II:**120, 121; **III:**153, 155
  French explorations of the Atlantic **I:**134
  headright **I:**158
  indentured servitude **II:**175
  Indian Removal Act **IV:**198
  Iroquois **I:**185
  James I **I:**192
  Jamestown **II:**181–182
  labor/labor movements **II:**198
  Lane, Ralph **I:**203
  Maryland **II:**220
  Massachusett **I:**233
  Massachusetts **II:**225
  mercantilism **II:**231
  Mississippian **I:**245
  monarchy, British **II:**240
  Monardes, Nicholas **I:**247
  Natchez **I:**259
  Native American religion **I:**260
  New South **VI:**265
  Northwest Coast Indians **II:**275
  Opechancanough **II:**279
  Parsons' Cause **II:**281, 282
  plantations **V:**308
  plantation system **II:**297
  Rolfe, John **II:**334–335
  St. Mary's City **II:**342
  slavery **III:**390, 392; **IV:**347; **V:**363

society, British American **II:**365
  South **VIII:**366
  Spanish colonies **II:**371
  trade, domestic and foreign **II:**393
  Virginia **II:**399, 400
  Wyatt, Sir Francis **II:**427
tobacco advertising ban **X:**376*c*
Tobacco Inspection Act **II:**86
tobacco lawsuits **X:351–353,** *352,* 381*c*
Tobacco Road (Caldwell) **VIII:**219
Tobias, Sheila **X:**133
Tobin, Dan **IX:**310
Tocqueville, Alexis de **IV:**413*c*
  Brown, William Wells **V:**46
  medicine **IV:**248
  science and technology **IV:**335
Todd, Francis **V:**164
Todd, George **V:**317
Todd, John Payne **III:**280
Todd, Lawrence **VII:**286
Togo **I:**103
To Have and Have Not (Hemingway) **VIII:**220
Tohono O'odham **II:**176
Tohopeka, Alabama **IV:**190, 277–278
Tojo, Hideki **VIII:**226, 229
To Kill a Mockingbird (Lee) **IX:**194
Tokyo, Japan **VI:**272–273
Tokyo Bay, Japan **IV:**298; **VII:**130
Tokyo bombing raids (March 9–10, 1945) **VIII:**48, 167
Tokyo Rose **VIII:**311
Tokyo Round (GATT negotiations) **X:**150, 151
Tolan, Eddie **VIII:**372
Toledo, Don Francisco de **I:**3
Toledo, Ohio **VIII:**377
Toleration Act (Maryland) **II:**220
Toli Tenegela **I:**330
Toll, Robert C. **VI:**116
Toll House Cookies **VII:**149
Tolman, Richard **VIII:**283
Toltecs **I:364–367,** *366,* 395*c*
  Aztecs **I:**18
  Chichén Itzá **I:**71–72
  Cholula **I:**74
  Itzcóatl **I:**190
  Maya **I:**235
  Nahua **I:**257
  Nahuatl **I:**258
  Quetzalcoatl **I:**309
  Tabasco **I:**351
T-O maps **I:**271, **367**
tomb(s) **I:**250
Tombigbee, Alabama **IV:**126
Tomb of the Unknown Dead of the Civil War **V:**17
Tomb of the Unknown Soldier **V:**17
"Tom Dooley" (Kingston Trio) **IX:**259

Tomlinson, Ray **X:**181
Tomochichi **II:392**
Tom Swift stories **VII:**315
Tom Thumb (locomotive) **IV:***314*
  Baltimore & Ohio Railroad **IV:**44
  economy **IV:**131
  industrialization **IV:**200
  railroads **IV:**314
  science and technology **IV:**333
Tonawanda Reservation **V:**295
Tongues of Jade (Laurence) **IX:**349
Tonquin **IV:**35
Tonti, Henri **II:**137
Tontine Crescent (Boston) **III:**65
tools **II:**385
Tools, Robert **X:**224, 320
Toombs, Robert A. **V:**104–105, **389; VII:**380
Toomer, Jean **VII:**136, 181
Topiltzin **I:**364
Topographical Bureau **V:**57
Topographical Engineering Corps **V:**407
Tora Bora caves, Afghanistan **X:**12
Torah **I:**33
Tordesillas, Treaty of **I:367–368,** 396*c*
  Alexander VI **I:**6
  Azores **I:**17
  Brazil **I:**34
  Cabot, Sebastian **I:**45
  Grotius, Hugo **I:**146
  Leo X **I:**210
  Portuguese seaborne empire **I:**300
  Spice Islands **I:**345
  Vitoria, Francisco de **I:**379
To Reclaim a Legacy (Bennett) **X:**245
To Renew America (Gingrich) **X:**152
Tories. *See* Loyalists
Tornado (Spanish warship) **VI:**377
Toronto, Ontario **IV:**300; **VII:**334–335
torpedoes
  Confederate navy **V:**83
  Mallory, Stephen R. **V:**247
  science and technology **V:**342
Torrijos, Herrera Omar **X:**269, 270
Tortilla Flat (Steinbeck) **VIII:**219, 374
tort law **VII:**391
torture **I:**182; **II:**239; **III:**345
Toscanelli, Paolo dal Pozzo **I:**68, 295
Toscanini, Arturo **VII:**219; **VIII:**252
Total Abstinence Society **IV:**233

"total war" strategy
  conscription **V:**90
  Lincoln, Abraham **V:**237
  rules of war **V:**338
  Sherman, William T. **V:**355
  tactics and strategy **V:**382
  Union army **V:**403
Totonac **I:**96
Touch of the Poet, A (O'Neill)
  VIII:220
Tourgée, Albion W. **V:389–390;**
  VI:225, 284
touring companies **VII:**96
tourism **IX:318–319**
  commemoration **IX:**66
  recreation **X:**303
  Sunbelt **X:**338
Touro Synagogue **III:**236
Tousey, Sinclair **V:**239
Tovar, Pedro de **I:**92, 168
Tower Commission **X:**184, 258,
  353–354
Town Act of 1662 (Jamestown)
  II:183
Town and the City, The (Kerouac)
  IX:36, 173
town council. *See cabildos*
Towne, Laura **V:**312
Townley, Arthur C. **VII:**241
Townsend, Francis E. **VIII:394–**
  395
  Coughlin, Father Charles E.
    VIII:88
  elderly **VIII:**107
  Long, Huey P. **VIII:**223
  New Deal **VIII:**270
  Social Security Act
    VIII:364
  Union Party **VIII:**401
Townsend, Kathleen Kennedy
  IX:172
Townsend Movement **VIII:**107
Townsend Plan **VIII:**364, 394
Townshend, Charles **III:**412
Townshend Duties **III:412–413,**
  459*c*, 460*c*
  American Revolution **III:**18
  Bernard, Sir Francis **III:**49
  Boston Massacre **III:**58
  Boston Tea Party **III:**58
  Coercive Acts **III:**100
  Dickinson, John **III:**137
  economy **III:**145
  Franklin, Benjamin **III:**173
  Laurens, Henry **III:**255
  Lee, Richard Henry **III:**260
  North, Frederick, Lord
    III:320
  Pitt, William **III:**337
  Quartering Act **III:**352
  resistance movement
    III:365, 366
  tariffs **III:**406
  Tea Act **III:**408, 409
Toynbee Hall (London, England)
  VI:121, 327
Toyota **IX:**27; **X:**35

Trachtenberg, Alan **VII:**259
track and field **VI:**359; **VIII:**372
tractors **VII:**8, 83
Tracy, Spencer **VIII:**188
trade (domestic and foreign)
  II:392–393; III:413–415, *414,*
  464*c,* 465*c;* **VI:359–360,** 412*c;*
  VII:353–355, 408*c. See also*
  free trade
  Acadia **I:**2
  Acts of Trade and Navigation
    II:3
  Adams, John **III:**5
  agriculture **II:**11–14; **III:**11
  Akan **I:**5
  Alaska **III:**12
  Alaska, Russia in **II:**14–15
  alcohol **II:**13
  Ames, Fisher **III:**19
  animals **II:**22; **III:**22
  Apalachee **I:**11
  Attucks, Crispus **III:**37
  Azores **I:**17–18
  Barbary Wars **III:**45
  Berlin Decree **III:**49
  Bernard, Sir Francis **III:**49
  Bonaparte, Napoleon **III:**55
  Boston **II:**41
  Brazil **I:**35
  Bretton Woods Conference
    VIII:52
  Bristol **I:**37
  British Empire **II:**48, 49
  Burke, Edmund **III:**68
  Cadore Letter **III:**73
  Caribbean **II:**59
  Casa de Contratación **I:**63
  cash-and-carry **VIII:**63
  Catawba **II:**61
  Charleston **II:**63–64
  Chesapeake-Leopard affair
    III:88
  China trade **III:**88–89
  Choctaw **III:**89
  cities and urban life **II:**68;
    III:90
  Columbian Exchange **I:**82
  cotton **III:**122
  Croghan, George **II:**84–85
  crowd actions **II:**86
  Dawes Plan **VII:**72
  Declaration of
    Independence **III:**132,
    133
  Djenne-Djeno **I:**109
  Djibouti **I:**109
  Dutch East India Company
    I:115–116
  Dutch West India Company
    II:107
  East India Company **I:**117
  economy **II:**109, 110;
    III:145–147; **VII:**83–85;
    VIII:103; **IX:**98
  embargo of 1807 **III:**151–
    152
  Essex decision **III:**157

Florida **III:**166
Forbes, John Murray
  VI:131
Fordney-McCumber Tariff
  VII:112
foreign affairs **III:**168, 169
foreign policy **VII:**114
Franklin, Benjamin **III:**173
French Alliance **III:**177
French colonies **II:**135, 136
French Revolution **III:**179
fur trade **III:**183
Gaspée affair **III:**189
GATT **X:**150–151
Georgia **II:**147
Girard, Stephen **III:**195
globalization **X:**153
Gold Coast **I:**143
Great Depression **VIII:**158
Great Plains **III:**197
Greenville, Treaty of
  III:200
Guinea-Bissau **I:**148
Haiti **III:**203
Hancock, John **III:**209
Hausa **I:**156
Hawaii **III:**210
Hawley-Smoot Tariff Act
  VIII:163
Henry the Navigator **I:**161
Hopewell culture **I:**167
Hudson's Bay Company
  II:168
Hull, Cordell **VIII:**180
Huntington, Collis Potter
  VI:180
industrialization **IV:**199–200
Industrial Revolution
  III:224, 226
investments, foreign
  VII:152
Iroquois **I:**187
Jamestown **II:**181
Jay, John **III:**229, 230
Jay-Gardoqui Treaty
  III:230–231
Jay's Treaty **III:**231
Jefferson, Thomas **III:**234
Jews **III:**236
Johnson, Sir William **II:**188
Jolliet, Louis **II:**189
League of Armed Neutrality
  III:257
London **I:**215
LWV **IX:**187
Macon's Bill No. 2 **III:**280
Massachusetts **II:**224–225
mercantilism **II:**230–231
merchants **II:**231
Mexican immigration
  VII:202
Milan Decree **III:**297
Montagnais-Naskapi **I:**250
Morton, Thomas **II:**244
Mossi **I:**253
NAFTA **X:**259
NAM **VII:**225

Native Americans **III:**312
New Netherland **II:**264,
  266
New Orleans **II:**267
New York **II:**271–272
Nixon, Richard M. **X:**257
Non-Importation Act
  III:319
Non-Intercourse Act
  III:319
Northwest Coast Indians
  II:275
Ohio Company of Virginia
  III:323
Orders in Council **III:**325
Oyo **I:**282
Panama **I:**285
Pequot War **II:**289
Philadelphia **II:**292
presidency **VII:**269
privateering **II:**313
Quasi War **III:**352–353
Reciprocal Trade
  Agreements Act **VIII:**324
Revolutionary War **III:**369
Rhode Island **II:**333
rice cultivation **II:**334
rum trade **II:**338
Sahara **I:**324
salt trade **I:**324–325
Seville **I:**332
South Carolina **II:**369
Spanish colonies **II:**371
Stamp Act **III:**396
steel industry **IX:**300–301
Stuart, John **II:**378
Sugar Act **III:**401
tariffs **III:**406
Tenochtitlán **I:**354–355
Timbuktu **I:**359
Toltecs **I:**366
Tuareg **I:**370
Venice **I:**375
wage and price controls
  II:405
war and warfare **II:**407
West Indies **III:**436, 437
Westo **II:**411
Wingina **II:**417
women's status and rights
  II:446
trade barriers **X:**380*c*
  Clinton, William J. **X:**82
  economy **X:**110
  foreign policy **X:**142
  WTO **X:**372
trade deficits **X:**109
trade embargoes. *See* embargoes
trade preferences **X:**82
Trade Reform Act (1974) **X:**377*c*
trade regulations **X:**82
trade routes
  Calabar **I:**51
  Darfur **I:**104
  Islam **I:**188
  Mali **I:**225, 226
  Maravi **I:**231

Mecca **I:**238–239
Niger River **I:**271
Sahara **I:**324
Silk Road **I:**335
Sudan **I:**347
Trade Union Education League
  Foster, William Zebulon
   VII:117
  ILGWU **VII:**149
  labor/labor movements
   VII:172
trading posts
  Bosomworth, Mary Musgrove
   II:40
  Cherokee **III:**87
  Choctaw **III:**89
  Creek **III:**126
  forts **II:**133
  Mississippi River **V:**261
Trading with the Enemy Act
  VII:355–356
  conscription **VII:**63
  Greenwich Village **VII:**131
  journalism **VII:**160
  radical and labor press
   VII:285
  World War I **VII:**394
traditional conservatives **X:**93
"traditional family values." *See*
  "family values"
traffic lights **VII:**149
Tragedy of Lynching, The
  (Commission on Interracial
  Cooperation) **VIII:**23
T-rail **IV:**333
"Trail of Broken Treaties" march
  IX:319; **X:**376c
Trail of Tears **IV:377–378**
  Black Hawk War **IV:**56
  Boudinot, Elias **IV:**62
  Cherokee **IV:**85
  Choctaw **IV:**87
  cotton culture **IV:**108
  Creek **IV:**109–110
  Indian Affairs, Bureau of
   IV:197
  Indian Removal Act **IV:**199
  Jackson, Andrew **IV:**207
  Native Americans **IV:**273,
   275
  Nullification Controversy
   IV:282
  Ridge, John **IV:**324
  Ross, John **IV:**325
"Trails for America" **IX:**239
Train, George Francis **VI:**16, 346
Traits of American Life (Hale)
  IV:183
*Transactions of the American
  Philosophical Society* **III:**17
transatlantic flight **VII:**177
Transcendental Club **IV:**378, 379
Transcendental Law **IV:**376
transcendental movement
  IV:378–379, 413c, 415c
  art **V:**18
  Brook Farm **IV:**65

Emerson, Ralph Waldo
  IV:140
Fourier, Charles **IV:**162
Fuller, Margaret **IV:**169
journalism **IV:**210
literature **IV:**228
Peabody, Elizabeth Palmer
  VI:279–280
religion **IV:**320
Roman Catholicism **VI:**316
Seneca Falls convention
  IV:341
Thoreau, Henry David
  IV:376
transcontinental railroad **IV:**415c;
  V:444c, 446c
  business and government
   VI:56
  Chinese Exclusion Act
   VI:68
  Congress **V:**89
  Cooke, Jay **V:**93
  Crédit Mobilier **V:**96–97
  Deseret, State of **IV:**120
  exploration **IV:**146
  Huntington, Collis Potter
   VI:180–181
  immigration **V:**201
  migration **IV:**255
  Pacific Railroad Act **V:**293–
   294
  railroads **V:**321–322
Transcontinental Treaty. *See*
  Adams-Onís Treaty
transformational diplomacy **X:**310
transistors **IX:**352c
  computers **IX:**70; **X:**86
  science and technology
   IX:285
  technology **IX:**311, 313
transnational corporations (TNCs)
  X:153–154, 205
transportation **I:**271; **V:390–392,**
  391; **VIII:395–397,** *396*
  agriculture **VIII:**10; **IX:**7;
   X:19
  aircraft industry **VIII:**13
  air power **VIII:**16
  automobile industry
   VIII:35
  aviation **IX:**27–28
  Brotherhood of Sleeping Car
   Porters **VIII:**54
  business cycles **VI:**58
  cities and urban life **V:**65,
   66
  Civil Rights Act (1875)
   V:71
  Confederate army **V:**81
  government, state/local
   IX:137
  Halleck, Henry Wager
   V:182
  Hoosac Tunnel **VI:**176–177
  immigration **V:**199–200
  industrial development
   V:204–205

Interstate Highway Act of
  1956 **IX:**158–159
ladies aid societies **V:**228
Mississippi River **V:**261–262
Mississippi River war **V:**263
Pacific Railroad Act **V:**293–
  294
railroads **V:**321–322
science and technology
  X:319–320
technology **VIII:**389;
  IX:313
trade, domestic and foreign
  III:415
urban. *See* urban
  transportation
Vicksburg campaign **V:**416
World War II home front
  VIII:433
Transportation, U.S. Department
  of (DOT) **IX:**238; **X:**130
Transportation Act (1940)
  VIII:396
Transportation Building (World's
  Columbian Exposition) **VI:**347
Transportation Security
  Administration **X:**167
Trans-Siberian Railway **VII:**309
Transylvania Company **III:**460c,
  461c
  Boone, Daniel **III:**55, 56
  Cherokee **III:**87
  Dragging Canoe **III:**139
  Wilderness Road **III:**442
travel **II:393–394**
Traveler from Altruria, A
  (Howells) **VI:**226
Travelers Aid **VIII:**403
travel narratives **I:368–369**
  Battel, Andrew **I:**28
  Cieza de León, Pedro **I:**76
  Coelho, Jorge
   d'Albuquerque **I:**79
  Harriot, Thomas **I:**154–155
  India **I:**181
  literature **III:**268
  Moryson, Fynes **I:**252
  Peter Martyr **I:**290
  Purchas, Samuel **I:**306
  Ramusio, Giovanni Battista
   I:312
  Settle, Dionyse **I:**331–332
  shipwreck narratives **I:**334
  Stade, Hans **I:**346
Travels (Bartram) **III:**47–48, 463c
Travels (Mandeville) **I:**228
*Travels in New England and New
  York* (Dwight) **III:**143
Travels in the Interior of America
  (Maximilian) **IV:**61
Travers, William **VI:**177
Travis, Hark **IV:**381
Travis, William Barret **IV:379–380**
  Alamo, The **IV:**14
  Bowie, James **IV:**63
  Texas Revolution **IV:**375
Traynor, William J. **VI:**13–14

Treadwell gold mine **VII:**208
treason **III:**465c
  Arnold, Benedict **III:**30–31
  capital punishment **X:**66
  Supreme Court **VIII:**384
Treason of the Senate, The
  (Phillips) **VII:**217
Treasury, U.S. Department of the
  Chase, Salmon P. **V:**62
  Cobb, Howell **V:**76
  Emergency Banking Act of
   1933 **VIII:**113
  Executive Reorganization
   Act **VIII:**121
  Gallatin, Albert **III:**188
  Hamilton, Alexander
   III:206, 207
  Holocaust **VIII:**170
  Morgenthau, Henry T., Jr.
   VIII:244
  public health **VII:**276
  Pure Food and Drug Act
   VII:277
  Veterans Bureau **VII:**373
  Whiskey Ring **V:**429
Treasury Building **V:**425, 426
Treasury Department,
  Confederate **V:**259
Treasury Department, U.S.
  III:125, 188
Treasury Islands **VIII:**366
*Treaties Concerning Religious
  Affectations, A* (Edwards)
  II:114
*Treatise on the Intellectual
  Character, and Civil and
  Political Condition of the
  Colored People of the United
  States* (Hosea) **IV:**129
Treaty of 1835 **IV:**414c
Treaty of 1866 **IV:**326
treaty rights **IX:**241, **319–320**
Treblinka concentration camp
  (Poland) **VIII:**169–170
Tredegar Iron Works **V:**392
  industrial development
   V:205
  Richmond, Virginia **V:**335
  war contracting **V:**424
Treemonisha (Joplin) **VII:**158
Trenchard, John **III:**103
trenches **V:**341, 426
Trent, Council of **I:**110, **369–370**
Trent affair
  Bates, Edward **V:**31
  foreign policy **V:**150
  Seward, William H. **V:**348
  Sumner, Charles **V:**378
  Union navy **V:**405
Trenton and Princeton, Battles of
  III:415–416, 461c
  Beaumarchais, Pierre-
   Auguste Caron de **III:**48
  Brandywine, Battle of
   III:61
  Cornwallis, Charles, Lord
   III:120

Trenton and Princeton, Battles of
  (*continued*)
    Greene, Nathanael **III:**198
    Hamilton, Alexander
      III:204
    Hessians **III:**213
    Howe, Richard, Lord
      III:214
    Hull, William **IV:**192
    Knox, Henry **III:**248
    Knyphausen, Wilhelm,
      Baron von **III:**248
    Revolutionary War **III:**368
    St. Clair, Arthur **III:**377
    Washington, George
      III:431
    Wilkinson, James **III:**443
Tresca, Carlo **VII:**110
Très riches heures **I:**328
Tres Zapotes **I:**278
trial by jury **III:**51
Triangle Shirtwaist Company
  VII:324
Triangle Shirtwaist Fire **VII:**356,
  356–357, 405*c*
    Goldmark, Josephine Clara
      VII:127
    ILGWU **VII:**149
    Perkins, Frances **VIII:**293
    Shirtwaist Makers Strike
      VII:324
    Workmen's Compensation
      Act **VII:**392
triangle trade
    Caribbean **II:**59
    Massachusetts **II:**225
    Newport **II:**267
    Rhode Island **II:**333
    rum trade **II:**338
    slave trade **II:**358–359
tribal sovereignty **VII:**185
tribunals. *See* military tribunals
Trident Conference **VIII:**355
Triennial Convention **V:**331
Trigger, Bruce **I:**1
Trilateral Commission **X:**205
Trilling, Lionel **X:**252
Trimble, Isaac **V:**168
Trinidad (ship) **I:**223, 224
Trinity Church (Boston,
  Massachusetts)
    Brooks, Phillips **VI:**50
    La Farge, John Frederick
      Lewis Joseph **VI:**217
    Richardson, Henry Hobson
      VI:313
    White, Stanford **VI:**392
Trinity Church (New York City)
  II:194; **IV:**30
Tripartite Pact **VIII:**37, 141, 447*c*
Tripartite Union **VI:**4
Triple Alliance
    Aztecs **I:**18
    Tacuba **I:**352
    Tlaxcala **I:**362
Triple Crown **VI:**177
"triple wall of privilege" **VII:**383

Tripoli **III:**465*c*
    Barbary Wars **III:**45, 46
    Barlow, Joel **III:**46
    Chauncey, Isaac **III:**86
    Constitution, USS **III:**108
    Decatur, Stephen **IV:**114
    Essex, USS **IV:**144
    foreign affairs **III:**169
    Jefferson, Thomas **III:**233
    POWs **III:**346
Tripp, Linda **X:**82, 333
Tri-Quarterly review **X:**211
Trist, Nicholas P. **IV:**181, 253
Trois Rivières, Battle of **III:**81
trolleys **VI:**360; **VII:**92
troop surge **X:**188, 384*c*
Tropic of Cancer (Miller) **VIII:**65
Trotsky, Leon **VII:**308
Trott, Perient **I:**31
Trotter, William Monroe **VII:357**
Troubled Assets Relief Program
  (TARP) **X:**37
Troup, George M. **IV:**221
Troy, New York
    Garnet, Henry Highland
      IV:174
    NWTUL **VII:**231
    strikes **V:**374, 375
    Willard, Emma **IV:**401
Troy Female Academy **IV:**401
Troy & Greenfield Railroad
  VI:177
Truckee Lake **IV:**126
Truckee River **IV:**125
trucks **X:**36
True Blue Saloon (Chile) **VI:**67
*True Civilization, an Immediate
  Necessity* (Warren) **V:**295
True Confessions **VII:**160, 322
*True Discourse of the Present
  State of Virginia, A* (Hamor)
  II:162
*True History of the Conquest of
  New Spain (Mexico)* (Díaz del
  Castillo) **I:**106, 354
True Reasons (Morse) **III:**307
True Religion Delineated
  (Bellamy) **III:**317
True Story (magazine) **VII:**160
"true womanhood" **VI:**374
Truman, Harry S., and
  administration **VIII:**307, 448*c,*
  449*c;* **IX:**102, **320–321,** 321,
  351*c,* 352*c*
    Acheson, Dean **IX:**1, 2
    AEC **IX:**24
    African Americans **VIII:**4
    Americans for Democratic
      Action **IX:**13, 14
    Announcement of the
      Atomic Bombing of
      Hiroshima **VIII:469–
      471**
    Asia **IX:**21
    atomic bomb **VIII:**34, 35
    Baruch, Bernard M. **VII:**32;
      VIII:42

    Berlin blockade **IX:**39
    bombing **VIII:**48
    braceros **IX:**43
    Bradley, Omar N. **VIII:**51
    Brotherhood of Sleeping Car
      Porters **VIII:**54
    Bush, Vannevar **VIII:**57
    Byrnes, James F. **VIII:**60
    CIA **IX:**51, 52
    CIO **IX:**72
    civil defense **IX:**56
    cold war **IX:**62, 63
    communism **IX:**68
    Congressional Budget and
      Impoundment Control
      Act **X:**89
    conscription, end of **X:**89
    conservatism **IX:**74
    defense budget **IX:**83
    demobilization (WWII)
      VIII:91
    Democratic Party **IX:**85
    Dennis v. U.S. **IX:**86
    Dewey, Thomas E. **IX:**87
    domino theory **IX:**89
    Eisenhower, Dwight D.
      IX:100
    election of 1944 **VIII:**111
    elections **IX:**102, 103
    Europe **IX:**113
    Fair Deal **IX:**115–116
    Federal Employee Loyalty
      Program **IX:**119
    Flynn, Edward J. **VIII:**139
    Forrestal, James V. **VIII:**143
    Freedom Train **IX:**125
    FSA **VIII:**127
    Full Employment Bill
      VIII:145
    Gallup Poll **IX:**130
    government, state/local
      IX:137
    Grand Alliance **VIII:**156
    Harriman, W. Averell
      VIII:162
    Hershey, Lewis B. **VIII:**164
    Hillman, Sidney **VIII:**166
    Hiroshima and Nagasaki
      VIII:166–168
    Hiss, Alger **IX:**147
    Hopkins, Harry L. **VIII:**177
    hydrogen bomb **IX:**152
    Ickes, Harold L. **VIII:**184
    Internal Security Act (1950)
      IX:157
    Israel **IX:**160
    Jones, Jesse H. **VIII:**197
    King, Ernest J. **VIII:**202
    Korean War **IX:**177
    Latin America **IX:**184
    Leahy, William D. **VIII:**211
    Lend-Lease **VIII:**212
    liberalism **IX:**191
    MacArthur, Douglas **IX:**198
    Manhattan Project **VIII:**227
    Marshall, George C.
      VIII:233

    Marshall Plan **IX:**204
    McCarran-Walter Act **IX:**205
    McCarthy, Joseph R. **IX:**207
    Medicare **IX:**209
    medicine **VIII:**236; **IX:**210
    NATO **IX:**247
    New Deal **IX:**242
    NSC-68 **IX:**247
    Oppenheimer, J. Robert
      IX:251
    Point Four Program **IX:**257,
      258
    Potsdam Conference
      VIII:307, 308
    Progressive Party **IX:**264
    public health **IX:**265
    public housing **IX:**266
    Randolph, A. Philip
      VIII:321
    Republican Party **IX:**274
    Roosevelt, Franklin D.
      VIII:347
    Rosenberg, Julius and Ethel
      IX:280
    science and technology
      IX:285
    SEATO **IX:**292
    Soviet-American relations
      VIII:369
    States' Rights Party **IX:**299,
      300
    steel industry **IX:**300
    Stevenson, Adali E. **IX:**302
    Stimson, Henry L. **VIII:**375
    strikes **VIII:**378
    Submerged Lands Act
      (1953) **IX:**305
    Taft, Robert A. **VIII:**385
    Taft-Hartley Act **IX:**309
    Truman Doctrine **IX:**321
    union movement **IX:**323
    Urban League **IX:**325
    USHA **VIII:**404
    V-E Day **VIII:**405
    V-J Day **VIII:**406
    Wallace, Henry A. **VIII:**411,
      412
    WAVES **VIII:**418
    White Paper **IX:**343
    Zionism **VIII:**441
Truman Doctrine **IX:321–322,**
  351*c,* **359–361**
    cold war **IX:**63
    Freedom Train **IX:**125
    Johnson, Lyndon B. **IX:**164
    Korean War **IX:**177
    Middle East **IX:**214
    Progressive Party **IX:**264
    Truman, Harry S. **IX:**320
    White Paper **IX:**343
Trumbo, Dalton **IX:**147, 149, 223
Trumbull, John **III:416–417,**
  462*c,* 464*c*
    art **III:**32, 33
    Connecticut Wits **III:**104
    literature **III:**269
    West, Benjamin **III:**436

Trumbull, Lyman **V**:70
Truro Parish, Virginia **III**:292
truss bridges **VI**:47
Trusteeship Council (United Nations) **VIII**:402
Trustees of Dartmouth College v. Woodward **III**:291, 403
trusts **VI:361–365**, *363*, 409*c*
  business and government **VI**:57
  Industrial Revolution, Second **VI**:192
  Lloyd, Henry Demarest **VI**:227
  oil **VI**:271
  Sherman Antitrust Act **VI**:330
  Wilson, Thomas Woodrow **VII**:383
Truth, Sojourner **IV**:414*c*, 415*c;* **V:392–394**, *393*
  African Americans **IV**:9
  race and race relations **IV**:311
  woman suffrage **VII**:384
  women's status and rights **V**:437
Truxton, Thomas **III**:47
Trylon and Perisphere (1939 New York World's Fair) **VIII**:28–29
Tryon, William **III**:12, 321, 460*c*
Tshombe, Moise **IX**:4
tsunami (December 2004) **X**:384*c*
Tuareg **I**:324, 359, **370–371**
tubal ligation **X**:43
tuberculosis (consumption) **II:78–79**
  agriculture **VIII**:10
  alcohol **II**:16
  Cherokee **II**:65
  disease/epidemics **III**:138; **IV**:123; **V**:113
  Dix, Dorothea **IV**:124
  economy **II**:110
  medicine **VII**:198, 200; **IX**:211
  Native Americans **VII**:233
  population trends **VII**:266
  public health **VII**:274–276; **IX**:265
  science and technology **VII**:314
  society, British American **II**:367
  Spanish colonies **II**:373
  Sublette, William **IV**:359
  technology **IX**:313
  Thoreau, Henry David **IV**:377
  tobacco **II**:391
Tubman, Harriet **IV**:414*c;* **V**:*394*, **394–395**
  abolitionism **V**:3
  African Americans **IV**:9–10
  Underground Railroad **V**:397

Tucker, Jim Guy **X**:333
Tucker, Thomas **V**:1
Tudor dynasty **I**:159; **II**:240
Tufts University **VIII**:56
Tugwell, Rexford G. **VIII:397–398**
  Agricultural Adjustment Act **VIII**:5
  Berle, Adolf A., Jr. **VIII**:43
  Brain Trust **VIII**:51
  FSA **VIII**:127
  London Economic Conference **VIII**:221
  National Recovery Administration **VIII**:259
  Resettlement Administration **VIII**:338, 339
  unemployment **VIII**:399gd
Tuke, Samuel **IV**:124
Tukolor **I**:135
Tula **I**:364–367
Tulagi Island
  Coral Sea, Battle of the **VIII**:87
  Guadalcanal **VIII**:160
  Solomon Islands **VIII**:365
  World War II Pacific theater **VIII**:435
Tulane University Law School **VIII**:222
Tule Lake, California relocation camp **VIII**:194
Tullahoma campaign **V**:75
Tulsa, Oklahoma **VII**:283, 344
Tunis
  Barbary Wars **III**:45
  Barlow, Joel **III**:46
  Decatur, Stephen **IV**:115
Tunisia **VIII**:278, 431
Tunjur **I**:104
Tunnel Hill **V**:63
Tunney, Gene
  Dempsey, William Harrison "Jack" **VII**:76
  recreation **VII**:295
  sports and recreation **VII**:333; **VIII**:371
Tupelo, Battle of **V**:152
Tupí-Guaraní **I**:34
Tupinambá **I:371**
  Bahía **I**:26
  cannibalism **I**:58
  Léry, Jean de **I**:212
  Stade, Hans **I**:346
Tupper, Benjamin **III**:323
Tupper, Earl **IX**:122
Tupperware **IX**:122
Turell, Jane Colman **II:394**
Turgenev, Ivan **VI**:200, 219
Turkey
  Angell, James Burrill **VI**:15
  arms race **IX**:17
  Cairo Conference **VIII**:61
  cold war **IX**:63
  Crane, Stephen **VI**:85
  domino theory **IX**:89
  Europe **IX**:113

  Harding, Warren Gamaliel **VII**:135
  Jews **I**:196
  Leahy, William D. **VIII**:211
  Levant Company **I**:213
  Marsh, George Perkins **VI**:239
  Middle East **IX**:214
  printing press **I**:303
  Siberian Expedition **VII**:324
  Trading with the Enemy Act **VII**:355
  Truman Doctrine **IX**:321, 322
  Venice **I**:375–376
  Versailles, Treaty of **VII**:369, 370
  World War I **VII**:393
Turkey Company **I**:213
Turkish Americans **X**:189
Turkish wheat **I**:91
Turnbow, Hartman **IX**:220
Turner, Charles Yardley **VII**:251
Turner, Frederick Jackson **II**:39; **VI:365–366**
  Ely, Richard Theodore **VI**:115
  Gilman, Daniel Coit **VI**:148
  history **VII**:139–140
  World's Columbian Exposition **VI**:403
Turner, Henry McNeal **VI:366–367**
  African-American churches, growth of **VI**:4, 5
  Crummell, Alexander **VI**:87
  Liberia **VI**:223
  Tanner, Benjamin Tucker **VI**:351, 352
Turner, John **VII**:15
Turner, Nat **IV:380–382**, *381*, 412*c*
  abolitionism **V**:2
  Calhoun, John C. **IV**:69
  Civil War **V**:73
  Gabriel's Rebellion **III**:185
  labor/labor movements **IV**:219
  religion **IV**:318
  slavery **IV**:348; **V**:362
Turner, Richmond Kelly
  Mariana Islands **VIII**:228
  Nimitz, Chester W. **VIII**:274
  Solomon Islands **VIII**:365
Turner, Tina **X**:240
Turner, William **VII**:188
turning maneuvers **V**:341, 380
Turnvereine **V**:165
Turquoise Road **I**:366
Tuscarora **I**:185, 398*c;* **II:394–395**
  Iroquois **III**:227
  North Carolina **II**:273
  Tuscarora War **II**:395

Tuscarora War **II:395**
  Graffenried, Christopher, baron de **II**:154
  North Carolina **II**:273
  Tuscarora **II**:395
Tuskegee Airmen **VIII**:3–4, 27
Tuskegee Experiment **X**:381*c*
Tuskegee Institute, Alabama **VI**:409*c*, 411*c;* **VIII**:444*c*
  African Americans **VI**:7
  Carver, George Washington **VI**:63
  Eastman, George **VI**:105
  education, higher **VI**:111–112
  medicine **VIII**:236
  Washington, Booker T. **VI**:384
tutors **II**:112; **VI**:110
Tutsis **X**:102
"Tutti Frutti" **IX**:278
"Tuxedo Unionism" **IX**:323
Tuzultán, Guatemala **I**:206
TVA. *See* Tennessee Valley Authority
TV dinners **IX**:122, 286
TWA (Trans World Airlines) **IX**:319
Twachtman, John **VI**:275
Twain, Mark **V**:446*c;* **VI**:*367*, **367–368**, 409*c*
  cotton culture **IV**:108
  Gilded Age, The: A Tale of Today **VI**:145–146
  Harte, Bret **VI**:162
  literature **V**:240; **VI**:225, 226
  Reid, Whitelaw **VI**:305
Tweed, William Marcy "Boss" **VI**:*368*, 407*c*
  corruption, political **VI**:83
  immigration **V**:200
  journalism **V**:219
  New York City **V**:282
  Tilden, Samuel Jones **VI**:357
Tweed Ring **VI**:*368*, **368–369**
  corruption, political **VI**:83–84
  Gould, Jay **VI**:151
  Tilden, Samuel Jones **VI**:357
12th Army Group **VIII**:50–51
Twelfth Amendment **III:16–17**, 107, **151**, 465*c*
20th Air Force, U.S. **VIII**:27
Twentieth Amendment **VIII**:444*c*
20th Century-Fox **IX**:222; **X**:235
20th Century Limited (streamliner) **VIII**:396
20 Committee (Great Britain) **VIII**:118
20th Maine Regiment **V**:60, 167
20th Massachusetts Volunteer Infantry (Harvard Regiment) **V:186–187**

Twenty-fifth Amendment **IV**:383; **X**:138

Twenty-first Amendment **VII**:374; **VIII**:444*c*

Twenty-fourth Amendment **IX**:334, 356*c*

Twenty-Negro Law **V**:91

Twenty One (TV series) **IX**:65

Twenty-second Amendment **III**:107

27th Infantry **VII**:324

Twenty-seventh Amendment **X**:23

Twenty-sixth Amendment **X**:22, 376*c*

Twenty-Slave Law **V**:309

Twenty-third Amendment **X**:23

Twenty Years at Hull-House (Addams) **VII**:240, 297

Twice-Told Tales (Hawthorne) **IV**:229

Twide, Richard **I**:181, 182

Twi language **I**:13

2,4-D **VIII**:10

291 Gallery (New York City) **VII**:258–259

"Two Offers, The" (Harper) **VI**:160

Twopenny Act **II**:281, 282; **III**:53

"Two Sisters" **IV**:328

2001: A Space Odyssey (film) **IX**:224, 287

Two Treatises of Government (Locke) **II**:208

Two Years Before the Mast (Dana)
California **IV**:71
California Trail **IV**:77
Dana, Richard Henry **IV**:113

Two Years in the French West Indies (Hearn) **VI**:170

Tydings-McDuffie Act (1934) **VIII**:444*c*
Asian Americans **VIII**:32
immigration **VIII**:184
Philippine independence **IX**:256

Tyler, John **IV**:382, **382–383**, 414*c*
banking **IV**:47
Bell, John **V**:32
Calhoun, John C. **IV**:69
Clay, Henry **IV**:97
election of 1840 **IV**:139
foreign policy **IV**:155
Harrison, William Henry **IV**:186
Hollywood Cemetery **V**:192
Liberty Party **IV**:226
Mexican-American War **IV**:251
Van Buren, Martin **IV**:386
Webster, Daniel **IV**:393
Webster-Ashburton Treaty **IV**:394
Whigs **IV**:397
Wise, Henry A. **V**:434

Tyler, Royall **III**:411, **417**, 462*c*

Type 97 Alphabetical Typewriter (Japanese code machine) **VIII**:76

Typee (Melville) **IV**:229

typesetting **II**:134

Types of Mankind (Nott and Gidden) **IV**:311

typewriters **VI**:214, 284

typhoid fever
Alcott, Louisa May **VI**:10
disease/epidemics **V**:112, 113
environment **VI**:119
medicine **VII**:198
Mississippi River war **V**:264
population trends **VII**:266
public health **VII**:274
Washington, D.C. **V**:425

typhus **II**:399; **IV**:123; **V**:257

U

UAW. *See* United Auto Workers

Uber die Musik der Nordamerikanischen Wilden (On the Music of the North American Indians) (Baker) **VI**:255

U-boats
aircraft carriers **VIII**:12
armed forces **VII**:20
Atlantic, Battle of the **VIII**:33
Democratic Party **VII**:74
destroyers-for-bases deal **VIII**:94
foreign policy **VIII**:142
Lusitania, RMS **VII**:187–188
World War I **VII**:393

UC (Unemployment Compensation) **VIII**:364

UCV. *See* United Confederate Veterans

Udall, Stewart **IX**:344

UDC. *See* United Daughters of the Confederacy

UFCO. *See* United Fruit Company

UFW. *See* United Farm Workers

Ukraine **VIII**:431; **X**:142

Ulam, Stanislaw **IX**:152

Ulster plantation **II**:346–347

Ulster Scots. *See* Scots-Irish

Ultra intelligence (code) **VIII**:76

ultrarealism **VIII**:119

Ulysses (Joyce)
Baldwin, Roger Nash **VII**:31
censorship **VIII**:65
radical and labor press **VII**:285

UMA (United Mexican Students) **X**:166

Umpqua River
Fort Vancouver **IV**:159
Rocky Mountain Fur Company **IV**:325
Smith, Jedediah Strong **IV**:351

UMWA. *See* United Mine Workers of America

UN. *See* United Nations

Una, The (magazine) **IV**:404

unborn children **X**:289, 368

Unborn Victims of Violence Act (2004) **X**:171

Uncas **II**:222, 290–291

Uncertain Allegiance (Rice) **X**:309

"Uncle Sam" **IV**:176

Uncle Tom's Cabin (Stowe) **IV**:415*c*
abolitionism **V**:3
American Anti-Slavery Society **V**:15–16
Civil War **V**:73
entertainment, popular **VI**:116
Jackson, Helen Hunt **VI**:199
literature **IV**:227–229; **V**:239
religion **IV**:317
Stowe, Harriet Beecher **V**:374
theater **V**:387; **VI**:355
Weld, Theodore Dwight **IV**:396

Uncle Tom's Children (Wright) **VIII**:437

unconditional surrender **VIII**:62–63

Uncovered Wagon, The (film) **VII**:215

Underground Railroad **IV**:412*c*, 414*c*; **V**:397–398
abolitionism **V**:3
African Americans **IV**:9–10
African Methodist Episcopal Church **V**:5
Brown, John **V**:44
Brown, William Wells **V**:46
Christiana, Pennsylvania, riot **V**:65
Finney, Charles Grandison **IV**:151
fugitive slave laws **IV**:168
Garnet, Henry Highland **IV**:174
Langston, John Mercer **VI**:218
Mason-Dixon Line **V**:250
Mott, Lucretia **IV**:266
Pennington, James William Charles **V**:300
religion **IV**:317
slavery **V**:362
Society of Friends **V**:364
Still, William **IV**:357
Tappan, Arthur and Lewis **IV**:367
Tubman, Harriet **V**:394

Underhill, John **II**:105

"Under the Bamboo Tree" **VII**:353

Under the Horse Chestnut (Cassatt) **VI**:64

Under the Sea Wind (Carson) **IX**:50

Underwood-Simmons Tariff **VII**:359, 406*c*
elections **VII**:91
New Freedom **VII**:236
tariffs **VII**:350
Wilson, Thomas Woodrow **VII**:383

Underwood Tariff Act **VIII**:180

undue burden **X**:265

unemployment **VI**:407*c*; **VIII**:399–401, *400*, 443*c*, 444*c*; **X**:378*c*, 383*c*
African Americans **VIII**:3
Agricultural Adjustment Administration **VIII**:7
Amalgamated Clothing Workers of America (ACW) **VIII**:16
art and architecture **VIII**:29
big bands **VIII**:44
Black Cabinet **VIII**:46
Bonus Army **VIII**:48
business **VIII**:57
business cycles **VI**:58
children **VIII**:66
CIO **VIII**:82
cities and urban life **VIII**:68, 69; **IX**:55–56
civil liberties **VIII**:71
coal industry **VIII**:74
Congress **VIII**:79
conservatism **VIII**:84
CWA **VIII**:74
demobilization (WWII) **VIII**:91; **IX**:84
Democratic Party **VIII**:94
economy **III**:145; **VIII**:102, 103; **IX**:96, 98; **X**:107–111
elderly **VIII**:107
election of 1932 **VIII**:109
employment **V**:132
ERAA **VIII**:114
FAP **VIII**:129
Federal National Mortgage Association **VIII**:135
FEPC **VIII**:123
FERA **VIII**:132
fiscal policy **VIII**:139
Ford, Gerald R. **X**:139
GI Bill of Rights **VIII**:149
government **VIII**:152
Great Depression **VIII**:156, 158
Hawley-Smoot Tariff Act **VIII**:163
Hoover presidency **VIII**:174
Hopkins, Harry L. **VIII**:176
housing **VIII**:177
Ickes, Harold L. **VIII**:183
immigration **VIII**:184

Job Corps **IX:**161, 162
Keynesianism **VIII:**201
labor/labor movements
  VIII:205, 207
liberalism **VIII:**216
marriage and family
  VIII:230, 231
Mexican Americans
  VIII:237
Mexican Repatriation
  Program **VIII:**238
New Deal **VIII:**268
Norris–La Guardia Act
  VIII:277
NRPB **VIII:**261
NYA **VIII:**262
PECE **VIII:**309
politics (Roosevelt era)
  VIII:298
population trends **VIII:**304
POUR **VIII:**310
race and race relations
  IX:270
Reagan, Ronald W. **X:**300
Reaganomics **X:**302
recession of 1937–1938
  VIII:323, 324
refugees **VIII:**329
relief **VIII:**330, 332
Relief and Reconstruction
  Act **VIII:**333
Roosevelt, Franklin D.
  VIII:345
Social Security Act
  VIII:363, 454
steel industry **VIII:**373
strikes **VIII:**378
Third New Deal **VIII:**393
Thomas, Norman **VIII:**394
Tugwell, Rexford G.
  VIII:398
wage and price controls
  X:363
Wagner, Robert F.
  VIII:410
World War II home front
  VIII:432
Unemployment Compensation
  (UC) **VIII:**364
unemployment insurance
  VIII:445c
  liberalism **X:**207
  New Deal **VIII:**269
  Perkins, Frances **VIII:**293
  Social Security Act
    VIII:363, 364
UNESCO (United Nations
  Educational, Scientific and
  Cultural Organization) **X:**355
*Unexpected Legacy of Divorce,
  The* (Wallerstein) **X:**128
unfair labor practices
  ERA **X:**123
  NLRB **VIII:**259
  Wagner, Robert F. **VIII:**410
Unfunded Mandates Reform Act
  (1995) **X:**131

UNIA. *See* Universal Negro
  Improvement Association
uniforms **V:**398, **398–400,** 399
  common soldier **V:**78
  Confederate army **V:**81
  54th Massachusetts
    Regiment **V:**143
  industrial development
    V:205
  Shiloh, Battle of **V:**359
  Union army **V:**400, 401
  volunteer army **V:**419
  war contracting **V:**423, 424
  Zouaves **V:**441
Union army **V:400–404,** 402
  abolitionism **V:**4
  African-American regiments
    V:4
  Andersonville Prison,
    Georgia **V:**10–11
  Antietam, Battle of
    V:12–13
  Balloon Corps **V:**25
  Baltimore, Maryland, riots
    V:26
  Bentonville, Battle of **V:**34
  bounty system **V:**39–40
  Buell, Don C. **V:**48
  Bull Run/Manassas, First
    and Second Battles of
    V:49–51
  Chase, Salmon P. **V:**63
  Chattanooga, Battle of **V:**63
  Cold Harbor, Battle of
    V:76–77
  Confederate army **V:**82
  Confiscation Acts **V:**87
  Custer, George A. **V:**99
  desertion **V:**110, 111
  disease/epidemics **V:**112
  field fortifications **V:**140,
    141
  foraging **V:**148–149
  German-American
    regiments **V:**165–166
  Harpers Ferry, West Virginia
    V:186
  Harvard Regiment **V:**186–
    187
  immigration **V:**200, 201
  industrial development
    V:205
  Irish-American regiments
    V:205
  jayhawkers **V:**211
  Joint Committee on the
    Conduct of the War
    V:215
  letters **V:**233
  Medal of Honor **V:**255
  medicine **V:**256–258
  Milliken's Bend, Battle of
    V:260
  music **V:**274
  Native Americans **V:**278
  New Orleans, Battle of
    V:281

New York City draft riots
  V:284
Parker, Ely Samuel **V:**295
prisons **V:**314
race and race relations
  V:319
Revels, Hiram R. **V:**335
science and technology
  V:342, 343
Sherman's March through
  Georgia **V:**356–357
Shiloh, Battle of **V:**358–360
Sickles, Daniel E. **V:**360–
  361
slavery **V:**364
uniforms **V:**398–400
U.S. Christian Commission
  V:408
U.S. Military Academy at
  West Point **V:**409
U.S. Sanitary Commission
  V:411
veterans **V:**415
Vicksburg campaign **V:**417
volunteer army **V:**419
Wakeman, Sarah Rosetta
  V:422
war contracting **V:**423, 424
Warmoth, Henry Clay **V:**424
Washington, D.C. **V:**426,
  427
Wheeler, Joseph **V:**428
Wilderness, Battle of the
  V:432
Zouaves **V:**441, 442
Union Canal **IV:**79
Union Carbide **VII:**85
union contracts **IX:**352c
  business **IX:**47
  COLA **IX:**76–77
  economy **IX:**97
Union Fire Company **III:**227
Union Labor Party **VI:**220
Union Labor Press **VI:**220
Union League **V:404–405**
  Philadelphia **V:**303
  Reconstruction **V:**326
  Women's National Loyal
    League **V:**434
Union Mills **VI:**62
union movement. *See* labor unions
Union navy **V:405–407,** 406
  African-American regiments
    V:4
  Dahlgren, John A. B. **V:**101
  Farragut, David Glasgow
    V:137–138
  ironclads **V:**207
  Lincoln, Abraham **V:**237
  Medal of Honor **V:**255
  Mississippi River war **V:**263
  Monitor-Merrimack **V:**265
  New Orleans, Battle of
    V:280
  Porter, David Dixon **V:**311
  science and technology
    V:342

tactics and strategy **V:**381
Vicksburg campaign **V:**417
Welles, Gideon **V:**427
Union of American Hebrew
  Congregations **VI:**205, 308
Union of Needletrades, Industrial
  and Textile Employees (Unite!)
  VIII:188
Union of Soviet Socialist
  Republics (USSR). *See* Soviet
  Union
Union of Textile Workers
  VII:253
Union Pacific Railroad (UP)
  V:446c
  banking, investment **VI:**23
  Bridger, James **IV:**64
  business and government
    VI:56
  corruption, political **VI:**83
  Crédit Mobilier **V:**96–97
  Gould, Jay **VI:**151
  Harriman, W. Averell
    VIII:161
  Huntington, Collis Potter
    VI:180, 181
  immigration **V:**201
  lobbying **VI:**228
  Mormon Church **IV:**90
  Oregon Trail **IV:**286
  Pacific Railroad Act **V:**293,
    294
  railroads **V:**322; **VI:**301,
    302
  transportation **V:**391
Union Party **VIII:401**
  conservatism **VIII:**84
  Coughlin, Father Charles E.
    VIII:88
  election of 1936 **VIII:**109
  Long, Huey P. **VIII:**223
  Townsend, Francis E.
    VIII:395
unions. *See* labor and labor
  movements; labor unions
Union Society of Albany for the
  Improvement of the Colored
  People in Morals, Education,
  and the Mechanical Arts
  IV:295
Union Station (Washington, D.C.)
  VI:55, 56
Union Temperance Society of
  Moreau and Northumberland
  III:410, 465c
Union Theological Seminary
  VIII:394
Uniontown, Maryland **IV:**271
Union Trust Company **VII:**201
Union Volunteer Refreshment
  Committee **V:**228
UNITA (National Union for the
  Total Independence of Angola)
  X:85
"Unitarian Christianity" (Channing)
  III:419; **IV:**318
Unitarian Controversy **III:**419

Unitarianism **III:419**
  Adams, Hannah **III:4**
  Baldwin, Roger Nash
    VII:31
  Dix, Dorothea **IV:124**
  Emerson, Ralph Waldo
    IV:140
  female antislavery societies
    IV:147
  literature **IV:228**
  religion **IV:318, 320;**
    VII:297
United Aircraft **VII:165**
United Airlines **VII:165; IX:70**
United Arab Emirates **X:267**
United Auto Workers (UAW)
  VIII:445c; IX:352c
  AFL **IX:11**
  African Americans **VIII:3**
  automobile industry
    VIII:37; IX:26
  CIO **VIII:82; IX:71**
  COLA **IX:76, 77**
  labor/labor movements
    VIII:206, 207; X:201
  Murray, Philip **VIII:249**
  Reuther, Walter **VIII:339,**
    340; IX:275
  strikes **VIII:377**
United Colonies of New England
  II:436c
United Company of Philadelphia
  for Promoting Manufactures
  III:224
United Confederate Veterans
  (UCV)
  Civil War **V:75**
  common soldier **V:79**
  lost cause, the **V:244**
  monuments **V:268**
  veterans **V:415, 416**
United Conference of Mayors
  VIII:444c
United Daughters of the
  Confederacy (UDC) **V:407**
  Arlington National Cemetery
    V:17
  Cumming, Kate **V:98**
  Ladies Memorial
    Associations **V:229**
  lost cause, the **V:244**
  monuments **V:268**
  veterans **V:415**
United Farm Workers (UFW)
  IX:324–325, 357c
  Chávez, César Estrada
    IX:53, 54
  labor/labor movements
    IX:182
  Latino movement **IX:186**
  union movement **IX:324**
United Features **VII:159**
United Fruit Company (UFCO)
  Latin America **IX:184**
  trade, domestic and foreign
    VII:354
  UFW **IX:325**

United Glass Company **II:419**
United Kingdom. *See specific*
  countries, e.g. Great Britain
United Mastodon Minstrels
  VI:116
United Mexican Students (UMA)
  X:166
United Mine Workers of America
  (UMWA) **VII:359–360,** 403c;
  VIII:401–402
  AFL **VI:13; VII:11**
  Amalgamated Clothing
    Workers of America
    (ACW) **VIII:16**
  Anthracite Coal Strike
    VII:15
  Buck's Stove **VII:43**
  CIO **VIII:81**
  class consciousness **VI:73–**
    74
  coal industry **VIII:74, 76**
  Dubinsky, David **VIII:97**
  Fuel Administration
    VII:119
  labor, child **VI:212**
  labor/labor movements
    VII:170; VIII:206
  labor trends **VI:217**
  Lewis, John L. **VIII:212,**
    213
  Ludlow Massacre **VII:186**
  Mann-Elkins Act **VII:190**
  mining **VII:208–209**
  Mitchell, John **VII:210**
  Murray, Philip **VIII:249**
  NAM **VII:225**
  National Civic Federation
    VII:226
  New Unionism **VII:237**
  NWLB **VIII:262**
  Red Scare **VII:296**
  strikes **VIII:378**
United Nations (UN) **VIII:402–**
  403, 449c; **IX:353c**
  Africa **IX:3; X:16, 17**
  Albright, Madeleine K. **X:22**
  Asia **IX:21**
  Atlantic Charter **VIII:34**
  Baruch, Bernard M.
    VIII:42
  Bretton Woods Conference
    VIII:52
  Bunche, Ralph **IX:45**
  Byrnes, James F. **VIII:60**
  Carter, James Earl, Jr. **X:70**
  Congress **VIII:81**
  defense policy **X:101**
  demobilization (WWII)
    VIII:91
  Dulles, John Foster **IX:90**
  foreign policy **VIII:142;**
    X:143
  globalization **X:154**
  Grand Alliance **VIII:155**
  Hull, Cordell **VIII:180**
  isolationists **VIII:190**
  Israel **IX:160**

  Johnson, Hiram Warren
    VII:154
  Korean War **IX:177**
  Lange, Dorothea **VIII:210**
  Latin America **X:204**
  League of Nations **VII:175**
  liberalism **VIII:216**
  LWV **IX:187**
  MacArthur, Douglas **IX:197**
  Mariana Islands **VIII:229**
  Middle East **X:227, 229,**
    230
  militia movement **X:231**
  Morgenthau, Henry T., Jr.
    VIII:244
  Myrdal, Gunnar **VIII:253**
  Nimitz, Chester W.
    VIII:274
  nuclear proliferation **X:261,**
    262
  Paul, Alice **VII:254**
  Persian Gulf War **X:273**
  postwar planning **VIII:307**
  Powell, Colin L. **X:287**
  religion **IX:272**
  Roosevelt, Eleanor
    VIII:343, 344
  Roosevelt, Franklin D.
    VIII:346
  Soviet-American relations
    VIII:369
  Stevenson, Adali E. **IX:302**
  Taft, Robert A. **VIII:385**
  U.S. participation since 1968
    X:355–357, 356, 381c,
    384c
  Welles, Sumner **VIII:415**
  World War II **VIII:428**
  Yalta Agreement **VIII:468**
  Yalta Conference **VIII:439–**
    440
United Nations Atomic Energy
  Commission **VII:32**
United Nations Conference on
  International Organization
  VIII:402
United Nations Educational,
  Scientific and Cultural
  Organization (UNESCO)
  X:355
United Nations General Assembly
  VIII:402; X:355, 356
United Nations Human Rights
  Commission **VIII:343; X:135**
United Nations Interim
  Administration Mission
  (UNMIK) **X:200**
United Nations Relief and
  Rehabilitation Administration
  (UNRRA) **VIII:52, 209**
United Nations Resolution 1441
  X:383c
United Nations Security Council
  Africa **IX:4**
  Bush, George H. W. **X:53**
  Haiti **X:164**
  Iraq War **X:186, 187**

  Korean War **IX:177**
  MacArthur, Douglas **IX:198**
  Middle East **X:227**
  UN **VIII:402; X:355, 356**
  Yalta Conference **VIII:439–**
    440
United Negro Improvement
  Association **VII:344**
United Press **IV:209; VII:159,**
  160
United Service Organizations
  (USO) **VIII:403, 403–404,**
  447c
  Monroe, Marilyn **IX:223**
  music **VIII:252**
  recreation **VIII:329**
  women's status and rights
    VIII:424
United Society of Believers in
  Christ's Second Appearing
  IV:320
United States, USS
  Barry, John **III:47**
  Decatur, Stephen **IV:115**
  Quasi War **III:353**
  War of 1812 **IV:391**
United States Agency for
  International Development
  (USAID) **X:310**
United States Army Corps of
  Engineers **V:407**
  cartography **V:57**
  environment **VIII:116**
  internal improvements
    IV:202
  Lee, Robert E. **V:229**
  Manhattan Project **VIII:226**
  Mississippi River **V:261**
  OSRD **VIII:283**
  U.S. Military Academy at
    West Point **V:409**
  WAC **VIII:420**
United States–Chinese Treaty
  (1858) **V:443c**
United States Christian
  Commission (USCC) **V:407–**
  408
  ladies aid societies **V:228**
  letters **V:233**
  Moody, Dwight Lyman
    VI:249
United States Civil War
  Centennial Commission **IX:61,**
  62
United States Colored Troops
  (USCT)
  African-American regiments
    V:4
  Eaton, John, Jr. **V:120**
  54th Massachusetts
    Regiment **V:142**
  Union army **V:403**
United States Commission on
  National Security/21st Century
  X:152
United States Conference for
  Mayors **VIII:69**

United States Football League (USFL) **X:**330
United States Housing Act (1937). *See* Wagner-Steagall Housing Act
United States Housing Authority (USHA) **VIII:404, 445***c*
  cities and urban life **VIII:**70
  Congress **VIII:**80
  Federal Housing Administration (FHA) **VIII:**133
  housing **VIII:**178
  New Deal **VIII:**269
  PWA **VIII:**314
  Wagner, Robert F. **VIII:**410
United States International Exhibition **VI:**283–284
United States Magazine and Democratic Review **IV:**234
United States Marine Band **VI:**258, 339, 340
United States Military Academy at West Point **III:437,** 462*c;* **V:408–409**
  Alexander, Edward P. **V:**7
  André, John **III:**20
  armed forces **VII:**20
  Armistead, Lewis A. **V:**17
  Arnold, Benedict **III:**31
  Arnold, Henry H. "Hap" **VIII:**28
  Beauregard, Pierre Gustave Toutant **V:**32
  Bragg, Braxton **V:**42
  Buell, Don C. **V:**48
  Burnside, Ambrose E. **V:**51
  Chouteau family **IV:**88
  citizen-soldier **V:**68
  Custer, George A. **V:**98–99
  Davis, Jefferson **V:**103
  Early, Jubal A. **V:**119
  Eisenhower, Dwight D. **IX:**100
  Ewell, Richard Stoddert **V:**135
  Garnett, Richard B. **V:**163
  Gorgas, Josiah **V:**171
  Grant, Ulysses S. **V:**173
  Halleck, Henry Wager **V:**182
  Hancock, Winfield Scott **V:**183
  Hill, Ambrose P. **V:**189
  Hill, Daniel H. **V:**190
  Hood, John Bell **V:**195
  Hooker, Joseph **V:**196
  Howard, Oliver Otis **V:**197, 198
  Jackson, Thomas J. "Stonewall" **V:**209
  Johnson, Hugh S. **VIII:**196
  Johnston, Albert Sidney **V:**213
  Johnston, Joseph E. **V:**214
  Jomini, Antoine-Henri, baron de **V:**216

  Kościuszko, Tadeusz **III:**248
  Lee, Robert E. **V:**229, 230
  Longstreet, James **V:**241
  MacArthur, Douglas **IX:**197
  McClellan, George Brinton **V:**250
  McDougall, Alexander **III:**294
  McDowell, Irvin **V:**252
  McLaws, Lafayette **V:**253
  Meade, George Gordon **V:**253
  Pemberton, John C. **V:**297
  Pershing, John Joseph **VII:**258
  Pickett, George Edward **V:**305
  Rosecrans, William S. **V:**337
  Sampson, Deborah **III:**380
  Sheridan, Philip H. **V:**353
  Sherman, William T. **V:**354
  Stuart, J. E. B. **V:**375
  Thomas, George H. **V:**388
  uniforms **V:**398
  Union army **V:**400
  U.S. Army Corps of Engineers **V:**407
  Wheeler, Joseph **V:**428
  Whistler, James Abbott McNeill **VI:**389
  Wilson, Henry **V:**433
United States Military Railroad **V:**304
United States Military Telegraph Service **V:**385, 386
United States Mint **III:**372, 376
United States National Museum **IV:**84
United States Naval Academy at Annapolis **V:409–410**
  Dewey, George **VI:**97
  Halsey, William F. **VIII:**161
  King, Ernest J. **VIII:**201
  Leahy, William D. **VIII:**210
  Porter, David Dixon **V:**311
United States Navy. *See* Navy, U.S.
United States Postal Service **V:**233
United States Sanitary Commission (USSC) **V:***410,* **410–411**
  Bickerdyke, Mary Ann **V:**34
  disease/epidemics **V:**112
  Forbes, John Murray **VI:**132
  homefront **V:**193
  ladies aid societies **V:**228
  medicine **V:**257
  Olmsted, Frederick Law **V:**288
  women's status and rights **V:**437
United States Secret Service **V:**134
United States Service Society **V:**415

United States Shipping Board **VII:360–361**
  advertising **VII:**4
  armed forces **VII:**21
  Teapot Dome **VII:**351
United States Soldiers and Sailors Protective Society **V:**415
United States Strategic Bombing Survey **VIII:**48
United States Term Limits, Inc. v. Thornton **X:**131, 350, 381*c*
United States v. Booth **V:**443*c*
United States v. Butler **VIII:**382, 445*c*
United States v. C. C. Nash and Others **V:**412
United States v. Cruikshank **V:411–412**
  Enforcement Acts **V:**133
  Fourteenth Amendment **V:**157
  Ku Klux Klan Act **V:**225
  Ku Klux Klan cases **VI:**210
United States v. E. C. Knight Company **VI:**411*c*
  business and government **VI:**57
  Harlan, John Marshall **VI:**159
  Northern Securities Case **VII:**241, 242
  Sherman Antitrust Act **VI:**330
  Supreme Court **VI:**348
United States v. Eichman
  Brennan, William J., Jr. **X:**48
  flag burning **X:**136
  Scalia, Antonin **X:**316
  White, Byron R. **X:**369
United States v. Harris **VI:**210
United States v. Libellants and Claimants of the Schooner Amistad **IV:434–438**
United States v. Lopez **X:**161, 350
United States v. Microsoft **X:**147–148
United States v. Nixon **X:357–358**
  Burger, Warren E. **X:**51
  Jaworski, Leon **X:**193
  Nixon, Richard M. **X:**257
  Supreme Court **X:**338
  Watergate scandal **X:**367
United States v. Reese
  Enforcement Acts **V:**133
  Ku Klux Klan cases **VI:**210
  U.S. v. Cruikshank **V:**412
United States v. Susan B. Anthony **VI:**16
United States v. Turkette **X:**298
United States v. Virginia et al. **X:**381*c*
United States v. Washington Post **X:**376*c*

United Steel Workers of America (USWA)
  CIO **IX:**72
  labor/labor movements **X:**203
  steel industry **VIII:**374; **IX:**300
United Steelworkers v. Weber **X:**9
United Textile Workers (UTW) **VII:**173, 174, 253
United We Stand America (UWSA) **X:**272, 273, 304
Unity House **VII:**149
Unity Temple (Oak Park, Illinois) **VII:**395
UNIVAC computer **IX:**70, 353*c*
"Universal Community" **VI:**319
Universal Declaration of Human Rights **VIII:**344
Universal Exposition (Paris) **VI:**276
Universal Franchise Association **VI:**229
Universalis cosmographia **I:**381
Universalist Church
  Murray, Judith Sargent Stevens **III:**308
  religion **III:**361; **IV:**318
  religious liberty **III:**363
  spiritualism **IV:**355
Universal Negro Improvement Association (UNIA) **VII:361–362,** 408*c*
  DuBois, W.E.B. **VII:**81
  Garvey, Marcus **VII:**121
  Harlem Renaissance **VII:**136
  Liberia **VI:**224
  Malcolm X **IX:**198
  Muhammad, Elijah **IX:**226
Universal Peace Union **VI:**229
Universal Pictures **X:**235
"Universal Suffrage" speech (Kent) **IV:**412*c*
universe **VIII:**352
universities. *See* college(s); *specific universities*
University of Alabama **VIII:**45; **IX:**294, 355*c*
University of Berlin **VI:**120
University of California system **X:**9–10, 40–41
University of California at Berkeley **IX:**356*c*
  civil disobedience **IX:**58
  counterculture **IX:**78
  criminal justice **VII:**66
  education **IX:**100
  Free Speech Movement **IX:**125–126
  Friedan, Betty **IX:**126
  Gilman, Daniel Coit **VI:**148
  James, William **VI:**201
  Johnson, Hiram Warren **VII:**154

University of California at
Berkeley *(continued)*
Meese, Edwin C., III **X**:225
Savio, Mario **IX**:284
SDS **IX**:304
Steffens, Lincoln **VII**:339
University of California Medical
School at Davis **X**:40–41, 158
University of Chicago
Chautauqua Institute **VI**:66
education, philanthropy and
VI:112–113
football **VI**:131
Ickes, Harold L. **VIII**:183
James, William **VI**:201
Rockefeller, John Davison
VII:303
University of Halle (Germany)
VI:115
University of Heidelberg **VI**:115,
120
University of Kansas **IV**:243
University of Kansas School of
Law **VIII**:209
University of Kiel (Germany)
VII:39
University of Leiden **IV**:5
University of Leipzig (Germany)
VII:133
University of Maryland **VIII**:256;
IX:217
University of Maryland School of
Law **IX**:202
University of Michigan
affirmative action **X**:10
Angell, James Burrill
VI:14–15
Hamilton, Alice **VII**:133
medicine **VI**:244
University of Minnesota **VII**:330
University of Mississippi **IX**:355*c*
Faulkner, William
VIII:128
Meredith, James **IX**:213
White Citizens' Councils
IX:342
University of Munich (Germany)
VII:133
University of North Carolina
IX:227
University of Pennsylvania **II**:293
computers **X**:86
Henderson, Leon **VIII**:163
Kelley, Florence **VII**:164
medicine **VI**:244
Tugwell, Rexford G.
VIII:397
University of Pittsburgh **VII**:201
University of South Carolina
V:234; **VI**:358
University of Texas Law School
X:10
University of Utah **IV**:120
University of Virginia
Faulkner, William **VIII**:128
Jefferson, Thomas **III**:235
Madison, James **III**:284

McGuffey, William Holmes
IV:246, 247
Monroe, James **IV**:259
University of Virginia Law School
IX:171
University of Wisconsin
Ely, Richard Theodore
VI:115
history **VII**:139
La Follette, Robert M., Jr.
VIII:208
University of Zurich (Germany)
VII:164
unmarried mothers **X**:44, 45
Unmasking of Robert-Houdin, The
(Houdini) **VII**:142
UNMIK (United Nations Interim
Administration Mission) **X**:200
UNRRA. *See* United Nations
Relief and Rehabilitation
Administration
Unruly Calf, The (Homer) **VI**:*174*
Unsafe at Any Speed (Nader)
IX:357*c*
automobile industry **IX**:27;
X:35
consumerism **IX**:76
GM **IX**:133
literature **IX**:194
Nader, Ralph **X**:241
National Traffic and Motor
Vehicle Safety Act of 1966
IX:238
unskilled labor **VII**:146, 150
UP. *See* Union Pacific Railroad
Updike, John **X**:**358**, 370
Up from Liberalism (Buckley)
IX:74
Up from Slavery (Washington)
V:240; **VII**:384
Upjohn, Richard **IV**:30
Upjohn's Rural Architecture
(Upjohn) **IV**:30
Upper Silesia, Poland **VII**:370
Upshur, Ubel P. **IV**:383
Upward Bound **IX**:335
uranium **VIII**:227; **X**:261, 262
Urban Institute **X**:350
urbanization **I**:389; **VII**:143
Urban League **IX**:**325–326**
Economic Opportunity Act
(1964) **IX**:95
education **VIII**:106
Harlem Renaissance
VII:136
urban life. *See* cities and urban
life
urban redevelopment **IX**:56,
220–221, **326–327**
urban reform **VII**:**362–363**
child labor **VII**:52
children **VII**:399
criminal justice **VII**:67
elections **VII**:89
Johnson, Tom Loftin
VII:156
New Woman **VII**:240

politics (1900–1928)
VII:261, 262
progressivism **VII**:271
urban transportation **VI**:**360–361**,
361; **VII**:**363–365**, *364*
cities and urban life
VII:54–55
electricity **VII**:92
Johnson, Tom Loftin **VII**:156
Pingree, Hazen S. **VII**:261
politics (1900–1928)
VII:261
suburbanization/suburbs
VII:340
urban reform **VII**:363
Urbino, Raphael d' **I**:210
Uribe, Álvaro **X**:56, 144
Ursuline Convent burning
(Charlestown, Massachusetts)
anti-Catholic riots **IV**:23
Know-Nothing Party **IV**:214
nativism **V**:280
Uruguay **X**:206
Uruguay Round (GATT
negotiations) **X**:150, 151
USAAF. *See* Army Air Forces, U.S.
USAID (United States Agency for
International Development)
X:310
USA PATRIOT Act (2001)
X:**358–360**
Bush, George W. **X**:55
defense policy **X**:103
House of Representatives
X:170
USA Today **X**:219
USA trilogy (Dos Passos) **VII**:186;
VIII:219
U.S. Canadian Convention (1903)
VII:404*c*
USCC. *See* United States
Christian Commission
USCIR. *See* Industrial Relations
Commission
USCT. *See* United States Colored
Troops
USDA. *See* Agriculture, U.S.
Department of
USFL (United States Football
League) **X**:330
USGA (U.S. Golf Association)
VI:343
U.S. Geological Exploration
VI:208
U.S. Geological Survey (USGS).
See Geological Survey, U.S.
U.S.-German Peace Treaty (1921)
VII:408*c*
U.S. Golf Association (USGA)
VI:343
USHA. *See* United States Housing
Authority
U.S. Lawn Tennis Association
(USLTA) **VI**:342
U.S. Leadership Against HIV/
AIDS, Tuberculosis and
Malaria Act (2003) **X**:17

USLTA (U.S. Lawn Tennis
Association) **VI**:342
USO. *See* United Service
Organizations
Usonian designs (housing)
VIII:379
U.S. Open golf tournament
VI:343
U.S. Pharmacopoeia **IV**:123
USPHS. *See* Public Health
Service, U.S.
USSC. *See* United States Sanitary
Commission
USSR. *See* Soviet Union
U.S. Steel **VII**:**365–366**, 403*c*
American Liberty League
VIII:19
Carnegie, Andrew **VI**:62
CIO **VIII**:82
cities and urban life **VII**:54
Morgan, John Pierpont
VI:251
Murray, Philip **VIII**:249
Northern Securities Case
VII:241, 242
open shop movement
VII:247
steel industry **VII**:336–337;
VIII:373; **IX**:300
Steel Strike of 1919 **VII**:338
stock market crash **VIII**:376
strikes **VIII**:377
trusts **VI**:365
welfare capitalism **VII**:381
workers' compensation
VII:391
USWA. *See* United Steel Workers
of America
Utah **IV**:414*c*
abortion **X**:2
Compromise of 1850
IV:104
Deseret, State of **IV**:119–
120
Eccles, Marriner S.
VIII:101
elections, conduct of **VI**:113
exploration **IV**:145
immigration **IV**:193
Japanese Americans,
relocation of **VIII**:194
marriage and family **IV**:240;
X:215
migration **IV**:255
Mormon Church **IV**:90;
VI:252
Mormon War **IV**:262–264
Oregon Trail **IV**:285
overland mail **IV**:290
polygamy **IV**:303
popular sovereignty **IV**:304
population trends **X**:282
property rights **X**:290
religion **IV**:319; **VI**:308–
309
Utah Act **IV**:447
woman suffrage **VII**:384

women's status and rights
IV:403; VI:399
Young, Brigham IV:408
Utah Act IV:447
Utah beach VIII:276
Utah War IV:90, 121; VI:252
Ute Indians
Bent's Fort IV:55
Bridger, James IV:64
Carson, Kit IV:82
Deseret, State of IV:120
Indian Rights Association
VI:190
Utica, New York
chain stores VI:65
Conkling, Roscoe VI:80
Finney, Charles Grandison
IV:151
Free-Soil Party IV:163
"Utility Collection" IX:116
utility companies VII:93–94
Utley, Robert M. VI:376
Utopia, Ohio IV:392
utopianism VI:226, 371
Utrecht, Treaty of I:3; II:437c
Acadians II:2
Newfoundland II:259
Queen Anne's War II:324
South Sea Company II:370
Uttamatomakkin II:335
UTW. See United Textile Workers
UUNET (Internet service
provider) X:182
UWSA. See United We Stand
America; United We Stand
America (UWSA)
Uzama I:29

V

VA. See Veterans Administration
vacations VII:295; VIII:328;
X:303
Vaccination Assistance Act
IX:211
vaccines
medicine IX:211, 212;
X:222
public health IX:265
science and technology
VIII:351
technology IX:313
vacuum domicilium II:201
vacuum tubes VII:123, 403c
Vagabond King, The (Friml)
VII:218–219
vagrancy laws V:316
Vail, Alfred IV:264, 333
Vaillant, George I:277
Valcour Island, Battle of III:31,
81, 421
Valdez, Luis IX:186
Valdivia, Pedro de I:373
Valentino, Rudolph VII:97, 214
Valesh, Eva McDonald VII:285,
324, 367–368

Vallandigham, Clement L. V:414
Burnside, Ambrose E. V:52
civil liberties, Union V:70
Copperheads V:94, 95
elections V:126
homefront V:193
peace movements V:295
Valle, Pietro delle I:79–80
Vallejo, Mariano IV:49
Valley Forge III:421–423, 422,
461c
Continental army III:111
Kalb, Johann, baron de
III:245
Knox, Henry III:248
Marshall, John III:289
Monroe, James IV:258
Morristown encampment
III:306
Steuben, Frederick, baron
von III:398
Sullivan, John III:402
Washington, George
III:431
Valley of Mexico I:356, 364, 365,
367
Valparaíso, Chile IV:144
values. See ethics
Van Allen, William VIII:28
Van Buren, Martin IV:117, 385,
385–386, 413c
abolitionism V:3
American System IV:20
Amistad incident IV:22
anti-Masonry IV:25
banking IV:46–47
Benton, Thomas Hart IV:54
Calhoun, John C. IV:69
Caroline affair IV:81
Cass, Lewis IV:83
Clinton, DeWitt III:97
Democratic Party IV:117–
118; V:108
election of 1828 IV:135–136
election of 1840 IV:138, 139
foreign policy IV:155
Free-Soil Party IV:163–164
Harrison, William Henry
IV:186
Jackson, Andrew IV:206
Mexican-American War
IV:251
Oregon Treaty of 1846
IV:287
panic of 1837 IV:295
Polk, James K. IV:301, 302
Taylor, Zachary IV:368
Tilden, Samuel Jones
VI:357
Welles, Gideon V:428
Whigs V:397
Wilkes expedition IV:399
Vance, Cyrus X:66, 69
Vance, Zebulon B. V:414
Confederate States of
America V:86
conscription V:91

elections V:127
governors V:172
Heroes of America V:188
peace movements V:296
states' rights V:370
Vancouver, British Columbia
VIII:199
Vancouver, George I:274; IV:103
Vancouver Island
Canada VI:61
foreign policy IV:155
Fort Vancouver IV:159
Manifest Destiny IV:234
McLoughlin, John IV:248
Oregon Treaty of 1846
IV:287–288
Polk, James K. IV:302
Washington, Treaty of
VI:385
Vandalia, Illinois
economy IV:130
internal improvements
IV:202
National Road IV:271
Vandalia Company III:323
Vandenberg Resolution (1948)
X:259
Vanderbilt, Arthur X:47
Vanderbilt, Cornelius IV:386–
387, 414c; V:446c
Clayton-Bulwer Treaty
IV:98
economy IV:131
filibustering V:145
Gould, Jay VI:151
socialism VI:336
Walker, William V:423
Woodhull, Victoria VI:400
Vanderbilt, W. H. VI:23
Vanderbilt family VIII:373
Vanderbilt University
education, philanthropy and
VI:112
Garner, John Nance
VIII:147
Goldmark, Josephine Clara
VII:127
Vanderbilt, Cornelius
IV:387
Vandergrift, Alexander A.
VIII:365
Vanderlyn, John III:293
Van Devanter, Willis VIII:89,
382, 383
Van Dorn, Earl
Confederate army V:82
Corinth, Battle of V:95, 96
Pea Ridge/Elkhorn Tavern,
Battle of V:296, 297
Vane, Charles II:385
Vanessa (Barber) IX:228
Van Lew, Elizabeth V:134,
414–415
Van Lew, John V:414
Vann, Robert VIII:45
Van Nostrand Science Series
(McMaster) VI:242

Van Orden v. Perry X:216
Van Rensselaer, Kiliaen II:269,
331
Van Rensselaer, Maria Van
Cortlandt II:397
Van Ronk, Dave IX:121
vans (LTVs) X:36
Vanzetti, Bartolomeo. See Sacco
and Vanzetti
Vardaman, James K. VII:332
Vargas, Diego de II:318, 397–
398
Varieties of Religious Experience
(James) VI:201
Variety magazine IX:2
variety shows VI:117
variolation. See inoculation
Varney Airlines VII:28, 165
Varnum, James III:135
Vasari, Giorgio I:212
vasectomies X:43
Vasquez, Louis IV:64
vassals I:129–130
Vassar, Matthew VI:247–248
Vassar College
Blatch, Harriot Eaton
Stanton VII:38
education VI:109
FTP VIII:135
history VII:140
Kennedy, Jacqueline
IX:168
women's colleges VI:398
Vatican I:244
Vatican Council, Second IX:273
vaudeville VI:355; VII:368,
368–369
entertainment, popular
VI:116–117; VII:95
Gay Nineties VII:140
Johnson, Jack VII:156
music VI:257; VII:218
popular culture VII:263,
264
Tin Pan Alley VII:353
urban transportation
VII:363
Vaughan, John III:216
Vaux, Calvert V:288; VI:81
Vázquez, Tabaré X:206
VCR. See videocassette recorder
Veblen, Thorstein
Ely, Richard Theodore
VI:115
Galbraith, John Kenneth
IX:129
literature VII:180
Vector Analysis (Gibbs) VI:325
V-E Day VIII:405
Lend-Lease VIII:212
sports and recreation
VIII:373
World War II European
theater VIII:432
Vedder, Elihu VI:276
vegetables VIII:322
Velasco, Treaty of IV:330, 375

Velázquez, Diego de **I:**373–374
  Alvarado, Pedro de **I:**7
  art and architecture **VI:**19
  Aztecs **I:**21, 22
  Cortés, Hernán **I:**94
  Cuba **I:**100
  Grijalva, Juan de **I:**145
  Narváez, Pánfilo de **I:**258
  Sandoval, Gonzalo de **I:**325
  Veracruz **I:**376
Vella Lavella **VIII:**366
velodromes **VI:**35
venereal disease
  disease/epidemics **V:**112
  Hawaii **IV:**188
  medicine **VIII:**235, 236
  prostitution **V:**316
Venezuela
  Cuba **IV:**111
  El Dorado **I:**119
  Las Casas, Bartolomé de
    I:205
  Latin America **IX:**184;
    X:206, 207
  OPEC **X:**267
Venezuela boundary dispute
  VI:373
  Atkinson, Edward **VI:**22
  Bayard, Thomas Francis
    VI:28
  Cleveland, Grover **VI:**75
  Harrison, Benjamin **VI:**162
Venice, California **VIII:**150
Venice, Italy **I:**374–376
  Cabral, Pedro Álvares **I:**46
  Holy League **I:**165
  Islam **I:**189
  Ramusio, Giovanni Battista
    I:312–313
  Thevet, André **I:**357
Venice Company **I:**213
venta **I:**4
Venturi, Robert **IX:**20
VEP. *See* Voter Education Project
Veracruz, Mexico **I:**376; **IV:**414*c*
  Big Stick diplomacy **VII:**35
  cabildo **I:**41
  Cortés, Hernán **I:**96
  Escalante, Juan de **I:**123, 124
  foreign policy **VII:**114
  Grijalva, Juan de **I:**145
  Guadalupe Hidalgo, Treaty
    of **IV:**181
  Kearny, Stephen Watts
    IV:212
  King, Ernest J. **VIII:**201
  Mexican-American War
    IV:252
  Mexican Invasion **VII:**203
  Mexican Revolution
    VII:205
  New Spain **I:**267, 269
  Olmecs **I:**277
  Sandoval, Gonzalo de **I:**325
  Santa Anna, Antonio López
    de **IV:**330
  Scott, Winfield **IV:**336

Veracruz, siege of
  Gorgas, Josiah **V:**171
  Jackson, Thomas J.
    "Stonewall" **V:**209
  Meade, George Gordon
    V:253
Vergennes, Charles Gravier,
  comte de **III:**174, 177,
  423–424
Verhulst, Willem **II:**264
Vermont **I:**2; **II:**398; **III:**460*c*,
  463*c*; **X:**383*c*
  abolitionism **III:**1
  Allen, Ethan **III:**14–15
  anti-Masonry **IV:**25
  antislavery **III:**25
  citizenship **III:**93
  constitutions, state **III:**110
  Deere, John **III:**115
  deism **III:**135
  Ely, Samuel Cullick **III:**151
  fugitive slave laws **IV:**168
  gay and lesbian rights
    movement **X:**149
  Green Mountain Boys
    III:199
  Hartford Convention
    IV:186
  land riots **III:**254
  Lyon, Matthew **III:**277
  Maine Law **IV:**234
  marriage and family **X:**215–
    216
  Marsh, George Perkins
    VI:239
  religion **III:**361
  riots **III:**371
  Saratoga, surrender at
    III:380
  suffrage **III:**400, 401
  Willard, Emma **IV:**400
  Young, Brigham **IV:**407
  Young, Thomas **III:**457
Vermont Central Railroad **IV:**316
Verplanck Point **III:**216
Verrazano, Giovanni da **I:**377,
  377, 397*c*
  Abenaki **I:**2
  Acadia **I:**2
  Massachusett **I:**233
  New Jersey **I:**261
  New York **II:**269
  Norumbega **I:**274
Verrocchio, Andrea del **I:**211
Versailles, Treaty of **I:**251;
  VII:369–371, 407*c*, 408*c*
  Baruch, Bernard M. **VII:**32
  Dawes, Charles Gates
    VII:71
  Dawes Plan **VII:**72
  Democratic Party **VII:**75
  foreign policy **VII:**115, 116
  Hughes, Charles Evans
    VII:142
  Johnson, Hiram Warren
    VII:154
  League of Nations **VII:**175

Lodge, Henry Cabot
  VII:184
Naval Disarmament
  Conference **VII:**235
peace movements **VII:**256
presidency **VII:**269
public health **VII:**275
Republican Party **VII:**300
trade, domestic and foreign
  VII:354
Wilson, Thomas Woodrow
  VII:384
World War I **VII:**394
Versailles Peace Conference
  (1919) **IX:**90
Vertigo (film) **IX:**224
*Very Brief Account of the
  Destruction of the Indies
  (Brevísma relación de la
  destrucción de las Indias)* (Las
  Casas) **I:**206
Vesey, Denmark **IV:387–388,**
  412*c*
  Gabriel's Rebellion **III:**185
  labor/labor movements
    IV:219
  religion **IV:**318
  slavery **IV:**347–348; **V:**362
  Walker, David **IV:**389
Vesey, Joseph **IV:**387
Vespucci, Amerigo **I:377–378,**
  396*c*
  Brazil **I:**34
  "Mondo Nuovo" letter (1504)
    I:405–409
  New World **I:**270
  Ojeda, Alonso de **I:**277
  travel narratives **I:**368
  Waldseemüller, Martin
    I:381
Vetch, Samuel **II:**323
veterans (1950s–1960s) **IX:329–
330**
veterans (WWII) **VIII:**444*c*,
  448*c*
  demobilization (WWII)
    VIII:91
  GI Bill of Rights **VIII:**149–
    150
  housing **VIII:**177–178
  Patton, George S., Jr.
    VIII:291
  postwar planning **VIII:**306
  reconversion **VIII:**327
  suburbanization/suburbs
    VIII:380
  taxation **VIII:**387–388
veterans, Civil War **V:415–416,**
  446*c*
  Civil War **V:**75
  common soldier **V:**79
  conscription **V:**90
  Grand Army of the Republic
    VI:151–152
  Johnston, Joseph E. **V:**215
  Ku Klux Klan cases **VI:**210
  ladies aid societies **V:**228

Longstreet, James **V:**242,
  243
lost cause, the **V:**244
monuments **V:**267
Mosby, John Singleton
  V:271
New Orleans riot **V:**282
nurses **V:**286
Pacific Railroad Act **V:**293
railroads **V:**322
Society of Friends **V:**365
Taylor, Susie King **V:**385
Union army **V:**404
veterans, World War I
  VII:371
veterans, Korean War **IX:**329
veterans, Vietnam War **IX:**329–
330
veterans, World War I **VI:**410*c*;
  VII:371–373, 372
  American Legion **VII:**13–14
  citizenship **VII:**57
  presidency **VII:**269
  public health **VII:**276
  Soldiers' Bonus **VII:**331
  Veterans Bureau **VII:**373
  World War I **VII:**394
veterans, World War II
  consumerism **IX:**75
  economy **IX:**97
  Federal Housing
    Administration **IX:**119
  Latino movement **IX:**185
  migration **IX:**215
  veterans **IX:**329
Veterans Administration (VA)
  GI Bill of Rights **VIII:**149
  housing **VIII:**177–178
  suburbanization/suburbs
    IX:305
Veterans Bureau **VII:373–374**
  Harding, Warren Gamaliel
    VII:134–135
  politics (1900–1928)
    VII:262
  public health **VII:**276
  Soldiers' Bonus **VII:**331
  Teapot Dome **VII:**351, 352
  veterans **VII:**372
Veterans of Foreign Wars
  VII:371, 373
veto **X:361**
  Bush, George W. **X:**56
  Civil Rights Act (1866) **V:**70
  Constitution, United States
    III:107
  Constitutional Convention
    III:109
  constitutions, state **III:**110
  Ford, Gerald R. **X:**139
  Hayes, Rutherford B.
    VI:168
  Immigration Act (1917)
    VII:145
  impeachment of Andrew
    Johnson **V:**203
  presidency **VI:**290

VHS (Video Home System)
X:236, 317
Vibrio comma **IV:**121
Vice-Admiralty Courts **III:**326,
401, **424,** 465c
viceroys **I:**16, 17, 97, 268; **II:**371
"Vices of the Political System of
the United States" (Madison)
III:282
Vichy France
Casablanca Conference
VIII:62
North African campaign
VIII:277, 278
World War II European
theater **VIII:**431
Vicksburg, Battle of **V:**295
Vicksburg campaign **V:416–418,**
417, 445c
Blair, Francis Preston, Jr.
V:36
elections **V:**126
foraging **V:**149
homefront **V:**194
medicine **V:**257
Milliken's Bend, Battle of
V:260
Mississippi River war **V:**264
Pemberton, John C. **V:**298
Porter, David Dixon **V:**311
Sherman, William T. **V:**355
Warmoth, Henry Clay **V:**424
women soldiers **V:**435
Vicksburg National Military Park
V:276–277
Victoria (ship) **I:**60, 223, 224,
397c
Victorianism **VI:373–374**
cosmetics and beauty
industry **VII:**65
dime novels **VI:**98
Eakins, Thomas **VI:**104
entertainment, popular
VI:119
literature **VI:**225
sexuality **VII:**322
theater **VI:**354–355
Victor Talking Machine Company
VII:96, 97
"Victory Films" **VIII:**56
victory gardens **VIII:405–406,**
406
advertising **VIII:**1
marriage and family
VIII:232
women's status and rights
VIII:424
World War II home front
VIII:433
Victory magazine **VIII:**210, 286
Victrola **VII:**96. *See also*
phonographs/phonograph
records
video-capture cards **X:**319
videocassette recorder (VCR)
X:278–280, 317, 320
video games **X:**303

videos **X:**236, 283
Vienna, Austria **VI:**121; **VII:**118
Vietcong **IX:**330, 339, 357c
Vietnam **IX:**353c, 356c; **X:**381c.
See also North Vietnam; South
Vietnam
Asia **IX:**21
Dulles, John Foster **IX:**91
Eisenhower, Dwight D.
IX:100–101
foreign policy **X:**143
Lange, Dorothea **VIII:**210
Reagan, Ronald W. **X:**301
SEATO **IX:**292
Vietnamese immigrants **IX:**260;
X:33
Vietnamization policy **X:**361, 376c
Vietnam Veterans Memorial
IX:329–330, 332
Vietnam War **IX:330–332,** *331,*
357c; **X:**375c
Acheson, Dean **IX:**2
African Americans **IX:**6
Ali, Muhammad **IX:**9
Americans for Democratic
Action **IX:**14
anticommunism **IX:**14
Asia **IX:**21
Asian-American movement
IX:22
aviation **IX:**29
civil disobedience **IX:**58
cold war **IX:**64
communism **IX:**68
conscription, end of **X:**89
defense budget **IX:**84
Democratic Party **IX:**85
détente **X:**104
Dow Chemical Corporation
IX:90
Dulles, John Foster **IX:**91
Dylan, Bob **IX:**92
Eccles, Marriner S.
VIII:101
elections **IX:**104
Fellowship of Reconciliation
VII:109
folk music revival **IX:**121
foreign policy **X:**140
Gonzáles, Rodolfo "Corky"
IX:137
Gore, Albert, Jr. **X:**156
Harriman, W. Averell
VIII:162
Hayden, Tom **IX:**144
Humphrey, Hubert H.
IX:151
immigration **IX:**155
Johnson, Lyndon B. **IX:**163–
165
journalism **IX:**166
Kemp, Jack F. **X:**196
Kennan, George F. **IX:**167
Kennedy, Edward M. **X:**196
Kennedy, John F. **IX:**171
Kennedy, Robert F. **IX:**171
Kerouac, Jack **IX:**173

King, Martin Luther, Jr.
IX:175
Korean War **IX:**178
liberalism **IX:**191, 192
McCarthy, Eugene **IX:**205–
206
McGovern, George S. **X:**217
military-industrial complex
IX:216
Mondale, Walter F. **X:**233
movies **IX:**224; **X:**235
music **X:**238
NASA **IX:**231
New Left **IX:**244
O'Neill, Thomas "Tip" P., Jr.
X:267
Peace Corps **IX:**256
Pentagon Papers **X:**271, 272
popular culture **IX:**259
Quayle, J. Danforth **X:**293
Rankin, Jeannette **VII:**292
Republican Party **IX:**274,
275
rock and roll **IX:**279
Rumsfeld, Donald **X:**312–
313
SANE **IX:**283, 284
SDS **IX:**304
SEATO **IX:**292
"Silent Majority" Speech
(Nixon) **X:385–386**
sit-ins **IX:**291
Soviet Union **IX:**295
Spock, Benjamin **IX:**297,
298
teenagers **IX:**315
television **IX:**316
Thomas, Norman **VIII:**394
Twenty-sixth Amendment
X:354
veterans **IX:**329
wars of national liberation
IX:339
Young Chicanos for
Community Action
IX:350
Vietnam War (end of U.S.
involvement) **X:361–362,** *362*
AIP **X:**24
Albert, Carl B. **X:**21
antiwar movement, Vietnam
X:28–29
Asian Americans **X:**33
"Chicago Eight" **X:**73
Clinton, William J. **X:**79
Eagleton, Thomas F. **X:**107
economy **X:**108
Ford, Gerald R. **X:**139
Habib, Philip C. **X:**163
Jackson State protests **X:**192
Latin America **X:**204
Nixon, Richard M. **X:**257
North Vietnam **X:**260
political parties **X:**276
War Powers Act **X:**365
*Views of Society and Manners in
America* (Wright) **IV:**405

vigilantes **III:**394, 395
Viguerie, Richard **X:**24
Viking colonies **II:**258
Viking program **X:**327
Viking punch bowl (Tiffany and
Company) **VI:**19
Vikings. *See* Norse
Villa, Francisco "Pancho"
VII:405c, 406c
Big Stick diplomacy **VII:**35
foreign policy **VII:**114
Johnson, Hugh S. **VIII:**196
Mexican Invasion **VII:**203,
204
Mexican Revolution
VII:204, 205
Mitchell, William (Billy)
VII:211
Pershing, John Joseph
VII:258
Reed, Jack **VII:**296
Wilson, Thomas Woodrow
VII:383
Zimmermann telegram
VII:401
Village Funeral, Brittany (Pearce)
VI:19
Village of Equity anarchist
community (Ohio) **IV:**392
villages
Carib **I:**60
Florida **I:**131
Iroquois **I:**185–187
Villard, Henry **VI:**192, **374–375**
Villard, Oswald Garrison **VI:**384
Villard Houses (New York City)
VI:392
Ville de Paris **III:**379
Villiers, George **I:**192
Vincennes **III:**95, 96; **IV:**185
Vincent, John H. **VI:**66, 306
Vincent, Strong **V:**167
Vincent de Paul, Saint **IV:**344
Vincente de Fonseca, João
(archbishop of Goa) **I:**214
Vinland **I:**203–204, 272, **378,**
395c
Vinson Naval Act **VIII:**446c
Violence Against Women Act
X:382c
violence and lawlessness **VI:375–**
377, *376. See also* labor: strikes
and violence
Black Panthers **IX:**40, 41
entertainment, popular
VI:119
Great Strike of 1877 **VI:**154
Hamer, Fannie Lou **IX:**141
Hayden, Tom **IX:**144
lynching **VI:**229–231
New Left **IX:**244
Parks, Rosa **IX:**254
SDS **IX:**304
Voting Rights Act of 1965
IX:333
Violent Crime Control and Law
Enforcement Act (1994) **X:**161

Virginia **II:398–402,** 399*m*, 435*c*,
   436*c*; **III:**462*c*, 463*c*; **VII:**408*c*
   abolitionism **IV:**1; **V:**1
   African Americans **II:**5, 6;
      III:9, 10
   agriculture **II:**9, 11, 12;
      IV:10, 12; **V:**6
   Andros, Sir Edmund **II:**20
   Annapolis Convention
      III:23
   antislavery **III:**25, 26
   Appalachia **IX:**15
   architecture **II:**25
   Arnold, Benedict **III:**31
   Bacon's Rebellion **II:**31–32
   Berkeley, Sir William
      II:36–37
   Beverley, Robert **II:**37
   Bland, Richard **III:**52–53
   Boone, Daniel **III:**56
   Buck v. Bell **VII:**43
   Burgesses, House of
      II:50–51
   Byrd, William, II **II:**52–53
   Byrd family **II:**53
   Carter, Landon **II:**60
   Carter, Robert "King"
      II:60–61
   citizenship **III:**93
   civil liberties, Union **V:**69
   clothing **II:**72
   College of William and Mary
      II:74
   Compromise of 1850
      IV:104
   Confederate army **V:**82
   Constitution, ratification of
      the **III:**105, 106
   constitutions, state **III:**110
   Continental army **III:**111
   Continental Congress, First
      III:114
   convict labor **II:**80
   Cornstalk **II:**81
   cotton culture **IV:**107, 108
   Culpeper, Thomas, Lord
      II:87
   Dale, Sir Thomas **II:**89
   Declaration of
      Independence **III:**133
   "Declaration of Nathaniel
      Bacon in the Name of
      the People of Virginia"
      II:441–442
   disease/epidemics **II:**98;
      IV:122
   Dow, Lorenzo **IV:**126
   Dunmore, John Murray, earl
      of **III:**142
   Early, Jubal A. **V:**119
   economy **II:**109
   education **VIII:**105
   education, philanthropy and
      VI:112
   English Civil War **II:**116
   Enlightenment, American
      II:118

   environment **III:**155
   ethnocentrism **II:**122
   exploration **II:**124
   food **II:**130
   Fort Necessity **II:**132–133
   Fort Stanwix, Treaty of
      III:170
   fugitive slaves **II:**140
   Gabriel's Rebellion **III:**185–
      186
   Gates, Sir Thomas **II:**143
   Glorious Revolution **II:**149
   government, British
      American **II:**151–153
   governors **V:**171, 172
   Harpers Ferry, West Virginia
      V:185
   Harrison, William Henry
      IV:184
   Heroes of America **V:**188
   housing **II:**166–167
   humanitarianism **III:**217
   impeachment of Andrew
      Johnson **V:**202
   internal improvements
      IV:202
   Jackson, Thomas J.
      "Stonewall" **V:**210
   Jamestown **II:**181–183
   Jefferson, Thomas **III:**232
   Jews **III:**237
   Jim Crow laws **VI:**203, 204
   Johnson, Anthony **II:**186
   Johnson, Mary **II:**186–187
   King's Mountain, Battle of
      III:246
   labor/labor movements
      II:197–198; **IV:**219
   Ladies Memorial
      Associations **V:**229
   land **II:**201
   Langston, John Mercer
      VI:218
   lead mines **IV:**223
   Lee, Richard Henry **III:**260
   Lee, Robert E. **V:**230
   Letcher, John **V:**232
   Madison, James **III:**281–
      282
   Mason, George **III:**292
   McCormick, Cyrus Hall
      IV:243
   McCulloch v. Maryland
      IV:246
   mining **VII:**207
   miscegenation **II:**237; **V:**261
   Mitchell, William (Billy)
      VII:212
   monarchy, British **II:**240
   Monroe, James **IV:**258, 259
   mortality **II:**243
   Mosby, John Singleton
      V:270
   mulattoes **II:**246
   Native Americans **II:**252
   Newport, Christopher
      II:267–268

   Nullification Controversy
      IV:282
   Ohio Company of Virginia
      II:278; **III:**323
   Opechancanough **II:**278
   Parsons' Cause **II:**281
   plantations **V:**308
   population trends **II:**302;
      III:343
   postal service **II:**304
   Pott, John **II:**305
   Powhatan **II:**305
   Powhatan Confederacy
      II:307
   race and race relations
      IV:310
   Racial Integrity Act
      VII:284
   Randolph, Edmund **III:**358
   religion **III:**360, 361
   religion, Euro-American
      II:329
   religious liberty **III:**363
   Republican Party **IV:**323
   Revolutionary War **III:**368
   Richmond **V:**335–337
   Riedesel, Frederica
      Charlotte, baroness von
      III:370
   Rolfe, John **II:**334–335
   Sandys, George **II:**343
   Scots immigrants **II:**346
   Shenandoah Valley:
      Jackson's campaign
      V:349–351
   slave codes **II:**352
   slavery **III:**390–392; **IV:**344–
      345, 348
   slave trade **III:**393
   slave trade, internal **IV:**349
   Smith, John **II:**362
   society, British American
      II:365
   spinsters **II:**375
   suffrage **III:**401
   Susquehannock War **II:**380
   tactics and strategy **V:**381
   Teach, Edward **II:**385
   tenants **II:**387
   tobacco **II:**391
   travel **II:**393, 394
   Turner, Nat **IV:**380–382
   Tyler, John **IV:**382, 383
   violence and lawlessness
      VI:375
   Washington, D.C. **V:**425
   Washington, George
      III:429–430
   Wilderness, Battle of the
      V:432
   Wilkes expedition **IV:**399
   Wise, Henry A. **V:**434
   witches/witchcraft **II:**419,
      420
   wolves **II:**421
   women's status and rights
      II:423

   Wyatt, Sir Francis **II:**427
   Yeardley, Sir George **II:**430
   Yorktown, surrender at
      III:454–457
Virginia, CSS
   brothers' war **V:**43
   ironclads **V:**207
   Monitor-Merrimack **V:**265
   Peninsular campaign **V:**299
   science and technology
      V:342
   Tredegar Iron Works **V:**392
   Union navy **V:**406
Virginia and Kentucky Resolutions
   III:424
   Alien and Sedition Acts
      III:14
   Jefferson, Thomas **III:**234
   Madison, James **III:**284
   secession **V:**343, 344
   states' rights **III:**397
   Taylor, John, of Caroline
      III:408
Virginia and Truckee Railroad
   IV:105
Virginia Bill of Rights **III:**461*c*
Virginia City, Nevada **IV:**106
Virginia colony
   De La Warr, Lord **I:**104–
      105
   Drake, Sir Francis **I:**112
   Lane, Ralph **I:**203
   Roanoke **I:**320–322
   werowance **I:**383
Virginia Company of London
   II:402–403, 435*c*
   agriculture **II:**10
   Berkeley, Sir William
      II:36–37
   Bermuda Company **I:**30, 31
   Dale, Sir Thomas **II:**89
   environment **II:**120
   government, British
      American **II:**151
   Hakluyt, Richard, the
      Younger **I:**153
   Hamor, Ralph **II:**162
   indentured servitude **II:**174
   Jamestown **II:**181
   labor/labor movements
      II:198
   lotteries **II:**210
   monarchy, British **II:**240
   Sandys, Sir Edwin **I:**326
   Smith, John **II:**362
   Virginia **II:**398, 399
Virginia Convention **III:**211–212,
   281
Virginia dynasty **III:424–425**
Virginia Military Institute (VMI)
   X:381*c*
   Confederate army **V:**81
   Ginsburg, Ruth Bader
      X:153
   Jackson, Thomas J.
      "Stonewall" **V:**209
Virginian, The (Wister) **VII:**265

Virginia Normal and Collegiate Institute at Petersburg **VI**:219

Virginia Peninsula **V**:12

Virginia Plan **III**:463*c*
  Constitutional Convention **III**:109
  Madison, James **III**:282–283
  Randolph, Edmund **III**:358

Virginia Racial Integrity Act **VII**:282

Virginia Resolves **III**:**425**, 459*c*

Virginia Slave Code **II**:400

Virginia State Board of Pharmacy v. Virginia Citizens Consumer Council **X**:7

Virginia Statute of Religious Freedom **III**:282, 462*c*

Virginia v. United States **X**:153

Virginius affair **V**:175; **VI**:87–88, **377**, 407*c*

Virgin of Guadalupe **I**:270

virtue
  citizenship **III**:95
  Continental Congress, First **III**:114
  marriage and family **III**:287, 288
  republicanism **III**:364–365
  women's status and rights **III**:446–448

visas
  Asian Americans **X**:32
  immigration **X**:175
  refugees **VIII**:330

Vision for Space Exploration **X**:56

Visions of Cody (Kerouac) **IX**:173

visita **I**:268

Visiting Nurse Service **VI**:328

VISTA. *See* Volunteers in Service to America

Vitoria, Francisco de **I**:110, **378–379**

Vitruvius **I**:15

Viva Las Vegas (film) **IX**:225

Viviparous Quadrupeds of North America (Audubon) **IV**:38

Vizcaíno, Sebastián **I**:133

V-J Day **VIII**:166, **406–407**

Vladivostok, Siberia **VII**:324, 325

Vlag, Piet **VII**:193

VMI. *See* Virginia Military Institute

vocational schools/training
  African Americans **VI**:7
  Dewey, John **VII**:77
  education **VII**:87–88
  education, higher **X**:111, 112
  NYA **VIII**:263
  Washington, Booker T. **VI**:384
  Williams, Fannie Barrier **VI**:395

Voice of America **VIII**:312

Volcker, Paul **X**:109, 300

Volkswagen **IX**:26–27, 133, 354*c;* **X**:35

Vollmer, August **VII**:66

Volpe, Justin **X**:382*c*

Volstead, Andrew J. **VII**:374

Volstead Act **VII**:67, 273, **374**, 407*c*

Voltaire (François-Marie Arouet)
  deism **III**:134
  Dwight, Timothy **III**:143
  race and race relations **IV**:309

Voluntary Accident Relief Plan **VII**:391

voluntary associations **III**:173, 217

Voluntary Parenthood League **VII**:36

Voluntary Relocation Program **IX**:241

volunteer army **V**:**418–420**
  bounty system **V**:39
  Confederate army **V**:79–82
  Confederate States of America **V**:86
  conscription **V**:90, 92
  desertion **V**:110
  Halleck, Henry Wager **V**:182
  prostitution **V**:316
  Union army **V**:400, 402
  women soldiers **V**:435

Volunteers in Service to America (VISTA) **IX**:**332–333**, 356*c*
  Democratic Party **IX**:85
  Economic Opportunity Act (1964) **IX**:95
  Peace Corps **IX**:255
  Shriver, Robert Sargent, Jr. **X**:324

Volunteer's Journal **III**:80

Von Donop, Emit Kurt **III**:359

Von Holst, Hermann **VI**:242

Von Rundstedt, Gerd **VIII**:276

voodoo **IV**:317

"voodoo economics" **X**:52

Voorhees, Daniel W. **V**:94

Voorhis, Jerry **X**:256

Vorse, Mary Heaton **VII**:**375**
  Gastonia Strike **VII**:122
  Greenwich Village **VII**:130, 131
  modernism **VII**:212
  peace movements **VII**:256
  radical and labor press **VII**:285, 286

Voskhod space program **IX**:297

Vostok 1 (space capsule) **IX**:296

Voter Education Project (VEP) **IX**:190, 326

voter registration
  corruption, political **VI**:83
  elections, conduct of **VI**:113
  NAACP **X**:245

voter registration drives
  CORE **IX**:73
  King, Martin Luther, Jr. **IX**:174

Meredith, James **IX**:213
  MFDP **IX**:219

voter turnout **X**:116

voting age **X**:22, 23, 376*c*

voting rights **IX**:354*c. See also* African-American suffrage; suffrage; woman suffrage
  Amendments to the U.S. Constitution **X**:23
  Civil Rights Act (1957) **IX**:59
  Civil Rights Act (1960) **IX**:60
  Civil Rights Act (1964) **IX**:60
  feminism **X**:131–132
  Hamer, Fannie Lou **IX**:141
  Kennedy, John F. **IX**:170
  SCLC **IX**:293, 294
  SNCC **IX**:302–303
  Twenty-sixth Amendment **X**:354

Voting Rights Act (1965) **IX**:**333–334**, 356*c*
  African Americans **IX**:5
  Black Power **IX**:41
  Democratic Party **IX**:85
  Great Society **IX**:139
  Johnson, Lyndon B. **IX**:163
  King, Martin Luther, Jr. **IX**:174
  liberalism **IX**:191
  race and race relations **IX**:270; **X**:295
  SCLC **IX**:294
  segregation **IX**:288
  SNCC **iX**:303
  Southern Manifesto **IX**:294
  Twenty-sixth Amendment **X**:354

Voting Rights Act (1970) **X**:23, 354

voting systems **X**:169, 171

vouchers **X**:115

Voyage et Aventures de Lord William Carisdell en Icarie (Cabet) **IV**:67

Voyager II **X**:327

Voyager program **X**:327

Voyages (Champlain) **II**:206

voyageurs **II**:141

Vrais Pourtraicts et vies des hommes illustres (True Portraits and Lives of Illustrious Men) (Thevet) **I**:358

vulcanization **IV**:333

W

WAAC. *See* Women's Army Auxiliary Corps

Wabanaki Indians **I**:1; **II**:213

Wabash River **III**:95–96

Wabash v. Illinois **VI**:410*c*
  business and government **VI**:57
  Patrons of Husbandry **VI**:279
  railroads **VI**:303
  Supreme Court **VI**:348

WAC. *See* Women's Army Corps

Waco, Texas **X**:46, 231, 380*c*

Wade, Benjamin Franklin **V**:**421**
  amnesty, acts of **V**:9
  Fort Pillow **V**:153
  impeachment of Andrew Johnson **V**:202, 203
  Joint Committee on the Conduct of the War **V**:215, 216
  Kansas-Nebraska Act **V**:222
  Morrill Land-Grant Act **V**:269
  Radical Republicans **V**:320
  Republican Party **V**:334
  Wade-Davis Bill **V**:421–422

Wade-Davis Bill **V**:**421–422**, 445*c*
  Congress **V**:89
  Reconstruction **V**:325
  Wade, Benjamin Franklin **V**:421

Wadsworth, James W. **X**:123

Wagadu kingdom **I**:139

wage and price controls (1700s) **II**:384, **405**

wage and price controls (1940s) **VIII**:**409–410**
  black market **VIII**:46
  consumerism **IX**:76
  mobilization **VIII**:242
  NWLB **VIII**:261–262
  OPA **VIII**:282
  reconversion **VIII**:326

wage and price controls (1950–1953) **IX**:26

wage and price controls (1971–1973) **X**:108, 120, **363**, 376*c*

wage discrimination **VIII**:257

wages
  CIO **IX**:71, 72
  COLA **IX**:76–77
  employment **V**:132, 133
  54th Massachusetts Regiment **V**:143
  industrialization **IV**:201
  nurses **V**:286
  PCSW **IX**:262
  strikes **V**:374–375
  union movement **IX**:323
  volunteer army **V**:419

Wages and Hours Act. *See* Fair Labor Standards Act

Wagner, Richard **VI**:257

Wagner, Robert F. **VIII**:**410–411**
  antilynching legislation **VIII**:23
  Congress **VIII**:79
  Democratic Party **VIII**:93

Wagner, Robert F. *(continued)*
Employment Act of 1946
IX:106
housing **VIII:**178
labor/labor movements
VIII:206
medicine **VIII:**236
National Recovery
Administration **VIII:**259
NIRA **VIII:**256
NLRA **VIII:**257
PWA **VIII:**314
relief **VIII:**331
Smith, Alfred E. **VII:**326
Triangle Shirtwaist Fire
VII:356
USHA **VIII:**404
Wagner Act. *See* National Labor
Relations Act
Wagner-Murray-Dingall bill
VIII:410–411
Wagner-Rogers bill (1939)
VIII:330
Wagner-Steagall Housing Act
(1937) **VIII:**445c
cities and urban life
VIII:70
housing **VIII:**177, 178
public housing **IX:**266
USHA **VIII:**404
Wagner, Robert F. **VIII:**410
Wahoo Swamp, Florida **IV:**289
Wahunsonacock. *See* Powhatan
Waiilatpu, Oregon **IV:**398
Waite, Morrison R. **V:**412; **VI:**348
Waiting for Lefty (Odets)
VIII:218
"Wait 'Til the Sun Shines, Nellie"
VII:218
Wakefield, Ruth **VII:**149
Wake Island **VIII:**311
Wakeman, George **V:**261
Wakeman, Sarah Rosetta **V:422,**
435
Waksman, Selman **VIII:**234;
IX:218
Walcott, Charles Doolittle **VI:**141,
142, **379–380**
Wald, Lillian **VII:377**
Children's Bureau **VII:**53
NAACP **VII:**224
NWTUL **VII:**231
settlement houses **VI:**328
Walden: or Life in the Woods
(Thoreau) **IV:**376, 415c
literature **IV:**228
religion **IV:**320
Thoreau, Henry David
IV:376
transcendental movement
IV:379
Waldseemüller, Martin **I:**378, *381,*
381–382
Wales **I:**10, 395c; **II:**121
"walk against fear" **IX:**213
Walker, Madame C. J. **VII:**66,
403c

Walker, David **IV:389,** 412c
abolitionism **IV:**3; **V:**2, 3
ACS **IV:**17
Cabet, Étienne **IV:**67
Walker, Edwin **VI:**297
Walker, James **VI:**113
Walker, John G. (Confederate
general) **V:**13, 186
Walker, Johnny (drum major)
V:273
Walker, Joseph **IV:**144, 145
Walker, Leroy Pope **V:**155
Walker, Mary Edwards **V:**255,
258, *422,* **422–423**
Walker, Quok **III:**355
Walker, Samuel **IV:**101, 102
Walker, William **V:423,** 443c
Clayton-Bulwer Treaty
IV:98, 99
filibustering **V:**145
foreign policy **IV:**156
Manifest Destiny **IV:**235
Walker Commission **X:**73
Walker Isthmian Canal
Commission **VII:**250, 251
Walker Lake **IV:**145
Walker's Pass **IV:**145
Walker Tariff Act **IV:**414c
Walker War **IV:**120
walking **II:**394
Walking Purchase **II:405–406**
land **II:**201
Pennsylvania **II:**285
Teedyuscung **II:**386
Weiser, Johann Conrad
II:409
Wall, The (Hersey) **VIII:**164
Wallabout Market (Brooklyn, New
York) **VI:**391
Wallace, George C. **IX:**355c;
X:363–364
AIP **X:**24
assassinations **IX:**23–24
Democratic Party **IX:**85
elections **IX:**104
elections, presidential
X:116, 117
Great Society **IX:**139
liberalism **IX:**191
McGovern, George S. **X:**217
Nixon, Richard M. **X:**256
political parties **X:**277
Republican Party **IX:**275
SNCC **IX:**303
southern demagogues
VII:332
Southern Manifesto **IX:**294
Warren, Earl **IX:**337
White Citizens' Councils
IX:342
Wallace, Henry A. (1888–1965)
VIII:411–412, 445c; **IX:**352c
Agricultural Adjustment Act
VIII:5
agriculture **VIII:**9
Americans for Democratic
Action **IX:**13, 14

Carver, George Washington
VI:63
Democratic Party **IX:**85
Dewey, Thomas E. **IX:**87
election of 1940 **VIII:**110
election of 1944 **VIII:**111
elections **IX:**102
FSA **VIII:**127
Hopkins, Harry L. **VIII:**177
Jones, Jesse H. **VIII:**197
Keynesianism **VIII:**200
Progressive Party **IX:**263–
264
Reciprocal Trade
Agreements Act **VIII:**325
Social Security Act
VIII:363
Zionism **VIII:**441
Wallace, Henry C. (1866–1924)
Carver, George Washington
VI:63
McNary-Haugen Farm Bill
VII:195
Wallace, Henry A. **VIII:**411
Wallace, Lew **VI:**376, *380,*
380–381
Wallace, Mike **IX:**199
Wallace's Farmer **VIII:**5
Wallach, E. Robert **X:**225
Walla Walla, Washington **IV:**415c
McLoughlin, John **IV:**248
Whitman, Marcus **IV:**398
Whitman, Narcissa **IV:**398
Walla Walla Valley **IV:**398
Wallerstein, Judith **X:**128
Walling, William English **VII:**230,
231
Walloons **II:**264, 266, 269
Wall Street. *See* stock market
Wall Street Journal, The **X:**219
Wal-Mart **X:**58, 109
Walnut Street Prison
(Philadelphia) **III:**347
Walpole, Sir Robert
Blackstone, Sir William
III:52
commonwealthmen **III:**103
Pitt, William **III:**337
Whigs **III:**439
Walsh, Frank **VII:**145, 229
Walsh, Lawrence E. **X:364–365**
independent counsel **X:**179
Iran-contra affair **X:**184
North, Oliver L. **X:**258
Walsh, Lorena S. **II:**424
Walsh, Thomas J.
ERA **X:**123
Irish Americans **VIII:**188
religion **VIII:**334
Walsh-Healey Government
Contracts Act **VIII:**445c
Walsingham, Sir Francis **I:**152,
382
Walt Disney Company **IX:**246
Walt Disney World (Florida)
IX:89, 246
Walter, Francis **IX:**204

Walter, Thomas (composer)
II:247, **406**
Walter, Thomas Ustick (architect)
IV:30
Walter Reed Army Medical
Center **VII:**258
Walters, Vernon **X:**357
Waltham, Massachusetts **III:**226;
VI:216–217
Waltrip, Michael **X:**332
Wampanoag **II:**435c
King Philip's War **II:**193
Massachusetts **II:**223
Massasoit **II:**226
Metacom **II:**231–232
Pilgrims **II:**294
Plymouth **II:**298
Rhode Island **II:**332
wampum **I:**199; **II:406–407,** *407*
art **II:**26
Iroquois **II:**179
Narragansett **II:**249
Native Americans **II:**252
Pequot **II:**289
Pequot War **II:**289
Wanamaker, John **VI:**78, 96,
381–382
Wanamaker & Co. **VI:**382
Wanchese **I:382–383,** 398c;
II:274
Barlowe, Arthur **I:**28
Manteo **I:**229
Roanoke **I:**321
Wangara **I:**226
Wanghia, Treaty of **IV:**414c
Wannsee, Germany **VIII:**169
War Admiral (racehorse)
VIII:373
war and warfare **II:407–408**
Howe, George Augustus
II:167
New York **II:**272
Pequot War **II:**289–291
privateering **II:**313
scalping **II:**344
war bonds **VIII:412,** *412*
advertising **VIII:**1
banks **III:**43
children **VIII:**67
mobilization **VIII:**242
women's status and rights
VIII:424
World War II home front
VIII:433
war contracting **V:423–424**
War Council **VII:**21
Ward, Aaron Montgomery **VI:**237
Ward, Artemas **III:**65
Ward, Hamilton **VII:**303
Ward, Holcombe **VI:**342
Ward, John M. **VI:**26
Ward, John Q. A. **VI:**327
Ward, Lester Frank **VI:382–383**
Gilman, Charlotte Perkins
VII:125
literature **VII:**180
Social Darwinism **VI:**334

Ward, Nancy **II:408**
Ward, Samuel (1725–1776)
  II:333
Ward, Samuel (1814–1884)
  VI:228
Ward, Samuel Ringgold (1817–
  1866) **V:58**
War Democrats
  Congress **V:89**
  Democratic Party **V:109**
  elections **V:126**
War Department, Confederate
  Benjamin, Judah P. **V:33**
  Davis, Jefferson **V:105**
  impressment **V:204**
War Department, Union **V:368,**
  402
War Department, U.S.
  armed forces **VII:20**
  Army, U.S. **VIII:25**
  Army Act **VII:22**
  Bell, John **V:32**
  CCC **VIII:71**
  Dana, Charles A. **V:102**
  Davis, Jefferson **V:104**
  demobilization (WWII)
    VIII:91
  dollar-a-year men **VIII:96**
  Executive Order 9066
    VIII:120
  Freedmen's Bureau **V:160**
  Hershey, Lewis B. **VIII:164**
  Indian Affairs, Bureau of
    IV:196, 197
  Indian Affairs, Office of
    VI:188
  industrial development
    V:205
  Interior, Department of
    IV:201
  Kearny, Stephen Watts
    IV:212
  Knox, Henry **III:247, 248**
  Mississippi River war **V:263**
  Mitchell, William (Billy)
    VII:212
  movies **VIII:246**
  National Security Act of
    1947 **IX:237**
  peace movements **VII:257**
  Pinckney, Charles
    Cotesworth **III:336**
  Scott, Winfield **IV:336**
  Stanton, Edwin M. **V:368–**
    369
  uniforms **V:398–399**
  V-J Day **VIII:406**
  Washington, D.C. **V:425,**
    426
War Department Counter
  Intelligence Corps **VIII:186–**
  187
War Department General Staff
  VIII:76, 233
War Department Military
  Intelligence Division (WDGS/
  MID or G-2) **VIII:186**

Wardley Society **III:387**
Wardman, Ervin **VI:405**
Ward's Cove Packing Company v.
  Antonio
    affirmative action **X:9**
    Civil Rights Act (1991) **X:77**
    Rehnquist, William H.
      X:305
Ward's Island, New York **VII:158**
Ware, Charles Pickard **VI:255**
Ware, Henry **III:307, 419**
Warehouse Act (Illinois) **VI:101,**
  279
warfare
  Aztecs **I:19, 21**
  Chichén Itzá **I:72**
  Huron **I:172**
  Mississippian **I:245**
  Toltecs **I:365–366**
"warfare state" **IX:260**
War Hawks **IV:389–390**
  American System **IV:19**
  Calhoun, John C. **IV:68**
  Canada **III:79**
  Clay, Henry **IV:96**
  War of 1812 **IV:390**
Warhol, Andy **IX:19; X:30**
War Industries Board (WIB)
  VII:377–378
  AEF **VII:10**
  Baruch, Bernard M. **VII:32;**
    VIII:41–42
  dollar-a-year men **VIII:96**
  Fuel Administration
    VII:119
  Johnson, Hugh S. **VIII:196**
  military-industrial complex
    IX:216
  National Recovery
    Administration **VIII:259**
  presidency **VII:269**
  World War I **VII:393, 394**
War Is Kind (Crane) **VI:85, 227**
War Labor Board **VIII:249**
warlock **II:419**
War Manpower Commission
  (WMC) **VIII:412–413**
  FEPC **VIII:123**
  government **VIII:154**
  mobilization **VIII:241**
  NWLB **VIII:261**
  NYA **VIII:262**
War Message (1812) (James
  Madison) **IV:417–419**
Warmoth, Henry Clay **V:424–425**
Warm Springs, Georgia **VIII:347**
Warm Springs Reservation **VI:17**
Warner, Charles Dudley
  Gilded Age, The: A Tale of
    Today **VI:145–146**
  literature **VI:225**
  Twain, Mark **VI:367**
Warner, John **X:259**
Warner, Seth **III:199**
Warner, Susan **IV:229**
Warner Brothers **VII:216**
Warner Lambert Co. **X:7**

War of 1812 **III:466c; IV:390–**
  392, *391,* **411c**
  Adams, John Quincy **IV:5**
  Adams-Onís Treaty **IV:6**
  agriculture **III:11; IV:12**
  American Fur Company
    IV:18
  American System **IV:19**
  art and architecture **III:29;**
    IV:28
  Ashley, William Henry **IV:31**
  Astor, John Jacob **IV:34**
  Astoria **IV:36**
  Atkinson, Henry **IV:36**
  Baltimore, Battle of **IV:43**
  banking **IV:45**
  Bank of the United States,
    Second **IV:48**
  banks **IV:42–43**
  Barbary Wars **III:46**
  Becknell, William **IV:50**
  Benton, Thomas Hart **IV:53**
  Black Hawk War **IV:56**
  Bonaparte, Napoleon **III:55**
  Bonus Bill **IV:62**
  Cadore Letter **III:73**
  Calhoun, John C. **IV:68**
  Canada **III:79**
  Caroline affair **IV:81**
  Catholics **III:83**
  Chauncey, Isaac **III:86**
  Cherokee **III:87; IV:85**
  Chesapeake-Leopard affair
    III:88
  Choctaw **III:89**
  Chouteau family **IV:87, 88**
  Claiborne, William C. C.
    IV:95
  Clark, William **III:97**
  Clay, Henry **IV:96**
  Columbia River **IV:103**
  conscription **V:90**
  Constitution, USS **III:108**
  Creek **III:126**
  Crockett, Davy **IV:110**
  Dartmoor Prison **IV:113**
  debt, national **III:132**
  Decatur, Stephen **IV:115**
  Democratic Party **IV:117**
  Democratic-Republican
    Party **III:136**
  Drayton, William H. **IV:127**
  economy **IV:130**
  election of 1828 **IV:135**
  Era of Good Feelings
    IV:141
  Essex, USS **IV:143, 144**
  Essex decision **III:157, 158**
  Farragut, David Glasgow
    V:137
  federal income tax **VII:106**
  Federalist Party **III:164–**
    165
  foreign affairs **III:169**
  foreign policy **IV:154**
  Free Trade and Sailor's
    Rights **IV:165**

  French Revolution **III:179**
  frontier, the **III:182**
  Fulton, Robert **III:183**
  Ghent, Treaty of **IV:175–**
    176, **411c, 419–422**
  Girard, Stephen **III:195**
  Harrison, William Henry
    IV:185, 186
  Hartford Convention
    IV:186
  Houston, Sam **IV:190**
  Hull, William **IV:192**
  Indian Removal Act **IV:198**
  industrialization **IV:199**
  Industrial Revolution
    III:226
  Iroquois **III:228**
  Jackson, Andrew **IV:205–**
    206
  journalism **III:241**
  Kearny, Stephen Watts
    IV:212
  Keokuk **IV:213**
  Key, Francis Scott **IV:213**
  Lafitte, Jean **IV:220**
  Lake Erie, Battle of **IV:220**
  lead mines **IV:223**
  Macon's Bill No. 2 **III:280**
  Madison, Dolley Payne
    Todd **III:280–281**
  Madison, James **III:284**
  Madison's War Message
    IV:417–419
  Mason, Richard B. **IV:241**
  McCulloch v. Maryland
    IV:245
  migration **IV:253**
  Missouri Fur Company
    IV:258
  Monroe, James **IV:259**
  Mott, Lucretia **IV:265**
  mountain men **IV:266**
  National Road **IV:271**
  Native Americans **III:315;**
    IV:273, 275
  Native Americans in the War
    of 1812 **IV:276**
  neutrality **VII:235**
  New Orleans, Battle of
    IV:280
  Otis, Harrison Gray **III:326**
  panic of 1819 **IV:293, 294**
  panic of 1837 **IV:294**
  Pickering, Timothy **III:335**
  Pike, Zebulon Montgomery
    IV:300
  political parties **III:339**
  privateering **III:348**
  Prophet, the Shawnee
    III:349
  public land policy **IV:305**
  race and race relations
    IV:312
  Red Jacket **III:360**
  Sac and Fox **IV:327**
  Scott, Winfield **IV:336**
  secession **V:343, 344**

War of 1812 (continued)
  Seminole IV:338
  states' rights III:397
  Taney, Roger B. IV:365
  Taylor, Zachary IV:367
  Tecumseh III:409
  Thames, Battle of the
    IV:375
  Vanderbilt, Cornelius
    IV:386
  War Hawks IV:389
  Washington, D.C. III:429
  Webster, Daniel IV:393
  Webster-Ashburton Treaty
    IV:394
  Wilkinson, James III:444
War of Jenkins' Ear II:313,
  408–409
War of the Pacific (1879–1884)
  VI:67
War of the Worlds (radio
  broadcast) VIII:446c
  FCC VIII:131
  news media VIII:271
  public opinion polls
    VIII:313
  radio VIII:320
  Welles, Orson VIII:414, 415
War of the Worlds (Wells) IX:287
war on crime X:242
war on drugs
  Bennett, William J. X:41
  Bush, George H. W. X:52
  crime and punishment X:97
  foreign policy X:144
  Mexico X:226
  narcotics X:243
War on Poverty IX:335–336,
  357c
  Bilingual Education Act
    X:42
  CAP IX:68
  cities and urban life IX:56
  Democratic Party IX:85
  Economic Opportunity Act
    (1964) IX:95
  elections IX:104
  Galbraith, John Kenneth
    IX:129
  Gonzáles, Rodolfo "Corky"
    IX:136
  Great Society IX:139
  Harrington, Michael IX:142
  Head Start IX:144–145
  Job Corps IX:161
  liberalism X:208
  LWV IX:187
  Model Cities program
    IX:220
  NASA IX:231
  New Deal IX:242
  Shriver, Robert Sargent, Jr.
    X:323
  VISTA IX:333
war on terrorism
  Afghanistan War X:10–12
  Bush, George W. X:56

defense policy X:102–103
foreign policy X:143
Hamdan v. Rumsfeld X:164
Powell, Colin L. X:287
terrorism X:347
War Powers Act (1973) X:22, 365,
  376c
War Production Board (WPB)
  VIII:413–414
  automobile industry VIII:37
  Baruch, Bernard M.
    VIII:42
  Congress VIII:81
  dollar-a-year men VIII:96
  government VIII:154
  Hillman, Sidney VIII:166
  miracle drugs IX:218
  mobilization VIII:241, 242
  Nelson, Donald M.
    VIII:266, 267
  OPA VIII:282
  OPM VIII:283
  OWM VIII:286
  rationing VIII:322
  scrap drives VIII:354
  War Manpower Commission
    VIII:412
  zoot-suiters VIII:442
War Refugee Board (WRB)
  VIII:448c
  Holocaust VIII:170
  immigration VIII:184
  Jews VIII:196
  Morgenthau, Henry T., Jr.
    VIII:244
  refugees VIII:330
War Relocation Authority (WRA)
  Executive Order 9066
    VIII:121
  Japanese Americans,
    relocation of VIII:194
  Lange, Dorothea VIII:210
Warren (frigate) III:333
Warren, Earl IX:336, 336–337,
  353c
  assassinations IX:22
  Baker v. Carr IX:33–34
  Brennan, William J., Jr.
    X:47, 48
  Brown v. Board of
    Education IX:44
  Burger, Warren E. X:50
  Eisenhower, Dwight D.
    IX:101
  elections IX:102
  Engel v. Vitale IX:108
  gays and lesbians IX:131
  Marshall, Thurgood IX:203
  Meese, Edwin C., III X:225
  Miranda v. Arizona IX:219
  NAACP IX:232
  Oswald, Lee Harvey IX:252
  Reynolds v. Sims IX:276
  Supreme Court X:338
  Warren Court IX:337–338
Warren, Fred VII:325
Warren, George F. VIII:243

Warren, Gouverneur K. V:147,
  167
Warren, James III:427
Warren, John IV:333
Warren, Joseph III:427
  Gage, Thomas III:187
  Old South Church III:323
  Revere, Paul III:366
  Suffolk Resolves III:400
Warren, Joshua V:295
Warren, Josiah IV:392–393
Warren, Kemble IV:146
Warren, Mary Cole II:409
Warren, Mercy Otis III:427–428
Warren, Robert Penn IX:193–194
Warren, Samuel VII:58
Warren Association III:44
Warren Commission
  assassinations IX:22
  Ford, Gerald R. X:138
  Oswald, Lee Harvey IX:252
  Warren, Earl IX:337
Warren Commission Report
  IX:356c
Warren Court IX:337–338
  Baker v. Carr IX:33, 34
  Burger, Warren E. X:50
  Eisenhower, Dwight D.
    IX:101
  Heart of Atlanta Motel v.
    U.S. IX:146
  segregation IX:288
  Warren, Earl IX:337
War Revenue Act VII:378–379
  journalism VII:160
  presidency VII:269
  World War I VII:393
Warrior, Clyde IX:241
War Risk Insurance VII:262, 371
Warsaw, New York IV:413c
Warsaw ghetto uprising VIII:170
Warsaw Pact IX:353c; X:379c
  cold war IX:63
  Europe IX:112, 113
  Iron Curtain, collapse of
    X:188
  Soviet Union IX:295
War Service Committees VII:378
wars of national liberation
  IX:338–339
Wartime Civil Control
  Administration (WCCA)
  VIII:193
wartime contracts
  mobilization VIII:242
  OWMR VIII:287
  reconversion VIII:326, 327
Wartime Prohibition Act (1918)
  VII:272
Warwick II:150, 333
Warwick-Yorktown siege V:341
Wasatch Range
  Deseret, State of IV:119
  Mormon Trail IV:262
  Young, Brigham IV:408
Washburn, Cadwallader Colden
  VI:129

Washburn, William D. VI:100
Washington, Booker T. VI:383,
  383–384, 409c, 411c
  African Americans VI:7
  Atlanta Compromise speech
    VI:432–433
  Carver, George Washington
    VI:63
  DuBois, W.E.B. VII:80
  education, higher VI:111–
    112
  literature V:240
  NAACP IX:232
  Niagara Movement VII:240
  Trotter, William Monroe
    VII:357
Washington, Bushrod III:403
Washington, D.C. III:428,
  428–429, 463c; IV:411c;
  V:425–427; VII:444c
  Act Abolishing the Slave
    Trade in the District of
    Columbia IV:449
  Amendments to the U.S.
    Constitution X:23
  American Liberty League
    VIII:19
  antiwar movement, Vietnam
    X:28
  architecture III:29
  Arlington National Cemetery
    V:16
  assassination of Abraham
    Lincoln V:19–21
  banking VIII:40
  black market VIII:46
  Blair, Francis Preston, Jr.
    V:35–36
  Bonus Army VIII:48
  Brotherhood of Sleeping Car
    Porters VIII:54
  Bureau of Motion Pictures
    VIII:56
  Burnham, Daniel Hudson
    VI:55
  Bush, Vannevar VIII:56
  Byrnes, James F. VIII:60
  contrabands V:92
  corruption, political VI:83
  Coxey's Army VI:84
  Crittenden Compromise
    V:98
  Davis, Jefferson V:103
  Davis, Varina Howell
    V:105–106
  Declaration of
    Independence III:134
  demobilization (WWII)
    VIII:91
  dust bowl VIII:98
  Eakins, Thomas VI:104
  economy IV:130
  education, higher VI:111
  education, philanthropy and
    VI:112
  election of 1828 IV:136
  Ellington, Duke VIII:112

emancipation **V:**129
ERA **VII:**100
espionage **V:**134
FEPC **VIII:**123
foreign policy **IV:**154
Freedmen's Savings Bank
    V:159
Frémont, Jesse Benton
    IV:165
Ghent, Treaty of **IV:**176
Grant, Julia Dent **V:**173
Greenhow, Rose O'Neal
    V:178
gun control **X:**162
Halleck, Henry Wager
    V:182
Hancock, Winfield Scott
    V:184
Harvard Regiment **V:**186
Hershey, Lewis B. **VIII:**164
Hillman, Sidney **VIII:**165
Hooker, Joseph **V:**196
Hoover presidency
    VIII:175
Howe, Louis M. **VIII:**179
Hurston, Zora Neale
    VIII:181
Indian Rights Association
    VI:190
invention and technology
    VI:196
Jackson, Helen Hunt
    VI:199
Johnson, Lady Bird **IX:**163
Juneteenth **V:**219
Keokuk **IV:**213
Key, Francis Scott **IV:**213,
    214
King, Ernest J. **VIII:**202
Langston, John Mercer
    VI:218, 219
Lee, Jason **IV:**224
L'Enfant, Pierre-Charles
    III:260, 261
Lincoln, Mary Todd **V:**238
lobbying **VI:**228
Lockwood, Belva Ann
    Bennett McNall **VI:**229
Madison, Dolley Payne
    Todd **III:**281
Madison, James **III:**284
March on Washington
    (1963) **IX:**199–201
March on Washington
    Movement **VIII:**227–
    228
McClellan, George Brinton
    V:250
McDowell, Irvin **V:**252
migration **VIII:**239
Mitchell, William (Billy)
    VII:212
monuments **V:**267, 268
Morris, Robert **III:**306
Morse, Samuel F. B. **IV:**264
Mosby, John Singleton
    V:270

Muhammad, Elijah **IX:**226
NWP **VII:**230
Panama Canal **VII:**250
Paul, Alice **VII:**254
Pershing, John Joseph
    VII:258
popular sovereignty **IV:**307–
    308
population trends **X:**282
prostitution **V:**316
spiritualism **IV:**355
suburbanization/suburbs
    VIII:379
Sweet trial **VII:**344
Taylor, Zachary **IV:**368
Terrell, Mary Eliza Church
    VII:352, 353
UN **VIII:**402
Union army **V:**404
Valesh, Eva McDonald
    VII:367
Veterans Bureau **VII:**373
victory gardens **VIII:**405
Virginius affair **VI:**377
V-J Day **VIII:**407
War of 1812 **IV:**390, 392
Whitman, Walt **V:**430
Washington, George **I:**222;
    III:429–432, *430,* 461c–464c
    Adams, John **III:**5, 6
    alcohol **III:**13
    André, John **III:**20
    animals **II:**23
    anti-Masonry **IV:**25
    antislavery **III:**26
    Bache, Benjamin Franklin
        III:39
    banks **III:**42
    Barry, John **III:**47
    Braddock, Edward **II:**44
    Brandywine, Battle of
        III:61, 62
    Burgoyne, Sir John **III:**68
    Burr, Aaron **III:**69
    Capes, Battle of the **III:**79
    Chase, Samuel **III:**85
    Cherokee **III:**87
    Cincinnati, Order of **III:**90
    Clinton, Sir Henry **III:**99
    cold war **IX:**62
    Constitution, ratification of
        the **III:**105
    Constitutional Convention
        III:108
    Continental army **III:**111–
        112
    Continental army, mutinies
        of **III:**113
    Continental Congress, First
        III:113
    Continental Congress,
        Second **III:**115
    Conway Cabal, the **III:**118
    Cornplanter **III:**119
    Cornwallis, Charles, Lord
        III:120
    deism **III:**135

Delaware River forts **III:**135
Democratic Party **IV:**116
Democratic-Republican
    societies **III:**136, 137
Dorchester Heights **III:**138
environment **III:**154
Fallen Timbers, Battle of
    III:161
Farewell Address of George
    Washington **III:**162
Federalist Party **III:**164
Federalists **III:**166
foreign affairs **III:**168
Fort Necessity **II:**133
Fort Washington, capture of
    III:172
French Alliance **III:**177, 178
French colonies **II:**138
French Revolution **III:**179
Freneau, Philip **III:**180
Fulton, Robert **III:**182
Gates, Horatio **III:**190
Genêt, Edmond Charles
    III:191
Germantown, Battle of
    III:193–194
Greene, Nathanael **III:**198,
    199
Hamilton, Alexander
    III:205, 207
Harlem Heights, Battle of
    III:210
Harpers Ferry, West Virginia
    V:185
Howe, Sir William **III:**215
Independence Hall **III:**223
Industrial Revolution
    III:225
Iroquois **III:**228
Jay, John **III:**230
Jay's Treaty **III:**231
Jefferson, Thomas **III:**233
Jews **III:**237
Kalb, Johann, baron de
    III:245
Knox, Henry **III:**247, 248
Lafayette, marquis de
    III:253, 254
land **II:**202
Lee, Charles **III:**258, 259
Lee, Henry **III:**259
Lee, Robert E. **V:**230
L'Enfant, Pierre-Charles
    III:261
literature **III:**268
Long Island, Battle of
    III:271
Madison, James **III:**283
Marshall, John **III:**289
Medal of Honor **V:**255
Monmouth, Battle of
    III:299–300
Monroe, James **IV:**258
Morris, Gouverneur
    III:304
Morristown encampment
    III:306–307

Mount Vernon **II:**245
music **III:**309
Neutrality Proclamation
    III:315
Newburgh conspiracy
    III:316
New York City, fire of
    III:318
New York World's Fair
    (1939–1940) **VIII:**273
Ohio Company of Virginia
    II:278
Ostenaco **II:**280
Peale, Charles Willson
    III:333
Pickering, Timothy **III:**335
Pinckney, Charles
    Cotesworth **III:**335, 336
political parties **III:**338–339
popular culture **III:**341
Popular Front **VIII:**304
POWs **III:**345, 346
Pulaski, Casimir **III:**350
Randolph, Edmund **III:**358
republicanism **III:**365
Revolutionary War **III:**368
Ross, Betsy **III:**374
Rush, Benjamin **III:**376
Schuyler, Philip John
    III:384
Scott, Winfield **IV:**336
Seven Years' War **II:**348
Steuben, Frederick, baron
    von **III:**398
Stoney Point, Battle of
    III:399
Stuart, Gilbert **III:**400
Sullivan, John **III:**402
tactics and strategy **V:**380
theater **III:**411
Trenton and Princeton,
    Battles of **III:**415, 416
Truman, Harry S. **IX:**320
U.S. Military Academy at
    West Point **V:**408
Valley Forge **III:**421
Virginia dynasty **III:**425
Washington, D.C. **III:**428
Washington, Martha **III:**432
Washington Benevolent
    Societies **III:**433
Weems, "Parson" Mason
    Locke **III:**435
West Point **III:**437
Whiskey Rebellion **III:**440
White Plains, Battle of
    III:440
Yorktown, surrender at
    III:455
Washington, Margaret Murray
    VII:225
Washington, Martha **III:432–433**
    Arlington National Cemetery
        V:16
    Valley Forge **III:**423
    Washington, George
        III:430, 432

Washington, Pennsylvania **IV**:271
Washington, Treaty of **V**:175;
   VI:61, **384–385**, 407c
Washington, USS **IV**:21
Washington, William **III**:213
Washington Agreement **VII**:119
Washington Artillery **V**:81
Washington Benevolent Societies
   III:433
Washington College **IV**:246; **V**:232
Washington Conference on Naval
   Disarmament **VII**:379
      foreign policy **VII**:115
      Harding, Warren Gamaliel
         VII:135
      Naval Disarmament
         Conference **VII**:235
      peace movements **VII**:257
      presidency **VII**:269
Washington Daily News
   VIII:314–315
Washingtonians (temperance
   activists) **IV**:369
Washington Monument **VI**:239
Washington Navy Yard **V**:101
Washington Post, The **X**:219, 233
Washington Post March, The
   (Sousa) **VI**:339, 340
Washington Square (James)
   VI:200
Washington State
   abortion **X**:2
   Canada **VI**:61
   conservation/
      environmentalism **VI**:82
   Flynn, Elizabeth Gurley
      VII:109
   Foster, William Zebulon
      VII:116
   free speech fights **VII**:117
   IWW **VII**:147
   Japanese Americans,
      relocation of **VIII**:193
   Native Americans **X**:250
   Seattle General Strike
      VII:317
Washington State v. Glucksberg
   X:305
Washington *Telegraph* **IV**:136
Washington Territory **IV**:415c
Washington Times-Herald **IX**:168
Washington University **VII**:31
WASP. *See* Women Airforce
   Service Pilots
Waste Land, The (Eliot) **VII**:408c
Waste Makers, The (Packard)
   IX:76, 253
waste treatment **X**:131, 375c
Watauga River **III**:139
water **II**:16, 235
Water-Cure Journal **V**:139
watered stock **VI**:83
Waterford, New York **IV**:401
Watergate scandal **X**:365–367,
   366, 376c, 377c
   Albert, Carl B. **X**:22
   Burger, Warren E. **X**:51

conservative movement
   X:93
   Cox, Archibald, Jr. **X**:95
   economy **X**:109
   Ford, Gerald R. **X**:138
   Haig, Alexander M., Jr.
      X:163
   House of Representatives
      X:169
   impeachment of Richard M.
      Nixon **X**:178
   independent counsel **X**:179
   Jaworski, Leon **X**:192, 193
   media **X**:219
   Mitchell, John N. **X**:232,
      233
   Nixon, Richard M. **X**:257
   OMB **X**:266
   Ruckelshaus, William D.
      X:312
   Supreme Court **X**:338
   U.S. v. Nixon **X**:357
Waterloo, Battle of **III**:54
Waterman, Louis **VI**:196
water pollution **X**:376c
Water Quality Act (1965) **IX**:47,
   109, 356c
water rights **X**:290
Waters, Ethel **VII**:220
Waterworks Improvement
   Association **VII**:345
Waterworks Park, Detroit
   VII:345
Watie, Stand **V**:297, **427**
Watkins, Sam **V**:239
Watkins, William **IV**:17; **V**:184;
   VI:159
Watkins v. United States **IX**:337
Watres Act **VII**:29
Watson, Elkanah **III**:161, 466c
Watson, Gregory D. **X**:23
Watson, James D. **IX**:285, 314
Watson, John **III**:213; **VII**:4
Watson, Thomas Edward
   VII:379–380
   Bryan, William Jennings
      VI:52
   People's Party **VI**:282
   southern demagogues
      VII:332
Watson and the Shark (Copley)
   III:32
Watson-Parker Act **VII**:409c
Watt, James G. **X**:300, **367**
Watterson, Henry **VI**:43, **385–
386**
Watts uprising (1965) **IX**:339–
340, 340, 356c
   Great Society **IX**:139
   Model Cities program
      IX:220
   race and race relations
      IX:270; **X**:295
Waubaunsee County, Missouri
   VI:123
WAVES. *See* Women Accepted for
   Volunteer Emergency Service

Wa-Wan Press **VI**:255
Waxaklahun-Ubah-K'awil (Mayan
   ruler) **I**:90
Waxhaws, Battle of **III**:407
Waxman, Henry **X**:72
Way Down East (film) **VII**:132
Wayles, John **III**:210
Waymouth, George **I**:135
Wayne, Anthony **III**:433–434,
   464c
   Blue Jacket **III**:54
   Brandywine, Battle of
      III:62
   Fallen Timbers, Battle of
      III:161–162
   Georgia Expedition **III**:192
   Greenville, Treaty of
      III:200
   Harrison, William Henry
      IV:184
   Native Americans **IV**:273
   Pike, Zebulon Montgomery
      IV:300
   Pulaski, Casimir **III**:350
   Stoney Point, Battle of
      III:399
   Washington, George **III**:431
Wayne, John **VIII**:246; **IX**:224
Waynesboro, Battle of **V**:120, 352
WCAR. *See* Women's Central
   Association for Relief
WCCA (Wartime Civil Control
   Administration) **VIII**:193
WCTU. *See* Women's Christian
   Temperance Union
WDGS/MID (War Department
   Military Intelligence Division)
   VIII:186
We (Lindbergh) **VII**:178
WEAF radio (New York City)
   VII:160, 290
Wea Indians **III**:200
WEAL. *See* Women's Equity
   Action League
wealth
   banking **II**:32
   Charleston **II**:64
   horses **II**:166
   New Deal **VIII**:270
   *Recent Social Trends in the
      United States* **VIII**:323
   Spanish colonies **II**:371–
      372
   World War II **VIII**:428, 429
   World War II home front
      VIII:433
"Wealth" (Carnegie). *See* "Gospel
   of Wealth, The"
Wealth Against Commonwealth
   (Lloyd) **VI**:227; **VII**:303
Wealth Tax. *See* Revenue Act
   (1935)
weapons. *See* firearms
weapons inspections **X**:383c
   Bush, George W. **X**:56
   foreign policy **X**:143
   Iraq War **X**:186, 187

   Middle East **X**:229
   Powell, Colin L. **X**:287
weapons of mass destruction
   (WMD) **X**:384c
   Bush, George W. **X**:56
   defense policy **X**:101, 103
   Iraq War **X**:186, 187
   Middle East **X**:229
   Persian Gulf War **X**:273–
      274
   Rice, Condoleezza **X**:309
   terrorism **X**:346, 347
   UN **X**:356
"We Are Coming Father Abra'm"
   V:273
Weary Blues (Hughes) **VII**:136
Weather Bureau, U.S. **IV**:334;
   VI:386–387, 407c
Weatherford, William **IV**:109
Weathermen (Weather
   Underground) **IX**:340–341;
   X:367–368, 375c
   Leary, Timothy **IX**:188
   New Left **IX**:244
   SDS **IX**:304
Weaver, James B. **VI**:411c
   currency issue **VI**:89
   Greenback-Labor Party
      VI:155
   Lease, Mary Elizabeth
      Clyens **VI**:220
   People's Party **VI**:282
Weaver, John **VII**:42
Weaver, Randy **X**:231, 267
Weaver, Richard **X**:93
Weaver, Robert C. **VIII**:45, 255
Weavers, the **IX**:120–121
weaving **III**:445
Webb, Edwin **VII**:101, 318
Webb-Kenyon Act **VII**:406c
Weber, David **I**:32
Weber, Max **II**:322; **IX**:272
Weber and Fields **VI**:117
Web sites **X**:239
Webster, Daniel **IV**:393, **393–
394**, 412c, 414c
   Cass, Lewis **IV**:83
   Compromise of 1850
      IV:104
   Dartmouth College case
      IV:114
   election of 1840 **IV**:137,
      139
   Free-Soil Party **IV**:163
   McCulloch v. Maryland
      IV:245
   Nullification Controversy
      IV:283
   Oregon Treaty of 1846
      IV:287
   Pacific Railroad Act **V**:293
   Tyler, John **IV**:382, 383
   Van Buren, Martin **IV**:386
   Webster-Ashburton Treaty
      IV:394
   Whigs **IV**:396, 397
Webster, Joseph P. **VI**:257

Webster, Noah **III**:104, **434–435,** 462*c*; **IV**:134
Webster, Peletiah **III**:305
Webster-Ashburton Treaty **IV:394–395,** 395*m*, 414*c*
  Aroostook War **IV**:27
  foreign policy **IV**:154
  Oregon Treaty of 1846 **IV**:287
  Tyler, John **IV**:383
  Webster, Daniel **IV**:393
Webster v. Reproductive Health Services **X:368–369,** 379*c*
  O'Connor, Sandra Day **X**:265
  Rehnquist, William H. **X**:305
  White, Byron R. **X**:369
Wedderburn, Alexander **III**:174
Weddington, Sarah **X**:133
Weed, Thurlow
  Fillmore, Millard **IV**:149
  Greeley, Horace **V**:176, 177
  Massachusetts Emigrant Aid Society **IV**:242
  Whigs **IV**:397
"Weekend Passes" campaign ad **X**:168
Weeks, Edwin **VI**:275
Weeks, John D. **VII**:386
Weeks v. Southern Bell **X**:133, 247
Weems, "Parson" Mason Locke **III**:268, 429, **435**
Wefers, Bernie **VI**:359
Wegadugu **I**:252, 253
Weigel, George **X**:70
Weiland (Brown) **III**:64
Weill, Kurt **VIII**:252
Weimar Republic **VII**:370
Weinberg, Jack **IX**:126
Weinberger, Caspar **X**:100, 365
Weiner, Lee **X**:73
Weir, Benjamin **X**:183
Weir, Julian Alden **VI**:275; **VII**:23
Weir, Robert F. **VI**:389
Weisberg, Bernard **IX**:111
Weisbord, Albert **VII**:253
Weiser, Johann Conrad **II:409; III**:175
Weiss, Carl A. **VIII**:223
Weitzel, Godfrey **V**:403
Welch, Joseph **IX**:18
Welch, Robert **X**:93
Welch, Thomas **II**:124
Welch, William H. **VI**:148
Weld, Angelina Grimké **V**:434
Weld, Theodore Dwight **IV:395–396**
  abolitionism **IV**:3, 4
  American Anti-Slavery Society **IV**:15
  Foster, Abigail Kelley **IV**:161
  Grimké, Angelina and Sarah **IV**:180
  Tappan, Arthur and Lewis **IV**:366

Weld, William **X**:225
Welde, Thomas **II**:115
welfare **X**:381*c*. *See also* relief
  Clinton, William J. **X**:79–80, 82
  conservative movement **X**:93
  elections **IX**:104
  FSA **X**:128
  Goldwater, Barry **IX**:135
  Great Society **IX**:139
  liberalism **X**:207
Welfare Administration **VIII**:365
welfare capitalism **VII:380–381**
  American Plan **VII**:14
  Ford, Henry **VII**:112
  National Civic Federation **VII**:226
  social work **VII**:329
Welles, Gideon **V**:405, **427–428**
Welles, Orson **VIII:414–415,** *415*, 446*c*
  FCC **VIII**:131
  FTP **VIII**:136
  movies **IX**:224
  news media **VIII**:271
  public opinion polls **VIII**:313
  radio **VIII**:320
Welles, Sumner **VIII**:151, 180, **415–416**
Wells, Fargo and Company **IV**:290–291
Wells, Herman **IX**:176
Wells, H. G. **VIII**:446*c*
  radio **VIII**:320
  science fiction **IX**:287
  Welles, Orson **VIII**:414, 415
Wells-Barnett, Ida Bell **VI:387– 388,** *388,* 411*c*
  African Americans **VI**:7
  lynching **VI**:230–231
  NAACP **VII**:224
  NACW **VI**:259; **VII**:225
  Terrell, Mary Eliza Church **VII**:352
  women's status and rights **V**:438
Welsh, Herbert **VI**:190
Wendat **II**:178, 179
Wentworth, Benning **II**:260
werowance **I:383; II**:278, 362, 363
Wesberry v. Sanders **IX**:34
"We Shall Overcome"
  Birmingham confrontation **IX**:39
  folk music revival **IX**:121
  music **IX**:229
  sit-ins **IX**:291
Wesley, Charles **II**:409, 410, 413
Wesley, John **II:409–410,** *410*
  Asbury, Francis **III**:36
  Great Awakening **II**:155
  Methodism **III**:296, 297
  music **II**:247
  Whitefield, George **II**:413

Wesleyan Chapel (Seneca Falls, New York) **IV**:341
West, Benjamin **III:435–436**
  art **III**:32–33
  Earle, Ralph **III**:145
  Peale, Charles Willson **III**:332
  Trumbull, John **III**:416
West, Cornel **X**:14
West, Kanye **X**:174
West, Mae
  censorship **VIII**:65
  entertainment, popular **VII**:95
  movies **VIII**:245
  vaudeville **VII**:368
West, Thomas. *See* De La Warr, Lord
West Africa **I**:396*c*
  Fulani **I**:135–136
  horses **I**:169
  Mali **I**:225–226
West Bank
  Camp David accords **X**:64–66
  Israel **IX**:160
  Middle East **X**:227, 229, 230
Westbrook, T. R. **VII**:303
West Church (Boston) **III**:293
West Coast
  African Americans **VIII**:4
  Asian Americans **VIII**:32
  dust bowl **VIII**:98
  economy **VIII**:104
  enemy aliens **VIII**:115
  Executive Order 9066 **VIII**:120
  Forty-niners **IV**:160
  Ickes, Harold L. **VIII**:183
  Japanese Americans, relocation of **VIII**:193
  La Guardia, Fiorello **VIII**:208
  Lee, Jason **IV**:224
  migration **IV**:255
  Oregon Treaty of 1846 **IV**:286
  technology **VIII**:397
  zoot-suiters **VIII**:442
Westendorf, Thomas Paine **VI**:257
West End Street Railway (Boston, Massachusetts) **VI**:360
Western Air Express **VII**:28, 165
Western Conference **VI**:131
Western Defense Command **VIII**:121
Western Europe
  demobilization (WWII) **IX**:84
  Europe **IX**:113
  Marshall Plan **IX**:203–204, 359–361
  Middle East **IX**:214
  NATO **IX**:246, 247

western European immigration **VII**:227–228
Western Federation of Miners (WFM) **VII:381–382**
  Coeur d'Alene miners' strike **VI**:77
  Darrow, Clarence Seward **VII**:70
  Haywood, William Dudley **VII**:137
  IWW **VII**:146, 147
  labor/labor movements **VII**:170
  Ludlow Massacre **VII**:186
  mining **VII**:210
  workers' compensation **VII**:391
Western Independent Republican Committee **VIII**:183
Western Inland Lock Navigation Company **IV**:79, 141
Western Labor Union (WLU) **VII**:381
Western Museum (Cincinnati) **IV**:37
Western Railroad **IV**:316
Western Reserve **IV**:246; **VI**:218
Westerns **IX**:224
Western Sanitary Commission **V**:228
Western school (photography) **VIII**:30, 296
Western Stories **VII**:160
Western territories
  agriculture **IV**:10–12
  American Fur Company **IV**:18, 19
  American System **IV**:20
  art and architecture **IV**:28, 29
  Astor, John Jacob **IV**:35
  election of 1840 **IV**:138
  exploration **IV**:145–146
  Fort Leavenworth **IV**:158
  Forty-niners **IV**:160
  gold **IV**:179
  Gregg, Josiah **IV**:179
  internal improvements **IV**:202
  Kearny, Stephen Watts **IV**:212
  lead mines **IV**:224
  Lee, Jason **IV**:224
  Massachusetts Emigrant Aid Society **IV**:242
  Mexican-American War **IV**:252
  migration **IV**:254
  Mormon Trail **IV**:261
  Mormon War **IV**:263
  mountain men **IV**:266–267
  Native Americans **IV**:273
  New Madrid earthquake **IV**:280
  Oregon Trail **IV**:285
  overland mail **IV**:289–291
  panic of 1819 **IV**:293

Western territories (continued)
Permanent Indian Frontier **IV**:297
popular sovereignty **IV**:305–307
railroads **IV**:313, 314
Texas **IV**:370
Texas Revolution **IV**:373
War Hawks **IV**:389–390
War of 1812 **IV**:391
Weld, Theodore Dwight **IV**:395–396
Whigs **IV**:397
Willard, Emma **IV**:401
Young, Brigham **IV**:407
Western Union
communications **VI**:78
Industrial Revolution, Second **VI**:192
Ingersoll, Robert Green **VI**:193
invention and technology **VI**:196
Morse, Samuel F. B. **IV**:265
western United States
agriculture **VIII**:9
cities and urban life **VI**:71
communications **VI**:78
Crane, Stephen **VI**:85
currency issue **VI**:88
education, federal aid to **VI**:110
entertainment, popular **VI**:118–119
environment **VIII**:115–116
Farmer-Labor Party **VII**:105
federal income tax **VII**:106
free speech fights **VII**:117
imperialism **VI**:187
Indian Affairs, Office of **VI**:188–189
Irish Americans **VIII**:188
Langston, John Mercer **VI**:218
Lease, Mary Elizabeth Clyens **VI**:220
literature **VI**:226
migration **VIII**:240
National Reclamation Act **VII**:228, 229
New Unionism **VII**:237
population trends **X**:281–282
poverty **X**:286
property rights **X**:290
segregation **VII**:320
UMWA **VII**:360
West Germany. *See* Germany, Federal Republic of
West Gulf Blockading Squadron **V**:137, 263, 264
West Indies **III:436–437**
abolitionism **III**:2
African Americans **III**:8
agriculture **II**:11, 14
Barbados **I**:27

Barry, John **III**:47
Bingham, William **III**:51
Clinton, Sir Henry **III**:99
Columbus, Christopher **I**:84
conquistadores **I**:87, 88
Continental Congress, First **III**:114
Cuba **I**:100–101
Drake, Sir Francis **I**:111
Drake Manuscript **I**:113
foreign affairs **III**:168, 169
French Alliance **III**:177, 178
Freneau, Philip **III**:179
gold **I**:142
Grasse, François-Joseph-Paul, comte de **III**:197
Hamilton, Alexander **III**:204, 205
Harlem Renaissance **VII**:136
Jay, John **III**:230
Jay's Treaty **III**:231
Jones, John Paul **III**:238
Louisiana Purchase **III**:273
Moravians **III**:302
Paris, Treaty of (1763) **III**:331
pearl diving **I**:287
privateering **III**:347, 348
Quasi War **III**:352
Seville **I**:332, 333
slavery **II**:354
Spanish Armada **I**:344
tariffs **III**:406
trade, domestic and foreign **III**:413, 414
Yorktown, surrender at **III**:454
Westinghouse, George **V**:446c; **VI**:410c
Industrial Revolution, Second **VI**:191
invention and technology **VI**:195, 196
Tesla, Nikola **VI**:353, 354
Westinghouse Corporation
AEC **IX**:25
New York World's Fair (1964) **IX**:246
popular culture **VII**:265
radio **VII**:288, 289
science, invention and technology **VII**:150, 151; **VIII**:352
Westo Indians **II:410–411,** 429–430
Weston, Edward **VIII**:296
Weston, Thomas **II**:294
West Orange, New Jersey **VI**:194
Westo War of 1680 **II**:411
West Point. *See* United States Military Academy at West Point
West Roxbury, Massachusetts **IV**:379
Westside Community Schools v. Mergens **X**:122

West Side Story (Bernstein) **IX**:228
West Side Story (film) **IX**:225, 259
West Virginia **V**:444c
Appalachia **IX**:15
Byrd, Robert **X**:61
oil **VI**:271
population trends **X**:282
Rosecrans, William S. **V**:337
tobacco suits **X**:352
UMWA **VII**:360
violence and lawlessness **VI**:375
West Virginia State Board of Education v. Barnette **VIII**:448c
westward expansion **VI**:175, 177
Wetamo **II**:411
Wetherald, Richard **IX**:286, 356c
Wetumpka. *See* McIntosh, William
Weyler y Nicolau, Valeriano **VI**:88
Weyrich, Paul
conservative movement **X**:93
Moral Majority **X**:234
think tanks **X**:349
WFL (World Football League) **X**:330
WFM. *See* Western Federation of Miners
Wharton, Edith **VI**:200; **VII**:179; **VIII**:218
Whately, Thomas **III:437–438**
What Is Conservatism (Meyer) **IX**:74
What We Talk about When We Talk about Love (Carver) **X**:211
"What We Want" program **IX**:40
wheat **I**:17–18
agriculture **II**:12–14; **IV**:10–13; **VI**:9, 10
Maryland **II**:220–221
Pennsylvania **II**:287
trade, domestic and foreign **VI**:360
Wheat, Chatam Roberdau **V**:441
Wheatley, Phillis **III:438, 438–439,** 460c
African Americans **II**:7; **III**:8
Hammon, Jupiter **II**:162
literature **III**:268
religion, African-American **II**:328
Wheatstone, Charles **IV**:333
Wheeler, Burton K. **VIII**:416
America First Committee **VIII**:17
politics (1900–1928) **VII**:262
progressivism **VII**:271
PUHCA **VIII**:313
Republican Party **VIII**:337

Seattle General Strike **VII**:105
Teapot Dome **VII**:352
Wheeler, Candace **VI**:356
Wheeler, George Montague **VI**:141
Wheeler, Joseph **V:428–429,** *429*
Orphan Brigade **V**:288
Sherman's March through Georgia **V**:357
Wheeler, Wayne **VII**:374
Wheeler-Rayburn Act. *See* Public Utility Holding Company Act
Wheeling, Virginia
internal improvements **IV**:202
migration **IV**:254
National Road **IV**:271
railroads **IV**:316
Wheelock, Eleazar **II**:91, **411–412**; **III**:62
Wheelwright, John **II**:170, **412**
Whewell, William **IV**:334
Whig Party **II**:153; **III:439**; **IV:396–398**, 413c, 414c; **V**:443c
abolitionism **V**:3
American System **IV**:21
anti-Masonry **IV**:25
art **III**:33
Ashley, William Henry **IV**:33
Bates, Edward **V**:30
Burke, Edmund **III**:68
Cass, Lewis **IV**:83
Catholics **III**:83
citizenship **III**:92
Civil War **V**:73
Clay, Henry **IV**:96, 97
commonwealthmen **III**:103
Conkling, Roscoe **VI**:80
Continental Congress, First **III**:113
Crockett, Davy **IV**:110
Democratic Party **IV**:118; **V**:108, 109
Douglas, Stephen A. **V**:114
education **IV**:133
election of 1840 **IV**:137, 139
elections **IV**:125
Fillmore, Millard **IV**:149, 150
foreign policy **IV**:155
freemasonry **III**:176
Free-Soil Party **IV**:163, 164
Freneau, Philip **III**:179
fugitive slave laws **IV**:168
Green Mountain Boys **III**:199
Harlan, John Marshall **VI**:159
Harrison, William Henry **IV**:184, 186
Henry, Patrick **III**:211
Herndon, William H. **V**:187
Jackson, Andrew **IV**:207
Jews **III**:236

Julian, George Washington **V**:219

Kansas-Nebraska Act **V**:221, 222

Know-Nothing Party **IV**:214, 215

labor/labor movements **IV**:218

Liberty Party **IV**:226

Lincoln, Abraham **V**:235

Livingston, William **III**:271

Mann, Horace **IV**:237

Mexican-American War **IV**:251

Moore's Creek Bridge, Battle of **III**:301

Mormon Church **IV**:89

nativism **V**:280

Nauvoo **IV**:278

Oregon Treaty of 1846 **IV**:287

Otis, James, Jr. **III**:326

panic of 1837 **IV**:294, 295

Penobscot campaign **III**:333, 334

political parties **III**:338

Polk, James K. **IV**:301

Republican Party **IV**:322; **V**:332

Scott, Winfield **IV**:336

Stephens, Alexander Hamilton **V**:371

suffrage **III**:401

Taylor, Zachary **IV**:368

theater **III**:411

Tyler, John **IV**:382

Van Buren, Martin **IV**:385–386

Van Lew, Elizabeth **V**:414

Webster, Daniel **IV**:393

Weld, Theodore Dwight **IV**:396

women's status and rights **III**:445, 446

Wyoming Valley Massacre **III**:449

Whip Inflation Now (WIN) **X**:109

Whirling Dervishes **I**:348

whiskey
alcohol **III**:13
rationing **VIII**:322
temperance movement **III**:410

Whiskey Rebellion **III**:439–440, 464c
alcohol **III**:13
Brackenridge, Hugh Henry **III**:60
Democratic-Republican societies **III**:137
Hamilton, Alexander **III**:207
Husband, Herman **III**:218
Lewis, Meriwether **III**:261
riots **III**:371
Washington, George **III**:431

Whiskey Ring **V**:429–430
corruption, political **VI**:84
Grant, Ulysses S. **V**:175
Ingersoll, Robert Green **VI**:193
Internal Revenue taxes **VI**:194

whistle-blowers **X**:315

Whistler, Anna **VI**:390

Whistler, James Abbott McNeill **VI**:388–390, 389, 407c
Aesthetic movement **VI**:3
art **V**:19; **VI**:19
Chase, William Merritt **VI**:66
illustration, photography, and graphic arts **VI**:184
painting **VI**:276
U.S. Military Academy at West Point **V**:409

White, Alfred Tredway **VI**:390–391, 408c
Brace, Charles Loring **VI**:45
environment **VI**:120
housing **VI**:179
progressivism **VI**:294

White, Andrew (missionary) **II**:412–413

White, Andrew Dickson (education reformer, diplomat, author) **VI**:391–392
Ely, Richard Theodore **VI**:115
Gilman, Daniel Coit **VI**:148

White, Byron R. **X**:369
Engel v. Vitale **IX**:107
Escobedo v. Illinois **IX**:111
Roe v. Wade **X**:311
Supreme Court **X**:339
Warren Court **IX**:337

White, Clarence **VII**:258

White, Edward **IX**:231, 297

White, Elijah **IV**:187

White, Ellen Gould Harmon **VI**:307

White, Garland H. **VI**:4

White, George L. **VI**:255

White, Harry Dexter **VIII**:52

White, Horace **VI**:43

White, Hugh Lawson
Bell, John **V**:32
Van Buren, Martin **IV**:386
Whigs **IV**:397

White, John **I**:383–384, 398c
Bry, Theodor de **I**:37
Dare, Virginia **II**:90–91
Gilder, Richard Watson **VI**:147
Harriot, Thomas **I**:156
Lane, Ralph **I**:203
Native American religion **I**:261
North Carolina **II**:274
population trends **I**:298
Roanoke **I**:321, 322
Secotan **I**:329

White, Stanford **VI**:392, 409c
art and architecture **VI**:18
Richardson, Henry Hobson **VI**:313
Saint-Gaudens, Augustus **VI**:321
sculpture **VI**:327

White, Walter **VIII**:416–417
antilynching legislation **VIII**:23
civil rights **VIII**:72
FEPC **VIII**:123
March on Washington Movement **VIII**:227
NAACP **VIII**:255
Roosevelt, Eleanor **VIII**:343

White, William Allen **VII**:134; **VIII**:77

White Caps **VI**:376

"White Christmas" **VIII**:252

White Citizens' Councils **IX**:254, 294, 341–342

"White City" (World's Columbian Exposition) **VI**:55, 403

White Collar (Mills) **IX**:217

white-collar work
business **IX**:47
economy **IX**:97
labor/labor movements **VII**:169; **IX**:181, 182
union movement **IX**:324

Whitefield, George **II**:413, 413–414, 437c
camp meetings **III**:77
Dartmouth College **II**:91
Davenport, James **II**:91
Frelinghuysen, Theodorus Jacobus **II**:135
Great Awakening **II**:155
Protestantism **II**:315
religion **III**:360
Tennent, Gilbert **II**:388
Wesley, John **II**:410
Wigglesworth, Edward **II**:414

White Heron and Other Stories, A (Jewett) **VI**:202

White House, the **IV**:411c
Kennedy, Jacqueline **IX**:169
L'Enfant, Pierre-Charles **III**:261
Lincoln, Mary Todd **V**:238
Washington, D.C. **V**:425, 426

White House counsel **X**:225

White House Office on Environmental Policy **X**:246

White House tapes
Cox, Archibald, Jr. **X**:95
impeachment of Richard M. Nixon **X**:178
Jaworski, Leon **X**:193
Nixon, Richard M. **X**:257
U.S. v. Nixon **X**:357
Watergate scandal **X**:366–367

White Indians **II**:86; **III**:255

Whiteman, Paul
entertainment, popular **VII**:97
Gershwin, George **VII**:124–125
music **VII**:220

"White Negro, The" (Mailer) **IX**:37, 194

White Oak Road, Virginia **V**:14

White Paper (State Department report on China) **IX**:20, 342–343

White Plains, Battle of **III**:440–441
Fort Washington, capture of **III**:172
Hamilton, Alexander **III**:205
Howe, Sir William **III**:215
Revolutionary War **III**:368

White Plains Hospital (New York) **VII**:312

"White Rabbit" (Jefferson Airplane) **IX**:230

White River **IV**:146

Whitesboro, New York **VI**:87

White Star Line **VI**:186

white supremacists **VII**:406c
anti-Semitism **VII**:17
corruption, political **VI**:83
Democratic Party **V**:110
Ku Klux Klan **V**:223–225
race and race relations **VII**:282
Rhodes, James Ford **VI**:312
Tillman, Benjamin Ryan **VI**:358

Whitewater investigation **X**:380c
Clinton, Hillary Rodham **X**:77
Clinton, William J. **X**:82
impeachment of William J. Clinton **X**:178
independent counsel **X**:179
Starr, Kenneth **X**:332, 333

Whitgift, John **I**:307

Whitman, Christine Todd **X**:371

Whitman, Malcolm **X**:342

Whitman, Marcus **IV**:398–399
Fort Vancouver **IV**:159
McLoughlin, John **IV**:248
Whitman, Narcissa **IV**:399

Whitman, Narcissa **IV**:159, 248, 399

Whitman, Walt **IV**:415c; **V**:430, 430–431
art and architecture **IV**:28
literature **IV**:229; **VI**:226–227; **IX**:195
Manifest Destiny **IV**:234
nurses **V**:285

Whitman College **VIII**:96

Whitney, Anita **VII**:343

Whitney, Eli **III**:441, 441–442, 463c, 465c
abolitionism **V**:1
agriculture **III**:11; **IV**:11

Whitney, Eli (*continued*)
cotton **III:**123
cotton culture **IV:**107
economy **III:**146
industrialization **IV:**199
Industrial Revolution
III:225–226
mass production **VII:**194
science and technology
III:385
slavery **III:**390
Whitney, Eli, Jr. **IV:**101
Whitney, Josiah D. **VI:**207, 208, 253
Whitney, Richard **VIII:**357
Whitney, Silas **IV:**313
Whitney, Willis **VII:**123
Whitney family **VIII:**373
Whitney Museum (New York City) **VIII:**29
Whitney v. California **VII:**42, 343–344
Whitneyville, Connecticut **IV:**101
Whittaker, Charles **IX:**33, 337
Whittier, John Greenleaf **II:**203
American Anti-Slavery
Society **IV:**15
Jewett, Sarah Orne **VI:**203
Weld, Theodore Dwight
IV:396
WHO. *See* World Health
Organization
Who, the **IX:**121, 259
Whole Earth Catalog **IX:**110
whooping cough **X:**222
Who's Afraid of Virginia Woolf?
(Albee) **IX:**193
Who's Afraid of Virginia Woolf?
(film) **X:**278
Who Wants to Be Millionaire? (TV
show) **X:**344
Why Change Your Wife? (film)
VII:97
Why England Slept (Kennedy)
IX:169
Why We Fight (film) **VIII:**61, 62, 246
"Why Women Should Vote"
(Addams) **VII:**420–424
WIB. *See* War Industries Board
Wichita, Kansas **VI:**220
Wickard, Claude **VIII:**405
Wickersham, George W. **VII:**67
Wickersham, Joseph **IX:**8
Wide, Wide World, The (Warner)
IV:229
Wide Awake Clubs **V:**333
Widmar v. Vincent **X:**122
widows **VII:**405c
gender **II:**144, 145
marriage and family **III:**288
women's status and rights
II:423, 424; **III:**446
Wiegand, Charmion von **VIII:**31
Wi-Fi **X:**319
Wigfall, Louis T. **V:**431–432
Wiggin, Kate **VII:**265

Wiggins, Ella Mae **VII:**122
Wiggins, James Russell **X:**357
Wiggins Amendment **X:**123
Wigglesworth, Edward **II:**414
Wigglesworth, Michael **II:**414–415
Wight, Peter **VI:**54
wigwams **I:**233; **II:**24, 166
Wilberforce, Ontario **IV:**295
Wilberforce, William **III:**127
Wilberforce University
African Methodist Episcopal
Church **V:**5
education, higher **VI:**112
Terrell, Mary Eliza Church
VII:352
Wilbraham, Massachusetts
IV:224
Wilcox, Orlando **V:**13
Wild and Scenic Rivers Act of
1968 **IX:**237, 271, **343–344,**
357c
Wild Angels, The (film) **IX:**225
Wildcat (Seminole chief) **IV:**338
wildcat strikes **X:**201
Wilde, Lady Jane **VI:**222
Wilde, Oscar **VI:**19
Wilde, William C. Kingsbury
VI:222
Wilder, Laura Ingalls **VI:**392–393
Wilderness, Battle of the **V:432**
Burnside, Ambrose E. **V:**52
Early, Jubal A. **V:**119
Grant, Ulysses S. **V:**174
Hancock, Winfield Scott
V:184
Hill, Ambrose P. **V:**190
homefront **V:**193
Lee, Robert E. **V:**231
Longstreet, James **V:**242
Meade, George Gordon
V:254
Overland campaign **V:**291
Wilderness Act (1964). *See*
National Wilderness
Preservation Act of 1964
Wilderness Road **II:**124; **III:442,**
461c
Wilderness Society **IX:**108, 240
wildlife protection **X:**90
Wild One, The (film) **IX:**117
Wild West shows **VI:**116,
118–119
Wiley, Bell **V:**110
Wiley, Harvey **VII:**277
Wilfong, George **IV:**188
Wilhelm II (kaiser of Germany)
VII:338
Wilkerson, James **VII:**292
Wilkes, Charles
exploration **IV:**146
foreign policy **V:**150
Union navy **V:**405
Wilkes expedition **IV:**399–400
Wilkes, John **III:**337, **442–443**

Wilkes expedition **IV:**146, 399, 399–400
Wilkes Land, Antarctica **IV:**400
Wilkie, Sir David **IV:**29
Wilkins, Roy **IX:**293, **344–345**
Wilkinson, James **III:443–444**
Burr, Aaron **III:**70
Claiborne, William C. C.
IV:95
Pike, Zebulon Montgomery
IV:300
Scott, Winfield **IV:**335
Willamette River
exploration **IV:**146
Fort Vancouver **IV:**158
Lee, Jason **IV:**224
McLoughlin, John **IV:**248
migration **IV:**255
Oregon Trail **IV:**286
Willamette University **IV:**224
Willamette Valley
Applegate, Jesse **IV:**26
exploration **IV:**145
Oregon Treaty of 1846
IV:287
Willard, Emma **IV:**184, **400–402,**
401
Willard, Frances **V:**445c; **VI:**296,
393–394, 394, 399, 408c
Willard, Jess
Dempsey, William Harrison
"Jack" **VII:**75, 76
Johnson, Jack **VII:**155
sports and recreation
VII:333
Willard, John **IV:**400, 401
Willard, Samuel **II:**415
Willey, Norman **VI:**77
William I (king of England) **I:**304;
III:102–103
William III (king of England,
Scotland and Ireland)
British Empire **II:**48
Dominion of New England
II:102
Glorious Revolution **II:**150
monarchy, British **II:**240
William and Mary College
IV:382
William L. Sublette Company
IV:32
Williams, Aubrey **VIII:**45, 46,
262, 263
Williams, Bert **VI:**117
Williams, Eunice **II:**58
Williams, Fannie Barrier **VI:**394–395
Williams, George Washington
VI:395–397
Williams, Hank **VIII:**252
Williams, Harrison A. **X:**5, 321
Williams, Hosea **IX:**270
Williams, James Douglas **VI:**161
Williams, John **II:**93
Williams, Nelson **IV:**333, 381
Williams, Peter **III:**26; **VI:**5
Williams, Peter, Jr. **IV:402; VI:**87

Williams, Roger **I:**229; **II:415–417,** *416,* 435c
Baptists **II:**33
Canonicus **II:**57
ethnocentrism **II:**122
Massachusetts **II:**223
Rhode Island **II:**332–333
Winthrop, John **II:**418
Williams, Tennessee **IX:**193, 258,
351c
Williams, William Carlos **VII:**179,
212
Williams Act (1968) **X:**57
Williamsburg, Battle of
Early, Jubal A. **V:**119
Hancock, Winfield Scott
V:183
Hill, Ambrose P. **V:**189
Longstreet, James **V:**241
Peninsular campaign **V:**299
Pickett, George Edward
V:306
Williamsburg, Virginia **II:**401;
III:142
Williams College (Massachusetts)
VIII:119
Williams-Steiger Act. *See*
Occupational Safety and
Health Act
William Watts Sherman House
(Newport, Rhode Island)
*VI:*19
William Wilson & Son Company
V:255
Willich, August **V:**165
Willing, Thomas
Bank of North America
III:40
Bingham, William **III:**51
insurance **III:**227
Willkie, Wendell L. **VIII:417,**
447c
CIO **VIII:**82
election of 1940 **VIII:**110
election of 1944 **VIII:**111
Ickes, Harold L. **VIII:**183
isolationists **VIII:**190
Johnson, Hugh S. **VIII:**197
labor/labor movements
VIII:207
Lewis, John L. **VIII:**213
Luce, Henry R. **VIII:**224
Murray, Philip **VIII:**249
politics (Roosevelt era)
VIII:300
Republican Party **VIII:**338
Roosevelt, Franklin D.
VIII:346
Taft, Robert A. **VIII:**385
Tennessee Valley Authority
VIII:392
Willoughby, Sir Hugh **I:**272
Willow Place Chapel **VI:**327, 390
Willow Run, Michigan **VIII:**14–15
Wills, Bob and the Texas Playboys
VIII:250

Willstown, Alabama **IV:**342
Wilmington, North Carolina
    lynching **VI:**230
    Moore's Creek Bridge,
        Battle of **III:**301
    violence and lawlessness
        VI:375
Wilmot, David
    abolitionism **V:**3
    Democratic Party **IV:**118
    Free-Soil Party **IV:**163, 164
    Wilmot Proviso **V:**432, 433
Wilmot Proviso **IV:**414*c*; **V:432–
433**
    abolitionism **V:**3
    Civil War **V:**73
    Democratic Party **IV:**118
    Fillmore, Millard **IV:**150
    Free-Soil Party **IV:**163
    Guadalupe Hidalgo, Treaty
        of **IV:**181
    popular sovereignty **IV:**304
    Taylor, Zachary **IV:**368
WILPF. *See* Women's
    International League for Peace
    and Freedom
Wilson, Alexander **III:**155; **IV:**37
Wilson, Charles E. **IX:**216
Wilson, Edmund Beecher
    VII:314
Wilson, George **IV:**388
Wilson, Henry **V:433**
    espionage **V:**134
    Freedmen's Savings Bank
        V:159
    Free-Soil Party **IV:**164
    Medal of Honor **V:**255
Wilson, James (1742–1798)
    III:174, 403, **444–445**
Wilson, James (1835–1920) **VI:**63
Wilson, James H. (1837–1925)
    V:76
Wilson, Joan Hoff **VII:**115
Wilson, John **II:**82
Wilson, Joseph **X:**72, 179
Wilson, M. L. **VIII:**5
Wilson, Pete **X:**176
Wilson, Sloan **IX:**47
Wilson, Teddy **VIII:**169
Wilson, Thomas Woodrow
    VII:382–384, 383, 405*c*–407*c*
    Adamson Act **VII:**2
    AFL **VII:**12
    Americanization **VII:**13
    Arlington National Cemetery
        V:17
    armed forces **VII:**20
    Baruch, Bernard M. **VII:**32;
        VIII:41–42
    Big Stick diplomacy **VII:**35
    Brandeis, Louis Dembitz
        VII:41
    Budget and Accounting Act
        VII:44
    Cannon, Joseph Gurney
        VII:48
    chain stores **VI:**65

citizenship **VII:**57
civil liberties **VII:**58
Clayton Antitrust Act
    VII:59
Committee for Public
    Information **VII:**59
communism **IX:**67
Congress **VII:**61
conscription **VII:**62
Coolidge, Calvin John
    VII:64
Dawes, Charles Gates
    VII:71
Democratic Party **VII:**74,
    75
direct election of senators
    VII:78
dollar-a-year men **VIII:**96
domino theory **IX:**89
elections **VII:**91
elections, presidential
    X:116
Ely, Richard Theodore
    VI:115
Espionage Act **VII:**101
FCA **VIII:**125–126
Federal Farm Loan Act
    VII:106
Federal Reserve Act
    VII:107–108
Federal Trade Commission
    Act **VII:**108
Fellowship of Reconciliation
    VII:109
foreign policy **VII:**114, 115
"Fourteen Points" speech
    VII:427–430
free speech fights **VII:**118
Fuel Administration
    VII:119
Howe, Louis M. **VIII:**179
Hughes, Charles Evans
    VII:142
Hull, Cordell **VIII:**180
Immigration Act (1917)
    VII:145
Industrial Relations
    Commission **VII:**145
Jones Act (1916) **VII:**157
labor/labor movements
    VII:170
League of Nations **VII:**175
lobbying **VII:**181
Lockwood, Belva Ann
    Bennett McNall **VI:**229
Lodge, Henry Cabot
    VII:184
Lost Generation **VII:**185
Ludlow Massacre **VII:**187
"Make the World Safe for
    Democracy" speech
    VII:424–427
Mexican Invasion **VII:**203
Mexican Revolution
    VII:204–205
Mooney-Billings case
    VII:213

National Defense Act
    VII:227
National Park Service
    VII:228
neutrality **VII:**235–236
New Freedom **VII:**236
New Nationalism **VII:**237
NWLB **VII:**229
NWP **VII:**230
Nye committee **VIII:**279
open shop movement
    VII:247
Palmer, Alexander Mitchell
    VII:249
Paul, Alice **VII:**254
peace movements **VII:**256
politics (1900–1928) **VII:**262
Preparedness **VII:**267
presidency **VII:**268–269
Progressive Party **VII:**270
progressivism **VII:**271
Prohibition **VII:**272
Railroad Administration
    VII:290–291
Rankin, Jeannette **VII:**292
Red Scare **VII:**296
Republican Party **VII:**300
Roosevelt, Franklin D.
    VIII:344
rural life **VII:**306
Sedition Act **VII:**318
Selective Service Act **VII:**321
Siberian Expedition **VII:**324
socialism **VII:**328
Steel Strike of 1919
    VII:338–339
Taft, William Howard
    VII:348
tariffs **VII:**349–350
taxation **VIII:**387
trade, domestic and foreign
    VII:354
Trading with the Enemy Act
    VII:355
Trotter, William Monroe
    VII:357
UN **VIII:**402
Underwood-Simmons Tariff
    VII:359
Versailles, Treaty of
    VII:369–371
Volstead Act **VII:**374
War Industries Board
    VII:377, 378
Watterson, Henry **VI:**386
woman suffrage **VII:**385
Workmen's Compensation
    Act **VII:**392
World War I **VII:**393, 394
Zimmermann telegram
    VII:401
Wilson, Valerie Plame **X:**72, 179
Wilson Dam **VIII:**392–393
Wilson-Gorman Tariff **VI:**411*c*
    Allison, William Boyd **VI:**12
    business and government
        VI:56

Congress **VI:**80
federal income tax **VII:**106
Internal Revenue taxes
    VI:194
tariffs **VI:**352
Wilsonian Internationalism
    VII:115–116
Wilson Meat Company **VII:**198
Wilson's Creek, Battle of **V:**313,
    317
Wimbledon **VIII:**372
WIN (Whip Inflation Now) **X:**109
Winchell, Walter **VIII:**272
Winchester, Battle of
    Ewell, Richard Stoddert
        V:135
    Jackson, Thomas J.
        "Stonewall" **V:**210
    Shenandoah Valley:
        Jackson's campaign **V:**350,
        351
Winchester, James **IV:**185
Winder, John H. **V:**68, 314
Windows operating system
    X:381*c*
    computers **X:**87
    Gates, William Henry, III
        X:147
    science and technology
        X:318
Wind River Mountains **IV:**31, 354
wine **III:**13
Wingate, George **X:**248
Wingina (Roanoke sachem) **I:**382;
    II:274, 417
Wingino (Secota chief) **I:**203
Wings of the Dove (James)
    VII:179
Winnebago Indians **II:**273; **IV:**36,
    57
Winnemucca, Sarah **VI:**280,
    397–398
Winnsboro, South Carolina
    IX:123
Winslow, John **V:**7
Winsor, Justin **VI:**224
Winter of Our Discontent, The
    (Steinbeck) **VIII:**374–375
Winter Quarters (Omaha,
    Nebraska)
    Deseret, State of **IV:**119
    Mormon Church **IV:**89, 90
    Mormon Trail **IV:**261
    Young, Brigham **IV:**407
Winthrop, John **II:417–418,** *418*
    Bradford, William **II:**44
    Dudley, Thomas **II:**103
    government, British
        American **II:**151
    Hutchinson, Anne Marbury
        II:170
    jeremiads **II:**184
    Massachusetts Bay Company
        II:225
    "Model of Christian Charity"
        II:439
    postal service **II:**304

Winthrop, John, Jr. **II:**76, 77
Winthrop College **VI:**358
wireless networks **X:**319
wireless telegraphy **VII:**151
WIRES (Women in Radio and
    Electrical Service) **VIII:**420
wiretaps **VII:**409c; **X:**359–360,
    365, 366
Wirt, William
    anti-Masonry **IV:**25
    McCulloch v. Maryland
        IV:245
    Native Americans **IV:**275
Wirtz, Lenny **X:**303
Wirz, Henry
    Andersonville Prison,
        Georgia **V:**11
    monuments **V:**268
    prisons **V:**315
    Wallace, Lew **VI:**381
Wisconsin **IV:**412c, 413c
    abolitionism **V:**1
    agriculture **IV:**10; **V:**6
    Atkinson, Henry **IV:**36
    disease/epidemics **IV:**122
    Dred Scott decision **V:**116,
        117
    economy **IV:**130
    education, federal aid to
        VI:110
    Forty-niners **IV:**160
    Harrison, William Henry
        IV:184
    immigration **IV:**195
    internal improvements
        IV:202
    lead mines **IV:**223
    lumbering **IV:**231
    McCarthy, Joseph R. **IX:**206
    migration **IV:**254
    Non-Partisan League
        VII:241
    Patrons of Husbandry
        VI:279
    Pike, Zebulon Montgomery
        IV:300
    railroads **IV:**316
    Republican Party **IV:**321
    Seattle General Strike
        VII:105
    Siberian Expedition
        VII:325
    Strang, James Jesse **IV:**358
    Taylor, Zachary **IV:**367
"Wisconsin Idea" **VII:**173
Wisconsin Public Service
    Commission **VIII:**392
Wisconsin Volunteer Infantry
    V:273
Wisconsin v. Yoder **X:**307
Wisconsin Woman Suffrage
    Association (WWSA) **VI:**51
Wise, Henry A. **V:433–434**
    Hollywood Cemetery **V:**192
    Meade, George Gordon
        V:253
    Petersburg campaign **V:**301

Wise, Isaac Mayer **IV:**319; **VI:**205,
    308
Wise, John **V:**25
Wise, Stephen S.
    Jews **VIII:**196
    Judaism **VI:**205
    religion **VII:**298
Wistar, Caspar **II:418–419**
Wister, Owen **VII:**265
witchcraft **I:**172, 384, **384–385;**
    II:419–421, 420, 437c
    crime and punishment
        II:83
    Massachusetts **II:**223–224
    Mather, Cotton **II:**227
    midwives **II:**234
    Nurse, Rebecca **II:**275–276
    Parris, Samuel **II:**281
    Popé **II:**301
    popular culture **III:**341
    Tituba **II:**390
    Willard, Samuel **II:**415
    women's status and rights
        II:425
Witherspoon, John **III:445**
Without Sanctuary **VI:**230
Witness (photographic exhibit)
    VI:230
Witt, Shirley **IX:**241
Wittenmyer, Annie **V:**408, 438
Wizard of Oz, The (film)
    VIII:247, 328
Wizard of the Nile, The (Herbert)
    VI:170
WLS radio (Chicago, Illinois)
    VIII:250
WLU (Western Labor Union)
    VII:381
WMC. *See* War Manpower
    Commission
WMD. *See* weapons of mass
    destruction
WNBA (Women's National
    Basketball Association) **X:**331
WNYC radio (New York City)
    VII:160
Wobblies. *See* Industrial Workers
    of the World
Wöhler, Friedrich **IV:**332
Wokokan Island **I:**203
Wolcott, Oliver **III:**125, 207
Wolfe, James **II:**421, 438c
    Carleton, Guy **III:**81
    French colonies **II:**138
    Monckton, Robert **II:**241
    Seven Years' War **II:**348
Wolfe, Thomas **VIII:**219, 443c
Wolfe, Tom **X:369–370**
    journalism **IX:**166
    literature **IX:**194
    LSD **IX:**196
Wolfowitz, Paul **X:**252
Wolfskill, William **IV:**145
Wolfson, Warren **IX:**111
Wolof **I:**69, 330
Wolsey, Thomas **I:**74, 159
wolves **II:421–422**

Woman, Church, and State (Gage)
    VI:137
Woman as Force in History
    (Beard) **VII:**140
Woman in the Nineteenth Century
    (Fuller) **IV:**169, 379
woman labor **II:214–215,** 217
Woman Rebel (journal)
    birth control **VII:**36
    Greenwich Village **VII:**131
    radical and labor press
        VII:284
    Sanger, Margaret **VII:**312
    women's status and rights
        VII:388
Woman's Advocate **IV:**404
Woman's Bible **VI:**399
Woman's Journal **VI:**172
Woman's Medical School,
    Northwestern University
    VII:133
Woman's National Liberal Union
    VI:137
Woman's Pavilion (Philadelphia
    Centennial Exposition)
    VI:284
Woman's Pavilion (World's
    Columbian Exposition)
    Cassatt, Mary **VI:**64
    Hayden, Sophia Gregoria
        VI:165–166
    World's Columbian
        Exposition **VI:**402
Woman's Peace Party
    Catt, Carrie Lane Chapman
        VII:50
    Hamilton, Alice **VII:**133
    peace movements **VII:**256
*Woman's Point of View, Some
    Roads to Peace* (Blatch)
    VII:38
*Woman's Record: or, Sketches of
    All Distinguished Women from
    "the Beginning" till A. D. 1850*
    (Hale) **IV:**184
woman suffrage **IV:**414c; **VI:**407c,
    408c; **VII:384–386,** 406c
    Amendments to the U.S.
        Constitution **X:**23
    Anthony, Susan B. **VI:**15–
        16
    Anthony, Susan B. speech on
        VI:413
    anti-suffragists **VII:**18
    Blackwell, Antoinette Brown
        VI:39
    Blatch, Harriot Eaton
        Stanton **VII:**38
    Bowles, Samuel **VI:**43
    Bradwell, Myra Colby **VI:**47
    Brown, Olympia **VI:**51
    Cary, Mary Ann Shadd **V:**58
    Catt, Carrie Lane Chapman
        VII:50
    citizenship **VII:**56–57
    elections **VII:**89
    feminism **X:**131–132

Flynn, Elizabeth Gurley
    VII:109
Gage, Matilda Joslyn **VI:**137
Garrison, William Lloyd
    V:164
Hamilton, Alice **VII:**133
Harper, Frances Ellen
    Watkins **VI:**160
Hooker, Isabella Beecher
    VI:176
Howe, Julia Ward **V:**198
Johnson, Hiram Warren
    VII:154
marriage and family
    VII:191
Mitchell, Maria **VI:**248
NACW **VII:**225
NAWSA **VII:**223
New Woman **VII:**239
NWP **VII:**230
NWSA **V:**277
NWTUL **VII:**231
Palmer, Alexander Mitchell
    VII:249
Paul, Alice **VII:**254
Philadelphia Centennial
    Exposition **VI:**284
Pinchot, Gifford **VII:**260
politics (1900–1928)
    VII:261, 262
Progressive Party **VII:**270
radicalism **VII:**287
Rankin, Jeannette **VII:**292
Shaw, Anna Howard
    VI:328
socialism **VII:**327
Stanton, Elizabeth Cady
    V:369, 370
Stone, Lucy **VI:**345–346
Supreme Court **VII:**343
Tarbell, Ida Minerva
    VII:349
Terrell, Mary Eliza Church
    VII:352, 353
Wells-Barnett, Ida Bell
    VI:388
"Why Women Should Vote"
    (Addams) **VII:420–424**
Willard, Frances **VI:**393–
    394
Williams, Fannie Barrier
    VI:395
women's status and rights
    V:436, 437; **VI:**399;
    VII:386–388
Woodhull, Victoria **VI:**400,
    401
World War I **VII:**394
YMCA/YWCA **VII:**397
Woman Suffrage Amendment
    VII:254
Woman Suffrage speech (Anthony,
    1871) **VI:**413
Woman Voter **VII:**286
Women Accepted for Volunteer
    Emergency Service (WAVES)
    VIII:418, 424

Women Airforce Service Pilots
(WASP) **VIII:418–419**
Army Air Forces, U.S.
VIII:27
WAVES **VIII:**418
women's status and rights
VIII:424
Women and Economics (Gilman)
VII:125, 388
Women in Publishing (language
guidelines) **X:**133
Women's Armed Services
Integration Act **VIII:**418, 421
Women's Army Auxiliary Corps
(WAAC) **VIII:**418–420
Women's Army Corps (WAC)
VIII:419–421, *420*
Army, U.S. **VIII:**26
WASP **VIII:**419
women's status and rights
VIII:424
Women's Auxiliary Ferrying
Squadron **VIII:**419
Women's Central Association for
Relief (WCAR)
disease/epidemics **V:**112
ladies aid societies **V:**227–
228
nurses **V:**285
U.S. Sanitary Commission
V:411
Women's Christian Temperance
Union (WCTU) **VI:**408*c*
Harper, Frances Ellen
Watkins **V:**184; **VI:**160
New Woman **VII:**239
Prohibition **VII:**272
Prohibition Party **VI:**295,
296
Shaw, Anna Howard **VI:**328
temperance movement
IV:370
Volstead Act **VII:**374
Willard, Frances **VI:**393, 394
women's status and rights
V:438; **VI:**399
women's colleges **VI:398,** 400
Women's Committee of National
Defense **V:**50
"Women's Declaration of 1876"
VI:16
Women's Economic Equity Act
(1984) **X:**135
Women's Equity Action League
(WEAL) **IX:345–346; X:**132,
133
Women's Era Club **VI:**388
Women's Exchange **VI:**18
Women's Flying Training
Detachment **VIII:**419
Women's International League for
Peace and Freedom (WILPF)
VII:386
Carnegie Endowment for
International Peace
VII:49
foreign policy **VII:**115, 116

Hamilton, Alice **VII:**133
NAWSA **VII:**223
peace movements **VII:**256
Rankin, Jeannette **VII:**292
Terrell, Mary Eliza Church
VII:353
women's status and rights
VII:389
women's liberation movement
feminism **X:**132
Steinem, Gloria **X:**334
women's status and rights
IX:348
Women's Loyal National League
VI:16
Women's Medical College of
Philadelphia **IV:**184, 250
Women's Medical College of the
New York Infirmary **VI:**40, 400
Women's National Basketball
Association (WNBA) **X:**331
Women's National Loyal League
V:434–435, 436
women's network **VIII:421–422**
Democratic Party **VIII:**93
Dewson, Mary **VIII:**95
Perkins, Frances **VIII:**293
Roosevelt, Eleanor
VIII:343
women soldiers **V:**422, **435–436**
Women's Organization for
National Prohibition Reform
(WONPR) **VII:**274
Women's Political Union (Great
Britain) **VII:**385
Women's Relief Corps **V:**385
Women's Rights Project **X:**152
women's status and rights
II:422–426, *424;* **III:445–448,**
447; **IV:402–405,** 414*c*, 415*c;*
V:436–438, 445*c;* **VI:399–400,**
408*c;* **VII:386–389,** 387, 405*c,*
406*c,* 408*c;* **VIII:422–425,** *423,*
444*c;* **IX:346–348,** *347,* 355*c;*
X:370–371, 375*c,* 378*c,* 381*c*
abolitionism **IV:**3; **V:**3
abortion **X:**1–5
Adams, Abigail **III:**3
Adams, Hannah **III:**4
Adkins v. Children's Hospital
VII:3
affirmative action **X:**10
Afghanistan War **X:**12
AFL **VI:**13
African Americans **IV:**7;
IX:5; **X:**13
agriculture **II:**9; **III:**11;
IV:11
aircraft industry **VIII:**15
alcohol **II:**16
Aleut **II:**17
Algonquin **II:**18
Amendments to the U.S.
Constitution **X:**23
American Anti-Slavery
Society **IV:**15–16
American Revolution **III:**19

Anthony, Susan B. **VI:**15–16
art **II:**26
Aztecs **I:**20–21
baby boomers **X:**39
Baptists **II:**33
baseball **VII:**33–34
Berkeley, Lady Frances
II:36
birthrates **X:**44
Black Power **IX:**42
Blackwell, Antoinette Brown
VI:39
Blatch, Harriot Eaton
Stanton **VII:**38
Bloomer, Amelia **IV:**59–60
Bradford, Cornelia Smith
II:44
Bradwell, Myra Colby **VI:**47
Brandeis, Louis Dembitz
VII:41
Brent, Margaret Reed **II:**47
Brown, Olympia **VI:**51
Butler, Benjamin Franklin
V:53
Byrd, Robert **X:**61
Cable Act **VII:**47
camp followers **III:**77
Carib **I:**60
Carter, James Earl, Jr. **X:**68
CCC **VIII:**71
Chautauqua Institute **VI:**66
children **VIII:**67
Christian Science **VI:**69
cities and urban life **II:**68;
III:92
citizenship **III:**94–95;
VII:57
Civil War **V:**74
Clinton, William J. **X:**80
clothing **II:**71–73
Colden, Jane **II:**74
cold war culture **IX:**65
consumption **II:**79
corn **II:**80
criminal justice **VII:**67
crowd actions **II:**86
Declaration of Sentiments
(Seneca Falls convention)
IV:441–443
Democratic Party **VIII:**93
Dewson, Mary **VIII:**95
Dickinson, Anna E. **V:**111
domesticity **II:**100–101
Douglass, Frederick **V:**116
dress **VII:**79–80
economy **II:**110; **IV:**131
education **III:**148; **IV:**134;
V:125
education, higher **X:**112
Edwards, Sarah Pierpont
II:114–115
EEOC **IX:**110
elections, conduct of **VI:**113
elections, presidential
X:118
electricity **VII:**93
employment **V:**133

Enlightenment, American
II:118
entertainment, popular
VI:116
environment **II:**119
ERA **VII:**100; **X:**123–124
espionage **V:**134, 135
Ewe **I:**126
Expatriation Act **VII:**103–
104
family life **X:**127
female antislavery societies
IV:147–148
feminism **X:**131–135
fertility **II:**125–126
Flynn, Elizabeth Gurley
VII:109, 110
folk music revival **IX:**121
food **IX:**122
Foster, Abigail Kelley
IV:161–162
Fourteenth Amendment
V:157
Franklin, Ann Smith **II:**134
Franklin, Deborah Read
II:134
Friedan, Betty **IX:**126–127
Fuller, Margaret **IV:**169
Gage, Matilda Joslyn **VI:**137
gays and lesbians **IX:**131,
132
gender **II:**144–145
gender gap **X:**150
Glorious Revolution **II:**149
Goldmark, Josephine Clara
VII:127
Great Awakening **II:**155–
156
Great Plains **III:**197
Grimké, Angelina and Sarah
IV:180
Hale, Sarah Josepha **IV:**184
Hamilton, Alice **VII:**133
Harper, Frances Ellen
Watkins **VI:**160
Hayden, Sophia Gregoria
VI:165, 166
Hemings, Sally **III:**210–211
Higginson, Thomas
Wentworth **VI:**171
history **VII:**140
Hoar, George F. **VI:**173
homefront **V:**192
homespun **V:**194
Hooker, Isabella Beecher
VI:176
House of Representatives
X:171
Howe, Julia Ward **V:**198
humanitarianism **III:**217
Hume, Sophia Wigington
II:169
Huron **I:**172
Hutchinson, Anne Marbury
II:170–171
ILGWU **VII:**149
immigration **IV:**195

women's status and rights
  (continued)
    Indian Removal Act **IV**:198
    Industrial Revolution
      III:224, 225
    Iroquois **I**:185, 186; **II**:180
    Islam **X**:189
    Jews **I**:197
    Johnson, Hiram Warren
      VII:154
    Johnston, Henrietta Deering
      II:188
    Kelley, Florence **VII**:164
    Knight, Sarah Kemble
      II:195
    Knights of Labor **VI**:209
    labor/labor movements
      II:199–200; **IV**:218;
      IX:181–182
    ladies aid societies **V**:227–
      228
    Ladies Memorial
      Associations **V**:229
    land **II**:202
    Langston, John Mercer
      VI:218
    La Raza Unida **IX**:183
    Latin America **X**:205
    Latino movement **IX**:185,
      186
    Lennox, Charlotte Ramsay
      II:204
    liberalism **VIII**:214, 216
    Libertarian Party **X**:209
    literature **IV**:229; **IX**:194;
      X:212
    Lockwood, Belva Ann
      Bennett McNall **VI**:228–
      229
    LWV **IX**:186–187
    lyceum movement **IV**:231
    magazines **VI**:235
    Mali **I**:226
    manufacturing and industry
      II:214
    marriage and family **II**:216–
      219; **III**:286–289; **IV**:238,
      239; **V**:248–249; **VII**:191–
      192; **VIII**:230–232;
      IX:201–202; **X**:213
    McCrea, Jane **III**:293
    Mead, Margaret **VII**:197
    medicine **II**:230; **IV**:249–
      250; **VII**:200
    mestizaje **I**:241
    midwives **II**:234
    Mitchell, Maria **VI**:247–248
    Montagnais-Naskapi **I**:250
    Mott, Lucretia **IV**:265–266
    movies **VIII**:246
    Muller v. Oregon **VII**:217–
      218, **417–420**
    Murray, Judith Sargent
      Stevens **III**:308
    Murray, Pauli **IX**:227
    music **X**:240
    NACW **VII**:225

New Amsterdam **II**:257
New Deal **VIII**:270
New Netherland **II**:266
news media **VIII**:272
New Woman **VII**:238
New York **II**:271
New York City **II**:272
NOW **IX**:236; **X**:247–248
nurses **V**:285
NWLB **VIII**:262
NWSA **V**:277
O'Connor, Sandra Day
  X:265
Osborn, Sarah Haggar
  Wheaten **II**:279
Paul, Alice **VII**:254
PCSW **IX**:261–262
Pelosi, Nancy **X**:271
Perkins, Frances **VIII**:293–
  294
Philadelphia Centennial
  Exposition **VI**:284
Phillips, Wendell **IV**:299
"The Pill" **IX**:257
Pinckney, Elizabeth Lucas
  II:295; **III**:336
politics (Roosevelt era)
  VIII:300
population trends **III**:342–
  343; **VIII**:306
pornography **X**:284
poverty **III**:344; **X**:285
Powhatan Confederacy
  II:307
Prohibition **VII**:273–274
pro-life/pro-choice
  movements **X**:288–289
prostitution **VII**:315–316
Protestantism **II**:316
public health **VII**:276
Quakers **II**:321, 322
race and race relations
  III:357
radical and labor press
  VII:285
Reformation **I**:318
relief **VIII**:333
religion **IV**:317; **VIII**:334;
  IX:273
Remarks to the Fourth
  World Conference
  on Women (Albright)
  X:405–407
Revolutionary War **III**:369
Richards, Ellen Henrietta
  Swallow **VI**:312–313
Riedesel, Frederica
  Charlotte, baroness von
  III:370
Roe v. Wade **X**:311–312,
  387–390
Roosevelt, Eleanor
  VIII:342–343
Rosie the Riveter **VIII**:347–
  348
Ross, Betsy **III**:374
rural life **III**:375

Sampson, Deborah **III**:379–
  380
Sanger, Margaret **VII**:312–
  313
Schlafly, Phyllis **X**:316–317
science and technology
  V:343
SDS **IX**:304
Seneca Falls convention
  IV:340–342, **441–443**
service sector **IX**:289
sexuality **VII**:322
shipbuilding **VIII**:359
slavery **IV**:347
Smith, Joseph, Jr. **IV**:354
Social Security Act
  VIII:364
society, British American
  II:365, 366
South Carolina Regulation
  III:395
space exploration **IX**:297
Spanish colonies **II**:372,
  373
Spanish immigration **II**:375
spinsters **II**:375
sports and recreation
  VII:335; **VIII**:372;
  IX:299; **X**:331
Stanton, Elizabeth Cady
  V:369, 370
Starbuck, Mary Coffin
  II:377
Steinem, Gloria **X**:334–335
Stone, Lucy **VI**:345–346
suburbanization/suburbs
  VIII:380; **IX**:306
suffrage **II**:380; **III**:401
Sufism **I**:348
Supreme Court **VII**:343
Tappan, Arthur and Lewis
  IV:367
Tarbell, Ida Minerva
  VII:349
temperance movement
  III:410; **IV**:369, 370
tenants **II**:387
Terrell, Mary Eliza Church
  VII:352–353
Thomas, M. Carey **VI**:356
travel **II**:394
Truth, Sojourner **V**:393, 394
Turell, Jane Colman **II**:394
unemployment **VIII**:399–
  400
United Daughters of the
  Confederacy **V**:407
U.S. Christian Commission
  V:408
U.S. Sanitary Commission
  V:411
Valesh, Eva McDonald
  VII:367
Vietnam War **IX**:332
Virginia **II**:400
Walker, Mary Edwards
  V:422–423

Ward, Nancy **II**:408
Warren, Mary Cole **II**:409
Warren, Mercy Otis
  III:427–428
Washington, Martha
  III:432
Weathermen/Weather
  Underground **IX**:341
*Webster v. Reproductive
  Health Services* **X**:368–
  369
Weld, Theodore Dwight
  IV:396
Wells-Barnett, Ida Bell
  VI:387, 388
Wetamo **II**:411
"Why Women Should Vote"
  (Addams) **VII**:420–424**
Willard, Emma **IV**:400–401
WILPF **VII**:386
Wilson, Thomas Woodrow
  VII:384
witches/witchcraft **I**:384;
  II:419, 420
Women's National Loyal
  League **V**:434
Woodhull, Victoria **VI**:400
World War II **VIII**:427–429
World War II home front
  VIII:432, 433
WPA **VIII**:425
Wright, Fanny **IV**:405
YMCA/YWCA **VII**:397
Women's Strike for Equality
  feminism **X**:132
  NOW **X**:247
  Steinem, Gloria **X**:334
Women's Strike for Equality
  (1970) **IX**:127
Women's Studies programs
  feminism **X**:133, 134
  multiculturalism **X**:236
  NOW **X**:247
Women's Trade Union League
  VII:356
women' strike for equality **X**:132
"Women's war" **VI**:295, 408c
Wonder, Stevie **IX**:229
Wonderful Wizard of Oz, The
  (Baum) **VI**:90
Wonderland (Coney Island, New
  York) **VII**:263
WONPR (Women's Organization
  for National Prohibition
  Reform) **VII**:274
Wood, Abraham **II**:124
Wood, Ed **IX**:224
Wood, Fernando **V**:94, 283
Wood, Gordon **II**:166
Wood, Grant **VIII**:31
Wood, Leonard
  armed forces **VII**:20
  Preparedness **VII**:267
  Rough Riders **VI**:317
Wood, Natalie **IX**:225
Wood, Robert E. **VIII**:17
Wood, William **II**:426

woodblocks **I**:303
Woodhull, Claflin and Company
  VI:400
Woodhull, Victoria **VI**:**400–402**,
  401, 407*c*
  Beecher-Tilton scandal
    VI:30
  Hooker, Isabella Beecher
    VI:176
  Lockwood, Belva Ann
    Bennett McNall **VI**:229
  socialism **VI**:336
  women's status and rights
    V:438; **VI**:399
Woodhull and Claflin's Weekly
  VI:407*c*
  Beecher-Tilton scandal
    VI:30
  magazines **VI**:235
  socialism **VI**:336
  Woodhull, Victoria **VI**:400,
    401
"Woodnotes" (Emerson) **IV**:140
Woodrow Wilson Foundation
  VII:115
Woods, Arthur **VIII**:309
Woods, Tiger
  recreation **X**:303
  sports and recreation **X**:331,
    332
  television **X**:344
Woodson, Carter **VII**:140
Woodstock music festival (1969)
  X:**371–372**, 375*c*
  folk music revival **IX**:121
  music **IX**:230
  popular culture **IX**:259
  sexual revolution **X**:322
Woodstock Ventures, Inc. **X**:371
Woodville, Richard Caton **V**:18
Woodward, Bob
  Burger, Warren E. **X**:51
  media **X**:219
  Mitchell, John N. **X**:233
Woodward, C. Vann
  literature **V**:239
  multiculturalism **X**:237
  segregation **VII**:319
Woodward, Ellen S. **VIII**:95
Woodward, George **V**:94
Woodward College **IV**:246
Woody Guthrie Memorial Concert
  IX:93
Wool, John E. **IV**:233
Woolcott, Alexander **VII**:180
Woolen Act (England) **II**:3, 214
Wooley, Mary **VII**:386
Woolman, John **II**:**426–427**
  abolitionism **II**:1–2
  Benezet, Anthony **II**:35–36
  Quakers **II**:323
Woolson, Albert **V**:416
wool trade **I**:66
Woolworth, Frank W. **VI**:65
Woolworth department store sit-in
  (Greensboro, North Carolina)
  IX:290, 291, 354*c*

Worcester, Massachusetts
  Dix, Dorothea **IV**:124
  Foster, Abigail Kelley
    IV:161
  Massachusetts Emigrant Aid
    Society **IV**:241, 242
  railroads **IV**:314
  women's status and rights
    IV:404
Worcester v. Georgia
  Cherokee **IV**:85
  Native Americans **IV**:275
  Trail of Tears **IV**:378
Worcester Women's Rights
  Convention (1850) **VI**:171
Worden, John L. **V**:207, 266
Wordsworth, William **IV**:379
Work, Henry Clay **V**:273; **VI**:257
work, household **VII**:125, 192,
  389–391, *390*
Workers' Alliance **VIII**:130
workers' compensation **VII**:**391–
  392**, 406*c*
  citizenship **VII**:57
  Hamilton, Alice **VII**:133
  Johnson, Hiram Warren
    VII:154
  National Civic Federation
    VII:226
  New Unionism **VII**:238
  occupational health and
    safety **VII**:243
  Pinchot, Gifford **VII**:260
  politics (1900–1928)
    VII:262
  progressivism **VII**:271
  Triangle Shirtwaist Fire
    VII:357
Workers' Health Bureau of
  America **VII**:244
Workers' Party **VII**:311
Workingmen's Benevolent
  Association **VI**:248, 249
Workingmen's Party
  immigration restrictions
    VI:187
  labor/labor movements
    IV:218
  Socialist Labor Party **VI**:336
  strikes **V**:375
Working Women's Protective
  Union of New York **V**:133;
  VI:215
Workmen's Compensation Act
  VII:**392–393**, 406*c*
  muckrakers **VII**:217
  New Freedom **VII**:236
  Wilson, Thomas Woodrow
    VII:383
work-relief **VIII**:364
Works Progress Administration
  (WPA) **VIII**:*425*, **425–426**,
  445*c*
  advertising **VIII**:1
  art and architecture **VIII**:31
  Black Cabinet **VIII**:46
  children **VIII**:67

cities and urban life
  VIII:69
Congress **VIII**:81
conservatism **VIII**:84, 85
ERAA **VIII**:114
FAP **VIII**:128
FBI **VIII**:130
FERA **VIII**:133
FMP **VIII**:134
folk music revival **IX**:120
FTP **VIII**:135
FWP **VIII**:136
Henderson, Leon **VIII**:163
Hopkins, Harry L. **VIII**:176
Johnson, Hugh S. **VIII**:196
literature **VIII**:220–221
marriage and family
  VIII:231
Murray, Pauli **IX**:227
music **VIII**:250
Native Americans **VIII**:264
New Deal **VIII**:269
NYA **VIII**:262
popular culture **VIII**:301
recession of 1937–1938
  VIII:324
recreation **VIII**:327
relief **VIII**:332, 333
Roosevelt, Eleanor
  VIII:343
Second New Deal **VIII**:356
Social Security Act
  VIII:363
transportation **VIII**:395,
  396
Welles, Orson **VIII**:414
World and the Individual, The
  (Royce) **VI**:319
World Anti-Slavery Conference
  (1843) **V**:301
World Anti-Slavery Convention
  (1840)
  American Anti-Slavery
    Society **IV**:16
  female antislavery societies
    IV:148
  Liberty Party **IV**:226
  Mott, Lucretia **IV**:265
  Seneca Falls convention
    IV:341
World Bank
  Bretton Woods Conference
    VIII:52
  business **IX**:46–47
  Eccles, Marriner S.
    VIII:101
  economy **VIII**:105
  foreign policy **VIII**:142
  postwar planning **VIII**:307
WorldCom **X**:59, 315
World Conference on Women
  speech (Albright) **X**:**405–407**
World Congress of Representative
  Women **VI**:402
World Council of Churches
  IX:272

World Court
  Carnegie, Andrew **VI**:63
  Carnegie Endowment for
    International Peace
    VII:49, 50
  Coughlin, Father Charles E.
    VIII:88
  Johnson, Hiram Warren
    VII:154
  League of Nations **VII**:175
  Lodge, Henry Cabot
    VII:184
  peace movements **VII**:257
World Disarmament Conference
  VIII:**426–427**, 443*c*
  foreign policy **VIII**:140
  Hoover presidency
    VIII:174
  London Naval Conference
    VIII:222
World Football League (WFL)
  X:330
World Health Organization
  (WHO) **IX**:212; **X**:6, 7, 222
World Heavyweight Boxing
  Championship **IX**:9, 10, 356*c*
"World of Tomorrow" (New York
  World's Fair) **VIII**:273, 446*c*
World Parliament of Religions
  (1893) **VII**:297
World Party for Equal Rights for
  Women **VII**:254
World Peace Foundation **VII**:115
World's Columbian Exposition
  (Chicago, 1893) **VI**:*195*, *402*,
  402–403
  art and architecture **VI**:19;
    VII:18, 19
  Beach, Amy Marcy Cheney
    VI:29
  Burnham, Daniel Hudson
    VI:54, 55
  Carver, George Washington
    VI:63
  Cassatt, Mary **VI**:64
  Cody, William Frederick
    VI:77
  entertainment, popular
    VI:117
  environment **VI**:120
  Hall, Granville Stanley
    VI:158
  Hayden, Sophia Gregoria
    VI:165
  Industrial Revolution,
    Second **VI**:191
  Joplin, Scott **VII**:158
  Olmsted, Frederick Law
    V:288
  painting **VI**:276
  Pan-American Exposition
    VII:251
  Richards, Ellen Henrietta
    Swallow **VI**:313
  sculpture **VI**:327
  Sullivan, Louis H. **VI**:347
  Tesla, Nikola **VI**:353

World's Columbian Exposition
(*continued*)
  Tiffany, Louis Comfort
    VI:356
  Victorianism **VI:**374
  Wells-Barnett, Ida Bell
    VI:388
  Williams, Fannie Barrier
    VI:395
World Series **VII:**407*c;* **X:**380*c*
  baseball **VII:**33
  DiMaggio, Joe **VIII:**96
  sports and recreation
    VIII:370
World's Fair (1904) **IV:**94
World's Fair (1939–1940). *See*
  New York World's Fair (1939–
  1940)
World's Temperance Convention
  (1853) **VI:**39
World Tomorrow, The **VII:**109
World Trade Center attacks
  (2001). *See* September 11,
  2001, terrorist attacks
World Trade Center bombing
  (1993) **X:**80, 346, 380*c*
World Trade Organization (WTO)
  X:372, 380*c,* 382*c*
  economy **X:**110
  foreign policy **X:**142
  GATT **X:**151
  globalization **X:**154
World War I **VII:**393–394, *394,*
  406*c,* 407*c*
  Addams, Jane **VII:**3
  advertising **VII:**5
  AEF **VII:**10–11
  AFL **VII:**12
  African Americans **VIII:**2
  Agricultural Adjustment Act
    VIII:5
  Agricultural Marketing Act
    VII:5
  agriculture **VIII:**8–9
  Americanization **VII:**13
  American Legion **VII:**13
  armed forces **VII:**20
  aviation **VII:**28
  Balloon Corps **V:**26
  banking **VIII:**39
  Baruch, Bernard M. **VII:**32;
    VIII:41–42
  baseball **VII:**33
  Bennett, James Gordon, Jr.
    VI:33
  Black, Hugo L. **VIII:**45
  blitzkrieg **VIII:**47
  blues **VII:**39
  Bonus Army **VIII:**48
  Borah, William E. **VIII:**49
  Bradley, Omar N. **VIII:**50
  Bryce, James **VI:**53
  Budget and Accounting Act
    VII:44
  Bureau of Motion Pictures
    VIII:55
  Cable Act **VII:**47

Carnegie, Andrew **VI:**63
Catt, Carrie Lane Chapman
  VII:50
censorship **VIII:**65, 66
cities and urban life **VII:**55
citizenship **VII:**57
civil liberties **VII:**57–58
code breaking **VIII:**76
COLA **IX:**76
Committee for Public
  Information **VII:**59
conscription **VII:**62
Coolidge, Calvin John
  VII:65
cosmetics and beauty
  industry **VII:**65
Dawes, Charles Gates
  VII:71
Debs, Eugene Victor **VII:**73
Democratic Party **VII:**74
dollar-a-year men **VIII:**96
domino theory **IX:**89
Dow Chemical Corporation
  IX:89–90
dust bowl **VIII:**97–98
economy **VII:**84, 85
education **VII:**88
Ely, Richard Theodore
  VI:115
Espionage Act **VII:**100, 101
ethnic organizations
  VII:102
Expatriation Act **VII:**104
Farmer-Labor Party
  VII:105
Faulkner, William **VIII:**128
Federal Farm Loan Act
  VII:106
federal income tax **VII:**107
Fordney-McCumber Tariff
  VII:112
foreign policy **VII:**114–116;
  VIII:140
Forrestal, James V. **VIII:**143
Foster, William Zebulon
  VII:117
free speech fights **VII:**117
Fuel Administration
  VII:119
Gentlemen's Agreement
  VII:123
German Americans
  VIII:149
Gilman, Charlotte Perkins
  VII:125
Goldman, Emma **VII:**126
Great Depression **VIII:**157
Great Migration **VII:**127
Greenwich Village **VII:**131
Halsey, William F. **VIII:**161
Harding, Warren Gamaliel
  VII:134
Harlem Renaissance
  VII:136
Haywood, William Dudley
  VII:137
Hershey, Lewis B. **VIII:**164

Hillman, Sidney **VIII:**165
Holmes, Oliver Wendell
  VII:141
Hoover, Herbert C.
  VIII:171
Hoover presidency
  VIII:173
immigration **VII:**143, 144
Immigration Act (1917)
  VII:145
Industrial Revolution,
  Second **VI:**191
intelligence tests **VII:**148
investments, foreign
  VII:152
investments, foreign, in the
  United States **VI:**197
IWW **VII:**147
Johnson, Hugh S. **VIII:**196
Jones Act (1917) **VII:**157
journalism **VII:**160
Kennedy, Joseph P.
  VIII:200
King, Ernest J. **VIII:**201
Knox, Frank **VIII:**202
labor/labor movements
  VII:171
La Guardia, Fiorello
  VIII:208
Landon, Alfred M. **VIII:**209
League of Nations **VII:**175
Leahy, William D. **VIII:**211
liberalism **VIII:**214
Lodge, Henry Cabot
  VII:184
Lost Generation **VII:**185
Lusitania, RMS **VII:**187
MacArthur, Douglas **IX:**197
"Make the World Safe for
  Democracy" speech
  (Wilson) **VII:**424–427
Marshall, George C.
  VIII:232–233
The Masses **VII:**193
McNary-Haugen Farm Bill
  VII:195
Middle East **IX:**214
migration **VII:**206, 207
military-industrial complex
  IX:216
mining **VII:**209
Mitchell, William (Billy)
  VII:211
modernism **VII:**212
Mooney-Billings case
  VII:213
movie industry **VII:**216
muckrakers **VII:**216
NAM **VII:**226
National Civic Federation
  VII:226
National Origins Act
  VII:227
National Recovery
  Administration **VIII:**259
nativism **VII:**233, 234
NAWSA **VII:**223

neutrality **VII:**235
New Nationalism **VII:**237
New Unionism **VII:**238
New Woman **VII:**239, 240
Nimitz, Chester W.
  VIII:274
Non-Partisan League
  VII:241
NWLB **VII:**229
NWP **VII:**230
Nye committee **VIII:**278,
  279
open shop movement
  VII:247
Palmer, Alexander Mitchell
  VII:249
Passaic Strike **VII:**252
peace movements **VII:**256
Pershing, John Joseph
  VII:257
Polish Americans **VIII:**297
politics (1900–1928)
  VII:262
popular culture **VII:**265
population trends **VII:**266,
  267
Preparedness **VII:**267
presidency **VII:**269
progressivism **VII:**271–272
Prohibition **VII:**272
public health **VII:**275, 276
Quota Act **VII:**279
race and race relations
  VII:283
radical and labor press
  VII:285
radicalism **VII:**287–288
radio **VII:**288
Railroad Administration
  VII:291
Red Scare **VII:**296
Reed, Jack **VII:**296
relief **VIII:**332
religion **VI:**307
rules of war **V:**338
Sacco and Vanzetti **VII:**311
Schenck v. U.S. **VII:**313
science, invention and
  technology **VII:**150, 151,
  315
scrap drives **VIII:**354
Seattle General Strike
  VII:317
Sedition Act **VII:**318
Selective Service Act
  VII:321
Sheppard-Towner Act
  VII:323
Sinclair, Upton **VII:**326
socialism **VII:**328
Soldiers' Bonus **VII:**331
Sousa, John Philip **VI:**339
sports and recreation
  VII:334
steel industry **VII:**337
Steel Strike of 1919
  VII:338

Stimson, Henry L. **VIII:**375
submarines **VIII:**378
Supreme Court **VII:**342, 343
Sweet trial **VII:**344
Taft, Robert A. **VIII:**385
Taft, William Howard **VII:**348
tanks **VIII:**385
tariffs **VII:**350
taxation **VIII:**387
Tennessee Valley Authority **VIII:**392
Terrell, Mary Eliza Church **VII:**352–353
Thomas, Norman **VIII:**394
trade, domestic and foreign **VII:**354
Trading with the Enemy Act **VII:**355
Truman, Harry S. **IX:**320
USO **VIII:**403
U.S. Shipping Board **VII:**360
U.S. Steel **VII:**366
Versailles, Treaty of **VII:**369, 371
veterans **VII:**371
Veterans Bureau **VII:**373
victory gardens **VIII:**405
Vorse, Mary Heaton **VII:**375
War Industries Board **VII:**377–378
War Revenue Act **VII:**378–379
White, Alfred Tredway **VI:**391
WILPF **VII:**386
Wilson, Thomas Woodrow **VII:**383
woman suffrage **VII:**385
women's status and rights **VII:**389
Zimmermann telegram **VII:**401
World War II **VIII:427–429,** 447*c;* **IX:**352*c;* **X:**379*c,* 381*c*
ACLU **VIII:**17
advertising **VIII:**1
AFL **VIII:**19
African Americans **VIII:**3; **IX:**4
Agricultural Adjustment Act **VIII:**6–7
Agricultural Adjustment Administration **VIII:**8
agriculture **VIII:**10–11; **IX:**8
aircraft carriers **VIII:**12–13
aircraft industry **VIII:**14
air power **VIII:**15–16
Alaska statehood **IX:**8
America First Committee **VIII:**16–17
amphibious warfare **VIII:**19–20

Anglo-American relations **VIII:**20–21
antimonopoly **VIII:**23, 24
anti-Semitism **VIII:**24–25
Arlington National Cemetery **V:**17
Army, U.S. **VIII:**25
Army Air Forces, U.S. **VIII:**26
Arnold, Henry H. "Hap" **VIII:**28
art and architecture **VIII:**29–31
Asian-American movement **IX:**21
Asian Americans **VIII:**32
Atlantic Charter **VIII:**34, 461
atomic bomb **VIII:**34
automobile industry **VIII:**35–37
Axis **VIII:**37–38
baby boom **IX:**31
Baldwin, Roger Nash **VII:**32
Bankhead-Jones Farm Tenant Act **VIII:**39
Baruch, Bernard M. **VII:**32; **VIII:**42
Bataan Death March **VIII:**42
Berle, Adolf A., Jr. **VIII:**43
big bands **VIII:**44
Black Cabinet **VIII:**46
black market **VIII:**46
blitzkrieg **VIII:**47
bombing **VIII:**47–48
Borah, William E. **VIII:**50
Bourke-White, Margaret **VIII:**50
Bretton Woods Conference **VIII:**52
Bridges, Harry **VIII:**53
Buck v. Bell **VII:**44
Bureau of Motion Pictures **VIII:**56
Bush, Vannevar **VIII:**56
business **VIII:**57–59; **IX:**45–47
Byrnes, James F. **VIII:**60
Cairo Conference **VIII:**61
Capra, Frank **VIII:**61, 62
Casablanca Conference **VIII:**62
cash-and-carry **VIII:**63
Catholics **VIII:**63, 64
CCC **VIII:**71
CEA **IX:**77
censorship **VIII:**65
child labor **VII:**53
children **VII:**400; **VIII:**66, 67
CIA **IX:**51
CIO **VIII:**82
cities and urban life **VIII:**70
civil liberties **VIII:**71
civil rights **VIII:**72, 73

Civil War **V:**74
coal industry **VIII:**75
code breaking **VIII:**76
COLA **IX:**76
commemoration **IX:**66
communism **IX:**67
Communists **VIII:**78
Congress **VIII:**78–81
conscientious objectors **VIII:**83
conscription **VII:**63
conservatism **VIII:**83, 85
conservative coalition **VIII:**86
consumerism **IX:**76
convoys **VIII:**86, 87
"Day of Infamy" speech (Roosevelt) **VIII:**466
demobilization (WWII) **VIII:**91
Democratic Party **VIII:**94
Disney, Walt **IX:**88
Dole, Robert **X:**104
dollar-a-year men **VIII:**96
Douglas, William O. **VIII:**97
dust bowl **VIII:**99
Eccles, Marriner S. **VIII:**101
Economic Bill of Rights **VIII:**102
economy **VIII:**102, 104–105; **IX:**96–97
education **VIII:**107
Eisenhower, Dwight D. **IX:**100
elderly **VIII:**108
election of 1940 **VIII:**110
enemy aliens **VIII:**114
espionage **VIII:**116–118
Ethiopia **VIII:**118
Executive Order 8802 **VIII:**120, 465–466
Executive Order 9066 **VIII:**120–121, 466–467
exploration **IV:**146
FAP **VIII:**129
fashion **IX:**116
Faubus, Orval **IX:**117
FBI **VIII:**130
FCC **VIII:**131
Federal National Mortgage Association **VIII:**135
Fellowship of Reconciliation **VII:**109
FEPC **VIII:**123
fireside chats **VIII:**138
fiscal policy **VIII:**139
flag burning **X:**135
FMP **VIII:**134–135
Ford, Gerald R. **X:**137
Ford Motor Corporation **IX:**122
foreign policy **VII:**116; **VIII:**141–143
Four Freedoms **VIII:**143, 461–465

Freedom Train **IX:**125
FSA **VIII:**127
Full Employment Bill **VIII:**145
FWP **VIII:**136–137
gays and lesbians **VIII:**147, 148; **IX:**131
GI Bill of Rights **VIII:**149
GM **IX:**133
Goldwater, Barry **IX:**135
Goodman, Benny **VIII:**151
Good Neighbor policy **VIII:**152
government **VIII:**154
Grand Alliance **VIII:**155
Guadalcanal **VIII:**159–160
Guthrie, Woody **VIII:**160
Harriman, W. Averell **VIII:**161–162
Henderson, Leon **VIII:**163
Hersey, John R. **VIII:**164
Hershey, Lewis B. **VIII:**164
Higgins, Andrew J. **VIII:**165
Hillman, Sidney **VIII:**166
Hiroshima and Nagasaki **VIII:**166, 469–471
Hiss, Alger **IX:**146
HOLC **VIII:**171
Holocaust **VIII:**170
Hoover, Herbert C. **VIII:**173
Hopkins, Harry L. **VIII:**177
housing **VIII:**177–178
Hull, Cordell **VIII:**180
Ickes, Harold L. **VIII:**184
immigration **VIII:**184
intelligence **VIII:**186
Irish Americans **VIII:**189
isolationists **VIII:**190
Italian Americans **VIII:**190
Jaworski, Leon **X:**193
jazz **VIII:**195
Jews **VIII:**195
Jones, Jesse H. **VIII:**197
Jones Act (1916) **VII:**157
Kaiser, Henry J. **VIII:**199
Kellogg-Briand Treaty **VII:**165
Kennedy, John F. **IX:**169
Kennedy, Robert F. **IX:**171
Keynesianism **VIII:**200, 201
Knox, Frank **VIII:**202
Korean War **IX:**177
Korematsu v. U.S. **VIII:**203
labor/labor movements **VIII:**205, 207
Landon, Alfred M. **VIII:**209
Lange, Dorothea **VIII:**210
Leahy, William D. **VIII:**211
Lend-Lease **VIII:**211
Lewis, John L. **VIII:**213
Life magazine **VIII:**217
Lilienthal, David E. **VIII:**217
Lindbergh, Charles Augustus **VII:**178

World War I (continued)
   literature **VIII**:218, 219–
      220; **IX**:193
   London Economic
      Conference **VIII**:221
   Luce, Henry R. **VIII**:224
   MacArthur, Douglas
      IX:197–198
   Manhattan Project
      VIII:226–227
   March on Washington
      Movement **VIII**:227
   Marines, U.S. **VIII**:229–230
   marriage and family
      VIII:231–232; **IX**:202
   Marshall, George C.
      VIII:232, 233
   Marshall Plan **IX**:203–204,
      359–361
   McCarthy, Eugene **IX**:205
   McCarthy, Joseph R. **IX**:206
   medicine **V**:257; **VIII**:234,
      236; **IX**:212
   Mexican Americans
      VIII:237
   Mexican Repatriation
      Program **VIII**:238
   Middle East **IX**:214
   migration **VIII**:239–240;
      IX:215
   military-industrial complex
      IX:216
   miracle drugs **IX**:218
   Mitchell, John N. **X**:233
   Mitchell, William (Billy)
      VII:212
   mobilization **VIII**:240–242
   monetary policy **VIII**:244
   Monroe, Marilyn **IX**:222
   Morgenthau, Henry T., Jr.
      VIII:244
   movies **VIII**:245, 246
   Munich Conference
      VIII:248
   Murray, Philip **VIII**:249
   music **VIII**:249, 252
   NAACP **VIII**:255
   Native Americans **VII**:231;
      VIII:264; **IX**:240
   Nazi-Soviet Pact **VIII**:266
   Nelson, Donald M.
      VIII:266
   New Deal **VIII**:268, 270
   news media **VIII**:272
   Nimitz, Chester W.
      VIII:274
   NLRB **VIII**:259
   NRA **X**:249
   NRPB **VIII**:261
   NWLB **VIII**:261–262
   Paul, Alice **VII**:254
   Philippine independence
      IX:256
   Polish Americans **VIII**:297
   politics (Roosevelt era)
      VIII:300
   popular culture **IX**:259

population trends **VIII**:304–
   306; **IX**:260
POWs **VIII**:310
presidency **VIII**:309
propaganda **VIII**:311
public health **IX**:265
public housing **IX**:266
public opinion polls
   VIII:313
race and race relations
   IV:312; **VIII**:317, 319
Randolph, A. Philip
   VIII:321
Rankin, Jeannette **VII**:292
reconversion **VIII**:326
refugees **VIII**:329–330
relief **VIII**:333
religion **VIII**:334–336
Revenue Act of 1942
   VIII:341
RFC **VIII**:326
Roosevelt, Eleanor
   VIII:343
Roosevelt, Franklin D.
   VIII:334–336, 344–346
Rosenberg, Julius and Ethel
   IX:280
Rosie the Riveter **VIII**:347–
   348
rubber **VIII**:348
Sanger, Margaret **VII**:312
science and technology
   VIII:351; **IX**:284–285
scrap drives **VIII**:354
Selective Service **VIII**:357,
   358
shipbuilding **VIII**:359
Smith Act **VIII**:361
socialists **VIII**:362
Social Security Act **VIII**:365
South **VIII**:367
sports and recreation
   VII:335; **VIII**:370–373
steel industry **VIII**:373–374
Steinbeck, John **VIII**:374
strikes **VIII**:377–378
submarines **VIII**:378–379
suburbanization/suburbs
   VIII:379, 380
Sunbelt **VIII**:380–381
Supreme Court **VIII**:384
Taft, Robert A. **VIII**:385
tanks **VIII**:385
Tarawa **VIII**:386
taxation **VIII**:386, 388
technology **VIII**:389, 397
Teheran Conference
   VIII:390
television **IX**:315
Tennessee Valley Authority
   VIII:393
Third New Deal **VIII**:393
Thomas, Norman **VIII**:394
TNEC **VIII**:391
transportation **VIII**:396
Truman, Harry S. **IX**:320
Truman Doctrine **IX**:321

Truman's Announcement of
   the Atomic Bombing of
   Hiroshima **VIII**:469–471
UMWA **VIII**:402
UN **VIII**:402
unemployment **VIII**:400–
   401
union movement **IX**:323
V-E Day **VIII**:405
Versailles, Treaty of
   VII:370
veterans **IX**:329
victory gardens **VIII**:405
V-J Day **VIII**:406
WAC **VIII**:419–421
Wagner, Robert F. **VIII**:410
Wallace, Henry A. **VIII**:411
War Production Board
   VIII:414
WAVES **VIII**:418
Wheeler, Burton K.
   VIII:416
Wilkins, Roy **IX**:344
Willkie, Wendell L.
   VIII:417
women's status and rights
   VIII:423, 424
Yalta Agreement **VIII**:467–
   469
Yalta Conference **VIII**:439
Zionism **VIII**:441
zoot-suiters **VIII**:442
World War II European theater
   VIII:429–432, *430*
   air power **VIII**:15–16
   amphibious warfare
      VIII:20
   Army, U.S. **VIII**:25
   Army Air Forces, U.S.
      VIII:26
   bombing **VIII**:47
   Bradley, Omar N. **VIII**:50
   Bulge, Battle of the **VIII**:54
   Casablanca Conference
      VIII:62
   Italian campaign **VIII**:191
   Marines, U.S. **VIII**:229
   Mauldin, Bill **VIII**:233
   mobilization **VIII**:241
   Normandy, invasion of
      VIII:275
   North African campaign
      VIII:277
   Patton, George S., Jr.
      VIII:291
   Pyle, Ernie **VIII**:315
   second front **VIII**:355
   Teheran Conference
      VIII:390
   V-E Day **VIII**:405
   War Manpower Commission
      VIII:413
   World War II **VIII**:428
World War II home front
   VIII:432–434
   Asian Americans **VIII**:32
   black market **VIII**:46

censorship **VIII**:66
children **VIII**:67
civil liberties **VIII**:72
mobilization **VIII**:241–242
NRPB **VIII**:261
OCD **VIII**:281
OPA **VIII**:282
public opinion polls
   VIII:313
radio **VIII**:319
rationing **VIII**:322–323
recreation **VIII**:327, 328
World War II **VIII**:428,
   429
World War II Pacific theater
   VIII:434–437, *436*, 448c
   aircraft carriers **VIII**:12
   air power **VIII**:15, 16
   amphibious warfare
      VIII:20
   Army, U.S. **VIII**:25
   Army Air Forces, U.S.
      VIII:26
   atomic bomb **VIII**:35
   Axis **VIII**:38
   bombing **VIII**:48
   Cairo Conference **VIII**:61
   Casablanca Conference
      VIII:62
   code breaking **VIII**:76
   Guadalcanal **VIII**:159–160
   Halsey, William F.
      VIII:161
   Hersey, John R. **VIII**:164
   Higgins, Andrew J.
      VIII:165
   Hiroshima and Nagasaki
      VIII:166
   Iwo Jima **VIII**:192
   Japanese Americans,
      relocation of **VIII**:194
   King, Ernest J. **VIII**:202
   Lend-Lease **VIII**:212
   Leyte Gulf, Battle for
      VIII:214
   Manchuria **VIII**:225
   Mariana Islands **VIII**:228
   Marines, U.S. **VIII**:229,
      230
   Midway, Battle of **VIII**:238
   mobilization **VIII**:241
   Nimitz, Chester W.
      VIII:274
   North African campaign
      VIII:277
   Okinawa **VIII**:287
   Philippines **VIII**:294
   Potsdam Conference
      VIII:307
   shipbuilding **VIII**:359
   Solomon Islands **VIII**:365
   Soviet-American relations
      VIII:368
   Tarawa **VIII**:386
   Teheran Conference
      VIII:390
   V-E Day **VIII**:405

War Manpower Commission
VIII:413
World War II **VIII:**427
Yalta Conference **VIII:**439
World Wide Web (WWW). *See
also* Internet
business **X:**59
Gore, Albert, Jr. **X:**157
Internet **X:**181–183
music **X:**239
pornography **X:**284
science and technology
X:319
Worth, William J.
Gregg, Josiah **IV:**179
Pemberton, John C. **V:**298
Seminole War, First/Second
IV:339
Wouk, Herman **X:**212
Wounded Knee, South Dakota
occupation (1973) **X:**376*c*
AIM **IX:**13
Native Americans **X:**250
treaty rights **IX:**319
Wounded Knee massacre
VI:410*c*–411*c*
Bright Eyes **VI:**49
Native Americans **VI:**262
religion **VI:**310
Sioux wars **VI:**331
Wovoka **VI:**309–310, 410*c*
Wozniak, Stephen **X:**87, 318
WPA. *See* Works Progress
Administration
WPB. *See* War Production Board
WRA. *See* War Relocation
Authority
WRB. *See* War Refugee Board
Wren, Christopher **II:**25, 74
Wrenn, Robert **VI:**342
Wright, Benjamin **IV:**79, 141
Wright, Cleo **VIII:**318
Wright, Donald R. **II:**7
Wright, Edward **I:**262, 334
Wright, Fanny **IV:405–406**
Wright, Fielding **IX:**299
Wright, Frank Lloyd **VII:395;**
VIII:445*c*
art and architecture **VII:**19;
VIII:28; **IX:**20
New York World's Fair
(1964) **IX:**246
suburbanization/suburbs
VIII:379
Wright, Harry **VI:**25, 26
Wright, Henry **IV:**161
Wright, James C., Jr. **X:**151, 170,
372–373
Wright, Martha C. **IV:**341; **V:**436
Wright, Richard **VIII:437,** 447*c*
African Americans **VIII:**3;
IX:5
Baldwin, James **IX:**34
FWP **VIII:**137
literature **VIII:**219, 221;
IX:194
Wright, Silas **IV:**149

Wright, Susan Weber **X:**381*c*
Wright brothers **VII:395–396,**
404*c*
aviation **VII:**28
invention and technology
VI:196–197; **VII:**150
technology **IX:**313
writing **I:**234, 236
writ of habeas corpus **X:**164
writs of assistance **II:**224; **III:**219,
326, **448–449,** 459*c*
writs of mandamus
Judiciary Act (1789) **III:**242
Marbury v. Madison
III:285
Marshall, John **III:**290, 291
Wrong Man, The (film) **IX:**224
WSM radio (Nashville, Tennessee)
VIII:250
WTO. *See* World Trade
Organization
wunderkammer **I:**42, 43
WWJ radio (Detroit, Michigan)
VII:160
WWSA (Wisconsin Woman
Suffrage Association) **VI:**51
WWW. *See* World Wide Web
Wyandot Indians **II:**170
Clark, George Rogers
III:95
Fallen Timbers, Battle of
III:161
Greenville, Treaty of
III:200
Hull, William **IV:**192
Native Americans **IV:**273
Wyant, Alexander Helwig **VI:**275
Wyatt, Sir Francis **II:427**
Wycliffe, John **I:**315
Wye River Memorandum **X:**83
Wyeth, Nathaniel J. **IV:**145, 224,
406
Wyfliet, Cornelius **I:**274
Wygant v. Jackson **X:**9
Wykoff's Academy (Connecticut)
VI:78
Wynne, Angus, Jr. **IX:**317
Wyoming **II:**85
Cody, William Frederick
VI:76–77
conservation/
environmentalism **VI:**82
Deseret, State of **IV:**120
Donner party **IV:**125
elections, conduct of **VI:**113
exploration **IV:**144–146
immigration **IV:**193
Japanese Americans,
relocation of **VIII:**194
oil **VI:**271
Smith, Jedediah Strong
IV:350
woman suffrage **VII:**384
women's status and rights
V:437; **VI:**399
Wyoming Valley Massacre
III:449–450

Wyoming Valley Wars **III:**371,
450
Wythe, George **III:**232; **IV:**96

X

X-Files **X:**35
Xibalba **I:**236
Xicallanco **I:**351
Xicotencatl the Elder **I:387**
Xicotencatl the Younger **I:387**
X-ray machines **VII:**403*c*
GE **VII:**123
medicine **VIII:**234
Pan-American Exposition
VII:251
science and technology
VIII:351
XYZ affair **III:451,** 464*c*
Bache, Benjamin Franklin
III:39
Federalist Party **III:**164
foreign affairs **III:**168
foreign policy **IV:**153
Gallatin, Albert **III:**188
Gerry, Elbridge **III:**194
Pickering, Timothy **III:**335
Pinckney, Charles
Cotesworth **III:**335, 336
Pinckney Treaty **III:**336
Quasi War **III:**353
Talleyrand-Périgord, Charles-
Maurice de **III:**405

Y

yacht racing **V:**367
YAF. *See* Young Americans for
Freedom
Yale, Elihu **II:429,** 429
Yale College/University **II:429**
Austin, Stephen F. **IV:**39
Calhoun, John C. **IV:**68
Connecticut **II:**78
Douglas, William O.
VIII:96
Dwight, Timothy **III:**143
education **IV:**134
education, higher **VI:**111
Edwards, Jonathan **II:**113–
114
Ellington, Duke **VIII:**112
Evans, Walker **VIII:**120
football **VI:**130–131
Goldmark, Josephine Clara
VII:127
Harriman, W. Averell
VIII:161
Hersey, John R. **VIII:**164
King's College **II:**194
libraries, public **VI:**224
Luce, Henry R. **VIII:**224
Marsh, Othniel Charles
VI:240
medicine **VI:**244

Morse, Samuel F. B. **IV:**264
Pinchot, Gifford **VII:**260
religion **IV:**317
science and technology
VI:326
Taft, Robert A. **VIII:**385
Taft, William Howard
VII:347, 348
Trumbull, John **III:**416–
417
Yale, Elihu **II:**429
Yale Divinity School **IV:**318
Yale Report (1828) **IV:**134
Yale University Law School
IX:227
Yalta Agreement **VIII:467–469**
Yalta Conference **VIII:439–440,**
440, 448*c*
Byrnes, James F. **VIII:**60
foreign policy **VIII:**142
Grand Alliance **VIII:**155–
156
Harriman, W. Averell
VIII:162
Hiroshima and Nagasaki
VIII:168
Hopkins, Harry L. **VIII:**177
Leahy, William D. **VIII:**211
Polish Americans **VIII:**297
Roosevelt, Franklin D.
VIII:346, 347
Soviet-American relations
VIII:369
Soviet Union **IX:**295
Teheran Conference
VIII:391
UN **VIII:**402
Yamacraw Indians **II:**147, 392
Yamamoto, Isoroku **VIII:**291–292
Yamasee Indians **II:429–430**
South Carolina **II:**370
Yamasee War **II:**430
Yamasee War **II:430,** 430, 437*c*
Yancey, Jimmy **VIII:**250
Yancey, William Lowndes **V:**146,
345, **439–440**
Yangtze River **VIII:**141
"Yankee Doodle" **III:**309, **453**
Yankton Sioux Indians **IV:**84
Yap Treaty **VII:**408*c*
Yaqui Indians **IV:**267
Yarbrough, ex parte **VI:**210
Yarbrough, Joseph **VI:**210
Yatenga **I:**252
Yates, Abraham **III:453–454**
Yates v. United States **IX:**337
Yawata steel plants (Japan)
VIII:48
Yax Ch'aktel Xok (Mayan ruler)
I:358
Yax-K'uk'-Mo' (Mayan ruler) **I:**90
Yax Pasah (Mayan ruler) **I:**90
Yazoo claims **III:**291, 359, **454**
Yeardley, Sir George **II:**50, 279,
430
Year of American Travel, A
(Frémont) **IV:**165

yellow-dog contracts **VIII**:444c
  labor: strikes and violence
    VI:213
  NLRA **VIII**:257
  Norris–La Guardia Act
    VIII:277
yellow fever **I**:107, 108; **II:431**;
  III:463c; **VI**:408c
  Allen, Richard **III**:16
  Brown, Charles Brockden
    III:64
  Carey, Mathew **III**:80
  cities and urban life **III**:91;
    VI:71
  disease/epidemics **II**:99,
    100; **III**:138; **IV**:122–123;
    V:112
  Girard, Stephen **III**:195
  Jones, Absalom **III**:238
  Kearny, Stephen Watts
    IV:212
  Lake Erie, Battle of **IV**:221
  Lining, John **II**:205
  medicine **III**:295
  mortality **II**:243
  Rush, Benjamin **III**:376
  science and technology
    VII:314
  Seton, Elizabeth Ann **IV**:343
Yellow Hand **VI**:76
yellow journalism **VI:405**, 411c
  Bennett, James Gordon, Jr.
    VI:33
  Hearst, William Randolph
    VII:138
  journalism **VII**:158
  newspapers **VI**:267
  Pulitzer, Joseph **VI**:297
"Yellow Kid, The" **VI**:405; **VII**:138
"Yellow Peril"
  Gentlemen's Agreement
    VII:123
  Great White Fleet **VII**:130
  Root-Takahira Agreement
    VII:305
  Russo-Japanese War
    VII:309
Yellow Stone **IV**:84
Yellowstone National Park **VI:**120,
  407c
  conservation/
    environmentalism **VI**:81,
    82
  environment **VI**:119; **VII**:98
  national military parks
    V:276
  National Park Service
    VII:228
Yellowstone River
  American Fur Company
    IV:18
  Ashley, William Henry **IV**:31
  Atkinson, Henry **IV**:36
  Clark, William **IV**:96
  exploration **IV**:146
  Missouri Fur Company
    IV:257

Yellowstone River Basin **VI**:85
Yellow Submarine (film) **IX**:225
Yellow Tavern, Battle of **V**:99, 376
"Yellow Wallpaper, The" (Gilman)
  VII:125
Yell Rifles **V**:75
Yeltsin, Boris
  ABM Treaty **X**:28
  Clinton, William J. **X**:81
  foreign policy **X**:142
  Soviet Union, breakup of
    X:326
yeomen **V**:349
Yep, Laurence **IX:349**
Yersina pestis **I**:293
Ying-Yai Sheng-Lan (Ma Huan)
  I:225
Yippies
  "Chicago Eight" **X**:73
  counterculture **IX**:79
  Weathermen/Weather
    Underground **X**:341
YMCA. *See* Young Men's Christian
  Association
Yom Kippur War. *See* Arab-Israeli
  War (1973)
Yoncalla Valley **IV**:26
York, Herbert **IX**:152
York, Pennsylvania **III**:116
York River **III**:457
Yorktown, siege of (1862) **V**:251
Yorktown, surrender at **III:454–
457**, *455*, 456*m*, 462*c*
  Capes, Battle of the **III**:79,
    80
  Clinton, Sir Henry **III**:99
  Continental army **III**:112
  Cornwallis, Charles, Lord
    III:119, 121
  Cowpens, Battle of **III**:124,
    125
  French Alliance **III**:177,
    178
  Grasse, François-Joseph-
    Paul, comte de **III**:197
  Hamilton, Alexander
    III:206
  Knox, Henry **III**:248
  Lafayette, marquis de
    III:253–254
  POWs **III**:346
  Revolutionary War **III**:368
  Rochambeau, Jean-Baptiste-
    Donatien de Vimeur,
    comte de **III**:372
  Steuben, Frederick, baron
    von **III**:398
  Tarleton, Banastre **III**:407
  Vergennes, Charles Gravier,
    comte de **III**:423
  Washington, George **III**:431
  West Indies **III**:436
Yorktown, USS **VIII**:238, 314
Yoruba **I:389–390**
  Ewe **I**:125
  Niger River **I**:271
  Oyo **I**:281–282

Yosemite National Park **VI**:410c
  conservation/
    environmentalism **VI**:82
  environment **VII**:98
  Muir, John **VI**:253, 254
  National Park Service
    VII:228
Yo Soy Joaquín (Gonzáles) **IX**:136,
  137, 357c
Yost, Charles **X**:357
You Can't Go Home Again (Wolfe)
  VIII:219
You Have Seen Their Faces
  (Bourke-White) **VIII**:50
Youma (Hearn) **VI**:170
Young, Andrew
  African Americans **X**:14
  South Africa **X**:325
  UN **X**:357
Young, Brigham **IV:407–409**, *408*
  Brannan, Samuel **IV**:63, 64
  California Trail **IV**:78
  Deseret, State of **IV**:119, 120
  exploration **IV**:145
  Mormon Church **IV**:89–90;
    VI:251, 252
  Mormon Trail **IV**:261, 262
  Mormon War **IV**:263, 264
  Nauvoo **IV**:279
  religion **IV**:319; **VI**:308–309
Young, Ewing **IV**:81, 145
Young, John **IV**:188, 211
Young, Lester **VIII**:169
Young, Thomas **III:457**
Young, Whitney M. **IX**:326
Young, William **II**:287; **VII**:311
Young America Movement **IV**:234
Young Americans for Freedom
  (YAF) **IX**:74, **349–350**
Young Chicanos for Community
  Action **IX:350**, 357c
Young Citizens for Community
  Action **IX**:350
Younger, Cole
  entertainment, popular
    VI:118
  Quantrill, William Clarke
    V:317
  violence and lawlessness
    VI:376
Young Lords **IX**:357c
  Hispanic Americans **X**:166
  Latino movement **IX**:185
  Puerto Ricans **IX**:268
Young Men's Christian Association
  and Young Women's Christian
  Association (YMCA and
  YWCA) **VII:397–398**, *398*
  children **VIII**:67
  cities and urban life **VII**:55
  Comstock, Anthony **VI**:79
  education **VI**:110
  Moody, Dwight Lyman
    VI:249
  recreation **VII**:294
  Social Gospel **VI**:335
  Still, William **IV**:357

  Sunday, William Ashley, Jr.
    VII:342
  USO **VIII**:403
  Wanamaker, John **VI**:381,
    382
Young Men's Hebrew Association
  VIII:195
Young Men's Municipal Reform
  Association **VI**:227
Young Men's Republican Union
  V:93
Young Negroes' Cooperative
  League **IX**:32
Youngs, John **II**:431
Young's Point **V**:260
Youngstown, Ohio **IV**:246
Young Turks **X**:138
youth. *See* children
*Youth, Its Education, Regimen and
Hygiene* (Hall) **VI**:158
youth gangs **X**:97, 243
Youth International (Yippie) Party.
  See Yippies
Yucatán Peninsula **I**:390
  Aguilar, Francisco de **I**:4
  Aguilar, Gerónimo de **I**:4–5
  Alvarado, Pedro de **I**:7
  Chichén Itzá **I**:71–73
  Córdoba, Francisco
    Hernández de **I**:90
  Cortés, Hernán **I**:94
  Cozumel **I**:98
  Grijalva, Juan de **I**:145
  Guerrero, Gonzalo **I**:147
  Maya **I**:234, 235
  Mexico **I**:243
  New Spain **I**:267
  smallpox **I**:341
  Tabasco **I**:351
  Velázquez, Diego de **I**:374
Yugoslavia
  cold war **IX**:63
  Europe **IX**:112
  Soviet Union **IX**:295
  Truman Doctrine **IX**:321
  Versailles, Treaty of **VII**:370
  Yalta Agreement **VIII**:469
Yugoslavia, former Republic of
  X:381c
  Dayton accords **X**:99
  defense policy **X**:102
  Kosovo **X**:199–200
Yukon River **VI**:208, 209
Yuma Indians **III**:74; **IV**:70;
  VII:233
Yúngé Pueblo **I**:327
Yup'ik **II**:177

Z

Zacatecas **I**:243, 267, **391**
Zacharias, Ellis M. **VIII**:143
Za dynasty **I**:14
Zahniser, Howard **IX**:108
Zaldívar, Juan de **I**:279
zambaigo **I**:64

Zambia **I:**231
zambo **I:391–392**
   casta paintings **I:**64
   castas **I:**65
   mestizaje **I:**241
   mestizo **I:**242
   New Spain **I:**269
ZANU (Zimbabwean African
   National Union) **X:**16
Zapata, Emiliano **VII:**204, 205,
   405*c*
Zapotec Indians **I:**250
Zapruder, Abraham **IX:**22
ZAPU (Zimbabwean African
   People's Union) **X:**16
Zar'a Ya'qob (emperor of
   Ethiopia) **I:**124
Zarqawi, Abu Masab al- **X:**187,
   188
Zea mays. See corn
Zeila **I:**109–110
Zeisberger, David **II:433**

Zen Buddhism **IX:**272
Zenger, John Peter **II:433–434,**
   437*c*
   De Lancey, James **II:**93
   Hamilton, Andrew **II:**161
   journalism **III:**240
   newspapers **II:**268
   New York **II:**271
Zerrahn, Carl **VI:**29
Ziegfeld, Florenz **VII:**95–96, 405*c*
Zigler, Edward **IX:**145
Zimbabwe **X:**84
Zimbabwean African National
   Union (ZANU) **X:**16
Zimbabwean African People's
   Union (ZAPU) **X:**16
Zimmermann, Arthur **VII:**401
Zimmermann telegram **VII:401,**
   407*c*
   foreign policy **VII:**115
   neutrality **VII:**236
   World War I **VII:**393

Zinzendorf, Niklaus Ludwig von
   III:302
Zionism **VIII:441**
   Jews **VIII:**195
   Judaism **VI:**205
   Lazarus, Emma **VI:**219
Zion's Cooperative Mercantile
   Institution **IV:**408
Zola, Émile **VI:**200, 225
zoology **I:**139; **III:**384
*Zoology of the Voyage of the
   Beagle* (Darwin) **VI:**122
zoonosis **X:**6
zoot-suiters **VIII:441–442,** 448*c*
   children **VIII:**67
   Mexican Americans
      VIII:237
   migration **VIII:**240
   race and race relations
      VIII:319
   World War II home front
      VIII:433

"Zoot Suit Riots" **VIII:**319,
   441–442
Zouaves **V:441–442,** *442*
   music **V:**273
   uniforms **V:**398
   Wallace, Lew **VI:**381
Zuara, Eanes de **I:**160–161
Zuikaku (Japanese sip) **VIII:**87
Zumárraga, Juan de **I:392–393**
Zuni Indians **I:**393**, 393–394**
   art and architecture **I:**13
   Coronado, Francisco **I:**92
   Hopi **I:**168
   New Mexico **I:**264
   Pueblo **I:**305
Zurara, Gomes Eannes de **I:**337,
   339
Zwicker, Ralph **IX:**18
Zwingli, Ulrich **II:**148
Zworykin, Vladimir K. **VII:**151;
   IX:315